THE
CAMBRIDGE
GUIDE TO

WOMEN'S WRITING
IN ENGLISH

Lorna Sage

ADVISORY EDITORS

Germaine Greer
University of Warwick

Elaine Showalter
Princeton University

CAMBRIDGE
UNIVERSITY PRESS

PUBLISHED BY THE PRESS SYNDICATE OF THE UNIVERSITY OF CAMBRIDGE
The Pitt Building, Trumpington Street, Cambridge, United Kingdom

CAMBRIDGE UNIVERSITY PRESS
The Edinburgh Building, Cambridge CB2 2RU, UK   http: www.cup.cam.ac.uk
40 West 20th Street, New York, NY 10011–4211, USA   http: www.cup.org
10 Stamford Road, Oakleigh, Melbourne 3166, Australia

First published 1999

Printed in United Kingdom at the University Press, Cambridge

Typeface Lexicon A (*The Enschede Type Foundry*) 8.25/10.5pt   *System* QuarkXPress   [SE]

A catalogue record for this book is available from the British Library

Library of Congress cataloguing in publication data

Sage, Lorna.
     The Cambridge guide to women's writing in English / Lorna Sage;
advisory editors, Germaine Greer, Elaine Showalter.
         p.   cm.
     ISBN 0 521 49525 3 (hardback). – ISBN 0 521 66813 1 (paperback)
     1. English literature – Women authors – Dictionaries.   2. Women and
literature – English-speaking countries – Dictionaries.   3. Women and
literature – Great Britain – Dictionaries.   I. Greer, Germaine, 1939–   .
II. Showalter, Elaine.   III. Title.
PR111.S24   1999
820.9'9287'03 – dc21   98-50778   CIP

                     ISBN 0 521 49525 3 hardback
                     ISBN 0 521 66813 1 paperback

Preface

This book's guiding assumption is that all writings have a place, a history and a character. From the beginning we decided that this should apply to the entries as well, and that, however brief, they should be attributed. My contributors have given the style in which the *Guide* describes women's writing in English over the centuries a special liveliness and concision. They themselves also convey something of the diversity of the contemporary scene. They include distinguished writers of fiction, poetry and drama, alongside writers at the beginnings of their careers, graduate researchers and well-known academic critics and scholars, freelances of all kinds, and literary journalists. They are men as well as women, and of very different generations, too – almost seventy years separate my oldest contributor from my youngest. What they have in common is that their enthusiasm, and their pleasure as readers in the writers and writing they describe, persuaded them to put their information at the service of a work of reference.

The largest share of space has been given to entries on authors, followed by texts, followed by entries on kinds of writing, genres and sub-genres, general terms and large labels like 'postmodernism'. These last sketch out some of the projections employed in our maps of writing. The *Guide*'s coverage reflects the spread of literacy, and the legacy of the ex-empire of English. In concentrating on women's writing, in fact, you stress the extent and pace of change, for the scale of women's access to literary life has reflected and accelerated democratic, diasporic pressures in the modern world. Nothing stays still, the past itself changes under the eye of the present, and competing paradigms of writing – what most counts and why – suggest how ambivalent we have become about any claim to common ground. Focus on 'modernism' and 'postmodernism' and you are likely to talk about textuality in terms of breaking the sequence, exilic experience, the arts and crafts of evading sexual, social, national definition. Focus on 'postcolonialism' and you put the gender and the geography back into the accounts rendered, you revisit identity. There are many Englishes in 'English', and one consequence of *that* is that the literatures of Canada, or Australia, or South Africa, or India have their own internal contemporary cultures, values, markets. Which means in turn that much of the writing that matters in those countries is not necessarily published elsewhere.

It was all the more important, then, that the *Guide*'s contributors should come – intellectually and imaginatively, not always literally – from everywhere that there's a significant body of writing in English. This made a lot of difference to the choice of authors we eventually covered, and even more to the texts that are cross-referenced for most major figures, and many minor ones too. The canonical texts and set-books are here, but so are a whole range of less well-known works, from off the beaten track. One way to use this book is simply to read on past the person whose name you already knew and looked up, or the text whose title rang a bell, from what you can place to what you can't. You can start to do that on almost any page, and since the entries are arranged alphabetically, not by century or region, you'll find yourself in undiscovered country quite fast. The *Guide* is also a closet reading-list, and it's bigger on the inside than it looks from the outside. Readers travel. British novelist Iris Murdoch, who has died just as we are going to press, described in her first fiction *Under the Net* in 1954 the seduction of this – 'Starting a novel is like opening a door on a misty landscape, you can still see very little, but you can smell the earth and feel the wind blowing . . .' I hope we don't in the future settle exclusively for separate guides to American literature or Australian Literature or English Literature or Irish Literature. Excellent and comprehensive as they'll be, their boundaries won't have this permeability, this global projection that the history of the language has landed us with – where our differences are (paradoxical as it may sound) more readable than they are in more close-up focus.

We are divided by the dream of a common language: this applies to the anglophone world, but also, by symbolic extension, to women writers themselves. Works in translation – women's writings that have exerted incalculable influence across languages – are represented here, of course; and so are authors whose texts themselves stage dialogues between languages, like Chicano writers in the United States, Maori writers in New Zealand and Caribbean writers. And this is where you come to the edge of this book's world (which is after all flat, a projection on paper), and have to look for other maps, and other guides. Which is as it should be. For everything that's here, there's a great deal that's not: reference books may strive to be comprehensive and reliable, certainly this one has, but they can never be definitive, not only because we're not at the end of this history, but also because our picture of the past gets more and more populous. Here's just one example of who's not here: Anne Hunter. She was a late eighteenth-century London lady, wife of surgeon John Hunter, and the composer Haydn set several of her poems to music. She also wrote a libretto, which was not performed until 1993, for Haydn's *Creation*, based on Milton's *Paradise Lost*. Anne Hunter's text plays some suggestive games, punning on Eve's name ('The dewy Eve, the tempting fruit'), though on the whole she's as sweetly conformist as Milton might have wished: 'God view'd his works sublime / Which now complete were made / With an approving eye . . .' However, the story did not finish there, as we know. Such lost earlier writers, whose work helped create our world, can become once again part of the living record. We have no ready-made mythic connection with them (all daughters of Eve), but they are there to be rediscovered, re-read, reprinted. Anne Hunter is only just off the map: Fanny Burney was a guest at her musical parties, and the *Creation* libretto is in the Library of the Royal College of Surgeons of England.

Little by little, literature became a suitable profession for a woman during the eighteenth and nineteenth centuries. You can trace the nature of the social pressures involved by reading between the lines of many of the life-stories here. When a father or a husband died leaving no provision, when business ventures failed, or extravagance undermined the family finances, *then* decent women were allowed – allowed themselves – to write for a living. Otherwise, said Mary Brunton, whose novel *Self-Control* (published anonymously in 1811) seems to have influenced Jane Austen – well, a lady would as soon go in for rope-dancing. But they did, they did. In fact, rope-dancing isn't a bad metaphor for the precarious business of supporting yourself by writing, even now. Although women writers' life-stories take very different shapes these days, living by literature is no simple matter. For example – many of the women in these pages are teaching creative writing, in schools, colleges, prisons, all over the world; it's a job that figures large in a surprising number of living writers' careers, and something we take for granted. Is this is a development that's merely incidental to creative work and the inner processes of authorship? Or is it changing the relations between writers and readers, all of this passing-around of the role of author in workshops? Is writing becoming less of a solitary activity?

A *Guide* like this one can't answer such questions, though it can map out the grounds for asking them. Writing about writing certainly became less lonely for me in the process of editing it. I'm grateful to my contributors for that, first of all. Also to the Advisory Editors Germaine Greer (who wrote the entry on Sappho) and Elaine Showalter (who wrote the entry on the *fin de siècle*). I asked them for help more often than advice, I'm afraid, and they were generous in providing it. And I owe particular thanks to Alison Stuart, Kate Webb, Lynda Thompson, Mary Ellen, Kate Sillence, Rupert Hodson and Jeanetta Pollok, all of whom helped to research the book, make sense of the materials, uncover gaps, cope with copy, and assemble the final text; and to my editor at Cambridge University Press, Caroline Bundy, who has seen the book through from beginning to end.

Lorna Sage

Note to the reader

Entries are listed in alphabetical word by word order. Mc is alphabetized as Mac and St as Saint. Names of authors, titles of books, movements, terms and so forth in headwords are in **bold** type. Titles or names in SMALL CAPITALS in the course of the text indicate that they have a separate entry elsewhere in the Guide.

A name or part of a given name which is unused is placed in round brackets: e.g. **Byatt, A(ntonia) S(usan)**, or **Stowe, Harriet (Elizabeth) Beecher.** Where a writer is known by more than one name or adopted a different name during her life, the alternative name appears in square brackets after the more familiar one, e.g. **Burney, Fanny [Frances]**, or **Wharton [née Jones], Edith (Newbold).**

To avoid making the prose stilted, text in small capitals may not correspond exactly with the headwords of the entries referred to – for example, the word BIOGRAPHER indicates a cross-reference to the entry for **biography**; the word CHILDREN signals an entry on **children's books.**

A

Abbess of Crewe, The (1974) MURIEL SPARK'S fourteenth novel is a characteristically elegant and economical satire on politics, and, in particular, surveillance, inspired largely by the Watergate affair. In the Benedictine Abbey at Crewe, the sinister and manipulative Sister Alexandra has recently triumphed in the elections for Abbess, aided by a secret inner circle of loyal nuns, and by her extensive and closely monitored network of listening and viewing devices. Her supremacy is threatened, however, by her defeated rival, Sister Felicity, who has fled the Abbey following the bungled robbery of her silver thimble by representatives from a nearby Jesuit Order, and who is now engaged in unmasking Alexandra's misdemeanours to the press and television. The Abbess's struggle for control of the Order, in the course of which she continually asserts that she and her cohorts are operating in the realm of mythology, and are therefore not subject to everyday laws, echoes Spark's perennial interest in the nature of charisma, the conflict between personal will and the larger forces of history, and the battle between good and evil, particularly within a religious setting. AC

Abdullah, Mena 1930– Australian poet and short-story writer who explores the overt tensions and hidden delights of an Indian upbringing in rural Australia. Born in Bundarra, New South Wales, to sheep-farming immigrant parents, she was among the first in the country to write of ethnic difference at a time when the White Australia Policy was still active. 'The Red Koran' (1954), her first published poem, draws on the disparity between location and inheritance to inform the bush ballad with Indian folklore. Appearing in the *Bulletin* in 1954, it was anthologized in *Australian Poetry* (1955) as was her poem 'The Prison' (1957).

Her elliptical short stories are vivid with landscape and tradition and tell of the quest for identity and enchantment in an unfamiliar land. 'What was to be done with a dark-faced Indian child who was a second-generation Australian?' asks 'Grandfather Tiger' (1956). Although all but three of her stories – collected in *The Time of the Peacock* (1965) – were 'in collaboration with' the poet, Ray Mathew, it is generally thought that he was more an influence than a co-author. JAH

Abra (1978) JOAN BARFOOT's first book, later reissued in Britain as *Gaining Ground* (1980), won the Books in Canada First Novel Award. Dealing with the betrayals of domesticity, it shows the female protagonist searching for an identity separate from that of her husband and family. Although conditioned to be dependent, and even though nothing is more frightening than freedom and uncertainty, Abra nevertheless flees a world in which her sole function seems to be circumscribed by a socially constructed role of wife and mother. Leaving the suburban security of husband and children, she goes to live in an isolated cabin, free from human contact, clocks and mirrors. Through a chosen life of self-sufficiency and the immediacy of living in close contact with nature, Abra gains physical strength and sharpened senses. Once deeply in touch with herself, she is ready and able to re-evaluate her life and account for her actions when her daughter tracks her down. In this women-centred fiction, Barfoot, in REALISTIC and intense detail, shows the protagonist's achievement of the inner peace and strength that formerly eluded her. SM/PRH

Acker, Kathy 1948–97 Avant-garde American novelist, *enfant terrible* of the subcultural POSTMODERN scene. Acker grew up in the midst of the counter-culture: in New York, mixing with the FLUXUS group and underground film-makers and studying Classics at Brandeis University, then on the West Coast, where she continued her studies at the University of California at San Diego and was married to Peter Gordon (actually her second marriage) in the seventies. During this period she had various jobs, ranging from secretary to sex show performer.

Often dubbed a 'punk' novelist, her early trilogy, comprising *The Childlike Life of the Black Tarantula* (1973), *I Dreamt I Was a Nymphomaniac: Imagining* (1974) and *The Adult Life of Toulouse Lautrec* (1975), constructs an aggressive, vulnerable, abject persona out of disparate materials: fiction, poetry, pornography, film, true lives and childhood memories. William Burroughs is a strong influence, along with Sade, Bataille, the surrealists and the *nouveau romanciers*. In the 1980s Acker divided her time between London and Paris. *Great Expectations* (1982), a schizophrenically cracked BILDUNGSROMAN, and BLOOD AND GUTS IN HIGH

THE

ENGLISH BREAD-BOOK.

"In no way, perhaps, is the progress of a nation in civilisation more unequivocally shown, than in the improvement which it realises in the food of the community."

Eliza Acton: title-page of *English Bread Book* ('In no way, perhaps, is the progress of a nation in civilisation more unequivocally shown, than in the improvement it realises in the food of the community'), 1857.

SCHOOL (1984), the picaresque confessions of a whore who meets up with Jean Genet, attracted mainstream attention, including charges of plagiarism and pornography. At this time she also diversified into other media, writing the screenplay for the film *Variety* (1983) and the libretto for an opera, *The Birth of the Poet* (1985). Her work isn't always hostile to narrative; *EMPIRE OF THE SENSELESS* (1988) and the earlier *Kathy Goes to Haiti* (1978) are shaped by relatively accessible plots. Stories and fragments from her career are collected in *Hannibal Lecter, My Father* (1991). Acker may be viewed as a formalist exploiting the death of the author or a frighteningly compulsive seeker-after-identity within the patriarchal symbolic. She died of cancer at the age of forty-nine.   MO'D

Ackland, Valentine [Mary Kathleen Macrory Ackland; 'Molly Turpin'] 1906–68 British poet who strode about her Dorset home in breeches with a rifle. Her trade-mark Eton crop was the result of an act of defiance on the morning of her disastrous brief marriage to Richard Turpin. Ackland's confident personality hid insecurity about her work: her verse was

loose-formed and slight, and her output was small. She became convinced that she could only write 'properly' when experiencing emotional despair, a conviction that conflicted with the happiness she found after 1930 in her 'marriage' to novelist and poet SYLVIA TOWNSEND WARNER. Together they produced *Whether a Dove or a Seagull*, dedicated to Valentine's hero, Robert Frost, who was embarrassed by it. The individual poems were left anonymous, but this failed to deflect critical attention from their authorship, with unfortunate consequences for the lesser writer. Valentine's later life was characterized by restless searching after meaning, in human rights issues, religion and love-affairs.   JLB

Acton, Eliza 1799–1859 Considered Britain's first modern cookery writer because of the exactness of her recipes, which remain eminently practical today. She was both educator and food reformer, ahead of her time in advocating healthy eating and simple cooking. Her work remained in print until 1918 when ousted by that of MRS ISABELLA BEETON.

Eliza grew up in Ipswich in East Anglia where her father was a partner in a brewery and wine business. Aged 18, Eliza and a friend founded a boarding school in Suffolk, offering 'a course of education combining elegance and utility with economy'. She left after four years, though she may have begun writing poetry at this time for some was published during the 1820s. Ill health led to her living in France where she developed a lifelong admiration for French cooking. It's thought she became engaged to a French officer whose infidelity caused her to return home, possibly with an illegitimate daughter who was brought up by her sister.

During the 1830s Eliza approached her publisher with 'further fugitive verses' but Mr Longman suggested she write a COOKERY BOOK instead. *Modern Cookery, in all its Branches* (1845) was the result. In 1855 an expanded edition appeared, *Modern Cookery for Private Families*, described by ELIZABETH DAVID as 'the greatest cookery book in our language'; in its preface the author complains of being much plagiarized. Eliza's only other work, *The English Bread Book* (1857), was published just two years before her death in London due to premature old age.   GH

Adam[s], Jane [Jean] 1710–65 British poet and teacher born in Renfrewshire, Scotland. Being orphaned at an early age she went into domestic service for a local minister, using his library to educate herself. Her religious poems, often deeply pious and didactic, were collected and published in Glasgow in 1734 as *Miscellany Poems, by Mrs Jane Adams, in Crawfordsdyke*. Her enthusiasm for ameliorating the social position of women was evinced by her founding of a girls' school in Scotland. She was reported to have closed this for six weeks in order to walk to London to meet Samuel Richardson, whose *Clarissa* had so moved her. She died in Glasgow's poorhouse, having been admitted as an impoverished vagrant. Much of her work has been ignored since her death, and she remains best known for being the supposed author of the song, much admired by Burns, 'There's nae luck aboot the house'. ELER

Adam Bede

Adam Bede (1859) Extraordinarily popular when it first appeared, this novel by GEORGE ELIOT is set in the Midlands at the beginning of the 19th century. Its scenes of rural life and detailed characterization have often led it to be described as a quintessentially 'REALIST' novel, along with Eliot's other works.

The plot is based around four main characters: Adam Bede, the village carpenter, Hetty Sorrel, the woman he loves, Arthur Donnithorne, the local squire, and Dinah, the methodist preacher. The relationship of Hetty, who is seduced by flattery and attention, with Arthur reaches a tragic conclusion when she is imprisoned for infanticide, and 'some fatal influence seems to have shut up her heart against her fellow-creatures'. Like other novels by Eliot, *Adam Bede* was conceived as a moral book in which all the main characters learn through suffering, so that Adam becomes worthy enough to marry the caring Dinah, Arthur comprehends the consequences of his actions, and Hetty's confessional to Dinah allows her to both give and receive forgiveness. RDM

Adam-Smith, Patsy (Patricia Jean)

Adam-Smith, Patsy (Patricia Jean) 1924– Australian author best known for her popular historical and autobiographical works. Established her name with *Hear the Train Blow* (1964), an account of her childhood in rural Victoria, where her father worked as a railway fettler and her mother as a station-mistress. Two subsequent books, *There was a Ship* (1967) and *Goodbye Girlie* (1994), have extended her life story, covering her time with the Voluntary Aid Detachment during World War II, her six years as the first woman articled as an able seaman on an Australian coastal trader, and her later experiences living in the outback. Her time working in adult education in Hobart and as a manuscripts field officer for the State Library of Victoria led to an interest in writing the life stories of others, especially of people working in extreme conditions. These include *Moonbird People* (1965), *Outback Heroes* (1981) and *The Shearers* (1982). She has also produced several works relating to Australian war-time experiences, including *The Anzacs* (1978), *Australian Women at War* (1984) and *Prisoners of War: From Gallipoli to Korea* (1992). In addition, she has written or edited several histories and other studies of the railways of Australia as well as works based on Tasmanian history, such as *Heart of Exile* (1986), on the Irish political prisoners sent there in the early 19th century. Adam-Smith describes her life and her writing as being driven by a need for independence and freedom, which is 'the sweetest thing and I ran headlong into it'. EW

Adams, Abigail Smith

Adams, Abigail Smith 1744–1818 Wife of John Adams, second president of the United States from 1797 to 1801. Married in 1764, she bore four children who survived to adulthood: Abigail (b. 1765), John Quincy (b. 1767, US president 1825–9), Charles (b. 1770) and Thomas (b. 1772). Consistent with the cultural norms of her era, Adams regarded writing for a public audience as inappropriate for a woman; her considerable private correspondence, however, much of which was addressed to her husband during the long separations occasioned by his responsibilities as a statesman, offers a unique insider's view of the events that led to the establishment of the new nation and is commonly regarded by historians as the most thorough accounting of the Revolutionary period available from a woman's perspective.

Her most celebrated letter was written to her husband in 1776 after she learned he would take part in crafting the Declaration of Independence. She points out the problematic paradox of the Southern congressional delegates' simultaneous advocacy of liberty and defence of slavery and then writes, '[I]n the new Code of Laws which I suppose it will be necessary for you to make I desire you would Remember the Ladies ... Do not put such unlimited power into the hands of the Husbands. Remember all Men would be tyrants if they could. If ... attention is not paid to the Ladies we are determined to foment a Rebellion, and will not hold ourselves bound by any Laws in which we have no voice, or Representation.' The letter's humorous tone and sophisticated consideration of political issues suggest the egalitarian nature of the couple's relationship. Adams's letters to her husband, along with her voluminous correspondence with friends and family, provide an early look at an American women's literary tradition that links gender equity with the national political morality. VC

Adams, Anna

Adams, Anna 1926– British poet born in West London who celebrates the force of nature and writes with a remarkable empathy for the natural and human worlds. Adams trained as an artist and ceramicist at Harrow Art School and Hornsey College of Art. She worked as an art teacher, casual farm labourer and pottery designer, and divides her time between Horton-in-Ribblesdale and London. Her work distrusts both biography and the personal pronoun – a calculated and impassioned aesthetic which draws strength from the examples of the poets ELIZABETH BISHOP and Charles Tomlinson. She published *A*

Journey Through Winter in 1969 and has pursued a prolific career since. Her rate of productivity is driven by a high-pressured awareness of mortality. In the very moving *A Reply to Intercepted Mail (A Verse Letter to W.H. Auden)* (1979), she tells how, following a sudden life-threatening illness in 1960, she 'begged for time', the medicine partly being 'poetry'. The qualities inherent in the prose of *Island Chapters* (1991) and *Life on Limestone* (1994) are her ear for the cadences of speech, precise observation, wit and compassion. These skills become even more concentrated in her poetry. She published *Green Resistance: New and Selected Poems*, in 1996.   DM

Adams, Glenda 1940– Australian novelist and short-story writer, born and educated in Sydney. She studied languages at the University of Sydney, before travelling first to Indonesia and then settling in New York in 1964, where she studied creative writing at Columbia University. Adams taught fiction-writing in New York and travelled in Europe, remaining an expatriate until her return to Sydney in 1990. Adams has written several novels, including *The Tempest of Clemenza* (1996), *Longleg* (1990), *Dancing on Coral* (1987) and *Games of the Strong* (1982), in addition to two collections of short stories, *The Hottest Night of the Century* (1979) and *Lies and Stories* (1976). She has won several major Australian literary prizes, including the 1987 Miles Franklin and New South Wales Premier's awards for *Dancing on Coral*, and the 1991 Banjo Award and 1990 Age Book of the Year Award for *Longleg*. Adams has written in both NATURALISTIC and highly stylized modes, with *Games of the Strong* and some stories from *The Hottest Night of the Century* using experimental and allegorical forms. These elements are uncomfortably combined in her novel, *The Tempest of Clemenza*, which follows the emotional relationship of a mother and her dying adolescent daughter as they pursue their lives in the USA, while at the same time telling a GOTHIC and highly layered tale of the mother's own upbringing in Australia.   MLA

Adams, Hannah 1755–1831 American writer, historian. Considered the first professional American writer, Hannah grew up in Medfield, Massachusetts, and came to her scholarship through economic necessity and intense curiosity. Educated at home because of poor health and her father's financial difficulties, Adams read every book in her father's library and even learned Greek and Latin from the occasional boarders her father took in. During the Revolutionary War she helped support her family by making lace and tutoring, but also began laboriously researching theology and history. For a long time the only woman allowed in the Boston Athenaeum, she was so intense in her studies that the librarian claimed he often could not induce her to leave during his lunch hour. Adams's

first book, *A Compendium of the Various Sects Which Have Appeared From the Beginning of the Christian Era to the Present Day* (1784), was her answer to Broughton's terribly biased *Dictionary of Religions*. Adams's book sold out its subscription list, but her contract returned most of the money to her publisher. Subsequent editions, printed under shrewder contracts, increased her income and allowed her to compile several expanded editions. Research for her *Summary History of New England* (1799) was so demanding that it caused her temporary blindness. The volume was a comprehensive history from the Mayflower to the Constitution, which she was in the process of abridging as a textbook for sale to schools when Jedidiah Morse published his own textbook version. The result was a ten-year litigation, with heated theological and philosophical battles, which ended in 1814 in Adams's favour. Following *The Truth and Excellence of the Christian Religion* (1804), a series of portraits of exemplary Christian laymen, she published the sympathetic *History of the Jews* (1812). Her final work, *Memoir* (1832), was written to support her ailing younger sister.   SP

Adams, Sarah Flower 1805–48 Poet and hymn-writer, born at Great Harlow, Essex. When her father died in 1829 she lived with the family of W.J. Fox, and contributed articles to his literary journal, the *Monthly Repository*. In 1834 she married William Bridges Adams. Her principal work, *Vivia Perpetua, a Dramatic Poem*, a play about its heroine's conversion to Christianity, was published in 1841 and a long poem in ballad metre, entitled 'The Royal Progress', appeared in the *Illuminated Magazine* for 1845.

She wrote numerous unpublished poems on social and political subjects and composed several hymns which were set to music by her sister, and used in the services at Finsbury Chapel. She was drawn to dramatic writing and even considered acting as a profession, but much of her work was devotional and lyrical rather than dramatic in form. She is best known for her hymn 'Nearer, my God, to Thee'.   RS

Adcock, Fleur 1934– New Zealand poet, editor, translator. She gained an MA in Classics from Victoria University of Wellington, New Zealand. Having had an English childhood, Adcock made Britain her permanent home in 1963, and worked as a professional librarian for the Foreign and Commonwealth Office in England until 1979. In 1996 she was awarded the OBE for her contribution to New Zealand literature.

Although frequently cited for its cool restraint, Adcock's detached voice is distilled from an underlying emotional intensity. Her subject matter spans personal relationships and ecological, political, historical and gender concerns. She uses an assured lyrical voice and biting wit:

Fleur Adcock: extract from manuscript of 'The Soho Hospital for Women', 1975.

I write in praise of the solitary act:
of not feeling a trespassing tongue
forced into one's mouth, one's breath
smothered, nipples crushed against the
ribcage, and that metallic tingling
in the chin set off by a certain odd nerve . . .

There is much to be said for abandoning
this no longer novel exercise –
for not 'participating in
a total experience' – when
one feels like the lady in Leeds who
had seen *The Sound of Music* eighty-six times . . .

('Against Coupling')

More recently, Adcock has focused on women's experience through an array of fictional voices, as in 'Mary Magdalene and the Birds': 'Tricks and tumbles are my trade, I'm / all birds to all men. / I switch voices, adapt my features, / do whatever turn you fancy. / All that is constant is my hair: // plumage, darlings, beware of it'. Her diction, accessible and declarative, derives from the anti-academicism and irony of Movement aesthetics, and she is at ease with traditional principles – her work fuses casual speech and various stanzaic forms for its rhythmic energies.

An early interest in FAIRY TALE and allegory (*The Eye of the Hurricane* (1964) and *Tigers* (1967)) shifted to realistic documentations of urban and domestic scenes, although Adcock still explores poetry as narrative fiction in futuristic works such as 'Gas' (*HIGH TIDE IN THE GARDEN* (1971)).

Much of Adcock's work uses the perspective of the ambivalent outsider – a position overtly aligned to issues of immigration and national identity, from *High Tide in the Garden* (1971) to *Time Zones* (1991), a title that refers both to geographical regions and to the hauntings of memory.

Her editorial and translation work intensified in the 1980s and 1990s, and included *The Oxford Book of Contemporary New Zealand Poetry* (1982), *The Faber Book of Twentieth Century Women's Poetry* (1987), Grete Tartler's *Oriental Express* (1989), Daniela Crăsnura's *Letters From Darkness* (1991), and (with Jacqueline Simms) *The Oxford Book of Creatures* (1995). The Eighties also saw the appearance of her *Selected Poems* (1983) and *The Incident Book* (1986), which retrospectively traces Adcock's role as outsider to its origins in her English childhood. *Looking Back* (1997) extends her fascination with personal and ancestral history.   EJN

Adeline Mowbray (1804) This was the third novel by AMELIA OPIE and tells the story of a girl brought up in a free-thinking environment by a philosophical mother. Unaware that her parent's opinions are strictly theoretical, Adeline defies convention by attempting to live by the principles she has been taught. She lives openly with her handsome young lover, Glenmurray, in accordance with the free-thinking rejection of marriage. Adeline boldly and nobly defies the public odium until, after the death of Glenmurray, she is finally brought to see the error of her ways by the intervention of a Quaker. By the end of the novel she is able to die, reconciled to God and social convention.

The characters of Adeline Mowbray and Glenmurray have been widely identified with MARY WOLLSTONECRAFT and William Godwin, with whom Amelia Opie was intimate in the 1790s. While Adeline is sympathetically portrayed as moral but misguided, the novel can be seen as an attack on the Godwinian attitude to marriage. It has thus been allied to the reaction against radical, 'jacobin' ideas, despite its criticism of intolerance, bigotry and slavery.   LBe

Adventures of David Simple, The (1744) SARAH FIELDING's first and most famous novel was praised for its 'vast Penetration into human Nature'. Acclaimed by Richardson, Johnson and the BLUE-STOCKINGS, it was included with other classics in the *Novelists Magazine* (1782) and commended in CLARA REEVE's *THE PROGRESS OF ROMANCE* (1785). However its sentimental philosophy, its emphasis on tender feelings and moral predicaments, and its pessimistic conclusion that selflessness is inevitably defeated by worldly ambition, delayed modern recognition. The guileless hero's quest to found an ideal community 'without any selfish and separate Interest' encounters self-seeking cynics and tragic set-backs. The only real survivor is Cynthia, whose spirited complaints that the intellectual aspirations of clever girls are thwarted, and that a wife is no more than an 'upper Servant', possibly echoed her author's own frustrations. Sarah's brother Henry wrote a complimentary preface and edited the second edition, which she followed with two sequels.   LMT

African Laughter: Four Visits to Zimbabwe (1991) In this political TRAVEL NARRATIVE DORIS LESSING's ambivalence about her exile from Africa prompts a rethinking of time. Her desire to belong in Africa appears doomed to collide with the violence of the COLONIAL past and an eternal POST-COLONIAL present. Fracturing the linear colonial/post-colonial framework imposed on Africa's history enables an imaginative means of belonging.

African Laughter appears to be a straightforward REALIST excursion into four visits to Zimbabwe (1982–92). Although chapter divisions reflect the time periods of each visit, the simple device of merging time frames through retrospection and anticipation, of informed comment on events which occurred in her absence, creates a pervasive presence for the exiled self which enables a kind of belonging. Lessing's fascina-

tion with Zimbabwe's rock formations offers a more complex questioning of time. The rupturing of 'historical time' through the medium of 'ageless' geographical features alludes to an elusive relationship with landscape beyond the dynamics of ownership and appropriation. It hints at an ambivalent aesthetics of desire encompassing the yearning, both for time as a referent in the making of identities, and for its opposite, the negation of time to free the self.   C-AM

Age of Innocence, The (1920) EDITH WHARTON's Pulitzer-Prize-winning novel describes the disillusionment of its thoughtful, conformist hero with the stifling manners and mores of 19th-century New York society. The significantly named Newland Archer marries the charming but conventional May and, believing that 'Women should be free . . . as free as we are', he unsuccessfully attempts to raise her out of their trivial and confined sphere only to discover instead his increasing attraction to her disgraced cousin, Countess Ellen Olenska. Vibrant with thwarted passions and necessary renunciations, prompted by a refusal to 'behave like people in novels', the relationship between Newland and Ellen nevertheless owes something to Henry James's microcosmic representations of the stormy FIN DE SIÈCLE affair between the civilizations of Puritan, young America and of ancient, decadent Europe, although the 'innocence' of the younger culture is shown throughout the novel to be only mythical. By the end of the novel an older, widowed Newland reflects on the liberating potential of rapid technological and cultural change, but, crippled by the values of the old society, he ultimately renounces Ellen.   MM

Agnes Grey (1847) ANNE BRONTË's first novel, published under the pseudonym 'Acton Bell', depicts the life of a clergyman's daughter whose circumstances force her to become a governess. The first-person narrative presents an uncompromising satire on middle-class social behaviour, exemplified by two families, the Bloomfields and the Murrays. Their moral vacuity, self-indulgence and habitual failure to support their governesses in matters of discipline are contrasted with Agnes's own strict and unyielding ethical attitudes. The protagonist finally finds happiness through marriage with Mr Weston, the curate, who has always stood by her through her years of servitude. The book was partly inspired by Brontë's own experience as a governess to the Ingham family at Blake Hall, Mirfield, in 1839, where she was unfairly dismissed after only one year, and to the Robinson family at Thorpe Green Hall between 1841 and 1845. In the Preface of the second edition of her later book *THE TENANT OF WILDFELL HALL*, Brontë vigorously defends this outspoken portrayal of the deprivations of the governess class.   NBP

Aguilar, Grace 1816–47 British novelist. Aguilar was the first woman to write in English about Judaism. Enormously popular, many of her works were translated into foreign languages. Educated at home by her Spanish immigrant parents, Aguilar was ill and, by some accounts, dominated by her mother for most of her short life. Seven of Aguilar's novels were published posthumously by Sarah Dias Fernandes Aguilar. By looking at composition rather than publication dates, Aguilar's writing career can be divided into three phases. The first one is of Historical ROMANCE. This includes *Vale of Cedars*, a romance set during the Inquisition. The central characters are practising Jews who must hide their faith behind both a metaphorical veil and a literal vale (a valley of cedars). Her second phase is translation, theology and BIOGRAPHY. It is this phase that has garnered the most critical attention. These works include *Israel Defended* (1838), a translation from the French on the emancipation question; *The Spirit of Judaism* (1842) which explores the humanistic spirit anchoring Jewish rituals; and *Women of Israel* (1844), a collective biography of women who appear in the Bible and the Talmud. This last work was still being given as a Sunday School prize as late as the 1950s. Her final phase is one of moral and DOMESTIC FICTION. Her two most popular works come from this time: *Home Influence* (1847) and *A Mother's Recompense* (1851). In these works, Aguilar seems to be advocating both the Victorian ideal of motherhood and the restricted freedom of women.   RB-S

Aidoo, Ama Ata [Christina] 1942– Ghanaian playwright, novelist, short-story writer and poet, born in the Fanti-speaking region of Central Ghana. She studied and later taught at the University of Ghana, was Minister for Education in the Ghanaian government in the 1980s, and has also lived and taught in Zimbabwe and the United States. While at the University of Ghana in 1964 she produced her first play, *Dilemma of a Ghost*, which dramatizes a young African-American woman's search for a homeland and the conflict between her western individualism and an African emphasis on community and family. Aidoo's second play, *Anowa* (1969), takes up similar issues in a 19th-century Ghanaian setting and in terms of the conflict between a young African woman's desire for romance and equality and her husband's quest for status and wealth. Both plays focus on women who desire to be sisters and comrades, and both set that female desire for equality and comradeship in the context of slavery and inequalities of wealth and class. Aidoo's drama and fictions draw on an innovative mixture of African and European (especially Brechtian) techniques in their use of dialogue, chorus, music and oral story-telling.

Aidoo is now better known in Europe and North America for her fiction. Her collection of short stories, *No Sweetness Here* (1970), is remarkable for the variety of its styles, techniques and narrative voices, frequently of rural men and women whose lives have been disrupted by colonization, war and racism. Her experimental novel, *OUR SISTER KILLJOY: Confessions of a Black-Eyed Squint* (1977), explores the ways in which language, western education and the glamour of material goods from the West seduce the younger generation of Ghanaians. Aidoo's fiction engages with issues which are crucially important to the health and identity of the emerging Ghanaian nation, but they do so with a lively humour, compassion and subtlety unusual in writing from Ghana.

In the 1980s and 1990s, Aidoo published two collections of poems, *Someone Talking to Sometime* (1985) and *An Angry Letter in January* (1992), and a number of children's books. Yet another change in style and direction was signalled by a ROMANCE, *Changes* (1991), awarded the 1992 Commonwealth Writers Prize for Best Book (Africa), which explores the dilemmas of contemporary urban professional women in Ghana.   CLI

Aiken, Joan (Delano) 1924– British writer of historical ROMANCES, thrillers and imaginative adventure-fiction for children (see CHILDREN'S BOOKS). Born in Sussex, the daughter of American poet Conrad Aiken, she was educated at home and read widely (especially AUSTEN, Scott, the BRONTËS, Dickens and Poe, whose influences are apparent). She supported her children as a copy-writer after her first husband died in 1955, before winning acclaim for several juvenile mysteries including *The Wolves of Willoughby Chase* (1962), a FAIRY TALE set in a Britain ruled by descendants of Bonnie Prince Charlie and haunted by ravening wolves. Many stories rely on fantasy and magic: *A Necklace of Raindrops and Other Stories* (1968) features egg-laying houses and flying pies baked with sky. Her adult novels of intrigue (*A Cluster of Separate Sparks,* 1972) and regency romances (*The Five-Minute Marriage*, 1977) indulge the romance of place. She has written four companion books to the novels of Jane Austen. (*Eliza's Daughter* (1994) invents a story for Willoughby's misguided victim from PRIDE AND PREJUDICE; *Emma Watson* (1996) rewrites Austen's fragment, *The Watsons*.) Recent children's fiction (*Cold Shoulder Road*, 1995) continues familiar themes of mysterious disappearances, child abduction and miraculous rescue. Aiken remarried and lives in Sussex and New York.   LDo

Albatross Muff, The (1977) BARBARA HANRAHAN's 'fantastic' novel troubles Dickensian England with a lost dreamscape of Australia. Mama, daughter Stella and ex-convict maid Moak travel from Australia, after Stella's father falls from his horse and becomes a bloodied corpse, to the oppressively gendered and class-ridden world of Victorian England. Here Mama's friend Pensa languishes on a couch, giving birth to a series of babies that disappoint if they are girls and die if they are boys. Albatross, shot on the voyage, cast a malign shadow over events: girls lapse into madness, there are numerous deaths, and Stella, antipodean and therefore vulnerable, becomes the victim of a predatory patriarch in her quest to recover the perfect body of the father. Throughout, deformed and diseased bodies resist the Victorian ideal, and slums lurk around the corner from 'well-groomed' London, though an idyllic female space in Wales offers refuge. Edith, a Mariner figure, writes to 'soothe the past': through her and references to Coleridge, Dickens and CHARLOTTE BRONTË, Hanrahan plays with literariness, confusing the distinctions between real and imaginary, magical and rational.   CM

Alcott, Louisa May 1832–88 American novelist and short-story writer. Nothing in her early life could have prepared Alcott for the success she eventually achieved with the publication of LITTLE WOMEN. As the daughter of the Transcendentalist philosopher Amos Bronson Alcott she was brought up within the formidably high-minded milieu of the 19th-century Massachusetts intelligentsia, and was principally taught at home by her father in preference to an orthodox schooling. She herself began a career in teaching in order to shield her family from the effects of Bronson Alcott's eccentric improvidence. When their circumstances worsened she took in sewing and worked as a general maid, before volunteering as a Union Army nurse at the outbreak of the Civil War.

During this period she began to write a series of violently SENSATIONAL magazine stories – 'I think my natural ambition', she declared, 'is for the lurid style. I indulge in gorgeous fancies and wish that I dared set them before the public.' Employing various pseudonyms, Alcott continued to produce such adult fare, with its murderous, drug-addicted heroines, long after she had made her reputation as a children's writer. The nature of this dual identity was only exposed during the 1940s, when Madeleine Stern and Leona Rostenberg successfully penetrated her various literary disguises.

After the Civil War, Alcott made the first of several visits to Europe, where she tried unsuccessfully to interest a London publisher in the manuscript which eventually became Little Women. Published in 1868, the novel, set against a background of a Yankee household managed by the mother while the father is absent fighting for the Union, was instantly popular, providing the author with the affluence and security earlier denied her. Just as Marmee, wise, benign matriarch of the March family, is based on Alcott's mother, so her four daughters – socially adventurous Meg, artistic

Amy, angelic Beth, and Jo, whose literary hankerings are buoyed up by irrepressible high spirits – are all in some sense autobiographical refractions, or else based on Alcott family originals. To Jo, most plainly her creator's *alter ego*, three more books – GOOD WIVES, *Little Men* and *Jo's Boys* – were devoted, and though Alcott claimed to be tiring of 'providing moral pap for the young', her fame continues to rest securely on her achievements in this genre.

Despite obvious concessions to mid 19th-century sentimentality, her stories are firmly grounded in contemporary American life, never demanding that we view their heroines as anything more than ordinary girls of their period. Identification and republication of Alcott's adult potboilers, including a recently discovered novel, *The Chase*, have created a fresh context for feminist criticism of her writings for the young. JK

Alden, Isabella (Macdonald) [Pansy] 1841–1930 American CHILDREN's author and popular religious novelist. She was born in Rochester, New York, and educated by her father and at boarding schools. After publishing her first story in a local paper at the age of 10, she set out as a schoolgirl to explain Christianity to children in *Helen Lester*, which won a prize from the Christian Tract Society and was published under her penname 'Pansy' in 1865. In 1866 she married Presbyterian minister Gustavas R. Alden. They had a son whose ill health prompted them to move first to Winter Park, Florida, and later to Palo Alto, California. Alden was active in the Sunday School movement, the Young People's Society for Christian Endeavour, the Chautauqua movement, and the Women's Christian Temperance Union. In addition to writing for and editing several religious magazines, she wrote or edited nearly 150 books, most of them for children. Her Chautauqua novels, beginning with *Four Girls at Chautauqua* (1876), helped to establish Christian summer camps. Her most popular novels were a series based on her own experiences *Ester Ried: Asleep and Awake* (1870), *Ester Ried Yet Speaking* (1883), and *Ester Ried's Namesake* (1906), but the works considered her most important were a life of Christ, *The Prince of Peace* (1890), and a retelling of Christ's life in a modern setting, *Yesterday, Framed in To-Day* (1898). By 1900 her books were selling worldwide, translated into many languages, at the rate of 100,000 per year. Alden left an unfinished autobiography, *Memories of Yesterday*, completed by her niece Grace Livingston Hill.   JSG

Aldrich, Bess (Streeter) [Margaret Dean Stevens] 1881–1954 American novelist and short-story writer. Daughter of pioneer settlers, she was born in Cedar Falls, Iowa, attended local schools and the Iowa state teachers' college, and taught for six years in Iowa and Utah. In 1907 she married Charles S. Aldrich, a

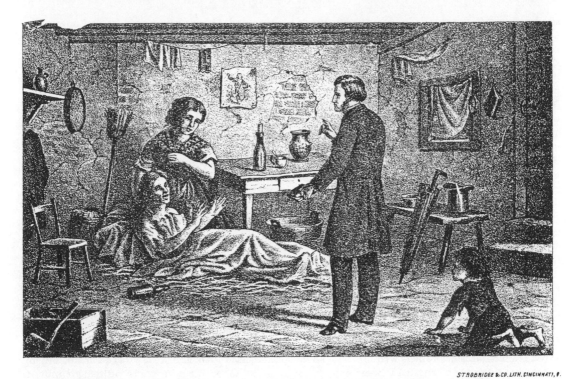

O LORD DON'T LET TODE EVER TOUCH A DROP OF RUM! Page 20.

STROBRIDGE & CO. LITH. CINCINNATI, O.

Isabella Alden: 'O Lord don't let Tode ever touch a drop of rum!', illustration from *Three People*, 1873.

banker and lawyer, with whom she settled in Elmwood, Nebraska, and had four children. She began publishing short stories in 1911 and after her husband died, in 1925, she wrote to support the family. Her ten novels, beginning with *The Rim of the Prairie* (1925), concentrate on the settlement of the Mississippi Valley region. In her bestselling *A Lantern in Her Hand* (1928), Aldrich pays tribute to her pioneer mother. The heroine of *Miss Bishop* (1933; filmed 1941) dedicates her life to teaching after being disappointed in love. *Song of Years* (1939) chronicles the growth of Cedar Falls into an industrial city. The title character of *The Lieutenant's Lady* (1942) is a 19th-century army wife living on the frontier. Aldrich wrote over 150 short stories concentrating on small-town family life, collected in *The Man Who Caught the Weather* (1936), *Journey into Christmas* (1949), *The Bess Streeter Aldrich Reader* (1950) and *A Bess Streeter Aldrich Treasury* (1959).   JSG

Aldrich, Mildred [H. Quinn] 1853–1928 American journalist born in Providence, Rhode Island, and raised in Boston. After graduating from high school in 1872, she taught in an elementary school in Boston. She wrote for the Boston *Home Journal*, *Arena*, the *Boston Journal* and the *Boston Herald*, and founded and edited

The *Mahogany Tree*, a weekly journal of ideas. By 1904 she had moved to France and was supporting herself as a foreign correspondent for American magazines. She also translated French plays into English and negotiated rights for US productions of French plays. In 1914 she moved to a cottage in Huiry outside Paris, from which she wrote eyewitness accounts of the Battle of the Marne. These are collected in *A Hilltop on the Marne* (1915), a bestseller considered her most important work. Other writing about World War I appears in *On the Edge of the War Zone* (1917), *The Peak of the Load* (1918), *When Johnny Comes Marching Home* (1919) and her Foreword to *The Letters of Thomasine Atkins (WAAC) On Active Service* (1918). *Told in a French Garden* (1914) is a collection of stories told in imitation of Boccaccio. Aldrich received the French Légion d'Honneur in 1922 for influencing the US to enter the war. A close friend of GERTRUDE STEIN and ALICE B. TOKLAS, she appears in Stein's THE AUTOBIOGRAPHY OF ALICE B. TOKLAS (1932).   JSG

Aleramo, Sibilla 1876–1960 Pseudonym of Rina Faccio, Italian writer, poet, political and social activist, who became known throughout Europe with her novel, *Una Donna* (1906; *A Woman at Bay*, 1908) the semi-autobiographical account of her marriage to an abusive husband and her eventual decision to leave, which meant the loss of her son. A controversial and shocking novel for its time, it was compared to Ibsen's *A Doll's House*. Aleramo had been seduced by a worker, Ulderico Pierangeli, at Porto Civitanova Marche where she was employed as a book-keeper, and forced into marriage in 1893. Aleramo did not write another novel until 1919, *Il Passaggio*, which was a revision of *Una Donna*, and included details of her affair with the writer Giovanni Cena. She then published a collection of her poetry, *Momenti* (1920), and two volumes from her JOURNALS, *Diario di una donna: Inediti 1945-60* and *Un amore insolito: Inediti 1940-44*, were published posthumously in 1979 and 1978 respectively, as well as essays concerned with female subjectivity and autonomy. Although she was known in the Italian press chiefly for her love-affairs with other writers, Aleramo became an activist for political and social change, travelling to Eastern-bloc countries at the behest of the Italian Communist party. SD

Alexander, Cecil Frances 1818–95 Religious poet and hymn-writer, the author of 'There is a green hill far away . . .', the carol 'Once in Royal David's City', and 'All things Bright and Beautiful'. Her family owned large estates in County Wicklow and County Tyrone in Ireland. Her brothers went to Oxford and she and her sisters were educated at home. As a young woman, she wrote a book of stories with Harriet Howard, the daughter of Lord Wicklow. She was committed to the High Anglican views of the Oxford Movement and wrote pamphlets for Newman and Keble as well as books of verse and prose for children. In 1850 she married William Alexander, rector of Termonamongan in County Tyrone (later Archbishop of Armagh and Primate of All Ireland), and later bore four children. When her husband was created Bishop of Derry and Raphoe, Frances set up a home for fallen women there. RS

Alexander, Meena 1951– Indian poet, novelist, essayist and critic. Born in Allahabad, into a Christian family, the author moved to Sudan with her family at the age of 5. She began writing poetry and publishing at a very early age. When she was 17, she went to the English Midlands, to Nottingham, where she completed a Ph.D. on *Women in Romanticism*, published in 1989. Later she returned to India to teach in Delhi and Hyderabad. In 1979 she married an American and moved to New York, to teach creative writing at Columbia University, and Women's Studies at Hunter College.

She has published many volumes of poetry including *The Bird's Bright Ring* (1976), *I Root My Name* (1977), *Stone Roots* (1980), *House of a Thousand Doors* (1988) and *River and Bridge* (1995). Much of her poetry deals with the issues of origins, displacement and female identity. She is highly praised for the intense lyrical quality of her writing. She has also written several novels. The first one, *Nampally Road* (1991), is a short novel set entirely in India. *FAULT LINES* (1994), her best book so far, is a memoir in which Alexander creates her leading figuration of the 'fault lines'. These are areas of fraction created by multiple uprootings through countries, languages and time.

In *The Shock of Arrival. Reflections on Postcolonial Experience* (1996), Alexander further explores the condition of migration and cultural displacement, fusing poetry, prose and critical thinking. Her novel *Manhattan Music* (1997) has an autobiographical content, and it narrates her life as a diasporic Indian writer, a married woman and a mother, a professor and a poet in the multicultural New York of the 1990s. SPo

Alexander, Mrs [Annie French Hector] 1825–1902 Originally from Ireland, this well-travelled author wrote over forty novels, many dealing unadornedly with matters of kinship, inheritance and obsession with money. *The Snare of the Fowler* (1892) details both the disappointment of someone who narrowly misses a large legacy and the predicament of a supposed heir dispossessed when he discovers that a woman, initially thought to be illegitimate, is entitled to inherit. Similarly, *Her Dearest Foe* (1876) is about a property dispute, though the dispute is resolved when the two combatants marry.

The young Annie French travelled extensively with her parents before they finally settled in London. However, it seems that, on marrying the explorer, merchant and archaeologist Alexander Hector in 1858, her nomadic life continued. She claimed to have written nothing between marriage and her husband's death in 1875. However, her best-known novel, *The Wooing o't*, was published in 1873.

As a widow, she wrote to support her four children and once again travel was on the agenda. The family lived in France and Germany in 1876–82 and in St Andrews in 1882–5, the former locations providing material for novels such as *The Frères* (1882). Her final novel, *Kitty Costello* (1904), is semi-autobiographical. EMH

Alford, Edna 1947– Canadian short-story writer, editor and teacher whose conventional REALIST stories scrutinize their characters' apparently mundane lives. Alford grew up in a working-class neighbourhood of Saskatoon where she went to school, before marrying and having a son. Her literary career began around the time she won a scholarship at 15 to attend a summer writing programme in Saskatchewan, and includes short-story collections: *A Sleep Full of Dreams* (1981), for which she was named co-winner of the Gerald Lampert Award, and *The Garden of*

Eloise Loon (1986). In addition to her own writing, Alford has contributed significantly to the development of other writers in Canada through her involvement with *Dandelion*, the literary magazine she co-founded and co-edited with JOAN CLARK (1975–80), with the aim of giving young writers in the prairie region greater access to publication. More recently she was appointed fiction editor of *Grain* magazine (1990). She has also edited short-fiction collections by Canadian writers such as Bonnie Burnard and Rachel Wyatt; co-edited the anthology of women's writing, *Kitchen Talk*, with CLAIRE HARRIS; and taught creative writing throughout western Canada. She is a member of the editorial board of Coteau Books and is Associate Director of the Writing Studio Program at the Banff Center for the Arts. On the subject of producing works of art or what Alford describes as 'home-made light' she states, 'I don't actually believe that I create. It seems to me that what I do is behold. And in some sense, I guess I am responding to the human longing to behold.'   SEP

Alias Grace (1996) In her ninth novel, MARGARET ATWOOD makes a fictional return to her fascination with early Canadian history and her former 'heroine', SUSANNA MOODIE. During her visits to the Provincial Penitentiary in Kingston and Toronto's Lunatic Asylum, Moodie wrote of Canada's 'star attraction', the 'celebrated murderess', Grace Marks, convicted of the Kinnear-Montgomery murders in July 1843. Whilst Grace's accomplice, James McDermott, was hanged, she was imprisoned until her Pardon in 1872. Atwood takes such verifiable facts and extends the mystery of Grace's crime into the realms of historical fiction: 'I have not changed any known facts, although the written accounts are so contradictory that few facts emerge as unequivocally "known".' This is a novel which questions the truth of writing (and history) alongside the 'origins' of the female subject whose crime is seen to relate directly to issues of sexuality. Pre-Freudian medical speculations abound as to the origin of Grace's 'madness': Atwood's exploration of mesmerism and dream work reflects the 19th century's fascination with mental illness, whilst her POST-MODERN approach questions its textual validity. Grace's own story is sewn into a 'quilted' narrative, each section introduced by a different illustrative 'block' or pattern, hinting at past memories and future freedoms.   MRE

Alkali, Zaynab 1950– The first novelist to bring a Northern Nigerian female perspective to Nigerian literature. Born in Borno State, Northern Nigeria, her family had belonged to a devoutly Muslim ethnic group until her father moved the family to a predominantly Christian village shortly before her birth,

a fact reflected in the background of conflicting belief systems in her fiction. She graduated in English from Ahmadu Bello University in 1973, and took her MA in African Literature in English there in 1979. She is married with six children and lectures in English and African literature at the University of Maidiguri in Borno State. Through a detailed evocation of village ritual, routine and idiom, her first novel, THE STILLBORN (1984), charts the lives of its female protagonists in a period of cultural contradiction and confusion in gender roles. Of her second novel, *The Virtuous Woman*, (1986), she has said it was 'deliberately moralistic . . . I feel our children are in desperate need of morals.' In 1995, she co-edited an anthology of fiction and poetry, *Vultures in the Air: Voices from Northern Nigeria*.   WJB

All my Pretty Ones (1962) Nominated for a National Book Award in 1963, ANNE SEXTON's second volume of poetry explores experiences of death, loss and grief, signalled in the title words from Shakespeare's *Macbeth*. The poems attempt to fulfil Kafka's proposal, the epigraph to the volume, that books should arouse a suicidal urge within the reader, breaking the 'frozen sea within'. The opening poem, 'The Truth the Dead Know', begins this examination by dealing with Sexton's deceased parents. 'Lament' discloses a consequent desire to control death: 'I think I could have stopped it, / if I'd have been as firm as a nurse.' 'A Curse Against Elegies' berates those who disturb and idealize the dead; and 'Housewife' suggests death's many guises for women, killed into submission by society. The associated subjects of religion and spirituality are treated in 'Young', 'The Starry Night', and 'For God while Sleeping', attempting to go beyond existence into a mythological realm, alternately pursued in 'The Black Art' where poetry becomes a dark entrance to forbidden knowledge.   EM

All Passion Spent (1931) VITA SACKVILLE-WEST's portrait of recalcitrant old age is a mixture of polemic and fantasy. Although often considered a fictional expression of the constraints on women's creativity identified by VIRGINIA WOOLF in A ROOM OF ONE'S OWN (1929) (Sackville-West attended Woolf's 1928 Cambridge lectures, the genesis of that work), the novel also explores the conflict between private artistic fulfilment and public duty. Lady Slane, at 88, the recent widow of an eminent statesman, rejects, to their amazement, her family's 'sensible' plans for her remaining years. Renting a cottage in Hampstead, she surrounds herself with idiosyncratic elderly new acquaintances, and reviews her life. In her judgement, the thwarting of her youthful hopes of becoming a painter was not wholly attributable to gender politics,

COVER·&·TITLE·PAGE·DESIGNED·BY·GRACE·BARTON·ALLEN

Elizabeth Akers Allen: title-page of *The Sunset Song and Other Verses*, 1902.

but also to the contemporary 'rift between the worker and the dreamer'. A vast bequest from an eccentric admirer proves a final test of her integrity. The issues raised are leavened with lyrical reminiscences of travels in Persia and India, and passages of deliciously sly humour aimed at Lady Slane's all-too-grown-up, hypocritical children.   WAP

Allan, Mabel Esther 1915–98 Young people's author, who also wrote as 'Jean Estoril', 'Anne Pilgrim' and 'Priscilla Hagon'. Despite life-long eye problems, she published over 150 novels and more than 300 short stories, printed her poems, autobiography and TRAVEL accounts and maintained a lively correspondence with admirers worldwide. Born in Cheshire to a non-bookish family, bored by a perfunctory education in private schools, she nevertheless resolved extremely young to be an author. During World War II, working in the Women's Land Army, teaching in infant schools, and putting on displays of country dancing, she per-

sisted with her writing. After years frustrated by wartime publishing conditions, she saw *The Glen Castle Mystery* appear in 1948. Success allowed more of the travel which so enriched her novels (*The Background Came First*, 1988). She embraced many genres – including thrillers, adventures, the inner-city Liverpool 'Wood Street' books, BALLET NOVELS (most famously, the 'Drina' series) and progressive school stories, which she described as 'Self government, self discipline and no games' (*To Be An Author*, 1982). Always open to new ideas, she remained constant in her respect for individuals and her writing remained refreshingly free from pious orthodoxies.   PEK

Alleine, Theodosia d. before 1685 British memoirist, who was born in Somerset, the daughter of a preacher. After marrying a kinsman, radical minister Joseph Alleine, in 1659, they taught together at a school in Taunton until her husband's removal in 1662 under the Acts of Uniformity. Alleine's BIOGRAPHY of her husband describes his ensuing bouts of imprisonment and ill-health, and provides an interesting early account of the struggle between wifely obedience and the need for a loving companion: 'I know nothing I could complain of, but that he was so taken up, that I could have but very little converse with him.' Along with MARGARET CAVENDISH, DUCHESS OF NEWCASTLE, Alleine is remarkable for being one of the very few women in the 17th century to write her autobiography. This appeared in the composite *Life* in 1672.   RDM

Allen, Elizabeth (Chase) (Taylor) Akers [Florence Percy] 1832–1911 American poet and editor. She was born in Strong, Maine, and suffered abuse and neglect after her mother died when she was 4. Educated at Farmington Academy, she began working at the age of 13 and writing under the pseudonym 'Florence Percy' at the age of 15. In 1851 she married Marshall Taylor, whom she divorced after he abandoned her and their daughter. She became an assistant editor of the *Portland Transcript* and, following publication of her first book, *Forest Buds, from the Woods of Maine* (1856), regularly contributed to *Atlantic Monthly*. From 1859 to 1860 she travelled in Europe as a news correspondent. In 1860 she married Benjamin Akers, who died the following year. During the Civil War she worked as a government clerk in Washington and tended wounded soldiers. Her poem 'Rock Me to Sleep' (*Saturday Evening Post*, 1860), a plaintive cry to a dead mother, was set to music and gained widespread popularity during the war. She married Elijah Allen in 1864. Later verse was collected in *Silver Bridge* (1886), *The High Top Sweeting* (1891), and *The Sunset Song* (1902). Late in life she wrote an autobiography of her financial life, bitterly recounting how all her husbands exploited her.   JSG

Allen, Paula Gunn 1939– Native American poet, critic and novelist concerned with the re-establishment of the importance of women in Native American tradition. She was born into a multi-lingual family of Laguna Pueblo, Sioux, Scottish, German and Lebanese ancestry and is related to the writer LESLIE MARMON SILKO. She grew up in the land between the Laguna Pueblo and Acoma reservations in New Mexico. Educated at a convent school and at the Universities of California and New Mexico, following a Professorship at the University of California, Berkeley, she became Professor of English at the University of California at Los Angeles.

Her novel *The Woman Who Owned the Shadows* (1983), written from the perspective of a woman recovering from mental collapse, is the first novel by and about a Native American woman. It is constructed from fragments of memory and includes diverse forms such as interior monologues, letters, doctors' notes and divorce papers. She has written books of criticism, including the groundbreaking *The Sacred Hoop: Recovering the Feminine in American Indian Traditions* (1986) in which she expresses the need for Native Americans to recognize 'our amazing ability to endure, recover, restore our ancient values and life ways, and then blossom'. She has also edited critical anthologies, the most notable of which, *Spider Woman's Granddaughters: Traditional Tales and Contemporary Writing by Native American Women* (1990), won the 1990 American Book Award. In 1994 she published an anthology in two volumes called *Voice of the Turtle: A Century of American Indian Fiction* (1994). Although she is prolific as a poet, she is best known for her prose writings. She is sometimes discussed as a lesbian writer and cites GERTRUDE STEIN and AUDRE LORDE amongst her influences. MAB

Allfrey, Phyllis Shand 1915–86 Journalist, politician and writer, who was born, and lived, in Dominica. She was active in the British Fabian Society, started the Labour Party in Dominica in 1955 and, when she was expelled from that, started the opposition Dominica Freedom Party. Allfrey became the first woman minister in the short-lived West Indian Federation in 1958. She was editor of the daily newspaper, the *Dominica Star*, and published four collections of poetry and a novel. Her short stories and a second novel may yet be published posthumously.

Allfrey's poetry is not widely available but her novel, *The Orchid House*, continues to be read and was recently adapted for television. A member of the tiny white population of Dominica, Allfrey captures the disintegration of the old social order of the plantation system in her novel and points the way to reconstruction via an alliance across racial and social boundaries. The novel argues that the white landowning class must align themselves politically with the black masses and insists on the collective power of women working together to overthrow the decaying power of the patriarchal COLONIAL order. Writing at a time when West Indian writing was the domain of male, black, writers, Allfrey remains an important, pioneering, literary figure. DdeCN

Allingham, Margery (Louise) 1904–96 British writer of thrillers and DETECTIVE STORIES, notable for charm as well as for excitement. Like many of her coevals – DOROTHY L. SAYERS, NGAIO MARSH – Allingham was at times a little in love with her hero, Albert Campion, but, far more than Sayers, she allowed him to change and grow as her work proceeded, not least because she needed him to be more complex and damaged. She herself had a conventional education and married young.

Campion appears in the majority of her books, as a comparatively conventional matinée-idol sleuth in *The Crime at Black Dudley* (1929) and rather more interestingly in her novels of the late 1930s, such as *Dancers in Mourning* (1937) and *The Fashion in Shrouds* (1938). These last two are interesting not only for their detailed depiction of small closed worlds disrupted by murder, but in their sense of the extent to which the disruption is not merely the sudden violent deaths but the breach of that trust on which daily life in small communities of colleagues is based.

World War II produced a sequence of spy thrillers – *Traitor's Purse* (1942) stands out – which have, at their best, a paranoid quality, a sense of urgency and menace. The latter stage of her career produced fluent but forgettable psychological thrillers in which Campion's urbanity was that of the physician as much as the sleuth. Closely linked to these in theme, yet entirely different in its effect, is *The Tiger in the Smoke* (1952) which bursts the usual format wide open by setting Campion in ineffectual opposition to a charismatic psychopath in a wrecked post-war London of bombsites and dark shadows. It is Allingham's most remarkable book and one in which she chooses – as she rarely does – to stretch the limits of her chosen form.

She was at her most assured when being witty; of the more comic Campion books, the best is perhaps the last, *More Work for the Undertaker* (1948), where her usually snobbish portrayal of comic cockneys acquires an elegiac tone. A class she had patronized had surprised her by their courage and sacrifices, and the jokes acquire an edge, not least at her own expense. RK

Allnutt, Gillian 1949– British poet whose versatile use of rhyme and vowel music is distinctive in her generation of post-feminist poets and poetics. Allnutt was born in London, received a convent and grammar-school education and studied Philosophy and English

13

at Cambridge. She has taught in further and adult education, and was poetry editor for *City Limits* before moving to County Durham to live and work. During her time in London she lived in squats, short-life and co-op houses, and involved herself actively in the Women's Arts Alliance Poetry Workshop from 1976 to 1980. Her experimental pamphlet, *The rag and bone man's daughter imagines a happy family* (1978), and first major book, *Spitting the Pips Out* (1981), were helped into existence by the support she received from other women writers. Her follow-up work, *Lizzie Siddall: Her Journal (1862)* (1985), is a successful sustained attempt to inhabit the mind of the ironmonger's daughter who eventually married Rossetti.

She co-edited the controversial anthology *The New British Poetry* in 1988. Allnutt had by this time left London for the North-East: 'to a self-imposed exile in which I hoped I might learn to stop leaving'. Her subsequent collections – particularly *Blackthorn* (1994) and *Nantucket and the Angel* (1997) – demonstrate a deepening of spiritual consciousness and lyric authority. Her stance owes much to the thorny grace and example of Anna Akhmatova (whom she acknowledges as her 'adoptive godmother'). Allnutt's boldly poetic syntax, often rooted in past models, is a significant venture in British POSTMODERNISM.   DM

A.L.O.E. (A Lady of England) [Charlotte Maria Tucker] 1821–93 This English writer of hymns, poetry and evangelical fiction never married, living in her parents' home until 1869 and with a brother until 1875. She spent the remaining eighteen years of her life as a missionary in India. Only beginning to publish her writings after her father's death in 1851, she nevertheless produced over 140 works. A gifted linguist, she translated some of these titles into Urdu and Punjabi as aids to her mission work.

Some of her books, for example *Battling With the World* (1904), are conventional stories about Christian children combating adversity. Such books are full of improving conversations and biblical quotations. However, the best of her writing is allegorical in nature. One such allegory is *The Crown of Success: or, Four Heads to Furnish* (1862), an often-amusing tale in which four children are each left to furnish a room whilst their mother is out. The rooms in question are, metaphorically, the 'four heads' of the title.   EMH

Alther [née Reed], Lisa 1944– American comic novelist from Kingsport, Tennessee, who after going north for college, marriage and work in publishing, wrote a raucous fiction that became a much-loved bestseller. *Kinflicks* (1976), the story of Tennesseean Ginny Babcock's evolution from southern belle to hippy, lesbian separatist and suburban housewife, is a ribald, jaunty satire of the cultural and sexual manners of the

1960s and early 1970s. *Original Sins* (1981) drew on similar material with equal success; with *Other Women* (1984) she continued to show a punchy irreverence and an ability to bring lesbian stories into the mainstream that invite comparison with fellow Southerner RITA MAE BROWN, who has praised her work. Married at 22 to a doctor, she moved to rural Vermont where she raised her daughter and wrote full time, journalism as well as fiction. Her 1990 novel *Bedrock*, set in a Vermont town of fallen industry and backwoods perversion, was described as 'a southerner's version of northern gothic'. *Five Minutes in Heaven* (1995) recounted a displaced Southern woman's emotional and sexual development, and included a passage of 1960s description which showed that hedonistic spirit to be one with which she has an ongoing affinity.   SB

Alvarez, Julia 1950– Poet and novelist. Originally from the Dominican Republic, Alvarez escaped with her family to the United States in 1960 when her parents fled the secret police of the Trujillo dictatorship. Her best-known work is *How the Garcia Girls Lost Their Accents* (1991), a collection of linked stories that look at the split lives of the four Garcia sisters as they shuttle back and forth – literally and metaphorically – between the Dominican Republic and the United States. She is also the author of two books of poetry, and two additional works of fiction: *In the Time of the Butterflies* (1995), a historical novel which recounts the 1960 assassination of the Mirabal sisters by the Trujillo dictatorship, and *Yo!* (1997), which continues the story of one of the characters from *How the Garcia Girls Lost Their Accents*.   SMSt

Alvi, Moniza 1954– British poet Moniza Alvi was born in Lahore, Pakistan. She was educated at the Universities of York and London, training as a teacher. She became Head of English at Aylwin School in London, and in 1995 married Robert Coe.

Alvi's poetry came to public notice in 1992 when she co-won the Poetry Business prize. *Peacock Luggage*, a pamphlet, was subsequently published by Smith Doorstop of Huddersfield in 1992, and her first two collections, *The Country at My Shoulder* (1993) and *A Bowl of Warm Air* (1996), by Oxford University Press. *The Country at My Shoulder* was well received – it was chosen for special marketing in 1995 under the banner of 'New Generation Poets'. Observers of the new British poetry scene began grouping Alvi with a rising generation of Asian women writers in Britain, including MEERA SYAL and SUJATA BHATT. Her ear for cadence also recalled the 'Persian' lyricism of MIMI KHALVATI. With hindsight, these groupings appear to be socio-critical wish-fulfilment – Alvi is on record as saying 'the poems that do not concern my Asian background are equally important to me . . . I have written about

Pakistan partly because it was, in the first instance, a fantasy.' Indeed, she left Pakistan for England when only a few months old. She writes an economical free verse that has a disarming sense of artlessness, though the apparent 'innocence' of her voice disguises a strong intellectual drive to explore and come to terms with her dual cultural worlds, their languages and pressures.   DM

American In Paris, An (1940) *New Yorker* correspondent GENÊT [JANET FLANNER] was one of the most well-known characters of the Left Bank, and her memoirs and journalism are among the most vivid accounts of early 20th-century European cultural life. Part of this legacy is *An American In Paris* in which Flanner maps the parameters of the social, cultural and political life between the two world wars. Her virtual camera moves in a panoptical manner, recording as well as criticizing the figures and events that marked the interwar period. Portraits of artists and writers like Picasso, Stravinsky, Isadora Duncan and EDITH WHARTON are featured alongside portraits of Elsa Sciaparelli, renowned for the sweaters she designed, and the Papin sisters who, while working as housemaids, brutally murdered their landlady, Mme Lancelin, and her daughter. This spectacular parade offers a taste of the Zeitgeist and culminates in a satirical profile of Hitler's rise to power.   MPe

Ana Historic (1988) Poet DAPHNE MARLATT's first novel shares the concern with the lesbian feminist 'salvaging' of patriarchal language evinced also in her poetry and in the work of some of her Canadian contemporaries, among them NICOLE BROSSARD.

While grieving for her dead mother Ina, the first-person narrator, Annie, is searching for and finding her place in a lineage of women. She re/writes the lives of three women: her mother's story; that of Mrs Richards, who appears in three brief lines in the civic archives of Vancouver; and the script of her own life. The stories of women are found 'in the gap between two stories', in the interruptions and absences, beyond the categorization of fact and fiction. The reclaimed female language does not follow any linear order but consists of 'words that flow out from within' the female body, signifying the interconnectedness of women, across generations, over history, linked by blood and birth – and by desire. Annie's re/search leads her to Zoe, and in their love-making they read each other 'into the page ahead'.   CES

Anderson, Barbara 1926– New Zealand novelist and short-story writer noted for her acute observation and sharp irreverent eye for absurdity. Her background is upper middle-class Anglophile New Zealand: her husband was vice-admiral of the Royal New Zealand Navy. She began writing when she was 60 and success with a collection of short stories, *I Think We Should Go Into The Jungle* (1989), was followed by five widely acclaimed novels between 1991 and 1996.

Anderson has said that she is fascinated by the *modus vivendi* of marriage and family life, and she probes these institutions with a mixture of sharpness and tenderness that recalls JANE AUSTEN, with perhaps a dash of JOANNA TROLLOPE in her easy familiarity with the pre-occupations of the middle classes. *Girls' High* (1991) portrays the love-lorn staff of a girls' school, while the next novel, *Portrait of the Artist's Wife* (1992), winner of the NZ\$ 20,000 Goodman Fielder Wattie Award, is a breezily humorous and sometimes bleak picture of well-off, white New Zealand. *All The Nice Girls* (1992) is set on a New Zealand naval base in the 1960s and draws partly on the author's own experience as a navy wife.

The plot of *The House Guest* (1995), about an English tutor's investigations into the life of a dead poet (reminiscent of A. S. BYATT's novel POSSESSION), is a vehicle for the author's sharp wit and eye for the bizarre. In *Proud Garments* (1996) Anderson casts a sardonic eye on marriage and family relationships, sometimes with the sardonic detachment of a Mr Bennet, but also with some admiration for those whose response to the absurdity of life is a stoic determination to make the best of it.   RB

Anderson [née McCubbin], Doris 1921– A journalist, novelist and activist, born in Medicine Hat and raised in Calgary, Alberta. She attended the Calgary Normal School and the University of Alberta, and after two years teaching in country schools moved to Toronto where she worked in advertising and journalism, becoming editor of *Châtelaine* magazine (1957–77). As the daughter of a working mother in the 'dirty thirties', and a working mother to three sons herself, she experienced many of the challenges and problems facing women; she changed *Châtelaine* from a typical 'women's magazine' focused on health, beauty, fashion and cooking into one combining those subjects with serious feminist discussion of birth control, battered babies, divorce laws, equal pay for work of equal value, child care, lesbianism, women's prisons, sexual harassment, and patriarchy in religion, schools and unions. Anderson wrote many influential editorials, one of which was instrumental in pressing the government of Canada to establish the Royal Commission on the Status of Women (1967–70). She was appointed president of the Canadian Advisory Council on the Status of Women (1979–81), a job that came to a precipitous end when she resigned because of a conflict over the inclusion of women and women's issues in the constitutional negotiations in 1982. From 1982–4, she was president of the National Action

Committee on the Status of Women (NAC). Among her many awards, Anderson has been made an Officer of the Order of Canada.

She wrote three novels – *Affairs of State* (1988), *Rough Layout* (1981) and *Two Women* (1979) – which did not achieve great critical acclaim. *The Unfinished Revolution: Status of Women in Twelve Countries* (1991) was based on her travels and interviews. Her autobiography, *Rebel Daughter*, was published in 1996. For Anderson, women are more 'focused and practical' than men. Her autobiography ends with this question: 'Isn't it time women stopped holding up half the sky and began making at least HALF the decisions right down here on earth?'   GHN

Anderson [née Mason], Ethel 1883–1958
Australian essayist, short-story writer and poet. She was born in Leamington, England, whilst her Australian parents were visiting Britain, and grew up on her grandfather's property in Picton, New South Wales. Educated initially at home by governesses, she later attended Sydney Church of England Girls' Grammar School. After marrying an officer in the British Army, she lived in India for a number of years and moved back to Australia when he took up a diplomatic post there in 1926.

She considered herself to be chiefly a poet and, at a time when Australia had 'not become acceptable to other English-speaking nations', fused the two cultures to which she belonged 'to perform for Australia, the service the Nature poets . . . have done for England'. In *Sunday at Yarralumla* (1947) she evokes English Sunday languor and Australian lushness, and in *Squatter's Luck* (1942, enlarged 1954) she celebrates both the people and the landscape of Australia. However, she is best remembered for her fiction and in particular for her arch but incisive discontinuous narrative, *At Parramatta* (1956). Set in the 1850s it comments on patriarchal power and exposes male foibles by drawing parallels with the seven deadly sins.   JSte

Anderson, Jessica 1916– Born in Queensland and brought up in Brisbane, Australian novelist Anderson has lived for much of her life in Sydney. After many years working in radio, her first novel, *An Ordinary Lunacy*, was published in 1963, followed by *The Last Man's Head* (1970), a foray into DETECTIVE FICTION. *Tirra Lirra by the River* (1978) was the first of Anderson's novels to be published in Australia and is also her most famous and critically acclaimed work; it won the Miles Franklin Award and the Australian Natives' Association Literary Award. *The Impersonators* (1980) also won the Miles Franklin Award and the NSW Premier's Award. Her more recent novels are *Taking Shelter* (1989) and *One of the Wattle Birds* (1994).

Anderson's best-known novels – *The Commandant* (1975), *Tirra Lirra by the River* and *The Impersonators* – have been referred to as novels of expatriation, and all involve journeys between Australia and Europe. In *Tirra Lirra by the River*, in particular, the physical journey to London of the protagonist, Nora Porteous, is a metaphor for her personal and creative development. Anderson's vivid portrayal of location is most clear in her short-story collection *Stories from the Warm Zone and Sydney Stories* (1987). The first section of the collection, an autobiographical short-story cycle set in Queensland, is her most poignant evocation of her childhood home while the second section of the collection consists of three stories about Sydney – 'the only place', Nora says in *Tirra Lirra*, 'where I ever felt at home'.   SS

Anderson, Margaret (Carolyn) 1886–1973 As editor from 1914 to 1929 of the American avant-garde literary magazine, *The Little Review*, Anderson was one of the 'movers and shakers' who opened a window for modern art. Born in Indianapolis, and raised in Columbus, Indiana, Anderson succinctly remarked 'I liked my home and disliked my family.' She escaped as soon as she could to Chicago and founded *The Little Review* on a shoestring. She fended off a takeover bid from AMY (LAWRENCE) LOWELL, and sought support from well-heeled society matrons. She was joined by Jane Heap as assistant editor in 1916 ('You're the buzz and I'm the sting', Heap said), and moved the magazine to New York the following year. She published Pound, and through him came to be a vehicle for the writers (Eliot, Lewis, Joyce) he was assembling under the banner of modernism. 'One can trust M.C.A.', Pound wrote of Anderson, 'to die on the bayonets, but not bring up the water and hard tack.' The moment of bayonets came in 1918 when she began to publish Joyce's *Ulysses*. Anderson was prosecuted in 1920 and fined $100 for publishing an obscenity. The *New York Times* did not defend her. The magazine was moved to Paris in 1923, where Anderson became a disciple of the mystic Gurdjieff. She published two volumes of autobiography, *My Thirty Years' War* (1930) and *The Fiery Fountains* (1953), and edited *The Little Review Anthology* (1953).   EH

Anderson-Dargatz, Gail 1963– Canadian short-story writer and novelist who grew up on a farm in central British Columbia. She worked as a reporter for the local newspaper, then studied Creative Writing at the University of Victoria where she was instructed by the Canadian novelist Jack Hodgins.

The short fiction collected in *The Miss Hereford Stories* (1994) barely hints at the suspense contained in the novel *The Cure for Death by Lightning* (1996), a supernatural story set in central British Columbia in 1941. Its 15-year-old heroine, Beth Weeks, comes of age into a rural culture contested by two spiritual spheres: the stifling Protestant mores that dominate the local town and the First Nations cosmology evident on the nearby reserve. The native elder and storyteller Bertha Moses provides an empowering model for Beth by lending a decidedly feminist interpretation to the stalking of the community by Coyote, the native trickster figure. Beth's awakening takes place against the backdrop of World War II, making *The Cure for Death by Lightning* a story about women resisting the intertwined patriarchal projects of war and colonization. The narrative is haunted by the spectre of incest, with the father's actions synecdochic for the abuses of patriarchy. Magic realist influences of Hodgins, Isabelle Allende, and especially Laura Esquivel are prominent. The novel has been translated into several languages and has become an international bestseller. Anderson-Dargatz's next novel, *A Recipe for Bees* (1998), tells of a day in the life of its aged protagonist, Augusta, who lives with her husband Karl in an apartment on Vancouver Island. Augusta makes sense of their long marriage by narratively revisiting its 1940s beginning on an isolated sheep ranch in the interior of British Columbia, her need for companionship beyond the marriage, her affair with another man in the nearby town, and the ensuing decades during which she and Karl raised the daughter fathered by the lover. In the 1960s Augusta had come to terms with herself, her husband and her difficult daughter by taking up bee-keeping, just as her mother had done a generation earlier. By the end of the current recounting of her life's story Augusta is able to forgive Karl 'his inadequacies, just as he had forgiven hers so many times in the past'. While there is no suggestion that Augusta's death is imminent, by telling the story she has put her affairs in order.

After several years dairy farming near Parksville on Vancouver Island, in 1997 Anderson-Dargatz and husband Floyd bought a 160-acre farm near Millet, Alberta, with the proceeds from *The Cure for Death by Lightning*.   JBM

Angelou, Maya [Marguerite Annie Johnson]

1928– African-American autobiographer and poet whose work gives testimony to the power of African-Americans to endure, and whose life gives testimony to the expression of immense and varied talent. Her best-known works are the five volumes of her autobiography which describes a life notable for its many traumas. The first and most famous volume, *I Know Why the Caged Bird Sings* (1970), describes her experiences as a victim of child rape and the murder of the rapist by her uncles, which turned her mute for five years. The later volumes of her autobiography record her struggle to overcome involvement in violence, drugs and prostitution to become a mother, poet, civil

rights activist, dancer, actor, singer, producer, composer and journalist.

Angelou left Arkansas for San Francisco during adolescence and then moved to Brooklyn where she met PAULE MARSHALL and James Baldwin. In the 1960s she went to Africa and lived in Ghana and Egypt where she was the editor of the *Arab Observer*. She is historically notable as in 1993 she became the first woman and the first African-American to read her poetry, at the request of President Clinton, at a Presidential Inauguration. She has been nominated for the Pulitzer Prize for Poetry, but despite the critical praise for *Just Give Me a Cool Drink of Water 'for I Die* (1971) and *And Still I Rise* (1978), has never won it. The title poem of *And Still I Rise* encompasses Angelou's commitment to life and the resistance of oppression:

> Bringing the gifts that my ancestors gave,
> I am the dream and the hope of the slave.
> I rise.

Her acting and stage career includes being a dancer in the 1950s European tour of *Porgy and Bess* and a role in the television series *Roots*. She has written a television series called *Black, Blues, Black* (1968) and film scripts: *Georgia Georgia* (1971) and *Sister Sister* (1979). She has also written a stage play *Moon on a Rainbow Shawl* (1988). Her seventieth birthday was marked by the publication of her collected poems, *Even the Stars Look Lonesome* (1998).   MAB

Anger, Jane fl.1589 Proto-feminist polemical writer.

While her name need not be pseudonymous, it conveniently denotes her stance and tone. Her pamphlet, *Jane Anger her Protection for Women* (1589), was probably written in response to the misogynist *Book: his Surfeit in Love* (c.1588), and thus participates in a small-scale 'woman controversy', using her 'anger' as a literary motif. Anger argues that the bad women of history are counterbalanced by bad men, and blames men for women's wilfulness. She is scathing on the subject of male infidelity, and condemns men as seducers who 'rob women of their honour undeservedly': 'ravenous hawks . . . who devour us'. She notes that English law allots 'terrible laws' to punish sexual offenders, but that these 'will not serve to restrain men'. Anger defends women's speech, and argues that written as well as spoken male language poses a threat to women, as men make 'their pens the executioners of their barbarous manners'.   JC

Anne of Green Gables (1908) L. M. MONTGOMERY's

first and strongest novel describes a Prince Edward Island orphan adopted by Matthew and Marilla Cuthbert, an ageing brother and sister seeking a boy to help with their chores. They are mistakenly given a girl whose vivid imagination enriches their lives and proves more valuable than practical help. There is a cost, however, for Matthew's death is caused partly by overwork. Once again, Anne's sterling qualities provide compensation and she abandons her career plans in order to stay home with Marilla. The appeal of Montgomery's freckled, red-haired character has never diminished. She has been the subject of numerous films, plays and musicals. The house described in the novel has become a literary shrine drawing tourists from all over the world. Although the book would normally fall into the young adult category, its appeal includes all ages and levels of sophistication. Literary critics treat it seriously as a *Künstlerroman*. Anne's relationship with her kindred spirit, Diane Barry, is often invoked in books dealing with female friendship, notably in MARGARET ATWOOD's *Cat's Eye*.   JG

Annie John (1983) JAMAICA KINCAID's short novel (recounted in the first person but not explicitly autobiographical) deals with an imaginative young girl growing up in Antigua. Annie John's intellectual gifts and her obsession with death set her apart from her social surroundings, and when her passionate, richly sensuous relationships with her mother and her schoolfriends gradually wear off she is left feeling isolated and disillusioned. Despite her youth, she is a diligent observer of the people she is close to and a shrewd judge of their motives, yet her compassion for them (especially for her father and for her less gifted peers) usually outweighs her scorn for their limitations. The exception to this rule is her mother, whose dazzling beauty and apparent hypocrisy she finds difficult to overlook or forgive (though Kincaid drops hints that forgiveness will come with emotional and physical maturity). When Annie John leaves Antigua for England at the end of the book, the reader registers both her satisfaction at having outgrown her place of origin and her wariness of the 'emptying out' that this displacement may produce.   BWB

Anthony, Susan Brownell 1820–1906 American reformer, editor. Raised in a Quaker household committed to the ideas of equality and service, Susan was educated in her father's mill school and began teaching in 1839. Moving to her family home in Rochester, New York, in 1849, she devoted herself to social work and reform. Her first cause, temperance, led her directly to women's rights when she was denied permission, on the basis of her gender, to speak at a temperance society meeting. In 1851, she met ELIZABETH CADY STANTON, and they formed a working friendship that would be the driving force behind the feminist anti-slavery movement and the campaign for women's right to vote. They fought fiercely for passage of the Thirteenth Amendment (1865), and thereafter turned their energies toward

women's suffrage. From 1868 to 1870, they published the *Revolution*, a journal focusing on women's rights, improved working conditions and equal marriage laws, and whose motto was 'Men, their rights, and nothing more; women, their rights, and nothing less'. In 1869, she and Stanton founded the National Woman Suffrage Association. In 1872, Anthony was arrested for trying to vote. While awaiting her trial, she toured central New York arguing that the Fifteenth Amendment granted women the right to vote because it guaranteed the rights of 'citizens'. 'We appeal to women everywhere', she said, 'to exercise their too long neglected "citizen's right to vote".' From 1881 to 1886, she and Stanton, together with Matilda Joslyn Cage, wrote the first three volumes of *History of Woman Suffrage*. She was president of the National American Woman Suffrage Association from 1892 until 1900, but did not live to see women granted the vote.   SP

Antin, Mary (Grabau) 1881–1949 Antin's *The Promised Land* (1912) is the most widely read account by a woman of the American immigrant experience. Born in the *shtetl* of Plotzk in Russian Poland, Antin accompanied her parents when they emigrated to Boston in 1884. She attended Girls' Latin School, and Columbia University, marrying a professor there. Her first book, *From Plotzk to Boston* (1899), a description of family life in the Jewish Pale and of immigration, was written in Yiddish when Antin was 11. She was welcomed in Brahmin Boston as a child prodigy, 'a queer, thin little thing, . . . overdressed for the occasion and with dreadfully frizzed hair'. Antin's is one of the very few accounts of immigration actually written by a child. Her principal work, *The Promised Land*, first serialized in the *Atlantic Monthly*, retold her family's story, in greater detail, and celebrated America as offering salvation to her people. It was followed in 1914 by *They Who Knock at Our Gates: A Complete Gospel of Immigration*. After several years as a popular lecturer and advocate of patriotism and assimilation during World War I, she suffered a nervous breakdown, withdrew from the lecture circuit, and did not write again.   EH

Anzaldúa, Gloria 1942– Self-styled 'Latina-Chicana dyke feminist writer', Anzaldua is an important feminist theorist of the late 20th century. *This Bridge Called My Back: Radical Writings by Women of Color* (1981), co-edited with CHERRIE MORAGA, received the Before Columbus Foundation's American Book Award and consolidated the importance of women of colour in the feminist movement. The anthology was followed by *BORDERLANDS/LA FRONTERA* (1987), an equally influential text that blends history and folklore, personal reflection and essay, prose and poetry, and several different languages and dialects in an effort to negotiate the 'borderlands' that define, trouble, and finally empower identity. In 1990, Anzaldua edited *Making Face, Making Soul / Haciendo Caras: Creative and Critical Perspectives by Women of Color*. In the tradition of *This Bridge Called My Back*, this second anthology brings together women from a wide variety of backgrounds in the common project of rejecting culturally prescribed masks and establishing new voices. More recently, Anzaldua has come to focus more specifically on issues of sexuality, receiving the Sappho Award of Distinction in 1992 and editing an issue of *Signs: Journal of Women in Culture and Society* entitled 'Theorizing Lesbian Experience' in 1993. She is also the author of two bilingual CHILDREN'S BOOKS: *Friends from the Other Side/Amigos Del Otro Lado* (1993), which tells the story of a friendship between a Mexican-American girl and a Mexican boy, and *Prietita and the Ghost Woman / Prietita y La Llorona* (1996), which rewrites the story of La Llorona.   SMSt

Appachana, Anjana 1958– Indian short-story writer and novelist whose first volume of short fiction, *Incantations and Other Stories* (1991), marked her out as a distinctly new voice among Indian fiction writers in English. She received her schooling in Gwalior, and graduated in English from Lady Shri Ram College, New Delhi. After an MA in Sociology from Jawaharlal Nehru University she worked in Delhi for five years before going to Pennsylvania State University to do an MFA. She describes herself as 'belonging to India but (now) living in Tempe, Arizona' with her husband and daughter, Malavika.

Sympathy and satire co-exist in her writing, a matter-of-fact tone concealing the seething intensity. Stories from her first volume have been anthologized many times, the latest inclusion being in *The Vintage Book of Indian Writing* (1997), edited by Salman Rushdie and Elizabeth West. Her second and major work is a 516 page novel, *Listening Now* (1998), in which seven overlapping narratives of seemingly ordinary women in Delhi and Bangalore trace an intricate design, dark and smouldering with untold secrets and submerged guilt. She writes in a ruthlessly REALISTIC mode woven with strands of irony and humour.   MMu

Archer, Robyn 1948– Australian Robyn Archer, born in Adelaide, has distinguished herself as a stage performer as well as a writer, in a varied career. Most of what she has written she has also performed, with a consistent emphasis on sexual politics. In common with many other Australian feminists, Robyn Archer is associated with left-wing politics and sympathy for the working class. Her satirical examinations of patriarchy's treatment of women and her sympathetic portrayals of female heroism and victimhood have been conveyed in shows such as the 1979 *A Star is Torn*, where her powerful and adaptable singing voice enabled her to interpret and celebrate earlier female singers such as Bessie Smith, Judy Holliday and Janis Joplin. As a singer she has specialized in the work of Kurt Weill and Bertholt Brecht. She has repeatedly exploited cabaret as a political tool: her 1990 *Cafe Fledermaus* was one example, as was her earlier *The Pack of Women* (1981). Archer continues to write and perform, but has also developed a career as an arts administrator. She was director of the National Festival of Australian Theatre (Canberra) from 1993 to 1996, and 1988-2000 director of the prestigious Adelaide Festival. She has written two plays: *Il Magnifico*, about Lorenzo de Medici, and *The Conquest of Carmen Miranda*; a CHILDREN'S BOOK, *Mrs Bottle Burps* (1983); and three books based on her most popular cabaret shows. Robyn Archer has a broad range of talents and has been as successful as a theatre director, singer, actor and arts administrator as she has as a writer for the theatre.   HTh

Archibald, Edith Jessie 1854–1936 Canadian feminist, biographer and novelist. She was born in St John's, Newfoundland, attended private schools in London and New York City, and married a distant cousin who owned a mine and became president of the Bank of Nova Scotia in Halifax. During the 1890s she was active in the non-confrontational suffrage movement and served as president of the Women's Christian Temperance Union (1892–6) and the Halifax Local Council of Women (1896–1906). During World War I, she worked with the Red Cross. In 1917 she led a suffrage delegation to the legislature. She wrote fiction for periodicals and published a life of her father, Sir Edward Mortimer Archibald, a diplomat (1924). Her play *The Token*, staged in Halifax in 1927 and later rewritten as a novel (1930), follows several romantic couples through contrasting settings – a Cape Breton mining community, French smugglers' islands, St John's and Boston.   JSG

Arendt, Hannah 1906–75 German-Jewish philosopher and political scientist. Arendt went to Marburg to study philosophy and at the age of 18 became the lover of her teacher, Martin Heidegger (then 35, already married and writing his master work, *Being and Time*), whom she was later to refer to as 'the secret king of (modern) thought'. Later she left for Heidelberg to study with Karl Jaspers, under whose supervision she wrote her doctoral dissertation on Saint Augustine's concept of love. It reveals her other great influence: Rahel Varnhagen, a German-Jewish BLUESTOCKING who maintained a celebrated salon in Berlin at a time (1790–1806) when intellectual Jews mixed with non-Jewish writers and intellectuals. Arendt, like Varnhagen, was obsessed with modern Jews' 'world-lessness' due to their self-exile from the gilded ghetto of the Jewish middle class and the uncertainty of their place in Gentile society.

With Hitler's rise to power, Arendt emigrated to

Paris, in 1933, and was immersed in Jewish relief activities until 1941, when she fled to America, where she lived (in New York) for the rest of her life. *The Origins of Totalitarianism* (1951) made her famous, and controversial, because she argued that Stalinist Russia and Nazi Germany were functionally the same. She was resented by the left for the ease with which her arguments were co-opted to bolster the Western position in the Cold War. In her most important completed theoretical work, *The Human Condition* (1958), she adapted some of Heidegger's key ideas. She sought consistently to dignify the idea of political life as against the contempt for the worldly world of most philosophers, Heidegger included.

Eichmann in Jerusalem: A Report on the Banality of Evil (1963) is her best-known book. It began as a series of *New Yorker* articles on the trial of Adolf Eichmann, the Nazi bureaucrat in charge of the deportation of Jews to the concentration camps. She brought down on herself the rage of old friends and of the organized Jewish community in America. She argued that, far from being monstrous according to our conventional romantic and religious ideas of evil, Eichmann represented a new kind of monstrosity: normal, ordinary, at worst ludicrous and incapable of thought. She said that many fewer Jews would have gone to their deaths had the Jewish community's leaders not provided the enemy with so much information and aid. During her last decade she surprised those who had thought of her as basically conservative by her sympathetic essays on the student movement against the war in Vietnam. She wrote at length about the crisis of authority, in this respect as in others deeply influencing the left-wing German social philosopher Jurgen Habermas.

Although she came late to the English language, she proved to be a gifted writer in the tradition of Jewish ironists like Heinrich Heine. She had many literary friends, including MARY MCCARTHY, W.H. Auden, and Robert Lowell. MLK

'Ariadne' fl.1696 Playwright about whom nothing is known, except that she wrote the comedy, *She Ventures and He Wins*. Staged at Lincoln's Inn Fields in September 1695, it was published a year later as the work of 'a Young Lady'. The play employs a number of contemporary themes and motifs, including a heroine disguised in boy's clothes, the testing of her husband-to-be, and, in the sub-plot, a bed-trick and the gulling of a country booby. There are several similarities with APHRA BEHN's plays, including THE LUCKY CHANCE (1686), and 'Ariadne' claims in her Prologue to have been inspired by both Behn and KATHERINE PHILIPS. Although the anonymous writer suggests that a favourable reception for her first play may make her 'ambitious enough to be known', no other play has been attributed to her, although it is possible that she wrote the uncredited *The Unnatural Mother*, which appeared in 1697. RDM

Ariel (1965) SYLVIA PLATH's second (and posthumous) volume of poetry. Edited and rearranged by Ted Hughes, and containing the poems Plath wrote in the period leading up to her suicide in 1963, *Ariel* caused a literary sensation. It includes her most notorious works, such as 'Daddy', 'Lady Lazarus', the Bee Sequence and 'Edge'. The most reductive and vulturous readings treat it as little more than an exceptionally eloquent suicide note. However, closer attention discovers that it is witty as well as grim, invigorating as well as chilling, and stylish as well as violent.

Its range is panoramic. It is concerned with the nature of power at work in history and in language – and the ways in which it both shapes and jeopardizes our personal identities and relationships. Particularly interesting to feminists is the way in which the domestic realm – sanctified in the fifties as the place where women could find their ultimate fulfilment – is represented as a kind of GOTHIC nightmare. The speaker of 'Stings' protests:

> I am no drudge
> Though for years I have eaten dust
> And dried plates with my dense hair.
> And seen my strangeness evaporate,
> Blue dew from dangerous skin

These are challenging poems, semantically, emotionally and politically. The language is active and aggressive, dense and intense, dirty and difficult. As Plath herself wrote, 'I really don't think poems should be all that chaste'. AFT

Armour, Rebecca Agatha (Thompson) 1845–91 Canadian novelist, educator and historian. She was born in Fredericton, New Brunswick, the oldest of four daughters of Irish immigrants. Her father was a grocer. Educated at teachers' college, she taught locally from 1864 to 1873, then in southern New Brunswick, where she was honoured as one of the best female teachers. She married John G. Thompson, a carriage maker, in 1885. In 1880 she published a series of sketches, 'Landmarks of Old Fredericton,' in the Fredericton *Capital*. The St John *Telegraph* serialized her HISTORICAL NOVELS (e.g. *Lady Rosamond's Secret*, 1878; *Sylvia Leigh*, 1880; and *Marguerite Verne: or, Scenes from Canadian Life*, 1886), in which SENSATIONAL plots unfold against a backdrop of local colour and regional pride. Her fiction remains of interest for its rich depiction of New Brunswick social life during the 19th century. JSG

Armstrong, Jeannette 1948– Okanagan Native Canadian poet, novelist and educationalist, concerned with the contemporary revision and restoration of

Native Canadian tradition. Brought up on Penticton Indian Reserve, British Columbia, she was educated at Okanagan College. Her writing provides a critique, from the perspective of Native Canadian traditional teachings, of the self-destructiveness and violence in native communities and is influenced by modern poetical techniques and narrative devices. Her first two published books are CHILDREN's fiction, *Enwhisteekwa Walk in Water* (1982) and *Neekna and Chemai* (1984). She has since become best known for her novel *Slash* (1985 and revised 1988) which provides a fictionalized account of the Native American cultural and political movement of the 1970s and 1980s from the perspective of a young Native man. Her first book of poetry, *Breath Tracks*, was published in 1991 and explores issues of traditional teachings in the contemporary context, and the boundaries between personal, cultural and representational identities. In 1993 she edited a critical anthology, *Looking at the Words of Our People: An Anthology of First Nation Literary Criticism*. As the director of En'owkin Native Education Centre (associated with the University of Victoria, British Columbia) she inaugurated the only creative writing course for native peoples in Canada.   MAB

Aron, Geraldine 1948– Prolific Irish playwright and lyricist of international reputation whose work has been performed in many languages. She was born in Galway and educated there and in London. She has lived in Zambia, Zimbabwe and South Africa, and, since 1989, in Britain. Her first play, *Bar and Ger*, opened at the Space Theatre in Cape Town in 1975, and has since been performed in fourteen languages; it was filmed in 1985. *Zombie* (1978) is a rock opera which also premiered at the Space. She has developed a special relationship with Druid Theatre Company in Galway, where many of her plays have been produced, including *Bar and Ger*, *The Stanley Parkers*, *A Galway Girl* (1979) and *The Donahue Sisters* (1990). *Same Old Moon* (1985) is a funny and bitter coming-of-age story with a matriarchal twist. She has written song lyrics and a number of screenplays, as well as adapting several of her plays for broadcast by the BBC and the South African Broadcasting Corporation.   CL

Arranged Marriage (1995) CHITRA BENERJEE DIVAKARUNI's collection of short stories won the 1996 American Book Award. As the title suggests, the pivot around which many of the stories revolve is the cherished Indian institution of arranged marriage and how the changing times affect it. All the stories start *in medias res*, making the reader plunge into long-enwoven lives which have now reached a climax. The climax often consists in the acknowledgement of a crisis: women who are caught between two worlds, the traditional Indian life – vivid and comforting – left

behind, and the more ruthless American life offering possibilities and risks.

The characters shift between roles as dutiful obedient wives and daughters and as career-orientated, emancipated women. Divakaruni conveys the emotional turmoil of her heroines and renders poignantly the kaleidoscopic reality of migrant lives. In this wide array of stories the writer does not offer ready-made solutions. Drinking to our 'precious, imperfect lives' is the book's closing line. No real catharsis is found but only adjustments and compromises.   SPo

Arrowsmith, Pat 1930– British poet, novelist and anti-war activist. She was the organizing secretary for the first Aldermaston March for Nuclear Disarmament in 1958 and went to prison ten times between 1956 and 1977 for non-violent protests. From 1977 she worked for Amnesty International. Her autobiographical memoir, *I Should Have Been a Hornby Train* (1995), reflects all of this, along with her feminism and her lesbianism, as do her various collections of terse, passionate poems, notably *Thin Ice* (1984). Her novels are similarly straightforward and committed; *Jericho* (1965) dealt with a group of activists in a peaceful picket of a nuclear weapons establishment and their eventual success – it contains intelligent observation of activist sub-cultures and the internal pressures of small groups. *The Prisoner* (1982) is a portrait of a selfish middle-class woman reduced to petulance by being bed-ridden; it is not only through direct preaching, but also through a capacity for unlikely sympathies, that Arrowsmith's work reflects her politics.   RK

Ascham [née Howe], Margaret fl.1535–90/2 Wife of the educationalist Roger Ascham. He married Margaret, twenty years his junior, in 1554; they had three sons. After her husband's death in 1568, Margaret oversaw the publication of his educational treatise *The Schoolmaster* (1570), which included praise of the academic accomplishments of women like ELIZABETH I and LADY JANE GREY. Margaret added a prefatory epistle to Sir William Cecil, Elizabeth I's chief minister, in which she asserted the public importance of scholarship in general and of her husband's work in particular. Just as Cecil has used his own learning 'to the good service of the Queen's Majesty and your country', so her husband's work will contribute 'to the common weal': 'Good I trust it shall do'. Striking a more personal note, she mentions that Ascham has left not only herself as his widow but also 'a great sort of orphans', and she hopes for Cecil's continued beneficence to 'me and my poor children'.   HH

Ashbridge, Elizabeth Sampson Sullivan 1713–55 Quaker minister and autobiographer. Born in England to Anglican parents, she eloped at the age of

THE FIRST PAGE OF THE ORIGINAL MANUSCRIPT

Daisy Ashford: the first page of the original manuscript of *The Young Visiters*, 1919.

look at COLONIAL life from the disenfranchized perspective of a woman who survived indenture and domestic abuse on the road to spiritual fulfilment. VC

Ashford, 'Daisy' [Margaret Mary Julia] 1881–1972 This English child-author first became known to the reading public with her story *The Young Visiters or Mr Salteenas Plan*. Written in 1890 when Ashford was 9, it remained unpublished until 1919, when it was printed complete with the original idiosyncratic spelling. An immediate success, it remains her best-known work. Dramatized in 1920, it was made into a musical in 1968 and into a film in 1984. A comedy of manners in every sense of the term, *The Young Visiters* centres on Mr Salteena – who is 'not quite a gentleman but you would hardly notice' – and his plan to become 'the real thing'. This amusing tale concludes with details of the matrimonial circumstances of all the major characters – Mr Salteena himself 'found relief in prayer' whilst his friend the Earl 'decided to offer [his marriage] up as a Mortification'.

However, Ashford's writing career extended from the age of 7 through to the age of 15, her earliest efforts being dictated to her father who wrote them down verbatim. A number of these other pieces were lost but those that survived were published in *Daisy Ashford: Her Book* (1920). EMH

Ashton, Helen (Mrs Arthur Jordan) 1891–1959 English middlebrow novelist and daughter of a successful barrister, Ashton nursed during World War I and later qualified as a doctor. But she then abandoned her medical career on marriage in 1927 and turned to fiction. She published some twenty-two novels, several with a medical setting. She drew on her own experiences nursing in France in *A Background for Caroline* (1928), a delicately traced account of a girl whose life is blighted by diffidence and timidity. With her fourth novel, *Dr Serocold* (1930), she achieved success. Thereafter books appeared almost annually, the majority novels of manners, very much of their period, elegantly written and with an eye for detail that gives them value as conversation pictures of their author's time. She also wrote fictionalized biographies of William and DOROTHY WORDSWORTH (1938), Henry Vaughan (1939), JANE AUSTEN (1949) and LETITIA LANDON (1951), skilfully weaving into her narrative her subjects' own published words and ideas. Of her hospital novels, *Yeoman's Hospital* (1944) was filmed in 1951 as *White Corridors*. CT

Ashton-Warner [née Warner], Sylvia (Henderson) 1908–84 Charismatic personality, polemical writer and teacher, who made her name through several semi-autobiographical novels about her work with Maori children in backblocks New

14 but was almost immediately widowed and spent the next five years in Ireland, where she began her search for spiritual fulfilment. She emigrated to the Colonies as an indentured servant and after three years of suffering at the hands of a cruel master married a schoolteacher named Sullivan. Following her exposure to the tenets of Quakerism, Ashbridge converted and, against her husband's wishes, joined the Friends. Sullivan objected to the Quaker tradition of female ministry, but, despite his emotional and physical abuse, frequently occasioned by drunkenness, Ashbridge persevered in her devotion, and Sullivan expressed Quaker convictions before he died. She later married Quaker Aaron Ashbridge, but in 1753 travelled to Ireland to preach, where she died. Her autobiography, *Some Account of the Fore Part of the Life of Elizabeth Ashbridge, . . . Written by her own Hand Many Years Ago* (1774), resembles contemporary Quaker conversion records, but offers in addition a unique

Zealand schools. Always controversial, Ashton-Warner had battles with school inspectors and the Department of Education about her innovative methods of teaching children to read. However, following publication of *Spinster* (1958), and *Teacher* (1963), her methods found acceptance overseas: in the 1970s she held workshops in America, gaining followers who acclaimed her as a seminal thinker. Ashton-Warner's literary reputation stems from her recognition that unconscious forces drive the artist: her temperamental, hypersensitive heroines, as in *Myself* (1967) and *Three* (1971), are capable of grand passions and creative feats. It was her autobiography, however, *I PASSED THIS WAY* (1979), which brought her long-awaited recognition in New Zealand, where she had felt 'a prophet without honour'. Like JANET FRAME's use of writing to extend life's imaginative possibilities, Ashton-Warner's problematic conflations of autobiography and fiction can often be attributed to heightened powers of invention. Lynley Hood's *Sylvia! The Biography of Sylvia Ashton Warner* (1988) effectively exposes many of the inconsistencies that contributed to her personal mystique, but for many she continues to symbolise the voice of an age: the prophetic determination to be fully creative.

JMW

Askew, Anne *c*.1521–46 English Protestant martyr, who left a dynamic account of her interrogation and imprisonment for heresy by Henry VIII's bishops and councillors. After she was burned at the stake for refusing to recant her reformist faith, the Protestant propagandist John Bale published her narrative in 1546 and 1547 as *The First*, and *The Latter Examinations of Anne Askew*. Her story immediately became popular, and it is estimated that during Edward VI's reign 3,500 copies of Askew's examinations were in circulation.

The *Examinations* represent one of the earliest forms of autobiography in English. Askew boldly narrates a story of herself at a time when the acceptable form of writing for women was translations. She creates a devout and courageous protagonist – Anne – who gives learned responses to her interrogators and refuses to be manipulated by their questions. In one case Anne corrects the logic of her interrogator, demonstrating the ill-conception of his analogy. In another, ironically drawing upon scripture used by contemporaries to circumscribe the role of women, she explains she has no answer for the priest because 'Solomon sayth that a woman of few words is a gift of God'. When learning and wit fail to defend her and the examiners subject her to torture by the rack, Anne heroically endures the pain, commenting wryly, 'I lay still and would not cry'. Even under physical duress she withstands temptations to deny her reformist beliefs and to betray her women friends at court.

GG-R

Asquith [née Charteris], Cynthia Mary Evelyn 1887–1960 English diarist, BIOGRAPHER, writer and compiler of fiction. Daughter of a titled aristocrat. Asquith was a beauty painted by McEvoy, Sargent and Augustus John. After a privileged youth, in 1910 she married Herbert Asquith, a barrister and second son of Prime Minister Herbert Asquith, and bore him three sons. Her posthumously published extensive 1915–18 DIARY reveals not only her active social life and war work but also how her brothers' war deaths and the agonizing discovery of autism in her eldest son, John (b.1911), clouded her life. After the war, her husband having been incapacitated by his military service, she became the family's support. Besides CHILDREN'S BOOKS, she wrote columns in *The Times*, compiled ghost-story collections such as *The Ghost Book* (1926) and *When Churchyards Yawn* (1931) – sometimes including her own stories pseudonymously – and published the novel *Spring House* (1937). Also J.M. Barrie's private secretary for twenty years, she wrote his biography, *Portrait of J.M. Barrie* (1954), as well as her own memoirs, *Haply I Remember* (1950) and *Remember and Be Glad* (1952), and a life of Sonja Tolstoy (1960).

HB

Assignation, The (1988) JOYCE CAROL OATES calls the forty-four very short stories in this collection 'miniature narratives'. In them, minimalism is employed (paradoxically) in rich and varied ways, from the use of blank space and sparse punctuation to a focus on apparent non-events and ordinary lives. Although not explicitly linked, the stories contain recurrent themes, including the psychological effects of illness, especially terminal; adolescent sexual initiation; chance encounters with strangers or past acquaintances; and giving lifts in cars. Like so many Oates creations, many of these characters are desperate and inarticulate; all are isolated. These are not the only very brief stories by Oates; others are collected in *Where Is Here?* (1992), and both volumes contain stories previously published in journals as well as new material. The minimalist form is well suited to Oates's persistent desire to represent the importance of the everyday: the stories' pared-down, breathless quality forces the reader to share the characters' bewilderment and to look for meaning in the supposedly minor or marginalized.

KSi

Astell, Mary 1666–1731 British religious and political controversialist, a Tory wit and proto-feminist. The Astells were Newcastle-on-Tyne gentry, 'Hostmen' in the coal trade who were losing their ancient monopoly over a booming business. Hostmen were royalists and religious conservatives – convictions Mary inherited. She was tutored by her uncle, who had been at university in the heyday of Cambridge Platonists More and Cudworth, and it was as a Stuart sympathizer,

High Anglican and Platonist that Astell made her mark after moving to London in 1688.

She survived with help from (among others) the Archbishop of Canterbury; in 1692 she settled to celibate life in Chelsea, then almost a country town. She had written poetry, but found her vocation in prose: a dialogue in letters with John Norris, the last Cambridge Platonist holding out against Cartesian rationalism and empiricism. This high-minded correspondence was published in 1695. Meanwhile she published anonymously Part I of *A SERIOUS PROPOSAL TO THE LADIES* (1694, Part II 1697) urging the establishment of Protestant convents, communities of gentlewomen offering space for the life of the spirit. Though no seminary was founded, Astell was a mentor to other women intellectuals, from ELIZABETH ELSTOB to LADY MARY WORTLEY MONTAGU. Her arguments were so wittily, austerely conservative that she contrived to pamphleteer without losing caste. *Some Reflections on Marriage* (1700) again challenges 'masculine empire' – 'though the order of the world requires an *outward* respect and obedience . . . yet the mind is free'. She is a practised ironist: 'All famous arts have their origin from men, even from the invention of guns, to the mystery of good eating.' Fiercely articulate heroines in novels by Defoe (*Roxana*, 1724) and Richardson (*Clarissa*, 1747–8) echo Astell's arguments against marriage. After the early 1700s pamphlet wars, Astell fell silent, though she was instrumental in founding the girls' charity school in Chelsea, which taught literacy and practical skills. She died of cancer at 65.   LS

Astley, Thea

Astley, Thea 1925– One of Australia's foremost writers and one of the first women writers there to be published to critical acclaim. Born in Brisbane, Astley was educated at the University of Brisbane and has since lived in Queensland, Sydney and, more recently, rural New South Wales. Astley's first novel, *Girl with a Monkey*, was published in 1958 and her most recent novel, *The Multiple Effects of Rainshadow*, in 1996. In the intervening years she has written ten other novels, a short-story collection (*HUNTING THE WILD PINEAPPLE*, 1979), a short-story cycle (*It's Raining in Mango*, 1987) and two novellas published together as *Vanishing Points* (1993), almost all of which – with the exception of *A Boat Load of Home Folk* (1968) and *BEACHMASTERS* (1985) – are set in rural Australia, and, most commonly, Queensland. Astley's mythical Queensland towns such as Allbut, from *An Item from the Late News* (1982), and Mango, the location of her short-story collection and cycle, are 'second-rate Eden[s]', the goals of escapees and losers and also sites of danger for those on the fringes of society.

Astley is known for her powerful, almost baroque language. She forces her words to capture the wild drama of the landscape of northern Queensland, and the brutal cultural climate which she perceives in rural Australia, and particularly the north. Her overblown language – 'the garden and the barbaric leafy shape and sheen with its succulent pulpy cannibal gobbling of heat and moisture' (*Hunting the Wild Pineapple*) – is matched by her acerbic, cynical humour, directed particularly at the hypocrisy of the Catholic Church and, increasingly, at the violent male world of rural Australia. In Astley's earlier writing she adopted male personae because she believed that it was the only way to validate her writing within a culture 'that believed that women had no brains'. Her later works have seen her write from a more distinctly female and feminist point of view: 'I come from a long line of men. This country tells me this . . . Well, women enter into it, but peripherally' (*An Item from the Late News*).

Thea Astley has won the Miles Franklin Award for *The Well Dressed Explorer* (1962), *The Slow Natives* (1965) and *The Acolyte* (1972). She won the Patrick White Award in 1989.   SS

Aston, Constance [Constantia], later Fowler

Aston, Constance [Constantia], later Fowler c.1617–1660s Youngest daughter of Sir Walter Aston of Tixall, Staffordshire, and sister to poet GERTRUDE ASTON (THIMELBY), Constance is best known for the body of letters she wrote during the 1630s to her brother Herbert (himself an amateur poet) whilst he accompanied their father on an embassy to Madrid. Constance's letters, which largely concern themselves with arranging the relationship between, and eventual marriage in 1638 of, Herbert and KATHERINE THIMELBY (also an occasional poet), are particularly noteworthy for the lively and individual voice of Constance herself and the sense of drama she brings to the affair. Clearly deeply fond of her brother, she also develops an intimate female friendship with Katherine and seems to revel in the 'secrecy' of the relationship's early stages, arranging messengers and deploying coded references, sometimes in the form of exquisite ciphers and illustrations.

Constance married Walter Fowler (date unknown). Her commonplace book, in which she collated work by eminent authors of the day and by her family, survives in the Huntington Library in California. Certain poems in the book have been attributed to Constance herself but there is no firm evidence on this matter. It is as an epistolary writer of skill and vigour that she is most significant.   JS

Aston, Gertrude, later Thimelby

Aston, Gertrude, later Thimelby c.1615–70 17th-century poet, unpublished during her lifetime. Eldest daughter of Sir Walter Aston, head of a prominent family in Tixall, Staffordshire. This highly literary family acted as patrons to Michael Drayton, and Richard Fanshawe wrote several poems about them (in one, 'A Dreame', describing the two sisters Gertrude and CONSTANCE ASTON as 'Tixall swans'). Gertrude was the chief poet of the group, writing a body of texts on family subjects – such as births, weddings and deaths – between 1630 and the 1650s. She clearly had a sense of herself as a writer, although engaged in the tropes of modesty and humility common to women authors of the time: for example, in 'To the Lady Southcote on Her Wedding Day' she begins: 'If 'mongst the happy number this day crowd / To kis your hand, my humble pen's alowd'. Author of several extremely touching elegies. Married Henry Thimelby (whose family also engaged in literary pursuits) in the late 1630s / early 1640s. Henry died young, however, and in her grief, Gertrude, a converted Catholic like many of her close relatives, retired to the convent of her sister-in-law WINEFRID THIMELBY in Louvain, France, where she later died.   JS

Atherton [née Horn], Gertrude (Franklin) 1857– 1948 American novelist who wrote prolifically about a variety of themes, from women's opportunities in California to expatriation to classical history. Atherton came from a well-to-do San Francisco family, but because of her parents' divorce and social ostracism, she spent a rather neglected youth shuttling between boarding schools and the family ranch. She considered then-provincial California a 'hole'. At 17, she eloped with George Atherton (her mother's suitor), and, though they had two children, the marriage was an unhappy one. Her first novel, *The Randolphs of Redwoods*, was published in 1883. This was the first of many California-based ROMANCES, including *The Californians* (1898) and *The Splendid Idle Forties* (1902). After George's death in 1887, Atherton moved between New York and Europe, returning to California in 1931. She achieved her first critical success in turn-of-the-century London, and she remained a prominent novelist in America until the 1930s. *Black Oxen* (1923) was a bestseller dealing with New York's postwar obsessions with youth and sexuality; it became a successful movie. Although the 1906 San Francisco earthquake and fire destroyed Atherton's early papers, she wrote an autobiography, *Adventures of a Novelist*, in 1932. She was the first to be named 'California's most distinguished woman', in 1940.   KW

Atkinson, Diana ?– Canadian novelist who was born and raised in Vancouver, Canada, and studied in Montreal at the Concordia University. Her first novel, *Highways and Dancehalls* (1995), takes the form of the private journal of Tabitha, a stripper who travels across Canada in a journey of self-discovery. Exploring as it does the realities of female experience in the underbelly of Canadian society, *Highways and Dancehalls* is a brutal tale, confronting romanticized

on-the-road narratives with the horrors of female life under patriarchy. Yet it is simultaneously lyrical, humorous and triumphant, telling 'the story of what happened when a stripper, after picking up her G-string from the carpet, went back to her room and reached for a pen instead of a drink'. Atkinson can be placed within a growing tradition of contemporary Canadian women's writing which subverts, rewrites and ironically plays with notions of TRAVEL and that self-discovery associated with pilgrimage and interior/exterior journeying (see, for example, ARITHA VAN HERK, PAULETTE JILES and NICOLE BROSSARD).   CSt

Atkinson, Louisa 1834–72 Australian writer, whose *Gertrude the Emigrant*, published in Sydney in 1857, was the first novel published by an Australian-born white woman. It transforms elements of the conventional women's novel (the orphaned heroine who must find her own way in the world, the exemplar of Christian living, the search for a suitable husband) into a COLONIAL tale of life both in towns and on outback stations, featuring adventures associated with station life, such as bushfires and encounters with Aboriginal people. Although Atkinson's foremost talent was as a journalist and naturalist who illustrated her own work, her fiction constitutes a considerable achievement. Among her five later novels, *Tom Hellicar's Children* (repr. 1980) shows both the strengths and the weaknesses of her serialized fiction: economical, often striking, character sketches in unevenly paced and developed narratives. This tale of a widow and her children separated and oppressed by viciously venal executors draws on the experience of Louisa's own mother. It is the vehicle for some strong feminist statements on the combination of misogyny, social powerlessness and personal timidity that so often shaped women's lot.   SMS

Atwood, Margaret (Eleanor) 1939– Versatile and prolific Canadian poet, novelist, essayist and critic, and unquestionably one of that country's most important writers. Her upbringing, though happy, lacked any social structure – summer meant uprooting and following her entomologist father around the wilds of northern bush country – and the dual identity it fostered has informed both the imagery and ideas in her work. She discovered an emerging cadre of Canadian poets while studying for a BA at the University of Toronto and self-published her first collection of poems, *Double Persephone* (1961), in her final year. A stint at Harvard where she earned a master's degree and began, but did not complete, a Ph.D. on 'The English Metaphysical Romance', inadvertently helped to crystallize her thinking on the shape of Canadian culture. *The Circle Game* (1966), a collection of poems that introduced readers to what would become familiar

Watercolour by Margaret Atwood (Archive label: Atwoods as birds), 1974.

Atwoodian themes of escape, transformation and identity, won the prized Governor General's Award for Poetry and officially launched her career as a writer.

Over the next six years, she published four more books of poetry, including THE JOURNALS OF SUSANNA MOODIE (1970), and her first novel, THE EDIBLE WOMAN (1969). Atwood's work began to receive international critical attention in 1972, with the publication of her novel SURFACING and her influential critical analysis of Canada's literary tradition to date, SURVIVAL: A Thematic Guide to Canadian Literature. Both books played with many of the same themes, in particular the notion of a victim complex – 'not only the Canadian stance towards the world, but the usual female one'. Predictably, most Canadian reviewers saw Surfacing as a nationalist treatise while Americans treated the book as a feminist or ecological statement.

Her first best-selling novel, THE HANDMAID'S TALE (1985), diverged most dramatically from previous work, depicting the eerily plausible dystopia of Gilead, and containing a dedication to her ancestor who was hanged as a witch (but survived). An artist of many talents, Atwood has designed the covers of some of her own poetry collections and, in the seventies, published a cartoon strip which satirized the very subjects that characterized her early work – Canadian nationalism and sexual politics. When visual art figures in her work, most obviously in Cat's Eye (1988), it serves to reinforce her obvious belief in the inability of myths and systems to impose order on reality. Characters in novels like the romantic parody Lady Oracle (1976) and the POSTMODERN FAIRY TALE The Robber Bride (1993) show a secret desire – but ultimate inability – to find refuge in systems, patterns and accepted visions that

contradict the reality of a fractured and multiple experience of self. Atwood is a master of genre trickery – all her novels allude to, yet subvert, traditional genres. ALIAS GRACE (1996), a re-telling of history from the murderess's viewpoint, is one of a string of Atwood's novels employing that most compulsively readable – and confusingly deceptive – form of narrative, the fictionalized autobiographical mode. Her own autobiographical comments are often just as illusory; while her self-analyses are wry and sardonic, she is cynical about comparing fiction with life: 'As an artist, your first loyalty is to your art.' With each successive publication, Atwood moves farther away from earlier tendencies toward didactic REALISM and deeper into an increasingly self-conscious, mirror-laden POST-MODERNISM.   SLK

Aubin, Penelope 1679–1731 Influential British novelist who published a handful of poems in 1708 before plying the products of her wit on Grub Street and Drury Lane. Although the details of her biography are scant, she was of Catholic origin and married sometime before publishing her first novel in 1721: *The Strange Adventures of the Count de Vinevil and His Family*. Often categorized with JANE BARKER and MARY DAVYS as a writer of pious polemics, her seven novels in seven years suggest a savvy knowledge of the literary fashions of her day. She was a translator of French novels, and her own fiction reflects the influence of the emotionally heightened, formulaic French ROMANCE. To this style, she adds a Catholic morality, a focus on conjugal fidelity and an unabashed intent to warn her readers of the dangers of excessive love and lust. Strikingly, she preached these moral lessons from a public pulpit in the York Building near Charing Cross. Her only play, *The Humours of the Masqueraders* (1733), was staged unsuccessfully shortly before her death.   JRS

Auel, Jean 1936– American writer born in Chicago where she studied Business Administration. Her extremely popular sequence of novels about prehistoric hominid life starts with *The Clan of the Cave Bear* (1980), and continues with *The Valley of Horses* (1982) and *The Mammoth Hunters* (1985). She uses contemporary scientific ideas about the evolution of modern humans and the different capacities of Neanderthals both for their own sake and as gendered metaphors; her Cro-Magnon heroine is reared by gentle yet brutish Neanderthals, among whom she is something of a Cinderella figure, yet from whom she learns lessons about gender roles and ways of relating to the natural world which she will take with her when she moves into a broader human society. Auel is often sentimental and novelettish, and yet the real concern of her books, both with the popularizing of scientific ideas and with her views about feminism and the environment, gives them a force which transcends her limitations of technique.   RK

Aurora Leigh (1857) In this nine-book _Künstlerroman_ in blank verse, ELIZABETH BARRETT BROWNING developed her views on poetry and the position of women. The narrator and title character, an aspiring poet, rejects familial duty and the courtship and patronage of her cousin Romney Leigh to pursue her art. Aurora's narrative, which has a complicated structure that moves between flashback and present-tense description, in part follows Romney's life, particularly his interest in a poor seamstress, Marian Erle. Marian's story – in a melodramatic twist, she is drugged, raped and impregnated – is integral to Browning's feminist programme: Aurora overcomes her disapproval of the unwed mother and invites Marian to share her home. This female-centred domestic idyll does not last – Aurora and Romney marry in the end. Although recent critics have contended that this marriage compromises the work's feminism, the ending is not entirely conventional: the pair form a marriage in which Aurora's intellect and art supersede her domestic role. In her dedication, Browning called _Aurora Leigh_ 'the most mature of my works, and the one into which my highest convictions upon Life and Art have entered'.

                                                            KW

Austen, Jane 1775–1817 English novelist of the first rank, her reputation resting on a lifetime's work of six novels. Born in Steventon, Hampshire, a clergyman's daughter and second-to-youngest of eight children – six boys, two girls – she was educated for the most part at home, but was well read, and versed in the classics. On her father's retirement the family moved to fashionable Bath (she is reputed to have fainted at the news, though whether from shock or pleasure is not made clear) but returned to Hampshire after his death in 1815. With her mother and sister Cassandra – a small family of modest means – she lived briefly at Southampton, and then at Chawton near Alton, until her death at the age of 41. She died, it is said, of Addison's disease, and is buried in Winchester Cathedral. She did not marry, had no children, and the sum total of her earnings from writing, as far as it can be told, was some £750. The novelist and critic Walter Scott admired her work, as did the Prince Regent, but she received no special recognition in her lifetime. Her literary reputation has grown with the decades, and her life, however short of event it might seem on the surface, is now the subject of many biographies and much speculation. Cassandra's action in burning many of the letters she received from Jane, lest they portray her sister as anything other than gentle and admirable, succeeded only in adding fuel to the biographical fire.

Jane Austen: 'Offended two or three young ladies', illustration from _Pride and Prejudice_, 1894 edn.

A miniaturist, finding that '3 or 4 Families in a Country Village is the very thing to work on', Austen seemed for a time to attract only the more genteel of readers, but her novels are now the stuff of Hollywood and TV adaptation. There is no wonder in this: the universality of her themes, the clarity of her characters and the liveliness of her plots are a boon to those mining the past for our entertainment. But it is the manner of the writing itself, exhilarating and charming as it is, which so endears her to readers. In her use of language she is precise, witty, ironic and polished. The age she wrote in was notable for the elegance of its prose; even so, she excels. To describe her work as a comedy of manners, as is often done, is to diminish it. The novels are underpinned by a strong moral SENSIBILITY, and, though much concerned with the trivialities of courtship and marriage, in the words of Hilaire Belloc, 'send a message from her sex to mine'.

The novels, in order of publishing, are: _SENSE AND SENSIBILITY_ (1811), _PRIDE AND PREJUDICE_ (1813), _MANSFIELD PARK_ (1814), _EMMA_ (1816), and _PERSUASION_ and _NORTHANGER ABBEY_, published posthumously in 1818. They are judged, however, to have been written in a rather different order: _Pride and Prejudice_ (originally entitled _First Impressions_) was begun in 1796, when she was twenty-one, and _Sense and Sensibility_ and _Northanger Abbey_ in 1797. A delightful collection of juvenilia includes _Love and Friendship_, _Lady Susan_ and _The Watsons_. _SANDITON_, a novel unfinished at her death, is an unfinished fragment of some 70,000 words.   FW

Jane (Goodwin) Austin: 'Here's a poor creature freezing to death', illustration from *Cipher: A Romance*, 1869.

Austin, Jane (Goodwin) 1831–94 American historical and children's novelist (see HISTORICAL NOVELS) and short-story writer. She was born in Worcester, Massachusetts, and educated in private schools in Boston. Her mother was a poet, her father a lawyer and historian descended from Mayflower Pilgrims. In 1850 she married Loring Henry Austin, with whom she had three children. Between 1859 and 1892, she published more than twenty books, mostly fictional accounts of American history for young readers. In *Dora Darling* (1864), the heroine defies her Confederate male relatives by joining the Union Army as a provisioner. *Cipher* (1869), a SENSATION novel, is dedicated to Austin's friend LOUISA MAY ALCOTT. Her best-known books are about the Pilgrims: *A Nameless Nobleman* (1881), *Standish of Standish* (1889), *Dr Le Baron and his Daughter* (1890), *Betty Alden* (1891) and *David Alden's Daughter and Other Stories of Colonial Times* (1892). In *Nantucket Scraps* (1882), she combined sketches of current everyday life with local history and legends.   JSG

Austin [née Hunter], Mary 1868–1934 American essayist and fiction writer who centred her life and art in the landscapes and cultures of the arid Southwest. Born in Illinois, she drew her love for nature and books from her father, whose death in 1878 left her grieving deeply. In 1888, after graduating from Blackburn College, she moved with her mother to southern California's San Joaquin Valley, a shift she found liberating. She taught in school, studied the desert, and committed herself to 'write of the West', as she explained in her autobiography, *Earth Horizon* (1932). At 22 she married Stafford Wallace Austin and the following year published her first two short stories; by 1903 she had assembled her first book, *The Land of Little Rain*, the lyrical collection of desert sketches for which she is still best known. Years of prolific writing followed, as she separated from her husband and moved first to Carmel, then Europe. Between 1910 and 1924 she shuttled between California and New York, finally settling in Santa Fe, New Mexico. Austin wrote with a naturalist's eye and a feminist's insight, translating her creative energies into activism by speaking out on behalf of birth control, water rights, and both Native American and Hispanic art. In all her work, from her novels of California like *The Flock* (1906), to her frank study of marriage and female creativity in *A Woman of Genius* (1912), to her CHILDREN'S BOOKS, she investigated in meticulous detail the impact of environments – natural and social alike – on those who inhabit them.
                                                                     WG

Australian Aboriginal narratives The indigenous people comprise now, 200 years after colonization, only a few per cent of the population of (what has for 100 years been called) Australia. It is in this context that, since the late 1960s, a new type of writing has been flowering: prose narratives by Aboriginal women. These narratives constructing cultural identity are hybrid, with a combination of strains producing a variety of blooms. If their genre had to be summarized in one word, it might be 'faction'; for its practitioners mix autobiography, life-writing, history and fiction – but almost invariably with an emphasis upon a reading effect of truth to experience.

These books evoke the experience of 'living black' in rural or station communities, missions and reserves, where Aboriginal people were often the backbone of the workforce, and/or in urban communities where they have frequently existed as fringe dwellers. They endorse, almost without exception, Arthur Corunna's opinion in SALLY MORGAN's MY PLACE (1987): 'The trouble is that colonialism isn't over yet.' In fact, the entry of Aboriginal writers into prose/fiction has brought with it scrutiny of who has power and authority in the production of texts. There has been much debate about the use of Aboriginal or standard English, the extent and style of editing, and the relationship of written to oral discourses. Not all is deadly seriousness: one common and characteristic textual strategy is a sly and subtle, often wry or ironic humour.

Monica Clare's *Karobran*, posthumously published in 1978, is usually called the 'first Aboriginal woman's novel'. A key role these narratives play is the voicing of silenced history. Labumore (Elsie Roughsey), throughout *An Aboriginal Mother Tells of the Old and the New* (1984), reiterates the importance of the maintenance of identity for cultural survival. Mabel Edmund in *No Regrets* (1992) offers stories 'of old Islander beliefs' from Queensland. Mumshirl recalls in *An Autobiography with the Assistance of Bobbi Sykes* (1981) how she learnt to see through her grandfather's eyes – 'you only get the message if you watch'. Work and the family are sites of repeated conflict between colonized and colonizers, with the removal of children a common theme – as it was a common historical fact. *Caprice – A Stockman's Daughter* (1992) by Nugi Garimara (Doris Pilkington), describes surviving the missions and their 'hard work, discipline and the bible'. Glenyse Ward's *Wandering Girl* (1987), also set in Western Australia, is the story of a domestic servant's resistance; its dust-jacket comments: 'This is a hidden story, and its telling is long overdue.'

A dialectic between speech and silence is at work. Withholding of information and the avoidance of direct questioning have been features of Aboriginal resistance. But the narrator/historian of *My Place* advocates exposure, against the diffidence born of experience in older generations: 'someone's got to tell. Otherwise things will stay the same.' RUBY LANGFORD GINIBI's refusal of the expected self-representation as 'respectable' Aboriginal woman and mother in *DON'T TAKE YOUR LOVE TO TOWN* (1989) was predictably received censoriously in some quarters.

Two works that further push out the boundaries of Aboriginal 'faction' are Alexis Wright's *Plains of Promise* (1997) and Melissa Lucashenko's *Steam Pigs* (1997). Both move in the direction of fiction while retaining an aura of the authority of experience. Aboriginal people have been forced to 'know their place' in the white colonizer's scheme of things (hence the bitter pun in Morgan's title); they have, nonetheless, found within many institutions a place from which to stand and speak, this becoming a crucial strategy of resistance.

CF

Australian Girl, An (1890)

CATHERINE MARTIN's first novel was published anonymously in London and received enthusiastic reviews. The heroine, Stella Courtland, resembles JANE AUSTEN's EMMA in her sharpness of social analysis, beauty and initial resistance to marriage, yet displays a greater literary awareness, religious sensibility and national consciousness: '"I am an Australian . . . Australia is not a colony; it is a continent, a great country where generations have already lived and died."' Martin's sardonic characterization of the new generation of Melbourne 'aristocrats', whose society Stella is forced to frequent, is balanced by memorable descriptions of her family home, 'Fairacre', in Adelaide, and the home-station at Lullaboolagana. Tricked into marrying her childhood sweetheart, Stella's passage into womanhood is marked by a severe nervous breakdown which appears to ratify her previous aversion to marriage as a state of imprisonment: '"I am in a wide, great, empty corridor, where my footsteps make a strange sound . . . at the end there are great cages with iron bars in front, strong iron bars, for there are wild creatures behind them."'

MRE

Autobiography of Alice B. Toklas, The (1933)

GERTRUDE STEIN's sole bestseller is one of the most amusing of 20th-century autobiographies, presented through the persona of Stein's beloved lifelong companion, ALICE B. TOKLAS. *The Autobiography* is significant not only for the insights it provides into Stein's theories of writing, mind and history, but as one of the key documents describing the triumphant emergence of MODERNIST painting and writing in Paris in the first years of the century. Consisting of a mesh of detailed anecdote and affectionate individual portraiture, Stein describes the development of her own artistic practice in relation to that of her friends, Picasso and Matisse, who, aside from Toklas and Stein, are the two key figures in the text. Concerned as well with the genesis and publishing history of Stein's own work, and especially *Three Lives*, THE MAKING OF AMERICANS and TENDER BUTTONS, the *Autobiography* is one of the definitive accounts of bohemian Paris up to and including the arrival of the 'lost generation', the modernist, expatriate American authors whose practice owed so much to Stein's innovatory techniques.

KF

Avison, Margaret 1918–87 Canadian poet, reviewer and scholar, author of three collections, twice recipient of the Governor General's Award for Poetry. Her father was a minister; she was born in Galt, Ontario, was raised in western Canada, and returned to Toronto where she received her BA, MA and ABD, and subsequently lectured in English. She began writing in 1939, and is associated with important poetic groups and publications in both Canada (Alan Crawley's *Contemporary Verse*, 1940-1952) and the United States (Cid Corman's *Origin*, 1957). Her personal reticence and distrust of biographical literary interpretation has left little information beyond the record of multiple linguistic undertakings, friendships with literary figures, and her religious conversion of 1963. Her first volume, WINTER SUN (1960), established her growing reputation and influence, while the following two (THE DUMBFOUNDING, 1966, and *sunblue*, 1978) reflect and incorporate her Christian sensibility as well. Both before and after her conversion, her poetry tends to concern itself particularly with confronting 'the swimmer's moment at the whirlpool', where those 'who dare the knowledge . . . are whirled into the ominous centre' of vision and understanding. 'Nobody stuffs the world in at your eyes', she writes. 'The optic heart must venture.'   FD

Awakening, The (1899) KATE CHOPIN's second novel narrates heroine Edna Pontellier's struggle to transcend the constrictions of leisure-class marriage to a successful Creole businessman and the dutiful travails of motherhood. Her determination not to be limited to the 'mother-woman' role involves learning to swim (the novel is suffused with ocean imagery) and neglecting decorum to gamble, paint and experiment romantically and sexually with men; her relationship with her close friend Adele Ratignolle is also charged with intense ambivalence. At once archetypal and richly circumstantial in its details of late 19th-century Creole life in New Orleans and the holiday haven of Grand Isle, its transgressive plot has much in common with Flaubert's *Madame Bovary* and Tolstoy's *Anna Karenina*, while the existential selfhood which Edna seeks anticipates SYLVIA PLATH's *THE BELL JAR* (1963). *The Awakening*'s scandalized reception virtually ended Chopin's career. Since the 1960s, however, the novel has entered the canons of American and feminist fiction. A 1981 film version, entitled *The End of August* (dir. Bob Graham), attracted the 'local colour' label which Chopin worked so hard to throw off.   MO'D

Awfully Big Adventure, An (1989) BERYL BAINBRIDGE's twelfth novel, set in an atmospherically dreary 1950s Liverpool, charts the fortunes of Stella, a 16-year-old who is plunged into the tawdry values of theatrical life when she lands a job in a rep. company. A naive and impressionable observer of the theatre's petty jealousies, misplaced passions and sexual infidelities, Stella's voice is fresh and immediate. Her desire to escape from her lower-middle-class existence into a bohemian world is a flawed but endearing one. Her initial crush on Meredith Potter, the homosexual director, is subsumed by her sexual initiation with P. L. O'Hara, a notorious womanizer and star of the new production of *Peter Pan*. The drama climaxes when O'Hara discovers the truth behind his involvement in both Stella's and her absent mother's life. The plot is the material of tragedy, but around it Bainbridge weaves a darkly comic web. *An Awfully Big Adventure* was filmed in 1994, with a cast that included Alan Rickman and Hugh Grant.   CS

Ayres, Ruby M(ildred) 1883–1955 Immensely prolific and commercially successful British writer of anodyne, formulaic, but jaunty ROMANCE fiction, in which plots that uphold conservative sexual and class values are played out by stereotypical heroes and heroines. Ayres was masterly at reading her market and keeping it supplied with reassuringly 'good, clean love stories' that first challenged and then reaffirmed the virtue of their heroines. She wrote about 150 novels and countless serials and stories for popular newspapers and magazines. At her peak in the 1920s and 1930s, many novels were updated and reissued into the 1970s. Some were filmed.

A sampling of titles reflects her emotional colouring – the titillating: *Unofficial Wife* (1937); the sentimental: *From This Day Forward* (1934); the sinister: *A Loveless Marriage* (1921); the earnest: *A Man of His Word* (1916); and the pathetic: *The Man Who Lived Alone* (1950). All have the requisite happy ending.

Daughter of an architect, she married a London insurance broker at the age of 26; they had no children.   LDo

Ayscough, Florence Wheelock 1878–1942 American writer, translator and lecturer who tried to demystify Chinese culture for a Western audience. Born in Shanghai to a Canadian father and an American mother, her family moved to Boston when she was 11. Returning to China in 1897, she married Francis Ayscough, an Englishman with a British importing house in Shanghai, and began studying Mandarin. The Ayscoughs moved to New Brunswick, Canada, in 1923, but continued to visit China regularly. After her husband's death in 1933, Ayscough settled in Chicago with her second husband, Harley Farnsworth MacNair, a university professor and fellow Sinologue.

Often vexed by the West's interpretations of her beloved birthplace, Ayscough depicted vividly her own vision of China by interspersing her fiction and non-fiction with autobiographical anecdotes and by employing a simple writing style. She collaborated with AMY LOWELL, a friend since childhood, and her Chinese teacher Nung Chu, to translate the poems of several popular Chinese poets in *Fir-Flower Tablets* (1921), the work for which she received the most critical recognition. Her theory of translation explicitly critiqued Western artists' growing but amateurish interest in Chinese art. The translator of Chinese poetry, she argued, must be able to analyse the pictorial representation of a written Chinese character in addition to the character's various meanings and associations. VM

B

Bâ, Mariama 1929–81 Senegalese novelist and feminist, who was the winner of the first Noma Award for African Literature for *Une si longue lettre* (*So Long a Letter*), published in 1980. Written in the form of a journal letter from a recently widowed woman addressed to her closest woman friend, this novel eloquently recounts the emotional pain and sense of abandonment she felt when her husband announced that he was taking a second and much younger wife. The experience of the narrator, who decides that she has no option but to remain within this polygamous marriage, is contrasted with that of her friend, Aissatou, who in similar circumstances left her husband to embark upon a career in the civil service.

Mariama Bâ's second novel, *Un chant écarlate* (*Scarlet Song*) was not quite completed at the time of her tragically early death from cancer in 1981. This novel recounts an affair and marriage between a Senegalese student from a working-class background and a French woman student, the daughter of an aristocratic diplomat. The marriage shatters upon the rocks of cultural difference; here again a second wife (this time Senegalese) leaves the first one stranded, while her husband justifies his actions in the name of African tradition and cultural nationalism.

Bâ was educated in Islamic and French schools, was a primary school teacher, and the mother of nine children. Married to a former Senegalese Minister of Information (from whom she was later divorced), she was active for many years in national and international feminist movements.   CLI

Backwoods of Canada: Being Letters from the Wife of an Emigrant Officer, The (1836) A collection of letters, written by CATHARINE PARR TRAILL to her mother in England between the years 1832 and 1835, which recount the author's experiences as a Canadian pioneer. Though contending with unfamiliar climates, wildlife and living conditions, Traill presents the details of her early years in her adopted country in a surprisingly cheerful tone, alternating between episodic story-telling and more contemplative ruminations. The latter include appreciative, though imperialistic, descriptions of her native neighbours, and a celebration of the freedom from social constraints she enjoys as a 'bush-settler'. Compared to the more melodramatic language used by her sister SUSANNA MOODIE in her book *ROUGHING IT IN THE BUSH, OR LIFE IN CANADA*, Traill's narrative voice is practical and optimistic: 'I must say, for all its roughness, I love Canada.' An edition published in 1929 added Traill's spirited denunciation of the Mackenzie Rebellion of 1837, her humorous account of 'Bush Weddings,' and numerous recipes, including, of course, one for maple sugar.   SLK

Bacon [née Cooke], Anne, Lady 1528–1610 Translator, and one of the famously learned daughters of Sir Anthony Cooke. The others included MILDRED CECIL, Lady Burghley; Lady Elizabeth [Hoby] Russell; and Lady Katharine Killigrew – all writers. She was fluent in several languages and may have tutored Edward VI. Her translation from Italian of fourteen Calvinist sermons by Bernardine Ochine (published *c*.1550) was dedicated to her mother, remarking with respectful satisfaction that 'it hath pleased you, often, to reprove my vain study in the Italian tongue'. In around 1557 she became the second wife of Sir Nicholas Bacon (d. 1579); they had two sons, Anthony and Francis. After Bishop John Jewel's *Apology of the Church of England* appeared in Latin in 1562, she translated it into English (published 1564). Her highly accurate version of this founding text of the Anglican Church was widely read and much admired. She wrote spirited letters deploring plays and masques, defending the rights of Non-conformists, and giving affectionate but vigorous advice to her distinguished sons. She became senile in her later years.   HH

Bacon, Delia Salter 1811–59 American novelist, critic. Born to Congregationalist ministers in the Ohio Territory, Delia returned with her family to Connecticut when the mission failed. Educated for one year at CATHARINE BEECHER's school, Bacon and her sister tried and failed to establish a private school of their own. She went on to moderate success as a lecturer on literature and history, and published her first book, *Tales of the Pilgrims,* in 1831. By 1845, she was obsessed by her theory that Shakespeare's plays were actually written by Francis Bacon and Sir Walter Raleigh, among others. Granted a fellowship to research her theory, she sailed to England in 1853.

Briefly taught by Carlyle and then dismissed for her unwillingness to do research, she became increasingly isolated and destitute. In 1856, irrationally convinced that proof for her theory lay in Shakespeare's tomb, she tried to have it opened. Hawthorne came to her aid by securing her a publisher and even writing the introduction to her book, *The Plays of Shakespere Unfolded* (1857). In 1858, violently insane, she was brought back to a mental institution in Connecticut.　　SP

Bad Sister, The (1978) EMMA TENNANT's novel is at once a delayed flowering of the anti-establishment, progressive, feminist, ambience of the late 1960s and one of its most devastating critiques. Tennant makes extra-textual use of James Hogg's *Confessions of a Justified Sinner* (1824). Here, Calvinism is replaced with an amalgam of Laingian analysis and militant feminist separatism; film critic Jane Wild is dragged by the mysterious Meg into a world of self-justifying murderousness. The framing narrative makes clear that nothing we are told is necessarily true – but Tennant appears to be taking a moral stand against all ideologies which include hatred and blame. The devil, Meg, has the best tunes, taking Jane into dreams and phantasmagoria which are, simply, beautiful and terrifying; Tennant's next novel, WILD NIGHTS (1979) takes this dream-GOTHIC even further, but lacks *The Bad Sister*'s tension between mundane humane urgency and gorgeous danger.　　RK

Bagnold, Enid (Algerine) 1889–1981 Educated in England, Germany, Switzerland and France, Bagnold studied painting with Walter Sickert, served as a driver with the French Army, and worked as a nurse during World War I. She is best known for her novels *Serena Blandish* (1924) and *National Velvet* (1935) which was adapted for both stage (1946) and film. Once given the title 'that disagreeable chit' by VIRGINIA WOOLF, Bagnold was friendly with many society people of her day. She came under attack for her naive views of Nazism, which placed her amongst the pro-German faction of the Establishment at the beginning of World War II. In many ways her work was marred by the fact of her society connections, which often became an obstacle to any objective in-depth critique. Her most successful play was *The Chalk Garden* (1956) which ran for over 650 performances in the West End. The play examines the development of a child and a garden, both starved of nourishment and overseen by an aristocratic and eccentric old lady. For critic Kenneth Tynan it was 'the finest artificial comedy to have flowed from an English pen since the death of Congreve', a play which somehow marked the end of an era; other critics noted the similarity between Bagnold's style of dialogue and Chekhov's. Her plays include *The Last Joke* (produced in 1960) and *The Chinese Prime Minister* (1964). Bagnold was awarded the CBE in 1976.　　MBG

Bailey, Hilary 1936– British writer and editor Bailey studied English at Cambridge. Her first short stories appeared in *New Worlds*, the SCIENCE-FICTION magazine published by her then husband, Michael Moorcock; Bailey herself later became editor of *New Worlds*. She also edited *Bananas*, the 1970s avant-garde fiction magazine with EMMA TENNANT. Her first novel, *Polly Put the Kettle on*, is a roman à clef about *New Worlds*, and its rickety finances; it celebrates the canny endurance of its much put-upon heroine – Bailey's central characters, most notably in the blockbusterish *All the Days of my Life* (1984), are rarely victims and always survivors. A number of her novels, rather more successfully than those of Tennant in this vein, are sequels to other novels, notably *Miles and Flora* (1997), her sequel to Henry James's *The Turn of the Screw*, and *After the Cabaret* (1998), which deals with the war-time adventures of Christopher Isherwood's Sally Bowles. Perhaps Bailey's most thoughtful and inventive works are the two HISTORICAL NOVELS *Cassandra, Princess of Troy* (1993) and *The Cry from Street to Street* (1992) in which a prostitute, rich from Californian gold, searches desperately for a feckless old friend in Jack the Ripper's London, unaware that her name is that of his final victim. Bailey is at her best when dramatic irony and consequent suspense overlay her facility.　　RK

Baillie, Lady Grisell [Grizel] 1665–1746 Scottish poet and patriot, whose early life became part of Scottish legend. In *Metrical Legends of Exalted Characters* (1821), JOANNA BAILLIE relates how Grisell, as a twelve-year-old child, passed secret messages to the imprisoned Jacobite, Robert Baillie, and later smuggled food to her father, Sir Patrick Hume, when he was forced into hiding. After managing the family during their exile in Holland, Grisell declined the offer to become maid of honour to the Princess of Orange, and instead married Robert Baillie's son, George. They settled in Scotland but also held fashionable parties in London. From her childhood, Baillie wrote prose and verse. Her popular Scottish songs first appeared anonymously in collections such as Allan Ramsay's *The Tea-Table Miscellany* (1723–40). She is particularly well known for the popular Scots song, 'And werena my heart licht I wad dee' (pub.1726). Fragments of other poems and songs were found after her death by her daughter, Lady Murray, whose account of her parents' life, *Memoirs*, was published in 1822.　　RDM

Baillie, Joanna 1762–1851 Scottish dramatist and poet. She was sent to school in Glasgow at the age of 10, where she developed skills in acting. After her father's death, the family moved to London in 1784.

In London, Joanna published a volume of poems, *Fugitive Verses*, which was well received. In 1798 she published, again anonymously, the first volume of her *Plays on the Passions* in which each drama explores the effect of one particular passion: *Basil*, a tragedy on love, and *De Montfort*, a tragedy on hatred, were the most successful. Sir Walter Scott was at first suspected of being the author and the two writers became life-long friends. *De Montfort* was produced by John Kemble and Mrs Siddons at Drury Lane Theatre in 1800.

In 1802 she and her sister moved to a house in Hampstead which became a meeting place for many literary figures of the day. She published a second volume of *Plays on the Passions* in 1802, *Miscellaneous Plays* (1804), a third volume of *Passions* in 1812 and a second volume of poems, *Metrical Legends of Exalted Characters*, in 1821. Her most successful drama, *A Family Legend* (1810), based upon a Scottish feud, was brought out under Scott's auspices at the Edinburgh theatre. She continued to write until she was over 80 years old.

RS

Joanna Baillie.

Bainbridge, Beryl 1934– English novelist and short-story writer, born in Crosby near Liverpool. The latter has continued to feed her imagination, providing the settings for *The Dressmaker* (1973), a grimly comic tale of love and murder among the sand dunes of the Mersey estuary during World War II, and for *An Awfully Big Adventure* (1989), which is a fictionalized version of Bainbridge's own experiences as an assistant stage manager at the Liverpool Playhouse in the late 1940s. The city is also the setting for *Young Adolf* (1978), which has Adolf Hitler working as a waiter at the Adelphi Hotel in the early years of the century; and its heroic maritime past can be seen as an influence in her two novels of Edwardian adventure: *The Birthday Boys* (1991), about Scott's fatal last expedition to the South Pole, and *Every Man for Himself* (1996), about the sinking of the *Titanic*, which was shortlisted for the Booker Prize and the Whitbread Award.

Bainbridge has an eye for bizarre detail and an ear for unintentionally comic, self-betraying dialogue. Her earlier novels, *A Weekend with Claude* (1968), *The Bottle Factory Outing* (1974) and *Injury Time* (1977) are black comedies incorporating unexpected disasters, slightly feminist in tone and with characteristically accident-prone heroines. Some of these were reissued in the 1980s when she had a popular success with her portrait of Victorian murder, *Watson's Apology* (1984). In 1986 her publishers, Duckworth (where her long-standing friend and editor, ALICE THOMAS ELLIS, was the wife of the publisher), brought out *Filthy Lucre*, an illustrated juvenile romance of the sea which she wrote when she was 13. Despite the historical and factual basis for much of her work, Bainbridge is an idiosyncratic writer who projects a strong persona, familiar to readers from her many interviews and from her rather rambling columns for the *Spectator* and the *Evening Standard*. Specializing in irony and oblique criticism of society, her writing is always piquant and original, though sometimes scrappily plotted, a weakness which is apparent in her *Collected Stories* (1984). LD

Baker, Elizabeth 1876–1962 British dramatic author who caught public attention with her 1909 play *Chains*. Baker had early associations with innovative theatres like the Manchester and the Birmingham Repertory companies. Her 1912 play *Edith*, about familial reaction to the discovery that the family business has been left to the estranged but business-like daughter rather than the pompous son, was produced by the Women Writers Suffrage League. Baker was interested in women's relationship to the work economy in general and this is reflected in a number of plays such as *Miss Tassey* (1910), *Partnership* (1917) and *Miss Robinson* (1918). Early career experience as a typist influenced her critical portrayal of the poor conditions of clerical work. She was equally critical of the limited expectations of lower-middle-class women, questioning the choice of marriage as a career and the ideology of separate spheres. Often presenting marriage as a strait-jacket for both sexes, Baker toyed with the theme of intermarriage between the classes and questioned capitalism as a positive economic strategy (*The Price of Thomas Scott*, 1913). She also wrote for many well-known journals and magazines of her day. MBG

Baker, Louisa Alice 1858–1926 New Zealand novelist, writing under the pseudonym 'Alien', born in

Warwickshire, England. Her family arrived in New Zealand as assisted immigrants in 1863. When she was 18 she married, and had two children. She wrote a column for women under the name 'Alice' and one for children – 'Dot's Little Folk' – in the *Otago Witness* before moving to England in 1894, leaving her husband behind. Her early novels contain many ideas of the current women's movement. *A Daughter of the King* (1894) is about a woman's right to leave an unhappy marriage and to search for 'the secret of woman's power'. In *The Majesty of Man* (1895) the heroine is strongly attracted to the leader of a celibate separatist sisterhood. But all the novels end in a celebration of marriage. In *Wheat in the Ear* (1898) the heroine's teacher and mentor, a celibate suffragist, has been instrumental in getting New Zealand women the vote in 1893, dies, and the heroine ends up with a ruggedly handsome farmer. Later novels like *A Maid of Mettle* (1913) have a stroppy heroine in a conventional ROMANCE plot. She published sixteen romantic novels and from 1903 wrote a letter from England by 'Alien' for the *Otago Witness*. She felt that the New Zealand setting of many of her novels meant she was not recognized – 'So it seems with colonial artists, they are bred under the Southern Cross, held cheaply there – and labelled in London.'   AM

Baldwin (Cuthrell), Faith [Amber Lee] 1893–1978
American popular novelist, born in New Rochelle, New York, and educated in Brooklyn and Berlin, where she lived during the first two years of World War I. She married Hugh Hamilton Cuthrell in 1920 and had four children. She began writing as a child; her juvenile poems were published in the *Christian Advocate*. During her lifetime, she published nearly a hundred books, including two books of poems and four CHILDREN'S BOOKS. Her fiction was published in such popular magazines as *Good Housekeeping*, *Pictorial Review*, *McCall's* and *Woman's Home Companion*. Novels originally serialized in these magazines were republished as books, starting with *Mavis of Green Hill* (1921). *Alimony* (1928), a bestseller, established her success as a sentimental novelist. *Office Wife* (1930) and *Weekend Marriage* (1932) became films. Other titles include *White Collar Girl* (1933) and *He Married a Doctor* (1944). *Testament of Trust* (1960) offers semi-autobiographical sketches.   JSG

Balfour, Mary ['Mary of Belfast'] 1775?–1820? Irish
poet and dramatist. The daughter of a Church of Ireland clergyman, Balfour was probably born in Derry. Following the death of her parents, she supported herself and her sisters by keeping a school in Limavady and later in Belfast.

An enthusiast for the revival of Gaelic music and literature, Balfour was a member of the Harp Society in Belfast, and contributed eight poems to the 1809 edition of Edward Bunting's *General Collection of Ancient Irish Music*. *Hope, a Poetical Essay: With Various Other Poems*, which appeared under her own name in the following year, was based on Balfour's researches into Irish language and folklore. The collection included loose translations from Gaelic such as 'In ringlets curl'd thy tresses flow' and 'The dew each trembling leaf inwreath'd', as well as the ballad 'Kathleen O'Neill', based on the legend of the banshee of Shane's Castle.

Balfour later turned this subject into a play. *Kathleen O'Neill*, 'a grand national melodrama', incorporating songs and a comic subplot, was staged in Belfast, and published anonymously in 1814. Balfour herself died in Belfast in about 1820.   RR

Balkan Trilogy, The Set in 1939–41, these books are
based on OLIVIA MANNING's experiences as the young wife of a British Council lecturer in war-torn Budapest. The first two volumes, *The Great Fortune* (1960) and *The Spoilt City* (1962), follow the escapades of numerous idiosyncratic and unforgettable characters, from the outbreak of war to the fall of Budapest. In the final volume, *Friends and Heroes* (1965), Greece becomes a temporary haven, until the proximity of the fighting precipitates their escape to Africa's comparative safety. Manning's colourful portrait of this insecure ex-patriate British community identifies characters by habits, gestures or possessions, and is often tinged with comic pathos. The problematic relationship of newly-weds Guy and Harriet Pringle unfolds against an unstable political background of assassinations and changing allegiances. Despite Guy's apparent indifference, Harriet chooses marriage and responsibility instead of the personal freedom of a love affair. The petty squabbles and intrigues of their social circle, expressed in dialogue with a wealth of knowledge and awareness of the period, become a microcosm for wartime politics.
                                    MET

Ballard, Martha Moore 1735–1812 New England
midwife and diarist. Born in Oxford, Massachusetts, Moore married Ephraim Ballard in 1754 and had nine children. The family moved to Hallowell, Maine, in 1777, where Ballard remained until her death in 1812. Because Ballard's husband was perceived to have Loyalist sympathies, the family suffered confiscation and destruction of some of their property during the Revolutionary War. However, the DIARY rarely displays bitterness or distrust; rather, the entries are consistently practical, apparently factual, often sympathetic toward the townspeople. The diary recounts her struggles in harsh weather, through rugged terrain and across the river, to reach patients in labour. The writing is often terse but revelatory, as in

the entry for 18 January 1796: 'Clear and pleasant. I was Calld from Mrs Moore to Steven Hinkleys wife at 10 hour morning. Shee was delivered at 11 of a son. I part drest the infant and was Calld to return to Mrs Moore. Find her more unwell. Shee was delivered at 4 hour 30 minutes of a son. The Children were the first Born of their mamys. I returnd home at 8 hour Evening. Brother Ebenezer Moore sleeps here. I made Bids, washt dishes, swept house, and got supper. I feel som fatagud.' Ballard's steady, pragmatic recording of her daily routines provides a view of domestic life in an Early Republic outpost and presents valuable information concerning midwifery and other medical practices performed by women in the period.   LCa

ballet stories During the 1930s, London, with its energetic young company at the newly built Sadler's Wells Theatre, became an important centre for ballet. On the wave of interest in the rising British dancers, and in the sensational season of the Ballets Russes de Monte Carlo, Arnold Haskell's *Balletomania* (1934; subtitled 'The Story of an Obsession') became a bestseller. NOEL STREATFEILD's *Ballet Shoes* (1936), written for children, is the most famous of the first generation of novels centring on the life of the ballet school. Unlike the male 'balletomanes', obsessively fascinated with the graceful bodies of beautiful women, Streatfeild wrote from the viewpoint of young dance pupils, in training for a tough profession, setting the pattern for many later writers. From the 1940s to the 1960s, readers could follow, among others, the 'Belle of the Ballet' books (from *Girl* magazine), LORNA HILL's 'Wells' and 'Dancing Peel' series, MABEL ESTHER ALLAN's 'Drina' and Linda Blake's 'Laura'. In these, and in non-series stories, audiences grew to expect the revelation of the heroine's vocation, her struggles to join a school, the looming audition, her set-backs and anxieties, her relationships with other students, the recognition of her unique talent, and her arrival at the title of Ballerina, with the accolade of a professional name.

Detractors emphasize the narcissistic gratifications of these novels, and their inculcation of a stereotypically 'feminine' conformity, but from the start ballet stories offered girls their own kind of quest narrative. The lessons of the wise, multiaccented, charismatic, teacher and the comradeship of the international ballet school opened out perspectives beyond the limits of the nuclear family and the provincial sphere, providing unusual models of ambition, dedication and self-interest, even ruthlessness, in the pursuit of the chosen art. From the 1970s, writers have kept to the paradigm, though gradually shifting the emphasis to explore more directly the pressures of a dancer's life. In novels by Jean Richardson, RUMER GODDEN, Jean Ure or Mal Lewis Jones, and others, readers meet more openly voiced questions about sexuality, injury, abuse,

eating disorders, racism, family expectations. All these, and the continued popularity of the earlier series, suggest the genre is far from exhausted.   PEK

Bambara, Toni Cade 1939–95 African-American fiction writer, critic and film maker whose political activism informs her work. Born in New York City, she was brought up in a politically aware family and was educated at Queen's College and New York City College and worked as an occupational therapist and a social worker in Harlem. In the 1960s she became involved in the Black Arts Movement, and also taught on the SEEK access programme for Puerto Rican and black students with BARBARA CHRISTIAN until 1969.

In the 1970s she began to concentrate on her writing and was involved with the organization of women's groups, for which she travelled to Vietnam and Cuba. She wrote two collections of short stories, *GORILLA, MY LOVE* (1972) and *The Sea Birds are Still Alive* (1977) and two novels, *The Salt Eaters* (1980) and 'If Blessings Come' (which has remained unpublished). She edited two anthologies of stories by African-American women writers including the pioneering *The Black Woman* (1970) which established her as an important figure in the development of the profile of African-American women's writing.

TONI MORRISON has been closely involved with her work and acted as editor at Random House during the publication of *The Salt Eaters*. The writing of Bambara and Morrison shares many concerns including the influence of jazz, storytelling and vernacular tradition, and the recovery from trauma through memory and collective mothering.

Bambara wrote an important introduction to ZORA NEALE HURSTON's *The Sanctified Church* (1983) and the introduction to GLORIA ANZALDÚA's and CHERRIE MORAGA's *This Bridge Called My Back* (1981). She was predominantly involved in film making during the last decade of her life, during which she wrote a script for a television documentary on W. E. B. du Bois and was involved in the production of a documentary about the bombing of the MOVE black movement by the Philadelphia police. After her death, her notes on black film making were published as *Deep Sightings and Rescue Missions*, which is edited and prefaced by Toni Morrison.   MAB

Bandler, Faith 1923– Eminent novelist, writer and campaigner for Aboriginal causes in AUSTRALIA. Born in Tumbulgum, northern New South Wales, Bandler left school at 15 to work as a cook and dressmaker, and then spent three years in the Women's Land Army during World War II. In 1956, with Pearl Gibbs, she formed the Aboriginal-Australian Fellowship (her 1983 work *The Time Was Ripe* is a history of this organization) and she was instrumental in the establishment of the Federal Council for the Advancement of Aboriginal and Torres Strait Islanders (FCAATSI), a peak Aboriginal organization operating 1958–72, serving as general secretary in 1970-3. *Turning the Tide* (1989) is Bandler's 'personal history' of FCAATSI.

Her literary work must be read in this context of activism and political involvement, within a tradition articulating the complex genealogy of Aboriginal identities and the need to reclaim history. Her best-known works, *Wacvie* (1977) and *Welou, My Brother* (1984), are based on the lives of her family, brought as slaves from Vanuatu to work on the Queensland cane fields in the late 19th century. She has also published a children's book, *Marani in Australia* (with Len Fox) (1980).

In 1976 Faith Bandler refused an MBE. In 1984 she accepted a medal of the Order of Australia.   BO

Banks [née Varley], Isabella 1821–97 English novelist whose works described life in her native Lancashire during the early decades of industrialization. Her family had been prosperous Manchester entrepreneurs, but when Isabella was a child her father's health and business both failed, and her mother supported the family by taking in sewing and lodgers. Isabella operated a school before her marriage in 1846 to George Linnaeus Banks, a newspaperman and poet. Isabella wrote for her husband's newspapers and had eight children (five of whom died young); she began writing novels when her husband's poor health, physical and mental, forced her to support the family. She published both a volume of poetry written with her husband, *Daisies in the Grass*, and her first novel, *God's Providence House: A Story of Old Chester*, in 1865. Her most successful book, *The Manchester Man* (1876), which tells the story of a conscientious working-class orphan who rises in the world and eventually marries the upper-class woman he loves, was based in part on her family's stories of industrializing Manchester. The novel includes a graphic description of the Peterloo Massacre of 1819, and reveals Banks's sympathy for the plight of the working classes during the years of the Napoleonic Wars, when food was scarce. Among her other novels, most published under the name Mrs George Linnaeus Banks, were *Stung to the Quick: A North Country Story* (1867), *More than Coronets* (1882), *Forbidden to Marry* (1883), *A Rough Road* (1892) and *Bond Slaves* (1893).   KW

Banks, Lynne Reid 1939– British novelist born in London to Jewish parents. She was evacuated to Canada during World War II. As a child she wanted to become an actress and trained for the stage at RADA after which she went on to become one of the first women television news reporters in Britain. In 1959 she published her first novel, *The L-Shaped Room*, which was later turned into a film. Very much in the style of the new British REALISM, *The L-Shaped Room* deals with a woman's struggle for independence in the still very restricted society of the late 1950s and early 1960s. Like NELL DUNN's *POOR COW* and SHEELAGH DELANEY's *A TASTE OF HONEY*, *The L-Shaped Room* became an iconic tale of women's condition in the mid 20th century. Banks has written many books for teenagers and young adults, including *I, Houdini* (1979), *The Indian in the Cupboard* (1980) and *The Fairy Rebel* (1988). Of these the most successful is *The Indian in the Cupboard*, which was made into a film in 1997.   JHB

Bannerman [née Watson], Helen Brodie Cowan 1862–1946 Scottish-born writer of CHILDREN'S BOOKS from a staunchly Calvinistic background, Bannerman spent most of her married life in India, where her husband was a doctor in the Medical Service. Her fame rests on her first book, *The Story of Little Black Sambo* (1899), which grew from a story told to her small daughters. This is a FAIRY TALE for the very young: its setting a jungle more Indian than African, its hero a little black boy of apparently African origin who during a walk encounters and outwits four hungry tigers. The tigers fight among themselves before melting into ghee, which is used to cook a feast of pancakes. The book enjoyed immediate success, but Bannerman, who had sold the copyright for £5, never profited from it. It was widely translated and, despite being attacked for racism, has rarely been out of print since.

Bannerman went on to write and illustrate a further eight infant books, some of which were used as school readers. All are notable for their improbable plots, and many for their conspicuously gory illustrations. Typical of these are *The Story of Little Black Mingo* (1901) and *The Story of Little Black Quasha* (1908). A tenth book, *The Story of Little White Squibba*, was compiled from unfinished notes and jottings by her daughter, and published posthumously in 1966 partly in order to establish Bannerman's non-racist credentials.   CT

Bannon, Ann 1937– American writer and head of the linguistics department at California State University, Sacramento. She is best known for a sequence of six novels – *Odd Girl Out* (1957), *Women in the Shadows* (1959), *I am a Woman* (1959), *Journey to a Woman* (1960), *The Marriage* (1960) and *Beebo Brinker* (1962). Like much other lesbian writing of their period, even PATRICIA HIGHSMITH's *The Price of Salt* (published as by Claire Morgan and later reissued under Highsmith's own name as *Carol*), they were originally published looking like soft-core pornography for the male market, with sensational glossy cover art, while being widely read by lesbians on the basis of word-of-mouth recommendation. Bannon's rather sentimental and lugubrious novels form a linked sequence featuring three overlapping characters and cover a college affair, the Greenwich village bar scene of their time and the later troubled marriage of one of the three. They also featured Beebo Brinker, a memorable early portrait of a butch, which caused much comment when the books were reissued, in more appropriate packaging, during the eighties when butch–femme roleplay was the subject of much debate about its alleged power imbalance and imitation of heterosexual behaviour.   RK

Barbalet [née Hardy], Margaret 1949– Australian writer born in Adelaide, spent part of her childhood in Tasmania before returning to South Australia, where she married Jack Barbalet, with whom she had three sons. In 1979, after a period in Papua New Guinea, she moved to Canberra. Trained as a historian, Barbalet published her first book, *The Adelaide Children's Hospital 1876-1976* (1975) before leaving South Australia. Her first novel, *Blood in the Rain* (1986), was an exploration of the inner lives of a brother and a sister abandoned by their mother. *Steel Beach* (1988) was published before Barbalet joined the Australian foreign service, and her third novel *Lady, Baby, Gypsy, Queen* (1992), appeared the year after the publication of her highly successful CHILDREN'S BOOK, *The Wolf* (1991). The critic Helen Daniel has noted Barbalet's 'vitality and intensity', and her use of 'striking images that open out into elusive and unexpected meanings'.   SDo

Barbauld [née Aikin], Anna Laetitia 1743–1825 British poet, educator and critic who maintained a lifelong loyalty to Unitarian ideals of peace and liberty. Her father taught languages and *belles-lettres* at the important Dissenting centre of Warrington Academy, where from an early age she conversed with prominent radicals. Some of her earliest poems are addressed to Warrington tutors William Enfield and Joseph Priestly. She persuaded her father to teach her the 'abstruser languages' and contributed anonymous hymns to *Essays on Song-Writing* (1772), edited by her brother, John Aikin. When ELIZABETH MONTAGU asked her to collaborate in forming a school for girls she famously refused, arguing 'My situation has been peculiar and would be no role for others'. From 'Corsica', the opening poem of her début volume (*Poems*, 1773), to her controversial *Eighteen Hundred and Eleven* (1812), Barbauld's poetry combines unusual and forceful imagery with a moral vision of equality. Her comments on women's freedom tend to be oblique and ironic, rather than overtly feminist. 'A Summer Evening's Meditation' (*Poems*) provides an interesting successor to ANNE FINCH's 'Nocturnal Reverie', extending the female imaginary into the stratosphere

of astronomical space, the 'glories of a world unknown'. While Johnson and Wordsworth fêted Barbauld's early talent, they disapproved of her educational work, which after her marriage (to Rochemont Barbauld in 1774) dominated her life. However, her *Lessons for Children* (1778) were revolutionary in increasing levels of literacy, combining easy words with pictures to create a successful teaching medium. She was a broad-ranging literary critic, editing the poets William Collins and Mark Akenside and a substantial critical edition of *British Novelists* (1810), which includes several of her female precursors. On Barbauld's death her niece, the poet Lucy Aikin, collected her work, adding a memoir (1825).   ESE

Barber, Mary *c.*1690–*c.*1757 Irish poet, and a leading member of Swift's 'female senate', the circle of friends which also included CONSTANTIA GRIERSON and LETITIA PILKINGTON. Barber began to write poetry, as she declared, 'chiefly to form the minds of my children', but possibly also as a means of livelihood – her husband, a woollen draper, was apparently unsuccessful in business.

Barber published two poems in Dublin in 1725, one in praise of the Viceroy, Lord Carteret, and, anonymously, 'A Widow's Address'. In 1730 she visited England in search of literary advancement, but the trip was dogged by misfortune. Her *Poems on Several Occasions* (1734) were well received by the critics, but brought little financial reward, she suffered severely from gout, and was briefly imprisoned on a charge of importing allegedly subversive material. Her financial problems were eased when Swift agreed to donate the manuscript of his *Polite Conversation* (1738) to be published for her benefit, but her health remained poor. She returned to Dublin, where she died.

A number of Barber's works appeared in *Poems by Eminent Ladies* (1755), and her work was highly regarded by contemporaries – she was described by Swift as 'the best poetess of both kingdoms'. Subsequent assessments were more cautious: *The Cabinet of Irish Literature* (1902) described her poetry as 'pleasant and not inelegant'. However, recent critics have seen her as an enemy of hypocrisy and injustice in works such as 'An unanswerable apology for the rich', in which she mocked the charitable pretensions of the affluent.

> No man alive could do more good,
> Or give more freely, if he could.
> He grieves, whene'er the wretched sue,
> But what can poor Castalio *do*?
> Would Heaven but send ten thousand more,
> He'd give – just as he did before.   RR

Barclay, Florence [Charlesworth] 1862–1921 English romantic novelist whose Edwardian bestseller

The Rosary (1909) sold millions. She attributed her sense of mission to her family's 1869 move from Surrey rectory to Limehouse parish. She was educated by her father, and in 1881 married his curate, Charles Barclay. After honeymooning in Palestine they settled in Hertford Heath, where Barclay would divide her time between eight children and parish duties, including training the choir. In 1905, convalescing from illness, she wrote her first two novels, *The Wheels of Time* (1908), and *The Rosary*. In this JANE EYRE variant, plain, stout, contralto Jane self-sacrificingly rejects her handsome suitor who falls in love with her singing; his subsequent blindness, and her incognito nursing reunite them. The novel's adroit synthesis of spirituality and eroticism against a country-house comedy background, presented in a style more respectable and literate than that of CORELLI earlier or DELL later, attracted readers across the board. Later novels, including *The Mistress of Shenstone*, *The Following of a Star* (both 1911) and *The White Ladies of Worcester* (1918), maintained her success. Barclay saw her novels as providing an extended field for spiritual enlightenment, accepting lecture invitations in Europe and America only from religious organizations, and answering her fan-mail assiduously. She died of bronchitis in 1921.   AT

Bardwell, Leland 1928– A poet, dramatist and fiction-writer, musician and editor, born to the rich and distinguished Hone family of Irish artists and writers, but early turning her back on Protestant class privilege in Ireland in favour of socialist politics and living. She often focuses in her work on the lives of poor Protestants in the Republic, having shared this position as a single parent of six children. More than any other Irish woman writer, she creates characters or poetic personae living at dangerous edges of society and human life: sexual risk, madness, incest, obsession, pain in reckless relationships. Her work treats themes of family pain, cruelty, rebellion, poverty, and the struggles of gifted, tormented outcasts. In one of her published volumes of poems are these opening lines of a poem entitled 'Obituary for Leland Bardwell': 'Lea-land- there was no shelter there; / no shelter from the cutting North'. This kind of bleak but intense experience informs her novels as well: *Girl on a Bicycle* (1977), *That London Winter* (1981), *The House* (1984), *There We Have Been* (1989), and a volume of short fiction, *Different Kinds of Love* (1987). Despite the sombreness of these themes, however, her work is marked by an extraordinary compassion. She is also one of Ireland's most generous promoters of other artists' works, founding the poetry journal *Cyphers* with EILÉAN NÍ CHUILLEANÁIN, Macdara Woods and Pearse Hutchinson, and devoting herself to editing volumes of schoolchildren's poetry, and creating festivals and other artistic events.   CStP

Barfoot, Joan 1946– Canadian novelist whose fiction maps the changing roles of women in contemporary Canada. She received her BA in English Literature from the University of Western Ontario in 1969 and worked for many years as a journalist for the *Free Press* in London, Ontario. Her first novel, *Gaining Ground* (1978), originally published as *ABRA*, won the Books in Canada Award for the best first novel of the year and tapped into the Canadian motif of locating the self's authentic state in relation to the wilderness. Her second novel, *Dancing in the Dark* (1982), takes the 'mad housewife' as its main theme and depicts the murderous results of marital betrayal; it was made into a film of the same name. Her other novels include *Duet for Three* (1985), *Family News* (1989), *Plain Jane* (1992), *Charlotte and Claudia Keeping in Touch* (1994) and *Some Things About Flying* (1997). Though her early work is more consciously feminist, she continues to take as her focus the domestic space, figuring it variously as treacherous, deadly, confining or lonely. Her protagonists include a lonely 'spinster' who trawls personal advertisements for love, betrayed wives who react with violence or grief, and illicit lovers who understand that their particular griefs are neither acceptable to, nor understood by, society at large.   HSM

Barker, Elspeth 1940– British novelist, educated in Scotland and then at Oxford University. She married the poet George Barker in 1963 and then moved to Norfolk where she raised five children and taught classical languages at a girls' boarding school. She published her first novel, *O Caledonia!*, in 1991 – a dark, GOTHIC novel about a childhood in the Scottish Highlands. The novel opens with 16-year-old Janet dead at the foot of the stairs of Auchnasaugh castle. Who killed her? The novel, while unravelling the story that leads up to the death, contains darkly comic and magic set-pieces which drew comparisons with ANGELA CARTER's stories in THE BLOODY CHAMBER, especially in the way the novel uses symbolism to represent the adolescent Janet's developing sexuality. Barker won the David Higham Literary Prize and the Angel Literary Award for the novel, as well as being short-listed for the Whitbread First Novel Prize.   JHB

Barker, Jane 1652–1732 Coterie poet and professional novelist, spinster and staunch royalist, her oeuvre reflects the struggle of sustaining her controversial personal and political convictions. Educated by her brother, she spent her youth writing poetry from her home in Wilsthorpe, Lincolnshire, much of which was published in the volume *Poetical Recreations* (1688) by friends at Cambridge. Her father, Thomas Barker, held office in the court of Charles I and her mother's family, the Connocks of Cornwall, fought valiantly for the Stuarts during the Civil War. Barker fled England for

France in 1688 when the events of the Glorious Revolution drove James II from the throne. In her poetry she celebrates James as 'prince, and Hero, King, and Glorious Saint' and dedicated a volume to his son. In France, she converted to Roman Catholicism, a choice that would result in the double taxation and forced registration of her English property. In 1704, she returned to England where she lived with her niece, who left her two children under her aunt's care when she eloped with her second husband. In 1713 Barker turned to the London literary marketplace to augment her insufficient annuity. She published four works of fiction before her death in 1732, five years after returning to France.

Her political poetry, two short novels, and eclectic collections of poetry, recipes and short tales – A PATCH-WORK SCREEN FOR THE LADIES (1723) and The Lining to the Patch-Work Screen (1726) – combine conservative politics with radical views of female education and the virtues of escaping 'the Pow'rs of Men's almost Omnipotent Amours'. In the quasi-autobiographical personae of Fidelia and later Galesia, Barker explores the psychological and social spaces of a remarkable life of piety, resistance and exile.   JRS

Barker, Pat 1943– Educated at grammar school in the North-east of England and at the London School of Economics, this prize-winning novelist taught history before the births of her son and daughter (her husband is Professor in Zoology at Durham University). Her work is especially interesting for changes in the kind of fiction which is committed to socialist and feminist principles. Her first novel, UNION STREET (1982), won immediate recognition. Its serial narration of women's struggling, impoverished lives was refined in Blow your House Down (1984), set in the threatening context of serial killers such as the 'Yorkshire Ripper'; the voice of experience here is less controlled by the perspective of the social worker than in Union Street. In work always attuned to contemporary and historical socio-political issues, after The Century's Daughter (1986) she turned from an obviously woman-centred perspective to exploring masculine subjectivities in the complex contexts of private and large-scale conflict and aggression, beginning with The Man Who Wasn't There (1989), the fantasies of a young boy about his absent father after World War II.

This shift to 'cross-gendered writing' produced her most recognized success, the World War I trilogy beginning with Regeneration (1991) and ending with THE GHOST ROAD (1995 winner of the Booker Prize), whose finest volume may be The Eye in the Door (1993 winner of the Guardian Prize). In the betrayals, failures and achievements represented in the 'Regeneration Trilogy', differences and complicities in class, sexual and power relations are exposed. The

1914–18 European context of lost lives and beliefs is juxtaposed to comparable losses in the culture of the Solomon Islands, investigated by the medical and anthropological researcher W.H.R. Rivers. In reviews there was disgust at the 'dirty realism' (interrupted by lyrical moments), but mainly celebration of what was seen as a return to 'documentary REALISM'. However, she is as concerned as any POSTMODERNIST with the uncanny, and also doubles imaginary characters and events with historical figures such as the poets Siegfried Sassoon and Wilfred Owen, Dr Rivers (who treated Sassoon, among others, for 'shell-shock'), and with the cases recorded by Rivers. Like the fictional and bisexual character, Billy Prior, whose ambiguities become central in this trilogy, Barker's writing is both brutal and sensitive.   EJ

Barlow, Jane 1857–1917 Irish novelist, poet and short-fiction writer. Born in Clontarf, she was the daughter of a Church of Ireland minister who later became Vice-Provost of Trinity College, Dublin. Although famously shy and almost reclusive, Barlow was nevertheless a prolific and extremely popular writer in her day, credited with an eye for detail and an ear for the nuances of Hiberno-English, of which she was one of the earliest exponents in literature. Her representations of the speech of people who were not of her class are inevitably flawed and revealing of the politics of the time. Her early poems were published in the Dublin Magazine, but it was the publication of Bog-Land Studies (1892) – followed by such works as Irish Idylls (1892), Strangers at Lisconnell (1895), A Creel of Irish Stories (1897), Flaws (1911) and Irish Ways (1909) – which brought her to the attention of the wider reading public.   LM

Barnard [née Lindsay], Lady Anne 1750–1825 Scottish poet, memoirist and letter writer. Ann's elderly father, the fifth Earl of Balcarres, left the rearing of his eleven children to his stern young wife. Educated by her tutor in Fife, Anne regularly visited Edinburgh and moved in literary circles. The scandalous bankruptcy and flight of her sister Lady Margaret's banker husband brought Anne to London, and the sisters' Berkeley Square home became a fashionable salon frequented by Pitt, Burke, Walpole, Sheridan and others.

A lifelong writer, Anne is remembered for 'Auld Robin Gray' (1772), a ballad set to a traditional Scottish tune. Its young narrator, forced to marry an ancient herdsman, pines for her true love: 'The woes of my heart fa' in showers frae my ee, / Unkenned by my gudeman, who soundly sleeps by me.' Published anonymously, the ballad enjoyed an immense vogue – a 'lovely maniac' sings it in WOLLSTONECRAFT'S THE WRONGS OF WOMAN. Years later, after her friend Sir Walter Scott revealed her as the ballad's author, Anne wrote two inferior continuations.

Drawing by Djuna Barnes of Lillian Russell.

At 42, Anne 'stood the world's smile' and married Andrew Barnard, a 30-year-old half-pay officer. Through her influence, Barnard was appointed colonial secretary to the governor of the Cape of Good Hope. Anne's account of her five years in South Africa, along with her drawings, was published posthumously in the *Lives of the Lindsays* (1840). After Barnard's death in 1807, Anne spent her remaining years with her sister in London. Regrettably, her strict injunction against publication has kept much of her writing, including eighteen volumes on London life, in manuscript form. JHP

Barnard, Marjorie 1897–1987 Australian novelist, historian and one half of the writing partnership 'M. Barnard Eldershaw', formed with FLORA ELDERSHAW whom she met while studying at Sydney University. Born into a middle-class Sydney family, Barnard graduated with first-class honours and the university medal in History but was prevented by her father from travelling to England to take up a postgraduate scholarship at Oxford. Instead she trained as a librar-

ian, a profession she followed until 1950. In 1928, Barnard Eldershaw's *A HOUSE IS BUILT*, a HISTORICAL novel set in early Sydney, shared the *Bulletin* novel prize with KATHARINE SUSANNAH PRICHARD'S *COONARDOO*. Four further novels followed, including *The Glasshouse* (1936) and *Plaque with Laurel* (1937), more satirical studies of the contemporary Australian writing scene, and their most ambitious work *TOMORROW AND TOMORROW AND TOMORROW* (1947). A novel within a novel, this enfolds a realist study of life in Sydney in the decades leading up to World War II within a futurist frame. The two women also collaborated on historical studies and on *Essays in Australian Fiction* (1938) which provided some of the first extended criticism of Prichard, HENRY HANDEL RICHARDSON and CHRISTINA STEAD.

Under her own name, Barnard published a collection of short stories, *The Persimmon Tree* (1943); she regarded the title story, now an acknowledged classic, as her best work. Other titles published after Eldershaw's death include *A History of Australia* (1962) and a BIOGRAPHY of MILES FRANKLIN (1967). During the 1940s Barnard had a passionate love affair with fellow writer Frank Dalby Davison. She never married and spent the last thirty years of her life living with a friend, Vera Murdoch. A selection from her letters is included in *As Good as a Yarn with You* (1992), edited by Carole Ferrier. EW

Barnes, Djuna 1892–1982 American MODERNIST whose expatriate years in Paris were the inspiration for *NIGHTWOOD* (1936), a novel that brilliantly evokes a whole abject carnival of bisexual, cross-dressing, louche and lesbian life. This mistresspiece was the climax of Barnes's writing career. She wrote little after her return to the States in 1939, although she lived to a great age in sick and cantankerous solitude in Greenwich Village.

She was born on a farm in Cornwall-on-Hudson. Her father Wald was a self-styled visionary who lived in polygamous fashion with his wife Elizabeth (Djuna's mother) and his mistress Fanny, and their tribe of children. The household was dominated by Wald's mother, Zadel, journalist, suffrage campaigner and medium, who had honed her Boston-bohemian style in 1880s London as a friend of Lady WILDE and ELEANOR MARX. Zadel shared a bed and risqué jokes with her granddaughter Djuna. However, when Wald divorced her mother in 1912, Djuna left with her for New York, and never looked back except in mockery and anger. The West she loathed, she once said with grand dismissiveness, because 'it personifies everything in my father that I hated – Mark Twain – Bret Harte – Walt Whitman sort of thing – Ezra Pound and his hick-prune-chewing prose.'

By contrast, her own style was intensely urban. In

New York she quickly found her niche as a journalist, interviewing street-people, artistes and performers, rabble-rousing preachers and doubtful politicians. In 1921 she was posted to Paris, and launched on a radiant decade in which she flirted with NATALIE BARNEY's high-toned lesbian set, mocked in THE LADIES ALMANACK (1928), and – the same year – published a first autobiographical novel, RYDER. Her emotional life centred on her doomed love-affair with American sculptor Thelma Wood. Thelma's promiscuous, self-immolating style at once appalled Barnes and mirrored her. Thelma was Nightwood's muse: the title plays on her name, 'Nigh T. Wood'. But the book is an inventory of dark desires. Its main spokesperson, Matthew O'Connor, is based on a real-life 'character', Dan Mahoney, transvestite doctor to the expat. underworld.

Nightwood was partly written at Hayford Hall, an English country house which Peggy Guggenheim rented; there Barnes met EMILY COLEMAN, who was instrumental in encouraging her to finish the book, and in persuading T.S. Eliot to publish it. Barnes herself had expected (and got) rejections from publishers – 'they all say that it is not a novel; that there is no continuity of life in it, only high spots and poetry – that I do not give anyone an idea of what the persons wore, ate or how they opened and closed doors.' But while nothing in Nightwood is ordinary, it conveys a pungent sense of its human menagerie. WILLA MUIR described its quality very well – 'You have entered into every kind of human distortion ... you have a genius for imaginative empathy.'

Barnes had made her life over into her work; the only finished writing of her later years, the poetical drama The Antiphon (1958), harked back to her family background. 'My talent is my character, my character my talent, and both an estrangement', she wrote in 1963, with characteristic succinctness and finality.   LS

Barney, Natalie Clifford 1876–1972 American lesbian poet, playwright, novelist and essayist. After spending her early years in Cincinnati, Ohio, she was educated at finishing schools in the USA and Europe. Her father was a railroad heir, her mother an accomplished painter. After complying with her father's wish that she come out as a debutante, she went to France (1897) where she became legendary as a seductress of women. GERTRUDE STEIN, DJUNA BARNES, RADCLYFFE HALL, COLETTE, and Remy de Gourmont all based characters on her in their writings. Barney's father tried to suppress her first book of poems, Quelques portraits-sonnets de femmes (1900), which her mother illustrated. When he died in 1902, Barney's inheritance allowed her to settle comfortably into Parisian bohemian life. She wrote prolifically about lesbianism and, for over sixty years, beginning in 1909,

held salons that brought together international artists and intellectuals, including Valery, Proust, Cocteau, Wilde, Rilke, Pound, Eliot, Hemingway, Fitzgerald, MINA LOY, EDITH SITWELL, Colette, Barnes, and Stein (whose THE MAKING OF AMERICANS she translated into French). In 1927 she founded the Académie des Femmes, a forum for the presentation of women's writing, art and dance. Her writings include wartime scenes, Pensées d'une amazone (1920); a GOTHIC novel, The One Who is Legion or A.D.'s After-Life (1930); epigrams, Nouvelles Pensées de l'amazone (1939); and memoirs, Aventures de l'esprit (1929), Souvenirs indiscrets (1960) and Traits et portraits (1963), with portraits of writers and artists she knew. During World War II, she lived in Italy and supported the Fascists.   JSG

Barrell, Maria (Weylar) fl.1788–90 English poet, dramatist and polemical writer, she lived in London and Isleworth, and published in periodicals under the name 'Maria'. As Maria Weylar she also claimed to have written Reveries du Coeur, or Feelings of the Heart (1770), which combines polemic with poetry. From about 1785, with her soldier-husband absent in America and two children to feed, she was imprisoned for debt. This occasioned a number of works, including the pamphlet 'British Liberty Vindicated: Or A Delineation of the King's Bench Prison' (1788), and her theme became one of loyalty to British liberty but complaint about her country's treatment of its prisoners. A preface to her play, The Captive (1790), is dedicated to the Prince of Wales and argues that, whilst the British were disgusted by France's Bastille prison, similar conditions greeted those confined within British gaols; the system did not help to rehabilitate debtors, nor allow them to pay their debt to society. The play itself depicts sentimental scenes, such as the dying husband and the misery of his virtuous wife, and claims that those who fall on hard times through no fault of their own are punished in the severest terms: 'O! savage laws that laid my Heartly low, and is insolvency so great a crime that man must die, because he is in debt?'   RDM

Barrett, Browning, Elizabeth see BROWNING, ELIZABETH BARRETT

Barrington, Margaret 1896–1982 Irish novelist and short-fiction writer, critic and journalist. Born in Donegal, she married Edmund Curtis in 1922 and then divorced him to marry writer and novelist Liam O'Flaherty, whom she had met through the Irish Statesman, where both published short fiction. Following her separation from O'Flaherty, she went to live in London where she continued to write and became editor of the women's section of the Labour Party newspaper, Tribune. Her novel My Cousin Justin (1939) gives an account of growing up as a Protestant in an idyllic Ireland before World War I, overshadowed toward the end by a growing awareness of sectarian division and limitations on the lives of girls and women.

Following the outbreak of World War II she returned to Ireland where she finally settled in Cork. Much of the material written at this period of her life remains unpublished. A collection of short stories, *David's Daughter Tamar* (published posthumously, 1982), portrays Barrington's concern with social and political issues, as do many uncollected stories such as those published in the *Bell*. Along with many other Irish writers, she experienced the negative effects of censorship (she was denounced from the pulpit following the publication of her short story 'Colour'). She articulated a vigorous anti-censorship position in her contribution to the censorship debate in the *Bell* in 1945.   LM

Bartlett, Elizabeth 1924– British poet whose work

is remarkable for its painfully truthful insights into people's lives. Born in Deal in the mining region of Kent, Bartlett was educated at Dover School for Girls and married Denis Perkins in 1943. Despite an early success at the age of 19, in Tambimuttu's *Poetry London*, Bartlett did not publish again until her mid-fifties. She worked for sixteen years as a medical secretary, and later in the home help service, drawing upon these experiences to construct the world of her poems. It is an intensely and uncompromisingly physical world of blood, bowels, sickness and vomit, in which people are often deranged. Bartlett has stated 'I am drawn to people with maimed personalities because I know I am one myself' – her poetry was originally stimulated by a five-year stint of psychoanalysis.

The strength of her poetry derives from its humane curiosity and compassion. These qualities very much inform her first volume, *A Lifetime of Dying* (1979), which draws on poems from the previous forty years, and includes material from consultants' notes and social work reports. *Strange Territory* (1983) and *The Czar is Dead* (1986) continue to probe the uncomfortable worlds of the doctor's office and the overstretched social services. Material from two small press publications, *Instead of a Mass* (1991) and *Look, No Face* (1991), was incorporated in *Two Women Dancing: New and Selected Poems*, edited by CAROL RUMENS the same year.   DM

Barton, (Barbara) Anne [Roesen Righter] 1933–

American-born academic and critic of Renaissance drama and Romantic poetry. She was born in New York, educated at Bryn Mawr and Cambridge, and has worked in England continuously since 1960: Fellow of Girton (1960–72), Professor at Bedford College, London (1972–4), first woman Fellow of New College, Oxford (1974–84) and Professor of English at Cambridge since 1984. Since *Shakespeare and the Idea of the Play* (1962), Barton has been a *doyenne* of English Shakespearean studies: a leading expositor of the comedies (notably in the widely read introductions of the *Riverside Shakespeare* and a Penguin *Tempest*) and an important influence in expanding performance of non-Shakespearean drama in the Royal Shakespeare Company's second house, The Swan. Her criticism is noted for its command of the totality of English drama before 1700. *Ben Jonson, Dramatist* (1984) expounds all Jonson's stagework and rescues the late plays; its arguments on dramatic character and onomastics are pursued across time in *The Names of Comedy* (1990). The formidable *Essays, Mainly Shakespearean* (1994) gathers influential work of increasingly historicist emphasis: its introduction gestures reticently at critical autobiography.

A substantial second writing career appears in Barton's sustained essay work for the *New York Review of Books*: highlights include a trenchant account of the new historicist methods of Stephen Greenblatt, and a body of essays on Romantic authors, notably Byron and Clare.   JFM

Barton, Clara Harlowe 1821–1912 American

humanitarian and teacher. Best known as the founder of the American Red Cross, Barton was born in Massachusetts and began teaching at the age of 15. She taught for eighteen years, before moving to Washington, D.C., in 1855, where she became the first woman to hold a full-time position in the Patent Office. When Civil War broke out, she immediately began to care for the wounded soldiers. Often the first person to attend the sick and dying, she herself would distribute the food, blankets and supplies donated to her. She was involved in many major Civil War battles.

In 1869, she went to Europe and attended soldiers during the Franco-Prussian War. She also met with members of the International Committee of the Red Cross, who enlisted her aid in getting the United States to sign the Geneva Convention of 1864. When she returned to the United States in 1873, she began working to establish an American chapter of the Red Cross, which was duly founded in 1881. She served as its first president until her resignation in 1904, and is credited with expanding the scope of Red Cross activities to include peacetime aid to the victims of natural disasters. Her DIARIES are held in the Library of Congress; her only published works are histories of the Red Cross (*The Red Cross*, 1898, and *A Story of the Red Cross: Glimpses of Field Work*, 1904) and a small autobiography for children, entitled *A Story of My Childhood* (1907).   SP

Bassett [née Roper, Clarke], Mary c.1522–72

Translator, eldest daughter of MARGARET ROPER, and granddaughter of Sir Thomas More. She continued the family traditions of female scholarship and devout Catholicism, and her choice of works shows a strong sense of family identity and intimacy. Between 1547 and 1553, as Mary Clarke (wife of Stephen), she translated into English the first five books of Eusebius's Greek *Ecclesiastical History*, which her mother had translated into Latin. She presented a manuscript copy to Queen MARY I, who showed her favour as a fellow-Catholic, and gave her a court post in 1557. By this time she had married James Bassett. Her translation from Latin to English of *An Exposition of a Part of the Passion*, written by her grandfather while imprisoned in the Tower, was published with More's works in 1557 and was much admired. However, she was said to have resisted publication because she undertook it 'but for her own pastime and exercise'. HH

Bates, Katharine Lee 1859–1929 American educator, poet, TRAVEL WRITER and CHILDREN's writer. She was born in Falmouth, Massachusetts. Her family moved to Grantsville after her father, a minister, died when she was still an infant. She was educated at public schools and earned AB and AM degrees from Wellesley College (1880, 1881), having spent a year studying at Oxford University. From 1885 to 1925, she was an Instructor in English at Wellesley. Her reputation as a writer came to rest on a single poem, the patriotic hymn 'America the Beautiful', which first appeared in 1895 in the *Congregationalist*, but she published, in all, six collections of poetry, including *America the Beautiful and Other Poems* (1911). She also wrote juvenile fiction (*Rose and Thorn*, 1889; *Hermit Island*, 1890) and travel books (*In Sunny Spain*, 1913). Through her teaching and her college and high school textbooks, most notably *American Literature* (1898), she was a force in the modernization of American pedagogy, seeking to inspire students' appreciation of literature and its relevance to their lives. JSG

Bathurst, Anne *c.*1638–96/7 British visionary and diarist. She was brought up in a highly religious atmosphere and spent much of her childhood reading the Bible and praying with her sister. At the age of 17 she rejected the doctrine of Election and later joined the sect of JANE LEAD. In her thirties, Bathurst became obsessed with the idea of knowing God. She began to keep a DIARY of her visions in 1678 when she claimed to have been visited by an angel. Her writing is passionate and hyperbolic, and she frequently employs explicit sexual imagery: 'O Love! Love! how am I imbellished sick with Divine Sweetness more than marrow or fatness. My Beloved has placed himself within me, as if the Earthen vessel were stretched beyond its wonted bigness.' Her diary and letters survive in manuscript form and are kept in the Bodleian Library. RDM

Bathurst, Elizabeth *c.*1655–85 Quaker polemicist who was sickly from childhood but developed a gift for moving public assemblies. She made a preaching tour to Bristol at a time of persecution, and was imprisoned in the Marshalsea. In her twenties she published *An Expostulatory Appeal* (1679?), then *Truth's Vindication* (1679), a carefully structured defence of the Quakers which combined theological erudition with personal and PROPHETICAL passages. George Whitehead reported that 'the meanness and weakness of her person' led some to doubt her authorship. Bathurst herself asserted that she had not 'fondly desired to get my name in print, for 'tis not inky character can make a saint', but 'for some time I have not been mine own'. *Sayings of Women* (1683) described and quoted significant biblical women, to show that 'women receive an office in the truth as well as men'. After her early death, *Truth Vindicated* (1691) combined Bathurst's collected works with memorials by family and friends, one of whom said in praise that 'her mind was directed and turned inward'. HH

Battier [née Fleming], Henrietta 1751–1813 Irish poet, now acknowledged as one of the most gifted authors of satirical verse in late 18th-century Ireland. Born in County Meath, Henrietta married Major John Battier when she was just 17. In 1783–4 she visited London, where she appeared as an amateur on the Drury Lane stage, and met Samuel Johnson, who encouraged her literary ambitions.

Returning to Dublin, Battier established a niche for herself as a commentator on contemporary controversies, often accepting commissions to versify on a specific topic. For instance, her 'Lines Addressed to the late Lord Clifden', included in her collection *The Protected Fugitives* (1791), appealed for mercy for the abductors of two teenage heiresses, and was composed at the request of the sister of one of the accused, while *The Kirwanade* (1791), published under the pseudonym 'Patt Pindar', was a masterful exercise in vituperation directed at Revd Walter Blake Kirwan, a celebrated Dublin preacher. Battier also campaigned for political reform in works such as *The Gibbonade, or Political Reviewer* (1793–4), *The Marriage Ode Royal* (1795) – a work in the style of Dryden, which ridiculed the Prince of Wales – and *An Address on . . . the Projected Union* (1799), which opposed the imminent abolition of the Irish Parliament.

Although modest in her estimate of her own work – she pronounced herself 'a better housewife than poet' – Battier defended her status as a professional author: 'I wrote for profit, and Fate added fame.' Described by Thomas Moore as 'acute, odd, warm-hearted and intrepid', she was a notable figure in Dublin literary, political and social life during the 1790s, but her fortunes declined in later years, and she died in poverty in Dublin. RR

'Battle Hymn of the Republic, The' (1862) This poem was JULIA WARD HOWE's supreme contribution to the war effort. Her *Reminiscences* (1899) record her aimless longing to serve 'our great battle' against the evils of slavery, and the inspiration which struck her in the night, after attending a review of the troops. Used to nocturnal 'attacks of versification', Howe scribbled down her stanzas in the dark, to avoid waking the baby. With 'John Brown's Body' still in her mind from the day with the soldiers, she diverted the tune to the Book of Revelation. Recalling UNCLE TOM'S CABIN, a decade earlier, her poem has a visionary sweep, thundering with the notes of the Day of Judgement, as the Lord – 'the Hero, born of woman' – makes His Second Coming in the cause of the Federal armies. The slaughter is the vintage of 'the grapes of wrath', the fires of the camps are altars to justice; the march to battle is the march to everlasting life. In the apocalyptic convulsion of the Civil War, still only in its beginnings, this blazing faith in the triumphant righteousness of the fight turned images of potential disaster into promises of eternal glory. PEK

Battlefields (1939) Published in the troubled period immediately before the outbreak of World War II, MARY GILMORE's seventh major collection of poetry maintains earlier ambivalences toward warfare, but the balance here is less towards praising the heroism of war's soldiers ('For Anzac, 1939') and more toward attacking those addressed in 'To the War-Mongers'. Forceful criticism of the churches as proponents of war, as in the title poem, results in part from anger felt by socialists like Gilmore against the Catholic Church for its role in the Spanish Civil War ('Spain', 'Barcelona'). In a wider sense, however, Gilmore engages with other social and political battlefields. Her attacks on poverty ('Unskilled', 'Widows' Pensions') are sharpened by the experiences of the Great Depression, while she continues the forays – begun in *The Wild Swan* (1930) and *Under the Wilgas* (1932) – into what would become major battles of the late 20th century, those of environmentalists against land degradation and species loss ('I Saw the Beauty Go') and those for recognition of the dispossession and maltreatment of AUSTRALIA's indigenous peoples ('Aboriginal Themes', 'Truganini'). JStr

Baumgartner's Bombay (1988) ANITA DESAI's novel reconstructs the multitudes of India echoing the far-off drama of World War II. It is told through the eyes of Hugo Baumgartner, a German Jew who has escaped Nazi persecution in Europe and has come all the way to India to live in a squalid apartment behind Bombay's Taj Hotel. From his childhood memories in pre-war Berlin, and throughout his business activities first in Calcutta then in Bombay, Baumgartner remains an underdog, as much as the homeless Indian families camped on the sidewalks. His hermit life has reduced itself to looking after a dozen stray cats in his apartment. Aside from his friend Lotte, a has-been cabaret singer who shares his exile status, he has no companions and he does not belong anywhere. He slowly retreats even from language, speaks reluctantly with foreigners and loathes venturing outside his living space: a man from a cultivated German family who ends up as a marginal figure both for his country and for India. As Desai demonstrates, Baumgartner's fate is shaped by forces beyond his control. SPo

Bawden [née Mabey], Nina (Mary Kark) 1925– British REALIST novelist and writer of CHILDREN'S FICTION whose 20 adult novels and 17 works for children are largely concerned with the 'myths, half-truths, fancies and deceits that make up family history'. *The Peppermint Pig* (1975) and *Carrie's War* (1973) are contemporary children's classics, the latter inspired by her experiences as a war evacuee in South Wales. These also informed *Anna Apparent* (1972), an examination of the adult outcomes of ill-treatment and deprivation in childhood. *A Woman of My Age* (1967) examines feminist themes of entrapment. *Circles of Deceit* (1987) was shortlisted for the Booker Prize. *Family Money* (1991) attacks Thatcherism in a familial context. Dark and suspenseful, her work nevertheless incorporates humour and is as concerned with the spirit of survival as it is with human failings (and those of the welfare state). She attended Somerville College, Oxford (where she belonged to the Labour Club and debated with Margaret Thatcher), and spent ten years as a magistrate. *In My Own Time: Almost an Autobiography* (1994), discusses the influence of oral history on her development as a writer. She is a Fellow of the Royal Society of Literature. LDo

Baynton, Barbara 1857–1929 Dissident Australian short-story writer and novelist. Although in her dotage she invented stories about her birth and early life, she is believed to have been born and raised in outback New South Wales, the child of Irish bounty immigrants. In 1880 she married the first of her three husbands, a member of a family of small land holders in which she worked as a governess. After producing three children and enduring harsh bush conditions for seven years, she was abandoned by her husband who ran off with her cousin – a devastating experience which would later fuel her creative writing. Her second marriage in 1887 in Sydney, to Thomas Baynton, a seventy-year-old retired surgeon, secured her financially for life and introduced her to literary and academic circles in which she was described as 'robust and vigorous, overflowing with vitality'. Her literary output was small but significant. In her six short stories, begun in 1896 and collected under the title *BUSH STUDIES* in 1902, and novel, *Human Toll* (1907), she details the physical and psychic horrors of outback life, especially for women who suffer indifference, brutality and misery at the hands of selfish, vicious and predatory men. After Thomas Baynton's death in 1903 she utilized her considerable business acumen by investing in antiques, furniture and jewellery. She also became the chair of the directors of the Law Book Company of Australasia. With homes in Sydney and London, she was a celebrated literary hostess, known for her devastating wit, caustic tongue and forceful personality. Her brief marriage to her third husband, the fifth Baron Headley, in 1921, came to an end when he suffered bankruptcy and she returned to Melbourne.

Her frequently anthologized stories like 'The Chosen Vessel', 'Squeaker's Mate' and 'Billy Skywonkie' defy idealized bush nationalism, typified in the celebrated works of Henry Lawson. Baynton's stories were neglected in her lifetime and lost to view until being recovered by nervous reviewers in the 1960s. A rare talent, her reputation has been revived since the 1980s with a new, appreciative audience of feminist readers and deconstructive critics. KS

Bayou Folk (1894) KATE CHOPIN's first short-story collection was well received, although many reviewers approved of it on a wave of fashionable enthusiasm for 'local colour' fiction. But, drawing on her years living in upper Louisiana, in the Cane River country near Natchitoches, Chopin was already tapping into regional material for her own ends. Most of the twenty-three stories had been separately published, in a variety of newspapers, and children's and adult magazines, including the newly founded *Vogue*. Gathered together, with some additions, they highlighted Chopin's repeated interest in characters trapped in larger histories: the trauma of the Civil War in 'Ma'ame Pélagie' and 'Beyond the Bayou', the power of a violent husband in 'In Sabine', the force of class lines in 'At the 'Cadian Ball', the grip of sentiment in 'A Visit to Avoyelles'. In several sketches, Chopin suggests that will or passion can break down social and psychological barriers. But in 'Désirée's Baby', with its further racial twist, she brought these elements together, in a tragic and shocking form. This story, with the equally haunting 'La Belle Zoraïde', stands out for many readers, now as at first, as the most powerful in the collection. PEK

Beach, Sylvia 1887–1962 American bookseller, founder of Shakespeare and Company, Paris, in 1919; and publisher of James Joyce's *Ulysses* (1922). She was born in Baltimore, Maryland, to a Presbyterian minister, grew up in New Jersey, where her father's

Princeton parishioners included presidents Woodrow Wilson and Grover Cleveland, and first lived in Paris at 14. A permanent resident by 1917, she opened her own bookshop and lending library in 1919. Hung with photographs of Wilde, Whitman and Poe, and stocked with English and American fiction and literary magazines, Shakespeare and Company attracted both French authors – André Gide (who bought *Moby-Dick*) was one of Beach's first subscribers – and 1920s expatriates. Ezra Pound and James Joyce arrived in Paris in 1920 and became her close friends; Wyndham Lewis, T.S. Eliot, Ernest Hemingway, Scott Fitzgerald, Thornton Wilder, Sherwood Anderson and GERTRUDE STEIN would follow.

Beach did not intend to be a publisher, but it is as a publisher she is best remembered today. After VIRGINIA and Leonard WOOLF rejected Harriet Shaw Weaver's appeal to have the Hogarth Press publish Joyce's *Ulysses*, Beach arranged for her old-line stationers, Darantière of Dijon, to bring out the book. Shakespeare and Company would continue to publish Joyce's work-in-progress, and to introduce young writers through well-publicized readings, until the bookshop was forced to close in 1941. After the war, Beach wrote her memoirs and sold her papers to American university libraries. Her ashes are buried in Princeton. AMD

Beachmasters (1985) THEA ASTLEY's tenth novel represented a departure from her focus on Australian society as she turned her attention to contemporary politics in the Pacific. She had written about the Pacific islands before, in her *A Boatload of Home Folk* (1968) but as little more than a setting for the activities of white Australians. *Beachmasters* confronted the growing native independence movements there, and gives an account of a failed attempt to throw off the British and French colonizers in a fictional island, Kristi. The complexity of multiple allegiance is dramatized in the narrative of Gavi Salway, a mixed-race member of a planter family, who initially helps the rebels, only to be appalled when they murder an old friend of his family. Astley writes parts of the novel in Seaspeak, her version of pidgin, as a comment on the language oppression of English and French. But, for all her distaste for the injustices of colonialism, her perspective must remain with her European characters and she lavishes on them her habitual wit and irony. SPL

Beard, Mary Ritter 1876–1958 American historian, anti-war activist, labour reformer, and feminist whose work critiques the discourses of feminism as well as anti-feminism. Born in Indianapolis, Indiana, Beard earned her Ph.B. from DePauw University and briefly attended Columbia graduate school. In 1900 she married Charles Austin Beard who became a prominent

Columbia University professor of history and political science. She frequently collaborated with her husband on such popular and influential books as *The Rise of American Civilization* (2 vols., 1927).

Beard agitated for the rights of working women, helping to organize the shirtwaist workers' strike of New York City in 1909–10. Although she worked for the woman-suffrage amendment, she did not support the Equal Rights Amendment. She argued that the discourse of equal rights did not take into account women's differences and only encouraged women to become equally culpable participants of a flawed society. In her best-known work, *Women as Force in History* (1946), she further criticized the language of subjection, maintaining that woman has always possessed power and has participated equally in the creation of civilizations – even if the story of woman's power has been ignored by historians. Dedicated to the recovery of this story, she helped to create the ill-fated World Center for Women's Archives (1935–40).   VM

Beattie, Ann 1947– American short-story writer and novelist who satirizes the infectious vacuity of popular culture and investigates the resulting 'world of alienation, sadness, conflict'. With one's identity consistently muddled by magazine and film, 'you've got to figure out', she writes in the novel *Love Always* (1985), 'whether you're a phony or a real person'.

Born in Washington, D.C., she was educated at American University and the University of Connecticut, and has taught at the universities of Virginia and Harvard. 'In the process of writing', she explains, 'I try to figure out how to present the underpinnings of the dress without demystifying the fabric.' Her other novels include *Falling in Place* (1980) and *Another You* (1995), a campus satire. She has also published several collections of short stories, *The Burning House* (1983) and *Where You'll Find Me* (1987) among them.

Asked by her editor to 'step out of the literary world to confront the art world', Beattie wrote a book-length critique of the American artist *Alex Katz* (1987). This was followed by an essay, 'Agreeable Accomplices', in *Flesh and Blood: Photographers' Images of their own Families* (1992), in which she confesses that 'like a lot of artists, I sidestep solving mysteries by presenting alternative mysteries'.   JAH

Beaufort, Lady Margaret, Countess of Richmond and Derby 1443–1509 English translator of religious texts and literary patron. The great-granddaughter of John of Gaunt, Duke of Lancaster, she married three times. Her first husband was Edmund Tudor, half-brother of Henry VI. She had one son by that marriage (the future Henry VII) but no other children. Her life was one of religious dedication, self-

discipline and self-sacrifice. Indeed her translations can be seen as an exercise in, as well as expression of, piety. The first is of book 4 of Thomas à Kempis's *The Imitation of Christ*, perhaps the most influential devotional work in the Christian tradition. The second is of a text less well known today, but nonetheless popular in the Middle Ages and Renaissance, *Speculum Aureum* (*The Mirror of Gold*). Lady Margaret Beaufort's interest in humanist scholarship is demonstrated further in her patronage of not only John Fisher, Bishop of Rochester, but also the two early printers, William Caxton and Wynkyn de Worde. In addition to her translations, a number of letters written by Lady Margaret Beaufort also survive.   DW

Beauvoir, Simone de (Lucie Ernestine Marie Bertrand) 1908–86 French philosopher, novelist, essayist, autobiographer, biographer and foundational 20th-century feminist theorist. One of the greatest intellectual forces of her century, and a life-long challenger of conventions, Simone de Beauvoir was born in Paris into a French bourgeois family of declining fortunes. She followed her early education – at a second-rate Catholic girls' school – with a brilliant student career which culminated in her triumph as the youngest student (and one of only a handful of women) ever to pass the highly competitive *agrégation* in Philosophy in 1929. While preparing for this examination, which secured her place in the elite ranks of the French teaching profession, Beauvoir met Jean-Paul Sartre, her life-long friend, lover, and fellow-philosopher, whose thought she powerfully influenced. A legendary couple, crucial for the development of French existentialism, Beauvoir and Sartre achieved iconic status as socially and politically engaged 20th-century intellectuals.

After teaching in secondary schools in Marseilles, Rouen and Paris in the 1930s, Beauvoir published her first novel, *She Came to Stay*, in 1943. Densely worked in terms of her original treatment of the concept of the Other and of the mechanisms of intersubjectivity, this deeply philosophical novel achieved popularity for its portrayal of a sexual triangle and as a picture of contemporary Parisian life. From this time, Beauvoir earned her living from her writing. Her novels, *The Blood of Others* (1945) and *All Men Are Mortal* (1946); important philosophical essays, *Pyrrhus et Cinéas* (1944) and *The Ethics of Ambiguity* (1947); a play, *Les Bouches inutiles* (1945); and an extended sociopolitical account of her travels in America, *America Day by Day* (1948) – all precede her most influential work, the classic of feminist thought, THE SECOND SEX (1949). In it, famously, Beauvoir argues that the female condition is not fixed, but a result of concerted, historical efforts to define woman as the Other, a status which women have themselves largely accepted. 'One is not born, but rather becomes, a woman', argues Beauvoir in the key statement of *The Second Sex*. Beauvoir's extensive analyses of woman's historical, social, religious, aesthetic and biological history all contribute to an argument which insists that women must reject essentialist definitions of themselves as Other, and assume the rights and duties attendant on their status as full Subjects. The sex/gender divide that Beauvoir's theory suggested has been important for subsequent feminist writers.

In the 1950s and 1960s Beauvoir continued to produce fiction (*The Mandarins* (1954) won the Prix Goncourt), but much of her time was spent writing her four-volume autobiography, now regarded as a classic. She first declared herself a feminist in 1972, after spending many years in the international limelight as the major female existentialist thinker and as a campaigner on issues such as the Algerian and Vietnam wars. She devoted much of her time in her last years to various feminist causes and generously gave assistance to young female scholars. Sartre died in 1980; Beauvoir in 1986. They are buried together in the Montparnasse Cemetery in the quarter of Paris in which Beauvoir was born and spent most of her life.   KF

Becker Wives, The (1946) a novella by MARY LAVIN, set in Dublin in the early 20th century. The story focuses on the bourgeois and somewhat 'lacklustre' Becker family. Throughout, Lavin draws attention to the ways in which personal aspirations are challenged in relation to social identity. Flora and Honoria, wives of the two younger brothers, Theobold and Samuel Becker, are linked by the reality of illusion. The artistically gifted but infertile Flora becomes obsessed by the pregnant Honoria and in her imagination changes places with her as a means of establishing her own identity as a 'real' woman. Metaphors of slimness and roundness are superimposed in the narrative to draw attention to the paradoxes associated with women and beauty and Lavin exploits these images to great effect. The story unfolds to reveal the pattern of inherited madness, the cause of Flora's dilemma, which serves to question the outer material reality of the Becker household and the inner reality of human frailty.   EF

Beckett, Mary 1928– Was born in Belfast and lived in Northern Ireland until her marriage in 1956. As an unmarried primary teacher in her twenties, she had early success as a short-story writer. But when she married, she moved to Dublin and raised five children, only returning to writing when her children were grown and the 'Troubles' of the North galvanized her into writing Northern lives as a way of promoting understanding among audiences distant from the North and impatient with Catholic resistance.

Her first book of short stories, *A Belfast Woman* (1980),

focuses on 'small', private lives of women – straitened, often joyless lives, though the characters are tough and resilient, too, as in the title story, when an elderly Dublin widow tries to run away for the day to Belfast, but is stopped by 'bombs on the line' and has to return home: 'She would never let them know where she'd gone; if she were very careful . . . Belfast would still be there for her.' This kind of independent, stubborn strength informs the working-class woman in Beckett's 1987 novel, *Give Them Stones*.

With *A Literary Woman* (1990), a collection of stories set in Dublin, Beckett leaves behind the ordinary and invents one of Irish literature's oddest grotesques, a character whose own abused life leaves her wanting to destroy others'. 'I believe in God', says Miss Teeling. 'Only a fool wouldn't believe in God. So many nasty things could not happen accidentally . . . Oh He is mighty and He can do great things but I am an independent operator. I can compete in my own small way.'
                                        CStP

Bedford, Jean (Gladys Agnes) 1946– Australian novelist. Born in Cambridge, England, but moved to Australia with her family as a child and grew up in the Victorian countryside. She trained as a school-teacher and also worked as a journalist before becoming a full-time writer in the 1980s. Her first publication, a collection of stories called *Country Girl Again* (1979), was issued by the feminist publishing house Sisters. It draws on her own background in tracing some of the destructive effects of rural life on women while also questioning whether the supposedly freer, sexually liberated city of the 1970s offers a better alternative. Autobiographical material is also evident, though used in a more deliberately playful and self-referential manner, in *Colouring In: a Book of Ideologically Unsound Love Stories* (1986), co-written with Bedford's long-time friend, the literary agent Rose Creswell. As the sub-title suggests, this offers comically ironic portraits of two best friends, Iris and Sal, as they party and change sexual partners in 1980s Sydney.

Bedford is, however, probably best known for her first novel, *Sister Kate* (1982), a rewriting of the story of the iconic 19th-century Australian bushranger Ned Kelly from the perspective of his sister, part of the attempt during the 1980s to put women back into the still resolutely masculinist 'Australian legend'. *If With a Beating Heart* (1993) also rewrites history from a woman's perspective, the focus here falling on CLAIRE CLAIRMONT, Byron's lover and MARY SHELLEY's step-sister, during her tumultuous years living with the Shelleys. Other novels include *Love Child* (1986), based on her mother's life, and *Lease of Summer* (1990). Since 1991, Bedford has also produced a series of crime novels, featuring Anna Southwood, private investigator, brave to the point of foolhardiness and on the side of the battler: *Worse than Death* (1991), *To Make a Killing* (1992) and *Signs of Murder* (1994). *Now You See Me* (1997) is a psychological thriller on the very current topic of child abuse, which intercuts the narrative with passages from the killer's diary.   EW

Bedford [née von Schoenebeck], Sybille 1911–
German-born British novelist, biographer and journalist. Bedford was educated in Italy, France and England and became a talented linguist. She covered the Auschwitz Trial in Frankfurt at the end of World War II. Her first published novel, *A Legacy* (1956), concerning the marriages between two rich German families, was partly based on her own background. Her book *The Best We Can Do* (1958) is an almost verbatim account of the courtroom proceedings in the trial of John Bodkin Adams, an ill-considered prosecution brought against a doctor who was held to have killed an elderly patient with morphine and heroin. 'There is no way out', she wrote. 'The prisoner in the dock is committed to his deed, committed irrevocably to one course between two points: the wheels are moving, nothing – nothing on earth can stop them – and the wheels are going one way only, towards a verdict.' *The Faces of Justice: A Traveller's Report* (1961) reflected her continuing interest in the relentless nature of judicial procedures.

In 1930 Bedford had met Aldous Huxley, when they were both living in Sanary in the South of France, and they became friends. Many years later she would write Huxley's BIOGRAPHY – her major work, admiring, but revealingly exhaustive, 'a labour of love . . . done in a spirit of detachment'. The first volume was published in 1973; the second in 1974.

In 1979 Bedford became vice-president of PEN and her autobiographical novel, *Jigsaw: An Unsentimental Education*, was published in 1989.   RH

Beecher, Catharine Esther 1800–78 American
essayist, polemicist, educator. Raised in Litchfield, Connecticut, Catharine was trained early in the domestic duties of a large household. Her mother's death left her in charge of seven children, and four more after her father, the Reverend Lyman Beecher, remarried. Her crusading zeal in reforming women's education led her to found female seminaries, write textbooks, train teachers and deliver lectures with such energy that she suffered recurrent nervous collapse. Her main influence, however, was as the author of such generative works as *A Treatise on Domestic Economy* (1841) and *The American Woman's Home* (1869), written in collaboration with her equally prolific younger sister, HARRIET BEECHER STOWE. Elevating the household arts to both a 'domestic science' and an evangelic calling, the Beechers sanctified the American housewife as the nation's ideal Christian guide.   BF

Beer, Patricia 1924– British poet, born into a
Plymouth Brethren family in Devon. Educated at Exmouth Grammar School, she took a First in English at Exeter University and a B. Litt. ('The Sermons of Henry King') at Oxford. She taught English in Italy (including at the University of Padua and the British Institute in Rome) for seven years, then at Goldsmith's College, University of London, in 1962–8. Her first volume of poetry was *Loss of the Magyar* (1959), 'affected by the poetry of the Thirties . . . all too clearly', she later said. *Just Like the Resurrection* (1967) followed, revealing Beer's wit ('Here I come, the poet Drayton, / Quite convinced of my salvation') and her capacity to find significant meaning in ordinary experience. *The Estuary* (1971) includes 'In Memory of Constance Markiewicz', commenting equivocally on Yeats's poem on the same subject and suggesting Beer's guarded views on feminism more generally:

> Yes, she became opinionated
> And shrill, but had a longer funeral
> Procession than most of us will have.

Poems (1979), *The Lie of the Land* (1983), *New Poems* (1988), and *Collected Poems* (1988) followed. *Friend of Heraclitus* (1993) includes a series of twelve sonnets on locations in the South-West and a set of brief imagist verses: 'Poet's minds make the best filters; they deal in fragments', she said. The rhyming couplets of 'Sequence', from Beer's *Autumn* (1997), record her near-fatal illness in spare language but offer a measure of reassurance in their wit. Beer has also published an autobiography, *Mrs Beer's House* (1968), and some literary criticism, including *Reader, I Married Him* (1964), on female characters in JANE AUSTEN, CHARLOTTE BRONTË, ELIZABETH GASKELL and GEORGE ELIOT.   FJO'G

Beet Queen, The (1986) The second in German-
American and Chippewa Indian LOUISE ERDRICH's epic North Dakota tetralogy relates the struggle for survival of immigrant Poles and Germans in the small town of Argus. Beginning in 1932 with Mary and Karl Adare's abandonment by their mother, Adelaide (she flies off with The Great Omar, 'Aeronaught Extraordinaire') and their arrival by boxcar to live at the butcher's shop belonging to their aunt and uncle (but Karl runs away at the last moment), *The Beet Queen* weaves a chequered tapestry of fragmented, damaged yet enduring lives. Erdrich shifts adeptly between first- and third-person narration, harsh NATURALISM and lyrical myth, and absurd coincidence and iron fate. The novel's highly contrived conclusion, when Celestine's and Karl's unruly child Dot is (almost) crowned 1972 Sugar Beet Queen, promises yet refuses any simple happy ending. The tensions between the Indian culture of the Turtle Mountain tribe and the

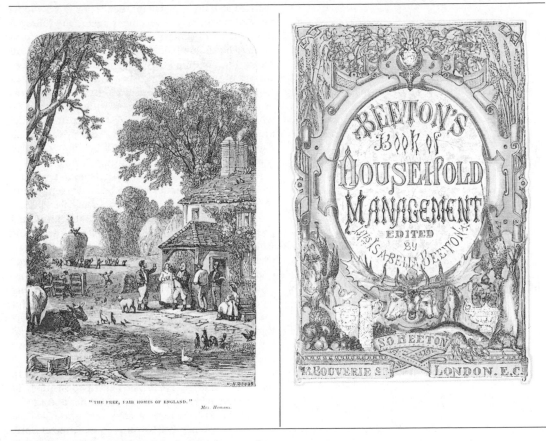

Isabella Beeton: frontispiece ('The free fair homes of England') and title-page of *Beeton's Book of Household Management*, 1861.

white intruders, which underpin the series, circumscribe the border community's gruelling existence.

MO'D

Beeton [née Mayson], Isabella (Mary) 1836–65 Britain's most famous cookery author. Her *Book of Household Management* (1861) was an immediate success and, radically revised, stayed in print for a century. Today, Mrs Beeton is synonymous with straightforward, economical cooking, and new books still appear under her name.

She was born in London, and, following her mother's second marriage to Henry Dorling, she became the eldest of twenty-one children – a large family even then. Educated in London and Heidelberg, she was proficient in French and German.

When Isabella, aged 20, married Samuel Orchart Beeton, a shrewd young publisher, she knew little about practical cooking and employed a cook. Yet after a few months Isabella was contributing the cookery, and fashion, pages to Samuel's magazine, *Englishwoman's Domestic Magazine*. Within a year a large COOKERY BOOK was planned, which first appeared monthly in the magazine in 1859, making it accessible and affordable to a wide cross-section of readers.

The book itself is a compendium of household, medical and legal advice – how to engage servants and so on – and curious facts and fables about food, with 1500 recipes, many of them submitted by the magazine readers or culled from better books such as ELIZA ACTON's. Isabella described herself correctly as the editress of the work, but it is nonetheless impressive as a record of the aspirations of the Victorian middle classes: these days it would be termed a 'life-style bible'. And it was accomplished swiftly and conscientiously – Isabella claimed to have tested all the recipes – by a novice writer.

Her two other books, *The Englishwoman's Cookery Book* (1863) and *Dictionary of Everyday Cookery* (1865), never achieved the popularity of her first work.

Isabella's married life was blighted by tragedy; two of her four sons died young and she died of puerperal fever aged 28.

GH

Behn, Aphra 1640–89 British novelist, playwright, poet and translator who was also a Tory apologist and

MISCELLANY,

Being A

COLLECTION

O F

POEMS

By several Hands.

Together with

REFLECTIONS

O N

MORALITY,

O R

SENECA UNMASQUED.

LONDON: Printed for *J. Hindmarsh*, at the *Golden Ball* over against the *Royal Exchange* in *Cornhil*, 1685.

Miscellany edited by Aphra Behn, with her translation of *Reflections on Morality or Seneca Unmasqued*, 1685.

wit, and a proto-feminist. She was baptized Aphra Johnson in the Kent village of Harbledown on 14 December 1640. Her father was a barber and freeman of the city of Canterbury; her mother descended from the gentry and wetnurse to the Culpepper family. Behn, according to a memoir published soon after her death, wrote poetry 'from the earliest age'. In 1663 she travelled with her family to Surinam where she became deeply involved in colonial politics and in a public affair with William Scot, son of the regicide Thomas Scot who had been executed on Charles II's restoration, and whose relatives were planters in the colony. Behn's family returned to London after a few months and Scot went to join English dissidents in Holland. Almost immediately Aphra must have

married a German merchant, Behn, but was a widow by 1666 when, as a government agent, she followed Scot to the Low Countries to try to get him to inform against his fellow conspirators, and the Dutch, in return for a pardon and money to pay his debts. For their assignations and correspondence they used names from the French romance *L'Astrée*: 'Celadon' for Scot and for Behn herself the soubriquet 'Astrea', by which she was known for the rest of her literary life. She returned from this bungled enterprise in such debt that she was threatened with prison, while Scot himself assisted the Dutch to capture Surinam.

Behn now took the conscious decision to try to live by her pen. Some money was to be made from poetry but if she was serious about supporting herself as a writer she would have to write for the commercial theatre. Her first play *The Forc'd Marriage* opened at the Duke's Theatre in September 1670. It was followed by some twenty others, many – like THE LUCKY CHANCE (1686) – most ingeniously plotted. Meanwhile she continued to write poetry, bringing out anthologies of her own and her friends' work. When the two major theatre companies merged in 1682 and new productions were severely cut Behn turned to prose, publishing the first part of her three-decker novel LOVE LETTERS BETWEEN A NOBLEMAN AND HIS SISTER in 1684. In 1688 she drew on her experiences in Antwerp for the brilliant *The Fair Jilt*, and her trip to Surinam for her masterpiece: OROONOKO. Some of her output (she described it as 'Tory farce or doggerell') was rewarded by the court. When her patron, James, Duke of York, who had praised her most commercially successful play, THE ROVER, became king in 1685, Behn celebrated his coronation with a baroque ode of over 1,000 lines. She clearly expected some royal return – a pension or a house. James's reign lasted only three years and in 1688 he fled the country. Behn, already in poor health, mourned that she was 'ruin'd in the universal turn', but the arrival in London of his daughter Mary began to reconcile her to the new regime. Five days after the joint coronation of Mary and her husband William, she died and was buried in Westminster Abbey. Her name appears in the burial register as Astrea. MD

Bell, Gertrude 1868–1926 British archaeologist, Arabist, writer, TRAVELLER, alpine climber, intelligence officer, diplomat, king-maker and founding member of the Women's Anti-Suffrage League. Above all an outstanding figure in Middle Eastern power politics. During and after World War I, when Ottoman rule was overthrown in Mesopotamia, she stood beside T. E. Lawrence in his struggle for Arab independence.

She was born at Washington Hall, County Durham, her family's wealth deriving from the steel and iron industry. As a BLUESTOCKING Victorian miss she pioneered women's higher education (often considered 'against Nature') and from Lady Margaret Hall won a brilliant First in Modern History. After sampling the glitter and fritter of a London Season she began to travel widely. In Persia, as if sensing her future, she studied Turkish, Farsi and Arabic. A young love affair was quashed by her father, whom she adored and never disobeyed. Consolatory years followed, two round-the-world journeys, Bayreuth for the Festival, climbing in Switzerland or the Rockies and the splendours of the Delhi Durbar, until a brief journey to the Jebel Druze revealed her true destiny – archaeology, the desert and its people.

Never one to do things by half she spent a year in Paris cramming under Reinach the celebrated archaelogist, and in 1905 set out alone, save for a scant Arab escort, on her first expedition deep into the unknown and dangerous Syrian desert, seeking traces of Babylonian ruins. Her book *The Desert and the Sown* records this adventure. It is in her fascinating *Letters* (1930), however, that we glimpse the real woman, witty, romantic, steely brained and pig-headed.

In 1913, in London, she had renewed a casual acquaintance with distinguished soldier 'Dick' Doughty-Wylie. An overwhelming love affair ensued. Gertrude, at forty-five, was famous, and reckless. Dick was married, had scruples and held back. They exchanged fevered letters, meeting, repining and renouncing, but their love was never consummated. Dick was killed at Gallipoli, and awarded a posthumous VC, and Gertrude, in anguish, wrote of 'pacing the floor of hell'.

Little mattered now, except Arab causes. To the Arabs she had become 'Al Khatun', their Great Lady. In the early days of World War I, the British appointed her to the Military Intelligence Bureau in Cairo. In 1917, in Baghdad, she settled in a small house, dividing her time between the Archaeological Museum which bears her name, and work as Oriental Secretary to successive High Commissions. She attended the Paris Peace Conference of 1919, and Churchill's Cairo Conference of 1921. Her influence was decisive in the choice of the Amir Faisal Ibn Husain as king of the newly created Iraq. He was her protégé, she doted on him, furnished his palace (from Waring and Gillow) and pronounced on politics and protocol, though some British ladies jibbed at curtseying to an *elected* king.

But gradually, Faisal began to stand alone. Gertrude knew she had outlived her uses. In the savage July heat of 1926 she was found dead of an overdose of sleeping pills. Suicide, it was said. Enormous crowds swarmed into Baghdad for her funeral.   LB

Bell, The (1958) IRIS MURDOCH's fourth novel is a deceptively light comedy that centres on Imber Court, a lay Anglican community in the Gloucestershire countryside, and the spiritual, sexual and psychological dilemmas that afflict its inhabitants. As the novel opens, Dora Greenfield journeys from London to Imber to rejoin her estranged husband Paul, a cold and aggressive art historian who is there studying 14th-century manuscripts. Once arrived, she becomes entangled in the complicated lives of the community's adherents, including its leader Michael Meade, a repressed and guilty homosexual; would-be nun Catherine Fawley; her brother, the dissolute and wayward Nick; and a young and impressionable Christian, Toby Gashe. With Toby, Dora formulates a secret plan to drag the lake for the Abbey's long-lost bell, whose tolling, as legend has it, foretells a death. The bell's discovery, together with a series of bizarre and prohibited couplings, does indeed precipitate disaster, ending with Nick's suicide and the community's dissolution. As in many of her early novels, Murdoch's preoccupation with the difficulty of working out a coherent moral philosophy in the face of desire, temptation and guilt is a central theme.   AC

Bell Jar, The (1963) Poet SYLVIA PLATH's only novel was patently autobiographical. Published in the year of her suicide, it enhanced the aura of doomed genius that surrounded her after death. It describes a provincial scholarship student's summer internship in New York working on a women's magazine, where she stews with curiosity and anxiety about sex and work. News of an academic rejection leads to a suicide attempt and a spell in a mental hospital. *The Bell Jar* combines hard-eyed, worldly wise humour with poetic and often bitterly amusing evocations of accidie, hyper-sensitivity and mental suffering. The narrator is torn between two role models: cynical, daredevil Doreen who goes out with a wolfish DJ and gets so drunk she vomits on the carpet; and Betsy, who is sensible but a lot less fun. Likewise, she veers between Buddy Willard, the humourless boy from her hometown who wants her to be pure, and an older professor who deflowers her and gives her a haemorrhage. *The Bell Jar*'s evocations of insulin, shock treatment and the ambience of life in a mental hospital have a brutal luminosity which has not been dimmed by time.   KE

Beloved (1987) TONI MORRISON's fifth novel, dedicated to the memory of 'Sixty Million and more' slaves, was written, she said, out of her desire 'not to allow for the confirmation of a national amnesia'. It is set in Kentucky in the mid 1800s. The main protagonist, Sethe, a black woman with 'iron eyes', performs a mourning rite over the grave of her baby, Beloved. This murdered daughter – killed by Sethe herself to save her from slavery – is a mark of the history of which there are no records. The plot brings her back to life, and the prose of the narrative melts down into a terrifying poetry of possession, only returning to the daylight of the present when her hungry spirit is appeased. The novel speaks of the impossibility of the exact representation of history, which is nevertheless saved from perdition, a tree of scars on Sethe's back being a sign of the suffering, pain and violence inflicted on her people. Through an act of story-telling Sethe reconciles her dead baby's desire for knowledge and memory with her own need to let go of the troubled past.

In 1988, *Beloved* was awarded the Pulitzer Prize for Fiction.   JZ

Benedict, Ruth 1887–1948 American anthropologist. She went to Vassar and later studied Anthropology with Guy Boas at Columbia – one of three famous women pupils, the others being ZORA NEALE HURSTON and MARGARET MEAD. Like Mead, her pupil and sometime lover, Benedict saw anthropology as both scientific discipline and source of progressive ideology. If human nature was mutable, social improvement was definitively possible; in *Patterns of Culture* (1934), a study of various native American and Polynesian societies, she argued that tribal cultures, far from being 'primitive', are rich and complex. Her clear and precise prose made her an effective popularizer. She can be seen as an early advocate of multi-culturalism; she also makes an argument for sexual pluralism – she had recently left her husband for a woman. *Race* (1940) is a swingeing attack on pseudo-scientific racism and a call to America to set its house in order. It has been argued that there is a tendency toward an over-simplifying cultural essentialism in her own work, particularly in *The Chrysanthemum and the Rose* (1946), her study of Japanese culture written during World War II when she was working for the Office of War Information. Benedict had tremendous influence on the way that the USA saw other cultures; like Mead, she was a moralist as much as a scientist.   RK

Benefactor, The (1967) This novel by SUSAN SONTAG is at one level a sustained exercise in literary pastiche. What is echoed in the style of the book is not so much a single author or work as a tradition of European literary sensibility, the BILDUNGSROMAN. The subject of the *Bildung* in this case is a first-person narrator, Hippolyte, who decides that he will live his life under instruction from his dreams. What this means is resisting the desire to interpret his dreams, and, in this way, the novel echoes Sontag's famous essay, *Against Interpretation*. Dreams are not an enigmatic presentation of the passions so much as a resource for leading life according to a will which will go beyond good and evil. This stylish, clever novel declares Sontag's affiliation with European modernity. It is at once a declaration of her difference from home-spun American culture and the confident assertion of a cosmopolitan American intellectual in its deft use of a European style.   JCo

Bennett, Louise 1919– Jamaican poet, performer, short-story writer. Louise Bennett has been writing and performing poetry since her youth, but her 'dialect verses' were then regarded as part of the oral tradition and it was difficult for her to find a publisher. It was only after a radio performance of her work that she was given an opportunity to publish by the *Sunday Gleaner* newspaper. Her weekly column of poetry on topical issues quickly gained popularity and 'Miss Lou' was soon a household name in Jamaica. Her first collection, *(Jamaica) Dialect Verses*, was published in 1942. In 1945, a scholarship to study at the Royal Academy of Dramatic Art in London gave her the opportunity to develop her dramatic skills and she worked as a resident artist at the BBC before returning to Jamaica in 1955. By the 1960s nation language poetry was beginning to receive serious critical attention and an anthology of Bennett's works, *Jamaica Labrish* (1966), helped to establish her status as a writer. Her *Selected Poems* (1982) and collected stories, *Anancy and Miss Lou* (1979), have since brought her work to an international audience. Bennett's poetry has been central in establishing the value of nation language and orality in Caribbean writing. Her work on Jamaican folklore and songs, which she has studied and collected for many years, is also of national importance. She has received many awards including the Gold Musgrave Medal, the MBE and an honorary doctorate from the University of the West Indies.   AD

Benson, Stella 1892–1933 English experimental novelist who used fantasy modes to explore contemporary alienation and loneliness. Born into a Shropshire landowning family, and educated by governesses, in 1914 she finally broke from the constraints of her county background and chronic ill health to work in London for the United Suffragists branch of the Women's Suffrage movement. She described her first novel, *I Pose* (1916), an allegory of gender relations, as 'post-Impressionist'. Her war work for the Charity Organization Society in Hoxton, and as a land-girl in Berkshire, provided material for *Living Alone* (1919), a fantasy about witches in wartime. In 1918, on medical advice, she travelled to California, and taught English Composition at Berkeley, before moving on to Hong Kong and then China, where she taught English. In 1921 she married James O'Gorman Anderson, an Irish customs official in Chungking. Thereafter she lived in China, experiencing great loneliness, and from 1931 campaigning against child prostitution. *The Poor Man* (1922) is a satirical fantasy of San Francisco bohemian life. *The Little World* (1925) collects sketches of America and China. Her major novel, *Tobit Transplanted* (1931; American title *The Faraway Bride*), draws on biblical narrative and folktale to describe the alienation of White Russian refugees in Manchuria. She died of pneumonia in 1933. Benson's novels were critically well received; she was admired by MANSFIELD and REBECCA WEST, and WOOLF saw her as a serious rival. Her writing is distinctive in its use of fantasy and whimsy to treat urgent social, political and psychological topics. AT

Bentley, Phyllis 1894–1977 British regional novelist who also wrote extensively on Yorkshire authors, particularly the BRONTËS. Born in Halifax, Yorkshire, the sole daughter of a textile manufacturer, she lived with her parents until World War I offered the opportunity to work in London at the Ministry of Munitions. Her autobiography, *O Dreams, O Destinations* (1962), discusses single women without income and the difficulties resulting from living with parents. She returned to London to work once again during World War II. During the 1930s and 1940s she made several trips to the USA for lecture tours – once braving German submarines. She is best remembered for a series of novels that follows the fortunes of a Yorkshire textile family, the Oldroyds. The first in this group is *Inheritance* (1932) and the last is *A Man of His Time* (1966). Her only novel set outside Yorkshire, *Freedom Farewell* (1936), was a decided failure. In addition to novels, Bentley also regularly produced articles, reviews and TV scripts. In 1949, the University of Leeds awarded her an honorary degree, and in 1970 she was granted the OBE. Never married, she resided in Halifax until her death. RB-S

Beresford [neé File], Anne [Anne Ellen Hamburger] 1928– British poet, born in Redhill and educated at the London Central School for Dramatic Art. She worked for a number of repertory companies and for BBC Radio, marrying the poet and translator Michael Hamburger in 1951. She has two daughters and a son. Anne Beresford has published many volumes of poetry and has been closely connected with *Agenda* magazine, publishing both poems and reviews. Her fine *Landscape With Figures* (1994) and *Selected and New Poems* (1997) are Agenda Editions.

David Storey has commented how closely Beresford's poems remind the reader of a devotional 'Book of Hours' – 'mystical in its origins, religious in its aspirations, psalmic in its asperity and concision'. However, in a revealing 'self-review' in the *Rialto* in 1998, Beresford commented, 'these are not religious poems. A Deity or God stands behind as a backbone to life, a critic to her struggle for an understanding of the impossible.' Beresford's self-perception as reluctant mystic, as truth-teller – 'like a Cassandra, speaking truth no one will believe' – recalls the stance of KATHLEEN RAINE. Beresford's poetics, however, has

more edge, thanks to its intelligence, its empathy for people and the first-hand vitality of the poet's imagination, particularly marked in a sequence such as 'Fragments From a Torn Tapestry' from *Landscape With Figures*, which has the sharpness and liveliness of *The Canterbury Tales*. DM

Beresford-Howe, Constance 1922– Canadian novelist and short-story writer, author of eight works of fiction published between 1946 and 1985. She was born in Montreal and did her BA and MA at McGill University. Her first three novels (1946, 1947 and 1949) deal with important phases of self-development in the lives of her young heroines. The fourth, *My Lady Greensleeves* (1955), written after she had taken her Ph.D. at Brown in 1950, weds some of her scholarly interests with her interest in dealing with the daily life of women: the novel is about an actual 16th-century divorce in England. Much occupied with her teaching, first at McGill University and then at Ryerson Polytechnique in Toronto, she did not publish again until 1973 when her most famous work, THE BOOK OF EVE, appeared. In this as in the novels that followed in 1977 and 1981, she deals with convention-breaking behaviour in middle-class women. *Night Studies* (1985) probes the difficult and unhappy lot of night students and their teachers at an urban college, a locale with which this author had long been familiar. Constance Beresford-Howe was married in 1960, has one son, and retired in Toronto in 1987. FD

Berkeley, Sara 1967– One of the most celebrated of young Irish poets. Born in Dublin she was educated at Trinity College and the University of California, publishing her first collection when she was just 19. Berkeley's collections include: *Penn* (1986), *Home Movie Nights* (1989), *Facts About Water* (1994) and her short stories, *The Swimmer In The Deep Blue Dream* (1991). She has contributed translations from Irish into English for the anthology *The Bright Wave* (1991). Often there is nothing specifically Irish about her poetic territory and poems are typically set against backgrounds of desert or seascape where she explores identity, offering release through water and flight. Comparable with a younger generation of Irish women poets such as EAVAN BOLAND, NUALA NÍ DHOMHNAILL and MEDBH MCGUCKIAN, her work is also evocative of American CONFESSIONAL poets such as SYLVIA PLATH and Robert Lowell. Her writing bears the traces of emigration, as it invokes America as much as Ireland. Having lived in both London and America, in 1992 she went to work as a technical writer for a software company in San Francisco. SFu

Berridge, Elizabeth 1921– English novelist and short-story writer whose works typically focus on personal crises in the lives of predominantly middle-class English characters. The daughter of Albert and Phyllis (née Drew) Berridge, she grew up in Wandsworth, where her father was an estate agent. After studying French and German privately in Switzerland and attending Regent Street Polytechnic in London, Berridge married the writer and publisher Reginald Moore in 1940. The couple lived in a remote cottage in Wales throughout World War II, working on a collection of stories by men and women in the Forces. Though she worked briefly at the Bank of England and then as a journalist and book critic, for Berridge 'being a writer is a way of life', and she vividly recalls correcting the proofs of her first story 'sitting up in bed with a day-old son in a cottage hospital in Hertfordshire'. She began writing fiction in the forties – *House of Defence* (1945), *The Story of Stanley Brent* (1945), *Selected Short Stories* (1947) and *Be Clean, Be Tidy* (1949) – but Berridge is best known for the three darkly comic novels she wrote in the sixties: *Rose Under Glass* (1961), *Sing Me Who You Are* (1967) and *Across the Common* (1964), which won the *Yorkshire Post* Award for Best Novel of the Year. At the centre of this work is 'The Hollies', a Victorian villa which for the protagonist, Louise, is both a shelter from the world and a manifestation of the burden of the past. Berridge explores themes of time and memory and the difficulty of breaking free from the past while finding the courage to live in the present. Other works include *Family Matters* (1980), *Run For Home* (1981), and *People at Play* (1982) which features the experiences of Stanislaus Spolianksi, a Pole living in London.   LCo

Berry, Mary 1763–1852 English editor, diarist, society figure, born in Yorkshire. Berry's mother died when she was 4 and she was educated by her grandmother and later, a governess. In 1783, with her younger sister Agnes, she travelled to Europe where she began the JOURNAL which she was to keep assiduously for the rest of her life. Due to a series of family complications, she was deprived of the large fortune she had always presumed to inherit. Berry still longed to participate in the social life of fashionable London and the friendship of Horace Walpole (whom she met in 1788) enabled her to do so. Walpole purchased a house for Berry and her sister and maintained an affectionate correspondence with them until his death – in one letter he refers to Berry as 'suavissima Maria' and in another signs himself 'Horace Fondlewives'. Upon Walpole's death, Berry was entrusted with his books and manuscripts and edited his *Works* in 1798.

In her later years, Berry found herself at the centre of a large social circle, and enjoyed the friendship of MADAME DE STAËL and other literary figures. She published an unpopular play, *Fashionable Friends* (1802), wrote *A Comparative View of the Social Life of England and France from Charles II to 1830* (1828–31), essentially an aristocratic chronicle of manners, and edited Madame du Deffend's *Letters* in 1810. Her *Works* were published in 1844, and in 1865 an edition of her journals and collected correspondence appeared.   KD

Bersianik, Louky [Lucile Durand] 1930– Francophone Canadian novelist, satirist, playwright, poet, and writer and researcher for Radio Canada. Bersianik is a committed feminist, a dedication exemplified by her adoption of a pseudonym breaking with patrolinear tradition. Her major concerns are male–female relations, the demythologization and deconstruction of psychoanalytical theories and Greek philosophy. The coinage of new words and disruptive writing are characteristic of her work. Born in Montreal, Quebec, she obtained a doctoral degree from Université de Montreal and taught Creative Writing at Montréal universities. In Paris (1953–60) she studied French Literature at the Sorbonne and took additional classes in radio and TV at CERT.

She became the mother of a son, and first published four CHILDREN's stories, but is best known for her first novel, the utopian SCIENCE FICTION bestseller *L'Euguélionne* (1976), criticizing psychoanalytical theories, the sexism of the French language and patriarchal society as viewed by a female extraterrestrial, the 'Euguélionne'. Howard Scott's imaginative English translation, *The Euguelion* (1996) won the 1997 Governor General's Award for Translation. The film *Firewords / Les Terribles Vivantes* (1986, director Dorothy Todd Hénaut) focuses on Bersianik and the Quebec feminist writers JOVETTE MARCHESSAULT and NICOLE BROSSARD. Her second novel, *Le Pique-Nique sur l'Acropole* (1979), a feminist spoof on Plato's *Symposium*, is a spin-off of a year spent on Crete. Phallogocentric philosophy is also criticized in her important feminist essay 'Les Agénésies du vieux monde' (1982), republished together with other essays in *La Main tranchante du symbole* (1990). Her novel *Permafrost* (1997) is the first of a series called *Les Inenfances de Sylvanie Penn*.   DMM

Besant [née Wood], Annie 1847–1933 English orator, journalist and author. Passionate and charismatic, Besant experienced a series of spiritual upheavals in a life devoted to social reform. Born in London to Irish parents, she left home after the death of her father to study with the evangelical Ellen Marryat. At the age of 16, Besant was an ardent Christian who flagellated herself and prayed fervently.

By 28 she had lost her faith, left her clergyman husband (with whom she had borne two children) and joined Charles Bradlaugh, the crusading atheist, as a member of the National Secular Society. Here she attracted large audiences with her lectures and pamphlets, including *Why I Became an Atheist* (1877). At 30 she was publicly tried with Bradlaugh for publishing an 'obscene' book on contraception and lost custody of her children. By the age of 36 she converted to socialism and befriended George Bernard Shaw who considered her the greatest orator of her time; she published many of her lectures in her magazine *Our Corner*. Her crusading journalism introduced her to the plight of London match girls and in 1888 she organized their first strike. The first version of her *An Autobiography* (1893) recounts her campaign for social justice.

At 42 she converted to Theosophy, a spirituality based on contact with the occult. Soon thereafter she moved to India where the movement was headquartered to establish schools, embark on a political career, launch the journals *Commonweal* and *New India*, and eventually be named president of India's National Congress.   MAD

Beth Book, The (1897) In the third part of her trilogy, SARAH GRAND draws on the formula which secured her international fame with *The Heavenly Twins* (1893): a tomboyish heroine whose comic exploits subvert patriarchal power structures. A cross between Grand's anarchic Angelica (one of the twins) and the social purist Ideala (in the novel with that title, 1888), Beth is also a self-portrait of the author, who, in vivid descriptions of the Irish and English countryside, girls' boarding schools and feminist rallies, retraces her own progression from child rebel to prominent NEW WOMAN writer and suffragist activist. The text offers a sharp critique of mothering, and continues Grand's crusade against marital and medical oppression, taking issue with vivisection and the Contagious Diseases Acts. Exploding the conventions of the *Künstlerroman*, Grand encodes artistic as sexual energy in metaphors of the wave and the room-as-womb, and self-confidently distances herself from *FIN-DE-SIÈCLE* aestheticism by placing female writing in a separate artistic tradition. The programmatical ending rewards Beth with public and private success, blurring the boundaries between feminist art and political activism.   AH

Betham (Mary), Matilda 1776–1852 English poet, DIARIST and compiler. Daughter of the Revd William Betham, noted antiquarian and genealogist, she was sent to school 'only to learn sewing and prevent too strict application to books'. In 1797 she published *Elegies and Other Small Poems*, a collection of translations and fashionable sentimental verse on British historical subjects. Unable to secure a London marriage, Matilda endeavoured to support herself through portrait painting, Shakespearean readings, and literary projects. Popular, though considered irritable and unstable by some, she befriended ANNA LAETITIA

BARBAULD, Coleridge, Charles and MARY LAMB, the 'Ladies of Llangollen' (see ELEANOR BUTLER and SARAH PONSONBY), HANNAH MORE and other literary figures. After six years of labour, she published *A Biographical Dictionary of Celebrated Women of Every Age and Country* (1804), a work with the foresight to include MARY WOLLSTONECRAFT. Other publications include a second volume of *Poems* (1808), and *The Lay of Marie: A Poem* (1816), a verse account of the 13th-century Anglo-Norman minstrel, containing scholarly appendices on female troubadours and translations of Marie's lays. Family problems and a possible nervous breakdown forced her into the country for several years, but she returned to London in the 1830s and resumed her place in literary circles until her death.

JHP

Bethell, (Mary) Ursula 1874–1945 New Zealand poet. Born in England, Ursula Bethell grew up in Rangiora, New Zealand, before her later tuition at Oxford, Geneva and Dresden, in languages, painting and music. A strongly compassionate Christian, Bethell worked for the disadvantaged through both the Anglican organization the Grey Ladies, and the New Zealand Soldiers' Club in London. She often repeated the journey between Europe and New Zealand, until she took up permanent residence in New Zealand with her companion, Effie Pollen, after World War I.

Bethell's first collection was published under the pseudonym 'Evelyn Hayes'. This reticence over public exposure accords with the nature of her first compositions, initially written for an overseas friend, and not for publication. The characteristic style of *From a Garden in the Antipodes* (1929) is similarly understated. In it Bethell charts wider seasons, registered in local geographic forms and her labour as a gardener. Her diction is lucid, spare, evokes a shared colloquial speech, and combines subtle elegy with gently Shakespearean wit: she articulates pressing questions of human mortality, and care for all living things, through her tending to the plants and soil of one of our 'small fond human enclosures'. Bethell's religious beliefs are firmly grounded in her pragmatic gardener's sense, as in 'Bulbs':

> All these lovely lilies, I wish that they would grow with
>   me:
> No other flowers have the texture of lilies.
> The heart-piercing fragrance, the newly alighted
>   angel's
> Lineal poise'

Bethell's linguistic tastes range from scientific and botanical terminology to words rich with classical or Old English inflections. *Time and Place* (1936) and *Day and Night* (1939), after Effie Pollen's death, display an increased formal and rhetorical register. Bethell now displays Christian Humanist concerns through grand abstraction and scriptural cadences. The metaphorical, connotative role of her imagery is heightened; general statement and sweeping views predominate over the intimate, close-focus of her first volume. This sombre and commemorative tone locates Bethell's final work within devotional traditions.   EJN

Bethune, Mary Jane McLeod 1875–1955 African-American educator, journalist and activist. She was born near Mayesville, South Carolina, the fifteenth of seventeen children of former slaves. She was educated at a Presbyterian mission school for black children in North Carolina and at the Moody Bible Institute for Home and Foreign Missions in Chicago, but the Presbyterian Church rejected her application to become a missionary to Africa because of her race. She taught in Georgia and South Carolina, then in 1898 married Albertus Bethune; they had one son and separated after eight years. She founded two mission schools; the second, established in 1904, became Bethune-Cookman College in 1923. Bethune was its president from 1929 to 1942. She headed the National Association of Colored Women (1924–8) and founded the Federal Council on Negro Affairs, the National Council of Negro Women (which she served as president from 1935 to 1949), and *Aframerican Women's Journal*. She served F.D. Roosevelt's presidency as Director of Negro Affairs in the National Youth Administration and, allied with Eleanor Roosevelt, contributed much to the desegregation of government employment and the creation of the Fair Employment Practices Commission. Having convinced the Women's Army Auxiliary Corps to integrate, she served on the twelve-member Committee for National Defense under Truman and acted as a consultant for the Conference to Draft a United Nations Charter. Her writings include columns for the *Pittsfield Courier* and *Chicago Defender*; 'A Century of Progress of Negro Women' (1933), 'A College on a Garbage Dump' (1941) and other of her essays and speeches have been anthologized.   JSG

Betts, Jean 1952– New Zealand co-author (with William Shakespeare) of *Ophelia Thinks Harder*. Betts inherited Left-wing theatrics from her father, a founder member of London Unity Theatre. Her brilliant transposition of *Hamlet* differs from other adaptations – like Tom Stoppard's *Rosencrantz and Guildenstern are Dead* and *The (Fifteen-Minute) Dogg's Troupe Hamlet* – because of its feminist base and the flexibility of its borrowings. Here intertextuality extends not only to *Hamlet* (Ophelia gets all the soliloquies), *Macbeth*, *A Midsummer Night's Dream*, *Julius Caesar*, *Othello*, *Henry V*, *Love's Labour's Lost* and the sonnets, but to A.E. Housman and Samuel Beckett. Saint Joan appears as one ghost and Ophelia's mother, advising wifely self-disparagement, as another; a serious (feminist) analysis of Virginity ensues from the now-scholarly Rosencrantz and Guildenstern. This feminist pastiche was created for the centennial of women's suffrage in New Zealand in 1993, ten years after Betts's Shakespearean co-authored play, a reworking of *A Midsummer Night's Dream* as a riposte called *The Revenge of the Amazons* (1983).   JD

Between the Acts (1941) VIRGINIA WOOLF's last novel, finished only few weeks before her suicide and published posthumously, describes the annual amateur theatrical performance of Miss La Trobe's pageant by the local people of a remote English village on a hot June day in 1939. La Trobe's spectacle, a modern adaptation of court masques, is inscribed within a carnivalesque structure which explores through theatrical representation the relation between past, present and future. The author subverts the 'rules' of representation, as the future looks bleaker and the present becomes estranged from the past. La Trobe's ambitious project is put under continual strain as she undertakes to reactivate the audience's consciousness through a chronological account of English history. The reader will discover brilliantly written, breathtaking moments where author, actors and spectators commune to generate the buried anxiety and violence looming behind Woolf's ultimate writing practice as the world is about to plunge into chaos. Woolf's three-dimensional approach – play, poetry, prose – illustrates the dialogical approach which motivates the enunciation of the text.   AA

Beveridge, Judith 1956– Australian poet whose work concentrates on the natural world, especially celebrating her sense of its pattern, order and intricate design. A resident of Sydney, she was born in London and arrived in Australia in 1960. Beveridge has worked variously in the library and education sectors, and has been active in several writers' and publishing groups. Her first book of verse, *The Domesticity of Giraffes* (1987) was highly acclaimed, winning the prestigious Mary Gilmore Award, and the 1988 Premier's Prizes in both New South Wales and Victoria. Her second volume, *Accidental Grace*, published in 1996, was long awaited and enjoyed similar critical approval. Animals – both native and exotic – figure prominently in Beveridge's work, with her grief for the caged giraffes of the title poem of her first volume tempering to a perhaps more complex, if still wounded, view of the relationships between man and animals in the elephant poems in her second collection. Throughout her work she attempts to locate the consolations of design and endurance in what appears to be a chaotic and cruel world. Later poems, in which her experiences of motherhood figure, continue in this vein.　　　　　MLA

Bevington, L(ouisa) S(arah) 1845–95 Poet and political writer, was born and grew up in London, possibly in a Quaker family, certainly in one long-associated with radical causes, and was encouraged by her father to write. In 1876, she brought out, under the name of 'Arbor Leigh', a short pamphlet of poetry entitled *Key Notes* revealing a scepticism about orthodox religion and a buoyant belief, partly the result of her Darwinism, in human progress – 'Upward! upward, O man! for Progress can never die.' Thereafter, she became a convinced opponent of Christianity, publishing an essay in the *Nineteenth Century* on 'Modern Atheism and Mr Mallock' in 1879. She published *Poems, Lyrics, and Sonnets* in 1882, a year before her brief marriage to the Munich artist Ignatz Guggenberger. As she grew older, Bevington became increasingly interested in anarchism which she defined in *Anarchism and Violence* (1896) as 'the removal of all the enervating restrictions . . . which have hitherto hindered the individual from developing his self-controlling tendencies in spontaneous obedience to the inevitably social and peaceful instincts of his own humanity'. She published *Liberty Lyrics*, a mixture of zesty poetry about political freedom and more conventional celebrations of love, in 1895.　　　　　FJO'G

Beyond the Glass (1954) follows FROST IN MAY, *The Lost Traveller* and *The Sugar House* as the last in ANTONIA WHITE's sequence of autobiographical novels. Clara Batchelor is now 22, separated from her husband Archie and, since they are both Catholic, seeking an annulment of the unconsummated marriage. She returns to her parents, Claude, a Classics teacher and scholar, whose faith and reason Clara reveres and whose disapproval she dreads, and Isabel, beautiful, elegant and demonstrative, who fears Clara's disapproval. Clara and Richard Crayshaw fall in love at first sight, almost before first sight, since they communicate by telepathy. They plan to marry but Clara collapses with a severe mental illness, is certified insane and admitted to the Nazareth Royal Hospital (based on the Bethlem Asylum, now the Imperial War Museum, where White herself was a patient). She recovers in less than a year, despite a pessimistic prognosis, to find that Richard has married. The novel acutely depicts Clara's imprisonment in institutions – family, Church, mental hospital and (still powerfully present) convent school – which both support and abuse her.　　　　　PMar

Bhatt, Sujata 1956– Indian English poet who writes of the loss and gains of the diasporic Indian woman and examines the role of language in this sense of dislocation. Born in Gujarat, educated in the USA, living in Germany, she finds herself heir to Gujarati, her mother tongue, as well as European languages. Gujarati figures prominently in both her collections, present in the original Devnagari script. This works as a visual correlative for her attempt to hold on to her Indian language to protect her integrity. The title of her first collection, *Brunizem* (1988), is a new word compounded from French and Russian to refer to the dark brown prairie soil found in the three continents in which she has lived and which form her poetic landscapes. *Brunizem* and *Monkey Shadows* (1991) cover a wide range of themes from the erotic to the political but the voice is always personal and often passionate.　　　　　GJVP

Biddle, Hester [Esther] c.1629–96 British PROPHETIC writer of the Civil War period. She grew up as an Anglican and lived in Oxford, then London, where she joined the Quakers. In 1655 she published two identical diatribes against the Universities of Oxford and Cambridge, in a visionary style which merges her voice with God's: 'Woe to thee city of Oxford, thy wickedness surmounteth the wickedness of Sodom; therefore repent whilst thou has time, lest I consume thee with fire'. *A Warning from the Lord God* (1660) was directed at London: the metropolitan woman is compared with the Whore of Babylon as she passes by the poor 'in thy gaudy apparel, and outstretched neck'. Other publications include *The Trumpet of the Lord* (1662), which rebuked the 'high and lofty ones' of the Parliamentary government for their neglect of the poor; and *A Brief Relation* (1662), which describes her robust self-defence when on trial for preaching. After imprisonment in Newgate in 1665 for speaking in the street, she published nothing more.　　　　　HH

Bildungsroman The genre originated in late 18th-century Germany, where the bourgeois concept of *Bildung* merged Enlightenment ideals of moral education and psychological self-development. From its prototypes onwards – Wieland's *Agathon* (1766) and Goethe's *Wilhelm Meisters Lehrjahre* (1795/6) – the Bildungsroman charted the sometimes illustrious, but (according to Hegel) often also quite formulaic, journey from the hero's youth to maturity, from individuation to social integration. As a representation of the male subject in a man's world, the genre did not at first lend itself easily to the quest of heroines: women assisted male development or became 'rewards' for achieved goals.

JANE AUSTEN's *EMMA* (1816), however, could be considered a tentative exploration of the idea of self-development in a heroine, and the scene where Jane paces the corridor in CHARLOTTE BRONTË's *JANE EYRE* (1847) ('[women] suffer from too rigid a restraint, too absolute a stagnation') indicates how readily the Bildungsroman accommodates criticism of social and literary confinements. Yet what would become the marriage-or-death yoke for late 19th-century heroines also offered a loophole of greater literary permissiveness: if nothing else, problematic heroines (Anna Karenina, Emma Bovary, Effi Briest, Maggie Tulliver, Lily Bart) could at least develop transgressive social and sexual tendencies before their fatal end.

Early 20th-century women writers did not only go further in their social criticism but clearly tested the viability of the genre for contemporary women's lives. In THE VOYAGE OUT (1915) VIRGINIA WOOLF actually preferred her heroine dead rather than trapped in a conventional marriage. MAY SINCLAIR'S THE LIFE AND DEATH OF HARRIET FREAN (1922) is a decided 'no' to even the remote possibility of a female Bildungsroman, whereas SYLVIA TOWNSEND WARNER'S LOLLY WILLOWES (1926) celebrates the female potential waiting to be explored outside convention. DOROTHY RICHARDSON'S PILGRIMAGE (1915-38) employs the stream-of-consciousness technique to portray the gender-specific difficulties on the journey toward selfhood. Later, DORIS LESSING (THE CHILDREN OF VIOLENCE, 1952–69 and THE GOLDEN NOTEBOOK, 1962) and MARY MCCARTHY (THE GROUP, 1963) would take up the genre again to rediscover the inevitable failure of the female quest for political and personal goals.

A version of the female Bildungsroman is the 'novel of awakening', named after KATE CHOPIN'S novella THE AWAKENING (1899). Here self-development usually sets in where the compliant 19th-century heroine was supposed to be no longer of interest – long after the wedding. This variant flowered into the most popular genre for women's writing in the 1970s: the feminist Bildungsroman. Its political agenda of emancipation and liberation also provided open-ended narratives for the reader's own utopian rewriting of women's lives (MARGARET ATWOOD, SURFACING, 1972; MARILYN FRENCH, THE WOMEN'S ROOM, 1977; FAY WELDON, DOWN AMONG THE WOMEN, 1972). RITA MAY BROWN (RUBYFRUIT JUNGLE, 1973) and ALICE WALKER (THE COLOR PURPLE, 1983), while working along these lines, paid specific attention to lesbian and racial issues. These fictions also stimulated feminist academic interest in the Bildungsroman, partly celebrating its appropriation for women and partly contesting its usefulness for women's agendas.

In the 'post-feminist' era the female Bildungsroman-as-social-critique has become slightly unfashionable: strong, independent and self-aware heroines who populate the fiction of both male and female writers seem to indicate that development is no longer the aim of, but the precondition for becoming, a major fictional character.   PUR

Binchy, Maeve 1940– Irish journalist, novelist and dramatist. Born and educated in Dublin, she graduated from University College Dublin. After teaching for eight years, she began her journalistic career with the *Irish Times* for which she writes a weekly column. She is equally adept at dealing with serious or frivolous topics; the psychiatrist Professor Anthony Clare describes her as an unassuming,'sagacious therapist'. Her good-humoured column considers a wide range of contemporary concerns from the 'the histrionic pretence' of friends of the terminally ill, to the need for Aer Rianta (who don't care 'if we take off or land on an emu as long as we use their airports') to restore airport buggies. Her short stories and novels such as *Light a Penny Candle* (1982) and *Firefly Summer* (1989) are the fictional extensions of her column. Her sensitive treatment of the ordinary and the everyday, her knowledge of her readers and her ability to respond to, and satisfy, their readerly needs, have made her a bestselling author. While her early stories are set nostalgically in Ireland of the 1950s and 1960s, *Tara Road* (1998) deals with relationships in the maritally unstable 1990s. Her television play, *Deeply Regretted By* (1979), won the Best Script Award at the Prague Film Festival, while *The Lilac Bus* (1984) and *Echoes* (1985) have both been dramatized for television and *Circle of Friends* (1990), an exploration of loyalty and friendship, is a major film.   BHu

biography Biographies of women written by women have constituted an essential groundwork in women's history-writing. 'We think back through our mothers if we are women', wrote VIRGINIA WOOLF in *A ROOM OF ONE'S OWN* (1929), and if those 'mothers' were in any way breakers of the conventional female mould, that thinking-back was generally feminist.

In China in 64 BC the first book of women's history was *Biographies of Several Thousand Women*. In medieval Europe, accounts of early Christian women martyrs were followed by CHRISTINE DE PIZAN'S championing of virtuous and gifted women *c.* 1400 and by nuns' accounts of their spiritual 'mothers'. The first collective biography of women by a named English woman writer was *Sketches of the Lives and Writings of the Ladies of France* by ANN THICKNESSE, published by subscription in 1780 – 'in France not less than four hundred women have been renowned for their literary talents'. And in the Revolutionary period, 1790–1815, feminist contributions to the collective biography of women were compiled in Britain by Elizabeth Benger, MARY ROBINSON (under the pseudonym of Anne Frances Randall), MARY HAYS, MATILDA BETHAM, MARY PILKINGTON and Lucy Aikin. The American 'Separate Spheres' feminist, SARA JOSEPHA HALE, compiled her monumental and seminal *Woman's Record – All Distinguished Women [from Eve] till AD 1850* in 1853, coinciding with the inception of the organized

A

BIOGRAPHICAL

DICTIONARY

OF THE

CELEBRATED WOMEN

OF

EVERY AGE AND COUNTRY.

By MATILDA BETHAM.

London:

PRINTED FOR B. CROSBY AND CO. STATIONERS' COURT, LUDGATE-HILL;
TEGG AND CASTLEMAN, WARWICK-LANE; AND E. LLOYD,
HARLEY-STREET, CAVENDISH-SQUARE.

1804.

Frontispiece and title-page of Matilda Betham, *A Biographical Dictionary of the Celebrated Women of Every Age and Country*, 1804.

Women's Movement in America and Britain. *Distinguished Indian Women* were commemorated by Mrs E. F. Chapman in 1895. In the 20th century, collective biographies of British feminists have been compiled by Olive Banks (1985 and 1990) and, much more selectively, by MARGARET FORSTER in *Significant Sisters* (1984), while Jenny Uglow's *Dictionary of Women's Biography* courageously attempted worldwide coverage from Ancient Egypt to the 1980s.

As women are increasingly acknowledged to have contributed to their societies, so do they figure in national biographical collections edited by women – e.g. Jessie Carney Smith's *Notable Black American Women* (1992 and 1996) and *The Book of New Zealand Women – Ko Kui Ma Te Kaupapa*, edited by Macdonald, Penfold and Williams (1991). Women's resistance to Nazism has

been recorded in Vera Laska's *Women in the Resistance and the Holocaust* (1983). 'Exemplary Lives' may seem like outmoded piety now but we still seek out exemplars and mould-breaking women's lives do have a place in the story.

Predictably, the most common subjects for women's biography before 1800 were royal and aristocratic women and religious martyrs. The 20th-century feminists' ignorance of much early women's historical/biographical writing may be explained by the almost total loss of that faith which had once animated women's testimonies to their religious heroines, whether early Christian, Lutheran, Protestant Anglican, Catholic, Quaker, Huguenot, Methodist, Scottish Calvinist or Jewish. Such figures were later joined by women writers, singers, actresses and artists, and, as the 19th century allowed women into more interventionist public spheres, by women social reformers, educationists and medical missionaries active in almost every corner of the earth hitherto unexplored by Westerners. Most

19th-century women chroniclers of such pioneers treated their heroic women subjects with uncritical awe.

The writing of full-length biographies of individual women by women in English may be said to have been inaugurated by ELIZABETH GASKELL's testimony to CHARLOTTE BRONTË as a Heroine of Letters – and personal fortitude – in 1857. Significant later 19th-century biographies were published in the 'Famous Women' series by Roberts Bros., Boston – including Emma Pitman on Elizabeth Fry, MATHILDE BLIND on GEORGE ELIOT, CHARLOTTE YONGE on HANNAH MORE and Florence Fenwick Miller on HARRIET MARTINEAU. Among women contributors to Leslie Stephen's and Sidney Lee's first edition of *The Dictionary of National Biography (1885-1901)* Jennet Humphreys, who wrote 47 entries on women, and Lee's sister Elizabeth, who wrote over 100 should not be forgotten. Other 19th-century British writers of women's biography worth re-discovering are Louisa Costello, JULIA KAVANAGH, Matilda Betham-Edwards and Lina Eckenstein. Certain works of biography by women, e.g. JOSEPHINE BUTLER's *Recollections of George Butler* (1892), Henrietta Barnett's *Canon Barnett: His Life, Work and Friends* (1918) and Margaret Macmillan's *Life of Rachel Macmillan* (1927) – not to mention KATE MILLETT's *Sita* (1976) – included significant elements of autobiography.

During the 20th century, the writing of full-length, individual biographies of women by women has so burgeoned that Patricia Sweeney's annotated bibliography (1993) is needed for reference and overview for Britain alone. Four works of more than national interest and significance that may be singled out are Mary Stocks's *Eleanor Rathbone* (1947), Elzbieta Ettinger's *Rosa Luxemburg. A Life* (1987), Deirdre Bair's *Simone de Beauvoir* (1990) and Sara Parkin's *Life and Death of Petra Kelly* (1994). Some of the most controversial recent biographical writing by women has focused on women writers – on EMILY DICKINSON, CHRISTINA ROSSETTI, WILLA CATHER, VIRGINIA WOOLF, SYLVIA PLATH, ANNE SEXTON and CHRISTINA STEAD. The woman artist is seen as a heroine of creativity, despite all the sociocultural and familial forces ranged against her; controversy arises when she is also depicted as less than admirable – as in ANNE STEVENSON's study of Plath – or when clues found in her work allegedly reveal suppressed experience or desire – as in Christina Rossetti. Among interesting discussions of women writing about women are Ascher's, De Salvo's and Ruddick's *Between Women* (1984); Elizabeth Young-Bruehl's 'The Writing of Biography' in *Mind and the Body Politic* (1989); and Gail A. Hornstein's 'The Ethics of Ambiguity: Feminists Writing Women's Lives' in *Women Creating Lives: Identities, Resilience and Resistance* (1994), edited by Franz and Stewart. Both the reading and the writing of biographies of women by women flourish – despite recent theoretical and POST-

MODERNIST assaults on narratives of character and personal development.

How a feminist woman biographer may be sympathetic toward, but not uncritical of, her [woman] subject – and how to respect her right to some remnant of privacy in an age that demands to know 'all' – are still contested areas. Women's writing of biography has moved from the SPIRITUAL to the intellectual to the social and now includes the intimately personal – but there are obvious limitations to any human's total understanding of another, and the Talmudic precept 'Do not do to another what you would not wish done to yourself' might serve as a useful motto for all of us who attempt to interpret another personality and sum up another woman's life.   SO

Bird, Carmel 1940– Australian fiction writer who explores, with a quirky wit, the spiritual possibilities beneath a mainly female domestic culture. Bird was born in Launceston, Tasmania, and educated at the University of Tasmania before settling in Melbourne in 1963. In her early work, Bird expressed a fascination with the culture of the Catholicism of her family, particularly that of her grandparents' generation, and her first novel, *Cherry Ripe* (1988), plays whimsically with the image of the Sacred Heart, which dominated many Australian Catholic households until the 1960s.

In her twenties, Bird made her living as a high-school teacher. She has married twice and has one daughter. Since the early 1980s she has worked mainly as a teacher of fiction-writing and she has published two guides for beginning writers. For a time, she co-edited the literary magazine *Fine Line*.

Her short stories offer a mix of autobiography, essay and speculative fiction, while her most ambitious novels explore the threatening world beneath the surface of her female characters' lives. *The Bluebird Café* (1990) plays with the dominant Tasmanian myths of loss and shows a clear POSTMODERN consciousness. *The White Garden* (1995) uses recent scandals about the use of 'deep sleep' therapy as a starting point for the entry into the memories and dreams of her characters. She says 'this paradoxical merging of the bad and the beautiful, this invisible line between what's evil and what's good – this is my territory'.   SPL

Bird, Isabella (Lucy), later Bishop 1831–1904 British writer and traveller, related to William Wilberforce who worked for the abolition of slavery. In childhood she suffered from ill health and in later years was advised to find a better climate. This opened the way for her, while visiting Australia, to strike out on her own to the Sandwich Islands. She loved the violent clashes of nature, its storms, volcanoes and hurricanes and was totally unafraid of travelling alone.

Isabella journeyed through the Wild West, meeting

Jim, a rough frontiersman, 'the soul of chivalry', who wanted to marry her, though she refused him. All her adventures were reported to her beloved sister, Henrietta, in England, and these letters form the basis of books published by John Murray, numbering over twenty. *The Englishman in America* appeared in 1856; in 1875, *The Hawaiian Archipelago*; *Unbeaten Tracks in Japan* in 1880; *The Golden Chersonese* was published in 1883; and *The Yangtze Valley and Beyond* in 1899. She gave medical help where she could and visited isolated missions.

In 1881 she married, and admitted she would like to visit New Guinea, but 'she was married now and it was hardly a place you could take a man to'. Five years later she was widowed and became a more determined traveller than ever. She went to India, Turkey and Persia and from Kurdistan to Trebizond. In 1904, at the age of 73, she was preparing to travel to China when she died. MEW

Bird in the House, A (1970) The fourth book of MARGARET LAURENCE's five-volume 'Manawaka' cycle, which creates a fictional small-town community partly based on the author's hometown of Neepawa, Manitoba.

The 'semi-autobiographical fiction' of *A Bird in the House* recounts the life of Vanessa McLeod from roughly the age of 6 to adolescence. Set in the thirties, the Manawaka society and the effects of the Depression are presented through the eyes of a perceptive child. Although sometimes called a novel or an *Entwicklungsroman* (formation novel), the book is really a short-story cycle of eight stories dealing with different episodes from Vanessa's life. They are told in the first person: the reader learns of Vanessa's encounters with birth, death and love from an older narrator, who is looking back on her childhood experiences and feelings.

Like Laurence's other books, *A Bird in the House* wittily and humorously depicts life's small and great joys, sorrows and humiliations. TP

Bird of Night, The (1972) SUSAN HILL's commitment to the GOTHIC is confirmed in this portrayal of one man's inexorable descent into madness, and a world of nightmares, hallucinations and despair. In this complex and retrospective narrative, Harvey Lawson explains how he cared for the poet Francis Croft until his madness became too unpredictable, using disturbing entries from Francis's notebooks. Although Lawson believes that security, normal human companionship and protection can treat insanity effectively, the end is bleak; Francis becomes a danger to himself, and, despite Lawson's vigilance, commits suicide in church.

Hill's use of figurative language is sophisticated. The bird of night whose hooded face frightened Croft becomes an omen of evil; he regards himself as a bird

of night. A Janus metaphor unifies the narrative. The poem which assures Croft's reputation is 'Janus'; the extreme moods encapsulated by Croft's swings between elation and depression are Janus-like. In old age, Lawson is Janus-faced with the researchers who want Croft's notebooks; as his own death approaches, he honours his promise and burns them. MET

Birds and Other Stories, The (1963) This collection of short stories by DAPHNE DU MAURIER was first published as *The Apple Tree* in 1952. It was a new departure for Du Maurier, in which she experimented with neo-GOTHIC motifs. These stories reveal, as Du Maurier herself suggested, her own psychological and emotional obsessions. The original title story, 'The Apple Tree', relates the story of a man who becomes obsessed. He is convinced that an apple tree represents his recently deceased wife and seeks to destroy it. In the end, having cut down the tree, he trips over the roots and becomes trapped in the snow. 'The Little Photographer' tells the story of a rich and married woman who, in order to preserve her ideal of a loveless, merely sexual affair with a photographer, commits murder. 'The Birds' recounts the deadly invasion of a small seaside town by lethal hordes of birds. The apocalyptic tale ends with one of the characters contemplating 'how many million years of memory were stored in those little brains . . . , now giving them this instinct to destroy mankind with all the deft precision of machines'. Daphne du Maurier disapproved of Alfred Hitchcock's 1963 film version, *The Birds*. NBP

Birds Fall Down, The (1966) This novel, the last that REBECCA WEST completed, follows on thematically from various of her non-fiction works, notably *The Meaning of Treason*, dealing as it does with the discovery, early this century, by a young Anglo-Russian woman, of the extent of the overlap of personnel between the secret police and the revolutionary underground. She comes to realize how much her reactionary grandfather and a young revolutionary whom she befriends have in common – 'Were men perhaps no good?'; idealism seems irrevocably caught up with bloodshed. It is a sinister and powerful meditation on fanaticism, and on the complexities of loyalty, which is also showily ironic about the optimism with which the new century was greeted and what the century actually delivered. Here, as in other late fiction, West applies prickly hindsight to a concretely evoked portrait of the period of her own childhood. RK

Birds of America (1971) MARY McCARTHY's fifth novel, begun in 1964, was her personal favourite, though its critical reception was unfavourable (the *New York Times* headlined its review 'Frozen Foods a New Villain'). Peter Levi – the 19-year-old son of a

refugee intellectual and a beautiful, opinionated musician, studying in Europe – is attractive, sensitive, decent and uninteresting. McCarthy's title invokes James Audubon's series of watercolours published between 1827 and 1838, of birds in their natural habitat, and the novel praises old-fashioned American virtues: domestic skills, Jamesian fastidiousness, 'taste' as a moral imperative; and attacks the unquestioning belief in equality, in a style reminiscent of De Tocqueville two centuries earlier. Peter's own commitment to equality is shattered in Rome, where he dissociates himself from the 'mob of tourists' – 'Garbage dumped by planes and sightseeing buses, with guides and storekeepers diving for them like scavenger gulls'. In a startling final scene, Peter is delirious in hospital and Kant himself appears at the foot of his bed. The philosopher (who is minutely described) announces the death of God, and (worse) the death of Nature.   TC

Birdsell [née Bartlette], Sandra (Louise) 1942–
Canadian writer of short stories and novels, whose ethnically and religiously diverse upbringing manifests itself in her fiction. Often called a 'Mennonite writer', she was, in fact, raised in a crowded household divided by Catholic and Mennonite allegiances, and often balked at the restrictions of small-town life. She left school at fifteen, returned briefly, and married young in 1959. She had two children in quick succession and eventually settled in Winnipeg. She was divorced in 1984. Her early publications were mainly limited to articles and short stories which appeared in local newspapers. In the late 1970s, she took a creative writing class led by Robert Kroetsch, which helped her transform the oral tales of her youth into polished pieces of fiction. Partly as a result of Kroetsch's support, she published her first collection of short stories, *Night Travellers,* in 1982, followed closely by the linked collection, *Ladies of the House,* in 1984. Two novels followed: *The Missing Child* (1989), and *The Chrome Suite* (1992), partly based on her sister's death when they were both children. She is a founding member of the Manitoba Writers' Guild and has won a number of literary prizes for her work, including the Marian Engel Prize in 1993.   HSM

Birtles [née Toll], Dora (Eileen) 1903–94
Australian TRAVEL writer, novelist, CHILDREN'S author and journalist whose work is forged out of an indefatigable spirit of adventure. She was born in Wickham, New South Wales, and read Oriental History at the University of Sydney, where she met her husband, Bert Birtles. In 1932, after a spell of teaching, she embarked on a voyage in a cutter from Newcastle to Singapore, keeping a diary which she later wrote up whilst living in an old horse-drawn caravan in Surrey. The journal was published, to critical acclaim, as *Northwest by North* in 1935 and re-issued in 1985.

In London, where she was the English correspondent for the *Newcastle Sun* (1932–4) and a fashion journalist, she joined the International Women's League against War and Fascism and was apprehended for initiating a peace protest in the House of Commons. She also wrote an unpublished novel, *Lovely, Lousey London,* about her time in a lice-ridden attic in the capital. She continued to travel throughout Europe and Asia and was one of the first Australians to live in and write about Greece. She returned to Australia, prompted by the threat of war and the desire for a family. 'I think being a mother is more important than writing', she said.

By turns inspired and frustrated by her two young sons, she composed the children's novels, *Pioneer Shack* (1947) and *Bonanza the Bull* (1949), and completed her most successful work, *The Overlanders* (1946; Re-issued 1987). The novel of the film (one of the first of the genre) she had originally researched for its scriptwriter and director, Harry Watt, *The Overlanders* follows wartime cattle-trekkers across an outback threatened by Japanese attack.

Although describing herself as 'an ordinary housewifely feminist', she was an active member of the Fellowship of Australian Writers and a friend of MILES FRANKLIN. Later visits to Yugoslavia, Russia, New Guinea, China and Afghanistan combined her wanderlust with her left-wing political convictions.   JAH

Bishop, Elizabeth 1911–79
American whom James Merrill called 'the poet's poet's poet', Bishop is one of the most cited literary influences of our time. She grew up in Nova Scotia, and lived in Florida and Brazil, landscapes which appear in her work more as a part of the dramatic action than as just scenery. For Bishop, observation is animated by an excited consciousness of the perceptive act, what she herself called in reference to Gerard Manley Hopkins, 'the releasing, checking, timing and repeating of the movement of the mind'.

NORTH AND SOUTH (1946) declares this interest in its opening poem, 'The Map':

> Land lies in water, it is shadowed green.
> Shadows, or are they shallows, at its edges
> showing the line of long sea-weeded ledges
> where weeds hang to the simple blue from green.

Bishop characteristically includes the moment of speculation, 'or are they shallows', reminding us of the *active* nature of looking. This adjustment, a double-take that focuses our attention, also moves the poem lightly from the representational to the real, which are further bridged by repetition and rhyme.

The orderly, firm tone of this poem is reminiscent of Herbert, whom Bishop greatly admired. Like him, the force of feeling in her work is matched by an imperturbable lucidity. Her judgement and control are such that it is surprising to realise how extreme her effects can be: veering scales, hallucinatory acuity and metaphorical leaps. Bishop's metrics are an embedded version of the sprung rhythm she liked in Hopkins. They do not interfere with her voice but charge and sustain it through long narrative sweeps.

Bishop's early work shows an interesting resistance to consciousness with poems about sleep, wishful disorientation and coming-to. Countering this is the intense scrutiny she learned in part from MARIANNE MOORE, who helped her to shape and discipline her curiosity. *A COLD SPRING* (1955) shows Bishop expertly composing and arranging details that ground some more abstract philosophical truth.

> The bight is littered with old correspondences.
> Click. Click. Goes the dredge,
> and brings up a dripping jawful of marl.
> All the untidy activity continues,
> awful but cheerful.

Another poet vital to Bishop was Robert Lowell, whose extreme autobiography perhaps prompted her to explore her own childhood. *Questions of Travel* (1965) is divided into 'Brazil' and 'Elsewhere', intensely localized portraits of her present and childhood homes. The title poem asks '"*Is it lack of imagination that makes us come / to imagined places, not just stay at home?*"', as if Bishop is weighing the benefits of experience against the cost of not belonging.

Bishop, patient and particular, published four small collections, each a decade apart. Her last book, *Geography III* (1976), is a distillation of her themes of memory, possession, perception and place. She struggled against fear and ill health to remain receptive to experience and never lost her imaginative excitement: 'I really don't know *how* poetry gets to be written. There is a mystery and a surprise, and after that a great deal of hard work.' (See POEMS, NORTH & SOUTH – A COLD SPRING.)   LG

Black, Clementina 1853–1922 English novelist and essayist whose writing formed part of her feminist and pro-labour activism. Black, who never married, was the eldest daughter of a solicitor's large and intellectual family (among her sisters was the translator CONSTANCE GARNETT). At 22, Clementina published her first story, 'The Troubles of an Automaton', followed by *A Sussex Idyll* (1877) and *Orlando* (1880). Black moved to London with two sisters in 1879, and during the 1880s moved in some progressive and literary circles; she was particularly close to the poet AMY LEVY. She also began her political activism: she made speeches, led strikes and published numerous articles on trade unionism and working women's rights. She continued to write fiction, including *Miss Falkland and Other Stories* (1892), *An Agitator* (1894) and *The Pursuit of*

Camilla (1899). *The Linleys of Bath* (1911), a history of that family in the 18th century (her favourite literary period), was her most widely read work.   KW

Black Beauty: His Grooms and Companions: The Autobiography of a Horse (1877) ANNA SEWELL's only novel.

Published as 'Translated from the Original Equine, by Anna Sewell', the novel is the best-known animal autobiography. A CHILDREN's classic, it was first written for people who worked with horses. 'Its special aim', Sewell wrote, 'being to induce kindness, sympathy, and an understanding treatment of horses.' Influenced by Sewell's Quaker beliefs, the novel contains messages against cruelty, smoking, alcohol, war and working on Sunday. The novel's didacticism is balanced by the story of its hero's life. Of thoroughbred stock, Black Beauty falls on increasingly hard times as his beauty and worth is ruined by human mistreatment and he is sold on. Notable are the scenes of Black Beauty as a London cab horse and his relationships with other horses, particularly the feisty mare, Ginger, whose death has been called one of the saddest moments in literature. Pirated in America in 1890 the novel broke publishing records and is said to be one of the top ten best-selling novels in English. It came to be recommended by the Royal Society for the Prevention of Cruelty to Animals and was instrumental in the abolition of the bearing rein.   AEG

Black Lamb and Grey Falcon: The Record of a Journey through Yugoslavia in 1937 (1941) REBECCA WEST said her writing expressed 'an

infatuation with human beings' and this, her longest work, exemplifies her passionate curiosity about the human condition. West's range is vast: she ruminates brilliantly on art, philosophy, feminism, history, religion, literature and politics in this innovative, exploratory narrative threaded together by her 'infatuated' record of Yugoslavia in the late 1930s. Writing on the eve of World War II, West also proffers stringent criticism of a Western Liberalism which permits the appeasement of Hitler. A Black Lamb's wanton sacrifice and the defeatist myth of a Grey Falcon are two of the many symbols which Yugoslavia 'reveals', as her anti-Fascist polemic develops, enlivened by lyrical descriptions of landscape and feeling. *Black Lamb*, once a classic for serious travellers, was reprinted during the 1992–5 Yugoslav conflict as a guide-book and historical document. It is also an invaluable key to Rebecca West, proving the marvellous female power of, in VIRGINIA WOOLF's words, 'her tenacious and muscular mind'.

JL

Black Opal (1921) KATHARINE SUSANNAH PRICHARD's third fictional work and her first attempt to incorporate political concerns with the literary

construction of individual characters. These include owner-miners, overseas corporate representatives, *femme fatales*, the Australian squattocracy and bush characters generally. Political and personal conflicts are explored through the main protagonists, Michael Brady, Sophie Rouminof, 'Potch' Heathfield and the New York gem buyers, Dawe and John Armitage. Sophie is referred to as 'the storm-centre' and instigates most of the action. She has experienced the glamorous New York lifestyle, and revelled in its affluent decadence, but recognizes its corrupt, self-seeking foundations. She prefers the earthiness and community spirit of the opal fields, and settles for the inarticulate and simple 'Potch' rather than the wealthy sophisticate, John Dawe. Given the hardship and isolation of mining life described (and witnessed) by Prichard, this seems an extreme choice. However, the metanarrative in the novel is the passion, not just for black opal, but for being your own 'master' and prefigures Prichard's increasingly political stance in all of her remaining novels.   JN

Black Tickets (1979) The brief pieces and more developed stories in American JAYNE ANNE PHILLIPS's first major collection form a poetic and disturbing collage. She inhabits voices and styles with disarming technical assurance, while her subjects range from subtle anatomies of family feeling to the morbid yet casual excesses of sexual obsession, drug addiction and murder. Struggles for power are everywhere evident, often with a sado-masochistic streak. Five narrators offer differing perceptions of Dude and Rita's combustible affair in the gritty 'El Paso', a kind of literary country-and-western song which celebrates the power of cliché. In 'Home', a young woman staying with her divorced mother dreams that her father tried to abuse her as a child; her mother's own sexual frustration pours out after she hears her daughter having sex with an old boyfriend. The closing story 'Gemcrack', by contrast, is the chilling testimony of a psychopath who shoots women, with encouragement from an uncle who, it seems, lives in his head.   MO'D

Blackburn, Helen 1842–1903 Irish suffragist, lecturer and author. Brought up on Valentia Island, County Kerry, Blackburn moved with her family to London in 1859, where she became involved in the campaign for women's rights. She was secretary from 1874 to 1895 to the National Society for Women's Suffrage, and from 1880 to 1895 to the Bristol and West of England Suffrage Society. From 1881 until her retirement in 1895 she was editor of the feminist journal *Englishwoman's Review*.

In 1881 Blackburn published *A Handbook for Women Engaged in Social and Political Work*. Her concern with female employment was also evident in her *Handy Book*

of Reference for Irishwomen (1888), in which she encouraged the development of home industries, and in her opposition to protective legislation, which she feared would threaten the livelihood of working-class women.

Blackburn's moderation was condemned as 'timidity' by some later feminists. However, she left an enduring legacy in her *Record of the Women's Suffrage Movement in the British Isles* (1902). Arguing that 'the effort to bring political liberty . . . forms part of the continuity of history and must be treated as such', she offered a historical account of the female experience from the medieval period, as well as an insider's view of the evolution of the Women's Movement in her own time.

Though she lived for most of her life in England, Blackburn retained strong links with feminists in Ireland. A supporter of the Irish Women's Suffrage and Local Government Association, she spoke at meetings in Dublin in 1891 and 1895, and when she died in 1903 the IWSLGA described her as 'the warmest and most strenuous friend our Irish society has ever had'.   RR

Blackburne, Elizabeth Owens [Elizabeth Casey] 1848–94 Irish novelist, poet and biographer. Born in Slane, County Meath, in 1873 Elizabeth moved to London. Under the pseudonym 'Elizabeth Owens Blackburne', she published a number of novels, many of them with Irish themes or settings. They include *A Woman Scorned* (1876), *Molly Carew* (1879), *The Glen of the Silver Birches* (1880) and *The Heart of Erin* (1882). She also produced poetry, journalism, a collection of short stories – *A Bunch of Shamrocks* (1879) – and a two-volume biographical work *Illustrious Irishwomen* (1877).

According to Blackburne, *Illustrious Irishwomen* was inspired by 'silent patriotism' and by an ambition to 'preserve the names and achievements of some of the more gifted daughters of Erin', and it includes BIOGRAPHIES of subjects as diverse as the mythical Queen Macha, the Ladies of Llangollen (see ELEANOR BUTLER and SARAH PONSONBY), Charlotte Brooke and FELICIA HEMANS. Although Blackburne was not a trained historian, she based her research on 'some years of reading' of manuscript sources in archives in Dublin and London, and her use of original documents makes this a work of continuing usefulness.

Although Blackburne's earlier novels enjoyed some success, her career subsequently went into decline, and she returned to Dublin, where she died in a house-fire.
                                                        RR

Blackwell, Alice Stone 1857–1950 American poet, BIOGRAPHER and feminist. She was born in Orange, New Jersey, the only child of suffragist LUCY STONE and niece of Elizabeth Blackwell, the first American woman physician. She attended Boston University. At first resisting her mother's cause, she later became a prominent reformer, promoting not only suffrage but also temperance, anti-vivisection, anti-racism, aid for immigrants and opposition to Tsarist oppression in Russia. She led the reconciliation of rival suffrage organizations, the National Woman Suffrage Association and the American Suffrage Association, and helped to found the League of Women Voters. She compiled a weekly column of suffrage news items that was distributed to 1,000 newspapers and, for thirty-five years, edited *Woman's Journal*, the periodical her mother founded. In addition to writing articles and pamphlets arguing the cause of suffrage, Blackwell translated Armenian, Yiddish, Hungarian, Spanish and Russian poetry. Late in her life she became a radical socialist. JSG

Blackwell, Antoinette Brown 1825–1921 American minister and reformer who in 1853 became the first woman in the United States to be ordained in the Protestant ministry. At the precocious age of 9, Blackwell joined her family's liberal congregational church in Henrietta, New York. While earning a literary diploma at Oberlin College she met her lifelong friend, activist LUCY STONE. She successfully completed Oberlin's Theological Seminary in 1850, even though as a woman she was refused institutional support and official recognition. In 1856 she married Samuel Blackwell, Stone's brother-in-law, and brother of the physician Elizabeth Blackwell.

Soon after her ordination at the orthodox congregational church of South Butler, New York, Blackwell began questioning denominational doctrine and subsequently gave up her position. In an effort to become 'a preacher for the people', she offered non-denominational Sunday sermons in a rented New York hall from 1859 to 1860. More successful on the lecture circuit, she became a popular orator of women's rights, temperance and abolition. After 1908 she acted as the pastor emeritus for a New Jersey Unitarian Society church.

Throughout her career she remained committed to reconciling Christianity with equal rights for women. After the rise of Darwinism many of her essays and books, most notably *The Sexes Throughout Nature* (1875) and *The Physical Basis of Immortality* (1876), attempt to accommodate science to woman's rights and her Christian beliefs. Also interested in writing fiction, she published at least one novel, *The Island Neighbors* (1871), and a book of poems, *Sea Drift* (1902). VM

Blackwood, Caroline 1931–96 Caroline Blackwood, daughter of the Marquis and Marchioness of Dufferin and Ava, was born into the Anglo-Irish nobility, spent her childhood in Northern Ireland, was sent to an English boarding school and became a journalist. Her first and second marriages, to the painter Lucian Freud

and the composer Israel Citkowitz, ended in divorce. Her third husband, the poet Robert Lowell, encouraged her in creative writing. Blackwood categorized the pieces in her first book, *For All That I Found There* (1973), as 'Fact', 'Fiction' and 'Ulster'. The three (not entirely distinct) headings cover the rest of her work. She wrote novels, *The Stepdaughter* (1976), *Great Granny Webster* (1977), *The Fate of Mary Rose* (1981), *Corrigan* (1984), and a collection of stories, *Good Night, Sweet Ladies* (1983). She produced a COOKERY BOOK, *Darling, You Shouldn't Have Gone To So Much Trouble* (1990), in collaboration with Anna Haycraft (the novelist ALICE THOMAS ELLIS who, with her husband Colin, was Blackwood's first publisher). She also wrote books about the Duchess of Windsor (*The Last of the Duchess*, 1995), the Women's Peace Movement occupation of Greenham Common near the Cruise nuclear missile base (*On the Perimeter*, 1984) and hunting (*In the Pink*, 1987). Blackwood's subjects are trapped (sometimes voluntarily) in almost unbearable situations: physical and mental illness, hospital, destructive families, bereavement, terminal boredom. She suggested that the troubles of Northern Ireland might be the inhabitants' protest against their tedious 'internment' in the province and *Great Granny Webster* shows the disintegrating stately home of her own childhood as a tragicomedy of changelessness. Her characters include her daughter as a patient in a Burns Unit, the paralysed and helpless Duchess, a concentration-camp survivor and many desperate wives and husbands. She casts a cold eye on every kind of atrocity and reports it with merciless elegance. PMar

Blais, Marie-Claire 1939– Prolific Francophone Canadian novelist, playwright and poet associated with a new era of Quebec fiction, writes dark visions of contemporary poverty, sadistic Catholicism, betrayed innocence in a barbaric world, French/Quebec cultural (colonial) relations and lesbianism. A critical view from the underside runs through her books together with the search for reasons for our existence. In a narrative style reminiscent of VIRGINIA WOOLF's use of stream-of-consciousness, she invents phantasmagoric landscapes, experimenting with language and method, blending real and surreal, lyric symbolism and street-talk.

Born in a working-class district of Quebec City, Blais left convent school at 15 to work in a shoe factory due to her family's financial difficulties. Later she studied French Literature in Canada and then in Paris as a Canada Council and Guggenheim Fellow (1962), sponsored by Edmund Wilson, an experience partly reflected in *Une Liaison parisienne* (1975) (*A Literary Affair*, 1979). The US sculptor Mary Meigs portrays their life together in Quebec, the USA and France in *Lily Briscoe* (1981) and *The Medusa Head* (1983). Blais won immediate

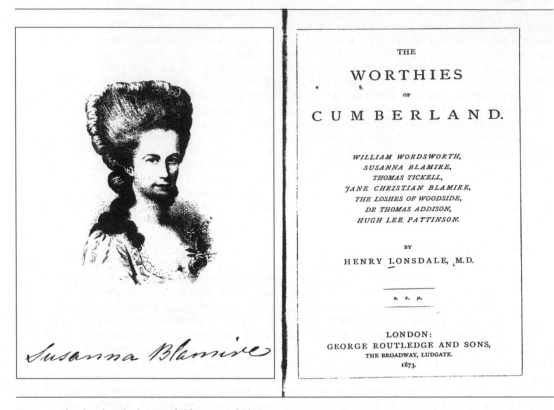

THE

WORTHIES

OF

CUMBERLAND.

*WILLIAM WORDSWORTH,
SUSANNA BLAMIRE,
THOMAS TICKELL,
JANE CHRISTIAN BLAMIRE,
THE LOSHES OF WOODSIDE,
DR THOMAS ADDISON,
HUGH LEE PATTINSON.*

BY

HENRY LONSDALE, M.D.

o. e. μ.

LONDON:
GEORGE ROUTLEDGE AND SONS,
THE BROADWAY, LUDGATE.
1873.

Susanna Blamire: frontispiece and title-page of *The Worthies of Cumberland*, 1873.

international recognition (France-Québec and Médicis Prizes) with *Une Saison dans la vie d'Emmanuel* (1965) (*A Season in the Life of Emmanuel*, 1966), a study of repressed life in rural Quebec. Blais published in various genres and collaborated with NICOLE BROSSARD, FRANCE THÉORET and others in *La Nef des sorcières* (1976). She received Governor General's Awards for *Manuscrits de Pauline Archange* (1968), a semi-autobiographical trilogy about female adolescence in Quebec, illustrated by Mary Meigs, *Le Sourd dans la ville* (1979) (*Deaf to the City*, 1980) and *Soifs* (1995), a fantastic extrapolation of the world approaching the millennium. The near future is also the topic of *L'Ange de la solitude* (1989), a description of eight lesbians founding utopia. In 1980 Blais was appointed a member of the Order of Canada.   DMM

Blamire, Susanna 1747–94 'The Muse of Cumberland', is the author of songs such as 'The Nabob', 'What Ails this Heart o' Mine?' and 'The Chelsea Pensioners'. Her long poetic *tour de force*, 'Stoklewath; or, the Cumbrian Village' (*c.* 1780) celebrates 18th-century village life and everyday domestic activity in simple, affectionate language. With wry humour and striking natural imagery, Blamire empha-

sizes the ephemerality of human life and memory. The poem details the enormous human price of warfare but also portrays romantic love as a source of unhappiness, alienation and tragedy. Although English by birth, Blamire embraced Scottish language, manners, music and legends during a six-year stay in the Highlands, when she began writing songs in Scottish dialect. Few Blamire poems saw print during her lifetime, but many became popular as songs or circulated widely in manuscript and in commonplace books. In 1842, nearly half a century after the poet's death, a collected edition of her work appeared, with some poems in standard English, and others in Cumbrian or Scottish dialect, including lyrics, ballads, epistles and elegies.   PRF

Blanch, Lesley 1907– Although British writer Lesley Blanch called *Journey Into the Mind's Eye* (1968) an autobiography, it owes much of its attractiveness to the romantic cloud with which she clothes historical fact. Like the four subjects of her most successful book, THE WILDER SHORES OF LOVE (1954), she had early romantic yearnings for the Caucasus and the Levant, and she created a remarkable Oriental environment for herself in Garavan, outside Menton, where her collection of books and objects, tragically destroyed by fire in the spring of 1994, was shown to perfection. Little is

The-four women who form the subject of this book might be described as northern shadows flitting across a southern landscape. ~~Each~~ All of them belonged to ~~a~~ the fast-greying ~~West~~ climate ~~of~~ nineteenth-century Europe, where its twentieth-century disintegration of women, as such, was already foreshadowed. Yet although of different natures, backgrounds + origins, all had this in common — each found, in the East, glowing horizons of emotion + daring which were, for them, now vanishing from the West. And each of them, in her own way, used love as a means of individual expression, of liberation ~~+ of fulfilment~~, ~~with~~ fulfilment within that radiant periphery.

Lesley Blanch: an extract from the manuscript of *The Wilder Shores of Love*, 1954.

known of her earlier life: she does not appreciate the prying eyes of a biographer. A friend and contemporary of NANCY MITFORD she preferred to live in France after World War II. In 1945 she had married French novelist and diplomat Romain Gary; together they made a glamorous couple, as much at home in New York as in Paris, with literary friends and correspondents all over the world. They parted company in 1962.

As well as the biographical *Sabres of Paradise* (1960) and *Pavilions of the Heart* (1974), she wrote two COOKERY BOOKS, *Round the World in Eighty Dishes* (1956) and *From Wilder Shores: The Tables of My Travels* (1989); neither was strictly confined to cookery, and, like her other writing, they combined the exotic with the matter-of-fact, TRAVEL with personal reminiscence, kitchen mundanities with flights of fancy. It is perhaps surprising that her only novel, *The Nine Tiger Man* (1965), was relatively unsuccessful: but she needed a biographical bedrock to create her unique atmosphere of ROMANCE. In *Pierre Loti: Portrait of an Escapist* (1983) she did just that once again, recounting the life of a most flamboyant orientalist with 'the habit of faraway places'.   JSS

Blavatsky, Helena 1831–91 Spiritualist, philosopher, psychic researcher, self-reinventer, holder of seance salons, founder of Theosophy. Helena Petrovna von Hahn was born in Russia. Her father was an artillery captain, her mother a sometime novelist who died of tuberculosis at 28, in 1841. Her father began a second family and she was raised in St Petersburg and on country estates by her grandmother. A sickly and foul-tempered child, Helena was happiest when left alone with books. To avoid attending a ball at 16, she scalded herself with boiling water so badly, on purpose, that she was in bed for the next six months (reading alchemy). When her family made her marry, at 17, their old friend Nikifor Blavatsky, she had to be forced to the wedding, and fled her husband three months later. The next nine years of Blavatsky's life are a cipher. She spent time in Constantinople, travelled in Egypt, and there began smoking the hashish and opium she would use all her life. She may have gone to India.

In 1858, at 27, Blavatsky resurfaced in Russia. Fascinated with Eastern religions, particularly Hinduism and Buddhism, and with American spiritualism (spirit 'rapping'), she read widely about – and then practised – hypnotism and levitation. In 1873 she moved to New York to be nearer the leading lights of the American spiritual movement, particularly Henry Olcott. Together, she and Olcott formulated their ideas of Theosophy – an esoteric version of Buddhism with increasing amounts of Christianity added, purporting to be not *a* religion but, all-encompassingly, *religion*. She went to India in 1878 to found a headquarters in Adyar and then moved to London, where she would publish *The Secret Doctrine* (1888; two vols.; 1,500 pages). Blavatsky held weekly advice sessions and seances at her home at 17 Lansdowne Road; a young W. B. Yeats attended. She died in May 1891, but the Theosophical Society remains in Adyar (with a branch office in California) and there are thousands of members worldwide.   AMD

Bleecker, Ann Eliza 1752–83 Early American writer. Bleecker loved books despite her lack of formal education and maintained her literary interests in the frontier-like setting of Tomhanick, New York, after marriage in 1769. The Revolution brought domestic upheaval, loss and a lingering illness that eventually led to her death. Her extant fiction, letters and poetry were gathered in *The Posthumous Works of Ann Eliza Bleecker, in Prose and Verse* (1793) by her daughter, who wrote Bleecker's memoir. Although she claims Bleecker wrote primarily for the entertainment of friends, the volume's preface also notes that she had several works published in the *New-York Magazine*.

Bleecker's letters display an often playful voice which recounts news from politics to neighbourhood gossip. The poems in the volume use typical 18th-century forms (e.g., rhymed couplets) and conventions (e.g., pastoral settings and references to Greek gods) and range widely from a rendering of the story of Joseph to verses praising revolutionary generals Montgomery and Washington. Fiction in *The Posthumous Works* includes 'The Story of Henry and Anne', an immigration tale in which a poor yet honourable family suffers persecution by a landlord in Germany and finds paradisaical community in the New World. Included in the volume but also published on its own, her most popular work was THE HISTORY OF MARIA KITTLE (1797). It was one of the first fictional works of the CAPTIVITY genre, using GOTHIC and sentimental elements as well as anti-Indian propaganda.   KMP

Blessington, Marguerite, Countess of 1789–1849

Irish-born editor and novelist. Her 'silver-fork' novels and Annuals appealed enormously to mid-Victorian tastes, but neither her list of illustrious contributors nor their idealized sentiments could give her social respectability. Sold into marriage at 14, she later lived with various protectors, including the Earl of Blessington, whom she married in 1818 after her husband's death. Soon after her first book, *The Magic Lantern* (1822), their *ménage à trois* with her stepson-in-law, Count D'Orsay, effectively exiled the 'Blessington Circus' to Europe. She published her Genoa *Conversations with Lord Byron* in 1834. After Blessington's death (1829), she supported herself and D'Orsay in London by writing ten hours a day, fitted around brilliant salons (almost exclusively male). 'Write', she briskly advised the young Disraeli, 'write *write* no matter what, so that you do but write'. She produced sixteen books, innumerable magazine pieces, and gossip columns, while simultaneously editing four fashionable Annuals, *The Book of Beauty* (1834–49), *Gems of Beauty* (1836–40), *Flowers of Loveliness* (1836–41) and *The Keepsake* (1841–50). Her last *Keepsake* and novel, *Country Quarters* (1850), appeared after she died, bankrupt and exhausted, in Paris.   MSM

Blind, Mathilde 1841–96 Poet, BIOGRAPHER, translator and editor whose works engage strongly with political and scientific issues of the Victorian period. Born in Mannheim, she was the daughter of a Jewish banker (Cohen) but took the surname of her mother's second husband, Karl Blind, a political writer and revolutionary who led the 1848-9 Baden Insurrection. The family were forced to seek refuge first in Belgium and then in London, where they received such political visitors as Louis Bland, Garibaldi and Mazzini (Mathilde published her 'Recollections of Mazzini' in 1891). Mainly self-educated, Blind was a highly independent woman who remained single, lectured on female franchise and women's education, and travelled extensively by herself. Heavily influenced by the Romantics, she published a biography of Shelley (1872) and edited Byron's letters and poems (1886). Blind was drawn to strong women and wrote biographies of GEORGE ELIOT (1883) and Madame Roland (1886), as well as translating Marie Bashkirtseff's *Journal* (1890). Two trips to the Scottish Highlands inspired her poems *The Prophecy of St Oran*, a story of a monk's love for a Pictish woman, and *The Heather on Fire*, an attack on the clearance of crofters' communities from Highland estates. In 1889 she published her epic poem based upon Darwin's evolutionary theory, *The Ascent of Man*. Other collections include *Dramas in Miniature* (1891), *Songs and Sonnets* (1893) and *Birds of Passage* (1895). On her death, she left money to Newnham College, Cambridge, to found a scholarship for Language and Literature.   SA

Bliss and Other Stories (1920) MODERNIST pioneer KATHERINE MANSFIELD's second short-story collection includes some of her finest pieces. The almost novella-length 'Prelude' (written 1915–17), which cemented her reputation as an important writer, fluidly renders the experiences, perceptions and fantasies of three generations of the Burnell family womenfolk as and after they move house. At times almost a symbolist prose poem, presided over by the barbed great aloe in the garden, its mobile free indirect discourse reveals the cruelties and repressions of patriarchal family life. 'Je Ne Parle Pas Français' is the convoluted monologue of decadent charlatan Raoul Duqette, a victim of sexual abuse who in turn has become an abuser himself. The commerce between art, sex and ethics also informs the title story, 'Bliss', a scathing satire on a seemingly liberated London set, centred on the emotions and desires of the (as it transpires) betrayed Bertha. These, and some of the other, slighter stories, feature stylistic (and arguably thematic) innovations as bold as those of James Joyce, GERTRUDE STEIN, VIRGINIA WOOLF and DOROTHY RICHARDSON.   MO'D

Blixen, Karen see DINESEN, ISAK

Blood and Guts in High School (1984) Denounced by some critics as obscene, KATHY ACKER's sixth novel offers a caustic attack on what she sees as the obscenities of patriarchy and capitalism, through its representation of women's repression and alienation. It tells the story of a young girl called Janey who is rejected by her father, imprisoned by a slave trader who teaches her how to be a whore, masochistically pursues a famous author in order to learn how to write, and ultimately dies of cancer (ironically, like Acker herself). This was Acker's first text to be accepted by a mainstream publisher and the first to bring her work critical attention, not always favourable: the brutally frank and disturbing representation of sex and violence caused controversy. The use of plagiarism and intertextuality, together with a montage of drawings and 'dream maps', gives the text a highly experimental style. POSTMODERN in impetus, in terms of both form and theme, it reflects Acker's interest in ideas explored by French feminists about the relationship between language, sexuality, the body and power.   EP

Bloody Chamber, The (1979) ANGELA CARTER continues the demythologizing project of her earlier fiction in this collection of short stories which take traditional FAIRY TALE as their point of departure. Deconstructing the patriarchal structures of the original tales, Carter is able to reverse their repressive gender dynamics, and offer alternative figurations of female sexuality and desire. Bluebeard's wife senses her 'potentiality for corruption' in the title story, Beauty recognizes her own beastliness in 'The Tiger's Bride' and Red Riding Hood lies down with the Wolf in 'The Company of Wolves'. These GOTHIC tales develop, in fictional terms, the discussion of the sexual politics of sadomasochistic attraction in Carter's polemical essay, *The Sadeian Woman* (1979).

'The Lady of the House of Love' began as the radio play *Vampirella* (1976) and Carter also adapted *The Company of Wolves* (1980) and *Puss in Boots* (1982) for radio. She later co-scripted a film version of *The Company of Wolves* with director Neil Jordan in 1984; its graphic werewolf transformations marking a shift in emphasis from fairy tale to horror.   CCr

Bloom, Valerie 1956– Poet, dramatist, CHILDREN's writer. Born Valerie Wright in Clarendon, Jamaica, she trained at Mico College, before returning to the school where she herself was educated, Frankfield Primary and High School, to teach English, Speech, Drama and Economics. Three of her plays and several poems and speeches were awarded prizes in the Jamaican National Festival.

She made her début in London as performer of her own poetry at the First International Fair of Black and Third World Books in 1982. In the tradition of the popular Jamaican poet Louise Bennett, she brings to life through her poetry an array of characters, sharply and wittily observed, and exploits the nuances and appeal of Jamaican patois. Although often humorous and tragi-comic, her poems can also carry a strong political message. The performance is heightened by her use of a few simple costumes and props to convey different generations and types of Jamaican and black British women. Her first volume of poetry, *Touch mi, Tell mi!*, was published in 1983 while she was studying for a degree in English and African and Caribbean Studies at the University of Kent, where she was subsequently awarded an Honorary MA for her achievements as a poet in 1995. Her selected spoken works are recorded on cassette tape, *Yuh Hear Bout?* (1997). Valerie Bloom has also written a number of books for children: *Duppy Jamboree* (1992), *Fruits* (1997) and *New Baby* (1999).   CLI

Bloomer, Amelia Jenks 1818–94 American reformer, editor. Born in Homer, New York, Amelia entered into social reform by writing articles for her husband's paper, the *Seneca County Courier*. In 1849, she began publishing the periodical *Lily*, in which she focused on the temperance movement, while also advocating women's suffrage, education, employment opportunities and dress reform. 'Bloomers', the modified skirt and trousers which were named after her, were in fact created by Elizabeth Smith Miller, and remained popular until they were seen to detract from the focus on women's rights. From 1852 until her death, she lectured around the country, always emphasizing the idea that the country's health was dependent on women's participation in politics, through a combination of education, suffrage and temperance. 'With her mind and body fully developed', she wrote, 'imbued with a full sense of her responsibilities, and living in the conscientious discharge of each and all of them, she [woman] will be fitted to share with her brother in all the duties of life.'   SP

Blower, Elizabeth c.1763–after 1816 English novelist and poet. Little is known of the life of Elizabeth Blower. She was born in Worcester, an area notorious for election violence, and her gentleman father appears to have attached himself to an unsuccessful independent Parliamentary candidate. Perhaps as a result, the family fell on hard times, and Elizabeth began writing novels to earn money. The author also appears to have worked as an actress in Ireland for five years and in London from 1787 to 1788. Published when she was between the ages of 17 and 25, her four works are *The Parsonage* (1780), *George Bateman* (1782), *Maria* (1785) and *Features from Life: Or, A Summer Visit* (1780). Her first novel is EPISTOLARY and satirizes popular fictional styles. Reviews were favourable two

Bluestocking: frontispiece to the *Female Spectator*, vol. 1, 1744–6.

years later when Elizabeth published poems and *George Bateman*, which includes dialogue in dialect and an insightful account of electioneering. Her later novels contain further examples of Blower's skill in concocting social satire and comedies of manners. *Features from Life* embraces the vogue for sentimentalism and chronicles a virtuous rural marriage broken by the seductions of London life.   JHP

Bluest Eye, The (1970) TONI MORRISON's short first novel is a distillation of the potent rage and poetry which find more elaborate expression in her later work. As elsewhere, her central subject is the spiritual wounds endured by black Americans. Here, it is the white physical ideal doing the damage: eleven-year-old Pecola Breedlove is crippled by an ineradicable conviction of her own ugliness, and prays every night for blue eyes. The novel's opening ironically juxtaposes the blemishless 'Dick and Jane' children's story with the statement that Pecola is carrying her father's child. Morrison describes Pecola's undoing in intricate

alternating narratives, one concerning the two sisters who befriend Pecola, the other tracing the cruel history of her embattled parents, Cholly and Pauline ('Mrs Breedlove' to her own children, 'Polly' to the white family that employs her). Set in 1941 in Morrison's native Lorain, Ohio, the novel's vivid childhood moments give it a personal tone similar to that of *SULA*; characteristic Morrisonian flourishes include a trio of whores called China, Poland and The Maginot Line. Though the novel describes a child broken on the back of her parents' disappointments, it is graced throughout by a stark and remarkable beauty.   SB

bluestocking A learned or literary woman. The phrase was originally used to abuse Puritans of Cromwell's 'Little Parliament' in 1653. It was revived in 1756 when the eccentric scholar Benjamin Stillingfleet notoriously appeared at one of ELIZABETH MONTAGU's assemblies wearing the worsted blue stockings worn by working men, instead of the more socially acceptable white silk. The term came to be applied more generally to all Montagu's visitors, who included Dr Johnson, James Boswell, Edmund Burke, David Garrick, Sir Joshua Reynolds, Horace Walpole, CATHERINE MACAULAY, Lord Lyttleton, the Earl of Bath and, later, FANNY BURNEY and HANNAH MORE. The initial cultivation of 'bluestocking philosophy' by a select group of aristocrats and professional authors might be seen as the social expression of an Enlightenment belief in freedom of enquiry. As Hume observed, 'The more the refined arts advance, the more sociable men become.' He emphasized that 'Particular clubs and societies are everywhere formed', where 'both sexes meet in an easy and sociable manner' (*Essays Literary and Moral*). Montagu and Mrs Vesey both campaigned to replace card-playing with literary conversation at evening parties. Montagu seated her guests in a large semi-circle, while Vesey preferred more informal, scattered groups: to her, Hannah More addressed her complimentary poem, *The Bas Bleu* (1786), which joins FRANCES BOSCAWEN to these two bluestocking hostesses.

Patronage played an important part in spreading bluestocking ideas. Montagu's shrewd management of her husband's coal mines in Northumberland ensured great wealth. After his death in 1775, she built Montagu House, a mansion in Portman Square where her parties continued on a grand scale. She held annual May Day entertainments for London chimney sweeps on her front lawns. The interior was lavishly decorated by Angelica Kauffman, founder member of the Royal Academy. James Barry's important series of paintings for the Society of Arts, 'The Progress of Human Knowledge and Culture' (1784) includes a group portrait which gives pride of place to Montagu, by then well known as 'Queen of the Blues'. She is depicted as a generous benefactor of the poor, with Johnson point-ing at her example in approval.

Montagu's most profound legacy was to forge a public identity for the female intellectual as a socially useful individual, through both her own scholarship and her encouragement of other women. She corre-sponded wittily with ELIZABETH CARTER, who wrote, 'I may make my fortune very prettily as Mrs Montagu's owl.' Montagu granted her an annuity and they travelled together on the continent, Carter's fluency in languages being something of a curiosity at European courts and spa towns. Montagu's *Essay on the Writings and Genius of Shakespeare* (1769), in which she powerfully refuted Voltaire's criticisms of the bard, consolidated her reputation as a critic. By the 1770s, 'bluestocking' began to refer specifically to women. Recent research has revealed the enormous and incre-mental increase in women writers during the second half of the 18th century – a radical epistemic shift. Their success was a cultural phenomenon, provoking a spurt of eulogies, anthologies and dictionaries of women writers. Richard Samuel's portrait of *The Nine Living Muses of Great Britain* (1779, now in the National Portrait Gallery Collection) provides a powerful visual image of a group of professionals of national standing: Angelica Kauffman, Elizabeth Carter, ANNA BARBAULD, Elizabeth Sheridan, Catherine Macaulay, Elizabeth Montagu, ELIZABETH GRIFFITH, Hannah More and CHARLOTTE LENNOX. These women corre-sponded and met with each other, forming a critical community who read each other's work. Their com-bined output was voluminous – poetry, educational texts, history, philosophy, political pamphlets, drama, novels and Shakespeare criticism. Their professional achievement challenged traditional stereotypes of female accomplishment, drawing attention to the need for equality between the sexes. While these women had few legal rights, they demonstrated their right to 'the life of the mind'. Writing provided a route to autonomy and the control of one's income. 'Who would not be a bluestockinger at this rate?' wrote Fanny Burney in her diary in 1780.

Education and morality were central to the blue-stocking project. Montagu's sister SARAH SCOTT wrote an EPISTOLARY NOVEL, *Millennium Hall*, which developed the earlier feminism of MARY ASTELL's *SERIOUS PROPOSAL TO THE LADIES*, offering a utopian vision of a harmonious female community which, secluded from the public gaze, pursues a virtuous life through various arts, manufactures and acts of charity. Another important precursor of the bluestockings was the Anglo-Saxon scholar ELIZABETH ELSTOB, grammarian of 'the mother tongue', who, after the closure of her charity school, was governess to the Duchess of Portland, a youthful correspondent of Montagu's. The widespread use of the term 'bluestock-ing' by the 1790s was coterminous with the rise of women's education and self-advancement. Barbauld's best-selling *Lessons for Children* (1778) and Hannah More's Sunday-school system were revolutionary in improving literacy levels throughout Britain. WOLLSTONECRAFT was influenced by Macaulay's *Letters on Education* (1790) when she wrote her most famous work, *A VINDICATION OF THE RIGHTS OF WOMAN* (1792), which can be read as an extension of bluestocking ideals.

The combined social and intellectual prominence of so many intelligent women was greeted with suspi-cion and disgust by many literary men. 'Bluestocking' became a term of comedy and abuse, echoing earlier distrust of learned women's 'slipshod' appearance and morality. Satires include Richard Polwhele's vitriolic *Unsex'd Females* (1798), which rails against female learn-ing in all areas, from botany to astronomy. Polwhele tapped post-revolutionary fears of contamination by radical female writers such as HELEN MARIA WILLIAMS. Byron's more whimsical *The Blues: A Literary Eclogue* (1821) sketched Montagu as 'Lady Bluebottle'. 'I have an utter aversion to *blue-stockings*. I do not care for any woman who knows even what *an author* means' wrote Hazlitt (*Table-talk*, 1822). Such prejudice from established figures, with their influ-ence in the press and publishing houses, can be held largely responsible for the original bluestockings' fall from public view and for the rising tendency for women authors to adopt masculine pseudonyms. By the end of the 19th century, as women renewed their campaign for equality in education, 'bluestocking' remained a label for the learned female, suggesting primness of attitude, plain features and political inter-ests. The term persists as an awkward stereotype, too often revealing men who continue to find intelligence in a woman remarkable. As the original bluestockings are brought to light again, perhaps the term will come once more to denote intellectual women who pursue an active life within a community of equals.　　ESE

Blume [Sussman], Judy

Blume [Sussman], Judy 1938– American novelist, whose honest, humorous, confessional stories are bestsellers with young readers worldwide. Growing up in a Jewish family in New Jersey, with friends, festivals, summer camp, enjoying school for sociability rather than study, she had a less outwardly turbulent child-hood than that of many of her characters. Married to her first husband in college, while graduating in Education, she spent some years looking after her young children, coming to writing in her late twenties. After much dis-couragement she published *Iggie's House* – about a newly interracial neighbourhood – when she was thirty. Certain that young people need understanding, even in the most stable families, and criticizing the 1950s as a time when 'we were all pretending we had no problems'

(*Memory Book*,1988), she has made speaking openly the hallmark of her fiction. The day-to-day dramas, disappointments and complications of growing up are as important to her stories as the more controversially taboo 'issues' – menstruation (*Are You There God? It's Me, Margaret*, 1970), wet dreams (*Then Again, Maybe I Won't*, 1971), teenage sex (*Forever*, 1976), violent death (*Tiger Eyes*, 1981) – which gained her notoriety.

Though many adults disapprove, young readers respond powerfully to her frankness, writing to her, in their thousands, often asking for advice about painfully difficult lives. Her royalties from the tactfully selected *Letters to Judy* (1986) go toward her Kids' Fund – a practical charitable foundation for youth-centred projects. But novels are her main channel of communication. She fills her fiction with young writers, like Sally J. Freedman in her most autobiographical story (*Starring Sally J. Freedman As Herself*, 1977), and through their diaries, letters, fantasies, confessions and jokes, encourages readers to take the first step in assuming responsibility for their own lives – getting the problem told. Campaigning against censorship, speaking for Planned Parenthood, but, above all, writing her fiction, Judy Blume has pioneered new territory for young people.   PEK

Bly [née Russell], Carol 1930– American essayist, social critic and short-story writer born in Duluth, Minnesota, and educated at Wellesley College and the University of Minnesota. Married to and divorced from poet Robert Bly, she has taught extensively, including stints at Hamline University, Carlton College, the University of Minnesota Creative Writing Program and the University of Iowa. Founder of COMPAS Literary Post, a teaching/writing programme for senior citizens. She has received writing awards from the Bush Foundation and the Minnesota State Arts Board. In the early 1970s Bly began writing essays that evolved into the collection *Letters from the Country* (1981). She has published several other collections of essays including: *The Passionate, Accurate Story*: *Making Your Heart's Truth into Literature* (1990), *Bad Government and Silly Literature* (1986), *Backbone* (1985) and *An Ethics Reader* (1985). Her most recent books include: *The Tomcat's Wife and Other Stories* (1991), which won the Friends of American Writers Award, and *The Life of an Ordinary Woman* (1990). Three of her stories from *Backbone* were developed into the critically praised film, *Rachael River*. She has also edited, or contributed to, such anthologies as *Everybody's Story: Writing by Older Minnesotans* (1987) and compiled *Changing the Bully Who Rules the World: Reading and Thinking about Ethics* (1996).
                                                          MRA

Blyton, Enid (Mary) 1897–1968 English writer who published over 600 books for children. Born in London and educated at a private school, she trained as a teacher and briefly taught in Kent before spending four years as a governess. In 1917 her first poem was published and she continued to write poems, stories and articles for publication in magazines such as *Teacher's World*. In 1924 she married Hugh Pollock with whom she had two children and began devoting herself solely to writing. In the 1940s she briefly used the pseudonym 'Mary Pollock'. After divorcing, she married Kenneth Darrell Waters in 1943.

In 1926 Blyton began editing *Sunny Stories* which became synonymous with her name and which contained her stories and serials. A successful children's writer by the outbreak of World War II, she went on to become a phenomenon of both output and popularity (see CHILDREN'S BOOKS). In 1951, her peak year, she published thirty-seven titles. Her books included a number of series: the 'Noddy' books for younger children; adventure and detective series such as the 'Famous Five' and the 'Secret Seven'; the school series 'Malory Towers' and 'St Clare's' as well as fantasy books such as *The Magic Faraway Tree* (1943).

Her work has provoked controversy which was at its most heated in the 1960s and 1970s. Her books were accused of sexism, racism, middle-class prejudice and poor quality, and this caused some librarians effectively to ban them. Her work has, however, maintained its huge popularity with children.   AEG

Boatman, The (1957) Canadian JAY MACPHERSON's slim volume of poetry, which won the Governor General's Award, presents in six sections a hermetic, occasionally enigmatic universe, and considers a wide range of subjects, from sexual love to spiritual rebirth. Macpherson's idiosyncratic syncretism freely blends classical and biblical elements in tones that shift from archaic poetic to colloquial contemporary. Allusive and epigrammatic, the erudite rhymed verse (judged 'one of a kind' by MARGARET ATWOOD) invokes the patterns of folk songs, fables and – as the final section, 'The Fisherman', suggests – playful riddles. *The Boatman* introduces a complex series of linked images – sea, egg, fish, ark, cave – and figures spanning from striving 'anagogic man' Noah to Mary Magdalene and the Cumaean Sibyl. Set in a decidedly postlapsarian time ('the world is foul'), the poems, some of which were published as early as 1948, express longing for a prelapsarian epoch when 'the world was first a private park'. Through a Christian humanist lens, Macpherson's poems focus on the possibility of spiritual transformation, re-connection with nature, and renewal of order and community – for the poet, the reader and humanity.   BJG

Bobbin Up (1959) By DOROTHY HEWETT, this is often seen as the first Australian industrial novel to focus centrally upon women workers. It has some twenty female characters and follows many of them home from the textile factory, the Jumbuck Spinning Mills in Sydney, to show also the diverse privations and aspirations of their domestic lives. The women's interactions in the workplace lead up to a determined sit-in strike with which the novel concludes.

One of the main characters, Nell, a militant in the Communist party, has some similarities to Hewett herself in the 1950s, the time of the novel. In her autobiography, *Wild Card* (1990), while recognizing that the party helped women to develop confidence and abilities in many areas of activity, Hewett looks back on her novel as overly constrained by the prescriptions of socialist REALISM. It was nonetheless daring and radical in terms of its language, and its expression of female autonomy, personal and political desire, and solidarity, and remains of great interest for these features.

Bobbin Up was Hewett's first novel; after a long career of poetry and play-writing a second, *The Toucher*, appeared in 1993.   CF

Bodichon, Barbara Leigh Smith 1827–91 English painter, pamphleteer, philanthropist and political activist, co-founder of Girton College. Barbara Smith was born in Sussex in 1827 to Benjamin Leigh Smith, a wealthy distillery owner and later MP, and Anne Longden, who worked for a milliner. Her parents lived together as man and wife, but never married. She and her brothers and sisters were educated at home by a Swedenborgian tutor, with little discipline but surrounded by much wealth. Throughout her life, Bodichon would acknowledge the power her money gave her to pursue causes and actions she deemed important. She married Eugene Bodichon, a French Algerian doctor, in 1857 after a disappointing affair with John Chapman, the (married) editor of the *Westminster Review*, and the couple lived between England and Algiers until Barbara's health confined her to London and Scalands, her cottage near Hastings. Bodichon had no children.

Women's education was Bodichon's chief cause. In 1849, after travelling through Germany with two female friends, unchaperoned, to hike and paint, she began art classes at the newly founded Bedford College for Women. However, she was more interested in lecture formats and administration than in painting. The Portman Hall progressive elementary school, operating until 1864, was the first of her increasingly successful ventures in education. The last of these was Girton College. Opened by EMILY DAVIES in a house in Hitchin in 1869, Girton was moved to Cambridge in 1873 after Bodichon arranged for and oversaw the construction of a campus. She persuaded GEORGE ELIOT, a close friend since the early 1850s, and other prominent women to help to fund Girton, and when she died she left most of her estate to the college.

Bodichon's political activities were feminist and progressive: she supported the Married Women's Property Bill in her swiftly selling, aptly titled *A Brief Summary in Plain Language of the Most Important Laws in England Concerning Women* (1854) and organized the Married Women's Property Committee. Bodichon's great ability to bring together committees and draft petitions for circulation was seminal to all future 19th-century feminist activity in England.   AMD

Body of this Death (1923) LOUISE BOGAN's first volume of poetry, published when she was 26, thematically coheres around the failures, disappointments and disillusionment of romantic love. Tonally ironic and bitter, sometimes slipping into self-pity, these lyrics move through loss, betrayal, obsessive desire and fear toward rupture, resistance, solitude and a dangerous freedom. While some have found internalized masculinism in Bogan's representations of the sexes, notably in the well-anthologized *Women* and *Medusa* (Bogan's lyrics are for the most part clearly gendered and heterosexual), one can also find ironic critiques of men's and women's acculturation in this poetry of struggle. Bogan's defiant female speakers often claim some measure of liberation from the entrapments of men and the illusions of heterosexual love. These poems lean toward MODERNIST formalism and the metaphysicals in their strict compactness, their intensity, their brevity. The title comes from St Paul, who begs release from the source of sin; Bogan's entrapping body seems less obviously sinful, but no less a body of death in the pain it delivers where pleasure had been hoped for.   SC

Body of Water, A (1990) 'Not one story has achieved its being in my hands for nearly two years now', laments Australian writer BEVERLEY FARMER in her book's opening pages. Concerned that perhaps 'an anxious rigidity about forms is part of the problem', Farmer determines to forge a new way of writing, marking a departure from the conventional narratives and structures of her previous work. In *A Body of Water*, subtitled 'A Year's Notebook', she exposes and examines the construction of her work even as she is creating it. The sources she draws on as she writes are juxtaposed in a kaleidoscopic series of images and ideas. These disparate influences include Buddhism, philosophy and fragments of fiction and poetry by other writers, as well as those aspects of the author's day-to-day existence that inform her art, such as love, sexuality, friendships and the natural environment. The resulting poems and short stories, contained within the text, are multifaceted and open-ended.   AL

Boehmer, Elleke 1961– South-African-born British-based writer and academic whose novels signal the limitations of both white South African consciousness and the white novel form under apartheid. Both her 'heroines' in *Screens Against the Sky* (1990) and *An Immaculate Figure* (1993) are characterized by passivity, their failure to see and to act. Boehmer focuses on their partial or retarded vision, especially in relation to black history. This is intensely self-conscious writing. Boehmer signals her own entrapment in a particular form of writing 'pendulous' with its own guilt, self-consciousness and anguish. Writing against the realism which has characterized the liberal South African novel, she attempts to open a regenerative space for South African writing, recalling some of the fictional strategies of J. M. Coetzee.

Boehmer has also produced a number of academic works, including *Colonial and Postcolonial Literature* (1995), a history of the writing of empire and of writing that grew out of opposition to empire. She considers new nationalist literatures of former colonies and the POSTCOLONIAL search for self-definition, and shows how, though bearing the attractions of the exotic, the marginal and the other, migrant literatures also participate reassuringly in aesthetic languages familiar to Anglo-American culture. SN

Boesing, Martha 1940– American playwright and director who in 1974 co-founded, and became artistic director of, 'At the Foot of the Mountain' in Minneapolis, a major feminist theatre that for two decades collaboratively created plays incorporating ritual and theatre, with Boesing as principal playwright. She explores women's quest for validation in *Love Story for an Amazon* (1976) and *Rites of Love and Defiance* (1983), and examines archetypal and actual mothers and daughters in *The Story of a Mother* (1977, 1987), her best-known work, which combines ritual and consciousness-raising interaction with the audience. Some works depict the politicization of women, including *The Mothers of Ludlow* (1983), while others satirize popular myths of women, such as *Dora Du Fran's Wild West Extravaganza* or *The Real Low Down on Calamity Jane* (1979). *Raped: A Woman's Look at Brecht's 'The Exception and the Rule'* (1976) deconstructively incorporates narratives of rape victims into Brecht's framework. The production toured extensively and was revived in 1987. Boesing and her company have often interwoven environmentalist and feminist critique, most notably in *Ashes Ashes We All Fall Down* (1983), an examination of nuclear issues, and *River Journal*, an ecological chronicle of a river (1975, revived in 1995). SBB

Bogan, Louise 1897–1970 American critic and MODERNIST lyric poet. She was born in Livermore Falls, Maine, to working-class Irish-American parents, and attended Girls' Latin School in Boston, where she began writing poetry. After one year at Boston University, she turned down a scholarship from Radcliffe to marry Curt Alexander (1916). They had one child and separated in 1918. Bogan moved to Greenwich Village, where she joined a lively literary community. Her second marriage to poet Raymond Holden ended in divorce (1925–37).

By 1921 Bogan had published poems in *New Republic*, *Vanity Fair* and *Poetry*. Unlike other modernists, Bogan avoided formal experimentation, writing usually rhymed stanzas with strictly controlled rhythms. She also avoided leftist politics, which attracted many writers during the 1930s. Though praised as a 'masculine' poet, she insisted on mental differences between men and women, as in her poem 'Women' (1923):

> Women have no wilderness in them,
> They are provident instead,
> Content in the tight hot cell of their hearts
> To eat dusty bread.

Her poems were collected in BODY OF THIS DEATH (1923), *Dark Summer* (1929), *The Sleeping Fury* (1937), and *Poems and New Poems* (1941). In 1931 she became poetry editor of the *New Yorker*, a position she held for thirty-eight years. Commissioned to write a summary of American poetry in 1951 (*Achievement in American Poetry, 1900-1950*), she was one of few critics of her era to praise 19th-century women poets, noting that they kept the 'line of feeling' alive in poetry. In 1960 she collaborated with poets Archibald MacLeish and Richard Wilbur in assessing the first publication of EMILY DICKINSON's complete poems (*Emily Dickinson: Three Views*). Other critical writings are collected in *Selected Criticism: Poetry and Prose* (1955) and *A Poet's Alphabet* (1970).

From the 1940s to the 1960s, Bogan taught at New York University, the University of Chicago, and elsewhere. She was poetry consultant to the Library of Congress in 1945–6 and in 1948 served on the committee that awarded the Bollingen Prize to Ezra Pound. She received a lifetime achievement award from the National Endowment for the Arts (1967). For *The Blue Estuaries* (1969), her final collection, Bogan chose only 105 poems. Her correspondence with HARRIET MONROE, RUTH BENEDICT, MAY SARTON and others was collected posthumously in *What the Woman Lived* (1973) and an 'autobiography' pieced together from essays in *Journey Around My Room* (1980), both by Ruth Limmer. JSG

Boland, Bridget 1913–88 Playwright and prolific writer of screenplays, Boland, the daughter of an Irish politician, was convent-educated and then went on to receive a degree in Politics, Philosophy and Economics from Oxford in 1935. She began film scripting in 1937 and, during World War II, produced morale-boosting plays for the troops. Her best-known screenplays are perhaps *This England* (1941 – co-written with A.R. Rawlinson and Emlyn Williams), *The Prisoner* (1955) and *Anne of a Thousand Days* with John Hale (1970). Boland claimed that – unlike most women writers – she did not thrive on domestic themes. Indeed her first successful play, *The Cockpit* (1949), set her apart from the majority of writers of her era, regardless of gender. Here, she experimented with the environment of the theatre building itself, and with theatre as a metaphor. Set in a German provincial theatre at the end of the war, the action happens around the audience as well as on the stage, in a play which examines the experiences of Europe's displaced persons and the British handling of repatriation. Boland's exploration of racial difference and the ways in which social crises eventually bring people together was unsentimental and in many ways ahead of its time. In *The Prisoner* (1954) Boland dealt with the destruction, by psychiatric interrogation, of a one-time hero of the Resistance by his interrogator. In private life Boland was a keen GARDENER: *Old Wives' Lore for Gardeners* (1976), co-written with her sister, was a bestseller.   MBG

Boland, Eavan 1944– Irish poet and critic, born in Dublin, the daughter of the artist Frances Kelly and F.H. Boland, the diplomat. When the family moved to London, the young Boland experienced a sense of rupture and exile which has helped to shape her later development as a poet. Her early collection, *New Territory* (1967), was an accomplished and confident début, while her literary journalism marked her, early in her career, as an intellectual force.

Boland's direction as a poet changed with the publication of *In Her Own Image* (1980), a collection which explores aspects of specifically female experience. In 1982, both *The Journey* and *Night Feed* appeared, extending the new parameters of Boland's poetic practice, and declaring an acceptance of the ordinary, the domestic, and the suburban as legitimate subject matter for Irish poetry.

Throughout the eighties Boland was involved in a series of writing workshops sponsored by Arlen House, and, typically, articulated a defence of the concept of workshops against the criticism of the literary establishment. During this period she also began to articulate her position in relation to the traditions of canonical Irish poetry, and her influential pamphlet *A Kind of Scar: The Woman Poet in a National Tradition*, appeared in 1989. Here Boland interrogates the presumptions and assumptions of Irish poetry and argues for the radical shift in perspective achieved when people (in this instance women) who have previously been the 'passive objects of a work of art have . . . become the authors of it'. This theme is developed in *Outside History* (1990).

Boland occupies a unique position in Irish letters. Her importance as a voice is uncontested, but in retaining a consciously critical position in relation to the canon she has inevitably altered and extended it. While her identity as an Irish woman poet is central in her work and crucial to it, she is not, in any sense, a parochial or merely 'local' poet. Her imagery is strongly visual and draws on her knowledge of painting as well as historical and classical allusion. She acknowledges the influence of contemporaries from many different cultures. She continues to question the nature and possibilities of poetry in a more radical investigation of the complex relationship between art and life, notably in *In a Time of Violence* (1994).

> Make of a nation what you will
> Make of the past
> What you can -
>
> There is now
> A woman in a doorway.
>
> It has taken me
> All my strength to do this.
>
> Becoming a figure in a poem.
>
> Usurping a name and a theme.
> "Anna Liffey"   LM

Boleyn, Anne 1507–36 Letter writer and patron; second queen of Henry VIII. She was brought up at the French court; after her return to England in 1522 her admirers included the poet Sir Thomas Wyatt. By 1527 the King was writing her passionate love letters, 'wishing myself (specially an evening) in my sweetheart's arms, whose pretty dukkys [breasts] I trust shortly to kiss'. His efforts to divorce CATHERINE OF ARAGON culminated in the schism from Rome and the founding of the Church of England.

From 1529 Anne had her own court apartments. Her patronage of Protestant thinkers and politicians was instrumental in furthering the Reformation in England, and her letters to the King and his ministers display both eloquence and a political temperament.

Henry finally married the pregnant Anne in 1533; however, the child proved to be not the desired son, but a mere girl (later ELIZABETH I). After a miscarriage and a stillbirth Anne was charged with adultery and incest and was beheaded. Henry immediately married Jane Seymour.   HH

Bolton, Isabel [Mary Britton Miller] 1883–1979 After a not especially distinguished career under her own name as writer of a novel, and five volumes of poetry, for children, American writer Miller turned in her sixties to adult fiction. The three New York novels – *Do I Wake or Sleep?* (1946), *The Christmas Tree* (1949) and *Many Mansions* (1952) – share slightly contrived melodramatic plots with a technically admirable stream-of-consciousness technique. Lovers betray each other over bisexuality or wealth; the well-intentioned are trampled by the ruthless and greedy; human life proves endlessly fragile. Miller's impressionism is at once ornate and humane – she evokes the comedy of the frustrated vulnerability of her characters while making their betrayals venial in their essentially tragic context. Growing eye problems restricted her writing thereafter; in 1966, she published *Under Gemini*, a memoir of her childhood and a drowned twin sister, and in 1971 *The Whirligig of Time*, a valedictory novel about old age and friendship.   RK

Bolton, Sara (Knowles) 1841–1916 American poet, novelist, biographer and reformer. Born in Farmington, Connecticut, she grew up on a farm. When her father died in 1852, she and her mother moved to Hartford, Connecticut, where she attended Hartford Female Seminary. After graduating in 1860, she taught briefly. In 1866 she married Charles Edward Bolton, with whom she shared a commitment to the cause of temperance, which she promoted in *The Present Problem* (1874). From 1878 to 1881 she worked on the editorial staff of the Boston *Congregationalist*. Her poems are collected in *Orlean Lamar and Other Poems* (1864), *From Heart and Nature* (1887) and *The Inevitable* (1895); her short stories in *Stories of Life* (1886). She also wrote educational BIOGRAPHIES, including *Girls Who Became Famous* (1886), *Some Successful Women* (1888), and *Famous Leaders Among Women* (1895). Her son, Charles K. Bolton, edited her memoirs, *Sarah K. Bolton, Pages from an Intimate Autobiography* (1923).   JSG

Bolton, Sarah Tittle (Barrett) 1814–93 American poet and journalist, born on a farm in Newport, Kentucky, and raised in Indiana. Educated in local schools in Madison, Indiana, she published her first poems in the Madison *Banner* when she was 14. She married Nathaniel Bolton, later founding editor of the *Indiana Democrat*, in 1831. They lived near Indianapolis and had two children. Bolton was active in the Women's Rights movement and the campaign for married women's property rights. Her best-known poem, 'Paddle Your Own Canoe' (1851), urges self-reliance and addresses the causes of antislavery and women's rights. Living in Europe from 1855 to 1858, she corresponded for the *Cincinnati Commercial*. Her husband died in 1858; in 1863 she married Judge Addison Reese of Canton, Missouri. They separated after two years and she returned to Indianapolis. Her verse is collected in *Poems* (1865), *Life and Poems of Sarah Tittle Bolton* (1880), and *Songs of a Lifetime* (1892).   JSG

Bone Scan (1988) GWEN HARWOOD's fourth major collection of poems was the last entirely overseen and arranged by her. While her final illness casts its shadow here, it is one characteristically variegated: matter-of-factly recognized and defied when her activities as fisherwoman evoke the inevitable future of 'death's hook in my jaw'; exuberantly and wittily figured in the *revenant* Crab of 'Night and Dreams' (a worthy continuation of earlier poems of night thoughts and night voices); or simply and strangely luminous in the title poem. Luminosity is a key quality: if it 'beguiles' Harwood's dreams, it also enables memory to restore to the light of the present the childhood world (comical, poignant and ethically fraught) of 'Class of 1927'. And it is a 'charm of light' that suffuses her concluding section, the Pastorals in which the Brisbane-born lover of brilliant sunlight, music and Wittgensteinian word-games celebrates a new (but not supplanting) love affair, not only with the softer seas and skies of Tasmania but also with 'the pure, authentic speech / that earth alone can teach'.   JStr

Book of Eve, The (1973) The protagonist and narrator of Canadian CONSTANCE BERESFORD-HOWE's much-acclaimed novel is Eva, a 65-year-old woman who – because she is now the recipient of a monthly old-age pension – can leave the stultifying life of a middle-class housewife trapped in a destructive marriage for a humble, solitary life in a basement apartment in working-class Montreal. She supplements her meagre pension by scavenging for objects to sell to a pawn shop. However, she is not unhappy with her choice, as shown in a letter which she imagines writing to God: 'Do You realise, I wonder, what submerged identities women like me can have?'

Although Eva recounts her story with considerable wit and humour, her autonomy comes at the cost of illness, poverty and painful memories recollected in solitude, and the almost complete renunciation of her relationship with her son and beloved grand-daughter. On the other hand, her search for self-expression brings her some happiness and sensual pleasure in a love-affair with a sybaritic Hungarian eccentric, her junior by some years. Beresford-Howe, while not identifying herself as a feminist, was aware of the issues feminists were addressing in the 1970s; she is also ironically aware of the contradictions between Eva's desire for freedom and her desire for romantic love.   GHN

Book of Margery Kempe, The (*c*.1430) KEMPE's strikingly idiosyncratic *Book* is one of the two most important Middle English works by women (the other is by JULIAN OF NORWICH). Though often claimed as the first autobiography in English, it is part plea for saintly recognition, part record of her experiences as a woman determined to dedicate her life to Christ while remaining a married lay member of her community. Kempe recounts her conversations with Christ, her religious education, and her journeys within England

and across Europe to Jerusalem, Rome, Compostella, and Prussia. Much of the narrative is concerned with her many difficulties in gaining acceptance for her new spiritual career. The *Book*'s refusal to distance visionary experiences from their social dimensions has provoked controversy ever since the lost manuscript resurfaced in 1934. Kempe describes without embarrassment her attempts to persuade her husband to stop having sex with her so that she might live spiritually chaste, and records the contempt heaped upon her apparently bizarre practices of weeping and 'roaring' (they still elicit contempt). The *Book* was nearly not written. Its prologue details the work's complex genesis, evidence of the difficulties experienced by an illiterate lay woman in gaining entry into the privileged world of writing.   REv

Boothby, Frances fl.1669 British playwright, who claims in her only known work, *Marcelia: or the Treacherous Friend* (1669), that she was related to Lady Yate of Harvington, in Worcestershire. Boothby's play is the first wholly original drama written by a woman to be professionally produced; it follows KATHERINE PHILIPS's two translations, *Pompey* (1663) and *Horace* (1668), and precedes APHRA BEHN's first play, *The Forc'd Marriage*, by over a year. A somewhat cynical tragi-comedy, *Marcelia* concerns a virtuous but proud woman who is manipulated, abused and betrayed by all those around her, including her brother and a jealous lover. Although the play received a modest success, no other works have been attributed to this writer. Her life is shrouded in mystery, and so little was known about her that in 1691 the writer of the *Account of the English Dramatic Poets* was not sure whether she was alive or dead.   RDM

Borden, Mary (Lady Spears) [Bridget Maclagan] 1886–1968 American and English novelist and journalist born in Chicago, daughter of a businessman. She was educated at Vassar. Her marriage to George Douglas Turner, with whom she had three children, ended in divorce. In 1918 she married English baronet, MP and diplomat Edward Spears; they had one son. During both World Wars, she ran award-winning field hospitals for the French army at her own expense, for which she was given the Croix de Guerre and made a member of the Légion d'Honneur. She recounted her wartime experiences in *The Forbidden Zone* (1929) and *Journey Down a Blind Alley* (1946). Her fiction concentrated on upper-class life but also took up war themes. *Sarah Gay* (1931) treats a nurse's wartime love affair; *For the Record* (1950) enters the mind of a secret agent; in *Martin Merriedew* (1952), a pacifist is tried for treason.   JSG

Borderlands/La Frontera: The New Mestiza (1987) GLORIA ANZALDÚA's text investigates and enacts interrelated aspects of cultural hybridity. She combines a confessional mode with the role of cultural critic, in a discourse which resembles that of North American radical feminism, but which is more complex and catholic in its range. Using her self as a site of psychic and cultural enquiry, she describes the 'borderland' and 'mestiza' experience. She characterizes this as living with contradictions and ambiguity, since it is on the Tex/Mex borderland that two major self-consistent but mutually habitually incompatible frames of reference collide. This binary model is yet more complicated since, as Anzaldúa reminds us, Mestizos (Chicanos) are 70–80 per cent Indian.

Anzaldúa's project in this book is to transform the constant culture shock of this collision, and to transform the sense of worthlessness and marginality, into a new sense of numinosity. She incorporates Aztec and Catholic myths and Mexican legends into a psychic and cultural ritual of regeneration, which stands as a blueprint for cultural shifts, bridges and growth in the 21st century. The book incorporates phrases and passages in Chicano Spanish.   HMD

Bornholdt, Jenny 1960– New Zealand poet. Her first collection, *This Big Face* (1988), was followed by *Moving House* (1989), *Waiting Shelter* (1991) and *How We Met* (1995). She is a co-editor of an anthology of New Zealand love poetry, *My Heart Goes Swimming* (with husband Gregory O'Brien, 1995) and *The Oxford Anthology of New Zealand Poetry in English* (with Gregory O'Brien and Mark Williams, 1997).

Her poetry is characterized by clear simple statement, playful and humorous language games, and slippages of a POSTMODERN kind which nevertheless always return the reader to some sense of real experience and real value. Bornholdt writes about the self and about its relationships, with a consciousness of the defining function of the conventions of language, of both a literary and a non-literary kind. She is interested in the interrogation of rhetoric and cliché, often by giving mock-literal readings from which she then teases a perverse but ultimately valid meaning. All her collections show experimentation in form – from lengthy prose poems to very short pieces which use folk-song as a formal inspiration.

Bornholdt's work is widely read outside the normal readership of poetic slim volumes: 'Instructions for how to get ahead of yourself while the light still shines' has appeared on a poster on Wellington buses, 'Scrub cut' can be found on the wall of a hairdressers', and her poem 'Wedding Song' which begins:

Now you are married
try to love the world
as much as you love
each other

has become a standard at wedding ceremonies. Selected poems, *Miss New Zealand*, were published in 1997. JSt

Boscawen, Frances 1719–1805 Englishwoman said by contemporaries to be the best letter-writer of her age. Her correspondents included HANNAH MORE, ELIZABETH MONTAGU and MARY DELANY. The wife of Admiral Boscawen, Lord of the Admiralty, she was a central figure of the BLUESTOCKING circle. Her evening salons were attended by prominent literary figures and she was lauded among polite society for her learning and conversation. The mother of five, two of her sons were to die abroad in 1769 and 1774. After the death of her husband in 1761, Edward Young dedicated his poem *Resignation* to her. In *Sensibility* (1782), also dedicated to Boscawen, HANNAH MORE eulogized her friend's maternal affection and social virtues:

> Still for you your gentle stars dispense
> The charm of friendship and the feast of sense
> Yours is the bliss, and Heav'n no dearer sends
> To call the wisest, brightest, best, your friends.

Boscawen's copious correspondence remains uncollected. KD

Boston [née Wood], L(ucy) M(aria) 1892–1990 English children's writer whose trans-historical 'Green Knowe' novels influenced later children's fantasy writers. Born in Southport, Lancashire, she was educated at a Quaker school in Sussex, finishing school in Paris, and Somerville College, Oxford. During World War I she served as a nurse in France, marrying in 1917 and having one son. She spent time in Europe as a painter after the 1935 dissolution of her marriage and in 1939 bought a Norman manor house at Hemingford Grey in Huntingdonshire, which inspired most of her novels.

She began writing in her sixties and her six-novel Green Knowe series, beginning with *The Children of Green Knowe* (1954), centres on a manor house and children from various periods of the house's existence. The novels combine a strong sense of place and the natural world with time-travel fantasy and the theme of continuity and change. *A Stranger at Green Knowe* (1961), which excludes the fantasy element, won the Carnegie medal. Boston's other children's books include *The Castle of Yew* (1965) and *The Sea Egg* (1967). She also wrote novels for adults: *Yew Hall* (1954) and *Persephone* (1969), and autobiographical works. AEG

Boswell, Annabella 1826–1916 Australian DIARIST. Born Annabella Innes, at Bathurst, New South Wales, after her father's death she moved to Port Macquarie to live with her uncle, the police magistrate Archibald Innes. She is best known for *Annabella Boswell's Journal*

(1965), an abridged account of her *Some Recollections of My Early Days Written at Different Periods* (1908), which focuses on her time at Port Macquarie, giving a rare and delightful account of domestic life in New South Wales in the 1840s. She recalls, for example, a notoriously bug-infested inn on the road from Bathurst to Sydney, where 'One traveller declared he had been dragged out of bed, another kept up a continual fight to prevent himself from being devoured alive, and a nervous lady, being left alone with her invisible tormentors, could think of no expedient save that of ringing a small hand-bell all the weary night to frighten them off.' A second work, *Further Recollections of My Early Days in Australia* (1911), has been republished as *Annabella Boswell's Other Journal 1848-51*. EW

Bottle Factory Outing, The (1974) BERYL BAINBRIDGE's novel helped shift British writing during the early 1970s toward a dark and edgy comic tone, and away from social REALISM's (comfortable) occupation of the centre-ground (i.e., north London). The Bottle Factory is an Italian peasant community embedded, but certainly not 'integrated', in an exact somewhere north of the river. By an expert trick of style, grotesque black comedy is seamlessly inserted into the low mimetic; the result is the paradox of a *farrago* which, at every point, commands the power of observation.

Thin, spacy Brenda – a victim – and fat, dominant Freda huddle into fragile alliance. The enigmatic plot is a version of Poe's 'The Cask of Amontillado' – with 'Rubensesque' Freda (her neck broken on the Outing in Windsor Park by Irishman Patrick, Manager Rossi, or fancyman Vittorio) stuffed at the last into a sherry barrel from Santander and marked 'unsatisfactory'. VS

Bottome, Phyllis 1884–1963 British writer, the daughter of an English mother and American father, known for her opposition to Nazi Germany and her interest in the psychiatry of Alfred Adler. In the 1914–18 war she worked in the Ministry of Information with John Buchan and published an adventure story, *The Dark Tower* (1916). She married Alban Ernan Forbes-Dennis in 1917. Bottome was resident in Germany when Hitler, who regularly ate in the same café as she did, rose to power. She studied with Adler in Vienna, organizing food distribution for European refugees, before returning to England where she organized public lectures on the threat of Fascism. Her most famous novel is the anti-Fascist, *The Mortal Storm* (1937). She wrote a BIOGRAPHY, *Alfred Adler: Apostle of Freedom* in 1939. *Within the Cup* (1943) is a novel about the life of a Viennese psychiatrist, Rudi von Ritterhaus, who seeks refuge in England from Nazi persecution. Bottome was a friend of Sinclair Lewis, GERTRUDE ATHERTON, Max Beerbohm and Ezra Pound. She published three autobiographical volumes, *The Challenge* (1942), *Search for a Soul* (1947) and *The Goal* (1962). MJ

Boucherett, (Emilia) Jessica 1825–1905 An early English feminist, editor and essayist. Boucherett was born in Lincolnshire and read widely, including HARRIET MARTINEAU and the *English Woman's Journal*. She moved to London in 1859. Along with BARBARA BODICHON and ADELAIDE PROCTER, that same year, she founded the Society for Promotion of Employment for Women and helped to finance a school that taught clerical skills to classes of twenty women. The journal she established, *Englishwoman's Review* (1866–1910) was amalgamated with the *English Woman's Journal*, and she held the post of editor from 1866 to 1870. Boucherett also wrote numerous essays on women's issues, especially concerning the right to paid employment – suggesting many positions that could be opened to them. For older women she favoured domestic service. She was an outspoken SUF-FRAGIST and campaigned for the Married Women's Property Act. Her most influential essays include 'The Condition of Women in France' (1867) and 'Provision for Superfluous Women' (1868). Despite her seeming radicalism, she was a political conservative, and in 1899 she and HELEN BLACKBURN founded the Freedom of Labour Defence League, which was against legislation designed to protect women workers. RB-S

Bourke-White, Margaret 1904–71 A leading American photographer, Bourke-White was author of numerous books of reportage, some in collaboration with other writers. Bourke-White was the first photographer hired by Henry Luce's *Fortune* magazine, and in 1936 she joined the staff of *Life*. She travelled across the world in the 1930s, from the Oklahoma dust bowl to the Sudetenland, taking pictures, and doing interviews. What she heard, and sensed, as well as what she saw, made her into a writer. Her books are, in total, an extended account of her travels. *Eyes on Russia* (1931) was an account of a journey across Russia in 1930. Bourke-White travelled with the writer Erskine Caldwell (whom she briefly married) and collaborated with him on *North of the Danube* (1939) and *Say, is This the USA* (1941). She was the only western photographer present in Moscow when the Germans attacked in 1941, and published *Shooting the Russian War* in 1942. Her *They Called it 'Purple Heart Valley'* (1944) was an account of the US Army in the Italian campaign. Germany after the war was recorded in *Dear Fatherland, Rest Quietly* (1946). An autobiography, *Portrait of Myself*, appeared in 1963. EH

Bowen, Elizabeth 1899–1973 Anglo-Irish novelist, born in Dublin and taken at the age of six weeks to Bowen's Court, the family home in Cork, whose history she wrote in 1941. Bowen was educated in England and lived for a long time with her mother on the south coast, but she continued to spend long periods at Bowen's Court, which she inherited on her father's death in 1930, and she always saw herself as part of romantic Ireland as well as prosaic England. After two collections of short stories and a novel, *The Hotel* (1927), published before she was 30, she wrote *The Last September* (1929), which is still regarded as a classic Irish 'big house' novel, in which the conflicting loyalties of the Ascendancy are dissected against a background of post-treaty troubles in the South of Ireland. The fiction she wrote during World War II – the feverish *THE HEAT OF THE DAY* (1949) and some fine stories of the London Blitz, in particular 'Mysterious Kor' and 'In the Square' – continued to draw nourishment from an atmosphere of the collapse of civilization. Bowen's formal prose style is displayed, in elegantly comma'ed-off qualifications, in works such as *To the North* (1932), *THE DEATH OF THE HEART* (1938), 'Summer Night' and 'A Love Story', which contrast rocketing passion and cold, repressed emotion. In an essay on JANE AUSTEN, she wrote that it was a fallacy to suppose that writing about life with the lid off was more interesting than writing about life with the lid on. Her last completed novel was *EVA TROUT* (1968).

Like VIRGINIA WOOLF, whom she knew and liked, Bowen was one of the first woman writers to be regarded as a public figure. Always rather grand and stylish in appearance, she gave broadcasts and lectures and gave interviews to magazines (there is an interesting photograph taken of her with the young, very respectful SYLVIA PLATH who was interviewing her for *Miss* magazine in the United States in the 1950s). She was awarded the CBE and made a Companion of Honour. Her reputation has continued to grow, helped by Victoria Glendinning's biography *Elizabeth Bowen: Portrait of a Writer* (1977). Recently there has been new research published about her love affair with the writer Sean O'Faolain (a supporter of the new Ireland, who wrote that Bowen's novels had as their subject 'the kid and the cad') and about her intelligence-gathering missions for the British government in neutral Ireland during World War II. LD

Bowen, Marjorie [Gabrielle Margaret Vere Campbell] 1888–1952 Prolific British writer of historical ROMANCES and BIOGRAPHIES. Educated at home in various London boarding-houses by her mother, a thwarted actress, she read history and Smiles's *Self-Help* as defence against her genteel hard-up family's turmoils. She studied art at the Slade and in Paris where, at 16, she wrote the bestselling *The Viper of Milan* (1906), a romance of Renaissance intrigue. Graham Greene claimed its picture of 'perfect evil

79

walking the world' was seminal in forming his own world-view. *The Glen O'Weeping* (1908), a Glencoe romance, sustained her themes of a world of arbitrary violence, and powerful men seeking to manipulate that violence, explored in a succession of historical romances. She married twice, to Zeffrino Emilio Costanzo (1912–16), and to Arthur Lang in 1917, and had three sons. She adopted two pseudonyms, 'George Preedy' from 1928, who shared the romances and wrote a biography of WOLLSTONECRAFT, *This Shining Woman* (1937); and 'Joseph Shearing' from 1932, who wrote mostly historical whodunnits. She also wrote plays and CHILDREN'S BOOKS. Her autobiography, *The Debate Continues* (1939), suggests disappointed ideals and dissatisfaction with her own commercial adaptability. AT

Bowering, Marilyn 1949– Canadian writer of stories, poems and plays. She was born in Winnipeg, Manitoba, grew up in Victoria, British Columbia, is married with one child, and has lived in Greece, Scotland, the Queen Charlotte Islands and Spain. Her first book of poetry (*The Discovering of Newfoundland*) appeared in 1972, and she has since published nine collections of poems, two novels and a play. She is best known for her 1980 volume SLEEPING WITH LAMBS and her multi-media work about Marilyn Monroe, *Anyone Can See I Love You*. Her poems are mirrors through which she views a variety of subjects, employing both distortion and the macabre in order to capture her impressions. She has an MA in Creative Writing, lives currently in Sooke on Vancouver Island, teaches Creative Writing part-time at the University of Victoria, and works on-line for Writers in Electronic Residence for Canadian schools, where she feels she can help young people 'keep up respect for creativity, for literature, for the individual, and steer clear of too many straight lines'. FD

Bowles, Caroline (later Southey) 1787–1854 English poet and essayist who, dogged by financial difficulties, applied to Robert Southey with the manuscript of *Ellen FitzArthur: A Metrical Tale*, which he admired, and which was published in 1820. It established her reputation for powerful pathos. Her heroine, seduced and abandoned, is treated sympathetically and without judgement, even if her prodigal return ends tragically. Her essays *Chapters on Churchyards* (1829), originally published in *Blackwood's Magazine*, enhanced her reputation. More poems were published: *The Widow's Tale* (1822); *Tales of the Factories* (1833), an early enlightened protest against harsh working conditions; and *The Birthday* (1836), semi-autobiographical and critically acclaimed. Meanwhile, her correspondence with Southey led to collaboration – on the poem 'Robin Hood' (1847) – and finally, in

1840, to a brief – and unhappy – marriage. Bowles wrote no more after Southey's death in 1843, but their correspondence – more congenial than their marriage – was published posthumously as *The Correspondence of Robert Southey with Caroline Bowles* (1881). LMT

Bowles [née Auer], Jane 1917–73 American original who, with a few short works, earned herself a place alongside other American innovators such as GERTRUDE STEIN and CARSON MCCULLERS. Born in Long Island to Jewish parents, she married the writer Paul Bowles and with him lived an adventurous life, sexually and geographically: their affectionate open marriage was conducted across New York, Paris and Tangier. Their circle of friends included Truman Capote and Tennessee Williams, both of whom were devoted fans of her work.

Her only novel, TWO SERIOUS LADIES (1943), is singular in every respect: its abrupt and absurd comedy, its plotless structure of patterns and repetitions, and above all the distinctive, wise-child voices of its central characters. The two ladies experience feverish enthusiasms and dark hysterias as they pursue separate adventures across New York and Panama. Yet underneath the bright disjointed surface lurk serious, melancholy reflections on morality and fear and the 'great danger of losing the whole world once and for all'. Equally eccentric characters populate her short stories, *Plain Pleasures* (1966), including the troubled spinster sisters of 'Camp Cataract'.

Her single play, *In the Summer House* (1951), which Williams called 'the most original play I have ever read', expresses the paradoxes of her writing. Its first act dramatizes with unnerving hilarity the conflict between a despairing mother and her sinister daughter, but none of the various endings she tried worked and the second act feels unresolved. A combination of a stroke, problems with alcohol, and her passionate but mostly doomed affairs with women contributed to an unending writing block; she left unfinished a more naturalistic novel 'Out in the World' and another play. After various breakdowns she spent the last years of her life in and out of a clinic in Spain, where Paul loyally visited her and where she died in 1973. Her collected work was published as *My Sister's Hand in Mine* in 1978, so that what McCullers called her 'curious, slanted and witty style' could move and discomfit a new generation of readers and writers. SB

Boylan, Clare 1948– Irish journalist, short-story writer and novelist. Born and educated in suburban Dublin, she describes her childhood as 'very isolated'; consequently she and her sisters – encouraged by their unconventional mother – created their own fantasy world by 'telling and drawing stories, listening to the wireless and going to the pictures'. She began her journalistic life in the *Irish Press* before becoming editor of *Image* magazine and greatly increasing its literary content. Short stories from her collections, *A Nail in the Head* (1983) and *Concerning Virgins* (1989), have been widely anthologized and adapted for radio and screen. Her first novel, *Holy Pictures* (1983), was followed by *Last Resorts* (1986) and *Black Baby* (1988), a humorous story which draws on the religious practice of 'buying black babies' to aid missionary work. Many of her stories explore the social and sexual tensions within her young, female protagonists; in spare, elegant prose she focuses on oblique aspects of objects and personalities with a child's studied attention. *Room for a Single Lady* (1997) evokes Dublin in the 1950s as three impressionable girls encounter the lodgers who come to their poverty-stricken home: 'our house absorbed Miss Taylor like dust or cobwebs in a corner'. 'A willingness to lay open oneself' coupled with technique and an elusive element that 'outreaches' the writer's personality, is how she defines the art of the fiction-writer in *The Agony and the Ego* (1993). BHu

Boyle, Kay 1903–92 American novelist, essayist, poet, translator and one of the most politically active writers of her generation. The multi-talented Boyle studied music at the Cincinnati Conservatory of Music, and Architecture at the Ohio Mechanics' Institute. She moved from St Paul, Minnesota, to New York in 1923 and published her first poem, 'Morning', in the literary magazine *Broom*, edited by Harold Loeb. Soon after, she married a Frenchman, Richard Brault, and moved to Paris where she remained for almost two decades, during which time she divorced and married Laurence Vail, the former husband of Peggy Guggenheim. A surfeit of novels were written in the 1920s, including *Plagued by a Nightmare*, *Year Before Last*, *Gentlemen, I Address You Privately*, and *My Next Bride*, all reflecting her experiences as an expatriate in France. In 1943 she divorced for the second time and remarried Baron Joseph von Franckenstein with whom she remained until his death in 1963. Though primarily a writer of prose fiction she also taught creative writing at San Francisco State University in 1960, as well as at other colleges and universities in the United States. Winner of several Guggenheim Fellowships and O. Henry Awards for her short stories 'The White Horses of Vienna' (1935) and 'Defeat' (1941), she also wrote such novels as *Monday Night* (1938), *Avalanche* (1944), *The Underground Woman* (1974), and *Death of a Man* (1989), as well as the *Autobiography of Emanuel Carnevali* (1967) and a revision of Robert McAlmon's memoirs, *Being Geniuses Together, 1920-1930* (1968), and a collection of short stories entitled *Fifty Stories* (1980). A bonafide activist, Boyle spearheaded movements related to civil and human rights, nuclear disarmament and the Vietnam War. Her contribution to the Citizens'

Mission to Cambodia (1966), prompted by United States' expansion into Southeast Asia, contained a series of diaries, correspondence and articles related to the aims of the members. Her later work includes the translation of René Crevel's novel, *Babylon* (1985). Her *Collected Poems* were published in 1991. MRA

Boyle, Mary (Louise) 1810–90 Anglo-Irish writer of prose and verse for her own pleasure and for friends in the aristocracy. Her father was Vice-Admiral Courtney Boyle, her great-grandfather the Earl of Cork and Orrery, an ancient Irish title. She lived in fashionable London and had 'close and tender' friendships with Tennyson, Dickens, Thackeray, Browning and Landor among others. She was not prolific, nor entirely literary. Three of her publications were catalogues of portraits at Longleat, Panshanger and Hinchingbrook; nonetheless D. J. O'Donoghue included her verse in *The Poets of Ireland* in 1912.

The State Prisoner, a lively Regency tale, appeared in 1837, followed by *The Forester* (1839) and in 1844 a verse-drama, *The Bridal of Melcha: A Page from Ireland's Early History*, which A.S. Allibone in *A Critical Dictionary of English Literature 1859-71* considered 'a tale skilfully wrought and abounding in passages of great beauty'. Her popular poem 'My Father's At The Helm' appeared in a collection of verse edited by the Marquis of Northampton. In 1865 came a novel of the Crimean War, *Tangled Weft*, but her *chef d'oeuvre* was *An Imperfect Narrative of the Gay Doings and Marvelous [sic] Festivities Holden at Althorp* (1857) on the coming of age of Earl Spencer's son, Viscount Althorp. Written in pseudo-medieval style and luxuriously printed, it described the three-day celebrations, including banquets for 1,200 people and a ball lasting till dawn. *Mary Boyle, Her Book*, edited in 1890, related the reminiscences of a life richly enjoyed and lived to the full. MEW

Brackett, Leigh (Douglass) 1915–78 American writer of SCIENCE FICTION, crime fiction and screenplays. She was one of the first women writers to become popular in sf magazines with planetary ROMANCES in the style of Edgar Rice Burroughs, to which she brings her own combination of frenetic action and passionate regret – swords clash as dust whispers in the beds of Martian canals. Typical of her work is *The Sword of Rhiannon* (1953). Her early novellas often feature a series hero, Eric John Stark, who also appears in the smoother and more considered Skaith trilogy – *The Ginger Star* (1974), *The Hounds of Skaith* (1974), *The Reavers of Skaith* (1976).

Although her *noir* crime fiction is unremarkable, her distinguished Hollywood career included two Raymond Chandler adaptations – *The Big Sleep* (1946), on which she collaborated with William Faulkner, and *The Long Goodbye* (1973) – as well as the Western *Rio Bravo*

(1958), and *The Empire Strikes Back* (1979) for which she received a posthumous Hugo Award.   RK

Brackley [née Cavendish], Elizabeth, Viscountess 1626–63 Daughter of William Cavendish, Duke of Newcastle, and his first wife, Elizabeth Bassett. Stepdaughter to MARGARET CAVENDISH (née Lucas) (see DUCHESS OF NEWCASTLE) and sister of LADY JANE CAVENDISH. Member of a highly literary family which practised both patronage and creative writing, particularly in the dramatic sphere. Married, aged 15, to John Egerton, Viscount Brackley (future Earl of Bridgewater), who also had theatrical origins: he played the role of the Elder Brother in John Milton's *A Masque Presented at Ludlow Castle 1634*. All of this may have contributed to the Cavendish sisters' interest in the dramatic genre. At the outbreak of the English Civil War (1642–9), Jane, Elizabeth and Frances Cavendish found themselves under siege at the family estate at Welbeck Abbey. Their mother died in 1643 and the sisters ran the estate alone until it was taken by force by Parliamentarian troops in 1644. Many of Jane and Elizabeth's collaborative literary productions date from this time. The sisters co-authored a masque, *A Pastorall*, which, with its antimasque of witches, owes much to court masques of the early Stuart period, in particular Ben Jonson's 1609 *Masque of Queens*. Their co-written play *The Concealed Fancies* is of particular interest to feminist scholars. Whilst there is no recorded performance the play evidences an understanding of the genre and is also important due to the allusions it makes to the sisters' real predicament. The plotline revolves around three cousins trapped by Parliamentary troops in a castle.

Elizabeth, like her elder sister Jane Cavendish, wrote poetry. One extant poem is a moving elegy for her son who died at just 29 days old: 'On my Boy Henry'. Elegies for children who have died in infancy are understandably common in the canon of early modern women writers. Elizabeth also wrote devotional works and an autobiography, collected and published by her husband following her death.   JS

Bradbrook, Dame Muriel (Clara) 1909–93 English scholar–critic, Cambridge professor, and Mistress of Girton College. Born Wallasey, Cheshire, she spent her undergraduate career and much of her entire later life at Girton, and wrote its centenary history, *The Infidel Place* (1969). Her literary sympathies were large: monographs included studies of the Ralegh circle, *The School of Night* (1936); *Andrew Marvell* (with Megan Lloyd Thomas, 1940); *Ibsen the Norwegian* (1946; Norwegian was a language she acquired in wartime Board of Trade service); and *Malcolm Lowry* (1974). An important friendship was sustained with KATHLEEN RAINE.

Four volumes of *Collected Papers* (1982–9) sum up Bradbrook's enthusiasms: volume II (1982) collects work on *Women and Literature 1779-1982*.

Her chief work lay in well-contextualized study of English Renaissance drama, Shakespeare at its centre, in a long run of six volumes (1934–76, gathered in 1979 as *A History of Elizabethan Drama*). A densely circumstantial study of *John Webster, Citizen and Dramatist* (1980) adds a valuable pendant. Her criticism's busy knowledgeableness occasionally overwhelms its lucidity: among major scholars of Renaissance literature she had the least idea of what paragraphs were for.

JFM

Braddon, Mary Elizabeth 1835–1915 Perhaps the best-known woman sensation novelist of the 1860s, had a lengthy career as a bestseller. The London-born Braddon began writing, and subsequently went on the stage, to support her mother. *Three Times Dead* appeared in 1860 (reissued as *The Trail of the Serpent*, 1861), but her first success was LADY AUDLEY'S SECRET (1862), the prototypical women's SENSATION NOVEL, with its upwardly mobile, bigamous and murderously inclined heroine. Throughout the 1860s Braddon wrote ceaselessly to support her partner (the publisher William Maxwell), his wife (domiciled in a lunatic asylum), and the children of both unions. *Aurora Floyd*, *John Marchmont's Legacy* and *Eleanor's Victory* (all 1863), *Henry Dunbar* and *The Doctor's Wife* (both 1864) and *Birds of Prey* (1867) all dealt with sensational subjects, and featured headstrong, independent women who engaged in duplicity and deception for reasons (noble or reprehensible) often related to a father with a criminal or disreputable past (her own father, a feckless solicitor, was abandoned by her mother when Braddon was four). *The Doctor's Wife*, which contains a wonderful satirical portrait of a male sensation writer, reworks Flaubert's *Madame Bovary*, evidence of both Braddon's penchant for recycling other people's plots, and her aspiration to be a Balzac as well as a penny-a-liner. A prolific contributor to magazines (*All The Year Round*, *Reynold's Miscellany*, *Temple Bar*, the *London Journal*), Braddon was also a successful magazine editor (Maxwell's *Belgravia*, 1866–76, and the *Belgravia Annual*, 1867–76). Her novels were reissued throughout the century in cheap and railway editions, and some (most notably *Lady Audley's Secret*) were adapted for the stage. She later abandoned sensationalism for a more psychological focus.   LP

Bradley, D.H., Katherine Harris see FIELD, MICHAEL

Bradley, Marion Zimmer 1930– American writer of SCIENCE FICTION and fantasy, much of it characterized by vivid action and portrayals of mood that are always intense and often purple. Most of her sf from 1962 onwards takes place in a lost planetary colony, Darkover, where human beings, after interbreeding with aliens, acquire psychic powers. Many of her tales are swashbuckling ROMANCES, but the later ones in particular take on feminist and gay themes in a manner that is attractively thoughtful, while often indulging reader fantasies of being Amazon swordswomen and the like. Many of her more recent, and rather more popular, fantasy novels tend to place a radical feminist gloss on mythological material. *The Mists of Avalon* (1983) assumes a background of Mother Goddess worship to the activities of the women of the Arthurian cycle, while *The Firebrand* does the same for the Trojan War. When young, she wrote a number of novels, many with lesbian themes, for the pulp paperback market; *The Catch Trap* (1979), a circus novel featuring rival gay male trapeze artists, has its admirers.

RK

Bradshaigh, Lady Dorothy (Bellingham) 1706?–1785 Her emotive, argumentative and (despite her strict Christian morality) flirtatious correspondence drew from Samuel Richardson the most detailed and revealing explanations of his literary purposes. Married to Sir Roger Bradshaigh after a nine-year courtship and settled at Haigh Hall in Lancashire, she was less intellectual and more aristocratic than Richardson's other favourite correspondents. She first wrote to him anonymously to protest at the tragic ending of *Clarissa*. Enthusiastically responding (but refusing to alter his plot), he begged for a meeting with his ardent reader, but had to wait until she had viewed him from a distance, and departed, before she finally agreed. His ideal reader – engrossed, impressionable, virtuous – she identified with the trenchant Charlotte in *Sir Charles Grandison* (agreeing to write one of her letters), while he relied on her commentary, even asking for her amendments to *Pamela* and *Clarissa*. Her sister, Lady Echlin, became another favourite, but it was Lady Bradshaigh he called his 'most beloved and revered' correspondent. Her letters were published in Richardson's *Correspondence* (1804), edited by ANNA LAETITIA BARBAULD.

LMT

Bradshaw, Maire 1943– Irish poet and feminist. Bradshaw was born in County Limerick, and educated at Laurel Hill Convent, the *alma mater* of KATE O'BRIEN, and went to live in Cork, where she became involved in the feminist movement. She also runs, and teaches in, poetry workshops and is active in organizing readings and meetings of poets and writers. She was commissioned to write a poem 'First Citizen / Free Woman' to celebrate the conferring of the freedom of Cork city on Dr Mary Robinson, Ireland's first woman president. Bradshaw is a founding member of the Cork Women's Poetry Circle and Tigh Fhili (Poet's House). Her work is anthologized in *The Box under the Bed* (1986), a collection of writing from Cork women writers, which proceeded with encouragement from EAVAN BOLAND. Her collection *Instinct* (1988) explores the relation of language to power, gender and relationships in a somewhat classical feminist voice.

MSu

Bradshaw [née Jeffereyes], Mary Ann (Nugent) Cavendish *c.*1758–1849 Irish author of two HISTORICAL NOVELS, whose recurring themes of female intrepidity and marital discord echo the circumstances of her own life. In 1784 Mary Ann Jeffereyes married George Frederick Nugent, Earl of Westmeath, by whom she had several children. In 1796, immediately following her divorce from Nugent, she married Augustus Cavendish Bradshaw.

Bradshaw's first novel, *Memoirs of Maria, Countess d'Alva* (1808), is set in the 16th century, against the background of the Spanish Armada. Its heroine is assertive and resourceful, and her husband, the villain of the story, is a Spanish spy.

The theme of a woman escaping from an unhappy marriage also features in Bradshaw's second novel, *Ferdinand and Ordella: A Russian Story* (1810), set in the time of Peter the Great. A further insight into Bradshaw's resentment at the limitations placed on women's scope for action is provided by the introduction to this work, in which the author laments male contempt for female abilities.

RR

Bradstreet [née Dudley], Anne 1612–72 Colonial America's most celebrated poet emigrated from England to Boston in 1630, at the age of 18. Used to a well-appointed life, Anne Dudley Bradstreet found COLONIAL existence a trial to which she submitted with religious obedience.

Bradstreet's poetic efforts date from soon after her arrival in America. Her early poems look to Europe in matters of both form and content, but when she turned to her own life in the New World, she found her voice. Her CONFESSIONAL lyrics encompass the variety of experience of life in New England. They range from the homely – as when she addresses lines of love and longing to her husband, 'absent upon Publick employment' – to the philosophical (for example, the classical logic underlying such poems as 'Contemplations'). They address domestic concerns and religious ones, matters of church disputes as well as personal faith, the troubles 'between Old England and New' as well as the 'Vanity of all worldly things'. Bradstreet mingles humility with searching questions; her work constitutes the continuing efforts of a devout Puritan to live not only under God's difficult and largely inscrutable will, but also with the harsh unpredictability of colonial existence, against the rolling backdrop of colonial politics.

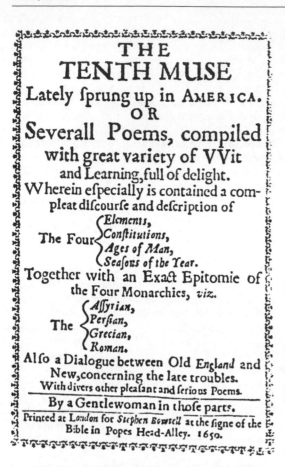

Anne Bradstreet: title-page of *The Tenth Muse*, 1650.

Bradstreet's brother-in-law took a collection of her verse with him to London in 1647 – most likely surreptitiously – and the poems were published in 1650 as THE TENTH MUSE LATELY SPRUNG UP IN AMERICA. They were well received, and the ambivalent author (she describes her book as a 'rambling brat') gained a reputation as a noted poet. Bradstreet's fame clearly affected her artistic stance. She corrected many of her published poems for a second edition which appeared after her death, and wrote a number of other poems and prose pieces with the expressed idea that they would survive her. Her work has indeed endured. Contemporary feminist critics have paid special attention to the tensions and oppositions in Bradstreet's poetry and prose, finding in her work a rich artistic account of women's experience in colonial America. LC

Brand, Dionne 1953 – Canadian-Caribbean poet, fiction-writer and political activist. She was born in Trinidad and moved in 1970 to Canada where she has lived ever since, and in her work there is a constant mediation between the two locations. She is a fiercely political writer, her central themes are race, her lesbian identity and the recovering of black women's histories. Her collections of poetry include *'Fore Day Morning* (1978), *Primitive Offense* (1983), *Chronicles of the Hostile Sun* (1984), *No Language is Neutral* (1990) which mixes slave history and Caribbean women's voices with contemporary meditations on life as a black in Canada, and *Land to Light On* (1997) which won her the Governor General's Award. Brand writes large, flowing, *bricolage*-like poems, heavily influenced by ADRIENNE RICH, and, like Rich, exposes the interlacings of history, politics and sexuality in the day-to-day world.

She has also written a collection of stories, *Sans Souci and Other Stories* (1988), and a political and lesbian novel in a Caribbean idiom, called *In Another Place, Not Here* (1996). She is also the author of many non-fiction works, including *Bread Out of Stone* (1994), which she subtitled 'Recollections, Sex, Recognitions, Race, Dreaming, Politics' and *No Burden to Carry* (1991), an oral history of black working women. She has co-authored and co-edited many works including *Rivers Have Sources, Trees Have Roots, Speaking of Racism* (1986), *We're Rooted Here, They Can't Pull Us Up* (1994) and *Grammar of Dissent* (1994). She can be said to have the politics, concerns and style of the radical feminists of the 1970s, which formed her political identity. She strongly believes that writers can and should change the world. Hers is a radical pan-black-women vision, and, while she tends to romanticize black history and the black past, her ultimate aim is to use memory as an aid to creating a peaceful, collective and egalitarian future.

ATe

Brand, Mona (Alexis) 1915– Australian dramatist. Mona Brand has written extensively for theatre on topical social and political issues with over twenty-five plays performed in Australia, England, Eastern-bloc countries, India and China. She travelled and worked in Europe in 1948–54, married poet and journalist Len Fox in 1955, worked in Hanoi in 1956–7, and thereafter in Sydney where her work has mainly been produced – in the Left-wing Sydney New Theatre. Despite consistently good reviews, professional production in Australia has eluded Brand.

Her first play, *Here Under Heaven* (produced 1948, published 1969), depicting prejudices against Aboriginal and Asian individuals, reveals a consciousness ahead of its time. *Strangers in the Land* (1952, published 1954), set in Malaya, deals with British colonialism. Both plays were professionally produced in translation in Eastern-bloc countries from 1954.

Other published plays reflect her sustained interest in social justice, inequity and political bias. *On Stage Vietnam* (unpublished, 1966), with Pat Barnett, uses Brechtian stage techniques but intentionally appeals to humanitarian feelings. *Here Comes Kisch!* (1984), an experimental cinematic play, dramatizes the plight of Egon Kisch. This Czech journalist, who opposed the Nazi regime which Australia then supported, was denied entry to Australia in 1934. *Flying Saucery: Three Plays for Young People* (1981) has had successful productions.

Other works include over twenty unpublished plays, adaptations for radio and television, five novellas (*Daughters of Vietnam*), poetry and autobiography (*Enough Blue Sky*). ILB

Brandt, Di [Diana] 1952– Canadian poet, essayist, editor and teacher, known for her poetic and prose challenges to the patriarchal family and religious structures in which she was raised as a Mennonite in Reinland, Manitoba, as well as, more recently, for her exploration of ideas/feelings about mothering. Growing up in a farming community where she spoke three different languages, Brandt left home at 17 to pursue her education in Winnipeg. Here she experienced a huge sense of 'culture shock', the effects of which she began to explore through her poems and discussions with 'hiatus', a group of women writers that included Smaro Kamboureli and KRISTJANA GUNNARS. Married in 1971 and later divorced, with two daughters, she has taught creative writing and English at the University of Winnipeg and more recently at the University of Windsor. Her first collection of poems, *questions i asked my mother* (1987), created a scandal in her community and won the Gerald Lampert Award. She has since published three more collections, *Agnes in the sky* (1990), *mother, not mother* (1992), and *Jerusalem, beloved* (1996), which won the 1996 Canadian Authors' Association National Poetry Award. Brandt has also published a collection of essays, *Dancing Naked: Narrative Strategies for Writing Across Centuries* (1996). She co-edited *Contemporary Verse 2* (1985-8) and poetry for *Prairie Fire*. Acknowledging the influence of Mennonite poet Patrick Friesen and West-Coast writer DAPHNE MARLATT, Brandt sees poetry as 'revolutionary. It puts the power of language back where it belongs, inside each living body . . . It throws us into action.' SEP

Brassey [née Allnutt], Anna (Annie), Baroness 1839–87 British traveller and authoress. She married, in 1860, Thomas, 1st Baron Brassey, who was elected Member of Parliament for Hastings, and her charm and ability as a leader of society were a great help to him. Lady Brassey loved to travel and wrote many accounts of her voyages, for the benefit of her friends. Her earliest books were printed for private circulation: *The Flight of the Meteor* in 1869 and *A Cruise in the Eothen* in 1872, both about TRAVEL, to the Mediterranean, Canada and the United States.

The book with which her name is always associated,

Anna Brassey on board the *Sunbeam*, 1886.

and which had an astonishing and immediate success, was *The Voyage in the Sunbeam*, published in 1878. This was an account of a voyage round the world in her yacht the *Sunbeam*: it reached a nineteenth edition in 1896, and was translated into French, German, Italian, Swedish and Hungarian. The drawings by the Hon. A.Y. Bingham are not the least of its attractions, one showing Lady Brassey at her desk in her cabin wearing an elaborate teagown. She was not disturbed by the nakedness of natives nor by the burning of open fires in the cabin grates.

The Voyage of the Sunbeam is virtually her only major work. She left England in 1886 on her last voyage and died at Brisbane on 14 September 1887, aged 48: she was buried at sea, at sunset on that day. MEW

Brazil, Angela 1868–1947 Mention the GIRLS' SCHOOL STORY, and the first name that springs to everyone's mind is that of Angela Brazil. She was born in Preston, Lancashire; educated at Ellerslie College, Manchester; and made her home in Coventry from 1911 until her death thirty-six years later. Her first full-length BOOK FOR CHILDREN, *A Terrible Tomboy*, was published in 1904; and then, in 1906, came THE FORTUNES OF PHILIPPA and the start of an incomparable career. Not that Angela Brazil got into her stride as a school-story writer straight away; it wasn't until about 1911 or 1912 that her distinctive manner came into full blossom. This, as is well known, includes some preposterous (but enjoyable) plot-making, the upholding of schoolgirl honour, some emphasis on sports, a lot of high jinks and much egregious slang: 'Miss Jones is a stunt, as jolly as you like'; 'How ripping! Oh, I say! This is top-hole!'

The schools which followed the early *Miss Kaye's* (1908) were on the whole progressive – no educational experiment goes untried, whether it's callasthenics, self-expression, various guilds and leagues or different styles of teaching. A good deal of botanizing goes on in the books ('"I believe it must be the butterfly orchids!" cried Jean'). Schools are located in manor houses, on clifftops, moors, in moated granges and so forth, and in all these picturesque settings many schoolgirl friendships 'flame to red heat', thrilling adventures occur and drastic character-moulding is got under way. After the fusty tone of late 19th-century school fiction, the Brazil atmosphere positively overwhelmed the reading public with sunniness and light. The author, it's true, was altogether too avid in her assumption of schoolgirlishness, embracing the conventions she initiated in a way that laid her open to the attentions of later parodists ('Sixteen jolly faces . . . grinning under sixteen school hats': that sort of thing). Among her fifty-odd stories of school life – *The New Girl at St Chad's*, *For the School Colours*, *Joan's Best Chum*, and so on – however, you will find some that can stand rereading. And Angela Brazil deserves great credit for having taken her chosen genre to monumental heights, and pointing the way forward for a host of other writers.   PC

Breeze, Jean 'Binta' 1956– Jamaican poet and performer. Jean 'Binta' Breeze grew up in Sandy Bay, rural Jamaica, and later moved to Kingston where she studied at the Jamaican School of Drama and became involved in Sistren, a women's theatre collective. In the early 1980s Breeze moved to the hills to live as a Rastafarian but, dissatisfied with aspects of this life, took a job for the Jamaica Cultural Development Commission. She began performing her poetry in 1981 and her first collection, *Answers*, was published in 1983. Her contacts with fellow performing poets, Mutabaruka in Jamaica and Linton Kwesi Johnson in Britain, led to recordings of her work and Breeze soon had a reputation in Jamaica and Britain as the first woman Dub Poet. Although her subsequent collections, *Ryddim Ravings* (1988), *Spring Cleaning* (1992) and *On the Edge of an Island* (1997), have strengthened this reputation, the complexity and subtlety of her poetry have more importantly helped to redefine 'dub' as a genre. In an article 'Can a Dub Poet be a Woman?' (1990), Breeze discusses her work and the gender politics of dub, stating that 'my politics were shaped by my personal experiences and those of the people round me in their day-to-day concerns'. Breeze divides her time between Jamaica and Britain and, in addition to writing and performing her poetry, she works as an actress, dancer, choreographer, director and recording artist.   AD

Brendt, Linda, see JACOBS, HARRIET

Brett, Dorothy Eugenie 1883–1977 British artist and memoirist, best known for her association with D.H. Lawrence. Born in London to a Belgian mother and an English viscount father, she utilized the single name 'Brett' after her studies at the Slade School of Art, where using only surnames was the practice. At various times, besides the Lawrences she could number among her intimate friends (often also those with whom she had fallen out) DORA CARRINGTON, Mark Gertler, OTTOLINE MORRELL, KATHERINE MANSFIELD, Gilbert Murry and VIRGINIA WOOLF. Together with the Lawrences and MABEL DODGE LUHAN, she helped found a utopian community at Taos, New Mexico, in 1924; the local scenery and Indians became the subjects of her more distinguished painting thereafter. Her memoir, *Lawrence and Brett: A Friendship* (1933), her only book, is couched entirely in the present tense and bespeaks her adulation of Lawrence. Lawrence may have modelled the character Hilda Blessington, added to *The Boy in the Bush*, on Brett; deaf like Brett, she too is willing to emigrate with the hero to serve him.   HB

Brett, Lily 1946– Australian poet, fiction writer and essayist. She came to Melbourne in 1948 as a post-World-War-II migrant from Germany, with her parents, Polish Jews whose experiences as concentration-camp victims and survivors largely generate her writing. Brett writes about the effects of the Holocaust on the present, the impact of loss and displacement. To negotiate the ambiguous familial experience of children of concentration-camp survivors and of an autobiographical mother–daughter relationship which is intensely bound to history, Brett employs a variety of textual stategies and forms. Her poetry is spare, direct and confronting. In 1986 her poem *Poland* won the Mattara Poetry Prize and her first book, *The Auschwitz Poems* (1987), won the C.J. Dennis Prize for Poetry. *Poland and Other Poems* (1987) was followed by other volumes, including *Mud in My Tears* (1997). The short stories in *What God Wants* (1991) and *Things Could be Worse* (1992) use a wry humour as a means of subverting suffering, pain and loss, a mode also used in her novel *Just Like That* (1994). *In Full View: Essays* (1997) provides honest and often amusing accounts of the writer's wrestling with a self forced to live with a fractured past. Many of the essays are based in New York, where

Brett now resides with her children and husband, Australian painter David Rankin, whose drawings illustrate several of her volumes of poetry.   MF

Brewster, Elizabeth 1922– Canadian poet and fiction writer. She was born in New Brunswick, educated at the University of New Brunswick, Radcliffe College (AM 1947) and the University of Indiana (Ph.D. 1962). She also took a degree in Library Science from the University of Toronto and worked as a librarian and sometime teacher of creative writing during her early years. From 1972 to 1990 she was a member of the English department at the University of Saskatchewan.

Over the years she has maintained a steady publication record, most often with the small Ottawa publisher, Oberon Press. As well as the separate volumes of poetry, Oberon published *Selected Poems, 1944–84* and, ten years later, *footnotes to the book of job* (1985). The latter, which contained new work and selections from *Entertaining Angels* (1988), *Spring Again* (1990) and *Wheel of Change* (1993), was short-listed for the Governor General's Award. She has also published novels – *The Sisters* (1974) and *Junctions* (1983) – and several volumes of short fiction. Although in the last few years she has written works designated as autobiographies, she has in fact 'been writing autobiography all my life'. Brewster's writing is characterized by a feisty, uncompromising independence of mind often concealed beneath a decorous surface.   JG

Bride Price, The (1976) Nigerian writer BUCHI EMECHETA's novel traces the thorns strewn on the path of traditional girlhood and subsequent womanhood. Set in Nigeria in the aftermath of World War II, *The Bride Price* is the story of Aku-nna ('father's wealth'), so named because in this society, boys are so highly prized that bearing only one is equated to infertility and the worth of a girl is only measured in terms of the size of bride wealth she would fetch for her father. It is about the challenges posed by conformity to a traditional sex role in the face of change. The novel centralizes the doomed love relationship between Aku-nna and Chike, an educated man born into an ostracized family of slaves. It employs irony in its exploration of the clashing models of tradition and modernity. No clear-cut resolution is offered. Aku-nna and Chike elope to another village where they live happily until Aku-nna dies in childbirth, thus hauntingly fulfilling the traditional myth that a girl whose bride price is not paid dies in childbirth.   PMM

Bridge, Ann [Mary Anne Dolling Sanders, Lady O'Malley] 1891–1974 British popular novelist. Born in Surrey, the seventh of nine children of a wealthy English entrepreneur and his American wife. She was educated at home before studying at the London School of Economics. In 1913 she married Sir Owen St Clair O'Malley, a British diplomat with whom she had three children. Her husband's diplomatic career took her initially to China, the inspiration for the first of her twenty-six published books, the novel *Peking Picnic* (1932), which won her the *Atlantic Monthly* Prize.

She took a pseudonym to protect her husband's career. His postings included Yugoslavia, the source for Bridge's *Illyrian Spring* (1935) – a novel set on the Adriatic coast which inspired cruises around Dubrovnik by British and American tourists – and Hungary, the setting for *A Place to Stand* (1952), based on Bridge's experiences in wartime Budapest. The main character in *Singing Water* (1946), a novel set in northern Albania, is a thinly disguised EDITH DURHAM. Several of Bridge's works have Iberian settings, inspired by her travels. In addition to romantic and adventure novels, Bridge wrote short stories, CHILDREN's fiction and autobiographical works, including an account of her successful campaign to reinstate her husband when he was asked to resign because of alleged speculations in French currency. After his retirement, the couple lived in Ireland and England.   VG

Brinsmead, Hesba (Fay Hungerford) 1922– Australian CHILDREN's author who came to prominence with her first novel, *Pastures of the Blue Crane* (1964), which won several awards and, unusually for its time, included an exploration of racial issues. Brinsmead is, however, probably best known for her 'Longtime' series, four books based on her experiences of growing-up in a remote part of the Blue Mountains of New South Wales. These include *Longtime Passing* (1971), *Once There was a Swagman* (1979), *Longtime Dreaming* (1982) and *Christmas at Longtime* (1984). Her love of the bush also led her to write about environmental issues, again before these became widely popular in children's writing. *A Sapphire for September* (1967) deals with a battle against real-estate developers; *Isle of the Sea Horse* (1969) with the threat to the Great Barrier Reef from increased tourism; and *I Will Not Say the Day is Done* (1983) with the attempt to save Tasmania's Lake Pedder. Brinsmead is no longer writing but her novels, of which over twenty have been published, remain popular because of her insights into children's experiences and her skilful evocations of both familiar and unfamiliar landscapes.   EW

Brite, Poppy Z. 1967– American Novelist, who looks from her photos like a demented Louise Brooks, poses as a Goth-and-cyberpunk ANNE RICE, and translates the latter's cosmic Vampire epics back into a social medium – the drifting homosexual teenage society of the South – and specifically into a sinisterly overripe

New Orleans. Her novels, *Lost Souls* (1992) and *Drawing Blood* (1993), also draw on the realism of Stephen King, using the vampire tag to explore the lost lives of lower-middle-class teenagers in towns called things like 'Missing Mile'. These novels, the stories in *Swamp Foetus* (1995) and her later *Exquisite Corpse* (1996) exoticize and eroticize the orgiastic and violent transfer of bodily fluids between androgynous young males – rock-guitarists and singers, cartoonists and computer-hackers – employing precisely fetishized parallels between vampirism or necrophilia, heroin-mainlining and male gay sex. Women exist; but they are not at the heart of these heartlessly florid, three-way transactions.   VS

Brittain, Vera (Mary) 1893–1970 British chronicler, novelist, journalist and poet whose feminism and pacifism informed her eclectic body of work. Born into a paper-mill-owning family who suffered from 'the terrible respectability of the middle classes' in Newcastle-under-Lyme, Staffordshire, Vera was educated first at St Monica's School, Surrey, and went up to Somerville College, Oxford, in 1914. Her studies were interrupted by World War I when she enlisted as a VAD nurse in 1915, serving in London, France and Malta until 1918. Her experiences as a woman in war and the death at the front of her fiancé, Roland Leighton (1915) and her only brother, Edward (1918), set the foundations for her unrelenting pacifism, already expressed in *Verses of a VAD* (1918). She returned to Somerville in 1918 to read History, 'because college seemed the one thing left out of the utter wreckage of the past'. She fictionalized her post-war experiences at Oxford in *The Dark Tide* (1923). At Somerville her close intellectual and emotional collaboration began with WINIFRED HOLTBY. They moved to London upon graduation in 1921, where they both wrote, lectured for the League of Nations Union and joined the feminist Six Point Group. With *Testament of Friendship* (1940) she commemorated Holtby's short life and the 'loyalty and affection between women'. In 1925 Brittain married George Catlin, the political philosopher, and their unconventional 'semi-detached' union permitted both to pursue their own careers. As her pacifism became progressively more radical she joined the Peace Pledge Union (1936), served as vice-president of the Women's International League of Peace and Freedom, invited adversity with her condemnation of the bombing of enemy cities in *Seed of Chaos* (1944), and participated in sit-ins with the Campaign for Nuclear Disarmament in the 1950s.

While Brittain wrote over twenty-five books, it was her autobiographical writings which secured her reputation as a spokeswoman for her generation. *TESTAMENT OF YOUTH* (1933) was acclaimed as 'the war book of the women of England'; *Testament of Experience* (1957) chronicled her anti-war activities; and she was working on *Testament of Time* when she died.   JVG

Broad Arrow, The (1859) This novel by CAROLINE LEAKEY (OLINE KEESE) predates by fifteen years the more famous Australian convict novel, Marcus Clarke's *For the Term of His Natural Life*. It recounts the experiences of a female convict of genteel background, Maida Gwynnham, who is wrongly transported to Van Diemen's Land (Tasmania) for child-murder. Her seduction and betrayal by her lover, Norwell, have embittered Maida, but she is softened and converted by her position as convict servant for the Evelyn family. Still struggling against the shame and mortifications of a convict existence, she dies alone but at peace in the prison hospital. Norwell is thoroughly punished for luring Maida into sexual transgression and forgery. His pregnant wife dies on learning of his past, and his attempted restitution is frustrated by Maida's death. The novel is full of Christian righteousness, but less conservative in its criticism of the corrupt and corrupting operations and social effects of the convict system.

SKM

Brodber, Erna 1940– Jamaican novelist, sociologist and historian. Born in rural Jamaica, she was educated at regional and North American universities before returning home to teach at the University of the West Indies. Her research there resulted in a fascinating documentation of oral testimonies and histories of 'Freemen in Jamaica, 1904–44'. Her academic training and publications, commitment to preserving the memories of community elders, and interest in psychology and psychiatry, have filtered into her literary writing: 'My sociological effort and therefore the fiction that serves it . . . has activist intentions: it is about studying the behavior of and transmitting these findings to the children of people who were put on ships on the African beaches and woke up from this nightmare to find themselves on the shore of the New World.'

Her intricately structured novels feature female protagonists struggling with the after-effects of this historical trauma. *Jane and Louisa Will Soon Come Home* (1980), originally conceived as a 'case study' for Abnormal Psychology students, details the healing of a 'dissociative personality': a young woman whose connections to her ancestral community have been fractured by social and sexual pressures. Therapeutic re/membering and immersion in folk-practices reconnect her to the community, a theme which recurs in Brodber's prize-winning *Myal* (1998). In this novel, however, fragmentation is exacerbated by the deracinating experience of living in the United States. Increasingly, Brodber explores 'links between the way of life forged by the people of two points of the black diaspora – the Afro-Americans and the Afro-Jamaicans', nowhere more so than in *Louisiana* (1994). Connections – between classes and races in the

Caribbean, between the Caribbean and African-American diaspora, and between spiritual and physical modes of being – are central to her work. Her lyrical prose reveals with affection and humour the profound resources of Caribbean peoples, their languages and culture.   EO'C

Broner, E.M. 1930–

As a feminist novelist, American E.M. Broner creates didactic fictions of 'female heroes' designed to guide and inspire; as a literary scholar, she seeks heroic examples in the lives of MARGARET FULLER and VIRGINIA WOOLF, among others. Broner grew up in Detroit in a left-wing family that educated her in the politics of organized labour and Jewish persecution. Inspired by ELLEN MOERS's *Literary Women: The Great Writers*, Broner was inspired to reclaim gynocentric modes of narrative, writing the novel *Her Mothers* (1975) as what she calls 'a very conscious counter Telemachus'. Broner's style is lyrical and spare, dispensing with many traditional aspects of narrative and plot. Her most successful work emits a haunting poetry reminiscent of that of GERTRUDE STEIN.

Broner's feminism and her religious sensibility complement each other. In *A Weave of Women* (1978), Broner indicts the effects of Jewish patriarchy in spiritual, familial and political life, focusing on the efforts of a group of exile and native Israeli women to form a utopian community in Jerusalem. In this novel, as in her life, Broner creates feminist religious rituals that link her not only to Fuller but to such feminist spiritual thinkers as MARY DALY. Countering her pessimism about the status of women in contemporary social and political life, Broner reaches to the past and to visions of the future for alternative visions of female identity and empowerment.   MG

Brontë, Anne 1820–49

British novelist and poet, sister of CHARLOTTE and EMILY BRONTË. Unlike her sisters, she was not sent away to school, but educated at home in Haworth, Yorkshire until 1836. She was perhaps more influenced than her sisters by her aunt, Elizabeth Branwell, who was a Wesleyan. She manifested strong religious feeling throughout her life, and Charlotte described her as 'naturally sensitive, reserved and dejected'. In 1834, with her sister, Emily, she created the imaginary kingdom, Gondal, and together they wrote numerous tiny books of Gondal stories. In 1836, she was sent for one year to Roe Head school where she suffered, and recovered from, a crisis of faith. In 1839, she became governess to the Ingham family at Blake Hall and was subsequently employed by the Robinson family in Thorp Green, near York. Her time with the Robinsons was disrupted, however, by the arrival of her brother Branwell as tutor to the family: his affair with Mrs Robinson resulted in their both being sent back to Haworth in 1845. In 1846,

Charlotte arranged for a volume of the sisters' poems to be published, but it was not successful. In her first novel, *AGNES GREY* (1847), Anne used her own and her sisters' experiences as governesses to draw attention to the abuses then often suffered by single, educated women making their own livings.

All the sisters used pseudonyms: Anne's was 'Acton Bell'. Charlotte explained that 'the ambiguous choices [were] dictated by a sort of conscientious scruple at assuming Christian names positively masculine, while we did not like to declare ourselves women, because – without at that time suspecting that our mode of writing and thinking was not what is called "feminine" – we had a vague impression that authoresses are liable to be looked on with prejudice'. This vague impression was soon confirmed. Through the character of Huntingdon in her second novel, *THE TENANT OF WILDFELL HALL* (1848), Anne graphically depicted the alcoholism that she saw destroying Branwell, and the book scandalized reviewers with its 'profane expressions, inconceivably coarse language, and revolting scenes and descriptions' (*Sharpe's London Magazine*). This novel is now considered her masterpiece. Not constricted by the conventional 19th-century limitations on female imagination, her writings challenged the dominant idea of 'womanhood' with their intense and painful accounts of female experience. After the deaths of Branwell and Emily in 1848 she became ill with tuberculosis. Charlotte and a friend took her to Scarborough, hoping that sea air would help her, but she died there aged 29.   CPe

Brontë, Charlotte 1816–55.

Charlotte was the third of six Brontë children, a year older than her brother Branwell (her closest imaginative companion in childhood), two years older than EMILY and four years older than ANNE. Their mother died when Charlotte was 5; at 9 she became the eldest child, on the deaths of her sisters Maria and Elizabeth from TB, exacerbated by the privations of the Clergy Daughters' School. Charlotte would be the most outgoing and long-lived of her family. Compared with other contemporary women writers (HARRIET MARTINEAU or ELIZABETH GASKELL, both of whom she came to know), she still seemed shy, savage, prickly and intensely private. Nonetheless she saw more of the world than Emily or Anne: after the Clergy Daughters, she attended and taught at Roe Head School, where she made lifelong friends (Ellen Nussey, Mary Taylor); and (first with Emily, later alone) she attended the Pensionnat Heger in Brussels (1842–3) where she found a mentor in M. Heger – and lost him when her essays (and her feelings) became passionate and demanding. Back home at Haworth, she published with her sisters *Poems* under the names 'Currer, Ellis

Charlotte Brontë: frontispiece of Clement K. Shorter, *Charlotte Bronté and Her Circle*, 1896.

and Acton Bell', in 1846. That same year she finished her novel, *The Professor* (1857, rejected in her lifetime), and in 1847 completed JANE EYRE, which was published to immediate acclaim and notoriety.

Reviewer ELIZABETH RIGBY accused 'Currer Bell' of coarseness, code for crude strength of feeling, and lack of delicacy and altruism. Jane Eyre's 'I' was hungry, self-absorbed: the very use of the first-person narrator harked back to the GOTHIC. That this 'I' belonged to a mere governess compounded the offence. Such a woman's BILDUNGSROMAN was almost a contradiction in terms. Plain Jane gave off an ambivalent message, rather as Charlotte herself had done ten years earlier, when she wrote confiding her ambition to the poet Southey. She received crushingly fatherly advice: 'Literature cannot be the business of a woman's life ... The more she is engaged in her proper duties, the less leisure she will have for it'; and replied that she had plenty of duties, but that hadn't cured her – 'In the evenings I confess I do think.'

Her next novel, SHIRLEY (1849), had a social theme, but touched the same nerve – 'Is there not a terrible hollowness, mockery, want, craving, in that existence which is given away to others, for want of something of your own to bestow it on?' In VILLETTE (1853) narrator Lucy Snowe's enigmatic, negative style of self-assertion ('I was no bright lady's shadow') creates one of the most lurid inner worlds of the 19th-century novel. It's a masterpiece of loneliness, and it was the first work she conceived in isolation. All her siblings were dead, Branwell of drugs and drink, Emily and Anne of TB. In *Villette* she re-counts her emotional capital – and her heroine ends bitterly alone. Charlotte, however, would not: in 1854 she married her long-time suitor Arthur Nicholls, and died pregnant at 38, possibly of typhoid.

Charlotte wrote of Emily, 'An interpreter ought always to have stood between her and the world.' Elizabeth Gaskell felt the same about Charlotte, and her 1857 *Life* portrayed her as the very type of the woman writer as heroine. *Jane Eyre* has become common property, like a FAIRY TALE. It has inspired endless re-writings, and fed the imaginations of writers of popular ROMANCE. This is despite Charlotte Brontë's exigent 'I'. '*I am not like you*' she wrote to one of her closest friends, insisting on her inalienable individuality.   LS

Brontë, Emily Jane [Ellis Bell]

1818–48 The fifth of the six Brontë children, Emily is the most intriguing and mysterious because biographical information about her is sparse. She made few excursions away from the Haworth Parsonage. At the age of 6 she briefly attended the infamous Clergy Daughters' School at Cowan Bridge which hastened the deaths of her two oldest sisters. Eleven years later she spent four months at Roe Head School and taught for a short time at a school in Halifax. She accompanied her sister CHARLOTTE to the Pensionnat Heger in Brussels, but when the sisters came back after several months to attend their aunt's funeral, Charlotte returned to Belgium alone. Rooted in her surroundings, reclusive and solitary, Emily delighted in the bleak moors with their wildlife and atmospheric tumult. Her last two years were overshadowed by the upheaval caused in the family by the drunken rampages of her brother Branwell. His self-destruction resulted in his death in September 1848. Emily, refusing medical treatment, died of tuberculosis three months later.

Her writing started early, inspired by the arrival of a box of toy soldiers around which the children wove imaginary adventures. With her sister ANNE, Emily composed the Gondal saga, writing down stories and poems about its inhabitants. This secret play, with its literary component, continued long after childhood. It was her discovery of Emily's poems in 1845 which motivated Charlotte to publish a year later a collection of poems by the three sisters under the pseudonyms of 'Currer, Ellis and Acton Bell'. Although Emily contributed only 21 poems to this book, she wrote over 200 poems which have subsequently been collected in various editions.

It is, however, on her single novel, WUTHERING HEIGHTS (1847), that her reputation stands. The story

An extract from Emily Brontë's diary, 1845.

describes the love and hatred which plays itself out between the inhabitants of two neighbouring but different houses – the sedate Lintons of Thrushcross Grange and the chaotic Earnshaws of Wuthering Heights. The plot is set in motion when the head of the Earnshaw family brings back from Liverpool a foundling boy. Heathcliff, whose dominant emotion is an overwhelming passion for his adoptive sister, seizes control of the Earnshaw estate and takes revenge for the loss of his love by sadistically tormenting both the Linton and Earnshaw survivors. The disregard for social convention which characterized Emily's life extended to her writing, and she ignored the literary conventions of her day. In doing so, she not only unleashed powerful raw emotions but also produced a GOTHIC novel that was ground-breaking in its non-linear structure and use of shifting narrative viewpoints. These she achieved through two narrators – Lockwood, a stranger, and his housekeeper, Ellen Dean. A literary descendant of Pandarus and Juliet's nurse, she is part wise-woman ('There is not a book in this library I have not looked into') and part meddling busybody. It is to her role as interpreter and participant, and her mixing of first- and second-hand information with hearsay that the novel owes its complexity.

Contemporary reviewers found the book 'wild, confused, disjointed and improbable' and the subject matter so 'coarse and loathsome' that Charlotte Brontë was impelled to jump to her late sister's defence, unnecessarily explaining that 'it was hewn in a wild workshop, with simple tools, out of homely materials'. The combination of uncurbed energy and innovative technique accounts for its enormous influence on later novelists. These include such different practitioners as William Faulkner (who tacitly acknowledged his debt in 'A Rose for Emily') and JEAN RHYS, who found her subject matter for WIDE SARGASSO SEA in JANE EYRE, but her narrative art in Wuthering Heights.   JG

Brooke, Emma Frances 1845 or 1859?–1926 NEW WOMAN novelist and champion of women's rights. Brooke was born in Cheshire and educated at Newnham College, Cambridge. In 1879 she moved to London, where she studied at the London School of Economics. She was a member of the Fabian Society from its inception in 1884, and was secretary of the Karl Marx Club in Hampstead, which became the Hampstead Historic.

Brooke was also an associate of the Men and Women's Club, formed in 1885 to discuss matters 'connected with the mutual position and relation of men and women'. She joined the Fellowship of the New Life commune, which was run according to utopian ideals. In 1898 she published her *Tabulation of the Factory Laws of European Countries*, analysing the working conditions of women and children in particular.

Brooke used the pseudonym 'E. Fairfax Byrrne' for some of her early works: *Milicent. A Poem* (1881), *A Fair Country Maid* (1883), *Entangled* (1885) and *The Heir Without Heritage* (1887). Her best-known novel, *A Superfluous Woman*, appeared in 1894, at the time when New Woman fiction was in vogue. She published seventeen books, the last of which was *The House of Robershaye* (1912).

Brooke believed that many women dreaded motherhood and argued that rearing children should be recognized as work for the state, meriting financial support: 'In this women's question it cannot be solved unless women be allowed distinctly to work out for themselves their own idea of what their duty or ideal is.'   SF

Brooke, Frances 1724–89 English novelist, dramatist and translator. Born in Lincolnshire, Brooke and her sister were brought up by relatives after the deaths of their parents. Brooke's writing career began in 1755, with her weekly periodical, the *Old Maid*. In 1756, she published *Virginia, A Tragedy*, a play which Garrick rejected and which was never subsequently produced.

Christine Brooke-Rose: 'But then to Herodotus the world would have the exact shape of the human brain', illustration from *Amalgamemnon*, 1984.

In the same year she married the Reverend John Brooke and later travelled to Canada, where her husband was posted as chaplain to the garrison of Quebec. Brooke continued to write, translating Madame Riccoboni's *Letters from Juliet, Lady Catesby to her friend, Lady Henrietta Campley* (1760) and publishing her first EPISTOLARY NOVEL, THE HISTORY OF LADY JULIA MANDEVILLE (1763). Her *History of Emily Montague* (1769) is generally regarded as the first Canadian novel. In Quebec, Brooke also translated Framery's *Memoires de M. le Marquis de S. Forlaix* (1770), a sentimental novel, and Milot's *Elements de l'histoire d'Angleterre* (1771). On her return to England, she was involved in the management of the Haymarket Opera House with her friend, the actress Mary Ann Yates, and wrote a number of plays, including *Rosina* (1783), *Marian* (1788) and *The Siege of Sinope* (1782) which was produced at Covent Garden. Her novel of 1777, *The Excursion*, includes a thinly veiled personal attack on Garrick for his rejection of the work of a young dramatist. Her final novel, *The History of Charles Mandeville* (1790), a sequel to her work of 1763, was published posthumously. The narrative style of her later work was more witty and lively than that of her early novels and in ANNA LAETITIA BARBAULD's *British Novelists* (1810), she is named as the first author 'who wrote in a polished style'.   KD

Brooke-Rose, Christine 1923– British experimental novelist and critic, born in Geneva and brought up in Belgium and in England. During World War II, she vetted German communications at the British decoding centre at Bletchley Park. In her 1996 anti-autobiography, *Re-make*, she wrote of 'the otherness of the other learnt young, the real war ... from the enemy viewpoint ... the writer does that, learning to imagine the other'. At Bletchley she met, married and parted from her first husband. After the war, she studied Philology at Oxford, married Polish writer and intellectual in exile Jerzy Peterkiewicz, and worked as a freelance literary journalist. Her first novel, *The Languages of Love*, was published in 1957; her first – more impressive – work of literary criticism, *The Grammar of Metaphor*, in 1958.

Her early novels were ironic tales of manners and mores. In *The Dear Deceit* (1960), using a male narrator, she told the story of her English father, who had died in 1934, and had (it turned out) once been a monk in an Anglican Order, stolen the plate, and been sent to prison. (With bizarre symmetry, her mother, after the war, had become Sister Mary Anselm in a Benedictine convent in London.) Brooke-Rose the writer, convinced that only the text mattered, in practice as well as in theory, became, with *Out* (1964), a 'new' novelist, akin to Robbe-Grillet and SARRAUTE, whose reflexive fictions she admired. She set herself formal puzzles – *Between* (1968), about a love-affair between simultaneous translators, eschews the verb 'to be' – and played with writing's graphic surface. At the end of the decade, when her marriage foundered, she took up HELENE CIXOUS's invitation to teach at Paris VIII, where she became Professor of English Language and Literature in 1975. THRU, published that same year, played with Parisian ideas in fictional form.

Her critical books included *A ZBC of Ezra Pound* (1971) and *A Rhetoric of the Unreal* (1981) – the latter's interest in the structural features of fantasy and SCIENCE FICTION evident in her fictions *Amalgamemnon* (1984), *Xorandor* (1986), *Verbivore* (1990) and TEXTERMINATION (1991). All of these are playful and parodic, and, while she remains a structuralist and a MODERNIST, her version of textuality has become less neutral. In 'Illiterations' (collected in *Stories, Theories and Things*, 1991) she talked openly for the first time about gender, and the priestly exclusiveness of the male avant-garde. Her own work is determinedly demystificatory, at once self-conscious and movingly personal. *Next* (1998), about the London homeless, denies itself the use of the verb 'to have', and its characters have no 'I' except when they are talking to each other, speaking for Brooke-Rose's tireless wit and intransigence.   LS

Brookner, Anita 1928– English novelist and art historian concerned with fine moral discriminations and careful aesthetic distinctions. The only child of a businessman and a retired professional singer, Brookner grew up in a middle-class London suburb, Herne Hill, in a family of successful Polish Jewish immigrants (her father had changed his name from 'Bruckner'). The Brookner household included her grandparents and an uncle as well as her parents, and a range of servants. In the 1930s, the Brookners took in Jewish refugees. Brookner has described her parents as 'silent, stoical . . . and very unhappy'. Schooling allowed a welcome escape from the claustrophobia of home. Her education at James Allen's Girls' School in Dulwich was followed by an undergraduate degree in History at King's College London, and a doctorate in Art History at the Courtauld Institute. After studying in Paris, Brookner embraced an academic career which included lecturing at the University of Reading from 1959 to 1988, and serving as the first female Slade Professor at Cambridge in 1967-8. Finally, she secured a readership at the Courtauld Institute (where the distinguished scholar – and notorious spy – Anthony Blunt particularly encouraged her), retiring in 1987. In the 1960s, she nursed her elderly parents until her mother's death in 1969. They died disappointed that their daughter never married.

Brookner's has been a teaching and writing life. As an art historian she published books on Watteau (1968), Greuze (1972) and David (1980), before turning to fiction at the age of 53. Her first novel, *A Start in Life*, appeared in 1981. Since then, she has produced a book each year. Her most successful novel, HOTEL DU LAC, appeared in 1984 and won the Booker McConnell Prize for Fiction. Her many book reviews in the *Spectator* mark her skill as a literary journalist. She was awarded the CBE in 1990.

Concentrating on intimate ethical dilemmas attendant on solitude and betrayal, Brookner's fiction invites comparison with the work of BARBARA PYM, ELIZABETH TAYLOR, ROSAMOND LEHMANN and ELIZABETH BOWEN. An exquisite stylist, Brookner nevertheless insists that a 'novel should have a moral lesson'. Her ethical orientation, melancholy emotional register, and attentiveness to social decorum place her in the tradition of English psychological fiction. The same qualities attract hostility on charges of preciousness and hyper-gentility. In a period when the fiction of quiet inwardness has become unfashionable, Brookner remains one of its most distinguished practitioners.   KF

Brooks, Gwendolyn 1917– Born in Kansas, she
went to live in Chicago, which was an inspiration for her writing. Brooks was the first black writer to win a Pulitzer Prize, for *Annie Allen* (1949). In an age when black women writers were largely ignored in the black (and white) literary world, Brooks's many honours and her genius made her the exception, breaking ground for future generations. She graduated from Wilson Junior College (1936), married (1939), had two children, taught in several universities, was a publicity director, and has gained the American Academy of Arts and Letters Award, Guggenheim fellowships and honorary doctorates. She has been Library of Congress consultant in poetry, edited and published the *Black Position* journal, was poet laureate of Illinois in 1968 and founded a publishing house – The David Company – in Chicago.

Brooks is best known for her poetry for the people, 'plain black folks', including *A Street in Bronzeville* (1946) and *The Bean Eaters* (1956). Her novel *Maud Martha* (1953) illustrates the imaginative stoicism of an ordinary Black American woman. An autobiography, *Report From Part One* (1972) (comparable to HURSTON's *Dust Tracks on a Road*, [1986]), represents her as supported by her family in her writing, volatile, and proud of her blackness: 'When I was a child it did not occur to me, even once, that the black in which I was encased (I called it brown in those days) would be considered, one day, beautiful . . . I always considered it beautiful.' It is a prose poem, a fragmented text of short sections on travel; autobiography; introductions by other black, male writers in the tradition of authentication from slave narrative history; letters; book reviews; and so on. The fragmented discontinuities of form draw from the tradition of variety, of family and community voices speaking through African-American writing, contrasting with her travelled but settled life, in terms of family, friends and community. Hers is an essentially urban life without the oral storytelling traditions of the more rural writers such as Hurston. It is a positive celebration of the Black female self; a model to balance those of subordination and suffering.   GW

Brophy, Brigid 1929–95 English novelist, essayist and
polemicist, educated at, and expelled from, St. Hugh's College, Oxford. The defining aspect of Brophy's work is her dandyism, a love of fireworks and display which drew her to the subjects of her three major non-fiction studies, Mozart (in *Mozart the Dramatist*, 1964), Aubrey Beardsley (in *Black and White*, 1968) and Ronald Firbank (in *Prancing Novelist*). In each of these studies, she points to the combination of rococo ornamentation and underlying classical form, and to the deep seriousness and hard work implicit in apparent frivolity and facility. In each case, she argues that what has been seen as effete is actually tough-minded; there is in these books an implicit critique of traditional masculinity and a sense of how things might profitably be otherwise. In some ways, these are her most successful works because her passionate and perverse identification with her subjects, and her love of their works, makes these critical biographies her most emotional books. Her love of formalism can make her novels rather cold affairs, particularly *In Transit* where her refusal definitively to gender, or otherwise situate, her protagonists makes them less rather than more interesting. Her first novel, HACKENFELLER'S APE, discusses animal rights and space travel in a talky polemical vein. Her first collection of essays, DON'T NEVER FORGET, came out in 1966. Brophy had many strong convictions such as vegetarianism, and held and expressed them with a forcefulness that sometimes undercut their effectiveness, but never their sincerity. Perhaps her best novel, *The Snow*

Ball (1964), works because of its intertextual links with Mozart's *Don Giovanni*: in the course of an 18th-century masquerade, a couple flirts, a younger couple explore infidelity, another man dies and, we come to feel, human life is revealed as made up of the constant reiteration of unacknowledged cultural archetypes. *Palace Without Chairs* (1978) is a Ruritanian farce which quite cleverly exploits reader expectations by juxtaposing the likable with the upsetting; she cleverly avoids, and therefore effectively hints at, direct satirical portraiture of the British royal house. As an activist on behalf of her profession, she was, with MAUREEN DUFFY, largely responsible for the introduction of the Public Lending Right. RK

Brossard, Nicole 1943– Born in Montreal, Quebec, French-Canadian writer Nicole Brossard has published prolifically since 1965 – collections of poetry, novels, a play, essays and several pieces for radio. She was co-founder and editor of the cultural journal *La Barre du Jour* (1965) and *La Nouvelle Barre du Jour* (1977) and co-director of the film *Some American Feminists* (1986). She also co-founded *Les Têtes de Pioche*, the radical feminist journal, between 1976 and 1979, and established the feminist press L'Intégrale. She has won numerous awards, including the Governor General's Award for poetry in French for *Mécanique jongleuse* (1975) and *Double Impression* (1984); the Harbourfront Festival Prize; and Le Prix Athanase-David. Brossard is a continuing and active participant in international conferences on literature, writing and feminism. She was the president, for instance, of the Third International Feminist Book Fair in Montreal in 1988.

Brossard is one of the leading avant-garde writers to have emerged from the 1960s political tensions in Quebec and has become a major agent of the province's *nouvelle écriture* which subverts and disrupts literary and social orthodoxies. Her work is part of the feminist literary scene in Quebec which embraces and celebrates concepts of *l'écriture féminine* and lesbian difference, writing the female body and desire in exhilarating and erotic texts in her explicitly stated project of 'writing in the feminine'. Mixing the personal and the political and effacing genres in an inventive and innovative textualization, Brossard's writing revolves around a metaphorics which includes spirals and the city, the body and skin. Mobility is a further feature of her aesthetic: *Picture Theory* is a novel of lesbian love moving from Curaçao to Montreal, from New York to Paris, whilst *Mauve Desert* simultaneously traces Mélanie's driving across the Arizona desert and the quests of reading, textuality and translation. Brossard's own work has been translated widely by, for instance, Barbara Godard, Susanne de Lotbinière-Harwood and Patricia Claxton, and includes *French Kiss* (transl. 1986); *Lovers* (transl. 1986); *Mauve Desert* (transl.

1990); *Picture Theory* (transl. 1991); and *Baroque at Dawn* (transl. 1997). Her essays on lesbian culture and writing are collected in *The Aerial Letter* (transl. 1988).

CSt

Broster, D. K. (Dorothy Kathleen) 1878–1950 English HISTORICAL NOVELIST, particularly popular in the 1920s and 1930s for her trilogy about events during and after the 1745 Jacobite Rebellion: *The Flight of the Heron* (1925), *The Gleam in the North* (1927) and *The Dark Mile* (1929). Broster moved from Cheltenham Ladies' College to St Hilda's College, Oxford, where she read History. Her first two novels, *Chantemerle: A Romance of the Vendean War* (1911) and *The Vision Splendid* (1913 – about the Tractarian Movement), were written with her friend, Gertrude Winifred Taylor. There was a break during World War I, when Broster worked in France in a Franco-American hospital, but she thereafter established herself as secretary to the Regius Professor of History at Oxford, and fifteen novels followed at regular intervals until 1947, when *The Captain's Lady* became one of her most successful works. A volume of poetry, *The Short Voyage* was published posthumously in 1951.

The novels are marked by scrupulous attention to historical detail. The characterization is simple and heroic. In the Jacobite trilogy, the friendship between the Scottish and English 'enemies', Ewan Cameron and Keith Windham, is shown to hinge on their shared values: they are both 'gentlemen' who despise anything 'womanish'. However, despite this predictability, there is great pace to the narratives and depth and colour to the settings. Broster seemed not to mind being taken by many readers to be a man. Though she wrote for an adult audience, she is now often included in guides to CHILDREN's literature. VP

Broughton, Rhoda 1840–1920 Bestselling novelist with a reputation for 'fast' heroines and sexually daring plots. Born in Denbigh (North Wales), the youngest of the four children of the Reverend Delves Broughton, she spent her childhood in a Staffordshire manor house which provided the setting for several of her novels. In 1863, following the death of her father, who had educated her in classics and given her free access to his extensive library, she returned briefly to Wales before going to Oxford, where she moved in literary and academic circles. Her writing career began in 1867 with *Not Wisely But Too Well*, serialized in the *Dublin University Magazine* (edited by her uncle Sheridan Le Fanu), and *Cometh Up As A Flower*, which reworks SENSATION themes and also anticipates the marriage problem novels of the 1880s and 1890s with its free-spoken heroine who sacrifices her love for a handsome young soldier for the legalized prostitution of marriage to a rich older man in order to help her family. The tension between love and duty, the pleasures and pains of unwise love and the (readerly) pleasurable pains of the lingering deaths of beautiful young women are staples of Broughton's plots in *Red As A Rose Is She* (1870), *Goodbye Sweetheart* (1872), *Nancy* (1873), *Belinda* (1883) and *Doctor Cupid* (1886). In later years Broughton moved away from her earlier sensational style and preoccupations: *A Beginner* (1894), *Dear Faustina* (1897), *Foes in Law* (1900) and *Lavinia* (1902) were among the one-volume novels which she produced after the collapse of the three-decker.   LP

Brown, Pam(ela Jane Barclay) 1948– Australian poet, prose writer and performance artist, who has experimented since the 1970s with a mix of artistic media. She was born in Seymour, Victoria, and grew up on various military bases in Queensland, being educated mainly in Toowoomba and Brisbane. Brown was active in the feminist movement in Sydney from the early 1970s, participating in feminist writing collectives, theatre groups and even a feminist band called Clitoris Band. Her output has been prolific, with half a dozen books of poetry in the 1970s, four substantial collections of poetry and prose pieces in the 1980s and four more in the 1990s, including a *New and Selected Poems* in 1990.

Brown's early work was playful, impromptu and sometimes tricky. She moved from verse forms into short prose pieces, based on the paragraph, in the early 1980s, but has recently returned to poetry of an increasingly abstract kind. Her work has always resisted the conventional structures of the well-made poem or the short story. While feminist ideology has been an evident driving force, she chooses to write poetry and prose precisely because they are 'practically invisible in this heroic, nuclear-Sylvester-Stallone-video-computer-body-organ-transplant-oriented culture. And this is the culture I try to chip away at in my work'.   SPL

Brown, Rita Mae 1944– American novelist, poet and essayist. She grew up orphaned and impoverished in Florida and Pennsylvania, and was expelled from Florida University for Civil Rights Movement activism (she later graduated in History at New York University). *RUBYFRUIT JUNGLE* (1973), a narrative of lesbian feminist self-discovery, exposes the patriarchal power structures underlying hetero-romance, which subordinate women. Molly Bolt, a politicized lesbian, makes choices about her own sexuality. A fighter, she announces: 'Let's stop this shit. I love women. I'll never marry a man and I'll never marry a woman either. That's not my way. I'm a devil-may-care lesbian.' But she finally rejects the Women's Movement of the time as divisive because it refuses a pro-lesbian stance and is bleak, projecting an unsupportive, submissive view of women. This reflects Brown's experiences of the separatism of the National Organisation of Women (NOW), from which she resigned in 1970. She uses humour and revises history, recuperating women's experiences, concentrating on a Southern tradition of women's moral influence in *Six of One* (1978) and *Southern Discomfort* (1982). *Sudden Death* (1983) exposes the undercurrents of women's tennis, and *High Hearts* (1986) recuperates the history of brave Southern women who fought, disguised as men, during the Civil War. Other works including *The Hand That Cradles the Rock* (1971) and *Songs to Handsome Women* (1973), also revise representations of women while later works such as *Rest in Pieces* (1994) and *Murder She Meowed* (1997) start to move into the crime genre as the vehicle for a critique of misrepresentations of women.   GW

Brown, Rosellen 19?– American writer who teaches creative writing at the University of Houston. Her novels deal effectively but crudely in long-term consequences and in memory – *Tender Mercies* (1978), for example, sentimentally depicts the gradual regeneration of an alcoholic country-and-western singer under the influence of the religion of his second wife. *Civil Wars* (1984) tries to be a panorama of the South and of the aftermath of the Civil Rights struggle and is effective in its portrait of a burned-out white activist and the racist niece for whom he and his wife find themselves responsible, less so in its attempt to deal with the broader issues of sexual politics that come to the fore in the breakup of his marriage. *Before and After* (1992) unsatisfactorily loads its debate about guilt and innocence; the small town which reacts badly to a family whose son is accused (rightly) of murder is crudely portrayed as intolerant. Brown's fictions have many felicities but are unsatisfactory; her short-story panorama of a neighbourhood, *Street Games* (1991), has some effective impersonations of character and idiolect, but relies heavily on class and ethnic stereotypes. Her poems are collected in *Some Deaths in the Delta* (1970), *Cora Fry* (1977) and *The Pillow Book of Cora Fry* (1994).   RK

Brown Girl, Brownstones (1959) PAULE MARSHALL's partly autobiographical first novel deals with the burdens and opportunities of being a second-generation Barbadian-American. The novel's heroine, Selina, grows up in a household that submits to the will of Silla, the mother who intends to do whatever it takes to own a house. Indeed, the entire community of Barbadian immigrants in Brooklyn, New York, in the late 1930s and 1940s seems to have been motivated by the premise that owning real estate is as vital to life in the United States as breathing. Selina's desire to shape her developing sense of self is presented against this backdrop of familial obligation and communal expectation. She will be her own woman like her mother, but she reserves the right to envision a different world. Marshall's woman-centred novel predates the Women's Movement. The re-issue of this novel by the Feminist Press at the City University of New York in 1981 signalled the acknowledgement of its author's contribution to women's writing in multiple contexts: American, Caribbean, POST-COLONIAL and Third World.   KO

Browne, Frances ['The blind poetess of Donegal']

1816–79 Irish poet, novelist and author of stories for children. Born in Stranorlar, County Donegal, Frances was one of twelve children of the local postmaster. Although blinded by smallpox in infancy, she managed to acquire an education. Her first poem was published in 1840 in the *Irish Penny Journal*, and her work later appeared in periodicals such as the *Keepsake*, *Hood's Magazine* and the *Athenaeum*.

Browne's first volume of poems, *The Star of Atteghei*, appeared in 1844, and Sir Robert Peel was sufficiently impressed to grant her a pension of £20 a year. In 1847, together with a sister who acted as her secretary, she moved to Edinburgh. She later settled in London, where she died in 1879.

Despite her disability, Browne was a prolific author, who published short stories, essays, reviews and poems, as well as a number of novels. These included *My Share of the World: An Autobiography* (1861), *The Exile's Trust* (1869) and *The Foundling of the Fens* (1886). Her collection of stories for children, *Granny's Wonderful Chair and its Tales of Fairy Times*, was a bestseller on its first appearance in 1857. In 1877 FRANCES HODGSON BURNETT reproduced some of the tales in *Stories from the Lost Fairy Book*, reviving interest in Browne's own version. Reissued in 1880, *Granny's Wonderful Chair* quickly established itself as a classic of 19th-century CHILDREN'S LITERATURE.   RR

Browning, Elizabeth Barrett

1806–61 British poet who believed passionately that poetry should engage in the issues and problems of its day. She was born at Coxhoe Hall, near Durham, on 6 March 1806, the eldest of the twelve children of Edward Moulton (who later changed his name to Barrett) and Mary Graham. She grew up on her father's estate in Herefordshire, a country house with stained glass and Moorish turrets, standing in a park. Largely self-educated at home, Elizabeth could read Homer in the original at 8 years old, which was when she began to write poetry. She completed an epic poem, 'Battle of Marathon', when she was 13, and her father had it privately printed.

At 15 Elizabeth injured her spine in a riding accident so seriously that she had to spend years on her back. When she was 20 her mother fell ill at the same time as her father's business began to collapse. After her mother's death the family moved to Sidmouth and later to London where Elizabeth lived a reclusive life, dogged by illness. In 1838 she was sent to Torquay to improve her health and here in 1840 her brother tragically drowned in Babbicombe Bay, which, she claimed 'gave a nightmare to her life for ever'.

In 1841 she returned to London to almost complete sick-bed reclusivity, overseen by her father who refused to allow visitors. During this time, with her lap-dog Flush at her feet, she read books in almost every language, wrote articles for the *Athenaeum*, contributed to a modern rendering of Chaucer and published one of her most famous poems, the 'Cry of the Children', in response to the report of the commissioners appointed to investigate child employment.

In 1845 she began a secret correspondence with Robert Browning and in 1846 the couple were secretly married and left for Italy where they finally settled in Florence, where their son was born in 1849. For many years she was best known for her SONNETS FROM THE PORTUGUESE, a sonnet sequence which traces the development of her love for Robert Browning, presented as if it were a translation from Portuguese. Sonnet 43 begins: 'How do I love thee? Let me count the ways.' In Italy she wrote 'CASA GUIDI WINDOWS' (1851) about Italian liberation, and her verse-novel, AURORA LEIGH (1857), which she called 'the most mature of my works, the one into which my highest convictions of work and art have entered'. Robert Browning wrote about the poem: 'My wife used to write it and lay it down to hear our child spell, or when a visitor came in it was thrust under the cushions then. At Paris, a year ago last March, she gave me the first six books to read, I never having seen a line before. She then wrote the rest and transcribed them in London, where I read them also. I wish in one sense that I had written it and she had read it.'

Aurora Leigh, a story about its heroine's struggle to make a career for herself as a writer, is remarkable for its passionate and often fierce challenge to the social conventions and expectations that smother female creativity.   RS

Bruce, Mary Grant

1878–1958 One of Australia's most popular and prolific writers for children (see CHILDREN'S BOOKS). She wrote thirty-eight books in all but is most famous for her fifteen 'Billabong' novels, published from 1910 to 1942, which tell the story of the Linton family who live on a sheep station in Victoria. The first of this series, *A Little Bush Maid*, initially appeared in episodic form in the *Age*, and introduces Jim and Norah Linton, their father David and friend Wally. In two of the later books, *From Billabong to London* (1915) and *Jim and Wally* (1916), the location moves to Europe during World War I and Bruce recalls her own experiences of living in Ireland and England.

Nevertheless, at the heart of the Billabong books is Bruce's strong evocation of a rural utopia as the Australian ideal.

Bruce's work is strongly steeped in the 'bush myth' and the ideals of mateship, and her influence shaped the self-perception of generations of young readers. Her portraits of Aboriginals and of the Chinese are shocking to contemporary readers but relatively liberal for the period, as is her portrayal of her female protagonist. Norah, a tomboy heroine, is capable and independent but she is eventually domesticated by marriage to Wally. Mary Grant Bruce's other works include a collection of Aboriginal myths, *The Stone-Axe of Burkamukk* (1922), prefiguring the later use of Aboriginal stories in Australian children's literature by writers such as PATRICIA WRIGHTSON.   SS

Brumby Innes (1927) KATHARINE SUSANNAH PRICHARD's play won the Australian Triad competition in 1927 for its 'originality of subject, atmosphere, characterization, virility and technique' but remained unperformed for forty years on account of its 'sordid' content. Like its novelistic counterpart – COONARDOO – the drama is set on a lonely cattle station in the North-West and relates the sexual relations between a stockman, Brumby Innes (based on the real-life Brumby Leake), and his female 'mares': the Aboriginal girl, Wylba, and his white wife, May. Prichard's sympathetic portrayal of the harassed Aboriginals is balanced by an astute honesty in her treatment of sexual matters: there is no moral judgement, for example, of Brumby's aggressive denial of romantic love. Prichard's control of structure, tempo and character are distinctively 'orchestrated' throughout: from the opening corroboree (the first to be dramatized) to the closing dance with Brumby and Wylba re-united to the strains of the domestic gramophone.   MRE

Brunton, Mary 1778–1818 British novelist, born on Barra, Orkney, where her education was sporadic and conventional. She nevertheless read poetry and prose and practised translations from an early age. In around 1798 she married the Reverend Alexander Brunton, who later became Professor of Oriental Languages at Edinburgh University, and they studied history and philosophy together. Given contemporaneous views of the woman writer as imbuing SENSIBILITY and morality, her two completed novels, *SELF-CONTROL* (1811) and *Discipline* (1814), are significantly titled. Although claiming that 'I would sooner exhibit as a rope dancer' than enter the literary marketplace, the first of her novels appeared anonymously in 1811, dedicated to JOANNA BAILLIE, the Scottish poet and dramatist. Its heroine seeks Christian martyrdom, eventually ending up in the Canadian wilderness, whilst the later novel centres on a woman who needs to be re-educated

and taught virtue. Brunton's ambitious plan to write a series of moral novels was cut short by her death in childbirth. She left behind the unfinished *Emmeline*, which condemns a well-meaning woman for leaving her loveless marriage to marry another man. This was published by her husband in 1819, along with letters, criticism and other miscellanea. Several critics have argued that Brunton's work directly influenced JANE AUSTEN.   RDM

Bryher 1894–1983 English editor and author known for her contribution to MODERNIST literary and film culture. Born Annie Winifred Ellerman to prominent, wealthy parents, she sought to disavow her original name's social cachet – as well as its overt femininity – by legally changing it to 'Bryher' in remembrance of one of the Scilly Isles, where she had vacationed as a child. Despite two marriages – to the writers Robert McAlmon (1921–7) and Kenneth Macpherson (1927–47) – her primary relationship was with the female author H. D., with whom she lived from 1919 to 1946.

Fascinated by film, Bryher founded and helped to edit *Close Up* (1927–33), an international and interdisciplinary publication that, as the first theoretical film journal, made a groundbreaking case for the cinema as an intellectually fertile enterprise. Bryher also published a book on Soviet silent cinema, and collaborated on several experimental films, including *Borderline* (1930) with Paul Robeson. In the 1950s and 1960s she turned to HISTORICAL FICTION, producing novels set in periods of cultural transformation – from the invasion of the Roman Empire by Germanic tribes, to the Norman Conquest, to the Battle of Britain. At the core of Europe's artistic and intellectual network, Bryher encouraged and shepherded many fellow writers, including MARIANNE MOORE and DOROTHY RICHARDSON.   RE

Buck, Heather 1926– British poet whose direct and simple style, and unpretentious but convincing wisdom, has won her many advocates, including ANNE STEVENSON and Peter Levi. Buck emerged slowly from a generation that included Stevenson herself, as well as ELIZABETH BARTLETT. She began to write when she was 40 – a result of Jungian analysis – and has published three books of poems with the pioneering small press, Anvil. Buck's first collection, *At the Window* (1982), recounts an inward journey through pain, loss, fear and the shadow of age toward rebirth and a quickening of love and spirit. Its closing biblical sequence of poems about Tobias is a fine synthesis of prayer and affirmation, both uncompromisingly undramatic and sensuous.

The Sign of the Water Bearer (1987) continued this modest trajectory, making vivid recreations of things remembered and quiet statements about life or the mind or the poem. 'Shadow Figures for Carl Gustav Jung' exemplifies the strategy and is, at once, a mixture of honesty, honest freedom, and perfect control or moral balance. *Psyche Unbound* showed greater range of subject – Buck opened her poems to the nature of war, as well as more familiar themes of faith, childhood, art and people. More recent work explores the presences that deepen our daily lives – perceptions of mortality and of the life of the spirit – through imagery firmly rooted in the world of the senses. DM

Buck, Pearl Sydenstricker 1892–1973 American novelist, short-story writer, biographer, essayist. The daughter of Presbyterian missionaries, Pearl was born in West Virginia and raised in China. She graduated from Randolph-Macon Women's College in Virginia in 1914 and returned to China, where in 1917 she married agricultural expert John Losser Buck, gave birth to one daughter and adopted another.

Her first book, *East Wind: West Wind* (1930), was immediately popular. Her second, THE GOOD EARTH (1931), tells the story of Chinese farmer Wang Lung and follows his family from poverty to wealth, while sympathetically chronicling the suffering and trials along the way. Its style combines the King James Bible with traditional Chinese narratives. *The Good Earth* became an instant American bestseller and won the Pulitzer Prize. Pearl followed it with the sequels *Sons* (1932) and *A House Divided* (1935). In 1936, she published BIOGRAPHIES of her mother and her father, entitled *The Exile* and *Fighting Angel*, notable for their sensitivity to her parents' circumstances and perspectives.

Having returned to the United States in 1934, she divorced John Buck and married Richard J. Walsh, her publisher. Together they adopted eight American-Asian children. In 1938, she became the first woman and the third American to be awarded the Nobel Prize in Literature. The Nobel Committee praised her especially 'for rich and genuine epic descriptions of Chinese peasants and for masterpieces of biography'. The American critical establishment was hostile to her being awarded the Prize, on the grounds that she had written too few books, was too much of a popular writer, and had been an expatriate. Buck defended her writing as influenced by the Chinese style of simple storylines.

Although she produced well over a hundred more books in all genres, her writing became increasingly didactic as her humanitarian work increased. In 1949, she founded Welcome House, to assist in the adoption of Asian-American children and, in 1964, she created the Pearl S. Buck Foundation, to support American-Asian children in Asia. At her death in 1973, there were twenty-five book manuscripts awaiting publication. SP

Bulstrode [Boulstred], Cecilia [Cicely] 1584–1609 Wit and courtier. As one of the Twickenham coterie of Lucy Harington, Countess of Bedford, she engaged in satirical and aphoristic exchanges called 'news'. Her 'News of my Morning Work' appeared in *A Wife* (1614), a collection of poems, characters and news by Sir Thomas Overbury and others. 'M[ist]ris. B' relates 'That women's fortunes aspire but by others powers. That a man with a female wit is the worst Hermaphrodite . . . That all this is news only to fools.'

Ben Jonson attacked Bulstrode in his 'Epigram on the Court Pucell [= Whore]', where he complained that 'with tribade [= lesbian] lust she force[s] a muse', although her 'news' is 'Equal with that, which for the best news goes'. However, when she died aged 25 his elegy hymned 'Sell Boulstred' as an exemplary virgin. She was also elegized by Donne, the Countess of Bedford, and others. HH

Burchill, Julie *c.*1960– Waspish, self-publicizing *enfant terrible* of English journalism and popular cultural criticism. Burchill grew up a working-class only child in Somerset, moving to London to work for the *New Musical Express* (after submitting a review of Patti Smith's *Horses*) in the heyday of punk rock. Aged 18 she co-authored *The Boy Looked at Johnny* (1978), an insider's reflections on punk, with her partner Tony Parsons; their later divorce was acrimonious. In the eighties she worked for *The Face*, the *Sunday Times* and the *Mail on Sunday*, among others, writing on subjects ranging from penises, beards and Lads to Madonna, Mrs Thatcher and Princess Diana. Her books from this period include *Damaged Gods: Cults and Heroes Reappraised* and *Girls on Film* (both 1986), a racy anatomy of actresses in Hollywood, and a voguish shopping and bonking novel, *Ambition* (1988). Some of her most representative journalism is collected in 1992's *Sex and Sensibility*. In that year also she co-founded, with her husband Cosmo Landesman and others, the *Modern Review: Low Culture for Highbrows*; a 1993 article transcribed her 'fax war' with the equally confrontational American critic Camille Paglia. MO'D

Burdekin, Katherine 1896–1963 British novelist whose feminist anti-fascist dystopian fiction has been rescued by feminist critics. Born into an upper-middle-class Derbyshire family and educated at Cheltenham Ladies' College (1907–13), though not allowed to study at Oxford, she married Australian barrister Beaufort Burdekin in 1915. Her service as a VAD nurse during World War I inspired her pacifism, which, together with her critique of the 'cult of masculinity', provided the themes for *Quiet Ways* (1930) and *Proud Man* (1934).

After the failure of her marriage in 1922, Burdekin settled in Cornwall with a woman friend and together they raised her two daughters and lived the life of 'eccentric country gentlewomen'. She published ten novels, but is best remembered for the proto-Orwellian *Swastika Night* (1937), written under the pseudonym 'Murray Constantine', which describes the futuristic world of a male-supremacist Hitlerdom where women are mere breeding animals. JVG

Burford, Barbara 1946– British writer, who broke new ground in black British women's writing when she brought out her anthology *A Dangerous Knowing: Four Black Women Poets* in 1984. A mother and an active feminist, she is committed to medical research, writes poetry, prose including SCIENCE FICTION, and plays, such as 'Patterns', which was commissioned by the Changing Women's Theatre and performed in 1984. In 'Women Talking', she expresses the power of black women together:

And we are mistresses
of strong, wild air,
leapers and sounders
of depths and barriers.

Her work challenges and refuses stereotypes of black women as victims, celebrating energies, love and lesbian relationships. Her short stories in *The Threshing Floor* (1986) follow women's lives in the ancient Kent city of Canterbury, exploring lesbian relationships and creativity. Other stories appear in *Everyday Matters: 2* (1984). In 'Miss Jessie' from this collection, a seemingly exhausted, kindly, maternal cleaner, 'invisible to the great mass of people' in the station in which she works, misnamed and ignored, takes home a Norwegian student ostensibly to care for, bath and feed him, surprisingly inheriting her Priest father's roles as she treats the young man (one of many?) as a sacrificial bullock. This is a culture-laden piece of horror. Burford also edited *Dancing the Tightrope: New Love Poems by Women* (1987). GW

Burger's Daughter (1979) Novel by Nobel-Prize-winning author NADINE GORDIMER. The burger of the title is Lionel Burger, son of an Afrikaner Nationalist family who turned to become a member of the Communist Party of South Africa. His daughter Rosa rejects her father's political legacy, which seems to negate the possibility of a private life, by going to Europe – only to return to accept the challenges of the South African political situation. Gordimer shows Rosa moving beyond the position her father was able to articulate – namely one in which private life and political commitment are mutually exclusive. Rosa, unlike her father, manages to forge a synthesis between the personal and the political. Like a number of Gordimer's other heroines, she makes for herself a personal identity which is valued as authentic pre-cisely because it is grounded in, and forged by means of, her political engagement. CCo

Burke, Janine [Carmel Brigitte] 1952– Australian art historian, critic and novelist, who has been important in developing a feminist understanding of visual and literary art in Australia. Burke was born and grew up in Melbourne. She has been active in the feminist movement since the 1970s, and was founding member of the collective which produced the feminist art magazine, *Lip*. Burke trained in Fine Art, and by the early 1980s had established herself as an art critic, publishing her landmark study of Australian women artists in 1980.

She began to find art criticism 'very inhibiting' and moved to fiction-writing. Her first novel, *Speaking* (1984), experimented with the use of women's voices as the sole medium for story-telling. Burke says that she was looking back at the era of the 1970s and 'the way ideas had changed people's lives during that time . . . These ideas of change and transformation and confrontation seem to be things I return to in all my novels.' Her understanding of the visual arts and the art world informed both *Second Sight* (1986) and the ironic *A Company of Images* (1989). Her most recent novel, *Lullaby* (1994), shows a self-conscious interest in writing as an art form. SPL

Burnett, Frances (Eliza) Hodgson 1849–1924 Manchester-born novelist, dramatist and short story writer whose children's classics – THE SECRET GARDEN (1911), *The Little Princess* (1905), *Little Lord Fauntleroy* (1886) – outlive her adult fiction, which includes early REALIST novels that prompted comparison with GASKELL, ELIOT and Dickens (see CHILDREN'S BOOKS); and ROMANCES for which she traded critical acceptance for popular appeal.

She immigrated, aged 16, to Tennessee with her widowed mother and siblings after the failure of the family business and soon began writing for ladies' journals. She married Swan Burnett in 1873 (divorced 1898) and entered the 'world of actual literature' with *That Lass o' Lowrie's* (1877), *Through One Administration* (1883) and other fiction that examined industrialism, working-class poverty, Anglo-American ideals, and modes of female power. Publication of the notorious *Little Lord Fauntleroy* (which she also dramatized) brought her enormous fame and proved to be the turning point in her abandonment of earlier realist approaches in favour of children's and popular adult fiction. She was notable in her effective use of dialect, and the best romances have daringly unconventional heroines (*A Lady of Quality*, 1896); some (*The Making of a Marchioness*, 1901) are adept social comedies. The best children's fiction is keenly perceptive of the child's view of loneliness and neglect (hardships, however,

Fanny Burney.

which are always redeemed through love, especially love of nature, and purposeful living). Her memoir, *The One I Knew the Best of All* (1893) is among her most interesting explorations of pastoral themes.

From 1887, she moved between Britain and America, becoming an American citizen in 1905 (she remarried in 1900 and divorced again in 1902). She died at her home on Long Island, a wealthy and eccentric celebrity with a love of fantasy and happy endings: 'With the best that was in me I have tried to write more happiness into the world.'   LDo

Burney [d'Arblay], Fanny [Frances] 1752–1840 British novelist, DIARIST and playwright, known for her witty reflections on her social milieu and her heroine-centred fiction. Daughter of the upwardly mobile musician and writer Charles Burney and his wife Esther Sleep, she began writing during her London childhood. Her mother's death when Frances was 10 was followed by her father's remarriage; the stepmother was unpopular with his six children. The young Burney mixed in high social and literary circles, and the actor and manager David Garrick was a close family friend. She combined a notorious shyness in public with a liveliness shown to family, close friends, and in her writing.

Burney's journal, begun in 1768 and continued throughout her life, was often cast in letters to her sister Susan. Acknowledging authorship of EVELINA (1778) after the novel's great success, she was favourably noticed by Samuel Johnson and Hester Thrale (see HESTER LYNCH PIOZZI). A second novel, *Cecilia* (1782), was also well received. In contrast, Burney's plays never gained a public, despite the enthusiasm of successive theatre managers. Her father and a fatherly friend, Samuel Crisp, squashed her plans to produce her first comedy, *The Witlings*. During her unhappy stint at court as an attendant to the Queen (1786–91), she worked on four tragedies: *Edwy and Elgiva*, the only one staged, was withdrawn after one performance at Drury Lane in 1795. In the late 1790s and early 1800s she wrote three comedies, but none were performed. Burney married Alexandre d'Arblay, a French émigré, in 1793; their son was born in 1794. Her court pension and the proceeds from her third novel, CAMILLA (1796), supported the family. From 1802 to 1812 she lived in France, and after her return published her final novel, THE WANDERER (1814). In her later years she wrote memoirs of her father.

Burney's novels combine satirical sketches of modern manners with serious sentiment. They focus on 'A Young Lady's Entrance Into the World' (subtitle of *Evelina*) and associated 'Female Difficulties' (subtitle of *The Wanderer*): difficulties which increase in magnitude from the comic social embarrassments of her first novel to the displacement, isolation, poverty and persecution suffered by her final heroine. She excels at delineating character through speech, whether the staccato miserliness of Cecilia's rich guardian ('Don't visit often; always costs money. Wish I had not come now; wore a hole in my shoe; hardly a crack in it before'), or the casual irreverence of Camilla's friend Mrs Arlbery, who discourages her romantic attachment to Edgar Mandlebert ('I do not wish to see her surrounded by brats, while a mere brat herself'). Though her later novels contain narrative too solemnly didactic for today's tastes, their powerful social analyses are increasingly valued. Her letters and journals include accounts of public scenes, like audiences with George III and a sight of Napoleon, and unshrinking renditions of personal experiences like her mastectomy. Burney's varied oeuvre, combining a strong comic sense with a pessimistic analysis of female social identity, gives us some of the best accounts we have of her time and place.   JSp

Burns, Joanne 1945– Australian poet. Born in Sydney, where she still lives, working as a teacher to support her habit: poetry writing. Now recognized as one of Australia's best prose poets, Burns has been regularly published since the 1960s, and issued her first collection, *snatch*, in 1972. The titles of some of her later collections give a good idea of her quirky humour and concentration on the often mundane facts of life in a big city toward the end of the 20th century: *ratz* (1973), *adrenalin flicknife* (1976), *ventriloquy* (1981), *blowing bubbles in the 7th lane* (1988), *on a clear day* (1992), *penelope's knees* (1996), *aerial photography* (1998). As these titles also indicate, Burns has persisted in the use of lower-case, long after it has ceased to be a fashionable way to write poetry. For her, it is part of an attempt to make poetry more humble, to bring it down to earth, as are her use of the prose-poem form, strongly vernacular language and interest in contemporary popular culture. These same qualities, along with the wit and humour of her work, have also contributed to Burns's success as a performance poet. More recently, however, she has become interested in writing longer sequences, such as 'mere anarchy', included in *aerial photography*.   EW

Burr [née Edwards], Esther 1732–58 Daughter of the New England theologian Jonathan Edwards, and mother of the politician Aaron Burr, Esther Burr's JOURNAL was first published in complete form in 1984. Burr's family had played a distinguished role in New England (her great-grandfather had been a founder of Connecticut, her father was a founder of Yale College), and she had received an education far superior to that given to most women in the 18th century. At the age of 20 she married Aaron Burr Sr, a Presbyterian pastor who, in 1746, had been elected president of the newly founded College of New Jersey (later Princeton University).

Her journal, which she dismissingly described as 'these broken, confused, jumbled thoughts', was written as a letter-journal, addressed to her friend Sarah Prince, of Boston, from October 1754 to September 1757. Her aim was not, in the great tradition of Puritan self-scrutiny, to interrogate the state of her soul. It is a more intimate and domestic document, recording the family life of a leading Presbyterian pastor, as well as observing the growth of her children. The framework through which Burr viewed her daily life was that of evangelical Christianity, and it is her faith and her need to accept God's will which give us a complex picture of the way religion effected an integration between the diverse roles she played, and the various levels of her life.   EH

Burton, Catherine 1668–1714 Autobiographer born at Bayton, near Bury St Edmunds in Suffolk. Her unwavering faith and religious conviction made her an exemplum of piety and community service. In 1694, she took up holy vows in the convent of the English Teresian nuns at Antwerp where she was repeatedly elected Mother Superior and became known as Mother Xaveria of the Angels. Following her death, the Jesuit Father Thomas Hunte compiled an account of her 'exemplary life, singular industry and care in keeping

up the spirit of their Order'. This collection, which fortunately includes her own writings, remained in manuscript until 1876 when it was edited by Henry James Coleridge with the title *An English Carmelite*. In the autobiography, the largest portion of the volume, Burton claims to have been instructed by St Xaverius to write 'my life and the favours God had done me', a task about which she expresses 'great affliction and anxiety'. However unwilling, Burton presents a complex account of the dynamics of ecclesiastical and communal authority, a nun's visionary faith and a woman's struggle to become the writer of her own life.   JRS

Burton [née Arundell], Isabel, Lady 1831–96 English TRAVEL WRITER who began her career as her husband's amanuensis and concluded it by writing her (possibly romanticized) autobiography and his BIOGRAPHY. The convent-educated Isabel came from an aristocratic Anglo-Catholic family. She married Richard Burton, an explorer, Arabist and a non-Catholic, in 1861 despite her family's objections. She shared her husband's travels and literary life, helping with the publication of his books, especially his translation of the *Arabian Nights*. She wrote two travel narratives: *The Inner Life of Syria* (1875) and *Arabia, Egypt, India* (1879). When Richard Burton died in 1890, she burned his translation of an erotic Persian text (because of its sexual content), and other papers. She based her *Life of Sir Richard Burton* (1893) on his journals and some memoirs he had dictated. *The Romance of Isabel, Lady Burton, Told In Part by Herself* appeared posthumously in 1897, edited by W. H. Wilkie.   KW

Bush (Banks), Olivia (Ward) 1869–1944 American poet and playwright, born on Long Island, New York, to parents of African and Native American descent. Her mother died when she was an infant and she was raised by an aunt in Providence, Rhode Island, where she received a high-school education. In 1889 she married Frank Bush. They had two children and were later divorced. She contributed to *Colored American Magazine* and self-published *Original Poems* (1899) and *Driftwood* (1914), which includes prose sketches of the waterfront and poems addressing white and black public figures. Later she directed plays for a Boston community centre. Her Easter pageant, *Memories of Calvary*, was published in 1915. She married Anthony Banks, ran a drama school with him in Chicago, then returned to New York to teach drama. Her plays fostering African-American and interracial culture, *Indian Trail*, *Shadows* and *A Shantytown Scandal*, were not produced in her lifetime.   JSG

Bush Studies (1902) BARBARA BAYNTON's famous short stories subvert the images of Australia projected by male writers of the 1890s: a predominantly male rural community defined by an egalitarian code of mateship. Baynton's stories (with the exception of 'Scrammy 'And') concentrate on the female experience of the bush, which is uniformly negative. Baynton's female characters struggle to survive in the face of the isolation and privation of their lives and against the prevalence of male violence. In 'Squeaker's Mate' the title character, paralysed by a falling tree when doing the work of a man, must endure the neglect of her husband and the arrival of his new woman. In Baynton's most famous story, 'The Chosen Vessel', a young woman, left alone by her cruel husband, barricades herself and her child against a swagman trying to force entry into her hut. Mistaking the sound of horses' hooves for possible salvation she escapes, only to be raped and killed by her attacker. The brutal REALISM of Baynton's stories combines with her use of GOTHIC horror, particularly in 'The Dreamer', to create a collection of considerable power.   SS

Busman's Honeymoon (1937) This is the last of DOROTHY L. SAYERS's full-length Lord Peter Wimsey stories. In it, he at last marries his Harriet, in a final courtship and wedding which we learn of through the EPISTOLARY exchanges between characters who have become old friends through the previous novels. Sayers commented that while 'a love interest is only an intrusion upon a detective story', in this book the opposite might be said to be true. The newly wed Wimseys' idyll in their Hertfordshire cottage is broken by the discovery of the corpse of their shady landlord in the cellar and the farcical local investigation which ensures involving the detective skills of the reluctant hero, who of course solves the mystery in the end. The novel *is* undoubtedly a love-story, and Wimsey's evolution, from the dilettante detective of the earlier novels to the middle-aged man sobbing in the arms of his wife on the morning of his prey's hanging, is complete.
                                                JLB

Busy Body, The (first performed in 1709) SUSANNA CENTLIVRE's successful comedy which, after initial problems with the rehearsal and the first performance at the Drury Lane Theatre, London, became very successful. The play, a witty intrigue comedy, depicts by stock means the plottings of two young couples, Miranda and Sir George Airy, Isabinda and Charles, against their fathers and guardians. The main character, though, is Marplot – the busybody – who through his inquisitiveness and eagerness to know everybody's secrets, repeatedly nearly mars the lovers' undertakings completely. The couples therefore have to oppose and outwit not only their adversaries but also their friend. *The Busy Body* ends happily but on a reflective note with Sir Jealous:

By my example let all parents move,
And never strive to cross their children's love;
But still submit that care to Providence above.

The play was initially performed thirteen times at the Drury Lane and, enthusiastically supported by the likes of David Garrick, held the stage until the late 19th century.   NBP

Butala [née Le Blanc], Sharon 1940– Canadian short-story writer, essayist and novelist who celebrates the lives of women in the rural communities of south-west Saskatchewan. She grew up in the northern village of Nipawin, one of five daughters of a French-Canadian father and a mother of English Protestant descent. She studied English and Art at the University of Saskatchewan, married, and taught for a decade in Nova Scotia.

After her second marriage to a rancher and her move to the Cypress Hills region of southern Saskatchewan she began her steady outpouring of fiction. Her collections of short stories, *The Queen of the Headaches* (1985) and *Fever* (1990), and her trilogy of novels, *The Gates of the Sun* (1986), *Luna* (1988) and *The Fourth Archangel* (1992), richly evoke the beauty of the land, the changing world of the farms and ranches, and the struggles of women to live and be creative in adverse circumstances. Her SPIRITUAL AUTOBIOGRAPHY, *The Perfection of the Morning: An Apprenticeship in Nature* (1994), was enormously popular and brought a wider readership, beyond the regional, for all her work. *Coyote's Morning Cry*, a short collection of meditations, appeared in 1995. Butala was instrumental in establishing The Wallace Stegner House as a writers' centre in the small town of Eastend, close to the Butala ranch. Because of its association with her work, a large part of the ranch has been purchased for preservation as a provincial park.   JG

Butcher Shop, The (1926) JEAN DEVANNY's first novel was initially banned in her home country of New Zealand on the grounds of indecency, and later in Australia, Boston and Nazi Germany. When interviewed she expressed her disappointment but stated 'I am not surprised my book has been banned . . . I know it is horrible, brutal, revolting. But life is brutal – brutal to women, working women . . . The title is chosen because the woman is butchered. It is a materialistic conception of history. Only a scientific Socialist will fully comprehend my object.' Devanny's analysis of women and class is at times confused and over-theorized yet her explicit representations of female sexuality and the overall boldness of her socialist ideas indicate a strength of social criticism common to New Zealand writing. Set on an isolated sheep-station ('Maunganui'), the novel relates the claustrophobic consequences of Margaret Messenger's affair with her husband's new worker, Glengarry, culminating in the death of the two men. The locale is well drawn with some strong metaphoric connections between animals, economic attitudes, sex and death, whilst Tutaki, the Messengers' friend, exemplifies Devanny's sympathy toward the Maori people.　　　MRE

Butler, Eleanor, Lady 1739–1829 Irish DIARIST, letter-writer and one of the 'Ladies of Llangollen'. Born into an aristocratic Catholic family, she was educated at a French convent before returning to the family home in Kilkenny. Still unmarried at 29, she developed a close friendship with SARAH PONSONBY, then a 13-year-old schoolgirl. Ten years later, in 1778, Butler and Ponsonby caused a scandal when they eloped together, setting up home in a cottage in Llangollen in North Wales.

Their life together, recorded in journals and in voluminous correspondence, was planned in accordance with the contemporary ideal of retirement promoted in works such as SARAH SCOTT's *Millennium Hall*, and based on study and self-improvement, simple living and SENSIBILITY. They indignantly denied suggestions of lesbianism, but their relationship and mode of life attracted widespread interest, and they were described as 'the two most celebrated virgins in Europe'.

Proud, quick-tempered and politically conservative, Lady Eleanor was generally regarded as the dominant partner, and the initial inspiration for the retirement was probably hers. However, the balance of power in the relationship shifted during the final years of her life, when, feeble and almost blind, she became increasingly dependent on the tenderness and commonsense of her 'beloved Sally'.　　　RR

Butler, Gwendoline 1922– British novelist, best known for DETECTIVE FICTION, born in south-east London and educated at Haberdashers' Aske's Hatcham School and Lady Margaret Hall, Oxford. Married Lionel Butler (d.1981), vice-principal of St Andrew's University and later principal of Royal Holloway College, London. Butler's first novel, *Receipt for Murder*, was published in 1956. She is a striking and prolific author whose work includes HISTORICAL and neo-GOTHIC fiction, as well as the more straightforward detective writing for which she is best known. She has two main series characters, Commander John Coffin of London's 'Second City' (Docklands) Police Force and – writing under the name 'Jenny Melville' – Charmain Daniels, the first policewoman in the genre (*Come Home and be Killed* was published in 1962) to break away from the cartoon-strip image previously associated with the type. First in the (imaginary) Thames Valley town of Deerham Hills, and then in Windsor, Charmian Daniels tackles many instances of gruesome

and demented wrong-doing, while at the same time rising steadily in her profession. The Coffin novels, likewise, are distinguished by intricate plotting, a grimly humorous approach and some nicely judged macabre ornamentation, including detached bodily parts, congealing pools of blood and the odd decaying rat. A bracing element – the author's tone – gets between the horrors envisaged and their potentially disturbing impact. The murderous instinct, in both the Butler and the Melville series of investigations, is often traced back to some kind of sexual aberration; but the whole drift of the novels is recreational rather than clinical, and their distinctive atmosphere, compounded of jauntiness and menace, procures an enthralling effect.　　　PC

Butler [née Grey], Josephine (Elizabeth) 1828–1906 English activist who campaigned for the rights of women, especially prostitutes who, under the 1864–9 Contagious Diseases Acts, were forced to undergo medical examinations for syphilis as a means of preventing disease among the prostitutes' clients, the British armed forces. The Ladies' National Association, headed by Butler, campaigned successfully for repeal of the Acts.

Butler's father, John Grey, was a prominent Northumbrian agricultural reformer and abolitionist, whose daughters were well educated at home. In 1851 Josephine married George Butler; they moved to Oxford, where she felt stifled by social conservatism: her memoirs record that she argued with men there over the morality of ELIZABETH GASKELL's novel *RUTH*. The Butlers eventually settled in Liverpool, where she turned to charitable work with destitute and fallen women after her daughter Eva's death in 1864. Her work moved gradually from the local to the national stage. She fought for women's higher education, gaining prominence in 1868 with her first pamphlet, *The Education and Employment of Women*. In 1869 she became head of the Ladies' National Association's campaign against the Contagious Diseases Acts, to which she objected on 'moral and religious, but also on constitutional and scientific grounds'. Butler's politics were grounded in the idea that women had the right and duty to defend Christian morality, but she also challenged Victorian gender roles, particularly the idea that women belonged in the domestic sphere.

Butler's public speaking and political writing on various subjects continued after the 1883 suspension of the Contagious Diseases Acts; she also wrote biographical notices of her father in 1869, and of her husband in 1892. Her *Personal Reminiscences of a Great Crusade* appeared in 1896.　　　KW

Butler, Octavia 1947– African-American writer of SCIENCE FICTION born in Pasadena, California, and

Mary Francis Butts: line drawing by Jean Cocteau, 1926–7.

matic sequel. Butler, who also writes short stories, is a difficult and rebarbative writer, whose message-oriented fictions are at once impressive and emotionally gruelling.   RK

Butler, Sarah ?–1735? Irish novelist, whose work was an early example of reviving interest in Gaelic culture and civilization. Little is known of Butler's life, but she may have been a member of the aristocratic Butler family of County Kilkenny. Although the Butlers had been among the most prominent of the Norman invaders of Ireland, they had subsequently integrated into local society, becoming, it was said, 'more Irish than the Irish themselves'. Certainly, Butler's work demonstrates a familiarity with Gaelic culture, and defends the native against the victorious English civilization.

Butler's *Irish Tales, or Instructive Histories for the Happy Conduct of Life*, a novel in ten parts, was among the earliest examples of Irish romantic fiction. The stories deal, according to the author, with 'heroic love, and all the patriot virtues', and in researching them she claimed to have consulted historians such as Geoffrey Keating and Peter Walsh, and to have studied 'those many transactions which made up the lives of the most potent Monarchs of the Milesian Race in that ancient Kingdom of Ireland'. *Irish Tales* appeared in 1716; it was reissued in 1719 and again, as *Milesian Tales*, in 1727. RR

Butterfly Ward, The (1976) MARGARET GIBSON's first collection, bearing her married name Gilboord, was critically acclaimed, awarded the City of Toronto Award, and reissued under the name Gibson by Oberon Press in 1994. It consists of six stories, two of which are set in the women's wards of mental hospitals. The title story is a lyrical account of a group of female patients routinely given shock therapy, insulin injections and lobotomies. 'Ada' describes a murderous attack by a lobotomized patient on another patient who belittles her efforts to remain creative. 'Making It' presents an exchange of letters between a former mental patient and a talented female impersonator. Gibson's intensity and first-hand experience of mental illness bring freshness to the theme that the declared insane often have more humane qualities than do the functioning members of contemporary society.

'Making It' was the basis for the 1977 film, *Outrageous*, directed by Richard Benner and starring Gibson's friend, Craig Russell, as the story's female impersonator. 'Ada' was made into a film for CBC-TV from a script by Gibson and Claude Jutra.   JG

Butts, Mary Francis 1890–1937 English novelist, poet, critic and short-story writer. Born in Dorset, she led a bohemian existence which took her to Paris, which she evokes in a story, 'Mappa Mundi', and where

raised by strict Baptist women. She first came to prominence with the 'Patternist' series from 1976 onwards – this series of novels, not published in order of their internal chronology, deals with the long-term consequences of the breeding programme of an African bodychanger, Doro, through the era of slavery and on into an apocalyptic plague-ridden post-human future. Butler deals with slavery and with gender issues most explicitly in *Kindred* (1979) in which a time-travelling black woman is repeatedly called upon to save the life of her slave-owning white ancestor in order to guarantee her own existence; savage moral ironies abound. These issues recur, along with broader environmental concerns and issues of power and responsibility, in the disturbing *Xenogenesis* sequence – *Dawn* (1987), *Adulthood Rites* (1987) and *Imago* (1989) – in which a few humans who have survived Earth's ecological collapse are more or less compelled to interbreed with three-sexed aliens, who want their more useful genes; the sequence portrays humanity as hopelessly flawed by aggression, and the aliens as not only radically different, but genuinely superior. *The Parable of the Sower* (1995) deals again with environmental collapse through the eyes of a young messianic protagonist whose empathetic powers both empower her and make her suffer. *The Parable of the Talents* (1998) is a the-she was friendly with notables such as Ford Madox Ford and Jean Cocteau. She and her first husband, John Rodker, were also briefly members of Aleister Crowley's occult community in Italy. She initially hoped for 'a poet's success', but in 1921 the serialization in the *Little Review* of her first novel, *Ashe of Rings* (begun in 1916 and published as a whole in 1925), launched her career as a prose writer. Amazingly prolific given her short and eventful life, she produced a book of stories (*Speed the Plough*, 1923), two novels with Grail motifs (*Armed with Madness*, 1928, and *The Death of Felicity Taverner*, 1932), two more HISTORICAL NOVELS – (*The Macedonian*, 1933, and *Scenes from the Life of Cleopatra*, 1935) – and an autobiography (*The Crystal Cabinet*, 1937). This output is prodigious, given Butts's hectic life, which included numerous emotionally draining love-affairs with both men and women, spells of drug dependency, a nervous breakdown and poverty. Her posthumous book, *Last Stories* (1938), was withdrawn from publication because of a threatened libel suit. Her reputation has been revived recently, partly through the efforts of a young scholar named Nathalie Blondel.　　　　　　　　　　　　　　　BWB

By Grand Central Station I Sat Down and Wept

(1945) Drawing heavily on classical myth and biblical imagery – the title invokes the 'Rivers of Babylon' psalm – ELIZABETH SMART's ten-part prose poem fictionalizes her love-affair with the married poet, George Barker, in America at the start of World War II. Dense in metaphor and allusion, the rhythmic narrative is relentless in its communication of passion and suffering, of the 'kisses whose chemicals are even more deadly if undelivered'. Although it's a tale of martyrdom, an elegy for the doomed wife and the eventually rejected lover, the book is an ardent celebration of the ephemeral yet transformative joys of love and nature. After all, Smart decrees, 'there is no beauty in denying love'.

Re-issued twenty-one years after its first appearance, this emotive, blissfully obsessive book has enjoyed cult status ever since. BRIGID BROPHY much admired it; ANGELA CARTER, deploring and deriding its passive lyricism, suggested instead, 'By Grand Central Station I tore off his balls'.　　　　　　　　　　JAH

Byatt [née Drabble], A(ntonia) S(usan) 1936–

English novelist, short-story writer and critic. A.S. Byatt was born in Sheffield, the elder sister of MARGARET DRABBLE. Educated at The Mount School, York, she read English at Newnham College, Cambridge. After a year at Bryn Mawr College, Pennsylvania, as an English-Speaking Union Fellow, and a year of post-graduate work at Somerville College, Oxford, Byatt embarked on a career which encompassed writing, literary criticism and teaching posts at the Central School of Art and Design, and University College, London. She became a full-time writer in 1983, and was created a CBE in 1990.

Byatt has become one of the most widely respected and senior figures in postwar literary fiction, despite some critical reservation about the effect of her work's high intellectual content on its aesthetic quality. Drawing on the moral seriousness and density of the 19th-century novel, perhaps in particular the work of GEORGE ELIOT, her writing is allusive and metaphorical, blending REALISM with aspects of MODERNIST and POSTMODERNIST fictional styles, and characterized by an interest in both arts and science.

Her first novel, *Shadow of a Sun*, was published in 1964, and explored the effect of a novelist on his daughter; *The Game* (1967) followed the difficult relationship between two sisters, one a bestselling novelist and the other an Oxford don. In 1979, she published *The Virgin in the Garden*, the first novel in a projected tetralogy; to date, *Still Life* (1985) and *Babel Tower* (1996) have followed. Set in Yorkshire in 1952–3, *The Virgin in the Garden* centres around a production of a new verse drama, *Astraea*. The brilliant and precocious Frederica takes the part of ELIZABETH I and, despite the large cast of intricately drawn characters, she remains the central figure of subsequent novels. *Still Life* follows her progress to Cambridge, and also focuses on the frustrated ambitions of her sister, Stephanie. *Babel Tower* intersperses Frederica's attempts to escape a brutal marriage and forge her own career with an account of an obscenity trial.

This ambitious and highly complex series of novels can be seen as Byatt's most important fictional project, but it was eclipsed by the enormous success of *POSSESSION* (1990), which won the Booker Prize. A beautifully-constructed story of literary detective work, it concerns the efforts of two scholars to piece together the interlinking lives of two fictional Victorian poets, Randolph Henry Ash and Christabel LaMotte. *Possession* reflects Byatt's interest in the 19th-century intellectual consciousness, a theme which featured in two novellas, published as *Angels and Insects* in 1992.

Byatt has also published four collections of short stories, and her critical works include an acclaimed study of IRIS MURDOCH, *Degrees of Freedom* (1965). Selected writings, *Passions of the Mind*, appeared in 1991.　　　　　　　　　　　　AC

C

Cable, [Alice] Mildred 1878–1952 and **French, Francesca** 1871–1960 British TRAVEL WRITERS who worked for the China Mission. Cable, a Guildford draper's daughter, who studied medicine at London University, met French and her elder sister Evangeline, both educated in Geneva, in Hwochow where the trio ran a successful girls' school from 1902. In 1923 the Mission granted the trio's application to carry the faith to the Gobi Desert, where they travelled and taught till 1938. They lectured on the Gobi on their leaves in Britain, and Cable and Francesca wrote a series of books, including *Through Jade Gate to Central Asia* (1927) and *A Desert Journal: Letters from Central Asia* (1934), based on letters smuggled out in fragments to evade censorship and then reassembled. Their major work, *The Gobi Desert* (1942), written after war enforced a permanent return to Britain, summarizes their travels as a single journey. It won medals from the Royal Scottish Geographic Society and the Royal Central Asia Society for its contribution to geographic knowledge; it is also a spiritual allegory, an elegy for Western Christians' 'loss' of China, and a feminist enquiry into the possibilities for changed conditions for the women of Central Asia. In a sustained emphasis on collaboration and self-abnegation, the trio's individual personalities are seldom mentioned in the books, never in *The Gobi Desert*, and they are presented as one and indivisible. They settled together in Dorset, for the rest of their lives, frequently travelling to campaign energetically for the Bible Society.   AT

Cadigan, Pat 1953– Working name of US SCIENCE FICTION writer Patricia K. Cadigan, now resident in Britain. She made her name in the field partly by editing the magazine *Shayol* (1977–85), partly by short stories from 1978 onwards. *Patterns* (1989) collects this early work, often assimilated to cyberpunk. Cyberpunk was usually a boy's game; Cadigan added a mature perception of where this game left women – she is often cited by theorists like Sadie Plant as being as prophetic as William Gibson. Where women in Gibson's novels are either naive resourceful waifs or genial psychotics, Cadigan portrays competent fallible survivors. *Mindplayers* (1987) and *Fools* (1992) are near-future thrillers which play, somewhat formulaically, with inventive scenarios about the engineering of

human personality. The longer *Synners* (1989) involves real individual and social jeopardy as infant Artificial Intelligences derived from computer viruses mature at the expense of the human beings interfaced with the machines they inhabit. Where the other two novels focus on the limited perceptions of their protagonists, *Synners* makes thrilling use of multiple viewpoints to create suspenseful pace and kaleidoscopic locales.   RK

Caesar, Mary 1677–? The wife of MP and Tory conspirator, Charles Caesar, her five-volume journal, written between 1724 and 1741, displays wide-ranging interest in politics, poetics, and the lives of prominent public figures. In it, she copies Whig and Tory ballads, comments on literary works and records the details of her many correspondences and friendships. She had a special relationship with Alexander Pope, exchanged many letters with him, and commented on manuscript copies of his work. Although rough and sometimes disjointed, her journal reveals insight, a sense of whimsy and good humour, and a creative mind. Herself a poet, she authored a four-line verse which was for generations mistakenly attributed to Pope. His opening, 'On all-accomplished Caesar! on thy shelf / Is room for all Pope's works – and Pope himself', invited her response:

> Tis true great Bard Thou on my shelf shall lye
> With Oxford, Cowper, Noble Strafford by.
> But for thy Windsor a New Fabrick Raise
> And there Triumphant sing thy soverain's Praise.

She would have been chagrined to learn that critics misinterpreted 'Caesar' and 'soverain' as references to George II, not to 'accomplished', Mary and *her* valued 'soverain', James II.   JRS

Caffyn [née Hunt], Kathleen 'Iota' 1853–1926 Irish novelist and short-story writer. Born in County Tipperary to Louisa Goring and William Hunt of Waterloo House, she was educated at home by English and German governesses. At the age of 21 she left for nurse's training in London. Early in her nursing career she met and married Stephen Mannington Caffyn, surgeon and writer. The couple emigrated to Sydney in 1880, and in 1883 moved to Melbourne where Kathleen helped found the District Nursing Society of Victoria and began her literary career with occasional contributions to Australian newspapers and with the composition of her first and most successful novel, *The Yellow Aster* (1894), which was published in London after the Caffyns' return in 1893. The novel's echoes of Zola and Ibsen created a minor scandal and 'Iota' became for anti-feminists a byword for the dangerous excesses of the NEW WOMAN. She was a frequent contributor to literary journals and published sixteen more novels – none matching the success or notoriety of the first – including *Children of Circumstance* (1894), *A Comedy of Spasms* (1895) and *Dorinda and Her Daughter* (1910), the last being one of only two of her works to draw upon her twelve years in Australia.   MO'C

Caird [née Alison], (Alice) Mona 1854–1931 British novelist and essayist who achieved notoriety in the 1880s and 1890s through her anti-marriage polemics. Her family was Scottish gentry, and in 1877 she married James Caird, a Scottish landowner; they had one son. She lived in London and Scotland, and was part of the progressive literary milieu of the 1890s. Early novels (published under the pseudonym 'G. Noel Hatton') were unsuccessful, but she became well known in 1888 with her *Westminster Review* article 'Marriage', which sparked a heated public debate by arguing that marriage was a failure. In 1889 she published (under her own name) a melodramatic feminist novel, *The Wings of Azrael*, followed by *A Romance of the Moors* (1891). Her essays were collected in *The Morality of Marriage* (1897). Her best-known novel, THE DAUGHTERS OF DANAUS (1894), portrays a talented woman thwarted by her marriage and family. She took on the system of marriage again with *The Stones of Sacrifice* (1915), but she also wrote anti-vivisection books, a fantasy, a TRAVEL book, and the SCIENCE FICTION story *The Great Wave* (1931), her last novel. KW

Califia, Pat 1954– American lesbian polemicist and writer of fiction. Brought up a Mormon, Califia studied psychology at San Francisco State University and the University of San Francisco. Active on the anti-authoritarian side in the 1980s debates within feminism about censorship and lesbian sadomasochism, she produced witty polemics, many of them collected in *Public Sex: The Culture of Radical Sex* (1994); there is a pronounced utopian strain in her feminism. She wrote the advice column in *The Advocate*, the largest US lesbian and gay newspaper, and wrote and edited lesbian sex manuals, such as *Sapphistry* (1980) which stressed safe sex and sexual diversity. The erotic short story collection *Macho Sluts* (1988) is redeemed from the programmatic or arousing by conceptual wit and elegant refusal of standard expectations. A rather less successful novel *Doc and Fluff* (1990) draws heavily on SCIENCE FICTION tropes and therapy as its eponymous couple move through a devastated America. RK

Calisher, Hortense 1911– American fiction-writer and reviewer. She was born in New York City and educated at Hunter College High School and Barnard College, where she studied Philosophy. After graduating in 1932, she worked as an investigator with the New York Department of Public Welfare, gathering experiences that later appeared in her fiction. In 1935 she married Heaton B. Heffelfinger, an engineer; they had two children and later divorced. In 1959 she married novelist Curtis Arthur Harnack; from 1971 to 1986, they lived at Yaddo Artists' Colony in Saratoga Springs, New York, where he was the director.

She began publishing in the *New Yorker* in the 1940s and thereafter contributed widely to literary periodicals. Her first collection of stories (some autobiographical), *In the Absence of Angels*, appeared in 1951; later collections include *Tale for the Mirror* (1962), *Extreme Magic* (1964) and *Saratoga, Hot* (1985). Calisher's stated aim in her cool but shocking short fiction is to serve up 'an apocalypse . . . in a very small cup'. Her slow-paced but finely crafted novels range from sexual farce (*Queenie*, 1971) and ribald tale (*The Bobby-Soxer*, 1986) to SCIENCE FICTION (*Journal from Ellipsia*, 1965) and space odyssey (*Mysteries of Motion*, 1983). Calisher has taught in several universities in the United States and Europe, served as president of American PEN (1986) and the American Academy of the Institute of Arts and Letters (1987-90), and received numerous prestigious grants. Her autobiographical works include *Herself* (1972) and *Kissing Cousins* (1988).   JG

Callaghan, Mary Rose 1944– Irish novelist born and educated in Dublin. She taught in Ireland and England, and then lived for twenty years between Ireland and the United States, before moving back with her husband to settle in Bray, Co. Wicklow, Ireland.

Callaghan's novels feature a female protagonist whose emotional turmoil and entanglements are portrayed with zany wit and a light touch. Collectively, they provide a snapshot history of feminist consciousness in Ireland in the last thirty years – appropriately, three were published by the Irish feminist presses, Arlen House and Attic. The backdrop to *Mothers* (1984), centering on the pregnant protagonist's decision whether or not to choose motherhood, was the 1983 campaign to make abortion in the Republic of Ireland unconstitutional as well as illegal. *Emigrant Dreams* (1996) dramatizes the female narrator's vacillating belief in testimonies of incest and domestic violence, undermined by what she perceives as American political correctness. The present is counterpointed with the equally ambivalent past by the narrator's missions to record her family history in Irish-American politics. *The Awkward Girl* (1990) , a BILDUNGSROMAN unfolding a young woman's troubled personae from 1960's schoolgirl to semi-successful artist and early death, is complemented by the narrower focus on adolescent dilemmas – such as family relationships – of *Confessions of a Prodigal Daughter* (1985) and *The Last Summer* (1997).

The strength of Callaghan's fiction lies in humorous insight – focused through the protagonist's self-consciousness, hostage to her own or her family's eccentricity – which throws a powerful light on Irish middle-class conformity and hypocrisy. The later novels expand the milieu to the United States and England. She has also written a young adult novel, *Has Anyone Seen Heather?* (1990) and a biography, *Kitty O'Shea* (1989).   JFG

Callwood, June 1924– Born in Chatham, Ontario, she began her career as a journalist on the *Brantford Expositor* and became a reporter for the Toronto *Globe and Mail* where she was a columnist from 1975 to 1977 and from 1983 to 1989. She has also been a freelance journalist since 1946. June Callwood has written about and taken part in actions regarding drug addiction, social justice, homelessness, AIDS and women's issues. She has co-written and written numerous books: *The Law is not for Women* (with Marvin Zuker, 1976), *Emma: The True Story of Canada's Unlikely Spy* (1984), *Twelve Weeks in Spring* (1986), *Jim: A Life with Aids* (1988), *The Sleepwalker* (1990), *National Treasures* (1994) and *No Easy Answer* (1995). In *Emma*, she writes about a case of injustice from the stand-point of civil libertarianism. *Twelve Weeks in Spring* describes how the friends of Margaret Frazer, a terminally ill retired teacher, organized themselves to look after her so that she could die at home.

Callwood has also worked on radio and TV, hosting for CBC the series, 'Human Sexuality' and 'Generations' (1966), 'In Touch' (1975–8), and, for Vision TV, 'National Treasures' (1991–6) which formed the basis of her book by the same title. Activism, an important part in Callwood's life, informs her writings. She has been the director-founder of Nellie's Hostel for Women (1974–8 and 1986–92), of Jessie's Centre for Teenagers (1987–9) and of the Casey House Hospice (1992–3). She has received sixteen honorary doctorates, the Order of Ontario (1988) and is an Officer of the Order of Canada.   GHN

Cambridge, Ada 1844–1926 Australian poet and prolific serial novelist. She grew up in England, the daughter of a Norfolk gentleman farmer, and was educated at home by governesses, with a brief period at boarding school. In her early twenties she published two volumes of hymns. In 1870 she married George Cross, an Anglican clergyman, and travelled with him to Australia.

Cambridge's life in Australia was the conventional routine of the Anglican clergyman's wife – bearing and caring for children, assisting in the parish, and settling her family in one country rectory after another as they moved around rural Victoria. But she soon began publishing stories in the Victoria press – the first was 'Up the Murray' in 1873. By the end of her life she had published two books of poetry, two books of reminiscences, more than twenty novels in book form and numerous other newspaper serials.

The evidence of her poetry and later novels – that she engaged with contemporary arguments about women's rights, the place of religion and economic justice – may be overlooked given the volume of conventional ROMANCES she wrote. Cambridge called herself a 'Meredithian' because of her admiration of George Meredith's novels, and her most ambitious novel, *A MARKED MAN* (1890), takes its cue from Meredith's *The Ordeal of Richard Feverel*. At her best, Cambridge is witty and satirical; her characters, even when most committed to social justice, are likely to encounter practical obstacles to their ideals. In *A Woman's Friendship* (1889), for example, her two women reformers are forced to confront their own sexual weakness; and her hero in *A Marked Man* fails to implement the liberal ideals he espouses. These two novels, with *MATERFAMILIAS* (1898) and her poetry, establish Cambridge's claims as a major figure of late 19th-century Australian literature.   SPL

Cameron, Anne 1938– Canadian poet, novelist and screenwriter also known as 'Cam Hubert', born in Nanaimo, British Columbia. Her books include *Dreamspeaker* (1978), *Daughters of Copper Woman* (1981), *How Raven Freed the Moon, How the Loon Lost her Voice* (1985), *Child of her People* (1987) and *Spider Woman* (1988). *Dreamspeaker* won the 1978 Gibsons Award for Literature and the screenplay won the Canada Film Award for Screenplay in 1977. She has described as her 'main wish in this life' that 'women would stop volunteering ... and, instead, use their energy to just go out in the streets . . . and YELL'. Female emancipation, empowerment and escape are major themes of *The Journey* (1986), set in the Canadian West in the 1800s and telling the story of Anne and Sarah fleeing from patriarchy across the plains. Heroines here can stride and ride, shoot and bash, in an attempt to 'solve the problem of women taking action in a world which is hostile to action-taking females'. Her books celebrate West-Coast native myths, weaving together mythic and imaginary characters and exploring the spiritual and social power of women. However, although her earlier stories draw from native Canadian myth, she has subsequently stated her reluctance to use this native Canadian voice. Her more recent works draw from goddess and Amazon mythology, and include *Stubby Amberchuk and the Holy Grail* (1987) and *Women, Kids and Huckleberry Wine* (1989).   CSt

Camilla, Or, A Picture of Youth (1796) The third novel by FANNY BURNEY, *Camilla* explores the characteristic Burney themes of social and financial embarrassment, in a story that combines wit and satire with moralizing social comment. It also contains one of the most priggish and unattractive heroes in 18th-century fiction. Camilla is playful, beautiful, lively and intelligent, but also vain and impulsive. She has to learn, in the course of a long novel, to keep control of both her passions and her money, enabling her eventually to obtain the approval of the virtuous Edgar Mandlebert, and with it the dubious privilege of his hand in marriage. In its reorientation of fictional didacticism toward issues of manners, financial prudence and self-restraint, and in the character of its austere and exacting hero, *Camilla* clearly foreshadows the work of JANE AUSTEN. Despite ambivalent reviews on first appearance, the novel was a great financial success, and the copyright sold for £1,000.

LBe

Campbell, Hazel D(orothy) 1940– Jamaican short-story writer who began writing the short stories about Kingston life for which she is known in the early 1970s. Her first collection, *The Rag Doll and Other Stories*, was published in 1978. Two additional collections have appeared since: *Woman's Tongue* (1985) and *Singerman* (1992). Campbell's deceptively simple fiction explores the function of religion and compassion in healing the shattered cultures of the Caribbean. It is a fiction which, under the veil of social commentary, depicts characters who must find their own path to resurrection amidst the chaos and sense of doom of a fractured society. One of her best and most representative stories is 'See Me in Me Benz An T'ing (Like the Lady Who Lived on That Island Remote)'. Campbell has published various tales for CHILDREN, chief among them *Tilly Bummie and Other Stories* (1993) and a series commissioned by UNESCO to incorporate health concepts into reading skills materials, which includes *Sharon's Song* (1988), *Walk Good: 'Mind Makka Juk You'* (1988, a booklet on AIDS prevention), and *Juice Box and Scandal: Three Stories on the Environment* (1992). Campbell lives in Kingston, where she works as a teacher and public relations officer.

LP-G

Campbell, Maria 1940– Saskatchewan-born First Nations orator and film writer who interweaves historical narrative and autobiography to convey 'what it is like to be a half-breed woman living in Canada'. Her first autobiographical novel, HALFBREED (1973), charts her move from childhood on the edge of an oral-based hunter–gatherer community to her subsequent battles with urban isolation, racism and drug abuse. This book has been extremely influential on subsequent First Nations writers in Canada, and has provided a vocabulary to challenge cultural stereotypes. After the publication of two revisionary histories for CHILDREN in First Nations schools, *People of the Buffalo* (1976) and *Riel's People* (1978), Campbell collaborated with the non-Aboriginal actress, Linda Griffiths. The 'theatrical transformation' of Campbell's life and the fraught emotional exchanges that took place between Griffiths and Campbell during the play's production are detailed in *The Book of Jessica* (1989). Campbell views her writing as inseparable from the community of First Nations people she writes for. This is exemplified by *Stories of the Road Allowance People* (1995), a poetry collection that combines Métis dialect and story-telling conventions to re-animate the cultural traditions of Métis and First Nations people.

SCM

Campbell, Marion 1948– Australian novelist, whose fiction offers a playful critique of feminist theory. Several critics regard her second novel, *Not Being Miriam* (1988), as the most challenging feminist novel by an Australian, yet it hardly surpasses the verve and brilliance of her first, *Lines of Flight* (1985).

Campbell was born in Sydney. Her father, a scientist, died in an accident in 1952 and her schoolteacher mother took the family to live in Perth. Campbell studied French at Australian universities, and spent 1971-2 in Provence. This experience of the aftermath of French student radicalism of the late 1960s contributed to her depiction of the period in *Lines of Flight*. She returned to Perth, teaching in high schools and then at Murdoch University. In 1974 she gave birth to a son, and in 1990 she had a second child, a daughter.

Her two novels participate in the feminist debate about form and power by means of narratives and language which constantly signal the act of creation. She says, 'I always had trouble writing too much fiction into academic stuff and romancing certain ideas when I write fiction, of writing poetry when I'm meant to be doing prose, of painting when I'm meant to be writing. It's one big borderline disorder from which I try to create patterns.' Campbell has also written two pieces for performance: *Dr Memory in the Dreamhome* (1990) and *Ariadne's Understudies* (1992).

SPL

Campbell, Meg 1937– New Zealand poet. Born in Palmerston North, New Zealand, she left her acting career to marry the poet Alistair Te Ariki Campbell in 1958 (after his divorce from New Zealand poet FLEUR ADCOCK). A combination of post-natal depression after her first child, stress and bipolar depression led to a nervous breakdown. Campbell spent twenty-one years (1958–79) coping with psychiatric illness, including treatment by electro-convulsive therapy (ECT). She began writing poetry while in Porirua Psychiatric Hospital. In March 1978 her first poem, 'Solitary confinement', was published in the New Zealand

Listener and she was on the road to recovery. In 1981 she won the PEN Best First Book Award for Poetry with *The Way Back*. It was followed by *A Durable Fire* (1982), *Orpheus and Other Poems* (1990) and *The Better Part* (1998). Campbell's poetry is marked by CONFESSIONAL candour, a strong voice and good humour. She examines the treatment of women in mental institutions with sympathy and wit. Other themes include familial and personal relationships, the landscape (particularly the Kapiti coast where she and her husband raised four children) and challenges to the male God. She employs FAIRY TALE and personae from Polynesian mythology to address issues of gender, sexuality and social role.

AM/JMcK

Cancer Journals, The (1980) AUDRE LORDE's courageous work on her survival of breast cancer is as much a powerful polemic on the American medical establishment as it is a memoir. Lorde frequently figured herself as embattled, calling herself a 'black woman warrior poet', and cancer was one of her most pernicious enemies. The JOURNAL entries, from before and after her mastectomy, describe her fear and pain with rage, humour and a passionate honesty. They alternate with essays in which Lorde radically challenges the assumptions that post-mastectomy women should have a prosthesis, and that cancer sufferers have illness-prone psychologies (a notion also critiqued in SUSAN SONTAG's *ILLNESS AS METAPHOR*). In a work bold for its time, Lorde honoured her feminist commitment to shattering destructive silences. 'My silence had not protected me. Your silence will not protect you.' In its eloquence and directness the book was a great help to other cancer sufferers, and was augmented by Lorde's later reflections on her ongoing struggle against cancer in *A Burst of Light* (1988), published four years before the disease finally won its long battle over this vital American poet. – SB

Cannan, May Wedderburn 1893–1973 British poet, novelist and memoirist, best known for poetry of World War I. Born in Oxford of Scots parents, she was prevented from training as an actress by the outbreak of war. She had joined the Red Cross Voluntary Aid Detachment when she was 18; when Britain entered the war, three years later, she helped set up a hospital in a local school. She spent a month as a volunteer worker in a soldiers' canteen in Rouen, France, in addition to doing volunteer nursing, and in 1918 she began work in intelligence in the War Office in Paris. After the war she worked at King's College, London, and at the Athenaeum Club as assistant librarian, the first woman to hold that position; she also married Brigadier P.J. Slater, an admirer of her poetry, after having lost a fiancé to pneumonia in 1919. Supportive of those who fought, she published three books of

non-modernist poems: *In War Time* (1917), *The Splendid Days* (1919) and *The House of Hope* (1923), all with themes of patriotism, male sacrifice and female loss; one novel, *The Lonely Generation* (1934); and an unfinished, posthumously issued memoir, *Grey Ghosts and Voices* (1976).

HB

Cannibal Galaxy, The (1983) The title of CYNTHIA OZICK's second novel refers to Europe perceived as a carnivorous monster eating its unwanted children. Although the event of the Holocaust is not described directly, it functions as a bleak memory in the life of its main protagonist, Principal Joseph Brill. Brill's life is an attempt to reconcile the high culture associated with the France of his childhood with the 'middleness' of America. However, the novel goes beyond such oppositions, which are put in question by a number of women that appear in Brill's life. Presenting the dilemmas concerning the proper structure of education and the notion of achievement faced by Principal Brill, Ozick raises issues about the relationship between genius and gender as well as that between nature and nurture. Although Brill seems to lose out in his attempt to rationalize the world, the novel does not postulate a straightforward shift from reason to feeling; instead, it teaches one to follow the attitude of 'the unsurprise of surprise', which excludes certainty, and leaves room for the unpredictable. JZ

Cannibals and Missionaries (1979) MARY McCARTHY's last novel, reflecting ruefully once again on the shortcomings of the liberal imagination. A Boeing 747 carrying a delegation of millionaire art collectors and liberals bent on investigating conditions under the Shah is hijacked en route to Iran. The hijackers are led by a Dutch former art student, Jeroen, who ransoms the owners for their priceless old masters, and the story hinges on the hijackers' dilemma: how to convert the value of the works of art into the political purpose of forcing the Hague out of NATO? It is a novel of ideas, short on thought and personality. McCarthy herself described her own dilemma in a letter to her friend HANNAH ARENDT: 'It is sad to think that one's fictions, ie one's creative side, cannot learn anything. I have learned, I think, but they, or it, haven't.' The voice she used so brilliantly in her essays, journalism and memoirs is muted in the fiction. TC

Cannon, Moya 1956– Irish poet. Cannon exemplifies some of the best-quality work produced by the 1990s generation of those successive waves of women poets who have challenged and energized Irish writing since the 1970s. Born in Dunfanaghy, County Donegal, Cannon studied History and Politics at University College, Dublin, and at Corpus Christi College, Cambridge, before going on to teach in a school for adolescent travellers in Galway. In her collections *Oar* (1990) and *The Parchment Boat* (1997), Cannon's keynote theme is redemption through states of loss. She focuses intensely on landscape and language as an intersecting network of desire and power. Her work explores the fragile balance between experiences of alienation and of grace, in poems which first resist then gradually admit human presence, including that of the speaker. Her recent work demonstrates a more honed political attentiveness to the intersections between the aesthetic act and the inheritance of colonization. The earlier dominance of a revelatory tone in her writing yields toward the more spacious and celebratory voices of accidental epiphany as a condition of faith:

> ... today I brought back
> three bones of a bird,
> eaten before it was hatched
> and spat or shat out with its own broken shell ...
>
> There are things which can neither be written, nor
>   spoken, nor read; ...
>
> the bones hold in their emptiness
> the genesis of the first blown note.
> ('Scríob').   CCI

captivity narrative Considered one of the few distinctively American literary genres, the 17th- and 18th-century captivity narrative chronicles an Indian raid on a COLONIAL settlement, followed by the details of the author's captivity and eventual return to the colonial community. MARY ROWLANDSON's 1682 publication of *The Soveraignty and Goodness of God, Together With the Faithfulness of His Promises Displayed: Being a Narrative of the Captivity and Restauration of Mrs Mary Rowlandson* is the first printed account of New English captivity, and served to define the genre. The primary goal of the captivity narrative is didactic; prior to printing, many captivity narratives were first told as embedded narratives within sermons. The narrative explains why God visited hardship on the community, and suggests that the release of the captive is evidence of his or her salvation. Thus, the account testifies to both the awful wrath and the mercy of God. Colonial readers were also interested in the first-hand accounts of native American life, and many captivity narratives offered detailed descriptions of native society, its rituals, foodstuffs and other intimate aspects of daily life. Additionally, the vivid and often lurid tales of the Indian raid and the emotional trials of captivity, followed by the dramatic release, had great appeal for colonial society which was devoid of fiction. Captivity narratives served as heroic tales, the heroes being members of their own community of believers.

While many of the captivity narratives authored by both men and women follow a codified format, there is variation in these accounts. Hannah Dustan's captivity narrative (1701), included in Cotton Mather's *Magnalia Christi Americana*, describes how she effected her release by killing and scalping her captors. ELIZABETH HANSON's *God's Mercy surmounting Man's Cruelty, Exemplified in the Captivity and Redemption of Elizabeth Hanson* (1728) highlights French and Indian viciousness, at the expense of downplaying the role of God's providence. Mary Jemison's *A Narrative of the Life of Mrs. Mary Jemison Who Was Taken by the Indians in the Year 1755 When Only About Twelve Years of Age and Has Continued to Reside Amongst Them to the Present* (1824) speaks with great fondness of her adoption by the Seneca and many happy years of married life within the tribe.

Captivity narratives continue to influence 19th-century fiction from James Fenimore Cooper's *The Deerslayer* to Herman Melville's *Typee*. However, many 19th-century women authors appropriate this genre to new purpose. LYDIA MARIA CHILD's heroine in HOBOMOK (1824) willingly marries a native American man and lives among his people, while CATHERINE SEDGWICK's HOPE LESLIE (1827) revises the traditional captivity plot to include the enslavement of native Americans by European colonists, the willing adoption of Puritans into native tribes, and the captivity within English society of Puritan women who are married to Indian men.   DZB

Carbery, Ethna (Anna Johnston MacManus)

1866–1902 Irish poet. Born into a middle-class Catholic Belfast family with a strongly nationalist background, Anna Johnston began to publish poetry when she was still at school. Most of her poetry is patriotic in tone, and she also published versions of Irish legends. She had a close friendship and political and literary association with ALICE MILLIGAN. Widely published in journals, periodicals and newspapers, Johnston collaborated with Milligan to produce two magazines, first the *Northern Patriot* (1895) and subsequently the *Shan Van Vocht (An tSean Bhean Bhocht* / The Poor Old Woman), which they edited and produced jointly from 1896 to 1899. Both magazines had political as well as literary aspirations and content. Her style was accessible, romantic and balladic. She was a vice-president of Inghinidhe na hÉireann (Daughters of Ireland), an organization of nationalist working women formed in 1900. Books include *The Four Winds of Eirinn* (1902) and *In the Celtic Past* (1904). Her work is featured with that of Alice Milligan and Seumas MacManus, together with an introduction by the latter, in *We Sang for Ireland* (1950).   LM

Carey [née Jackson, Payler], Mary, Lady 1609/12–

1680 Writer of religious meditations and poems of

maternal grief. Daughter of Sir John Jackson of Berwick, she lived fashionably until, at 18, a serious illness precipitated religious conversion. Her first husband, Sir Pelham Carey, had died by 1643, when she married George Payler, although she continued to call herself Carey. Payler was a Parliamentary paymaster and they spent the Civil War travelling between garrison towns. Although one child survived from her first marriage, and two from her second, she had lost five others by 1652. In 1653 she began to assemble in one manuscript volume her prayers, poems and meditations. Like ANNE BRADSTREET, she wrote a number of poems on the deaths of babies, combining grief with stoical submission to God's will. In 'Upon the sight of my abortive birth' (1657), she lovingly mourned 'A little embryo; void of life, and feature', but concluded that it was God's return for the 'dead fruit' of her inadequate worship. HH

Carey, Rosa Nouchette 1840–1909 Author of forty-one 'DOMESTIC' NOVELS and continuously in print from 1868 to 1924, this English writer neither married nor worked outside the home. Never living independently from immediate family, she spent six years bringing up her widowed brother's children. Her novels reflect this life-experience, focusing on home and family rather than male employments and political activity.

Conservative in outlook, Carey's novels nevertheless give credence to female experience, providing a positive response to the supposed 'spare woman problem' and treating housekeeping and woman's caring role as real work. Also notable are Carey's sympathetic portrayals of women suffering from mental illness. Several novels suggest that mental health can be maintained through the 'control of the will' as advocated by the alienist Henry Maudsley, admixed with a strong religious faith.

Stylistically, Carey may be likened to CHARLOTTE YONGE, ELLEN WOOD and Annie S. Swan, writers who also have a connection with Carey in that they were editors of journals which published her work. *Heriot's Choice* appeared in Yonge's journal, the *Monthly Packet*, in 1877–9. Wood accepted shorter fiction for the *Argosy* and her son Charles, editor after her death, serialized *The Mistress of Brae Farm* in 1896. Likewise, Swan published the opening chapters of *Other People's Lives* (1897) in the *Woman at Home*.

From the 1880s, reviewers increasingly regarded Carey's fiction as old-fashioned, though she still commanded respectable sales. Her association with the Religious Tract Society may have further eroded her reputation as a serious writer. Ironically, posterity has attributed to Carey four SENSATION NOVELS, published 1895–1900, under the pseudonym 'Le Voleur'.

EMH

Carleton, Mary 1633?–73 British pamphleteer, actress, bigamist and thief. Extensive portions of her life remain undocumented, largely because of her many aliases, such as Moders, Carlston, Kirton and De Wolway. Born in Kent, she first married a shoemaker, Thomas Stedman of Canterbury. Arriving in London in 1663 she masqueraded as a German princess, marrying again, this time John Carleton, relative of a Southwark innkeeper. In June 1663 she appeared at the Old Bailey on charges of bigamy. These charges were dropped and she was exposed as being, despite her protracted protestations to the contrary, not a German princess but a petty criminal from Canterbury. The Carletons had her arrested, and her subsequent articulate appearances in court were widely celebrated. Some of the many pamphlets which appeared at that time are ascribed to her. *The Case of Madam Mary Carleton*, for example, combines diverse genres and discourses manipulated for its author's self-promoting ends, presenting forcibly the frustrations of the disenfranchized woman. Her success in literary and courtroom role-playing did not transfer to the commercial stage, however. In 1664 she took the lead – disastrously, according to Pepys – in *The German Princess*, a play centring on her escapades and derived from Thomas Porter's *A Witty Combat*. She went briefly to Holland, but in 1671 was transported to Barbados. Convicted of petty theft, she was executed at Tyburn in January 1673. ELER

Carlin, Vuyelwa (Susan) 1949– British poet, born in South Africa and raised in East Africa, she spent her adulthood in Shropshire, a landscape she says 'has sunk into my soul'. She married Brian Wigston in 1969, and has one daughter and one son. She graduated in English from Bristol University in 1972, and worked as a secretary, an artist's model and a House Mother at Bedstone College.

Carlin's breakthrough as a poet came in 1990 when she featured in the primarily Anglo-Welsh anthology *Seren Poets 2*. Her selection was distinctive for the richness and quirkiness of her syntax, qualities celebrated again when the poet and critic Michael Hulse reviewed her first collection, *Midas' Daughter* (1991) – 'the work of a voluptarist, wordsmith, hex, the best first collection for years'. A second collection, *How We Dream of the Dead*, in 1995 was less noticed despite the bold diction and polyvalent subject matter. Her relatively low profile in contemporary British letters is probably due to her being published by the excellent but small press, Seren, not often distributed outside Wales. Yet, like the work of her English contemporary MAGGIE HANNAN, the approach to Vuyelwa Carlin has to be one of surrender to her effects. Neither poet allows the reader to play safe. When that includes the rejection of 'the rational, the linear, the sequential', Carlin's poetry demands and rewards the reader's attention. DM

Carlyle, Jane Welsh 1801–66 British letter-writer, literary hostess and conversationalist. She is remembered, perhaps surprisingly, as a writer, though the all-absorbing work of her life was her forty-year marriage to Thomas Carlyle. The precocious only child of a Scottish doctor, Jane went to local schools in East Lothian, but, unusually for her sex, was allowed a classical education. Her beauty, vivacity and charm hid a powerful mind and a sharp wit, both of which appealed to Carlyle, whom she eventually married after much demur in 1826. He had, she said, 'a towering intellect to command me'. There was unhappiness and frustration in this marriage, despite the deep friendship at its centre; Jane channelled her creative energies into brilliant letters, 3,000 of which survive; they deal, not with her own role, nor with wider women's issues, but with keenly observed domestic and social life – revealing a novelist's talent for story-telling. She matched Carlyle in intellect but seems not to have felt the need to match him in achievement. Far from suppressing her literary development, Carlyle begged her in vain to write fiction. Her closest friend, GERALDINE JEWSBURY, wrote of 'the quixotism you have for sacrificing yourself': certainly Jane worked assiduously at providing Carlyle with conditions in which *he* could write. Their Chelsea house attracted a wide literary circle, including Tennyson, John Stuart Mill and Dickens. Leigh Hunt wrote about her in the poem 'Jenny kissed me'. Her death in 1866 was sudden. She had told Dickens that she would finish a novel. He wrote, 'How often I have thought of that unfinished novel. No-one now to finish it. None of the writing women come near her at all.'   VP

Carpathians, The (1988) JANET FRAME's interest in the twin functions of memory and point of view provides the framework for her tenth novel. Set in the quiet suburban town of Puamahara, New Zealand, it traces the arrival of Mattina Brecon, a wealthy New Yorker, and her subsequent immersion in the strange events of Kowhai Street. Her interest in the newly discovered Maori legend of the Memory Flower—the town's main source of pride and tourism—is complicated by the new-found force of the Gravity Star. Together they form an unsettling influence upon her and all her immediate neighbours; her world begins to shift dimension, logic becomes overturned and the nearby Tararua mountains become as near and far as the distant Carpathians. 'Was that her discovery during her visit to the "far country"? Mattina wondered. A shift of language, of landscape, of time and space? . . . Perhaps the only answer lay in the birth of a new language from a new way of thought.' These familiar themes of Frame's are granted new points of view within this cross-cultural exploration.   MRE

Emily Carr: illustration from her autobiography, *Growing Pains*, 1946.

Carr, Emily 1871–1945 To her neighbours, Canadian Emily Carr was the eccentric keeper of a boarding house who took her monkey shopping each morning; to others she was already known as a painter; to First Nation people she was Klee Wyck, 'the laughing one'. Born to a settler family in Victoria, she trained as a painter in San Francisco and Europe, but returned to spend the rest of her life in British Columbia. In the initial stages of a painting she tried to 'word' her experience, 'peeling' a sentence to achieve immediacy. She is now probably Canada's most famous woman painter, but her books provide a vivid child's view of the settlement of British Columbia, soon after the Gold Rush, and a painter's account of its effect on the people of the First Nation. *KLEE WYCK* describes living in their villages; other books of idiosyncratic autobiography include *The Book of Small*, *The House of All Sorts*, *Growing Pains*, *The Heart of a Peacock* and *Hundreds and Thousands*. Gender roles in settler life are evoked with startling clarity through Small, the embodiment of Carr as a child. Father builds fences, but Small is happiest singing in the Cow Yard or sticking her head through thorny hedges to discover the wild side. She finds it in D'Sonoqua, a totem: 'She seemed to be part of the tree itself, as if she had grown there at its heart, and the carver had only chipped away the outer wood so that you could see her.'   ASm

Carrington: extract from a letter to Lytton Strachey, December 1920.

Carr, Marina 1964– Irish playwright whose work ranges from Beckettian probings into gender absurdities to a dark and savage neo-REALISM. She was brought up in the north midlands, near Tullamore, and read English and Philosophy at University College Dublin. Her father, Hugh Carr, is a playwright and novelist. She worked in America as a teacher before returning to Dublin. First performed was *Low in the Dark* (1989), in which motherhood as the defining aspect of gender difference is playfully sent up. Curtains, a character whose body is invisible to the audience, narrates the irreconcilability of male and female in the voice of the story-teller which recurs in Carr's plays: 'Long after it was over, the man and woman realised that not only had they never met north by north east or south by south west, much worse, they had never met.'

The *Deer's Surrender* (1990) was commissioned and performed by the Gaiety School of Acting. *This Love Thing* (1991) is a series of witty sketches on sexual manners; it was staged in Dublin and Belfast. In it, Jesus, Mary Magdelene, Michaelangelo and others romp through deliciously implausible romantic situations. After the unwelcoming reception given to *Ulalloo* (1991) at the Peacock Theatre, Carr visited Romania as a writer-in-residence, and returned to Dublin with *The Mai* (1994). The eponymous heroine is beautiful and successful, yet the shadow cast by the failure of her marriage consumes her. Four female generations of her family inhabit the play, each struggling with the promise and disillusion of romantic love. *Portia Coughlan* (1996) is a tragedy of epic emotional power, written phonetically in the dialect of County Offaly. The speech coruscates with demon ferocity as Portia obliterates every possibility of love except reunion with her dead twin, Gabriel. In *By the Bog of Cats* (1998) tragedy and hilarity are yoked together in a story inspired by *Medea*. Of her future, Carr recently remarked, 'I plan to live to be ninety, so that's – twenty-five plays.' CL

Carrington (Dora de Houghton) 1893–1932 British painter and peripheral member of the Bloomsbury group. The fourth of five children born to middle-class parents, she was educated at Bedford High School and the Slade School of Fine Art in London. She was neither an intellectual nor a published writer, but she read widely, wrote magnificent illustrated letters, kept a journal throughout her life, and has recently been recognized as a very talented and original painter. Encouraged by the atmosphere of sexual equality at the Slade, she rebelled against her Victorian upbringing, cropped her hair, and became known as 'Carrington', an androgynous personality which she developed through wearing trousers, and, later, exploring her bi-sexuality. She was introduced to Bloomsbury by a fellow art student, Mark Gertler, with whom she had a romantic relationship. At the home of LADY OTTOLINE MORRELL, she met and fell in love with Lytton Strachey, with whom she was to live for the rest of her life, notwithstanding his homosexuality and her marriage to Ralph (Rex) Partridge in 1921. Upon Strachey's death in 1932, Carrington committed suicide.

Carrington's letters, described by VIRGINIA WOOLF as 'completely unlike anything in the habitable globe', were published in David Garnett's *Carrington: Letters and Extracts from her Diaries* (1970). She appears as a character or caricature in numerous works of fiction including D. H. Lawrence's *Women in Love* (1921) Aldous Huxley's *Crome Yellow* (1921), and Gilbert Cannan's *Mendel* (1916). MCJ

Carswell [née MacFarlane], Catherine 1879–1946 Scottish writer whose novels challenged the conventional roles available for middle-class women at the turn of the century. She studied music at the Frankfurt Conservatory and attended classes at Glasgow University at a time when women could not enrol for a degree. Her first marriage to Herbert Jackson ended when he tried to kill her and was declared insane. With Donald Carswell, she had a successful partnership, both professionally and privately.

Literary journalism provided her main income. Notoriously, Carswell was sacked from the *Glasgow Herald* for a favourable review of D. H. Lawrence's *The Rainbow*. She and Lawrence swapped manuscripts and he influenced the development of her first novel. The style of *Open the Door!* (1920) shifts between 19th-century REALISM and a fragmented, early 20th-century experimentation. In this, and in her second

And I give a little shiver because suddenly I know,

I know in my water, my ancient water, that something will happen, today
- something nice, something nasty, I don't give a ~~monk~~ monkey's. Just as
long as something happens to remind us we're still in the land of the living.

Seventy five today.

I don't believe it.

BOOM... BOOM... BOOM...

Not the end of the world, ducky. That soft, velvetty, metallic boom
rises up from down below. My sister, slave of a custom that predates our
birth, has just assumed the attitude of J. Arthur Rank to beat the brass gong
in the entrance hall, announcing breakfast.

Angela Carter: extract from manuscript of *Wise Children*, 1992.

novel, *The Camomile: An Invention* (1922), her heroines attempt to escape the confines of Calvinistic Glasgow life by fleeing toward self-realization, either as a woman or as an artist.

In order to have the privacy to write, Carswell hired various rooms, keeping the addresses secret. She planned two more novels; both were abandoned. The need to earn money by literary journalism got in the way. 'All I need is to be financed for a year or two', she told a friend, but even that was out of reach. Her autobiography, *Lying Awake*, was published posthumously in 1950.   JH

Carter, Angela 1940–92 Her picaresque speculative fictions and elegantly rude versions of FAIRY TALES were a startling new achievement in fiction by British women. Their revisionary 'demythologizing' was influenced by surrealism, and the 'situationist' cultural activism of 1968. She was also a notable essayist, of feminist and socialist persuasion. Her father was a journalist from Scotland; her mother, grammar-school-educated, gave up work in a department store after marriage; she and her brother spent the war years in Yorkshire, and grew up in south London. Carter started work reporting for a local newspaper, married (1960), and studied at Bristol University (1962–5), preferring medieval allegories to moralized 19th-century novels.

Three early novels (*Shadow Dance*, 1966; *Several Perceptions*, 1968; and *Love*, 1971) retain aspects of REAL-ISM, and a critical attitude to femininity which she later called 'male impersonation'. Her second novel, THE MAGIC TOYSHOP (1967), already recoils from captivation by images geared to 'masculine' desire. She claimed that she was politicized as a woman by the activism of 1968, and by Japan, where she lived between 1969 and 1972 (when her divorce became final), financed by literary prize money, work as a bar-girl, and cultural journalism for *New Society*. Her essays expose contemporary culture with animus and enjoyment (*Nothing Sacred*, 1982; *Expletives Deleted*, 1992). FIREWORKS (1974) includes her most avant-garde narrative experiments, but two stories also draw directly on her Japanese experiences. Later, her cultural history, *The Sadeian Woman* (1979), reread Sade in the light of modern debates about sexual force and reciprocity.

She taught creative writing in the USA and Australia, as well as in Britain. In 1977 she began her association with the feminist press Virago, and formed another base in south London with Mark Pearce (their son was born in 1983). *Heroes and Villains* (1969) had confirmed a popular following among fans of GOTHIC fantasy, and was followed by a series of speculative fictions: THE INFERNAL DESIRE MACHINES OF DR HOFFMAN (1972), *The Passion of New Eve* (1977), NIGHTS AT THE CIRCUS (1984). She produced further collections of stories: THE BLOODY CHAMBER (1979) and *Black Venus* (1987), in which feminist challenges to traditional icons and narratives fuse with the will, evident earlier, to be as bold as the boys. Her 'walk on the wild side' took critical and cultural theory, including psychoanalysis and ethnography, in its stride.

" Emily Mayfield all the day
Sits and rocks her cradle alone." Page 18.

Alice Cary: 'Emily Mayfield all the day / Sits and rocks her cradle alone', illustration from a posthumous edition of *The Poetical Works of Alice and Phoebe Cary*.

Interest in her work increased after her early death from cancer at 51. Her radical concerns made her fictions a gift for academic studies of sexuality, gender as masquerade, and 'POSTMODERN' parody. Late novels (*Nights at the Circus* and *Wise Children*, 1991) were welcomed as more benign than the scandals of *The Passion of New Eve* and *The Sadeian Woman*; here fascination with screen idols is extended to other performance artistes, especially in the circus and music hall.

She took a scholarly interest in folk and fairy tales, and experimented with radio plays. Neil Jordan's film *The Company of Wolves* (1984) drew on stories from *The Bloody Chamber*; *The Magic Toyshop* was filmed for Granada TV by David Wheatley (1987).   EJ

Carter, Elizabeth 1717–1806 Poet, translator and letter-writer. Her father, Revd Dr Nicholas Carter, taught Elizabeth Greek, Hebrew and Latin. She later added Portuguese and Arabic. Family friend Edward Cave published her verse in the *Gentleman's Magazine* in 1734 and introduced her to Johnson, with whom she became firm friends, writing two essays for his periodical, the *Rambler*. Cave published her *Poems on Particular Occasions* (1738), which are uniformly accomplished but markedly restrained. 'Ode to Wisdom', originally circulated in manuscript, was included in Richardson's *Clarissa*, unattributed (he later apologized). Further editions of her *Poems* (1762 and 1776) added comic and emotional work to the solemn and classical.

Carter first translated Crousaz's *Examination of Mr*

Pope's Essay on Man (1738), followed by Algarotti's Italian handbook, *Sir Isaac Newton's Philosophy Explain'd for the Use of the Ladies* (1739). Her major translation, *Epictetus, All the Works* (1758), printed by Richardson, remained the standard scholarly text until the beginning of this century; it earned her £1,000 in her lifetime. Its stoic advocacy of the conquest of passion through self-command is developed in the writings of BARBAULD and WOLLSTONECRAFT. Carter preferred reading women writers and was proud of her unmarried state. Her correspondence (1741–70) with fellow-BLUESTOCKING CATHERINE TALBOT was published in 1809, along with her letters to Mrs Vesey. She was also a close friend and correspondent of ELIZABETH MONTAGU, with whom she travelled on the continent. A tireless scholar, famous for taking snuff to stay awake for long hours of study, she was revered by the literary luminaries of her day. Toward the end of her life she encouraged the younger writers HANNAH MORE and JOANNA BAILLIE.   ESE

Cartland, Barbara 1901– English popular novelist and celebrity, often dubbed 'The Queen of Romance'. Cartland's gentry upbringing was blighted by financial crisis and her father's death in World War I; her mother, Mary Hamilton (affectionately known as Polly), shaped her dedication to work as a social and religious mission. A debutante in 1920s London, she wrote about her upper-class milieu in a *Daily Express* gossip column and in her first novel, *Jigsaw* (1925). This novel set the pattern for her chaste vision of romantic love which she developed, as part of a broader Tory politics, in literally hundreds of fictions; BIOGRAPHIES of historical figures; self-help, health and advice books for women – such as *Touch the Stars: A Clue to Happiness* (1935), *You – In the Home* (1946), *Look Lovely, Be Lovely* (1958) and *Men Are Wonderful* (1973); and several autobiographies, of which *We Danced All Night 1919-1929* (1970) is the best known. Her own first marriage, however, to printing scion Alexander George McCorquodale, ended bitterly in 1932; her second, to his cousin Hugh, lasted until his death in 1963. She undertook welfare work during World War II (in which she lost both her brothers), worked for the St John Ambulance Brigade and served as a Conservative County Councillor for Hertfordshire. Since the 1970s she has become the brand name for a ROMANCE empire, publishing up to twenty-four novels annually and marketing perfume, fabrics and items of home decoration. She was made a Dame of the Order of the British Empire in 1991.   MO'D

Cary, Alice 1820–71 American poet and writer of REALIST fiction, born on a farm near Cincinnati, Ohio, fourth of nine children. Cary had little education but began writing early in her life – she started publishing poetry in periodicals, including the abolitionist *National Era*, in 1838. She and her sister PHOEBE CARY achieved national recognition when Rufus Griswold included them in *The Female Poets of America* (1849). Following publication of *Poems of Alice and Phoebe Cary* (1850), the sisters used their literary earnings to move to New York City. Their Sunday evening receptions drew the New York literati. Cary became president of the first American women's club and filled a poetry column in the *New York Ledger*. Her prose sketches are collected in *Clovernook: Or, Recollections of Our Neighborhood in the West* (1852), *Clovernook, Second Series* (1853) and *Pictures of Country Life* (1859), and reprinted in *Clovernook Sketches and Other Stories* (1987). JSG

Cary [née Tanfield], Elizabeth, Lady, Viscountess Falkland 1585–1639 Renowned as the first woman to write a tragic drama in English, *The Tragedy of Mariam* (printed 1613) and a long narrative with inset blank-verse speeches, *The History of the Life, Reign and Death of Edward II* (c. 1627–8). She is also said to have written religious verses and translated classical texts, though none survive. She translated from the French *The Reply of Cardinal du Perron* to James I (1630), a major work of Catholic polemic. Much is known about her life from her daughter's BIOGRAPHY, *The Lady Falkland, Her Life* (published in 1861).

Cary had a strict upbringing but one which allowed her access to education. She was able to read fluently in French, Spanish, Latin and Hebrew. Married Sir Henry Cary in 1602. Her husband became Lord Deputy of Ireland in 1623 and the couple had eleven children between 1609 and 1624. Elizabeth had shown an interest in Catholicism as early as 1605, and in 1626 she converted, with great scandal, to Rome, which brought her into conflict with the strict Protestantism of her husband. This reached a head in Ireland where she witnessed his brutal suppression of Catholics, and, when she formally converted in 1625, he dismissed her back to England. He had her placed under house arrest and tried to take custody of the children but the Privy Council decided in her favour. A form of reconciliation seems to have taken place between the couple in the early 1630s when Cary nursed her dying husband.

The Tragedy of Mariam, a Senecan-style drama intended to be spoken aloud rather than performed on a public stage, whose source is Josephus's *Antiquities of the Jews*, offers an unusual account of the Herod–Mariam relationship in that it is seen from the woman's perspective. The text has much to say on the subject of marriage and has been read for details of Cary's life. It is certainly notable for its complex and ambiguous female protagonist. JS

Cary [Rande], Mary c.1621 – after 1653 PROPHETIC writer of the Civil War period. She was a Fifth Monarchist who believed that the godly could justly use the 'material sword' to establish the New Jerusalem. Following *A Sword in Season* (1647) and *The Resurrection of the Witnesses* (1648), she published *The Little Horn's Doom and Downfall* (1651), which envisaged a new godly commonwealth in which wives would have equal property rights with their husbands, and the idle and profane rich would not be tolerated. Cary presented as 'a pencil, or pen' guided by the hand of God. Her three dedicatees were female; she identified 'pious, precious, prudent, and sage matrons, and holy women' as the guardians of the new order. In a preface she explained that, although she continued to publish as Cary, her surname had changed to Rande, presumably by marriage. In *Twelve Humble Proposals* (1653) she urged the new Parliamentary government to make the needs of the poor their first concern, and to place an upper limit of £200 on annual income. HH

Cary, Phoebe 1824–71 American poet, who was born on a farm near Cincinnati, Ohio, sixth of nine children. She had little education and few books but began writing in her teens, publishing a popular hymn, 'Nearer Home', at the age of 18. She and her sister ALICE CARY gained national recognition when Rufus Griswold included their works in *The Female Poets of America* (1849) and helped them publish *Poems of Alice and Phoebe Cary* (1850). Following Alice to New York City in 1850, Phoebe assumed the homemaker role in their household, which for 20 years was a literary centre. Phoebe published *Poems and Parodies* (1854) and *Poems of Faith, Hope, and Love* (1868), edited *Hymns for All Christians* with Dr C.F. Deems (1869), and worked briefly with SUSAN B. ANTHONY's suffrage paper, the *Revolution*. While both sisters held abolitionist views, Phoebe's poetry is more often directly political ('Homes for All', 'Harvest Gathering'). Her poems on women's issues strike notes of anger and sensuality, while her parodies exhibit a wry wit. Luxury editions of the sisters' last poems (1873) and *The Poetical Works of Alice and Phoebe Cary with a Memorial of Their Lives* (1877) appeared posthumously. JSG

Casa Guidi Windows (1851) A long political poem in two parts, which records ELIZABETH BARRETT BROWNING's reaction – from the windows of Casa Guidi, where she lived in Florence – to the Italian political situation from 1848 to 1851. The first half of the poem displays Browning's enthusiasm and hope for the success of the Italian risorgimento in its struggle for the unification and liberation of Italy. Encouraged by the reforms of Grand Duke Leopold II and Pope Pius IX, Browning defines and celebrates her political heroic ideal, the Christian-artist-teacher whom she believes must lead Italy to eventual democracy by educating its people. She sympathetically describes the suffering of the Italian people and condemns the romanticization of their struggle, particularly in the form of tragic female figures.

The second half of the poem reflects Browning's disillusionment over the abandonment of the liberal struggle by both Pio Nono and Leopold – (the latter of whom capitulated to the Austrian forces), England's lack of intervention, and the failure of the people of Tuscany to pursue revolution more ardently.　　MCJ

Caspary, Vera 1904–87 American popular novelist, playwright and screenwriter. Caspary, who called the 20th century 'The Century of the Woman', bore witness to her feminism in her writing and political activity. Born to a middle-class German-Jewish family in Chicago, Caspary claimed her independence early, determined to differ from her sister, who married for social standing and disdained Chicago's Russian-Jewish immigrants. The versatility Caspary developed in her first career, advertising, took her into journalism, where she worked for MacFadden Publications' physical culture, true-crime and confessional magazines. Having moved from Chicago to Greenwich Village, Caspary began publishing novels in the mid 1920s. Like other popular female novelists of the twenties, Caspary embraced the diverse issues of her day, including racial passing (*The White Girl*, 1929), Jewish assimilation (*Thicker Than Water*, 1932) and premarital sex (*Music in the Street*, 1930). Caspary achieved her greatest literary, cinematic and stage success with the murder mystery *Laura* (1943), which she patterned after the novels of Wilkie Collins.

Caspary became increasingly involved in the Left in the thirties and forties, collaborating with the socialist writer Samuel Ornitz, joining her local Communist writers' cell, and fundraising for the anti-Fascist movement in Spain. During World War II, she spoke on behalf of European Jews to Jewish-American women's clubs. Although no longer a Party member after her move to Hollywood, Caspary was 'graylisted' in the early 1950s; while she was never formally blacklisted or subpoenaed by the House Un-American Activities Committee, her career suffered and she spent much of the fifties in Europe. Her autobiography, *The Secrets of Grown-Ups* (1979), charts her transition from NEW WOMAN to Party member to successful screenwriter.

MG

Cassady, Carolyn 1923– American Beat-generation survivor and memoirist. Born in Michigan, USA, a distant descendant of Sir Walter Scott, she graduated from Bennington after World War II with a Fine Art degree, and a Theatre Arts MA from Denver University. At Denver she met Neal Cassady, Jack Kerouac and Allen Ginsberg – the 'Beat poets' – and married Neal in 1948. They had three children. As with many women Beat writers, Cassady's main work takes the form of memoirs. Her work first appeared in *Rolling Stone* and *Heart Beat: My Life with Jack and Neal* (1976; filmed 1980). *On The Road: Years with Cassady, Kerouac and Ginsberg* (1990) expands on these years, depicting a wife and mother, before the days of the feminist movement, finding her own place in the essentially male-dominated Beat movement, from the days of their early struggles, through the fame of *On the Road* – Kerouac's Beat masterpiece – and into the days of the hippy movement where Neal Cassady drove Ken Kesey's 'Merry Pranksters' bus. The book chronicles challenges to her middle-class values with these wild men of poetry, her stoic coping with Neal's philandering and drug abuse and life with her three children. In the 1980s Cassady moved to live and work in London.　　GW

Castillo, Ana 1953– An American poet, novelist, essayist and translator; a native of Chicago. Castillo's writing is unique in the sophistication with which it blends indigenous Mexican myth and symbolism, magic realism, feminist thought and experimental technique. She is best known for *The Mixquiahuala Letters* (1986) – an EPISTOLARY meta-NOVEL tracing the history of a female friendship, which received an American Book Award from the Before Columbus Foundation – and *So Far From God* (1993), which received the Carl Sandburg Literary Award, and tells the story of the female members of a New Mexican family in an experimental collage of family recipes, folk cures, mysticism and dry humour. *So Far from God* also playfully mimics, rewrites, and thus comments upon, Steinbeck's *Tortilla Flat* in terms of both general tonal structure and representation of Mexican-Americans.

Castillo's second novel, *Sapagonia: An Anti-Romance in 3/8 Meter* (1988), creates a politically metaphorical mestizo homeland, and *Loverboys* (1996) is a collection of short stories. Her collection of essays, *Massacre of the Dreamers: Essays on Xicanisma* (1994), has been influential in its incorporation of indigenous Mexican myth, practice and symbolism. *Goddess of the Americas / La Diosa de las Americas* (1996), a variety of stories, poems and essays that she edited in 1996, explores the cultural, historical and personal impact of Our Lady of Guadalupe.　　SMSt

Castle Rackrent (1800) The first and probably most famous work by MARIA EDGEWORTH, *Rackrent* has been described as the first regional novel and was the direct inspiration for Walter Scott's *Waverley*. Through the history of successive generations of the Rackrent family, it provides a satirical portrait of the manners of the Irish landowning class in the 18th century. The lavish Sir Patrick, the litigious Sir Murtagh, the negligent Sir Kit and the improvident Sir Condy all contribute to the progressive decline in the Rackrent fortunes, which is narrated by the old Catholic retainer, Thady Quirk. Thady's slavish devotion to the Rackrents may be read as consciously or unconsciously ironic, but the ultimate irony of the novel is that the final ruin of the old family is not brought about by an outsider but by Thady's son, Jason. The satire of the novel is therefore juxtaposed with an elegiac tone describing the decline, while criticizing the effects, of the old Irish way of life. The anthropological aspect of the text was developed by the inclusion of a glossary to explain Irish words and customs to English readers. LBe

Cather, Willa Sibert 1873–1947 American novelist, poet, short-story writer and journalist. Born into a farming family in Virginia, at the age of 8 she moved to Red Cloud, Nebraska, a prairie town of pioneer immigrants that would provide her with material for her greatest novels. After a degree at the University of Nebraska, she began a career as teacher and journalist, and she wrote for a variety of magazines and newspapers, including *McClure's Magazine* which she edited until 1912. She then left to become a full-time fiction-writer.

Her first publication was a collection of poems, *April Twilight* (1903), and her second, *The Troll Garden* (1905), initiated a series of short-story collections. Throughout a long, productive career, she produced twelve novels, more than sixty stories and several volumes of critical essays. However, it is for the series of novels focusing on her beloved Nebraska that Cather will be remembered: *O PIONEERS!* (1913), *The Song of the Lark* (1915), *MY ÁNTONIA* (1918), the Pulitzer-Prize-winning *One of Ours* (1922) and *A Lost Lady* (1923). Her later work, which in recent years has attracted more attention, uses symbolic means to explore the pressures of modern life upon traditional ways and values, featuring historical treatments of the Catholic Church in New Mexico and Quebec (*DEATH COMES FOR THE ARCHBISHOP*, 1927, and *SHADOWS ON THE ROCK*, 1931) and slavery in antebellum Virginia (*Sapphira and the Slave Girl*, 1940). A Catholic, Cather never married, and enjoyed a series of deep friendships with women. She is claimed by some feminist critics as a lesbian writer, though others note that she never supported any woman-centred political line or group. She died in New York and was buried in New Hampshire. She is recognized as one of America's greatest writers.

Cather has been praised for her evocation of pioneer Mid-Western life, tracing the hardships, cultural challenges and emotional lives of immigrants working an unforgiving land. Using both male and female narrators, Cather's work spans that period of American history in which the frontier closed and generations of new immigrants sought to establish a new, hybrid identity within a shifting, unstable society. She created characters who have a keen sense of history and wish to establish and understand familial and spiritual roots. As Hermione Lee expresses it, she evoked 'landscapes of the mind' by an imagination working through 'memory, distance, and loss'. The workings of memory are crucial to most of her great novels and stories, and the problem of journeying – literal and symbolic – is central. As Eusabio says (*Death Comes for the Archbishop*), 'Men travel faster now, but I do not know if they go to better things.'

Cather's literary models were writers who had a complex version of REALISM – Flaubert, Henry James, and SARAH ORNE JEWETT, the only woman writer she warmly befriended and admired. She criticized women's writing for its 'sex consciousness', claiming women were 'so horribly subjective', and launched a ferocious attack on KATE CHOPIN's novel, *THE AWAKENING*. Torn between a 'masculine' tradition of the epic and pastoral she admired and her own independent female vision, Cather produced a body of work that is both realist and ROMANTIC, regional and national. Her best fiction interrogates without nostalgia the meanings of community, roots, gender and ethnicity, as the nation erupted from its rural past into modernity. HT

Catherine of Aragon 1485–1536 Patron and Henry VIII's first Queen. She helped introduce to England new humanist thinking on women's education: between 1523 and 1538 seven such treatises were published under her influence, including one by the Spanish humanist Juan Luis Vives, who assisted in the tuition of her daughter Princess Mary (MARY I).

When Henry VIII discarded her in favour of ANNE BOLEYN, Catherine earned wide admiration for her dignified endurance. To a spiritual adviser she wrote that 'in the time of this my solitude and the extreme anguish of my soul . . . I confess to you that I am consumed by a great desire to be able to die.' To an intercessor at court she conveyed polite gratitude for the King's concession that Mary be sent 'to some place nigh me, so as I do not see her'; but pointedly asked that 'you shall always say unto his highness that the thing which I desired was to send her where I am'. HH

Cato, Nancy [Nancy Norman Fotheringham] 1917– Australian poet, environmentalist, journalist and prolific writer of popular HISTORICAL fiction who dramatizes the genealogy of Australian families against a backdrop of the country's physical, social and cultural development. She was born in Adelaide and worked as a journalist and art critic for the *Bulletin* and for the *Adelaide News* between 1936 and 1958. By the time she left to become a full-time writer, she had already had two collections of poetry published: *The Darkened Window* (1950) and *The Dancing Bough* (1957).

All the Rivers Run (1958), her début novel, was the first of three charting the course of a mother's 'rebelliousness, wanting to work and being hampered by children'. This is a central Cato theme: female characters who 'try not to be limited by their sex'. It was followed by *Time, Flow Softly* (1959) and *But Still the Stream* (1962). In 1978, the trilogy was abridged by Cato, issued in a single volume, and became a bestseller. A film version appeared soon afterwards.

Among her other novels, *Green Grows the Vine* (1960), *Brown Sugar* (1974), *Forefathers* (1983) and *The Heart of the Continent* (1989) are the best-known. Her works of non-fiction include *Mister Maloga* (1976), an account of Daniel Matthews's River Murray mission to the Aborigines, and *The Noosa Story: A Study in Unplanned Development* (1979). JAH

Cavendish, Jane, Lady, later Cheyne 1621–69

Daughter of William Cavendish, Duke of Newcastle and his first wife Elizabeth Bassett. Stepdaughter to MARGARET CAVENDISH (see DUCHESS OF NEWCASTLE) and therefore part of a literary family, both in terms of artistic patronage and authorship. At the outbreak of the English Civil War (1642–9), Jane and her sisters, Elizabeth Cavendish (VISCOUNTESS BRACKLEY) and Frances, found themselves under siege at the family estate at Welbeck Abbey. Their mother died in 1643 and the sisters ran the estate alone until it was taken by force by Parliamentarian troops in 1644. Many of Jane and Elizabeth's literary productions (the most significant of them collaborative) date from this period. The sisters co-authored a masque, *A Pastorall,* which owes much to early Stuart court masques. Their co-written play *The Concealed Fancies*, with its plot concerning three cousins under siege from Parliamentary troops, alludes to the sisters' real-life predicament in the 1640s. Jane was also the author of letters plus several poems, including an elegy on her sister's death written after her own marriage to Charles Cheyne, later Viscount Newhaven, in 1654. JS

Cecil [née Cooke], Mildred, Lady Burleigh 1526–89

Eldest daughter of Sir Anthony Cooke who had been tutor to Edward VI. Like her sisters – Katherine Cooke Killigrew, ANNE COOKE BACON and Elizabeth Cooke Hoby (later Russell) – Mildred wrote poetry, letters and translations. She married William Cecil, Lord Burleigh, in 1545. He was one of the most powerful men in Elizabethan England and this gave Mildred political influence as well. Roger Ascham described her as one of the most learned ladies in England. She was particularly skilled in Greek and wrote translations, some of which survive, including a transcription of a sermon by St Basil (now in the British Library). She was also reported, in an anonymous BIOGRAPHY of her

husband, published in 1600, to have translated 'a peece' by the 4th-century St John Chrysostum. Whilst devotional works of this nature were an accepted literary pursuit for women, this translation may have been more controversial since Chrysostum was quoted by both Protestants and Catholics alike in the debates over transubstantiation.

Significant politicians and humanist thinkers of the day corresponded with Mildred and several of her letters survive. These indicate her shrewd political acumen as well as rhetorical skill. JS

Cellier, Elizabeth fl.1678–88

Pamphlet writer, activist and midwife who was born in London of good Protestant stock, and later converted to Catholicism in reaction to the excesses of the Civil War. During the time of the 'Popish Plot' she chronicled the torture of Catholics in Newgate gaol. Her organization of political meetings led to an intrigue to discredit the Whig party, nicknamed the Meal Tub Plot because evidence implicating Cellier and others was found 'between the pewter in my kitchen'. After successfully defeating a charge of treason in 1680, she wrote and sold from her house *Malice Defeated*, which outlined conditions in prison and led to a further accusation of libel. This resulted in heavy penalties, including several periods in the pillory and, as a result, Cellier was much satirized in contemporary pamphlets. In 1687 she published *A Scheme for the Foundation of a Royal Hospital ... and such for the Maintenance of a Corporation of skillful Midwives*. This pamphlet was submitted to James II and argued for the establishment of a midwives' union to protect the (female) profession from being taken over by (male) physicians. Its implementation was stopped by the King's flight from the throne and Cellier herself may also have gone into exile. RDM

Centlivre, Susanna ?–1723

British playwright whose most popular comedies were played throughout the 18th and 19th centuries. Conflicting contemporary sources name her father either as Rawkins or as Mr Freeman of Holbeach, Lincolnshire. Unverified stories of her early life have her joining strolling players and spending time at Cambridge University in male disguise. By 1700 she was part of a circle of writers and actors in London. She first published as Susanna Carroll, apparently using a surname acquired in a short-lived marriage; she became Centlivre on her 1707 marriage to a cook in the royal household. Centlivre wrote nineteen plays, including three farces. Her greatest successes were *The Gamester* (1705), a comedy claiming a moral aim in line with current ideas of stage reform; THE BUSY BODY (1709), an intrigue comedy featuring the good-natured bungler Marplot; *The Wonder! A Woman Keeps a Secret* (1714), a fast-paced comedy of young lovers, jealousy and true female friendship; and *A Bold Stroke for a Wife* (1718) whose hero's many disguises include one that created a common catch-phrase: 'the real Simon Pure'. Centlivre's comedies make brilliant use of stage techniques and rely on swift, dazzlingly complex action more than verbal wit. In ideology they are firmly Whig, and both George I and the Prince of Wales acknowledged her support for the Hanoverian dynasty by commanding performances of her plays.

JSp

Ceremony (1977) In LESLIE MARMON SILKO's second novel, her protagonist, Tayo, is a returning World War II veteran, suffering from a sickness that white doctors are unable to diagnose or cure. Set in and around Laguna Pueblo, New Mexico, the novel tells the story of Tayo's quest for a cure. He is guided through a purification ceremony by a Navaho medicine man, Old Betonie, who helps him to see the extent to which his individual sickness is connected to a much larger pattern of 'witchery'.

Silko was criticized for revealing too much about Pueblo Indian beliefs – the novel's full significance depends on them. Tayo's nausea is not just that of a separate individual, but is connected to tribal malaise, and beyond that to a global destructive force. The book's structure enacts interconnectedness, including the connection between nuclear testing at White Sands, New Mexico, in the early 1940s, and the first atomic bombs dropped on Hiroshima and Nagasaki. Silko's story-telling represents the strength of cultural hybridity, combining traditional techniques and patterns with a far-reaching, investigative mode of writing.

HMD

Cervantes, Lorna Dee 1954– Poet and editor, a fifth-generation Californian of Mexican and native American (Chumasch) descent, best known for the hugely anthologized 'Poem for the Young White Man Who Asked Me How I, an Intelligent, Well-Read Person Could Believe in the War Between the Races'. *Emplumada* (1981) was a recipient of the 1982 American Book Award, and *From the Cables of Genocide: Poems on Love and Hunger* (1991), recipient of the Patterson Poetry Prize and the Poetry Prize of the Institute of Latin American Writers. Her poetry is widely recognized as having articulated the feminist concerns of 'el movimiento', the Chicano Rights Movement of the 1970s, and her editing has been crucial in sponsoring the work of such writers as Gary Soto, SANDRA CISNEROS and Luis Omar Salinas. Cervantes founded *MANGO*, a cross-cultural literary magazine, as well as the MANGO Publications press, with the intent of providing a space for the work of Chicano/a writers. She has also founded and edited *Red Dirt*, a biannual, cross-cultural poetry journal. Cervantes has been the recipient of two National Endowment for the Arts poetry fellowships.

SMSt

Chambers, Jane 1937–83 American playwright known for her realistic, poignantly humorous depictions of lesbian women leading quiet, dignified lives that are thrown into crisis, often when the 'normal' is ironically reversed with the 'abnormal'. Her early plays include *Eye of the Gull* (1971 revised in 1991), *Deadly Nightshade* (1971) and *Random Violence* (1972). *Eye of the Gull* is a tribute to the love between two of Chambers's friends and the disabled sister they take as their child into the East-coast lesbian guest-house they manage. In Chambers's most produced play, *Last Summer at Bluefish Cove* (1982), a closeted, married woman unknowingly rents a cabin in a lesbian resort, suddenly becoming a misfit within the norm of the majority, but ultimately realizing her own homosexuality as she is accepted into Bluefish Cove. Here the lesbian community becomes a surrogate family, as in *A Late Snow* (1979) and *My Blue Heaven* (1981). Chambers's last play, *Quintessential Image*, unfinished at her death in 1983, departs from domestic REALISM, presenting a dialectic of lesbian experience versus society's image of the lesbian. This mass-media image is a constructed identity imposed on the real women, making them doubt their experience and their love for each other.

SBB

Chandler, Elizabeth Margaret 1807–34 American Quaker abolitionist, poet and essayist, born in Centre, Delaware. Orphaned at nine, she was raised by her grandmother and aunts in Philadelphia, where she attended the Friends' school. She began writing poetry as a child and, by the age of 16, was publishing anonymously in periodicals. At nineteen she became the editor of the women's column in the anti-slavery periodical *Genius of Universal Emancipation*. Through her poems, hymns, fictional letters, allegories and essays, she urged American women to follow the lead of English anti-slavery women, reject slavery, and boycott products of slave labour. Chandler is credited with providing the conceptual basis for an organized American women's abolitionist movement by defining forms of activism consistent with 'femininity' based on free women's sisterhood with enslaved women. In 1830 she moved to the Michigan wilderness where she founded the state's first anti-slavery society and corresponded for the Boston *Liberator*. Her poems were collected posthumously in *Poetical Works of Elizabeth Margaret Chandler* (1836).

JSG

Chapel Perilous, The (1971) This partly autobiographical play by Australian DOROTHY HEWETT dramatizes a feminist quest for freedom and autonomy.

Elizabeth Margaret Chandler: frontispiece and title-page of *Poetical Works*, 1836.

Sally Banner, who says 'I believe in the blood and the flesh as being wiser than the intellect', refuses to bow down to the authority figures whose large masks are onstage for the entire play: the Headmistress, the Canon and the religious Sister Rosa. Her aggressive sexuality both fascinates and repels the many men who love her but cannot avoid judging her as a whore. Employing poetry, music, ritual and symbolism in a deliberate rejection of dramatic naturalism, partly influenced by Brecht and Elizabethan dramatists, *The Chapel Perilous* was immediately recognized as an important challenge to the traditional well-made play, and to ideas of masculine heroism. Sally Banner represented the female artist whose creativity required total liberation from sexual and social constraints. Buffeted and apparently repeatedly defeated in a turbulent life, Sally never consents to victimhood, asserting an indomitable spirit, passion and courage, finally achieving wisdom and peace.   HTh

Chapone [née Mulso] , Hester 1727–1801 Essayist, poet and BLUESTOCKING whose precocity (she wrote a romance, aged 9) caused her jealous mother to suppress further literary activity. After her mother's early death, however, she continued her strenuous self-education while managing her father's household. At 23, she impressed ELIZABETH CARTER with her 'uncommon exactness of understanding', and Samuel Richardson with her sparkling repartee. He called her 'the little spitfire' and she was thought to have inspired his liveliest female characters, although Mrs Donnellan blamed her lack of 'politeness of manners' for his characters being not 'so really polished as he thinks them to be'. In her prolific correspondence with Richardson she argued against strict parental discipline at a time when, perhaps not uncoincidentally, her father opposed her attachment to John Chapone, another of Richardson's intimate circle. The couple were prevented from marrying until 1760; Chapone died the same year, and left her grief-stricken.

Admired by Dr Johnson, she contributed to the *Rambler* (no.10, 1750), while he included her elegant poetry in his *Dictionary*. Her 'Story of Fidelia' appeared in Hawkesworth's *The Adventurer* (1753), John Duncombe complimented her 'genius' and 'goodness' (as 'Delia') in *The Feminiad* (1754) and she wrote a prefatory ode to Carter's *Epictetus* (1758). Later, FANNY BURNEY referred to her 'conversational power' and 'uncommon ugliness'. To her friend ELIZABETH MONTAGU she dedicated her acclaimed *Letters on the Improvement of the Mind* (1773) on female self-education. *Miscellanies in Prose and Verse* followed in 1775, the didactic *A Letter to a New-Married Lady* in 1777, while *Works and Life*, which included her correspondence with Richardson and Carter, was published posthumously in 1807.   LMT

Chapone, Sarah (Kirkham) 1699–1764 Her anonymous *Remarks on Mrs Muilman's Letter to the Right Honourable the Earl of Chesterfield*, which censured the 'SCANDALOUS MEMOIRIST' CONSTANTIA PHILLIPS for her lack of contrition, attracted Richardson who described the mid-century memoirs as 'Women's Poison' needing just such an 'Antidote'. Chapone admitted authorship and he printed the pamphlet in 1750. Already a fervent admirer of Richardson's novels, she now became an intimate correspondent who was not afraid to differ from him occasionally, especially regarding the limits of women's independence, and he praised her as one of the best of female writers. Her childhood friend MARY DELANY called her an 'intrepid spirit' and she probably wrote the feminist-inclined *Hardships of the English Laws in relation to Wives* (1735). She was married to a clergyman who, with their four children, was also drawn into Richardson's orbit; their son married another member of his circle, the BLUESTOCKING Hester Mulso (see HESTER CHAPONE).   LMT

Charades (1988) Australian novelist JANETTE TURNER HOSPITAL's highly intellectual POST-MODERN novel is the story of Charade, who has arrived in Boston in search of her father. Like Scheherezade, Charade tells her lover, Koenig, a new story every night: stories of her own childhood in Queensland, and the stories of her mother Bea, her father Nicholas Truman, Katherine and the mysterious Verity Ashkenazy. The multiplicity of the stories Charade tells points to Hospital's emphasis on the unreliability of narrative and the fluidity of location. Places conflate and dislocate: Charade thinks 'I might fall right through Toronto to Queensland.' Throughout the novel Hospital destabilizes her own narrative, as she focuses on the Zundel trial in Toronto (which raised the question of the truth of the Holocaust), on Verity's identity and on Charade's own parentage. The final image of Charade's rejection of the one father for her multiple mothers, and her realization of the futility of the search for certain truth, is a powerful evocation of the '*necessity* of uncertainty', and of its rich possibilities.   ss

---

THE

MERCER,

O R

Fatal Extravagance :

BEING A TRUE

NARRATIVE

Of the LIFE of

Mr. *Wm.* DENNIS.

MERCER, in *Cheapfide*, LONDON.

The Occurrences herein related, are well worthy the Obfervation of the READER, and proper to be Regarded, by every Mechanick in *Great Britain*.

Written by Mrs. CHARKE, Author of the Life of *Henry Dumont*, Efq; And Mifs *Charlotte Evelyn*, &c. &c.

LONDON.
BAILEY, PRINTER (Nᵒ. 110,)
Leadenhall 'treet.

Charlotte Charke: title-page of *Narrative of The Life*, (1755).

Charke, Charlotte 1713–60? Playwright, actress and strolling player, whose wry and racy *Narrative of the Life* (1755) describes her (mis)adventures, imprisonments, disguises (often as a man), disastrous business ventures and struggle to support her child. Her autobiography renders a subtler, more complex and ironic subjectivity than her father Colley Cibber's self-portrait in his *Apology* (1740), and made a significant contribution to representations of interiority in the novel.

At first successful, acting at Drury Lane and Lincoln's Inn Fields, her career foundered after she parodied Cibber, actor–manager and poet laureate, in Henry Fielding's political satires at the Haymarket. Her play *The Art of Management* (1735) was suppressed for its attack on theatre-manager Fleetwood, while *The*

Carnival (1735) and *Tit for Tat* (1743) were not printed. Deserted by her husband, disowned by her father and desperate for money, her autobiography was immediately popular and serialized in the *Gentleman's Magazine*. But two novels, *The History of Henry Dumont* (1756) and *The Lover's Treat* (1758), failed to save Charke from dying, aged 47, in poverty.   LMT

Charles [née Rundle], Elizabeth 1821–89 English writer whose HISTORICAL NOVELS on Christian themes were among the most popular religious fiction of the 19th century. Elizabeth was the daughter of John Rundle, MP for Tavistock, and she was educated at home. She was devout from childhood, and in her autobiography, *Our Seven Homes* (1896), she describes her religious beliefs and influences, including her attraction to the Oxford Movement. Her first book, *Tales and Sketches of Christian Life in Different Lands* (1850), appeared shortly before her marriage to Andrew Paton Charles. She wrote her most successful book, *The Chronicles of the Schonberg-Cotta Family*, depicting the life of Martin Luther, in 1863, after a magazine offered her £400 for a serial. Charles later wrote that she felt she had found her 'vocation' in writing religious stories 'born of a genuine historical enthusiasm, and of a simple, sacred human duty.' Among Charles's other works are *The Diary of Mrs Kitty Trevylyan* (1864), *Winifred Bertram and the World She Lived In* (1866), *Against the Stream* (1873) and *Joan the Maid* (1879), a portrait of Joan of Arc. She also wrote nonfiction, including *The Women of the Gospels* (1867), *Three Martyrs of the Nineteenth Century* (1885) and many hymns.   KW

Charles, Gerda 1914–96 Gerda Charles began writing in her forties, when an essay for an evening class was published in the Morley College magazine and she was encouraged to attempt a novel, *The True Voice* (1959). Four more followed in about a decade. An orthodox Jew, Charles describes *The Crossing Point* (1960) as her 'Jewish novel' but, as well as her realistic portrait of a North London Jewish family and their rabbi, she proposes a symbolic reading of the Jew as typifying all the oppressed. Charles's definition of oppression is a wide one. The hero of her last novel, *The Destiny Waltz* (1971), wishes for 'the ability to extend the boundaries of pain'. The victims who inhabit these marginal territories are starved by social deprivation and tortured by humiliation and neglect. Bernard in *A Slanting Light* (1963) is not invited to the first-night party of his own play. The heroine of the war-time novel, *A Logical Girl* (1966), sees the injustice of life in the misalliance of her favourite GI and identifies herself with the Jews and her sister-in-law with Hitler. Charles received several literary prizes and critical praise for her moral seriousness and acuity.

Increasingly, however, reviewers were exasperated by the self-pity and self-esteem of her characters and the author's endorsement of them.   PMar

Charlesworth, Maria (Louisa) 1819–80 English writer of religious tales, mostly intended for children. Charlesworth was the daughter of a clergyman and helped him with his parish duties, working with the poor, and for a time, running a mission and a 'ragged school'. She described her experiences in two books, *The Female Visitor to the Poor* (1846) and the fictionalized *Ministering Children* (1854), which was aimed at children and used widely as a Sunday-school prize. Charlesworth hoped the story would teach children by example; she wrote in an 1867 preface: 'Difficulty being sometimes felt in training children to the exercise of those kindly feelings which have the Poor for their object, it was thought that an illustrative tale might prove a help ... [in] calling forth and training the sympathies of children by personal intercourse with want and sorrow, while as yet those sympathies flow spontaneously.' *Ministering Children* was followed in 1856 by *Africa's Mountain Valley*, a biographical sketch of a missionary to Africa and by several other books for children, among them *A Sequel to Ministering Children* (1867), *Oliver of the Mill* (1876) and *Sunday Afternoons in the Nursery, or Familiar Narratives from the Book of Genesis* (1885).   KW

Charlotte Temple (1791) Sentimental novel by SUSANNA ROWSON. First published in England as *Charlotte, A Tale of Truth*, and in 1794 in the United States, it has gone through over 200 editions and is considered the first American bestseller. Loosely based on Rowson's family, *Charlotte Temple* was intended 'for the happiness of that sex whose moral and conduct have so powerful an influence on mankind in general.'

Army lieutenant Montraville and his deceitful friend Belcour meet 15-year-old Charlotte and her devious teacher, Mlle La Rue. Convincing them to elope, the soldiers sail with them to America, where Montraville leaves Charlotte and marries the wealthy Julia Franklin. Montraville determines to support Charlotte secretly, but through an elaborate intrigue orchestrated by Belcour, he is convinced to abandon her forever. Seduced, betrayed and penniless, Charlotte is thrown out into the street. Refused entry to La Rue's home, she gives birth in the servants' rooms, where her father, who has come to America to bring her home, finds her dying. A repentant Montraville, having sought death in vain at Temple's hands, kills Belcour in a duel, and the Temples raise Charlotte's daughter Lucy back in England.   SP

Charnas, Suzy McKee 1939– American SCIENCE FICTION and fantasy novelist, prominent in the seventies wave of feminist fabulation. Born in Manhattan of artist parents, she was educated at Barnard College and New York University. In the 1960s she worked for the US Peace Corps in Nigeria and taught in New York, before marrying, moving to Albuquerque, New Mexico, and becoming a full-time writer. To date she remains best known for her earliest novels, the uncompromising *Walk to the End of the World* (1974) and *Motherlines* (1978), which grew out of the imaginative and political energies sparked off by the Women's Liberation Movement and were compared to works by URSULA LEGUIN, JOANNA RUSS and MARGE PIERCY among others. The former depicts a post-apocalyptic, patriarchal dystopia in which women ('fems') are a brutalized slave class; the latter reworks the Amazonian stereotype in contrasting the lifestyles of two all-woman tribes. These harsh allegories on gender relations were followed by *The Vampire Tapestry* (1980), a collection of novellas which startlingly naturalizes the vampire figure as predator. Charnas's subsequent fictions include *Dorothea's Dream* (1986) and the *Sorcery Hill Trilogy* (1985–9) for younger readers.

MO'D

Chase, Mary Ellen 1887–1973 American author and educator. The second of eight children, Chase was born in Blue Hill, Maine, into a family whose roots could be traced back to before the American Revolution, and which had lived in Blue Hill for three generations. Much of her work is set in Maine and focuses on its tradition and people. She graduated from the University of Maine at Orono in 1909, and spent the next eight years teaching and writing CHILDREN'S BOOKS. After earning her Ph.D. from the University of Minnesota, she continued teaching: in 1926, she took up a post at Smith College, where she remained an influential and much-beloved professor for thirty years. She published thirty-five books, in many genres, including the best-selling novel *Windswept* (1941), as well as autobiographical reminiscences, biographies, essays, criticism and biblical studies. Much of her work was critically acclaimed, and she has been compared to authors as diverse as SARAH ORNE JEWETT, WILLA CATHER, Henry James and William Dean Howells. SP

Chavez, Denise 1948– Fiction writer, playwright, editor. A native of New Mexico, Chavez sets her work in the American Southwest, and her characters are founded in this cross-cultural context. She is best known for her fiction, which is powerfully experimental and introspective, at times bordering on the surreal. Her novel, *Face of an Angel* (1994), winner of the 1995 American Book Award, paints the portrait of a Mexican-American waitress and writer composing in turn 'The Book of Service', a text of lessons on female life thinly disguised as a handbook for waitresses. *The Last of the Menu Girls* (1986) juxtaposes a series of highly interior and introspective short stories from the perspective of the same young female character struggling to come to grips with her identity. Chavez has written many plays, performing her one-actor *Women in the State of Grace* throughout the United States, and has edited or co-edited several anthologies, including *Shattering the Myth: Plays by Hispanic Women* (1994). She has also written fiction (*The Woman Who Knew the Language of Animals*, 1992) and drama (*The Flying Tortilla Man*, 1975) for children. SMSt

Cheke [née Hill, McWilliams], Mary, Lady ??–1616 Courtier and epigrammatist. She married first, in around 1547, the scholar Sir John Cheke (1514–57); then Henry McWilliams (but continued to be known as Lady Cheke). She was one of ELIZABETH I's most intimate attendants throughout her reign. In the late 1590s she was provoked to verse by an epigram by Sir John Harington. Apparently an ignorant preacher had glossed the text 'there was a certain man' to mean that although no man in the present was certain, there was once a man who was. Harington quipped, 'But yet I think in all the Bible no man / Can find this text: there was a certain woman.' Lady Cheke replied that this 'argues men are blind', and gave several biblical examples of certain women. She concluded that the preacher should blush to be confuted by a woman, 'Yet for his comfort one true note he made / When there was now no certain man he said'. The two poems exemplify the fashion for witty poetic exchanges at Elizabeth's court. HH

Cheney [née Foster)], Harriet Vaughan ?–1854? American and Canadian poet, CHILDREN's writer, novelist and religious writer. She was born in Boston to novelist HANNAH WEBSTER FOSTER; her father was a minister. Both she and her sister, novelist Eliza Foster Cushing, emigrated to Canada. Together they authored *The Sunday School, or Village Sketches* (1820) and cultivated other Canadian women writers as editors of the *Snow-Drop* (1847–51), a magazine about female roles and domestic responsibilities for girls aged 6–12. Cheney contributed tales with US, Canadian and Indian settings to the *Literary Garland*. She published two fictional accounts of the Pilgrims with a background of Indian warfare, *A Peep at the Pilgrims* (1924) and *Rivals of Acadia, an Old Story of the New World* (1827), and a work on Christ, *Confessions of an Early Martyr* (1846), the only book published with her name. JSG

Chéri (1920) and **The Last of Chéri** (1926) Novels by COLETTE. Beautiful, vain and egocentric Chéri has the good fortune to misspend his youth with the mature Lea, turn-of-the-century, Parisian 'grand cocotte', 'proud of thirty years devoted to radiant youths and fragile adolescents'. Despite profound and genuine affection, the inevitable ensues and even the pleasures of uninhibited sex and a relationship free of commitment are defeated by convention and youth. In *The Last of Chéri* tragedy overtakes Lea in the form of decline into old age – 'she ceased to belong to any assignable sex' – and Chéri in that of intense malaise and post-war depression. Colette's deceptively light style packs its punch in two bitter dénouements while the contrast between the sensual hedonism of the first story and the weariness and vulgarity which the characters have assumed in the second, eloquently reflects the atmosphere of both periods. *Plus ça change*, Colette's streetwise, independent ladies cope with life's vicissitudes while the men founder without emotional props.   EL

Cherry, Frances 1937– New Zealand novelist and short-story writer. After the breakup of her marriage in 1978, Cherry (with five children) moved onto the solo mother benefit and began teaching creative writing workshops. In 1988 she began a correspondence writing school. Her gutsy, satirical feminist short-story collection, *The Daughter-In-Law and Other Stories* (1986), contained a story, 'Waiting for Jim', about a husband who was cooked to death by his wife in a home sauna and which was made into a successful short film, 'One Man's Meat'. Her lively REALIST novel, *Dancing with Strings* (1989), tells of the ending of a marriage, the frustration and consolation of children and the discovery of lesbian alternatives, which can be both worse and better than their heterosexual predecessor. *The Widowhood of Jacki Bates* (1991) follows a middle-aged wife's discoveries about herself after her husband's death. Cherry's fictions are set in the Wellington area where she grew up and still lives.   AM

Cherryh, C. J. 1942– Working name of US writer of fantasy and SCIENCE FICTION Carolyn Janice Cherry, a prolific and occasionally clumsy writer, whose work is characterized by a strong tragic worldview and a capacity to enter into the mindset of imagined alien or supernatural creatures. A classicist by training, she is fascinated by the insights of anthropology and of sociobiology – her leonine aliens live in prides and her lupine aliens in packs, but their cultures are dominated by shame or guilt. Her tendency to proliferate series is not just pot-boiling; she returns to locales to conduct further thought-experiments on her material. A singleton fantasy of magic, amnesia and betrayal, *Fortress at the Eye of Time* (1995) is one of her more sustained works and typifies her tendency to depict protagonists adopted into cultures into which they can never fit; this is a metaphor for her can-do instinctual feminism.   RK

Chesnut, Mary Boykin Miller 1823–86 Chesnut is best known for her Civil War DIARY which recounts her experiences and observations during the years of the Confederacy. Wife of James Chesnut, Jr, United States senator from South Carolina, she moved in the highest circles of Confederate society, Jefferson and Varina Davis being the Chesnuts' closest friends and political allies. Thus, her *Diary* is both personal and political, as it chronicles the chaotic drama of the Confederacy, and discusses the highest ideals and the critical self-assessment of the Southern leadership.

A complex woman, Mary Chesnut was devoted to Confederate supremacy, but was also an abolitionist: 'God forgive us but ours is a *monstrous* system, and wrong and iniquity'. She claimed hyperbolically that Southern women 'hate slavery worse than MRS STOWE'. Additionally, like many mid 19th-century women authors, Chesnut conflated her concerns about racial inequality with her interest in women's rights: 'There is no slave after all like a wife.'

Not a bona fide diary, this text was adapted from her journal entries from February 1861 to July 1865, which were never intended for publication. In the years 1881–4, Chesnut reworked a portion of this material, which was published in 1905 as A DIARY FROM DIXIE. Ben Ames Williams edited a 1949 edition of her *Diary*, and later used Mary Chesnut as a character in his novel, *House Divided*.

Chesnut herself, a native of Camden, South Carolina, was well positioned to chronicle the drama of Confederate society and leadership. Daughter of Stephen Decatur Miller and Mary Boykin Miller, she was educated in the home and in a Charleston boarding school where she became friendly with the daughters of the South's wealthy planters. Her father, a lawyer and politician, served as state senator, governor, then United States senator; thus, the family home was filled with political debate and an eye to the life of the nation. Her 1840 marriage to James Chesnut, Jr, state senator and subsequently United States senator, allowed her to continue her interest in political life in both Charleston and Washington, D.C.

In addition to her *Diary*, Chesnut wrote a draft of a semi-autobiographical novel, *The Captain and the Colonel*, her first, rough attempt at fiction. Her second novel, *Two Years of My Life*, concerns her remove from her Charleston boarding school to her father's plantation on the Mississippi frontier. The extant pages of a third novel, *Manassas*, indicate that this, too, was largely autobiographical.   DZB

Chidley, Katherine fl. 1626–45 British writer whose writings advocating religious toleration and separation from the national church contributed to the religious and political controversies of the Civil War. In 1626 she married Daniel Chidley in Shrewsbury, but by the 1640s she was in London and involved in religious and political polemic. In his *Gangraena*, an attack on

Civil War sects, Thomas Edwards said Chidley spoke with 'violence and bitternesse against all Ministers'. Certainly, her first publication, *Justification of the Independent Churches of Christ* (1641), advocates separation from the Church of England, arguing that 'the Congregation of the Saints' ought not to be subject to earthly powers, let alone the 'evills' of that Church. She supports her authority by quoting 1 Samuel 17, 45: 'I come to thee in the name of the Lord of Hosts.' She also cites the story of Jael, who 'took a naile of the tent' and nailed her husband's head to the ground '(for he was asleep and weary)' (*Judges* 4.21). Chidley attacks Edwards in *A New-Yeares-Gift or a Brief Exhortation to Mr Thomas Edwards* (1645). In 1649 and 1653 she may have been involved in petitioning for the release of the Leveller John Lilburne. SW

Child [née McWilliams], Julia (Carolyn) 1912–

American COOKBOOK author, television chef and major protagonist in the gastronomization of the USA during the second half of the 20th century. Well-born and comfortably raised in Pasadena, California, she graduated from Smith College in Massachusetts, worked in Asia for the US government during World War II, and subsequently married her urbane colleague, Paul Child.

In Paris with Paul, a Foreign Service officer assigned to that city in 1948, Child fell 'hopelessly in love with French food at . . . first bite'. She studied eagerly with distinguished French chefs and was befriended by Simone Beck and Louisette Bertholle, upper-middle-class Parisians with whom she opened a small cooking school. Their French cookbook for Americans, *Mastering the Art of French Cooking* (mainly the work of Beck, Child and their editor), was published in New York during 1961, the year the Childs came home from Europe.

This long, literate, dazzlingly exact and organized volume taught the flavours, techniques and fundamental principles of 'expert French home-style cooking', and placed that cooking firmly within 'the Here', using ordinary ingredients 'from the American supermarket'. Enthusiastic and unintimidating – 'Above all, have a good time' – the book, without precedent in the USA, captivated an increasingly affluent nation discovering exotic food via airline travel, a growing trickle of ambitious gastronomic writing, and the publicity surrounding René Verdon, President Kennedy's White House chef.

In 1963, Child became 'The French Chef' on PBS, America's then-minimal-budget educational television network. Her lofty height, reassuring patrician warble and down-to-earth authority as she bumbled her way through serious cooking and snatched success from recurring culinary mishap fascinated her growing public. For a country of dedicated self-improvers, 'she took the fear out of cooking', declared a contemporary. During the 1960s, 'Julia', as she is known to admirers, became a household name.

Mastering the Art of French Cooking, volume II (1970), by Child and Beck without Bertholle, continued the theme selectively. Child's subsequent recipe books, highly polished television, and extensive magazine journalism have taken her clear, meticulous approach beyond France to the 'melting pot' of modern American food, whose diversity she has helped to create. AWS

Child, Lydia Maria (Francis) 1802–80

Abolitionist, novelist, journalist, writer of CHILDREN'S BOOKS and women's self-help manuals. Born into a baker's family in Medford, Massachusetts, Child and her brother Convers were the family intellectuals. But while Convers was able to go on to Harvard, Child educated herself to be a teacher, and, as her writing career developed, taught in school in Maine and Massachusetts. Her first political work, *The First Settlers of New-England: or, Conquest of the Pequods, Narragansets and Pokanokets* (1829), was written as a pedagogical dialogue between a mother and her children.

Though her childhood was unhappy, Child had imbibed her family's Revolutionary-era egalitarian beliefs. Her first novel, HOBOMOK (1824), a ROMANCE set in Puritan Massachusetts, hinges on the marriage of the white heroine and the Indian of the title. In keeping with contemporary prejudices, Hobomok cedes the heroine and their child to a white man, and virtually vanishes from the scene. But the novel's racial politics were radical enough to draw down charges of 'bad taste' from critics. The novel opened doors for her in Boston's literary world, where she met David Lee Child, whom she married in 1828. While the two supported each other's political beliefs, it was Lydia Child who had to manage their financial support, and her level-headed and hugely successful *American Frugal Housewife* (1829) household advice book was written from experience. Though childless and in a difficult marriage, Child became an early and immensely influential voice of domestic ideology and a highly respected authority on childhood and motherhood, especially through her periodical the *Juvenile Miscellany* (founded 1826), *The Little Girl's Own Book* (1831) and *The Mother's Book* (1831).

From 1830, when the Childs joined William Lloyd Garrison's anti-slavery movement, abolition became Child's calling, and accounts for the largest category of her book-length publications, though her convictions jeopardized her livelihood. With the appearance of *An Appeal in Favor of That Class of Americans Called Africans* (1833), immediately recognized as a central work, *The Mother's Book* fell out of print, subscriptions cancelled in protest led her to give up the *Miscellany*, and her own

Boston Athenaeum membership was rescinded. For two years, Child edited the *National Anti-Slavery Standard*, and served as conduit and editor for HARRIET JACOBS's *Incidents in the Life of a Slave-Girl* (1861). In addition to Child's lifelong and widely influential commitment to abolition and to Indian advocacy, she promoted women's rights through the biographies and histories she wrote for the Ladies' Family Library (1832–5). PCr

'Children of Violence' A sequence of five novels by DORIS LESSING, comprising *Martha Quest* (1952), *A Proper Marriage* (1954), *A Ripple from the Storm* (1958), *Landlocked* (1965) and *The Four-Gated City* (1969). Described by its author as 'a study of the individual conscience in its relation with the collective', this epic quintet tells the story of Martha Quest, from her childhood in colonial Southern Rhodesia to her part in an apocalyptic vision of the world at the end of the twentieth century. Throughout, Lessing portrays Martha's struggle to achieve liberation, both from constricting psychological states and from her specifically female role as a wife and mother, and her attempts to understand and engage with larger historical and political realities.

During this odyssey, Martha escapes the farmstead of her childhood for a more vital urban life, only to find herself frustrated by marriage and social mores. The breakdown of her heroine's marriage and her subsequent involvement with a Communist group during World War II allows Lessing to explore the possibilities and limitations of political action, especially as it conflicts with the individual will. In the final book, Martha finds herself in post-war London, with Europe shattered by war, the Cold War and the nuclear age about to start. Lessing's acute analysis of this ideologically desolate period sits alongside her powerful rendition of mental and psychological breakdown. AC

children's books Women's involvement with children's writing developed from their initial role as primary educators in the nursery. Many women from all stations of life were the first, often the only, teachers their children knew, a prominent example being Jane Johnson (1706–59), wife of a Buckinghamshire vicar. From their ranks emerged, in the latter part of the eighteenth century, women such as Anna Barbould, poet and educator, whose work was both published and influential. Enlightened radicals like Barbould and MARIA EDGEWORTH were criticized for their rationalism by writers who feared that purely entertaining fiction, still a relatively young medium, was becoming unavailable to children. This debate had flourished since the publication, in 1749, of the first children's novel, *The Governess*, by SARAH FIELDING. Even at that date people were questioning the whole-

someness of FAIRY TALES which had been annexed, along with some adult fiction, by children for whom they had not been originally intended. In 1839 Catherine Sinclair observed that children now seemed to be so over-educated that the notion of reading for pleasure was becoming foreign to them. Sinclair's *Holiday House* was the first DOMESTIC NOVEL for children and established a trend. Throughout the 19th century, fantasy was largely the province of male writers; women concentrated chiefly on REALISTIC tales of home life and, latterly, school days, an exception being JEAN INGELOW whose maverick SCIENCE FICTION story *Nineteen Hundred and Seventy-Two* was published in 1872.

In COLONIAL and POST-COLONIAL societies the bulk of reading material was initially imported from Britain. In America, James Janeway's *A Token for Children* (1671–2) influenced the creation of pious and proselytizing little girls in such books as *The Wide, Wide World* (Elizabeth Wetherall 1850), and the Elsie Dinsmore stories of Martha Finley Farquharson (1867 onwards). In 1868 LOUISA MAY ALCOTT decisively broke the mould with the first of the 'LITTLE WOMEN' quartet and her influence can be observed on both sides of the Atlantic in the lively family stories of Sarah Chauncey Woolsey (SUSAN COOLIDGE), JULIANA EWING and EDITH NESBIT, which can also trace their ancestry to CHARLOTTE YONGE's *The Daisy Chain* (1857). A number of English children's writers were Evangelical Christians as opposed to the Calvinists of New England, a major example being MARY MARTHA SHERWOOD and a minor one, Charlotte Maria Tucker (1821–93) who wrote as A.L.O.E. (A LADY OF ENGLAND). The notion that *publishing* books – as opposed to writing them – was a dubious pursuit for a woman persisted well into the 19th century and numerous female writers sought anonymity in the words 'A Lady', often averring that their works had been devised initially for use with their own children, thus distancing themselves from any declared intent to make money out of them. Charlotte Yonge, concurring heartily, handed over her income to her father.

Throughout the 19th century many magazines carried, or devoted themselves to, children's fiction, the most notable being *St Nicholas* (1874–1943), edited in the United States by Mary Mapes Dodge, herself author of *Hans Brinker or The Silver Skates* (1865). An indifferent novelist, she was a superlative editor, eliciting contributions from the best and most popular of writers including Rudyard Kipling, Alcott, and Susan Coolidge, whose *What Katy Did at School* (1873) was the first girls' boarding school story worthy of the term. As the century drew to a close the School Story (see GIRLS' SCHOOL STORIES), for both sexes, became a major genre, the heavy and over-heated works of L.T. Meade being superseded by those of ANGELA BRAZIL, which posited an environment where girls were seen to enjoy an active life and a degree of autonomy impossible in the company of boys, and developed a racy, slangy style of dialogue. Rarely realistic, although appearing to be so, Brazil's books continued to spawn imitations into the 1950s, and they still emerge from time to time. Ethel Talbot was a prolific practitioner but, like several of her contemporaries, wrote also about working girls, a subject of appeal to older readers at a time when the school leaving age was 14. The Girl Guide movement furnished an accessible background to many novels and short stories in annuals of the 1920s and 1930s. Modern critics who lament the dearth of strong female characters in the fiction of the first half of the 20th century tend to overlook such genre works which, although seldom literary or memorable, were usually literate and entertaining.

The tendency of little girls to fall in love with horses first found expression in Joanna Cannan's *A Pony for Jean* (1936). The book is dedicated to her daughters who, as Josephine, Christine and Diana Pullein-Thompson, effectively established the 'PONY BOOK' genre. At about the same time, NOEL STREATFEILD published *Ballet Shoes*, initiating a preoccupation with the performing arts which informed children's fiction through the middle decades of the 20th century – possibly the only genre which ENID BLYTON refrained from essaying. The 1950s and 1960s saw a flowering of new talent that broke away from the constraints of loco-parental guidance that had obtained in mainstream fiction since the decline of Nesbit's free-range families and the school/adventure story. Children's fiction began to evolve as a serious literary phenomenon, in which writers were accepted as serious stylists – though this was short-lived in Britain, today's critics and reviewers being more swayed by content than form. Rosemary Sutcliffe and Jill Paton Walsh specialized in historical fiction, JOAN AIKEN in fantasy, PHILIPPA PEARCE in novels and, importantly, the short story.

In the United States, where children's fiction has long been recognized as a bona fide literary form, the family story continued to flourish in the hands of Eleanor Estes and Elizabeth Enright, continuing with the contemporary novels of Katherine Paterson and Betsy Byars. America and all the post-colonial societies by this time boasted their own established traditions of children's writing, with many of the books travelling back to the UK. URSULA LE GUIN's *Earthsea* books, for instance, have been in print in America and Britain since they were first published in 1968, although her fiction for younger children is less well known here. But the avid curiosity about Europe evinced by 19th-century American writers has been replaced by a depressing parochialism. Works fail to cross the Atlantic in either direction, but chiefly westward, on the grounds that they are 'too English'. The British themselves, meanwhile, although willingly exposed to North American culture, and fairly receptive to such Australian writers as PATRICIA WRIGHTSON, ROBIN KLEIN and NADIA WHEATLEY, are appallingly resistant to anything attempting to enter from Europe.

A strong line of female author–illustrators has descended to the present day from the enduringly popular BEATRIX POTTER whose *The Tale of Peter Rabbit* was first published commercially in 1902, through Kathleen Hale whose books about Orlando the Marmalade Cat have enjoyed a revival. Young children and adults are able to share an appreciation of an illustrator. Text is always more problematic. The contemporary trend for books to be sold in readily identifiable series has resulted in children being less able to associate a book with its author than with the typography on the jacket, but this situation is probably as transient as any other. New writers continue to establish themselves and children continue to read in spite of doom-laden submissions to the contrary. JMM

Childress, Alice 1920–94 African-American playwright, novelist, short-story writer and actress on Broadway, in film and on television, who was known for her creation of characters, mostly black women, whom she called 'losers' (if measured by social status, power, money or education), but who have wit, compassion, a strong sense of reality and the courage not to capitulate to injustice.

In the early 1950s Childress wrote the column 'A Conversation from Life' for *Freedom*, Paul Robeson's Harlem newspaper. The column's speaker was Mildred, a clear-eyed, witty domestic servant. Childress became the first black woman to have a play produced Off Broadway – *Trouble in Mind* (1955) – which won an Obie Award. The play depicts an interracial cast rehearsing a play about a lynching. The protagonist, a black actress, exposes the historical racism in American theatre, including that of the white director and the cast, who learn that their hypocritical liberal attitudes allow racism to continue. Tommy in *Wine in the Wilderness* (1969), akin to Mildred but with even less education and money, is a strong, outspoken type reminiscent of Sapphire in the *Amos and Andy* radio series. Tommy teaches middle-class blacks a lesson in authenticity, kindness and their shared history.

Wedding Band: A Love–Hate Story in Black and White (1966, televised in 1973), Childress's best-known play, depicts a love relationship between a black woman and a white man in a small South Carolina town in 1918, when interracial marriage was banned by law. The couple, who have lived together for a decade, are not heroic or defiant but gentle and passive: Herman is afraid to move North because of his domineering mother, while Julia is resigned to moving from shanty to shanty. Finally, their love allows them to reject the petty racism of both blacks and whites. Though not sensational, the play offended blacks and whites who were against interracial love and marriage. Childress also wrote the children's play, *Hear It for the Queen* (1976), and later in life turned to novels, notably *A Hero Aint Nothing But a Sandwich* (1980), adapted later as a film.   SBB

Childwold (1976) JOYCE CAROL OATES's novel, set around Eden Valley, scene of her earliest writings, describes familiar Oates material: people living on the margins of American society, and the violence and complexity of their everyday lives. Its form is contrastingly lyrical: Oates describes it as 'a prose poem in the form of a novel, or a novel in the form of a prose poem'. The plot derives from the gradual unfolding of character through multiple narration. The reader distinguishes five perspectives: Laney, a 14-year-old girl living with her family in a chaotic, rundown farmhouse; Kasch, a brooding 40-something intellectual, sexually obsessed with Laney; Arlene, Laney's mother, addicted to abusive relationships and producing babies; Joseph, Arlene's father, plagued by disordered memories and senility; and Laney's brother Vale, a violent, disfigured Vietnam veteran. The Kasch–Laney relationship reworks Nabokov's *Lolita*, and the parallels include Kasch's liturgical wordplay: 'Childwold/Childwood/Childwide/Childworld'. The multiple narration, demanding on the reader, makes the focus broader and more compassionate than Nabokov's work, however, and reinforces the novel's point that life is too messy to be controlled.   KSi

Chinaberry Tree, The (1931) JESSIE REDMON FAUSET's third novel is often dismissed as a simple, sentimental representation of African-American life, at odds with the dominant concerns of the Harlem Renaissance. The novel's central characters confront the sexual and social orthodoxies of their middle-class environment in Red Brook, New Jersey: Sarah Strange (Aunt Sal) is ostracized for her loving (but unsanctioned) relationship with a prominent white man; their daughter, Laurentine, is beautiful but isolated in her ambiguous social standing; and Aunt Sal's vivacious, aspirant niece, Melissa, has her unfounded faith in her own legitimacy (and destiny) destroyed when she nearly elopes with her half-brother. Both Laurentine and Melissa face the stigma of inherited sin as they search for an adult female role in their community. Although the novel ends in happy resolution, its overtly sentimental form incorporates a powerful examination of racial and sexual identity. Fauset exposes the constraining and divisive fiction of 'bad blood', highlighting the tensions between external notions of lineage and the desires and struggles of modern African-American women.   AG

Cholmondeley, Mary 1859–1925 British writer most widely known for her novel, RED POTTAGE (1899). Although Cholmondeley published eight novels, two collections of short stories and a memoir, none of her other works rivalled the celebrity of this sensational and satiric novel. Cholmondeley wrote *Red Pottage* in London where she moved with her father, a Shropshire clergyman, when he retired.

The eldest daughter of eight children, she had assumed management of the family household at the age of 16 because of her mother's chronic ill health. Around the same time she began writing in earnest, and at 28 she published her first novel, a detective story called *The Danvers Jewels* (1887).

Cholmondeley's satire of the provincial clergy in *Red Pottage* provoked vehement denunciation of the novel in some circles. However, the novel's notoriety may be equally due to its engagement with the issues and debates associated with the NEW WOMAN, a social and cultural figure of the 1890s castigated and celebrated for her transgression of Victorian gender and class norms. Through the doubled heroines of *Red Pottage* – Rachel who pursues a doomed love-affair, and Hester, a writer struggling to complete her masterpiece in the stifling atmosphere of her clergyman brother's house – Cholmondeley explored the issues of female sexuality and vocation, recurring topics in late-Victorian debates about the New Women, and in the New Woman novel, a popular sub-genre of the period.

Cholmondeley wrote and published work until 1921 when she suddenly fell ill. She never fully recovered, and died at home at the age of 66.   EC

Chopin, Kate 1850–1904 American novelist, short-story writer, poet, DIARIST and essayist broaching controversial themes concerning women's experience, race and sensuality. She was born in St Louis, Missouri, to a Creole mother and a father of Irish descent, and after his death in 1855 received an unorthodox schooling from her great-grandmother before attending a local Academy. She married Oscar Chopin – 'the right man' – in 1870; they lived in New Orleans and had five sons, before moving to a village in northwest Louisiana. An independent streak so far most obvious in cigarette-smoking persisted on widowhood in 1882, when she managed some of Oscar's businesses. In 1884 she returned to St Louis, and began writing professionally.

Her stories set in up-state Louisiana appeared in local journals, then national magazines such as the *Century* and *Atlantic*. Exploring three racial groups –

Creoles, Acadians, Afro-Americans – their success reflected the vogue for 'local colorists', though she protested against the provincialism and sentimentality this label implied. They were untypical in their affirmative power and poise, lack of condescension, risqué themes and improper women. Asked by the *Century*'s editor to tone down a heroine she responded with revision, due irony and an obligingness that would abate – 'I have tried to convey the impression of sweetness and strength, keen sense of right, and physical charm beside.' Significant influences included European thinkers and writers, realists Flaubert and De Maupassant (whom she translated) especially; also iconoclastic contemporaries – authors, editors, artists, women friends – in St Louis's progressive intellectual circles and salons.

Twenty-odd stories appeared in *Vogue*, a new magazine in the 1890s catering for 'seasoned souls'. She published a short-story collection, *A NIGHT IN ACADIE*, in 1897. In her privately printed first novel, *At Fault* (1891), Chopin's non-judgemental treatment of women's passion, divorce and alcoholism proved too much, leading to rejection of a second novel which she thereupon destroyed. The first of three collections of short stories, *BAYOU FOLK* (1894), established her national reputation; the third, *A Vocation and a Voice*, was turned down in 1900, following the notoriety of her novel *THE AWAKENING* (1899). This radical narrative of a discontented wife and mother had ironies often overlooked; its sensuous economy and arresting ending met with great hostility and – mostly much later – feminist appreciation. KC

Christian, Barbara (T.) 1943– The most established African-American feminist literary critic and educationalist. She was born and brought up in the US Virgin Islands where she taught at the College of the Virgin Islands. She continued her education at Marquette University, Wisconsin, and Columbia University, New York, where she gained a doctorate in Contemporary British and American Literature. Whilst in New York she administered and taught for the SEEK programme for the promotion of access for black and Puerto Rican students to New York City College. She is best known for her critical texts *Black Women Novelists: The Development of a Tradition 1892-1976* (1980), for which she won the American Book Award, and *Black Feminist Criticism: Perspectives on Black Women Writers* (1985). Her critical practice involves textual analysis rather than theory and is influenced by an understanding that literature functions as a means of cultural promotion and survival. She has written and edited critical works on black women's writing and is particularly known for her work on ALICE WALKER. She has been awarded a Professorship in African-American Studies at the University of California,

Berkeley, and has edited a critical series on women writers for Rutgers University Press. MAB

Christie [née Miller], Agatha 1890–1976 Agatha Christie remains the pre-eminent DETECTIVE novelist of the 20th century. It's well known that she is the world's third best seller (only surpassed by Shakespeare and the Bible), and that no considerations of age, intelligence, social grouping or nationality restrict her appeal. Born Agatha Miller in Torquay, Devon, she married Archibald Christie in 1914, and published her first novel, *The Mysterious Affair at Styles*, in 1920. This, which introduced the retired Belgian detective Hercule Poirot to an avid readership, adumbrated her amazing capacity for subterfuge and labyrinthine plotting; and in truth she is not so much a novelist as the inventor of a novelty, a peculiarly intricate and fascinating type of literary puzzle. *Styles* was an immediate success; but it wasn't until 1926 and *THE MURDER OF ROGER ACKROYD* with its splendidly audacious ending, that her reputation was consolidated. In the same year occurred the single most dramatic episode in her own life – as a consequence, probably, of stress due to her mother's death and her husband's infidelity, she walked out of her Surrey home and disappeared. The ensuing press speculation didn't rule out foul play; but Agatha Christie turned up in Harrogate over a week later, having booked herself into a hotel using the name of her husband's mistress. It was an odd departure for someone who, before and after, showed an aversion to personal publicity – and indeed detested public occasions of all kinds.

In 1930 Agatha Christie married her second husband, the archaeologist Max Mallowan, and created – in *THE MURDER AT THE VICARAGE* – a striking new series detective, Miss Jane Marple of St Mary Mead. With her fragile and fluttery exterior masking a powerful capacity for observation and deductive logic, Miss Marple – the archetypal English spinster – exemplifies the device of least-likely-person-as-sleuth (never mind murderer). The best of the Marple stories – *The Body in the Library* (1942), for example, or *The Moving Finger* (1943) – rank with the best of Poirot (which might include almost everything from *Roger Ackroyd* to the late 1940s, but especially *Peril at End House* (1932), *The ABC Murders* (1935), and *Ten Little Niggers* (1939)) as absolute *pièces de résistance* of the genre. Certainly Agatha Christie has never been surpassed in the area of craftsmanship; she makes the most of the artifice inherent in detective writing, and provides, in book after book, the most staggering instances of prestidigitation. Even her story-book settings and playing-card characters have a certain decorativeness and charm – and if the flatness, not to say ineptitude, of her literary style is the price you have to pay for all the superb entertainment, then it seems worth paying.

(Only in the execrable last novels, *Elephants Can Remember* (1972), for example, or *Postern of Fate* (1973), does she lose her grip altogether.) As a bonus, with the Agatha Christie novels, you learn a good deal about social customs and assumptions of the middle classes in the second quarter of the 20th century – but these detective stories are best read simply for their sureness of configuration and inspired bamboozlement.   PC

Chronicles Of Carlingford, The The collective title by which MRS OLIPHANT's sequence of novels set in an English provincial town are known. The series began with two novellas, *The Rector* and *The Doctor's Family* (1863), and was swiftly followed by *Salem Chapel* (1863), an account of the progress of a young dissenting minister, who cannot reconcile his duty to God with duty to the Chapel elders; this novel is marred by an unnecessary sensationalist subplot. In *The Perpetual Curate* (1864), Mrs Oliphant turned her attention to the established Church, and dealt with the career, matrimonial and spiritual, of a High Church curate whose future seems to be in the hands of three evangelical aunts. The most critically acclaimed of the series is *Miss Marjoribanks* (1866) which charts the progress of an unsentimental girl who sets out to run the town's social life. Q. D. Leavis saw this dryly ironic and witty book as bridging the gap between JANE AUSTEN and GEORGE ELIOT. Mrs Oliphant's last chronicle of Carlingford was *Phoebe Junior* (1876), a quietly subversive novel whose purposeful and pragmatic heroine rises above her lowly origins to marriage with a rich, but malleable, bore. All these novels are distinguished by Mrs Oliphant's portrayal of spirited, disciplined and determined women and their less capable, and often less courageous, male counterparts.   CT

Chudleigh [née Lee], Mary, Lady 1656–1710 English poet and essayist, whose witty invectives against the state of marriage won her great acclaim. Such barbed sentiments as 'Wife and Servant are the Same, / But only Differ in the Name', suggest that her own marriage to Sir George Chudleigh of Ashton was unhappy and unfulfilling. Her first publication, *The Ladies' Defense* (1701), sharply answers a misogynist sermon by John Sprint and enters into a public conversation on the nature of femininity and female education. Widely read in poetry, history and philosophy, Chudleigh suffered the loss of a favourite daughter and was herself plagued by illness. In 1703, she published an edition of her *Poems* and became a successful essayist. Pieces on such topics as Knowledge, Pride, Friendship and Solitude lack the verve and energy of her poetry but similarly encourage female rationality in the face of 'treacherous Man'. Like her contemporary, MARY ASTELL, whom she greatly admired, Chudleigh's oeuvre encompasses an exclu-

sive world of female experience, suffering and struggle. She died at fifty-five, having written several plays and translations which were never published.   JRS

Churchill, Caryl 1938– Prolific and polemical British dramatist whose experiments with form combine with social commentary. Born in London, Caryl Churchill spent some of her early years in the Lake District before moving with her parents to Canada, to Montreal, where she lived from 1948 to 1955. She attended Montreal's Trafalgar School, but returned to the United Kingdom to read English at Oxford University. Whilst at Oxford, her plays *Downstairs* (1958) and *Having a Wonderful Time* (1960) were performed by student groups. For a decade after leaving Oxford, the majority of her output was plays for radio, including *The Ants* (1962), *Lovesick* (1966) and *Identical Twins* (1968). A commission by the Royal Court Theatre, London, led in 1972 to the production of the stage play *Owners*, a parable of society's attitudes to gender and ownership. Strongly influenced by EVA FIGES's *PATRIARCHAL ATTITUDES*, it was this play that marked a turning point in Churchill's career, and an indication of her future as a playwright at the forefront of her generation. Further connection with the Royal Court as a writer-in-residence saw the development of *Objections to Sex and Violence* (1975).

Her collaborative work in the 1970s with the theatre companies Monstrous Regiment and Joint Stock resulted in several plays, notably *Light Shining in Buckinghamshire* (1976; set in the English Civil War and concerning issues of property and community), *Vinegar Tom* (1976; about the persecution of witches in 17th-century England) and *CLOUD NINE* (1979; which juxtaposes issues of colonialism and patriarchy). Her Obie-Award-winning *TOP GIRLS* (1982) counterposes REALISTIC and imaginary scenes depicting women's roles in society and the results of 'success' within it. Amongst her later works are *SERIOUS MONEY* (1987; a satire in rhyming couplets set in the Stock Exchange), *Lives of the Great Poisoners* (1992) and *The Striker* (1994). Throughout her writing, Churchill probes the structure of society and issues of gender, often using historical or mythical settings to debate contemporary context. Her themes derive much from her association with the feminist and collectivist ideologies of the 1970s, while the group-led nature of her plays, and their use of song and refrain, is in the Brechtian style.

CS

Churchill, Sarah, Duchess of Marlborough 1660–1744 Essayist and letter writer, she was prudently introduced into court circles by her parents, where she became a maid of honour. Her meeting with the future Queen Anne when she was aged about 13 was to result in an intimate but tempestuous relationship. A determined, wilful and ambitious woman, she married John Churchill in 1678 and bore him eight children, five of whom survived. Both took up highly influential positions in the court but, given the volatile political situation, it is not surprising that their fortunes were constantly fluctuating; the Duchess in particular was much lampooned by contemporaries like DELARIVIÈRE MANLEY. Aside from her political career and her part in the building of Blenheim Palace, the Duchess's claim to be 'a kind of author' is borne out by the eventual publication in 1742 of her *An Account of the Conduct of the Dowager Duchess of Marlborough*, co-written with several others, including Nathaniel Hooke. Although unpublished during her lifetime, her *Memoirs* and personal and political correspondence are vivid and well-written.   RDM

Chute, Beatrice Joy 1913–87 American fiction writer, her first novel appeared when she was only nineteen. While writing under the pseudonym, 'B. J. Chute', she published over fifty sports stories for boys, including such novels as *Blocking Back* (1938), *Shattuck Cadet* (1940) and *Camp Hero* (1942), which acquired a devoted following of boys who thought she was a man. After she abandoned formula writing for boys, she began writing a number of stories for romance magazines such as *McCall's*, *Redbook* and *Woman's Home Companion*. Though she had written a number of short-story collections, including *The Blue Cup and Other Stories* (1957), *One Touch of Nature and Other Stories* (1965), Chute was better known for novels such as *The Moon and the Thorn* (1961), *Story of a Good Life* (1971), *Katie: An Impertinent Fairy Tale* (1978) and her most successful novel the lyrical pastoral fantasy *Greenwillow* (1956), which reflects her warm affection for the woodlands and lakes of Minnesota. In 1960, *Greenwillow* was produced as a musical in New York with the book by Lesser Samuels, scored by Frank Loesser and starring Anthony Perkins. The last work she completed before her death was *The Good Woman* (1986).   MRA

Cimarron (1930) EDNA FERBER's best selling novel opens with a vivid description of the day of the 1889 Oklahoma Run when 2 million acres in the former Indian Territory were handed over to the first (white) settlers fast enough and ruthless enough to stake their claim, and ends as the new state strikes oil. Ferber's fast-moving narrative centres on Yancey Cravat, an idealistic lawyer, sharpshooter and newspaper editor, and his wife, Sabra, delicately reared but a willing pioneer. Neither however is depicted stereotypically: Yancey for all his heroics is deeply flawed, his impractical aspirations being further undermined by Sabra's innate conservatism, evinced in the imposition of her version of civilization on their shanty town. Ferber has said that few people had recognized her intention to write 'a

malevolent picture of what is known as American womanhood', but hoped that this would be comprehended 'in another day'. The novel was outstanding for its time in its sympathetic portrayal of the dispossessed native Americans.

Cimarron has been filmed twice: in 1931, director Wesley Ruggles (Oscar, Best Picture), and in 1960, director Anthony Mann.   WAP

Cisneros, Sandra 1954– Chicana short-story writer and poet whose genre-crossing work explores the multiple experiences of Mexican-American women in the United States. Raised with six brothers in a series of working-class neighbourhoods in Chicago by her Mexican father and Mexican-American mother, she spent much of her childhood moving with her family from house to house and also back and forth to Mexico. Though she began writing at the age of 10, she didn't discover her subject until the late 1970s in graduate school, where she decided to 'write about something my classmates couldn't write about': her barrio childhood. That decision eventually produced THE HOUSE ON MANGO STREET (1984), a lyrical story of the personal and artistic development of a young Chicana struggling to reconcile selfhood, community and creativity amidst racial, sexual and economic oppression. In 1987 Cisneros published her second volume of poems, *My Wicked Wicked Ways* (her first, the chapbook *Bad Boys*, had appeared in 1980), a collection offering a complementary yet ironized narrative of development that carries the voice of *Mango Street* into a defiantly transgressive adulthood. With *Woman Hollering Creek and Other Stories* (1991) she brought her postnationalist feminism to the Texas borderlands in a book of tales that provocatively mingles genres, languages and cultures. *Hairs: Pelitos*, a bilingual version of a chapter from *Mango Street*, illustrated for children, came out in 1994, as did *Loose Woman: Poems*, an exuberant volume at once rowdy and tender, erotic and political. 'I'm Pancha Villa', the title poem declares – 'Beware, honey.'   WG

Cixous, Hélène 1937– French writer, intellectual and political activist, working in the area of sexual difference, feminism, literary theory and philosophy. Author of nearly thirty books of poetic fiction, eight plays and numerous critical essays on Joyce, Freud, Tzvetaeva and the Brazilian writer CLARICE LISPECTOR. Cixous was born into a Jewish-German family in Oran, Algiers, which she left in 1955 for Paris. Having obtained a diploma in English, she embarked upon a teaching career. She then became Professor of Literature at the experimental Université de Paris VIII, which she helped found in 1968.

Cixous's version of 'the feminism of difference' has been enormously influential for Anglo-American feminist literary critics. Her work, orientated toward overcoming the patronizing, masculine, or 'phallogocentric' bias in Western thought, reflects her multicultural background and her interest in the heterogeneity of women's psychosexual experience. Her influential essay 'The Laugh of the Medusa', translated into English in 1976, introduces her concept of *'l'écriture féminine'* (feminine writing). Asserting women's right to repossess their bodily pleasure and its links with creativity, Cixous managed to combine poetic style with rich residues of affection and thought: 'Write! And your self-seeking text will know itself better than flesh and blood, rising insurrectionary dough kneading itself, with sonorous, perfumed ingredients.' Her literary experiments, intended to demonstrate a link between libidinal energy and artistic creativity, have given way to a series of innovative practices in both academic and non-academic writing. Femininity functions for Cixous as a paradigm for a new ethics, one that would leave behind the male logic of property and individualism for the sake of infinite spending: 'I is never an individual. I is haunted. I is always, before knowing anything, an I-love-you.' Other works in translation include *To Live the Orange* (1979), *Angst* (1985), *The Newly Born Woman* (1986) and *Three Steps on the Ladder of Writing* (1993). JZ

Clairmont, Clara Mary Jane ('Claire') 1798–1879

MARY SHELLEY's step-sister, wandered with the Shelleys around England and Italy (1814–22). A brief liaison with Byron (1816) resulted in the birth of a daughter, Allegra (1817–22), whom, to her bitter regret, she was persuaded to surrender to the poet. A marriage-scorner, she lived mostly on the continent, governessing in Russia and finally settling in Florence; posthumously, she inspired Henry James's 'The Aspern Papers' (1888). Speculation concerning her relationship with P. B. Shelley and her reputation as tempestuous muse and irritant have obscured her genuine talents. But, while few traces of her literary projects survive, editions of her *Journals* and *Correspondence* (Stocking, 1969 and 1995) and Gittings's and Manton's biography (1992) have revealed a progressive teacher, an independent woman with a gift for languages (including, uncommonly for 1820, German) and a vivid letter-writer. NC

Clampitt, Amy 1920–1992 American poet. She was a

New Yorker, the daughter of a prairie settler family, who came suddenly to prominence at the age of 53 with the publication of her first, miraculously accomplished, book, *The Kingfisher* (1983). Over the next decade, until her death in 1992, she produced four more books of poetry, for which she gained several prizes, visiting professorships, and a Macarthur fellowship which allowed her to buy a modest house in Massachusetts.

The title of her first book, *The Kingfisher*, alludes to the dense, passionate writing of Victorian poet and priest, Gerard Manly Hopkins; and she has something herself of what she calls a 'Miltonic rocketry of epithet'. 'Sunday Music' parallels the domestic act of sewing on patches with the texture of the Allegro from Handel's 'Concerto Grosso':

> The Baroque sewing machine of Georg Friedrich
> going back, going back to stitch back together
> scraps of a scheme that's outmoded.

But this is ironically 'modern': the real subject of the poem is the nature of historical change and, cunningly, Handel goes forward by going back. The reader is led through dense chains of parallelism and appositional phrasing, only to find that the ostensible subject of the poem, by a lateral shift, has metamorphosed into something else. She is frankly a late romantic, following Keats (whom she calls a 'fairweather scavenger of what pleases the eye') and the Keatsian side of Hopkins, into her own American heritage (Wallace Stevens and Hart Crane), tracing through them the desire to coax out of the natural object 'that glimpsed inkling of things / beyond systems' ('Sed de Correr'). Clampitt's obsession with the (geological, botanical) naming of parts, makes language's technical vocabularies give something back to the common tongue.

The characteristic effect of this rich style is gained through an unusual foregrounding of syntax which critics have labelled 'baroque'. This air of suspension disguises the clever metrics of the poem – Clampitt is often writing a form of heroic blank verse, but whose *enjambement* is so rigorous one no longer notices. The metaphysics of Romanticism's confrontation with the natural world is suspended, weightlessly, in webs of doubtful syntax – miming back immediately the reader's perception – which often seem a commitment to sheer process. The effect is not to naturalize, however, but to make and re-make resonant objects of contemplation out of the humblest event:

> An ordinary evening in Wisconsin
> seen from a Greyhound bus. VS

Clara Morison (1854) Australian CATHERINE

HELEN SPENCE's first and best novel was one of the first about Australia written by a woman. In this Cinderella plot, the orphaned heroine, gentle, middle-class Clara, is unfeelingly sent off alone from England to Adelaide where she is forced into service to survive. She discovers cousins in the Elliott family, and ultimately marries the grazier Charles Reginald. The novel ranges well beyond its DOMESTIC settings and ROMANCE plot to include vivid letters from the gold-diggings in Victoria, sharp and amusing satire of false gentility and snobbery, and a vigorous defence of COLONIAL society. In particular it champions the colony's rejection of class divisions based on birth and wealth, instead eulogizing the respectability achieved through hard work and education. It provides a fascinating picture of early Adelaide, and possesses a second heroine, Margaret Elliott, a self-portrait of Spence, who chooses a single life of work toward legal and social reform. This domestic and largely urban novel represents an important feminine and feminist alternative to the masculine bush stereotypes of the later 19th century.   HTh

Clark, Eleanor [Warren] 1913–96 American fiction and non-fiction writer. The daughter of a mining engineer, Clark was raised in Roxbury, Connecticut, and educated in convent schools in France and Italy before she graduated from Vassar College in 1934 to begin her literary career. Working as an editor and translator, she authored short stories, novels and in-depth TRAVEL essays. In 1952 she published *Rome and a Villa* to critical acclaim and married Robert Penn Warren. After the birth of their two children, they continued to travel frequently to Europe. Clark's best work, *The Oysters of Locmariaquer* (1964), which won a National Book Award, is about more than French *belon* oysters. In describing a fishing village in Brittany, she reveals a moral passion for order and meaning derived from lives rooted in an exacting *métier* and in a particular place. From the vantage of an idealized pastoral community, Clark, in a voice as acerbic as it is lyric, critiques American culture in a way that echoes the New England tradition of Ralph Waldo Emerson and Henry David Thoreau. Awarded two Guggenheim Fellowships, she was also elected to the National Institute of Arts and Letters.
                                                                BF

Clark, Joan 1934– Canadian writer of fiction for adults and children. Born in Liverpool, Nova Scotia, Clark grew up there and in other parts of the Maritimes. After graduating from Acadia University she attended the University of Alberta and worked as a schoolteacher. For many years Clark lived in Calgary where she was co-founder, with EDNA ALFORD, of the literary magazine *Dandelion*, and an active member of a literary community which included CLAIRE HARRIS. Clark was shortlisted for the Governor General's Award for *The Victory of Geraldine Gull* (1988), a novel which explores the relationship between a Eurocanadian artist and the northern First Nations community in which she temporarily resides.

A compelling story-teller, Clark rejects the view that CHILDREN's literature is separate or radically different from adult literature, asserting that 'the difficulty of any story has to do with what is being risked, with how the story shifts and slides, with problems of craft

rather than genre'. This belief is exemplified in her award-winning novel for children, *The Dream Carvers* (1995), about a young Norse boy who 'disappears' during an incident in her adult novel, *Eiriksdottir, A Tale of Dreams and Luck* (1994). Since the early 1980s, Clark has lived in St John's, Newfoundland, where she writes full-time.   DF

Clarke [née Novello], Mary (Victoria) Cowden 1809–98 English scholar and novelist whose work on Shakespeare, ranging from an authoritative concordance to inventive tales about his characters, was aimed at making the playwright's works more accessible. Mary Cowden Clarke was the daughter of composer Victor Novello, and grew up surrounded by the literati of the Regency: Charles and MARY LAMB and Leigh Hunt were family friends. Mary was educated at home and in France, and, at 19, married Charles Cowden Clarke, a 41-year-old writer and publisher who moved in the same literary social circles as her father.

In 1829, Mary began work on her *Concordance to Shakespeare*; it was not completed and published until 1844–5, when it appeared in monthly parts. She continued her work on Shakespeare with the collection *Shakespeare Proverbs* (1848) and THE GIRLHOOD OF SHAKESPEARE'S HEROINES (1851–2), a collection of stories imagining the early lives of Shakespeare's women. The Cowden Clarkes collaborated on two other projects focusing on Shakespeare: an inexpensive annotated edition completed in 1868 and *The Shakespeare Key: Unlocking the Treasures of His Style* (1878). The couple remained part of English literary circles until they moved to Italy in 1856, and in 1878 they published their *Recollections of Writers*, describing their friendship with Hunt, the Lambs, Charles's close friend John Keats, and Charles Dickens, among others.

Mary Cowden Clarke also wrote fiction, including *Kit Bam's Adventures* (1849) – a collection of stories for children – and *A Rambling Story* (1874) – a novel for adults. Among her BIOGRAPHICAL works are *World-Noted Women* (1858), sketches of historical figures ranging from SAPPHO to FLORENCE NIGHTINGALE; an 1864 life of her father; and a privately printed biography of her husband, written in 1887, ten years after his death. Cowden Clarke's autobiography, *My Long Life*, was published in 1897.   KW

Clarke [née Owenson], Olivia, Lady c.1785–1845 Irish dramatist and author of parodies and comic verse. Born in Dublin, Olivia's childhood as the daughter of a feckless actor–manager was an insecure and peripatetic one. Her mother died when she was only 2 years old, and Olivia was cared for by her elder sister SYDNEY OWENSON, later the novelist Lady Morgan. After leaving boarding school, she spent some time with her father, who managed a travelling repertory company, and then became a governess. She was saved from poverty by marriage in 1808 to a Dublin physician, the 'tiny, seductive and most respectable' Sir Arthur Clarke, by whom she had three daughters. The couple enjoyed a secure place in Dublin society, and Olivia was now able to offer a home to her charming but disreputable father.

Clarke's play, *The Irishwoman*, a comedy in five acts, was successfully produced on the stage in Dublin, and published in 1819. However, her chief talent was for comic and satirical verse, and her poems were published in periodicals such as *Metropolitan Magazine* and the *Athenaeum*. *Parodies on Popular Songs*, featuring traditional Irish airs, as well as one by her father, appeared in 1836.

Although ten years younger than her sister, it was Olivia who died first, in 1845. The 'precarious youth' through which both had struggled had laid the basis for a lifelong intimacy, and Sydney mourned not only a 'noble-minded and affectionate sister', but also the friend to whom she had confided the triumphs as well as the disappointments of her own more flamboyant literary career.   RR

Clausen, Jan 1950– American poet and fiction writer born and raised in the Pacific North-West. In 1973 she moved to New York, where she was active in feminist publishing, radical political organizations and community groups. She was co-founder of *Conditions* magazine and ran the lesbian publishers Long Haul Press. In 1981 she received a National Endowment for the Arts Fellowship. Her poetry, fiction and criticism have appeared widely in a range of periodicals and anthologies and explore issues of lesbian identity, politics and desire. Her books include *Mother, Sister, Daughter, Lover* (1980); *A Movement of Poets: Thoughts on Poetry and Feminism* (1982); *Duration* (1983); *Books and Life* (1988); and *The Proserpine Papers* (1988). In particular, she writes around issues of lesbian mothering. Hence her first novel, *Sinking, Stealing* (1985), reappropriated on-the-road narratives to explore issues of lesbian parenting, telling the tale of the bereaved Josie's flight with her female lover's child across country by Greyhound bus.   CSt

Cleeve, Lucas [Adeline Georgina Isabella Kingscote] 1860–1908 Prolific British novelist. She was the only daughter of the diplomat Sir Henry Drummond Wolff MP. According to 'Who's Who' she attended Oxford University, but this has been queried. She was 'a great traveller and linguist', who enjoyed riding and cycling. After her marriage to Lt. Col. Howard Kingscote in 1885, they lived in India and had three children.

As 'Mrs Howard Kingscote' she published *Tales of the Sun, or, Folklore of Southern India* (1890, in collaboration) and *The English Baby in India and How to Rear It* (1893). Under her pseudonym she wrote around sixty novels. The most famous, *The Woman Who Wouldn't* (1895), was a deliberate response to Grant Allen's bestseller: 'If one young girl is kept from a loveless, mistaken marriage, if one frivolous nature is checked in her career of flirtation by the remembrance of Lady Morris, I shall perhaps be forgiven by the public for raising my feeble voice in answer to *The Woman Who Did*.' Cleeve's first edition sold out in three weeks, and some of its reviews amounted almost to libel. She died in Switzerland, having settled there after separating from her husband.   SF

Cleghorn, Sarah 1876–1959 American poet, author, reformer. Born the fifth of six children, four of whom eventually died, Cleghorn spent her early years in Wisconsin and Minnesota. After her mother's death, when Cleghorn was 8, the family moved to Manchester, Vermont, where she lived for the rest of her life, with occasional trips to New York and Europe. Raised in a devout Episcopalian household interested in poetry and intellectual inquiry, she was educated at the local Burr and Burton's Seminary, graduated in 1895 and spent the following year studying Philosophy and Literature at Radcliffe College.

She published her first stories and poems in 1897, and began printing 'letters to the editor' on causes as diverse as workers' rights, Christian charity and anti-vivisection. After the death of her father in 1913, she joined the Socialist party, and became a pacifist and a vegetarian. Her autobiographical second novel, *The Spinster*, was followed closely by her first book of poetry, *Portraits and Protests*, including what she called her political 'burning poems', the last of which extols 'Comrade Jesus'. Over the next decades, while teaching at the communitarian schools Brookwood and Manumit, she took up the causes of the Labour Movement and women's suffrage, writing a memoir of the World War I years, an alternative American history for children, and a second book of poetry. Her sensitive and charming autobiography, *Threescore* (1936), was perhaps her most popular work.   SP

Clerke, Ellen Mary 1840–1906 Versatile Irish writer and linguist. She and her sister, the astronomer Agnes Mary Clerke, were born in Skibbereen, County Cork, lived in Dublin briefly, but ultimately made London the home to which they returned from their many European tours. The sisters lived in Italy from 1870 to 1877, a sojourn of importance to Ellen Mary who immersed herself so deeply in the culture's language and literature that she contributed, in perfectly idiomatic Italian, a series of stories to Florence periodicals. No discipline or literary genre appears to have been closed to Clerke. She wrote for the journal of the Manchester Geographical Society and made regular editorial contributions to the *Tablet*, often commenting knowledgeably on the complex religious and political problems facing contemporary Europe. She shared with her sister an interest in making scientific discoveries and principles accessible to the general reader and published valuable pamphlets on popular astronomy, including *The Planet Venus* (1893). She translated into English a collection of Italian essays and poetry, *Fable and Song in Italy* (1899), and published a collection of her own poetry, *The Flying Dutchman* (1881), as well as a novel, *Flowers of Fire* (1902), remarkable for its recreation of the eruption of Vesuvius.   MO'C

Clifford, Anne, Lady, later Countess of Dorset, Pembroke, and Montgomery 1589–1676 Diarist.

Her work records a lifelong legal struggle to reclaim family lands which she considered rightfully hers. This brought her into conflict not only with her husbands (she married Richard Sackville in 1609 becoming Countess of Dorset, and Philip Herbert in 1630 becoming Countess of Pembroke and Montgomery) but with King James VI and I himself. Intriguingly her DIARIES from 1617 record how James's wife, Anna of Denmark, supported Clifford behind the scenes, advising her 'not to trust [the] matter absolutely to the king, lest he should deceive [her]'. As well as offering an invaluable record of court life, masques, meetings with the monarch and all, the diaries and daybooks provide a remarkable insight into the daily life of a woman of élite rank, juxtaposing such disparate elements as a child's nosebleed with accounts of Star Chamber speeches by the King. The tensions of Clifford's marriages are obvious ('in the afternoon my lord and I had a great falling out') and she appears to have spent much of her time in relative isolation at her husbands' country estates. She famously evoked the Psalms in describing herself at Knole, the Sackville estate in Kent, as being 'like an owl in the desert'.

Clifford clearly had a strong sense of self, further evidenced by her commissioning late in life of the so-called 'Great Picture' which hangs at Appleby Castle in Cumbria. The portrait depicts her as both a younger and older woman, surrounded most obviously by her books (the titles of which are clear), thereby emphasizing her intellect and learning. As a child she was tutored by the poet Samuel Daniel. She was an important patron of the arts and is famously described, along with her mother, Margaret, Countess of Cumberland, in AEMILIA LANYER's poem *Salve Deus Rex Judaeorum* (1611). Her land-rights case was ultimately successful and she immediately left her second husband spending the rest of her years in her northern castles. In the 20th century VITA SACKVILLE-WEST edited her female ancestor's remarkable autobiographical writings.   JS

Cliffs of Fall (1963) SHIRLEY HAZZARD's first collection of short stories, most of which had previously been published in *New Yorker Magazine*, covers Hazzard's favourite themes of love and misguided love, art, creativity and moral distinction, within the world of the personal relationships of the European and Anglo-American middle classes. While not interconnected, the stories all focus on minute, acute perceptions of isolated, introspective characters, on their sense of being at odds with the world around them, and their desires for love and beauty.

The source of the collection's title in Gerald Manly Hopkins's 'O the mind, mind has mountains; cliffs of fall / Frightful, sheer, no-man-fathomed. Hold them cheap / May who ne'er hung there', while referring explicitly to key metaphors in the title story, encapsulates the concern of all ten stories with the persistence of poetic insight in the inner drama of individual lives and relationships.   BO

Clift, Charmian 1923–69 Australian columnist,

novelist and short-story writer famed for her weekly newspaper articles on the pleasures and perils of suburban living. Born in New South Wales and named by her English father after Cleopatra's attendant in Shakespeare's play, she served in the Women's Army during World War II and began her journalistic career on the Melbourne *Argus* in 1946. She married the writer George Johnston and they collaborated on three novels, the first of which, *High Valley* (1949), was a critical success.

After three years in England oppressed by 'the gloomy monstrous weight' of London, they settled on the Greek island of Hydra. Here, whilst Clift was writing a novel, *Honour's Mimic* (1964), and her journals of Aegean life, *Mermaid Singing* (1958) and *Peel Me a Lotus* (1959), the couple argued frequently and drank heavily. 'I have always been attracted by the wrong roads', she later confessed.

The family returned to Australia in 1964 and Clift began her weekly column in the Women's Section of the *Sydney Morning Herald*. Quirky and anecdotal, her articles were influenced by VIRGINIA WOOLF and aimed at the 'common reader'. They soon gained a large following at a time when the traditional newspaper essay was being superseded by the New Journalism of young America. 'I don't think it is my business to educate or elevate', she said of her work. 'I suppose all that any writer asks, apart from a labourer's wage, is the knowledge that he is in communication with responsive people.' Her own column never failed to elicit a large and favourable response. IMAGES IN ASPIC, a collection of short essays, was published in 1965.

She was, however, desperately struggling to cope with the increasing demands of her popularity whilst also trying to look after her sick husband and three children. Exhausted and depressed, she committed suicide in July 1969.   JAH

Clifton, Lucille 1936– American poet and fiction writer born in Depew, New York, to a working-class family, she went on to study at the State University of New York at Fredonia, then at Howard University. While raising six children she gained attention in the late 1960s after publishing her first book, which positioned her in the Black Arts Movement. Her collections include: *Good Woman: Poems and a Memoir* (1987), *Quilting: Poems 1987–1990* (1991) and *The Book of Light* (1993) which offers a range of voices; characters we might think we know (many of them biblical) are re-invented and speaking to us – sometimes it's Superman:

> Lord
> man of steel,
> i understand the cape,
> the leggings, the whole ball of wax.
> you can trust me.

Sometimes it's Leda, Ruth, Samson; or just an ordinary mortal:

> The woman walks into my dreams
> dragging her old habit.
> i turn from her, shivering,
> to begin another afternoon
> of rescue, rescue.

There is a spiritual tenor to Clifton's voice but the presence of God does not stultify; it liberates the poems in expressions of discovery, joy and sanctuary from the difficult world.   ACH

Clive [née Meysey-Wigley], Caroline 1801–73 British novelist and poet. She felt that her childhood was unhappy because she had contracted infantile polio as a small child and remained lame, and was otherwise unattractive too, though intelligent and well-read. Her ambition was to become a writer, especially a poet, but her first venture into print was a small volume of sermonlike essays under the pen name 'Paul Ferrol'. When nearly 39 she published a book of poems, and a few months later married the man she had worshipped for nine years: her clergyman, the Revd Archer Clive, to whom she bore a son and a daughter in a happy marriage lasting thirty-three years. Her great success as a writer was the novel *Paul Ferroll* (1855), admired among the intelligentsia and even translated into French but shocking to ordinary readers because it is the tale of a wife murderer whom the novel vindicates, even allowing his ever-loving daughter to arrange his escape from prison on the eve of execution. (The novel also allows him to quell a workers' riot by having the ringleaders summarily executed.) A sequel, *Why Paul Ferroll Killed His Wife* (1860), extenuates his guilt even more.   HB

Clive [née Raftor], Catherine (Kitty) 1711–85 Comedy actress and singer. The daughter of an impoverished Irish lawyer, Kitty joined the company at London's Drury Lane Theatre at the age of 17, and quickly graduated from minor to leading roles. One of her early successes was as Polly in *The Beggar's Opera*, a part which she regarded for many years as her own, resisting management's attempts to assign it to rival actresses.

Assertive on her own behalf, Clive was also vociferous in defence of her profession, and in 1744 championed actors' rights in *The Case of Mrs Clive*. Described by a colleague as 'passionate, cross and vulgar', she was also respected for her wit, intelligence and artistry. Admirers included Handel, Samuel Johnson and the theatre historian Victor, for whom she was 'this laughter-loving, joy-exciting actress'.

In 1749–50 Kitty appeared in her own play, *The Rehearsal* (published 1753), but her performance, in a 'breeches' part, was poorly received. She wrote three other farces, *Every Woman in her Humour* (1760), *Sketch of a Fine Lady's Return from a Rout* (1763) and *The Faithful Irishwoman* (1765), none of which was well reviewed. She continued, however, to dominate the Drury Lane stage, acclaimed for performances such as Lady Wishfort in *The Way of the World* and Widow Blackacre in *The Plain Dealer*.

In 1769, with her reputation still at its height, Clive retired from the stage and moved to a cottage in Twickenham owned by her friend, Horace Walpole, where she died in 1785.   RR

Cloud Nine (1978–9) CARYL CHURCHILL's twenty-fifth performed play was written for Joint Stock Theatre Group after a workshop in which writer, director and actors explored sexual politics, including 'the parallel between colonial and sexual repression'. Churchill incorporated in the two-act structure the distance between the 'conventional, almost Victorian expectations' of sex and marriage the members of the company had inherited and their own changes and discoveries. Act 1 takes place in British Africa in 1879. Clive is both colonial administrator and autocratic ruler in his household. There are 'troubles' among the natives but the Victorian family ostensibly supports a benign tyranny, loyal to God, Queen, Empire and Father. This respectable façade masks adultery, homosexuality, pederasty and desperate frustration. Highlighting the hypocrisies and distortions, Clive's wife, Betty, who 'wants to be what men want her to be', is played by a man; his black servant, who 'wants to be what whites want him to be', by a white man; his homosexual son, on whom masculinity is imposed, by a woman. Act 2 takes place in England a century later but only twenty-five years have passed for the characters. Betty has left Clive, and their children are experimenting with open and fluid relationships. Most characters are now played by actors of their own sex.   PMar

Cluysenaar, Anne (Alice Andrée) 1936– Poet, Irish by nationality, who was born in Brussels. She was educated at Trinity College, Dublin, where she won the Vice-Chancellor's Prize. After reading English and French, she studied Linguistics at Edinburgh University. She then became reader and writer to Percy Lubbock, and held a number of academic appointments in universities in Ireland, Scotland and England. The most striking of these was at Sheffield Hallam from 1976 to 1987, where she chaired the Verbal Arts Association and closely involved herself with a number of educational initiatives for the wider community, especially The Poetry Society's Poets-in-Schools project. She is recognized as one of the early activists in the subsequent poetic renaissance centred on Sheffield, Manchester and Huddersfield. She married Walter Freeman Jackson in 1976 and has three step-children. Cluysenaar went on to live and work mainly in South Wales as a freelance song writer and tutor of creative writing.

Her poems – 'meditations on precisely those gaps and silences where lives meet and separate, where writing begins and ends' – were showcased in one of Faber and Faber's influential 'Poetry Introduction' anthologies. She published two major volumes with Carcanet – *Double Helix* (1985) and a new and selected poems, *Timeslips* (1997). *Double Helix* was 'started into being' by the death of the poet's mother. It eloquently records her family history reaching back over three generations and is thought by many of her readers her most sustained and impressive work. Where *Double Helix* drew substantially on past lives, Cluysenaar's later poems look to her own future using experimental strict-verse forms and the language of the new science. Other works include an *Introduction to Literary Stylistics* (1976) and the 1977 Carcanet edition of the *Selected Poems* of Burns Singer – a poet like Cluysenaar and contemporary PAULINE STAINER – much concerned with metaphysical explorations of biology.   DM

Cobbe, Frances Power 1822–1904 Indefatigable Irish essayist and lecturer, outspoken feminist, and dedicated anti-vivisectionist. Born in Dublin, she was instructed at home, then sent to Brighton, where her education, frivolous and 'shallow' compared to her brothers', roused Cobbe's early resentment of sexual inequality. While still living with her parents, she wrote *Essays on the Theory of Intuitive Morals* (1855), which, though published anonymously, resulted in a falling-out with her religiously conservative father. After his death in 1857, she left home and began to travel throughout Europe and the East. After settling in England, she became involved with Mary

Carpenter's 'Ragged School' movement in Bristol. Her work with underprivileged girls decisively compelled her advocacy of women's rights. Her impassioned discourse on behalf of women and other victims of injustice rang through innumerable lecture halls and was regularly featured in the leading periodicals of the day.

Cobbe was persuasive as well as prolific; her pamphlet *Wife Torture* (1878) influenced that year's Matrimonial Causes Act. Into the 1870s she continued to discuss women's issues, including equal access to education, the problems of marriage and the imperative need for suffrage, in works like *Why Women Desire the Franchise* (1877), though her focus in this decade shifted somewhat to the issue of vivisection. The aggressive candour that characterizes her feminist discourse also distinguishes her sometimes brutally explicit anti-vivisectionist writing, examples of which can be found in *The Moral Aspects of Vivisection* (1875) and *False Beasts and True* (1876). She founded both the Anti-Vivisection Society of London and the British Union Anti-Vivisection Society. In addition to her many articles, lectures and pamphlets, late in life she wrote her autobiography, *The Life of Frances Power Cobbe, by Herself* (1894). With her companion Mary Lloyd she retired in 1884 to Wales where she remained until her death.

MO'C

Cobbold [née Knipe], Elizabeth *c.*1767–1824 English poet, novelist and editor. Elizabeth grew up in London, Liverpool, and Manchester, where she published *Poems on Various Subjects* (1783) and the well-received *Six Narrative Poems* (1787) dedicated to Sir Joshua Reynolds. In 1790, she was widowed only six months after marrying elderly invalid William Clarke of Ipswich. Using the name 'Clarke', Elizabeth published a novel set in the Middle Ages, *The Sword, or Father Bertrand's History of his Own Times* (1791). Marrying wealthy Ipswich brewer John Cobbold, she entered a household of fourteen children and eventually added seven more of her own. Intrigued by natural history, Elizabeth became a skilful painter of flowers and an active philanthropist. Under the pseudonym 'Carolina Petty Pasty', she published *The Mince Pye: An Heroic Epistle* (1800), mocking C.S. Pybus's *The Sovereign* and dedicated to popular cookbook author HANNAH GLASSE (see COOKERY BOOKS). Elizabeth edited *Poetical Attempts* (1803) to assist the cottager poet Ann Candler, and she contributed poetry to *The Chaplet* (1807), a volume she may also have edited, and to the periodical *Ladies' Fashionable Repository* (from 1809). Twenty years of verse Valentines to friends were collected as *Cliff Valentines* (1813, 1814), and her *Poems* were published posthumously with a memoir in 1825.   JHP

Coelebs in Search of a Wife (1808) The first and only full-length novel of the evangelical HANNAH

MORE represents her attempt to reclaim the novel as a didactic, moral and Christian form. The structure is similar to that used by SARAH FIELDING in THE ADVENTURES OF DAVID SIMPLE and follows the adventures of Charles, the 'Coelebs' or bachelor of the title, as he searches for a wife who will be able to live up to his exacting standards. The resulting adventures expose the financial, moral and religious failings of society. Charles is horrified by the general lack of morality, and the refusal of the upper classes to pay their debts, but he is also scandalized by religious practices that differ from More's evangelical Anglicanism, attacking Calvinism, antinomianism and latitudinarianism alike. He is eventually married to Lucilla Stanley, his equal in virtue, pomposity and doctrinal correctness. Although the moral tone of More's work is not really to the modern taste, *Coelebs* was popular throughout the 19th century, and was a major influence on JANE AUSTEN's *MANSFIELD PARK*.   LBe

Cofer, Judith Ortiz 1952–

Originally from Puerto Rico, Judith Ortiz Cofer writes in a range of genres and for a double audience – teens and adults. She has written poems, essays, stories, novels and memoirs. *The Latin Deli: Prose and Poetry* (1993), for example, collects stories, essays and poems into a tactile collage of a girlhood caught between longings for Puerto Rico and the reality of a New Jersey barrio. In addition, Ortiz Cofer has written several poetry chapbooks, two full collections of poetry – *Reaching for the Mainland* and *Terms of Survival* (both 1987) – and an autobiographical novel, *The Line of the Sun* (1989). She has written books for teen readers as well, including *Silent Dancing: A Remembrance of a Puerto Rican Childhood* (1990) and *An Island Like You: Stories of the Barrio* (1995).   SMSt

Coke, Mary, Lady 1726–1811

British journal writer, and youngest daughter of John, Duke of Argyll and Greenwich, and Jane Warburton. Given only a scanty education by her parents and encouraged in her temper tantrums, she married the profligate Earl of Leicester, Edward, Viscount Coke, in 1747; the marriage may never have been consummated. Practically abandoned in Norfolk, she saw herself as a romantic heroine and, once her husband died in 1753, she imagined that the Duke of York, the youngest brother of George III, was in love with her; although a friend, he was put off by her delusional manner. Coke is now remembered for her JOURNALS, written as letters to her sisters, Lady Dalkeith and Lady Strafford (1766–85); and, after the latter's death, Lord Strafford (1785–91). These provide a useful commentary on 18th-century mores and closely observed thumbnail sketches of leading members of society. The journals of 1766–74 were privately published in four volumes by her family in 1889, whilst those of 1775–91 have never been published.   RDM

Cold Comfort Farm (1932)

The heroine of STELLA GIBBONS's comic first novel (Femina Vie Heureuse Prize, 1933) is Flora Poste. Orphaned at the age of 19, Flora invites herself to stay at Cold Comfort Farm with her distant relatives the Starkadders. Here she begins work '"Collecting material"' for 'a novel as good as *PERSUASION*' and also imposing AUSTEN-like tidiness and order over the chaotic and uncivilized lives of the Starkadders. Through a series of fairy-tale transformations Flora reforms the farm and its occupants and breaks the tyranny of Aunt Ada Doom, who has terrorized the household for decades since witnessing, as a child, 'something nasty in the woodshed'. The novel's humour derives from this unlikely combination of (rural) fantasy with sound (urban) practicality, as well as its exaggerated consciousness of its own fictionality. Gibbons, like Flora, is acutely and satirically aware of the medium she works in: adopting the conventions of the travel guide she grades her writing against a three-star rating as an aid to readers which 'ought to help the reviewers, too'.   AS

Colegate, Isabel 1931–

English novelist in whose work a powerful sense of place is always present. Tension derives from the unexpected impact of drama on the lives of her characters, who are drawn with intelligence and wit. Colegate also has an intense feeling for times other than her own. Victorian Bath, Edwardian country life and London between the two World Wars have all been vividly evoked in her fiction. She is the daughter of Arthur Colegate, MP, and Winifred Worsley, and is married to Michael Briggs, company director and long-time chairman of the Bath Preservation Society; they have three grown-up children, and live near Bath in an 18th-century castle whose ground plan was inspired by the Ace of Clubs.

Colegate finished her first novel at the age of 18 and 'when I was about twenty-three the great Jonathan Cape read one and accepted it for publication. It was later rejected by one of his editors but he gave me confidence.' It was in 1958 that she published her first book – *The Blackmailer*. Subsequent novels include *Statues in a Garden* (1964), *Orlando King* (1968), *Orlando at the Brazen Threshold* (1971) and *Agatha* in 1973 (afterwards reissued as the 'Orlando Trilogy' (1984); *The Shooting Party* (1980); *The Summer of the Royal Visit* (1991); and *Winter Journey* (1995).

The Shooting Party (which brought her national recognition when it won the W.H. Smith Literary Award in 1981 and was made into a successful film) is finely crafted with a plot in which an untoward invasion by hostile elements threatens the fabric of an Edwardian household. The narrative is shot through with humour. The subtlety and sophistication of Colegate's writing draws here as elsewhere on a profound knowledge of the Country-House way of life.

She says 'I am not at the centre of such life. It is much easier to see things if you are on the periphery, but I do know the smells and sounds.'   SJ

Coleman [née Holmes], Emily 1899–1974 American novelist and poet, born in Oakland, California, and raised in Hartford, Connecticut. Her father was an insurance executive; her mother suffered from mental illness and died young. She graduated from Wellesley College in 1920 and married Loyd Ring Coleman, a psychologist, in 1921 (they divorced by 1931). After the birth of their son in 1924, she had suffered puerperal fever and mental collapse, experiences on which she based much of her later poetry and fiction (including her surrealist novel, *The Shutter of Snow*, 1930). In 1926, as a correspondent for the *Chicago Tribune*, she went to Paris where her poems were published in *transition*, a leading modernist literary magazine. Though she published little and her poems remain uncollected, she exerted a strong influence on other writers through her intense, passionate personality. Her friends included ANTONIA WHITE and DJUNA BARNES. In 1928, she spent a year as EMMA GOLDMAN's secretary in San Tropez. There she met Peggy Guggenheim, who recounted their long friendship in *Out of This Century* (1979). In 1939 Coleman returned to the States where she lived with an Arizona rancher before converting to Catholicism in 1944. In 1953 she moved to England, where she lived in Stanbrook Abbey from 1957 to 1968. She spent her last years at DOROTHY DAY's Catholic Worker Farm in Tivoli, New York. Many of her writings, including a second novel, 'The Tygon', remain unpublished.   JSG

Coleridge, Mary (Elizabeth) 1861–1907 English poet, novelist and critic who descended from an acclaimed literary family, with Samuel Taylor Coleridge as her great-great-uncle and SARA COLERIDGE her great-aunt. Born in London, she was educated at home by W. J. Cory, ex-Eton-schoolmaster and poet, and knew Tennyson, Browning and Ruskin, who were among her family's literary friends. From 1895 to 1907 she taught literature at the Working Women's College. She wrote articles for several periodicals including CHARLOTTE YONGE's *Monthly Packet*, the *Monthly Review* and the *Times Literary Supplement*. Her first novel was *The Seven Sleepers of Ephesus* (1893), a dream-like work much admired by Robert Louis Stevenson. Her next novel, a ROMANCE based on the life of Gustav III of Sweden, called *The King with Two Faces* (1897), established her reputation. Coleridge published three further novels, but it is now widely held that her talents lay primarily in poetry. Encouraged by Robert Bridges who offered to edit her poems, she published *Fancy's Following* (1896), enlarged and retitled *Fancy's Guerdon* (1897), under the pseudonym 'Anodos'

Sara Coleridge.

('the wanderer'). Her verse is concentrated and powerful, some poems showing a pre-Raphaelite influence whilst others prefigure the techniques and subject matter of early 20th-century poetry. The accomplished poem 'The Other Side of the Mirror' is perhaps her most famous work. Coleridge also published a collection of essays, *Non Sequitur* (1900) and (posthumously) a life of Holman Hunt (1908). Her literary remains were published as *Gathered Leaves* in 1910.   SA

Coleridge, Sara 1802–52 Fiction writer, poet, translator and editor, daughter of Samuel Taylor Coleridge and his wife Sara Fricker. She published a three-volume Latin translation when she was 19 and followed that with a book-length translation from 16th-century French. In 1829, she married her first cousin, Henry Nelson Coleridge, and spent most of the next decade pregnant and in precarious physical and mental health. Increasingly she turned to opium to treat severe depression. For the instruction of her children, she began writing short poems, eventually published as *Pretty Lessons in Verse for Good Children* (1834). The book went through five editions in five years. The death of Samuel Taylor Coleridge, then considered a dissolute, self-indulgent, plagiarizing poet, gave her new purpose. She began rehabilitating her father's reputation by editing much of his work, writing introductions or appendices explaining, defending and qualifying her father's ideas. Eventually she remade him into the respected philosopher and Victorian sage whose work was canonized. Meanwhile, she produced *Phantasmion* (1837), a book-length FAIRY TALE interspersed with sensuous poems revealing the inner life of her characters. At her death, she was said to have left thousands of pages of unpublished manuscripts. PRF

Colette [Sidonie-Gabrielle Colette] 1873–1954

In the old catalogue of Cambridge University Library, Colette could only be found under 'Gauthier-Villars (mme)'. Some telling irony there, since the woman writer who had three husbands and eventually chose the patronymic as her one and only pen-name was indeed, as she told in *My Apprenticeships*, pushed or coerced into writing by Henri Gauthier-Villars, alias Willy, her first entrepreneurial husband, who claimed authorship, or co-authorship, of the hugely successful school-girl 'Claudine' novels.

She was the friend of Pierre Louys, Debussy, NATALIE BARNEY, Proust, Ravel, Cocteau, Giono, a woman of many incarnations and many lives from Belle Epoque Paris to World War I, the post-war years, World War II and its post-war years: the author of novels, stories, novellas, prose poems, plays, memoirs, autobiographies, librettos spanning over half a century. She frequented many milieux from *demi-monde* to *beau monde*, sequentially child-wife, bored housewife, actress, mime, music-hall artiste touring the provinces, much-photographed belle, food lover, animal lover, lesbian mistress of the Marquise de Bel boeuf, journalist, occasional war correspondent, society wife to newspaper editor-in-chief Henri de Jouvenel, divorcee who had an affair with her stepson, successful writer who fell in love with a third husband young enough to be her son and ended demanding larger advances than André Gide and, from the wheelchair to which arthritis had confined her, spotting Audrey Hepburn in a Côte d'Azur hotel to play Gigi. But it isn't so much Colette's protean self as her unconventionality, her sexiness, her not fitting any writerly model which may explain why it was not till after World War II that she gained full recognition from Anglo-American women writers. KATHERINE MANSFIELD stands out as the one in the twenties with the nous to be influenced by the author of CHÉRI (1920). Since World War II Colette's influence on English-language women writers has become all-pervasive: one only has to think of ANGELA CARTER or MICHÈLE ROBERTS.

Colette's voice is unique, elusive, concise, sensuous, graceful, euphonic. It continuously refreshes and renovates metaphors. She writes about love, in all its forms and stages, its triangles, jealousies, savageries, wild generosities – and 'blanks'. She writes about gardens and orange groves and springs and dawns and courtesans and left-bank lesbians and the lost, big-hearted girls of music-hall sidelights. She writes of high and low: of possession and incest and doubles and murder and suicide, of resilience and survival and female friendship and the strange intercourse of humans and animals. Few writers have accessed as she does the subliminal, the pre-oedipal, the realm of the senses. Reading her is sharing in her passion for life, fuelled by what her writing made into the legend of an idyllic childhood in Sido's, the mother's house, in the Burgundy village of Saint-Sauveur-en-Puisaye: 'I inhabit forever a country that I have lost.' That passion endured: marooned by arthritis on her chaise-longue, her 'raft' as she called it, her hearing and sight impaired, Colette wonders in her last book, *The Blue Lantern*, whether life, the splendour of life, is diminishing. It isn't, she replies: 'Patience, I'm the one who is drifting away'. NWJ

Collector of Treasures, The (1977)

These short stories arose directly from BESSIE HEAD's daily life in Serowe, Botswana, as she herself says in an interview with Lindsay Mackie. They depict the lives, hopes and problems of rural village women from different walks of life whom she met on her 'Boiteko' garden project, and collecting interviews for *Serowe*. But though they have 'oral' sources, these 'Village Tales' should not be mistaken for the elaborate Setswanan oral literatures. Realist cameos, they depict characters such as Dikeledi, a dressmaker and 'collector of treasures'; Life, an ex-prostitute from Soweto forced to return to the village after Independence; and the traditionally minded Johanna. Head, having moved outside the country, anticipates biographical work by black women writers beginning to appear in South Africa at this time. In America, Head's work on women caught the eye of ALICE WALKER and Michelle Cliff, both of whom dedicated books to her in tribute (*You Can't Keep a Good Woman Down* and *Abeng*). HLR

Collier, Jane 1709?–1754?

British writer of wit and invention, author of a savage parody of conduct literature, *An Essay on the Art of Ingeniously Tormenting* (1753). Daughter of an improvident rector and philosopher who died penniless, Collier was keenly aware of the difficulties facing the single woman and her bitter experience of dependency is reflected in her *Essay*. Focusing on the imbalance of power in domestic relationships, she argues cynically that authority over others is most effective when it manipulates the affections.

Listed by Richardson as one of the superior women who advised on his writing of *Clarissa*, she also collaborated with SARAH FIELDING on *The Cry* (1754), an allegory which contrasts truth and slander, and intervened with Richardson on Sarah's behalf over corrections to *The Governess* (1749). She was much appreciated by her literary friends. Henry Fielding inscribed a favourite book to her 'as a Memorial . . . of the highest Esteem for an Understanding more than Female, mixed with Virtues almost more than human'; and Richardson wrote to Sarah after her death, 'Don't you miss our dear Miss Jenny Collier more and more? I do.'   LMT

Collier, Mary *c.*1689–1762 Keen of mind and virtually self-taught, she pioneered the tradition of female working-class poetry in England. The publication of her influential poem, *The Woman's Labour: An Epistle to Mr Stephen Duck* (1739), seems not to have relieved her from her labour as laundress, domestic servant and field-hand in England's West Country. An autobiographical preface to her *Poems on Several Occasions* (1762) describes 'poor but honest Parents' who taught her to read, and her demanding but single life allowed her crucial time for studying and observing the plight of women around her. The *Epistle to Duck* engages stylistically (imitating the neoclassical epistle form) and thematically (enumerating the demands of a labouring life) with his masculinist account of working-class experience. Introducing a crucial gender consciousness, her work meditates on the nature of competing female labours: menial, social, familial and, above all, literary. Her appeals to a higher authority, be it religion or the monarchy, suggest both a conservative politics and a potentially radical attempt to claim for women the privileges of a fading social order. Her appeals to education as an equalizing, empowering force echo MARY ASTELL, although she remains carefully class-conscious, always distinguishing between 'poor Woman-kind' and the married women whom they serve. She died in 'Piety, Purity, and Peace', in the hamlet of Alton.   JRS

Collins, An (Anne) Writer of *Divine Songs and Meditacions* (1653). The preface offers us scant autobiographical material on Collins's sickly childhood and present state: 'Being through weakness to the house confin'd'. *Divine Songs* expresses the author's efforts to rise above the physical restraints of her ill health and explore the poetic gift, which has 'enflamed my faculties'. She suggests that this is a humble, private offering to other suffering Christians. The 'songs' express the joy of those who have found communion with God, not always in the easiest or pleasant poetic terms, but always devoutly. Her text incorporates poetic investigations of scripture and the vanity of earthly things, and includes 'A Song composed in the time of the Civill War'. *Divine Songs* concludes with five meditations and verses on Ecclesiastes. GERMAINE GREER suggests that Collins was anti-Calvinist, in *Kissing the Rod* (Virago, 1988), which includes extracts of *Divine Songs*.   SMcK

Collins, Jackie 1941– Bestselling ROMANCE novelist who details the glitz and glamour lifestyles of the Californian jetset. Born in London, Collins was reputedly writing fiction by the age of 8. Expelled from school at 15, she travelled to Los Angeles hoping to become a film actress. Instead, after a short-lived marriage to Wallace Austen and a second to Oscar Lerman, she published her first novel, *The World is Full of Married Men*, in 1968; it was an instant bestseller. (*The World is Full of Divorced Women* (1975) carried an ironic echo in its title.) Her novels set in swinging London, *The Stud* (1970) and its sequel *The Bitch* (1979), were made into British films starring her sister Joan. Collins's style is racy, colloquial and street-wise; her characters live life in the fast lane of the media and business milieux which she knows intimately. She frequently writes romans à clef, as in the trilogy *Hollywood Wives* (1983), *Hollywood Husbands* (1986) and *Hollywood Kids* (1994). Completed in 1996, her 'Lucky Santangelo Quartet', with its upwardly mobile, powerdressing heroine, has much in common with novels by Judith Krantz, Shirley Conran and Sally Beauman. Several of her books have been adapted into TV mini-series.   MO'D

Collins, Merle 1950– African-Caribbean writer who was born in Grenada and has lived in Britain and the United States. She has published short stories, poetry, novels and a wide range of essays on Caribbean culture. Collins was active in Grenada's National Women's Organization and in the London-based 'African Dawn'.

Collins's writing is committed to documenting the historics and struggles of Caribbean people, within the region and in their various diasporic contexts. Her first novel, *Angel*, offers a detailed re-telling of the history of a revolutionary socialist government in the Caribbean, and its demise (based on the Grenadian reality). The novel presents an account of these events which insists on the complex realities of 'the folk' and on their centrality as agents in the region's history. Alongside this endorsement of the folk is the consistent use and celebration of Caribbean Creole culture, reflected, at the level of form, in the widespread inscription of features of orature (proverbs, popular sayings, biblical quotes, fragments of calypso) within her texts, and made dramatically clear in Collins's compelling performances of her work. In her second novel, *The Colour of Forgetting*, and in her poetry, Collins continues to destabilize the boundary between 'the oral' and 'the scribal'.   DDeCN

Collyer, Mary Mitchell 1716/17 – 1762/3 Novelist, translator and proprietor – with her husband, Joseph Collyer the elder – of a small bookstore and circulating library in London. Collyer's work foreshadows both the novel of SENSIBILITY and a later, Romantic enthusiasm for the natural world. *The Virtuous Orphan* (1735), her translation of Marivaux's *La Vie de Marianne*, later released as *The Life and Adventures of Indiana* (1746), abridges large portions of the original and adds a sentimental, Richardsonian ending in which Marianne's seducer repents and marries her. Collyer's EPISTOLARY NOVEL, *Letters from Felicia to Charlotte* (1744, 1749), offers enthusiastic depictions of natural beauty, as the Londoner Felicia travels and finds love in the countryside. Until 1761, with the publication of her influential translation of Salomon Gessner's *The Death of Abel*, Collyer's works were all published anonymously. A translation of Klopstock's *Messiah*, unfinished at her death, was completed by her husband. Collyer came to the notice of BLUESTOCKINGS ELIZABETH MONTAGU and ELIZABETH CARTER, in part because, as she stated in 1761, she wrote 'to contribute to the support and education of my children'. JGr

colonial writing While never as numerous or as powerful as male colonialists, British women working as social reformers, missionaries, journalists and teachers, or travelling, as well as in the more conventional roles of wives and mothers, played an important part in establishing and forwarding the imperial project, and in writing about that project from their own different perspectives.

Women's colonial involvements became especially widespread and their writing increasingly prominent during the latter half of the 19th century, encouraged by movements at home – especially campaigns for greater women's representation – and also by the new domestication of the empire emerging out of a variety of developments: attractive emigration deals, the growth of colonial urban centres, the consolidation of crown rule in India as well as the scramble for Africa, and eugenicist attempts to safeguard the racial purity, and the sexual probity, of white men. Therefore, while colonization centrally involved the domination of colonized men and women by European men, it also increasingly drew European women into activities which positioned them both alongside their male counterparts, *and* in juxtaposition with the colonized.

Because of their relative absence from official imperial discourses, it was long assumed that colonial women, whether settler or itinerant, co-operated in upholding colonial structures of race and class privilege. More recently, however, questions have been raised by historians and literary scholars concerning the extent to which women's views and identifications in fact coincided with those of men. Certainly colonial women writers were never called upon, nor offered themselves, as the defining voices of the British empire; there was no female Kipling. Yet while colonial women writers, of travelogues and letters as well as poetry and fiction, may have reproduced the approaches, style and stock images of imperial writing by men, at the same time their perspectives, in particular their terms of address, do not run in parallel with male writing. On the grounds of their position as women, of related or overlapping experiences of submission and marginalization, they at times express a personal involvement with native people, especially with colonized women. Energetic women travellers such as GERTRUDE BELL, ISABELLA BIRD and MARY KINGSLEY, for instance, with whose names the term 'colonial writing' is often associated, record native customs and recount their parleying with intriguing local personalities even as they express their firm belief in the spread of British justice.

Differently from the TRAVEL WRITERS, novelists such as the Anglo-Indians MAUD DIVER, Alice Perrin and the prolific FLORA ANNIE STEEL, were concerned to give memorable literary shape to their colonial experience – an experience which was located at the very heart of empire, and was form-giving for other colonial regions. Each one of these women writers owes a considerable debt to Kipling, yet they also express distinctly different interests and anxieties. These differences, such as Alice Perrin's acute though inconsistent insights into the mutual incomprehension between cultures in the sub-continent, may to an extent relate to the writers' oblique perspectives on colonial power. Divergent perspectives are particularly characteristic of the achievement of Flora Annie Steel whose short-story portraits of individual Indians can be at once judgemental and sympathetic. Due perhaps to their status as mainstream colonial writers of Kenya, ambivalence seems less easy to discern in the mid 20th-century White Highlands memoirs of ELSPETH HUXLEY and ISAK DINESEN, with their predictable racist stereotypes of Africans, yet here too are found moments of identification with individual native Kenyans.

Based on many years' residence, Anglo-Indian and Kenyan colonial writing was by and large produced in Europe, and written from a European perspective. For settler writers in the white colonies of the empire, who form another important constituency of colonial women writers, the option of a retreat 'home' was often not available. Writers of 'bush' and backwoods fiction, such as the Australians BARBARA BAYNTON and MILES FRANKLIN, the South African OLIVE SCHREINER and, to an extent, the cosmopolitan New Zealander KATHERINE MANSFIELD, as well as writers of journals and memoirs, such as the Canadian Victorians SUSANNA MOODIE and CATHERINE PARR TRAILL, confronted problems of perspective and definition generated by their attempts imaginatively to inhabit an unfamiliar land. This unfamiliarity importantly included the competing presence of indigenous peoples on 'European' land. It testifies to their own painful sense of marginality to the masculine ethos of settler survival, that several women settler writers developed strong, influential feminist voices, as well as openly questioning the brutalizing effects of white dominance.

It would be inaccurate to speak of women writers from among colonized peoples at the time of empire as colonial. But it is also important not to forget that during imperial times, and in the medium of the then imperial language, English, women such as the late 19th-century Indian poets TORU DUTT and SAROJINI NAIDU, the 1930s Caribbean writer UNA MARSON, or the 1950s South African autobiographer NONI JABAVU, were seeking self-expression in writing, using figurative devices that were borrowed from colonial texts, and yet were also subtly reinflected by being adapted to fit very different cultural and gender perspectives. EBo

Color Purple, The (1982) Celie, the main character in ALICE WALKER's third novel, communicates with God in an EPISTOLARY gesture meant to recall the cry of the ancestral slave mother that none but God heard. Raped by her stepfather, separated from her children and her sister, and abused by her husband, Celie begins reversing the assault on her mind and body by writing letters to God. Writing, like the quilting done by Celie and Sofia, is presented as a therapeutic and self-affirming activity. At the core of this Pulitzer-Prize-winning novel is the assertion by Celie that she may be poor, black and ugly, but 'I'm here'. To protect this increasingly assertive self from further exploitation, Walker turns her into a successful businesswoman with a house of her own, and to make her being here worthwhile her children and beloved sister are brought back to her. Family reunion takes place on the 4th of July: Celie and her family celebrate each other when fellow Americans are busy celebrating their independence. KO

Come in Spinner (1951) Taking its title from the wartime gambling game of Two-Up, this collaborative creation between DYMPHNA CUSACK and Florence James is written against the propaganda and sloganeering of late World-War-II Sydney. Regardless of the severe censorship which accompanied its initial serial publication shortly after the war, the novel attracted considerable controversy. Focused on the employees of a downtown beauty parlour, the narrative seamlessly merges REALISM and ROMANCE as it moves rapidly from crisis to crisis. The overwhelming presence and influence of American servicemen offers an immediate and significant counterpoint to its portrayal of the role of women in the formation of an Australian national identity. Issues such as female sexuality, prostitution and abortion were not accommodated fully until

James reworked the manuscript for republication in 1988. Adapted into a mini-series shortly afterwards, the novel attracted a new readership. In both the original and subsequent editions, the dissection of social mores and double standards within the narrative suggests a subdued but persistent anarchic and agitational motivation. CE

Compton, Jennifer 1949– Australian dramatist, poet and story writer. Born in Wellington, New Zealand, but moved to Australia in 1972 and now lives in the country south-west of Sydney with her husband and two children. In New Zealand she trained as an actor and first achieved recognition with her play *Crossfire* (1976), originally called *No Man's Land*, which moves between two different time settings, 1910 and 1975, to question women's roles as wives and mothers and the impact feminism has had on them. Her other stage plays include *They're Playing Our Song* (1978), *Barefoot* (1994) and *The Big Picture* (1998). She has also written many plays for radio and in the 1970s wrote some episodes of the highly regarded ABC TV series *Certain Women*. Her poetry and stories have appeared in many literary magazines, with her first collection of poems, *From the Other Woman* (1993), praised for its creation of effective voices and personae. In 1995 she won the Robert Harris Poetry Prize with 'Blue Leaves'. Her second collection, *Aroha* (1998), has been published in England. EW

Compton-Burnett, Ivy 1884–1969 English novelist whose writing on the difficulties and tensions of Edwardian family life frequently reflected the history of her own large and contentious family. Compton-Burnett was the eldest of the seven children of Dr James Compton Burnett and his rather dictatorial second wife, Katharine Rees (who added a hyphen to the family name). Ivy was educated at private schools and Royal Holloway College, where she took a second in Classics. She then returned home (at her mother's behest) to teach her four younger sisters. Ivy became head of the family upon her mother's death in 1911, and relations between Ivy and her sisters became so strained that when the four girls moved to London in 1915, they refused to let Ivy live with them. Compton-Burnett had in any case been closer to her brothers, but one, Guy, died in 1905, and the other, Noel, was killed in World War I. She later claimed that her first novel, *Dolores* (1911), with which she was unhappy, had been largely Noel's work. Her two youngest sisters died of drug overdoses in 1917, and Ivy nearly died of influenza in 1918.

After this difficult period, she moved to London with a friend, Margaret Jourdain, a prominent interior decorator and historian of furniture; they lived together until Jourdain's death in 1951. It is not entirely clear whether the two had a sexual relationship (they maintained separate rooms), but they were constant companions. The move brought greater stability for Compton-Burnett, and, beginning in the mid-1920s with PASTORS AND MASTERS (1925), she wrote and published regularly, producing twenty novels, most with intentionally similar titles. Her novels were noted for privileging dialogue over psychological exploration or exposition of plot. The brittle, bantering tone of *Brothers and Sisters* (1929), about an incestuous family and its overbearing matriarch, is rather like that of her contemporary Evelyn Waugh. Novels followed nearly every other year, including *Men and Wives* (1931), *More Women than Men* (1933), *A HOUSE AND ITS HEAD* (1935), *Daughters and Sons* (1937), *A Family and a Fortune* (1939), *Parents and Children* (1941) and *Elders and Betters* (1944). The settings of her works, and her lack of engagement with MODERNIST forms and innovations, often led to their being viewed rather unfairly as retrograde; VIRGINIA WOOLF said there was 'something bleached about Miss Compton-Burnett'. (Ivy, for her part, thought Woolf a snob.) Compton-Burnett's work with dialogue, however, was innovative in its own right, and her treatments of selfishness, power struggles and criminality, while domestic in setting, were hardly prudish in their implications about human nature, of which she took a rather dim view. In *Two Worlds and Their Ways* (1949), for instance, a character comments, 'We have done our best', only to be answered, 'We have done nothing.' He replies: 'Well, that is usually people's best . . . Their worst is something quite different.' Although Compton-Burnett's novels were not always critical successes, *Mother and Son* (1955) won the James Tait Black Memorial Prize; among her other honours, Compton-Burnett was made a Dame of the Order of the British Empire in 1967.   KW

Comyns, Barbara 1909–92 English novelist whose eclectic education and odd assortment of jobs gave rise to a unique writing style which blends a child-like naivety with stylistic innovation. Comyns's education by a series of governesses and life in a chaotic household with her deaf mother provided ample material for her humorous yet macabre novels. They combine everyday images with magically realistic portraits of insects resurrected from the dead, women levitating or chairs covered in human skin. Descriptions of her various jobs as artist's model, dog breeder and vintage car dealer lend quirky authenticity to her fiction. Her first novel, *Sisters by a River* (1947), utilizes the 'mistakes' of a child's writing – some the result of Comyns's haphazard education, others added by her editor – in order to explore a child's view of the complex, often violent, adult world. Written initially for her own children, it had remained unpublished until it was partly serial-ized by the magazine *Lilliput*. Comyns' second novel, *Our Spoons Came From Woolworths* (1950), is considered more than semi-autobiographical. The author of eleven books, she is best known for her novel *The Vet's Daughter* (1959), which has been adapted for radio and the stage.   HSM

confessional poetry Characterized by explicit narratives of personal experience, this style of poetry is most closely associated with certain American poets writing after World War II. Its literary provenance may lie in the work of poets such as Theodore Roethke, though confessional poet ANNE SEXTON claimed W. D. Snodgrass's explorations of his marital struggles and eventual collapse in *Heart's Needle* were the much-needed catalyst for her own voice. But Sexton also suggested that undergoing pyschotherapy was the flame which ignited her creativity. This was an experience shared by many of the post-war poets associated with Confessional poetry; Robert Lowell and SYLVIA PLATH, like Anne Sexton, went through treatments for depression and their poems often reflected battles with mental illness.

Confession was noted as a new idiom for poetry in that writers explored their relationship to themselves and others in the kind of detail that had historically (deliberately) been suppressed. While poets have always used verse to document their emotional terrain, the innovative poems of the Confessionals did not disguise the intimate, deeply personal particulars of the writer's life. Sylvia Plath's work often related her world to more general issues in history and/or culture (such as in 'Daddy' and 'Lady Lazarus'), while Anne Sexton offered even more intensely autobiographical studies (e.g. 'In Celebration of my Uterus', 'Wanting to Die', 'Pain for a Daughter'). These two poets particularly gained both devoted audiences and merciless criticism from some (most notably male) reviewers, such as the well-established poet James Dickey. The expressive, self-focused work of Plath's and Sexton's poems (particularly Sexton's TO BEDLAM & PART WAY BACK and Plath's ARIEL) met with resistance and even hostility from some critics who were uncomfortable with the intimacy rendered in the poems: their details of sex, the body, anger and illness. Because Plath and Sexton were writing at a point in history (which saw great emphasis on female domesticity following World War II) when a woman was expected to find total fulfilment as wife and mother, these poems met (male) hostility as they fought to make their place in the world. Sexton's well-known 'To John, Who Begs me not to Inquire Further' posits a kind of defence of Confessional poetry, as she counters her writing teacher's admonitions not to be so self-revealing in poetry. She quotes Schopenhauer: 'Most of us carry in our hearts the Jocasta who begs Oedipus not to inquire further.' She, like the other Confessional poets, is an Oedipus who must confront the truth, however ugly.

The other writers usually associated with the genre are John Berryman and ADRIENNE RICH. Berryman, like Plath and Sexton, committed suicide, but Adrienne Rich has continued to write poems which have become less 'confessional' over the years; moving toward larger spheres of discussion, starting with *Diving into the Wreck* (1973), which merges the personal with the political. Although some of the more revelatory poems of the Confessional genre have not stood the test of time, it is acknowledged that the Confessional poets of the 1950s had a profound influence on contemporary poetry, particularly in America. Many young writers today are perhaps unaware that the emotional vernacular of contemporary poetry was unavailable before the Confessional poets, because their unique idiom seems now so familiar.   ACH

Conlon, Evelyn 1952– The Irish author was born in rural Monoghan, and makes use of this landscape and Catholic girlhood in her 1989 BILDUNGSROMAN, *Stars in the Daytime*. A single mother of two children, she has been both a teacher and a writer of CHILDREN'S BOOKS as well as an active cultural critic and journalist. One of the founders of Irishwomen United in 1975, she continues to be active in Women's Movement politics, and her wide experience of women's victimization and resistance informs all her fiction. Harsh insight combines with adroit humour in a pungent style, as in this arrival of Dymphna with 'great noise and bosomly confidence': 'Sure sign something's really gone wrong when you're calling on us. You must have fucked up badly if it's time to call in the women.' 'Jesus', [thinks Rose], 'she didn't get that confidence rubbing up and down men's legs.'

Besides *Stars in the Daytime*, she has published collections of short fiction – *My Head is Opening* (1987), a gathering of stories, and *Taking Scarlet as a Real Colour* (1993) – as well as a second novel, *A Glassful of Letters* (1998).
     CStP

Conservationist, The (1974) Arguably Nobel-Prize-winning author NADINE GORDIMER's most innovative book, as far as form is concerned. In it she draws on Zulu mythology to create a richly symbolic field of reference. The protagonist, Mehring, is an urban Afrikaner, who owns a farm; through him, Gordimer explores a particular kind of response to land, one that is framed by the concept of land as privately owned – an approach to the land here seen as representative of a white, European relationship to the South African land. Mehring's antagonist is the dead body of a black man, which keeps resurfacing from its shallow burying place on his farm, claiming as a symbolic representative its ownership rights to the land. The novel reveals the moral corruption of Mehring and his kind, and is prophetic about the return of the land to those with a prior claim to it. A storm at the end of the novel can be read as an indication of the end of Mehring's time, although the novel shows him incapable of imagining what is to come.   CCo

Constantine, Murray see BURDEKIN, KATHERINE

Convent of Pleasure, The (1668) MARGARET CAVENDISH's most famous play (see DUCHESS OF NEWCASTLE) takes up contemporary debates about the single woman and female education. It centres on Lady Happy, a rich and aristocratic woman who argues that 'Men . . . make the Female sex their slaves; but I will not be so inslaved, but will live retired from their Company.' Founding a convent that is self-sufficient and a place of sensual pleasure, she takes with her all those Ladies 'whose Births are greater than their Fortunes, and are resolv'd to live a single life, and vow Virginity'. In a play-within-a-play, men are portrayed as uncaring, brutal and vicious, whilst those who try to assail the convent's walls are depicted as drunken fools. The convent is, however, infiltrated by a Prince who disguises himself as a woman; his love for the heroine is reciprocated, although the cross-dressing device leads the bewildered Lady Happy to ask, 'But why may I not love a Woman with the same affection I could a Man?' Eliciting much critical analysis of its explicit lesbianism, rejection of male society and promotion of female power, the play swiftly concludes once the Prince's true identity is revealed and the anticipated marriage takes place.   RDM

Conway [née Finch], Anne, Viscountess 1630?–79 Author of a posthumously printed text on natural philosophy, *The Principles of the Most Ancient and Modern Philosophy* (1692), and involved in a life-long correspondence with Cambridge philosopher Henry More, on the subject of, amongst other things, the theories of Descartes. Born into a prominent political family of gentry standing – her father had been Speaker of the House of Commons – she married into the Anglo-Irish aristocratic Conway family. Her father-in-law, the 2nd Viscount, to whom she wrote a series of letters, was interested in literature and science, and his sister LADY BRILLIANA HARLEY was also a significant letter-writer. This intellectual family context clearly acted as a stimulus to Conway. There was apparently a laboratory at her home, Ragley Hall, and she was learned in Greek, Latin and mathematics.

Conway's brother introduced her to More whilst he was a Cambridge undergraduate. Although many of her letters to More do not survive, it is clear from those on his side that their debates on Cartesian philosophy were far-reaching; she herself refers to the subject in one letter, in which she challenges Descartes's theory of colours, as 'our old controversie'. Conway was an exception in her age, a woman with access to education of the highest order (More's epistolary communications have been described as a correspondence degree for a woman denied access to university), and her influence on More was significant and enduring. She appears to have been an intensely private person, suffering ill health much of her life. She begged More to keep their correspondence private (he did however dedicate one of his philosophical treatises to her) and her own scientific writing only came into the public domain after her death.   JS

Conway, Jill Ker 1934– Australian scholar and writer, born at Hillston, New South Wales, Conway left Australia in 1960 for the USA, with a brilliant degree in History. She completed a doctorate in history at Harvard, taught at the University of Toronto where she became a vice-president, was the first woman president of Smith College, and has been a visiting scholar at the MIT since 1985. A mineral company director, Conway was named one of *Time*'s 1986 twelve Women of the Year. Her acclaimed autobiography, *The Road to Coorain* (1989), deals with her isolated but initially idyllic childhood; her desperate fight alongside her father to save their loved property from drought; her difficult school years, and increasingly bitter relationship with her mother. It finishes with her agonized decision that she must leave Australia to grow emotionally and intellectually. Not a feminist writer, Conway is nevertheless acutely aware of women's social positioning. When her application for a traineeship in Foreign Affairs was refused on the assumption that she would soon marry, she writes of her recognition that her 'sex rendered [her] merits invisible'. A second autobiographical work, *True North* (1994), covers Conway's life in America. She has published several books on the experience of American woman.

DB

Cook, Eliza 1817–89 Self-educated London working-class poet. Eliza Cook was the youngest of the eleven children of a tinman and brazier from Southwark. Her mother died when she was 15. She began to publish her verses in literary magazines in her teens, and they were collected in *Lays of a Wild Harp* (1835) and *Melaia, and Other Poems* (1838). She was hailed as a new Burns. In 1849 she established *Eliza Cook's Journal* which ran until 1854 with a wide circulation and was filled with her own work – essays on contemporary issues and editorials with titles such as 'The Health of the Skin' and 'Chemistry in the Kitchen'. She never married and had strong views on the degradation of women in marriage.

Her poetry was most popular in the 1850s, but by the

end of the century its naivety went out of fashion. Cook's later life was dogged by ill health and she survived on a Civil List Pension granted her in 1864. Her poetry is simple in form, utilizing rhyming couplets and a regular metre and it was this simplicity that ELIZABETH BARRETT BROWNING criticized, implying on several occasions that Cook was an apt name for this poet. She wrote a number of poems on themes of social injustice and about the conditions of the labouring poor, many of them sentimental and pious. Like poetry by other Victorian women poets, hers is a curious mixture of piety, patriotism and radical social critique.   RS

Cooke, Rose Terry 1827–92 American poet and writer of REALIST/regionalist fiction. She was born on a farm near Hartford, Connecticut. Her father was a banker and a congressman. After graduating from Hartford Female Seminary in 1843, she taught for five years, then received an inheritance that allowed her to devote herself to writing. Her first story was published in 1845 and her first poem in 1851. In 1873 she married Rollin H. Cooke, a widowed banker with two daughters, whose business failures used up her savings. Needing the income, she wrote for leading periodicals, both adults' and children's, including *Atlantic, Harper's, Our Young Folks* and *St Nicholas*. She published two collections of poems (1861, 1888) and two novels, *Happy Dodd* (1878) and *Steadfast* (1889). Short-story collections include *Rootbound* (1885), *Sphinx's Children and Other People* (1886), and *Somebody's Neighbours* and *Huckleberries Gathered from New England Hills* (1891). A precursor of local-colour realists SARAH ORNE JEWETT and MARY WILKINS FREEMAN, Cooke wrote stories with regional settings and authentic dialect. Her critical view of Puritanism, rejection of Romantic literary conventions and sympathetic portrayals of women have given her fiction enduring interest.   JSG

cookery books Cookery books, which, after all, are instructional manuals for the preparation of food, may seem unlikely candidates for consideration as a literary genre. Their very usefulness suggests that they belong with other utilitarian volumes such as telephone directories or computer guides. But, when approached for evidence of women's experiences, some cookery books rise above their ostensible purpose and inform not only about the preparation of foods, but about the people who cook and consume them, and about when and where they are eaten. Like other women authors, those who write cookery books have voices that express joy, dread, ambivalence and any other human emotion or attitude that can be found in literary genres.

In one manner or another, the voice of authority is what usually prevails in cookery books. Kept out of the

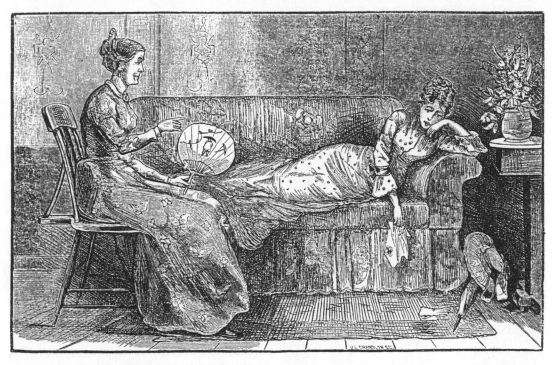

Rose Terry Cooke: 'The heroine learns her father was a drunk', frontispiece of *Happy Dodd or, 'She hath done what she could'*, 1878.

public sphere, many women in the 19th, and the first half of the 20th, century were relegated to writing about cooking, child-rearing and other domestic subjects. Men wrote on cooking too, but while male cookery-book writers wrote for the professional kitchen, women writers were addressing the woman at home. Some 19th-century women nonetheless managed to make lasting impressions by offering information in commanding voices that projected images of mature managers of complicated households. In the United States, LYDIA MARIA CHILD in her *American Frugal Housewife* (1832) extolled the virtues of parsimony through such alarmingly practical tips as keeping eggs fresh for three years or ordering children to pick and sell blackberries rather than 'wearing out their clothes in useless play'. The voice she projects leads readers to believe that Child is an experienced homemaker and mother of a large brood of children. In fact, she wrote the book in the first year of her marriage and was childless. A passionate anti-slavery activist, Child earned her living through her pen, and found in the genre of cookery-book writing a formula that met with social approval and financial success, for the book has remained in print until this day. Similarly, ISABELLA BEETON, compiler of the famous *Book of Household Management*, an authoritative tome on the proper running of a home, was not what she

seemed. Only 29 years old at the time of her death, Mrs Beeton was hardly the middle-aged instructress her reader imaged her to be, at the time her book was published in 1861 and ever since. In fact, much of the writing of her classic may have been produced by others – but Mrs Beeton has come to signify the voice of domestic authority in the average British kitchen.

But some writers have made a striking impact on their readers with voices that are more authentic representations of themselves. IRMA ROMBAUER's classic *The Joy of Cooking* surpassed its rivals in popularity in part because the writer's voice brings humour, comfort and encouragement to its readers, and not just guidance. JULIA CHILD, who is perceived as bringing those same qualities to her cooking instruction, achieves that reputation more through her showmanship on television than through her written recipes, which tend to be formal, precise and thorough.

With some women authors, writing about food reaches another level, more truly approaching art. ELIZABETH DAVID and M. F. K. FISHER use food to evoke places and to present insights about human behaviour in the manner of novelists. Both hold particular views about food and what it represents. Through their descriptions of dishes, meals or social gatherings around food, they each establish a unique voice, sometimes passionate, often witty and always critical of what they see and hear, and, most of all, of what they taste.

At the same time that individual women writers

Cookery books: title-page by David Gentleman for Patience Gray's *Plats du Jour*, 1957.

have created cookery books to support themselves, women volunteer groups have produced recipe collections to support community organizations. Prompted in the 1860s by the impulse to assist Civil War veterans or their widows and orphans, American women began to offer for sale small regional cookery books made up of recipes contributed by the members of their groups, a custom that has become a standard way for voluntary women's organizations to raise funds for local causes. The sheer abundance of these books makes them important resources for understanding not only what foods women were cooking and serving, but how their charitable deeds benefited. Similarly, though far fewer in number, cookery books produced in Great Britain by the Women's Institute, which spread from Canada to England in 1915, provide information about the foods that were produced and cooked by country-women from all parts of the nation. A thoughtful reading of these cookery books can extract women's history that has been ignored or misunderstood. BH

Cookson, Catherine 1906–98 Prolific, highly successful novelist born and based in the North-East of England. Her first, autobiographical book, *Our Kate* (1969), deals with the stigma of illegitimacy. Cookson was an adult before learning that her 'sister' was actually her mother and this casts its pall over the fiction. She began writing in her forties and has published over eighty books, including, latterly, poetry and memoirs, and even an LP of songs. South Tyneside is designated 'Catherine Cookson Country'. Selling worldwide and adapted fairly lavishly for television, her work is often read simply as formulaic heterosexual romance. Some is: notably the multi-volumed sagas; the historical 'Mallen' series (1973–9) and the contemporary 'Bill Bailey' (1986–8) series. She alternated between modern and historical settings, succeeding more in the often rather well-reconstructed past. She often recycled the conventions and even plots of Victorian High Realism, integrating working-class experience with warmth and a commonsense humanism. *The Man Who Cried* (1979) contains the best of her writing on tensions bound up in class and sexuality. Elsewhere heroines are too perfect; the tobacconist's daughter in *The Wingless Bird* (1991), for example. Yet there were always flashes of insight in the sometimes garrulous tone. *My Beloved Son* (1991) is not without its moments of grim wit and pithiness. PM

Coolbrith, Ina (Josephine Smith) 1842–1928 American poet, born in Nauvoo, Illinois, a niece of Joseph Smith, founder of the Mormon Church. Her father died when she was an infant; her mother remarried and renounced Mormonism. In 1849 her stepfather moved the family to California in search of gold. Ina attended Los Angeles schools and studied the only two books she owned, works of Shakespeare and Byron. In 1859 she married an iron-works owner; she divorced him in 1861. Their only child died an infant. In 1865 she took her mother's maiden name, Coolbrith, and moved to San Francisco. She became the only female member of the Bohemian Club, held weekly salons for travelling artists and writers, and was co-editor with Bret Harte of *Overland Monthly*. A librarian from 1874 to 1906, she guided the reading of young Jack London and Isadora Duncan.

Coolbrith had begun publishing poetry as a teenager and by the 1870s had received critical acclaim in the USA and England. She became California's first Poet Laureate in 1915. Her best work describes western nature in tight, sensuous lines:

> The skies that thrill and woo you,
> That torture and undo you,
> That lure and hold you so –
> And will not let you go!

> ('My Cloth of Gold').

Her poetry is collected in *A Perfect Day* (1881), *The Singer by the Sea* (1894), *Songs from the Golden Gate* (1895), and *Wings of Sunset* (1929) which includes 'Concha', a long first-person narrative mixing Spanish with English, about a young Chicana's struggle with orthodox religion and prescribed gender roles.   JSG

Coolidge, Susan (Sarah Chauncey Woolsey)

1835–1905 American CHILDREN'S AUTHOR, short-fiction writer, poet and editor. She was born into a highly educated family in Cleveland, Ohio, attended private schools there and in New Hampshire, and moved to New Haven, Connecticut, in 1855. She worked in hospitals during the Civil War. After her father's death in 1870, the family lived for two years in Europe, then moved to Newport, Rhode Island, near the home of Woolsey's friend HELEN HUNT JACKSON. She began writing that year while vacationing with Jackson, and in 1871 published a collection of stories for girls, *The New Year's Bargain*, under her 'Coolidge' pseudonym; numerous other collections of poems and stories followed. She also edited personal writings of FANNY BURNEY (1880) and JANE AUSTEN (1892) and compiled *A Short History of the City of Philadelphia* (1887). Her most popular books are comparable to LOUISA MAY ALCOTT's chronicles of the March sisters – a series following the adventures of lively Katy Carr from childhood to adulthood, partially based on Woolsey's own life (*What Katy Did*, 1872; *What Katy Did at School*, 1874; *What Katy Did Next*, 1886; *Clover*, 1888; *In the High Valley*, 1890).   JSG

Coonardoo (1929) Written from first-hand experience of outback life at Turee station, Western Australia, KATHARINE SUSANNAH PRICHARD's fifth novel relates a love-affair between a white station-owner and an Aboriginal girl. It was greeted with shock by Australian readers despite sharing first place in the *Bulletin*'s 1928 competition. In *Coonardoo* Prichard breaks new ground by placing the Aborigine centre-stage in the Australian writing tradition rather than relegating her to its margins. Her use of naturalistic detail is balanced by a symbolic framework in which Coonardoo – 'the well in the shadow' – signifies the exploitation of black women by white men and the failure of a new love-based relationship between the races. Prichard's socialism is evident on all fronts – the portrayal of colonial brutality, land relations, careful research into Aboriginal life – yet her vivid portrayal of female sexuality is weakened by a reliance on primitive Romanticism in which woman becomes synonymous with the land itself.   MRE

Cooper [née Haywood], Anna Julia 1858–1964

Celebrated as the first black feminist for raising consciousness about the place of black women in American society. Exposing the fact that black women were not allowed to participate in the social and political movements that supposedly represented them, she wrote in *A Voice From the South by a Black Woman of the South* (1892), 'The colored woman of today . . . is confronted by both a woman question and a race problem, and is as yet an unknown or an unacknowledged factor in both.' In this first and only book Cooper criticizes Women's Movement leaders SUSAN B. ANTHONY and Anna Shaw for refusing admittance to a 'cream-colored applicant' (Cooper herself) seeking to join their women's culture club. And to her black male contemporaries advocating political and social equality, she warns 'every attempt to elevate the Negro . . . prove[s] abortive unless so directed as to utilize the indispensable agency of an elevated and trained womanhood'. Cooper insists that black women's agency only develops through access to higher education and teaching jobs in the schools and churches.

Though Cooper herself knew such prominent figures as Frederick Douglass and W. E. B. DuBois, she was not recognized by these same leaders as a spokesperson for the black cause. Despite a lack of public support from her male contemporaries, she went on to be the school principal at Washington's Dunbar High School, where she also taught Latin. At the age of 57 she adopted five orphaned children, and at 67 earned a doctorate from the University of Paris, being the fourth American black woman to receive a Ph.D.   GG-R

Cooper, Edith Emma see FIELD, MICHAEL

Cooper, Lettice (Ulpha) 1897–1991

Prolific British novelist, often on provincial subjects, biographer of Dickens, Stevenson and GEORGE ELIOT, and writer of popular stories for CHILDREN, who is best known for her novels set in the North, *The New House* (1936) and *National Provincial* (1939), and for *Fenny* (1953), a story of failed romantic love in Florence. Born in Eccles in Lancashire, she read Classics at Lady Margaret Hall, Oxford, before joining the family engineering firm, and working in a centre for the unemployed. In 1939 she went to London to work for *Time and Tide*.

A lifelong socialist – the miners' strike of 1971–2 is the background of a late novel, *Snow and Roses* (1976) – Cooper shared a flat amicably with her Conservative sister, Barbara, for thirty years. Her literary reputation declined after *Fenny*. Lettice Cooper was President of PEN, fiction reviewer for the *Yorkshire Post*, and founded the Writers' Action Group, which secured Public Lending Right for authors in 1978.   MJ

Cooper, Susan Fenimore 1813–94

American novelist, nature writer, editor and philanthropist. She was born in Mamaroneck, New York, daughter of the novelist James Fenimore Cooper, for whom she acted

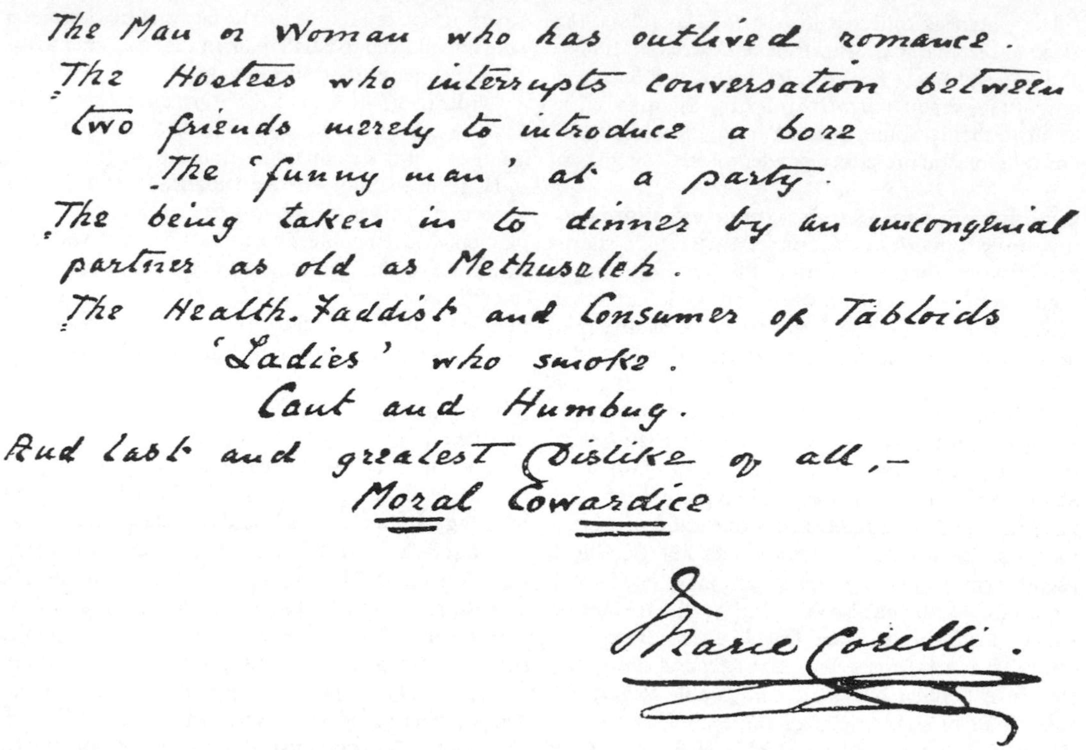

The Man or Woman who has outlived romance.

The Hostess who interrupts conversation between two friends merely to introduce a bore

The 'funny man' at a party.

The being taken in to dinner by an uncongenial partner as old as Methuseleh.

The Health-Faddist and Consumer of Tabloids

'Ladies' who smoke.

Cant and Humbug.

And last and greatest Dislike of all,—

Moral Cowardice

Marie Corelli.

Marie Corelli: an extract from 'My dislikes', *Lady's Realm*, 1897.

as copyist during her twenties and thirties. She was educated by tutors and in private schools in New York City and Europe, where her family travelled from 1826 to 1833. On their return, they settled in Cooperstown, New York. Cooper's novel, *Elinor Wyllys* (1845), appeared under the pseudonym 'Amabel Penfeather' with a preface written by her father.

Her *Rural Hours: Or, Some Chapters on Flowers, Birds, and Insects* (1850), a journal of a year's observations, was glowingly received in the United States and England and reprinted nine times from 1850 to 1876; an abridged version was published in 1887. Praised by Henry David Thoreau well before he published *Walden*, *Rural Hours* gained Cooper a permanent place as a pioneering naturalist. The first American woman to publish an extended work on nature, she chronicled geologic and human history and described animal and plant life, noting the diminishment of certain species and warning about the profligate use of natural resources. She compiled a posthumous collection of her father's work, *Pages and Pictures, from the Writings of James Fenimore Cooper*, in 1861. After the Civil War she founded a hospital and an orphanage.   JSG

Cope, Wendy 1945– Wry, crowd-pleasing English poet and accomplished parodist. Born in Erith, Kent,

and educated at private schools in Ashford and Chislehurst and at St Hilda's College, Oxford, where she read History, Cope then became a primary school teacher and later deputy head in London. After the appearance of her first collection, *Across the City*, in 1980, she achieved widespread commercial and critical success with the publication of *Making Cocoa for Kingsley Amis* (1986), which was reinforced by *Serious Concerns* in 1992. An acerbic chronicler of the everyday 'clutter of urban life', including lonely-heart columns, fridge magnets and her own royalty statements, she also achieves a comedic poignancy, notably in her love poetry. Unrepentantly populist (berating a reviewer in 'Serious Concerns' for accusing her of being both 'witty and unpretentious'), she mocks the male tradition of poetry, while displaying her own virtuosity within the strictures of form. She has also written for children (*Twiddling Your Thumbs*, 1988), edited an anthology of women's poetry (*Is that the New Moon?*, 1989) and has been presented with the Cholmondeley Award (1987) and the American Academy of Letters Michael Braude Award for Light Verse (1995).   CS

Corelli, Marie [Mary Mackay] 1855–1924 Bestselling British novelist whose SENSATIONAL melodramas and ROMANCES appealed to a surprising cross-section of turn-of-the-century readers. Daughter of Scottish balladeer and journalist Charles Mackay, she had a lonely childhood near Box Hill, but her father's indulgence was an important factor in her romantic temperament. Her first novel, *A Romance of Two Worlds*, was an unexpected bestseller when it appeared in 1886, launching an unparalleled publication record. She had a profuse imagination, and wrote more than twenty-five books. *Ardath* (1889) and *The Soul of Lilith* (1892) are curiously esoteric approaches to Victorian science and archaeology, while *Barabbas* (1893) was an enormously popular but controversial retelling of the crucifixion. Many of Corelli's novels blatantly attack the moral emptiness of the British aristocracy (as in *Thelma*, 1887), or oppose male infidelity and female purity in violently melodramatic narratives (*Vendetta!*, 1886; *Wormwood*, 1890; and *The Murder of Delicia*, 1896). Perhaps her most famous book is THE SORROWS OF SATAN (1895), a vindictive fantasy attacking late-Victorian publishing practices. Throughout her career, she engaged in fierce battles with literary critics and reviewers. Her fall in popularity was sudden and total after World War I and her reputation as a low-status author of bestsellers has hardly been disputed. Still, her success had a lasting impact on the publishing industry and on generations of readers, who found her narrative energy and moral confidence irresistible. She died of a heart attack in Stratford-upon-Avon in 1924.   ARF

Corke, Helen 1882–1978 English educator and writer. She served as an assistant mistress from 1905 to 1919 in Croydon and as a headmistress at Kelvedon from 1919 to 1928 and also wrote history textbooks. Her autobiography, *In Our Infancy* (1975), tells how she met Croydon fellow-teacher D.H. Lawrence in 1908 and, because he had helped her to resolve her grief, allowed him to base his second novel, *The Trespasser* (1912), on her 'Freshwater Diary' account of a summer 1909 affair with her married violin-teacher lover who later committed suicide. Lawrence's novel closely follows her account and incorporates some of her sentences, but expands the story's context. She saw the manuscript in process, although not the final revision before printing, and approved of Lawrence's rendering. Her other writings on Lawrence include criticism in *Lawrence and 'Apocalypse'* (1933), the memoir *Lawrence's Princess* on Jessie Chambers (1951), and the biography *D.H. Lawrence: The Croydon Years* (1965). Besides books on history and economics, she also published the novel *Neutral Ground* (1933) and poetry, *Songs of Autumn* (1960), both of which include autobiographical material.   HB

Cornford, Frances Crofts (Darwin) 1886–1960 English poet and translator, associated with the Georgian school, friend and elegist of Rupert Brooke and Edward Marsh, but, especially in her later poems,

offering a sharp, witty, bleak perspective, particularly on the lives of anonymous women. The poem for which she is best known is 'To a Fat Lady Seen from the Train'. Cornford, an only child, was born, lived and died in Cambridge, in a world of academic privilege and pastoral serenity which her poetry both celebrates and questions. She was the grand-daughter of Charles Darwin, the daughter of a Newnham College fellow, and the wife of a classical scholar. Her two eldest children also acquired national reputations. John, poet and Communist, died in the Spanish Civil War. Cornford's first volume, *Poems*, came out in 1910; seven volumes followed, three illustrated by her cousin Gwen Raverat, one by Eric Gill and two by her artist son, Christopher. VIRGINIA WOOLF encouraged her throughout the 1920s, and the Hogarth Press published her *Different Days* (1928). She worked with Esther Salaman on *Poems from the Russian* (1943) and with Stephen Spender on translating Paul Eluard's *Le Dur désir de durer* in 1950; her *Collected Poems* in 1954 was the choice of the Poetry Book Society; in 1959 she was awarded the Queen's Medal for Poetry. Praised by Stephen Spender and other fellow writers, she was included by FLEUR ADCOCK in her 1987 anthology of *Twentieth Century Women's Poetry* as 'an important neglected older poet'.   VP

Cornwell, Patricia D. 1956– Contemporary American crime novelist whose investigator, Dr Kay Scarpetta, richly inhabits the once male preserve of tough crime fiction. Cornwell was born in Miami to an unstable mother who 'gave' her and her brothers to evangelist Billy Graham; her first publication, *A Time of Remembering* (1983), is a biography of Graham's wife Ruth Bell, and her fiction is imbued with a well-nigh Manichean sense of human good and (especially) evil. Studying at Davidson College in North Carolina, she met and married a much older English lecturer; they later divorced. After police reporting for the *Charlotte Observer*, she spent six years as a computer analyst at the Virginia Chief Medical Examiner's office, during which time she invented her acknowledged *alter ego*, Scarpetta, the office's fictional celebrity Chief Medical Examiner and FBI forensic pathologist. The bleak *Postmortem* (1990) opens the series with Scarpetta pursuing a serial sex killer in a millennial United States where violence, perversion and horror are endemic. A popular and critical success – it garnered five awards – it was followed at yearly intervals by *Body of Evidence*, *All That Remains*, *Cruel and Unusual*, *The Body Farm*, *From Potter's Field* and *Cause of Death*. Life imitated art in 1996 when it was alleged that Cornwell had had an affair with FBI agent Marguerite Bennett; she later admitted this, prompting attention to the treatment of gays in her work. Her first non-Scarpetta novel, *Hornet's Nest*, was published in 1997.   MO'D

Costello, Louisa Stuart 1799–1870 TRAVEL WRITER, poet, novelist and artist. Louisa was born in Ireland but on the death of her father, an army officer, in 1814, the family moved to France, where she studied art and contributed to the family income by painting miniatures.

At 16 she published *The Maid of the Cypress Isle, and Other Poems* (1815), followed in 1825 by *Songs of a Stranger*. Admirers of her work included Thomas Moore, to whom she dedicated her *Specimens of the Early Poetry of France* (1835). Costello was also a novelist and a BIOGRAPHER: *Memoirs of Eminent Englishwomen* appeared in 1844, and she returned to this genre in her *Memoirs of Mary, the young Duchess of Burgundy* (1853) and *Memoirs of Anne Duchess of Brittany* (1855).

However, Costello's reputation was principally based on her travel-writing, which drew on her expertise in the fields of history, art and literature, and which coincided with the new English middle-class vogue for foreign travel. *A Summer Amongst the Bocages and the Vines* appeared in 1840, and was followed by *A Pilgrimage to Auvergne* (1842), *Bearn and the Pyrenees* (1844), *Falls, Lakes and Mountains of Wales* (1845) and *Venice and the Venetians* (1845).

Awarded a Civil List annuity of £75 in 1852, Costello retired to Boulogne, where she died.   RR

Cotters' England (1966) This is CHRISTINA STEAD's second novel of the working-class, an English counterpart to SEVEN POOR MEN OF SYDNEY. Begun in the late 1940s, and based on socialist friends from Newcastle-upon-Tyne, it offers a powerful analysis of the failure of the working class to achieve radical change after World War II. The central figure, the journalist Nellie Cotter, is one of Stead's flawed socialists. Once a strike leader, she now feeds on the misery of 'poor frail waifs' and jealously opposes all who claim to be able to promote social change. Through the Cotters the novel counts the physical and psychological cost of the hungry years of the Depression. The darkly domineering Nellie and her brother Tom, locked destructively together, are both predatory and charming. Episodes set in the parents' Newcastle home, the 'chamber of horrors', offer damning images of the family as a destructive institution, comparable to those of THE MAN WHO LOVED CHILDREN. Equally pervasive and harmful is the English attachment to the past: 'so old baronial, so out of date'. Though the Cotters and their like muddle on, and the narrator withholds comment, the gloomy judgement of Stead the outsider is unmistakable.   ABl

Couani, Anna 1948– Writer and publisher of poetry and prose fiction, was born a third-generation Australian of Greek and Polish parents. Her writing is a complex play of non-narrative structures and collage effects which eschews genres of fiction, non-fiction and poetry. Couani claims to write from her 'own ideological condition rather than an implicit received one', drawing critical attention to the politics of production and reception by publishing her work exclusively with small presses. She also runs Sea Cruise books, a small press which concentrates on women writers. Couani's interest in experimental writing and community writing and publishing, and her concern with identity, authorship and place, have highlighted theoretical issues of marginality in Australian writing. Her publications include *Italy* (1977), *Were All Women Sex Mad? and Other Stories* (1982) and *The Train* (1983). Couani has co-edited two collections of experimental writing; *Island in the Sun: An Anthology of Recent Australian Prose* (1980) with D. White and T. Thompson, and *Telling Ways: Australian Women's Writing* (1988) with Sneja Gunew. *The Harbour Breathes* (1989) combines photomontages by co-author Peter Lyssiotis with Couani's poetry and prose poems.   MF

Countesse of Mountgomeries Urania, The (1621) With this long and eclectic ROMANCE, LADY MARY WROTH produced probably the earliest piece of prose fiction by an English woman writer. It was withdrawn six months after publication. The sequel never appeared, after contemporaries like Lord Edward Denny (later Earl of Norwich) objected to Wroth's depiction of real-life characters. Whilst the title cites Sir Philip Sidney's romance *The Countess of Pembroke's Arkadia* and the text borrows from other, earlier literary works, it clearly rewrites traditional romance conventions. Wroth shifts the narrative focus from male to female characters and concentrates on the social and political impotence of early 17th-century women. Figures such as Pamphilia, Lindamira and Bellamira seem to represent Wroth's multiple selves and speak of the difficulty of reconciling her own lives as a courtier and writer. Other protagonists such as Urania, a character who already appears in Sidney's text, are complex and assertive women who contest the restrictions of their age.   NBP

Country Between Us, The (1981) CAROLYN FORCHÉ's second volume after *Gathering the Tribes* established her as a voice of conscience: in Susan Griffin's phrase, as 'one of the greatest political poets of our time'. Forché's territory in many of the poems was one of the most fraught for Americans in the early Reagan years – El Salvador – and her dramatic subjects include the atrocities she learned of during her time there. Her form, which she described as the 'first-person, free-verse, lyric-narrative poem', emphasized the importance of the poet's bearing witness. As one poem testifies, 'There is nothing one man will not do to another.' Her passionate humanism and cool commitment prevent the work from seeming sensational, as does her inclusion of more personal testimonies: the volume encompasses both the human ears a Salvadoran colonel spills on a table to shock her, and lyrical, melancholy scenes of European travels and her childhood Michigan. Accolades for the collection, which was widely read, came from fellow political poets such as DENISE LEVERTOV and Jacobo Timerman, who likened Forché's powerful, sensual work to Neruda's.   SB

Country Girls, The (1960) In EDNA O'BRIEN's first novel, Caithleen describes her upbringing in downtrodden, rural Ireland, as she and her companion Baba mature from the eponymous country girls into aspiring young women searching for life and love. The novel's simple, but painterly, descriptions richly evoke a familiar yet dream-washed world in which humdrum disaster coalesces with fragile optimism. The 'enchantment of life' is repeatedly frustrated by disillusion. Growing up in the shadow of her abusive and alcoholic father, Caithleen's childhood is brought to an abrupt end by the death of her mother. Bereavement, abandonment and loss are juxtaposed against escape and endurance – Caithleen finds solace in the arms of the seedy Mr Gentleman and solidarity in her intense, if ambivalent, friendship with Baba. The two successfully contrive their expulsion from the restrictive Catholic convent, leaving behind their rustic roots for the promise and glamour of Dublin.

The novel forms the first part of a trilogy with *Girl with Green Eyes* (1962); (previously THE LONELY GIRL), and *Girls in their Married Bliss* (1964).   CCr

Country of the Pointed Firs, The (1896) Like GASKELL'S CRANFORD, SARAH ORNE JEWETT's novel is a connected sequence of stories, narrated by a visitor to a small community, a declined maritime village on the coast of Maine. The nameless woman writer, on a summer retreat to get her work done, finds herself drawn more and more intimately into the lives and the landscape of Dunnet Landing. Jewett uses the tiny village, the scattered homesteads and the beautiful shores and islands of this lonely coast to explore the nature of human connections, and to evoke the unique inner worlds of individuals. Above all, in Almira Todd, the community herbalist, and her wonderfully independent old mother, Mrs Blackett, and in stories of the long-dead hermit, Joanna, she creates characters of mysterious force, with sustaining strengths drawn from ancient sources of wisdom. Never losing touch with the everyday, in this novel and its short sequels, Jewett found a descriptive power and a poetic cadence that suggested alternative ways of communicating women's experience and relationships.   PEK

Couvreur, Jessie ('Tasma') 1848–97 Born in London and raised in Tasmania, she divorced her first husband and went to Europe where she worked as a journalist and lecturer, and married Auguste Couvreur, a Belgian political journalist.

Her first novel, UNCLE PIPER OF PIPER'S HILL (1889), had already been a success in serial form in the *Australasian*, and was equally so in Britain and Europe, despite its un-exotic setting in Melbourne in the 1880s. The advent of snobbish English cousins to the establishment of Uncle Piper, a butcher who had made his fortune on the goldfields, provides 'Tasma' with golden opportunities for social satire combined with the sentimental appeal of a central child character, the romance of several courtships and the spice of a rebellious BLUESTOCKING heroine. Laura is something of a NEW WOMAN, in that she questions social mores and conventional religion. In this novel all the characters who are capable of learning manage to grow by the experience, and end up with the right partner; their stories are accompanied by leisurely and interesting reflections on passion and true love, and on the consolations of religion contrasted with Laura's and George's modern 'materialism'.

The puzzle about Tasma as a novelist is the difference between *Uncle Piper*, deservedly her most admired novel, and the other five which followed in quick succession. *In Her Earliest Youth* (1890), *The Penance of Portia James* (1891), *Knight of the White Feather* (1892), *Not Counting the Cost* (1895) and *A Fiery Ordeal* (1897) are all melodramas concerned with unhappy marriages. Their heroines hardly qualify as types of the 'New Woman' of the 1880s and 1890s, except for some details like their extensive education and lack of religious faith: none is motivated by the desire for an independent career, and they object not so much to the institution of marriage itself as to their misfortune in the marriage lottery.   SMS

Couzyn, Jeni 1942– South African-born poet, who left for England in 1966 and later went to live in Canada. Her reputation is greatest outside South Africa, although her work has at times retained a South African feeling. Her work combines personal and political themes, and has been published in six volumes: *Flying* (1970), *Monkeys' Wedding* (1972), *Christmas in Africa* (1975), *The Happiness Bird* (1978), *House of Changes* (1979) and *Life by Drowning: Selected Poems* (1983). This last, her most recent volume, includes some poems from her earlier collections, but also an entirely new sequence of poems on pregnancy and childbirth. She has also published a collection of poems by others under the title *The Bloodaxe Book of Women's Poetry*, in which some South African poets are included. The style of Couzyn's work ranges from lyrical to narrative; her themes are varied, including

memories of childhood, reflections on daily life, and poems with a strong social concern. CCo

Cowley, Hannah 1743–1809 British writer of popular comedies. A bookseller's daughter from Tiverton, Devon, she moved to London with her husband and helped support their children through writing. David Garrick staged her first play, *The Runaway*, in 1776 before retiring from Drury Lane. Cowley's thirteen plays, appearing in 1776–94, included two tragedies and one farce. Her best work adapted and refined Restoration comic conventions; SUSANNA CENTLIVRE and APHRA BEHN were among the authors she used. *The Belle's Stratagem* (1780) draws on plays by George Etherege and William Wycherley, replacing their rake-heroes' control of the action with supremacy for the clever, witty yet modest heroine, a character-type especially prominent in Cowley's work. She was a prolific poet, and as 'Anna Matilda' engaged in poetic exchanges with 'Della Crusca' (Robert Merry). This sentimental 'Della Cruscan' poetry was later satirized by William Gifford. In 1801 she retired to Devon, where she revised her plays for her three-volume *Works* (published posthumously in 1813). JSp

Cowley, Joy 1936– New Zealand novelist, short-story writer and prolific CHILDREN's writer. Cowley's novels for adults from 1968 focused on the limited and repressive life of New Zealand *pakeha* (white) society, both in parent–child and male–female relationships. *Man of Straw* (1970) was a lucid tragic story of a girl growing up in a constricting family and community. Since then she has written over 350 books for early readers, picture story books for younger children, stories and novels for young people and plays for adults to act for children. Her CHILDREN'S BOOKS are set in New Zealand and the Pacific – 'I see a national identity emerging through our children's literature' – and in 1990 she received a commemoration medal for services to New Zealand. Her novel *The Silent One* (1981) won the New Zealand Children's Book of the Year, and *Bow Down Shadrach* (1991) won the AIM Prize (for children). Cowley married in 1956 and had four children; is now in her third marriage and lives in a sea-side settlement, Kenepuru, near Picton, but travels widely. In 1997 she published her complete short stories for adults, written from the 1960s on. AM

Cowman, Roz 1942– Irish poet. Cowman's poetry characteristically inverts the given perspective in communal myths, FAIRY TALES and religious beliefs, using vivid spare imagery ('my father's crotch / moved like simmering stew' – 'Catskin's Song') in order to develop the author's pervasive sense of the *unheimlich* which threatens states of too-readily embraced security. Born in Cork, Cowman was educated at the Loreto

Convent in Clonmel and at University College Cork. She won Ireland's unofficial national prize for an emerging poet, the Patrick Kavanagh Award, in 1985. She works as a teacher and has three children. The poems of her collection *The Goose Herd* (1989) were aptly described on its back cover by EAVAN BOLAND as being 'far less witnesses than participants in the experiences they recount . . . mak[ing] a fascinating intersection between a bleak spirituality and a lyric strength'. This is a dark collection, reflecting the reversals suffered by the movement for women's liberation in the 1980s in Ireland in its recurrent focus on the threat of a larger patriarchal power planning, controlling and ultimately undermining women's sense of achieved liberation: 'all the giants invisible, / at work behind the scenes' ('Peanuts'). CCl

Craig, Edith (Edy) 1869–1947 English woman of the theatre, the eldest child of the actress Ellen Terry and the architect and designer William Godwin. The couple split up shortly after financial pressures forced them to leave their Hertfordshire retreat and Terry to return to the stage in 1874. From that time, most of Craig's life was dominated by the powerful presence of her mother.

Debarred from her chosen career as a pianist by the early onset of rheumatism, Craig returned from musical training in Berlin to act with her mother and Henry Irving in the Lyceum company in 1890. Finding that work uncongenial, she turned to costume design and production work. She became a leading figure in the Actresses' Franchise League, where she produced Cicely Hamilton's *How the Vote Was Won*. She also organized a number of feminist pageants, work which inspired the character of Miss La Trobe in VIRGINIA WOOLF'S *BETWEEN THE ACTS* (1941). Craig also founded the Pioneer Players, with whom she produced 150 plays from 1911 to 1921. Bernard Shaw wrote of this group that, 'by singleness of artistic direction, and unflagging activity, [it] did more for the theatrical vanguard than any of the other coterie theatres'.

After her mother's death in 1928, Craig devoted herself to perpetuating the actress's memory. She persuaded Shaw to allow the publication in 1931 of his correspondence with Terry, co-edited *Ellen Terry's Memoirs* (1932) with her companion Christopher St John, and turned Terry's former home in Smallhythe, Kent, into the Ellen Terry Memorial Museum. GM

Craik, Dinah (Maria) Mulock 1826–87 Prolific English writer of novels, essays, short stories and poetry. Educated at home, with an impecunious father, at 13 she helped her mother run a school. At 19 she wrote to support herself and two younger brothers. After her marriage to George Lillie Craik in 1865 she insisted, against his wishes, on continuing writing.

Her novels are deeply moral, with Christian virtue and hard work rewarded. The best-known is JOHN HALIFAX, GENTLEMAN (1856), which is narrated by Craik's favourite figure, the crippled outsider (a metaphor for the role of the female in society?). Other novels include *Olive* (1850 – about a deformed heroine), *The Half-Caste* (1851), *Agatha's Husband* (1853), *A New Year's Gift to Sick Children* (1865), *Two Marriages* (1867), *A Noble Life* (1866 – about a crippled little earl), *The Woman's Kingdom* (1869) and *The Little Lame Prince* (1875); most praise female self-reliance and show the dangers of marriage. In *A Life for a Life* (1859), a double narrative questions accepted gender roles. In *Mistress and Maid* (1863), the eponymous pair make a living first by school-teaching and then by shop-keeping. Craik occasionally dealt with social issues. In her essays, especially *A Woman's Thoughts about Women* (1858), she examined the professions open to single women, particularly teaching. Contemporary reviewers – male and female – could be condescending about her 'lack of education' – though her circle included ELIZABETH GASKELL and JANE CARLYLE.   VP

Cranford (1851–3) ELIZABETH GASKELL's stories of 1830s life in a small market town, based on childhood experiences in Knutsford, originally appeared at irregular intervals in *Household Words*, while Gaskell wrote RUTH simultaneously. AUSTEN's preoccupation with the financial exigencies of single women, and MARY MITFORD's exploration of parochial politics in *Our Village*, inform Gaskell's depiction of a community of spinsters and widows, and *Household Words* specialized in the pathos of incomplete or vestigial families. The central figure, Miss Matty Jenkyns, has survived all her family, and an early abortive romance. Gaskell's treatment, however, emphasizes the resiliences and co-operative strengths of her women without men, as well as their regrets and anxieties. Muted indications of social change, as the community proclaims resistance while tacitly accepting increased class mobility, are complemented by emphasis on the vanishing traces of personal history; in one episode Miss Matty remembers her family while burning their letters. *Cranford* has suffered from a reputation for fragrant charm, but Gaskell's assured treatment of the epiphanic episode make these among the best Victorian short stories.   AT

Crapsey, Adelaide 1878–1914 American poet. Crapsey was the third of nine children born to Algernon Crapsey, an Episcopalian minister in Rochester, New York. She was educated at Kemper, an Episcopal boarding school in Wisconsin, and at Vassar College, where she was class poet and from which she graduated in 1901. Alternating teaching with travel through Europe, Crapsey spent the next ten years writing poetry and studying metrics and prosody in earnest. Returning to teach at Smith College in 1911, she was diagnosed with tuberculosis, which was not discovered by her family until 1913, when they sent her to a sanatorium in Saranac Lake, New York. Here she began working on cinquains, a simple poetic form which Crapsey created. Similar to Japanese haiku, the cinquain is a five-line poem, with two syllables in the first line, four in the second, six in the third, eight in the fourth and two in the fifth. She was praised for her pre-Imagist style:

I know
Not these my hands
And yet I think there was
A woman like me once had hands
Like these.

Crapsey's single volume of poetry, *Verse*, was published posthumously in 1915, as was *A Study in English Metrics* (1918).   SP

Crawford, Isabella Valancy 1850–87 The first important woman poet to write in Canada, her work is noted for its vivid celebration of natural beauty. In 1858 she emigrated from Dublin, the city of her birth, with her parents and her eleven siblings to the pioneer village of Paisley, deep in the Canadian wilderness. Her father, Paisley's first physician and the township's treasurer, taught the children at home, instructing them in the classics as well as in French and Italian literature. Despite unusual intellectual encouragement and picturesque surroundings, from early on Isabella's life was one of suffering and sacrifice, the dominant themes of her mature work. In 1864, following the deaths of nine of the children and Dr Crawford's trial and conviction for misappropriation of public funds, the family moved to the village of Lakefield in the Kawartha Lakes district of Ontario. They relocated again to Peterborough where Isabella's father died in 1875 and where her lone surviving sister died in 1876. Crawford and her widowed mother then moved to Toronto where they lived in a small apartment over a grocery store until Isabella's death.

In this impoverished setting she began to write in earnest to supplement the small allowance provided by her uncle. She dedicated the only volume of verse published in her lifetime, at her own expense (and at a financial loss), *Old Spookses' Pass, Malcolm's Katie, and Other Poems* (1884), to this benefactor. Otherwise, the short fiction and poetry produced in the last decade of her life appeared in Toronto newspapers and American periodicals. Her poetry, reflecting the influence of the Romantic tradition, is characterized by evocative descriptions of the Canadian wilderness and by moving narratives of the hardships endured by simple, hardworking men and women. Her *Collected*

Poems appeared posthumously in 1905. She died of heart failure at the age of 36.   MO'C

Crocker, Hannah Mather 1752–1829 Boston moralist author and matron of a Masonic lodge of women, Crocker's goal was the cultivation of the female mind. She authored religious texts, reform tracts and feminist essays, including *A Series of Letters on Free Masonry* (1815) and *The School of Reform, or Seaman's Safe Pilot to the Cape of Good Hope* (1816), and articles in the *Centinel*, a Boston Masonic publication. In *Observations on the Real Rights of Women, With Their Appropriate Duties, Agreeable to Scripture, Reason and Common Sense* (1818), Crocker acknowledges 'moral and physical distinction of the sexes agreeably to the order of nature, and the organization of the human frame', yet she asserts that 'the wise Author of nature has endowed the female mind with equal powers and faculties, and given them the same right of judging and acting for themselves, as he gave to the male sex'. Crocker argues from the authority of biblical history that 'under the Jewish dispensation, the man should rule over her', but that 'woman [was] restored to her original right and dignity at the commencement of the christian dispensation'. Crocker is the granddaughter of Cotton Mather and daughter of Revd Samuel and Hannah Hutchison Mather. Well-read, having inherited most of the Mather family library, she began authorship following the 1797 death of her husband, Joseph Crocker.
                                                                  DZB

Croker [née Shephard], B.M. (Bithia Mary) 1850–1920 Prolific writer of ROMANTIC, COLONIAL novels. The daughter of a Church of Ireland rector, she was born in County Roscommon, Ireland, and educated in England and France. Following fourteen years in India and Burma with her army officer husband, she published her first novel *Proper Pride* (1883), which was popularized by Gladstone having been seen reading it. A self-reflexive, skilled prose-stylist, Croker produced some forty novels in thirty-seven years, many of which were translated into French and German. Although they promote traditional values, her novels provide astute and sympathetic readings of colonial societies in India and Ireland. In *Lismoyle* (1914), the Anglo-Irish Ascendancy is sensitively described as 'a heritage perilously near to its dark moment of eclipse', while the ambiguous position of the Anglo-Indians dictates the theme and background of *Pretty Miss Neville* (1883) and *Her Own People* (1903). *The Road to Mandalay* (1917) was made into a film, and a dramatized version of *Terence* (1899) ran for two years in the USA. Despite the widespread appeal of her witty, light-hearted stories, she complained that her native land had consistently ignored her and had never acknowledged her as 'an Irish novelist'.   BHu

Crommelin, May [Maria Henrietta de la Cherois] 1850–1930 This TRAVEL WRITER and author of forty-two novels was born into a landed Irish family that migrated to England in the 1880s, due to ill health and 'land troubles'. Her father disapproved of her writing and, whilst under his roof, she always worked away from his sight. Following her parents' deaths and her brother's return to Ireland, she moved to London.

Crommelin's books often closely parallel her travels. *Orange Lily* (1879) is set in her birth-place, Ulster; *Joy* (1884) is located on Dartmoor, place of her first English home; and *Cross-Roads* (1890) suggests first-hand knowledge of France and Italy. The non-fictional *Over the Andes From the Argentine to Chili [sic] and Peru* (1896) chronicles her tour of South America. Other pieces, fiction and non-fiction, were the fruit of visits to relatives in Holland.

Reviewers were ambivalent. Some deemed that her descriptions of scenery were 'word-painting of rare fidelity' and that 'the idea of Duty [was her] keynote'. However, a novel such as *Goblin Gold* (1885) could be dismissed as 'not a successful addition to shilling fiction'. She eventually returned to the family estate in Ireland where she ended her days in total obscurity.
                                                                  EMH

Crompton (Lamburn), Richmal 1890–1969 English novelist, whose sequence of forty collections of stories portraying the exploits of schoolboy William Brown brought her the kind of fame she would have preferred to earn as a writer of adult fiction. Educated at the Clergy Daughters' School, Warrington, and at Royal Holloway College, she spent some years teaching Classics at Bromley High School, until poliomyelitis forced her to retire in 1923. The previous year had seen the publication of *Just William*, a dozen magazine stories featuring the disaster-prone but always well-intentioned boy hero modelled on her nephew Tommy Disher. Though Crompton continued to produce serious novels, largely set against suburban backgrounds and tackling issues of status and money (the last of these, *The Inheritor*, appeared in 1960), it was through William and his world that her shrewdest perceptions of English bourgeois society were filtered. With sly acidity she mocked the pretensions, aspirations and speech habits of the professional classes among whom she lived, in a house on Bromley's outskirts, built with the help of increasingly successful 'William' sales. Though the author's moral awareness never abandons her, and such values as loyalty, compassion and determination are strongly inculcated, her continuing popularity rests on the skill with which she encourages her readers to applaud William's anarchic assaults on the pomposity and inherent silliness of grown-ups.   JK

Crosby, Caresse (Mary Phelps Jacob) 1892–1970
Founder of the Black Sun Press with Harry Crosby, she
was a luminary in the American expatriate community
between the world wars. 'Polly', as Mary Jacob was
called, was of 'good' family in New York and was a
debutante in the 1914 season in London. A sign of
rebelliousness came later that year when she cut away
the bottom of her boned corset and tied two handker-
chiefs together with pink ribbons, thus inventing the
brassière. (She later sold the patent for $50.) After a
failed marriage to a Boston socialite, she married
Harry Crosby, banker and wayward nephew of J.
Pierpont Morgan. They moved to Paris, where Crosby
gave Polly a new name, 'Caresse', which she retained. In
addition to publishing Hart Crane's *The Bridge*, and
works by Joyce and MacLeish, the Black Sun Press
ensured a vivid place for the Crosbys in the Paris expatriate community. After Crosby's murder-suicide in
1929, Caresse kept the Black Sun Press going until 1937,
when she remarried. After divorcing in 1950, Crosby
wrote her autobiography, *The Passionate Years* (1955),
and rented a 350-room castle in Italy, which she ran as
an artists' colony.   EH

Cross, Amanda see HEILBRUN, CAROLYN

Cross(e), Victoria 1868–1952? British author of racy
novels. Victoria Cross(e) was the pseudonym of a
woman known variously as Vivian Cory, Vivian Cory
Griffin and Annie Sophie Cory. She dropped the 'e'
from her name after Queen Victoria died. Cross grew
up in India, but after her father's death she travelled
the world with her uncle, then retired to Monte Carlo
to live with female friends. One of her sisters was the
poet LAURENCE HOPE (Adela Nicolson), and
another was Isabell Tate (editor of the *Sind Gazette* in
India).

Cross's short story 'Theodora: A Fragment', first
published in the *Yellow Book* in 1895, describes the
heroine's eyes, full of 'the hot, clear, blinding light of
passion'. Her writing was frequently denounced by
reviewers because she wrote frankly about sexual feelings. The first novel, *Consummation*, was retitled by the
publisher John Lane. It was volume 18 of his 'Keynote'
series, and was called *The Woman Who Didn't* as a
deliberate response to Grant Allen's controversial bestseller of the same year, 1895, *The Woman Who Did*. Her
most successful work was *Anna Lombard* (1901), in which
the heroine persuades her husband to permit her to
continue her pre-marital affair. Cross produced
numerous popular novels about sex and adultery, with
provocative titles such as *The Night of Temptation* (1912)
and *Electric Love* (1929). One critic complained that she
believed 'life means love-making'. Her last novel was
Martha Brown, MP (1935), a utopian fantasy in which
England is ruled by women.   ST

Cross, Zora 1890–1964 Australian poet and novelist
born in Brisbane, Queensland, trained as a teacher,
later working as an actor, as an editor of a theatre
journal – the *Bohemian* – and as a freelance journalist.
Songs of Love and Life (1917), written to her *de facto*
husband, the poet David McKee Wright, attracted
attention for their sensuous enjoyment of passion
touched with spiritual awareness. The sonnets ran into
four editions in two years and an English edition followed in 1930. Their bold celebration of love may have
been responsible for some of the acclaim, but the verse
at its best approaches the knotty lyrical strength of the
sonnets of ELIZABETH BARRETT BROWNING. Love is
the central force of all Cross's poetry, including 'A Song
of Mother Love' (1916), 'The Lilt of Life' (1918), *The City
of Riddle-mee-ree* (1918) – a collection of verse for children – and in the moving 'Elegy on an Australian
Schoolboy' (1921), which commemorates her younger
brother killed in World War I. The exploration of
different kinds of love is continued in many of her
short stories published in Australian periodicals and
anthologies, and her three novels: *Daughters of the Seven
Mile: The Love Story of an Australian Woman* (1924), *The
Lute-Girl of Rainyvale: A Story of Love, Mystery and
Adventure in North Queensland* (1925) and *This Hectic Age*
(1944). Cross's 'An Introduction to the Study of
Australian Literature' (1922) is an early brief criticism
of a selection of Australian colonial and contemporary
poets. It is written with the same original and thoughtful perception of people and values which characterizes all her work.   EPe

Crothers, Rachel C. 1878–1958 American playwright, actress, producer, director and screenwriter.
She was born in Bloomington, Illinois; both parents
were doctors. After graduating from high school in
1891, she studied elocution in Boston, then returned to
Bloomington where she taught. In 1897 she moved to
New York, enrolled in Stanhope-Wheatcroft School of
Acting, and became an instructor. By 1902, the one-act
plays she wrote for her students attracted critical
notice. In 1906 she launched a long, successful career as
a playwright and director for the New York stage, creating roles for such leading actresses as Tallulah
Bankhead and Gertrude Lawrence. The growing film
industry, beginning with the silents, extended her
audience; at the height of the era of strong women
stars, two of her plays became vehicles for Joan
Crawford (*Susan and God*, 1940; *When Ladies Meet*, 1941).
Crothers used her prominent position in the theatre to
organize relief efforts during the Depression and the
World Wars.

Her first Broadway production, *The Three of Us* (1906,
filmed 1914), followed by *Myself Bettina* (1908) and *A
Man's World* (1909, filmed 1918), began a series of plays
she characterized as 'a Dramatic History of Women'. *He*

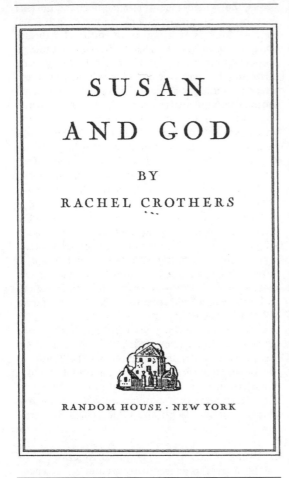

S U S A N
A N D   G O D

BY

R A C H E L   C R O T H E R S

RANDOM HOUSE · NEW YORK

Rachel Crothers: title-page of *Susan and God*.

and She (1911) depicts a woman sculptor who gives up a commission to devote herself to her troubled daughter. *Ourselves* (1913) ascribes prostitution to the sexual double standard. *Young Wisdom* (1914) satirizes radical views of gender relations. During the 1920s she took on youth rebellion and the flapper with *Nice People* (1921, filmed 1922) and *Mary the Third* (1923). Her social comedies of the 1930s (*As Husbands Go*, 1931; *When Ladies Meet*, 1932, filmed 1933 and 1941) depict jaded sophisticates coping with the consequences of sexual freedom. Her award-winning last play, *Susan and God* (1937, filmed 1940), concerns a woman's self-glorification through religion. JSG

Crozier, [Lorna] Uher 1948– Author of ten books of poetry, winner of the Governor General's Award for Poetry. She was born in Swift Current, Saskatchewan, and was inspired by prairie writer Sinclair Ross to 'realize someone from my area could actually be a writer'. 'I have lived on the prairie / all my life', she writes in an early poem,

have rubbed
the silver-green of sage
into my skin crushed the leaves
in my hair laid them
on the eyelids of my lover.

Under her married named of Lorna Uher, she published her first book of poems (*Inside Is the Sky*, 1975) and four subsequent volumes, including *No Longer Two People* (1979), poems written with and to the poet Patrick Lane, with whom she has lived following the breakup of her marriage in 1978. She has an MA in Creative Writing from the University of Alberta, has been much sought after as teacher and writer-in-residence, has taught in the Creative Writing Program at the University of Victoria, and has participated in the Writers In Electronic Residence Program for Canadian schools. She is noted for her frank and often humorous love poetry, and for arresting imagery drawn from nature. FD

Cruise O'Brien, Kate 1948–98 Irish novelist, short-fiction writer, columnist and editor. Born in Dublin, the youngest daughter of Conor Cruise O'Brien and Christine Foster. Related through her father to the Sheehy sisters and through her mother to Robert Lynd, Cruise O'Brien was always quick to demonstrate independence of mind and never afraid to voice an unpopular opinion in her journalism. She was a regular reviewer for the *Listener* and other publications, and a columnist with the *Irish Independent* for ten years.

The stories in her first collection, *A Gift Horse* (1978), which won the Rooney Prize, often reflect the perspective of an outsider refusing to conform to convention in thought, behaviour or feeling. Her first novel, *The Homesick Garden*, came out in 1991, but in 1993 she set aside an unfinished second novel to take up a position as literary editor of Poolbeg Press. Here she quickly developed a reputation as an influential editor with a keen eye for new talent and a willingness to take risks in bringing projects in which she believed into print. Early in 1998 she was credited with being responsible for 'approximately 80% of Irish-published fiction currently available in Dublin bookshops'. Her sudden death following a brain haemorrhage shocked the world of Irish letters. LM

Cry of a Stone, The (1653–4) One of six PROPHETIC texts by Fifth Monarchist ANNA TRAPNEL. She communicated the prayers and spiritual songs which are the core of the book during a twelve-day trance in January 1653, which began while she awaited the outcome of the trial of another Fifth Monarchist, Vavasour Powell. The book was transcribed by a

'Relator', but its preface is a brief SPIRITUAL AUTO-BIOGRAPHY narrating Trapnel's discovery of her vocation as God's 'handmaid'. Central to *The Cry* is the imagery of four horns (representing four world monarchies) from the book of Daniel. It associates Cromwell, whom Trapnel had previously praised as a second Gideon, with the fourth horn of Daniel's prophecy, describing him as one who has 'backslidden' and is now grieving God's elect. Yet Trapnel's apocalyptic imagery anticipates the destruction of this new status quo and the establishment of a fifth monarchy of the Saints.   PJB

Cry to Heaven (1982) Like Balzac's 'Sarrasine', which so enchanted Roland Barthes in *S/Z*, GOTHICIST ANNE RICE's third novel concerns gender confusion and a victimized castrato. In 18th-century Italy, teenager Tonio Treschi is abducted and castrated by his 'brother' Carlo's henchmen to prevent him or his offspring from succeeding to the patrician power of their aristocratic Venetian family. The melodramatic, labyrinthine yet, ultimately, functional plot chronicles Tonio's struggles to become the finest performer of his age and to take revenge on Carlo. Written in Rice's habitually expansive, ornate, languorous prose, simultaneously serious and camp, *Cry to Heaven* gives the author full reign to detail the castrato subculture, the result of a ban on women from opera and church choruses in the Papal territories, while homing in on her favoured themes of the marginal group and the perverse (biological or social) family. Eroticism, violence and death are closely interlinked in the novel's incestuous conflicts; perversion here resides in the heart of the normal.   MO'D

Culleton, Beatrice see MOSIONIER, BEATRICE

Cullwick, Hannah 1833–1909 English maidservant and diarist, mistress and later wife of Arthur Munby, barrister and poet, for whom she wrote the diaries. Their 54-year relationship only became public after both were dead. Cullwick was born in Shropshire, the daughter of a housemaid and a saddler, and began full-time work aged 8. She became variously a lower servant, nurserymaid, scullion, kitchenmaid and maid-of-all-work. Cullwick subverts the Cinderella story: she relished hard work, rejoiced in the servitude to Munby ('Massa'), and refused to become middle-class. The seventeen diaries (1854–73) she wrote at Munby's command, were, for her, not a *liberation*, but the worst drudgery of all. She stopped when they married in 1873. They give a forthright, detailed account of the servant's life, revealing how Cullwick saw her work as essentially Christian: 'if I was a lady and had such a lot o' fine things, I should be afraid I was never humble enough in God's sight'.   VP

Cummins, G(eraldine) D(orothy) 1890–1969 Irish playwright, novelist and psychic whose early interest in women's suffrage and theatre was shared with her collaborator, SUZANNE R. DAY. They wrote several successful plays together. For ten days in 1920 she was married to the poet Austin Clarke. Later, she wrote fiction based on peasant life in her native Munster: *The Land They Loved* (1919), *Fires of Beltane* (1936) and *Variety Show* (1959). Her gift for comedy displays the influence of SOMERVILLE AND ROSS, and in 1952 she published a biography of the former, who was a close friend. She worked as a journalist in London, and increasingly devoted her energies to establishing contact with the dead through automatic writing. *Swan on a Black Sea* (1965) is a study of her psychic experiences. In 1943 she claimed to have received advice from Theodore Roosevelt warning Franklin D. of a US conspiracy. She died in Cork. A large number of unpublished and unperformed plays and other papers are held at the Cork City Archive.   CL

Cummins, Maria Susanna 1827–66 A leading light of the 'd–d mob of scribbling women', as Hawthorne ungallantly described the DOMESTIC and sentimental novelists of mid-century America, Cummins shared with STOWE, STEPHENS and SOUTHWORTH the full warmth of popular approval. In a literary career which lasted a decade, Cummins published four novels, beginning with her greatest success, *The Lamplighter* (1854), followed by *Mabel Vaughan* (1857), *El Fureidis* (1860) and *Haunted Hearts* (1864). Published when she was 27, *The Lamplighter* became a sentimental favourite, selling on average 5,000 copies per week for two years. By the end of the first year after publication, it had sold 70,000 copies, placing Cummins in the highest rank of bestsellers.

From a family long established in Massachusetts, Cummins's precocious literary interests were encouraged by her father. She was sent to the school in Lenox, Massachusetts, run by Mrs Charles Sedgwick, where she met and was encouraged by her school mistress's sister-in-law, the novelist CATHARINE MARIA SEDGWICK. The key to her success lay in Cummins's wholehearted endorsement of conventional moral values, and a mastery of the formula for domestic fictions. She had great skill in showing the usual routines of domestic life, meals as they were put on the table, and the dresses which an average suffering heroine might wear. 'We enter into their home struggles, and we rejoice when they gain victory' (ELIZABETH GASKELL). Cummins did not marry and continued to write until her health failed in 1866.   EH

Cunard, Nancy 1896–1965 Poet, political organizer and editor, the daughter of Sir Bache Cunard, the shipping magnate, and his wife, Maud. Her radical politics and flamboyant personal life caused her estrangement from her wealthy family. She was often dismissed as a rich dilettante but is now recognized as a pivotal figure of the avant-garde between the world wars.

In Paris in the 1920s Cunard was associated with imagism and surrealism. A gifted poet and translator, her early poems were published in the collections, *Outlaws* (1921) and *Sublunary* (1923). Her long poem, *Parallax*, was published by the Hogarth Press (1925). The Hours Press, which she founded (1928), published key MODERNIST figures including LAURA RIDING, Ezra Pound, John Rodker, Roy Campbell, Robert Graves, Louis Aragon, Richard Aldington and Samuel Beckett. Cunard's relationship with a black musician, Henry Crowder, led to her writing *Black Man and White Ladyship* (1931). She became treasurer of the campaign to defend 'the Scottsboro boys', who were accused of raping a white woman, and compiled the monumental anthology, *Negro* (1934), a compendium of 'the struggles and achievements, the persecutions and the revolts against them, of the Negro people'.

Cunard visited Spain to offer support to the Republican forces during the Spanish Civil War and made friends with the Chilean consul in Madrid, Pablo Neruda. On her return to England she co-edited *Authors Take Sides in The Spanish Civil War* (1937) with Edgell Rickword. In World War II, she produced and edited an anthology, *Poems for France* (1944), dedicated to the French Resistance, which was published in French by La France Libre, the Free French publishing house, and translated and republished in English after the war. Cunard wrote memoirs of two friends, Norman Douglas (*Grand Man: Memories of Norman Douglas*, 1954) and George Moore (*G.M.: Memories of George Moore*, 1956). Her account of her time at the Hours Press, *Those Were the Hours*, was published posthumously in 1969. Cunard's behaviour in public was often volatile and she was frequently the subject of scandal. In 1960 she had a nervous breakdown and was committed to Holloway Sanatorium, near Virginia Water in Surrey. She spent her final years in France and died in Paris.   MJ

Cuney-Hare, Maud 1874–1936 American musicologist and writer. She was the daughter of prominent Texas politician, Norris Wright Cuney, and his wife, Adelina. Norris and Adelina were educated mulatto children of white slaveholders. Maud Cuney's childhood in Galveston, Texas, was refined and sheltered; her father recited Shakespeare, her mother was an accomplished vocalist.

Cuney attended Boston's New England Conservatory of Music. While there, she met the young W.E.B. DuBois, who was then studying at Harvard. The two were briefly engaged, and always remained friends. DuBois arranged publication of the biography

Cuney-Hare wrote about her father, *Norris Wright Cuney: A Tribute of the Black People* (1913), through the National Association for the Advancement of Colored People (NAACP). Cuney-Hare was music editor of the NAACP's *Crisis* magazine for years.

Cuney endured a difficult marriage to a doctor who expected her to pass for Spanish with him. She left him, and they eventually divorced; the story appears anecdotally in MARY CHURCH TERRELL's autobiography in the chapter 'Crossing the Color Line'.

Cuney-Hare compiled a poetry anthology in 1918, and wrote a play called *Antar of Araby* (1930). Her comprehensive ethnomusicological study, *Negro Musicians and Their Music* (1936), appeared just before she died of cancer in Boston, where she had been living with her second husband, William Parker Hare, since 1904.

LMC

Cusack, Dymphna 1902–81 Australian writer born in New South Wales, Dymphna Cusack published twelve novels and eight plays, although there were many more unpublished plays for stage, television and radio. A member of the Left during the politically conservative mid-century years in Australia, Cusack's work expressed her lifelong concern with social injustice, focusing on disadvantaged groups such as women, Australian Aboriginals and the working-class poor. She was a social realist writer for whom the political ends of literature seemed more important than the artistic means, yet her work was accomplished, widely published and admired, and reached enormous audiences for the time.

Her novel *Jungfrau* (1936) and most-performed play, *Morning Sacrifice* (1950), dealt frankly and sympathetically with female sexuality and powerlessness. Novels and plays like COME IN SPINNER (1951, written with Florence James) and *Shoulder the Sky* (1950), which criticized male wartime heroics, and her play *Pacific Paradise* (1955), an anti-nuclear protest, were typical in their support for the Peace Movement and for their belief in the goodness of ordinary people. Cusack's writing gave voice to many powerless and victimized characters, particularly women and non-European racial representatives, and she had the courage to air such 'silenced' issues as abortion. Her work was translated and published in many former socialist bloc countries. Dymphna Cusack's was a brave and important voice in Australian literature at a time when her own struggle to live from her writing mirrored the difficulties faced by her decent, ordinary characters who were ennobled by their struggle for justice. HTh

Cusk, Rachel 1967– British novelist whose arch, ironic voice, psychological insight and old-fashioned wordiness have provoked comparisons with JANE AUSTEN and Henry James. Born in Canada, she grew

up in Los Angeles and in the UK (in East Anglia) before reading English at Oxford. Her first Novel, *Saving Agnes* (1993), is semi-autobiographical, telling the tale of a young Oxford graduate grappling with love and loneliness in London. It won the Whitbread First Novel Award and was widely praised for its emotional intelligence, wit and sparkling lightness of touch. Still 26, Cusk was hailed by *The Times* as 'the outstanding discovery of the year'.

The response to her second novel, *The Temporary* (1995), was more muted and Cusk's attempt to move into less familiar territory – the manipulative behaviour and snobbish aspirations of a working-class temporary secretary – less convincing. Her acute observation and skill in depicting the nuances of self-consciousness and embarrassment are still in evidence, but her highly idiosyncratic prose style lacks the dry humour of *Saving Agnes* – 'She had been disappointed by the park, for having decided to grace the art of contemplation with her indulgence in it, it had not occurred to her that the proper accoutrements for its execution would fail to present themselves'. Few would guess that this sentence was written half-way through the 1990s by a writer still in her twenties. Some reviewers praised her 'exquisite lyricism'; others found it affected.

Cusk describes herself as a comic novelist, and her third novel, *The Country Life* (1997), aimed at a more commercial readership, is a return to more comic form.
CP

Custer, Elizabeth Bacon 1842–1933 American chronicler. Born in Monroe, Michigan, Elizabeth met George Armstrong Custer in 1862, while he was on leave from Civil War duty. They corresponded by letters for the next year and were married in February 1864. Elizabeth travelled with Custer to the Virginia front, and, after the war, to Texas, Kansas and the Dakota Territory. When she learned of his death at

Little Bighorn in 1876, she found herself without any income. She moved to New York and began immediately to write her reminiscences of her life with 'the General'. In 1885, she published *Boots and Saddles*, about their life in the Dakotas. Consciously avoiding political controversy, she focused on her experience of the army life, trials on the frontier and domestic difficulties. Her presentation of Custer is always positive, and she emphasizes the strength of army relationships in response to hardship. The popularity of *Boots and Saddles* inspired her to write two more books about their earlier experiences, *Tenting on the Plains* (1887) and *Following the Guidon* (1890). More importantly, it made her the sole authority on Custer and her version of events became the standard American myth about Custer until after her death at the age of 90. SP

Custom of the Country, The (1913) EDITH WHARTON's satirical epic of the new 20th-century United States plots the rise and fall of civilizations through the social trajectory of devastating Undine Spragg. Like Thackeray's Becky Sharp, or (later) MARGARET MITCHELL's Scarlett O'Hara, Undine is an opportunist, a survivor and a conqueror, advancing single-mindedly, acquiring and discarding husbands, non-maternal, beautiful. A crudely refined product of Apex City, somewhere out West, Undine embodies the values Wharton's fiction largely deplores, but in spite of her depradations, the novel makes room for her energies. The genteel leisure-classes of Old New York are a worn-out line, paralleled in Europe by the inbred aristocratic French. In her own divorce, writing, work and relationships, Wharton was negotiating her own final escape from these airless upper-class rooms. In her novel, however, she leaves Undine dangerously confined, ornamental and empty. The country, clearly, needs fresh customs, different models of gender. Even new money acquires only the old forms, failing to invent new kinds of being. PEK

D

da Cunha [née Patel] Nisha 1934– Passionate theatre buff and reclusive short-story writer, began writing in 1986 after resigning her job as Professor of English at Bombay University. A Gujarati married to a Goan, she grew up and was educated abroad, graduated from Newnham College in Cambridge, travelled widely but spent the better part of her adult life as a teacher in Delhi and Bombay. Her sensibility was shaped by two powerful factors: a mother who refused to learn English, and a father who was largely self-taught. Nisha herself exemplifies the cosmopolitanism of a modern Indian writer.

Her stories are imbued with aspects of grief, or grieving, and her protagonists are invariably female. *Old Cypress* (1991), her haunting first anthology, and *The Permanence of Grief* (1993) are about loss of many kinds – a home, a country, a mother, a daughter, the safe and familiar – and about the strength of women. Both are memorable for the ineffable sadness with which she delineates the interior landscapes of her characters. *Set My Heart in Aspic* (1997) confirmed her as a writer who resists easy categorization, but her prose is marked by an almost old-world quality: quiet, reflective, intensely private. RM

Dacre, Charlotte c.1772–1825 English poet and GOTHIC novelist (born as Charlotte King), published in 1798 a book of poems called *Trifles of Helicon*, with her sister Sophia, who was also a novelist. Her poetry was influenced by the Della Cruscans, a late 18th-century school of poets. Using the pseudonym 'Rosa Matilda', from 1802 to 1815, she wrote occasional verse for the *Morning Post*. Between 1806 and 1809, she gave birth to three children fathered by Nicholas Byrne, the editor of this London daily newspaper, whom she married later in 1815. As Charlotte Dacre she published four novels – *Confessions of the Nun of St Omer* (1805), *Zofloya or The Moor* (1806), *The Libertine* (1807), *The Passions* (1811) – and a volume of poems entitled *Hours of Solitude* (1805).

Dacre is most well known as the author of the lurid Gothic novel, *Zofloya*, which was an influence on P.B. Shelley's *Zastrozzi*. In recent years, it has been appreciated in its own right as a hybrid of ANN RADCLIFFE's Female Gothic and the horror fiction of Matthew 'Monk' Lewis. When it was first published, a reviewer for the *Literary Journal* accused the author of 'being afflicted with the dismal malady of maggots in the brain'. Its interest today is for the issues it raises in regard to race, gender, class and feminine evil. After the heroine murders her husband by slow poison and hurls her female rival down a precipice, she is murdered by her lover, the moor, Zofloya, who reveals himself to be Satan. Dacre's husband was murdered after her death by a mysterious figure in a black crepe mask. The identity of the murderer is one of the many unanswered questions surrounding Charlotte Dacre and her circle. MM-R

Dallas, Ruth 1919– New Zealand poet and CHILDREN'S AUTHOR. Dallas wrote nine volumes of poetry between 1948 and 1979. Her *Collected Poems* appeared in 1987.

Her early writing is concerned with landscape of a particularly local kind, the south of the south island of New Zealand – 'Savage grasses / That bristle in a beard' – and her identification with it: 'Now I know it is I who exist in the land', she writes. Her perspective is framed by a sense of history, particularly in regard to the women of 19th-century settlement, whom she commemorates with admiration but without sentiment in the poem 'Pioneer Woman with Ferrets':

> She is monumental
> In the treeless landscape.
> Nonchalantly she swings
> In her left hand
> A rabbit,/Bloodynose down,
> In her right hand a club.

Dallas is also a noted author of children's literature, playing a pivotal role in the establishment of an authentic New Zealand voice. She describes her experience of reading as a child as 'an English storybook world unrelated to life as I knew it'. Instead she sets out to give New Zealand children an experience which reflects their world and its past, 'primeval forests and cleared fields', most notably in her sequence *The Children of the Bush* (1969), *The Wild Boy of the Bush* (1971), *The Big Flood in the Bush* (1972) and *Holiday Time in the Bush* (1983).

Dallas continues to write and develop as a writer. Recent influences are Chinese literature and electronic music, both sources of inspiration which provide what she describes as 'more freedom of thought without losing discipline'.   JSt

d'Alpuget, Blanche 1944– Australian novelist and BIOGRAPHER. Born in Sydney; her father was a well-known journalist and she also worked in journalism in the 1960s. After her first marriage, to an Australian diplomat, she lived outside Australia for several years, including four in Indonesia and one in Malaysia. These experiences provided some of the background for her first two novels. *Monkeys in the Dark* (1980), set in Indonesia during the last days of the Sukarno regime, centres around a doomed love affair between an Australian woman and a radical local poet. The prize-winning *Turtle Beach* (1981) deals with part of the aftermath of the Vietnam War, as Chinese refugees arrive in Malaysia. Its heroine, the journalist Judith Wilkes, again gets involved in an unhappy relationship with a local man; her story is counterpointed with that of Minou, an ex-Saigon bargirl now married to an Australian diplomat. *Winter in Jerusalem* (1986) also features a woman writer in an exotic and politically troubled locale – here, however, she is engaged in a search for her long-lost father. *White Eye* (1993) was a marked departure for D'Alpuget; a well-paced thriller on the theme of biological warfare and genetic manipulation, it is set in the Australian bush. D'Alpuget has also written biographies of a leading Australian judge, Sir Richard Kirby (*Mediator*, 1977) and of the former Australian Prime Minister, Robert J. Hawke (1982), whom she was later to marry.   EW

Daly, Ita 1945– Irish novelist and short-story writer. Daly was born in County Leitrim and lived there until her family moved to Dublin, when she was 13. She received a BA, majoring in English and Spanish, an MA and a teaching diploma from University College Dublin and taught in secondary schools for eleven years before she turned to writing full-time. She is married to the novelist and literary editor David Marcus, and they have one daughter, Sarah. Her short stories were collected in *The Lady with Red Shoes* (1980). She has won two Hennessy Literary Awards and the *Irish Times* short-story competition. Daly's novels, *Ellen* (1986), *A Singular Attraction* (1987), *Martina* (1989) and *All Fall Down* (1992), display a wry and observant sense of humour and although her protagonists tend to be solitary and emotionally closed, the authorial distance and the irony with which they are often treated provides relief. Considered a writer's writer, she plays with the expectations of traditional genres, particularly those of ROMANCE in *Ellen*.   MSu

Daly, Mary 1928– North American radical feminist philosopher, academic and theologian, whose writings continue to enrage and inspire. Her early work, including *Natural Knowledge of God in the Philosophy of Jacques Maritain* (1966) and *The Church and the Second Sex* (1968), entered into debate with contemporary Catholic theology, but *Beyond God the Father* (1973), as the title indicates, marks her movement away from the Catholic tradition toward a female spirituality which is enunciated through punning word-play. She broke completely with academic traditions of theology in the influential *Gyn/Ecology: The Metaethics of Radical Feminism* (1978) which, together with the satirical *Webster's First New Intergalactic Wickedary of the English Language* (1987), written with Jane Caputi, established Daly's reputation as an original and humorous polemicist. Her argument in *Gyn/Ecology* was elaborated in *Pure Lust: Elemental Feminist Philosophy* (1984) and continued in her idiosyncratic autobiography, *Outercourse: The Be-Dazzling Voyage. Containing Recollections From My Logbook of a Radical Feminist Philosopher (Be-ing an Account of My Time/Space Travels and Ideas – Then, Again, Now and How)* (1993).

Born in Schenectady, New York, she has taught at the University of Fribourg, Switzerland, where she gained doctorates in Philosophy and Theology, and at Boston College, Massachusetts. *Pure Lust* declares her as 'unconfined by the teachings of church and man' and she is an influential voice in contemporary feminist spirituality and radical lesbian politics.   RW

Danby, Frank [Julia Davis Frankau] 1864–1916 ROMANTIC novelist and art historian, born in Ireland. Her father, an artist, moved the family to London where she worked as a journalist and married Arthur Frankau, a wealthy merchant, in 1883. Influenced and encouraged by George Moore, she published *Dr Phillips* (1887), the first of fourteen novels. She also produced three competent and well-regarded art histories and co-founded The Independent theatre. She rebelled against the moral strictures imposed by lending libraries: her themes of illicit love-affairs and amoral aesthetes drew comments such as 'daring' and 'unconventional' while *The Times* described her novels as 'unpleasant studies of ill-behaved and disagreeable people'. Varying in the depth of their characterization and the intricacies of their plots, her novels reveal her cultural heritage, being frequently peopled by Jewish and Irish protagonists; Sinclair Furley, in *A Babe in Bohemia* (1889), is an Irish aesthete 'whose mental excreta soiled every word that percolated through the laboratory of his diseased imagination', while *Pigs in Clover* (1902), which is foregrounded against the Boer War and features two Jewish half-brothers, was described in *The Times* as a *succès de scandale* because of its 'brilliant portrait and caricature of a well-known and unfortunate "aesthete"'.   BHu

Dane, Clemence [née Winifred Ashton] 1888–1965 Educated in England, Germany, Switzerland and at the Slade School in London, Dane was one of the few playwrights of either sex to find continued success throughout the inter-war years and beyond. Originally an actress, she was a prolific writer of essays, articles and novels as well as plays. Her novels include *Regiment of Women* (1917), *Legend* (1919) and *Broome Stages* (1931). In her social tract *The Woman's Side* (1926) she reproached women for what she saw as their unwillingness to participate actively in public affairs. Both her dramatic texts and her journalism investigate women's cultural role. The play *A Bill of Divorcement* (1921) examines intergenerational difference and eugenics and was an instant success, later made into a film starring the young Katherine Hepburn. Others of Dane's plays, such as *Granite* (1926) and *Cousin Muriel* (1940), were written with particular actresses, such as Sybil Thorndike, in mind. Her plays were often written from a woman's perspective, with male roles of secondary importance.

Dane was also an accomplished sculptress and painter. Her portrait of her close friend Noel Coward is well known and Coward gives favourable mention of her poem *Trafalgar Day* (1940) in his autobiography. Dane adapted numerous novels and plays and during the late 1920s and early 1930s wrote DETECTIVE stories with Helen Simpson, such as *Printer's Devil* (1930) and *Re-enter Sir John* (1932). Elected president of the Society of Women Journalists 1940–2, Dane worked during the early 1940s alongside H.G. Wells as a member of the British Screen Writers Association. Awarded the CBE in 1953, she found success in the United States as a screen writer and still took up the occasional stage role until her death in 1965. Her reminiscences, *London Has a Garden*, were published in 1964.   MBG

Dangarembga, Tsitsi 1960–

Zimbabwean who studied Medicine and Psychology, then film in Germany; the first black Zimbabwean woman to direct a feature film, *Everyone's Child* (1996). She is best known for her only novel to date, NERVOUS CONDITIONS (1988). The book's epigraph is taken from Sartre's introduction to Fanon's *The Wretched of the Earth*: 'The condition of native is a nervous condition'. The novel's nervous conditions are those of a group of Shona women and girls in colonial Rhodesia. The pressures of being doubly colonized, by Shona patriarchy as well as by white supremacism, create a bond of love and humour between the women as they try to negotiate a place for themselves. The feisty opening sentence sets the tone of the narrator, Tambudzai: 'I was not sorry when my brother died.' Her brother's death gives Tambu a chance of a Western education, though this proves another trap; she escapes from her father's view of 'the real tasks of feminine living' to encounter her cousin's descent into madness, provoked by Western constructions of Africa: 'She rampaged, shredding her

history book between her teeth ("Their history. Fucking liars. Their bloody lies.")'. In this refreshingly unpredictable novel, Tambu often enjoys herself; the pleasure of the traditional women's bathing place in the river is balanced against her incredulous joy at her first bath in a tub with taps. As Tambu resolutely searches for the 'self I expected to find', her cousin regresses to a foetal position, hinting at the complexity for Zimbabwean women of identity rather than reflecting an image.   ASm

Daniel Deronda (1876)

GEORGE ELIOT's last novel, published in 1876 (initially in eight parts from February to September). Its principal female character is Gwendolen Harleth, a difficult and frequently selfish character, who marries the aristocrat Henleigh Grandcourt to protect herself, her mother and her sisters from approaching poverty. The marriage founders, in part because of Grandcourt's relationship with his mistress and their children, although Gwendolen is aware of the alliance when she marries him. Gwendolen seeks comfort in an intense spiritual relationship with Daniel Deronda, at first assumed to be an illegitimate cousin of Grandcourt, and later revealed to be the son of a famous Jewish singer. Two of the key developments of the novel are Grandcourt's death by drowning and Gwendolen's guilt at her failure to help him, and Daniel's involvement with a young Jewish singer, Mirah, and her brother Mordecai, a fervent and highly intelligent Jewish nationalist. The novel closes with Deronda marrying Mirah and pledging himself to the Zionist cause.

Daniel Deronda is possibly Eliot's most ambitious and most flawed work. Examining issues of race and religion, artistic and ethical commitment, inheritance and responsibility, its most striking feature is the contrast between its English and Jewish characters.   AC

Daniels, Sarah 1957–

British feminist playwright, best known for her confrontational *Masterpieces* (1983), which made a direct connection between economic exploitation in the sex industry, and the dangerous collusion of the polite middle classes. It showed how everyday patriarchal conventions uphold sexually oppressive norms which dehumanize women. In this play representations of individual pin-up girls and other women involved in the sex industry echoed topical debates, with lines and slogans like 'Looking at pictures never hurt anyone' and 'the growth industry for the eighties'. The central character, Rowena, comments that there are indeed problems with an industry and attitudes which 'condone the idea that half the human race are mere objects with suitable orifices'. The particularly shocking connection with 'Snuff' movies and the almost inevitable, but inevitably misunderstood, violent reaction emptied some early performances.

Daniels's earlier work includes *Penumbra*, *Ma's Flesh is Grass* and *Ripen Our Darkness* (1981), performed like much of her work at the Royal Court where she was writer-in-residence in 1984. Another controversial play, *The Devil's Gateway* (1983) deals with a working-class mother leaving her nurturing role for Greenham Common women's peace camp. *Neaptide* (1986) considers lesbians coping with prejudice. Other plays deal with women's work and rights in different ages, including *The Gut Girls* (1989) about 19th-century women slaughterhouse workers whose self-sufficiency is threatened by a philanthropic lady's attempts to turn them into domestic servants.   GW

D'Arcy, Ella 1856?–1939 British short-story writer, novelist and translator best known for her affiliation with the *Yellow Book*. Born in London of Irish parents, D'Arcy grew up in the Channel Islands and received part of her education in Germany and France. She studied Art at the Slade School in London but was forced to abandon painting when her eyesight failed.

Instead she began writing; her stories appeared in ten of the thirteen issues of the *Yellow Book*, for which she served as an 'unofficial' assistant editor. Working closely with editors Henry Harland and John Lane, D'Arcy helped open up the periodical to female contributors such as VICTORIA CROSS(E), E. NESBIT and CHARLOTTE MEW. Her own stories were gathered in two volumes, *Monochromes* (1895) and *Modern Instances* (1898). 'The Pleasure Pilgrim', her most provocative work, rewrites Henry James's *Daisy Miller* (1887). She also published a novel, *The Bishop's Dilemma* (1898), and in 1924 a translation of André Maurois's fictionalized biography of Shelley, *Ariel*. To her friend NETTA SYRETT she was 'clever and amusing', but 'the laziest woman I ever met'.   MAD

Dargan [née Tilford], Olive [Fielding Burke] 1869–1968 American poet, playwright and novelist. She was born in Grayson County, Kentucky, to parents who were both teachers and had been abolitionists. In 1879 the family moved to the Missouri Ozarks where her parents founded a school; in 1882 they founded another school in Arkansas. Olive began teaching at the age of 14, then attended Peabody and Radcliffe colleges on scholarship. She married Pegram Dargan in 1898. They moved to New York to pursue writing careers, then in 1906 to a farm in Almond, North Carolina. Her first two books, *Semiramis* (1904) and *Lords and Lovers* (1906), both closet dramas in verse, met with quick success. From 1911 to 1914 she lived in England where she supported union and feminist causes and published three books, *The Mortal Gods and Other Dramas* (1912), *The Welsh Pony* (1913) and *Path Flower*

and Other Verses (1914). After her husband drowned in 1915, she settled in the North Carolina mountains. Critics considered *Highland Annals* (1924), local-colour sketches about mountain people, her best work, but she most directly expressed her socialist and feminist views in proletarian novels she published under the pseudonym 'Fielding Burke' (*Call Home the Heart*, 1932; *A Stone Came Rolling*, 1935; *Sons of the Stranger*, 1947). Her last book of poems, *The Spotted Hawk* (1958), won three awards; her late fiction is collected in *Innocent Bigamy and Other Stories* (1962).   JSG

Dark [née O'Reilly], Eleanor 1901–85 Australian novelist, born in Sydney, the only daughter of Dowell O'Reilly, writer, teacher and failed politician. Her childhood was marked by a keen awareness of literary and socialist issues. Following work as a secretary and early publication as poet and short-story writer, her marriage in 1922 to Dr Eric Dark, the pioneering physiotherapist, marked the beginning of a new life in the Blue Mountains. Their home at Katoomba (which can now be visited), provided the requisite peace and quiet required to fulfil Eleanor's dual ambition as both writer and home-maker. Her self-imposed isolation, broken only by one visit to the States, suggests a dislike of the public gaze, but can be taken as a marker of her immense self-reliance, humility and love of nature.

Dark's early novels represent an early Australian form of MODERNISM, combining internal monologue, compressed time-spans and localized settings (PRELUDE TO CHRISTOPHER, 1934; *Return to Coolami*, 1936; *Sun Across the Sky*, 1937; and *Waterway*, 1938; as well as her 1945 'novel of ideas', *The Little Company*), but it was her monumental 'HISTORICAL TRILOGY' – *The Timeless Land* (1941), *Storm of Time* (1948), *No Barrier* (1953) – which finally secured her position as one of Australia's foremost novelists. The factual accuracy and the authenticity of its story-lines were so effective that in her 1965 preface she wrote: 'This book has borrowed so much from history that it seems advisable to remind readers that it is fiction.' A parable-like conflict between tribal and 'civilized' society attains new heights in Dark's saga, displaying an early regard for the plight of the Aborigines, a sensitive awareness of the inhumanities of the penal system, a sympathetic portrayal of the colonial élite, and throughout, a superb exposition of the Australian landscape. Detailing a time-span of twenty-five years, from the First Landing to the crossing of the Blue Mountains, it remains the best-documented 'history' of Australia's colonial origins, and a clear indication of Dark's nationalism, socialism and pro-female concerns. The publication of *Lantana Lane* (1959) introduced yet another stylistic departure; based on the Darks' own farming experiences in Queensland, it is a humorous, loosely connected series of essays and short stories.   MRE

Darville, Helen 1971– Australian novelist at the centre of the 'Demidenko affair'. When her first novel, *The Hand that Signed the Paper*, was published in 1994, the author was known as 'Helen Demidenko'. Demidenko was an identity constructed over several years, through which the author presented herself as the daughter of an Irish mother and a Ukrainian father. In articles, short stories and public appearances, she elaborated on her Ukrainian background. Demidenko's novel was supposedly based on her family's oral history, and the author described her work as 'faction'. The novel begins in present-day Australia and is framed by the narration of Fiona Kovalenko, whose uncle has been charged with war crimes. Through the narratives of the older Kovalenkos, the novel describes both the family's suffering during the famine of the 1930s and Ukrainian participation in the Holocaust: the belief that Jewish communists are responsible for the famine leads to the characters' brutal collaboration with the Nazis.

Debate raged over the question of whether this historically inaccurate perception belonged to the novel as a whole. Accused of anti-semitism, *The Hand* won three major Australian literary awards, including the Miles Franklin Award, before Helen Demidenko was exposed as Helen Darville, the Australian-born daughter of English migrants. Allegations of plagiarism followed. They could not be sustained, but the novel does borrow heavily from historical and other sources. The whole affair provoked controversy in Australia over the significance of authorial authenticity, the judging of literary prizes and the politics of multi-culturalism.
CPr

Daryush, Elizabeth [Bridges] 1887–1977 English poet who identified herself with metrical experiment. Daughter of Robert Bridges, Poet Laureate 1913–30, she was educated at home in Berkshire, and from 1907 lived mostly in Oxfordshire. Her first volumes of poems were *Charitessi* (1911), and *Verses* (1916). The austere titling of *Verses*, resumed in *Verses II* (1932) to *Verses VII* (1971), indicates Daryush's emphasis on form; her preface to her *Collected Poems* (1976) is exclusively concerned with metre. She studied Persian and published translations of Persian poetry in *Sonnets from Hafiz and Other Poems* (1921). In 1923 she married Ali Akbar Daryush, a Persian government official; they lived in Persia until returning to Oxfordshire for good in 1927. Daryush saw her distinctive achievement as her experiments with syllabic metre, where 'the fixed element is no longer time but number; the integrity of line and syllable is challenged by the stress-demands of sense and syntax'.

In the 1930s her poetry became increasingly responsive to contemporary social and political crises, and she found syllabic metre's tensions expressive of her anxieties. Her most famous poem, the sonnet 'Still Life', uses syllabic metre to hint delicately at impending catastrophe, while describing an upper-class breakfast table. It appeared in the uncharacteristically titled *The Last Man and Other Poems* (1916); Daryush later rejected the title poem, the monologue of Earth's last survivor after global war, as crudely explicit, and returned from social concerns to her main subject, the natural world. She had earlier repudiated her pre-1930s poems as archaic and self-consciously poetic. Her slim *Collected Poems* is her rigorous selection, and arrangement, of poems unrejected by her. Yvor Winters, Roy Fuller and Donald Davie all championed her dedicated precision in matching metre and situation exactly. AT

Das, Kamala 1934– Indian English poet who brought a new atmosphere of honesty into women's poetry in India with her forthright treatment of sexuality. Born in matriarchal Kerala to an aristocratic family on her mother's side, Das is creatively bilingual – writing mostly poetry in English and mainly prose in Malayalam. Her mother, Balamani Amma, was a well-known poet in Malayalam. Her father's job with a British automobile firm took the family out of Kerala.

Das grew up in Calcutta and spent her vacations, as well as lived for a few years, at her maternal grandmother's house in Malabar and this house haunts her poetry as a lost inheritance. Educated in various schools, including a Roman Catholic convent with its emphasis on sin, Das was only 15 when she was married to a relative who worked in Bombay. The marriage was a disaster from the first night and motivated her poetry which she began to send out for publication from the time she turned 18, when she was already a mother.

Her poems, starting with *Summer in Calcutta* (1965) and *The Descendants* (1967), reflect a dualism between soul/innocence/childhood and the conscious mind/awakened body/adulthood and speak of her disappointment in marriage as well as in lovers. A CONFESSIONAL poet, she has herself said that '[A] poet's raw material is not stone or clay, it is her own personality.' Her poems celebrate her sexuality even as they lament its inadequacy, display pride in her conquests and ability to make men love her even as they mock the lovers. She has tried to link this personal poetry about various affairs to the perennial metaphoric quest for Krishna, the eternal lover. Ultimately her poems are about the self, and the search for, and construction of, identity. This attempt is continued in prose writing as well, mainly in her autobiography, *My Days* (1976), which fuelled public imagination as well as indignation, serialized as it was in a Bombay tabloid. This book helped in the construction of Das's image as a sex-driven guilt-ridden poet.

Das goes beyond conventional love poetry in that she confronts illness and aging and death even as she asserts her liberated sexuality. Her poetry does not flinch from the frailties and mortality of the body. One of her achievements is writing in an Indian English which is a correlative of her direct uninhibited manner of verse. She has also written socially committed poetry about communal tensions in India and Sri Lanka. Her collections include *The Old Playhouse and Other Poems* (1973), *Tonight, This Savage Rite* with Pritish Nandy (1979), *Collected Poems* vol. I (1984) and *Only the Soul Knows How to Sing; Selections from Kamala Das* (1996).

GJVP

Das, Mahadai 1955– Guyanese poet. Born to a poor rural family, Das has sought to link her artistic and political interests in all her work. As a member of the Messenger Group and the Cultural Division of the Guyana National Service, she sought to raise the profile of the Indo-Guyanese population in Guyana. Working in the late 1970s for the Working People's Alliance, Das continued her commitment to a multiracial society before studying in the USA. Serious illness prevented Das completing her studies and has made her work as a poet difficult to continue. The poetry in her three volumes, *I Want To Be A Poetess of My People* (1976), *My Finer Steel Will Grow* (1982) and *Bones* (1988), is often radical in both its exploration of a female Indo-Caribbean identity and its use of nation language. Das now lives in Guyana and has published several poems in the journal *Kyk-Over-Al*. AD

Elizabeth David in her kitchen, by John Ward, RA, frontispiece of *An Omelette and a Glass of Wine*, 1984.

Daughters of Danaus, The (1894) MONA CAIRD'S REALIST novel adapts the Greek myth of the Danaides, condemned for their marital insurrection to draw water from a well with sieves, in order to highlight the problems of the woman artist, prevented from realizing her gift by a hostile environment. A pianist and composer, Hadria Fullerton is pressurized by her mother into an unhappy marriage, whose social, sexual and maternal implications leave her severely depressed. All subsequent attempts at rebellion prove futile as Hadria realizes the extent to which women have internalized the duty of self-sacrifice. Her stark vision of a pit filled with women's bodies to allow the survivors to walk into freedom carries echoes of OLIVE SCHREINER'S allegory 'Three Dreams in a Desert' (*Dreams*, 1890). Hadria's mother, her frustration channelled into invalidism and domestic tyranny, illustrates Caird's critique of patriarchal mothering (*The Morality of Marriage*, 1897). The text presents central NEW WOMAN arguments through dialogue. Caird's uncompromising stance on marriage and motherhood, so anticipatory of modern radical feminist theory, shocked contemporaries. AH

Daughters of the House (1992) MICHÈLE ROBERTS'S sixth novel is a return to the semi-autobiographical focus of *A Piece of the Night* (1978), addressing the need for, and danger of, 'authentic' personal and collective histories. The book is intricately structured, each short chapter assigned a heading from the inventory which Léonie is constructing while waiting for her cousin, Thérèse, to arrive. The main middle section of the novel is written as a series of flashbacks which recount the relationship between Thérèse and Léonie, and their childhood in the family home in Blemont-la-Fontaine, a fictional Norman village. Following the traumatic death of Antoinette, Thérèse's mother, both girls have a vision of a woman in the woods, but it is Thérèse's more conventional account of the vision as the Virgin Mary which is endorsed by the Catholic hierarchy. Against the background of this sibling rivalry and its consequences, the novel charts the blurred divisions between fantasy and reality, memory and history. *Daughters of the House* was shortlisted for the 1992 Booker Prize. RW

David [née Gwynne], Elizabeth 1913–92 Elizabeth David's first work, *A Book of Mediterranean Food*, in 1950, made a profound impression on the British, who were heartily sick of wartime deprivations. Chefs and housewives alike were seduced by Elizabeth David's vision, and all memories of good pre-war English food were forgotten, along with austerity.

She had been sent to Paris at 16 to study at the

Sorbonne; while living with a Parisian family she became enamoured of their daily fare. From then on, throughout her career, she was to profess the superiority of French, Italian and Middle Eastern food. In 1939 she was living in Greece, and, when war broke out, she moved to Cairo where she worked for the Ministry of Information. In 1944 she married Englishman Anthony David, and followed him to India. The marriage did not last, and she returned to England alone in 1946. She shared a house in Chelsea with her sister Felicité from 1952 until 1986.

Her books changed in character as her scholarly nature asserted itself. *A Book of Mediterranean Food*, drawn from memories of Capri, Greece and Egypt, was followed by a second in the same genre, *French Country Cooking*, still with somewhat sketchy recipes. In 1954 *Italian Food* was published; for the first time she was able to research this thoroughly, subsidized by the Italian Tourist Board. A return to her discursive style followed with *Summer Cooking* (1955), and for the next five years she wrote articles for *The Sunday Times*, *Vogue*, *House and Garden* and the *Spectator*, while she researched *French Provincial Cooking* (1960), probably her best and most authoritative book. Sadly, this was to prove a watershed; from now on the nostalgia of her earlier writing was replaced by a more academic approach. A chapter in *French Provincial Cooking* starts : 'Peppers and onions are sizzling gently in a big frying pan, the goose dripping in which they are cooking giving off its unmistakable smell'; while a chapter in *English Bread and Yeast Cookery* commences: 'As already explained in the introductory notes to my chapter on the pizza and its variations'.

In 1965 she opened a cookware shop in Pimlico; this involved enjoyable trips to France, finding stock. *Spices, Salt and Aromatics in the English Kitchen* came out in 1970; this was intended as the first in a series on English food, but the project was abandoned. Her love of research now got the upper hand, and she found it almost impossible to bring a book to its close. After seven years she brought out *English Bread and Yeast Cookery* (1977), a massive tome sadly lacking in charm. By 1973 she had severed all connection with the shop. Her penultimate book, *An Omelette and a Glass of Wine* (1984), was a collection of articles and a welcome reminder of just how entertaining she could be: witty and perceptive, also abrasive and intolerant.

She was much honoured: the OBE in 1976, Chevalier du Mérite Agricole in 1977, Fellow of the Royal Society of Literature in 1982, and the CBE in 1986, but her last years were lonely; she quarrelled with publishers and mourned the death of her sister. Her last book, *Harvest of the Cold Months*, was completed after her death by her editor and friend, Jill Norman.   AB

Davidson, Lucretia Maria 1808–25 American child poet made famous by her prolific and precocious poetry, renowned beauty and early death in a sentimental culture that glorified childhood.

She was born in Plattsburg, New York, to a doctor-father who was barely able to support the family, and a poet-mother who was sickly and frequently confined to her bed. High-strung, Lucretia also suffered from ill health which worsened with the pressure of public examinations at boarding school as well as the pressures of being a child prodigy. Her parents encouraged, if not pushed, the literary efforts of Lucretia and their other poetically inclined daughter, Margaret Miller Davidson (1823–38), who also died young. Lucretia wrote over 300 poems, the longest being *Amir Khan* (first published in *Amir Khan and Other Poems* (1829)), a romantic tale about a young Christian woman and her Muslim suitor. Her last poem was an unfinished deathbed poem describing a fear of going mad. She died of tuberculosis at the age of 16.

'A Memoir of Lucretia Maria Davidson' by CATHARINE MARIA SEDGWICK, drawn in large part from Lucretia's mother's memoirs, was published in 1837 and later served as the introduction to the *Poetical Remains of the Late Lucretia Maria Davidson* (1841).   VM

Davidson, Robyn 1950– Australian TRAVEL WRITER and novelist whose determinedly idiosyncratic approach stems from her 'desire to be off hunting for new frontiers'. Brought up on a cattle station in Miles, Queensland, she studied Biology and, later, Japanese and Philosophy at Queensland University. Intent on resisting 'the great Australian drive towards homogeneity', she fled academe and settled in Alice Springs where she took an active interest in Aboriginal culture, worked in a bar, and trained camels for her first expedition, a 1,700-mile trek, alone with her dog, across the West Australian desert. In *Tracks* (1980), her bestselling account of the journey, and winner of the 1980 Thomas Cook Travel Book Prize, she marvels at the 'unearthly, prehistoric, mythological quality' of the landscape, and describes, with humility and wonder, the Aboriginal tribes she encounters. 'The deeper one can read their culture', she writes, 'the closer one comes to being able to imagine what it is to truly be "at home in the world".' *Ancestors* (1989), her highly praised first novel, also pursues themes of inheritance and belonging.

A selection of her travel articles appeared in *Travelling Light* (1989), including a recollection of ten days spent alone in the bush with a typewriter, a chronicle of a trip across America on a Harley-Davidson, and a critique of secularized Australia in 'The Mythological Crucible', first published in *Australia, Beyond the Dreamtime* (1987). 'Tough-minded women', she writes, 'are one of our principal exports.'

In *Desert Places* (1996), she joins a nomadic tribe in Rajasthan, India, on a year's migratory cycle. As in all her work, she sets the notion of a personal odyssey – the comprehension and communication, beyond language, of another culture's rites and dreams – within a political context, giving especial attention to issues of land ownership and national heritage.

As a writer 'scattered around the world . . . inhabiting realities antagonistic to each other, suspicious of each other', she sees her work and travel as 'a line of enquiry', a vivid and pertinent way of asking the question: 'which is paramount: our similarities or our differences?' JAH

Davie, Elspeth

Davie, Elspeth 1919–95 Scottish writer whose fiction comments ironically on the modern world. She was born in Kilmarnock and lived in England and Ireland before settling in Edinburgh. She attended Edinburgh College of Art and Edinburgh University, and taught painting. In 1939, she met her future husband, the philosopher George Davie. The meeting was a revelation: never had she enjoyed conversation so much.

This love of philosophical discussion and a painter's eye for detail are evident in her work. Davie tried to illuminate 'the strange, the desolating and the ludicrous'. Her dislike of modern consumerism is evident in *Providings* (1965), a novel in which the protagonist is pestered with jars of homemade jam by his mother. *Creating a Scene* (1971) foregrounds the social role of art. *Climbers on a Stair* (1978) and *Coming to Light* (1989) demonstrate Davie's complex relationship with Edinburgh, the beautiful buildings and aloof inhabitants. The social relevance of her work shows strong links with 19th-century literature.

She is perhaps best known for her short fiction collections: *The Spark* (1968), *The High Tide Talker* (1976), *The Night of the Funny Hats* (1980) and *A Traveller's Room* (1985). These stories take place in everyday settings: hospitals, motorway cafés, waiting rooms. In the course of apparently trivial discussions, ordinary characters reach small moments of epiphany. Davie believed that writers should 'talk other people's silences; they should be able to express things people find hard to tell, to grant them a kind of relief'. JH

Davies [née Touchet] Eleanor, Lady; Lady Audeley; later Douglas

Davies [née Touchet] Eleanor, Lady; Lady Audeley; later Douglas 1590–1652 An English Protestant and self-styled PROPHET who published over seventy tracts during the years 1625–52, all but one illicitly. To each of her tracts she boldly signed her name and, following the model of prophets in the Old Testament, addressed her prophecies to King and Parliament, threatening divine judgement if they should ignore her message.

Husband, King and Bishop attempted suppression of Lady Eleanor's works. Both of her husbands burned her writings. Charles I brought her before the court of High Commission in 1633, which immediately ordered her to prison. And Archbishop Laud, whose appointment she had protested, burned some of her books. Despite several imprisonments and a forced committal to Bethlehem Hospital, she continued to publish.

Eleanor attributed her prophetic gift to an experience in 1625 when the prophet Daniel came to her from heaven and told her things that had remained 'closed up and sealed till the time of the end' (Daniel 12:9). Her writing draws heavily upon the books of Daniel and Revelation. GG-R

Davies, (Sarah) Emily

Davies, (Sarah) Emily 1830–1921 English campaigner for women's higher education and suffrage, who was born into a clerical family. She spent much of her early life confined to home and a small social group, but met BARBARA BODICHON in 1859 and discovered the Langham Place circle. She was briefly editor of the *English Women's Journal*, and she founded the London Schoolmistresses' Association in 1866. Campaigning on behalf of women's admission to medical school, she wrote *Medicine as a Profession for Women* (1862), contending that 'Medicine [w]as eminently suitable for women of the middle-class.' In *The Higher Education of Women* (1866), her most important work, she argued that confining a woman's role to the family was 'radically inconsistent with the divine order' and that 'its action on society is profoundly demoralising'. She believed in essential differences between male and female, but deplored the 'arbitrary judgments not based on reason' which prevented women receiving a good education. FRANCES POWER COBBE declared 'the book can't fail to do good'. The following year Emily Davies established a college for women, in Hitchin, stressing the importance, in her *Some Account of a Proposed New College for Women* (1868), of a liberal, mind-expanding education for 'young women of the wealthy class'. The college moved to Cambridge in 1873, becoming Girton College. Thereafter, Emily Davies became prominent in the Suffrage Movement in which she argued against militant action. Her collection of essays and speeches, *Thoughts on Some Questions Relating to Women, 1860-1908*, was published in 1910. She voted for the first time in a general election two years before her death. FJO'G

Daviot, Gordon

Daviot, Gordon 1897–1952 Born Elizabeth Mackintosh in Inverness, Daviot qualified as a physical training instructress in Birmingham before becoming a prolific writer of short stories, plays and DETECTIVE novels, the latter written under another pseudonym, 'Josephine Tey'. Daviot took the West End by storm with John Gielgud's production of her historical play *Richard of Bordeaux* (1933), which ran for over 450 performances. Despite receiving good notices her next play, *The Laughing Woman* (1934), loosely based on the relationship between French sculptor Henri Gaudier and Sophia Brzeska, only had a relatively short run. The play focuses on the relationship between gender, creativity and domestic life more than it concerns itself with biographical detail. Similarly her next play, *Queen of Scots* (1934), examines closely the specific relationship of women to state power and proscribed notions of femininity. In the 1940s and early 1950s Daviot (as Josephine Tey) wrote her best-known novels, *The Franchise Affair* (1948, successful as both film and novel) and *Daughter of Time* (1951). Personally, she was undramatic – described by one theatre critic as 'serious in aspect and quietly dressed'. Her duel literary career as novelist and playwright was cut short by her early death.   MBG

Davis, Angela (Yvonne) 1944– African-American political radical, philosopher and campaigner for human rights who pioneered the demands of non-white working-class women to reshape first-wave feminism. Her powerful commentaries on race, class and gender focus upon issues such as education, slavery, rape, domestic work and reproductive rights. Born in Birmingham, Alabama, Davis attended Elisabeth Irwin High School, New York, before studying Philosophy with Herbert Marcuse at Brandeis University. After graduate study with Theodor Adorno at the Institut für Sozialforschung in Frankfurt, and with Marcuse again at the University of California, San Diego, she became an Assistant Professor of Philosophy at the University of California, Los Angeles.

In 1969 Davis travelled to Cuba to fight for prisoners' rights, provoking Governor Ronald Reagan and the University of California Regents to try to fire her from her UCLA post on charges of communism and conspiracy, accusations on which she was acquitted, along with two other charges of murder and kidnapping, both carrying the death penalty, in 1972. A member of the Communist party since 1968, she is part of the National Alliance Against Racist and Political Repression, the National Political Congress of Black Women and the National Black Women's Health Project. Davis has taught at Berkeley, Santa-Cruz and San Francisco. Her publications include *The Black Woman's Role in the Community of Slaves: Lectures on Liberation* (1970), *If They Come in the Morning: Voices of Resistance* (1971) and *Angela Davis: An Autobiography* (1974). *Women, Culture and Politics* was published in 1989.   EM

Davis, Margaret (Thomson) 1926– Highly popular Scottish novelist born in Bathgate in the West Lothian. Davis was educated at the Albert Secondary School, is divorced and has one son. Over the years she has contributed over 200 short stories to women's magazines in Britain and overseas. Davis published her first novel in 1972 – *The Breadmakers*, the first of 'the

Glasgow Trilogy' of the same name; the sequels, rapidly following in 1973, are *A Baby Might be Crying* and *A Sort of Peace*. Many novels swarmed after, including *A Woman of Property* (1991), the sprightly *Kiss Me No More* (1995), a 'tobacco lords trilogy' (1994) and the autobiographical *The Making of a Novelist* in 1982.

Davis has her designs on the general reader – the popularity of her output is worth celebrating and her formula is well executed, her writing direct and readable. Those of a POSTMODERN bent will find much to appreciate in the emotional palaver and play of stereotype. However, the author's reliance on an agenda of propriety and coercion may seem retrogressive. Male characters are usually feckless or drink-prone when not being bold and one-dimensional; their wives are trollopy or feeble – except the heroine of *Breadmakers*, Catriona MacNair, who simply has to put up or shut up about her failed dreams.   DM

Davis, Mollie (Mary Evelyn) Moore 1852–1909 American poet, novelist and short-story writer. She was born in Talladega, Alabama, and grew up on a Texas plantation until the Civil War. She learned to ride, shoot and swim with her brother and was educated at home by her parents. Her first book, verse about the Confederate experience in the Civil War, *Minding the Gap* (1867), went through five editions. In 1874 she married Thomas E. Davis, formerly a Confederate Major, then editor of a New Orleans periodical. In 1880 they moved to New Orleans, where their home became a centre of social and intellectual life. Mollie Davis presided over a literary circle called the Geographics and a literary club called Quarante. Her poems and sketches were published in *Harper's* and other periodicals. Her stories were collected in *In War Time at La Rose Blanche* (1888) and *An Elephant Track* (1896); she also published novels, *Under the Man-Fig* (1895), *The Wire Cutters* (1899), *The Queen's Garden* (1900) and *The Little Chevalier* (1903). The stories on post-bellum southern life led a craze among white readers for 'negro dialect' tales. Davis's poetry is collected in *Poems* (1872) and *Selected Poems* (1927).   JSG

Davis, Natalie Zemon 1928– American social historian whose pioneering work on 16th-century France helped to initiate a sophisticated approach to the study of culture and identity, attentive to the multiple intersections of belief and custom within early-modern societies. Studying both contemporary narratives and the symbolic languages of ritual and gesture, Davis has sought to uncover 16th-century cultural practices, with a particular emphasis on gender and religion, as seen in her first ground-breaking book *Society and Culture in Early Modern France* (1975). *The Return of Martin Guerre* (1983), researched originally for the film version of the story, intertwines her scholarship on the 'hidden

" IS YOU DONE WHIPPED DE YANTEES ? " ASKED LITTLE PERCY.

Mollie Moore Davis: '"Is you done whipped de Yantees?" asked little Percy', illustration in *In War Times at La Rose Blanche*, 1888.

world of peasant sentiment and aspiration', with the extraordinary tale of masquerade involving Martin, his wife Bertrande and the impostor Arnaud du Tilh. Davis's focus on intersecting identities in *Martin Guerre* also shapes her projects in both *Fiction in the Archives: Pardon Tales and their Tellers in Sixteenth-Century France* (1987) and *Women on the Margins: Three Seventeenth-Century Lives* (1995), where she traces 'varied lives, but produced within a common field'. Educated at Smith College (BA 1949), Radcliffe College (MA 1950) and the University of Michigan (Ph.D. 1959), she has since taught at Brown University, the Universities of Toronto and California at Berkeley, and Princeton. A prolific scholar, she has served on the editorial board of several distinguished journals, and founded and co-edited *Renaissance and Reformation*.   RL

Davis, Rebecca (Blaine) Harding 1831–1910

American short-story writer and novelist who exposed the darker side of mid-century industrialization. Born into an upper-middle-class household, she lived for a few years in Alabama before moving with her family in 1836 to the burgeoning iron-mill city of Wheeling, Virginia. After being educated at home, she attended a girls' seminary in Pennsylvania from which she graduated valedictorian in 1848. For the next decade she

helped to manage the Harding home and tutor her younger siblings. But she also nurtured her artistic ambitions, and by the late 1850s was contributing reviews, editorials and poems to the Wheeling *Intelligencer*.

In 1861 she published her first and most powerful story, LIFE IN THE IRON-MILLS, a grimly realistic novella of the stunted lives of immigrant factory labourers. It was an instant success, bringing her wide recognition, literary connections, and, indirectly, a spouse, when in 1863 (having published yet another fictional critique of industrial capitalism, *Margret Howth: A Story of To-Day* (1862)) she married an admiring correspondent, Philadelphia newspaper editor L. Clarke Davis. She continued to publish regularly, though increasingly to satisfy her new family's financial needs rather than artistic ones, crafting stories for popular magazines as well as high-culture journals. While she is best known for her work on industrialization, her prolific writings – fuelled by her interest in both the art of the 'commonplace' and the 'story of to-day' – touched in often pioneering ways a broad range of contemporary topics, including the Civil War and the position of the freed slaves (*Waiting for the Verdict*, 1868), insane asylum abuses (*Put Out of the Way*, 1870), political corruption (*John Andross*, 1874) and, frequently, the conflict between a woman's domestic duties and her professional aspirations. She was a keen ironist, a critic of transcendental idealism, and both a REALIST and a NATURALIST before the heyday of either. As writer and social historian she influenced such contemporary figures as William Dean Howells and ELIZABETH STUART PHELPS. Her later admirers include TILLIE OLSEN, whose rediscovery of *Life in the Iron-Mills* in the 1970s brought the long-forgotten Davis fresh critical recognition.   WG

Davys, Mary 1674–1732 Irish poet, novelist and playwright. Born in Dublin, she and her schoolmaster husband, Revd Peter Davys, were part of Swift's literary circle. On her husband's death in 1698 she moved to York, and embarked on a literary career.

Davys's novel *The Amours of Alcippus and Lucippe*, for which she was paid 3 guineas, appeared in 1704, followed by *The Fugitive* (1705), which was dedicated to Esther Johnson. Her play *The Northern Heiress* was staged at London's New Theatre in 1716, and she was able to open a coffee house in Cambridge on the proceeds. Other works included *The Reform'd Coquet* (1724), a cautionary tale of a girl who dares to defy the mores of patriarchal society, and *The Accomplish'd Rake* (1727).

Like the hero of her sharply observant depiction of literary life, 'The Modern Poet', Davys

thought it hard he should a scene run through
Of beggary, and be insulted too,

and in the preface to her *Works* (1725) she attacked those who questioned the right of women to earn their own living. As she pointed out, 'a woman left to her own endeavours for twenty-seven years together, may well be allow'd to catch at any opportunity for that bread, which they that condemn her would very probably deny to give her'. Conscious, however, of her equivocal status, she insisted on her own respectability as 'the relict of a clergyman', and on the 'purity' of her works. Davys's assessment of her own achievement was characteristically realistic. Of her writings she remarked that 'I never was so vain, as to think they deserv'd a place in the first rank, or so humble, as to resign them to the last'.   RR

Dawbin [née Hadden], Annie Baxter (Anna Maria) 1816–1905 Australian DIARIST who chronicled 19th-century settlement in the town and in the bush. She was born in Exeter, England, into the family of an army major who had fought at Waterloo, and went to school in London. She arrived in Van Diemen's Land in 1835, the newly married wife of Andrew Baxter, a lieutenant responsible for a convict transport. When he left the army they established a farm at Yesabba but her journal records their increasing marital disharmony, his frequent stays away from home, and her flirtations. Following Baxter's suicide she married Robert Dawbin in 1857, but this second marriage was equally unsuccessful.

Through her personal journals covering almost thirty-four years, which have been published in part as *A Face in the Glass* (1992), the details of personalities and communities in 19th-century Australia spring vividly to life. She published *Memories of the Past, By a Lady in Australia* (1873) but this account of her life, written from the distance of old age, lacks the immediacy of her journals in which she spontaneously confided her deepest feelings.   JSte

Dawson, Jennifer 1929– English novelist whose elliptical, blackly funny and rebarbative books explore the lives of the disoriented, from war-time evacuees to mental patients to 1960s squatters. She grew up in Camberwell, south London, studied History at Oxford, and – after dictionary-making at the Clarendon Press, and social work – Philosophy at University College London. Her first novel, *The Ha-Ha* (1961), is the stunned, hilarious, first-person narrative of Josephine, sectioned in a mental hospital with a dubious diagnosis of schizophrenia, trying to learn to suppress her sexuality and her uncontrollable laughter at the absurdity of nice people with 'the knack of existing'. *The Ha-Ha*, which won the 1962 James Tait Black Memorial Prize, was adapted for television and radio, and republished by Virago Press in 1985 with an afterword by Dawson – '"Does mental illness really exist?" parts of the New Left were asking . . . "Are mental institutions part of the social control of women?" feminists were asking . . . It is ironically painful, looking back, to see how these genuine questions have been exploited by present-day *laissez-faire* political looters who see in psychiatric "slum clearance" the economic advantages of . . . development.'

This clear-eyed bitterness characterizes Dawson's later fiction, and probably accounts for its relative neglect. Her novels become more garrulous, but rather in the manner of CHRISTINA STEAD, another committed and difficult writer who took the corruption of ideals for granted. *The Strawberry Boy* (1976) is about racism, particularly on the liberal Left; *The Upstairs People* (1988), short-listed for the Fawcett Prize, follows war-time evacuees to rural Wales where the murderous craziness of their urban family romance is acted out. Dawson's main cause for many years was the Campaign for Nuclear Disarmament, and this novel makes connections between anti-Semitism, woman-hating and the climate of fear created by nuclear weapons, which combine to produce the collective abjection that fascinates and horrifies her: 'People were all talking about Hiroshima . . . and it seemed now that we must all lie as close to the ground as possible lest we attract the attention of restless powers . . . it was not just us women who would have to lie so low.'   LS

Day, Dorothy 1897–1980 The conversion experience is central to the understanding of American religion, and throughout American culture the forms of conversion (especially into and out of radical politics) give a vocabulary for understanding dramatic swings in the inner life. Dorothy Day, author of novels and autobiographies, who spent years as a political activist, made perhaps the most dramatic conversion in this century. After studying at the University of Illinois in Chicago, Day went to New York, and worked for The Masses. She was imprisoned for her militant suffragism and was on the fringes of the Provincetown Players, sharing their hard-drinking riotousness. Day had a daughter with her common-law husband, and published a novel *The Eleventh Virgin* (1924). She became a convert to Catholicism (*From Union Square to Rome*, 1938) and in her mid-30s founded the Catholic Worker movement (and newspaper), and advocated an influential blend of 'personalist action', anarchist pacificism, voluntary poverty and conservative theology. Day founded a nationwide chain of charitable houses of refuge for the poor. She was a leading figure in the opposition to the war in Vietnam. A finely written memoir, *The Long Loneliness* (1952), omitted much of the tumultuousness of her early life. John Cardinal O'Connor proposed Day's sanctification in 1997. EH

Day, Marele 1947– Australian crime-fiction writer. Day was born and lives in Sydney, and the city figures as a vital, often threatening, yet seductive location of meaning, as well as a setting, in her feminist crime stories (see DETECTIVE FICTION). These parody the hard-boiled private-eye sub-genre and spin off the work of Peter Corris, the most popular contemporary Australian crime writer. Day has a BA(Hons.) degree, and has worked as a teacher, researcher and freelance editor.

Day's hero is Claudia Valentine, an ironically witty detective whose children live in Queensland with their father. Day's second novel, *The Life and Crimes of Harry Lavender* (1988), has a celebrated opening which demonstrates the quite conventional but entertaining twists Day achieves from her use of a female detective to manipulate readers' genre and gender expectations. A toughminded detective with a hangover wakes in typically sleazy surroundings beside an unknown blonde. It is truly surprising when it becomes clear that this detective is a woman. Day won the 1993 Shamus Award, Best Private Eye Paperback USA, for *The Last Tango of Dolores Delgado* (1992). A prolific and successful crime writer, Day is one of a group of well-known Australian women writing contemporary feminist crime fiction. Her writing is influenced by the techniques of *film noir*, and she has edited a book on *How to Write Crime* (1996). DB

Day, Suzanne R(ouvier) 1890–1964 Irish playwright, suffragist, novelist and ornithologist born in Cork and best known for her collaborations with GERALDINE CUMMINS, with whom she founded the Munster Women's Franchise League, and wrote three plays for the Abbey Theatre. *Broken Faith* (1913) is an expressionist family tragedy, lifted by the selfless heroism of the wife; it was castigated by critics for its negative representations of male behaviour. *Fox and Geese* was their greatest success. A farcical comedy of peasant manners, the colourful dialogue is in the style of SOMERVILLE AND ROSS. Biddy, the mother of a shy bachelor, says of men, 'They're like throut [*sic*] on the line, but faith they comes aisy enough to your hand and you playing them nicely.' Day also wrote independently of Cummins. Her plays *Out of a Deep Shadow* (1912) and *Toilers* (1913), on the life of female sweatshop workers, were produced in Dublin. Her novel *The Amazing Philanthropists* (1916) was based on her experiences as a poor-law guardian. She went as a nurse to the French Front in 1916, and gave her impressions in *Round About Bar-le-Duc* (1918). *Where the Mistral Blows* (1933) is a historical guide to Provence. She died in London where, during World War II, she had been a member of the Fire Service. CL

D'Costa [née Creary], Jean 1937– Jean D'Costa is the Caribbean woman who has most consistently written novels for children, beginning with *Sprat Morrison* whose main character has endeared himself to two decades of children in Jamaica and the wider Caribbean (see CHILDREN'S BOOKS).

She was born in Kingston, capital city of Jamaica, but grew up as a country girl, moving with her parents, both elementary-school teachers, from one school to another in rural Jamaica. It was Somerton, a district in St James, which was to have the most lasting effect on her and make her forever appreciative of things rural, an appreciation which is evident in the excitement with which she captures details of rural living.

Sprat Morrison (1972) was written for children coming into adolescence in Jamaican schools and having little reading material which spoke to their own lives. *Escape to Last Man's Peak* (1976) and *Voices in the Wind* (1978) were aimed at the same audience. In 1980 she edited (with Velma Pollard) *Over Our Way*, a collection of short stories for schools, including two of her own stories.

D'Costa read English at the University of the West Indies and Oxford University, and lectured at the University of the West Indies and Hamilton College in upstate New York. Her academic writing has been in both Caribbean Linguistics and Caribbean Literature.

In 1997 she went to live with her journalist husband, David, in Florida, where she continues to indulge her 'love for writing, for finding out things, for dark humour, for cats, for being difficult'. VEP

De [née Rajadhyaksha], Shobha 1948– Indian writer of popular fiction. Shobha De's work mirrors the changing lifestyles and aspirations of urban, middle- and upper-class India, caught between a deep-rooted tradition and a globalized modernity. Her own experiences, first as a successful model, and then as founder-editor of film and society magazines, gave her a unique vantage point from which to observe the glitzy, if sometimes sordid, ways of Bombay's *haute monde*. It was in the journalistic phase of her career, spanning the 1970s and 1980s, that she established a reputation for a no-holds-barred writing style. Her colloquial English, interspersed with Hindi and Martathi usage, had the immediacy of spoken language for a section of English-speaking Indians.

De's transition from provocative journalist to popular novelist was therefore remarkably smooth. When her first novel, *Socialite Evenings* (1988), appeared, it was an overnight bestseller. This was later acknowledged as a triumph of packaging and marketing, not just of the book but of its attractive author as well. Since then De has written six other works of fiction in much the same vein, all of them laced liberally with sex. Indeed, much of her appeal lies in her ability to Indianize the sexual idiom of Western pulp fiction. Not surprisingly the media labelled her the Jackie Collins of India: De has been quick to capitalize on her image as archpriestess of sex. *Surviving Men* (non-fiction, 1997) is replete with advice on female sexuality.

PP

de Cleyre, Voltairine 1866–1912 American poet and feminist–anarchist activist. She was born in Leslie, Michigan, and graduated from a convent school in Ontario. She wrote sketches under several pseudonyms, including Fanny Forester, for the *Progressive Age*. Following the 1887 conviction of five labour leaders for the Haymarket bombing in Chicago, she converted to anarchism and began lecturing for the American Secular Union and the Woman's National Liberal Union. She spent much of her life in Philadelphia, where she tutored immigrants. She helped found the Ladies' Liberal League in 1892 and contributed to EMMA GOLDMAN's journal *Mother Earth*. Her political poems were widely published and translated into several languages; she also translated works from French and Hebrew. She opposed stereotyped gender roles and rejected marriage, bearing a son with James B. Elliot. In 1897 she toured France and Britain lecturing for labour organizations. In 1902 she survived an attempted assassination and refused to press charges against her attacker.

JSG

de France, Marie fl. *c*.1170–80 The works of Marie de France, usually dated *c*.1170–80, belong to the flowering of French vernacular poetic narrative, alongside the Arthurian ROMANCES of Chrétien de Troyes and the original version of *Le Roman de la Rose* by Guillaume de Lorris (*c*.1220–30). Marie's favoured poetic modes are *Fables* and *Lais*, written in technically brilliant octosyllabic couplets – relatively short narratives, yet complex in plotting and in dramatizing sexual and ethical problems of court life. Marie is interested both in the interpretation of classical legend and in the writing of oral Celtic narrative (the 'Breton lays'). She writes for an audience whose interests converge with hers, and which she characterizes as courtly.

Does Marie's work properly form part of the history of French or of Anglo-Norman literature? The question is of historical importance, but it has a certain artificiality in literary terms; her work emerges from the cultural milieu of northern France and is addressed to sophisticated Francophones. The fact that she names herself as Marie *de* (from) France probably indicates that she was based in England; and the King in whose court she wrote is generally taken to be Henry II (who spoke only French, no English, spent much of his time fighting in France and was technically vassal to the King of France). In the late 12th century, then, here is a courtly woman writer in the English court with the confidence to name herself, whose popularity is attested by a (jealous) contemporary and whose work, though pious, is determinedly secular in orientation, dealing with lovers' worldly concerns and issues of rule and misrule. Only in *Eliduc* do the women heroes retire to monasteries, and it is their bond of friendship that takes them there.

In the history of writing in England, Marie can be seen as a major precursor of Chaucer, who, in the late 14th century – and writing now in English – has a comparable confidence in fiction, and whose treatments of gender and power in *The Canterbury Tales* include 'The Franklin's Tale' – identified as an old Breton lay and so a tribute, whether Chaucer knew it or not, to Marie de France (Chaucer certainly knew English translations from Marie's *lais*, such as *Lanfal* and *Frêne*.) Marie's tales, like Chaucer's, are concerned with good and bad marriage and with good and bad kingship, the relations of mutuality between men and women and the wise government of the state; readers are drawn into the social debate which such texts both embody and represent. In this, Marie's French fictions anticipate Chaucer's English ones by two centuries.

DL

de Groen, Alma 1941– Alma de Groen can be grouped, along with DOROTHY HEWETT, as one of the foremost women playwrights to emerge out of the 1970s 'new wave' of Australian theatre. She was born in small-town New Zealand and lived in England and Canada before coming back to Australia. Her plays

Voltairine de Cleyre: frontispiece and title-page of *Selected Works*, 1914.

reflect current intellectual concerns and ideas, and, in particular, feminist discourses. They have been very successful theatre productions as well as being critically acclaimed. De Groen, inspired by Sydney theatre in the 1960s, began writing when her daughter was aged 2. Her early plays include: *The Joss Adams Show* (1970), an absurdist exposé of battered-baby syndrome; *The After-life of Arthur Cravan* (1973), featuring a dissatisfied man who reinvents himself; *Perfectly All Right* (1975) and *Going Home* (1976), both showing the traps of domesticity; and *Chidley* (1977), about the historical figure. De Groen's comedy *Vocations* (1981) depicts a writer, Joy, married to the philanderer Godfrey, and her friend the actor Vicki, who cohabits with the biologist Ross, as they try to reconcile their artistic ideals with traditional female roles. The characters discuss feminist ideas as Ross tries to trap Vicki into motherhood and Joy tries to assert her independence. While De Groen skilfully communicates the feminist arguments through the dramatic situations, she cleverly critiques theatrical form in the text. The acclaimed THE RIVERS OF CHINA (1987), which is considered one of the important plays of the decade, won the 1988 Premier's Literary Awards for Drama in New South Wales and in Victoria. Combining two plots, it explores complex questions of identity and sexed bodies; a future of female domination and oppressed men which reverses the violence of patriarchal power relations is juxtaposed with the early 1920s world of a tubercular KATHERINE MANSFIELD yearning for self-knowledge. A doctor in the future, Rahel, tries to save a suicidal man by giving him Mansfield's identity through hypnosis, underscoring ideas about how the social order manifests through the gendered body and experiences of self. *The Girl Who Saw Everything* (1991), winner of the 1993 national drama award (AWGIE) for Best Stage Play, has a middle-aged female historian, author of a successful book on biological determinism, and her husband witness a hit-and-run accident. Recently, De Groen has written two radio plays, *Stories in the Dark* (1995) and *Available Light* (1997). PT

de Kok, Ingrid 1951– South African poet living and working in Cape Town. De Kok was born in the Western Transvaal and was educated in Johannesburg, Cape Town and at Queens, Canada. She lived for some time in Canada and has now resettled in Cape Town, where she works at the University of Cape Town as director of adult education. Her first volume of poetry was entitled *Familiar Ground* (1988). Her second volume is called *Transfer* (1997) and, like her first, interweaves the personal and the political. It echoes many of the themes South Africans are currently obsessed with, such as the nature of memory and forgetting, and the meanings of mourning and reconciliation. Her academic work continues the concerns of her poetry. Together with KAREN PRESS she edited a collection of responses to Albie Sachs's paper on culture 'Preparing Ourselves for Freedom', called *Spring is Rebellious: Arguments about Cultural Freedom* (1990).   CCo

de la Pasture [née Bonham], Elizabeth (Lydia Rosabelle), afterwards Lady Clifford 1866–1945
British novelist and dramatist. Born in Naples, the daughter of HBM Consul for Calais, she married firstly Henry de la Pasture of Llandogo Priory, Monmouthshire, and secondly, in 1910, Sir Hugh Clifford, a distinguished colonial civil servant.

By then she was a well-known writer: her first publication was *The Little Squire* in 1893, followed by *The Toy Tragedy* in 1894. One of her most successful books was *Adam Grigson*, written in 1899, which dealt with the conflict between money and standing in country society, and used characters of real liveliness: *The Man from America*, in 1905, showed amusing familiarity with American idiom. Both her plays, *The Lonely Lady of Grosvenor Square* and *Peter's Mother*, were performed at major London theatres, the latter also at Sandringham by command of King Edward VII.

After her marriage, her life with her husband in his official position in West Africa prevented her writing further, but in 1918 she edited an account of their life, on behalf of the Red Cross, entitled *Our Days on the Gold Coast*. Of seventeen items recorded, nearly all ran into several editions.   MEW

de la Ramee, Marie Louise see OUIDA

de la Roche, Mazo 1879–1961 Canadian novelist.
Born Mazo Roche in Newmarket, Ontario, to an invalid mother and and a ne'er-do-well father of Irish descent, Mazo reinvented herself with an illustrious French ancestry. The centre of her life was her cousin, Caroline Clement, who became her life-long companion, amanuensis and muse. They adopted two children and achieved a luxurious life in baronial manors in England and Canada, attended by a retinue of servants. The core of their existence was a secret unwritten play invented by Mazo, shared with Caroline, and continued throughout their adult lives. Related to the play as a parallel creation was Mazo's prolific literary output.

Although Mazo had published fiction from an early age, it was not until 1927 when she won the Atlantic Monthly prize, that she achieved success. She leapt to prominence with JALNA, the first of her sixteen novels about the the Whiteoaks of Jalna, an Ontario landowning dynasty. The series made her one of the most popular novelists of the 20th century. However, the critical acclaim earned by the first 'Jalna' novels waned as, encouraged by her publishers in the US and Britain and by avid readers around the world, she drew out the sexual exploits of her Whiteoak clan long after she had tired of them. She tried to publish on other subjects – children's books, novels and a reticent autobiography, but her fans clamoured for more adventures of the Whiteoaks. Her work and life together reveal an interesting tension between the need to write an orthodox heterosexual plot and the desire to inscribe in her fiction her own non-traditional life.   JG

de Lafayette, Madame (Marie-Madeleine de la Vergne) see LA FAYETTE, MADAME DE

de Pizan, Christine *c*.1365 – *c*.1434 Leading vernacular writer of her time, whose works show an extraordinary range of learning and of genres, including political theory, military strategy and polemical defence of women. Of Italian gentry stock, de Pizan was brought up in France by her humanist father who insisted that she be well educated. After the death of her husband she supported herself and her family in Paris, first by producing luxury manuscripts for aristocratic women and then by original writing. During the 1390s she participated in the so-called *querelle de la rose*, a three-year debate seeking to rethink the position of women in western literary tradition and culture.

One of de Pizan's sons lived in England, and her best-known work, the *Cité de Dames* (*Book of the City of Ladies*, 1405), was being read there (in French, amongst an educated élite) within a decade of its composition. It was popular with English women book-collectors. Chaucer's granddaughter, Alice, owned a copy and so probably did Cecily Neville, wife of Richard of York. This work describes the building of a mythical *polis*, the City of Ladies, as a bulwark against misogyny. Its bricks are three sets of exemplary stories, demonstrating women's virtue, strength and cultural contribution.

Five of de Pizan's works circulated in 15th-century English translations (all, ironically, by men, some of whom may not have known that she was the author): *The Letter of Cupid* (1399; Hoccleve, 1402); her bestseller *The Epistle of Othea* (*c*.1400; translated by Stephen Scrope, *c*.1440, for his step-father Sir John Fastolf, and also by Babyngton; used by Lydgate for crucial scenes in his *Troy Book* (*c*.1415); translated again in the sixteenth century (published Wyer, *c*.1540)); *The Moral*

Proverbs of Christine (c.1402; Woodville; published by Caxton, 1478); *The Body of Policy* (c.1406–7; anonymous); and *The Book of Faits of Arms and of Chivalry* (1406; translated for Henry VII by Caxton, 1489). Brian Anslay's famous English translation of the *Book of the City of Ladies* was published by Pepwell in 1521.   REv

de Souza, Eunice 1940– Indian English poet who combines a bareness of style and an ironic voice to express defiance of family, her religion, and tradition, as well as to chart her construction of her identity. She begins from an assertion of commonality with the mass of other Indians and their tradition(s), claiming especially the heritage of Marathi literature and culture and particularly the *bhakti* poetry of Tukaram. Born to a Goan Catholic family in Pune, Maharashtra, she satirizes the church, Catholic values, marriage, sexual prudery, hypocrisy and prejudice (both religious and colour). A teacher of English at St Xavier's College, Mumbai, she has written extensively on literature and culture. She has also written books for children.

Eunice de Souza's poems, collected in *Fix* (1979), *Women in Dutch Painting* (1988) and *Ways of Belonging: New and Selected Poems* (1990) – whether about her Catholic heritage as the early poems are, or about her claims to other Indian heritages or simply poems expressing a certain acceptance of her lot, as her later work does – exhibit a control over Indian English and its spoken rhythms which is rare among Indian English poets. Self-conscious her poems may be, self-pitying they are not. Ironic in tone and self-deconstructionist in their theme, her poems are feminist only in their awareness of repression and injustice to women and affinities to the mode of other women poets and not in any overt commitment. She has recently edited an anthology – *Nine Indian Women Poets: An Anthology* (1997).   GJVP

de Staël, Madame see STAËL, MADAME DE

de Vere [née Cecil], Anne, Countess of Oxford 1556–87 The daughter of Lord Burghley, ELIZABETH I's chief minister, who married Edward de Vere, Earl of Oxford, two weeks after her 15th birthday. In 1576 Oxford charged the virtuous and pregnant Anne with infidelity and returned her to her parents to be 'rid of the cumber'. They formally reunited in 1582, but a son born the following year did not survive. They had three surviving daughters.

Pandora by John Soowthern (1584) included 'Four Epitaphs made by the Countess of Oxford after the death of her young son, the Lord Bulbeck'. They share the same idiosyncratic versification as the other poems in *Pandora*, suggesting either that Soowthern wrote them in the Countess's voice or that the Countess imitated his model. They contain affecting expressions of maternal grief: 'Destinies and gods, you might rather have taken / My twenty years, than the two days of my son'.   HH

de Wolfe, Elsie (Lady Mendl) 1865–1950 Actress and interior decorator, daughter of an improvident New York physician, Elsie de Wolfe was sent to live with relatives in Edinburgh. After being presented at court, she acted in private theatricals, and on returning to New York was taken up by Pierre Lorillard and appeared in benefit performances. Elsie was handsome, talented and new, and made good copy for society editors. She began a long-term liaison with Elizabeth Marberry in 1887 and acted in Charles Frohman's company on Broadway. When her theatrical career faded, de Wolfe opened an office as the city's first interior decorator. Commissions flooded in from the 'Four Hundred', and de Wolfe was soon laying down the law in matters of taste. 'I loathe poverty', she said. 'I hate the sordid, the ugly, and the cheap.' *The House in Good Taste* (1913) set out her principles of decor. She led a wholesale purge of Victorian design, and, like EDITH WHARTON, championed 18th-century French furniture. A gossipy, unreliable autobiography, *After All* (1935), followed. She married Sir Charles Mendl in 1926, and lived rather grandly, all cocktail parties and amusing guests, at the Villa Trianon at Versailles in the years between the World wars.   EH

Death Comes for the Archbishop (1927) The tale of a young Catholic priest sent to New Mexico as a missionary reveals WILLA CATHER's efforts to reconcile the land with civilization in her writing. The title, taken from Holbein's series of religious woodcuts, the 'Dance of Death' (c.1525), heralds the novel's strong spirituality, carried by the central character, Father Jean-Marie Latour, and his loyal friend Father Joseph Vaillant. Latour, genteel and intellectual, and Vaillant, practical and keen, are sent from France to the comparably rugged land of the New World to re-establish Catholicism in Santa Fé, countering the corrupt Spanish priests and enthusing the Hopi and Navaho Indians. Wary of American 'infidels' who have colonized their religion and land, the townspeople cautiously accept the disciplined Latour, and he responds by remaining with them in retirement after Vaillant leaves for Colorado. Latour's greatest conversion is that of his own nature to one which respects and reveres the desolate landscape, a transformation symbolized by the fulfilment of his wish to construct a European-style cathedral out of the rock of New Mexico.   EM

Death Notebooks, The (1974) The eighth of nine volumes of poetry, *The Death Notebooks* deals with recurrent themes in ANNE SEXTON's work: childhood, female friendship, the death of her mother, the details of domestic life in post-war Middle America, mental breakdown, religious doubt and the desire for faith. Sexton commented: 'It is said that I am part of the so-called "CONFESSIONAL school". I prefer to think of myself as an imagist who deals with reality and its hard facts.'

She does so in a style which harnesses the resources of colloquial American speech but also employs a range of poetic forms: elegy, prayer – both intercession and celebration – surreal parody, and so on. She also commented: 'My poems are intensely physical.' Indeed, a striking characteristic of her work is the yoking together of the physical, overtly sensual or erotic with religious emotion. A fine example of this, and a poem she herself favoured, is 'The Fury of Cocks', which describes human sexuality and which she glossed as, 'I am saying in *that* is God.' Despite the colloquial, jokey surface of her work, she can therefore be placed centrally in a long tradition of New England verse.   HMD

Death of the Heart, The (1938)

In her fifth novel ELIZABETH BOWEN combines the leitmotivs characteristic of her fiction with astute social critique: the orphaned heroine, the Jamesian ambivalence of innocence, perennial homelessness and questions of female identity. Entering the London household of her stepbrother Thomas and his wife, Anna, orphaned 16-year-old Portia Quayne reveals this 'home' to be a mere contrived ménage where sophisticated interior design keeps disturbing emotions at bay. A multitude of maternal substitutions (for Portia as for most other Bowen heroines) parade a panoply of female rôles, demonstrating how inter-war femininity is still firmly tied to and dependent on Motherhood, in its flapperish denial as much as in its vision of the manipulative potential of the Freudian 'devouring mother'. The investigation of female subjectivity links Bowen to ROSAMOND LEHMANN and culminates in the rejection of the female BILDUNGSROMAN with EVA TROUT, partly a sixties rerun of *The Death of the Heart*.

The Death of the Heart was adapted for television by Granada in 1985, as a drama of adolescent sensibility.   PUR

Deerbrook: A Novel (1834)

HARRIET MARTINEAU's three-volume novel, celebrating home and domestic contentment, duty and love, tells the story of Edward Hope, a lonely country doctor, who agrees to marry Hester Ibbotson, a guest of the local Grey family, despite having fallen in love with Margaret, Hester's sister. Following their marriage, Hope's medical practice begins to fail, and Hester proves unbalanced and jealous. His patients reject his new methods and begin to abandon him, and he is accused of body-snatching

for medical purposes. However, he regains the admiration and trust of the villagers when he brings them through a serious fever epidemic. Hope's relationship with Hester is strengthened by this 'gracious piece of tribulation' and they become, we are left to suppose, happy together. The novel concludes with the narrator's tribute to Hope's exemplary commitment to his marriage, and his rise 'by dint of a religious discharge of duty towards [Hester], from self-reproach and mere compassion, to patience, to hope, to interest, to admiration, to love'. GEORGE ELIOT read *Deerbrook* in 1852, remarking that she was 'surprised at the depth of feeling it reveals', and Hope's marriage to Hester perhaps provided the idea for Lydgate's and Rosamund's marriage in MIDDLEMARCH, with its rather different outcome.   FJO'G

Deevy, Teresa [D. V. Goode] 1894–1963

Irish playwright whose hey-day was at the Abbey Theatre in the 1930s. She was born in Waterford City, one of thirteen children, and of eight daughters, none of whom married. Her education at University College, Dublin, was interrupted by the onset of Ménière's Disease. She completed her degree nearer home, at University College, Cork, and was, by that time, profoundly deaf. In London she studied lip reading and was impressed by the work of Shaw, Maeterlinck and Chekhov. Six of her plays were produced at the Abbey between 1930 and 1936. *Reapers* (1930) has disappeared. *In Search of Valour* (1931), *The King of Spain's Daughter* (1935) and *Katie Roche* (1936) all revolve around young women of remarkable vitality, whose poverty and social vulnerability make them think of marriage as the future. *Katie Roche* is a subtle mapping of the psychological and spiritual impact of marriage on an inexperienced woman. It has been twice revived. *Temporal Powers* (1932) is a painful tragedy of destitution, exemplifying Deevy's vivid dialogue and characterizations. In 1939 *Wife to James Whelan* was rejected by the Abbey. Later it was staged at the Studio Theatre Club, and broadcast on radio, and numerous radio plays followed, for Radio Eireann and the BBC. *Light Falling* (1948), a brief love story, effectively captures a momentary image of happiness; it was staged at the Peacock Theatre. From Dublin, Deevy returned to Waterford in the late 1950s, and died there.   CL

Defending Ancient Springs (1967)

Blake scholar KATHLEEN RAINE's critical study vigorously refutes the soul-killing materialism that she sees threatening to nullify not only academic and critical engagement with poetry, but, more alarmingly, the production of poetry itself. Taking her title from a poem by Vernon Watkins, Raine promotes her argument for the undervalued – if not utterly discounted – imaginative and spiritual dimensions of art through discussions of

Watkins and other poets, including David Gascoyne, Edwin Muir, Blake, Shelley and Yeats, as well as in larger-scoped meditations such as 'The Use of Beauty' and 'On the Symbol'. A poet herself, Raine cites writers who participate with her in 'symbolic language', and who share her neo-platonic mysticism and her belief in the primacy of myth and the 'unanalysable imaginative essence'. This *cri de coeur* militates against a fashionable capitulation to scientific positivism, a reductive and uninformed notion of 'realism' that simply revels in the profane and vulgar. Literature is doomed to irrelevancy, Raine warns, unless it realizes its function to urge us to perfection, to link us to the eternal.   MO'C

Delafield, E. M. [Edmee Elizabeth Monica Dashwood, née de la Pasture] 1890–1943 Prolific and successful British journalist, novelist, playwright and short-story writer. Delafield was the daughter of the popular novelist ELIZABETH DE LA PASTURE, and solidly of the English upper classes by birth and marriage, yet combined active membership of the social establishment (magistrate and stalwart of the Women's Institute) with a critical but humorous approach to that milieu in her literary output. Her principal characters are all drawn from the narrow world in which she herself moved, and though she consistently excoriates the emptiness and futility in contemporary women's lives, bound as they invariably were by husbands, children and domestic responsibilities, she stops short of advocating any drastic solutions. However much her heroines may bewail their lack of freedom or intellectual stimulation, Delafield herself seems ultimately to advocate stoical endurance.

Her best-known and most successful book, *DIARY OF A PROVINCIAL LADY* (1930), satirizes in journal form her own married life, as do its three sequels. The earlier and darker *Consequences* (1919; one of her own favourites) starkly depicts the life of a gauche debutante whose career ends in failure and suicide. More ironic, but with a similar theme, is *Thank Heaven Fasting* (1932) which chronicles an artless girl's increasingly desperate search for a husband, and the collapse of her romantic dreams. *Nothing is Safe* (1937) is an indictment of the harm done to children by over-easy divorce. In her last book, *Late and Soon* (1943), a middle-aged widow is reunited with her socially inferior first love.   CT

Delaney, Shelagh 1939– Born in Salford in Lancashire and educated at Broughton Secondary School, Delaney came into the public eye in her late teens with what remains an extraordinary play, *A TASTE OF HONEY* (1959). Produced by Joan Littlewood's Theatre Workshop company, the play transferred to the West End and ran for more than 350 performances. Later made into a film, Delaney's first play tackles mother–daughter relationships, class, race and sexuality using an experimental form in terms of both style and structure – a jazz trio break the fourth-wall convention by accompanying and heightening the action. Plays about the working class by the working class were still rare at this point, and Delaney, along with ANN JELLICOE, was amongst the few women to be recognized as significant by the male-dominated new generation of playwrights, which included Arnold Wesker and John Osborne.

Delaney's wit and insight were developed further in her second play, *The Lion in Love*, which found less favour with London audiences, perhaps because it is an altogether more difficult play to deal with, full as it is of pessimism and an unashamed lack of romanticism about the family as an institution. Delaney moved into screen-writing fairly soon after the poor reception of *The Lion in Love*, her best-known screenplays being *Charlie Bubbles* (1968) and *Dance With a Stranger* (1985). Seen by many as a proto-feminist playwright, working in a world of 'angry young men', Delaney foregrounds the female experience in much of her work. She has been given many awards including a BAFTA in 1963 and a Cannes Film Festival award in 1985.   MBG

Delany, Mary (Granville) (Pendarves) 1700–88 Delightful letter-writer with a wide circle of aristocratic and literary friends, including Jonathan Swift, Samuel Richardson and FANNY BURNEY. Her unhappy experience of being compelled by her family to marry, when 17, a wealthy 60-year-old whom she detested was echoed in (and perhaps inspired) Richardson's *Clarissa*. A BLUESTOCKING, she introduced Richardson to SARAH CHAPONE and Anne Donnellan, whom he numbered, with her, amongst the 'superior women' whose advice he sought.

Widowed in 1725, she turned down several suitors before marrying (happily, this time) Swift's friend Patrick Delany in 1743, though he was considered her social inferior. Dividing their time until his death in 1768 between Ireland (he was Dean of Down) and London, they were renowned for their hospitality. An admirer of Fanny Burney's novels, she even persuaded her close friend, the Duchess of Portland, to enjoy them (despite her horror of women novelists), and introduced Burney to the royal family with whom she was intimate, and who provided her with a house and pension. Late in life Delany became famous for her exquisite paper flower collages (later praised by Darwin), while her *Autobiography and Correspondence* was published in 1861.   LMT

Dell, Ethel M(ary) 1881–1939 Immensely successful British ROMANCE novelist of the 1910s, 1920s and

1930s who devised a winning formula for fast-paced, addictive, adventure narratives that injected religious and risqué elements into the machinery of popular romance. Idealized views of marriage, patriarchy and empire reassured her mainly conservative, female audience, while erotic overtones (conveyed through euphemism and florid metaphor) and highly dramatic plots (narrow escapes, abductions, duels and disfigurements) appealed to their taste for fantasies of female power. Her spirited heroines reject feminine helplessness (typical of earlier melodrama) to prove courageous in trying situations (*The Knave of Diamonds*, 1913; *The Lamp in the Desert*, 1919; *The Top of the World*, 1920; *The Gate Marked Private*, 1928; *The Prison Wall*, 1932; and *The Serpent in the Garden*, 1938). She published 30-odd novels (and numerous stories) which were reprinted into the 1950s and revised by BARBARA CARTLAND in the 1970s and 1980s. Her work was often reviled and parodied, but STEVIE SMITH and Q. D. Leavis admired her genius for generating narrative lust. 'Bad writing, false sentiment, sheer silliness, and a preposterous narrative are all carried along by the magnificent vitality of the author' (Leavis).

Daughter of a devout mother and businessman father, Dell began publishing in magazines shortly after leaving Streatham College for Girls and made her name with *The Way of an Eagle* (1912), which became an instant bestseller. She married at 41 and retired to rural Herefordshire, where she continued to publish until her death.   LDo

Delta Wedding (1946) Setting her novel on a 1920s' Delta plantation, EUDORA WELTY wanted to show family life 'that went on on a small scale in a world of its own'. Using a technique recalling MANSFIELD's 'Prelude' and WOOLF's TO THE LIGHTHOUSE, she moves in and out of the inner worlds of the numerous Fairchilds, as they prepare in their different ways for the first wedding in the youngest generation. Shellmound is a 'fragile, temporary' enclosure, already agitated by outsiders: first Robbie, a disconcertingly different sister-in-law, now Troy Flavin, the overseer and hillman whom Dabney is suddenly to marry. Welty's lyrical prose captures the shock-waves, in images, objects, visions of landscape, through the eyes of children, sisters, their mother, their aunts. Compulsively returning to a moment of near-collision, the story of the family on the track as the Yellow Dog train came along, the narrative subtly evokes the shivers of class-dismay, of sexual force, of rebellion against the family, and of fear of change.   PEK

Delynn, Jane 1946– American writer, librettist and journalist who studied at Barnard and the Iowa University Writers' Workshop. She covered the Second Gulf War for *Rolling Stone* and co-founded *Fiction* with Donald Barthelme and Mark Mirsky. She has collaborated on various music-theatre pieces, notably *Hoosick Falls* and *The Monkey Theatre*.

Her novels are characterized by a combination of sly humour and intermittent moral outrage and often deliberately put the reader in false positions. *Some Do* (1978) studies the failure of the student Left and the rise of feminism through the careers of a group of women friends, while *In Thrall* (1982) is a profoundly ambivalent discussion of a teacher–pupil affair. *Real Estate* (1988) satirizes the New York property boom of the yuppy era. *Don Juan in the Village* (1990) was a departure, an episodic novel of bar pick-ups and sexual boasting which refused feminist pieties about the moral superiority of lesbian sex.   RK

Denison [née Andrews], Mary Ann 1826?–1911 Prolific American novelist who wrote popular fiction. Born in Cambridge, Massachusetts, Denison's career as a professional writer began when she became a contributor to the *Boston Olive Branch* where her husband, Revd Charles Wheeler Denison, was assistant editor. Her first book, *Edna Etheril, the Boston Seamstress* (1847), initiated her long career as a novelist. Denison published over eighty novels, including *Gertrude Russell* (1849), *Home Pictures* (1853), *Opposite the Jail* (1859), *The Mill Agent* (1864), *That Husband of Mine* (1877). Her works combined popular forms such as murder mystery, adventure and suspense, with DOMESTIC FICTION themes that emphasized the importance of home life. A wide range of issues emerge in her novels, including class antagonism, slavery and temperance. Her books often hinge on astonishing revelations and bizarre occurrences. For example, in *Old Hepsy* (1858), the heroine who believes she is white discovers that her father is black and that her parents were half-siblings. However, Denison's writings also reaffirmed conventional moral codes and pious values, as in *Out of Prison* (1864) and *Victor Norman, Rector* (1873), which include depictions of the sinful temptations, but conclude with assertions of traditional moral codes.   CJ

Desai, Anita 1937– Distinguished Indian novelist and short-story writer, who grew up in a multi-lingual family with a German mother and an Indian father. Married with four children she divides her time between England, the United States and India. A sense of place has a special relevance for Desai. All her novels reflect a concern with spatial metaphors and her imagery is built upon cities and open spaces, islands and mountains which affect her characters who are uprooted or alienated figures, nomads or refugees, haunted by their own inner conflicts. Desai's world is full of violence, where the characters are constantly under pressure to test their survival skills.

Her first two novels, *Cry, The Peacock* (1963) and *Voices in the City* (1965), are very much in the stream-of-consciousness mode and treat parallel themes of loneliness and survival. The concerns are existential and the conflict is between involvement and detachment. Her third novel, *Bye, Bye Blackbird* (1971), marks a shift from this existential questioning and, moving the locale to London, focuses on problems of cultural nostalgia and alienation.

The next three novels concentrate on the loneliness and unfulfilment of human existence, specifically female existence. *Where Shall We Go This Summer?* (1975) is a novel about Sita's pursuit of the memories of childhood and her reconciliation with the subsequent disillusionment. In *Fire on The Mountain* (1977) Nanda Kaul retreats to her mountain home as an act of self-preservation, but is exposed to suffering and pain all the same. *Clear Light of Day* (1980), the story of four siblings, works through a contrapuntal plot, and places their lives against the background of the country's partition. Bim, the central woman protagonist, emerges as a strong independent woman, allowing Desai to choose for her next novel, *In Custody* (1984), a dominantly male world. *In Custody* is a self-reflexive work about art, its making and preservation, and is a tale told with humour and irony. *Clear Light of Day* and *In Custody* were both shortlisted for the Booker Prize.

BAUMGARTNER'S BOMBAY (1988) zeroes in on a German Jew who seeks refuge in India. *Journey to Ithaca* (1995), like *Baumgartner's Bombay*, approaches India through Europeans who are attracted to the mystic India, an attraction which is disruptive of their personal relationship. Her powerful character delineation, the tunnelling to the past through constant probing and her spatial framing of the narrative distinguish her work, which Desai places in the category of subjective writing.

Desai has also written for children and has published a volume of short stories, *Games at Twilight* (1979). Her work has been translated into several Indian and European languages.　　　JJ

Descending Figure (1980) LOUISE GLÜCK's fourth

volume of poetry evolves from the CONFESSIONAL style of her previous verse, developing a reticent and stringent mode of writing. The title echoes the musical term, which describes the repetition of an aural theme as it moves down the scale, signifying 'a kind of irrevocable darkening' reflected in 'Pietà' and 'The Drowned Children'. The book's three sections, 'The Garden', 'The Mirror' and 'Lamentations', give the sequence a crafted unity wherein themes and images are repeated, permitting each tightly constructed poem a greater use of understatement. This renunciatory style evokes anorexia nervosa in the five-part poem, 'Dedication to Hunger', where it becomes a metaphor for discipline in both poetry and the construction of the self. As the narrator states in the fourth part, 'The Deviation': 'it is the same need to perfect,/ of which death is the mere byproduct', revealing death as the paragon for which we all strive. Particularly is this true for woman, Glück suggests, who is reduced, like her poetry itself, by culture's control over her body, emotions and thoughts.　　　EM

Desert of the Heart (1964) JANE RULE's first pub-

lished novel is a rare achievement for its time. Its affirmative treatment of a relationship between two women holds a special place both in literary history and in the hearts of many readers who could find few positive representations of women-loving women before the NEW WOMEN's Movement.

The novel is set in Reno in 1958. Evelyn Hall, 40, an English professor, comes to the 'burning sand' of the desert for her divorce. Bisexual Ann Childs, 25 and a successful cartoonist, works as a change apron in a Reno gambling house. These two women question dominant moral conventions in a process of moral education in which they learn 'to make choices based on understanding rather than blind faith or great fear'. Rule targets the discourses of Christianity and of Freudian psychology, in which homosexuality is associated with damnation and sterility, or with immature narcissistic or mother–daughter love, respectively. The novel reworks these constructions through complex imagery and an exploration of what is conventionally considered 'natural' or 'nature', establishing a desiring lesbian subject in the process.

Rule's revision of cultural imagery is translated to concerns of the 1980s in Donna Deitch's film version, *Desert Hearts* (1986).　　　CES

Deshpande, Shashi 1938– Novelist and short-story

writer born in Dharwad, she is one of the major Indian writers in English today. Her father was the well-known Kannada writer Shri Adya Rangacharya, but educated as she was in Christian missionary schools, she never wrote in her mother tongue. She studied Economics in Bombay and graduated in Law from Bangalore. Later she obtained a diploma in journalism and an MA in English Literature. She lives in Bangalore with her husband, a consulting pathologist, and has two grown-up sons.

Shashi Deshpande started publishing short stories in magazines from 1970, but her first volume of stories – *The Legacy* – appeared only in 1978. Her first novel, *The Dark Holds No Terrors* (1980), delved into a woman's troubled relationships with her mother and her husband in an intricate psychological study of gender-specific guilt. Her second novel, *Roots and Shadows* (1983), traced interactions in a large sprawling joint family in a way that writers in English have not very often attempted. Shashi Deshpande's special quality is that, although she writes in English, she can evoke a non-westernized traditional ethos from the inside, as if she is writing in an Indian language, and only for an Indian audience. She is among the very few Indian English writers to have her novels translated into Indian languages.

Her fifth novel, THAT LONG SILENCE (1988), was published outside India (Virago, London) and this was the beginning of her international visibility. *That Long Silence* has been translated into German, Dutch, Danish and Finnish, and *The Dark Holds No Terrors* into Russian and German. Her subsequent novels, *The Binding Vine* (1993) and *A Matter of Time* (1996), explore different dimensions of women's experience in India, across class/caste divisions and also along the axis of time.

While accepting the Sahitya Akademi (National Academy of Letters) Award in 1990, Shashi Deshpande expressed her dissatisfaction with critics who felt compelled to use words like 'sensitivity' and 'sensibility' when discussing women writers, while she thought of her work in terms of strength.   MMu

Despard, Charlotte (French) 1844–1939 Suffragette leader, Irish independence campaigner, pioneering social worker among the London poor. She had already acquired some reputation as a writer before the death, in 1868, of her husband Maximilian, a businessman from her own Irish 'Horse Protestant' Ascendancy background. Converting to Catholicism, she dedicated her substantial resources to philanthropic projects in Battersea, challenging the idleness and inefficiency of local workhouse guardians. An ardent campaigner for female suffrage, she became suspicious of the attention-seeking tactics of the WSPU, finally breaking with its leader Emmeline Pankhurst in 1907 to found the Women's Freedom League.

During World War I Despard embarrassed her brother Field Marshall Sir John French by her vociferous pacifism. By 1918, when he became Viceroy of Ireland, she had espoused the cause of emerging republicanism. Her six novels, published between 1874 and 1908, are touched by a characteristically exalted vision of human capabilities, which transcends their limited technical range. The best is undoubtedly *The Rajah's Heir* (1890), a spiritual fantasy appealing to the vogue for Oriental mysticism, in which a young Englishman acquires the soul of an Indian Rajah, thereby equipping him to redeem the world. Despard's work as a journalist included founding the SUFFRAGETTE periodical, the *Vote*, and contributions to the Irish radical paper *An Phoblacht*. At her Dublin funeral, attended by prominent members of the IRA, the oration was spoken by Maude Gonne Macbride. JK

detective fiction This genre invites the reader to engage in the process of detection (most commonly of a murderer) through the interpretation of clues. It developed in the 19th century: the critic Walter

Benjamin argues this development was a response to the threatening anonymity of urban existence. Edgar Allan Poe's 'The Murders in the Rue Morgue' (1841) is one of the earliest detective stories and Wilkie Collins's *The Moonstone* (1868) is regarded as the first detective novel though, given the unstable boundaries between detective fiction, criminal biographies and memoirs, mystery stories and SENSATION fiction these 'origins' are necessarily somewhat speculative. Early women detective writers include Seeley Regester (1831–85) and Anna Katharine Green (1846–1935). Green's female detective, Amelia Butterworth, an elderly, inquisitive, upper-class spinster, has many echoes in subsequent detective fiction.

Sir Arthur Conan Doyle introduced the character of Sherlock Holmes in the 1890s. Holmes's powers of observation, recondite knowledges and prodigious logical capacities, particularly when set alongside his obsessions and addictions and his disturbing domination of his assistant, helped to make the peculiarities of the detective a central element of the fascination of detective fiction. BARONESS ORCZY created an 'armchair detective' in *The Old Man in the Corner* (1909) and a female detective in *Lady Molly of Scotland Yard* (1910).

The 1920s and 1930s have been described as 'The Golden Age of Detective Fiction'. The period was marked by a developing consciousness of the nature of the genre: the Detection Club, which drew up rules for detective fiction, was formed by a group of writers in 1929, and AGATHA CHRISTIE created her two most famous detective characters, Hercule Poirot and Jane Marple in the 1920s. Christie, a prolific and hugely successful writer, specialized in murders committed within specific and detailed social milieus, often rural and upper-class. NGAIO MARSH and MARGERY ALLINGHAM both wrote novels of deduction and social observation with charismatic gentlemen detectives. The most memorable gentleman detective of this period is DOROTHY L. SAYERS's Lord Peter Wimsey who appeared in a series of novels in the 1920s and 1930s. Initially a rather foolish figure, he is given greater levels of complexity after Sayers introduces the character of Harriet Vane, a writer with whom he detects and whom he is eventually to marry. Through these characters Sayers explores gender inequalities, class relationships and sexual tensions within her contemporary society. In the USA MARY ROBERTS RINEHART, who wrote detective fictions and romances, was the leading popular writer of this period. 'Nancy Drew', teenage detective and adventurer, was created by Edward Stratemeyer in 1929, but the series was then written by his daughter, Harriet Stratemeyer Adams: both used the pseudonym 'Carolyn Keene'.

British writer P. D. JAMES combines tightly structured plots with an interest in social tensions and personal psychological disturbance or unease. Her female detective, Cordelia Gray, was initially read as an icon of feminist independence when she appeared in *An Unsuitable Job for a Woman* in 1972, but seen as disappointingly passive when she featured in *The Skull Beneath the Skin* (1982). RUTH RENDELL, who is also British (and writes also as 'Barbara Vine'), tackles disturbing social and psychological issues, including anorexia, child abuse, pathological revenge and rape, in her detective novels. American PATRICIA HIGHSMITH's novels also explore dark and festering passions. Her *Strangers on a Train* (1950) was made into a film by Alfred Hitchcock in 1951: Raymond Chandler was one of the screen-writers on the film.

Chandler's and Dashiell Hammett's 'hard-boiled' detective fiction, featuring cynical yet vulnerable wisecracking detectives who encounter extremes of both violence and corruption, was to be very influential for many of the feminist detective writers who emerged in the United States in the 1980s. SARA PARETSKY's detective, V. I. Warshawski, lives alone though she does have a network of friends and a series of lovers. She is verbally witty and physically courageous: she is inevitably beaten up at some stage in each novel. Despite her encounters with violence, cruelty and corruption, she remains principled, compassionate and professionally competent. Marcia Muller's detective, Sharon McCone, and Sue Grafton's Kinsey Millhone are also assertive, acerbic and proficient private investigators.

Sara Paretsky founded the organization 'Sisters in Crime' to help women detective writers and to challenge gender inequalities more broadly. Feminist writers have found detective fiction a very fruitful genre in which to explore questions of power, transgression and violence. Typically these novels feature a female detective who encounters various forms of inequality and oppression both in the process of detection and in the details of her personal life. A significant number of feminist detective novels examine sexual relationships and identities as particularly and powerfully expressive of social inequalities. Barbara Wilson, KATHERINE V. FORREST, MARY WINGS and the British writer VAL MCDERMID all explore the extent to which lesbian communities, and specifically lesbian detectives, can offer some form of resistance to the violence and anger found in contemporary urban cultures. Wilson pushes her exploration of gender and sexual transgression further in *Gaudi Afternoon* (1991) where the detection involved is concerned as much with the impossibility of uncovering the truth of identities as with criminality.

A number of writers have seen the academic community as a particularly appropriate setting for fictions of violence and detection: perhaps because it is relatively small, enclosed, hierarchical and unusually verbal.

Detective Kate Fansler, created by Amanda Cross [CAROLYN HEILBRUN], is a wealthy and successful academic who detects out of a mixture of curiosity and of duty. The crimes she solves not only happen in universities, schools and literary institutions but are in a real sense created by the inequalities and rivalries of these institutions. VALERIE MINER's *Murder in the English Department* (1982) and British writer Joan Smith's novels featuring Loretta Lawson also explore the violent undercurrents of academic life.

Detective fiction remains a creative and popular literary genre. In recent writing the boundaries between detective fiction, thriller and crime fiction have become significantly more permeable. The conviction that violence and criminality represent a symptom of other forms of social pathology is particularly strong in recent detective writing.　　MS

Devanny, Jean [née Jane Crooks]

1894–1962 New Zealand novelist, political activist and Communist propagandist who married Hal Devanny, a miner, in 1911 and then became active in the Labour Movement. The Devannys moved to Sydney in 1929 and joined the Australian Communist party. Jean became national secretary of Workers' International Relief in 1931 – travelling to Berlin, Russia and throughout Australia – and President of the Writers' Association, but was expelled in 1936 on trumped-up sexual charges.

Devanny wrote short stories and twenty novels. Most notorious is *The Butcher Shop* (1926), banned on grounds of obscenity, but published in New York and Germany and selling 15,000 copies. Many like *Lenore Divine* (1926), *Dawn Beloved* (1928), *Riven* (1929), *Bushman Burke* and *Devil Made Saint* (1930) are out of print. Among the most inspired are those which demonstrate her ambivalence about benign colonization – the oppression of minority ethnic groups – and her belief in women's right to control their bodies. The 'sugar' novels of the mid 1930s, set in North Queensland, are about plantation life: *Sugar Heaven* (1936) concerns the 1935 cane-cutters' strike; her last novel, *Cindie* (1949), deals with racism over the issue of indentured labour, and the replacement of Kanaka and Chinese labour with white labour.

A social pioneer, Devanny's radical vision of woman's personal and political development, and of class struggle and change during the Depression, World War II and the Cold War, makes her work of historical and literary interest. But her writing came second to social and political issues. Her style is raw, even propagandist, at best showing flair and passion, at worst suggesting hastiness of composition. Her prodigious energy and prolific output, and some naivety in political matters, also worked against her, as her betrayal by the party which she had loyally served demonstrates.

Devanny's correspondence with Australian writers, MILES FRANKLIN, CATHERINE SUSANNAH PRICHARD and MARJORIE BARNARD has been collected in *As Good as a Yarn with You* (1992). Her gripping, uneven autobiography, partly an attempt to vindicate herself following expulsion from the Communist party, which she later rejoined but left again in 1949, was published posthumously as *Point of Departure* (1986). JMW

Devas, Nicolette 1912–87 Irish novelist and memoirist. Devas was born in County Clare in 1912, the daughter of Frank McNamara who was heir to Doolin House, a considerable country estate. After her parents separated she and her sister Caitlin, who went on to marry Dylan Thomas, were raised by their mother with the family of Augustus John in Fordingbridge in England. As a result of this she mixed with many literary and artistic people early in life. She was twice married, first in 1931, to Anthony Devas, a painter with whom she had two sons, and then, in 1965, to the artist Rupert Shepard. She studied at the Slade and had an abiding love of art throughout her life despite finding her forte as a writer, rather than as an artist. She wrote two novels: *Bonfire* (1958), which explores children's perspectives convincingly, and *Pegeen Cry-baby* (1986) which was privately published. Her most successful books, however, were the memoirs of her relationships with her father and Augustus John in *Two Flamboyant Fathers* (1966) and its companion work, *Susannah's Nightingales* (1978). MSu

Devlin, Polly 1944– Irish journalist, novelist and columnist. Devlin was born in County Tyrone in Northern Ireland into a family she has described as unusual in its closeness and in the inspirational vibrancy of her siblings. Her writing career kicked off in earnest when in 1964 she won the Vogue talent competition and moved to London to begin work for the same magazine. In this capacity she secured some journalistic coups, doing the first British interview with Bob Dylan, a controversial interview with Barbra Streisand, and the first profile of Seamus Heaney, the Nobel Prize-winning poet, and, incidentally, her brother-in-law. She has written widely for a number of magazines and newspapers and was awarded the OBE for her writing in 1992. She has published a collection of children's stories (*The Far Side of The Lough*, 1983), memoirs (*All of us There*, 1983) which were about growing up with her family on the shores of Lough Neagh, and *The Vogue History of Photography* (1979). Her novel *Dora, or Shifts of the Heart* (1990) resounds with literary and psychoanalytic echoes, but she remains best known as a journalist and columnist. MSu

Dharker, Imtiaz 1954– Indian poet, artist and documentary film-maker. She was born in Lahore, educated in Britain, and has lived in India since the 1970s, with her journalist husband, Anil Dharker. *Purdah* (1989), her first book of poems, is a biting and compassionate portrayal of women coping not only with oppressive traditions and social practices, but with the challenges of modernity and the demands of changing mores. From the struggling, lower-class 'Another Woman', doused with kerosene and torched to death in her husband's house to the more sophisticated, upperclass heroine of 'Battle-line', whose relationship with her partner is like that of two embattled countries, 'hunched against each other' like 'distrustful lovers', Dharker's women emerge as a victimized group regardless of differences in religion, caste, class or nationality. Ultimately, Purdah, or the veil, conveys not just the physical restraint and concealment of women, but their mental and psychological confinement and bondage as well. Her second book, *Postcards from god* (1994), has shorter, crisper, reflective poems. MP

di Michele, Mary 1949– Canadian poet, born at Lanciano, Italy, emigrated to Canada in 1955 and attended the University of Toronto (BA 1972) and the University of Windsor (MA 1974). She is Associate Professor of Creative Writing and English at Concordia University in Montreal, and has been writer-in-residence at various universities. Her lyric poetry reflects on her Italian-Canadian background, her family, love relationships and her political life. She has said of herself: 'I am a feminist. I am more interested in poems than in poetry, more interested in people than in poems. My primary ambition is to try to describe and illuminate life as experienced by women, and through writing to participate fully in human cultural history.' She is exploring ways in which novels, informal essays, creative non-fiction or 'anything with language in it, like film or scat singing' can be written as poetry. She has won several awards: the First Prize, CBC Poetry Contest (1980); the Silver Medal Du Maurier Award for Poetry (1982); the Air Canada Writing Award (1983); and the *Malahat Review* Long Poem Competition (1989). Her poetry has appeared in numerous literary journals and anthologies, and in collections like *Mimosa and Other Poems* (1981) and *Luminous Emergencies* (1990). *Stranger in You: Poems Selected and New* came out in 1995. GHN

Di Prima, Diane 1934– American poet born in Brooklyn to first-generation Italian-American parents; much of her work celebrates this vernacular:

> Brooklyn Navy Yard where everybody worked, to fall to
> pieces
> over Clinton Street
> and the plaster saints in the yard.

But she has also lived and worked in counter-culture communities such as Timothy Leary's psychedelic group and the 'Diggers' political community in San Francisco, where she also spent time with a Zen master in the late 1960s, forming a lasting interest in Buddhism. Her poetry also plays with form, with internal and external discord, with psychic states and mystical preoccupation:

> Is it not in yr service that I wear myself out
> running ragged among these hills, driving children
> to forgotten movies? In yr service
> broom and pen.
>
> ('The Loba Addresses the Goddess/ or The Poet as Priestess Addresses the Loba-Goddess')

Di Prima attended Swarthmore College but left to write, and her first collection, *This Kind of Bird Flies Backwards*, was published in 1958. She edited an underground literary newsletter with Leroi Jones (Amiri Baraka) called the *Floating Bear*, starting in 1961, for which they were both arrested on obscenity charges by the FBI. She also co-founded the New York Poet's Theatre and in the late 1960s she established the Poet's Press with Jack Kerouac, Allen Ginsberg and others. She was the most prominent woman in the Beat movement on both the East and West coasts of the United States, and her *Memoirs of a Beatnik* (1969, 1988) continues to find a wide audience. Other poetry collections include *The New Handbook of Heaven* (1963) and the popular *Revolutionary Letters* (1971), a study of the war in Vietnam and oppression. *Selected Poems: 1956-75* were published in 1975 and another selection, *Pieces of a Song*, in 1990. Her most recent collection is *Seminary Poems* (1991).

Di Prima co-founded the San Francisco Institute of Magical and Healing Arts, and began teaching there, in 1983.   ACH

diaries (journals) The diary or journal is a personal serial record of matters important to the diarist, ordinarily kept on a daily basis or nearly so; it takes in both happenings and perceptions according to the writer's preference; it may be impassioned or impersonal, focused on the diarist or on others, but gives us a sense of the diarist too. The diary may be seen as a literary work providing an individual perception of life that has been translated into words and images showing the process of living in a particular world. Reading the entries becomes an imaginative experience of participating in a diarist's life while the story unfolds each day, as formlessly as life itself, with the diarist become a character in verbal construct.

Along with letters, diaries have been women's most common form of writing in English over the centuries, evolving toward greater expressiveness since the inception of diary-keeping by both men and women in the Western world during the Renaissance. The diary form in English, born ultimately out of changing attitudes to the importance of individual perception, emerged during the second half of the 16th century as the male keepers of factual daily records and travel accounts increasingly added short personal comments to business and other regular-entry records kept as a duty, such as ships' or explorers' logs or military-campaign annuals. Under an impetus from religion, women became diary-keepers too; the oldest known diary in English may be that of LADY GRACE SHERRINGTON MILDMAY (1522–1620), who apparently kept a SPIRITUAL diary, no longer extant, from which between 1570 and 1617 she compiled a retrospect with religious meditations for her daughter. The earliest extant English diary proper may be that of LADY MARGARET DAKINS HOBY (1571–1633), a devout Puritan whose diary from 1599 to 1605 has survived in its original form to show the writer's religious zeal abating while her interest in the daily minutiae so typical of diaries increases. The 16th–17th-century diaries of conscience (religious soul-searching) prescribed by various Protestant Nonconformist or dissenting groups such as Puritans and Quakers (and, later, Methodists), which also issued models for the devout to follow, long remained central to the diary tradition in America, so many of whose settlers were dissenters. Although the diary of conscience eventually transmuted into the secular diary preoccupied with the inner life, as yet the secular diary typically focused on public events and persons more often than on the diarist and was more concerned with activities than feelings.

By the 18th century, diary-keeping had become a highly respectable form of writing that women were encouraged to undertake; keeping bound pocket diaries that allotted a space for each day had become regular practice, and some women even kept two diaries, expanding their laconic pocketbook jottings into fuller accounts. By now the diary was also flourishing as an eclectic form inclusive of both the public and the private and sometimes examining even consciousness closely, although most diaries remained factual records with scant subjective probing. The travel record continued to exist alongside the general diary; young gentlemen were encouraged to travel and keep an observant record from the 17th century on, and some hardy women also did so. During the 19th century, when women's diaries began to be published, British novelist FANNY BURNEY's *DIARY* (1752–1840), issued in 1842, was preceded by the travel diary of actress FANNY KEMBLE in 1835 (*American Journal*). Diarists became increasingly self-conscious about the literary quality of their records, and, beginning near the end of the 19th century, many women studied the effusive confessional *Journal of a Young Artist* of

Russian-born Frenchwoman Marie Bashkirtseff (1860–84, published in 1887) in an endeavour to imitate her frankness, much the way women would later take the candid six-volume *Diary* (published 1966–76) of French-born ANAIS NIN (1903–77) as model. But despite the importation by the early 20th century of the French *journal intime*, closely exploring the psyche, especially in its responsiveness to stimuli, the intimate confessional journal did not become widespread until the resurgent Women's Movement, beginning in the seventies, encouraged the keeping of an interior-focused journal as a tool of heightened feminist awareness and self-therapy.

What VIRGINIA WOOLF said of diarist Elizabeth, Lady Holland (1770–1845), an abused wife cut off from her children for adultery and with much to write about, she might have said of many other past diarists: 'it was not the purpose of her diary to follow her feelings closely, or indeed to record them at all, except to sum them up now and then in a businesslike way, as though she made a note in shorthand for future use'. Although diaristic reticence is not limited to females, good reasons exist historically for women to prefer objective narratives. Taboos of social censorship aside, past typical training for women has not taught them to accept or even understand their feelings but to concentrate on the feelings of others, and their working tool has been a male-devised language that may have stymied them. Yet whatever they may not have said, women's diaries have been important to them; they have kept them up even in difficult circumstances, such as pioneering westward in America or under bombardment on the continent during World War I. Some have expressly kept their diaries for their children's sake or as a family tradition or because their elders trained them to the habit, but beyond any conscious motivation diarists claim we may detect another impulse: the diarist's sense of her own importance, even when she focuses her entries on others rather than on herself. Diaries reinforce the sense of being someone whose tastes and perceptions matter. A woman's diary subliminally assures her that her existence is not justified only through serving as a reference point for others, especially males. Thus, even if the diary form is not specific to women and performs a comparable office for men, it has been especially important to females in patriarchal societies. HB

Diary from Dixie, A (1949) This edition of MARY BOYKIN CHESNUT's *Diary*, edited and revised by Ben Ames Williams, includes a more comprehensive selection from Chesnut's notebooks than the original extracts published in 1904/5. Written between 1861 and 1865, the *Diary* represents a chronicle of the Confederacy during the Civil War years, which she revised in the period 1881–4. Her journal finally comprised nearly fifty notebooks in which Chesnut observes the tragic consequences of secession for her intimate circle of friends, including prominent political and military figures of the South. Chesnut was in an ideal position to observe and narrate the impact war had on the South. She and her husband, James Chesnut Jr, were both from old southern families and James held a leading political and military role. Her informal style combines serious details of political and social upheaval alongside humorous anecdotes and gossip from her male and female acquaintances. Chesnut's intelligent and often outspoken narrative discloses her innermost thoughts on the impact of the War and, surprisingly, her anti-slavery sentiments. JP

Diary of Fanny Burney, The British novelist and diarist, spans 1768–1839 and consists of personal entries, letter journals (letters written over a period of time before sending) and additional personal letters. As first published in 1842 it lacked 1768–78, published in 1889 as her *Early Diary*. Burney wittily addressed herself at the outset as 'Nobody ... since to Nobody can I be wholly unreserved', but soon converted her diary to a letter journal for her sister Susan(na). By 1773 she was also writing for Samuel 'Daddy' Crisp, an adored family friend. She followed his advice to be spontaneous, but, though the tone of her writing is such, the entries were actually reconstructed from memory. A talented raconteur, to please Crisp and Susan she exerted herself to write the apparently artless, candid social comedy that makes the earlier diaries delightful to read. After Crisp's and Susan's deaths (by 1800) Burney's diary changed. Her 1802 journals from Paris are more stilted and pretentious. Her diaries of later years are quasi-literary productions composed from memory and notes to fulfil a promise to her husband to leave a record for their son. Between 1817 and 1838 she edited her manuscripts heavily and added retrospective commentary, probably anticipating the posthumous publication she did receive. HB

Diary of a Provincial Lady, The (1930) by E.M. DELAFIELD was first published as a weekly serial in the magazine *Time and Tide*. Its popularity gave rise to three sequels (1932–40). Delafield uses autobiographical material (she acknowledged 'mild likenesses' between her children and the *Diary*'s Robin and Vicky) to document a typical middle-class, inter-war Devonshire lifestyle characterized by difficult servants and deficient bank-balances. Working within the conventionally objective, unreflective style of women's DIARIES, the anonymous narrator uses the mass of quotidian domestic detail this generates to hint at the frustrations of provinciality and personal (literary) ambition buried underneath. Written in clipped, epigrammatic sentences suggestive of repressed emotion, the *Diary* probes its world with humour and detached irony, establishing from the opening sentence the tone of surreal – and comic – ordinariness which is this book's defining characteristic: '*November 7th.* – Plant the indoor bulbs. Just as I am in the middle of them, Lady Boxe calls. I say, untruthfully, how nice to see her, and beg her to sit down while I just finish the bulbs.'

AS

Diary of Virginia Woolf, The WOOLF kept a diary all her adult life. Even right at the end, she could note down that sausage and haddock were planned for lunch. She wrote her diary most days in the afternoons, and, as she filled up each manuscript book, had it bound. The charm of her diary is precisely that it is so unlike her novels, being full of herself and her thoughts and feelings, openly expressed rather than translated into high art. It's full of the 'I' that was a certain part of Woolf, the self that needed to drive off excess energy, to grumble and gossip, to experiment with phrases and images, to catch moods and perceptions as they flew past. Sometimes her diary seems like an artist's palette, on which she plays with and mixes colours. She herself suggested it might be like an old desk into which she might fling all kinds of bits and pieces, and to which she might return years later only to find that all the disparate fragments of material had coalesced into something formally pleasing. Taken as a whole, it charts her creative development against a background of the political and intellectual world in which she moved, and affords the reader extreme voyeuristic satisfaction.

MBR

Diaz, Abby Morton 1821–1904 American educator, reformer, essayist and CHILDREN's writer. She was born in Plymouth, Massachusetts. Her father, a shipbuilder and social reformer, moved the family to the Transcendentalist utopian community of Brook Farm, where she taught in the infants' school until 1847. She married Manuel Diaz in 1845 and supported their two sons when the marriage failed. Her first story was published in *Atlantic Monthly* in 1861. Educational children's stories initially published in the periodical *Our Young Folks* in 1867 became her best-known book, *The William Henry Letters* (1870), which she followed with two sequels. Her reform activities concentrated on women's household labour, a theme she explored in her novels, *The Schoolmaster's Trunk* (1874) and *A Domestic Problem* (1875). In 1877 she helped found the Women's Educational and Industrial Union of Boston. In the 1880s and 1890s she travelled as a union organizer and lecturer.

JSG

Dick, Kay [Jeremy Scott, Edward Lane] 1915– English novelist, critic, editor and sometime broadcaster. Dick was educated in English boarding schools

in Geneva, Switzerland and at the Lycée Français in London. For the first ten years of her career, she worked for publishing and bookselling firms in a variety of editorial, publicity and production positions, and under the pseudonym 'Edward Lane' she edited thirteen issues of the literary quarterly, the *Windmill*. While employed as assistant editor at *John O'London's Weekly*, she met STEVIE SMITH and later IVY COMPTON-BURNETT. Her friendship with these two writers led to what is her best-known work of non-fiction, *Ivy and Stevie: Ivy Compton-Burnett and Stevie Smith: Conversations and Reflections* (1971), a revealing and personal record of the work and characters of the two women. In addition to her novels, *By the Lake* (1949), *Young Man* (1951), *An Affair of Love* (1953), *Solitaire* (1958), *Sunday* (1962), *They: A Sequence in Unease* (1977) and *The Shelf* (1984), Dick published a work on the figure of Pierrot in the Commedia dell'Arte and edited several anthologies, ranging from the works of Edgar Allen Poe to interviews with writers gleaned from the *Paris Review*. Under the pseudonym 'Jeremy Scott', Dick compiled and edited numerous collections of stories of the fantastic, a subject which seems to hold a fascination for her, as well as works such as *Angels in Your Beer* (1979), *The Two Faces of Robert Just* (1980), *Hunted* (1980) and *Escape* (1981).

LCo

Dickens, Mary Angela 1863?–1948 British novelist born in London, the daughter of Charles Dickens Jr, the eldest son of the famous novelist. Her father had inherited the periodical *All the Year Round* from his own father upon his death in 1870, and Mary published her early stories in this journal. Mary Dickens produced most of her novels in her thirties – her most notable was *Cross Currents* (1891) which traces the unhappy progress of the love life of a young actress. *A Mere Cypher* followed in 1893, *A Valiant Ignorance* in 1894, and *Prisoners of Silence* in 1895. Dickens's style is sensational and sentimental, incorporating melodramatic revelations, murders and suicides. *Against the Tide* came out in 1897, and *On the Edge of a Precipice*, which deals with the exploitation of a young woman suffering from amnesia, in 1899. Dickens stopped writing fiction at the turn of the century.

CPe

Dickens, Monica 1915– British popular novelist, author of the 'Follyfoot' series. Her autobiographical *One Pair of Hands* (1939) traces her experiences as a cook-general, the only job her upbringing as a debutante had trained her for, she commented. During World War II she worked as nurse in a hospital, then in a munitions factory, finally returning to the source of her inspiration, a hospital. *Mariana* (1940) another semi-autobiographical work, followed, then *One Pair of Feet* (1942) – a hospital novel – and *The Fancy* (1943), based on aircraft factory work. Dickens contributed

Abby Morton Diaz: 'The welcome', illustration in *Lucy Maria*, 1874.

regularly to *Woman's Own* for twenty years, and worked with the RSPCA, from which derives her novel *Cobbler's Dream* (1963). The Samaritans were the inspiration for *The Listeners* (1970). Her writing springs from her work and her concern with social problems. *Kate and Emma* (1964) considers child abuse and *The Heart of the Islands* (1961) alcoholism and social deprivation. A contemporary interest in women's popular fiction has recently focused attention on Dickens's hospital novels where women wear a 'pure white halo' of a cap but refer to patients as 'Bladder Daddy' or a 'Gastric', thus injecting REALISM and humour into the representation of nurses as 'angels on the ward'. GW

Dickinson, Emily 1830–86 American poet. One of the great lyric poets of the English language, Emily Dickinson was born in Amherst, Massachusetts, a New England college town where her father was a prominent local lawyer. Highly educated for a woman of her era, Dickinson studied a modern curriculum of English and the sciences at Amherst Academy, then attended newly founded Mount Holyoke Female Seminary (later Mount Holyoke College) for a year before returning to Amherst, where she lived for the rest of her life, aside from short journeys. The informed, questioning intelligence and fearless emotional analysis of Dickinson's poetry contrast with a personal reticence that became reclusiveness: 'The Soul selects – her own Society' (*c.* 1862).

In the 1850s, New England culture had largely turned from Puritanism to the idealist Transcendentalism of Ralph Waldo Emerson, Henry David Thoreau and MARGARET FULLER. Dickinson loathed the 'magic prison' of Puritan belief, though some poems ambivalently long for heaven. She sometimes adopts Emerson's tropes of nature as transcendent 'Certainties of Sun – ', but other poems focus closely on the individual, often humble, object or act: a weed, a flower, the moment of death. Her pursuit of revelatory truth in object and act looks back to 17th-century metaphysical poets such as George Herbert, to Francis Quarles's *Emblems*, ANNE BRADSTREET and Edward Taylor. Like Shakespeare (a profound influence), she generated meaning through complex image clusters. Dickinson's short poems derived from ballad metre and the rhymed quatrain also link her poetics with hymnists such as Isaac Watts, and with children's poetry. When Dickinson fearfully asked Thomas Wentworth Higginson 'if my Verse is alive' in 1862, she was pushing out almost a poem a day, but knew that 'Civilization – spurns – the Leopard!' (the unconventional). Acknowledging her creative debt to female 'Tomes of solid witchcraft', Dickinson also identified strongly with contemporary women writers such as ELIZABETH BARRETT BROWNING, GEORGE ELIOT, the BRONTË sisters and GEORGE SAND.

Although she never married, Dickinson had passionately-felt relationships with both men and women. To bring her beloved friend Susan Gilbert closer, she urged her older brother Austin into his unhappy marriage with 'sister Sue'. Dickinson wrote poems of passion,

Emily Dickinson: extract from the 'fascicle' copy of her poem 'The Soul selects – her own Society', c. 1862, showing revisions.

poems whose speaker is bride or wife (she often wore an emblematic white dress). More depict anguish, loss, death: 'I felt a Funeral, in my Brain'; 'I heard a Fly buzz – when I died – '. The abject desire of her early 1860s 'Master' letters may have been addressed to the Revd Charles Wadsworth or the editor Samuel Bowles, but as Dickinson warned Higginson, 'when I state myself' as lyric speaker, it 'does not mean – me – but a supposed person'. Dickinson's broken or etiolated speaker (sometimes persona) acts as agency for the poems' drive toward pragmatic truths or paradoxes, their tone bitter, morbid, ironic, witty, playful or riddling.

Of Dickinson's 1,775 recorded poems, fewer than 20 were published during her lifetime. Abandoning the 'Auction' of publishing, she sent hundreds of poems to literary friends and family and also self-published, copying groups of poems into booklets or 'fascicles'. A posthumous poem selection by Higginson and Mabel Loomis Todd led to others, including her sparkling letters, but only since Thomas H. Johnson's 1955 edition of Dickinson's *Complete Poems* and his 1958 *Complete Letters* (with Theodora Ward), has her writing been fully available as she wrote it. Reading Dickinson is thus a modern act. Dickinson's condensed, image-studded line anticipates 20th-century imagist poetry, though her range is greater. Her terse ambiguities are inexorably 'modern', and her work, now widely read, has impacted powerfully on women poets such as SYLVIA PLATH and ADRIENNE RICH. HM

Didion, Joan 1934– Essayist and novelist whose cool intelligence has distinctively mapped the political and social cultures of America, particularly of her native California. Alert to the state's dignity and history – she comes from five generations of Californians on her mother's side – she is also blade-sharp on the absurdities and dangers of its excesses.

After working at *Vogue* in the 1950s she published her first novel, *Run River*, in 1963. The precision and acuteness of the essays in SLOUCHING TOWARDS BETHLEHEM (1968) established her as one of America's pre-eminent prose stylists; the title piece is a characteristically sceptical account of 1960s Haight-Ashbury culture. Her two 1970s novels, PLAY IT AS IT LAYS and A *Book of Common Prayer* (featuring her habitual atmosphere of ominous malaise and troubled female characters) were staple fictions of the American intelligentsia.

In 1964 she married the writer John Gregory Dunne, and they adopted a daughter, Quintana. Though the marriage had rocky periods, which Didion chronicled ('Writers are always selling somebody out', is a line of hers frequently quoted) they went on to become a major Hollywood couple, collaborating on screenplays including *Panic in Needle Park* (1971) and several on which little of their original work survived (*A Star is Born* and 1996's *Up Close and Personal*).

The 1980s found her exploring the extreme political cultures of Central America and Cuban exiles – in *Salvador*, *Democracy* (a novel) and *Miami*. ('Joan never writes about a place that's not hot', says Dunne.) She has described her own politics as a kind of highly moral libertarianism which she traces to the frontier mentality of her Sacramento origins. Her 1992 essays *After Henry* (*Sentimental Journeys* in the UK) probed the intersections of media, entertainment and politics; the book contains a searing reading of the culture of the Reagan White House. She observes with fascination the way democracy is perverted – the web of Iran-Contra conspiracies complicates the terse thriller *The Last Thing He Wanted* (1996), her first novel for twelve years. 'I'm a nag', she has said. 'I always think that I'm going to tell people exactly what's going on, and that they're going to listen.'   SB

Dike, Fatima (Royline) 1948– South African playwright, poet and short-story writer. She was born and grew up in Langa, Cape Town. In 1962 she was sent to St Anne's Catholic boarding school at Modimong where she discovered the English classics and read voraciously. She then attended Bafokeng High School in Phokeng. After matriculating she returned to Langa and worked in the family butchery and general store. In 1975 she began work as a stage manager at the Space Theatre – the first non-racial theatre in Cape Town. She began writing in response to the violence and oppression she saw around her in South Africa.

Her first play, *The Sacrifice of Kreli* (1978), was written during the student uprisings of 1976. It tells of the final stages of the Gcaleka people's resistance against the British in the Frontier Wars and contains allegorical references to the South Africa of the seventies. Her second play, *The First South African* (1979), is about a young man whose mother is black and biological father white. At first it seems he symbolizes the ideal citizen of a post-apartheid South Africa but then it becomes clear that he is a selfish opportunist who never really establishes a worthwhile identity. *The Crafty Tortoise*, performed in 1978, is a satirical piece where the native birds get their reward and the tortoise who tries to do them out of their birthright is brought to justice. *The Glasshouse* was first performed at the Space Theatre in 1979 and examines the meeting and clashing of cultures in a relationship between a middle-class, black woman and a rich, white woman.

Her poetry and short stories have been anthologized in various publications and include the poem 'Langa, My Love' in *Siren Songs* (1989), depicting the warm, happy years of growing up in Langa.   GMS

Dilke, Emilia (Francis Strong), Lady 1840–1904 British art historian who was born into a prosperous army family. She studied drawing at South Kensington and throughout her life knew many eminent men and women of letters. She published widely on French art, arguing for the relationship between artistic productions and wider political and philosophical movements. Her *Art in the Modern State* (1888) maintained that Renaissance ideals in 17th-century France had been checked by a redeveloping political absolutism. *French Painters of the XVIIIth Century* (1899) was the first of a series of books which examined how 'artistic development . . . corresponded to the renewal of human ideals by which the eighteenth century was distinguished'. Emilia Dilke was a prominent campaigner for trades unions for women from the 1870s, deploring the breakdown of family life she saw caused by poor wages. The posthumous *Book of the Spiritual Life* (1905) revealed her mystical interests and her belief that 'self-renunciation' was part of 'every call to lead the higher life'. She married Mark Pattison, Rector of Lincoln College, Oxford, in 1861 but the marriage was unhappy. He died in 1884 and, a year later, she married Sir Charles Dilke whose social fortunes, damaged by his divorce case, she spent much time trying to restore.
                                                    FJO'G

Dillard [née Doak], Annie 1945– North American poet, journalist and writer of inspirational autobiographical prose. She married the writer Richard Henry Wilde Dillard but divorced him in 1975, marrying novelist Gary Clevidence in 1980. Her prose works, *Pilgrim at Tinker Creek* (1974, winner of a Pulitzer Prize) and *Teaching A Stone to Talk: Expeditions and Encounters* (1982), are meditations on the natural world. Other prose writings include *Holy the Firm* (1977), *Living by Fiction* (1982), *Encounters With Chinese Writers* (1985), *American Childhood* (1987) and *The Writing Life* (1989). *Tickets For A Prayer Wheel* (1974), a collection of poetry, expands on her fascination with nature and the spiritual. In this focus on the specific in nature and its relation to the profound, both her poetry and prose may be considered part of an American literary tradition which stretches from writers such as Ralph Waldo Emerson, Henry David Thoreau and EMILY DICKINSON, through Robert Frost and AMY CLAMPITT. Her writing reiterates the notion, stated in *Pilgrim at Tinker Creek*, that 'our life is a faint tracing on the surface of mystery', while also asserting that 'the surface of mystery is not smooth . . . nor does it fit together'.   RW

Dinesen, Isak 1885–1962 Danish novelist and short-story writer, writing from 1934 on in English and translating her own works into Danish. Other pseudonyms: 'Pierre Andrezel', 'Tania B', 'Osceola'. Dinesen was born Karen Blixen (called 'Tanne' by her family) in Rungsted, Denmark, the daughter of Wilhelm Dinesen (an army officer who had been present at the Paris Commune, who had wandered alone in the North American wilderness, and who also wrote, under his own name and an Indian pseudonym, 'Boganis') and Ingeborg Westenholz. Wilhelm Dinesen committed suicide when Karen was 10 years old. Karen Blixen married her cousin, Baron Bror Blixon, in Finecke in 1914. From 1913 to 1921 she and Bror managed a coffee plantation in Kenya. After their divorce in 1921, Dinesen ran the farm herself until forced out by failing coffee prices in 1931. After the collapse of the farm and the death of her dashing lover, Denys Finch-Hatton, Dinesen returned to Denmark and began to write the brooding romances that would become the standard of her career. During World War II, Dinesen helped Jews to escape Hitler by opening her family estate at Rungstedlund as a 'runaway station'. Her later years were marked by chronic pain and a series of surgeries which, though they left her an emaciated invalid, did not prevent world renown and a triumphant tour of the United States in 1959. In 1962 Dinesen became a founding member of the Danish Academy. She died on 7 September of the same year in the home in which she was born.

Perhaps 'story-teller' would be the aptest description of her talents, which created a world of subterranean, mysterious forces more akin to mythology or medieval ROMANCE than to standard MODERNIST fiction. Most of her stories have intimately to do with the search for true identity, a concern which may also be reflected in her multiplicity of pen names. The acuity of her visual imagery and the compelling nature of her narrative gifts have allowed three of her works to date – *The Immortal Story*, *Out of Africa* and *Babette's Feast* – to be adapted into major motion pictures.

Other important publications include a play, *Sandhedens Haevn* (*The Revenge of Truth*), performed at the Royal Theatre, Copenhagen (1936); SEVEN GOTHIC TALES (1934), OUT OF AFRICA (*Den Afrikanske Farm*; 1937); *Winter's Tales* (1942); *The Ways of Retribution* (pseudonym: 'Pierre Andrezel'; 1944); *Babette's Feast* (1952); *Last Tales* (1957); *Anecdotes of Destiny* (1958). There are in addition a number of reviews and periodical publications, and a series of radio interviews collected under the title *Daguerreotypes* (1951).   DH

Dinner at the Homesick Restaurant (1982)

The ongoing traumas and undeniably strong bonds within dysfunctional families are once again the main concern of ANNE TYLER's ninth novel. As Pearl Tull lies dying, octogenarian and blind, the narrative of her youth, marriage and her three children's lives unravels in retrospect. The novel's structure pays homage to the polyphonies of VIRGINIA WOOLF's THE WAVES (1931)

and Faulkner's *As I Lay Dying* (1930) as each chapter switches perspective from one family member to another. The resulting multiplicity of character, event and point-of-view makes the novel more complex and less sentimental than her earlier fiction: everybody is 'weighted with other people's stories'. The leitmotivs of the Tull family are a bow-and-arrow accident, the father's desertion, and a ritualistic dinner that gets eternally deferred. 'Homesick' means sick *of* as well as sick *for* home and becomes metonymic for the conflicting desires Tyler's eccentric yet ordinary characters represent: neurotically saintly or understandably caddish, stiflingly domestic or forever on-the-road, nostalgically longing for the stability of blood ties or imprisoned by behavioural patterns. PUR

Diski, Jenny 1947–

British novelist, widely respected for her formidable intelligence and coolly disturbing narratives. Her own traumatic childhood, involving neglect, abuse and a nervous breakdown, has had a powerful impact on her work, causing her to return repeatedly to the themes of damage, fractured identity and psychic pain. At 14, she was rescued from a psychiatric hospital in Hove by DORIS LESSING, whose son had known Diski at school. She lived with her for four years and has acknowledged Lessing as an influence on her work.

In her controversial and shocking first novel, NOTHING NATURAL (1986), Diski portrays a woman caught up in a powerfully addictive sado-masochistic relationship. In her second, *Rainforest* (1987), she continues the theme of sexual obsession, intertwined with an exploration of solitude and chaos.

Diski's ideas about the patterns and beliefs that individuals construct to ward off chaos are further developed in *Then Again* (1990), which juxtaposes the life of a contemporary artist with that of a 14th-century Pole and victim of pogroms. It raises questions about faith, morality and the nature of time, revealing a vision that is profoundly pessimistic. This culminates in the choice of narrator for her third novel, *Like Mother* (1988): Nony, the baby without a brain, a potent symbol of emptiness and negation.

As if to anticipate accusations of unrelenting bleakness, Diski moves into new territory in her fifth novel, *Happily Ever After* (1991), a black comedy depicting a love affair in unconventional circumstances. Her themes remain the same, but her more recent fiction reveals an increasing preoccupation with the bizarre and a heightened sense of irony. A grim humour and sardonic wit pervade her next novel, *Monkey's Uncle* (1994), in which a grieving mother retreats to a strange internal world, and her short stories, *The Vanishing Princess* (1995), which involve weird excursions into wildly diverse worlds. *The Dream Mistress* (1996) is a return to more sombre form, a multi-layered exploration of dreams, identity and madness. 'I don't feel compelled to tell comfortable stories' Diski has said, 'For me, the fragmented narrative rings truer.' In 1997 she completed a non-fiction work, *Skating to Antarctica*. Part travelogue, part memoir, it continues to explore the links between fantasy and memory, families and sanity.　　　　　　　　　　　　　　　　　　　　CP

Dispossessed: An Ambiguous Utopia, The (1974)

In this SCIENCE-FICTION novel which won the Nebula, Jupiter and Hugo Awards, URSULA LE GUIN's narrative shifts through time and space in a manner that parallels her male protagonist's theory of a 'unified sequency and simultaneity of time'. The physicist, Shevek, leaves his home planet of Annares to develop his research on the sister world of Urras. Le Guin depicts two divergent worlds: Urras's capitalist society has extremes of wealth and poverty while the revolutionists who populate Urras's moon, Annares, live by anarchist/socialist theories of individual freedom aligned with the good of the whole. Le Guin's political and philosophical novel contrasts the paradoxes entrenched in both societies through flashbacks of the hardships suffered by Shevek on the arid Annares, while he enjoys the luxuries of the fertile Urras. She portrays Shevek's physical and spiritual voyage between the two worlds as a moral and psychological quest when finally he is forced to choose between his scientific career and his moral obligation to help the suffering under-class of Urras.　　JP

Divakaruni, Chitra 1956–

Poet and novelist who was born in Calcutta and moved to the United States at the age of 19. She received her degree in English from Wright State University in Ohio, and a Ph.D. from the University of California at Berkeley, also in English. She lives in San Francisco with her husband and two sons and teaches creative writing at Foothill College. For several years she has worked with battered and refugee women.

She has written several books of poetry: *Dark Like the River* and *The Reasons for Nasturtiums* (1990), and *Black Candles: Poems About Women from India, Pakistan and Bangladesh* (1991).

In 1995 she published the collection of short stories ARRANGED MARRIAGE which won critical acclaim and the 1996 American Book Award. These stories portray migrant Indians in America who are on the brink of decisive change. Their lives, poised on a fragile balance between old Indian dutifulness and free American spirit, will undergo a dramatic but positive transformation. Divakaruni succeeds in rendering the kaleidoscopic reality of migrant lives in a crafted prose.

Her first novel, *Mistress of Spices* (1997), combines the real magic of myth and the harsh urban language of American cities. It is a tale told by Tilo, a young Indian woman living in California who has been trained in the secret power of spices. She uses them to help out the local Indian women whose life stories swirl around her shop.　　　　　　　　　　　　　　　　　　　SPo

Diver [née Marshall], (Katharine) Maud (Helen)

1867–1945 British novelist, short-story writer, journalist and historian, whose work often explores the complexity of Anglo-Indian relationships. Born in India, into the family of a British officer in the Indian Army, she returned to the country of her birth following her education in England, and married a British Army officer herself in 1890. They left India in 1896 to live in England, but she maintained her connections with the country through her writing and through a wide circle of friends.

She was a popular and prolific writer who made her name with the first of her 'Indian Frontier Novels', *Captain Desmond VC* (1907). Despite the romantic theme in much of her fiction, she exposes matters of concern at a turbulent time in the history of the Raj – *Candles in the Wind* (1909) and *Lilamani* (1911) question racial intolerance and the fear of miscegenation. Of her works of non-fiction, *The Englishwoman in India* (1909) defends the British memsahib whilst also paying tribute to six Indian women, including CORNELIA SORABJI; and her final work, *The Unsung* (1944), celebrates the achievements of British engineers who constructed Indian roads and railways.　　JSte

Diviners, The (1974)

MARGARET LAURENCE's richest and most ambitious novel about her fictional town of Manawaka begins with the novelist Morag Gunn living beside a river that 'flowed both ways'. The story moves forward and back, probing early experiences that shaped her creativity, as well as witnessing the further unfolding of her adult life. The text is structured from short 'snapshots', 'memory-bank movies', stories Morag has been told, as well as tightly knit narration. Like other Laurence heroines, Morag's quest has been to shed her small-town prejudices and to appreciate the bizarre and loveable in the social outcasts around her, as well as to forge connections to her cultural history as a child of Red River Settlers. Jules Tonnerre, her first lover, becomes in some sense a model for this cultural search, and his Métis family story and songs about his heritage finally inspire Pique, the daughter he has fathered and whom Morag has brought up alone, to undertake her own quest. 'Look ahead into the past', thinks Morag at the end of the novel, 'and back into the future, until the silence.' She then returns to her house to 'set down her title', giving the search the dignity of divining. Silence follows: this was Margaret Laurence's last novel.　　FD

Dix, Dorothea Lynde 1802–87 American reformer. Raised in an extremely hard environment of religious zealotry and poverty, Dix left her parents when she was 12 to live with her grandmother in Boston. There she was educated and began teaching at the age of 15. Frailty and intermittent ill health forced her to limit her teaching, and to intersperse it with writing and travel. In 1824, she published the science textbook, *Conversations on Common Things*, which went through sixty editions. But it was in 1841, when she began teaching Sunday School at the East Cambridge House of Correction and saw the appalling conditions in which the inmates lived, that she found her true calling. She began publishing newspaper articles and lecturing all around the country, touring institutions wherever she went and agitating for better conditions for the inmates of prisons, asylums and poorhouses. Her detailed and thorough *Memorial to the Legislature of Massachusetts* (1843) resulted in an improved state institution for the mentally ill, and began her tour of the country, advocating change from state to state. She was made superintendent of Union nurses during the Civil War, but returned to touring the country's asylums and institutions until ill health finally forced her retirement in 1881 to the Trenton Hospital, the first state hospital she helped to found. SP

Dixie, Lady Florence 1857–1905 British TRAVEL WRITER, journalist, novelist and energetic social campaigner for causes ranging from Zulu nationalism, to Irish home rule, to women's rights, to vegetarianism. The youngest child of the 7th Marquess of Queensbury who died when she was 3, she spent an unconventional girlhood wandering around Europe and riding and hunting on equal terms with her brothers. After marrying Alexander Beaumont Churchill Dixie in 1875 and having two sons, she joined her husband on an expedition to South America, recounted in *Across Patagonia* (1880). Later she travelled to South Africa to report on the Boer War peace negotiations for the *Morning Post*; her observations were published as *In the Land of Misfortune* (1882).

She blended her activism with her literary talents in *Gloriana, or, The Revolution of 1900* (1890), a dream novel whose heroine resolves to tell little girls about 'all the wrongs that girls and women have to suffer, and . . . bid them rise as one to right these wrongs'. Gloriana assumes a male identity in order to pursue a gentleman's education at Eton and Cambridge before going on to become prime minister and introduce legislation to correct the inequality of the sexes. MAD

Dixon, Ella Hepworth 1855–1932 English fiction and TRAVEL WRITER, born in London, the daughter of William Hepworth Dixon (editor of the *Athenaeum*) and his wife, Marion (an occasional journalist). Details of her early life with her well-connected family are given in *'As I Knew Them': Sketches of People I Have Met Along the Way* (1930), which includes accounts of Oscar Wilde, Robert Browning, Henry James and George Meredith.

Dixon contributed short stories and travel pieces to the *World*, *Pall Mall Gazette*, *Ladies' Pictorial*, *Ladies' Field* and the *Yellow Book*, and began editing the eclectic journal the *Englishwoman* in 1895. Her early career was combined with a hectic social life: 'These journalistic activities were mixed up with a great deal of dancing and dining out; white tulle skirts and natty little laced-up bodices took the place of an evening of inky fingers.' In 1892, under the pseudonym 'Margaret Wynman', Dixon published *My Flirtations*, a series of comic sketches which light-heartedly examines women's economic imperative to secure a good marriage, a subject which is seen in a more troubling light in the short stories of *One Doubtful Hour, and Other Sidelights in the Feminine Temperament* (1904). Dixon is best known for THE STORY OF A MODERN WOMAN (1894), a harrowing account of a woman's attempts to survive economically and emotionally when left alone after her father's death. A tale of valiant and unrewarded courage, the novel's only hope for redemption is in women's helping each other to survive in a society which is founded on the 'acquiescent feminine smile'. GM

Dixon, Sarah fl. 1740 English poet of obscure origin, an annotated edition of her sole published work, *Poems on Several Occasions* (1740 in Canterbury), provides biographical detail and several poems, including a clipping of one, 'The Ruins of St Austin', which appeared in the Kentish Gazette in 1774. Subscribers to the *Poems* included Alexander Pope and ELIZABETH CARTER, and members of Dixon's niece's family, the De l'Angles. She received 'friendly correction' from her nephew John Bunce, vicar of St Stephen's near Canterbury, who encouraged her to turn her 'Employment of a youth of much Leisure' into a published volume. Pastoral verse and pious reflection, the poems in this collection reflect knowledge of classical literature and mythology and a concern for contemporary politics. Like many women poets of this period, she expresses loyalty to the House of Stuart – Charles I is 'the Saint, the Patriot, and the Prince' – and turns a satiric eye on the vanities of the present era. Humour, wit and an awareness of the everyday punctuate more conventional themes. Her 'A Receipt for an Extraordinary Dish' exploits a specifically female genre to enumerate the ingredients – 'little pumps, silk stockings', and 'a pound of powder' – of 'this thing we call a Beau'. JRS

Do With Me What You Will (1973) Set in the Detroit legal and media world of the 1960s and 1970, JOYCE

CAROL OATES's apparently sprawling novel explores the metaphysical idea that – as Elena, its beautiful, terminally withdrawn heroine puts it – 'all victims are guilty'. The startling rigour with which this Kafkaesque premise is pursued transforms dialogue and reportage alike – all social surfaces – into the meeting point of private dreams: tabloid dreams, largely, of rape and murder. Elena, her beauty created for profit by her mother and sold on to her husband, is the point at which this provincial society shows its real form. Refracted through the alienation of her absolute passivity, we view the dynamic careers of Elena's ex-model and hustler Mother, Ardis, who reinvents herself as a TV interviewer, her powerful top establishment lawyer husband Marvin Howe, and her lover, Jack Morissey, a tormented, idealistic ex-Civil Rights lawyer, as an insane and dangerous form of sleepwalking, which poses as 'normality'. The novel's title, taken from the legal plea of *nolo contendere* summarizes this metaphorical logic: offering absolutely no resistance, Elena awaits her own absolute destruction.   VS

Dobson, Rosemary (de Brissac) 1920– Australian

poet who has been admired as one of the country's finest poets since the appearance of her first volume of verse, IN A CONVEX MIRROR, in 1944, and throughout her distinguished fifty-year publishing career. Dobson was born in Sydney, educated in that city and at the Frensham School in Mittagong, and is now a long-term resident of Canberra, the Australian national capital. Dobson's father was the son of the 19th-century English poet Austin Dobson, and her sister Ruth was the first Australian woman career diplomat. In 1951, Dobson married Alexander Thorley Bolton (1926-96), whom she met when both worked with the Australian publishers, Angus and Robertson. Bolton's lifelong career in publishing culminated in the establishment of his own fine press, Brindabella Press, which published Dobson's *Untold Lives* in 1992. Dobson and Bolton shared a passion for art, design and printing, with Dobson studying under distinguished printmaker Thea Proctor in her youth and continuing her own art practice throughout her writing career and the raising of three children. Dobson's early artistic training informs much of her poetry. Many of her poems begin in contemplation of particular paintings, or are about the aesthetics and poetics of art. These ostensibly aesthetic considerations are very often implicated in Dobson's concerns with aspects of women's lives, including birth, grief and the vexed and complex relationship with what she calls her 'distaff side: / My mother, hers, and the long line backwards of women'.

Rosemary Dobson has been the recipient of many prestigious awards, including the Patrick White Award in 1984 (the year of her seventh major collection, THE THREE FATES), an Order of Australia in 1987, and both an Australia Council Emeritus Award and an Honorary Doctor of Letters from the University of Sydney in 1996. In addition to more than a dozen volumes of her own verse (one of which, *Child With a Cockatoo*, was translated into French and acclaimed by French critics), Dobson also published two volumes of 'versions' of Russian poems with her friend and colleague David Campbell in the 1970s, a novel for young adults, and several monographs and lengthy criticisms on Australian painting.   MLA

Dods, Mary Diana ('David Lyndsay') *c.*1791–*c.*1830

The illegitimate, erudite, freakishly masculine-looking daughter of a Scottish peer. She assumed a male authorial identity (1821–8), publishing in *Blackwood's Magazine* and literary annuals. *Dramas of the Ancient World* (1821), which remarkably, but without plagiarism, coincided in subject with Byron's contemporaneous *Cain* and *Sardanapalus*, brought her to the attention of the Shelley–Byron circle. Despite differing politics, Dods became (*c.*1825) the friend of MARY SHELLEY, who (1827) actively helped her to elope to Paris, in male attire, with a mutual friend, Isabella Robinson; the couple passed as 'Mr and Mrs Sholto Douglas'. Dods's *Tales of the Wild and the Wonderful* (1825) participated in the 1820s popularization of German fairy-tale. Until 1978, 'Lyndsay' was thought to be George Borrow; Betty Bennett's biography (1991) illuminated her life and career.   NC

Domestic Manners Of The Americans (1832)

FANNY TROLLOPE's first published work, a lively account of her protracted stay and travels in America. The first part deals with her stay in Cincinnati, but does not mention her business failure there, and the second with her wanderings in some of the eastern states. She set out for America with 'a little leaning to sedition', but returned an unenthusiastic conservative. Her comments on a more democratic society were of particular interest to an England then in the throes of debating an extension to the franchise.

Trollope's most memorable comments stem from her frontier experiences and her encounters with the uncultured masses rather than the sophisticated élite. She strongly deprecated the widespread habit of tobacco spitting. She noted and deplored the segregation of the sexes, which she saw as coarsening men and encouraging frivolity and prudery in women. She evinced a fascinated horror of evangelical Christianity and fundamentalist religion, and criticized the humbug of a people who boasted of liberty and freedom but saw no wrong in slavery and the confiscation of ancient tribal lands. But she admired what she could, was charmed by Washington and New York, and had a Romantic's eye for the flora and fauna and the grandeur of the landscape.   CT

domestic novel As its Latin source (*domesticus*; *domus*) suggests, 'domestic' signifies of/belonging to the home, house or household; accordingly, the English domestic novel, which sets the model for the genre in other literatures in English, portrays the social relations and daily life of a contained community – house, village, urban parish.

In the 18th century, as economic changes created the leisured middle-class woman, women writers, encouraged by the increased accessibility of books through subscription, devised fictional worlds that mirrored the lives of their readers. Inspired by conduct manuals, which catered to the emerging classes' desire for social guidance and household management, they valorized and codified the domestic and the feminine. The '3 or 4 Families in a Country Village' AUSTEN claims as 'the very thing to work on' sets the scene for her eccentric heroines' unpredictable responses to their scripted lives. Turning to dialogue, free indirect discourse, irony and understatement rather than descriptive summary, Austen refined narrative techniques that subsequently characterized the domestic novel.

In the Victorian period, ELIZABETH GASKELL'S gently ironic portrait of the 'elegant economy' of women in the quiet village of Cranford, and Anthony Trollope's dissection of clerical mores in the 'Barsetshire' novels continued the tradition. In the 1850s, as the decline of traditional, religious values roused their defence, CHARLOTTE YONGE, D.M. CRAIK and MARGARET OLIPHANT offered submissive heroines enshrined in the home, both sanctuary and moral centre. In GEORGE ELIOT'S and Charles Dickens's exposure of middle-class life and the interface of public with private world, we encounter a form of domestic REALISM. By the 1860s as the vogue of SENSATION fiction swept the country, the home became the repository of unsavoury secrets, and the family a structure of coercion. Reverting to Austen's preoccupation with manners, Henry James and EDITH WHARTON focused their attention on upper middle-class society and the consequences of marriage and money.

By the early 20th century, domestic novelists inspired by the NEW WOMAN and the SUFFRAGETTE movement made marriage the subject of rather than the solution to the plot (ADA LEVERSON, *The Little Ottleys*; E.M. Forster, *Howard's End*) and (re)viewed the household from the 'odd' perspective of the spinster, unwed mother or middle-aged wife. Between the World wars, while *Good Housekeeping* and the proliferation of suburbs beckoned the middle-class woman back into the home, E.M. DELAFIELD, Jan Struthers, E.H. YOUNG and IVY COMPTON-BURNETT directed a wry gaze upon the daily routine of the household. In the detective novels of AGATHA CHRISTIE, NGAIO MARSH and MARGERY ALLINGHAM, the sanctity of the home was threatened and then re-established. Although a MODERNIST experimentalist like VIRGINIA WOOLF did not shy away from incorporating domestic-novel conventions (dailiness, household tasks), other high modernists (Eliot, Pound) and the writers of social protest (Orwell, Auden, Spender), in their horror of domesticity, brushed aside the domestic novel. Thus, talented novelists (ROSAMOND LEHMANN, F.M. MAYOR, MAY SINCLAIR, SYLVIA TOWNSEND WARNER), although popular in their day, languished on the library shelves until recovered by Virago reprints. Writing after World War II ELIZABETH TAYLOR, BARBARA PYM, Molly Panter-Downes and Betty Miller viewed marriage, motherhood and war's disruption of the home through delicately structured and muted narratives.

In the aftermath of the 1970s feminist critique of the institution of marriage and housework, a more savage and POSTMODERN version of domesticity emerged in ALICE THOMAS ELLIS's mysticism, FAY WELDON's satire, ELIZABETH JANE HOWARD's 'Cazalet' chronicle, and ANITA BROOKNER's anatomy of solitude. The popular 'aga-sagas' of the 1990s, as penned by JOANNA TROLLOPE and her imitators, gestured toward the middle-aged woman's quest for fulfilment against a semi-rural backdrop where the well-equipped kitchen has replaced the Victorian hearth.　　KM/CBr

Don't Never Forget (1966) BRIGID BROPHY prefaced her first collection of print and broadcast essays with a characteristically vigorous declamation – 'as a matter of fact, my journalism *is* serious writing' – a tenet which is exemplified in the precision of her style as much as in the volume's subject matter. Contemporary perceptions of Brophy as an impassioned iconoclast were largely drawn from her deconstruction of received concepts of nature versus civilization. She deduced (notoriously) that women are more suited to polygamy than men, and one of her demands was for a new morality in marriage. From euphemism to pornography, her essays oppose censorship and are sharply aware of the relationship of language to morality. A follower of Freud and a fan of Wilde, Brophy states that 'wit is always some form of analysis'; her own *bon mots* illuminating as they amuse. She describes JANE AUSTEN's ivory as 'in fact a tusk, with which she gores deep into the essence of everything'. *Don't Never Forget* reveals Brophy herself to be more than a social commentator: an informed genre theorist and an incisive literary and cultural critic whose tastes and principles – like those of Shaw, another hero – are not determined by fashion.　　TY

Don't Take Your Love to Town (1988) The first book by RUBY LANGFORD [GINIBI] offered a new kind of autobiography – that of a working-class Australian

Aborigine who was part of the movement of Aborigines to the cities in the 1960s (see AUSTRALIAN ABORIGINAL LIFE-WRITING). The autobiography adopts a yarning style as Ruby tells the reader about the delights and trials of her life – growing up in rural northern New South Wales, marrying young to live an itinerant life around the countryside, and eventually moving to Sydney. The book provides a rare glimpse of conditions for rural workers in Australia in the years since World War II, and a strong account of the difficulties of Aboriginal people living in the inner city.

The familiar style invites readers to share Ruby's concern about her children and the importance of maintaining her family, but she challenges the values of white middle-class Australians with cheerful accounts of her various sexual liaisons. Her growing political awareness brings the autobiography to confront the problems of continued Aboriginal poverty and black deaths in custody.   SPL

Dooley, Maura 1958– British poet who grew up in Bristol, studied at York University, ran the Arvon Centre at Lumb Bank and the Literature Programme at the South Bank Centre and now lives in London as a freelance writer.

Dooley's often noted subtlety is, in fact, an unusual receptiveness. Her poems are alive with barely perceptible resonances, connections and signs. *Explaining Magnetism* (1991) is full of the paraphernalia of communication – bridges, telephones, airwaves and maps. These can also mislead or obstruct, leaving cities divided, people lost, calls unanswered and sentences suspended.

Dooley is always conscious of what goes into her surroundings. Her 1980s London is shaped by the enterprise culture, the rats in the Underground 'scratching over what's left'. Poems about Ireland explore current political tensions as well as immigration and collective disinheritance.

The gentleness of Dooley's voice comes from her careful handling of powerful feeling which, nonetheless, can erupt:

In the fiercest summer for years
gouts of sun sour milk in an hour,
rubbish simmers in streets which
steam with piss, swimming pools
pulse like tins of maggots
and all the time your postcards come.   ('Drought')

Kissing a Bone (1996) shows Dooley allowing herself more of this level of intensity. Her subjects are more charged: the stakes are higher, faith is more elusive and so means more when it can be found. Dooley concentrates her eye and voice to make powerful use of these tighter pespectives.   LG

Doolittle, Hilda, see H. D.

Dorcey, Mary 1950– Irish writer born in Dublin, who won the Rooney Prize for Irish Literature with her 1989 volume of stories, *A Noise from the Woodshed*, and succeeded in her desire to write of what she calls 'this second Ireland, this concealed Ireland, this Ireland that up to now has been silenced by emigration'. She has also been an important Irish feminist activist, being a founder in 1975 of the Women's Movement group, Irishwomen United.

Widely published in journals and anthologies, she has produced three published volumes of poems – *Kindling* (1982), *Moving Into the Space Cleared by Our Mothers* (1991) and *The River That Carries Me* (1995). Her sinuous voice explores the emotional nuances of a wide range of women's lives as lovers, citizens and friends, paying unusual homage to older women:

we daughters follow after
each one of us
moving into the space
cleared by our mothers.

Writing the ordinary moments of daily lesbian life, Dorcey wants the 'freedom to write openly about the subject [of lesbianism] in one's work, without it becoming one's whole identity', to write of women who are not condemned to having either a 'secret life or a notorious one'. Her special achievement, however, is writing lives of passion, as in this joyous coming together in *A Noise from the Woodshed*: 'And lying up there in the loft preoccupied with skin and bone and the in-between, you eventually got round to talking about all this, your tongues at last free to talk, the willows winding below, the sky flying in through the rafters, the goats bleating at the gate, you thought of all the others like this: the day and the women having them . . . more and more women having them – these days of languor and insurrection, armed to the teeth and undressed to kill, riding about backstreets and country lanes rescuing each other from race, class and creed.' Her 1997 novel, *Biography of Desire,* is a lyrical meditation on passion, love, betrayal, written in spellbinding counterpoint as two lovers wait for the decision of the third they both love.   CStP

Dorsey, Sarah Anne [Ellis] 1829–79 American novelist from the South who wrote popular fiction. Born on her parents' plantation in Natchez, Mississippi, Dorsey grew up among the southern planter aristocracy. After receiving a liberal education, she later married and settled on a plantation in Louisiana. Her first novel, *Agnes Graham* (1863), was serialized in the *Southern Literary Messenger* in 1863 and was later published in book form. She also published a biography of Louisiana's Confederate governor, Henry

Watkins Allen, in 1866. During the Civil War, the Dorseys' home was burned, and she and her husband retreated to Texas, an experience that inspired the fictional account in her novel *Lucia Dare* (1867). After the death of her husband, Dorsey returned to Mississippi to reside in a family estate where Jefferson Davis became her guest while he wrote *Rise and Fall Of the Confederate Government* (1881). Dorsey also published *Athalie* (1872), and her most famous novel, *Panola, A Tale of Louisiana* (1877), which depicts the life of a biracial heroine of white and native American descent. Her novels resemble much of the popular fiction of her time, incorporating intricate plots and subplots, disguises and mistaken identities, often all revolving around a central love plot.   CJ

Doudney, Sarah 1842–1926 British novelist and hymn-writer. The youngest daughter of G.E. Doudney, a Portsmouth soap-manufacturer whose family held strong religious convictions, she began to write when very young. Her subjects were pious in the extreme, and her early work was published by the Sunday School Union. In 1871 *Psalms of Life*, a collection of sixty hymns, appeared, as did *Under Grey Walls*, the first of a considerable number of stories published in the next thirty years. In many of these, illness, bereavement, death and repentance were paramount, but, at a time when the feminine world was in a state of seismic upheaval, she makes no reference to current agitation, the Rights of Women Convention, Mrs Bloomer or the ultimate liberator, the bicycle, apart from one reference to it as 'stealthy'.

In later years she wrote romantic stories for girls such as *Thy Heart's Desire* (1888), *Katherine's Keys* (1896) and *The Vanished Hand* (1896). Her style had become more robust and less proselytizing, but she still preferred a clergyman or preacher as hero, a rectory background and a suffering heroine. Edward Salmon in *The Nineteenth Century* says 'Her stories have little plot, characters and nature constitute her chief stock-in-trade.' Nevertheless she had a considerable vogue: some of her books reached several editions and eighty-seven items of her work are recorded. Her outstanding gift lay in conveying vividly the beauty of the countryside.   MEW

Douglas, Amanda Minnie 1851–1916 American novelist and short-story writer born in New York City and educated privately and at City Institute. From the age of 18 she participated actively in literary societies and wrote stories to help support her family, publishing in the New York *Ledger*, the *Saturday Evening Post* and the *Lady's Friend*. Beginning with *In Trust* (1866), which sold 20,000 copies, she published at least a novel a year. Her fiction promoted 'NEW WOMANhood' and emerging ideals of female competence and independence, while reinforcing domestic values. A recurring plot is one in which an impoverished heroine earns a new home through honest work: the heroine of *Home Nook* (1874) becomes an architect; in *Out of the Wreck* (1885) she becomes a businesswoman. Douglas wrote three series for children; *Larry* (1893) won an award for children's fiction from *Youth's Companion*. Douglas was a friend of LOUISA MAY ALCOTT and served as vice president of the New Jersey Women's Press Club.   JSG

Douglas, O. [Anna Buchan] 1878–1948 Daughter of a Free-Church minister, this Scottish author never married. A happy childhood was succeeded by a young-womanhood spent helping her father with his parish work. Her early experience informs her writing and she freely admitted to having drawn many characters from life. She is especially successful in depicting children.

Most of her novels chronicle everyday life in Scottish homes at a time when the Victorian DOMESTIC ideal was becoming less and less workable. Yet whilst reflecting a world in which the number of good servants was perceived to be on the decline and in which investment income was indeed uncertain, where war challenged the verities of religion and where new employment opportunities were taking women away from full-time domestic careers, the novels advocate traditional religious and family values. All levels of society are depicted but the main focus is upon the upper middle class.

O. Douglas began her writing career in earnest with her second novel, *The Setons* (1917). Set in Glasgow, this often-amusing tale begins in 1913 and concludes amidst the uncertainty of World War I. It was a great success and she began to receive correspondence from Scottish exiles all over the world. Significantly, it was re-issued in 1942. Also notable amongst her works is *The Proper Place* (1926), a poignant tale set immediately after World War I. O. Douglas wrote twelve novels in all, three of which were re-issued in a single volume under the title *People Like Ourselves* (1938).   EMH

Dove, Rita 1952– American poet and novelist who achieved considerable recognition for her Pulitzer-Prize-winning book of poems, *Thomas and Beulah* (1986). The poems explore her grandparents' relationship, offering their lives as representative of African-American experience in the middle of this century.

Born in Akron, Ohio, Dove's education included studies at Tübingen in Germany and the Writers' Workshop at Iowa University. Fluent in German, Dove is noted for her affection for languages, and the talismanic qualities of voice and words are central preoccupations in her poetry. Her other collections include *The Yellow House on the Corner* (1980), *Mandolin* (1982) and *Museum* (1983). She published short stories in *Fifth Sunday* (1985) and a novel, in 1992, entitled

Sarah Doudney: an illustration to a story in *Lady's Realm*, 1897, which seems to equate Cupid with Satan.

Through the Ivory Gate. Grace Notes (1989), which won the Ohioan Award for 1990, takes its title from music: the notes added to a basic melody. The poems are thus variations, in imagery and voice – she is Saul, 'On the road to Damascus', then Medusa, a mother, a schoolchild with Buckeye fruit. Her lyric poems are noted for their rendering of human experiences, from childhood to classic mythological struggles, such as Persephone and Demeter who appear in *Motherlove* (1995), a book of verse-drama. Also published is a *Selected Poems* (1993), which won an Ohioan Award. Dove's success is exemplified not only as the first woman (and the first African-American) Poet Laureate of the United States, but also as the first person to hold the post for two terms: 1993–5. ACH

Dowie, Ménie Muriel 1866–1945 British TRAVEL WRITER and novelist. Dowie was educated in her home city, Liverpool, but also in Stuttgart and France. She was an intrepid traveller. In *A Girl in the Karpathians* (1891) she urges: 'Give your whims a loose rein, follow the promptings of that queer live soul in you which always retains its affinity to simpleness and green-growing things, and be prepared to be thought very odd when you come back.' Dowie edited *Women Adventurers: The Lives of Madame Velazquez, Hannah Snell, Maryanne Talbot and Mrs Christian Davies* (1893) (see HANNAH SNELL). Her NEW WOMAN novel *Gallia* (1895) is a feminist classic, highlighting the importance of eugenic theory at the FIN-DE-SIÈCLE. The heroine does not choose to marry for love, but selects 'a fine, strong, manly man, full of health and strength'. MARGARET OLIPHANT attacked *Gallia* in her article

'The Anti-Marriage League'. Dowie's contributions to the *Yellow Book* are reprinted in *Some Whims of Fate* (1897). *The Crook of the Bough*, a satirical novel of 1898, describes contemporary attitudes to women in Turkey. *Love and His Mask* (1901) concerns the Boer War. *Things About Our Neighbourhood* (1903) is a compilation of Dowie's writing in *Country Life*.

In 1891 Dowie married Sir Henry Norman, MP, but they divorced twelve years later. She lived in India with her second husband, Major Edward Fitzgerald. Versions of her later life differ: it has been said that she returned to England to breed cattle and sheep; another account states that she became a society hostess. SF

Down Among the Women (1971) FAY WELDON's second novel is a bitter-sweet domestic satire which revolves around the trials and tribulations of a group of nine women. It documents the destructive effects of accepting the suffocating limitations of prescribed female roles which encourage women to betray each other in order to survive in a male-dominated world. Weldon also addresses class issues by highlighting how middle-class women tend to overlook or collude in the oppression of their working-class sisters. The characters are all flawed, male and female alike, but Byzantia, the youngest of the women, born into the period of Women's Liberation, rejects the views and attitudes of the older generation and demonstrates that change is possible. The novel combines the first-person narration of one of the characters looking back over her life with the voice of a third-person omniscient narrator who offers a pithy and witty commentary on the action. EP

Downes, Cathy 1950– New Zealand writer–performer of *The Case of Katherine Mansfield*. Cathy Downes was trained at Toi Whakaari, the New Zealand Drama School, and is internationally known for her dramatic monologue compiled from the journals, letters and stories of KATHERINE MANSFIELD. It was first performed at Theater De Kikker in Utrecht, Holland, in 1978 and subsequently in Edinburgh, London, the USA, Australia and for the Mansfield centennial in New Zealand in 1988 – nearly 1,000 performances. The piece opens with Downes as K.M. standing on her head in dinner-suit and tails, and includes the telling of one of the best-known Mansfield stories, 'The Doll's House', part of 'Prelude' and others.

Downes's subsequent play, *Farewell Speech*, adapted from a novel by the same name by Rachel McAlpine, was written and performed for the centennial of women's suffrage in New Zealand in 1993. JD

Downie, Freda 1929–93 British poet born in London and educated in Northampton, Australia and Kent. She worked for music publishers and art agents for many years and only began publishing her poems in the 1970s, in limited editions. Her first pamphlet, *Night Music*, appeared in 1974. Two full collections established her reputation as a poet of sharp, controlling intelligence: *A Stranger Here* (1977) and *Plainsong* (1981). She lived in Berkhamsted with her husband, mother and (for a while) an aunt. Her jobs were part-time and unexacting. She had, in her own words, 'become domesticated'. Friendships with local poets, such as George Szirtes, sustained her through some bleak times (she suffered several breakdowns and debilitating bereavements). Szirtes edited her posthumous *Collected Poems* in 1995; his Introduction links her aesthetic to that of STEVIE SMITH and JANE AUSTEN, and she certainly writes with an unsettling, contemplative wisdom. DM

Dowse [née Rosenthal], Sara (Dale) 1938– Australian novelist whose experience as an American Australian from a Jewish family has encouraged her to address public and international issues from a personal perspective. She was born Dale Rosenthal in Chicago, Illinois, to an actress mother and lawyer father. After a time in New York, she moved to Los Angeles where her mother, who had been a communist, and scriptwriter stepfather were caught up in the McCarthy investigation. These experiences, and those of her Jewish grandparents, form the basis for her novel *Sapphires* (1994). In 1958 she married an Australian footballer, John Dowse, and migrated to Sydney. They had four children before the marriage ended in the early 1970s. From 1974 to 1978 she headed the Office of Women's Affairs in Canberra, advising the Prime Minister on policy related to women.

Dowse wrote her first novel, *West Block* (1983), on the basis of this experience as a 'femocrat'. She has since worked from time to time as a television and film writer as well as a journalist. She gave birth to a fifth child in 1980.

Dowse's novels *Schemetime* (1990), *Sapphires* and *Digging* (1996) explore aspects of memory and the way in which the past influences the present. In her early work, she resisted what she called 'writing for effect', and much of its appeal lies in its sense of honesty and directness. Her later work, particularly *Sapphires*, demonstrates a growing versatility and willingness to take stylistic risks. SPL

Drabble, Margaret 1939– English novelist and biographer. Born in the professional English middle class and educated at the Quaker's Mount School, York, and at Newnham College, Cambridge. Drabble came to prominence in the 1960s with five novels, whose deceptively light accounts of the mundane lives of women of her age and class spoke to the condition of many readers by refusing to idealize her heroines and their aspirations. She published her first novel, *A SUMMER BIRDCAGE*, in 1963; her second, THE GARRICK YEAR (1964) takes an unillusioned look at motherhood; and the heroine of *The Millstone* (1965) has her child, and never tells the gay man who drunkenly impregnated her that he is the father; she feels profound ambiguities about her decisions and the economic security that makes them possible. The heroine of JERUSALEM THE GOLDEN (1967) escapes her dour Northern mother and joins the smart urban bourgeoisie as embodied in a family that befriend and seduce her; she is aware that she cannot afford loyalty to her mother's dismal world. *The Waterfall* followed in 1969. Some – not least, if only implicitly, Drabble's sister A.S. BYATT in her novel *The Game* (1967) – have criticized these early books as drawing too heavily on recognizable experience, not always Drabble's own.

Starting with *The Needle's Eye* (1972), Drabble moved on to more moralistic novels which dealt with society and social responsibility, rather than individuals, and indeed became full-blown 'State of the Nation' novels in *The Ice Age* (1977), *The Middle Ground* (1980) and the trilogy THE RADIANT WAY (1987), *A Natural Curiosity* (1989) and *The Gates of Ivory* (1991). This later manner was ludic, constantly addressing the reader and regularly name-dropping characters from earlier books. It used sensational genre material – e.g., in the trilogy, a serial beheader and a quest for a writer missing in Cambodia – to give the narrative mythic force, but only intermittently achieved real narrative force. At their occasional best, these novels portray landscape as a source of a sense of social continuity – Drabble has always admired, and wrote a short pamphlet on, Wordsworth; at her best, she transfers these epiphanies to the urban, as at the end of *The Needle's Eye* 'She liked the lion . . . It was gritty and cold, a beast of the people. Mass-produced it had been, but it had weathered into identity. And this, she hoped, for every human soul.' She has also always admired GEORGE ELIOT, from whose sense of what is lost to a community when an individual fails to fulfil their potential, much of what is most emotionally compelling in these novels derives.

Drabble wrote two biographies, one of Arnold Bennett (1975), whom she efficiently describes as a solid and underrated working novelist whose steady accumulation of emotionally telling detail is obviously what her later books aspire to, and of Angus Wilson, with whose vein of camp fantasy she is somewhat at sea. She edited the *Oxford Companion to English Literature* (1985) and has pursued a varied career as a traditional woman of letters and committee woman; if her later work has not always fulfilled early promise, it is perhaps because of high seriousness rather than its lack.

RK

Drake-Brockman, Henrietta (Frances York)

1901–68 Australian playwright, novelist, short-story writer and critic.

Henrietta Drake-Brockman, a Western Australian who drew on her outback experiences for her plays, short fiction, six novels and articles, was very active in literary circles, establishing the state branch of the Federation of Australian Writers (FAW) in 1938.

In a cultural climate of limited opportunity for the production of Australian drama, her plays enjoyed considerable success in the late 1930s and 1940s. One-act plays include *The Man from the Bush: A Burlesque* (1932) which skilfully dramatizes the naivety of a bushman giving away his year's cheque, his entire worldly wealth, only to find himself arrested for vagrancy. Drake-Brockman's experiences in the pearling town of Broome inform *Dampier's Ghost: A Comedy* (1933) and *The Blister* (1937).

Her full-length *Men Without Wives* (1938) won the 1938 New South Wales sesquicentenary competition. Its theme of women struggling with the harsh outback environment is resolved optimistically. There followed *Hot Gold* (1940), a full-length melodrama in three acts, set in the gold-mining town of Kalgoorlie; and *The Lion Tamer* (1948), a comedy wittily depicting Australian expatriates in London society. *The Turning Wheel* (1960) by her husband Geoffrey includes commentary on her life and work.

ILB

Dream of A Common Language: Poems 1974-1977, The

(1978) A collection of poems exploring the deep emotional and physical ties binding women. ADRIENNE RICH's intimate, conversational voice, which uses common, clear syntax and diction in each of the book's three sections, relies upon empty spaces between phrases both to create breath units and also to echo the historical silencing of women's voices that this collection sought to combat. The first section, 'Power', opens and closes with poems about the hazards of and restrictions on female power, cohering around motifs of splitting, wounding, hunger, desire and anger; '21 Love Poems' is a sonnet sequence, a celebratory exploration of lesbianism that weighs pain against comfort and pleasure, insisting on the role of the female body in poetry. 'Not Somewhere Else, But Here' struggles between the 'dismembered' physical body and the poetic attempt to remember it and thus to create an epistemology of the female body. Emphasizing the material lives of ordinary women, locating them in the here and the now, Rich seeks a way in which 'words are found responsible'.

SC

Dred: A Tale of the Great Dismal Swamp (1856)

HARRIET BEECHER STOWE's second anti-slavery novel was originally published in two volumes. *Dred* was written four years later than Stowe's UNCLE TOM'S CABIN and was immediately a phenomenal bestseller. Here Stowe shifts the emphasis of her story from the domesticity and passivity of the black characters, as portrayed in *Uncle Tom's Cabin*, to an image of noble resistance against slavery aided by a powerful faith. Her plot is overtly political and incorporates contemporary events including the lynching and rioting by the white mobs and the fears of an imminent slave revolt. In her mingling of REALISM, ROMANCE and satire, Stowe critiques the hypocrisy of the plantation owners and the clergy. She contrasts the utopian dreams of the white reformers with the Edenic refuge in the Carolina swamps offered by the eponymous Dred, a black prophet of mythic proportions. At the conclusion of the novel, with a flight from the violence of the slave states to relative safety in New York, civil war seems inevitable.

JP

Drinker, Elizabeth [Sandwith]

1735–1807 Pennsylvania DIARIST, chronicler of 18th-century daily life in the period of the American Revolution and the founding of the United States. Elizabeth Sandwith was born in Philadelphia to Irish Quaker parents. At least part of her education derived from study with Anthony Benezet, a Quaker teacher and abolitionist who established a school for girls, but she was also self-taught. Her life-long habit of reading in literature, biography, politics, medicine, theology, history and natural history is detailed in hundreds of DIARY entries and itemized book lists. She married well-to-do Quaker merchant Henry Drinker in 1761, and bore nine children, five of whom survived infancy.

Drinker began her voluminous diary in 1758, noting frequently that she finds herself 'in the reading and writing humour'. With the exception of those years in which child-rearing consumed her, Drinker sat down nearly every evening until her death in 1807 to record the events of her day. A determinedly private person, her focus throughout is on family life. But, like all families, the Drinkers were impacted by political and cultural events: British soldiers seeking quarters during the Revolutionary war, constant illnesses and evolving medical treatments, runaway slaves at the door, Philadelphia's emergence as a major multi-ethnic urban centre, Elizabeth's work to free Henry after his detention in 1777 for refusing to sign a loyalty oath to the rebel government, a new invention called the bathtub, factionalism in the Society of Friends, a daughter's elopement, household work. In the interactions of family members with governments, merchants, neighbours and each other, a richly detailed narrative evolves. Drinker maintained a Quaker plain-style prose, and shaped her anecdotal record for an audience of intimates. Though the diary was never intended to be printed, she knew it would be read aloud among friends and family. She had no desire 'to write or record any thing that might in a future day give pain to any one'. Keeping her judgements to herself, juxtaposing monumental communal events with the minutiae of household work, Drinker gathered a narrative of daily life that is only beginning to be unpacked by historians and literary scholars.   PLC

du Fresne, Yvonne 1929– New Zealander of Danish descent whose ancestors left South Jutland in 1876 following the 1864 Slesvig-Holstein War. Du Fresne writes about growing up among this Scandinavian community on the Manawatu Plains. *Farvel and Other Stories* (1980), Winner of the PEN International Best First Book of Prose Award, and *The Growing of Astrid Westergaard and Other Stories* (1985) – reprinted together in *The Bear from the North: Tales of a New Zealand Childhood* (1989) – feature her heroine, Astrid Westergaard. Secure in the embrace of her extended family (including Danish-Huguenots and Norwegian settlers), Astrid learns to balance her European inheritance – the romantic world of Danish legend – with the reality of her outsider status in New Zealand. Not only is she foreign, but during World War II she, like other Scandinavian immigrants, is mistakenly ostracized as German. Through the memories of her parents, Tante Helga, her Grandtante and their contemporaries, descendants of Jutland farmers who developed prosperous farms in the Manawatu, the stories affectionately recreate the world of Norse symbolism and mythology. Du Fresne also shows culture in transition linguistically, by drawing on the Danish language in her portraits of the older generation whose awkward English contrasts with Astrid's Kiwi idioms as she acquires a colonial identity.

The Book of Ester (1982) and *Frederique* (1987) are historical romances (see HISTORICAL NOVEL) about the Danish-Huguenots from Fredericia: Ester, born in New Zealand, must rediscover the life of the original Ester le Fevre who fled the Reformation into Denmark in 1660. The heroine of *Frederique* is Frederique D'Albret who has escaped the horror of the 1860s Slesvig-Holstein war to live in 19th-century, missionary New Zealand. Both draw extensively on Danish myths and legends. Most delicately evocative of place and past is *Motherland* (1996) in which Astrid Westergaard, now 50 and a well-known writer, returns to Denmark to rediscover her roots. Romance also flourishes, but the returning exile's communion with her country's history prevails. Writing in the 'abrupt, laconic, so-practical style of Danish storytelling', Du Fresne's exploration of the Danish–New Zealand relationship and openness to reconciliation is both spirited and magnanimous.   JMW

du Maurier, Daphne 1907–89 Bestselling English novelist, short-story writer and BIOGRAPHER strongly associated with Cornwall, where she set many of her stories and seventeen novels and lived much of her adult life, in a remote mansion that inspired Manderley in her bestselling novel, REBECCA.

Daughter of actor Gerald du Maurier, she was the second of three girls in an artistic, privileged and emotionally contradictory family. Her mother Muriel was distant; her father overly intimate and openly wishful she had been a boy, a feeling she shared. She had an early affair with her finishing-school teacher in Paris; and twenty years later, a passionate friendship with Ellen Doubleday (wife of the American publisher) and a sexual relationship with actress Gertrude Lawrence; yet she feared and disapproved of lesbianism, preferring to think of herself as 'a man in a woman's body'. She was also attracted, and attractive, to men; and one year after publication of her first novel, *The Loving Spirit* (1931), she married 'Boy' Browning, a career army officer and, later, courtier. They had three children and remained married, despite both having affairs, until he died in 1965.

At a time when literary MODERNISM and social REALISM were the celebrated modes of fiction, Du Maurier was an anti-realist who steadily produced inventive tales in the ROMANCE, GOTHIC and adventure traditions, reinstating plot in a context of psychological insight and suspense (qualities recognized by Alfred Hitchcock, who filmed *Rebecca* and her short story 'THE BIRDS' (1952)). It was a successful formula and *Jamaica Inn* (1936), *Rebecca* (1938), *Frenchman's Creek* (1941), *My Cousin Rachel* (1951) and many short stories have remained continuously in print. Her family history inspired several biographies. She also contributed to the study of Elizabethan and Jacobean history with books on statesman and polymath Francis Bacon and his brother Anthony (*Golden Lads*, 1975; and *The Winding Stairs*, 1976).

Although she disliked being called a romance writer and insisted she wrote not love stories, but about power struggles between women and men and the violence of repressed feeling, her enduring contribution has been as a storyteller with a genius for atmosphere generated by internal and external landscapes. The act of writing was for her a necessity – 'it's something to do with one's own development and passage through life'. She was made Dame of the Order of the British Empire in 1969 and died in her sleep at 82, after several years without real inspiration. Her last work, an autobiography, *Growing Pains: The Shaping of a Writer*, was published in 1977.   LDo

du Plessis, Menan 1952– South African writer from Cape Town whose work reflects the compulsive self-questioning of the white writer under apartheid. Her two novels, *A State of Fear* (1983) and *Longlive!* (1989), appeared at the height of the anti-apartheid struggle and during her own work as an anti-apartheid activist. Receiving a major literary award for her first novel, she caused a stir in the establishment of the time by immediately donating the funds to the United Democratic Front, widely recognized as the internal wing of the then-banned African National Congress which came to power in 1994.

Du Plessis's narrators are centrally concerned with the construction of an anti-apartheid identity, and fracture and contradiction are foregrounded as a means of interrogating 'privilege'. They seem to embody Memmi's figure of the 'colonizer who refuses' as living 'under the sign of a contradiction which looms at every step, depriving him of all coherence and tranquillity'. Identities are defined primarily in class terms, and gender disavowed in the face of other issues: Du Plessis does not see herself as having a 'specifically female voice'. Nonetheless, both texts are extremely gendered. Her writing often breaks into Afrikaans, asserted against the hegemony of English and as a sign of opposition to the complicity and romanticism of an English liberal political and literary tradition. It displays an ongoing concern with REALISM, according to which the writer should provide the solace of truth, of political faith, against collective trauma.   SN

Dubois [née Annesley], Dorothea 1728–74 Irish poet, novelist and playwright. As the eldest of three daughters of Ann Simpson and Richard Annesley, sixth Earl of Anglesey, Dorothea was born to a relatively privileged position. When she was 12, however, her father rejected her mother in favour of his housekeeper and, claiming that his marriage to Simpson was bigamous, he refused to support her or their children.

In 1752 Dorothea married a musician, Peter Dubois, by whom she had six children. She probably began writing as a means of livelihood, but an additional motive was to expose her father as 'a man absorb'd in vice and infamy'. *Poems on Several Occasions* (1764) included 'tales, fables, songs and pray'rs', as well as the autobiographical 'A True Tale', which described her parents' marriage, her father's desertion and his brutal rejection of her attempts at reconciliation. She dealt with the same events in *The Case* – a vindication of her recently dead mother – and in a novel, *Theodora* (1770).

The trauma of Dorothea's early life determined much of the content of her writing, and gave her an awareness of female disadvantage which was apparent even in lighter works. In 'The Amazonian Gift', for example, she reverses traditional gender roles, rejecting conventional feminine wiles in place of the more effective 'pistol, sword or gun':

> The pattern of the Spartan dame
> I'll copy as I can;
> To man, degen'rate man, I'll give
> That simple thing, a fan.

Dubois's other writings included two plays and a guide to letter-writing, *The Lady's Polite Secretary* (1771). Her literary pursuits, however, apparently brought her little profit, and she died in poverty in Dublin.   RR

Duckworth [née Adcock], Marilyn 1935– Prolific New Zealand novelist who charts her heroines' progress through marriage, divorce and children, with an eye for the unpredictable and an ear for the discordant. Women's entrapment in relationships as a metaphor for psychological confinement and their gestures toward escape are major preoccupations. Her publications fall into two phases. Heroines of early novels like *A Gap in the Spectrum* (1959), *A Matchbox House* (1960), *A Barbarous Tongue* (1963) and *Over the Fence is Out* (1969), struggling against parental control or passively submissive to dominating husbands, victims of fantasy or household blues, try to discover independence. Three of these early works are set in England where Duckworth and her sister, the poet FLEUR ADCOCK, spent a wartime childhood.

After a fifteen-year silence Duckworth published the prizewinning *Disorderly Conduct* (1984) in which her heroine, during the controversial 1981 Springbok tour, juggles the competing demands of her various children, their different fathers and her lovers. Other recent novels, introducing characters from across the social spectrum, investigate scenarios with a contemporary flavour: women's violence, lesbianism and incest (*Seeing Red*, 1993), baby snatching (*Leather Wings*, 1995), homosexuality, Alzheimer's Disease and the Women's Movement (*Message from Harpo*, 1989). Futuristic themes provide backgrounds for domestic drama and romance in *Married Alive* (1985) and *Pulling Faces* (1987). Duckworth's novels have an immediately recognizable tone, not just for their fey, collapsing, over-sensitive heroines, beset by mysterious ailments, or by alienating predicaments, but for the elegance and poise of the writing, the penetrating observations, the sharp dialogue. Although adept at describing the *grandeurs et misères* of the human heart, her outcomes provide a sharpened sense of the peculiarity of everyday life.

In addition to twelve novels, she has published poetry (*Other Lovers' Children*, 1975), short stories (*Explosions on the Sun*, 1989), a novella (*Fooling*, 1994), radio dramas and television scripts. She has also edited *Cherries on a Plate: New Zealand Writers Talk about their Sisters* (1996). Winner of the Literary Fund Scholarship in Letters (1961, 1972), the Katherine Mansfield Fellowship (1980), the New Zealand Book Award for Fiction (1984), she was awarded the OBE in 1987. JMW

Duff Gordon, Lucie, Lady 1821–69 British TRAVEL WRITER, translator and hostess of one of London's most celebrated 19th-century salons. The daughter of distinguished jurist John Austin and estimable translator and BLUESTOCKING Mary (née Taylor), Lady Duff Gordon travelled in distinguished intellectual circles throughout her life. As a child, she journeyed with her family to Germany and became fluent in the language. Her linguistic talent launched her literary career, when, in 1839, she published a translation of Barthold Georg Niebuhr's *Studies of Ancient Grecian Mythology*. In 1840 she married Sir Alexander Duff Gordon and established their home in Esher as a cultural and literary gathering place.

Though active with her translations of German and French works, Lady Duff Gordon suffered from consumption most of her life and suffered a severe attack in 1849 after the birth of her son, Maurice. In 1860 she left England in search of a more felicitous climate, and in 1862 settled in Cairo. She had remarkable insight into the cultural complexity of Egypt and made no secret of her contempt for English snobbery and condescension. Her reputation rests on her engaging works, *Letters from Egypt* (1865) and *Last Letters from Egypt* (1875), which reveal an active and critical imagination and a breadth of knowledge and interests. Beautiful, brilliant and highly unconventional, she was the inspiration for Tennyson's *The Princess* and the model for Lady Jocelyn in Meredith's *Evan Harrington*. She died in 1869 and is buried in the English cemetery in Cairo. LCo

Duffy, Carol Ann 1955– British poet born in Glasgow, who has lived in Staffordshire, Liverpool, Manchester and London. These regional shifts are reflected in Duffy's sensitivity to patterns of speech,

and in her themes of home and language which pivot on a sense of disenfranchisement: 'I remember my tongue / shedding its skin like a snake, my voice / in the classroom sounding just like the rest'.

Duffy's first collection, *Standing Female Nude* (1985), was followed by *Selling Manhattan* (1987), a book dominated by the disturbing dramatic monologues for which Duffy is well known. In these fluent and often darkly funny poems, the speaker – an American Indian, a fairground psychopath, a ventriloquist's dummy – is always somehow incapacitated by language.

The Other Country (1990) explores private and public loss through highly specific memories of childhood and satires of 1980s Britain:

> You will be knowing of Charles Dickens and Terry Wogan
> and Scotland. All this can be arranged for cash no questions.
> Ireland not on. Fish and chips and the Official Secrets Act
> second to none. Here we go.

Compressed syntax is a characteristic Duffy device. Language fragments under pressure: 'grown up. Just like that. Whoosh. Hairy.'

Widely imitated, this verbal interference is particularly potent in Duffy's work because language is also her subject. She even explores its texture in the lucent sensuality of her love poems:

> an animal learning vowels; not that I know
> I do this, but I hear them
> floating away over your shoulders, sticking
> to the ceiling. *Aa Ee ly Oh Uu*.

In *Meantime* (1993), her language is more concrete; the treatment of her familiar subjects, more abstract and atmospheric. These tensions are impressively judged.

Selected Poems (1994) included poems about 'The World's Wife', a sequence giving full rein to Duffy's fierce wit, for example 'Mrs Midas': 'And then he plucked / a pear from a branch, we grew Fondante d'Automne, / and it sat in his palm like a lightbulb. On.' LG

Duffy, Maureen 1933– In conscious echo of the way London, the city she writes most often about, contains and compacts endless heterogeneity, British writer Duffy's novels, plays, poetry and BIOGRAPHIES map life upon life with bold and often playful erudition. Each time she builds up a kind of frieze of interconnections, and from this a number of strands are plucked and revelled to their various conclusions. The writing seizes upon the love that can be salvaged from the fragments and the lopped-off ends of lives. In *Wounds* (1969), the first of her London trilogy of novels (continuing with *Capital* (1975) and *Londoners* (1983)), nameless lovers wind their dialogue through the other, more public threads of the novel. The endless tussle of their intimacy underscores everything else that goes on. In *The Microcosm* (1966), her marvellous, bricolaged novel about the London queer scene in the sixties, she ends by insisting on keeping, 'the idea of the totality of experience and knowledge at the back of our minds even though the front's busy'. The subjective is always measured up against the world out there. The work is filled with bravado: 'I'm just taking up my whole personality and walking quietly out into the world with it. We'll see what happens.'

She herself has campaigned for the rights of animals and authors, as well as bringing APHRA BEHN back to life in her ground-breaking biography *The Passionate Shepherdess* (1977). Her work reads like something triumphantly hard-won; Duffy reminds us that 'a working class author is one who is already working in a foreign language'. She celebrates liminality and the views it affords, the fluencies it can give. *Love Child* (1971) has a precocious, androgynous narrator, emblem of the ambiguous focalizers of each of Duffy's plots – all of their characters with feet in two or more worlds. Her very first book, *That's How It Was* (1962), sets us up immediately with this theme: that articulacy, as it gives you everything, robs you of what you had before. Again, though, her writing here is best when focused on the relationship at the heart of the novel – that between Paddy and her mother, their tricky and tender struggle to get by.   PM

Duggan, Eileen 1894–1972 Author of five volumes of verse (1921–51) who withdrew from Allen Curnow's anthology, *The Book of New Zealand Verse 1923–45*, because of his criticism of her work ('the whole effect is of an emotional cliché'). For decades she was in disrepute, for her sensibility was alien to the predominantly masculine New Zealand school of poetry. Although Duggan avoided the 'physiographical rhapsodies' of the '"landscape" school', her inheritance – Yeats and the 'Celtic twilight', the moral vision of Catholicism – seemed a tributary to the poetic mainstream. Her reputation, however, has recently staged a comeback. Her *Selected Poems* were published in 1994, and her affinity with the metaphysical poets acclaimed. To Michele Leggott her language and images are a rich source of inspiration. Duggan is essentially a lyric nature poet, although she also writes aphoristically: to her the sea is 'like some great winter bee, more sad than bold, that stumbles in the velvet of a flower'. Other depictions display a powerful rhythmic intensity:

> I was driving the cows and the frogs were soothsaying
> 'Woe, land and water! All, all is lost!'
> It was winter full grown and my bones were black in
>   me
> The tussocks were brittling from dew into frost.   JMW

Dumbfounding, The (1966) MARGARET AVISON's second volume of poetry continues the poetic investigation of 'The too much none of us knows' begun in WINTER SUN. This inquiry oscillates between an exploration of Christian spirituality and a questioning of perception itself. As the collection's title suggests, the aim here is to probe the inexplicable. Always deeply moral in tone, Avison's post-conversion poetry sheds much of its philosophical diction in order to experiment with the allusive aspects of parable, prayer and psalm. Using images that are enigmatic rather than illustrative, Avison communicates her spiritual vision of both urban and natural worlds without assigning definitive meanings to the universe she represents. Whereas Avison's early poetry frequently infuses landscape with philosophical content, the speaker in 'Pace' is content to record the movement of trees in a grove 'letting the ear experience this / discrete, delicate / clicking'. Avison nonetheless continues to esteem the 'dream of seeing' above ordinary sight. Characteristically, her meditations move from precise observations of the material world toward an unachieved and inarticulable spiritual epiphany.   IR

Dumont, Marilyn 1955– Métis poet, film producer and Native educator. A descendant of Métis leader Gabriel Dumont, Marilyn Dumont was born in Northeastern Alberta, Canada, to a large Cree- and English-speaking family. The tension and interplay between these two languages and cultures are formative influences on Dumont's imagination. As she writes in her first collection of poetry *A Really Good Brown Girl* (1996), 'Cree Language Structures and Common Errors in English book-end / my life.' The interstitial quality of Métis identity resonates throughout Dumont's poetry. Whether it is the 'White Judges' who look down on her people's 'halfbreed hides' or the 'full-blood' Native who gives Dumont's speaker '"this look", that says he's leather and I'm naughahyde', the problematic connections between race and identity continually resurface in her writing. Dumont challenges both native and white presuppositions – 'one wrong sound and you're shelved in the Native Literature section' – of how she should write. In 'Circle the Wagons', for example, Dumont exclaims, 'There it is again, the circle, that goddamned circle . . . [I]s there nothing more than the circle in the deep structure of Native literature?'

The differences between media also interest Dumont – she first pursued a successful career in film and video production before embracing her vocation as a poet. She recently completed a Master of Fine Arts degree at the University of British Columbia and works as a Native educator.   IR

Dunbar-Nelson, Alice (Ruth Moore) 1875–1935 African-American poet, short-story writer, essayist, journalist and educator who is best known for her romantic poetry. Born in New Orleans, the daughter of a seamstress and a merchant marine, Dunbar-Nelson pursued studies at Straight University (now Dillard University) and began a teaching career. One of her sketches, along with a photo, was published in the *Monthly Review* and caught the eye of another upcoming writer, Paul Laurence Dunbar, who wrote to her. They were married from 1898 to 1902. For eighteen years, she taught at Wilmington, Delaware's Howard High School, from which she was fired for participating in political activities. Dunbar-Nelson would continue to be an active voice in political and civic affairs, as well as a tireless member of the black women's club movement.

Her first book, *Violets and Other Tales* (1895), and her second, *The Goodness of St Rocque* (1899), were collections of sketches, essays, stories and poems. Her poetry often incorporates romantic themes and elevated poetic language, while her short fiction consists largely of local-colour pieces rich with depictions of her birthplace of New Orleans. Her later short fiction and her essays more directly address race and gender issues. Dunbar-Nelson contributed essays to newspapers and magazines, such as *Crisis*, the *Messenger* and the *Washington Eagle*. She was often in much demand as a lecturer and delivered a series of five lectures called 'Romances of the Negro in Our History' which called attention to the significance of African-American history. She also published and edited the *Wilmington Advocate* newspaper with her third husband, Robert J. Nelson. When she died, Dunbar-Nelson left behind two unpublished novels, 'This Lofty Oak' and 'Confessions of a Lazy Woman', as well as several screenplays, and a diary. CJ

Duncan, Sandy Frances 1942– Canadian author born in Vancouver, British Columbia, she attended the University of British Columbia (BA 1962; MA 1963). She writes fiction for children and for adults. Her fiction for adults has been widely anthologized from 1977 onwards; much of it is written with wit and with a clear feminist sensibility. She has published numerous books for CHILDREN and young people: *Cariboo Runaway* (1976), *Kap-Sung Ferris* (1977), *Dragonhunt* (1971), *The Toothpaste Genie* (1981 and 1991), *Finding Home* (1982), *Pattern Makers* (1981) and *Listen To Me, Grace Kelly* (1990). She is the author of *British Columbia: Its Land, Mineral and Water Resources* (1996). She was the co-founder and editor of (*f.*)*Lip* (1986–8), an avant-garde feminist literary journal, and she co-edited *Witness to Wilderness: The Clayoquot Sound Anthology* (1994). She is active in Canadian writers' associations and in PEN International. GHN

Duncan, Sara Jeannette [Sarah Janet, 'Mrs Everard Cotes', 'Garth Grafton'] 1861–1922 Canadian journalist, novelist and commentator on the politics of empire. Born in Brantford, the daughter of a merchant, she was educated at the Collegiate Ladies' College, County Model School and Toronto Normal School. Initially a teacher, she began publishing short pieces from 1880, and, unusually for a woman at that time, became a journalist working for the Toronto *Globe*, the London (Ontario) *Advertiser*, the *Washington Post* and the *Montreal Star*. Aged 27 she embarked on a world tour (1888–9) with fellow-journalist, Lily Lewis, and her dispatches to the *Star* were later re-published as *A Social Departure* (1890). In India she received a proposal of marriage from Everard Cotes, a museum curator, and she returned 18 months later to marry him – and to join the ranks of the 'memsahibs' whose way of life she was to mock in *The Simple Adventures of a Memsahib* (1893). She wrote editorials for the *Indian Daily News* as well as numerous novels. Her keenly observed commentaries on life in India, Canada and England reflect international politics, the marginality of women and social foibles with equal ironic detachment. *The Burnt Offering* (1909), a novel illustrating the dangers of British misapprehension of India, foreshadows E.M. Forster's *A Passage to India* (1924) – indeed, in 1912 Forster stayed briefly at the Cotes's home in Simla. Further works include her novel on Anglo-Canadian politics, THE IMPERIALIST (1904), and *Set in Authority* (1906). She died in Ashtead, England.

JSte

Duncombe [née Highmore], Susannah 1725?–1812 English literary illustrator and occasional poet. She was the daughter of Joseph Highmore, the famous painter, who undertook her education and instructed her in drawing. A member of the literary circle which surrounded Samuel Richardson during the 1740s and 1750s, her sketch of Richardson reading *Sir Charles Grandison* formed the frontispiece to his published correspondence, edited in 1804 by ANNA LAETITIA BARBAULD. In 1754 her suitor, John Duncombe, celebrated her talents in his *Feminiad*, a poetic catalogue of Britain's eminent and learned women. They were married in 1761. Duncombe wrote occasional verse (eight of her poems appeared in the 1763 *Poetical Calendar*) and provided illustrations for her husband's *History and Antiquities of Reculver and Herne* (1784), as well as other works. Her portrait of HESTER CHAPONE forms the frontispiece of Chapone's *Collected Works*. KD

Dunlop [née Hamilton], Eliza 1796–1880 Irish-Australian poet, who pioneered the study of Aboriginal culture. Born in County Armagh, Eliza was raised by her grandmother following her mother's death and her father's emigration shortly afterwards to India. She began writing as a girl, and her poems appeared in Irish magazines such as the *Dublin Penny*

Journal, and in *The Dark Lady of Doona* (1834), a novel by her cousin, William Hamilton Maxwell.

In 1838 Eliza moved with her second husband, David Dunlop, and four of her children to Australia, where Dunlop served as a police magistrate and held the post of Protector of Aborigines at Wollombi. Living in the Hunter Valley of New South Wales, Dunlop was able to pursue her interest in the culture and language of the Aborigines, and was the first person to attempt transliteration of Aboriginal songs and poetry. Her best-known poem, 'The Aboriginal Mother', based on the Myall Creek Massacre of 1838, was published in the same year in the *Australian*, and her works, on her nostalgia for Ireland and on the exploits of Australian explorers as well as on Aboriginal themes, appeared in other newspapers such as the *Sydney Gazette*, *Sydney Morning Herald* and *Maitland Mercury*. Some of her verse was collected in a manuscript, 'The Vase', which is now in the Mitchell Library, Sydney, and a collection of her poetry, *The Aboriginal Mother and Other Poems*, appeared in 1981.   RR

Dunmore, Helen 1952– English novelist and poet who has received numerous awards, from the Poetry Society for several of her collections, and, for her third novel, *A Spell in Winter*, the Orange Prize, for which, controversially, only women writers are eligible. Her work ranges across landscapes and time. Finland's icy spaces jostle, in poetry and prose, with Sussex gardens; the horrors of World War I with the dangerous deceits of the contemporary urban world.

When, in *Darkness in Zennor* (1993), D.H. Lawrence lectures Clare Coyne on the need to draw not the surface of a flower but its essence, we hear the expression of Dunmore's practice: a precision which allows to each object its particularity and integrity. Lawrence would approve too the unashamed sensuality of both poetry and prose, together with the insistent implication that those who refuse bodily pleasures are morally deficient. Celebration of food is, indeed, central: the prose oozes succulently with buttercream and summer puddings, lovingly stirred sauces and the simpler pleasures of rye bread and sausage.

All, though, is not glad revelry. The individual is seen in landscapes – of ice, water or sand – inimical to human needs. Nor is human nature unfailingly kind: the prose works are haunted by conspiracies and silences, suicide and killing. There is, though, an unsentimental insistence on survival, and love found in places and ways unexpected and unsanctioned.   EA

Dunn, Nell [Nell Mary Sandford] 1936– English writer; in the fifties she left her wealthy family to live in London, in working-class Battersea, where she wrote the choppy, dialogue-heavy sketches of the day-to-dayness of urban life which she published in the

New Statesman and shortly after, in book form as *Up the Junction* (1963). She immerses us in a world of detail – hot fish and chips and pissing behind vans – but the narrator's voice is sometimes curiously, coolly removed from what it narrates. The centrepiece and still heart of the book is the disquieting chapter detailing the birth of Rube's dead baby at home.

Dunn's best book is POOR COW (1967), a sad, slim novel, wonderfully of its time. Joy has a baby very young and, living from hand to mouth in the milieu described in the previous book, she takes up with a number of good-for-nothing men. The allowances of fiction get us closer to the characters this time and there is an enduring warmth in the relationship between mother and son. The opening scene casts the teenaged mother in an iconic light, which is carried through in the film made by Ken Loach (who also adapted *Up the Junction*). Her subsequent books have included novels, a book of interviews with women of the sixties (*Talking to Women*, 1965), and one with people making an effort at alternative lifestyles in the seventies (*Living Like I Do*, 1976). Her first play, STEAMING (1981), was very well received critically, and was made into a funny, arch film with Diana Dors and Vanessa Redgrave. A sequel to *Poor Cow*, *My Silver Shoes* made a belated but welcome appearance in 1996, proving that her work is best when it is close enough to documentary to beguile us with its candour, but far enough away to let the characters breathe. Dunn's fictions are valuable in their uncompromised insistence on putting experience that is outside of middle-class ordinariness back into literary fiction.

    PM

Durack [née Miller], Mary 1913– Australian novelist, BIOGRAPHER and CHILDREN'S writer. Durack was born in Adelaide into a famous pastoralist family, and spent her early years in the Kimberley region of Western Australia. During the 1930s she helped run the Durack cattle properties alongside her sister, Elizabeth Durack, the artist. *All-About: The Story of a Black Community* (1935) was the first of many collaborative publications for children; Mary wrote the text and Elizabeth illustrated it. Others include the fairy tale *Way of the Whirlwind* (1941), and *To Ride a Fine Horse* (1963). From 1937 to 1938 Durack was the columnist 'Virgilia' at WA Newspapers Ltd. Her major literary work is *Kings in Grass Castles* (1959), a pioneering saga of the Durack family from the moment of emigration to the death of Mary's grandfather in 1898; the sequel, *Sons in the Saddle* (1983), continues this history through to her father. *Keep Him My Country* (1955) is her only novel, relating an over-romanticized relationship between Stan Rolt, a white station owner, and a native girl, Dalgerie. Durack was awarded the OBE in 1966, and the DBE in 1978.   MRE

Duras, Marguerite [Donnadieu] 1914–96 French novelist, playwright and film-maker born in French Indochina (Vietnam) to a schoolteacher couple. Known outside France chiefly for her novel, *L'Amant* (Prix Goncourt, 1984; *The Lover*, 1985), made into a film by Jean-Jacques Annaud (1992), Duras's writing was, at first, associated with the group of the *nouveau roman*; it has also been argued that she is an existentialist; and (by feminist critics) that her work is concerned with alienation and absence, elided in the lyrical space of a style of 'écriture féminine'. Duras is consistently interested in the theme of sexual passion. The novel *Moderato cantabile* (1958), with its intense, detailed focus on the psychology of her characters, established her as one of France's foremost female novelists. This novel was one of many of her writings made into a film; she also wrote the original screenplay for Alain Resnais's film, *Hiroshima mon amour* (1959; English translation 1966). In the 1970s, she became known as a pioneer in avant-garde cinema with *India Song* (1975), which she wrote and directed, from a sub-plot of her novel *Le Vice-consul* (1965; *The Vice-Consul*, 1968). Her later work, *La Douleur* (1985), includes an enigmatic part-documentary narration of the nursing-back-to-life of her first husband, Robert Antelme, who was found in Dachau at the end of World War II by the Resistance leader 'Morland' (François Mitterand). She died in Paris.   SD

Durham, (Mary) Edith 1863–1944 British TRAVEL WRITER and ethnographer. Born in London as the eldest child of a prosperous surgeon, she studied art and went on to illustrate several volumes of the *Cambridge Natural History*, but spent most of the 1890s looking after her sick mother. As her own health deteriorated, her doctor suggested travel as a cure for depression, which led her to visit Montenegro and the Albanian lands in 1900. She returned to the Balkans on numerous occasions and went on to produce a series of books about the region, including her first, *Through the Land of the Serb* (1904); *The Burden of the Balkans* (1905), an account of her relief work in Macedonia and her first prolonged visit to Albania; *High Albania* (1909), a description of her journey among the mountain tribes of Northern Albania; and *Some Tribal Origins, Laws and Customs of the Balkans* (1927), an ethnographical study of Montenegro and northern Albania. Although initially captivated by the Montenegrins, Durham became an energetic campaigner for Albanian independence. By 1908 she appeared in the Foreign Office card index under 'Durham, Miss M.E.: Inadvisability of corresponding with'. In Albania she received the popular title of 'Queen of the Mountain People' and was welcomed by large crowds on her last visit in 1921. She continued to campaign for the Albanian cause until her death. In 1996, the Durham Gallery, devoted to her

ethnographic collections, opened at the Bankfield Museum in Halifax, England.   VG

Dutt, Toru 1856–77 Indian poet. She wrote and published poetry in English at a time when very few women in India had access to this language. She was born in an unusual Hindu family in Calcutta – highly literary and westernized – where it was customary for the children to go to England for higher education. A volume of poems written by members of the Dutt family, *The Dutt Family Album,* was published in London in 1870. Although Toru died at 21, her own two volumes of verse testify to an individual voice, and are very different from the merely competent versification of the other poets of the family.

Her father converted to Christianity in 1862, and Toru went to Europe with her parents and sister at the age of 13. Their only brother had already died of tuberculosis, the disease that was to claim the other siblings in the next few years. They spent a year at Nice where Toru learnt French well enough to translate nearly 200 poems into English (*A Sheaf Gleaned in French Fields,*1876) and to write a novel *Le Journal de Mademoiselle d'Avers* (published posthumously in Paris in 1879).They then spent three years in England and the two sisters attended the Higher Lectures for Women at Cambridge.

Returning to Calcutta in 1873 was an ambivalent experience for Toru. From her letters to a friend in England we know how much she missed the freedom she had enjoyed abroad, but her joy at the Indian fruits and flowers and the riot of colour in their large garden is celebrated in her poetry. Her sister Aru, who shared Toru's literary interests, died in 1874. Toru started learning Sanskrit 'in the hope', as she said, 'of being able to bring out another "sheaf" not gleaned in French, but in Sanskrit fields'. Her critical essays were published in the *Bengal Magazine,* the journal in which her unfinished novel, *Bianca or The Young Spanish Maiden*, was to be serialized after her death. Her best poems are to be found in *Ancient Ballads and Legends of Hindustan* (1882). Despite the sadly 'Orientalist' title (chosen by Edmund Gosse who accidentally discovered her work and published in London with an enthusiastic introduction), the poems remain fascinating today not only for their lyrical quality but also for the choice of the stories she renders in limpid narrative verse, foregrounding women and other marginal figures of society, low-caste men and children. Her most anthologized poems, 'Our Casuarina Tree' and 'Sita', do not retell old stories, but evoke metaphors of personal experience.   MMu

Dworkin, Andrea 1946– American radical feminist, author of fiction and non-fiction works, and anti-pornography activist. Born in New Jersey, Dworkin was educated at Bennington College and lived in

Amsterdam and Greece, before settling in New York. She has written nine books, while supporting herself through extensive public lecturing.

Dworkin's first book, *Woman Hating* (1974), introduces what would become the central concern of her work: the relationship between male violence and gender inequality. *Our Blood* (1976) and *Right-Wing Women* (1982) extend the analysis by exploring specific social effects of sexual violence. In the early 1980s, Dworkin turned her attention almost exclusively to the topic of pornography, beginning with *Pornography: Men Possessing Women* (1981). Later, in a work co-authored with American lawyer Catherine A. MacKinnon, *Pornography and Civil Rights* (1988), Dworkin and MacKinnon argue that pornography is best understood as an instance of sexual discrimination, and hence as a violation of women's civil rights. Anyone considering herself – or himself – 'injured' by pornography, they argue, ought to be able to bring a civil suit against its producers, rather than leaving prosecution to male-dominated professions such as the police and local government. Together, they took this discrimination theory to the courts, drafting anti-pornography ordinances in Indianapolis, Minneapolis and other American cities, which have served as models for such legislation around the world.

In addition to her many volumes of essays, Dworkin has published two novels, *Ice and Fire* (1980) and *Mercy* (1990). As controversial as her work has often been, critics have been virtually unanimous in hailing Dworkin's courage, her rhetorical virtuosity and her belief in the power of writing to effect social transformation. 'One must speak truth to power', she writes, 'against the silence created by the pain and despair of sexual abuse and second-class status.'   JGr

Dyer, Mary ?–1660 Memorialized as a Quaker martyr, her religious conviction was the defining force of her difficult life. The wife of William Dyer of Somersetshire, England, she travelled to America in 1635 where she became a follower of ANNE HUTCHINSON. Her loyalty to Hutchinson during the Antinomian Controversy inspired rumours that she had been cursed by God with a still-born, monstrous child. Living in England during the 1650s, she joined the Society of Friends and became a minister. When she returned to America to preach her new faith she faced constant persecution and threats to her life. Her arrest and eleventh-hour reprieve from the gallows (she literally had the noose about her neck) inspired a series of letters in which she censures the hypocritical policies of the Puritan leaders and expresses a brave willingness to die for her beliefs. In 1660 she stood behind her resolute, unwavering epistles by refusing to accept exile from Massachusetts in exchange for her life. On 1 June she was hanged in Boston and the story of her martyrdom, told in part through her courageous letters, has found a prominent place in accounts and histories of Quaker suffering.   JRS

E

Earle, Jean 1909– Anglo-Welsh poet, born in Bristol, who spent her youth in the Rhondda Valley and lived most of her adult life in Wales, latterly on the border near Shrewsbury. Her stories and articles appeared early in her career, but she published her first book, *A Trial of Strength* (1980), when she was 71, and went on to publish four further collections with the Welsh-based Seren Books. Her many prizes include the Welsh Arts Council Award.

Earle has a lifetime to draw on, but her nostalgia is rinsed in 'the intent look' and 'fierceness of thought' with which she views the world and her writing. *Visiting Light*, a Poetry Book Society Choice in 1987, shows Earle at her best – on the one hand raging for a Lawrentian purification of the world, on the other celebrating the common life and social experience of South Wales. Her Welsh rhetoric is leavened with wry wit making her somewhat overbearing diction more approachable and generous in spirit. Her *Selected Poems* in 1990 was followed up by the less substantial *The Sun in the West* in 1995.   DM

Earth and High Heaven (1944) Set in wartime Montreal, GWETHALYN GRAHAM's second novel chronicles the story of Erica Drake 'of the Westmount Drakes' and lawyer Marc Reiser, son of Jewish immigrants settled in northern Ontario, who fall in love despite social convention, family opposition and entrenched anti-semitism. This international bestseller won Graham a second Canadian Governor General's Award and the Anisfield-Wolf Award.

Erica is shocked when her enlightened father, Charles Drake, who has accepted a French-Canadian Catholic daughter-in-law, refuses to meet Marc. Drake's irrational opposition reveals possessiveness and prejudice. Marc, less shocked, is too diffident to fight Charles for Erica, appalled by the nastiness underpinning her privileged society. Eventually Erica's sister and Marc's brother intervene to effect a resolution.

The romance has strong elements of wish-fulfilment, for Graham's own relationship with a Jewish lawyer was thwarted by her 'liberal' father's opposition, and Marc is an idealized lover, but Graham's portrayal of the ethnic mosaic of pre-war Montreal – English, French, Jews – remains vivid and eloquent. This novel is also a love song to Montreal.   EB

East Lynne (1861) MRS HENRY WOOD's second novel, originally serialized in the *New Monthly Magazine*, January 1860 – August 1861, became immensely popular and was often presented in dramatized versions. A SENSATION-type melodrama, it ostensibly shows that adultery is the worst sin a married woman can perpetrate. Its carefully named heroine, Lady Isabel Vane, married to a lawyer who has rescued her from her father's bankruptcy and bought her former home, East Lynne, elopes in a passionate moment with a man whose child she bears; divorced by her husband, she is also deserted by her lover, later revealed to be a murderer. Assumed dead in the train wreck that kills his child, she returns disfigured and in disguise to East Lynne to serve as her legitimate children's governess and must endure having her son die in her arms without knowing her as mother. She herself dies after revealing her identity to her former husband and being forgiven by him. Feminist critics have seen Wood as secretly sympathizing with Isabel's desire to escape her passionless marriage.   HB

Eastlake, Elizabeth, Lady Rigby 1809–93 British writer of a notoriously scathing review of *JANE EYRE* in the *Quarterly Review* (December 1848). In the 1830s Elizabeth Rigby became a regular contributor to the *Quarterly*, writing on a dizzying array of topics: art, fashion, photography, lady travellers, children's books, and physiognomy. Her prose was known for its bite. G.H. Lewes noted its 'cutting sarcasm' and 'vigorous protest'.

Elizabeth Rigby's publication of a collection of letters written to her mother from Russia launched her career. This volume's popularity resulted in an immediate second edition entitled *A Residence on the Shores of the Baltic* (1841). Rigby's Russian sojourn also provided material for two works of fiction, *The Jewess* (1843) and *Livonian Tales* (1846).

In 1849 Rigby married Charles Eastlake who was shortly thereafter knighted. He later became Keeper of the National Gallery and president of the Royal Academy. Following her marriage, Rigby's work included translating G.F. Waagen's *Treasure of Art in Great Britain* (1845-7), and editing and completing ANNA JAMESON's *History of our Lord as Exemplified in Works of Art* (1864). In 1870, five years after her husband's death, Eastlake edited and published his *Contributions to the Literature of the Fine Arts.*   EC

Eccles, Charlotte O'Conor ['Hal Godfrey'] d. 1911
Irish journalist and novelist. A daughter of the founder of the *Roscommon Messenger*, she was educated in England, France and Germany. She began her journalistic career with the *Irish Monthly* and wrote articles on social issues such as the inadequacies of women's education and sexual prejudice in the workplace, for *Pall Mall Gazette*, *New York Herald* and *Blackwood's Magazine*. An authority on the social conditions of European peasants, her account of the appalling condition of women in a Viennese hospital (*Nineteenth Century*, Oct. 1899) revolutionized that hospital's treatment of its patients. Collaborating with Sir Horace Plunkett, she wrote and lectured throughout Ireland for the Board of Agriculture and Technical Instruction. According to a fellow-journalist, however, despite a promising start, Eccles 'drifted entirely into the background following the uprise of the NEW WOMAN's agitation' (*New Ireland Review*, March 1895). As a novelist she was best known for the humorous fantasy *The Rejuvenation of Miss Semaphore* (1897) in which a middle-aged woman consumes too much of a rejuvenating elixir. The critically acclaimed *Aliens of the West* (1904) was described by the *Daily Chronicle* as 'one of the best modern books of short stories on Ireland'.   BHu

Echoing Grove, The (1953) ROSAMOND LEHMANN's
penultimate novel challenges the critical judgement that her range is limited to analyses of feminine consciousness. In this intricately narrated account, set predominantly in the 1930s and 1940s, of the triangular relationship between a husband, Rickie Masters, his conventional wife, Madeleine, and his wife's bohemian sister, Dinah, it is Rickie's male consciousness that is most closely examined. Rickie is bewilderedly aware toward the end of the novel that 'a new thing is happening: men aren't any good to women any more', a realization all the more striking for being expressed during the London Blitz, subverting the accepted polarization of gender roles in wartime. Rickie dies unheroically from a perforated ulcer; the adulterous woman does not here pay. Many subsidiary characters also die, and death and madness are pervasive symbolic motifs, yet the overall tone is far from sombre. The framework of the reconciliation of the sisters after fifteen years' estrangement, tentatively remaking their lives after Rickie's death, offers hope of a new resolution for sexual differences.   WAP

Eddy, Mary Baker [Glover Patterson] 1821–1910
Founder of the Christian Science movement, author, editor. In ill health most of her life, Mary was educated at home. At 22, she married George Washington Glover, but when he died soon thereafter, leaving her pregnant and destitute, she was cared for by relatives. In 1853, she married Dr. Daniel Patterson, a dentist and homeopath. The marriage was an unhappy one, and her health declined seriously. In 1862, she consulted the mental healer Phineas P. Quimby, whose use of 'animal magnetism' to cure her made a disciple of Mary. She attributed her recovery from a spinal injury in 1866 to God's revelation, and this led her to develop the theology she published in *Science and Health* (1875), the textbook of Christian Science. In 1876, she founded the Christian Science Association; the following year, she married Asa Gilbert Eddy, one of her disciples (he died in 1882). The Mother Church was founded in Boston in 1892, although Eddy herself had retired to Concord, New Hampshire, three years earlier, due to her continued poor health. The basic tenets of Christian Science, as she later articulated them, are that 'eternal mind is the source of all being; there is no matter; sin, sickness, and death are illusions; and this was revealed to the world by Jesus Christ'. Eddy also advocated equality in property rights and suffrage for women, ordained female ministers, and even at one point referred to God as 'she'. Her belief in the written word was evidenced by her founding a monthly, a quarterly, a weekly and a daily journal. The latter, the *Christian Science Monitor*, remains a well-respected international newspaper.   SP

Eden, Emily 1797–1869 TRAVEL WRITER and novelist
who belonged to the English Whig aristocracy at the apogee of its self-confident assumptions of leadership in government and fashionable society. Her brother George, beside whom, with her sister Fanny, she lived devotedly throughout his exclusively bachelor life, sat in Parliament as Lord Auckland, and was rewarded in 1835 for services to his party by being appointed Governor General of India. Emily and Fanny accompanied him to Calcutta and spent the next seven years touring northern India at his side. A disastrous war on Afghanistan led to Auckland's recall, and both he and Fanny died in 1849.

Emily turned to fiction as a solace, and, despite her upbringing in a milieu which viewed writing for publication and profit as a middle-class vulgarity, produced *The Semi-Detached House*, a comedy of manners showing the positive influence of JANE AUSTEN in the buoyancy and crispness of its narrative and dialogue. Eventually published in 1859, it was an immediate success, encouraging her to issue *The Semi-Attached Couple*, a longer and livelier variant on similar themes, which she had written in 1830 as 'a tolerably faithful representation of modern society'. These novels, however enjoyable, now seem less interesting than the remarkable letters from India which Emily published in 1868 as *Up the Country*. These combine the stylistic brio and alertness to detail of her fiction with a consistently detached and sometimes critical view of British colonial attitudes, a perspective foreshadowing the widening gulf between ruler and subject in India which ultimately led to the Mutiny of 1857. Further collections of Emily Eden's letters were issued in 1869 and 1919. JK

Edgell, Zee 1940– The first Belizean writer to attain international recognition, Edgell was born in Belize City where she was educated. She trained as a journalist in both Belize and London, and one of her first jobs was to be a reporter for the *Daily Gleaner*, Kingston, Jamaica, between 1959 and 1962. From 1966 to 1968 she taught at St Catherine Academy in Belize City as well as being editor of the *Reporter*, a small newspaper based in the city. The urge to become a writer was felt early, although she started writing only after marrying Anvil Edgell, an American who was attached to CARE in Belize. Following her husband's work assignments, she spent many years overseas, in Nigeria, Afghanistan, Bangladesh, Somalia and the USA. Away from home she wrote *Beka Lamb* (1982), winner of the Fawcett Society Book Prize in 1982. Set against the background of Belizean society in the 1950s and alternating standard English with local creole, it is a BILDUNGSROMAN which charts the painful process of growing-up of the young female protagonist and reflects metaphorically Belize's journey toward independence.

After returning to Belize, Edgell was appointed by the government director of the Women's Bureau in 1981 and later director of the Department of Women's Affairs (1986–7). Her engagement in politics and women's issues is mirrored in her second novel, *In Times Like These* (1991). Generally considered more mature than *Beka Lamb*, it recounts the struggle of Pavana, a single mother, who returns to Belize with her twins to take up a government position. More personal issues of domestic violence and crimes of passion are explored in *The Festival of San Joaquin* (1997), told in a multi-layered narrative from a mestizo woman's point of view. PMa

Edgeworth, Maria 1768–1849 Highly influential and successful novelist and educational writer who nevertheless spent much of her life immersed in management of the family estate at Edgeworthstown in Ireland, and in educating an extended family comprising her father's twenty-two children. She was the eldest daughter of Richard Lovell Edgeworth, an enlightened landowner drawn to scientific experimentation and educational theorizing, and became his competent agent and accountant. Accused of domineering over his daughter's writing, her father also encouraged and enabled her, commissioning stories.

Maria Edgeworth.

In *The Parent's Assistant* (1796) and *Moral Tales for Young People* (1801) Edgeworth matched instruction with entertainment, creating a tension which continued to haunt her later novels. The Edgeworths' belief in the merits of 'education of the heart' for both sexes culminated in their co-authored influential *Practical Education* (1798).

Edgeworth's career as a novelist began, unaided by her father, with the brilliantly original and idiosyncratic CASTLE RACKRENT (1800), the first regional novel and a formative influence on Scott and Turgenev. Further tales celebrating Irish life were *Ennui* (1809), *The Absentee* (1812) and *Ormond* (1817). Edgeworth's prolific output expanded with her novels of fashionable and DOMESTIC life, beginning with *Letters for Literary Ladies* (1795) in defence of female education, and followed by *Belinda* (1801), featuring the psychologically complex and riveting Lady Delacour and the mannish and eccentric Harriott Freke, both designed as foils for the exemplary heroine whom Edgeworth herself condemned as 'that stick or stone'. An ambitious novel which tackled politics and professional life was PATRONAGE (1814), for which she was paid £2,100 (far more than AUSTEN received for EMMA or Scott for *Waverley*), which demonstrated her facility with male characterization. *Popular Tales* (1804), *The Modern Griselda* (1805), *Leonora* (1806) and *Tales of Fashionable Life*

(1809 and 1812) followed, while *Harrington* (1817) confronted anti-semitism. An influence on Austen who sent her a copy of *Emma*, Edgeworth was not a radical feminist like WOLLSTONECRAFT and always championed domesticity, but she consistently asserted her belief in women's intellectual and moral equality. Regretfully turning down an offer of marriage while on a visit to Paris in 1802–3 in order to remain at home with her father, she declared after his death in 1817 that her motivation for writing was gone. However she completed his *Memoirs* (1820) and wrote a last novel, *Helen* (1834), which later influenced GASKELL's *WIVES AND DAUGHTERS*. Visited by fashionable literary figures like Scott and feted in London and on the continent, she corresponded with distinguished writers like LAETITIA BARBAULD, ELIZABETH INCHBALD and ELIZABETH HAMILTON, and spent her last years enjoying her renown. LMT

Edginton, May 1883–1957 British novelist and dramatist. She married Francis Baily in 1912, having begun to write novels at the age of 26, and thereafter was both prolific and successful. Some of her stories were made into British and American films, one of the most famous being *Secrets*, written in collaboration with another contemporary playwright, Rudolph Besier, in which Mary Pickford starred in 1933. One of the most successful musicals of the inter-war period, *No! No! Nanette!* was based on her story, *His Lady Friends*.

The general tenor of her plots is indicated by some of the titles: *Emergency Wife, Experiment in Love, Oh! James!* and *Ladies Only*. Her stories were written between 1909 and 1955, and there are at least seventy recorded items: she was a constant contributor of short stories and serials to women's journals. She was a member of the Writers' Club of Cape Town and listed her interests as dancing, motoring, gardening and travelling. MEW

Edible Woman (1969) MARGARET ATWOOD's first published novel takes a sardonic look at male/female relations; she herself described it as 'protofeminist'. A young graduate, Marian, faces the choice between a dead-end career and marriage. Her response is one of alienation. She finds herself repelled by the 'thick sargasso-sea' of women's flesh and femaleness; at the same time food seems increasingly to be alive. She views herself in the third person, objectified, observing with curious detachment her body's progressive rejection of food. The novel is suffused with cannibalistic images, as Marian progressively perceives the world in terms of eaters and eaten. Even her job in market research sees women as consumers, a role she rejects in her involuntary anorexia. Through her relationship with Duncan (a sort of *alter ego* and anorexic mirror), and having left her job, she concludes that it is not she who consumes but her fiancé Peter who is

eating her. Asserting herself, she thoroughly frightens him off by baking him a woman-shaped cake. In ridding herself of both job and potential husband, she regains appetite, autonomy and energy. SAS

Edmond, Lauris 1924– New Zealand poet whose warm-hearted, accessible work is at its best when celebrating or mourning family events. Her literary career began late but made up for lost time. She was born in Hawkes Bay, trained as a teacher, and spent much of her early life in country towns. She married a fellow teacher and they had six children. In the early 1970s, with her family, she moved to Wellington, became editor of an educational journal, met other writers, and had her first collection of poems accepted. Before it appeared, in 1975, one of her daughters died. This tragedy tinged Edmond's subsequent poetry with a darker tone; beneath the often joyous celebrations of passing moments – her much-praised 'epiphanies' – there is a consciousness of transience and mortality. Reconciliation and the process of coming to terms with loss or change are important themes, together with birth, death, and love of all kinds. She is endlessly interested in people and their motives. Some of her work shows a questing eagerness to understand which can express itself, in its shallower moments, almost as naivety, but at its most profound achieves the status of wisdom. She is a poet of great emotional directness, whether writing from personal experience or as an observer. She shows little interest in verse-forms; her style is neutrally conventional, and the language relaxed and often colloquial, with an increasing use of self-deprecating wit.

After her late début she published prolifically, to considerable acclaim. Her *Selected Poems* (1984) won the Commonwealth Poetry Prize in 1985. Since then there have been five more collections, including *New and Selected Poems* (1991). Perhaps the strongest individual volume is *Seasons and Creatures* (1986), in which her technical skills for the first time matched her insights and descriptive power. She has also published a novel, *High Country Weather* (1984), set in 1950s rural New Zealand.

Her candid *Autobiography* (1994), first published in three separate parts (1989-92) and later condensed into one, caused a stir, not because it was particularly outrageous but because she wrote frankly about her family, her friendships and the long decay of her marriage, with its wider effects. (For many years she and her husband led separate lives, during which time she had several lovers, sometimes pseudonymous in her text but easily identified in such a small society.) Her serious motive in this undertaking was to chart her journey toward her emergence as a poet, and to document and validate her submerged, pre-literary life as a wife and mother in the years when, as she put it to fellow writers who had begun their careers early, she 'wasn't anywhere' – or so it appeared to those who saw women's domestic lives as unimportant. The autobiography and the poems have fed fruitfully into each other, with poems providing illustrations for the autobiography, while the long process of examining her life and times called up new material for poems.   FA

Edwardians, The (1930) VITA SACKVILLE-WEST's satirical evocation of the era before her own. This is a restless FIN-DE-SIÈCLE world in which the older generation, representing the quintessential complacency of the Edwardian aristocracy, with its private language, its insulated faith in its own traditions, and its sense of innate and impermeable separation from the middle class, is challenged by the sexually jaded young hero's infatuation with the pretty young wife of a doctor. At first, he finds her disingenuousness refreshing, while she is dazzled by her acquaintance with a 'real duke', whose life and milieu she has only glimpsed but longs to know better. Each falls for a myth which dissolves with collision of the two worlds at the Dowager's Christmas party. Teresa's artless imitations of the language and nonchalance of fellow-guests irritate rather than amuse Sebastian, an irritation which nevertheless strengthens his resolve to seduce her, a physical reality from which her genteel sensibilities ultimately revolt in a belated protest of virtue. The Edwardian era comes to an end; Sebastian's disillusion is almost complete, but for his family seat, Chevron, and all it stands for. The novel closes with an ironic anticipation of war, in which Tradition might serve gallantry better than experience.   JLB

Edwards, Amelia (Ann Blandford) 1831–92 Popular mid-Victorian English novelist who, later in her career, became well known for her scholarly work on ancient Egypt. Edwards was the daughter of an army-officer-cum-banker, and was educated at home. She was interested in writing (and indeed was published) at an early age, and began writing professionally when her family suffered a financial setback. She published stories in many periodicals, including *Chambers' Journal*, *Saturday Review* and Dickens's *Household Words*. Her first of eight novels, *My Brother's Wife*, appeared in 1855. *Barbara's History* (1864) established her reputation. The novel is a first-person narrative of a neglected girl who, grown up and happily married, comes to believe (wrongly, it turns out) that her husband is a bigamist; it combined several familiar mid-Victorian plot devices and was very successful. Other novels include *Hand and Glove* (1865) and *Debenham's Vow* (1870). In the early 1870s she published a travel book describing the Dolomites and set out on a trip up the Nile with a female friend. She was fascinated by Egypt and its history, and began researching

and excavating Egyptian archaeological sites. *A Thousand Miles up the Nile* (1877) was both a travel guide and a historical discussion of Egyptian culture and its artifacts, and sold very well. She later toured America lecturing on Egypt (publishing the lectures' substance as *Pharoahs, Fellahs, and Explorers* in 1891), helped to found the Egyptian Exploration Fund, and bequeathed money to establish an Egyptology chair at University College, London.   KW

Edwards, Matilda (Barbara) Betham 1836–1919 This erudite and versatile English author travelled extensively throughout her adult life, visiting places as exotic as Egypt and Algeria and publishing TRAVEL-books such as *Through Spain to the Sahara* (1868). However, she most often toured France and a significant proportion of her writing – fiction and non-fiction – depicts the French way of life. In recognition of this, the French Government awarded her the title of Officier de l'Instruction Publique de France in 1891.

At her best, she delineates landscapes with an almost photographic fidelity and sketches characters, real or imagined, in a manner that is perceptive but disconcertingly dispassionate. Thus, in her fictional chronicle of French life, *A Close Ring* (1907), the enclosed world of the Miot family is evoked vividly though without sentimentality. Similarly, in the short story *A Japanese Bride* (1881), the jealous wife's actions are described by an unimaginative fellow-character rather than an omniscient and sympathetic narrator. However, the plot of a longer tale, *Exchange no Robbery* (1882), is more sentimental in tone – two German foster-sisters exchange identities so that each can marry the man she loves – this perhaps indicating the occasional compromise on the author's part between her art and the requirements of her publishers. Amongst the best-known of Matilda Betham Edwards's novels during her lifetime were *Kitty* (1870) and *The Lord of the Harvest* (1889).   EMH

Edwards, Sarah Pierpont 1710–58 As a 13-year-old girl, the American Calvinist letter-writer and SPIRITUAL AUTOBIOGRAPHER Sarah Pierpont was celebrated in Revd Jonathan Edwards's tribute to her as 'a young lady in [New Haven] who is beloved of that Great Being'. Daughter of Revd James, and Mary Hooker Pierpont of New Haven, she married Edwards on 28 July 1727. Recognized for the elegant prose and profound religious sentiment in her correspondence with her daughters, ESTHER EDWARDS BURR and Mary Edwards Dwight, Edwards also authored the narrative of her 1742 conversion experience, which is included in the *Memoirs of Jonathan Edwards*. This essay expresses her immense joy in the knowledge of the presence of God in her life, and the intimacy of her relationship with the deity: 'He was mine and I his.' This narrative also discusses her understanding of the social imperative of spiritual regeneration: 'I felt a far greater love to the children of God, than ever before. I seemed to love them as my own soul; and when I saw them, my heart went out towards them, with an expressible endearedness and sweetness.'   DZB

Egerton, George (Mary Chavelita Bright, née Dunne)

1859–1945 Influential and controversial NEW WOMAN writer in the 1890s and exemplar of 'feminine modernity' to critics in the 1990s. Best known for KEYNOTES (1893), a series of 'psychological moments' exploring the 'enigma of woman', the title volume of a modish series of fictions by new writers published by John Lane. Born in Melbourne of Irish and Welsh parentage, Egerton's colourful, peripatetic youth provided her with fictional settings and subjects. Abandoning ambitions to become a painter to train as a nurse, she later eloped to Norway in 1888 (with Henry Higginson, a married friend of her father). She subsequently married the minor Canadian novelist George Egerton Clairmonte and, after her divorce, Reginald Golding Bright (a theatrical agent). In Norway she encountered Ibsen's plays, Knut Hamsun (whose novel, *Hunger*, she translated in 1899), drunken brutality (Higginson's) and the precariousness of the NEW WOMAN's situation, which inform her nineties fiction. The bleak, shocking stories in *Keynotes*, *Discords* (1894), *Symphonies* (1897) and *Fantasies* (1898) focus on struggling women, alone, or trapped in a marriage (or similar relationship) with inarticulate, imperceptive or drunken and brutal men. Self-consciously modern in form, they are impressionistic, allusive, episodic, making extensive use of dream, reverie and interior monologue. Egerton also wote an undervalued novel, *The Wheel of God* (1898) – the story of a young Irishwoman's struggle for independence as a writer and journalist in New York – and several unsuccessful plays, including *His Wife's Family* (1908), *The Backsliders* (1910) and *Camilla States Her Case* (1925).   LP

Egerton [née Fyge], Sarah (Field)

1668–1723 English poet, known principally for *The Female Advocate* (1686, 1687), and for poems in defence of women's rights. Grand-daughter of Valentine Fyge, London common councilman and Samuel Pepys's friend, and daughter of prominent apothecary, author and alderman Thomas Fyge, at about the age of 19 Egerton was banished from her London home for the 'crime' of publishing two editions of *The Female Advocate*, a response to Robert Gould's oft-printed, misogynist *Love Given O're* (1682). Egerton's rejoinder, signed 'S.F.', castigates clergymen, politicians, satirists and other male hypocrites, and sets forth in rhyme many commonplaces in the 'defence of women' genre; vindicat-

ing Eve, citing historical heroines and establishing gender equality in 'like Rational Souls'. Writing as 'Clarinda' or 'Larinda', Fyge recounts this 'banishment' and other elements of her life, including an unhappy first marriage to Edward Field, a lawyer, and her unrequited love for her husband's clerk, in *Poems on Several Occasions* [1703], published with commendatory poems by 'M.P.' (probably MARY PIX) and 'S.C.' (possibly SUSANNA CENTLIVRE). After Egerton unsuccessfully sued her second husband, Thomas Egerton, an elderly country clergyman, for divorce on the grounds of cruelty in 1703, the scandal became fodder for *The New Atalantis* (1709) by DELARIVIÈRE MANLEY, Egerton's former friend and fellow-contributor to *The Nine Muses* (1700), a collection of elegies on John Dryden. Egerton contributed another elegy on Dryden to *Luctus Britannici* (1700) and also composed an unpublished panegyric to Marlborough (1708). Her most anthologized poems, 'The Liberty' and 'The Emulation', defy the 'tyranny' of custom, marriage and public censure, and exhort women to 'attempt the Sciences and Arts'.   JSM

Eggleston, Kim

1960– Regional poet of the South Island, New Zealand, whose idiomatic, unadorned style matches her up-front, macho persona. Her settings are the pub or café and small towns like Picton, Greymouth on the West Coast, or the peninsula, Dunedin; her themes are the hardship endured by coal-mining communities, the difficulties of relationships, the heartlessness of nature. Violence is a fact of life, death comes quickly, and her essential intimacy with these facts of existence gives her work a bleak, nervous energy. Although her rhythmical fluency, terse tone and minimal punctuation suit performance, the content of her work argues for a private rather than a public readership. Eggleston's gestures toward escape from her provincial, rural realities by opting for the daring image, the romantic scenario, inevitably end in hard-nosed acceptance.

> My cigarette tastes like a cypress
> bending cool over the lagoon
> My legs are long enough
> to circle the moon.

Hers is a world close to nature, where compromise is rare. She has published *From the Face to the Bin: Poems 1978–1984* (1984), and *25 Poems: the Mist will Rise and the World Will Drip with Gold* (1985), and, with others, *The Whole Crack* (1987).   JMW

El Saadawi, Nawal (El Sayed)

1931– Egyptian writer, physician, activist and self-proclaimed 'historical social feminist' who first came to the attention of English readers with the translation of her non-fictional work, *The Hidden Face of Eve* (1980). El

Saadawi's many books include novels, short-story collections, plays, memoirs and scholarly books. She has also published innumerable articles in journals and newspapers both in her native Egypt and in the western world. The first part of her autobiography was published in Arabic in 1995.

For El Saadawi, writing constitutes a potent weapon, stronger in the fight against malaise than medicine itself. The recognition that poverty is the root cause of ill health for most patients in rural Egypt prompted her to stop practising medicine and take up writing. Her writings centre mainly on sex, politics and religion.

Her uncompromising critique of her culture; her exposition of the web of oppression woven by tradition, religion, patriarchy and a class system; and her analysis of male–female disparity as a tool for the oppressor are stances that have earned her animosity from the Egyptian government.

Her first work of non-fiction, *Women and Sex*, was banned on publication in 1970 and cost her her jobs as Director of Health in the ministry and editor of a health journal. For three months in 1981, she was imprisoned without trial. She was subsequently banned from television appearances, a ban which still holds to date. Not to be deterred, El Saadawi has continued to write, even using her difficulties as the subject of some of her works such as *Memoirs from the Women's Prison* (1987), *Woman at Point Zero* (1983) and *The Fall of the Imam* (1988). In 1982 El Saadawi founded The Arab Women's Solidarity Association for the advancement of Arab women. PMM

Elaw, Zilpha 1790?–? African-American evangelist and preacher who wrote a SPIRITUAL AUTOBIOGRAPHY. Born to free parents near Philadelphia, Pennsylvania, Elaw was put to service with a Quaker family by her father after her mother died when she was 12 years old. She records having visions of Christ in her teens and converting to Christianity soon after in 1808. Two years later, Elaw married, but the marriage was riddled with conflicts over her religious zeal. In 1817, Elaw attended her first religious camp meeting. Later, she exhorted a congregation and discovered that she had been called to preach by God. Despite objections from her husband and others, she began her own public ministry. She travelled into the South to preach, risking being sold into slavery. Her narrative, *Memoirs of the Life, Religious Experience, Ministerial Travels and Labours of Mrs Elaw*, is dedicated to the British Christian community where she spent five years, preaching. The narrative follows the conventions of traditional SPIRITUAL AUTOBIOGRAPHY, with a carefully chosen pattern of events that mirror her spiritual journey. Foremost in the narrative is her sense of self as an agent of the divine, and her bold defiance of socially prescribed racial and gender roles. CJ

Eldershaw, Flora 1897–1956 Australian novelist, historian, and one half of the writing team, 'M. Barnard Eldershaw', formed with MARJORIE BARNARD, whom she met at Sydney University. Born at Wagga Wagga, New South Wales, she grew up on a Riverina sheep station, and after graduating taught at a private girls' school from 1921 to 1940. During this period four of 'Barnard Eldershaw's' five novels, a collection of critical essays and other works were published. There has been debate about exactly what each woman contributed to the partnership; it has been claimed that Barnard did the actual writing while Eldershaw did more of the initial planning, but there is no firm evidence for this. Certainly, Eldershaw was more active in public life than Barnard, being President of the Sydney branch of the Fellowship of Australian Writers in 1935 and 1943 and a member of the Commonwealth Literary Fund Advisory Board, 1939–53. During World War II she worked for the Department of Reconstruction and later became a private industrial consultant before her early death. EW

Eldridge [née Stockfeld], Marian 1936–97 Australian writer. Born in Melbourne, Eldridge grew up in the Gippsland countryside, and graduated from the University of Melbourne. She married Kenneth Eldridge, and the couple had four children. Eldridge worked as a teacher before she published her first book, the collection of short stories *Walking the Dog* (1984), which gained the attention of overseas reviewers. James Cain wrote in the *New York Review of Books* that 'her writing resonates with life'. She published one more collection, *The Woman at the Window* (1989), before her only novel, *Springfield* (1992), a story of redemption concerning a young heroin addict and a Vietnam veteran. A later collection, *The Wild Sweet Flowers* (1994), reworked some of her earlier material in a new sequence which included additional stories. Before her death Eldridge gained a reputation for her narrative skill and her subtle, often poetic, revelation of character. SDo

Elfyn, Menna 1951– Internationalist poet, broadcaster and journalist, whose political commitments are always underwritten by her prior commitment to the Welsh language. Elfyn published six acclaimed poetry collections in Wales, including *Eucalyptus: Detholiad o Gerddi / Selected Poems 1978-1994* from Gomer in 1995. Her friend and mentor, the academic Tony Conran, called her 'the first Welsh poet in fifteen hundred years to make a serious attempt to have her work known outside Wales'. Newcastle publisher Bloodaxe Books, aware of her growing international reputation, published her bilingual *Cell Angel* the following year, giving her voice a wider airing. The book's title is double-edged: her cell is not just a prison –

Elfyn has twice been imprisoned as a result of Welsh nationalist protests – but also a place for contemplation, while her angel is both Eastern and Christian. Religion dances under the surface of her work. One of Elfyn's influences is the Catholic Utte Ranke, a woman who questions the basis of a religion founded on a cross, on suffering and on blood.

Elfyn's is essentially a communitarian and compassionate vision, her politics subtle, succeeding as parables rather than polemic. When she writes of her own imprisonment, she does so with a conscious conscience:

Nid Pasternak mohonof
Na Mandelstam ychwaith
Gallwn dalu fy ffordd o'r ddalfa
Teirawr a byddwn yn y ty.
[I'm no Pasternak
nor Mandelstam,
I could buy my way out of here,
Three hours and I'd be home.]

The point is that she didn't buy her way out.

Like her Irish-speaking contemporary NUALA NÍ DHOMHNAILL her work enacts dreams of nationhood. Yet, like Ní Dhomhnaill again, she is probably at her best when writing of personal matters. Elfyn's diction has been criticized for its 'difficulty' and this quality has been debated at the National Eisteddfod in Wales. Her cycle of poems dedicated to the memory of the Welsh historian Gwyn A. Williams elicited a troubled response from the judges in 1996. Their reservations concerning obscurity and 'dark wordiness' denied Elfyn the crown.　　　　　　　　　　　　　DM

Elgin, Suzette Haden 1936–　The working name of American poet, SCIENCE-FICTION writer and teacher of linguistics, Patricia Anne Suzette Wilkins Elgin, who in 1978 founded the Science Fiction Poetry Association. Much of her science fiction – the 'Coyote Jones' and 'Ozark' sequences, which overlap in *Yonder Comes the Other End of Time* (1986) – deals evocatively with a variety of locales, notably the magic-based hillbilly human colony of Ozark and the ultra-sexist Arabian world of *Furthest* (1971). They have ramshackle slightly flip conventional plots of derring-do on lost human colonies, unworthy of their emotional content and, in the Ozark books, real charm and lightness of touch. (*Furthest* is explicitly echoed in JOANNA RUSS's *The Two of Them* (1978) as a feminist text.) Elgin taught Linguistics at UCLA, San Diego, and her most influential sequence of sf novels, *Native Tongue* (1984) and *The Judas Rose* (1987), use linguistics as the basis of a fight back by women against a near-future misogynist dystopia: declared inferior by a Constitutional Amendment in 1991, women withdraw into their own intellectual space by creating their own language, and

are thus best equipped to deal with superior aliens when the latter, in the second book, arrive. From 1980 onwards, Elgin produced the slightly tongue-in-cheek self-help sequence *The Gentle Art of Verbal self-defense* and its sequels.　　　　　　　　　　　　　　　RK

Eliot, George [Mary Ann[e] Cross, née Evans]

1819–80 English REALIST novelist, poet, essayist and translator, Eliot believed that art could approach truth only through the faithful reproduction of ordinary human existence, describing her own complex narratives as 'simply a set of experiments in life'. The daughter of a self-educated estate manager and land agent, Eliot grew up in rural Warwickshire, attending local boarding schools from an early age. From 1837 she acted as her father's housekeeper, moving with him to Coventry in 1841. Here her friendship with a local freethinker, Charles Bray, and his family, stimulated Eliot's nascent doubt about conventional religious belief and precipitated her, in 1842, into a 'Holy War' with her father. Eliot examined her scepticism with reference to the German school of biblical criticism, translating, as her first mature publication, David Strauss's *The Life of Jesus* (1846), followed in 1854 by Ludwig Feuerbach's *The Essence of Christianity*. After her father's death, Eliot lived briefly in Geneva, returning, in 1850, to act as *de facto* editor of the *Westminster Review* under John Chapman's ownership. In London she met the philosopher and sociologist Herbert Spencer with whom she had a brief and unsuccessful romance. In addition, she wrote a series of essays for the *Review* in which she started to formulate the aesthetic based on the 'doctrine' of realism ('that all truth and beauty are to be attained by a humble and faithful study of nature') which would underpin her own writing career.

Eliot began her first short story in 1856, later theorizing her work as an example of the 'real and concrete' in art and undertaking to 'exhibit nothing as it should be' but rather 'some things as they have been or are, seen through such a medium as my own nature gives me'. This literary agenda was given essential encouragement by the writer and scientist G.H. Lewes, who cultivated the emotional and intellectual conditions under which Eliot flourished and with whom she lived from 1854 until his death in 1878. Ostracized by her family and by society for the irregularity of her union with Lewes (whose indissoluble first marriage precluded their own), Eliot rebuilt her reputation through a series of increasingly successful novels: *Scenes of Clerical Life* (1858) was followed by ADAM BEDE (1859), THE MILL ON THE FLOSS (1860), SILAS MARNER (1861), *Romola* (1863) and FELIX HOLT (1866). George Eliot also published two volumes of poetry (*The Spanish Gypsy*, 1868, and *The Legend of Jubal*, 1874) and a collection of character sketches (*Impressions of Theophrastus Such*, 1879), but it was the appearance of

MIDDLEMARCH (1871–2) and *DANIEL DERONDA* (1876) which confirmed her status as the greatest 19th-century English realist (VIRGINIA WOOLF described *Middlemarch* as 'one of the few English novels written for grown-up people').

The ambivalence of Eliot's own social position was undoubtedly reflected in her equivocal relationship to subjects such as the Woman Question or the public identity of the author. As 'George Eliot', however, she was a writer of profound intellect (but also notable warmth and humour), blending contemporary science and philosophy into a secular realist ethic based on the principle that 'if Art does not enlarge men's sympathies, it does nothing morally'. By the end of her life Eliot had written herself into national respectability. In 1880 she unexpectedly married her friend John Cross, twenty years her junior, but died eight months later aged 61. AS

Elizabeth I [Elizabeth Tudor] 1533–1603 Queen of England and writer of poetry, speeches, translations and letters. Daughter of Henry VIII and ANNE BOLEYN, she excelled in her Protestant humanist education. Aged 11, she translated Marguerite de Navarre's *Mirror of a Sinful Soul* (published 1548) as a gift for Catherine Parr. She translated Petrarch's 'Triumph of Eternity' sometime around her accession in 1558.

Elizabeth wrote most of her speeches herself, and several were published. Earlier speeches to Parliament asserted self-determination in the marriage question, while late in the reign the 'Golden Speech' mythologized the love between Queen and people. The words supposedly spoken as the Armada approached in 1588 – 'I know I have the body of a weak and feeble woman, but I have the heart and stomach of a king' – may not, unfortunately, be accurate (contemporary accounts differ).

Around fourteen poems attributable to Elizabeth survive. 'The doubt of future foes' (1569) refers to the security threat of MARY, QUEEN OF SCOTS, 'the daughter of debate'. A Petrarchan poem beginning 'I grieve and dare not show my discontent' is associated with the departure of the Duke of Anjou, Elizabeth's last potential husband, in 1582. Verses by Sir Walter Ralegh bemoaning the Queen's fickleness provoked an imperious reply: 'Ah silly pug, wert thou so sore afraid?' (1587). A book of *Devotions* in four languages, and a poem sung during the Armada victory celebrations, may also be Elizabeth's compositions. She translated works by Seneca, Boethius (1593), Plutarch (1598) and Horace (1598).

Elizabeth was extensively and inventively celebrated by contemporary writers, and inspired 17th-century women like AEMELIA LANYER and DIANA PRIMROSE. She often features in later fiction as a counter-type to Mary, Queen of Scots. HH

George Eliot: drawing of, by Princess Louise on her concert programme, 1877.

Elizabeth and her German Garden (1898) ELIZABETH VON ARNIM's first work, presented as the diary of 'Elizabeth' and based on her experiences on her husband's Pomeranian estate, owed its immense Edwardian popularity to its astute combination of GARDENING diary and feminist polemic. Elizabeth recounts a year spent replanting the neglected gardens of a German country-house. Detailed descriptions of planting successes and mistakes alternate with reveries in which Elizabeth discovers a lost self-awareness. As in BURNETT's *THE SECRET GARDEN*, the garden effects redemption; Elizabeth refuses to re-enter the house and resume the role of German housewife, instead finding independence and contentment outside with her three infant daughters. Her husband, the comically sexist 'Man of Wrath', perceives gardens as insignificant spaces appropriate for legal and political nobodies, but enjoys women's charming prattle, on which, indeed, the book banks heavily. Von Arnim's innovative and artful mix of gardening tips and domestic detail with feminist debate and commentary anticipates many later women's columns in newspapers. AT

Elliot [née Carnegie], Lady Charlotte 1839–80 British poet, was the daughter of Sir James and Lady

Charlotte Carnegie. Three years after the death of her first husband, Thomas Fotheringham, she published, as 'Florenz', *Stella, and Other Poems* (1867). The title work is a long dramatic poem which tells the turbulent story of the doomed love of an Italian patriot, Count Marone, for Stella, daughter of a Neapolitan nobleman. Marone's resolve to seek the distracting 'storm and the strife' of the battlefield after Stella's death echoes Tennyson's *Maud*. Other poems in the volume, such as 'Desolate', about a deserted lover, and 'The Prayer of the Penitent', about a speaker 'crouching at [God's] feet in abject shame', reveal a considerable interest in representing moments of intense and painful experience. She married Frederick Elliot, the son of an earl, in 1868 and published *Medusa and Other Poems* in 1878. This volume, dedicated to her husband, contains many short and melancholy pieces on time, love and death, while the title poem is a sympathetic account of the 'unspeakable woe' of Medusa before she is slain and her 'days of despair' are ended by Perseus. Fifty copies of *Mary Magdalene and Other Poems* (1880) were privately printed, as she had requested, after her death.   FJO'G

Elliott, Janice 1931–

English novelist and short-story writer whose always stylish work sometimes fails to deliver at the weight to which its doom-laden social context lays claim. In many of her twenty-four novels, elegantly written tales of middle-class angst have an insistent undertow of violent threat – of disconnection, disintegration and death, gestured at rather than realized. The technique succeeds when threat is not rendered by casual reference to terrorism, food riots and extinct whales but operates at story level. In *Figures in the Sand* (1994), the sense of civilization under threat, of death as always close, of the saving grace of sustained human affections and the small but crucial epiphanies it affords, is fully realized in the story of a general (of the second Roman empire: Elliott's apocalyptic visions are often set in a near future) in an outpost at the dangerous and abandoned edge of empire. Here metaphor fuses with the literal and characters and situation are well able to carry the weight of Elliott's concern with the central issues of the human condition.   EA

Ellis [née Lindholm], Alice Thomas [Anna Margaret Haycraft] 1932–

English novelist, publisher, journalist and non-fiction writer. Born in Liverpool, Alice Thomas Ellis's childhood was largely spent on the North Wales Coast, and several of her novels have Welsh settings. She was educated at Bangor Grammar School and Liverpool College of Art, and was briefly a postulant in a Liverpool convent, having converted to Roman Catholicism at the age of 19. She moved to London, and there met and married Colin Haycraft, at the time a director of Weidenfeld and Nicolson, and later chairman and managing director of the publisher Duckworth. Ellis served as a director and fiction editor at Duckworth, which published much of her earlier work, and also the work of BERYL BAINBRIDGE and CAROLINE BLACKWOOD.

Ellis's novels are spare, witty satires, drawing heavily on her preoccupation with Catholicism and feminism. Although they frequently have DOMESTIC settings, either in Wales or London, the novels are elegant and intelligent elaborations of the moral choices that face their characters, and occasionally have magical overtones. *THE SIN EATER*, published in 1977, was Ellis's first novel, and told the dark story of a Welsh patriarchal family. It was followed by *THE 27TH KINGDOM* in 1982 (the story of an ex-nun with miraculous powers, it was shortlisted for the Booker Prize), *Unexplained Laughter* (1985), *The Summerhouse Trilogy* (1991) (comprising *The Clothes in the Wardrobe* (1987), whose heroine was a young suburban girl on the brink of an unsuitable marriage, *The Skeleton in the Cupboard* (1988) and *The Fly in the Ointment* (1989)), *Pillars of Gold* (1992) and *This Rock* (1993). She is also the author of four volumes of columns about her family life, *Home Life* (1986–9), and *Serpent on the Rock* (1994), a personal view of contemporary Roman Catholic Christianity.   AC

Ellis, Edith (Lees) [Edith Mary Oldham] 1861–1916

English lesbian feminist novelist, essayist, short-story writer and playwright who advocated the moral and spiritual transformation of society on the basis of sexual freedom, tolerance and social equality. Close to OLIVE SCHREINER, ELEANOR MARX and Edward Carpenter, she married Havelock Ellis in 1891, recreating their open marriage in *Seaweed: A Cornish Idyll* (1898). Havelock Ellis, in *Sexual Inversion* (1897) and *My Life* (1939), presented her as an energetic and fiercely independent woman who nevertheless suffered from nervous disorders.

In *Attainment* (1909) Ellis took issue with the Fellowship of the New Life, whose secretary she had been in 1889–92. Her fictional and dramatic work provides local-colour sketches (*My Cornish Neighbours*, 1906; *The Subjection of Kezia*, 1908), while also reflecting on her early life (*Love-Acre*, 1914) and retracing periods of depression (*The Imperishable Wing*, 1911). In her essays and public lectures collected in *The New Horizon in Love and Life* (1921) and *Stories and Essays* (1924) she promoted a practical vision of class and sexual relations tinged with eugenic undertones; and celebrated Nietzsche, free-love advocate James Hinton and the socialist sexologist Edward Carpenter in *Three Modern Seers* (1910). Ellis died after completing two lecture tours in America.   AH

Ellis, Sarah Stickney [Mrs Ellis] 1799–1872

Conservative British moralist particularly associated

with 'separate spheres' ideology, which she manipulated to the benefit of women, Mrs Ellis had a varied career as writer, temperance activist and educationalist. Born to a prosperous Quaker farming family at Holderness in Yorkshire, she married the Congregationalist missionary William Ellis in 1837, when already an established author. Her first important work, *Pictures of Private Life* (3 series, 1833–7), a collection of short stories with moral themes, was prefaced by an *Apology for Fiction* in which she anticipated later writers' use of 'DOMESTIC realism'. *The Poetry of Life* (1835) followed with essays on aesthetics, and her first full-length novel, *Home or The Iron Rule* (1836), typically emphasized the role of the mother within the middle-class family. Her views on middle-class gender relations are most clearly seen in the conduct-books for which she is now mainly remembered. *The Women of England, Their Social Duties and Domestic Habits* (1839), the most important of these, went through twenty-four editions and was followed by three sequels. In her conduct-books and in her short stories with a temperance theme, *Family Secrets or Hints To Those Who Would Make Home Happy* (1842), a woman's moral influence exerted within the home becomes the defining feature of a Christian wife and mother: manipulation of men by women is a clearly discernible sub-text. Mrs Ellis's ideas were satirized by Thackeray and Jerrold in *Punch* and attacked by GERALDINE JEWSBURY.   HST.M

Elstob, Elizabeth 1683–1756 British Anglo-Saxon scholar, she was born in Newcastle-upon-Tyne. Her parents died while she was still young and, although prevented from furthering her studies by her uncle who thought one 'Tongue enough for a Woman', she went on to learn eight languages. Whilst living and studying alongside her clergyman brother, William, who had been educated at Eton, Cambridge and Oxford, Elstob was encouraged by the scholar George Hickes to publish her own work, including *An English-Saxon Homily on the Birthday of St Gregory* (1709) and *Rudiments of Grammar for the English Tongue ... with an Apology for the Study of Northern Antiquities* (1712). After her brother's death in 1715, she failed at running a school in Evesham, and her plight came to the attention of HESTER CHAPONE's mother who raised subscriptions for an annuity from several eminent women. Still unable to support herself, Elstob gave up writing and became governess to the Duchess of Portland's children. Her considerable scholarly achievements were recognized during her lifetime and had the effect of drawing attention to Anglo-Saxon studies as well as to the issue of female education. George Ballard's pioneering work, *Memoirs of Several Ladies of Great Britain Celebrated for their Writings* (1752), owed much to earlier lists of illustrious women begun by Elstob in 1709.   RDM

Emecheta, Buchi 1944– Nigerian novelist, born in Lagos, Nigeria. Emecheta is one of Africa's most acclaimed women writers, alongside BESSIE HEAD, AMA ATA AIDOO and FLORA NWAPA, whom she recognizes as her sisters in writing. Emecheta has enjoyed more success as a writer than any of her female African predecessors, due largely to the attention she has received from feminist critics, and has been able to live in London and 'keep my head above water' by writing since the 1970s. She has published thirteen novels – including THE BRIDE PRICE (1976), *The Slave Girl* (1977), THE JOYS OF MOTHERHOOD (1979), *Destination Biafra* (1982), *Double Yoke* (1982), *The Rape of Shavi* (1983), *A Kind of Marriage* (1986), *The Family* (1990) and *Kehinde* (1994). Autobiographical works include *Adah's Story* (1983) and *Head Above Water* (1986). She has also published a number of CHILDREN's books and numerous essays.

Emecheta has a reputation as one of Africa's most sustained and vigorous voices of direct, feminist protest. In her fiction she focuses on women's issues, and through her realistic portrayals of African women in Ibuza society, Emecheta exposes oppressive relationships that are sanctioned by Igbo myths and customs such as clitoridectomy and widow inheritance. However, she attributes her resistance to male dominance in African society not only to Western feminism but to oral traditions of story-telling and to the village organizations which have provided opportunities for African women to express their grievances. An advocate of global feminism, Emecheta aspires to a sisterhood between African and European women so that 'both of us together will hold hands and try to salvage what is left of our world from the mess the sons we have brought into it have made'.   GWh

Emelia see STOCKTON, ANNIS [BOUDINOT]

Emma (1816) The last novel to be published during her lifetime, this sophisticated comedy of manners is often regarded as JANE AUSTEN's finest. It records the progress of Highbury heiress Emma Woodhouse toward the marriage which will integrate her into the village's gentry community. Attractive, clever, wealthy and desirable, she is also, at the onset, spoiled, snobbish, wilful and misguided. The plot develops through romantic misrecognitions with painful consequences, for her and others: especially her orphan friend, Harriet Smith, whom she schemes to marry to the local vicar; and the silent, mysterious Jane Fairfax, whose caddish fiancé Frank Churchill uses Emma to deflect attention from their engagement. Austen develops the language of REALISM to anatomize, with wicked irony, the hierarchies of class and gender in a period when market relations were developing and a woman's place was being defined as wife and mother within the patriarchal family. The closing union between the novel's sentient centre, Austen's richest heiress, and its moral centre, the gentry capitalist Mr Knightley, cements the privileges of rank and property which her irony undermines but also reinforces.

The 1996 film of *Emma* emphasized the cruelty underlying much of Austen's dialogue; the British television version of the same year, by contrast, adopted a lighter comic tone. MO'D

Empire of the Senseless (1988) This was a breakthrough novel for KATHY ACKER, written on her revelation that it is impossible to write about a hypothetical freer society one doesn't actually inhabit. Paradise cannot be absolute, theory doesn't work. Her representation thus acquires the corporeal immediacy of Sadeian language: patch-worked by borrowed literary and journalistic discourses, without being too experimentally 'écriture féminine'. Having gone through the world of the oedipal myth, Abhor, part robot, part black, is thrown into another myth/place in a Paris taken over by Algerians in the revolution. Lost in a maze that is also, inevitably, politically controlled, she tries adopting nomadic identities as a sailor or a pirate, running away from and coming back to her partner, Thivai. Thivai starts his post-revolutionary narrative in the voice of Huckleberry Finn, while Abhor is like Ahab, as unfeeling as a fake leg because nothing is natural with her. He finally puts Abhor in goal, where she can become a great writer: a POST-MODERN female Sade the world needs. CY

Engel, Marian 1933–85 Canadian novelist and short-story writer born in Toronto, Canada. She studied at the Universities of McMaster and McGill; taught in Montreal and Montana; travelled widely in Europe; and worked in London and Cyprus before her return to Toronto in 1964. Her books include *Clouds of Glory* (1968), *The Honeyman Festival* (1970), *Joanne* (1975), *Bear* (1976), *The Glassy Sea* (1978) and *Lunatic Villas* (1981). *Bear* is the most notorious of these, a fable of Lou's island affair with a bear which won the Governor General's Award for fiction. Attempting 'to inscribe female sexuality on the wilderness', *Bear* stands as a seminal Canadian women's text, a furry, erotic, supremely unconventional tale which has acted as 'a guiding force' for writers such as ARITHA VAN HERK. Her work explores marriage, motherhood, woman's relationship to nature, family and sisterhood. Above all, she was concerned with gender divisions and rules, with the specificities of women's experience in a society which is 'completely sexually divided'. Against claims that 'gender is not a region', in 1978 she proclaimed 'try writing a novel from the other gender's point of view'. Engel's short fiction includes *Inside the Easter Egg* (1975) and *The Tattooed Woman* (1985). She also published two children's books, *Adventure at Moon Bay*

Towers (1974) and *My Name is not Odessa Yarker* (1977), and one non-fiction piece for *Islands of Canada* (1981). She was awarded the Order of Canada in 1982. CSt

Enormous Changes at the Last Minute (1974) The episodic pieces in Russian-Jewish-American GRACE PALEY's second short-story collection cemented her reputation as a genius of the genre. Set in the immigrant New York milieu in which she grew up, they combine formal innovation with a focus on moments of change in the humdrum but vibrant everyday lives of her quirky characters. Paley's breezy, fluid prose mixes pathos and irony within a resolutely optimistic frame. In the title story middle-aged Alexandra founds a community of pregnant women in her flat. There they bring up their children together, including her own, fathered by the idealistic young songwriter–taxi-driver Dennis. In a mysterious act of cultural reconnaissance, the narrator of 'The Long Distance Runner' jogs back to her childhood neighbourhood, now a decaying black ghetto, and moves in with the occupants of her old home. And in 'A Conversation with my Father', literary form itself becomes the subject, as a dying father tries to persuade his writer daughter to pen traditional stories with tragic closure. Despite his condition, she refuses, asserting that 'Everyone, real or invented, deserves the open destiny of life.' MO'D

Enough Rope (1926) A collection of epigrammatic and self-consciously tender poems, DOROTHY PARKER's first and bestselling collection of verse emerged from the sophisticated yet ostentatious New York of the 1920s. Speaking of death in a caustic manner, the volume conveys a sharp wit balanced by an underlying suicidal depression, drily portrayed in 'Résumé'. Parker's feminist plea to free women from imprisoning roles is enclosed within waspish and tragic narratives, the narrator equally pitiful and ridiculous within a glittering society marked by strained codes of politeness. Poems such as 'Chant for Dark Hours', 'Social Note' and 'General Review of the Sex Situation' bluntly reveal the differing expectations of men and women toward sexuality and love. Men are forever lascivious rascals who 'seldom make passes / At girls who wear glasses' ('News Item'), while women remain vapid and cautious, desperate for flattery. These acid portraits, loaded as they are with cynicism and deep bitterness, urge moral and social change as they wear down a speaker aware of the heavy emotional cost a woman pays for a razor-edged intellect.

EM

Enright, Anne 1962– Dublin writer, whose quirky wit has won her a reputation as one of the more interesting Irish newcomers. She studied in Vancouver, at

Trinity College, Dublin, and at the University of East Anglia, and worked in fringe theatre and television before becoming a full-time writer. Her striking collection of short stories, *The Portable Virgin* (1991), presented characters of spectacular strangeness, locked in a world they do not understand, where real communication seems impossible and bizarre behaviour arises out of desperation. Beneath the cool, epigrammatic surface, there is a strong sense, voiced by one of them, that 'Nothing is incomprehensible, when you know that life is sad.'

Her first novel, *The Wig My Father Wore* (1994), is a light-hearted subversion of the Annunciation in which a television producer falls in love with an angel and becomes pregnant. Enright uses this literal and metaphorical merging of the celestial and the down-to-earth to examine the traditional division between sacred and secular, alongside an affectionate portrayal of the complexities of family life. The resulting narrative is exuberant and erotic, a celebration of 'the astonishing web of the ordinary that keeps . . . the sun swinging in the sky'. CP

Ensing, Riemke 1939– New Zealand poet who emigrated from the Netherlands in 1951 and edited the pioneering anthology of New Zealand women's writing, *Private Gardens* (1975). Exile and her European heritage dominate Ensing's early volumes: *Letters* (1982), *Topographies* (1984) and *Spells from Chagall* (1987). But in *The KM File and other Poems with Katherine Mansfield* (1993) she celebrates the famous writer who also lived in two cultures by experimenting with intertextuality. Through glossing KM's texts, reproducing her autograph, photographs and sketches she conveys the impression of a dialogue. This form of collage emphasizes the fictionality of the texts and their multi-dimensionality as 'signatures' of the individual. *Dear Mr Sargeson* (1995), homage to New Zealand writer, Frank Sargeson, continues this practice. Ensing's fascination with art pervades her work, providing her with a significant European/antipodean matrix. *Like I have seen the green ladder climbing* (1995) responds to paintings by the artist Eion Stevens. JMW

Epanomitis, Fotini 1969– Australian novelist whose work combines magic realism, folk tale, and oral story-telling traditions. Her family migrated from Greece to Perth in the year of her birth. When she was 12, the family spent a year in the northern Greek village from which they came. Although both Greece and Australia shape her identity, Epanomitis maintains that she belongs to neither country. She has published short stories but is best known for her novel, THE MULE'S FOAL (1993), which conveys a rich sense of place but also the cultural dislocation often experienced by migrants. Set in a mythical Greek village, the novel evokes a magical and brutal world, in which mules give birth to foals and women to gorilla children, where people change sex and transmogrify into animals. While various periods of Greek history can be distinguished in the novel, Epanomitis describes its structure as non-linear and like a 'tapestry'. She writes in English although it is not her first language, and the novel incorporates directly translated Greek phrases such as 'when something or someone goes missing here, they say the earth eats'. *The Mule's Foal* won several prizes in Australia, including the Australian/Vogel Award and the Victorian Premier's Award. CPr

'Ephelia' fl.1678–82 British poet (or perhaps poets), author of *Female Poems on Several Occasions* (1679). 'Ephelia' praises APHRA BEHN, and it is likely that the two were acquainted: 'When first your strenuous polite Lines I read', declares 'Ephelia' in her poem 'To Madam *Bhen*',

> At once it Wonder and Amazement bred,
> To see such things flow from a Womans Pen,
> As might be Envy'd by the wittiest Men.

Her identity remains unknown but candidates include Elizabeth Mordaunt, a dubious attribution which was favoured by Edmund Gosse. It is possible that she was an actress or a courtier, apparently having a patron called 'Eugenia'.

Female Poems is a collection remarkable for its emotional and technical range. At its heart is a series of lyrics addressed to 'Strephon', the mysterious 'J.G.'. Charting a four-year relationship, the verses are at once witty and passionate. Verses in support of Charles II also appear in *Female Poems*, having first been published in 1678 as *A Poem to his Sacred Majesty on the Plot. Written by a Gentlewoman*. A play, *Pair-Royal of Coxcombs*, was performed at the same time, but only the sections reprinted in *Female Poems* survive. A verse broadside critical of Monmouth, *Advice to His Grace*, was circulated in about 1681 and ascribed to 'Ephelia'. Nothing is known of the elusive 'Ephelia' after this date, but the second edition of *Female Poems* (1682), containing additional verses by, among others, Rochester and Behn, may have been occasioned by her early death. ELER

Ephron, Nora 1941– American novelist, screenwriter, journalist, film director. Graduated from Wellesley College in Political Science, she started her career as reporter for the *New York Post* and wrote essays in *Esquire* and *New York* magazines, later collected in *Wallflowers at the Orgy* (1970) and *Crazy Salad* (1975). Her first novel, the amusing bestseller *Heartburn* (1983) – the plot of which is based on the break-up of the author's second marriage to the *Washington Post* journalist Carl Bernstein, famous for his role in exposing the Watergate scandal – was made into a successful screenplay and movie. In this work, as in her other writings, she expresses wry and perceptive observations on the relationships between the sexes. Though her tone is brilliant and ironical, and the effect often definitely hilarious, her treatment of the themes of love and sex, and of the adjustments and negotiations in the ever-evolving relationships between women and men, is deeper and more incisive than it may appear at first reading.

The daughter of two Hollywood screenwriters, since 1980 she has been working very successfully for the cinema: her first screenplay, which won an Academy Award nomination, was *Silkwood* (1983), followed by *When Harry Met Sally* (1989), which examined whether friendship is possible between a man and a woman sexually attracted to each other, and *Sleepless in Seattle* (1993), 'a cross-country romantic comedy with the charm of a Hollywood classic'. *Michael* (1996), is about an angel who is no saint.   MB

epistolary fiction Fictional narratives written in the form of letters were at their most popular during the 18th century, and played an important part in the 'rise' and wider definition of the novel. The 'familiar letter' establishes the novel's interest in the minutiae of subjective experience, and in the articulation of an individualized self. Private, yet written for a particular recipient, letters are not simply spontaneous expressions of feeling, but formalized, strategic performances, and epistolary fiction, offering multiple points of view, makes the difficulty and relativism of interpretation central to the process of novel-reading.

In 1785 Samuel Richardson was described, in CLARA REEVE's critical dialogue THE PROGRESS OF ROMANCE, as 'the first who wrote Novels in the Epistolary style'. But Richardson was preceded by a large number of epistolary fictions, many by women. APHRA BEHN's LOVE LETTERS BETWEEN A NOBLEMAN AND HIS SISTER (1684–7), popular throughout the 18th century, was the first English novel entirely in letters. This followed the great success of the *Lettres portugaises* (1669; trans. 1678), claimed to have been written by a Portuguese nun to the lover who had deserted her. Many of the popular seduction and scandal fictions of DELARIVIÈRE MANLEY and ELIZA HAYWOOD were told exclusively or extensively through characters' letters. At its inception, then, there was a strong association between the epistolary form and the expression of sexual desire – particularly of women's illicit or frustrated desires – an association already established within the classical tradition by Ovid's *Heroides*, verse epistles by abandoned heroines.

More generally, letters (including letter collections) feature prominently within the early 18th century's rapidly expanding print culture. In all kinds of proto-novelistic texts, letters – fictional or otherwise – are used as the sign of authenticity and immediacy. Periodicals quickly exploited possibilities for reader participation, encouraging (sometimes manufacturing) letters to the editor and versions of the modern agony column; the much-reprinted conduct book, *The Lady's New-Years Gift* (1688), by George Savile, Marquis of Halifax, establishes the epistolary address as a standard feature of advice literature; the characters in, for example, ELIZABETH SINGER ROWE's *Letters Moral and Entertaining, in Prose and Verse* (1728), work out their moral and amorous crises in letters to friends. In such texts, letters are a point of negotiation between public responsibility and private feeling, instruction and pleasure, didactic judgement and sympathy, actuality and fiction.

Richardson developed these fictional and proto-fictional uses of the letter to a point of great sophistication in *Pamela* (1740), *Clarissa* (1747-8) and *Sir Charles Grandison* (1753-4), in the preface to which he famously stressed the REALIST immediacy of this 'writing to the moment'. *Pamela*, written almost exclusively in the voice of the protagonist, evoked violently contradictory responses: Pamela's letters were seen both as an exemplary expression of feminine innocence, and, most famously in Fielding's parody *Shamela* (1741), as the calculated performance of a devious self-seeker. In *Clarissa*, the heroine's voice competes throughout with that of her libertine abductor, Lovelace. Their letters dramatize a gendered struggle for autonomy, interpretation and control – a dazzlingly complex development of the sexual power games in Haywood's seduction fictions.

It was Richardson's focus on female subjectivity, sensitivity and suffering, and the more straightforwardly moralistic tone of *Grandison*, which most directly influenced women's epistolary fiction of the 1770s and 1780s. In the novels of SENSIBILITY of ELIZABETH GRIFFITH and FRANCES BROOKE, for example, the heroines are distinguished by their capacity for refined, often self-sacrificial, feeling; and in FANNY BURNEY's *EVELINA* (1778), the heroine ultimately conforms to social expectations, though she does control the narrative through her letters. Richardson's more radical legacy returned through French fiction: Rousseau's *La Nouvelle Heloïse* (1761), like Laclos's cruel, sophisticated seduction fiction *Liaisons Dangereuses* (1782), was in part a response to *Clarissa*. In the politically turbulent 1790s, the illicit passion of Rousseau's sentimental heroine for her tutor became synonymous with French Revolutionary sympathies, and the letter form more generally with the expression of a dangerously radical individualism. WOLLSTONECRAFT's Maria in WRONGS OF WOMAN (1798) reads Rousseau in prison and defends her right to sexual autonomy in a letter to the divorce court judges.

A desire to avoid this controversial association with

radicalism is one possible reason for the marked decline of epistolary fiction (particularly by women) in the reactionary atmosphere of the early 19th century. JANE AUSTEN's parodic juvenilia suggest others: technical frustration with the awkwardness of narrating everything through letters, and impatience with epistolary fiction's tendency to reinforce a stereotype of women as reactive and passive.

In 19th- and 20th-century fiction, letters are an important resource at key moments – Darcy's letter in *PRIDE AND PREJUDICE* (1813) begins to change Elizabeth's view of him; letters are among the 'documents' which make up Bram Stoker's *Dracula* (1897). Full epistolary novels are rare. The most significant recent example is ALICE WALKER's *THE COLOR PURPLE* (1982) and it is interesting that, as in some of the earliest epistolary fiction, Celie's letters are an assertion of identity and control in a situation of threat and marginalization.   VJ

Erdrich, (Karen) Louise 1954–

American fiction writer and poet who crafts powerfully lyric stories of family, home and the search for belonging in native and white America. Part Chippewa, part French and part German-American, she grew up in a lower-middle-class family in Wahpeton, North Dakota. She began writing seriously in college at Dartmouth, where in 1972 she had matriculated with the first class of women students. After a graduate degree in creative writing, she returned at the age of 26 to Dartmouth as writer-in-residence, marrying that same year anthropologist Michael Dorris, who would serve as her most trusted reader, editor and collaborator until his suicide in 1997.

Her first two books appeared in 1984: *Jacklight*, a collection of poems, and *Love Medicine*, a richly imagined novel of the interlocking lives of five North Dakota families, told through a series of similarly interlocking first- and third-person narratives. Here she found both her technique and her terrain, following *Love Medicine* with a series of north plains novels – *THE BEET QUEEN* (1986), *Tracks* (1988), *The Bingo Palace* (1994), *TALES OF BURNING LOVE* (1996) and *The Antelope Wife* (1998) – each woven from its own complex story cycle and together comprising, in a fashion reminiscent of Faulkner's Yoknapatawpha fictions, an ongoing exploration of the lives and stories first introduced in *Love Medicine*. That novel itself was republished with four and a half new chapters in 1993, reflecting Erdrich's view that 'there is no reason to think of publication as a final process,' but instead as 'temporary storage'. She has published a second book of poetry (*Baptism of Desire*, 1989), a collection of essays (*The Blue Jay's Dance: A Birth Year*, 1995), a children's book (*Grandmother's Pigeon*, 1996), and, with Dorris, the best-selling novel *The Crown of Columbus* (1991). All her work

is edged with the ironic, mixed-blood perspective of belonging multiply, of being at once inside and outside. 'I'd be crazy to want to be anything else', she has said, 'Nor would . . . any Native writer who understands that through the difficulty of embracing our own contradictions we gain sympathy for the range of ordinary failures and marvels.'   WG

Escoffrey, Gloria 1923–

Born in Jamaica, Escoffrey is one of the island's foremost painters, involved in its artistic scene as critic and artist since 1943. After a first degree in Canada she studied at the Slade in England, returning to Jamaica some years later. She has taught art and literature, and been a regular art critic for *Jamaica Journal* since 1983. Her more recent reputation as a prize-winning poet began with a wide range of publications in journals, and was consolidated by two collections, *Loggerhead* (1988) and *Mother Jackson Murders the Moon* (1998). Escoffrey suggests her magic-realist poems can be related to her work as an artist, and her increasing use of symbolic and visionary elements in *Mother Jackson* bears this out. Yet her poems remain grounded in REALIST portrayals of rural Jamaica, telling 'the rockstone passion of a Jamaican country bumpkin / born and nurtured in Arcadia'.

A white Jamaican living in the predominantly black rural area of Brownstown, Escoffrey draws richly on island folk culture (the visionary persona of Mother Jackson is an example), whilst also being highly aware of European MODERNISM. The biblical, folk and literary influences that appear throughout her work are results of what she calls in 'Loggerhead' the 'voracious / . . . search of our dreaming selves for salacious connections' – connections re-rooted and steeped in local contexts, traditions and creoles. Escoffrey's work traces a search through word and image both for what she has termed the 'I-land' of the artist's internal geography, and for the strata of Island life and landscape she most often depicts.   HLR

Ethan Frome (1911)

EDITH WHARTON found 'the greatest joy' in writing this short novel, for many readers the most painful of her works. Intended as a counterblast to what Wharton saw as the 'rose-and-lavender' New England of JEWETT and FREEMAN, Starkfield's grim winter landscape mirrors the 'mute melancholy' of her characters' lives. Like *WUTHERING HEIGHTS* (1847), *Ethan Frome* deploys a city narrator who looks in on the lives of a remote community, and pieces together the story of Ethan Frome, and his isolated farmstead. Glimpsing FAIRY TALE and GOTHIC in the engineer's story – all gaps and guesswork – readers have endless scope for interpretation. Through the triangle of monosyllabic Ethan, his bitter wife, Zeena, and Mattie Silver, her charming cousin, Wharton explores desire, repression, barrenness, psychological deadlock. Though passion flares in the central section, Wharton's consummate use of the narrative frame produces one of the most shocking endings in her fiction, leaving readers with a devastating after-image of lives blasted, frozen and wasted.   PEK

Eva Trout: Or Changing Scenes (1968) ELIZABETH BOWEN's last completed novel is a 'POSTMODERN' and abject continuation of the themes of THE DEATH OF THE HEART (1938), an exploration of origins, gender and (sexual) identity. The fate of the outsize heroine, Eva Trout, enormously rich and disastrously innocent, suggests that any definition of identity is truly fishlike and 'slippery', any notion of a female BILDUNGSROMAN an impossible 'harlequinade'. Bowen employs her usual play with familial and sexual roles (the absent mother and the homoerotically tinged search for her substitute; the bisexual father; a gay guardian) with a keen eye for the absurd and satirizes both biblical and psychoanalytical ideologies of the family. Her style is now a determined departure from the novels of the interwar period, more abstract in dialogue, and the narrative enacts the fragmentations and incohesiveness of the grotesque female quest. Eva is ultimately shot dead by her adopted son Jeremy. Her search for origins is aborted – Bowen's last ironic comment on femininity in an inhospitable society.   PUR

Evans, Augusta Jane see WILSON, AUGUSTA JANE

Evans [née Congreve], Matilda [Maud Jeanne Franc] 1827–86 Australian author of fourteen novels with religious, temperance and DOMESTIC themes. Born into a London Baptist family of preachers, teachers and writers, she published in religious periodicals as a child. Her family emigrated to South Australia in 1852, where she worked as a teacher. Her first novel, MARIAN, OR THE LIGHT OF SOMEONE'S HOME (1859), and works such as *Vermont Vale* (1866) and *Silken Cords and Iron Fetters* (1870) promote a feminized religion, empowering to women. Widowed young, she supported her children by her teaching and writing. Influences on her work include *Pilgrim's Progress*, Evangelical tract narratives and the writing of SUSAN WARNER. Temperance themes are particularly prominent in *Minnie's Mission: An Australian Temperance Tale* (1869) and *Hall's Vineyard* (1875). Although all of her novels were set in South Australia and many of them were initially published or serialized there, they all appeared in many editions well into the 1920s from a British publisher, Sampson Low. Such works have been categorized as Anglo-Australian, not truly Australian. But her writing, since it is addressed to local readers and depicts settlers inhabiting land rightfully theirs, can be seen as doing the ideological work of 'Terra Nullius'.   MA

Evelina (1778) FANNY BURNEY's first novel unashamedly centralizes the agonies and triumphs of an inexperienced young girl's quest to reclaim her name and fortune. Her legitimacy and social position uncertain (she is disowned by her father on her mother's death), she overcomes numerous obstacles – vulgar relatives, libertine suitors, accidental association with prostitutes, near-disastrous misunderstandings – to succeed in winning back her father and marrying Lord Orville. Evelina's virtuous credentials – her innocence, artlessness and anxious correctness – generate comic, as well as threatening, confusions. Just as her heroine relied on male mentors to guide her toward prudence and to protect her endangered 'female delicacy', so Burney paid tribute to male precursors. Her picaresque ROMANCE plot harks back to Henry Fielding's similarly dispossessed Tom Jones, while her EPISTOLARY structure and intricate study of interiority recall Samuel Richardson, and her ribaldry and wit (however carefully dissociated from heroine and lover/mentor) evoke Tobias Smollet. By combining moral seriousness with satire and levity Burney raised the status of women's fiction. MARIA EDGEWORTH and JANE AUSTEN built on her achievement.   LMT

Evelyn [née Browne], Mary 1634–1709 British letter-writer, best known as the wife of 17th-century polymath, John Evelyn. Shared an important and lengthy correspondence from 1655 onwards with her son's tutor, Ralph Bohun. Raised in France, Mary spoke both French and Italian as well as being studied in mathematics and drawing. In 1647 she married Evelyn, an exiled Royalist at that point. She was 13; he was twice her age and seems to have been a strict husband in terms of expectations. He stressed in a book of marital instruction presented to her on their wedding day the importance of being a housewife over and above that of being a learned woman. Only one of the four sons born to the couple in the 1650s survived and Mary seems for the most part to have led an isolated life at her Sayes Court estate whilst her husband pursued one of public significance after the Restoration. Her friendship with Bohun appears to have offered some relief from this. He served as tutor to Jack Evelyn from 1655 to 1661 but maintained his correspondence with Mary long afterwards. At times he teases her for leading a domestic life when she might have been a significant intellectual. She stressed her view that 'Women were not bred to read authors' but elsewhere signalled that she imbibed something of the milieu in which she moved, describing herself as having lived 'under the roof of the learned, and in the neighbourhood of science'. She is an example of a woman who might have made more of that experience were it not for the restrictive views on women's education held by her husband and the society of the time.

Her daughter MARY EVELYN wrote poetry and devotional works.
JS

Evelyn, Mary 1665–85 Eldest daughter of John and MARY EVELYN (NÉE BROWNE), who wrote a long burlesque poem prior to her death at the age of 19 from smallpox. The *Mundus Muliebris: Or, The Ladies Dressing-Room Unlock'd and her Toilette spread* (published posthumously in 1690) prefigures 18th-century poetic satires by Pope and Swift on women's dressing-room habits. A catalogue of perfumes, ointments to keep hands 'plump, soft, and white', and vanities as embodied in the ever-present looking glass, the poem confirms the reputation for comedy that John Evelyn accords his daughter in his *Diary*, as well as providing a fascinating social document of the age and its attitudes toward appearance. Evelyn also recorded the pains his daughter took to educate herself. He discovered some of her devotional writings, the 'Miscellaneous Book of Meditations' (now housed in Christ Church College, Oxford), after her death.
JS

Everything that Rises Must Converge (1965) This collection was published after FLANNERY O'CONNOR's death, although some of the stories date as far back as 1956. Here, O'Connor deals largely with the frictions brought about by the increasing convergence of black and white people in a rapidly changing society, and the resulting fixations with achieving or maintaining status. As in the title story, social issues such as these are represented through their impact on the personal, particularly through conflict within families: mothers and sons are a key component of this collection. This inter-generational conflict is complicated by the even-handedness of the narrative, for, even if a young protagonist is successful in highlighting the culpable blindness of his elders, by assuming his own clarity of vision he implicates himself in self-deceptions at least equally profound. Beyond O'Connor's treatment of the social and the individual, her characteristic echoes of religious images lend an allegorical quality to the stories, where complex psychological characterizations of masochism, delinquency and self-delusion are paradoxically elevated to symbolic representations of Holy Fools, Demons and Pharisees.
MM

Ewing [née Gatty], J(uliana) H(oratia) 1841–85 British children's writer, who received, she said, a 'somewhat desultory' education from her mother, MARGARET GATTY, but had from childhood a great capacity for story-telling. Her first published story, 'A Bit of Green' (*Monthly Packet*, 1861), is a sentimental tale in which the (male) narrator learns the value of thankfulness from a dying, consumptive and lame young man. Thereafter she published tales for children prolifically, partly to help the family income, and, after her marriage in 1867 to Alexander Ewing, to help pay off her husband's debts. Her collected stories, *Works* (1894–6), form eighteen volumes. Almost all are moral tales, cheerfully praising well-behaved children and family virtues, and 'inculcat[ing] the love of animals'. They were, barely without exception, originally published in serials, including in her mother's *Aunt Judy's Magazine*. Ewing's story 'The Brownies' (1865) told of the race of little people who 'love dainties, play, and mischief' but, when 'useful and considerate . . . are a much-coveted blessing': it provided the name for the junior members of the Girl Guides. Reflecting on her 'household stories' in a brief essay, Ewing once summed up her ambitions as being to 'cultivate the Imagination' of the young and to teach 'high and useful lessons'.
FJO'G

Experts are Puzzled (1930) By LAURA RIDING, a work which deliberately defies generic classification. Part essay, part fable, part allegory, most of the book consists of series of short prose pieces, some complete in themselves, some presented as fragments of a larger work. The tone is forensic, detached and impersonal. Riding delights in paradox, contradiction and the reduction of arguments to absurdity. Some of the pieces, including the sketch which gives the book its title, read like diagnostic probes into a culture gone mad or sick. Yet the possibilities of escape are few. The act of writing itself becomes both metaphor and means for a detachment and alienation which constitute the best chance of cultural survival. The writing derives some of its energy from its wholesale resistance to the culture which surrounds it. But it is also animated by an intelligence which delights in playing with the possibilities of logical structure and literary form. *Experts are Puzzled* is a salutary reminder that POSTMODERNISM has been around for a lot longer than some people think.
JCo

Eye of the Story, The (1978) EUDORA WELTY's collection of her essays and reviews records a life-long meditation upon reading and writing. The marvellous title, taken from the essay on KATHERINE ANNE PORTER, captures Welty's respect for the force at the heart of a work. The Porter essay is a tribute to the writer who so encouraged Welty herself, but, like those on WOOLF, CATHER, AUSTEN and Chekhov – along with the 'Camp Fire Girls' and *The White House Cookbook* – it illumines both the life in the stories and 'the life that is the story's own'. Welty reflects on the image of the eye – of time or of memory, the vision of place, the power of perspectives, the landscape of fiction: 'Most good stories are about the interior of our lives.' For her readers, these essays enact narrative itself, 'the tracing out of a meaning', as Welty takes us with her, unfolding the journey into the story.
PEK

Eyles, Leonora (Margaret) 1889–1960 British journalist, newspaper columnist, novelist and crime writer. The first of her slum novels contrasting urban deprivation to rural freedom was the bestselling *Margaret Protests* (1919). *The Woman in the Little House* (1922) is an account of single motherhood in London's East End. Born into a family of pottery owners whose fortunes subsequently declined, her first job on leaving school was addressing envelopes in London. She emigrated to Australia as a domestic servant, returned to work in the Woolwich Arsenal during World War I, and for the charity Dr Barnardo's. Her first marriage was to Alfred William Eyles by whom she had three children, her second husband (1928) was David Murray. A lifelong feminist and socialist, Eyles was the first 'agony aunt' of *Woman's Own* and wrote several popular advice books including *Women's Problems of To-day* (1926), *Careers for Women* (1930), *Common Sense About Sex* (1933) and *Eat Well in War-time* (1940). *The Ram Escapes* (1953) is a fragmentary autobiography which ends as she is about to set sail for Australia.   MJ

F

Faderman, Lillian 1940– American literary scholar and historian of lesbianism. Raised in New York, she received her Ph.D. from UCLA, and has taught since 1967 at California State University, Fresno. She began her career co-editing two collections of American ethnic literature, *Speaking For Ourselves* (1969) and *From the Barrio* (1973). Her first work in lesbian history, *Lesbians in Germany* (1980), was soon followed by *Surpassing the Love of Men* (1981), an acclaimed study of five centuries of love between women. Far from being vilified, Faderman argues, passionate attachments between women were considered ennobling and honourable in prior centuries. Only after 1880, in the aftermath of sexology, did romantic friendship between women come to be seen as suspect, degenerate or even criminal. She has since published *Scotch Verdict* (1983), which chronicles the 1810 trial of two Scottish schoolteachers accused of lesbianism, and two more works of lesbian historiography, *Odd Girls and Twilight Lovers* (1991), a history of twentieth-century lesbians in America, and *Chloe Plus Olivia* (1994), an anthology of lesbian literature since the seventeenth century. JGr

Fage, Mary fl. 1637 wife of Robert Fage the younger, gentleman. Mary Fage wrote *Fames Roule: Or, the names of our dread Soveraigne Lord King Charles, his Royall Queen Mary, and his most hopefull posterity: Together with The names of the Dukes, Marquesses, Earles . . . of . . . England, Scotland, and Ireland: Anagramatiz'd and expressed by acrosticke lines on their names* (1637). This versified *Who's Who* dedicated to all the British royalty opens with the line 'Pardon powerfull Princes and potent Potentates my presumption, in pressing into your presence'. Her short anagrammatic poems continue to praise the 'High and Mighty'. Three of these offerings are addressed to women: to King Charles's three daughters, Mary, Elizabeth and Anne. The collection is believed to have been produced at the Fages' own expense, although it is not known whether Mary's extravagant literary flattery was ever financially rewarded by the dedicatees. Some restitution is perhaps found in the praise of Fage's work in a commendatory poem by Thomas Heywood. Heywood's acclaim of her 'Brave masculine spirit' takes on new meaning if we believe those who claim that the work was actually written by Robert Fage, who used Mary's name in an attempt to excuse what some may have considered a disappointing work. KTu

Fainlight, Ruth (Esther) 1931– American-born poet, short-story writer, playwright and translator. Fainlight was born in New York City, the daughter of a British father and an Austro-Hungarian mother, both of them Jewish; she had a brother, Harry, whose *Selected Poems* (1986) she edited after his death in 1982. Fainlight's family moved to Britain when she was a child, and she later attended Colleges of Arts and Crafts in Birmingham and Brighton. In 1951, she met the novelist Alan Sillitoe, and they married in 1959; they collaborated on a play, *All Citizens Are Soldiers* (1969), translated from Lope de Vega's *Fuenteovejuna*. During the early 1960s, Fainlight formed a close friendship with the poet SYLVIA PLATH, who dedicated her poem 'Elm' to her.

Fainlight published her first volume of poetry, *A Forecast, A Fable*, in 1958, and several further volumes have since appeared, including *Cages* (1967), *Poems* (with Ted Hughes and Alan Sillitoe, 1971), *The Region's Violence* (1973), *Sibyls and Others* (1980), *Selected Poems* (1987), *The Knot* (1990) and *This Time of Year* (1993). Her short-story collections include *Daylife and Nightlife* (1971) and *Dr Clock's Last Case* (1994). Fainlight's poetry combines a preoccupation with the complexity of daily reality with an intense realization of the almost mystical possibilities of poetry. Many of them also contain sharply observed portraits of the people about her. The immigrant experience of her mother's family and a remembered trip to Leningrad in 1965, in which she met the poet Anna Akhmatova, inspired her 1997 collection of poetry, *Sugar-Paper Blue*, which was shortlisted for the Whitbread Poetry Prize. AC

Fairbairns, Zoe 1948– British novelist and journalist, whose writing addresses feminist concerns through various forms of popular-genre fiction. As a writer she straddles the divide between 'literary' and 'popular' writing. Her early work includes the collaborative feminist short-story collection, *Tales I Tell My Mother* (1978) – also containing contributions from SARA MAITLAND, VALERIE MINER, MICHÈLE ROBERTS and MICHELENE WANDOR, whom

Fairbairns collectively introduces as 'women, writers, feminists and socialists'. She has written for the *Guardian* and the *New Statesman* and from 1983 to 1985 was writer-in-residence at Sunderland Polytechnic. Interested in, and supportive of, work by her contemporaries as well as fledgeling writers, she has tutored writing courses in a range of contexts, such as Holloway Prison, the City Literary Institute and the Arvon Foundation. After her first two novels, *Live as Family* (1968) and *Down: An Exploration* (1969), she experimented with SCIENCE-FICTION in *Benefits* (1982) and DETECTIVE FICTION in *Here Today* (1984). *Stand We At Last* (1983) employed the form of the HISTORICAL saga to examine the absences of women's history, while *Closina* (1987) recounted the lives of three very different women during the eighties, in the style of an airport blockbuster. Her work employs the narrative logic of the forms she engages with to discuss the complexity of women's lives; as she states, 'I am interested in the politics of relationships between men and women, and because I see them in a certain way, therefore I am a feminist – it is important to get it that way round.'   RW

Fairbank, Janet (Ayer) 1878–1951 American novelist. She was born in Chicago and attended private schools and the University of Chicago. In 1900 she married lawyer Kellogg Fairbank, with whom she had three children. A political activist, she held offices on women's committees of the Progressive Party and National Defense committees during World War I. She also served on committees for woman suffrage and the Democratic Party, and the board of a Chicago hospital. These activities placed a long gap between her first novel, *Home* (1910), and her second, *The Cortlandts of Washington Square* (1923), a HISTORICAL NOVEL giving a woman's view of the Battle of Gettysburg. This novel was the first in a trilogy including *The Smiths* (1925), runner-up for the Pulitzer Prize, and *Rich Man, Poor Man* (1936), following a family's history from the Civil War up to suffrage and the Progressive Party. *The Lion's Den* (1930) and *The Bright Land* (1932), too, feature characters involved in political issues. Her stories are collected in *Idle Hands* (1927).   JSG

Fairbridge, Dorothea (Ann) 1862–1931 South African COLONIAL author and conservationist. Cousin of Kingsley Fairbridge, the Rhodesian poet and founder of the Australian Fairbridge Farm Schools, Dorothea was the daughter of a 19th-century Cape parliamentarian and bibliophile, and her interests in 'Africana' are reflected in her life-work, the inventing of a national heritage for the new state of the Union of South Africa (1910). Early Cape history formed the subject of her first novel, *That Which Hath Been* (1910). Documentary work on this subject appeared in the

State, edited by members of Lord Milner's 'kindergarten'. An admirer of Milner, Fairbridge began the Guild of Loyal Women during the South African War (1899–1902), which became the Victoria League of her friend Violet Maxse (Lady Edward Cecil, later Viscountess Milner).

Her other novels include *Piet of Italy* (1913), *The Torch Bearer* (1915) and *The Uninvited* (1926). She wrote a school *History of South Africa* (1917), and in 1928 two travel books, *Along Cape Roads* and *The Pilgrim's Way in South Africa*. She edited LADY ANNE BARNARD's Cape diaries (1924) and the *Letters from the Cape* of LADY DUFF GORDON (1927), and produced two distinguished studies of old Cape Dutch farmsteads, *Historic Houses of South Africa* (1922) and *Historic Farms of South Africa* (1931). Schooled in London and much travelled, Dorothea Fairbridge typified the liberal Cape society that sought to establish the Union in 1910 on lines that would encourage imperial links, along with a conciliatory sense of national heritage.   PJM

Fairless, Michael [Margaret Fairless Barber] 1869–1901 English writer of popular devotional fiction. Born into a prosperous family of solicitors in West Yorkshire, she suffered all her life from poor health attributed to a weak spine. After her mother's death in 1891 she was financially independent and lost touch with most of her genteel family. Mary Emily Dowson, who was a religious writer associated with the Roman Catholic modernist movement, became her close friend. Fairless was eventually 'adopted' by the Dowson family in London, much to her family's disapproval. She took to writing only in the last two years of her life, when illness forced her to give up sketching and clay modelling. Her reputation rests mainly on a bestselling source of popular comfort, *The Roadmender* (1902). This was a collection of previously published sketches and a final chapter dictated on her death bed which were posthumously put into book form by her devoted friend and biographer, Dowson. They show the author in the unlikely persona of a roadmender relating simple events in his life. The narrative is interspersed with passages of natural description as well as classical, biblical and rustic homilies. In later sections the authorial voice becomes preoccupied with its own approach to the 'white gate' of death. The meditation on natural beauty and stoic acceptance of life's hardships were anticipated by her other posthumously published work, *Brother Hilarius* (1901). This depicts a young artist and monk who travels to acquire worldly knowledge and humility before becoming a Prior. During a plague he inspires fellow monks to tend the sick before dying peacefully himself.   JSpi

Fairly Honourable Defeat, A (1970) IRIS MURDOCH's thirteenth novel signals a new poise in her work: it uses an allegorical framework to question the apparent contingency of REALIST writing, but equally interrogates allegory through the refusal of the Christ-figure, Tallis, to accept such patterning. The 'magus' character, Julius King, returns from America to wreak mischievous havoc among well-meaning London intelligentsia, contending with good-but-absurd Tallis for the soul of the latter's estranged wife, Morgan, who is presented as both victim and, like Morgan le Fay, mischief-maker. Published in the same year as *The Sovereignty of Good*, it centres, as so often in Murdoch, on the writing of a book; through the destruction of Rupert, good-but-complacent writer and embodiment of Christianized Platonism, Murdoch seems to deconstruct her own 'metaphysical task'. The plot contains ROMANCE elements like the wager and the trial, and an operatic patterning reminiscent of *Cosi Fan Tutte*. Confrontations worthy of Dostoievsky are successfully transferred to South Kensington and transposed into wild social comedy. The diffident title subverts the final scene of Julius's triumph, and wryly implies a significance – even heroism – in messy, unenchanted human existence.

VP

fairy tale A misnomer, the fairy tale holds double-edged magic, and particularly so for women. Fairies are scarce in these tales, and, while reference to such creatures used to raise the question of belief just as 'ghost tales' continue to do today, fairy tales are, unlike myths and legends, fictional and often considered apart from faerie literature. But, like fairies, these tales perform magic. They have traditionally fulfilled complex, even conflicting, desires, and they have done so with ease, reassuring predictability, dazzling variety and adaptability. As simple actions, vivid metaphors, crisp outlines construct a world of possibility and transformation in the tales, the trajectory and desires of seemingly unpromising fairy-tale characters become not only codified but naturalized – for the hero's world and that of nature are presented as one and the same, and his or her success marks the restoration of natural and social order both. Thus, to scholar Jack Zipes, the fairy tale in the modern western world is the Barthesian myth par excellence in its disguise of its social project. In relation to gender, this social project has been to produce bold and entrepreneurial boys, silent and accepting girls, heterosexual scenarios with happy endings. And yet writer ANGELA CARTER could equally convincingly assert that precisely because it parades its artifice the fairy tale does not lie, and, because it is like a public dream, it speaks of invention, transgression and excess.

The pervasiveness of fairy tales and their highly individual-centred focus can help to explain this paradoxically normalizing and emancipatory func-tioning of the fairy tale in modern western cultures. But tracing a genealogy of the genre is also crucial, and here Zipes and Carter are in no disagreement: a bourgeois, literate, often collusive, and increasingly commodified child of the folktale, the fairy tale continues to embody maternal wisdom and resourcefulness as well as to reinvent new disguises for its survival and our pleasures in the wor(l)ds of the father–husband. In 'The Wise Little Girl', the heroine solves the tsar's riddle ('I want her to come neither on foot nor on horseback, neither naked nor dressed, neither with a present nor without a gift') by cleverly donning the logic of his words, then unmasks his injustice by fearlessly demanding 'common sense' from him, only to marry him in the end. This was Carter's declared favourite in her edited collection, *The Virago Book of Fairy Tales* (1990). But it is not one of the tales best known in the late 20th century: 'Cinderella', 'Snow White', 'Red Riding Hood', 'Beauty and the Beast' or 'Sleeping Beauty'. Scholars like MARINA WARNER, Jack Zipes, Maria Tatar, Ruth B. Bottigheimer and Kay Stone have, from quite diverse positions, sought to historicize the fairy tale, by actively linking the production of gendered representations within tales to their tellers, to the institutions of genre, and to their layered socio-historic meanings.

Told by women, as they often were in premodern times, tales of magic have been denigrated as 'old wives' tales'. Nonetheless, their symbols and knowledge have been recrafted and reinterpreted to shape the literary canon of fairy tales. This not-so-magic appropriation has marked the shift from folktale – as ordinary as 'potato soup' (Carter's analogy) or pasta alla carbonara – to the fairy tale's haute cuisine: a chef's signature dish. Women tellers, as oral 'informants', and women characters abound in this literary tradition, but their words are arranged, cut, embellished by Charles Perrault (*Les Histoires ou contes du temps passé*, 1697), the Brothers Grimm and Hans Christian Andersen in the 19th century, L. Frank Baum's *The Wizard of Oz* and Disney's glittery films and picture books in the 20th century – to list only the most prominent names. Ironically, it is to these appropriated words and mediated images – especially images – that women have looked for self-reflection. And, as the audience for fairy tales increasingly narrowed to children and women, the wise girl, the bawdy wife, the brave sister, the bold maiden were hidden away. Only Snow White and her (step)mother were left to face each other in the mirror, in that narrative economy of 'most popular' fairy tales (and girls) that rotates around marriage and compulsively rewards female innocence over knowledge.

But women have also written fairy tales, and more often re-written them: how do these tales relate to the canonized tradition? The answers are as varied as fairy

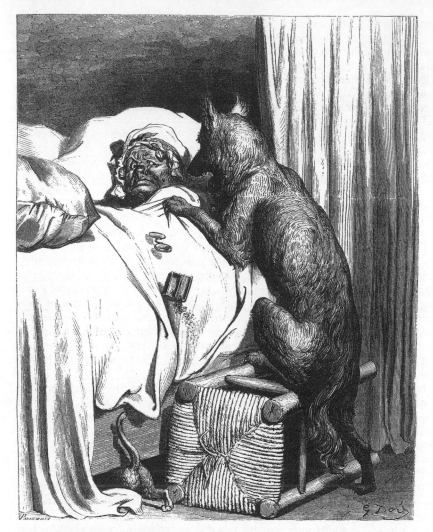

Fairy tale: Red Riding Hood, illustration by Gustav Doré from Charles Perrault's *Contes de fées*, 1872.

tales are – these ideologically variable desire machines which cast and break and recast their magic spells. For instance, Madame Le Prince de Beaumont's 'Beauty and the Beast' was produced in the context of the proliferation of early 18th-century French courtly women's clever and popular, but now hardly read, volumes of the *Cabinet des fées* – a tradition quite other than Perrault's and as rich as those of the Victorian, and the late 20th-century, fairy tales by women. But when 'Beauty and the Beast', later to become one of the most romanticized fairy tales of all, was first translated into English in 1761 in *The Young Misses Magazine*, it was read within the didactic context of its textual frame: a governess tells tales to young girls who face arranged marriages. Most characteristically, in CHARLOTTE BRONTË's *JANE EYRE*, 'Beauty and the Beast' (along

with 'Cinderella' and 'Bluebeard') works as a powerful sub-text both to bolster and to contain Jane's impish powers of transformation. And in popular ROMANCE novels that same dynamic is pushed to its extreme, more dangerously glamorous and misogynistic, effects.

Thanks to other women writers who embraced fairy tales with ambivalence and inquisitiveness (E. NESBIT and CHRISTINA ROSSETTI, CHRISTINA STEAD and JEAN RHYS), contemporary writers of fairy tales for children, like Jane Yolen, and for adults, like TANITH LEE or A. S. BYATT, can build on, and play against each other, plural traditions of this literary genre.

In the late 20th century, especially following the second wave of feminism in the 1970s, women writers have in a number of ways consciously sought to reappropriate the magic of the tale. Re-viewing, re-writing, re-reading have been key to this transformation. The poet ANNE SEXTON in *Transformations* (1971) broke the spell of the Grimms by showing their treasured stories to be haunted by greed, incest and violence. Olga Broumas (*Beginning with O.*, 1977) and Emma Donogue (*Kissing the Witch*, 1997) have re-vitalized relationships between women in fairy tales, shifting away from the tales' seemingly compulsory heterosexuality. Anthologies, like Ethel Johnston Phelps's *Tatterhood and Other Tales* (1978), Carter's two collections of *Virago Fairy Tales*, and Kathleen Ragan's *Fearless Girls, Wise Women and Beloved Sisters*, have greatly amplified and changed the common perception of roles available to women in fairy tales. JOY KOGAWA's *OBASAN* (1981), Suniti Namjoshi's experimental fictions, and CHITRA BANERJEE DIVAKARUNI's *Mistress of Spices* (1997) have in different ways questioned Orientalist readings of mystery and returned to Asian tales as metaphors for their own conflicted relations to both western culture at large and feminism. Most visibly and successfully, in their extensive oeuvres, British Angela Carter and Canadian MARGARET ATWOOD have imaginatively and subversively reworked the magic of Perrault and of the Grimms respectively, from a feminist or woman-centred perspective and in dialogue with both folk and literary traditions. These writers' explorations of fairy tales, especially of 'Bluebeard', have taken different directions and so have their strategies to counter the romanticization of fairy tales: from the dark shame of collusion to an invigorating and defiant laughter in Carter; from mythic strength to cutting irony in Atwood. Nevertheless, both writers have consistently mixed a high dose of curiosity, playfulness and intertextuality into their tales. Both Carter and Atwood have also written about fairy tales, calling attention to the range of fairy-tale heroines in the oral tradition, the room for experimentation paradoxically offered by this formulaic narrative, and the need to historicize our understanding of this seemingly timeless genre.

A 1998 collection, *Mirror, Mirror on the Wall: Women Writers Explore Their Favorite Fairy Tales*, offers a wide range of reflections on how wonder tales have shaped, and continue to be shaped by, women writers. If, as Marina Warner has argued, fairy tales 'offer a way of putting questions, of testing the structure as well as guaranteeing its safety, of thinking up alternatives as well as living daily reality in an examined way', women writers have many more fairy tales to (re)write. CB

Faithfull, Emily 1835–95 English activist and publisher. Trollope described her as 'that female Caxton of the Age'. The daughter of the rector at Headley, Surrey, Faithfull moved to London in 1859 and opened Victoria Press in 1860. Employing only female compositors, the Victoria Press printed, among other periodicals, the *English Woman's Journal*. The press's first book, *Victoria Regia*, was published in 1861. In the next year, the press was upgraded to a steam printing facility and Faithfull was appointed 'Printer and Publisher in Ordinary to Her Majesty'. Faithfull also founded and printed several magazines including the *Victoria Magazine* (1863–80) and *Work and Women* (1865–76), a penny weekly. Her only novel, *Change Upon Change*, was published by Victoria Press in 1868. It concerned women's work in the context of upper-class life. She made three lecture tours of the USA – the first in the early 1870s and two in the early 1880s – meeting with many suffragists. All her lectures had women's issues, particularly employment, as their common theme. In 1888 QUEEN VICTORIA presented her with an engraved and autographed portrait in recognition of Faithfull's unstinting service to women. In 1889 she was awarded a Civil List pension. RB-S

Falconer, Lanoe [Mary Elizabeth Hawker] 1848–1908 English writer of short fiction and rural vignettes. Despite several offers of marriage she continued to live in the comfortable Hampshire family home where she was born. From an early age she wrote for family entertainment, but only began submitting short pieces to journals for publication in the 1880s after her younger sister's marriage. Her successful short novel *Mademoiselle Ixe* (1891) was inspired by an account in *The Times* in February 1890 of the brutal ill-treatment of Madame Solnzoff-Kovalsky in a Russian prison. Its violent contents made it difficult to place until Fisher Unwin created his 'Pseudonym Library' within which to publish it. In *Cecilia de Noël* (1891) she introduced a spiritualist theme to her fiction by investigating the effect a ghostly apparition has upon a range of characters fortuitously gathered at a country house. Such sensationalist material then gave way to a series of descriptive pieces, collected as *Old Hampshire Vignettes* in 1907, in which the quaintness of the local rural poor was a favourite topic. JSpi

Fallon, Mary (Kathleen Mary Denman) 1951– Australian writer best known for her highly experimental *Working Hot* (1989). Published by the Melbourne feminist collective Sybylla Press, this radical exploration of lesbian sexuality won the award for new writing in the 1989 Victorian Literary Awards. Although notionally a novel, *Working Hot* employs a wide variety of literary forms: prose narratives, monologues, poems, letters, play scripts, even an opera libretto. There are also numerous intertextual references to other writers, including EVE LANGLEY, plus an abundance of playful literary puns and rapid switches between high and colloquial language registers. Fallon has also self-published two equally experimental works, *Explosion/Implosion* (1980) and *The Sexuality of Illusion* (1981) which, like *Working Hot*, uses a variety of literary forms to relate the aftermath of a lesbian love affair. Her plays include *Spill* (1987), a black comedy about media pornography, and *Laying Down the Law* (1985), about the Lindy Chamberlain trials. She was born in Queensland and grew up in Brisbane; subsequently she has lived in Sydney, London and Tasmania.   EW

Fane, Violet [Mary Montgomery Lamb] 1843–1905
English poet, novelist and shrewd commentator on the 'polite' society to which she belonged. Raised amongst the landed gentry, she married first an Irish landowner, Henry Singleton, in 1864. Her early articles on contemporary social foibles were published collectively in the *Edwin and Angelina Papers* (1878). There were also verse romances and several novels. In *Sophy: Or the Adventures of a Savage* (1881) she combines a romantic plot with lengthy comment on contemporary interests such as mesmerism and vegetarianism. In *Helen Davenant* (1889) the heroine marries a mad prince and travels to St Petersburg. She was a well-known figure in literary circles and W. H. Mallock's roman à clef *The New Republic* (1877) was dedicated to her. In the work, Fane appears as the sensational Mrs Singleton who flusters Mr Jenkinson, alias Benjamin Jowett, by her questions about the difficulty of translating the 'corrupt' Greek of ancient love poetry. In 1893 Fane married an old Etonian career diplomat, becoming Lady Currie upon his retirement and knighthood. She travelled with him to Rome and Constantinople and these new locations inspired later collections of poetry such as *Betwixt two seas . . .* (1900).   JSpi

Fanshawe [née Harrison], Ann, Lady 1625 – c. 1682
Author of *Memoirs* intended for private family circulation. Married Sir Richard Fanshawe in 1644. This was clearly an affectionate marriage: 'we never had but one mind throughout our lives'. The *Memoirs* (1665) are ostensibly an account of her late husband written for the benefit of their son, but like comparable texts (LUCY HUTCHINSON's account of her husband's life, for example) this BIOGRAPHY also functions as autobiography in many respects, not least regarding her travels. We learn of many adventures: the shipwreck she nearly endured, and her near-capture by pirates. Travel did not prove an easy task – in 1646 she notes: 'after having been pillaged and extreamly sick and bigg with child, I was sett a shore almost dead in the Iland of Silley' – but contributed to establishing a very public sense of self. She died some fourteen years after her beloved husband.   JS

Fanthorpe, U(rsula) A(skham) 1929– British poet
who was born in London and lives in Gloucestershire.

Fanthorpe taught English at Cheltenham Ladies' College for sixteen years before giving up her career in 1970 to become, eventually, a hospital clerk. These different lives are equally evident in her work which concerns itself largely with human and historical damage and disturbance while being both unaffected and erudite. Whatever the subject, Fanthorpe's detail and language are resolutely familiar. Like CAROL ANN DUFFY, her sensitivity to patterns of speech is shown in fine dramatic monologues as well as in the occasional use of splintered syntax, isolating a phrase or word.

Fanthorpe's first book, *Side Effects* (1978), explores hospital life with well-balanced compassion and detachment:

> The trolley's rattle dispatches
> The last lover. Now we can relax
> Into illness, and reliably abstracted
> Nurses will straighten our sheets.

Fanthorpe takes the patient's perspective while reminding us what an insular world illness can be.

Standing To (1982) makes overt links between the everyday and mythological worlds: dying patients reflect Charon, death's ferryman, in their gaze; the hidden rivers of London lead us to the Lethe and Styx. When Fanthorpe puts together a portrait of 'Four Dogs', they are her own pet, a Goya, Cerberus and the Egyptian deity Anubis.

In Fanthorpe's sixth collection (*Safe as Houses*, 1996), her allusions range from Virgil to Auden, Degas to Kierkegaard. The strongest poems here have a powerful strangeness. 'DNA' traces the genetic inheritance of King Arthur; 'Sirensong' compares a child's experience of the Blitz to the myth of fatal enchantment – 'some children / Are invaded for ever'.   LG

Farjeon, Eleanor 1881–1965 English CHILDREN'S WRITER and poet, celebrated for wry, original FAIRY TALES and light verse. Brought up in a bohemian Hampstead household, she read widely in her novelist father's 8,000-book library, later immortalizing this idyllic Victorian childhood in *A Nursery in the Nineties* (1935), with her writer brother, Herbert. Friend of Walter de la Mare (with whose work hers is often compared), of Christopher Fry and, more unexpectedly, of D. H. Lawrence (she helped type the manuscript of *The Rainbow*), she fell in love with the poet Edward Thomas, commemorating his death in *Edward Thomas: The Last Four Years* (1958). Farjeon began to write seriously after her father's death in 1903, publishing *Pan-Worship* in 1908 and *Dream Songs for the Beloved* in 1911. These were intended for an adult audience, as was *Martin Pippin in the Apple Orchard* (1921); however, the latter was reviewed as a CHILDREN'S BOOK and by 1930 she had become an established children's writer.

Nursery Rhymes of London Town (1916), *The Country Child's Alphabet* (1924), *Kings and Queens* (1932), *Magic Casements* (1941) and *Silver-Sand and Snow* (1951) give the flavour of picture-book innocence and English nursery whimsy for which she is famous. *The Little Bookroom*, published when she was 73 (1955), won the Carnegie Medal and the Hans Andersen Medal, and in 1965 an annual Eleanor Farjeon Award was established for 'distinguished service to children's books'. Her work still fascinates by its unassailable optimism, epitomized in her hymn, 'Morning Has Broken'. VP

Farmer, Beverley 1941– Australian novelist and short-story writer who was born in Melbourne and has lived in Greece, a setting in much of her writing and source of some of her characteristic preoccupations with migration, alienation and loneliness. She has written two novels: *Alone* (1980), which explores relationships lived in Melbourne's inner-city suburb of Cariton, and *The Seal Woman* (1992), in which a Danish widow returns to the Australia of her honeymoon in a journey both physical and spiritual. Its trajectory of self-discovery is typical of Farmer's writing. She has published two collections of short stories, *Milk* (1983) and *Home Time* (1985). Themes, characters and stories from both collections are inter-linked, the dislocation of migration a particularly important theme, explored through the breakdown of a Greek–Australian marriage. In stories such as 'Milk', 'Pumpkin' and 'The Captain's House', all set in Greece, Farmer describes, from the point of view of the foreign wife and daughter-in-law, the small but painful gaps and frictions in the domestic lives of three generations: 'Kyria Eirini bent over her eggplants arranged like small black boats in the pan, ladling the filling of onions and tomatoes more carefully than usual into each one: the pan would be on show in the baker's oven. Barbara would be annoyed with her for struggling down the hot road to the bakery with it, when they could have had something easy for lunch. The thought of Barbara's annoyance was almost as pleasant as the thought of how Andoni would carry the pan home, sucking his fingers coppery with oil when he arrived because he had picked at it on the way.' The concept of home is hauntingly explored in a variety of places, and a pattern of loss, particularly suffered by the women characters, whether due to death, the breakdown of a relationship, migration or simply the passage of time, is offset by the redemptive possibilities of personal growth. Farmer's compressed and affective prose has been likened to poetry in its effects, and she has won several fiction prizes. In 1990 she published *A BODY OF WATER*, a writers' journal organized in monthly instalments, reflecting meditatively on the craft of writing and the isolation of the writer. HTh

Farmer, Fannie Merritt 1857–1915 American COOKERY writer and teacher. Born in Boston, Massachusetts, and prevented by ill health from attending college, Fannie graduated from Mary Lincoln's Boston Cooking School in 1889. She soon became director of the school and published *The Boston Cooking School Text Book* (1896), drawing heavily upon Mrs Lincoln's works without acknowledgement. Farmer revised her text book in twenty-one editions before her death. Farmer's contribution to the new 'scientific cooking' was to simplify chemistry and nutrition for the middle-class housewife and to sanctify New England thrift as a principle of economics. Adopting a tone of objective authority, she advocated exact measurements and no-nonsense prose. A skilful businesswoman, she responded in five later books to changes in her targeted market by providing fancier and more fashionable dishes. Although an invalid, she died rich. BF

Farmer's Bride, The (1912) The publication of this love poem, in the *Nation*, 3rd February, brought CHARLOTTE MEW literary notice. Its theme of loneliness and disillusionment may reflect the unhappiness and frustration in her personal life; the poem is a farmer's personal meditation on his fey bride's efforts to escape him, and her refusal to consummate their marriage. H.W. Nevison, literary critic of the *Nation*, claimed the farmer's viewpoint was too sympathetic, but Mew believed the poem showed 'a rough countryman feeling and saying things differently from the more sophisticated townsman – at once more clearly and more confusedly'.

The free verse poem, without consistent metre or rhyme scheme, has six stanzas, varying from four to ten lines. The first three stanzas describe the situation; in the lyrical fourth stanza the farmer interrupts this account to describe his wife and reflect on her feelings for him. In the fifth stanza he considers the future, which precipitates an incomplete statement of his personal longing. The broken, repetitive last line indicates he may soon force a resolution of this intolerable situation, as any suggestion of metre breaks down under the weight of his extreme emotion. MET

Farr [Emery], Florence 1860–1917 British actress, writer, activist and journalist who worked in some of the most important literary movements of the 1890s. She went to Queen's College in 1877 but left to go on the stage. After a brief failed marriage to actor Edward Emery, she had intimate personal and professional relationships with both George Bernard Shaw and W.B. Yeats. Shaw wrote *Arms and the Man* for her, and Yeats wrote *The Land of Heart's Desire* for her. Farr and Yeats developed new ways of chanting poetry together. Farr learned embroidery under William Morris's daughter

May, and became involved in the occultist Golden Dawn. Her Aesthetic novel, *The Dancing Faun* (1894), has Wildean epigrams and an unexpected tragedy at the end in the style of JOHN OLIVER HOBBES. It describes everyone's relief when a woman murders a philandering cad. She also wrote *The Solemnization of Jacklin* (1912), articles defending prostitutes in the *New Age* (1907), and *Modern Woman: Her Intentions* (London 1910). Her unorthodox career concluded when she moved to Ceylon in 1912 to become principal of a girls' college. Like her contemporary, ELIZABETH ROBINS, Farr was a brilliantly gifted woman who turned her talents toward Ibsenism, Aesthetic fiction and radical social reform. TS

Farrell, Fiona [Fiona Farrell Poole] 1947– New Zealand short-story writer, novelist, poet and playwright. The winner of numerous New Zealand literary awards for her fiction since 1982, in 1993 Farrell won the New Zealand Book Award for Fiction for her first novel, *The Skinny Louie Book*. Growing up in the small South Island town of Oamaru, Farrell graduated from Otago University and completed an MA and M. Phil. in Literature at Toronto University. Her first collection of stories *The Rock Garden* (1989) contains twistings of historical 'truths' and of expected gender stereotypes. Her play, *In Confidence: Dialogues with Amy Bock* (1986), is based on a cross-dressing con-woman who in 1909 was imprisoned for marrying as a man. Farrell also wrote the entry on Bock for *The Book of New Zealand Women*. *The Skinny Louie Book* follows the lives of two sisters born in a small New Zealand town in the late forties. Its account of the life of one sister through the fifties to eighties is a detailed and perceptive sociohistorical study that shows Farrell the feminist historical 'faction' writer. But the book begins with the magic, mystical and comical virgin birth of one of the sisters, and this continues as a surreal minor theme to resurface in a vision of the apocalyptic future of a post-holocaust New Zealand in the 21st century. *Six Clever Girls Who Became Famous Women* is an interweaving of the stories of six schoolgirls in a small New Zealand town in the sixties and their adult lives in the mid nineties, in a more REALIST mode than her earlier fiction. Farrell is divorced, with two adult children, and lives in a tiny settlement near Akaroa in the South Island of New Zealand. AM

Farrell, M. J. see KEANE, MOLLY

Fault Lines (1994) MEENA ALEXANDER's lyrical memoir circles notions of identity, womanhood and ethnicity. From her description of Kerala, in South India, as her paradise lost, Alexander narrates with a highly poetic style the phases in her life which brought her across continents, cultures and languages. On the brink of turning 5, Alexander crossed the Indian Ocean to follow her father to Sudan. After becoming a precocious poet Alexander moved to Nottingham, England, for further education. She returned briefly to India, to Hyderabad, then married the American David Lelyfeld and moved to New York, where she teaches English and Women's Studies at Columbia University and Hunter College. Alexander's autobiographical novel is characterized by her inquisitive mood and persisting interrogation of the self. Scattered by multiple migrations and uprootings in an era of post-colonial turmoil, Alexander searches for her own place and identity in writing, where her idiosyncratic moods and telling of fragmentation can coexist. For this dissonant existential condition, Alexander adopted the metaphor of the book's title, the fault line. SPo

Fauset, Jessie Redmon 1882–1961 Harlem Renaissance novelist who was criticized in her day as an apologist for the black bourgeoisie, Jessie Fauset grappled with issues of racial identity and authenticity through the vehicle of the ROMANCE and marriage plots. While her four novels, *There Is Confusion* (1924), *PLUM BUN: A NOVEL WITHOUT A MORAL* (1929), *THE CHINABERRY TREE* (1931) and *Comedy: American Style* (1933), each treat the efforts of light-skinned, middle-class African-American characters to succeed despite their racial identities, the satiric edge of Fauset's style has often escaped its readers. Her novels subtly critique those whites and blacks who viewed race as an essential determinant of identity, and those, like white liberals or African-Americans who passed for white, who attempted to deny its power. Although in her first three novels, Fauset does not castigate those characters who pass for white, her final book, the savagely ironic *Comedy: American Style* demonstrates the effect on a family of the internalized racism of its light-skinned mother.

While formally Fauset remained indebted to the sentimental novel and genteel fiction, her personal commitments were to the politics of racial uplift. Fauset's personal history provided a vivid example of her advocacy for the intellectual achievements of African-Americans: possibly the first black female graduate of Cornell University, she took a Masters' in French at the University of Pennsylvania and then moved to New York as literary editor of the *Crisis*, the magazine of the NAACP. Working closely with W. E. B. DuBois, Fauset worked to promote black writers, wrote on the question of Pan-Africanism and other topics, and created *The Brownies' Book*, the children's section of the magazine, which she used as a forum to introduce black children to the richness of African-American history. MG

Fawcett [née Garrett], Millicent 1847–1929 English constitutional SUFFRAGE movement leader, reformer, writer. A Suffolk merchant's daughter, she attended school only from 12 to 15. Her sister Elizabeth's struggles to obtain medical training early inspired Millicent to work for women's causes. In 1867 she married Henry Fawcett, Professor of Economics at Cambridge and MP for Brighton, a blind man whose political secretary she became, and in 1868 bore a daughter, Philippa. Newnham College evolved from a lecture scheme originated in their drawing room. (In 1890 Philippa at Newnham placed above the senior wrangler in the mathematical tripos list, a significant achievement for a woman.)

A member of the first women's suffrage committee in 1867, Millicent increased public awareness by giving speeches, despite ridicule and hostility. She also laboured for married women's property rights. Although in 1886 she founded a separate suffrage society with Lydia Becker, she would reunite the movement as president of the National Union of Women Suffrage Societies (NUWSS) in 1897. From 1887 to 1903, she was member of the Liberal-Unionist group and a frequent speaker against Irish home rule; in 1901 she led a commission investigating concentration camps during the Boer War. She faced the post-war challenge of the newly formed, militant National Women's Social and Political Union (NWSPU) by publicly dissociating her constitutional organization because of NWSPU's violence. After Parliament enfranchised women in 1918, she resigned her presidency but continued working for fuller suffrage and extended legal rights and professional opportunities for women. Her writings include biographies of QUEEN VICTORIA (1895) and of JOSEPHINE BUTLER (1927) and a history of the movement, *Women's Suffrage* (1912), and *Women's Victory and After* (1918). In 1925 she was created a Dame of the British Empire. HB

Fear of Flying (1973) ERICA JONG's first novel was a feisty comic contribution to the male-dominated genre of sexual fiction. Writer Isadora Wing's nervous pursuit of the now infamous 'Zipless Fuck' ('a platonic ideal') centres on leaving her Freudian analyst husband, Bennett, for a racy affair with Laingian Adrian Goodlove. Jong's sophisticated confessional technique draws on the erotic picaresque tradition from Cleland to Nabokov and Roth to explore the contradictory desires – for love, sex, freedom and creativity – of her Jewish New Yorker heroine, who moves in circles where being in analysis has become a way of life. The novel's sexual frankness made Isadora, and even more Jong herself, the perfect stereotype of the liberated woman. Championed by the male establishment and reviled by some feminists for pandering to patriarchal fantasies, it tapped and informed changing sexual attitudes, becoming the tenth highest American fiction bestseller of the 1970s.

Fear of Flying spawned two sequels and, twenty years on, its apparatus was given a further, highly self-conscious spin in Jong's autobiographical memoir, *Fear of Fifty* (1994). MO'D

Feaver, Vicki 1943– British poet who was born in Nottingham and studied at Durham and University College, London. She now teaches at the West Sussex Institute in Chichester. Feaver's first collection, *Close Relatives* (1981), depicts a pivotal moment in family life. Motifs such as flowers and clean sheets carry the residue of their conventional meanings in poems that veer from appeasement to confrontation, from hope to admission, from a second honeymoon to a list of nine deadly female sins. Interestingly, it is never quite clear who is responsible or even from whom such accusation comes:

> He sends a postcard to the children
> Of Breughel's *Dulle Griet*:
> Mad-eyed, brandishing her saucepan,
> She reminds him of their mother.
>
> ('Pigeons and Cherubs')

Feaver expresses the gulf between expectation and reality through image and myth. Painters (Rubens, Bacon and Wyeth) are confronted and questioned but so, too, are their models. Judith, Circe, Esther are fascinatingly appraised. In all this, power is a central issue and it is subtly addressed.

The plain but gentle speaking of this early work is gone from *The Handless Maiden* (1994). Here, flowers are accomplices: 'Not the flowers men give women . . . but flowers / that wilt as soon as their stems / are cut . . . that remind us / we are killers, can tear the heads / off men's shoulders'. The vibrations of *Close Relatives* are seismic tremors now and Feaver has heightened her voice and language to match. She makes fine use of strongly accented rhythms and aural conflicts, such as that of sybillant hiss and conciliatory hush in 'The River God':

> . . . why he wants to smear
> their mouths and ears and stomachs
> with slime; why the water he shakes
> from his hair, that twists
> off his shoulders in the shower,
> glitters with sticklebacks, snails

Even at their most anguished, Feaver's poems are full of the pleasures of recognition and sensual joy. LG

Feinstein, Elaine 1930– English poet, novelist, translator and short-story writer whose influences are European, American, Russian and Jewish, and whose work is best understood when placed in this international context. An admirer of, among others, EMILY DICKINSON, Wallace Stevens, William Carlos Williams and Marina Tsvetayeva, she has forged a poetic voice that is both coolly intelligent and richly lyrical, lean and spare in an imagistic way, while structuring its thought through metaphors. She was one of the first poets in the 1960s to bring female, domestic, sexual content into verse, giving versions of female quests with a profound awareness of history, which she often mediated through myth.

In a Green Eye (1966) marked her out as a poet to be watched, and since then she has published ten collections. Her *Selected Poems* (1994) established her as a major contemporary poet, and *Daylight* came out in 1997. As well as producing her own work, she has translated that of others, notably in *The Selected Poems of Marina Tsvetayeva* (1971) which went into a fourth edition (1993) with new poems and a new introduction. She has written a biography of the Russian poet, *A Captive Lion* (1987), as well as a brief BIOGRAPHY of Bessie Smith (1986), and a book on *Lawrence's Women* (1993).

Feinstein is also a prolific and distinguished novelist, whose work has moved from the poetic-autobiographical, as in *The Amberstone Exit* (1972), to the more widely social-political, as in *The Border* (1984). Like her poems, her novels are characterized by their Jewish identification and profound feeling for history, and recently she has combined this with more popular saga forms, as in *Dreamers* (1994). Her interest in Brecht and Lawrence produced *Loving Brecht* (1992) and *Lady Chatterley's Confession* (1994). She has also written for television, stage and radio.   MBR

Felix Holt, The Radical

Felix Holt, The Radical (1866) GEORGE ELIOT'S novel, set in the Midlands in the 1830s, the time of the first Reform Bill, explores the tensions between social continuity and personal, political and cultural change. As a spirited artisan who vehemently informs his fellow-workers of their worth, the eponymous hero is radical in his desire to 'stick to the class I belong to' despite his education. In contrast to this vital world of protest and growth, Eliot introduces the moribund Transome family, sustained by dour tradition and vulgar materialism. The dynamic between these two moral outlooks is realized in Esther Lyon who undergoes an 'inward revolution' toward political awareness, prompted by Holt's passionate idealism. When she learns that she is the real heir to the Transome estate, she refuses the inheritance and marries 'the radical'. Holt's pledge to 'give up what other people call wordly goods' had thus inspired a transformation of Esther's social values, and ultimately Eliot's novel is less about political radicalism than the will toward personal development.   JAH

Fell, Alison 1944– Scottish novelist and poet whose early work is characterized by a marriage of socialist feminism and existentialist philosophy to lyrical style and dash, and whose later productions, less explicitly political, explore in depth the psychology of female artists, rebels and adventurers.

Fell first trained as a painter and sculptor, then co-founded the Women's Liberation Street Theatre Group, with whose members she wrote and performed short surrealist plays and happenings in the early 1970s. At the same time, as a journalist on *Ink* and on *Spare Rib*, she forged a writing style both passionate and polemical. All these traits merge in her fiction and verse. Her poetry collections include *Kisses for Mayakovsky* (1984), *The Crystal Owl* (1987) and *Dreams, Like Heretics* (1997). Her early novels like *Every Move You Make* (1984) and *The Bad Box* (1987) explore autobiographical material fictionalized through the use of realism and poetic prose. *Mer de Glace* (1991), which won the Boardman-Tasker Award, marked a turning-point in her writing, with its shift away from realism toward an interest in fragmented and layered narrative. This Fell took further in *The Pillow Boy of the Lady Onogoro* (1994) – which graphically explores themes of female sexual frustration, rage and revenge – and in *The Mistress of Lilliput* (1998). Desire powers all her best writing.   MBR

Fell, Margaret 1614–1702 A prolific Quaker pamphleteer and prophet (see PROPHECY), an Englishwoman from Lancashire, married to the barrister (later MP and judge) Thomas Fell. She and her household (but not her husband) converted to Quakerism in 1652 after hearing George Fox preach; thereafter her home, Swarthmoor Hall, was a centre of Quaker activity. Fell began to publish in 1655, and continued to do so for some two decades; her most famous work, *Women's Speaking Justified* (1666), was written during her four-year imprisonment under sentence of praemunire in Lancaster Castle. Whilst this was not the first Quaker work to defend women's preaching (*To the Priests and People*, for example, was published in 1655), it is striking for its authoritative, learned and rational tone. Her other work was similarly assured and ambitious, including a commentary on the entire Bible, and pamphlets aiming to convert Jews to Quakerism; after the Restoration, she campaigned vigorously against the persecution of Friends. More conservative than many other Quaker women writers, Fell was a powerful figure within the post-Restoration consolidation of Quakerism. Widowed in 1658, she married George Fox, a long-standing leader of the Quaker movement, in 1669.   HAH

Felman, Shoshana 19??– American feminist thinker whose work on literature and psychoanalysis is concerned to push the limitations of individual fields of study in order to create an interdisciplinary domain full of contrasting and colliding discourse. Within such a domain, 'truth' becomes untenable and unspeakable for Felman, and can only be performed through speech acts which seduce the subject rather than dominate with a repressive authority. Her primary interest is in madness and stems from its apparent ability to force boundaries and create sites of subversion, lying outside culture and challenging language as a medium of representation. Felman's ideas have been taken up by feminists, philosophers and literary critics alike, as well as those interested in psychoanalysis, for their power to reconfigure the past. Her books in English translation include *The Literary Speech Act* (1983), *Writing and Madness* (1985), *Jacques Lacan and the Adventure of Insight* (1987) and *What Does a Woman Really Want?* (1993). Felman is currently Thomas E. Donnelley Professor of French and Comparative Literature at Yale University.   EM

Female Friends (1975) FAY WELDON's third novel

concerns three friends, Marjorie, Grace and Chloe, and retrospectively relates the story of their unhappy lives and relationships. It focuses on the ways in which men exploit and undermine women in both the public and private spheres and, with her characteristic acerbic wit and typically sardonic tone, Weldon offers astute observations on how patriarchal oppression works on a psychological, sexual and economic level. However, the problematic relationship between her female characters suggests that women are complicit in their own subordination, as well as that of others. In particular, it points to the part that mothers play in social conditioning, and is scathing about snobbery. Although the main protagonists constantly criticize, irritate, and put men before each other, the text ultimately stresses the importance of taking responsibility on a personal and collective level, and celebrates sisterhood by illustrating how female friendship enables each of the women to change her life.   EP

Female Man, The (1975) JOANNA RUSS's feminist

SCIENCE-FICTION novel challenges the norms of gender identity by questioning women's position in variable pasts, presents and futures, all ironically depicted. Her subversive deconstruction of narrative forms, through her use of changing styles and content, produces a witty condemnation of patriarchal societies and their oppression of women. She breaks through the boundaries of conventional plot structure, time and place to create an open-ended, problematic fiction. Her novel offers possible parallel worlds inhabited by the four 'J's: Joanna, Jeannine, Janet and Jael, with a probable fifth voice that of the author herself. The four worlds are connected through the narrative of Alice-Jael Reasoner who, as the female man, is a parodic portrayal of the death-bringing, all-powerful, male hero. Russ's apocalyptic character is humorously depicted attempting to unite Joanna, Jeannine and Janet in her war to annihilate male domination in the disparate worlds.   JP

Female Quixote, The (1752) CHARLOTTE LENNOX's

novel was an immediate success, and much praised by contemporary male writers such as Richardson and Johnson. The lively heroine, Arabella, has been brought up by her widower father in an isolated castle. Left to her own devices, she fills her head with romantic notions taken from novels. After demanding that she marry her cousin, Glanville, her father dies, leaving her in the guardianship of her uncle. Like Cervantes's *Don Quixote*, on which it was based, the novel charts Arabella's adventures as she pursues life as a romantic vision. Believing all men to be seducers or heroes who have fallen in love with her, she constantly puts herself in moral danger, and has to be re-educated into the model of the perfect 18th-century lady before she is allowed to win Glanville. However, whilst written as a parody of romantic literature and to show the perils of female reading, the novel paradoxically charts how a woman can construct a world of excitement and adventure in which she is centrally placed.
                                                        RDM

Female Wits, The Title of an anonymous English

play which satirizes women dramatists of the late 17th century, as well as a generic term describing female writers of the period. Produced at the Drury Lane Theatre in 1696 and published in 1704, *The Female Wits: Or the Triumvirate of Poets at Rehearsal* centres on three identifiable writers whose inclusion indicates that they were well known as lettered women and dramatists. DELARIVIÈRE MANLEY is the main butt of the joke, appearing as 'Marsilia, a poetess that admires her own works, and a great lover of flattery'. CATHERINE TROTTER is 'Calista, a lady that pretends to the learned languages, and assumes to herself the name of critic'. The portrayal of MARY PIX is not quite so malicious; she appears as 'Mrs Wellfed', a 'fat female author', fond of drink, but also 'foolish and openhearted'.

At this time, women writers were roundly criticized for encroaching on what was seen as the male prerogative of writing. In contemporary satires, Pix was condemned for 'very pertinaciously, malipertly, unjustly, and peremptorily . . . unworthily, fraudulently, and sacrilegiously' writing fiction and plays, whilst Manley was described as 'usurping that Province of Poetry no ways belong or appertaining to her' and accused of writing 'like a self-conceived and opinionative Female'. A slight, misogynistic piece, *The Female Wits* is one of several roughly contemporaneous plays which ridicule female pretensions to learning, including the lost *The Poetess* (1667), Congreve's *The Double Dealer* (1693), and *Three Hours after Marriage* (1717), jointly written by Gay, Pope and Arbuthnot.

Based around the rehearsals of a thinly veiled version of one of Manley's plays, *The Female Wits* presents the central characters as mean-spirited, rancorous and envious of one another's achievements. In actual fact, women dramatists gave one another considerable support, commending female plays in prefaces and writing eulogistic verses. Catherine Trotter's play, *Agnes de Castro* (1695) – itself based on a translation by APHRA BEHN – was welcomed by a poem of support from Manley, whose play, *The Royal Mischief* (1696), in turn received verse tributes from Pix and Trotter. Clearly women saw themselves as part of a female literary tradition, and their mutual patronage anticipated later female groups like the BLUESTOCKINGS.

More than fifty plays attributed to women appeared in print between 1660 and 1710. Aphra Behn is perhaps the most renowned playwright, but Manley, Trotter, Pix, KATHERINE PHILIPS and SUSANNAH CENTLIVRE are also significant, along with lesser-known figures like 'ARIADNE', FRANCES BOOTHBY and ELIZABETH POLWHELE. These female dramatists were frequently grouped together as 'the Female Wits' and the term, by extension, came to be applied to the swelling ranks of women writers at the end of the 17th and into the 18th century. RDM

Feminine Mystique, The (1963) BETTY FRIEDAN's book heralded the most recent revival of the Women's Movement, through her analysis of the social and cultural pressures which blocked women from taking full advantage of civil and legal equality. She carried out surveys of women college students and of suburban housewives and also used evidence from women's magazines. Her analysis of the findings was that women in American society, post-World War II, internalized their own oppression and were agents of patriarchy working against their own fulfilment as individuals. She gave an account of a widespread frustration, depression and low self-esteem, which she identified as 'the problem that has no name'.

She defined the 'problem that has no name' as an identity crisis which young women had to face, and which, if they did not face it then, would be confronted later in life. It arose from 1950s social constructs of femininity, which centred on marriage, mothering and domesticity. She proposed that increased education for mature women would lead to their being more autonomous and developing more satisfying careers. HMD

Fenwick, Eliza fl.1795–1840 English epistolary writer and novelist. She married the editor, John Fenwick, from whom she separated in 1800. During the 1790s, Fenwick moved in the literary and radical circles of London and counted MARY WOLLSTONECRAFT, MARY HAYS, William Godwin and MARY ROBINSON among her friends. With Hays, she maintained a close correspondence which lasted over thirty years.

Fenwick was at Mary Wollstonecraft's bedside when she died in 1797 and cared for her daughter MARY SHELLEY during the first days of her life.

In 1795 Fenwick published *Secrecy, or the Ruin on the Rock*, a novel which explores the dynamics of female friendship and feminine desire in an EPISTOLARY NARRATIVE peppered with GOTHIC motifs. As well as collaborating with Godwin on his Juvenile Library, Fenwick wrote a number of CHILDREN'S BOOKS, which include *The Life of Carlo, the Famous Dog of Drury Lane Theatre* (1804), *Infantine Stories* (1810) and *Rays from the Rainbow* (1812). Fenwick taught as a governess in Ireland, moved to Barbados where she established a school with her daughter, and later settled in America. She died in Rhode Island. KD

Ferber, Edna 1885–1968 American fiction writer and playwright whose stories chronicled, in often sweeping detail, much of early 20th-century American social history. Born in Michigan, she moved frequently with her family in the wake of her father's business failures before settling in Appleton, Wisconsin. Yearning to be an actress but unable to afford elocution lessons, she took, at 17, a job as the first woman reporter for the *Appleton Daily Crescent*. 'I never had wanted to be a writer,' she recalled in her autobiography, 'But in those eighteen months . . . I learned to see, to observe, to remember; learned, in short, the first rules of writing'. A lifetime of words followed.

She published her first story ('The Homely Heroine') in 1910 and her first novel, *Dawn O'Hara*, in 1911. Popular success came with her Emma McChesney stories, magazine tales of a resourceful businesswoman, republished as three separate books in the early 1910s. Self-assured, hard-working, imaginative women – much like Ferber herself – would always occupy the centre of her fictions. From Emma she moved on to even greater successes, capped by her novels SO BIG (1924), for which she won the Pulitzer Prize (the first Jewish American woman to do so), *Show Boat* (1926), CIMARRON (1930) and *Giant* (1952). Ferber was attracted to stories not only of strong women but of the American landscape, and many of her best fictions are carefully researched (if not always flattering) sagas of regional locales, including Oklahoma, Texas and Alaska. She was also a collaborative playwright, penning with George Kaufman such works as *The Royal Family* (1928) and *Dinner at Eight* (1932), and many of her own writings were made into films or plays. An active member of the Algonquin Round Table, she spent most of her adult life in New York City. She died of cancer at 83. WG

Fergusson [née Graeme], Elizabeth 1737-1801 American poet and writer. The Graemes were Anglican gentry, with familial roots in Scotland, and prominent

Pennsylvanians. Her mother, Ann Diggs, was the step-daughter of Pennsylvania Governor, William Keith; her father was Thomas Graeme, a physician, and later Supreme Court Justice.

By the age of 15, Graeme was an amateur poet, exploring the problems of love and friendship. She had already adopted the pseudonym that she would use throughout her life, 'Laura'. In the 1760s, the Graemes began holding literary evenings at their home in Graeme Park, and, over the years, these evenings attracted Philadelphia's poets and writers, including Nathaniel Evans, Francis Hopkinson, John Dickinson, Dr Benjamin Rush and Elizabeth's life-long friend, Annis Boudinot (later, STOCKTON).

After her informal engagement to William Franklin, the illegitimate but acknowledged son of Benjamin Franklin, was broken, Elizabeth Graeme travelled to England in 1764. She wrote an exemplary JOURNAL of her travels, which, according to Benjamin Rush, was a 'feast to all who read it' – a manuscript considered lost until a portion of it was found in MILCAH MARTHA MOORE's commonplace book. Graeme's mother died while she was in England, so, when Graeme returned to Philadelphia, she presided over the salon at Graeme Park, bringing to it the wit and sophistication she had developed on her travels. This was now the most brilliant literary salon of the period when Philadelphia was called the 'Athens of North America'.

In 1772 Elizabeth Graeme secretly married Henry Fergusson, a Scotsman and newcomer to Philadelphia. When Henry Fergusson was accused of treason, he fled to England, in 1779, and the two never saw each other again. Because of Henry's loyalism, Graeme Park was confiscated after the Revolutionary War. Elizabeth Fergusson sought legal redress, arguing against the concept that a married couple had only one will – the husband's. Her 'proto-feminist arguments' can be seen in her many letters and documents to the General Assembly. Only after prodigious correspondence and through the intercession of her friends was part of her property restored to her. Elizabeth Graeme Fergusson wrote over 100 poems, and two unpublished book-length translations in verse: Fenelon's epic *Telemachus*, and a translation of the psalms.   CLB

Fern, Fanny [Sara Payson Willis] 1811–72 American journalist and novelist who negotiated between satiric social commentary and acceptably DOMESTIC subjects to become one of the best known writers in antebellum America. Born into a New England publishing family, she was well educated but discouraged by her father and brother from writing when the death of her husband left her penniless in 1846 with two young daughters. She remarried in 1849 under pressure from her family and was refused support when she left her husband in 1851. Two years later, after failed efforts as seamstress and teacher, she was a publishing celebrity with a bestselling first collection of articles, *Fern Leaves from Fanny's Portfolio* (1853), closely followed by other collections and an unconventional first novel, *Ruth Hall: A Domestic Tale of the Present Time* (1855), a notorious *roman à clef* whose heroine also achieves phenomenal success as a writer after years of isolation and struggle. The hypocrisies of the Calvinist Church and East Coast society, the double standard within and outside the family, and the failure of marriage to protect women's interests were abiding themes in her work. She re-married happily in 1856, the year she became the first female columnist for a major American newspaper – the *Ledger* – where she wrote exclusively for sixteen years until her death from cancer in 1872.   LDo

Ferrier, Susan 1782–1854 Novelist whose best-known work, *Marriage* (1818), contrasts, with sophisticated humour, Scottish rusticity and London refinement, romantic and prudent marriage and, following WOLLSTONECRAFT, rational and frivolous female education. Only remaining unmarried daughter of a Clerk of Session and manager of the Duke of Argyll's estate, she combined running his household with mixing amongst Edinburgh's fashionable, literary milieu which included Sir Walter Scott. She was influenced by MARIA EDGEWORTH's regionalism, but called her novel PATRONAGE (1814) 'the greatest Lump of cold Lead I ever attempted to swallow', and determined to leaven instruction with greater entertainment. However she humorously rejected the enthusiasm for blood-curdling GOTHIC of her original collaborator, Charlotte Clavering.

Admiring *Marriage* (which he thought a worthy successor to his *Waverly*) Scott ensured her later novels, *Inheritance* (1824), and *Destiny* (1831) which she dedicated to him, were well paid by publishers (she received £1,000 and £1,700 respectively). The didacticism of these later novels, although admired by contemporaries, has hampered re-appraisal. In later years, growing blindness prevented Ferrier from writing; her *Works* were published in 1841 and 1851, while her descriptions of visits to Scott appeared posthumously in the *Temple Bar Magazine* (1874).   LMT

Fidelia see GRIFFITTS, HANNAH

'Field, Michael' The shared pseudonym of English writers Katharine Harris Bradley (1846–1914) and Edith Emma Cooper (1862–1913), aunt and niece who collaborated in the writing of over twenty-five plays and eight volumes of poetry. The two women were constant companions from 1865 when Bradley, who had attended Newnham College, Cambridge, and the Collége de France, came to live with her invalid older sister and took over the care and education of her niece. In 1878 they moved to Bristol where they attended classes at University College and joined the Women's Suffrage Movement and anti-vivisection groups. Their first collaboration was *Bellerophon* (1881) published under the pseudonyms 'Arran and Isla Leigh'.

The first 'Michael Field' work was the tragedy *Callirrhoe* (1884), which was favourably received until it was revealed that the authors were two women. Encouraged by Robert Browning and Meredith, however, the women wrote many more plays, including *The Father's Tragedy* (1885), *Canute the Great* (1887) and *Attila, My Attila!* (1896), mostly drawing upon classical and historical subjects. In contrast, their more popular poetry demonstrates the influence of aestheticism in its sensuality and mysticism. *Long Ago* (1889) is based upon SAPPHO's poetic fragments and was clearly inspired by a recent translation of Sappho by Henry Wharton (1885) which restored the lesbian erotics to her work. A second volume, *Underneath the Bough*, appeared in 1893. Near the end of their lives both converted to Catholicism and their poetry developed the religious tone seen in *Poems of Adoration* (1912) and *Mystical Trees* (1913).

Both women died of cancer within months of each other. Their journal, published posthumously as *Works and Days* (1933), clearly reveals their mutual devotion.

SA

Fielding, Sarah 1710–68 British sentimental novelist and moralist, who nevertheless tackled contentious subjects like discordant families, incest and women's thwarted aspirations in fervent passages in her first novel, THE ADVENTURES OF DAVID SIMPLE (1744). With sympathetic satire she later explored, in *The Countess of Dellwyn* (1759), the subject of a wife's infidelity and subsequent powerlessness in the face of divorce proceedings. Involved in a family feud herself after her mother's death in 1718 when her maternal grandmother brought a lawsuit against her improvident father, Fielding, who never married, was keenly aware of her financial dependency on relatives and friends like philanthropist Ralph Allen. Maintaining a close and creative, if complex, relationship with her novelist brother Henry, she contributed to his writings while he wrote prefaces to her novels praising her 'Penetration into Human Nature'.

Driven to publish *David Simple* through 'distress of circumstances', it brought Fielding literary renown although it was at first assumed, due to its picaresque construction, to be by Henry. However, two sequels (in 1747 and 1753) draw closer to Samuel Richardson, both in EPISTOLARY style and in posing and questioning moral dilemmas debated in his novels. Sarah sustained her friendship with Richardson, though he was

Henry's arch-rival. Richardson praised her above Henry for her greater 'knowledge of the human heart' while also printing her works and encouraging subscribers, and she was the first to defend his *Clarissa* in an anonymous pamphlet (1749). An experimental writer, Fielding created the first CHILDREN'S NOVEL, *The Governess* (1749), collaborated with JANE COLLIER on a dramatic allegory, *The Cry* (1754), and, a self-taught classicist, translated *Xenophon's Memoirs of Socrates* (1762). Like her other writings, her last novels, *Cleopatra and Octavia* (1757) and *Ophelia* (1760), refuse to fit into any REALIST canon, delaying later recognition of her literary achievements.

LMT

Fiennes, Celia 1662–1741 British TRAVEL WRITER, daughter of the Puritan Parliamentarian Colonel Nathaniel Fiennes. She travelled extensively at a time when roads were rough and poorly signposted, sometimes alone, sometimes accompanied by her mother. She went by coach as she grew older, but preferred to undertake journeys on horseback, travelling about 1,000 miles in this way on her 'Great Journey' in 1698. During her travels she visited every county in England and some in Scotland, compiling a record of her journeys in 1702. This was first excerpted in a miscellany by Southey, and then published in full in 1888 as *Through England on a Side Saddle in the Time of William and Mary*. In her often minutely detailed writing the author recounts adventures such as encounters with highwaymen ('2 fellows ... truss'd up with great coates and ... pistolls') and describes the places she visited, their industries, and the religious meetings she attended. Since she undertook her travels professedly for reasons of health, her descriptions of spa towns are detailed, but she was of robust constitution, calmly describing the 'frogs and slow-worms and snailes' in her lodgings at Ely. Practically nothing is known of her after 1712 until her death in London in 1741.

ELER

Figes, Eva 1932– German-born experimental novelist and polemical feminist. Born to Jewish parents in Berlin, Eva Figes escaped with her family from the Nazi regime to the United Kingdom in 1939. Educated at Kingsbury Grammar School, London, and Queen Mary College, London University, she worked as an editor with various publishing companies and as a translator before becoming a full-time writer in 1967. Her first novel, *Equinox*, was published in 1966; her second, *Winter Journey* (1967), won the *Guardian* Fiction Prize. Her highly lyrical fiction turns from the English REALIST tradition toward a more continental European vision of the novel form, with identity and subjectivity taking precedence over plot. Interior monologue and a clear poeticism also indicate an affinity with VIRGINIA WOOLF, and Franz Kafka is another important influence, particularly in *Konek's*

Landing (1969). Later novels include *Days* (1974; adapted for radio in 1981), *Light* (1983; based on the life of Claude Monet), *The Seven Ages* (1986; which depicts 1,000 years of women's experience) and *The Tenancy* (1993) – many of which are overshadowed by the Holocaust whilst continually questioning notions of the self in writing.

Eva Figes is probably most well known for her classic of 1970s feminism PATRIARCHAL ATTITUDES (1970). Shortly predating GERMAINE GREER's *The Female Eunuch* and KATE MILLETT's *Sexual Politics*, *Patriarchal Attitudes* (1970) analyses with wit and vigour women's position in society, its historical and ideological pretexts, and the radical possibilities for liberation. Her attack on Freudian psychology is trenchant in the extreme. *Sex and Subterfuge: Women Novelists to 1850* (1982) is a critical study in which she interprets her subjects as reshaping the novel in a key period of its development, making the claim that 'on the whole the best of women's fiction tends to be short and compressed' – an epithet that could equally be applied to her own. She also wrote an autobiographical account of her war-time childhood experiences in *Little Eden* (1978), and *Tragedy and Evolution* (1976), a contextual examination of Greek and Renaissance drama.   CS

fin de siècle The French term *fin de siècle* literally means 'end of the century', but, unlike *fin de semaine*, or 'weekend', it implies much more than temporality. Originated in Paris in 1888, the term quickly spread to describe a wide range of anxieties about European civilization during the 1890s, and to suggest fears of decline, decay, disease, darkness and degeneration. Whether in Austria, where Max Nordau's best-selling treatise *Degeneration* (1892) linked social devolution to forms of avant-garde art; in France, where Zola wrote about the hereditary effects of alcoholism, venereal disease and criminality; or in England, where Hardy's 'Tessimism' expressed his tragic sense of human destiny, and Wells drew on scientific theories to imagine the end of the world, writers of the 1890s projected their fears of death onto the last years of the century. Women often appeared in the male fiction of the *fin de siècle* as agents of decline – femmes fatales, sphinxes, vampires, Salomes and even feminists whose desires for emancipation and equality seemed to threaten the continuity of the human race.

In one sense, the end of the century should seem no more alarming than the end of the week. But centuries inspire human mythologies and religious perceptions of time, and the historical events and cultural changes of the 1890s were experienced as crises and portents, just as in the 1990s, social and technological transformations are interpreted as signalling the collapse of the family, the end of nature, the death of literature and history, and the first signs of Armageddon. Yet looking back at the 1890s, we can see that this decade was one of the richest and most innovative periods in history, with epoch-making advances in science, technology, psychology, mass communications and the arts. By the year 1895, predictions of apocalypse were joined by images of renewal and rebirth, and hopes for the new century began to balance the fears.

In any case, women in the *fin de siècle* were never as despairing as men. While male artists, writers, politicians and scientists in the 1890s feared the degeneration of familiar structures and institutions, women writers had less to lose in the degeneration of old cultural forms and much to gain in the transformations of custom and authority. In the field of literature, the woman writer in the nineties, as MARGARET DRABBLE observed in 1991 in her introduction to a London exhibition of 1890s fiction, was so 'enterprising, bold and unconventional' that for women the decade was 'not an end but a beginning'. For *fin-de-siècle* women, the rhetoric of the 'new' was much more significant than the risks of losing the old.

In contrast to the gloom of Hardy and Gissing, Emmeline Pethick-Lawrence, the British suffragist who was part of this generation, recalled: 'It was a wonderful thing at that period to be young among young comrades, for the ninth decade of the last century was a time of expansion and vision. In spite of sordidness and insecurity in the lives of the poor, everything was on the upgrade … It was an era of religion and faith, and at the same time of intellectual challenge. We read, discussed, debated, and experimented and felt that all life lay before us to be changed and moulded by our vision and desire.' As the journalist Evelyn Sharp wrote in her autobiography, 'it was very heaven to be young when I came to London in the nineties. I arrived on the crest of the wave that was sweeping away the Victorian tradition . . . no hesitations or personal limitations could destroy the sense of escape I enjoyed.'

In the United States as well, women writers looked upon the coming end of the century with more optimism than men. Many women writers of innovative fiction made their début in the 1890s, including CHARLOTTE PERKINS GILMAN, KATE CHOPIN, WILLA CATHER and EDITH WHARTON. The decade also witnessed the birth of African-American women's writing, with Amelia Johnson's *Clarence and Corinne* in 1890, Emma Dunham Kelley's *Megda* in 1891, and FRANCES HARPER's *Iola Leroy* in 1892, and the emergence of a black feminist intelligentsia led by PAULINE HOPKINS, ANNA JULIA COOPER and MARY CHURCH TERRELL. In an essay on 'Woman in Literature' in 1891, Helen Gray Cone predicted a 'golden morrow' of great American women's fiction.

As we reach our own millennium, new prophets are once more predicting the decline of literature and the death of the novel, citing the effects of television, magazines and the computer culture. But once again, without claiming that utopia has arrived, women writers see a more hopeful picture, in which new voices and new stories are reaching wide audiences of readers, and the study of literature by women is a serious and established field of study. Whatever forms women's contribution to 21st-century literature may take, the experience of the past century suggests that it will be an age of beginnings rather than endings, of surprises rather than routines.   ES

Findlater, Jane Helen 1866–1946 and Mary Findlater 1865–1963

Scottish novelists and sisters who wrote powerful fiction about women's lives, some of it collaborative. They grew up in extreme poverty. Jane wrote her first novel, *The Green Graves of Balgowrie* (1896), an eloquent description of two sisters' wasted lives and unnecessary deaths, on discarded sheets of paper from the local grocer. She published four more novels and several short-story collections. Mary Findlater published six novels, including *The Rose of Joy* (1903), which describes an unhappy, inarticulate woman who becomes an artist after her husband betrays her – a novel admired by William James. Together, the sisters co-wrote *Crossriggs* (1908), about a vibrant Scottish woman forced to live without love; *Penny Moneypenny* (1911), which introduces 'Loren Weir', a sickly, charismatic man based on Robert Louis Stevenson; and *Beneath the Visiting Moon* (1923). The Findlaters also collaborated with 'Allan McAulay' and Kate Douglas Wiggin in *The Affair at the Inn* (1904) and *Robinetta* (1911). Friends and admirers included Henry James, MAY SINCLAIR, Rudyard Kipling and VIRGINIA WOOLF. The Findlaters used sophisticated MODERNIST literary structures to depict the private, passionate tragedies of obscure women, giving force and dignity to their heretofore untold struggles.   TS

Fine, Anne 1947–

Children's writer whose arch, unpatronizing and risky novels have won her an international following among children and adults (see CHILDREN'S BOOKS). Fine was born in Leicester and educated at the newly opened University of Warwick. She began her career teaching locally at Cardinal Wiseman Secondary School in Coventry from 1968 to 1969, marrying in 1968. In 1969 she worked as information officer for Oxfam before teaching at Saughton Prison in Edinburgh in 1971. Her breakthrough came in 1978 with the publication of *The Summer-House Loon*. Her reputation was further enhanced by the Hollywood adaptation of *Madame Doubtfire* (1987) as a major feature film by 20th Century Fox, starring Robin Williams.

Fine's hallmarks of high-readability, up-to-the-minute social REALISM and gritty dialogue are exemplified in *Doubtfire*. Three children torn between warring, divorced parents collude with the transvestite ruse of their father to be hired as their mother's cleaner – and they all live ambiguously after. Although wildly comic, the novel contains highly charged dialogue, and scalpel-sharp insights into adult relationships and the drives behind domestic violence (all feather-bedded by Hollywood).

Fine's fiction has gained many prizes. Her novel *Goggle Eyes* (1989) won the Guardian Children's Fiction Award and the Carnegie Medal, and was adapted by the BBC. *Flour Babies* (1992) won the Carnegie Medal and the Whitbread Children's Novel Award. Most of her books have been translated widely, notably into Welsh by Emily Huws. Fine also writes very well for adults. It is almost as if there is a darkening psychological pathway of experience through her books for different age-ranges. Her chilling adult fiction – for instance, *In Cold Domain* (1994) – is the logical outcome both for herself and for the reader who takes this journey with her.   DM

Fireworks: Nine Profane Pieces (1974)

The tales in ANGELA CARTER's first collection were written during her stay in Japan, where her avidity to estrange herself from the Same and experience the Other had brought her. The journalistic pieces written during this period reveal her shrewd observations as an amateur anthropologist, while three autobiographical pieces in the collection, dealing with her desperate affair with a young Japanese outsider, himself also a misfit, are oddly striking. The opening piece 'A Souvenir of Japan' is appropriately titled, as it combines the anthropological, detached quality with romantic feeling, giving a humorously lyrical effect like Japanese fireworks. In the other two autobiographical pieces she indulges theatrically in interweaving melancholy at the end of an affair with meditation on the narcissistic nature of craving love. The abyss of love, so keenly real to a misplaced *gaijin* (foreigner), required different kinds of narrative experiment. Having exorcized her mourning, she devises allegorical fables on the archetypal/savage styles of love in the other pieces. This is the real souvenir of Japan for her as a novelist, leading her to explore FAIRY TALES.   CY

First Stone, The: Some Questions About Sex and Power (1995)

Marking HELEN GARNER's venture away from fiction, this book sparked heated controversy on its publication in Australia, inciting a debate about the nexus between feminist discourses, sex and power. It recounts Garner's personally conducted investigation of a much publicized case of sexual harassment which had been brought by two young women students against the head of a residential college at an Australian university. Garner weaves various sources together in her quest to uncover the 'truth' of the affair, citing press reports, courtroom transcripts and interviews with selected 'witnesses'. In many ways an eloquent essay which attempts to defuse anticipated criticisms by recourse to a certain rhetorical reflexivity, Garner's construction of the affair seemed to her critics highly selective, unfairly weighted against, and even scandalous in its treatment of, the women and their supporters. Other commentators rallied to Garner's defence, charging these detractors with 'political correctness'. In a short essay, 'The Fate of *The First Stone*' (*True Stories*, 1996), Garner delivered a riposte to her critics. The debate was revived with the publication of *Bodyjamming* (ed. Jenna Mead, 1997), an anthology of essays critical of *The First Stone*.   BR

Fisher, M.F.K. 1908–92 A celebrated American essayist on gastronomy (see FOOD WRITING), was born Mary Frances Kennedy, the eldest daughter of a newspaper editor in Whittier, California. Mary Frances, as she preferred to be known, became a prolific writer; she produced twenty volumes of essays, memoirs and TRAVEL WRITING, compiled an anthology on feasting, a translation of Brillat Savarin's *La Physiologie du goût*, and contributed regularly to the *New Yorker*. She also wrote a novel, and, toward the end of her life, a book for children. Yet when she submitted her first article for publication in 1931 she sheltered behind her initials and her married name.

In 1929 and newly married to Al Fisher – the first of her three husbands – she moved to Dijon in Burgundy where Al was to complete his university studies. For Mary Frances, France was where she 'learnt to study and to think', and was happiest. *Long Ago in France – The Years in Dijon* (1991) and *Two Towns in Provence* (1964) reveal the enchantment that France held for her. The latter covers the period when she returned with her two daughters to live in Aix-en-Provence and Marseille.

Though ostensibly about eating, M.F.K. Fisher's powerful writing is concerned with all human needs. Her largely autobiographical style reveals her highly moral vision and her fascination with the unknowable. Characteristic of her unflinching professionalism is *Dubious Pleasures* (1988), a collection of her introductions to others' work enlivened by her later thoughts. Mrs Fisher's own favourite books were her Brillat-Savarin translation and *A Cordiall Water – A Garland of Odd and Old Receipts to Assuage the Ills of Man and Beast* (1961), yet it is the essays written during the 1940s in *Consider the Oyster, How to Cook a Wolf* and *An Alphabet for Gourmets* that established her reputation as one of America's most distinguished authors.   GH

Fitzgerald, Penelope 1916– English novelist. The daughter of Edward Knox, editor of *Punch* in the 1930s,

Fitzgerald was born in Lincoln and educated at Oxford. She began her writing career late with a biography of the Victorian painter *Edward Burne-Jones* (1975). Her first novel, *The Golden Child* (1977), a spy thriller involving the Secret Service and an exhibition of Egyptian treasure at the British Museum, was written in order to earn money when her husband was ill; she soon realized, however, that to make money from that sort of book meant writing a lot of them, and turned to more literary, less formulaic works.

Her novels tend to reflect periods in her own life, being set in a Suffolk bookshop (*The Bookshop*, 1978), on a Thames houseboat (OFFSHORE, 1979), in the BBC during the war (*Human Voices*, 1980, which contains a compelling character based on Louis MacNeice) and at the Italia Conti drama school (*At Freddie's*, 1982). All of these demonstrate Fitzgerald's elegant economy of style, her dry wit and human sympathy. In 1984, she published a biography, *Charlotte Mew and her Friends* (see CHARLOTTE MEW), which evoked drear late-Victorian Bloomsbury and Fitzrovia and the tragedy in a minor key that was Mew's life. She started on a biography of L.P. Hartley, but gave it up when she became aware that what she was finding out would cause pain to his sister, Norah. Fitzgerald is fond of creating fictional communities in which love or wickedness can flourish; her HISTORICAL NOVELS *The Beginning of Spring* (1988), which takes place in Moscow in the early years of the century, and *The Gate of Angels* (1990), which is set around a Cambridge college in the 1920s and whose Cockney working-class heroine is a thoroughly modern creation, are characterized by vivid scene-setting; *The Blue Flower* (1995), a fictionalized version of the life of the German poet Novalis, is full of a gentle undercutting of the Romantic temperament.

Fitzgerald, who lives in North London in a flat in her daughter's house, is a quiet, private person and a widely respected, well-loved writer. She won the Booker Prize with *Offshore* and has been short-listed several times since. In 1996 she won the newly established Heywood Hill Prize for 'a lifetime's contribution to the enjoyment of books'.   LD

Fitzgerald [Sayre], Zelda 1900–48 American writer, dancer and painter, whose life, reputation and art are still being disentangled from those of her husband, Scott. The indulged youngest daughter of an Alabama judge, she married Fitzgerald at 20, and the couple became icons of their generation, famous for their glamour, wildness and extravagance. Beautiful, witty and vivacious, she was model and muse for Fitzgerald's fiction, but, highly creative herself, worked on her own stories and paintings, publishing some of her writings under Scott's better-paying name.

In her late twenties, she revived an early talent for

dancing, pushing herself through arduous training to enter the ballet. Now receiving psychiatric treatment, she nevertheless completed *Save Me the Waltz*, and published it (1932) despite Scott's attempts to reserve its autobiographical materials for *Tender is the Night*. For Zelda, art was 'a glimpse of . . . honestly earned scars of battle' (letter, 1934). Now appreciated as a dazzling MODERNIST text, her novel explores the boundaries of the self and the extremes of inner experience. She continued working after Scott's death (1940) and through intensifying breakdowns, but died in a hospital fire in 1948. Her second novel remained unpublished.   PEK

FitzGibbon [née Rosling], Theodora 1917?–91 Born in London of Irish parents, FitzGibbon wrote almost thirty books, many of them on COOKERY. (She was Cookery Editor of the *Irish Times* for sixteen years.) Most innovative was a series starting with *A Taste Of Ireland* (1959), illustrated with photographs chosen by her second husband, Irish film maker and archivist George Morrison. *Food of the Western World* (1976) was a massive achievement, an encyclopedia which took her sixteen years.

Her best book is her first volume of autobiography, *With Love* (1982). This recounts her years in Paris and wartime London. In 1938 she had fallen in love with photographer/painter Peter Rose Pulham in the Café Flore. They lived together – first in Paris, then in London – for most of the war. In Chelsea they led a precarious existence, unable even to afford paper for Pulham to paint, dodging bombs and drinking in pubs with convivial friends like Caitlin and Dylan Thomas. In 1944 Theodora married Constantine FitzGibbon, then serving in the US Army; she later sailed to New York as a GI bride. By 1960 they had returned to Britain, but the marriage had soured, and Theodora married Morrison. They lived happily at Dalkey, near Dublin, until her death.   AB

Flanner, Janet see GENET

Fleming, Marjorie or Marjory [Margaret] 1803–11 Precocious Scottish diarist and poet who died of meningitis after an attack of measles. Praised for her honest spirit by Mark Twain, she has also been memorialized in the prestigious *Dictionary of National Biography*, the youngest subject with the shortest entry. Her DIARY keeping began in 1810, supervised by her cousin–tutor, who fortunately did not edit out its charming candour. With most minimal punctuation, the diarist writes of such matters as struggles with multiplication ('a horrible and wretch[ed] plaege') and with her temper and insubordination ('Isas health will be quite ruined by me it will indeed'), her preference for male dogs because their offspring are not drowned

(that 'is a hard case it is shoking'), and her fascination with the forbidden topic of love – 'but O I forgot Isabella forbid me to speak about love' – though she does speak, gleeful that 'a marade man' offered to kiss and marry her and that she loves a sailor. Topics for her poetry include MARY QUEEN OF SCOTS and an epitaph for three young turkeys: 'A direful death indeed they had, / . . . / But . . . [their mother] was more than usual calm. / She did not give a single dam.'   HB

Flesh and Blood (1994) This seventh novel marks MICHÈLE ROBERTS's return to the surreal and stylized fiction of *The Book of Mrs Noah* (1987) and *In The Red Kitchen* (1990). It is constructed as an interlocking series of short stories rotating around the central 'hinge' of 'Anon', a short incantatory stream of consciousness which plays with both language and identity. The novel begins with stories from Fred and Freddy and ends with Frederica's narrative, as notions of secure gendered or sexual identity are destabilized. Each story opens into another so the book appears to be a series of Russian dolls, but the reader is confounded in the desire to reach a central, unified core or 'solution' as the last story, like all its precedents, ends with the open-ended '. . . and into the next story'. This playful narrative lends itself to endless allusions in terms of both the structure and the content; it is about mothers and lovers, history and fiction; it is a story about stories.   RW

Fletcher, Alice Cunningham 1838–1923 American ethnographer. She was born in Havana, Cuba, and attended private schools in New York. She began her career studying Native American archaeological remains in the Ohio and Mississippi valleys, then studied the Omaha tribe in Nebraska. Appointed by the Secretary of the Interior, she oversaw allotment of farming lands among the Omaha, Winnebago and Nez Percé tribes between 1883 and 1893. She raised money for Native American education, and, through the Woman's National Indian Association, established a loan programme for Native Americans to purchase land and build homes. Her research resulted in *Indian Ceremonies* (1884), *A Study of Omaha Indian Music* (1893), *Indian Story and Song from North America* (1900), *The Hako: A Pawnee Ceremony* (1904) and *Indian Games and Dances with Native Songs* (1915). She was the first woman with a paid academic position at Harvard and served as president of the American Anthropological Society of Washington and vice-president of the American Folk-Lore Society.   JSG

Fletcher, Julia Constance [George Fleming] 1853–1938 American novelist, short-story writer and translator. Her father was a Presbyterian missionary who wrote about Brazil. She lived in Europe for most of her adult life and settled in Rome. Her first novel, *A Nile Novel* (1876), republished as *Kismet* (1877), tells of the romantic adventures of a Mid-western woman travelling in Egypt. *The Truth about Clement Ker* (1889) portrays a loveless marriage. *Mirage* (1877) depicts aesthetes in the Middle East. *The Head of Medusa* (1880) and *Vestigia* (1884) are set in Italy. Other titles include *Andromeda* (1885), *For Plain Women Only* (1885) and *Little Stories about Women* (1897). Fletcher's skilful narration and characterization, as well as her urbane wit, attracted such admirers as Oscar Wilde, who dedicated his prize-winning poem 'Ravenna' to her. She also translated the sonnets of Venetian poet Gaspara Stampa (1881) and *The Fantasticks* by French playwright Edmond Rostand (1900). JSG

Flower [née Bullen], Pat[ricia] 1914–77 Australian crime novelist and television script-writer. She was born in Kent, England, emigrating to New South Wales as a teenager with her family. In 1949 she married the painter, Cedric Flower, who collaborated with her on some of her later television scripts. She began to write crime novels in the 1950s, publishing at a rate of one every two years from 1958 until 1976. Her early novels followed the career of a detective, Inspector Swinton (see DETECTIVE FICTION), but her later works – such as *Cobweb* (1972), *Vanishing Point* (1975) and *Crisscross* (1976) – concentrated on the psychological states of criminals and their victims.

In the 1960s, she was one of the first Australian writers to move into television writing, and her plays featured regularly in the ABC Playhouse series, winning several awards. Her last years were marked by growing depression and she took her own life by drug overdose. SPL

food writing While receipt books and manuscripts date back to the 14th century, food writing as we know it began in the 1920s. Then, with society ladies competing to write COOKERY BOOKS and columns in the press, a new sophistication crept in. None of them could cook, but they were adept at training others. They also understood how to entertain their readers, and persuade them that housekeeping could be fun, rather than just a duty.

One of the earliest examples was Lady Jekyll's *Kitchen Essays* (1922), first published in *The Times*. Lady Jekyll was a sister-in-law of Gertrude, the horticulturalist. The Jekylls were highly cultivated, artistic and pillars of society, and Lady Jekyll was an acclaimed hostess. Another remarkable book was *The Gentle Art of Cookery* by Mrs HILDA LEYEL and Miss Olga Hartley (1925). Mrs Leyel went on to write six books on herbs, but this is her most celebrated, much admired by ELIZABETH DAVID.

While more classic receipt books were still being published, like *Minnie, Lady Hindlip's Cookery Book* (1925), and *A Book of Scents and Dishes* by Dorothy Allhusen (1927), these lacked the discursive style, and the wit, that made the others so appealing.

The 1930s produced more in this genre: *Lovely Food* by Ruth Lowinsky (1931) is printed on exquisite paper and illustrated with line drawings by her husband, the painter Thomas Lowinsky. Each chapter has a somewhat arch introduction: 'Supposing your husband has gone to America on business, this might be the first of a series of little dinners with a chosen friend.' Ruth Lowinsky was an amusing woman: an heiress who loved to entertain.

Other stylish and delightful books of the 1930s include Nancy Shaw's *Food for the Greedy* (1936), and *Lady Sysonby's Cook Book* (1935), with an introduction by Osbert Sitwell and illustrations by Oliver Messel. Ria Sysonby was a beauty, and renowned for her cuisine. Her husband, Sir Frederick Ponsonby, later Lord Sysonby, was private secretary to QUEEN VICTORIA, later to Edward VII. The Sysonbys were not rich; Ria wrote to make pin money, while other more affluent women like Lady Jekyll wrote for charity, or, like Ruth Lowinsky, for fun.

CONSTANCE SPRY was a friend of Ruth Lowinsky, and wrote the best of wartime cookery books: *Come Into The Garden, Cook* (1942). Despite its coy title, this is filled with cheerful good sense, and avoids dreary war-time substitutions. *The Constance Spry Cookbook* (1956), written with Rosemary Hume, is one of the great classics on English food, together with DOROTHY HARTLEY's *Food in England* (1954). But by now Elizabeth David's books were changing the course of food writing, and eating. *A Book of Mediterranean Food* (1950) came out while rationing was still in force, and pre-war British food was forgotten. It was twenty years before Mrs David wrote about English food, in *Spices, Salt and Aromatics in the English Kitchen* (1970).

JANE GRIGSON also wrote primarily about French food. Even today, much of the best food writing in English is about foreign food: either by Englishwomen living abroad, like Diana Kennedy in Mexico, or by foreigners living in Britain and writing about their homelands, like CLAUDIA RODEN on the Middle East, Anna del Conte on Italy, and Sri Owen on Indonesia. English food may be enjoyable to eat, but its simplicity is hard to write about, and often makes dull reading. The exotic has more appeal, especially now the British have become more adventurous in their eating habits.

Food writers are proliferating; the Guild of Food Writers, which began with a handful of members in 1984, now numbers over 300. AB

Foote, Mary Anna Hallock 1847–1938 American author and illustrator best known for her black-and-

Esther Forbes: frontispiece illustration of *A Mirror for Witches*, 1928.

Her manuscript autobiography, *Reminiscences*, appeared posthumously as *A Victorian Gentlewoman in the Far West* (1972). In 1971, Wallace Stegner memorialized her life in his Pulitzer-Prize-winning novel, *Angle of Repose*, which was performed as an opera in 1976. VM

For Love Alone (1943) CHRISTINA STEAD's novel succeeds in capturing the revolutionary ideality and largesse of adolescent female sexual desire, for which there are no correlatives in the world. Stead appropriates Joyce's male artist's odyssey of 'silence, exile, and cunning', telling it in reverse. Erotically taunted by her narcissistic father (Stead sent the book, savagely, to her own father), Teresa is a Saint-For-Love, already exiled in a claustrophobic, marriage-bound Australia, and her dreams of love are dreams of leaving for Europe. Jonathan Crow, her teacher in Sydney and chosen instrument of self-exile, turns out to be Death; but Teresa finds almost immediately on arrival in (sour, damp) London, her saviour, in her banker-boss. Desire rebounds from the dead to the energetic, (almost) understanding Quick, whom Teresa is careful to betray sexually, yet stay with.

The book is dense with allusion to allegory, epic and ROMANCE, and its great originality lies in its appropriation of the ambition of these poetic genres, not realism, as the only real pre-texts for the female BILDUNGSROMAN. VS

Forbes, Esther 1891–1967 American novelist, CHILDREN'S writer and historian. She was born in Westborough, Massachusetts. Her father was a judge, her mother a researcher of local history. After graduating from Bradford Academy in 1912, she studied History at the University of Wisconsin, then during World War I assisted the war effort by working as a farmhand in Virginia. From 1920 to 1926 she was an editor at Houghton-Mifflin. She married lawyer Albert Learned Hoskins in 1926 and divorced him in 1933, returning to her family home in Westborough. Forbes's research and writing skill established her prominence among HISTORICAL NOVELISTS with *O Genteel Lady* (1926), *A Mirror for Witches* (1928), *Miss Marvel* (1935), *Paradise* (1937) and *The General's Lady* (1938). She gained national recognition with a biography, *Paul Revere and the World He Lived In* (1942), which won the Pulitzer Prize for History, but her enduring fame rests on *Johnny Tremain: A Novel for Young and Old* (1943), a bestseller and Newbury Prize winner which became a school textbook and was filmed by Disney Studios (1957). The young hero, a disabled silversmith, comes of age during the American Revolution, learning responsibility amid tumult and tragedy. A Broadway musical, *Come Summer* (1969), was based on Forbes's novel *Rainbow on the Road* (1955), and a London dance company based a ballet on *A Mirror for Witches*. At

white woodcut illustrations of the West. Born to a Quaker farming family near Milton, New York, her drawing abilities were recognized at an early age; at 17, she attended the Cooper Institute School of Design for Women. In 1876, she married Arthur De Wint Foote, a civil engineer, pulling up her strong eastern roots in order to accompany him to mining towns in California, Colorado, Idaho and Mexico.

Once out West, she wrote frequently to her closest friends, the socialite Helena de Kay Gilder and her husband, Richard Watson Wilder, editor of *Century* magazine. The Gilders encouraged her to edit her letters which Richard published as 'A California Mining Camp' (1878). This began her literary career and a long relationship with *Century*. She enjoyed popular success and critical acclaim, illustrating her own books as well as books by Henry Wadsworth Longfellow, John Greenleaf Whittier, CONSTANCE FENIMORE WOOLSON and Rudyard Kipling. Risky mining ventures and her husband's drinking problem often made her the sole wage-earner for a family of three children. This necessitated a prolific output that included twelve novels and four short-story collections.

Pictures of the Far West, a series of eleven drawings accompanied by prose sketches, depict not the dangers of the frontier, but the security that comes from the development of settlements and the building of homes (*Century*, 1888-9). Her fiction was primarily ROMANTIC, although her final novels became increasingly REALIST. She died of arteriosclerosis at the age of 90 in Hingham, Massachusetts.

her death, Forbes left an unfinished study of New England witchcraft, a recurring interest.   JSG

Forbes [née Torre], Rosita (Joan) 1880–1967 British author and adventurer. Born in Lincolnshire, she married first Colonel Ronald Forbes whom she divorced; secondly, Colonel Arthur McGrath of County Clare. She was a lively, attractive member of fashionable society and an example of the new freedom offered to women in the years after World War I, determined to TRAVEL and visit every country in the world: she contrived to end the most gruelling journeys looking elegant, wearing jewellery and invariably a large picture hat.

Her prime interest was in Arabia and Arab affairs: in 1920 she says her Arabic is 'fairly good', and she was fearless in her search for adventure and the sun she worshipped. Her first book was about the Pacific and Eastern Asia – *The Unconducted Wanderer*, which appeared in 1919 – followed by *The Secret of the Sahara* in 1921. Later books were *Abyssinian Adventures* (1925), *Eight Republics in Search of a Future* (1933) about South America, *The Forbidden Road, Kabul to Samarkand* (1937), *India of the Princes* (1939) and, outstandingly, *These Men I Knew* (1940), which consisted of interviews with famous figures such as Stalin, Hitler and Mussolini.

Her own autobiographical reminiscences, *Gypsy in the Sun* (1944) were followed by two more books, *Island in the Sun* (1944) on the West Indies and *Sir Henry Morgan, Pirate* (1949). In all her books, together with an unquenchable interest in things feminine, she shows a deeply considered knowledge of world affairs and a sober regard for conveying the true picture as she saw it.   MEW

Forché, Carolyn 1950– American poet, born Carolyn Sidlosky in Detroit, Michigan. Her poetry explores history and language in personal and social nuances; from the body's investigation of an other to the shattering grief of war. She studies human survival in its accommodations: loss, beauty, pain and memory.

Forché attended Justin Morrill College at Michigan State University, and Bowling Green University in Ohio. Her first book, *Gathering The Tribes* (1976), won the Yale Series of Younger Poets for that year; in it Forché studies her ethnic origins vicariously reflected in native American experiences/voices. Her following collection, THE COUNTRY BETWEEN US (1981), won the Lamont Poetry Selection of the Academy of American Poets. This book, which primarily chronicles Forché's experiences in El Salvador in the late 1970s (during the civil war), won her much acclaim. Readers felt drawn to Forché's personal accounts of brutalities in El Salvador, particularly in light of the American government's indifference to atrocities there. Besides this particular theme, the book addresses Vietnam (poems

such as 'Joseph' and 'Selective Service') and offers other political and personal narratives. Forché works slowly and methodically as evinced by her work assembling and editing *Against Forgetting* (1993), an anthology subtitled *Twentieth Century Poetry of Witness*. And she has turned her considerable knowledge of languages to translation: of *The Selected Poems of Robert Desnos* and *Flowers from the Volcano* by Claribel Alegría. Her third collection of poems, *The Angel Of History* (1994), takes its title (and some concerns) from Walter Benjamin's *Theses on the Philosophy of History*. This last book shifts more in form than in subject; Forché's poems are still political, humanitarian in concern: 'It is worse than memory, the open country of death', but the lines extend so far they resemble prose. In Part 1 of this collection, she offers: 'Surely all art is the result of one's having been in danger, of having gone through an experience all the way to the end.' A postulation which may well represent Forché's poetry.   ACH

Forman, Charlotte 1715–87 Journalist, translator and probable author of a number of political essays signed 'Probus', which appeared between 1756 and 1760. Despite being 'well-born', the unmarried Forman lived alone in London during most of her adult life in extreme poverty, and was briefly imprisoned for debt in 1767. A self-proclaimed 'day labourer' of the literary profession, Forman translated the news from abroad for the *London Evening Post* and the *Gazetteer*. She is best known for the 'Probus' essays, more than 200 of which appeared in the *Gazetteer* and the *Public Ledger*, offering erudite but moralizing commentary on trade, commerce and international affairs. Her extended correspondence with John Wilkes, the renegade politician and satirist, provides graphic evidence of the struggles of an independent woman in the 18th century attempting to support herself by writing. As she wrote to Wilkes in 1769, 'I may as well hope, that in time, I shall become Queen of England, as expect to get a competency by the pen.'   JGr

Forrest, Katherine V. 1939– Canadian novelist, best known for her popular crime fictions featuring lesbian homicide detective Kate Delaware. Born in Windsor, Ontario, Forrest was educated at school and university in Detroit, Michigan, before studying at the University of California in Los Angeles, where she continues to live. She rose to prominence in the eighties wave of lesbian feminist crime writing (see DETECTIVE FICTION), alongside Barbara Wilson, VAL MCDERMID, MARY WINGS and others. Set in Los Angeles, the Kate Delaware series – which includes *Amateur City* (1984), *Murder at the Nightwood Bar* (1987), *The Beverly Malibu* (1989) and *Murder by Tradition* (1991) – powerfully reinflects police procedural conventions through its ongoing exploration of the contradictions raised by

Delaware's identity as a lesbian cop operating in a harsh, homophobic, patriarchal environment. Her other novels, *Curious Wine* (1983), *Daughters of a Coral Dawn* (1984), *An Emergence of Green* (1986) and *Flashpoint* (1994), also treat lesbian themes in a variety of genres. *Daughters*, for instance, draws on the codes of SCIENCE-FICTION and ROMANCE to depict the lesbian utopia of Maternas. She has also co-edited, with Barbara Grier, several collections of lesbian love stories.   MO'D

Forrest-Thompson, Veronica 1947–75 British poet born in Malaya, Veronica Forrest-Thompson grew up in Glasgow, and was a student then a teacher in Liverpool, Leicester, Birmingham and, most importantly, Cambridge where she met J.H. Prynne and the group that surrounded him. Forrest-Thompson married, but became estranged from, critic Jonathan Culler. She died in tragic circumstances during the 1975 Cambridge Poetry Festival.

Her output was inevitably small given the brevity of her life. Her *Collected Poems and Translations* (1990) includes all her mature poetry; her critical book *Poetic Artifice* (1978) contains, she wrote, 'the theory of which her poems are examples'. It presents a post-structuralist argument illuminated by practical criticism in the Empsonian tradition. Her poems in *twelve academic questions* (1970), *Language-Games* (1971) and *Cordelia or 'A poem should not mean, but be'* (1974) explore the conventions which make a poem a poem, and her work is celebrated for its linguistic panache and relentless analysis. 'Art' of poetry is certainly the emphasis, and she reacted strongly against the CONFESSIONAL and expressionist modes of poets like Ted Hughes, SYLVIA PLATH and Robert Lowell, preferring instead the work of poets such as Andrew Crozier and John Ashbery, where language itself is foregrounded.

The success of Forrest-Thompson's project in meshing linguistic philosophy and deconstruction often overshadows the fine achievement of her love poetry; in these poems she manages a balanced synthesis of form and emotion, as in the traditional 'The Garden of Proserpine' or the experimental and daring 'Pfarr-Schmerz (Village Anguish)'.   DM

Forster, Margaret 1938– English novelist, BIOGRAPHER and non-fiction writer. Forster was born in Carlisle, and her Cumbrian upbringing and identity have remained important to her, although she has lived mostly in London. She is married to the writer and broadcaster Hunter Davies. After reading History at Somerville College, Oxford, Forster began her career as a teacher in Islington, but became a full-time writer after the publication in 1964 of her first novel, *Dame's Delight*, an Oxford novel written from a disillusioned and critical standpoint. Forster's second novel, *GEORGY GIRL* (1965), is perhaps her most famous,

partly because it became a hit film. The story of a plain, difficult but highly intelligent girl and her selfish, spiteful flatmate, it was a remarkably frank and at times bleak examination of female sexuality and of motherhood. It signalled many of the themes in Forster's novels, which include the problems of women who break conventions, the relationships between women (especially within families and between mothers and daughters), social hierarchies and the relationships between the sexes.

A prolific writer, her other novels include *Mother Can You Hear Me?* (1979), *Private Papers* (1986), *HAVE THE MEN HAD ENOUGH?* (1989), *The Battle for Christabel* (1991) and *Shadow Baby* (1996). She has also written a history of feminism, *Significant Sisters* (1984), a family memoir entitled *Hidden Lives* (1995), a biography of ELIZABETH BARRETT BROWNING (1988) and a fictionalized account of her maid's life (*Lady's Maid*, 1990) and a life of DAPHNE DU MAURIER (1993), which attracted widespread acclaim and some controversy for its revelations about Du Maurier's lesbianism.   AC

Fortune, Mary 1833?–1912? Australian novelist, journalist and one of the first women in the world to publish DETECTIVE STORIES. Her own life is still something of a mystery, as are the exact dates of her birth and death. Born in Belfast, Ireland, as a child she travelled to Canada where she later married and had a son. In 1855 she and her son journeyed to Australia to join her father on the Victoria goldfields. She began publishing poetry in local newspapers and from the 1860s was a regular contributor to a popular fiction magazine, the *Australian Journal*. Initially, she wrote historical, romantic serials and comic sketches, under the pseudonym 'Waif Wanderer', as well as crime stories, as 'W.W.' From 1870 to 1909 she concentrated mainly on stories featuring a police detective; some of these were separately published as *The Detective's Album* (1871). A selection of her non-fictional journalism has been edited by Lucy Sussex as *The Fortunes of Mary Fortune*.   EW

Fortunes of Philippa, The (1906) ANGELA BRAZIL's first novel of school life established the formula which GIRLS' SCHOOL STORIES were to exploit until the 1950s. Like her Victorian predecessors in the field – COOLIDGE, EWING in *Six to Sixteen*, and L.T. Meade – Brazil here treated school life as part only of a 'rite of passage' novel. However, the main story – how motherless Philippa, returning from childhood in Brazil, adjusts to English life – is subordinate in interest to the idyllic school sections. Brazil introduces episodes characteristic of countless later stories: Philippa triumphs as Portia in the school play at short notice, rescues a hostile classmate from an enraged bull, and, most important, wins popular Cathy as best friend.

When her father completes her acclimatization by buying a seaside, downland manor-house, the characteristic locale of later fictional schools is discovered. The novel is transitional, paying more attention than later books to contemporary educational worries (Philippa has a breakdown through overstraining her intellect), but the genre's significant features are clearly evident.   AT

Fortunes of Richard Mahony, The (1917–29) In her trilogy, HENRY HANDEL RICHARDSON took as her subject the life of her father, an Irish-born doctor who came to the Victoria goldfields in the 1850s. A massive, carefully patterned and slow-moving narrative, it represents with unflinching psychological realism the life of a misfit who can never feel a sense of belonging anywhere, even during his years of prosperity. It is at the same time a searching study of a marriage. English-born Mary Mahony is a practical, earthbound being, unable to comprehend the metaphysical yearnings which matter so much to her husband, but fiercely loyal and loving. The first volume documents the material circumstances of colonial life; but succeeding volumes are tightly focused on Mahony's suffering. The writing is most powerful in the third, which traces the disintegration of Mahony's 'self', culminating in a memorable scene in the bush where his resistance to the temptation to suicide leads to his experiencing a moment of mystical insight. Richardson acknowledged the source of her central character, but recorded that 'the person who knew me best always maintained that, in my imaginary portrait of Richard Mahony, I had drawn no other than my own'.   JBa

Foster, Hannah (Webster) 1759–1840 Early American novelist. Little is known of the details of Foster's life; the author of two published works, she was born in Massachusetts, married in 1785, had five or six children, and died in 1840.

Foster's first work, *The Coquette: Or, The History of Eliza Wharton* (1797), remained popular through the early 19th century. The novel, 'founded on fact', was based on the story of Elizabeth Whitman of Hartford, Connecticut, who had died giving birth to an illegitimate child. While presenting the story of a woman's downfall through faulty judgement, Foster also exposes marriage as a market into which many men enter with the hopes of making their fortunes. She follows a Richardsonian model not only in theme, but also in the use of the EPISTOLARY form. While Foster claims that the novel's worth arises from its didactic value – a popular justification for novels in the early republic – she must also have known that it would be read for its details of seduction and betrayal.

Foster's second work, *The Boarding School: Or, Lessons of a Preceptress to her Pupils* (1798), presents ideas about female education through a series of lectures to pupils by a preceptress. The work counsels against reading novels (except, of course, those which teach moral improvement) and discourages romantic ideas about love and marriage. Although the text centred on a popular subject of the time – women's education – it was not a popular work.   KMP

Fothergill, Jessie 1851–91 English novelist whose fiction depicting strong female characters was often set near Manchester, the area where she spent most of her life. Jessie Fothergill was the eldest child of cotton merchant Thomas Fothergill, a Quaker who left the sect when he married non-Quaker Anne Coultate. Two of Fothergill's novels – *Healey* (her first novel, published in 1875) and *Kith and Kin* (1881) – focus on Quakers, and she was strongly influenced by her father's nonconformism. Thomas Fothergill died when Jessie was 15, and the family moved to an industrial area near Rochdale, which Fothergill loved despite what she called 'the out-of-the-worldness of it all'. Fothergill travelled to Dusseldorf for ten months in 1874, studying German and music. This visit provided the background for her third novel, *The First Violin*. Although at first she had some trouble finding a publisher, the novel, which ran as an anonymous serial in *Temple Bar* in 1878 and came out in book form later that year, became her most successful work. Its romantic plot and setting are atypical among her novels. Her other novels, including *Probation* (1879), *Peril* (1884), *Borderland* (1886) and *The Lasses of Leverhouse* (1886), were more closely focused on Fothergill's usual milieu; the latter, for instance, describes life in a cotton-mill town among a large and poor family, and seems to have been partly autobiographical. Fothergill, who suffered from chronic ill health, spent her last year at Rome, and died suddenly in Switzerland at the age of 40.   KW

Fountain Overflows, The (1956) is REBECCA WEST's most autobiographical novel and indeed, as a BILDUNGSROMAN set in South London in a family of high artistic aspiration and low income, it provides keys to many of West's beliefs and preoccupations. The child narrator, Rose, is fascinated by her parents, 'two springs, bursting from a stony cliff . . . joining to flow through the world as a great river' (fluvial imagery abounds; the title is from William Blake). Her musical Mamma is impoverished and looks 'like a scarecrow', yet advises her children, 'always believe that life is as extraordinary as music says it is'. Their wayward Papa sacrifices family funds to lost causes. 'I had a glorious father, I had no father at all', says Rose, which could describe West's own father, and, ironically, H.G. Wells, the father of their son, Anthony West. Yet Rose's discomfort with being a child, her complex identity as a musician and her developing sense of life take the book beyond autobiographical fiction. It is the first volume of a trilogy.   JL

Fountaine, Margaret Elizabeth 1862–1940 British lepidopterist and diarist, upper-middle-class and of staid background, was also a late-Victorian NEW WOMAN seeking freedom from conventional female roles. At 29 she became a roving collector of butterflies. Venturing into remote areas on horseback, refusing to ride sidesaddle and accompanied only by a guide or translator, she collected everywhere, often in the Middle and Near East. She formed a 25-year liaison with her Syrian interpreter, Khalil Neimy, and left to the Castle Museum at Norwich the Fountaine–Neimy collection of about 22,000 butterflies, along with her 12-volume 1878–1939 DIARY. Over 1 million words long, it was written up annually from notes into a skilful, often suspenseful, continuous narrative of her life and travels.   HB

Fowler [Felkin], Ellen Thorneycroft 1860–1929 This popular English writer's earliest publications were three volumes of verse, the first appearing in 1888. However, the success of her first novel, *Concerning Isobel Carnaby* (1896), persuaded her that fiction was her true forte.

The remainder of her best-known works followed on in rapid succession, these being *A Double Thread* (1899), *The Farringdons* (1900), *Fuel of Fire* (1902), *Place and Power* (1903) and *Kate of Kate Hall* (1904), this last written in collaboration with her husband. Nevertheless, she continued to write novels and short stories until 1926. Fowler's plots are certainly original. In *A Double Thread* a society beauty and heiress masquerades as her less fortunate (and long-dead) twin sister in order to be appreciated for herself rather than for her money; whilst in *Place and Power* a child rejected at birth lives to reproach his parents for their callousness on the very day that he is elected Prime Minister in preference to his politically ambitious father. Unfortunately the novels are marred by lengthy philosophical debates on the part of both characters and narrators, these weighing down her lively plots and, to some extent, obscuring her perceptive characterization.   EMH

Fowler, Karen Joy 1950– American writer with degrees from Berkeley in Politics and North Asian Studies who first came to prominence in the 1980s with short stories that combined stock SCIENCE FICTION motifs with a questioning feminist intelligence. This automatically made her controversial, a so-called New Humanist. Like others in what was not really a group, Fowler never disowned the description; she was primarily concerned to use SF material for its metaphoric and moral rather than its political or ethical resonances. Her 1986 collection, *Artificial Things*,

makes this clear even by its title; when Fowler introduces aliens, they are usually as an interrogatory Other whereby we perceive our own human flaws. In her first novel, *Sarah Canary* (1991), the dispossessed of C19 Washington project their yearnings onto a silent woman, probably an alien. *The Sweetheart Season* (1996) appears to abandon SF and fantasy altogether for a witty NATURALISTIC 1940s tale of small-town life, women's baseball and experimental cookery – in all of which, it transpires explicitly on the last page, the Goddess has been immanent.   RK

Frame, Janet 1922– New Zealand's most celebrated novelist who, from her earliest works, *The Lagoon: Stories* (1951) and OWLS DO CRY (1957), has criticized middle-class society and privileged the marginal: the mute, the disturbed, and artists. But her subversion of social norms extends to representing reality as liable to sudden collapse and language as prone to deception. A writer in the mirror, or non-realist, tradition, preoccupied with the meanings of death and transcendence, she constantly explores the borderline realms of existence. Instead of plot and character her fiction has a parable-like structure, although language is often an organizing principle, and the loss of language a recurring theme. Early, searing novels like *Faces in the Water* (1961) and *Scented Gardens for the Blind* (1963) draw loosely upon her experiences as a young woman in mental hospitals over eight years; and this out-of-time trauma habitually resurfaces as a metaphysics of absence to undermine the assumptions by which we understand reality. In *The Edge of the Alphabet* (1962) the quests of her protagonists end in failure or death; in *The Rainbirds* (or *Yellow Flowers in the Antipodean Room*) (1967) her hero comes back from the dead; in *A State of Siege* (1966) her heroine is haunted by an exterior, invisible presence, possibly a figment of her imagination; in THE CARPATHIANS (1988) provincial New Zealand society is invaded by a Gravity Star which destroys the concepts of time and distance.

Frame's later novels show a POSTMODERNIST influence. Complex narrative strategies, game-playing, deferred authorial responsibility, the collapse of fictional illusion combine with an ironic yet compassionate vision to offset the darkness that madness and death evoke. *Daughter Buffalo* (1972), LIVING IN THE MANIOTOTO (1979) and *The Carpathians* introduce multiple American and New Zealand settings and characters. But despite this increased fictionality, and her use of magical realism, surrealism and the fantastic, Frame remains close to MODERNIST or POST-COLONIAL concerns. She identifies the creative world of the imagination – represented either as childhood treasure, the artist who values memory, or the art which tells 'real' truths – as a source of value and insists that society's mythologies and collective memories be honoured. Memory apparently underpins the three volumes of autobiography published in the early 1980s. Filmed by Jane Campion as *An Angel at My Table* (1990), they brought her international fame; but as Frame compromises autobiographical 'truth' with the assumptions of fiction writing, any full understanding of her work will only emerge through investigating the features of all such genres which rely on the opposition between reported fact and invented fiction.

Frame has a significant academic readership and is an honorary member of the American Academy of Arts and Letters. She has written several volumes of short stories, including stories for children, many of which are now recognized as classics. Her verse in *The Pocket Mirror* (1967) also uses mirror imagery, collapses binary opposites to challenge categories of meaning, and introduces a thematic of difference to privilege the marginal.   JMW

Franc, Maude Jeanne see EVANS, MATILDA

France [née Henderson], Ruth 1913–68 New Zealand novelist and poet, who published two novels and two volumes of poetry. Her poetry, *Unwilling Pilgrim* (1955) and *The Halting Place* (1961), was published under the pseudonym 'Paul Henderson' and she tried to conceal her female identity as a poet. The editor of the magazine, the *New Zealand Listener*, which first published her poetry wrote in her obituary: 'In this country reviewers of poetry are often other poets. I have found among them a curious prejudice against the female of their species.'

Her first novel, *The Race* (1958), alternates between the men at sea on a yacht race from Wellington to Lyttelton during a storm and the women at home waiting for them. *Ice Cold River* (1962) concerns a family gathered to celebrate Christmas who have been cut off by a river in flood. Both novels focus on the emotions, fears and inadequacies and final survival strengths of the group members. In 1964 she published a children's book, *The Shining Year*, set in New Zealand, and at her death left an unpublished novel and memoir. A librarian before her marriage in 1934 to a professional boat builder, she had two sons.   AM

Francis [née Gittins], Ann 1738–1800 English poet and classical scholar. She was educated by her father, Revd Daniel Gittins of South Stoke (Sussex), in the classics and Hebrew and the DNB records that she became 'a competent scholar'. She married Revd Robert Francis, rector of Edgefield (Norfolk), and settled into a life that combined duties as mother and rector's wife with poetry and scholarship. *A Poetical Translation of the Song of Solomon, from the Original Hebrew, with a preliminary Discourse and Notes, historical and explanatory* (1781) was an imaginative, dramatized

translation that conveyed the eroticism of the *Song*. Later works include: *The Obsequies of Demetrius Poliorcetes: A Poem* (1785) based on a story from Plutarch; *A Poetical Epistle from Charlotte to Werther* (1788); and *Miscellaneous Poems, By a Lady* (1790). In 1798 she published an anti-Jacobin broadside ballad, *A Plain Address to My Neighbours*, which outlined the dire consequences that would follow a French invasion to liberate the British working class.   LBe

Frangipani Gardens, The (1980) In this menacing and highly symbolic GOTHIC novel, set in the Adelaide Hills, BARBARA HANRAHAN writes a 'double language' about the distortions and perversions that arise from being forced into gendered and class roles. The O'Brien clan, inhabitants of the Frangipani Gardens, slowly disintegrates as the Duke and Duchess of York voyage to Australia in 1927 to open the first parliament. Euphoria in Adelaide over the fairy-tale visit masks the grim underside of a society where unemployed men sleep with rats. Like the frangipani, with its scent of sweetness and decay, characters are 'masked', their surface perfection concealing monstrosity. The miniature Girlie, who was imprisoned in 'Papa's tyrant arms', is 'always two', painted perfection and viciously dangerous. Her brother Boy is emotionally crippled by being forced into a heterosexual mould. Innocents who enter the garden are threatened by sexual predation, though the painter Doll, apparently prissy and respectable, who folds undies on the line 'so you shouldn't see their private parts', can protect to some extent through art's power to envision and control.   CM

Franken, Rose 1895–1988 American writer Rose Franken's heroine, Claudia, whose marriage she chronicled over seven novels, earned her such popularity that Franken described her life before Claudia's creation as 'B.C.' Franken's B.C., however, was by no means an empty period of her life. Growing up in New York City's secular Jewish middle class in the early 20th century, Franken was educated at the School for Ethical Culture. Her first novel, *Pattern* (1925), was praised for her (partially autobiographical) analysis of how her heroine's overdependence on her mother proved an obstacle to adulthood and maturity. Franken's first Broadway play, *Another Language* (1932), challenged the Victorian stereotype of the mother as 'angel in the house'; selected for *The Best Plays of 1931 1932*, it was also made into a film starring Helen Hayes.

The conflict between appeasing and challenging her audiences may be seen throughout Franken's work. In her successful plays and novels, she masked her exploration of serious psychological issues through her engaging characters and plots. The first Claudia

Frontispiece from Mary Shelley's *Frankenstein*, 1831. 'By the glimmer of the half-extinguished light, I saw the dull, yellow eye of the creature open; it breathed hard, and a convulsive motion agitated its limbs . . . I rushed out of the room'.

novel, *Claudia and David: The Story of a Marriage* (1939), reiterated the concerns of *Pattern*: in the novel, heroine Claudia Naughton matures after her mother's death, but constantly grapples with her ambivalence toward marriage and sexuality. The novel, which Franken also produced and directed as a play, was a critical and commercial hit. Audiences were less approving when Franken treated social problems less tacitly. Her exploration of homosexuality, sexual repression and anti-Semitism in the drama *Outrageous Fortune* (1943) was such a critical and commercial failure that she returned to more pleasing fictions.   MG

Frankenstein: Or, The Modern Prometheus

(1818) MARY SHELLEY's first novel, a GOTHIC tale of Victor Frankenstein and the nameless monster he vivifies from charnel-house parts, continues to fascinate readers and attract critical attention. Frankenstein loses control of the monster by not only callously repudiating it for its ugliness but also refusing its demand for a mate to end its loneliness; the monster revenges itself by killing those Victor has loved. A Miltonic Adam according to Shelley's epigraph, the monster is born eager to love and fully appreciative of

what its Lockean senses teach it but embittered and corrupted by experience and expanding consciousness. The frame story of Frankenstein's parallel, explorer Robert Walton obsessively endeavouring to reach the magnetic North Pole, provides additional warning against the overweening, egotistical ambition that deflects males from Shelley's desiderata: close emotional ties to family and friends and the beneficent influence of nature. The monster has been construed both as Frankenstein's double and as Shelley's projection of her bleak sense of motherhood; her reference to the book as 'my hideous progeny' in her introduction to the revised edition of 1831 may also reflect her uneasy sense of being a female author in a patriarchal world.   HB

Franklin, Miles 1879–1954 Australian novelist, most famous for her first novel, *MY BRILLIANT CAREER* (1901), whose account of the frustrations of an ambitious young girl growing up in the bush, while not the straight autobiography many have assumed, had many resonances with her own life. She was born Stella Maria Sarah Miles Franklin in Talbingo, New South Wales, on her grandmother's property, a fifth-generation white Australian who was later to write extensively about her family's, and Australia's, pioneering past. In 1889 her family moved to a smaller and poorer property near Goulburn, New South Wales, the 'Possum Gully' of *My Brilliant Career*. Franklin's naive belief that publishing *My Brilliant Career* as 'Miles' rather than 'Stella' would conceal her sex and identity was shattered by Henry Lawson's preface to the first edition, which he also helped to cut, at the request of the publisher, William Blackwood. Despite this censoring of some of its more outrageous passages, *My Brilliant Career* brought notoriety to its young author, who was taken up by some of Sydney's leading literary and society figures. After failing to secure local publication of her even more outrageous sequel, 'The End of My Career', which included thinly disguised portraits of those she had met in Sydney, Franklin left for the USA in 1906.

Living mainly in Chicago, from 1908 to 1915 she worked with another Australian feminist, Alice Henry, in the National Women's Trade Union League. During World War I she served with a hospital contingent in the Serbian campaigns of 1917–18. Between 1919 to 1932 she lived and worked mainly in London, before returning to Sydney where she remained until her death. Although she continued writing plays and fiction for most of her life, much remained unpublished. In 1928, under the less-easily penetrable male pseudonym 'Brent of Bin Bin', she published *UP THE COUNTRY*, the first of six novels in a family saga which chronicles Australian bush life. Several other novels appeared under her own name including, in 1946 and extensively rewritten, the sequel to her first, *My Career Goes Bung*.

An ardent nationalist, Franklin worked tirelessly to promote Australian literature and assist other writers, both personally and through institutions like the Commonwealth Literary Fund and the Fellowship of Australian Writers. Much of this is recorded in her extensive correspondence, some of which has been collected in *My Congenials: Miles Franklin and Friends in Letters*. After *My Brilliant Career*, these letters remain perhaps her most lively and enduring pieces of writing. Having scraped and saved for most of her life, Franklin left her estate to found an award for Australian writers – the Miles Franklin, now Australia's most prestigious literary prize. Her own reputation has been greatly enhanced by the successful 1979 film version of *My Brilliant Career* directed by Gillian Armstrong, and by recent feminist re-readings of the Australian literary tradition. EW

Fraser [née Pakenham], Antonia, Lady 1932–

British BIOGRAPHER, broadcaster and DETECTIVE WRITER. Daughter of the politician, Lord Longford, and writer Elizabeth Longford, she was born into a family which boasts eight writers in three generations. Scholarly research is the family hallmark. She was educated at St Mary's Convent, Ascot, and at Lady Margaret Hall, Oxford. She married the politician Sir Hugh Fraser in 1956 and the playwright Harold Pinter in 1980. She is best known for her historical biographies of the Tudor and Stuart dynasties. Her *Mary Queen of Scots* (1969), for which she won the James Tait Black Memorial Prize, skilfully combined elements of fiction with biography, turning the book into an instant bestseller and popularizing the genre. Her other biographies include *Cromwell Our Chief of Men* (1973), *King James: VI of Scotland, I of England* (1974), *King Charles II* (1978) and *The Six Wives of Henry VIII* (1992). In 1977 Fraser introduced Jemima Shore, her female detective, in *Quiet as a Nun*. Jemima Shore has since appeared in over ten mystery stories including *Cool Repentance* (1982), *Oxford Blood* (1985) and *Political Death* (1996) and the books have been turned into a successful television series. JHB

Fraser, Sylvia (Myers) 1935–

Novelist and essayist, winner of the Canadian Authors' Association Award for Non-Fiction and the Library Association Book List Medal. She was born of working-class parents in Hamilton, Ontario, and experienced an unhappy childhood which she used as part model for her first heroine in *Pandora* (1972). She took her BA at the University of Western Ontario, worked as a journalist, was married in 1959 and divorced in 1977. *The Candy Factory* (1975) and *A Casual Affair: A Modern Fairy Tale* (1978) explore gender relations in the contemporary world, whereas *The Emperor's Virgin* (1980) deals with the live burial of a woman whose chastity is questioned in ancient Rome. The war novel *Berlin Solstice* was published in 1984. In her first work of non-fiction, *My Father's House: A Memoir of Incest and Healing* (1987), she bravely explores her long-repressed memories of incest. In 1994, she published *The Book of Strange: A Journey*, in which she attempts to come to terms with spiritual and paranormal events in her own life. She has taught writing and writing workshops and been much involved in organizations for the advancement of the arts. FD

Freeman, Mary Eleanor Wilkins 1852–1930

American regionalist writer of short stories, novels and CHILDREN's literature. She was born in Randolph, Massachusetts, daughter of a carpenter, and educated at Brattleboro High School, Mt Holyoke Female Seminary, and Mrs Hosford's Glenwood Seminary. When she was 15, the family moved to Brattleboro, Vermont, and began a disastrous economic decline. Her one sister and both parents had died by the time she was 31. Alone and impoverished, in 1884 she returned to Randolph where she lived for almost twenty years with her childhood friend Mary Wales. Literary successes rescued her from poverty; she earned money first with children's poems published in *Wide Awake*, then, in 1882, her first story for adults won a prize from the Boston *Sunday Budget*. Encouraged by editor Mary Louise Booth of *Harper's Bazaar*, she wrote short stories about New England, later collected in *A Humble Romance and Other Stories* (1887) and *A NEW ENGLAND NUN AND OTHER STORIES* (1891). These collections established her reputation as a 'local-color' writer, although she departed from the caricatures of her male contemporaries in the genre (Mark Twain, Hamlin Garland, Bret Harte), portraying her characters with dignity. She concentrated on the lives and viewpoints of women, most of them ageing, unmarried, poor and struggling fiercely for self-determination. In 1895 she began travelling, taking in Boston, Chicago and Paris. In all, Freeman published fourteen collections of stories and thirteen novels (the most successful of which was *Pembroke* (1894)), as well as children's books, poems and a play.

In 1902, after a prolonged and intermittent engagement, she married a non-practising physician, Charles M. Freeman, and moved to Metuchen, New Jersey. He was institutionalized for alcoholism in 1919 and they separated in 1921. In 1926 she received an award from the American Academy of Arts and Letters and, with EDITH WHARTON, was inducted into the National Institute of Arts and Letters. JSG

Freke, Elizabeth 1641–1714

Autobiographer and poet. Eldest daughter of Royalist gentry, in 1671, after a long courtship, she secretly married a second cousin, Percy Freke. The marriage was turbulent: she lived mainly at West Bilney in Norfolk, while Percy came over from his estate at Rathbarry in Ireland only when he wanted money for unreliable investments. They had one son, Ralph. Elizabeth's sister, Lady Frances Norton, wrote poetry and published books of classical quotations.

After Percy's death in 1706 Elizabeth wrote a JOURNAL beginning with their marriage. It records the effects on their lives of the Monmouth Rebellion and the Battle of the Boyne, and includes letters, inventories and poems. In the vivid 'Dialogue between the serpent and Eve', the serpent dwells on how the swelling, vermilion fruit bends into Eve's hand, and urges 'Come, pull and eat.'

A heated correspondence with the Bishop of Norfolk culminated in Freke's excommunication in 1714. Her 1913 biographer reported that 'Madam Freke' still figured in the folklore of Bilney.   HH

French, Anne 1956–

New Zealand poet whose first collection, *All Cretans are Liars*, was published in 1987. Her poetry, at its most characteristic, satirizes relationships between men and women, based often on the stereotype of 'the evader', the man who won't commit, filtered through a narrator who ruefully acknowledges women's complicity in their own betrayals.

Her focus is often self-consciously literary: a section of *The Male as Evader* (1988) is entitled 'The Language and Literature of Evasion'. And she is interested not only with how women confront romantic love, but how they write, and are written about within its rhetorical tradition. French sees the expectations of the canon and literary tradition as being irredeemably masculine, and its elitist and prohibitive strategies akin to the way men manipulate their relationships with women. In 'The lady fishermen', JANE AUSTEN, Mrs Melville, EMILY BRONTË, ELIZABETH BARRETT BROWNING and the New Zealand writer JANET FRAME are placed in the masculine world of fishing and hunting to subvert and undermine the stereotypes of the male author: 'Ludicrous. There's no tradition. / We'll just have to improvise (with improvements)'. The collection *Cabin Fever* was published in 1990, *Seven Days on Mykonos* in 1993 and *Boys' Night Out* in 1998.   JSt

French, Anne (Richmond Warner) [Anne Warner] 1869–1913

American writer from Minnesota who, at 18, married Charles Eltinge French, a 53-year-old Minneapolis businessman and began her writing career by compiling a genealogy entitled *An American Ancestry* (1894), dedicated to her son, Charles. That was just the beginning of a prolific writing career that included the publication of both novels and short stories. After spending two years in France, she wrote *His Story, Their Letters* (1902) before returning to St Paul to live; however, finding the Minnesota life too provincial, she soon returned to Europe where she spent the remainder of her life writing fiction, including some novels with provocative titles: *The Rejuvenation of Aunt Mary* (1905), *The Panther: A Tale of Temptation* (1908), *How Leslie Loved* (1911), *The Taming of Amaretti: A Comedy of Manners* (1915). She is probably best known for her lightly comic Susan Clegg stories, including *Susan Clegg And Her Friend Mrs Lathrop* (1904), *Susan Clegg and Her Love Affairs* (1906), *Susan Clegg and Her Neighbor's Affairs* (1906) and *Susan Clegg and a Man in the House* (1907), all of which focus on a series of conversations in which Miss Clegg gossips about the residents of a hospitable, though somewhat provincial, community.   MRA

French [née Edwards], Marilyn 1929–

American feminist best known for her first novel, the cultural landmark THE WOMEN'S ROOM. By 1977 'a gap opened between women's lib and women's lit', as Susan Faludi later wrote, and *The Women's Room* filled it, providing a compelling fictional counterpart to the ideas of BETTY FRIEDAN. In Mira Ward's evolution from frustrated housewife to Harvard graduate student amid the political ferments of the late 1960s (which closely paralleled French's own biography) thousands of American women found a depiction of their own circumscribed lives and a voice for the anger that would propel them toward change. The book galvanized readers but drew fierce criticism for, among other things, the two-dimensionality of its male characters. She continued to be criticized on this point in other novels: *The Bleeding Heart* (1980) and the intergenerational saga *Her Mother's Daughter* (1988). She has written and taught extensively, at Harvard and elsewhere; her non-fiction books are the essays of *Beyond Power: Men, Women and Morals* (1986) and *The War Against Women* (1992), a dense study of the origins of patriarchy. The 1990s saw publication of novels *Our Father* and *My Summer with George* (1996), a gentler depiction of romantic relations set in her native New York, where she lives.   SB

Frere, Mary Eliza (Isabella) 1845–1911

English writer and traveller, collector of South Indian folk tales. The eldest child of Sir (Henry) Bartle Frere, later Governor of Bombay and High Commissioner for South Africa, she went to a Wimbledon private school, but at 18 joined her father in Bombay. They travelled widely and in 1868 Frere published *Old Deccan Days, or Hindoo Fairy Legends, Current in Southern India*, with an introduction by her father. These twenty-four tales recorded conversations with an Indian ayah whom Frere presents as an equal, not as a servant. Referring to herself merely as 'the Collector', she writes in the

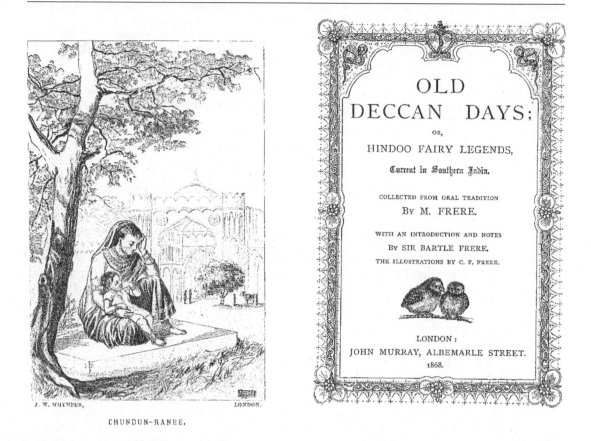

Mary Eliza Frere: frontispiece and title-page of *Old Deccan Days or, Hindoo Fairy Legends*, 1868.

preface of the similarity between Indian and European tales, anticipating the later structuralist approach of Vladimir Propp. She stresses the unexpected power of women in the stories, particularly in the astonishing tale 'Brave Seventee Bai', in which a wife takes over her husband's identity. The book went into five editions and initiated much new folkloric research. However, thereafter, all Frere produced was a sub-Shakespearean play, *Love's Triumph* (1869) and some religious poetry (1890). The Mary Eliza Frere Library in Girton College, Cambridge, contains manuscripts from her journey to the Holy Land in 1906–8.   VP

Friedan, Betty 1921– Illinois-born American feminist writer and social psychologist. Friedan was educated at Peoria schools then Smith College. A student of the Gestalt psychologist Kurt Koffka, she held a research fellowship at the University of California in Berkeley and was involved with early experiments in group dynamics, worked as a clinical psychologist and

in applied social research, and established the Community Resources Pool in which talented people from a variety of fields including science, the arts and politics work with schoolchildren. But she became famous with the publication of THE FEMININE MYSTIQUE in 1963 – a groundbreaking investigation of the social and cultural constructions of femininity. The book concentrates on 'the problem that has no name', women's questioning of life – 'Is this all?' – in the face of entrenched subordination and conditioning about what is 'feminine', leading to some suggestions about a new life plan which might enable women to think, speak out, expand their lives. Friedan has been visiting lecturer to Temple and Yale Universities and Queen's College and delivered numerous lectures worldwide winning the American Humanist Award in 1975. Her articles have appeared in *Harper's*, *Good Housekeeping*, *Mademoiselle*, *Reader's Digest*. Her other work includes *It Changed My Life* (1976) which charts the effects of *The Feminine Mystique*.   GW

From Man to Man (1926) Published posthumously, this philosophical novel by OLIVE SCHREINER is the outcome of some forty years spent inscribing her artistic vision and anti-imperialist socialist feminism into the story of two sisters – one an artist, the other a fallen woman – without being able to offer a resolution to the problems she raised. Experimental in form, the text combines typical plot elements of the NEW WOMAN novel with long essayistic reflections on art, interpersonal relationships and the politics of race and class. Drawing on John Morley's 'From man to man nothing matters but charity', Schreiner pleads for an ethic of humanitarian care to replace aggressive social Darwinism. Illustrating the destructive nature of personal power politics, the novel outlines the possibility of social change by contrasting the heroines' nurturing ethos with the injuries they suffer as a result of others' predatory behaviour, and breaks off at the precise turning point between 'old' and 'new' philosophies. Childbirth and room-as-womb metaphors establish a conceptual link between literal and literary mothering, while suggesting that the odds may be too heavily weighted against the woman artist who is also a wife and mother. AH

From The Fifteenth District: A Novella and Eight Short Stories (1979) The short fictions (there is no novella) in MAVIS GALLANT's fifth collection employ a polished and precise language of REALISM. Memory fuses with history in these uneasy stories, and the particular interprets the general; the rich imagery of detail is used to convey the vagary of more grandiose agendas. Of all her collections, this is the book in which Gallant reveals herself most clearly as a master of the short story – her economical prose, poetic density, precise imagery and uncanny ability to convey experience are impressive. In 'The Moslem Wife', Netta silently and politely fights against imprisonment within the 'portable-fence arrangement' of her marriage to Jack, finding freedom (and discovering her desire for it) only when World War II traps her in France and him in America with his young lover. Gallant's enduring empathy with social and political exiles and refugees is evident in the title story. As with most of her fiction, all of the short stories in this collection originally appeared in the *New Yorker*. SLK

Frost in May (1933) ANTONIA WHITE's first and most felicitous work of fiction. Nanda Grey, White's central character and the daughter of a convert, arrives at the Convent of the Five Wounds, Lippington, at the age of 9. (Antonia White herself, in similar circumstances, was sent to the Convent of the Sacred Heart at Roehampton in 1908.) Nanda's a spirited heroine; though susceptible to the glamour of Catholicism, she balks at the nuns' objective of breaking the will of every pupil in the interests of fostering a true spirituality. The whole suspect system comes under attack –

though without didacticism – as Nanda gradually distances herself from the more *outré* elements of Catholic teaching. ('"Now here's a nice little penance for someone", cried Mother Poitier gaily.'). The climax of the narrative occurs when Nanda, aged 14, is expelled – or at least required to leave – after an innocent but lurid story she's composed falls into the hands of the nuns. Before this point, though, the rather rarefied school atmosphere is beautifully evoked, with its traditions, its recreations, its alarms and restrictions. Written with exceptional clarity and lucidity, *Frost in May* is a minor classic of the GIRLS' SCHOOL-STORY genre. PC

Fugitive Pieces (1997) A first novel for poet ANNE MICHAELS, this acclaimed work of lyrical prose embraces such weighty subjects as memory, guilt, identity and loss. Disorienting images begin the memory narrative of Jakob Beer, a Polish Jew who escapes the Nazis by burying himself in the mud of an archaeological dig until smuggled to Greece by the geologist Athos. His rescuer's passion for language and fossils sets up Jakob's (and the novel's) project of excavating the past from the present, of grasping the 'gradual instant' of unearthed memories. The relationship between the physical and ephemeral world is reinforced when Ben, a Canadian meteorologist and son of Holocaust survivors, takes over the narrative voice in search of the now-dead poet Jakob's journals. Michaels's symbolic images and the parallel rhythms she weaves between the separate strata of the two men's stories are evocative. When self-consciously poetical, Michaels's intense prose can be somewhat overwrought; nevertheless, it serves both to affirm and to deny the capacity of language in a post-Holocaust world: 'There was no ordinariness to return to, no refuge from the blinding potency of things.' SLK

Fuller, Anne ?–c.1790 Irish novelist. Almost nothing is known of Fuller's background or personal life. She was the author of three novels, the first of which, *The Convent, or the History of Sophia Nelson* by 'a young lady', appeared in 1786. *Alan Fitz-Osborne* (1786), was a historical ROMANCE, whose knightly hero ends his life as a hermit after two women die for love of him.

The Son of Ethelwolf (1789), set during the period of Alfred the Great, was described by the *Monthly Review* as 'prose run mad'. Its heroine, Ethelswitha, disguises herself as a warrior in order to follow the King into battle, displaying 'an intrepidity which raised her above the character of her sex', and the hero's mother, reunited with him after a long separation, promptly dies in his arms: 'accustomed to misfortune, thy virtue had taught thee to support it without repining. Joy, long a stranger to thy soul, was the harbinger of death.' Fuller died of consumption near Cork in about 1790. RR

Fuller (Ossoli), (Sarah) Margaret 1810–50

American journalist, critic and feminist theorist. She was born in Cambridgeport, Massachusetts, oldest of nine children. Her father, a lawyer and legislator, educated her as young men were educated. When her father died in 1835, she assumed responsibility for her younger siblings' education. She became associated with the transcendentalists Ralph Waldo Emerson, with whose aid she founded the journal *Dial* in 1840, and Bronson Alcott, in whose school she taught from 1836 to 1837. Fuller became a leading figure in the Transcendentalist movement, an American philosophic school shaped by Platonism and German Romantic philosophy that emphasized intuition and direct experience as against rationalism and traditional authority. From 1837 to 1839, while teaching in Providence, Rhode Island, she began writing criticism and translating German literature. In 1839 she moved to Boston where she conducted a series of popular 'Conversations' for women at a bookshop. She was the first woman to study at Harvard and produced her first book, *Summer on the Lakes*, based on her research, in 1844. This book, which calls attention to exploitation of Native Americans, abuse of the environment, and mistreatment of pioneer women, prompted Horace Greeley to invite her to write for his newspaper, the New York *Tribune*. Her articles were collected in *Papers on Literature and Art* (1846).

Fuller's WOMAN IN THE NINETEENTH CENTURY (1845) is a landmark of feminist theory. Its call for the removal of gender barriers inspired participants at the Seneca Falls women's rights convention in 1848. Travelling in Europe as a foreign correspondent starting in 1846, Fuller met European writers and radicals – among them GEORGE SAND, the BROWNINGS and the Italian patriot Giuseppe Mazzini. She settled in Rome and involved herself in the cause of Italian revolution. In 1848 she had a son with Giovanni Angelo Ossoli, a nobleman who joined the short-lived Roman republican revolution. After the revolution failed, they fled to Florence. They apparently married in 1849. All three died in a shipwreck as they sailed into New York the following May. JSG

Fullerton, Mary (Eliza) ['Robert Gray', 'Gordon Manners', 'Alpenstock', 'E', 'Turner O'Lingo']

1868–1946 Australian poet, novelist and suffragette. The daughter of a selector, she was born in a bark hut in Glenmaggie, Victoria, where she was educated by her mother before attending the local state school. She read avidly amongst the books at home – in particular the Bible and the works of Milton, Shelley and Byron – and by the age of 11 had read *Paradise Lost* three times. Becoming a writer herself was therefore a natural process, and from an early age she contributed verse and prose to Australian periodicals. Her poetry was pub-

Margaret Fuller.

lished in *Moods and Melodies* (1908) and *The Breaking Furrow* (1921), but she is chiefly remembered for *Bark House Days* (1921), reminiscences of her childhood. She visited England in 1912 and returned there to live permanently in 1922. Like her close friend, MILES FRANKLIN, who lived with her in London for a while, she felt it necessary to publish pseudonymously to conceal her identity (and gender), and they managed each other's manuscripts and correspondence to provide yet another layer of anonymity between them and publishers. Although Fullerton published several novels, including *Two Women* (1923), *The People of the Timber Belt* (1925) and *Rufus Sterne* (1932), her fiction lacks the skill of her descriptive prose about the Australian bush, or that of her later poetry which appeared under the name 'E' in *Moles Do So Little With Their Privacy* (1942) and *The Wonder and the Apple* (1946).

JSte

Futehally, Shama 1952–

Indian fiction writer, who studied English Literature in her home city of Bombay and in England at Leeds University before returning to India to teach. Futehally's work so far remains an exploration of the limited manoeuvring space available to women and the deadening constraints imposed on their existence by a male-dominated society. The characters in her stories are pushed toward compromise, even if that involves the loss of a life-motivating idealism ('Waking Up') or life itself ('The First Rain'). A strong autobiographical element is present in her novel *Tara Lane* (1993), in which the women of an affluent business family desert the high moral ground, with a nagging sense of protest. Futehally's phrasing – 'The sea was appallingly long and shiny' – has an occasional strangeness not necessarily the effect of Indian language breaking in. Her 1994 translation of the *Songs of Meera* (a 16th-century female saint and poet of Rajasthan) had a mixed reception. VQ

G

Gág, Wanda 1893–1946 American artist and writer from Minnesota, who, at the age of 17, wrote in her diary, 'Draw to live; and live to draw' and knew of her calling at an early age. The oldest of seven children born and raised in New Ulm, Gág was best known as a commercial artist and author who was much admired for her self-illustrated CHILDRENS' LITERATURE. After the death of her father, the adolescent Gág sold bookmarks and contributed a comic strip to the Minneapolis *Journal* in order to support her family. Her first popular success was *Millions of Cats* (1928), which won her a Newberry Award and has been continually in print for seventy years and much translated. Her own version of *Snow White and the Seven Dwarfs* (1938) was a radical response to the Disney adaptation and *Growing Pains: Diaries and Drawings 1908-1917* depicts, in very emotional terms, Gág's early art school days, both in the Minneapolis and St Paul art academies. She also wrote *Gone is Gone; Or, The Story of a Man Who Wanted to Do Housework* (1933); *Nothing at All* (1941); *Snippy and Snappy* (1931); and several illustrated versions of the Brothers Grimm. MRA

Gage, Matilda Joslyn 1826–98 American suffragist and advocate for the social advancement of women. She was born in Cicero, New York, to Dr Hezekiah, and Helen Leslie, Joslyn, and was 18 years old when she married Henry Gage. At 26, she became active in the feminist cause when she attended the 1852 National Women's Rights Convention in Syracuse, New York.

Gage helped to organize the New York State Woman's Suffrage Association; she served terms as president of both the New York and the National Woman's Suffrage Association (NWSA). When SUSAN B. ANTHONY was prosecuted for voting in 1873, Gage lectured sixteen times in one month to win support for her.

Gage collaborated with Anthony and ELIZABETH CADY STANTON on numerous writing projects; in 1876 they started the *National Citizen*, a suffragist newspaper which Gage edited, and, in 1881, the trio produced three substantial volumes of the *History of Woman Suffrage*.

Gage was frustrated by purportedly biblical rationales for the subordination of women. She delivered a speech at the 1878 convention of the NWSA on the influential role of theology in determining women's inferior social status. The speech was so popular she expanded it into the book-length study *Woman, Church, and State* (1893). LMC

Gagnon, Madeleine 1938– Francophone Canadian poet, novelist and essayist, born in Amqui, Quebec. Educated at Université Saint-Joseph du Nouveau-Brunswick (BA 1959), Université de Montréal (MA 1961) and Université d'Aix–Nice (D.ès L. 1968). She taught literature at the Université de Québec à Montréal, and was later a guest professor and writer-in-residence there, and at the Université de Québec à Rimouski.

Madeleine Gagnon is an influential feminist writer and literary theorist in Quebec. She was part of the editorial collective of the journal *Chroniques* in the 1970s, and has been published in numerous feminist journals. Her work often integrates quotations from pop and 'high' culture. She has developed a form of discourse which she calls the 'fiction-essay', which combines fictional passages with poetry and discursive prose. She has also been an active participant in the political life of Quebec: during the 'Quiet Revolution' of the 1960s and early 1970s, she was active in the trade union movement and an active member of the influential Union des écrivains Québecois. At that time she wrote various 'collages' composed of both poetry and prose: 'Pour les femmes et tous les autres' (*l'Aurore*, 1974), *Poélitique* (1975), and *Retailles*, a prose poem (1977) and *Les Fées ont Soif* (1978), both with Denise Boucher. She also collaborated with HÉLÈNE CIXOUS and Annie Leclerc in a collection of feminist essays, *La Venue à l'écriture* (1977), and 'mon corps dans l'écriture', an essay on women's voice (*Autre*, 1978). In 1979 she published her first novel, *Lueur: roman archéologique*, a blend of literary theory, autobiography, prose and poetry around an 'archaeological exploration' of the origin of her own and women's language. Gagnon published several volumes of poetry which show the influence of psychoanalytic, feminist and nationalist ideas: *Pensées du Poème* (1983), *La lettre infinie* (1984), *Les Fleurs du Catalpa* (1986; Grand Prize, *Journal de Montréal*), *L'Infante immémoriale* (1987), *Chant pour un Québec lointain* (1991; Governor General's Award), and *La Terre est remplie de langage* (1993). In the late 1980s and the 1990s, Madeleine Gagnon moved from feminist REALISM to a psychoanalytical approach to literature focusing on mother–daughter relationships and influenced by the work of Cixous, Annie Leclerc, Michèle Montrelay and Luce Irigaray. Many of her texts have been collected in *Autobiographie 1 et 2* (1989) and *Toute écriture est amour* (1989).   GHN

Gaitskill, Mary 1954– American novelist. Educated at the University of Michigan, Gaitskill is the author of the novel *Two Girls, Fat and Thin* (1991) and the short-story collection *Bad Behaviour* (1988). Her work constantly alludes to, rather than being directly involved with, the debates about sexuality within feminism in the 1980s; her characters are never positive heroines and their involvement with issues like child abuse and sadomasochism is always seen complexly and often perversely. *Two Girls, Fat and Thin* sets off the awful childhoods and obsessional adulthoods of its two heroines against each other. Journalist Justine is crazy to succeed, Dorothy aims to be the perfect acolyte of an individualist guru wittily based on AYN RAND. Announcing itself by its title as portraiture, this is also one of the best fictional accounts of the late 1980s, efficiently deploying every aspect of New York life from brand-name junkfood to subway paranoia.   RK

Gale, Zona 1874–1938 American novelist, short-story writer, playwright and essayist known for her fiction depicting small-town Mid-Western life. Born in Portage, Wisconsin, the only daughter of Eliza (Beers) and Charles Franklin, Gale first published as a student at the University of Wisconsin. She worked in Milwaukee and New York City as a reporter, and later as a freelance short-story writer. Gale's early *Friendship Village* series carried Romanticism's traditions into the 20th century, portraying a warm, maternally centred home and cooperative community life. With *Birth* (1918) and *Miss Lulu Bett* (1920), the dramatic version of which won a Pulitzer Prize in 1921, her work became more socially relevant and REALISTIC.

In these later works and others, Gale depicted small-town life as full of meaningless ritual and guided by random forces. Eliza Gale repeatedly urged her daughter's return to the safety of Portage, but, more politically aware, Gale still went on to work tirelessly for Robert La Follette during his many Wisconsin campaigns. An admirer of Jane Addams and Hull House, Gale fought for women's rights, publishing 'What Women Won in Wisconsin' in the *Nation* (1922), describing what women had yet to win. In 1928, at the age of 54, she married Portage manufacturer William L. Breese. *Portage, Wisconsin and Other Essays* (1928) encompassed Gale's views on home, family and the evolution of her art. *Bridal Pond* (1930) includes short stories combining small-town sentiments with a literary realism that depicts the limitations in life.   LMu

Illustration by Wanda Gág from *Three Gay Tales from Grimm*, 1943.

Gallagher [née Bond], Tess 1943– American poet who writes with lyrical clarity about love and the landscape of her native Washington. Her early volumes, which include *Instructions to the Double* (1976), *Under Stars* (1978) and *Willingly* (1984), use a lush, elemental language to locate emotional moments in a natural, animated world; 1987's *Amplitude* collects the best of this early work. A dedicated teacher, Gallagher published her essays on poetry in the lucid and amiable *A Concert of Tenses* (1986), which includes a memoir about her alcoholic father. Her third marriage to American short-story master Raymond Carver was a vibrant, creative partnership; they inspired and supported each other as well as producing a joint screenplay about Dostoevsky (1985). With Carver's encouragement Gallagher also wrote a series of vivid homespun stories, collected in *The Lover of Horses* (1986). Carver's early death provided a melancholy role for Gallagher, which nonetheless made her more widely known, as editor and collator of his work and of much work about him. The elegiac poems in *Moon Crossing Bridge* (1992) canvas in mournful detail Carver's illness and death, while celebrating the spirit of their life together. She expanded on and republished an early sensual collection, *Passionate Kisses*, in 1994.   SB

Gallant, Mavis 1922– Montreal-born Canadian writer who went to live in Paris in 1950. Best known for her short stories (most of which appeared in the *New Yorker*) Gallant has also published novels – *Green Water, Green Sky* (1959) and the immensely comic *A Fairly Good Time* (1970) – a play, *What is to be Done?* (1982) and brilliant essays: *Paris Notebooks* (1986) describes the 'days of rage' in the spring of 1968 and the case of Gabrielle Russier.

Mavis Gallant was placed in a convent school a few weeks after her 4th birthday. She subsequently attended seventeen schools, with the result, she says, 'there's no milieu I don't feel comfortable in, that I don't understand'. Gallant's father died when she was a girl. Linnet Muir, her semi-autobiographical heroine, says, 'My father died, then my grandmother; my mother was left, but we did not get on.' Gallant spent most of her teenage years in New York with a psychiatrist and his wife and returned to Montreal at 18. Like Linnet Muir, she kept her stories in a picnic hamper. At 22 she got a job at the *Montreal Standard*: she says, 'Newspaper work was my apprenticeship', and again, 'I had amassed an enormous mental catalog of places and people, information that still seeps into my stories.' Also at 22, she married Johnny Gallant, a musician, briefly. In 1950 Gallant sent her first stories to the *New Yorker* (the second one was accepted), quit her job and left Montreal for Paris.

Gallant's early stories explore dislocation, disappointment, domestic disorder, gaps between parents and children. She also considers the ways lives are touched by politics and history. As she depicts characters, she also dissects nationality, whether Canadian, French, British, American, German. Her later stories, especially the four sequences which conclude her *Selected Stories*, trace characters' lives over decades and move past dislocation and disconnection to vitality, resolution, will and, in some cases (the Carette Sisters sequence, 'The Fenton Child') to family solidarity.

The best introduction to her writing is *The Selected Stories* (1996), which includes work from her first book, *The Other Paris* (1956), to *Across the Bridge* (1993). The stories are arranged chronologically by setting, emphasizing the importance of history.

Collections of stories include *My Heart is Broken* (1964), *The Pegnitz Junction* (1974), FROM THE FIFTEENTH DISTRICT (1979), HOME TRUTHS (Governor General's Award, 1981), *Overhead in a Balloon* (1985) and *In Transit* (1988).   EG

Galloway, Grace Growden ?–1789 American diarist

and correspondent. Grace Growden was raised with great social and economic privilege. In 1753, she married Joseph Galloway, member and sometimes Speaker of the Pennsylvania Assembly, whose wealth and position maintained her social status. Her DIARY (Part I: 17 June 1778 – 1 July 1779; Part II: 1 July 1779 – 30 September 1779) describes the physical, psychological and emotional hardships Galloway experienced as a Loyalist property owner cut off from her family and beset by confiscation and homelessness during the Revolutionary War. The writing illustrates Galloway's bitterness at her perceived abandonment by family and friends, especially after her husband evacuated to England with their daughter in 1778: 'my child is dearer to me than all Nature and if she is not happy or any thing shou'd happen to her I am lost . . . indeed I am concern'd for her father but his Unkind treatment

makes me easey Nay happy not to be with him and if he is safe I want not to be kept so like a slave as he allways Made Me in preventing every wish of my heart'. From 1778 to 1789, she descended into comparative poverty and her deteriorating health is recorded in diary entries relating her physical suffering and her estrangement from her social circle. Galloway died without recuperating any of the estates confiscated during the war, but they were partially recovered in later years and inherited by her daughter.   LCa

Galloway, Janice 1956– Scottish writer whose bleak

work satirizes male-dominated systems and charts the experience of being female in the West of Scotland. She was born in Ayrshire and studied Music and English at Glasgow University. In the late 1980s, she began to write short stories and was encouraged and influenced by James Kelman and Alasdair Gray. She gave up working as a teacher in 1990 and moved from Ayrshire to Glasgow, where she now lives with her son.

Surreal touches often encroach on her grim yet compassionate stories in *Blood* (1991) and *Where You Find It* (1996). She is best known for THE TRICK IS TO KEEP BREATHING (1989), which experiments with voice and form, and charts the disintegration of a woman's identity after her lover drowns, exploring how her loss exposes the terror and emptiness at her core. The acidic tone that was in some ways the strength of this first novel is somewhat dissipated in her second, *Foreign Parts* (1994), a tentative exploration of the friendship between two women.

Galloway foregrounds issues of identity and gender, against the backdrop of patriarchal, nationalistic Scotland: 'Scottish women have their own particular complications with writing and definition, complications which derive from the general problems of being a colonised nation. Then, that wee touch extra. Their sex. There is coping with that guilt of taking time off the concerns of national politics to get concerned with the sexual sort: that creeping fear it's somehow self-indulgent to be more concerned for one's womanness instead of one's Scottishness.' Despite these reservations, 'womanness' is central to all her fiction.

The Trick is to Keep Breathing was the most fêted novel by a Scottish woman for many years. Galloway's success made it possible for other Scottish women (such as A.L. KENNEDY and Alison Smith) to make their mark as writers in what had previously been a very male-dominated Scottish literary scene.   JH

García, Cristina 1958– Novelist Cristina García was

born in Havana, Cuba, and grew up in New York City. Her fictional style is often compared to that of Gabriel García Márquez and LOUISE ERDRICH for its employment of multiple voices, dream narrative, magical realism and the interpenetration of family and political history. Her first novel, *Dreaming in Cuban* (1992), tells the story of the Del Pino family as it evolves historically and metaphorically away from Fidel Castro and the ideals of the Cuban revolution. Her second novel, *The Agüero Sisters: A Novel* (1997), narrates the lives of two sisters, one who has escaped to the United States and a life of selling cosmetics, and the other who has remained in Cuba to become a skilled electrician. SMSt

Gardam, Jane 1928– British writer of quirky, exuberant social comedies for adults and children (see CHILDREN'S BOOKS). She frequently dramatizes the cross-over between the regular, 'grown-up' world and the world of the child or the mad person, lifting the lid on fastidiously correct, unremarkable lives. Daughter of a Redcar schoolteacher, she was educated in North Yorkshire until taking her degree in English in London in 1949. The north of England, with its wilder landscape and blunter ways, has inspired much of Gardam's best work, but she now lives in the south, which she portrays with equal comic acuity. After completing her Masters degree at London University, she worked in magazine editorial jobs until starting a family in 1955. Her travels with her husband inspired the story collection *Black Faces, White Faces* (1975), set in Jamaica. Her earliest work was written for teenagers: *A Long Way from Verona* (1971) and *Bilgewater* (1977) are emotionally convincing and quietly anarchic tales about growing up, and may constitute her most successful work along with the Booker-shortlisted *God on the Rocks* (1978), where Gardam shows her gift for capturing the untamed originality of youth and the consequences of repression in the name of evangelical belief. She is a connoisseur of cultural peculiarities, in particular the varieties of Englishness and the byways of religion. Accused of being a 'Muslin and tea-party writer' she responded, 'I'm more hair-cloth and gin.' Her Whitbread-Award-winning *The Queen of the Tambourine* (1991) portrayed the descent into madness of a pious, curtain-twitching Wimbledon housewife entirely in letters. Gardam's experiments with genre have included introducing drama into *Crusoe's Daughter* and adapting ghost stories, FAIRY TALES and ROMANTIC fiction. Her heroines identify with literary figures in *The Summer after the Funeral* (1973), *Bilgewater* and *Crusoe's Daughter* (1985). But her literariness and experiment stay grounded in character and incident. Her short-story collections for adults include *The Sidmouth Letters* (1980), *The Pangs of Love* (1983), *Showing the Flag* (1989) and *Going into a Dark House* (1994). Like her most recent short stories, Gardam's latest novel, *Faith Fox* (1996), pays a new attention to ageing and to relations between old and young. KE

Garden Party, and Other Stories, The (1922) This collection – KATHERINE MANSFIELD's third, and the last published in her lifetime – contains some of her most memorable and effective fiction. Many critics praise these stories for their supposedly 'feminine' qualities, such as delicacy, deliciousness and attention to detail. Such epithets may be accurate to a point, but should not obscure the fact that, in terms of narrative strategy, *The Garden Party* works at the cutting edge of MODERNIST innovation and, in terms of subject, has much greater range than is often assumed. For example, 'The Daughters of the Late Colonel' is a subtle and moving analysis of the ways in which patriarchal power structures and delimits the lives of women, even in the absence of a flesh-and-blood authority figure, operating through internalized 'shoulds' and 'oughts'. 'The Garden Party' is a superbly disturbing revelation of the suffering and squalor which underpins and threatens the privileged existence of the leisured classes. So, while Mansfield's writing is often beguilingly bright and effervescent, *The Garden Party* also produces disquieting *frissons* and biting ironies. AFT

gardening writers Women have written gardening books for money, for love (the love affair is with their own gardens), from an urge to express themselves or from a desire to instruct. But the first notable woman gardening writer wrote from wifely devotion: Jane Loudon helped her husband, John Claudius Loudon, edit the *Gardener's Magazine,* and published her own *Instructions in Gardening for Ladies* in 1840. When J.C. Loudon died, three years later, she poured out further gardening textbooks for 'ladies' and thus paid off some of the debts his *Arboretum* had incurred. Before her marriage, she had known nothing about gardening and saw herself as a novelist; she had already published what she called 'a strange, wild novel', *The Mummy,* in 1827.

Inside many a gardening writer, a novelist is longing to get out. This accounts for the career of ELIZABETH VON ARNIM: she began by writing vivacious impressions of life in her vast Pomeranian garden – *ELIZABETH AND HER GERMAN GARDEN* (1898) and *The Solitary Summer* (1899). When they became bestsellers, she left her garden behind her, along with her aristocratic husband, and took to fiction. But she had proved that a market existed for a woman's imaginative expression of her relationship with a garden, and thus started a genre still popular – for example, Mirabel Osler's *A Gentle Plea for Chaos* (1989).

Mrs C.W. Earle was an intelligent and independent-minded lady with a fluent pen and a Victorian belief in progress. At the age of 60, she discovered how much she enjoyed expressing her views on paper. Encouraged by her nieces, who included LADY CONSTANCE LYTTON (the future suffragette), she wrote monthly 'notes' about her garden, and about anything else that interested her: family life and its difficulties, the advantages of suburbs, picture exhibitions. But in the very first sentence of her first book she disclaimed any idea that this was a 'gardening book' (reliable gardening books were written by men; she advised anyone who wanted horticultural advice to turn to the work of William Robinson). Clearly she was not writing for money – indeed, her husband is reputed to have offered her £100 not to publish. But the money came; *Pot Pourri from a Surrey Garden* (1897), and its three sequels, were rumoured to have made her publishers, Smith Elder and Co., £30,000.

In the last year of the 19th century came Gertrude Jekyll's first book: *Wood and Garden*. She had every reason to write (except loyalty to a husband, since she was unmarried). She was passionately in love with her garden, Munstead Wood; she was a born teacher with a missionary zeal in propagating her original ideas about what good gardening was; she clearly enjoyed choosing the right descriptive words, just as she enjoyed designing the right tools and the right vases and taking the right photographs. And the money from her fifteen books and countless magazine articles cannot have come amiss in the wide acres of Munstead Wood.

The same was true, some years later, of VITA SACKVILLE-WEST. She, too, was deeply in love with her garden at Sissinghurst though entirely without Miss Jekyll's pedagogic fervour. But when, in 1946, the *Observer* invited her to write a weekly gardening column, she accepted, though she came to disparage her own journalism: 'Oh dear', she wrote in January 1957, 'I often say to myself as I sit down to this weekly article, what thin rubbish I do write.' Privately, however, she wrote to Harold Nicolson: '15 guineas a week is not to be lightly foregone'. The fact that her gardening columns, republished as hardbacks, became more widely read than anything else she wrote did not please her.

Following Vita Sackville-West's example, a whole school of women writers now advocates formal layouts, hedged compartments within gardens, careful colour-schemes. Others, like Margery Fish in *We Made a Garden* (1956) and later books, have re-discovered simple cottage flowers. Beth Chatto, a distinguished nurserywoman, has become the voice of ecological awareness; in *The Dry Garden* (1978) and *The Damp Garden* (1982) she suits plants to their environments.

As the 20th century closes, scores of women are writing gardening books and garden columns in the press. They keep pace with the burgeoning numbers of amateur gardeners who like to read about their hobby. Many are self-taught; they have learnt in their own gardens but, unlike the women gardeners of previous centuries, they now realize they are perfectly qualified to advise others.   DK

Gardner, Dame Helen (Louise) 1908–86 British critic, anthologist, editor of Donne, and the first woman (1966) to hold the Merton Chair of English Literature at Oxford. She was educated in north London and at St Hilda's, Oxford, to which (after Birmingham and London posts) she returned in 1941. Her strict scholarship, forceful Delegacy of the OUP and often overbearing manner dominated Renaissance studies in Oxford until her retirement in 1975. Pre-war research in medieval mystics and immersion in the learned Anglicanism of the T.S. Eliot school gave formidable depth to her editions of Donne's *Divine Poems* (1952, revised 1978) and *Elegies and Songs and Sonnets* (1965); other volumes also show her hand, though the textual collation on which she set such store is now overtaken in the *Variorum Donne*.

She read aloud supremely well, and helped introduce *Four Quartets* to a wartime public: later studies include *The Art of T.S. Eliot* (1949) and, with privileged access to the drafts, *The Composition of 'Four Quartets'* (1978). A wider public knew her best from anthologies, of which the *Penguin Book of Metaphysical Verse* (1961) and *The New Oxford Book of English Verse* (1973) are notable. Her humanism, seen to advantage in fine single essays on Shakespeare, turned pricklier in the Milton quarrels of the fifties and theory wars of the seventies. The nearest thing to critical credos are *The Business of Criticism* (1959) and the late, tired sallies of *In Defence of the Imagination* (1982). Her learned if occasionally tyrannous humanism did not include feminism.   JFM

Gare, Nene 1919–94 Australian writer, seen by some critics as having suffered neglect due to her support for 'traditional family values'. Born in Adelaide and educated at Adelaide Art School and later Perth Technical College and Murdoch University. Best known for her fiction written 'from the Aboriginal perspective', in particular *The Fringe Dwellers* (1961), which in turn is better known as the 1986 Bruce Beresford film of the same name. The novel concentrates on the tensions between white and Aboriginal inheritances in its central character, Trilby, who battles to escape a life of despair on an Aboriginal settlement. The short-story collection *Bend to the Wind* (1978) also concentrates on Aboriginal lives; Gare claimed that this was her most significant work.

Her other fiction is concerned with women's experiences of family life: *Green Gold* (1963), a novel based loosely on her experiences growing bananas at Carnarvon; *A House With Verandahs* (1980), a novel detailing the struggles of bourgeois family life in the 1930s and 1940s in Adelaide; and its sequel, *An Island Away* (1981), based on her experiences as wife of an Australian Army patrol officer in Papua New Guinea. *Kent Town* (1997), a collection of short stories based on her youth, was published posthumously.   BO

Garner [née Ford], Helen 1942– Australian novelist, short-story writer, scriptwriter and journalist, whose first novel, *MONKEY GRIP* (1977), was a turning point for Second Wave feminist publishing in Australia. Garner grew up in Geelong, Victoria, moving to Melbourne to attend the University of Melbourne in the 1960s. She taught in various Melbourne high schools until being dismissed for an explicit discussion of sex in answer to her students' questions. In 1968 she married the actor Bill Garner and they had one daughter, Alice Garner (now an actress). When this marriage ended, Garner lived in a series of group houses, supported by a single parent's pension. *Monkey Grip* provides a fairly autobiographical account of these experiences, but Garner's writing has a lyricism and a disciplined focus on detail which transcends its diary mode.

In 1980 she published two novellas, *Honour* and *Other People's Children*, which acutely observed the ideals and emotional failures of two groups of inner Melbourne characters. In *The Children's Bach* (1984), Garner used her observations of daily life to explore the emotional insecurities of her generation of urban intellectuals; a short-story collection, *POSTCARDS FROM SURFERS*, was published in 1985. After the failure of her second marriage, *Cosmo Cosmolino* (1992) seemed to express a dissatisfaction with REALISM. The bleakness of Garner's vision in this book is not alleviated by the intervention of the supernatural in the form of angelic beings. Her screenwriting has remained more securely based on realist observation, as in the television play *Two Friends* (1986), and the film *Last Days of Chez Nous* (1992).

In recent years, Garner has written more journalism, and she created considerable debate by publishing *THE FIRST STONE* (1995), her version of a sexual harassment case at a University of Melbourne residential college. While some have seen this as evidence of Garner's defection from feminism, the book's disregard of accepted feminist principles may be a sign of the intuitive (rather than ideological) nature of Garner's art. 'I work on feel and instinct to a certain extent', she has said, 'but I've learnt to trust my instincts.'   SPL

Garnett [née Black], Constance 1861–1946 English translator of Russian novels, whose work introduced the English literati and general public to 19th-century Russian literature. Garnett's interest in Russian could be traceable to family connections – her grandfather had been naval architect to Tsar Nicholas I – but as an adult living in London she moved in socialist intellectual circles, through which she met Russian expatriates. She was well educated in languages at home among her large intellectual family (including her sister CLEMENTINA BLACK), and earned a First in Classics at Cambridge in 1883, though as a woman she could not take a degree. She married Edward Garnett

in 1889 and their son David was born in 1892. Garnett travelled to Russia the following year, where she met Tolstoy. Her first translation (of Ivan Gontcharoff's *A Common Story*) appeared in 1894. During the nineties she concentrated on Turgenev (all of whose works she eventually translated); between 1901 and 1904 she translated Tolstoy's major writing. Her work continued until the mid-1930s, during which time she translated most of the works of Dostoevsky, Chekhov, Gogol, Ostrovsky, Gorky and Herzen. Although many of her translations are no longer the standard versions, she was instrumental in exposing the Anglophone world to Russian literature.   KW

Garrick Year, The (1964) MARGARET DRABBLE's second novel is an unblinking examination of the condition of marriage and maternity. Emma, the narrator, finds her marriage under strain when her husband accepts a season in a rep. company. She accompanies him from London to Hereford, their two small children in tow, leaving behind a modelling career and the offer of a television job. Caught in the tedium of provincial life and the vacuousness of the theatre, her relationship with her husband deteriorates further when she begins an affair with the talented, idiosyncratic director. But the affair seems born of chance and Emma's lassitude rather than of grand passion, and her analysis of her own actions is detached, almost existential in tone. The novel climaxes in a melodramatic scene where Emma is pinioned to the garage wall by the director's car, after which her physical recovery leads to a muted reconciliation. As a character study of a 'self-willed, distinct, determined woman', *The Garrick Year* is a social-REALIST miniature, redolent of the concerns of its time.   CS

Gaskell, Elizabeth Cleghorn (Stevenson) 1810–65 British novelist and BIOGRAPHER. Born in London, the youngest of eight children, Gaskell was brought up by an aunt in Knutsford, Cheshire. Her mother died when she was a baby; her only surviving sibling, William, was lost at sea. In 1832 she married the Unitarian minister William Gaskell: the Unitarian emphasis on responsibility and self-knowledge informs her writing. They had four daughters, and two sons who died in infancy. Gaskell's lively letters show her anxieties about balancing domestic life and writing, her love of gossip, her wide range of intellectual and literary friends, and her interest in current affairs.

Gaskell began her career by writing tales for Howitt's Journal. She produced some notable shorter fiction throughout her life, including 'The Grey Woman', 'Half a Life-Time Ago', 'Lizzie Leigh' and the novella, *Cousin Phillis* (1864). This story, like so much of her work, is set in the recent past, but refuses to countenance stasis, whether in the community, or in a young girl's relationship with her family. Gaskell was fascinated by the dynamics of social change. This is apparent in her two fictions set largely in Manchester, where she and her husband lived and moved among both industrialists and the urban poor. MARY BARTON (1848) and NORTH AND SOUTH (1855) are concerned with promoting increased communication between workers and employers. They suggest no real changes to the social structure, but ask that each side recognize the other's human capacity for understanding and compassion. In both novels, the most prominent character is a woman, who acts as a mediator between different social groups. Whilst powerfully treating social issues, both novels rely on melodrama and coincidence to propel their plots.

The controversial RUTH (1853) tackles the topic of the seduced woman trying to bring up her child in society: it is an attack on double standards, a plea for Christian forgiveness, and a demonstration of the redemptive power of motherhood. Active in supporting women writers, in promoting professional nursing training, and in encouraging women's emigration schemes, Gaskell was no separatist. Though CRANFORD (1853) has often been taken as a celebration of a community of women, it gently satirizes the naivety of their superficially hermetically sealed world. Like *North and South*, it first appeared in *Household Words*: Gaskell did not warm to Dickens's degree of editorial control.

Gaskell's close friendship with CHARLOTTE BRONTË ideally fitted her to write the latter's *Life* (1857). This uses correspondence and reminiscences in a very readable account of the latter's career, though it is conspicuously informed by a desire to present her as being as conventionally womanly as possible. *Sylvia's Lovers* (1863), set at the time of the Napoleonic Wars, treats sexual jealousy and the frustrations felt by a rural woman, in a bleak plot seemingly informed by Darwin's doctrine of the survival of the fittest. Gaskell's interest in contemporary science again appears in her final novel, WIVES AND DAUGHTERS (1866), which examines tensions between women with different standards of social conduct. She died, just before she could finish it, in the Hampshire house she bought with income from her writing.   KFl

Gatty [née Scott], Margaret 1809–73 British writer for children and expert on seaweeds, who was educated mostly by her clergyman father, A.J. Scott. In 1839, she married the Revd Alfred Gatty, and they had ten children, including JULIANA EWING. Her first book, *Recollections* (1842) of the life of her father, was jointly written with her husband.

In 1851, *The Fairy Godmothers*, her first collection of stories for children appeared, followed by *Aunt Judy's Tales* (1859), *Aunt Judy's Letters* (1862) and *Domestic Pictures and Tales* (1865). These stories have mostly middle-class DOMESTIC settings in which 'with so much drollery and amusement, there was sure to be mixed up some odd scraps of information, or bits of good advice'. The five series of *Parables from Nature* (1855–71), also children's stories, contain much specific information about natural history and also use nature to teach simple moral lessons – for instance, in 'Kicking' (1865), the importance of obedience: 'Happy the colts who learn submission without a lifetime of personal struggle!' In 1866, Margaret Gatty founded and edited the first periodical for girls in the Victorian period, *Aunt Judy's Magazine*, offering stories, music, emblems and natural history, and aimed at a genteel and leisured readership. It was admired but never financially successful. *The History of British Seaweeds* (1863) was her most substantial contribution to the adult study of natural history.   FJO'G

Gaudy Night (1935) The DETECTIVE STORIES of DOROTHY L. SAYERS introduce murder into closed communities; here, an Oxford women's college; hidden tensions are revealed alongside evidence. It is at once the most popular of her books and the slightest, considered as a puzzle, dealing with the resolution of the long-standing romance of series characters Lord Peter Wimsey, and Harriet Vane, whom he once cleared of murder. It turns on a dating piece of misdirection – the assumed reader is supposed to ignore servants as suspects. Like most 'classic' detective stories, it is a theodicy; the removal of threats to a perfect system and the uniting of lovers reveals that system as ever more perfect. For women of Sayers's generation, social snobbery and reactionary ideals sometimes appeared liberatory because they made it possible, by defining limits to sympathy, both to buy into a potentially hostile society and to concentrate on personal priorities.   RK

Gaunt, Mary 1861–1942 Versatile and prolific Australian-born writer, who was among the first generation of women writers to enter university studies (in Melbourne, in 1881), but did not graduate, having decided to earn her own living by writing. She had a brief marriage during her thirties, and after her husband's death in 1900 went to London to pursue her writing career. For the rest of her life she travelled widely collecting material for her considerable output of journalism, short stories, novels and TRAVEL books, such as *Alone in West Africa* (1912), which she illustrated with her own photographs. In her fiction she did not confine herself to the variations on ROMANCE narrative forms considered proper for women writers, but experimented with adventure stories, often centred on male characters. Her early novels published in the

1890s, *Dave's Sweetheart*, *Kirkham's Find* and *Deadman's*, employ elements of the Australian 'masculine romance', involving outback adventures in mining and cattle-raising.   SMS

Gearhart, Sally Miller 1931–

North American feminist writer and academic whose only novel, *The Wanderground: Stories of the Hill Women* (1979), offers a feminist vision of utopia. Born in Virginia, she went on to become Professor of Speech and Communication Studies at San Francisco State University. Her essay on 'The Womanization of Rhetoric' in *Women's Studies International Quarterly* (vol. II, 1979) called for a female model of communication, stating that 'Feminism is a source, a wellspring, a matrix, an environment for the womanization of communication, for the womanization of Western civilization.' Reprinted many times, *The Wanderground* may be read as the imaginative realization of that vision in a future where the essentialist distinctions between the genders are borne out by the Hill Women's mystical bond with the natural world and men's domination of the dystopian City. As a work of SCIENCE-FICTION/fantasy, *The Wanderground* has been overtaken by more recent feminist work in the genre but it is representative of a school of American feminist thought, with strong influences in radical lesbian feminist theory, theology and ecofeminism. MARY DALY cites Gearhart as one of a number of writers and artists who 'dream in female' in *Pure Lust* (1984).
                                          RW

Gee, Maggie (Mary) 1948–

British novelist, born in Poole, Dorset, whose M.Litt. in surrealism from Somerville College, Oxford, could very well have been the motivation for her fiction writing which is both experimental in form and darkly comical in substance. Stylistically compared with such writers as Nabokov and WOOLF, her maiden novel, *Dying, in Other Words* (1983) is an appropriate point of departure since it is as variegated in text as in content, strewn with such eccentric characters as a devious and deadly dairyman and which begins with the 'POSTMODERN' disclaimer that the novel is not 'a serious novel'. Her second novel, *The Burning Book* (1983), is a family saga following the lives of its members through both world wars and alludes to the holocaust that was Hiroshima and Nagasaki. The novel is in keeping with her avowed social and political interest as she was a member of the Society of Authors' Campaign for Nuclear Disarmament and, while a writing fellow at the University of East Anglia, edited the collection, *For Life on Earth: Writings Against War* (1982). The following decade was highly productive for her as she published *Light Years* (1985); *Grace* (1988); *Where Are the Snows* (1992); and *Lost Children* (1995). Her latest work is *How May I Speak in My Own Voice?* (1996). She has also written a tele-

play entitled, 'Handfast', and a radio play, 'Over and Out' (1984).   MRA

Gellhorn, Martha 1908–98

American journalist, war correspondent, novelist, playwright. Born into an influential family of St Louis enjoying a tradition of service and reform – both her grandmother and her mother were prominent in supporting civil rights – she was shaped by family philosophy.

Starting work as a journalist in 1937 with an article on the Spanish Civil War, she worked herself into a traditionally male-dominated profession, that of war correspondent, covering World War II in Normandy and in Italy, and, later, the Vietnam war, always defying risks and dangers, and even enduring torture, and travelling with untiring energy all over the world. At 82, in 1990, she went to Panama under cover as the *Daily Telegraph* thriller reviewer, and six years later she flew to El Salvador to support from there the cause of Brazilian street children. Her journalism is collected in *The Face of the War* (1959), *Vietnam: A New Kind of War* (1966), *Travels with Myself and Another* (1978).

A sentence she wrote concerning Ernest Hemingway, to whom she was married between 1940 and 1945, in a letter to her friend Eleanor Roosevelt – 'What you and I see as a lie, in a writer is called imagination' – may account for her relative lack of success as a novelist, compared to the enthusiastic approval met by her journalism. She wrote eight novels and a number of short stories, collected in *The Heart of Another* (1941), *The Honeyed Peace* (1953), *Two by Two* (1958) and *Pretty Tales of Fired People* (1966), all centred on her life-long concerns – justice, moral responsibility, action, the fulfilment of the independent woman – and, particularly in her earlier fiction, she relies perhaps too heavily on her journalistic approach and techniques. The protagonists of her novels are often strong, brave, idealistic women, and are obvious portraits of the author, a formidable character herself. Her later novels, *Liana* (1944), and particularly *The Wine of Astonishment* (1948), like many of the short stories, take the best from her journalism and also reveal an increasing maturity as a writer of fiction and successful experimentation with form.   MB

Gems [née Price], Pam(ela) 1925–

British playwright who has the rather unique distinction of creating works which have both feminist themes and mainstream audience appeal. Born of working-class parents in Bransgore, Hampshire, Gems was raised by women – both her grandmothers were widowed in World War I, and her father, Jim Price, died in the workhouse, leaving Elsie Mabel Price (née Annetts), alone to raise Pam and her two brothers. After serving in the Women's Royal Naval Service during World War II, Gems attended Manchester University, earning a degree in Psychology, shortly after which she married Keith Gems. She did not begin writing plays until her forties, when, after raising four children and working at a variety of odd jobs, she became involved in London's lunchtime theatre and wrote plays for the feminist collective, Almost Free.

In 1976, her play *Dead Fish* attracted attention at the Edinburgh Festival, and when it moved to London with the new title, *Dusa, Fish, Stas, and Vi*, enjoyed a long and successful run. Creating complex female characters whose lives are blighted by economic pressures and oppressive relationships with men, Gems nevertheless presents women who are funny, vital and supportive of each other. Her interest is in the particular difficulties faced by women, but she is also attentive to the ways rigid constructions of gender thwart all society's participants, stating, 'An all woman theatre wouldn't work. It would be chauvinistic and boring.' *Queen Christina* (1977) and *Piaf* (1978) were performed by the Royal Shakespeare Company, and other works include *The Treat* (1982) and *Aunt Mary* (1982). She adapted several dramas for the English stage, including Chekhov's *Uncle Vanya* (1979) and *The Cherry Orchard* (1984) and Ibsen's *A Doll's House* (1980). *Stanley* (1996) was a popular and critical success on Broadway and in London.   LCo

Genêt [Janet Flanner] 1892–1978 Daughter of a funeral director, she opted out of the funereal and provincial life of Indianapolis to become a novelist, translator and, for fifty years, a leading journalist with the *New Yorker*, authoring the popular 'Letters from Paris'. By the early 1920s, after a brief and perfunctory university career at the University of Chicago, followed by a brief and perfunctory marriage, she began a lesbian affair with Jane Heap who, for almost a decade, was her co-editor on the *Little Review*, which published the early work of James Joyce and Ezra Pound. In Paris she began another lesbian relationship with Solita Solano which lasted for twenty years, yet very little of her intimate relationships with women is revealed. Her private and personal lives were well separated and little of her insights into the lesbian life is revealed through her writing, though she was certainly privy to the gay life in Paris and even helped care for ALICE B. TOKLAS after GERTRUDE STEIN's death.

Of her first novel, *The Cubical City* (1926), allegedly a diatribe on American morality, she wrote, 'I am not a first class fiction writer . . . Writing fiction is not my gift.' There is little argument from the text which relies to a great extent on the elements of American realism. Her gifts were truly in the area of non-fiction and her keen insights into the arts and social fabric of Europe at the time, as well as the vivid portrayals of women, are seen in *London Was Yesterday 1934–39* (1975) and *Paris Was Yesterday* (1979) and her post-war letters,

Paris Journal vols. I and II (1965 and 1971 respectively). Though she published numerous other works, her primary interest and, indeed, her journalistic reputation was founded on her insights into the world of Parisian art and culture and her brilliant essays on World War II. See *AN AMERICAN IN PARIS* (1940).   MRA

Gentle, Mary 1956– British writer of SCIENCE FICTION and fantasy. Leaving school at 16, she completed a Combined Studies degree at Bournemouth in 1985 and did MAs in Seventeenth-Century and War Studies at Goldsmith's College and King's College, London. Her first novel, *Hawk in Silver* (1977), was a fantasy for young adults, but she made her name with two planetary romances somewhat influenced by URSULA K. LE GUIN: *Golden Witchbreed* (1983) and *Ancient Light* (1987). Her human adventuress wanders among the artifacts of a humanoid species's lost glory, failing to prevent catastrophe; the books have a deep sense of wistful gloom. Gentle found a voice uniquely hers in a group of novellas and two novels – *Rats and Gargoyles* (1990) and *The Architecture of Desire* (1991) in which the alchemical Rosicrucian studies of FRANCES YATES are united with a fast-moving perverse sensibility that draws on ANGELA CARTER and comic books. In a variety of worlds – a demon-ruled city of rats and men, a geomantically deranged London divided between Lady Protector and Restored Queen – the White Crow explores integrity, gallantry, dishonour and distress.   RK

Gentlemen Prefer Blondes (1925) ANITA LOOS's bestseller (subtitled *The Illuminating Diary of a Professional Lady*) purports to be the musings of a materialistic yet stubbornly naive young American woman whose sole purpose in life is to extract lavish gifts from her upper-class male admirers. The defiantly unliterary narrator claims that she has been encouraged to write by a 'gentleman friend' who, no doubt mindful of recent experiments in stream-of-consciousness storytelling, has informed her that if she 'put down all [her] thoughts it would make a book'. A satire on the hypocritical mores and strangely genteel aspirations of the 'flapper' generation as well as on MODERNIST literary pretensions, the book was an immediate success, applauded by such unlikely notables as James Joyce. While its satirical edge has been blunted by time, the psychology and career of the 'professional lady' (who finally marries a morally upright aristocrat with whose money she hopes to finance a male admirer's lubricious films) remain amusing.   BWB

Georgy Girl (1965) Set in 'swinging' London, MARGARET FORSTER's second novel deals with what were pressing issues for the sixties: unmarried motherhood, abortion and adoption. This dramatic comedy gives the eternal triangle motif an unusual twist. Outspoken emotional heroine George is convinced she is ugly and undesirable compared to her sexy but selfish flatmate, Meredith. When Meredith irresponsibly takes on marriage and motherhood, rejecting her baby Sara at birth, George adopts Sara, but becomes so committed that responsibility turns to martyrdom. Dissatisfied with the sexual fulfilment she once craved with Meredith's ex-partner Jos, George decides on a marriage of convenience with affluent James. Twenty years her senior, and known to George all her life as her parents' employer, James can give Sara a secure home. In this closely intertwined web of relationships Forster counts costs: Meredith, the rebellious sixties icon, only retains her freedom through emotional detachment, whereas George's unimaginative parents, their lives dulled by routine, are judged to deserve the freedom of retirement.

Forster and Peter Nichols co-wrote the screenplay for Silvio Narizanno's 1966 film; Lynn Redgrave played Georgy Girl. MET

Gerard [de Longgarde], Dorothea 1855–1915

Popular novelist who wrote on a wide range of controversial subjects. She was born into a Roman Catholic family in England. In 1886, she married Julius Longard de Longgarde, an Austrian Army officer, and lived in Galicia and Vienna with him. With EMILY GERARD, her younger sister, she wrote *Reata, Beggar my Neighbour, The Waters of Hercules* and *A Sensitive Plant* between 1880 and 1891. *Orthodox* (1891) depicts an Austrian aristocrat's affair with a Jewish girl, in which Gerard attempts to be fair but ends up excoriating Jews. *A Forgotten Sin* (1898) is an Aesthetic tale of a musician torn between his fair pure fiancée and a dark mesmeric opera singer; it shows the influence of OUIDA, DU MAURIER and Wilde. *The Eternal Woman* (1903) describes a NEW WOMAN, Clara Woods, who succeeds by modelling herself on Thackeray's anti-heroine Becky Sharp – though she reforms when she falls in love. Gerard is an interesting writer who experimented with new topics, though she often endorsed conservative resolutions. TS

Gerard [de Laszowski], (Jane) Emily 1849–1905

Popular writer who brought European concerns to a British audience. She was born into a Roman Catholic family in England. She became a lifelong friend of Princess Marguerite, whom she met in Venice when she was 15. Gerard married Chevalier Miecislas de Laszowski, a member of a Polish noble family, and lived with him in Galicia, Transylvania and Vienna. Her first book, *The Land Beyond the Forest: Facts, Figures and Fancies from Transylvania* (1888), was a well-received travel narrative of herself as an intrepid female adventurer. With DOROTHEA GERARD, her older sister, she wrote *Reata, Beggar my Neighbour, The Waters of Hercules* and *A Sensitive Plant* between 1880 and 1891. Gerard also wrote reviews of German literature, short stories, and six novels of her own, including *The Voice of a Flower* (1893) and *The Extermination of Love: A Study in Erotics* (1901). Her fiction is conservative but unusual in its combination of continental subjects, humour, and interest in contemporary debates. TS

Gerstler, Amy 1956–

An American poet and fiction writer, she has been involved in the literary and art scenes in California, with texts performed at the Museum of Contemporary Art (Los Angeles) and installations in both California and New York. Gerstler writes for *Art Forum* and other art publications and has published several books of poetry which include *The True Bride* (1986), *Nerve Storm* (1993) and *Crown of Weeds* (1997). Although there are fewer monologues in her later work, Gerstler's early poetry is characterized by dramatic voices which seem to siphon the thoughts of many individuals through one voice. They are POSTMODERN poems: cultured, raw and often surreal. They study autopsies, Lewis Carroll's Alice, V-E Day and Boy George: 'I'd give anything to be the limp, dripping form you stumbled from the lake with, draped over your pale, motherly arms, in a grateful faint, as your mascara ran and ran.' ACH

Gestefeld, Ursula Newell 1845–1921

American novelist. She was born in Augusta, Maine, married Theodore Gestefeld, and had four children. She studied Christian Science with MARY BAKER EDDY, who dismissed her from the church when she published *Statement of Christian Science* (1888), which Eddy took as an attack. Gestefeld responded with *Jesuitism and Christian Science* (1888), a pamphlet criticizing Eddy's claims to authority. She went on to establish her own authority by founding the Church of New Thought, the College of the Science of Being, and the Gestefeld Publishing Company, and publishing a monthly magazine, *Exodus* (1896–1904). In *The Builder and the Plan* (1901), she argues that reason and logic supersede the authority of any church or individual, a theme she translates to fiction in *The Leprosy of Miriam* (1894). Her popular novel *The Woman Who Dares* (1892) presents feminist analyses of marriage, sexuality and prostitution. JSG

Getting of Wisdom, The (1910)

HENRY HANDEL RICHARDSON's celebrated second novel traces the education – academic, social, emotional – of Laura Rambotham, eldest child of an impoverished up-country widow, at a girls' boarding school in Melbourne. The novel, drawing on Richardson's own experience, takes the innocent and intense Laura through a series of character-forming embarrassments and humiliations at the hands of both teachers and fellow-pupils, through which she learns to steer a course between stultifying conformity and the assertion of her own impetuous and colourful personality. Although uncomfortable with the mores of the school, she strives to conform, make friends and impress, and she develops a jealous passion for an older girl. Her efforts to shine are frequently disastrous and she is made to smart for her temerity and on account of her family's low social standing. Most of the characters are both thoroughly unpleasant and highly conventional in their aspirations and their fates. Laura by contrast strives, grows and retains her spirit, passion and curiosity. The wisdom of the novel's title proves profoundly ambiguous. SAS

Ghost Road, The (1995) This novel, the third in PAT BARKER's *Regeneration* trilogy, fuses imaginative fiction and historical fact in its examination of World War I. Interweaving the perceptions of W. H. R. Rivers, the neurologist who treated the poets Siegfried Sassoon and Wilfred Owen, with those of fictional Billy Prior, an army officer originating from a working-class background, Barker maps social and class differences and constructions of masculinity and sexuality onto her representation of war. The book not only recounts the grim reality of the fighting in France but, in describing Rivers's memories of his anthropological expeditions to Polynesia, foregrounds both the differences and the similarities between two diverse cultures in their experiences of conflict and death. A REALIST narrative which is wide-reaching in scope, the novel records the response of the British medical profession to the widespread, and often undetected, neurasthenia caused by trench warfare. But it is nonetheless philosophical in its concern with the ethics of combat and serves as a commentary on the propaganda which surrounded the 'war to end wars'. RCo

Gibbons, Kaye 1960– Novelist whose graceful stories of the American South have earned her a wide readership and many critical awards, including France's Knighthood of the Order of Arts and Letters. With *Ellen Foster* (1987) Gibbons created an apparently simple tale of a young girl's troubled family; the art was in the balance of humour and pathos, and its heroine's startling, direct voice. *A Virtuous Woman* featured an older male narrator, but with *A Cure for Dreams* and particularly the bestselling *Charms for the Easy Life* (1993) – which detailed four generations of Southern women – her work was pegged as 'women's fiction'. It's an unfortunately narrow description, as with her gift for character and voice she can bring to mind EUDORA WELTY – who has called Gibbons's work 'stunning'. She lives with her husband and their five children in

her native North Carolina, and regularly produces new work: *Sights Unseen* was published in 1995. SB

Gibbons, Stella (Dorothea) 1902–89 British journalist, novelist and poet. Copious reading and the creation of imaginary people and situations for the amusement of her younger brothers were her escapes from the dreariness of an unhappy home-life in a poor district of north London, and literary creation became second nature early in her life. Her doctor father had eccentric ideas about schooling, and she was educated at home by a series of governesses until she was 13, when she attended the North London Collegiate School for Girls. Precocious and spoilt, she fitted in badly until the success of her school stories and sketches made her popular. At 19, she went to University College London, where she took the journalism course, the only one of its kind at that time. After a first job as a decoder of cables with the British United Press, where she learnt her professional craft, she spent ten years on Fleet Street at various jobs, including dramatic and literary criticism and fashion writing. She also began publishing the first of many short stories and poems: *The Mountain Beast and Other Poems* appeared in 1930. Her published output was considerable and consistent for over four decades, including several novels – notably *Basset* (1934), *Miss Lindsey and Pa* (1936), *My American: A Romance* (1939), *The Matchmaker* (1949) and *A Pink Front Door* (1959). It is ironic therefore that her name is associated chiefly with just one work, her first novel, COLD COMFORT FARM (1932), a highly entertaining burlesque of earthy regional novels popular at the turn of the century, especially those by SHEILA KAYE-SMITH, MARY WEBB and D. H. Lawrence. It won the Femina Vie Heureuse Prize in 1933, and is generally considered a landmark of parodic writing. Her last book, *The Woods in Winter*, a novel, appeared in 1970. JLB

Gibbs, May 1877–1969 An Australian writer and illustrator of CHILDREN'S BOOKS, Gibbs was born in England and grew up in Perth. She settled in Sydney in 1913 after studying art in England and her first commission was illustrating the cover of Amy Mack's novel *Scribbling Sue*. During World War I, Gibbs produced postcards, gifts and calendars with images of Australian animals and birds to boost the morale of the Australian soldiers, and from this developed her signature gum blossom babies, naked cherubs who live in gum trees and are decorated with gumnuts or gum blossoms. The first of her illustrated books was published in 1916, and in 1918 the famous *Snugglepot and Cuddlepie* was published, telling the story of the adventures of the gum blossom babies as they outwit the 'big bad Banksia men'. Gibbs continued with her gum blossom babies in her illustrated weekly 'Bib and Bub' comic strip, published in the children's pages of *Woman's World* (to which MARY GRANT BRUCE also contributed) from 1925 to 1967. Gibbs was never interested in drawing the fairies of European fantasies, and her illustrations have been influential in the development of a distinctly Australian world for children. She was awarded the MBE in 1955 for services to Australian literature.   SS

Giberne, Agnes 1845–1939 This long-lived English writer of dismal evangelical tales for children also produced some immensely readable and highly regarded beginners' guides to scientific subjects such as astronomy and geology. She was born in India but the Giberne family left that country when she was very young. They subsequently lived at various locations around Europe before settling in England. Agnes Giberne was never obliged to undertake remunerative employment and, longevity being a family trait, she was still living under her father's roof at the age of 53!

Her evangelical tales such as *Floss Silverthorn: Or the Master's Little Handmaid* (1875) and *The Lost Found: Or, Brunhild's Trials* (1876) encourage morbid introspection on the part of the child-reader by representing every childish fault as a direct route to damnation and by emotively portraying the death or near-death of child-characters whose salvation is uncertain. However, her well-written scientific books, for example *Sun, Moon and Stars* (1879) and *The World's Foundations, or Geology for Beginners* (1881), make much pleasanter reading. Agnes Giberne was still publishing new fiction and non-fiction up until the 1920s.   EMH

Gibson, Margaret 1948– Canadian novelist and short-story writer who powerfully chronicles mental illness. Gibson has lived all her life in Toronto. Her formal education ended with high school and she has suffered from mental illness and has been hospitalized for long periods of time. The strength of her work comes from her authentic and precise rendering of those on the fringes of mainstream society. She focuses on mentally ill and abused women and all who have difficulty functioning in a bleak and pitiless world. Her stories endow society's outcasts with human qualities and explore their ability to establish relationships and find moments of happiness. She treats with particular tenderness the doomed efforts of dysfunctional people to become effective parents. THE BUTTERFLY WARD (1976), her first collection of short stories, garnered much attention and critical acclaim. Subsequent collections were *Considering her Condition* (1978), *Sweet Poison* (1993) and *The Fear Room* (1996). Gibson's first novel, *Opium Dreams*, was published in 1997. A new long story, *Desert Thirst*, appeared in the literary quarterly *Exile* in 1996, along with a portfolio of striking photographs of Gibson by John Reeves.   JG

Gilchrist, Ellen 1935– American novelist, short-story writer and poet. Gilchrist was born in Vicksburg in Mississippi, and both that Southern setting and her intense family life have proved enormous influences in all her books. Her writing career did not start until she was in her forties, by which time she had been married and divorced three times and had three children. At this point she moved to Fayetteville in the Ozarks, which also features prominently in her work.

Her first collection of short stories, *In the Land of Dreamy Dreams*, was published in 1981; it was followed by several more collections, including *Victory Over Japan* (1984) which won the American National Book Award, *Drunk with Love* (1986), *Light Can Be Both Wave and Particle* (1989), *I Cannot Get You Close Enough* (1990) and *The Age of Miracles* (1996). Her novels include *The Annunciation* (1983), *The Anna Papers* (1988), *Starcarbon* (1994) and *Sarah Conley* (1997); she has also published two volumes of poetry. Throughout, she has portrayed the difficulty of life in closely knit communities, particularly for women who seek to balance personal relationships with a rampant desire for freedom and creativity. One of her devices has been to people her stories and novels with a number of repeating characters, including the New Orleans orphan Nora Jane Whittington and, most autobiographically, Rhoda Manning, whose spirited battles in the face of life's trials have delighted many readers.   AC

Giles, Barbara 1912– Poet who was born in England, and moved to Australia with her family in 1923. Although she started both her tertiary education and her writing career late in life, Giles made up for lost time with a steady stream of publications from her mid sixties. She is a prolific poet: *Eve Rejects Apple* (1978) was followed by *Earth and Solitude* (1985), *The Hag in the Mirror* (1989), *A Savage Coast* (1993) and *Poems: Seven Ages* (1997). As her titles suggest, Giles's work concentrates on women's experience, ageing and the passing of time. Her approach to these subjects sparkles with humour; she has a sharp eye and an acerbic voice. In addition to her own writing – which encompasses novels for CHILDREN such as *Alex is my Friend* (1984) and *Gone Wild* (1990), translations, criticism and short stories – Giles has collaborated on several anthology projects for children, including a collection of short stories, *The Hat Trick* (1981), and one of verse by young people, *Of Human Being and Chestnut Trees* (1981), both edited by Giles, Michael Dugan and J.S. Hamilton. Giles is also a regular reviewer, was heavily involved with the magazine *Luna*, and was one of the initiators of the Victorian Pariah Press Co-operative, which has published a number of developing Australian poets.   MLA

Illustration of Caroline Gilman's summer house in *Recollections of a New England Bride and of a Southern Matron*.

Gilliatt [née Conner], Penelope (Ann Douglass)

1932–93 English short-story writer, novelist, playwright and critic. She was born in London. Her father was a successful barrister, but her parents separated when she was a child. Gilliatt was educated at Queen's College, London, and Bennington College, Vermont, after which she entered journalism, becoming features editor of British *Vogue*. From 1961 onwards, she was film critic of the *Observer*, and from 1967 to 1979 also worked for the *New Yorker*. Her second husband was the playwright John Osborne.

Gilliatt was the author of five novels: *One by One* (1965), *A State of Change* (1967), *The Cutting Edge* (1978), *Mortal Matters* (1983) and *A Woman of Singular Occupation* (1988). However, her short stories contained her best work. Her sophisticated, intellectual style, gift for dialogue and preference for character study over elaborate plotting enable her to achieve maximum impact over a short distance. Her collections include *What's It Like Out? and Other Stories* (1968), *Nobody's Business* (1972), *Splendid Lives* (1977), *Quotations from Other Lives* (1982) and *They Sleep Without Dreaming* (1985). Her talent for realizing psychological states and complex relationships also came to the fore in her most instantly recognizable work, the screenplay for the film *Sunday Bloody Sunday* (1972).   AC

Gilman, Caroline (Howard)

1794–1888 American journalist, novelist and poet. Her mother was from a prominent Boston family, her father a shipwright. She married Unitarian pastor Samuel Gilman in 1819, moved to Charleston, South Carolina, and had seven children. From 1832 to 1842, she published the first American weekly journal for young people, *Rose Bud* (later *The Southern Rose*), which made her the best-known woman writer of the South. Humorous sketches about the management of a middle-class household, written for the *Rose*, were republished as *Recollections of a New England Bride* (1834). Other publications include *Recollections of a Southern Matron* (1837), a chapter of which English journalist HARRIET MARTINEAU included in *Society in America* (1837); a book of housekeeping advice; *Love's Progress* (1840), a novel; children's books; and *Verses of a Lifetime* (1849). Her views on gender were progressive, but she justified slavery and supported the Confederacy during the Civil War.   JSG

Gilman, Charlotte (Anna) Perkins (Stetson)

1860–1935 US author, lecturer, sociologist, whose brilliant analyses of gender still hold. She was born in Hartford, Connecticut, to Mary A. Fitch Westcott – descendant of Rhode Island founder Stukely Westcott – and Frederick Beecher Gilman, nephew of novelist HARRIET BEECHER STOWE and feminist Isabella Beecher Hooker. Her father was a professional librarian, her intellectual model, perhaps a marital model as well since he left the family when Charlotte and her brother Thomas were about 6 and 7 years old respectively. The family, experiencing genteel poverty, moved from relative to relative in New England, neither her mother's skill at teaching young children nor her father's sporadic support providing financial security.

In 1884 Gilman married Charles Walter Stetson, a Rhode Island artist. His extant diary reveals a typically self-centred 19th-century husband. A daughter Katharine, born in 1885, seemed to precipitate what today would likely be diagnosed as postpartum depression. Gilman's condition gave rise to her masterwork, the short story 'THE YELLOW WALL-PAPER' (1892), though recent scholarship documents her unreliability regarding its creation, publication and reception history. Gilman went to Pasadena, California, to recover with the family of her best friend, Grace Ellery Channing, but relapsed upon returning east. Finally taking Katharine in 1888, she left Stetson, again staying in Pasadena. Eventually Stetson married Grace Channing, and Gilman sent Katharine to live with them in New York City. Between 1888 and 1900, Gilman practised reform, lecturing and journalism – the *Impress* (San Francisco) providing her with an informal apprenticeship. In 1900, after a three-year courtship correspondence (her letters extant, though not his), Gilman married her cousin George Houghton 'Ho' Gilman, an attorney. During this galvanizing period in her life, Gilman wrote a major sociological analysis, *Women and Economics* (1898), its insights on gender still provocative, though its views on evolution are now outmoded.

With Ho managing financial and legal matters, Charlotte launched the *Forerunner*, a magazine she alone wrote from November 1909 to December 1916. Each issue contained both fiction (her utopias, *Herland* (1915), and *With Her in Ourland* (1916)) and non-fiction serializations, a short story and numerous short pieces such as book reviews and editorials. Her goal in her writing was 'making better people'. In spite of racist and zenophobic attitudes, she remains an incisive thinker on gender relations. Her autobiography, *The Living of Charlotte Perkins Gilman* (1935), presents a life-story often in conflict with the record of her correspondence and journals.   CFK

Gilmore [née Cameron], Mary (Jean) 1865–1962
Australian poet and essayist whose lifelong commitment to the labour movement began during her first posting as a teacher in an outback mining-town. She became active in William Lane's utopian New Australia movement, and joined its unsuccessful Paraguayan experiment in communal living in 1896, returning to Australia with a husband and young son in 1902, after a period in Patagonia.

Her first collection, *Marri'd and Other Verses* (1910), was published after she had begun work on the Women's Page of the *Worker*. Her initiation of this project, which she edited until 1931, gave her a precarious financial basis for moving to Sydney. More importantly, it gave her a site in which she could pursue a succession of socialist and feminist causes and in which she could publish some of her own extraordinarily prolific output: radical 'Labour Verse', translations from Latin American poets and verse for children. Many of these have remained uncollected, for Gilmore, despite a modest insistence that she wrote 'verse' rather than 'Poetry', worked hard and selectively on her collec-

tions. The ballad-style social REALISM of *The Tilted Cart: A Book of Recitations* (1925) does relate to *Worker* poems, as well as to the prose re-creations of pioneering bush society in the popularly successful *Old Days, Old Ways* (1934) and *More Recollections* (1935), but other volumes show a wider and more ambitious scope of theme and style. THE PASSIONATE HEART (1918) and BATTLEFIELDS (1939) contain strong poems about women's experience of love and poverty and about war's wastefulness and suffering. *The Wild Swans* (1930) and *Under the Wilgas* (1932) forcefully acknowledge the destructive impact of pioneer settlement on the environment and its Aboriginal population.

Like many opinionated people, Gilmore was full of contradictions – witness her patriotic (even jingoistic) verse of World War II. She hungered for literary reputation, but was generous to other writers, and became a major figure in Sydney's literary culture, although her poetry became considered rather old-fashioned, so that she had difficulty in publishing her final collection, *Fourteen Men* (1954), although this still demonstrates the qualities which W.H. Wilde took as definitive in choosing *Courage A Grace*, the last line of 'Never admit the Pain', as the title for his biography of Gilmore.   JStr

Gilroy, Beryl 1924– Born in Guyana, Gilroy settled in
England in 1951, where she studied Education at the Universities of London and Sussex. She began writing in the 1960s, producing some fifteen titles for children about the experiences of young West Indian migrants in England (see CHILDREN'S BOOKS). In works like *New People at Twenty Four* (1973), *Once Upon a Time* (1975) and *Carnival of Dreams* (1985), Gilroy reconstructed the world of black child immigrants separated from their native climes and societies as their families forge new lives and communities in London.

In the 1980s Gilroy turned to adult fiction, publishing *Frangipani House* (1986) and *Boy Sandwich* (1989) to enthusiastic reviews. In *Frangipani House* Gilroy evokes the spiritual and historical significance of old age and ancestry through the use of the vicissitudes of old age as metaphor for the human condition and through the skilled interweaving of ritual and journey motifs. It narrates the journey of Mama King who, old and infirm, is placed in Frangipani House, a dreary rest home where she is nearly driven to madness by loneliness and anguish, and from which she escapes to the dangerous world of the homeless poor. In *Boy Sandwich*, Tyrone, a young man raised in London, 'sandwiched-in' by his family's protective circle, finds his world shattered when his grandparents are evicted to a callous and unresponsive institution. In an effort to find and assert his identity, he follows his grandparents to their native Caribbean, only to find that the answer does not lie in a return to the ancestral home.

Gilroy has also published two HISTORICAL NOVELS about early West Indian colonial history: *Stedman and Joanna: A Love in Bondage* (1991) and *Inkle and Yarico* (1996). *Black Teacher*, an autobiographical essay published in 1976, recounts Gilroy's experience as a teacher and headmistress in London.   LP-G

Giovanni, Nikki 1943– Born Yolande Cornelia Giovanni in Knoxville, Tennessee, she became politically active in left-wing and black-power organizations while studying at Fisk University. This concern is often reflected in her poetry, particularly in the early titles: *Black Feeling, Black Talk* (1967), *Black Judgment* (1969) and *Re: Creation* (1970). After the birth of her son in 1969 Giovanni wrote a book of children's poems: *Spin a Soft Black Song* (1970). Thereafter her work became more personal, as indicated by the following collection's title: *Gemini: An Extended Autobiographical Statement on my First Twenty Five Years of Being a Black Poet* (1976). This focus continues in *Love Poems* (1997):

> if i were a poet
> i'd kidnap you
> put you in my phrases and meter
> you to jones beach.

An album of her poetry set to music (mostly gospel) called *Truth Is On Its Way* brought her a large audience in the 1970s. Other collections include: *My House* (1972), *Cotton Candy on a Rainy Day* (1978), *Those Who Read the Night Winds* (1983) and a *Selected Poems* in 1996. A Professor of Creative Writing at Virginia Tech, Giovanni has won various awards in the course of her career.   ACH

Girl of the Period and Other Social Essays, The

(1883) The novelist and journalist ELIZA LYNN LINTON published articles on the Woman Question in the *Saturday Review* 1866–68, which were reprinted in two volumes. Linton had been rebellious in her youth, but became reactionary and anti-feminist. She provoked controversy in 1868 with her depiction of 'The Girl of the Period': a hedonistic, irresponsible, immodest creature with 'false red hair and painted skin'. Linton laments: 'The legal barter of herself for so much money, representing so much dash, so much luxury and pleasure – that is her idea of marriage.' Men turn to such girls for amusement, but have no desire to marry them. Linton compares them to prostitutes, although she prefers the 'unblushing honesty' of the latter. The extreme portraits of the traditional virtuous Englishwoman and the new Girl promoted the idea of an angel/whore dichotomy. Articles, jokes, new expressions and items of clothing were spawned. Linton was accused of exaggeration, especially as women had few options other than marriage.   SF

Girlhood of Shakespeare's Heroines, The (1850–

2) This highly successful work by MARY COWDEN CLARKE, one of the earliest professional writers on Shakespeare, was first published serially, before appearing as a five-volume collection. Following on five years after her *Concordance* to Shakespeare's plays, the book contains fifteen stories which describe the early life of selected Shakespeare heroines. In this way Cowden Clarke hoped to allow the reader or audience to imagine 'such situations as should naturally lead up to, and account for, the known conclusion of their subsequent confirmed character and afterlife'. Although the tales frequently deal with violent or sexual incidents, the biographical approach was popular with contemporary reviewers, who felt that these novels-in-miniature would appeal particularly to the younger reader. A shortened version was prepared by the author's sister, Sabilla Novello, in 1879, which left out much of the shocking material, although the full text was restored with a new preface in 1892.   RDM

girls' school stories The 'rosy, racy, healthy, hearty, well-grown set of twentieth-century schoolgirls' who burst upon the literary scene around 1912, in the pages of ANGELA BRAZIL, were almost without predecessors. True, a girls' school story of a kind had come into being in the late Victorian period, at the hands of Mrs J. H. EWING, L. T. MEADE and others; but it was an insipid creation, without gusto or merriment. The new century brought a new approach, in which entertainment was paramount and didacticism took a back seat (not that it ever evaporated altogether – the theme of 'character-moulding', for example, remains prominent in the genre, with one moral weakling after another acquiring a better attitude through games-playing, nearly coming a cropper, the influence of some upright contemporary, or whatever suits the plot).

Angela Brazil (1868–1947) was the first to invigorate this branch of girls' fiction, but it wasn't long before other authors began forging their individual contributions to the general store of exuberance and high jinks. Oxenham, Brent-Dyer, Bruce, Darch, Chaundler, Talbot, Smith, Gray, Elder, Moore, Wynne, Plunket... the list is endless. Elsie J. Oxenham (1880–1960) is best known for her 'Abbey' series – which mostly aren't school stories – but she also wrote some exemplary school fiction including the novels *Deb of Sea House* and *Dorothy's Dilemma*. Elinor Brent-Dyer (1894-1969) got into print in 1922 with *Gerry Goes to School*, and went on to create the famous 'Chalet' series, starting in 1925 and continuing right up until 1970 (fifty-eight titles in all), each school adventure coming furnished with its quota of life-saving exploits, natural and unnatural disasters (an avalanche, a landslide, two floods and a green dye which falls on someone's head), and bracing injunctions: 'In less than three years you should all be seniors and we don't like seniors who are as weak-kneed as all that.' Dorita Fairlie Bruce (1885-1970) is the fourth member of the peerless Brazil–Oxenham–Brent-Dyer–Bruce quartet, and she kept her end up with such splendid explorations of the world of school as *Dimsie Among the Prefects* and *Nancy Returns to St Bride's*.

The school story flourished between the wars, and indeed retained its popularity up until the 1950s, when other forms of juvenile literature gained the upper hand. In its heyday, it wasn't confined to hard covers; another notable outlet was established in the girls' 'story paper', beginning in 1919 with the *School Friend* and its serials featuring the girls of Cliff House (created and kept going by male authors under a variety of female pseudonyms). Even more colourful than mainstream school fiction, such long-running sagas provided unsurpassed diversion for more than one generation of readers. In general, though – whatever its provenance – the pattern was adapted, in the hands of one author after another, to accommodate adventure, mystery ('Who was the queer new girl . . . and who was it she met among the ruins of the desolate burnt-out wing?'), spy-catching (during both World Wars, but especially the second), Girl Guide activities and so on, alongside such staples as bosom friendships, fraught misunderstandings and predicaments of all types.

During the 1940s, the school story was taken up, not without vivacity, by the indefatigable ENID BLYTON (St Clare's, Malory Towers, and the *alma mater* of the 'naughtiest girl'); and at the same time the career of Nancy Breary, possibly the last and certainly the most ebullient of the traditional school-story writers, got under way. Nancy Breary's cheerful stories, though, contain the odd touch of self-mockery – and this indicates that the genre had begun to decline. There were, it's true, authors such as Mary K. Harris who attempted to resuscitate it by introducing a new realism and restraint, but without conspicuous success. They were up against the social climate of post-war England, not to mention the contemporary (adult) image of the schoolgirl as St Trinian's sexpot with macabre inclinations, a grotesque gym-tunic and regulation navy knickers which kept popping into view. The ordinary tale of madcap goings-on, or of prefects trying to bolster up a slackly run school, no longer struck a chord with adolescent readers, it seemed; and by the time the school story reappeared (as it did) it was in a guise that broke completely with the conventions of the past. PC

Glaister, Lesley 1956– Prolific British author of very finely focused, mostly first-person narrative adventures in the domestic GOTHIC. Born and educated in Wellingborough, she is the recipient of both Somerset

Maugham and Betty Trask Awards. Her first novel was *Honour Thy Father* (1991), followed by *Trick or Treat* (1991) and *Digging to Australia* (1992), which puts us uncomfortably back into the mind of an adolescent. The novel is an examination of a young woman's infatuation with an older man. As with all of the books, we are led right to the edge of danger, and aren't quite sure, by the end, whether we've been led back again to safety. *Limestone and Clay* (1993) has grown-up protagonists, staying together and disappointedly finding metaphors in landscape. Later books are *Partial Eclipse* (1994) and *The Private Parts of Women* (1996), which is a dark, polyphonic text, picking apart ideas of the different selves a woman is allowed to be. Inis has run away from her own family, and tries to befriend Trixie, an elderly victim of multiple personality disorder. The book skilfully examines everyday madnesses and brings the whole to a shocking climax. Glaister always manages to whip the mind-numbing and mundane into relentless, thriller-like tension. PM

Glasgow, Ellen (Anderson Gholson) 1873–1945 American fiction writer and essayist who unsettled the conventional romanticism of Southern fiction with what she called 'blood and irony'. Born in Richmond, Virginia, in a family with ties to both the Tidewater aristocracy and the new industrial south, she supplemented her brief formal schooling by reading widely, under the direction of her sister's husband (and through a subscription to the New York Mercantile Library), in science, economics, philosophy and literature.

She published her first story in 1895 at 22 and her first novel, *The Descendant*, in 1897. A flood of often best-selling novels followed, though it would not be until midway through her career (beginning with *Virginia* in 1913) that she began to tap the full measure of her talent for depicting strong women caught by, or struggling against, their expected roles. In the wake of a suicide attempt in 1918, she began to formulate what would become her most powerful novel, the story of the resolutely independent Dorinda Oakley in *Barren Ground* (1925). Now in her fifties, Glasgow's period of greatest creativity and critical acclaim lay before her, as she produced both her comic trilogy – *The Romantic Comedians* (1926), *They Stooped to Folly* (1929) and *The Sheltered Life* (1932) – and the family chronicle *Vein of Iron* (1935). *In This Our Life* (1941) brought a belated Pulitzer Prize, and in 1943 she published *A Certain Measure: An Interpretation of Prose Fiction*, a collection of her critical prefaces. She died in her home in Richmond at 72. WG

Glaspell, Susan 1876–1948 American playwright, novelist, short-story writer. Born in Davenport, Iowa, Glaspell graduated from Drake University in 1899, and went on to work as a reporter, but soon decided to

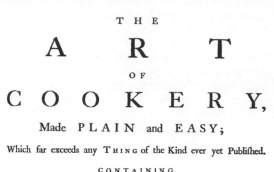

THE

A R T

OF

C O O K E R Y,

Made PLAIN and EASY;

Which far exceeds any THING of the Kind ever yet Publiſhed.

CONTAINING,

I. Of Roaſting, Boiling, &c.
II. Of Made-Diſhes.
III. Read this Chapter, and you will find how Expenſive a *French* Cook's Sauce is.
IV. To make a Number of pretty little Diſhes fit for a Supper, or Side-Diſh, and little Corner-Diſhes for a great Table; and the reſt you have in the Chapter for *Lent*.
V. To dreſs Fiſh.
VI. Of Soops and Broths.
VII. Of Puddings.
VIII. Of Pies.
IX. For a Faſt-Dinner, a Number of good Diſhes, which you may make uſe for a Table at any other Time.
X. Directions for the Sick.
XI. For Captains of Ships.
XII. Of Hog's Puddings, Sauſages, &c.

XIII. To Pot and Make Hams, &c.
XIV. Of Pickling.
XV. Of Making Cakes, &c.
XVI. Of Cheeſecakes, Creams, Jellies, Whip Syllabubs, &c.
XVII. Of Made Wines, Brewing, *French* Bread, Muffins, &c.
XVIII. Jarring Cherries, and Preſerves, &c.
XIX. To Make Anchovies, Vermicella, Ketchop, Vinegar, and to keep Artichokes, French-Beans, &c.
XX. Of Diſtilling.
XXI. How to Market, and the Seaſons of the Year for Butcher's Meat, Poultry, Fiſh, Herbs, Roots, &c. and Fruit.
XXII. A certain Cure for the Bite of a Mad Dog. By Dr. *Mead.*

BY A LADY.

L O N D O N:

Printed for the AUTHOR; and ſold at Mrs. *Aſhburn*'s, a China-Shop, the Corner of *Fleet-Ditch.* MDCCXLVII.

[*Price* 3 s. ſtitch'd, and 5 s. bound.]

Hannah Glasse: title-page of *The Art of Cookery Made Plain and Easy; Which far exceeds any Thing of the Kind ever yet Published*, 1747.

devote herself to fiction. She published several short stories, and in 1909 her first novel, *The Glory of the Conquered. Lifted Masks*, her first book of stories, came out three years later. In 1913, she married George Cook Cram, with whom she collaborated on plays in a group of writers that included DJUNA BARNES, EDNA ST VINCENT MILLAY and Eugene O'Neill. In 1914, they founded the Provincetown Players which became the major experimental theatre production group in the country. Glaspell's one-act play, *Trifles* (1916), is about a woman accused of murdering her husband: she never appears on stage, and her terrible life with him is explained by her two onstage friends. Glaspell rewrote *Trifles* as the award-winning short story, 'A Jury of her Peers'. To help fund the Provincetown Players, she continued to write stories and articles throughout the

1920s. Cook died in 1924 – a year after his death she published a romanticized biography of him, *The Road to the Temple* – and she married Norman Matson, from whom she was divorced in 1932. Her last play, *Alison's House* (1930), loosely based on EMILY DICKINSON's life, won the Pulitzer Prize. Her nine novels (including the 1942 *Norma Ashe* and the 1945 *Judd Rankin's Daughter*) and many of her stories are set in the Mid-West and explore issues of modernity and pioneer values. Writing for the stage, however, was the genre in which she made her most important contributions.   SP

Glass of Blessings, A (1958) The narrator of *A Glass of Blessings*, BARBARA PYM's fifth novel, is a latter-day Emma. Wilmet Forsyth, beautiful, elegant, well-off, married to a kind and successful civil servant, has little to vex her. But without children or career, her life, like that of a 19th-century middle-class heroine, revolves around her parish church and her mind is occupied with nostalgia for her war-time youth, hypothetical romance and the personalities of the clergy. Wilmet's romantic imaginings prove chimerical and she fails to detect the actual relationships developing in her family and parish. She comes to the understanding that her real life is 'a glass of blessings', the image used by the 17th-century religious poet George Herbert, for the profusion of divine gifts 'when God at first made man'. The phrase asserts the spirituality of the quotidian and of Pym's characteristic territory, ordinary lives charted with charity, accuracy and humour.   PMar

Glasse, Hannah 1708–70 Probably the bestselling COOKERY WRITER of her century and famously, but erroneously, considered the author of the phrase 'First Catch your Hare'. When most recipe books were written by professional male cooks and chefs, Hannah Glasse produced a work that lived up to its title: *The Art of Cookery made Plain and Easy* (1747). Not all her recipes were her own work: Hannah Glasse's innovation was to write not 'in the high polite style . . . for my intention is to instruct the lower sort'. Thus her clearly explained and mainly economical recipes for contemporary dishes won her a large audience of domestic cooks and kitchen maids.

Born illegitimately to Isaac Allgood and Hannah Reynolds, at only 16, Hannah secretly married John Glasse, a subaltern on half-pay; the marriage produced eight children. The financial misfortune that dogged her life may have prompted Hannah to write *The Art of Cookery*, compiled while she was in service in Broomfield, Essex. Early editions of the seventeen published give authorship to 'A Lady', though by 1751 Hannah reveals herself on the title-page as 'Habit Maker to Her Royal Highness, the Princess of Wales'. Unfortunately this enterprise resulted in bankruptcy in 1754 and in settlement Hannah had to sell the copyright of *The Art of Cookery*. Her other works, *The Compleat Confectioner* (1761) and *The Servant's Directory* (1760), never achieved the outstanding success of her first book.   GH

Glen, Esther 1881–1940 New Zealand CHILDREN'S WRITER. The Esther Glen Medal, an annual award for 'the most distinguished contribution to New Zealand Literature for children' was set up in 1945 in memory of her 'vigorous encouragement of the imaginative life of children'. The third of twelve children herself, Glen assisted her mother at home, then ran a kindergarten before becoming a freelance journalist. From 1925 to 1940 Glen wrote and edited the children's page of the *Christchurch Sun*, and later the *Christchurch Press*. As 'Lady Gay' she encouraged children to send stories, poems and pictures for publication.

In 1917 she published a children's novel, *Six Little New Zealanders* (the title echoing Australian ETHEL TURNER's highly successful *SEVEN LITTLE AUSTRALIANS*), and in 1926 its sequel, *Uncles Three of Kamahi*. *Six Little New Zealanders* is a lively story of childhood misadventures: the children's mother has to go 'Home' to England for medical treatment and the six children stay on their bachelor uncles' farm. With a very believable 12-year-old girl narrator, Ngaire, it's set on a sheep station in South Canterbury like the one where Glen and her siblings had spent holidays as children. As well as these two popular novels, Glen wrote *Twinkles on the Mountain* (1920) – a book of FAIRY STORIES – and *Robin of Maoriland* (1929) – a story of city family life.   AM

Glory Days (1988) ROSIE SCOTT's first novel, published shortly before she left Aotearoa/New Zealand, is in many ways her most successful. It sparkles with a wonderfully subversive humour and gusto sometimes missing from her later work, while being no less impassioned in the fight for social justice. Borrowing something of the mystery-thriller structure, it tells the story of the Rabelaisian artist, Glory Day, and her frenetic struggle to save herself, her art, and her Down's syndrome daughter, Rina, from the psychotic Roxy and the forces of ultra-conservatism. Her race against time becomes a journey into the past which enables her to come to terms with her present. There is Scott's usual cast of memorable and delightfully quirky characters, many of whom are outsiders, or 'people on the edge', as Scott calls them. These include the inimitable Glory herself; the aptly (if ironically) named transvestite, Grace; the splendidly sympathetic Rina; and Glory's staunch friends and neighbours, the Maori gangsters. Scott's background as a social worker enabled her to paint this world with vivid colours and uncompromising, but compassionate, REALISM.   LB

Glück, Louise 1943– American poet born in New York, she attended Sarah Lawrence College and Columbia University. Glück's poetry is primarily located in the domestic, but it is a jarred and rarely redeemed vortex into which these poems travel: 'What is the animal' / if not passage out of this life?' ('Horse'). A powerful, demanding engine drives the poems and as a result her writing is tight, intense and feels autobiographical without necessarily being so, because the 'I' is convincing and strong. She has been described as a 'post-CONFESSIONAL poet' and there is evidence for this in the intimations of wonder tinged with pain in much of her poetry. Her collections include *Firstborn* (1968), *The House on the Marshland* (1975) and *DESCENDING FIGURE* (1980) which like much of her writing, centres on loss, death and things broken.

In *Meadowlands* (1996) Glück interposes, in a richly charged, polyvocal sequence, the undoing of a contemporary marriage with the story of *The Odyssey*. Other titles include *Ararat* (1990), and Pulitzer-Prize-winning *The Wild Iris* (1992) in which Glück takes an unusual narrative form by positing the progress of a garden as the central conceit. Even flowers seem to speak in this intensely metaphorical study. There are biblical and mythological allusions, visceral and cerebral intensity: 'it wasn't possible any longer / to stare at heaven and not be destroyed' ('Trillium'). Glück won the National Book Critics Circle Award for *The Triumph of Achilles* (1985), perhaps her best-loved collection, in which she meditates on the death of her father: 'What were the Greek ships on fire / compared to this loss?' Other awards include Fellowships from the National Endowment for the Arts. Glück has taught at colleges in Vermont and North Carolina, and in 1994 she was appointed Poet Laureate of the State of New Hampshire.   ACH

Glyn [née Sutherland], Elinor 1864–1943 Novelist and scriptwriter. Alertness to the hankerings and illusions of the successive eras – Victorian, Edwardian, Jazz Age – through which she lived was the basis for Elinor Glyn's professional success. Brought up in Canada and Jersey with her sister Lucy, later a noted *couturiere*, she gained access, as a debutante, to the English country-house society which provided her with a husband, the Essex landowner Clayton Glyn, from whom she separated after eight years of marriage. The same world offered inspiration for her novels, beginning in 1900 with *The Visits of Elizabeth*. Eight years later she created a sensation with *Three Weeks*, the story of a whirlwind affair between the Queen of a Balkan state and a footloose Old Etonian. The fact that their relationship is fully consummated, the glamour and the fashionable décor made the novel an instant bestseller. Though always appealing to a mainstream readership, Glyn was pleased by the serious critical attention given to her later novels, especially *The Career of Katherine Bush* (1917), a cynical account of a freewheeling social climber's triumphant efforts to ensnare a Duke. After World War I, during which she worked as a war correspondent for Hearst newspapers in Paris, Glyn embarked on a career as a scriptwriter in Hollywood, triumphing with her screenplay for *It* (1927), starring Clara Bow, originally written as a novella defining modern sex appeal.　JK

Goblin Market and Other Poems (1862)

CHRISTINA ROSSETTI's second and best-known collection of poems is distinguished by lush, sensual imagery coupled with religious, allegorical and moral themes, audacious use of irregular rhyme and metre, as well as proto-feminist politics; it secured her place as one of the major poets of the Victorian era.

The title poem is a disturbing FAIRY TALE about two sisters, Laura and Lizzie, who live an idyllic life of virginal domesticity which is threatened by Laura's capitulation to the goblin's hawking of preternaturally delicious fruit. Slowly dying for another taste, Laura is saved by her sister Lizzie, who attempts to buy but refuses to eat the fruit. Resisting the force-feeding of the goblins, Lizzie rushes home so that Laura may lick the juices from her body. Laura is cured and she and Lizzie both marry and have children.

The volume also includes a selection of love poems, and religious and nature poetry. Rossetti depicts romantic love as a mutable and destructive force in the lives of women, particularly those who experience desire and pleasure outside of marriage. Her religious poems elevate the life of the spirit above that of the body, and the promise of the afterlife above worldly pleasures.　MCJ

Godden, Rumer 1907–98

British novelist born in India at the height of British colonial power, Rumer Godden lived there until the 1950s. Like RUTH PRAWER JHABVALA's, her relationship with India, though passionate, was ultimately and perhaps inevitably ambivalent, culminating in an incident in Kashmir where a servant tried to poison her and her children, forcing her to leave the country.

In a career spanning over sixty years Godden wrote over fifty books for adults and children as well as some twenty volumes of non-fiction and autobiography. Some of her most notable work for adults – *Black Narcissus* (1945) and *The River* (1946) – were successfully adapted for the screen. Perhaps most well regarded for her CHILDREN'S BOOKS, Godden won the Whitbread Prize for her novel *The Diddakoi* in 1972. Critics point to her thematic obsession with the conflicting needs of children and adults. She is sensitive to the suffering caused in children by parental neglect, yet, surpris-

ingly, she often shows the absence of a parent to be ultimately liberating, freeing a child to undertake the journey toward completion that Godden so values. In adult novels such as *An Episode of Sparrows* (1955) and *The Greengage Summer* (1958), and even more consistently in such books for children as *The Diddakoi, The Dolls' House* (1962), *Mouse House* (1957) and *Thursday's Children,* the independent struggle for personal fulfilment is rewarded.　JHB

Godwin, Gail 1937–

American writer of novels and short stories. Godwin grew up in Alabama and North Carolina, reared by her mother and grandmother; several of her early heroines reject their training as southern belles. Godwin studied Literature and obtained her Ph.D. at the University of Iowa. Two collections of short stories, *Dream Children* (1977) and *Mr Bedford and the Muses* (1984), are less interesting than the novels; Godwin deals in ambiguities and complexities which need space to develop.

Her earlier novels have a tendency to the schematic. The academic heroine of *The Odd Woman* (1974) attends a family funeral and decides to get rid of an unsatisfactory lover: so after a good deal of fascinating intellectual chat, she comes, patly, to see his work on the Pre-Raphaelites as essentially second-rate. Godwin's later novels, *Father Melancholy's Daughter* (1990) and *The Good Husband* (1995), are richer in their portrayal of mourning and of the mutual responsibilities of spouses and friends; there is a vein of the religious in both which never becomes sentimental but is treated merely as another aspect of life. Godwin has been underrated as a middlebrow feminist; she has a rare capacity for fair-minded characterization of the interestingly good.　RK

Golden Notebook, The (1962)

Hailed in the 1960s as one of the great feminist consciousness-raising novels, DORIS LESSING's sprawling novel represents her attempt to match the all-encompassing canvas of her 19th-century predecessors, Tolstoy and Stendhal. Informed equally by her Marxist principles and her interest in psychotherapy, Lessing argues that she conceived of the text as being centrally concerned with 'breakdown' in its conjoined social and personal forms, and was bemused when the book was received largely in terms of the ways it illuminated the contemporary 'sex war'. The narrative is divided into six parts: five differently coloured notebooks and a novel, each of which record one aspect of the experience of their author, Anna Freeman Wulf, who is suffering from writer's block. Each is a record of profound dysfunction, with the exception of The Golden Notebook itself, which is a collaborative document, written by Anna with her lover, Saul, which charts a way out of the corrupting egotism which characterizes the other notebooks and which forms the basis of Anna's culturally symptomatic paralysis.   KF

Goldman, Emma 1869–1940 Better known as 'Red Emma' she was a political agitator, anarchist and proto-feminist, writer, editor of radical literature, free-love advocate, and a future character in E.L. Doctorow's POSTMODERN novel, *Ragtime*. Born of Orthodox Jewish parents in tsarist Russia, soon after the assassination of Tsar Alexander II, a murder which fomented renewed anti-Semitism and unabated pogroms, she emigrated to the United States, settling first in Rochester, New York, in 1886. Her perfervid interest in the Chicago anarchist trials of 1886, in which the defendants were accused, convicted and eventually hanged on meagre evidence, prompted her to become a revolutionary: 'I had a distinct sensation that something new and wonderful had been born in my soul. A great ideal, a burning faith, a determination to dedicate myself to the memory of my martyred comrades, to make their cause my own.' After divorcing her husband and moving to New York City's Lower East Side, she eventually founded the organization Mother Earth (1906), which produced the country's major anarchist journal, which was meant to be a forum for presenting 'socially significant' art and social criticism. Mother Earth Publishing Association published 'radical' books on such subjects as sex, birth-control and, eventually, the 'Trial and Speeches of Alexander Berkman and Emma Goldman in the US District Court in the City of New York, July 1917', the trial which virtually ended her political career. Her positions on women, feminism and sexuality were all 'cutting edge' issues, though she was decidedly against a woman's right to vote, linking it with 'the sex question', both of which were, fundamentally, deeply rooted in patriarchal aspects of either governmental or gender repression. The diversity of her intellect is reflected in the diversity of her writings, from essays to autobiography (see *LIVING MY LIFE*, 1931), but she will always be recognized for her perfervid interest in writing about human rights and the oppression of women. In short, a woman who truly laid the social agenda for feminists to come.   MRA

Gom, Leona 1946– Poet and novelist, winner of the Canadian Author's Association Award for Poetry and The Ethel Wilson Fiction Award. She was born the child of homesteaders in Fairview, Alberta, and began writing at the age of 10. Her poetry focuses very much upon her background, avoiding 'All this romantic bullshit / about growing up on farms', but capturing image and experience in sharp and arresting language, wondering occasionally whether 'this jealous farm will let me go'. The first edition of the award-winning volume *Land of the Peace* (1980) contains sepia photographs of farm and family. Her more recent works are novels, and, particularly *Housebroken* (1986), reflect her feminist concerns. She published her first mystery novel, *After-Image*, in 1997. She has a B.Ed. and MA from the University of Alberta where she was writer-in-residence in 1987-8, has edited the magazine *Event*, and has been a teacher at Douglas and Kwantlen Colleges in British Columbia.   FD

Gone With The Wind (1936) MARGARET MITCHELL's sweeping epic of the American Civil War was awarded the Pulitzer Prize in 1937. It follows the fortunes of Scarlett O'Hara, southern belle and capricious heartbreaker, from adolescence to adulthood. Scarlett is the epitome of her bastardized name: a 'scarlet' woman whose on/off affair with Rhett Butler was immortalized by Vivien Leigh and Clark Gable in the 1939 film. Her character is that of a woman 'constitutionally unable to endure any man being in love with any woman not herself', and she rides roughshod over all the other characters in the novel in her pursuit of love. Rhett Butler is the only man with the means to tame her and yet he is the only man to whom she will not submit. The reader is invited both to admire and to despise Scarlett. Her practicality in war-time is admirable, while her amoral narcissism makes her seem at times abominable. *Gone With The Wind* paved the way for later pulp heroines, notably those of Shirley Conran and JACKIE COLLINS in the 1980s, poor shadows of Scarlett.   JHB

Gonne, Maud 1866-1953 Political activist, speaker and writer immortalized in the poetry of W.B. Yeats whose unrequited love for her first blossomed in 1889. The daughter of a British military officer stationed for long periods in Ireland, Gonne's childhood was financially comfortable, and remarkably unrestrictive. Despite her English origins, Gonne's passionate devotion to Irish Independence earned her the sobriquet 'Ireland's Joan of Arc'. Throughout her adult life, Gonne employed her legendary beauty and dramatic style to proselytize for Irish nationalism in speeches given throughout Europe, the US and the UK. In addition to having her activities covered in nationalist journals such as the *United Irishman*, Gonne was a regular contributor to the nationalist press.

Gonne embraced activism as well as speaking and writing. During the 1890s she was involved in famine relief efforts for evicted tenant farmers in the Western Counties. She also organized protests against the Queen's Jubilee visit to Ireland and participated in opposition to the Boer War. In 1900, she founded a woman's nationalist group, the Daughters of Erin. Later in her life Gonne became an advocate for prisoners' rights and pressed for better conditions for Irish children.   EC

Gooch, Elizabeth Sarah (Villa-Real) 1756–1804? Memoirist, novelist and poet who, although an heiress (her father was a wealthy Portuguese Jew), later wrote *An Appeal to the Public, On the Conduct of Mrs Gooch* (1788) from the Fleet Prison for debtors. She expanded on her tumultuous life in *The Life of Mrs. Gooch* (1792) written, in sentimental mode, 'more from the heart than from the head'. Married to a man only interested in her fortune (she failed to elope with another), who then accused her of infidelity and shipped her off to France, she rehearsed her bitter experience in five novels (1794-1804). She had been disowned by her family and supported by a series of lovers; her real misfortune, she argued, was her isolation. She re-established herself, however, publishing her poems in 1793, an essay collection – *Wanderings of the Imagination* (1795) – and completing Thomas Bellamy's novel *The Beggar Boy* (1801).

LMT

Good Behaviour (1981) Sharply comic twelfth novel of MOLLY KEANE (previously publishing as 'M.J. Farrell'), appeared after a gap of twenty-five years following her husband's death. The novel relates the demise of an Anglo-Irish household through the eyes of the massive and self-deceiving daughter of the house, Aroon St Charles, who craves love and eats. Family traditions of *sang-froid* and formality (wreaking irreversible damage on Aroon and her brother) mask suppressed passions and inadmissible desires, gradually revealed through Aroon's triumphantly ingenuous and unreliable narrative. Acute comic characterization gives unforgettable portraits – from Aroon herself, her chilly and distant mother and philandering father to the betrayed governess Mrs Brock, the impoverished sisters Nod and Blink and the self-regarding Major 'Wobbly' Massingham – yet Aroon's emotional isolation, her humiliations and defeats make for a painful comedy. Beginning with her mother's death, the novel is framed as Aroon's attempt to 'understand' through reconstructing the past. Readers' sympathies are manipulated through a variety of deceptions and self-deceptions which contribute to a mortal though covert struggle for power and, ultimately, revenge.

SSc

Good Earth, The (1931) PEARL BUCK's second novel won the Pulitzer Prize and sold millions of copies worldwide. Set in China, where Buck was raised, *The Good Earth* was ground-breaking in its REALISTIC depiction of Chinese peasant life for a Western audience. Narrated in limited-third-person, the events of the entire novel are filtered through the circumscribed awareness of Wang Lung, an uneducated farmer who rises and falls with circumstance and prospers through a combination of hard work, discipline and sheer chance. The forces of NATURALISM dictate Wang Lung's life, from his marriage to the ugly slave O-lan during the waning days of the Manchu dynasty at the end of the 19th century to his imminent death after the revolution. O-lan is the moral centre of Wang Lung's family, persevering, labouring, sensible and self-sacrificing, but Wang Lung fails to appreciate or even to know her, understanding only the power and endurance of the land. Critiquing the patriarchal values that create neither peace nor happiness, Buck ends the novel with Wang Lung's sons foolishly plotting to sell the land that has given them their place in life and their identities.

SC

Good Man Is Hard to Find, A (1955) FLANNERY O'CONNOR's first published collection helped vault her into the highest rank of fiction writers of her generation. The ten stories display her signature blend of provincial Southern grotesques, bizarre and often apocalyptic violence, and mysterious possibilities of redemption. O'Connor's dark sense of humour is evident throughout, as when – in her words – 'a lady Ph.D. has her wooden leg stolen by a Bible salesman whom she has tried to seduce' (in 'Good Country People'), or in 'The Life You Save May Be Your Own', where 'a tramp ... marries an old woman's idiot daughter in order to acquire the old woman's automobile'. But these off-centre dramas are always in the service of an anagogical sensibility rooted in O'Connor's devout Catholicism. Accordingly, the title story of the collection, in which a vacationing family is waylaid and murdered by an escaped convict called the Misfit, becomes an exploration of the workings of unrecognized faith in the lives of the murderer and the self-centred grandmother who, as 'the Misfit' puts it, 'would of been a good woman ... if it had been someone there to shoot her every minute of her life'. Such irreducible moments are, for O'Connor, the essence of her subject: 'the action of grace in territory held largely by the devil'.

LC

Good Morning, Midnight (1939) Taking its title from an EMILY DICKINSON poem, JEAN RHYS's fourth novel is set among the seedy haunts of the London and Paris *demi-monde,* and is narrated by its once-glamorous heroine, Sasha, as she wanders the city in search of love, work or a cheap room in which to live – a far cry from WOOLF's salubrious room of one's own. After a series of miserable encounters with squalid hotels and lurking degenerates, she announces, 'I want one thing and one thing only – to be left alone.' Nevertheless, in her bid to forget an unhappy past, she cannot resist the dark enchantment of the streets at night.

Written largely in the present tense and in Rhys's distinctively laconic prose, *Good Morning, Midnight*, in following its heroine's bibulous decline into middle age, also captures the urgency and anxiety prevalent on the streets of Europe on the eve of World War II. The novel was successfully adapted in 1957 for BBC Radio's Third Programme and was re-issued in 1967.   JAH

Good Terrorist, The (1985) This novel engages with one of DORIS LESSING's recurring themes: social responsibility. It is a critique of mindless activism, its narrative centred on an anarchistic group of social misfits who come together through the quasi-political occupation of a derelict house. The central character is the emotionally retarded Alice Mellings, whose unacknowledged motivation is to (re)create the family which she feels she has been deprived of. Alice struggles to hold together the disparate group of residents and organize them into restoring the house in the name of a militant, muddled but heavily sloganized political agenda to which they all more or less adhere. Lessing's mode in this novel is REALIST and the characters are fully delineated, but the shortfall between their political rhetoric and sloganizing and their understanding of either themselves, the issues they are fighting for or the nature of the enemy is strongly ironized. Eventually the tension between the political and social incoherence of the group and the individuals' powerful personal agendas leads to breakdown as they perpetrate the culminating act of violence.   SAS

Good Wives (1869) The second half of LOUISA MAY ALCOTT's LITTLE WOMEN focuses on the courtship and marriage of three of the four March sisters, and the characters' struggles to reconcile independence and ambition with love and domesticity. (The title *Good Wives* is used in Britain; in America the novels generally appear together as *Little Women*.) The novel opens with the wedding of Meg, the oldest sister, but focuses on restless second sister Jo. Alcott (purposely) disappointed readers by refusing to marry Jo to her close friend Laurie; instead, Jo moves to New York to write and live independently. There, she meets Professor Bhaer, an older German intellectual who encourages her to drop her sensational writing style. Jo leaves New York, however, to nurse her dying sister Beth, the scene of whose death is at the novel's emotional heart. Jo's depression does not lift until Professor Bhaer proposes at the novel's close, prompting some recent critics to suspect Alcott of undermining her feminist principles. But Jo's difficulties make much of the novel surprisingly bleak for CHILDREN'S FICTION; through this dark mood, the author criticizes traditional women's roles.   KW

Goodhue, Sarah Whipple 1641–81 Puritan woman of Ipswich, Massachusetts. In 1681, Sarah Goodhue was pregnant with twins and foresaw her 'sudden death'. In anticipation, she composed 'A Valedictory and Monitory Writing', one of only four texts attributed to women published in 17th-century New England. The 'Writing' adheres to Puritan beliefs and practices and emphasizes a strictly patriarchal family order, as when Goodhue exhorts her children to 'carry well to your father, obey him, love him, follow his instructions and example, be ruled by him, take his advice, and have a care of grieving him'. The 'Writing' includes a short poem in rhyming couplets that addresses each of her eight children by name and instructs each in their individual duty. The last part of the 'Writing' is directed to her husband, Joseph: 'Be courageous, and on the living God bear up thy heart in so great a breach as this.' 'A Valedictory and Monitory Writing' thus serves to underwrite Puritan tenets of family order while simultaneously expressing the impassioned desires of a dying wife and mother.   LCa

Goodison, Lorna 1947– Born in Jamaica where she continues to live, Lorna Goodison is a Caribbean poet who has published a collection of short stories and is also an accomplished painter.

Women often provide the starting point for Goodison's engagement with the world and her poems are rich with the detail of women's daily struggle for survival in Jamaica. In poems, such as 'Nanny', she also provides celebratory images of strong women who have triumphed over and refused their historically determined 'subject slot':

I was sent, tell that to history.

When your sorrow obscures the skies
other women like me will rise.

In the title poem from *I am Becoming My Mother* (1986), the sense of a female lineage claimed in 'Nanny' is again articulated:

Yellow/brown woman
fingers smelling always of onions

My mother raises rare blooms
and waters them with tea
her birth waters sang like rivers
my mother is now me

This sense of merging oneself with other women (even the dreaded mother of ADRIENNE RICH's *matrophobia*) operates in many of the poems to produce a kind of womanist groundswell which Goodison uses to authorize and empower her own poetic identity. As well as harnessing the power of women's voices, Goodison increasingly draws upon a range of other linguistic registers which might best be described as 'spiritual' (biblical, rastafarian idiom, psalms, prayers). In the poems in her third collection, *Heartease* (1988), this combination of voices is employed seamlessly to produce a powerful sense of Goodison, the poet, as a spiritually healing figure and *deliverer of the word*, providing a much-needed and sobering lyricism in an economically deprived region:

No judgement I speak
function is not mine
I come only to apply words
to a sore and confused time.   DdeCN

Gooneratne, Jasmine 1935– Academic, poet and novelist, born in Sri Lanka (then Ceylon). Gooneratne graduated in 1959 from the University of Ceylon and received her Ph.D. in English Literature from Cambridge in 1962, and married the physician Dr Brendon Gooneratne in the same year. She taught English Literature at the University of Ceylon from 1959 until 1972 when she migrated to Australia with her family; she later became Professor of English Literature at Macquarie University, and founding director of the Post-colonial Literatures and Language Research Centre. In 1981 she was awarded Macquarie University's first (and, to date, only) earned degree of Doctor of Letters. In 1990 she was made an Officer of the Order of Australia (AO) for her services to literature and education. As a critic, she has published books on JANE AUSTEN (1970), Alexander Pope (1976) and RUTH PRAWER JHABVALA (1983) as well as numerous essays and articles on POST-COLONIAL studies and on Sri Lankan literature in English.

Among her collections of poetry are *Word Bird Motif* (1971) and *The Lizard's Cry and Other Poems* (1972). She has written a memoir, *Relative Merits: A Personal Memoir of the Bandaranaike Family of Sri Lanka* (1986), and her novels *A Change of Skies* (1991) and *The Pleasure of Conquest* (1995) were both shortlisted for the Commonwealth Writers Prize. *A Change of Skies* won the 1992 Marjorie Barnard Literary Award for Fiction. It tells the story of the intercultural encounter of a Sri Lankan couple who settle in Sydney and adopt prejudices about Australia. *The Pleasure of Conquest* is set in the tropical island state of Amnesia which in 1996 seems to have come to terms with its imperial past. The symbol of Amnesia is a hotel where old colonial charm mixes with the latest high-tech conveniences and in whose lobby a horde of modern travellers pass through.   SPo

Gordon, Caroline 1895–1981 American novelist, short-story writer, critic. Born in Kentucky, Gordon was tutored in the classics by her father and later attended his school as the only female student. She graduated from Bethany College in 1916, and began teaching in high school. Introduced by Robert Penn Warren to the poet Allen Tate in 1924, she married Tate that year, and gave birth to their daughter, Nancy, in 1925. Gordon worked as secretary to Ford Maddox Ford until she and Tate left for Paris in 1928. In 1931, with the help of Ford, she published her first novel, *Penhally*, which followed the southern Llewellyn family through several genera-

tions of struggle with agrarian values and social change. Her second novel, *Aleck Maury, Sportsman* (1934), follows its hero, loosely based on her own father, as he tries to negotiate family and society through his love of hunting and fishing. Some of Gordon's more successful short stories have Maury as their hero. After her 1947 conversion to Catholicism, her novels became increasingly interested in issues of grace, as seen in *The Strange Children* (1951) and *The Malefactors* (1957). With Tate, she wrote a book of criticism, *The House of Criticism* (1950), which helped her later to write *How to Read a Novel* (1957). She and Tate went through a difficult divorce in 1959, after which she spent much of her time teaching in creative writing programmes around the country, and writing works increasingly focused on archetypal characters. Although she wrote only two books of short stories, they show her greatest artistry and control. Generally considered part of the literary Southern Renaissance, Gordon was also influenced by New Criticism, and in turn influenced writers like FLANNERY O'CONNOR and Walker Percy.   SP

Gordon, David see TEY, JOSEPHINE

Gordon, Mary [Catherine] 1949– American novelist considered by some a latter-day MARY MCCARTHY. She brought to life her rigorous Catholic upbringing in Long Island in her first novels, *Final Payments* (1978) and *The Company of Women* (1981), both praised for their combination of moral seriousness and sharp humour, and the elegance of the prose – which she modestly attributed in part to ELIZABETH HARDWICK, her mentor at Barnard College. Though she shifted territory in the urbane *Men and Angels* (1985), 1989's *The Other Side* returned with a generational saga of Irish immigrants. Her fictions show a deep engagement with sacrifice and salvation, and with the virtues and failures of love. 'It is for shelter that we marry and make love', says a character in *The Company of Women*; that her 1987 collection of stories is called *Temporary Shelter* may reflect her own history of two marriages (she has one child). She teaches at Columbia and writes essays, collected in *Good Boys and Dead Girls*; *The Rest of Life* (1993) was a volume of three novellas. Her fascination with paternal authority figures may have led to her decision to probe the myth she had of her own father, a Lithuanian Jew who converted to Catholicism, who died when she was 7. The resultant memoir, *The Shadow Man* (1996), is a painful exploration of the truth behind a man who lied and harangued, wrote anti-Semitic literature for Catholic papers – and who loved her passionately, 'more', he told her, 'than God'.   SB

Gordon, Ruth 1896–1985 Born in Massachusetts, Ruth Gordon was an actress, playwright, screenwriter, memoirist and novelist. Enrolling in the American Academy of Dramatic Art in 1914, Gordon débuted on both stage and screen in 1915, and continued to be succesful in both media for over seventy years. In 1921, Gordon married actor Gregory Kelly, who died in 1927. In 1929 Gordon and producer/director Jed Harris had a son, Jones Harris. In 1940, Gordon's play *Over Twenty-One*, about women on the homefront during World War II, was produced; it was filmed in 1945.

In 1942 Gordon married screenwriter and director Garson Kanin, with whom she would remain and collaborate the rest of her life. Together they wrote, between 1948 and 1952, several succesful screenplays about the 'battle of the sexes,' including *Pat and Mike* and *The Desk Set*, the now-classic vehicles for Spencer Tracy and Katharine Hepburn, as well as *A Double Life* and *The Marrying Kind*. Gordon continued to write independently as well, including an autobiographical play, *Years Ago*, produced in 1947 and rewritten as the screenplay *The Actress* in 1953. After 1943 Gordon acted less, until her triumphant return in *Rosemary's Baby* in 1967 inaugurated a series of roles playing eccentric old women that culminated in the cult hit *Harold and Maude*, in which she played the much older object of a suicidal young man's affection. Gordon published three memoirs, *Myself Among Others* (1971), *My Side* (1976), and *An Open Book* (1980), and a novel, *Shady Lady*.

SC

Gordimer, Nadine 1923– Eminent South African novelist and short-story writer, recipient of the Nobel Prize for Literature, who has provided an impressive in-depth fictional record of the phases of South African life from the inception of Apartheid rule in 1948 to its demise in 1994. Her early short stories and novels such as *The Lying Days* (1953) and *A World of Strangers* (1958) recorded in detail the texture of white sensibility in Johannesburg, and the experience of growing up in a cocoon of white privilege and prejudice on the Witwatersrand where vitality was glimpsed in the teeming black life of the cities and mines but whites were dedicated to gentility. Her protagonists, usually female, are the objects of a double-edged irony as they try to find effective lives for themselves as women and citizens in a servant-owning, patriarchal world. There is a strand of heroism in her work as young people in particular begin to break out of the prison-house of Apartheid society and forge links across different racial groups, whether in love, friendship or political action. The daily lives of South Africans, political trials and private betrayals, make up her subject matter.

In Gordimer's fiction the progressive politicization of South African society is echoed in the progressive subtlety of narrative modes and voices, from the social REALISM of the BILDUNGSROMAN to the poetic meditation of THE CONSERVATIONIST (1974) in which

the symbolic structure of ancient ritual sacrifice is put to new use to record the historical loss of the land by the original inhabitants and the materialism of an urban land-owning class. In BURGER'S DAUGHTER (1979), a post-Soweto-1976 novel, the verities of white liberalism and its inheritance are interrogated in the consciousness of a political martyr's daughter as she seeks to find a new synthesis of private and political loyalties. *July's People* (1981) is an economic parable of class, race and gender, presented in a political thriller mode. *A Sport of Nature* (1987) is a triumphalist novel showing the shifts of political alignment between exiled and internal political activists, and the links sexuality made between them. It is also Gordimer's take on post-feminism, showing that it may be parallel to a post-Apartheid sensibility.

In *My Son's Story* (1990) the novel of the inter-racial affair is put to new uses – the wife's perspective is not revealed, yet the lives of the adulterous couple show how private betrayals can hollow out both family affections and political effectiveness. In NONE TO ACCOMPANY ME (1994), the mixed new allegiances and cultural styles that developed in the wake of liberation are given form in a kind of swift notation that is the mark of Gordimer's later style, with a lyricism that records how the slow growth of the resistance movement in South Africa receives its fullest validation in the fact of mortality itself. Gordimer's fiction has shown how a white writer can give full expression to the ethical and emotional quandaries of those living under Apartheid by using her central voice or sensibility as an oblique recording device which is itself the focus of part of the political satire. The increasingly subtle ways in which her narratives have recoiled upon themselves have provided the technical means to express the complex suffering of a nation in turmoil and fighting against itself toward the healing forms of love and democracy.

CC

Gore, Catherine (Catherine Grace Frances Moody) 1800–61 English novelist and essayist, internationally acknowledged doyenne of so-called 'Silver Fork' fiction, whose knowing portrayal of smart society was given greater REALISM by a wealth of sophisticated allusion to the consumer trends and fashionable enthusiasms dominating the period between the death of George III and the accession of QUEEN VICTORIA. Daughter of a Nottingham wine merchant, Catherine Moody initially attracted notice in London literary circles as 'Miss Nevinson', whose conversation MARY RUSSELL MITFORD called 'the most dazzling and brilliant that can be imagined'. After her marriage in 1823 to Lieutenant Charles Gore she began writing novels (possibly to pay his debts) scoring her first real success in 1830 with *Women As They Are*, a skilfully calculated attempt at beating modish male society novelists like Bulwer Lytton and Theodore Hook on their own ground.

For the next decade she produced an average of two novels per year in this profitable genre, culminating in *Cecil or The Adventures of a Coxcomb* (1841) whose wistful backward glance at the world of Regency dandies was effectively a signal to her readers that Silver Fork's most accomplished practitioner was shutting up shop. 'My ormulu railroad', as she called it, had proved immensely lucrative, but Gore's unflagging grasp of contemporary trends dictated a new direction, and the later 1840s witnessed her metamorphosis into a Victorian novelist grappling with themes such as working-class poverty. Mrs Gore's influence on contemporaries has been consistently undervalued. Snobbish reactionary as she now appears (her anti-feminist novel *Mrs Armytage* gained notoriety in a celebrated murder trial) the sheer buoyancy of her inventiveness remains impressive.   JK

Gore-Booth, Eva (Selina) 1870–1926 Irish poet, playwright and activist in the causes of women's trades unionism, pacifism and women's suffrage. She was brought up at Lissadell in County Sligo, where her family were substantial land owners, their income, crucially, supplemented by further estates in industrial Lancashire; this connection, ironically, later turned out to be crucial to her political and imaginative life. She, and her famous sister Constance (later Markievicz), inherited the Gore-Booth reputation as relatively good landlords who were unusually aware, for their class, of Irish Ireland. She was, from childhood, a person of great spirituality, tall, ascetic and gentle, yet creatively energetic and ambitious. The defining moment of her life was in 1896, in Italy, when she met Esther Roper, a suffrage organizer from Manchester. She left the spacious confinements of Lissadell to share a life of political and social activism with Roper, first in Manchester and later in London. Her poetry and plays remain, for the most part, however, in the landscape and mythologies of County Sligo. *Unseen Kings* (1904) was produced at the Abbey Theatre in 1912. Her other plays (*The Buried Life of Deirdre*, *The Triumph of Maeve*, *The Sorrowful Princess*) and much of her poetry are a celebration of female subjectivity against a background of neo-Platonist and pacifist philosophy. Some of her most moving poems were addressed to Constance Markievicz in prison. Sadly, her letters to her sister were destroyed. Her final work was a study of St John's Gospel (1923). She died in London of cancer.   CL

Gorilla, My Love (1972) TONI CADE BAMBARA's first collection of short stories focuses mainly on the lives and voices of black women. 'Raymond's Run', for example, is a story told by a black girl, Hazel Parker, whose responsibility is to look after her older brother, Raymond. She earns the trust of her family because she tries to be nobody else but herself. This self-confidence comes through in the distinctive voice of the narrator. A mature namesake, Miss Hazel, tells the lead story, 'My Man Bovanne' (about not turning a blind eye on the needs of the elderly), while an adolescent Hazel is the narrator in the title story about adult insensitivity. The three Hazel stories set the stage for the ten first-person and two third-person narratives that follow: stories that either delineate taking responsibility for self, family and neigbourhood, or dramatize the consequences of shirking responsibility. Above all, the reader is impressed by portraits of young and mature women who may be poor, but are decidedly unapologetic about their race and gender.   KO

Gothic The rise of the Gothic novel (or ROMANCE) – with its haunted houses, wild mountainous landscapes and nightmare plots – is conventionally dated from the publication of *The Castle of Otranto* by Horace Walpole in 1764. Among the various, often rivalrous, versions of what the emerging genre of the novel was to be, the Gothic was by common consent the most sublime, the most disreputable and the most addictive and was widely disseminated via the new circulating libraries of the period. Its thematic currency was fear mingled with desire, its plots were openly obsessed with the workings of power (the suffering heroine and the Satanic villain were among its stereotypes), and it was recognizably the sub-text, or underside, or 'Other' of the styles of narrative associated with REALISM and rationalism in 18th-century culture. Key early texts are *Vathek* (1786) by William Beckford, THE MYSTERIES OF UDOLPHO (1794) by ANN RADCLIFFE, *The Monk* (1796) by Matthew Gregory 'Monk' Lewis, FRANKENSTEIN (1818) by MARY SHELLEY and *Melmoth the Wanderer* (1820) by Charles Maturin. Poetry and verse drama by the second generation of British Romantics – Byron, Shelley and Keats – also displays strong Gothic elements. The genre was hailed by the Marquis de Sade in 1800 as 'the necessary fruit of the revolutionary tremors felt by the whole of Europe' in the period of the French Revolution; it was parodied in *Nightmare Abbey* (1818) by Thomas Love Peacock, and in NORTHANGER ABBEY (written c.1800, published 1818) by JANE AUSTEN, and deplored by Wordsworth as decadent. Gothic has connections with pornography, fantasy, FAIRY TALES, ghost stories and SCIENCE FICTION. It has had from the beginning a suggestive relationship with rebellion, and particularly with the laying bare and transgression of gender roles, expressed (for example) through the appropriation and rewriting of the work of the 'fathers' of English letters, Shakespeare and Milton. When Mary Shelley called *Frankenstein* 'my hideous progeny' she was calling attention to the paradoxes surrounding the notions of female authorship and originality – for which she had found an especially suitable medium in the Gothic.

After its first hey-day Gothic became a recognizable sub-genre in both English and American fiction: in the work of James Hogg, Robert Louis Stevenson, Bram Stoker (*Dracula*) and Wilkie Collins in Britain; and of Charles Brockden Brown and Edgar Allan Poe in the USA. Gothic elements also appeared in the work of many major novelists – CHARLOTTE BRONTË, EMILY BRONTË, Charles Dickens, Herman Melville, Nathaniel Hawthorne and Henry James (*The Turn of the Screw*, 1898). In the 20th century, Gothic motifs have been increasingly associated with gender issues, and also with debates over the role of fantasy. Binary oppositions (fantasy/realism; patriarchy/subversion) are tempting, and in part obviously appropriate. However, the work of CHRISTINA STEAD (*The Saltzburg Tales*, 1934) and ISAK DINESEN (*SEVEN GOTHIC TALES*, 1934), and of many recent novelists – FAY WELDON (*REMEMBER ME*, 1976; *THE LIFE AND LOVES OF A SHE-DEVIL*, 1983), JOYCE CAROL OATES (*MYSTERIES OF WINTERTHURN*, 1984), ANGELA CARTER (*THE PASSION OF NEW EVE*, 1977; *THE BLOODY CHAMBER*, 1979) – calls into question this oppositional reading of Gothic, which makes it into a haunted annexe of the novel proper. The constructedness of bodies (the Frankenstein motif), and the spaciousness of the realms of Otherness, have become central issues. Carter's essay in cultural history, *The Sadeian Woman* (1979), takes a revisionist look at the supposedly timeless role of terror, to argue that 'flesh comes to us out of history', a history we are always reshaping.   LS

Gotlieb, Phyllis Fay (Bloom) 1926– Canadian poet, novelist and short-story writer, most famous for her SCIENCE-FICTION. Her father was a theatre manager and she was born in Toronto, received a BA and MA at the University of Toronto, married a computer scientist and has had three children. She has published four volumes of poetry, of which the best-known is *Ordinary, Moving* (1969), as well as two volumes containing both poetry and short stories, *Collected Works* (1978) and *Son of the Morning* (1983). The poems teem with characters and a chorus of voices, as well as calling upon her Jewish heritage and experimenting with form. She began writing science fiction in 1964, publishing the novel *Sunburst*, and then in 1976 her more famous *O Master Caliban*. She has, since then, published six further volumes of science fiction, most recently *Flesh and Gold* (1998). She is seen as one of the founding mothers of humane speculative fiction, presenting real people confronting complex social and metaphysical problems in a vividly imagined universe

of which she writes with love and celebration. As she says in an early poem, 'I only praise God for the light / and I take my sight / as I see it.'   FD

Goudge, Elizabeth 1900–84 Prolific English author of gentle, ROMANTIC novels with a deep-felt evocation of place. Born in Wells, Somerset, she subsequently lived in Ely, Cambridgeshire, and Oxford (where her father was Regius Professor of Divinity). Her Christian upbringing provided both the strong sense of morality and the setting of much of her work, as in her 'Cathedral Trilogy'. Educated at Grassendale School in Southbourne, Hampshire, and Reading University School of Arts, she entertained early hopes of becoming a writer, but her parents insisted she teach handicrafts on her return from Reading to Oxford. Her submission to her parents' will mirrors the virtuous sacrifices made by many of her characters. But she persisted with her ambitions, finding success and a loyal following with the publication of her first novel, *Island Magic* (1932), set on her mother's native Guernsey. Her bestselling novel, *Green Dolphin Country* (1944), was filmed as *Green Dolphin Street* by MGM in 1947. She combines in her writing an old-world charm, a moral order based on traditional English values and an almost magical sensuality in her depiction of the enchantment of the countryside. She also wrote HISTORICAL FICTION, CHILDREN'S BOOKS (notably *The Little White Horse* (1946)) and lives of Christ and Francis of Assisi. *The Joy of Snow* (1974), her autobiography, was a work that held out the promise, like her fiction, to dwell on the 'happy memories'. Toward the end of her life, she lived in Henley-on-Thames, devoting herself to her cottage and its garden.   CS

Gould, Hannah Flagg 1789–1865 American poet. She was born in Lancaster, Massachusetts, and lived most of her life in Newburyport. Her mother died when Gould was a child, and for many years she devoted herself to caring for her father, a Revolutionary war veteran. She began writing poetry in her thirties, first entertaining Newburyport citizens with mock-epitaphs of local celebrities, then contributing pieces to magazines and annuals. Her first book, *Poems* (1832), which included abolitionist verse, was published by her friends without her knowledge. It sold well, was reprinted in 1833 and 1835 and expanded in 1836. Ten other volumes followed between 1844 and 1870. In addition to children's poetry, she wrote religious, historical and commemorative poems. SARAH JOSEPHA HALE regarded Gould as an exemplary practitioner of female poetics, emphasizing humility, selflessness and uplifting emotions. Yet Gould's wit indicates that she viewed her role as a female cultural producer with irony, as in 'The Child's Address to the Kentucky Mummy':

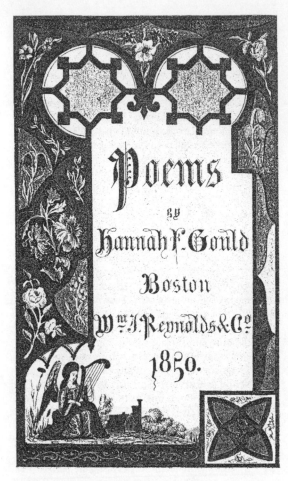

Hannah Gould: title-page of *Poems*, 1850.

And now, Mistress Mummy, since thus you've been
  found
By the world, that has long done without you,
... Be pleased to speak out as we gather around
And let us hear something about you.   JSG

Gour, Neelum Saran 1955– Indian English fiction writer whose humane faith-affirmative vision encompasses the absurdities as well as tragedies of life. Born to a Bengali mother and a Hindiphone father who was 'Hindu in persuasion and Islamic in culture' and a classical musician, philosopher and mathematician, and educated in a Catholic school run by German nuns, Gour received an eclectic heritage. Her doctoral thesis was on Raja Rao and she teaches at Allahabad University. Gour's fiction touches on her multiple heritages. She has an ear for Indian languages and tries to capture their rhythms in English. She records the residual spark of humane feeling which survives even the ravages of wars and riots. Her narratives work out the pattern in a situation in order to seek a larger significance.

Her published works include two collections of short stories – *Grey Pigeon and Other Stories* (1993) and *Winter Companions* (1997) – and a novel, *Speaking of '62* (1995).   GJVP

Govier, Katherine 1948– Canadian fiction writer, born in Edmonton, Alberta, who attended the University of Alberta (BA 1970) and York University (MA 1972). She has lived in Toronto, since 1971. Most of Govier's novels depict women finding their voices, exploring relationships and examining their past in order to make sense of their present. She has written that her central interest as a writer is character, how it is created and what events flow from the human personality. She acknowledges the importance of setting in her works, each of which is rooted in a 'strongly recognizable place'. Her collection of short stories, *Fables of Brunswick Avenue* (1985), is set in a district of Toronto; her novel, *Between Men* (1987), takes place in the Calgary Oil Boom. Her other novels are *Random Descent* (1979), *Going Through the Motions* (1982), *Hearts of Flame* (1991), and *Angel Walk* (1996), which is set in Britain before and during World War II. She has published two other collections of short stories, *Before and After* (1989) and *The Immaculate Conception Photography Gallery* (1994), and one TRAVEL anthology, *Without a Guide* (1994). In 1991 Govier was a founder of the Writers-in-Electronic-Residence Program which teaches creative writing and links professional writers with students in thirty high schools across Canada by telecommunications and modem. She has served as Canadian President of PEN. She has written for CBC radio and television.   GHN

Gowdy, Barbara 1950– Canadian novelist and editor born in Windsor, Ontario, who moved to Toronto in 1954. Influenced by the work of William Burroughs and Cormac McCarthy, Gowdy's fiction offers an insightful commentary on the themes of transgression, social violence and the fallout of the nuclear family. Far from being titillating or disgusting, however, Gowdy emphasizes the humanity of her characters and shocks the reader into questioning the bedrock of sexuality.

It was after travelling in Ireland and Wales that Gowdy published her first book *Through the Green Valley* (1988), a HISTORICAL NOVEL which is set in County Tyrone during the 18th century, and charts the escalation of violence within a close-knit community. In *Falling Angels* (1988), Gowdy offers a surreal portrait of three sisters growing up in the Toronto suburbs of the 1960s. Like *Falling Angels*, Gowdy's short-story collection *We So Seldom Look on Love* (1992) raises questions about gender and sexual identity in the late 20th century from the viewpoint of various human 'monstrosities'. The title story, 'We So Seldom Look on Love', was made into the award-winning film, *Kissed* (dir. Lynne Stopkewich), in 1996, a shadowy, yet tender look at female necrophilia. In *MISTER SANDMAN* (1995), Gowdy interrogates the family values of suburban Toronto, through the eyes of a mute child with bisexual parents and a sexually voracious sister. The concern with family structures is further explored in *The White Bone* (1998), a novel that explores the behaviour of the animal kingdom through the eyes of a female elephant.   SCM

Grace, Patricia 1937– New Zealand short-story writer and novelist whose first book, *Waiariki* (1975), was the first collection of stories by a Maori woman writer. She began writing while bringing up her children and teaching, and at a time when there was new receptivity in New Zealand to Maori culture. *Waiariki* was followed by *Mutuwhenua: The Moon Sleeps* (1980), a novel about exile within one's own country as Maori moved from their traditional homelands to the cities. *POTIKI* (1986), which describes how a Maori community retained their land and traditions against the onslaught of developers, was the winner of the fiction section of the New Zealand Book Awards, 1987. In *Cousins* (1993), as in her other fiction, the cultural and religious ethos of Maori society is portrayed as an integral part of, rather than an addition to, Maori life. Her writing has not typically dealt with the violence and despair that characterizes some aspects of Maori life in New Zealand, nevertheless her fourth collection of short stories, *The Sky People and Other Stories* (1994), marks a shift toward a darker, more disturbing environment.   RB

Graham (Erichsen-Brown), Gwethalyn 1913–65 Canadian writer who espoused human rights and racial tolerance. Born into an elite, liberal Toronto family – her mother was a suffragist, her father a lawyer who championed civil liberties – Graham suffered a lonely adolescence at private schools. The finishing school she attended in Lausanne, however, provided material for her first novel, *Swiss Sonata* (1938), set in 1935 and concerned with the growth of racial and national intolerance in Europe.

In 1931 Graham attended Smith College, leaving after a year for a short-lived marriage to a wealthy Canadian. In 1934 she settled in Montreal with her son Anthony. Following the publication of *Swiss Sonata*, which received the Governor General's Award, Graham became an advocate for refugees from Hitler. Her frustrated relationship with a Jewish lawyer in Toronto, strongly opposed by her father, inspired the plot of *EARTH AND HIGH HEAVEN* (1944), winning her a

second Governor General's Award along with international honours and recognition.

After a second failed marriage in the USA, Graham returned to journalism and television writing in Montreal. Her last book, co-authored with Solange Chaput-Rolland, was *Dear Enemies: A Dialogue on French and English Canada* (1963).   EB

Graham, Jorie 1951– An American poet who grew up in Italy and was educated at the Sorbonne and the Universities of New York, Columbia and Iowa. Graham's work reflects this cross-cultural experience, and an ontological preoccupation. She is a poet uniquely concerned with the various discourses of history, philosophy, language and science: 'This is the story of a beautiful lie' she begins in 'Reading Plato' (*Erosion*). Her first book, *Hybrids of Plants and Other Ghosts* (1980) won the Great Lakes Colleges Associate Award as the best first book of poems published that year. *Erosion* (1983) follows stylistically, but the spiritual search that marks her earlier work transmogrifies to a more cerebral study of language in her later books: *The End of Beauty* (1987), *Region of Unlikeness* (1991), *Materialism* (1995). In these the form becomes more disrupted and diction slightly more complex: 'No fate – cries the precipitate of something on the verge of – ' ('In the Hotel', *Materialism*). Also published is *The Dream of the Unified Field: Selected Poems*. In *The Errancy* (1997) Graham returns to a more lyrical form. Her other awards include the Morton Dauwen Zabel Award from the American Academy and Institute of Arts and Letters, as well as fellowships from the Macarthur Foundation, the Bunting Institute, and the Guggenheim Memorial foundation. Graham teaches in the Writers' Workshop at the University of Iowa.   ACH

Grand, Sarah (Frances Elizabeth McFall, née Clarke) 1854–1943 Active SUFFRAGE campaigner and member of the Women Writers' Suffrage League, was a notable contributor to the literature of the NEW WOMAN in the 1890s, in a famous exchange with 'OUIDA' (*North American Review*, 1894) and in novels portraying the New Woman as race-mother, orator, political activist, writer, hysteric and victim of male degeneracy. Grand scandalized critics with her frank portrayal of the horrors of the sexual double standard, but gained a wide readership for long novels of ideas such as *The Heavenly Twins* (1893), with its cross-dressing heroine, and its detailed treatment of syphilitic illness.

Marriage at 16 to a 39-year-old army surgeon allowed Grand to travel in China, Japan and the Far East, and exposed her to the male tyranny she later represented in her fiction. Grand launched her career with the anonymously published *Ideala* (1888), whose free-thinking heroine reads Thomas Huxley and lives

Sarah Grand: illustration from an article, 'The New Woman and the Old', *Lady's Realm* 8, 1898, in which she writes, 'The New Woman can be hard on men, but it is because she believes in him and loves him. She recognises his infinite possibilities. She sees the God in him, and means to banish the brute.'

with a man to whom she is not married. Grand's reputation rests mainly on *The Heavenly Twins* and THE BETH BOOK (1897), a long, often lyrical, sometimes dreamlike, narrative of its heroine's formation as an artist (as she comes to consciousness of the world and words), and then as a New Woman orator (following a horrific marriage to a debauched, tyrannical doctor who is also superintendent of a Lock Hospital for prostitutes and a vivisectionist, two causes which united various late 19th-century feminists).   LP

Grant, Elizabeth (later Smith) 1797–1885 Scottish autobiographer whose DIARIES, written in 1845–67 and published in 1898 as *Memoirs of a Highland Lady* (edited by Lady Strachey), give intensely evocative accounts of her childhood and travels. The family entourage – hypochondriac mother, lawyer father, relatives, nursemaids and governesses – travelled annually between London and the Highlands, the children thriving on the rich cultural mix. Unashamed of her 'rebellious spirit', Grant describes a disappointingly taciturn Walter Scott, and the wildly disorderly young Shelley. She responded to her father's bankruptcy by writing essays for *Fraser's* and *The Inspector* (1826–7) before they escaped their creditors by sailing to India where he became a judge. Grant's descriptions of her inner life (the conflict of renouncing her first love because of a family feud) and her outer (aboard ship, extravagant socializing, camping, and marriage in India) are equally compelling. Leaving India regretfully due to her husband's ill health, Grant set about improving conditions on their Irish estate, starting the first non-denominational school, and again writing for money with *Irish Journals* (1840–50).   LMT

Grass Is Singing, The (1950) Though the epigraph to DORIS LESSING's first novel comes from T.S. Eliot's

The Waste Land, the authoritative and ironic tone of Lessing's narration has little in common with the disjunctions of MODERNISM. The novel begins at the end, with the corpse of a farmer's wife, Mary Turner, who has been killed by her African servant, Moses. This removes any suspense and allows the reader to focus on the psychological portrait of a colonial marriage. The settlers' repressed fear of and fascination with Africans are expressed by Mary when she whips Moses; his 'amused contempt' and magnificent build provoke her but she eventually becomes dependent on him, and mad. The narrative remains external to all the black characters: 'what thoughts of regret, or pity . . . were compounded with the satisfaction of his completed revenge, it is impossible to say'. The emphasis is on the programmed hypocrisy and sterility of white settler society.   ASm

Gray [née Bailey], Dulcie 1920– British actress, playwright, novelist and theatre-writer. A nervous breakdown in the early fifties rekindled her interest in writing, partly as an antidote to insomnia when on tour. Kenneth Tynan's savaging of her first play daunted her into choosing a male *nom-de-plume* for her next, which, reworked as a musical, enjoyed brief success. She won critical acclaim for her crime novels which are characterized by attention to detail and an impressive quality of research, which extended to other areas of her work. Her book on British butterflies won the *TES* Senior Information Award in 1978. Her first 'straight' novel, *The Glanville Women* (1982), the story of a theatrical family spanning three generations, which addresses the problem of women's independence, was highly praised by REBECCA WEST, among others. She married actor Michael Denison in 1939, and the two have enjoyed a long partnership on and off the stage.   JLB

Gray, Oriel 1920– Australian dramatist. Oriel Gray wrote and acted for the Left-wing Sydney New Theatre from 1937 until her departure from the Communist Party in 1949. She was strongly influenced by American social realist playwrights. Appointed the first paid Australian playwright-in-residence (1942), Gray won numerous drama awards but failed to gain professional success in the conservative cultural and political climate of the 1950s and 1960s.

Her first full-length play, *Lawson* (1943), dramatizes several stories by the famous Australian writer, Henry Lawson; *Sky Without Birds* (1950) depicts prejudice against a Jewish immigrant in a small outback town; *Burst of Summer* (1959) explores the dilemma of an Aboriginal film star's plight after her brief success as the lead female actor of the film, *Jedda*. In 1955, Gray's *The Torrents* shared the Playwright's Advisory Board prize with Ray Lawler's *The Summer of the Seventeenth*

Doll. The Torrents, a comedy of manners set in the 1890s in an imaginary Australian mining town, focusing on conservation issues and the NEW WOMAN, was distinctly unfashionable in the fifties, gaining one amateur production. Unpublished until 1988, it was first staged professionally in 1996. It was adapted to television in the sixties and produced as a musical, *A Little Bit of Petticoat* in 1984.

Her work includes ten unpublished stage plays, political revues, radio drama, published children's plays, contributions to *Bellbird* (a popular television series), *Exit Left: Memoirs of a Scarlet Woman*, about her communist years, and a novel.   ILB

Gray, Patience 1917?– In the 1950s Gray worked as a researcher at the Royal College of Art and in the design studio of F.H.K. Henrion where she met Primrose Boyd. Three years after food rationing ended, Gray and Boyd brought out a modest paperback based on French *cuisine bourgeoise*, with beguiling illustrations by David Gentleman. *Plats du Jour* (1957) sold 50,000 copies in the first six months, beating ELIZABETH DAVID's books in popularity.

In 1958 Gray was made editor of the *Observer*'s first Women's Page; this lasted three years, then she left London to live with Flemish sculptor Norman Mommens as he travelled around the marble quarries of the Mediterranean. From this extraordinary life, a nomadic existence of over thirty years spent in remote impoverished regions, came her great book: *Honey from a Weed, Fasting and Feasting in Tuscany, Catalonia, the Cyclades and Apulia* (1986), where she describes their frugal life, eating local food cooked in traditional ways, as learnt from the peasants of the region. In the formidable nine-page bibliography, Gray writes: 'The weed from which I have drawn the honey is the traditional knowledge of Mediterranean people; the books cited can be regarded as the distillation of this knowledge.'   AB

Green, Dorothy 1915–91 Australian poet and woman of letters, Dorothy Green was a poet, essayist and critic who worked as a journalist, school teacher and university lecturer, and was married to H.M. Green, best known for his encyclopaedic *A History of Australian Literature* (1961) which she revised extensively and republished in 1985. Her poetry was published under the name 'Dorothy Auchterlonie' and appeared in three collections, *Kaleidoscope* (1940), *The Dolphin* (1967) and *Something to Someone* (1983). Her most significant critical work was a study of HENRY HANDEL RICHARDSON, *Ulysses Bound* (1973), revised and retitled *Henry Handel Richardson and her Fiction* (1986), which set the parameters for all subsequent research on this important Australian writer. Her essays in particular won her great respect for their cultural breadth and

Patience Gray: drawing by Soun Vannithone, 1998.

uncompromising moral probity, tackling questions of political responsibility and commitment amongst both readers and writers, insisting on the need for strong resistance to things such as nuclear armament. She showed an unflinching readiness to stand firm and speak out on issues of importance, unintimidated by her formal lack of power and unpopularity with those who supported government policies. Hers was an important voice in constituting and defining the role of the intellectual in Australian cultural life.   HTh

Green, Evelyn Everett 1856–1932 Primarily known today for her morally unexceptionable DOMESTIC fiction for girls, this prolific and versatile English novelist was educated in London at Bedford College and at the Royal Academy of Music. She later trained as a nurse but was obliged to leave the profession due to ill health. She then turned to writing, her nursing experience providing material for some of her novels. Much of her later life was spent abroad and she died in Madeira.

Though often characterized by an intrusive religious element, Evelyn Everett-Green's work is seldom dull. Her stories for CHILDREN, such as *The Secret of the Old House* (1890) and *Sweepie* (1904), contain credible child-characters of both sexes who participate in some exciting though plausible adventures. Nor do her novels for adult readers lack charm or topicality. *Eustace Marchmont* (1895) is set at the time of the 1832 Reform Bill but the major protagonists discuss the broader issue of universal suffrage; *The House of Silence* (1910) combines ROMANCE and SENSATION with a protracted debate about the ethics of authorship. Typical of her domestic and didactic tales for girls are *Vera's Trust* (1888) and *The Sisters of Silver Sands* (1904).

Evelyn Everett-Green also published under the name of 'Cecil Adair': one of her pseudonymous novels, *Gabriel's Garden* (1913), sold over 150,000 copies in her lifetime.   EMH

Greenaway, Kate [Catherine] 1846–1901 Prolific English illustrator and CHILDREN's writer whose depictions of innocent children in pastoral settings became extremely popular in the 1870s and 1880s. Greenaway's father was an engraver for the *Illustrated London News* who encouraged her interest in art from an early age. She studied at the National Art Training School at South Kensington (where she won several prizes), among other art schools. She began illustrating books and greeting cards in the 1860s, and published her own story, *Under the Window*, in 1878. John Ruskin admired her work and offered advice in a voluminous correspondence. Her art was wildly popular as well as critically acclaimed, and her style was widely copied in various forms, from wallpaper to designs for children's clothing. Her prominence as a children's artist and author was sustained by, among many other volumes, *Kate Greenaway's Birthday Book for Children* (1880), *Marigold Garden* (1885) and *Apple Pie* (1886), but she also illustrated books such as Ruskin's *Fors Clavigera* (1883–4) and produced yearly 'almanacks'. Greenaway also wrote Pre-Raphaelite-influenced sonnets, and turned rather bitterly to oil portraiture and other media in the 1890s after her vogue had passed, but she remains best known for her delicately outlined, prettily coloured drawings.   KW

Greenlaw, Lavinia 1962– English poet who writes detailed, distinctive observations of contemporary life and practices. Greenlaw was born in London, and brought up in London and Essex in a family of scientists and doctors. She has worked in publishing and arts administration and has held posts as poet-in-residence at the Science Museum, London (1995), and with a leading London Law firm (1997). Her initial publications, *The Cost of Getting Lost in Space* (1991) and *Love from a Foreign City* (1992), were followed by her first full-length collection, *Night Photograph* (1993). Using science as enabling strategy as well as subject, her poems explore the human dimension to the history of science and address questions of the status and ethics of knowledge. Although not explicitly political or feminist, her poetry, like that of ELIZABETH BISHOP, interrogates assumptions of the 'natural', challenging the authority of patriarchal constructions of reality. Her 1997 collection, *A World Where News Travelled Slowly*, expands such themes with poems exploring ideas of belonging, of comprehension and of varied attempts at communication. Her work maintains a detached, sometimes mildly ironic, style and a subtle mediation of tenderness.   AG

Greenwell, Dora 1821–82 English poet whose work was largely based on her strong religious and social conscience. She was the only daughter in a County Durham squire's large family, and was well educated at home. The family moved about after the sale of the estate for debts, but Greenwell eventually settled in Durham with her mother, where she did most of her writing. *Poems* (1848) marked her début, and was followed by *Stories that Might be True with Other Poems* (1850) and six more volumes, including two books of religious verse, *Carmina Crucis* (1869) and *Camera Obscura* (1876). Her poetry reveals thematic interests similar to those of other women poets of the time, especially CHRISTINA ROSSETTI (a friend): the poem 'Christina' depicts a fallen woman reformed by the title character's piety and charity. Other associates included JEAN INGELOW, with whom she collaborated on poetry for children, and the activist JOSEPHINE BUTLER. Greenwell's devotional prose, developed in such works as *The Patience of Hope* (1860) and *Two Friends* (1862), and her biographies of Lacordaire (1867) and John Woolman, a Quaker (1871), contributed to her high reputation in her day. She also published a number of polemical articles, primarily in the *North British Review*, on such issues as slavery, mental illness, religious education and the position of single women, in which she argued against injustice and intolerance. Toward the end of her life, Greenwell's health declined and she became less active in social causes, though she supported both anti-vivisectionism and women's suffrage.   KW

Greenwood, Grace (Sara Jane Clarke Lippincott) 1823–1904 Prolific contributor to the major 19th-century American magazines – among them, *Atlantic Monthly*, *Harper's New Monthly*, *Hearth and Home*, *New York Independent*, *New York Times*, *New York Tribune*, *Saturday Evening Post* – Greenwood also authored over twenty books. Greenwood's stories, novellas, and essays frequently worked within the sentimental culture of 19th-century America, her pseudonym invoking the language of flowers. However, she also wrote in differing modes. Her best-selling book, *Greenwood Leaves* (1850) includes not only sentimental sketches, but also TRAVEL narratives, literary criticism, art criticism, and realistic essays on courtship and marriage. *A Forest Tragedy, and Other Tales* (1856) offers HISTORICAL fiction set during the Revolutionary War that takes up the cause of the Oneida Indians, while *Records of Five Years* (1867) ranges from biographical, domestic idylls to Abolitionist treatises and portraits of exceptional Union soldiers and heroic northern women who supported the Union cause. Abraham Lincoln spoke of Lippincott as 'Grace Greenwood the patriot' because she devoted much time to visiting with and reading to Union soldiers. Greenwood was born in Pompey, New

York. In 1853, she married Leander K. Lippincott, with whom she edited the *Little Pilgrim*, and spent her married life in Rochester, New York.   DZB

Greer, Germaine 1939– Australian feminist author and English professor who wrote the bestselling *The Female Eunuch* and other polemical works on women's issues, as well as being a key figure in the revival of work by neglected women writers. After doing her Bachelor's and Master's degrees in her native land of Australia, Greer came to Cambridge for her Ph.D. in 1964, taking up a lectureship at Warwick University three years later. *The Female Eunuch* (1969) brought her to instant celebrity, with its crusading arguments for womens' freedom from oppressive stereotypes, its sexually liberated attitude and raunchy sense of humour, and its exhortation for women to 'not only equal men in the race for employment, but outstrip them'.

In the seventies, Greer turned to journalism, penning provocative editorials for the underground press, co-presenting a television series and writing for an improbable variety of magazines (including the medical journal *General Practitioner*, the satirical paper *Private Eye*, the counter-cultural magazine *Oz*, and respectable organs of the mainstream press such as the *Spectator* and the national papers). She had become Britain's most well-known feminist pundit. Her colourful journalism was offset by serious scholarship. Between 1980 and 1983 Greer was founder and director of the Centre for the Study of Women's Literature in Tulsa, Oklahoma. She also edited the uncollected verse of APHRA BEHN, put the 17th-century poet KATHERINE PHILIPS into print and edited an anthology of 17th-century women's verse. Her book, *The Obstacle Race*, restored a number of women painters to the mainstream of art history, but a later work, *Slipshod Sibyls* (1992), berated many women writers for succumbing to male flattery and failing to forge distinctive voices. In 1989, Greer was made Special Lecturer at Newnham College, Cambridge. In spite of her liberalism and feminism, Greer's respect for traditional families and ways of life was evident from the start of her career. *The Female Eunuch* invoked her experience of a traditional Italian peasant community, while her next book, *Sex and Destiny* (1984), defended the integrity of family structures in India and Africa and attacked the West's propagation of fertility control in third-world countries. *The Change* was an affirmation of the menopause as a natural cycle in womens' lives, and criticized society's attitude toward the subject. *Daddy, We Hardly Knew You* (1989) was another new departure, charting Greer's quest to uncover her father's shadowy past.   KE

Gregory [née Persse], (Isabella) Augusta, Lady 1852–1932 Irish playwright, theatre manager, translator, folklorist and major figure in the Irish cultural renaissance. She was born into the Anglo-Irish Ascendancy at Roxborough, County Galway, where she was a lonely child much interested in the stories told her by her nurse, Mary Sheridan. Her family was known for its proselytizing zeal on behalf of Protestantism, an imputation which haunted her even after she began publicly to espouse the republican cause. In 1880 she married Sir William Gregory, thirty-five years her senior. His estate at Coole Park was close to her family home, but he spent much of his life abroad, and was a former MP and Governor of Ceylon. She travelled widely with her husband, and after the birth of her only child, Robert, lived in Egypt where she supported the Egyptian nationalist movement and the cause of one of its leaders, Arabi Bey. He was the subject of her first pamphlet (1882). She fell in love with Wilfred Scawen Blunt, to whom she wrote a sequence of passionate sonnets. After the death of Sir William in 1892 she lived at Coole and became interested in the Irish language, and the folklore of the area, called Kiltartan. *Visions and Beliefs in the West of Ireland* was published in 1920.

In 1897 she, W. B. Yeats and Edward Martyn had conceived of a national theatre, which eventually became the Abbey Theatre. She made Coole Park a meeting place for the movers of the Irish cultural renaissance: she was a crucial agent in the recognition of Sean O'Casey's genius as a playwright, and her support of Yeats was constant during his long spells as house guest at Coole throughout his most productive years. She wrote dialogue for some of his early plays, such as *Cathleen Ni Houlihan* (1902). Her prolific and varied works for the theatre include skilfully wrought comedies (*Spreading the News*, 1904; *Hyacinth Halvey*, 1906; *The Workhouse Ward* and *The Rising of the Moon*, 1907); translations of Molière, Sudermann and Goldoni; 'folk history' plays (*The White Cockade*, 1905; *Dervorgilla*, 1907; *Kincora*, 1904 and 1909; *Grania*, 1911, which, controversially, was never performed in her lifetime) and the exquisite tragic threnody, *The Gaol Gate* (1906). Her range as a playwright sprang from what was, to her as she described it, 'the fascination of things difficult'. She translated and adapted the great Irish sagas and sought out and recorded the stories and cures of Biddy Early and others. Her son Robert, a talented stage designer, was killed in Italy in World War I. In 1927 she sold Coole Park to the government but continued to live there as a tenant and died there. The house was demolished in 1941. (See also her JOURNALS *1916–1930*.)   CL

Grenville, Kate 1950– Australian writer born in Sydney, Kate Grenville has published short stories, novels and handbooks on writing, her work everywhere informed by feminism and often exhibiting an exuberant, iconoclastic style that is both comic and satiric. Her collection of short stories, *Bearded Ladies* (1984), focuses on a variety of women and the unexpected, bizarre outcomes to their experiences. The novel *Dreamhouse* (1986) is a powerful portrait of a disintegrating marriage, narrated by the wife Louise Dufrey, in a style that borrows from the GOTHIC and is informed by psychoanalytic theory. JOAN MAKES HISTORY, published in Australia's bi-centennial year, is a satiric, feminist re-writing of Australia's 200 years of history from the point of view of a series of ordinary women called Joan. Grenville substitutes, for the grandiose masculine view of history as a series of public events, a celebration of the private, domestic and ultimately maternal experience of women whose presence was ignored in official accounts of significant historical events such as Australia's Federation. LILIAN'S STORY (1985), with its fat, rebellious heroine, Lilian, loosely based on a real-life Sydney eccentric, Bea Miles, suggests that non-conformity can be a powerful feminist strategy, one that Australia itself could well employ to break out of its colonial constraints. POST-COLONIAL and feminist theory reveals how radical is Grenville's symbolization of Australia as a 'mad' woman, freeing her and the nation she represents, from masculine desire and colonial respectability. Ten years later, Grenville published *Dark Places,* a version of Lilian's story told from the point of view of her father, Albion, who raped his daughter and had her incarcerated in an insane asylum, yet is revealed to be pitiably weak and defensive, a victim of his own psycho-sexual inadequacies. Kate Grenville's work is significant for its incorporation of feminist knowledge into powerful fiction that challenges the dominance of the masculine in Australian literary culture.   HTh

Greville [née Macartney], Frances 1726?–89

English poet and celebrated wit. Daughter of a wealthy Irish landowner, she was raised fashionably in London, admired for her beauty and considered formidable for her keen eye and sharp tongue. She probably inspired the forceful Mrs Selwyn in the novel *EVELINA* (1778) by her goddaughter FANNY BURNEY.

Eloping with the dashing but ruinously extravagant and inconstant Fulke Greville, Frances embarked on a life of financial insecurity and marital unrest. As Greville ravenously acquired art, refined Wilbury House, and gambled away his fortune, the couple became elegant nomads, staying with friends and connections at home and abroad. Greville, who squandered lucrative posts and diplomatic assignments, published in 1756 the well-received *Maxims, Characters, and Reflections*. More coherent than his other writings, the work was believed by Horace Walpole and others to have benefited from Frances's hand, but Greville jealously prohibited her taking credit or pursuing

writing. Despite this pressure, Frances's 'Prayer for [or Ode to] Indifference', a plea against SENSIBILITY, circulated among her friends and eventually reached print:

> Then take this treach'rous sense of mine,
> Which dooms me still to Smart,
> Which pleasure can to pain refine,
> To pain new pangs impart.

Probably spurred by the death of her son Algernon and her marital tribulations, the ode was immensely popular, frequently reprinted, and inspired several responses defending sensibility. Although eventually separated from Greville, Frances wrote in 1783, 'My pipe is broke, my muse is flown.' Descendants possess the manuscript of an unfinished novel and many poems.   JHP

Grey [Dudley], Jane, Lady [Jane I] 1537–54

Political sacrifice, and celebrated paragon of erudition and Protestant piety. She related that, whereas her parents taunted her 'with pinches, nips and bobs', time spent with her tutor was pure delight. She mastered numerous languages and corresponded with the theologian Heinrich Bullinger.

Her royal claim as cousin of Edward VI made her a pawn in a plot by the Lord Protector, the Duke of Northumberland. He married her to his son, Guilford, despite Jane's resistance, and proclaimed her Queen when Edward died in 1553. However, after nine days MARY TUDOR successfully took the throne and sent Jane and Guilford to the Tower, where they were eventually beheaded.

Jane wrote to her sister Katherine, 'trust not that the tenderousness of your age shall lengthen your life'; but urged, 'as touching my death, rejoice as I do, good sister, that I shall be delivered of this corruption, and put on incorruption'. John Foxe's *Acts and Monuments* records further writings and speeches.   HH

Grier, Syndey C. [Hilda Caroline Gregg] 1868–

1933 British popular novelist. The eldest daughter of Sara Caroline Frances (French) and the Revd John Robert Gregg, she was educated at home and at a private school and received an honorary degree from London University. After working as a teacher she started writing in 1881. Between 1894, when she published her first novel, *In Furthest Ind*, dealing with the adventures of a 17th-century Englishman in India, and 1925, the year of her last, *A Brother of Girls* (1925), she published roughly a novel a year, mostly about the exploits of English people in exotic foreign settings, with titles such as *His Excellency's English Governess* (1896), *The Prince of the Captivity* (1902), *A Royal Marriage* (1914) and *The Princess's Tragedy* (1918). Several of her novels were serialized in *Blackwood's* magazine.

Particularly popular was her sequence of ROMANTIC novels about an English aristocrat, Viscount Usk, who occupies the throne of the imaginary Balkan kingdom of Thracia, and his brother, Count Mortimer, who becomes involved in Balkan and Middle Eastern politics: *An Uncrowned King* (1896), *A Crowned Queen* (1898), *The Kings of the East* (1900) and *The Prince of the Captivity* (1902). Grier spent the last decades of her life in Eastbourne, where she had nursed her mother until her death in 1913.   VG

Grierson [née Crawley], Constantia 1705?–32

Irish classicist and poet. Born in Graiguenamanagh, County Kilkenny, to poor and illiterate parents, Constantia received some education from the local clergyman, and taught herself Hebrew, Greek, Latin and French. In about 1721 she moved to Dublin, where she studied midwifery under Dr Van Lewen, and met Van Lewen's daughter Laetitia (later Pilkington), to whom she addressed one of her most-anthologized poems. She became a leading member of Swift's circle of friends, and was particularly close to the poet MARY BARBER, who may have tutored her in history, theology and philosophy.

In 1724 Constantia married George Grierson, a printer, and abandoned midwifery in order to assist in his business. She edited a number of classical texts, including editions of Virgil, Terence and Tacitus, which were published by Grierson's press and which were widely praised for their scholarship.

Constantia wrote verses in Latin and Greek as well as in English, but few of these appeared during her lifetime. One poem, 'The art of printing', was distributed as a broadsheet in 1731, but she destroyed much of her work before her death, probably of tuberculosis, in 1732. Some of her poems were included in Mary Barber's *Poems* (1734), in the first volume of LETITIA PILKINGTON's *Memoirs* (1748) and in *Poems by Eminent Ladies* (1755), but others remain unpublished.   RR

Griffith, Elizabeth 1727–93 Playwright, actress and

novelist, born in Wales and brought up in Dublin, where she acted in Thomas Sheridan's theatre company from 1749. She secretly married Richard Griffith after a long correspondence, which she later transformed into *A Series of Genuine Letters between Henry and Frances* (1757). A witty blend of contemporary morality and plain speaking, Griffith's *Letters* gained widespread success, spurring her to move to London and write for a living. Her plays (predominantly comedies) were popular – *The Platonic Wife* (1765), adapted from Marmontal; *The Double Mistake* (1766); *A Wife in the Right* (1772); *The Times* (1779), adapted from Goldoni; and a revision of APHRA BEHN's OROONOKO (1800). She dedicated *The Morals of Shakespeare Illustrated* (1775) to David Garrick, her long-term employer, and cites

ELIZABETH MONTAGU's work as inspirational. 'Shakespeare is not only my Poet, but my Philosopher also', declared Griffith, extending Johnson's concern with Shakespeare's 'purely ethic' morals to highlight his 'general economy of life . . . domestic ties, offices and obligations', and showing particular interest in his heroines. She edited *A Collection of Novels* (1777) which included work by AUBIN, HEYWOOD and Behn. Her last works were spirited EPISTOLARY NOVELS, *The History of Lady Barton* (1771) and *The Story of Juliana Harvey* (1776). The return of a wealthy son from India removed the need to write.   ESE

Griffitts, Hannah 1727–1817 American writer, moral-

ist and wit, who wrote under the pseudonym, 'Fidelia'. Daughter of Philadelphia mayor Thomas Griffitts, and Mary Lloyd Norris, she was connected by birth and social ties to many of the most prominent Quaker families in the Philadelphia area. She never married, and asserted her happiness in the single life in letters and poetry. Her vocation was writing; she became the memorialist of the Quaker community in Philadelphia. Her efforts were encouraged by the poet SUSANNA WRIGHT, with whom she exchanged letters and poetry. The commonplace book of her cousin, MILCAH MARTHA MOORE, contains two exchanges of poetry between Wright and Griffitts. The Revolutionary War brought out the satiric side to Griffitts's pen. In 'the female Patriots', she celebrates 'the Daughters of Liberty in America', who point out the proper duty to men by using economic boycott to make their political point against British taxation policies. Her ridicule fell on Americans and British alike, though she singled out for special castigation those who led others astray by their rhetoric, like Thomas Paine, or by their behaviour, like the American women who danced at the masked ball given by the British in Philadelphia, 'the Meschiaza'. Though she lived long after the Revolutionary War, writing became increasingly difficult for her as rheumatism and then blindness disabled her. Griffitts chose not to publish her work, but instead circulated her poetry in manuscript among family and friends. Her niece, DEBORAH NORRIS LOGAN, wrote an account of her death.   CLB

Grigson [née McIntyre], Jane 1920–90 English

cookery writer (see COOKERY BOOKS). Grigson was born and brought up in Westmorland and was educated at Casterton School and Newnham College, Cambridge. After leaving university, she worked in art galleries, for publishers, and as a translator. She won the John Florio Prize in 1966 for a translation of Beccaria. In 1963, she married the poet and critic Geoffrey Grigson, who was fifteen years older than her. They collaborated on several children's books and she inspired some of Grigson's late love poetry. From 1968, she wrote cookery articles for the *Observer* and published a number of books celebrating good ingredients and traditional methods, including *Charcuterie and French Pork Cookery* (1969), *Good Things* (1971), *Fish Cookery* (1973), *The Mushroom Feast* (1975), a *Vegetable Book* (1978) and a *Fruit Book* (1982).

Although she has been compared to ELIZABETH DAVID, whom she admired, Grigson is much less dictatorial. She conveys warmth and enthusiasm, even when citing an obscure source or historical precedent – from John Evelyn, say, or HANNAH GLASSE – or when bemoaning some travesty of a good English dish such as Finan Haddock or parsnips. Her warmth and good-heartedness come through in everything she writes; it is characteristic of her personality that she is sometimes too lavish with butter, cream and sugar; when she says that a recipe is rich (as in Sussex Pond Pudding or mincemeat), she should be taken seriously. Many people have written about her great hospitality, both in Broad Town, Wiltshire, and in the Grigsons' French house in Trôo. She was kind and generous with her time and bravely continued to go about, meet people and work hard, even when undergoing the most unpleasant treatment for the cancer which caused her death. One of her great pleasures late in life was that her daughter, Sophie, was also a cookery writer, though in a different tradition.   LD

Grimké, Charlotte L. Forten 1837–1914 American
DIARIST, abolitionist, educator and poet. She was born in Philadelphia, third generation of a prominent African-American family who were active abolitionists, and, like other members of her family (e.g. Sarah Louisa Forten), she dedicated herself to proving the intellectual competence of African-Americans. Her mother died in 1840 and Forten grew up under the care of her grandfather James Forten and her uncle Robert Purvis, president of the American Anti-Slavery Society. She was educated by private tutors and at a private school in Salem, Massachusetts, where she joined the Female Antislavery Society. Upon graduating in 1856, she was appointed the first African-American teacher in Epes Grammar School of Salem. In 1854, she began writing the journals which became her best-known writing and established her as a forerunner of African-American women's literature. Covering the years 1854–64 and 1885–92, the five journals mingle accounts of a genteel woman's daily life with records of her bouts with illness and depression; ethnographic assays; observations about slavery, racism and social justice; and glimpses of famous people she knew (William Lloyd Garrison, William Wells Brown, LYDIA MARIA CHILD, John Greenleaf Whittier, Ralph Waldo Emerson). During the Civil War, she taught runaway slaves under the auspices of the Philadelphia Port Royal Relief Association, then, in

1862, moved to Port Royal, South Carolina, where she taught former slaves for two years, experiences she wrote about for *Atlantic Monthly* in 1864. In 1878, after moving to Washington, D.C., she married Revd Francis James Grimké, uncle of ANGELINA WELD Grimké. Their only daughter died in infancy.   JSG

Grimké, Sarah (Moore) 1792–1873 American femi-
nist and abolitionist. Born into the plantation aristocracy of Charleston, South Carolina, she received little formal education but secretly taught herself law in her father's library. Long frustrated by the constraints of southern womanhood, she fled at 28 to Philadelphia, where she converted to Quakerism. In the 1830s her younger and more outspoken sister ANGELINA Grimké (later WELD) drew Sarah into the public world of radical abolitionism, where they became the first women agents of the American Anti-Slavery Society. Sarah brought to this work a powerful intellect and a theological fervour, combining both in her anti-slavery pamphlet, *Epistle to the Clergy of the Southern States* (1836). But it was in her defiant articulation of women's 'inalienable' rights in *Letters on the Equality of the Sexes and the Condition of Women* (1837–8) that she found her most influential voice: 'I ask no favors for my sex . . . All I ask of our brethren is, that they will take their feet from off our necks and permit us to stand upright on that ground which God designed us to occupy.' Although her public career effectively ceased after Angelina's marriage in 1838, Sarah remained politically active until her death at 81.   WG

Grossmann, Edith Searle 1863–1931 New Zealand
novelist, involved with the suffragist movement in the 1890s. Born in Victoria, Australia, she came to New Zealand aged 15, graduated from Canterbury University College and taught before marrying in 1890. *In Revolt* (1893) and its sequel, *Hermione: A Knight of the Holy Ghost* (1907), tell of a young woman who marries a wealthy, alcoholic and dissolute squatter. She flees him and her children and becomes involved with the Women's Rightists in the States. Returning to Melbourne and setting up a women's commune, when the courts refuse a divorce she commits suicide rather than return to her husband. *Hermione* incorporates the ideas of the Woman Movement of the turn of the century, blending sexual purity and radical feminism and arguing that sexuality is the instrument of man's domination over woman and her body. Her last novel, *The Heart of the Bush* (1910), the story of a romance between a cultured Englishwoman and a rugged New Zealand farmer, is the only one of her four novels to be republished and a disconcerting sequel to her earlier feminism. She wrote nothing apart from some occasional journalism after 1910, and lived apart from her husband until her death in 1931.   AM

Group, The (1963) The sixth and most well-known novel by MARY MCCARTHY tells the story of eight women who graduate from the American university Vassar in 1933, charting the development of their lives and careers over a period of eight years. In the course of the novel, McCarthy explores the various intellectual, professional, social, sexual and emotional avenues open to them in the 1930s and early 1940s, highlighting in particular the double standards in operation between men and women. Her characters include the group's leader, Lakey, who travels to Europe and discovers her lesbianism; Kay, who embarks on a disastrous marriage, suffers a nervous breakdown and whose death, probably suicidal, closes the novel; Priss, married to a paediatrician and subject to all the latest child-rearing theories; and Polly, a nurse whose affair with a man under psychoanalysis allows McCarthy full rein to satirize that discipline. The novel's unflinching treatment of women's concerns, including sexual enjoyment, contraception and breastfeeding, provoked some discussion on publication, but contributed to its enduring popularity and significance. A film version appeared in 1966.   AC

Guest [Schreiber], Charlotte, Lady 1812–95 English linguist and DIARIST. An Earl's daughter, she learned quickly how to combine required social activity with private intellectual satisfactions. Largely self-taught, she mastered five languages in her teens and added Welsh after marrying John Guest, ironmaster, of Dowlais. Her translation of medieval Welsh legends, *The Mabinogion* (1838–49), done in intervals of childbirth, political campaigns, ironworks business and establishing local schools, was, Matthew Arnold pointed out, fundamental to the 19th-century Celtic revival. It was a source for Tennyson's *Idylls of the King*. 'Whatever I undertake', she wrote, 'I must reach an eminence in. I cannot endure anything in a second grade.' With her second husband, Charles Schreiber, she turned to collecting, and wrote scholarly annotated catalogues on *English China* (1885), *Fans and Fan Leaves* (1888–90) and *Playing Cards* (1892–5). Her journals (1822–91), intelligent and candid, are valuable for events of her time, but even more for what they reveal about the feelings and doubts which underlay Victorian self-discipline and drive.   MSM

Guiney, Louise Imogen 1861–1920 American poet and critic. She was born in Roxbury, Massachusetts, to Irish Catholic parents. Her father, a lawyer, politician and brigadier-general in the Civil War, died when she was 16. After graduating from a convent school in Providence, Rhode Island, she wrote to support herself and her mother, but although her writing was well received by key literary figures, it did not provide a living. She became postmistress of Auburndale,

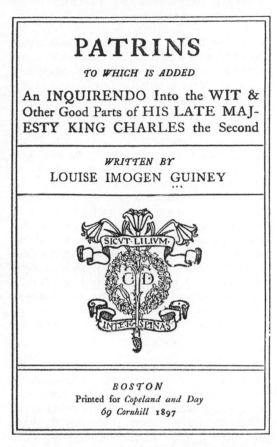

Louise Imogen Guiney: title-page of *Patrins*, 1897.

Massachusetts, in 1894 but resigned under sexist and anti-Irish-Catholic pressure. From 1899 to 1901 she worked in the Boston Public Library. She moved to Oxford, England, in 1901. In addition to poetry, she wrote scholarship and criticism, championing the Aesthetes (who advocated art's autonomy) and the 17th-century metaphysical poets. Her poetry collections include *Songs at the Start* (1884), *The White Sail* (1887), *A Roadside Harp* (1893) and *Happy Ending* (1909). She also published essays, short fiction, biographies and an anthology of Roman Catholic poetry, *Recusant Poets* (1938). Her skilful control of cadence and tone, together with her thematic concerns, brought her poetry close to Modernism, as in 'Monochrome':

> Our brooding sail is like the ghost
> Of one that served mankind,
>
> Who sad in space, as we upon
> This visionary sea,
> Finds Labour and Allegiance done,
> And Self begin to be.

MODERNIST poets LOUISE BOGAN and AMY LOWELL named Guiney as an influence.   JSG

Gunn [née Taylor], Jeannie 1870–1961 Australian novelist. Gunn was born and educated in Melbourne. Following employment as a teacher she accompanied her husband, Aeneas, to the Northern Territory where he had been appointed as manager to Elsey River Station. Her journey from Darwin to Elsey (250 miles south-east) and life at the station formed the basis of her semi-autobiographical novel WE OF THE NEVER-NEVER (1908). Despite rejection by six publishers within three months it became one of Australia's most popular books, selling over half a million copies. A film of the novel was released in 1982. *The Black Princess: A True Tale of Life in the Never-Never Land* (1905) was written for children and relates the affectionate relationship between 'Missus' (Gunn) and Bett-Bett, an Aboriginal girl. Gunn's charming portraits of outback characters and the remoteness of their lives were aimed mainly at a growing urban readership, presenting a faithful account of station life at the threshold of modern history. She was awarded an OBE for her services to literature and her work with injured soldiers during her later life.   MRE

Gunnars, Kristjana 1948– Canadian poet and fiction writer of Icelandic descent. Born in Reykjavik to a Danish mother and Icelandic father, Gunnars is equally fluent in English, Danish and Icelandic. She lived in the United States, graduating from the University of Oregon before moving to Canada, where she attended the Universities of Regina and Manitoba. Since 1989 she has taught creative writing at the University of Alberta.

During the 1980s she travelled back and forth between Iceland and Canada, publishing poetry about Iceland and Icelandic settlers in the prairie provinces – *Settlement Poems I and II*, *One-eyed Moon Maps*, *Wake-pick Poems* and *The Night Workers of Ragnarok*. She also produced a collection of short stories, *The Axe's Edge*. In 1989 she published a brilliant experimental work, *The Prowler*, designated for publishing purposes as a novel but, in fact, defying categorization by genre. It is an unpaginated work, consisting of 167 chapters or paragraphs, that combines autobiography and literary criticism. Gunnars followed that with other genre-blurring prose works, *Zero Hour*, *The Substance of Forgetting* and *The Rose Garden*. Besides her teaching and steady output of prose and poetry, she edits and translates the work of other Icelandic writers.   JG

Gunning [née Minifie], Susanna 1740?–1800 British novelist of sentiment and satire, herself the central character in a famed society scandal. In 1763, with her sister Margaret, she began a subscription list for her first novel, *The Histories of Lady Frances S – and Lady Caroline S –*. It achieved immediate popularity, and the twelve other novels she published between 1764 and 1800 were similarly successful. These included *Family Pictures* (1764), *Coombe Wood* (1783) and *Love at First Sight* (1797). Gunning's narratives follow the familiar sentimental theme of 'virtue in distress' – her heroines are orphans or social outcasts, innocent and friendless in a cruel world, pursued by villains through unlikely scenarios which are melodramatic and occasionally GOTHIC in style. Her writing was notorious for its particular brand of hyperbole, which Lady Harcourt caustically termed 'minific.'

In 1768 she married Captain John Gunning, brother of the celebrated beauties, though marriage did not bring all the social rewards she expected. Then, in 1791, she was involved in the series of misunderstandings, accusations and adulteries which Horace Walpole famously dubbed 'the Gunningiad' – a scandal which was followed with the avidity of a soap opera in the popular press and fashionable society. Gunning became estranged from her husband after allegations of his affair with a tailor's wife proved correct. She wrote a defence of her daughter, ELIZABETH PLUNKETT, whose reputation had been tarnished by the accusation that she had forged love letters in order to heighten her chances of an advantageous marriage. (*A Letter from Mrs Gunning, Addressed to his Grace, the Duke of Argyll*, 1791). In the *Letter*, Elizabeth appears, like the persecuted females of her mother's novels, as 'a suffering angel', an 'innocent darling' – a wronged sentimental heroine. Gunning's later writing was more barbed and satirical, and she increasingly and unashamedly drew on the events of her own life in her fictional plots.   KD

Gupta, Sunetra 1965– Indian novelist and scientist who was born in Calcutta and grew up in India and in several African countries. She took her degree in Biology at Princeton University and her Ph.D. at Imperial College, London before going on to do research on infectious diseases at Merton College, Oxford. She combines her career as scientist with that of a prolific writer.

Her first novel, *Memories of Rain* (1992, winner of the 1996 Sahitya Akademi Award) is a POST-COLONIAL reinterpretation of the Greek Medea. It is the story of a marriage between the Indian Moni and her English husband who is having a long-running affair with another woman. Finally Moni decides to return to Calcutta with her daughter, thus giving a different twist to the Greek tragedy. *The Glassblower's Breath* (1993) spans across one day through the streets of London. It is the narration of the sexual and personal self-discovery of an Indian woman, addressed by multiple narrators as 'you', and of the consequent macabre annihilation of her social circle. *Moonlight into Marzipan* (1995) is a story of scientific discovery. The Indian Promothesh steps into world celebrity when his wife's ear stud accidentally falls into an experimental solution, which gives vital catalysis. He is near the ultimate scientific miracle of turning light into food, a result that would rescue the subcontinent from poverty and famine. The discovery will bring the couple to London where their marriage, poised on a delicate balance, will disintegrate. Promothesh betrays his wife Esha with the Russian author Alexandra, who is meant to write his autobiography, and subsequently Esha commits suicide. The novel, which should have been about third-world male ingenuity, reinscribing the western capitalistic world, takes the form of an autobiography never written and ends up as a story of failure and damnation. Gupta's novels are not always easily accessible due to her virtuoso prose and intricate plot-lines. Her major accomplishment is to be found in her use of a highly visual and poetic style which transforms language into memory. SPo

Guy, Rosa 1925– Born in Trinidad, Guy grew up in New York City's Harlem, the setting for her many books for young adults. Beginning with *The Friends* (1973) – the first of a trilogy that includes *Ruby* (1976) and *Edith Jackson* (1976) – Guy's work offers richly complex examinations of young black men and women coming of age against the powerful forces of racism and cultural and class polarities of American society. *Ruby* drew controversy because of its focus on a love affair between two young women, although the novel centres on the protagonists' problematic family relationships and differing cultural backgrounds and the adolescent homosexuality is portrayed as a natural step toward maturity.

Between 1979 and 1987, Guy worked on a DETECTIVE SERIES featuring a streetwise Harlem teenager, Imanu Jones: *The Disappearance* (1979) functions as a symbolic study of the impact of poverty and prejudice on youth in the American ghettos; *New Guys Around the Block* (1982) and *And I Heard a Bird Sing* (1987) explore the theme of 'guilt by race' and offer commentary on victims, victimizers and social responsibility. *My Love, My Love, or the Peasant Girl* (1985), Guy's allegorical retelling of Andersen's 'The Little Mermaid', meshes the many strands of her West Indian heritage – oral tradition, calypso, Voodou, Catholicism and the luxuriant, sometimes violent, natural environment. It served as inspiration for the 1990 musical *Once Upon This Island*. Guy has also written three novels for adults: the autobiographical *Birds at My Window* (1966), written after the deaths of her husband and her friend Malcolm X; *A Measure of Time* (1983), an evocative chronicle of the disappearance of the 'village within' quality of Harlem; and *The Sun, the Sea, a Touch of the Wind* (1995), in which an American artist living in Haiti examines her troubled past. LP-G

H

H. D. (Hilda Doolittle) 1886–1961 American MODERNIST poet and novelist who writes in the spirit of the Greek poets and focuses on psychological, sexual and mystical themes. H.D. was the daughter of middle-class Moravians, a Protestant sect of intensely active missionaries. An adolescent sexual encounter with Ezra Pound, who recited poetry to her in a Pennsylvania forest, led to a brief engagement. In 1911 she travelled to Europe with her second love, Frances Gregg, and in 1913 she married Richard Aldington. Her first poems were published under the title 'H.D. imagiste' and her work was pivotal for the four annual Imagist Anthologies (1913–16).

During World War I, H.D.'s world fell apart: her marriage to Aldington collapsed, and she nearly died whilst giving birth to her daughter, Perdita, in 1919. In her novels *Palimpsest* (1926), *Asphodel* (1992) and *Bid Me To Live* (1960) and in her analysis with Freud in 1932 and 1933 she attempted to represent and understand these traumatic experiences. From 1919 her relationship with the millionairess, BRYHER, gave her the financial stability to pursue a range of artistic projects: she published *Hymen* (1921) and *Heliodora* (1924); she acted with Paul Robeson in the film *Borderline* (1930); she wrote pertinent articles for the film journal *Close Up* (1927–30); and she created experimental novellas such as *Kora and Ka* (1934). During World War II, H.D. wrote her most impressive poem, the epic *Trilogy* (1944–6), in which she adopts a mythical framework to structure the chaos and destruction fostered by war. In *Helen in Egypt* (1961), she uses the epic form again to re-write the myth of Helen of Troy. In 1960 H.D. received the recognition she felt she had been denied during her early life when she was the first woman to receive the American Academy of Art and Letters medal. HER, an autobiographical fiction written in 1927, was published in 1981. RP

Hackenfeller's Ape (1953) BRIGID BROPHY's first novel unites two of her lifelong passions, Mozart and animal rights, in a reworking of *The Marriage of Figaro* which explores 'homo sapiens' unremitting exploitation' of other creatures. *Hackenfeller's Ape* is the tale of caged monkeys, Percy and Edwina, and Darrelhyde, a gentle, slightly comic biologist keen to observe their remarkable mating ritual. Unfortunately, whilst Edwina lusts (wryly represented by a constant hunger for apples), Percy is prevented from lovemaking by his sense of captivity. Perceiving the ape's predicament (with recourse to *Figaro*), Darrelhyde feels a compassion which inspires his struggle against authorities who plan to fire the anthropoid monkey into space for military research. Each of the secondary characters to whom the Professor voices concern expresses a different opinion: his sister ranks human rights above animal welfare; a colleague defines evolution as 'man's exploitation of the weak'. Through open theoretical debate, Brophy raises all the objections against rights for animals and counters them with an endearing narrative which implores humans to act with the 'imagination, rationality and moral choice' which they uniquely possess. TY

Hacker, Marilyn 1942– American poet born in New York and educated at the Bronx High School of Science. Hacker's early work tended to the rhapsodic and surreal, in entire contrast to her mature work from *Presentation Piece* (1975) onwards, which was as deliberately mundane in much of its subject matter as it was formally highly structured in its use of traditional metres and stanzas. Sequences like *Love, Death and the Changing of Seasons* (1986), a series of sonnets punctuated by such other forms as villanelles, approached the personal journal in their detailing of lesbian love-affairs and her relationship with her daughter. There was a vein of inventive wit in her formalism – rhymes and assonances constantly exploited incongruity and her metrical regularity was often achieved by skin-of-her-teeth use of enjambement. *The Hangglider's Daughter* (1990) collected new work and a selection from earlier volumes. With her gay African-American ex-husband, the science-fiction writer and critic Samuel R. Delany, she edited the SCIENCE-FICTION anthology *Quark* for four volumes between 1970 and 1971. She edited the *Kenyon Review*. RK

Hale, Katherine [Amelia Beers Garvin, née Warnock] 1878–1956 Canadian poet, author and journalist. Born in Galt, Ontario, to a father of Scottish descent and a mother from the southern United States, she married John Garvin, a Toronto businessman who was also a respected critic, publisher and anthologist.

Before her marriage she was literary editor of the *Toronto Mail* and *Empire*. Between 1914 and 1950 she published six small volumes of poetry. In 1923 she published a selection of the work of ISABELLA VALANCY CRAWFORD, the 19th-century poet whose collected poems John Garvin had published in 1905. She also published a series of books on historic houses and Canadian cities – *Legends of the St Lawrence* (1928), *Historic Houses of Canada* (1952), *Canadian Cities of Romance* (1933), *This is Ontario* (1937) and *Toronto: Romance of a Great City*. (1956). She was an early supporter of MAZO DE LA ROCHE who admired her beauty and her social assets and saw her as a muse-figure. Hale remained one of De la Roche's few close women friends and confidantes.

JG

Hale, Sarah Josepha (Buell) 1788–1879 American editor, novelist, poet and essayist. She was born in Newport, New Hampshire, daughter of a tavern keeper, and educated by her mother and brother. She ran a school from 1806 to 1813, then married a lawyer, David Hale, who gave her the equivalent of a college education. Widowed with five children in 1822, she turned to writing for income. The success of her novel *Northwood* (1827) led to her becoming editor of *Ladies' Magazine* of Boston in 1828. In 1837, this journal merged into *Godey's Lady's Book* of Philadelphia. Hale's editorship (1837–77) made her one of the most influential American women of the mid 19th century, an arbiter of taste and a publicist for progressive causes such as women's education, property rights and professions. Yet she opposed women's suffrage and, after 1854, avoided the divisive topic of slavery. She edited or authored some fifty books, including *Poems for Our Children* (1830; 'Mary had a Little Lamb' appeared first in this Sunday-school book); *Three Hours; or, The Vigil of Love: And Other Poems* (1848); and *Woman's Record* (1854), an encyclopaedia of distinguished women throughout history, with the largest part devoted to living American women writers.

JSG

Halfbreed (1973) An autobiography by Métis writer, MARIA CAMPBELL, recounts the discrimination and racism to which Métis have been and, in some instances, still are subjected. Documenting community life, this book reveals an extended and mutually supportive Métis family – including the protagonist's Cree great-grandmother, Cheechum – which experiences the harsh realities of a life of few joys, limited material possessions and, often, utter poverty. Continued impoverishment, particularly after the death of the protagonist's mother and separation from Cheechum, encounters with an inhuman Canadian judicial system, school-sanctioned prejudice, racist attitudes and humiliation lead her to self-hatred, the vicious circle of alcohol, drugs and prostitution, and

Sarah Josepha Hale.

she succumbs to the image which an ignorant society has imposed upon native women. It is great-grandmother Cheechum, the spiritual centre of Campbell's family, who provides her with the mental fortitude required to overcome the degradation of her life, eventually leading to her work as a political activist. Despite the seeming despair in this book, humour and irony are often employed to overcome the dangers of an all-encompassing self-pity.

SM

Halkett [née Murray], Anne, Lady 1623–99 Autobiographer and religious writer. Her Scottish parents were tutors to the children of James I. She learned French, music, needlework and religion, and also medicine and surgery.

After an early romance with Thomas Howard she became involved with Colonel Joseph Bampfield. In 1648 he effected the escape from England of the future James II, whom Halkett disguised as a woman. Having learned that Bampfield had a living wife, she practised medicine in Scotland, and in 1656 married Sir James Halkett of Dunfermline. While pregnant she wrote *The Mother's Will to her Unborn Child*, now lost. As a widow she lived by teaching, then received a pension from James II.

Halkett left twenty manuscript volumes containing extensive religious meditations, some 'Instructions for Youth', and an autobiography (*c.*1677). Like other contemporary memoirs by Margaret Cavendish

Anna Maria Hall.

output was devoted to depictions of Irish life, often focusing on the peasantry (of English descent only – she abhorred the 'vulgar' Irish) – such as *The Groves of Blarney* (1883), *Lights and Shadows of Irish Life* (1838), *Stories of the Irish Peasantry* (1840) and *The White Boy* (1845) – she is frequently compared to MARIA EDGEWORTH, although she cites MARY RUSSELL MITFORD's *Our Village* as the inspiration for her own pastoral sketches. Her philanthropic activities included the founding of several hospitals and nursing homes and agitation on behalf of temperance.

MO'C

Hall, Radclyffe [Marguerite Antonia Radclyffe-Hall]

1880–1943 English novelist and poet, passionate advocate for tolerance of homosexuality, author of THE WELL OF LONELINESS (1928), the first novel in English to treat lesbianism sympathetically. A child of the privileged classes, she was born in Bournemouth, the youngest daughter of an American widow, Mary Jane Sanger (née Diehl), and an English socialite and playboy, Radclyffe Radclyffe-Hall. Her parents divorced shortly after Hall was born, but her mother soon remarried, settling with Hall and new husband Alberto Visetti, a singing teacher, in London. Educated sporadically by governesses and in day schools, Hall entered King's College London in 1898, but never completed her degree. In the same year, Hall received from her absent father a considerable inheritance, which she used to travel to Germany and to the American South, ultimately settling in London. There 'John', as she was always known, embarked on a series of love-affairs with women, including Mabel Veronica Batten ('Ladye'), who encouraged Hall's conversion to Catholicism, and with whom Hall lived until Ladye's death in 1916. In 1915, Hall met Una Troubridge, her lover and companion for the next thirty years.

In 1906, 'Marguerite Radclyffe-Hall' published the first of five poetry collections, *'Twixt Earth and Sky*. Early novels, including *The Unlit Lamp* (1924) and *Adam's Breed* (1926), received critical acclaim for their exploration of sexuality, spirituality and isolation – themes revisited in THE WELL OF LONELINESS, the most famous of Hall's seven novels. Often read as autobiography, the work's protagonist is Stephen Gordon, a novelist whose passionate love affair with *ingénue* Mary Llewelyn seems to promise relief from the pervasive alienation Stephen feels as an artist and a lesbian. Repeated rejection and morbid humiliation convince Stephen to 'sacrifice' Mary to a heterosexual marriage, rather than ask her to live as a lesbian in a homophobic society. For its bold portrayal of lesbian love, the work was found obscene – in spite of the objections of writers in the US and Britain – and banned in Britain until 1949. Despite its abject vision of homosexuality and its pathologizing vocabulary of

(DUCHESS OF NEWCASTLE) and LUCY HUTCHINSON this combines engaging personal narrative with records of public events. Halkett seeks to interpret all events, including romantic vicissitudes, in terms of a divine plan.

HH

Hall [née Fielding], Anna Maria

1800–81 Prolific, popular Irish author whose wide-ranging publications include novels, plays, short stories and children's literature, and who was a dedicated philanthropist. Born in Dublin, she was raised by her maternal grandparents in County Wexford. Though she settled in London permanently at the age of 15, she was often to return imaginatively to the picturesque landscape and populace that impressed her as a child. In 1824 she married the journalist and editor Samuel Carter Hall, whose periodical, the *Spirit and Manners of the Age*, published Anna Maria's first sketch, 'Uncle Ben'. Other vignettes of Irish life followed and were collected in her first published volume, *Sketches of Irish Character* (1829).

This initial success prompted a writing career that lasted for fifty years. Her next volumes, two readers for young children (*The Juvenile Forget-Me-Not*, 1829; and *The Chronicles of a Schoolroom*, 1830) and a HISTORICAL NOVEL *The Buccaneer*, 1832, attest to the author's versatility and energy. Because much of her literary 'inversion', it has remained the most widely read lesbian novel of all time, repeating its simple but trenchant demand, 'give us also the right to our own existence'.   JGr

Halligan, Marion 1940– Australian novelist and short-story writer, born in Newcastle, New South Wales, winner of a number of literary awards, and chairperson of the Literature Board of the Australia Council in 1992; Marion Halligan's work is characterized by studies of inward experience, particularly that of women. Her collections of short stories, *The Living Hothouse* (1988), *The Hanged Man in the Garden* (1989) and *The Worry Box* (1993), move between Australia, France and New Zealand, but also examine life in the academic and political capital of Canberra, the city in which she lives. Her novel *The Spider Cup* (1990), examines the breakdown of a marriage from the point of view of the abandoned wife, who flees from Australia to France, finally discovering a new sense of self. *Lovers' Knots* (1992) is constructed as a series of linked stories and traces the fortunes of a Newcastle family over the span of the 20th century. TRAVEL and FOOD are always important aspects of her writing, and her book *Cockles of the Heart* (1996) is an account of a culinary pilgrimage through France, while the book written with Lucy Frost, *Women Who Go To Hotels* (1997), develops these interests with enjoyable humour and relish. Her work often contains interesting alternations between the sensual, physical world, and subtle, ironic explorations of moods, emotions and relationships.   HTh

Hamilton, Cicely 1872–1952 British playwright, novelist, journalist, actress and TRAVEL WRITER who crusaded to free women from the 'idea of "destined" marriage [and] "destined" motherhood'. Her 'unhappy and frightened' childhood was spent most often separated from her parents: her father led a distinguished military career, while 'the parting of my mother came early in life' when she disappeared in mysterious circumstances. Hamilton was an actress in theatrical touring companies before she decided to earn her living as a professional writer, and, as such, produced six novels, nine plays and seventeen works of non-fiction. Her first success as a playwright was *Diana of Dobsons* (1908), a bitter-sweet comedy juxtaposing the experiences of women in the shop-girl class with those in the 'ornamental class'. From 1907 she was a dedicated suffragist and carved out her own space by forming the Women Writers Suffrage League with Bessie Hatton in 1908. Her suffrage plays included *How the Vote was Won* (1909) and *A Pageant of Great Women* (1910), but her most influential contribution to the cause was *Marriage as a Trade* (1909), where her 'contention is that woman, as we know her, is largely the product of the conditions imposed upon her by her staple industry' (see SUFFRAGETTE LITERATURE). During World War I she served with the Scottish Women's Hospitals, the WAAC and Concerts at the Front, and later became increasingly absorbed in the birth-control campaign and the international situation. True to her convictions, she never married, taking pleasure in the personal and professional company of women.   JVG

Hamilton, Elizabeth 1758–1816 Essayist and novelist, born in Belfast of an Irish mother and a Scottish father, both of whom died during her childhood. She was educated in a mixed school until the age of 13, and eventually moved to London where she made many friends, including Dr George Gregory and his wife who encouraged her to write, as well as JOANNA BAILLIE and MARIA EDGEWORTH. Becoming one of the leading literary lights of the time, she held weekly salons, gained a government pension and helped to found a Female House of Industry in 1809.

Always ambitious, by 1785 Hamilton had published a JOURNAL about her tour through the Highlands and written essays and poetry for the *Lounger*. She went on to publish three novels, all varying in style but highly popular. *Letters of a Hindoo Rajah* (1796) commemorates her recently deceased and beloved brother, and satirizes those philosophers and scientists who are unable to see the strength and efficiency of women. A satire on the Godwin circle, *Memoirs of Modern Philosophers* (1800), provides a veiled attack on MARY HAYS whilst praising MARY WOLLSTONECRAFT. Hamilton's last novel, *The Cottagers of Glenburnie* (1808), works on reformist principles, and uses the character of Mrs Mason to show how a community could be improved through the virtues of cleanliness, thrift and correct guidance. Hamilton also wrote a number of other works, including the highly influential *Letters on Education* (1801), which championed equality in the education of boys and girls, a biography of Agrippina, the *Wife of Germanicus* (1804), and *Letters Addressed to the Daughter of a Nobleman on the Formation of the Religious and Moral Principle* (1806).   RDM

Hamilton, Gail [Mary Abigail Dodge] 1833–96 American essayist, journalist and fiction writer. She was born in Hamilton, Massachusetts, daughter of a schoolteacher and a farmer, and completed her education at Ipswich Female Seminary in 1850. She taught physical education at Ipswich, Hartford Female Seminary and Hartford High School. In 1858 she moved to Washington where she began her writing career while serving as a governess. Early writings appeared in the abolitionist journal *National Era*. She co-edited *Our Young Folks* with LUCY LARCOM (1865–7) and in 1870 managed *Wood's Household Magazine*. Viewing authorship as a means to autonomy, she urged women to write. Writing journalism under her 'Hamilton' pseudonym, she applied witty and aggressive criticism to a broad variety of topics. Her books consist largely of collections of her writings for periodicals. She wrote on women's issues – *Woman's Wrongs, a Counter Irritant* (1868) and *Woman's Worth and Worthlessness* (1872) – and on authors' rights – *A Battle of the Books* (1870) – in addition to CHILDREN'S BOOKS, books on religion, and a TRAVEL book, *Wool Gathering* (1867). Her sister, H. Augusta Dodge, posthumously collected her letters in *Gail Hamilton's Life in Letters* (1901) and her poems in *Chips, Fragments and Vestiges* (1902). JSG

Hamilton [also Walker, née Leslie], Lady Mary

1739–1816 British novelist who campaigned for women's right to education in all her work. The youngest daughter of Alexander Leslie, fifth Earl of Leven and fourth Earl of Melville, in 1762 she married Dr James Walker, who later deserted her. In order to support herself, she wrote her first novel, *Letters from the Duchess de Crui* (1776), literally 'in her nursery'. After Walker's death, she married Robert Hamilton of Jamaica and settled in France. Hamilton's novels are predominantly EPISTOLARY, following conventional ROMANCE patterns. These are interspersed with sophisticated orations on education, philosophy and art, frequently plagiarizing works by other authors. Her most famous and successful book, *Munster Village* (1778), depicts the establishment of a utopian garden city by an aristocratic philanthropist. Hamilton's other novels are *Memoirs of the Marchioness de Louvoi* (1777), *The Life of Mrs Justman* (1782) and *Duc de Popoli* (1810). NBP

Hammick, Georgina 1939– English short-story

writer and novelist, renowned for her acute observation, compassion and wit. Born in Hampshire, she spent much of her childhood abroad before becoming a teacher and then helping to found the Hammicks Bookshop chain. Her first passion was poetry, but when the poems 'just went away' she turned to the short story. *People for Lunch* (1987) was a bestseller, unprecedented for a short-story collection, and Hammick was hailed as the Chekhov of the English middle classes.

This highly entertaining collection presents a range of characters, mostly middle-aged women, grappling with grief, loneliness, domestic crises and trips to the gynaecologist. All reveal Hammick's sharp talent for mimicry and complex explorations of social class. The title story, for example, is a touching and funny portrayal of a family in the aftershock of bereavement; 'Mad About the Boy', an account of a childhood obsession with Noel Coward, is about the ways in which disappointment is assimilated and made palatable. These themes continue in her second collection, *Spoilt* (1992),

which includes 'The Wheelchair Tennis Match', a moving depiction of the 'hairline crack' between 'everything being all right and everything being all wrong, for ever'.

Hammick's stories have been widely anthologized and broadcast. She has also edited *The Virago Book of Love and Loss* (1992), two themes that resonate throughout her work, and published one novel, *The Arizona Game* (1996), which tells the tale of a single mother struggling to come to terms with her past. Less tautly elegant than her short stories, it is nevertheless an impressive attempt to engage with the power of secrets, the failure of memory and the inadequacies of language. CP

Hampton, Susan 1949– Australian poet and prose

writer. Despite Hampton's relatively small publishing output, her work is well represented in anthologies of poetry and short fiction. She was born in rural New South Wales, and grew up in Newcastle before establishing herself in Sydney from the 1970s. A brief marriage in the early 1970s left her with one son. She taught at high schools and universities during the 1980s, specializing increasingly in writing theory and creative writing. For a few years, Hampton lived on a farm near Ballarat in Victoria, but she returned to city life in 1993, taking up a writing residence in Canberra and staying on to teach at the University of Canberra.

Hampton's poetry is distinguished by an appealing vitality and humour. In 1987, she co-edited *The Penguin Book of Australian Women Poets* with KATE LLEWELLYN, and she assisted RUBY LANGFORD GINIBI with her autobiography, DON'T TAKE YOUR LOVE TO TOWN (1988). Her first books, including *Costumes* (1982) and *White Dog Sonnets* (1987), offered poetry in the free-ranging style favoured by her male contemporaries; but *Surly Girls* (1989) worked across poetry and prose conventions, offering a collection of performance pieces, monologues and fables from contemporary lesbian culture. Hampton's feminism has directed her to formal concerns because 'deconstruction is always an intensely political activity for women, that is, more than playful/political'. Recently, she has changed tack again, working on a full-length novel. SPL

Hand, Elizabeth 1957– US writer of fantasy and

SCIENCE-FICTION, who studied Anthropology at the Catholic University in Washington. The sequence of baroque post-apocalyptic SF novels – *Winterlong* (1990), *Aestival Tide* (1992) and *Icarus Descending* (1993) – deal endlessly in masques, sinister waifs and decorative ruins; all three novels are paced with near-unbearable intensity. Her one pure fantasy, *Waking the Moon* (1994), is a campus novel in which the University of the Archangels and St John the Divine becomes the setting for a decades-long struggle between a sinister conspiracy of elderly men dedicated to the status quo and representatives of an older order based on theories about a primordial matriarchy. The heroine, not herself a joiner, rapidly discovers that there is little to choose between these forces in ruthlessness. Hand turns conceptual aspects of the plot on their head in a tricksy ending. *The Glimmering* (1997) portrays decadence and eco-collapse with energetic glumness. *Black Light* (1999), first of a diptych, vividly evokes the bohemia of Warhol's Factory and, like *Waking the Moon*, deals in secret societies and ancient mysteries. RK

Handfasted (1984) In 1879 CATHERINE HELEN SPENCE sent her manuscript to the *Sydney Mail* which was offering a £100 prize for a novel. It was dismissed for being 'too socialistic and dangerous' and 'calculated to loosen the marriage tie', and remained unpublished until 1984. It is set mainly in the utopian Commonwealth of Columba (founded in 1745 by Scottish settlers and named after Christopher Columbus and *colombe*, a dove): Spence's own brand of 19th-century socialist feminism is given free vent within the walls of this ideal 'lost world'. The attributes of this alternative 'evolutionary' model are best epitomized by the character of Liliard Abercrombie, whose loyalty to Columban mores, in particular the practice of trial marriage of a year and a day ('handfasting'), is severely tested when she pledges herself to Hugh Victor Keith (the novel's narrator), and accompanies him across Europe to Melbourne. Revealing influences from Spence's own literary background – mainly Scottish – it also implies the superiority of the Australian colonial model. MRE

Handmaid's Tale, The (1985) This disturbing 21st-century dystopia was a new departure for MARGARET ATWOOD, who had not adopted such an openly speculative style in prose before. The book is set in a Middle America where religious fundamentalists rule in the name of racial purity and procreation. In the born-again republic of Gilead (which owes something to Plato's *Republic* and more to the Old Testament's patriarchal order) everyone wears a uniform: Wives in powder blue, an army of Guardians in green who police the streets, Handmaids in scarlet who serve as concubines and surrogate mothers, and Commanders of the Faithful. The *Tale* reflects uncomfortably on the possible collusion of radical feminist puritans with other book-burners. In Gilead literacy is a carefully guarded masculine privilege. Offred, the scarlet nun who tells the story, can remember the time when women had access to words, to money, to the negotiable currencies of our messy, unappreciated present.

The Handmaid's Tale was made into a film (director Volker Schlöndurff, screenplay by Harold Pinter) in 1990; its picturesque images at odds with its bleak message. LS

Hands, Elizabeth fl. 1785–98 English plebeian poet and author of verse in a range of styles from the epic to pastoral and anti-pastoral. Details of her life are sketchy. In the dedication to her major work she described herself as 'born in obscurity, and never emerging beyond the lower stations in life' (1798). She was a servant for many years in the family of Mr Huddesford of Allesly and his daughter. By 1785 she was married to a blacksmith at Bourton-on-Dunsmore (Warwickshire) and the poem 'On the Author's Lying-In, August, 1785' indicates that she had at least one child, a daughter. Some of her early verse was published in *Jopson's Coventry Mercury* under the pseudonym 'Daphne', and attracted the attention of various local worthies, including masters from Rugby School. A subscription for the publication of a volume of verse attracted 1,200 names at 5 shillings each. *The Death of Amnon. A Poem. With an Appendix; Containing Pastorals and other Poetical Pieces* (1798) was favourably received, even though the title poem dealt with incestuous rape. While Hands clearly regarded the blank verse biblical epic *Amnon* as her most significant work, she is nowadays remembered for the lighter, more anti-heroic poems included in the volume, particularly those, such as 'A Poem, on the Supposition of an Advertisement appearing in a Morning Paper, of the Publication of a Volume of Poems, by a Servant-Maid', which deal with the anticipated reactions to her poetry. LBe

Hannan, Maggie 1962– British poet whose ingenious wordplay and innovative syntax have established her in the vanguard of a rising generation of poets for whom the language of poetry is of primary importance. Born in Wiltshire, Hannan worked as a stonemason and artist's model before moving to Hull in the late 1980s where she associated with the literary grouping centred on the magazine *Bête Noire*. In 1993 she was featured in the influential Bloodaxe anthology *The New Poetry*, a 'surprise inclusion' as she had published very little. Her first book *Liar, Jones* – the title and comma are typical Hannan – followed in 1995 and was shortlisted for the Forward Prize Best First Collection. She became a writer-in-residence on the Internet, moving to Newcastle-upon-Tyne in the 1990s.

Hannan's poetics are very much her own. Various groups, such as 'the Hull poets' and the L=A=N=G=U=A=G=E movement have attempted to co-opt her work to diversify their agendas; but Hannan fits no manifesto. Her single-minded pursuit of taut structure and bizarre verbal association, coupled with her ability to transmit these complex poems clearly and accessibly, have led to her being a standard-bearer. The sharpness of aesthetic, the exactions she sets herself, have much in common with the projects of the poets VERONICA FORREST-THOMSON and DENISE RILEY. In a time when high-profile anthologies of women's poetry appeared in Britain, her work has needed no special pleading. Hannan has – without any harm to her reputation – been excluded from the mainstream marketing exercises of the 1990s. DM

Hanrahan, Barbara 1939–91 Australian novelist and short-story writer, whose writing dramatizes the internal conflicts suffered by characters forced to choose between social expectations and their individual creative aspirations. Hanrahan is also known for her work as a printmaker and there is a close correlation between the visual immediacy of the prints and the world of her novels which are packed with intimate visual details and observations of the time in which they are set (for example, the usually Victorian world of her fantastic fiction). Hanrahan also creates intimate descriptions of the family home and of suburbia in her autobiographical novels.

She moved to London in 1962 where she started writing *The Scent of Eucalyptus* (1973), in an autobiographical trilogy (with *Sea-Green*, 1974, and *Kewpie Doll*, 1984), which details the childhood and adolescence of 'a SYLVIA PLATH girl from the fifties'. This first volume is infused with the GOTHIC overtones which predominate in the fantastic novels she produced in quick succession, starting with THE ALBATROSS MUFF (1977), *Where the Queens All Strayed* (1978), *The Peach Groves* (1979) and THE FRANGIPANI GARDENS (1980). In both the autobiographical and fantastic fiction the fevered dynamics of the family are seen through the eyes of the child – the child as voyeur. Hanrahan is drawn to recreating Adelaide's darker history for it provides a space in which to explore how the past inflects the present. Indeed, the past is seen as 'threading' through the present and 'both present and past are there reaching out to the future'. There is, in her attraction to the Victorian period, a fascination with the weird combination of the spiritual and the material it represents: her 'angels' are, as she suggested, 'weighed down in marble'.

Hanrahan's later novels *Dove* (1983), *Annie Magdalene* (1985), *Dream People* (1987) and *A Chelsea Girl* (1988), mark a return to REALISM, but the issues and concerns explored remain an extension of those examined in the fantastic fiction, namely the ties that bind women to the family, to history and to nation. JAM

Hansberry, Lorraine 1930–65 African-American playwright born to a Chicago family whose home was a centre for black intellectuals, artists and leaders of business and politics. Her father Carl Hansberry, a Civil Rights activist, legally challenged housing restrictions barring blacks, for which he became the target of white attacks, though finally winning a Supreme Court decision (Hansberry versus Lee) in 1940. This event was the basis for Hansberry's most famous play, A RAISIN IN THE SUN (1959), originally inspired by Sean O'Casey's *Juno and the Paycock*. After college Hansberry worked as a journalist and associate editor of Paul Robeson's Leftist newspaper *Freedom*. With *A Raisin in the Sun*, she became the first black, the first woman, and the youngest person to win the New York Critics Circle Award. Centred on a black family who dare to move from the Chicago inner city to a white suburb, *Raisin* hit the nerve of national outrage over recent terrorism against peaceful black demonstrators. Yet passages voicing the family's political awareness were deleted from the staging and film, and the political dimension of this play is still often underestimated. In spite of her intense commitment to civil rights, some militant blacks called Hansberry an 'Uncle Tom', a judgement later retracted. She was also prescient in seeing injustice toward women and gays before public awareness of it.

She left unpublished playscripts, filmscripts, notes for a play on MARY WOLLSTONECRAFT, and one scene of an opera about Toussaint L'Ouverture, the black leader of Haiti who freed the slaves and founded the world's first black republic in 1804. *The Drinking Gourd* (1960), a portrayal of the American slave system, was based on documentation and interviews with Civil War survivors, including Hansberry's grandmother. Written for television, it was judged as 'superb but too controversial' and the series was dropped. *The Sign in Sidney Brustein's Window* (1964) shocked Hansberry's followers because it centred on a white intellectual and on white injustice to other whites, a theme visible in other works whose main focus is on whites colonizing blacks who in turn oppress their own people, perpetuating a system of privilege and exploitation. *Les Blancs* (1983) documents colonialism's rise in Africa, with a plot based on *Hamlet* and the *Oresteia* but incorporating African performance elements. It shows, again presciently, that this economic system also destroys the land. 'The Arrival of Mr Todog' is a camp parody of *Waiting for Godot*, and ultimately rejects Beckett's existential resignation, while the play *What Use are Flowers?* (1983) is also a longer critique of Godot.

The Sign in Sidney Brustein's Window would have closed quickly, but stage and screen actors kept it open in homage to Hansberry who was terminally ill with cancer, finally letting it close on the day she died, 12 January 1965. Her former husband Robert Nemiroff later collected excerpts from her plays, notes, letters, speeches and interviews, and arranged them into the popular dramatic collage *To Be Young, Gifted and Black* (1969), the title of a speech she delivered in 1964 to the winners of the United Negro College Funds writing contest during an afternoon's release from the hospital. SBB

Hanson, Elizabeth Meader 1684–1741 New Hampshire Quaker, captured in an Indian raid in New Hampshire, purported author of a narrative of her captivity. Hanson was taken in an attack on her homestead in New Hampshire in 1724. Of her six children, two were killed immediately, and the others were marched to Canada with Hanson. She lived with her captors for several months but was sold to the French, from whom her husband ransomed her in 1725 after one year of captivity. Her narrative, *God's Mercy Surmounting Man's Cruelty*, published in 1728 by Samuel Keimer, a printer for the Society of Friends in Philadelphia, shares characteristics with the earlier women's CAPTIVITY NARRATIVES from the Puritan presses (see MARY ROWLANDSON and HANNAH SWARTON). Several critics have noted the extreme passivity detailed in the narrative, especially in Hanson's relationship to her Indian 'master' and have attributed it to her Quaker beliefs. In light of Quaker censorship practices, which sought to control and edit all the Society's publications, it is likely that *God's Mercy* is at least a production of several editors; the probability is that the narrative was 'taken from her mouth' by Samuel Bownas, a travelling Quaker preacher. LCa

Hanway [née Vergy], Mary Ann ?between 1756 and 1770 – ?1824 British novelist of whose life very little is known, she is thought to have married a near-descendant of the philanthropist Jonas Hanway in Middlesex in 1788. She published four novels which, in terms of style, hark back to an earlier 18th-century sentimental tradition, blending didactic and ROMANCE elements. The 1798 *Ellinor*, reminiscent in places of FANNY BURNEY'S *EVELINA* (1778), is subtitled *The World as It Is*. *Ellinor*, characterized in the author's preface as being 'offered to her fair country-women' as an antidote to the excesses of the GOTHIC genre or 'the *rage* for supernatural agency', was followed two years later by *Andrew Stuart* (1800). Critics generally concur that her two last novels, *Falconbridge Abbey* (1809) and *Christabelle* (1814), are her most successful. This latter work may be read as an early 19th-century Englishwoman's literary response to the French Revolution. ELER

Hardwick, Elizabeth 1916– American critic, fiction writer and book reviewer. Born in Kentucky and educated at the University of Kentucky, Hardwick came to New York in 1940 and remained there at the centre of an intellectual circle that included SUSAN SONTAG, MARY MCCARTHY, HANNAH ARENDT and others. She first attempted to get a Ph.D. at Columbia University and then to write novels. Finally she found her *metier* as a literary journalist, although her subject matter often extended beyond literature to a wide range of topics including popular culture, social criticism and political issues such as feminism and opposition to the Vietnam War. She was associated during the 1940s with the left-wing journal, the *Partisan Review*, was a founding editor in 1963 of the *New York Review of Books* and has been a regular reviewer for the *New York Times Book Review*. She also taught for several years at Barnhard College in New York City and is credited with influencing many younger women writers. In 1949 she married the manic-depressive poet Robert Lowell, with whom she had a daughter. Over the next twenty-eight years she cared for him during his numerous mental breakdowns and, through her own interests and contacts, influenced his work. He used her personal life and her letters in his poetry, most notably in his collections *History*, *For Lizzie and Harriet* and *The Dolphin*.

She has written three novels – *The Ghostly Lover* (1945), *The Simple Truth* (1955) and *Sleepless Nights* (1979). The third, and most successful, is a meditation on her past and present life, a blend of fact and fiction which resembles the essay form. She has published four collections of essays – *A View of My Own* (1962), *Bartleby in Manhattan* (1983), *Seduction and Betrayal* (1974) and *Sight-Readings: American Fiction* (1998). She has been praised as much for her lyrical personal style as for the content of her essays. She was given a life-time achievement award from the National Book Critics Circle and a Gold Medal for Belles-Lettres and Criticism from the American Academy of Arts and Letters. JG

Harford [née Keogh], Lesbia 1891–1927 Australian poet who put her socialist principles into practice by abandoning an early interest in free verse in favour of 'little fresh songs' accessible to 'the invisible people', the workers whose early morning journey to work went unwitnessed by middle-class ladies for whom eleven o'clock excursions to town were just one of 'a thousand ways / Of doing nothing all [their] days'. These poems drew on her experiences as a housemaid and clothing factory machinist, proletarian work deliberately chosen despite the persistent ill health resulting from a congenital heart defect and despite the fact that she was among the first women to graduate in Law from Melbourne University, where she became involved with the radical group the Industrial Workers of the World (the Wobblies). She published little in her lifetime and a complete collection of her poetry, *The Poems of Lesbia Harford* (1985), came only after feminist critics of the 1970s became interested in her exploration of the experience of gender-determined tensions in the spheres of political activism, writing and sexuality, whether lesbian, as in the early passionate attachment that caused her to write 'Would that I

were Sappho, / Greece my land, not this!' or, as in sub-
sequent relationships, heterosexual and finally wifely.
The revived interest also led to the publication of *The
Invaluable Mystery* (1987), her late (and temporarily
'lost') novel which places such themes in the context of
World War I.   JStr

Hariharan, Githa 1954– Indian novelist and short-
story writer who shot to fame when THE THOUSAND
FACES OF NIGHT won the Commonwealth Writers
Prize for the best first novel of 1992. She was born in
Coimbatore and grew up in Bombay and Manila. Her
BA in English is from Bombay University and she has
an MA in Communications from Fairfield University,
Connecticut. She worked in the Public Broadcasting
System in New York before returning to India to work
with a publishing firm as an editor. She lives in Delhi
with her two sons and her husband.

The Thousand Faces, which has been translated into
German, French and Spanish, traces a contemporary
woman's journey through experiences and relationships. Myths and metaphors interwoven with allusions to Indian classical music add resonance to the
narrative. Since then she has published a collection of
tautly structured stories of concentrated power – *The
Art of Dying* (1993) – and two novels, *The Ghosts of Vasu
Master* (1994) and *When Dreams Travel* (1998). *Vasu Master*
is intricately conceived, using fables and parables to
bring together the twin themes of teaching and
healing in a warm human story of a friendship
between a retired school teacher and a mentally
retarded child. *When Dreams Travel* takes off from *One
Thousand and One Nights*, blending dreams and awakening, past and present. Her stories have been included
in many anthologies including *The Vintage Book of
Indian Writing* (1997). In 1994 she herself edited *The
Southern Harvest*, a volume of stories in English translation from four major South Indian languages.   MMu

Harjo, Joy 1951– Born in Tulsa, Oklahoma, a Creek
(Muscogee) native American Indian and community
activist who attended the Institute of American Indian
Arts, then graduated from the University of New
Mexico in 1976. She has published several politically
engaged, spiritually resonant volumes of poetry: *She
Had Some Horses* (1983), *Secrets from the Center of the World*
(1989) and *In Mad Love and War* (1990), and also *The Last
Songs* and *What Moon Drives Me to This?* Harjo has taught
native American literature, written television scripts,
and travels, giving readings and workshops. She says
her work feeds on memory which enables cultural survival, her heritage nurturing her work as 'a delta in the
skin'. On the discovery of the body of Anna Mae
Aquash, a young Micmac American Indian Movement
member, Harjo writes polemically and lyrically of
anger, silencing and memory:

You are the shimmering young woman
                          who found her voice,
when you were warned to be silent, or have your body
    cut away
from you like an elegant weed.
    You are the one whose spirit is present in the
    dappled stars.
(They prance and lope like colored horses who stay
    with us
        through the streets of these steely cities. And I
    have seen them
nuzzling the frozen bodies of tattered drunks
                          on the corner.)

Her work draws on Native American myth and the
dominance of materialism in the 20th century. It is
concerned with the spiritual and the social – the dualities of modern life which she seeks to reconcile – and
is politically committed, exploring ways in which the
spirituality of the inner woman can reconcile contradictory states into a balanced harmonious whole.
Reinventing the Enemy's Language came out in 1989 and
her anthology, *Contemporary Native Women's Writing of
North America,* was reissued in 1997.   GW

Harley [née Conway], Brilliana, Lady 1600–43
Prolific letter-writer, most significantly during the
English Civil War (1642–9). Born at Brill in the
Netherlands (hence her striking name) where her
father held the post of lieutenant-governor, she
married Sir Robert Harley in 1623. For two decades she
was a regular letter-writer, both to her husband and
later to her son Ned. The letters she sent to the former
whilst he was stationed with the Parliamentary Army
provide a remarkable female perspective on the hardships and anxieties endured during the Civil War.
Harley is interested in 'publicke affaires' as she terms
them, recording in one letter the tensions 'betwne the
king and parliament' and in another the Kentish petition and the erecting of a maypole in Ludlow,
Shropshire, in opposition to Puritan edicts. Despite
the royalist sympathies of her own family (her brother
was Viscount Conway), Harley supported her
husband's pro-Parliamentary stance. Touchingly she
sends her son relief parcels of shirts, food and other
necessaries. One of her last letters talks of being threatened by royalist soldiers at her Brampton Bryan estate
(which she, like many women of her rank, was running
in her husband's absence) and of a heavy cold. Harley
in fact bravely endured a six-week siege of the property
only to die of influenza soon after.   JS

Harper, Frances Ellen Watkins 1825–1911 American
lecturer, activist, pioneer of African American literature. She was born in Baltimore, Maryland, to free
black parents. Orphaned at 3, she was adopted by an
aunt and uncle, who ran a school where she was edu-

cated until the age of 14. She joined the Underground Railroad in 1854, travelled as an anti-slavery orator and wrote for abolitionist newspapers. Her popular *Poems on Miscellaneous Subjects* (1854) ran to twenty printings. In 1860 she married Fenton Harper, a widower with two children. They had one child before he died in 1864. After emancipation, Harper travelled in the South lecturing on civil rights, education and economic opportunity. The poems in *Sketches of Southern Life* (1872) reflect hope for a new age. She participated in the Women's Christian Temperance Union and the American Women's Suffrage Association, white organizations in which she faced racism. She was director of the American Association of Colored Youth (starting 1893) and vice-president of the National Association of Colored Women (1896). Through a mixed-race heroine, *Iola Leroy: Or Shadows Uplifted* (1892, reprinted 1988) explores gender, race, identity and community from the Civil War through Reconstruction. Three earlier serialized novels (*Minnie's Sacrifice, Sowing and Reaping, Trial and Triumph*) were reprinted in 1994.　　　JSG

Harraden, Beatrice 1864–1936 British novelist and suffragist whose tales, often stories of love affairs between strangers, achieved early success. Harraden, the daughter of an importer of musical instruments and the ward of ELIZA LYNN LINTON, was educated in Germany and England, earning a BA from London University. Harraden's early stories were published in *Blackwood's*, and her first novel, *Ships that Pass in the Night* (written in 1893 and set among invalids in Switzerland), sold well. She wrote a number of other novels, among them *Hilda Strafford* (1897), *The Fowler* (1899), *Katharine Frensham* (1903) and *Interplay* (1908). She was a strong supporter of women's suffrage and became deeply involved with the Women's Social and Political Union (though she worried that the Pankhursts would fault her for lack of commitment to 'the cause'), for which she wrote pro-SUFFRAGE PAMPHLETS such as 'Lady Geraldine's Speech', a brief comic dialogue between educated pro- and anti-suffrage women. Harraden also wrote stories for children (some published in 1897 in *Untold Tales of the Past*), and lived for a time in California, writing (with one Dr William Edwards) *Two Health Seekers in Southern California* (1897), a guide to the area for invalids.　　KW

Harris, Claire 1937– Caribbean poet and editor who settled in Canada in 1966 after taking degrees in Jamaica, Dublin and Nigeria. Her poems combine the linguistic strategies of MODERNISM, Caribbean folktales and code-switching to create documentary collages that evoke the voices of black people living in various cultures. Her first book, *Translation into Fiction* (1984) translates the embodied experiences of African-Caribbean people into poetic language. *Fables From the Women's Quarters* (1984) won the Commonwealth Prize for Best First Book in 1984, and includes poems about the life of Rigoberta Menchu and Harris's experiences in Nigeria in the early 1970s. In *The Conception of Winter* (1989) she explores the enabling and dislocating effects of travel and migration during a flight to Barcelona. Using haiku and postcards, the speaker marks the historical connections between the Spanish slave trade and racism in contemporary Canada, and remembers her childhood in the Caribbean 'without embellishment or fantasy'. This search for an appropriate poetic voice for black women living in Canada is continued in *Drawing Down A Daughter* (1992), a narrative poem that explores the tensions between the speaker's life in Canada and her memory of the Caribbean, through a dialogue with her unborn child. Harris's 1996 collection of poetry, *Dipped in Shadows*, also speaks to women's communities in its engagement with difficult social issues, such as domestic abuse, racism and AIDS.　　SCM

Harry, J(an) S. 1939– Australian poet often described by other Australian writers as a 'poet's poet'. J.S. Harry was born in Adelaide, but has lived and worked in Sydney for many years, engaged in various occupations while publishing five volumes of poetry over a quarter-century: *The Deer Under the Skin* (1971), *Hold, For a Little While, and Turn Gently* (1979), *A Dandelion for Van Gogh* (1985), *The Life on Water and the Life Beneath* and *Selected Poems* (both 1995). Despite her relatively small output, and her reclusiveness, Harry's work is very highly regarded by critics, with her *Selected Poems* winning the 1996 New South Wales Premier's Award for Poetry. Harry's volumes have all been constructed around a small number of framework 'language' poems which set up a scaffolding for her considerations on the complexities and ambiguities of language. Harry's keen awareness of the limitations of words – and her highly intellectual engagements with Wittgensteinian and other philosophies – does not prevent her from using a chiselled and distilled language to detail her reverence for the natural world, or to provide sharp and often blackly humorous commentary on the social and political worlds, or indeed on her chosen vocation as a poet. Her poetry is complex and challenging, demonstrating sometimes breathtaking technical skill and precision, along with a palpable but unsentimental tenderness for the innocent, bewildered, deceived or dispossessed.　　MLA

Hartley, Dorothy 1893–1985 Born in Skipton, Yorkshire, Hartley devoted her life to recording the traditional crafts of rural England. An acknowledged draughtsman and photographer as well as historian, journalist and writer, she spent three years (1933–6)

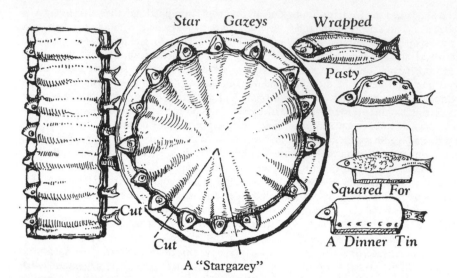

Star Gazeys Wrapped

Pasty

Squared For

Cut

Cut

A Dinner Tin

A "Stargazey"

'A Stargazey', line drawing by Dora Hartley in *Food in England*, 1954.

travelling round England on foot and bicycle, making sketches and photographs of ancient crafts like ploughing with horses and thatching haystacks, already in danger of dying out. She was inspired by the 16th-century Thomas Tusser's *Five Hundred Points of Good Husbandry*, which she later edited. The results were published weekly, in the *Daily Sketch*, later in book form, as *The Countryman's England* (1935). *Made in England* (1939) followed, then *Food in England* (1954). Her next great book was *Water in England* (1964). Like her other books, this is illustrated with her enchanting drawings; one depicts eighteen different types of drainpipe.

Her last fifty years were spent living near Llangollen, in Wales, by the famous Brunel aqueduct. In her last book, *The Land of England* (1979), she writes on keeping poultry: 'Hens were set upon clutches, went astray, went broody, vanished, or came back with a successful hatching, in the exasperating way common to all hens.' Between books, she painted, taught, lectured and wrote countless letters.   AB

Harvey, Caroline see TROLLOPE, JOANNA

Harwood [née Foster], Gwen(doline) 1920–95 Australian poet whose relatively late first collection, *Poems* (1963), established her immediately as a force to be reckoned with. Intellectual and passionate, elegiac and satirical, witty and tender, her reputation, and her list of literary awards, grew steadily with *Poems Volume Two* (1968), *Selected Poems* (1975), THE LION'S BRIDE (1981) and BONE SCAN (1988). Music was both her initial training and her abiding love, manifest not only in her

work as a librettist for several operas, and in her poetic themes and imagery, but also in poetic structures which are frequently reminiscent of the art of counterpoint and fugue. Marriage was responsible for introducing her to another abiding passion – a fascination with the linguistic theories of Wittgenstein. It also transported her from her native Brisbane – a habitat brilliantly evoked in *Blessed City: Letters to Thomas Riddell 1943* (1990) – to Tasmania. That island's remoteness from metropolitan literary circles possibly contributed to the success of the campaign of pseudonymous publishing she conducted during the 1960s, undeterred by the revelation of her identity as 'Walter Lehmann' as a result of a particularly mischievous pair of sonnets which embarrassed the *Bulletin* in 1961. Harwood described her themes as the old ones – 'love, friendship, art, memory' – and as a mistress of the memoir, the poem or prose piece that restores a lost past to the light of the present, she has made, among other things, a notable contribution to Australia's literature of childhood. The omission of landscape from her listing of themes may have been due to her resistance to identification with recognizably nationalist preoccupations; it certainly receives its due in the pastorals that become increasingly important in her later work. Her final collection *The Present Tense* (1995), is a spirited affirmation of life in the face of a death she knew to be imminent.   JStr

Have the Men Had Enough? (1989) MARGARET FORSTER's honest fictional exploration of the effects of Alzheimer's disease upon a sufferer and her family. Grandma's inevitable decline, and its primary effect of heightening existing family disagreements and tensions, are revealed through the contrasting viewpoints of Jenny, a stressed and guilt-ridden daughter-in-law, and her more tolerant but analytical teenage daughter, Hannah. Jenny and Hannah carry the narrative in alternating chapters of interior monologue, brightened by keenly observed comic moments, yet each asks searching questions about the nature of love, responsibility, duty and family loyalty. Although Forster is keen to show that, even in the progressive 1980s, women are still expected to shoulder the burden of care, and that care homes and geriatric wards are places where the elderly wait for death, her novel is more than a diatribe on the shortcomings of care provision. Exploring questions rather than offering answers, it is a compassionate portrayal of a family in crisis.   MET

Havergal, Frances Ridley 1836–79 British hymn writer and poet, was born into a clerical family. A precocious child, she wrote verse fluently from the age of 7 but received little organized education as her fragile health was thought to make this too risky. Devoting herself to God, she never married. From her first volume, *The Ministry of Song* (1869), the intensity of her spiritual nature was clear, as was her belief that writing religious poetry was an important vocation and that such verse, if it was to express 'the essence of existence', must arise from the 'tightest tension' of suffering. Her own hymns and poetry, including *Under the Surface* (poems, 1874), *Loyal Responses* (hymns, 1878) and *Life Echoes* (poems, 1883), gained a large Evangelical following; they emphasize the strong emotions of the Christian believer and reveal her personal devotion, exemplified in her still-popular 'Consecration Hymn': 'Take my life, and let it be / Consecrated Lord to thee'. She also wrote some playful 'Charades and Enigmas' and other poems for children, devotional prose and a small amount of hymn music. Her brief autobiography, chiefly recording the stages of her Christian belief, was included in her sister Maria's *Memorials of Frances Ridley Havergal* (1880). Frances Havergal's collected *Poetical Works* (2 vols., 1884) was also edited by Maria Havergal.   FJO'G

Hawken, Dinah 1943– New Zealand poet. Her first volume, *It Has No Sound and Is Blue* (1987), won the Commonwealth Best First Book of Poetry Award, and was followed by *Small Stories of Devotion* (1991) and *Water, Leaves, Stones* (1995). She has degrees in Social Psychology from State University of New York and in Creative Writing from Brooklyn College, and works in student counselling services at Victoria University, Wellington, where she lives with her husband. She began writing when she was 35, acknowledging ADRIENNE RICH's combination of the personal and political as 'a great influence' – 'I particularly loved THE DREAM OF A COMMON LANGUAGE – and I'm also very influenced by her prose.' Her lucid feminist

poetry – Jungian in its use of dream and myth – is concerned with gender oppression and women's spirituality:

> having broken the argument down and down
> we have come to a place in the text – a clearing –
> where a man and a woman have unexpectedly met.
> We have been led to believe, remember, that one,
> will take advantage of the other, as we have been led
> to believe that there is only one God.

Small Stories of Devotion contains prose poems, tiny narratives about gender relations, and includes poems and stories concerning the Sumerian goddess Inanna, while giving a strong sense of 'that slow green complacent place called home'.   AM

Hawkins, Laetitia Matilda 1759–1835 English novelist, memoirist and devotional writer. Daughter of biographer and musicologist Sir John Hawkins, she grew up in an affluent though rigorous atmosphere in London and Twickenham surrounded by the era's leading literary figures. Educated and employed as a copyist by her father, Laetitia never married but developed a lifelong interest in child-rearing and education.

Despite her father's fierce disapproval of novels, Laetitia at an early age anonymously published a novel concerning 'manners and situations of which I knew little but by hearsay'. While she apparently wrote several other anonymous volumes, the first work that can be securely attributed is *Letters on the Female Mind* (1793), a meditation on female capabilities and a retort to HELEN MARIA WILLIAMS's *Letters from France*. Conservative in nature, Laetitia's *Letters* allow the female intellect 'less strength but more acuteness' and 'concatenation of invention that disdains all limit'.

Eventually, she published a novel under her own name, *The Countess and Gertrude, or Modes of Discipline* (1811), followed by *Rosanne, or A Father's Labour Lost* (1814), *Heraline, or Opposite Proceedings* (1821) and *Annaline, or Motive Hunting* (1824). Each work follows an upright and idealized heroine struggling with a particular issue – education, atheism, candour vs subterfuge. Though widely read in their day, the novels today appear overly didactic and weighed down by essay-like asides and numerous footnotes. Her other works include a German translation, two memoirs of her childhood among literary circles, *Sermonets* (1814) written with her brother Henry, and *Devotional Exercises* (1823).   JHP

Hawks, Olive 1917–1992 British novelist, journalist and pamphleteer whose work has not received critical attention, due as much to its unremarkable style, didacticism and sentimentality as to the fact that the author was the Chief Woman's Organizer in Sir Oswald Mosley's British Union of Fascists. Educated at

THE

VICTIM

O F

PREJUDICE.

IN TWO VOLUMES.

By MARY HAYS,

AUTHOR OF
THE MEMOIRS OF EMMA COURTNEY.

VOL. I.

Her Trumpet Slander rais'd on high,
And told the Tidings to the Sky;
Contempt difcharg'd a living Dart,
A fide-long Viper, to her Heart;
Reproach breath'd Poifons o'er her Face,
And foil'd and blafted ev'ry Grace;
Officious Shame, her Handmaid new,
Still turn'd the Mirror to her View;
While thofe, in Crimes the deepeft dy'd,
Approach'd to whiten at her Side.

Moore's Female S....

LONDON:

PRINTED FOR J. JOHNSON, ST. PAUL'S CHURCH-YARD.

1799.

Mary Hays: title-page of *The Victim of Prejudice*, 1799.

Eltham Hill Secondary School, she joined Mosley's movement in 1933 and became a regular contributor to fascist publications. In 1939 she married fellow-fascist F.E. Burdett, but their marriage did not survive World War II and their internment under Defence Regulation 18B. She wrote her first novel in Holloway Prison: *What Hope For Green Street?* (1945) examined the struggle 'against all the evils of an obsolescent system of financial democracy' in London's East End. Abandoning the BUF's anti-semitism she collaborated on *Life Lies Ahead: A Practical Guide to Home-Making and the Development of Personality* (1951) with Jewish medical writer Dr Eustace Chesser, although her promotion of 'womanly training' suggested continued adherence to fascist ideals of female domesticity.   JVG

Hay, Elizabeth (Grace) 1951– Canadian short-story writer, novelist and radio personality, born at Owen Sound, Ontario, to Jean (Stevenson) and Gordon Hay. After earning her Bachelor of Arts at Victoria College, University of Toronto, in 1973, Hay worked for CBC Radio in Yellowknife, Winnipeg and Toronto until 1984. She then lived in Mexico, Brooklyn and Manhattan; in 1992 she moved to Ottawa. Her publications include a book of stories, *Crossing the Snow Line* (1989); two documentary novels, *The Only Snow in Havana* (1992) and *Captivity Tales: Canadians in New York* (1993); and another collection of stories, *Small Change* (1997). Hay states, 'My main writing concern is how to combine the real and the fictional: how to acquire the range fiction allows without losing the immediacy and urgency of autobiography, and by extension, biography and history.'

Thus, *The Only Snow in Havana*, written as historiographical metafiction, contrasts the emotional history of its protagonist with the predominantly economic history that she confronts in official discourse. As she reconstructs her travels from the Canadian north to New York, then to southern Mexico and back to Yellowknife, she becomes aware of the colours omitted from national histories: in this case, the shades of race, gender and class that are hidden behind the dominant Canadian whiteness.   JBM

Hays, Mary 1760–1843 Radical intellectual and writer in many genres including the essay, novels, letters, poetry and history. She was born into a dissenting family in Southwark, and raised by her widowed mother with her two sisters. A love affair with John Eccles, discouraged by her mother, ended tragically with his death in 1780. In 1792 she published *Cursory Remarks* under the pseudonym Eusebia, in which she defended the act of public worship against the censure of Gilbert Wakefield, a lecturer at the Dissenting Academy in Hackney. As a consequence she became part of the literary circle surrounding Joseph Johnson and met Godwin, Joseph Priestly, George Dyer, Thomas Holcroft and MARY WOLLSTONECRAFT, who was to become both a close friend and a powerful influence. In *Letters and Essays, Moral and Miscellaneous* (1793), she urged against oppression in religion, society and marriage. She began a lengthy correspondence with Godwin, asking his advice regarding her work, and confessing her unhappiness at her rejection by the Unitarian William Frend. Her first novel, MEMOIRS OF EMMA COURTNEY (1796), based partly on her own experiences, uses fictional autobiography to narrate the story of a woman who declares her passion for her lover to his face. The novel shocked contemporary audiences and Hays was cruelly parodied as Bridgetina Botherim in ELIZABETH HAMILTON's vicious satire, *Memoirs of Modern Philosophers* (1800). In her second novel, *The Victim of Prejudice* (1799), she rewrites the seduction narrative from a feminist point of view. *Appeal to Men in Great Britain on Behalf of Women* (1798), published anonymously, has been attributed to her; it urges the need to treat women as rational subjects. Her *Female Biography* (1803) and *Memoirs of Queens* (1821) both celebrate the achievements of women. She also worked as a teacher and retired in 1824 to London, where she died at 83.   PJW

Haywood, Eliza 1693–1756 Novelist, playwright, translator, journalist, poet and, briefly, publisher, Haywood was one of the most versatile, opportunistic and controversial writers of her time. Born the daughter of a London shopkeeper and without a classical education, she ostensibly chose the subject of love which, she explained, 'requires no Aids of Learning'. Her first novel, *Love in Excess* (1719), was an immediate bestseller, and more ROMANCES followed in quick succession. Notorious for the intensity of the erotic and emotional rapport with her (mainly female) readers, Haywood nevertheless used the seduction plot to attack the double standard and expose women's victimization.

Not given to autobiographizing like DELARIVIÈRE MANLEY, whose scandal fiction she emulated in her anti-Whig *Memoirs of a Certain Island* (1724), *The Court of Carimania* (1726) and *Adventures of Eovaai* (1736), Haywood left few clues about her private life. Married to clergyman Valentine Haywood (their son was baptized in 1711), in 1721 he announced her desertion and his refusal to pay her debts – hence her strenuous literary activity. Already an actress, her tragedy *The Fair Captive* was performed in 1721, while she acted in her own comedy *A Wife to be Lett* (1724), collaborated on a successful adaptation of Fielding's *Tragedy of Tragedies* (1733) and acted in his savagely anti-Walpole *Historical Register* (1737).

Attacks on Haywood by Swift, Richard Savage and Pope, who called her a 'shameless Scribbler' in *The Dunciad*, which she countered in *The Female Dunciad* (1729), possibly caused her relative silence in the 1730s, unless she wrote anonymously (as with *Anti-Pamela* (1741), her attack on Richardson's *Pamela*). Responding to a changing literary market she turned toward social and DOMESTIC concerns in her most successful periodical the *Female Spectator* (1744–6), and conduct books *The Wife* and *The Husband* (both 1756), while the erring but reformable heroine of later novels like *The History of Miss Betsy Thoughtless* (1751), prefigures the moral progress of FANNY BURNEY's and JANE AUSTEN's protagonists.   LMT

Hazzard, Shirley 1931– Australian writer, Hazzard was born and lived in Sydney until she went overseas with her family in 1947. Now an American citizen, she has not lived in Australia since. Hazzard's first return to Australia in 1976 and her negative impressions of its lack of cultural life were recorded in an authoritative account for the *New Yorker*. On a later visit in 1985, to deliver the annual ABC Boyer lectures, 'Coming-of Age in Australia', she was more positive. Australia is not a major influence in Hazzard's fiction. Only one short story, 'Woollahra Road', is set in Sydney, which provides one of several locations for her most acclaimed novel, *TRANSIT OF VENUS*, whose two major characters, sisters, are expatriate Australians. Hazzard's fiction is, however, marked by a sense of dislocation or placelessness, which characterizes much Australian fiction. A desire for love, which is for a secure sense of self and belonging, impels her heroine's quests. Hazzard worked as a clerk at the United Nations (1952–62) in New York and married American *litterateur* Francis Steegmuller (now deceased). The couple shared an intellectual and artistic life of great distinction, dividing their life each year between Manhattan and Capri.

Hazzard's ethical sensibility marks all her writing. Disillusioned in her idealistic expectations of the UN, her fervent opposition to the organization is the subject of one of her two long, non-fictional works, *Defeat of an Ideal* (1973). A sustained fictional satire, *People in Glass Houses* (1967), also focuses on the UN, whose New York building is the sterile setting for a series of minutely and wittily observed sketches of character and situation, rendered absurd by the satire. Hazzard's short fiction, collected in *CLIFFS OF FALL* (1963), and her novels deal with the significance of love, made poignant by its almost inevitable loss. Influenced by Flaubert and Turgenev and often traced by nostalgia, Hazzard's writing is elegant and compressed, powerful in its symbolic structures and psychological insights. Italy is at once a seductive and fickle setting for two short novels, *The Evening of the Holiday* (1966) and *The Bay of Noon* (1970), and several stories. *The Transit of Venus* (1980) is more structurally complex and extended than Hazzard's previous fiction, moving between Sydney, London, New York and Stockholm, patterned by elaborate literary allusions, and presenting coincidence, more to be found in life than in fiction, as its moral framework. When Caro Bell meets a man she had loved she feels 'in place of agitation . . . a sense of the long accident of life'. It won the 1980 National Book Critics' Circle Award and established her reputation as a major novelist. Hazzard's long-promised next novel has yet to appear.   DB

Head, Bessie 1937–86 South African/Botswanan novelist who chronicles the conflicts and hopes of a POST-COLONIAL Africa still rooted in its pre-colonial past. She was born in an asylum to a white mother whose 'illicit' union with a black man was deemed insane. Raised by foster parents, Head's illegitimacy was revealed to her in a brutal way and her mixed parentage compounded her sense of alienation. She writes with the unblinkered insight of the outsider. In South Africa she taught, wrote a newspaper column and became involved in Pan-Africanism. In 1964 she retreated from a suicide attempt and an unhappy marriage to teach in Botswana, where she held the precarious status of 'refugee' for the next fifteen years. Her first novel, *When Rain Clouds Gather* (1969), is an account of conflicting racial and social perspectives in a harsh new land: those of a black South African nationalist and a British agriculturist who try to modernize traditional subsistence farming in opposition to a Botswanan chief. *Maru* (1971) and THE COLLECTOR OF TREASURES AND OTHER BOTSWANAN VILLAGE TALES (1977) examined pre-colonial attitudes such as the oppression of one tribe by another, witchcraft and medicine murder. *A QUESTION OF POWER* (1974), her most original work and the one which brought her international recognition, is an autobiographical account of a coloured woman's mental breakdown and the psychological fragmentation induced by exile and racism. Like much of Head's work, it ends on a note of hope won from struggle: 'As she fell asleep, she placed one soft hand over her land. It was a gesture of belonging.' In 1979 Head was finally granted Botswanan citizenship and her writing reflected a new sense of serenity. Recorded interviews with members of her village provided the raw material for her last two books, *Serowe* (1981) and *A Bewitched Crossroad* (1984), both of which gave accounts of Botswanan history. However, her sense of isolation and unhappiness never left her and Head – hailed as one of Africa's greatest writers in her lifetime – died tragically at 49 from alcohol-related causes.   KE

Hearne, Mary fl.1718–19 Novelist whose libertine EPISTOLARY FICTIONS extol female passion and the pleasures of illicit love. Nothing is known of her life, and the name is possibly pseudonymous. *The Lover's Week* (1718), published for Edmund Curll and dedicated to DELARIVIÈRE MANLEY, follows the rapid-fire romance of Amaryllis and Philander, who meet, court, and 'Retire' to unmarried bliss in a country retreat, all in the course of six days. Like its sequel, *The Female Deserters* (1719), the work was published anonymously, 'by a Young Lady'. In 1720, both works were reprinted, again by Curll, in *Honour, the Victory; and Love, the Prize. Illustrated in ten novels by Mrs Hearne.* The novels are remarkable for their complete absence of moralizing discourse, their endorsement of female choice in amatory matters, and their unblushing celebration of 'the Joys of Love'.   JGr

Heart is a Lonely Hunter, The (1940) Published when she was 23, CARSON MCCULLERS's first novel is a haunting, poetic study of lonely people looking for love. Set in the deep South, where she herself grew up, it moves between the lives of four characters mysteriously – even mystically – drawn to deaf mute jewellery engraver John Singer. Roguish tomboy Mick Kelly dreams of becoming a concert pianist but has to go to work at Woolworth's to support her impoverished family. Drunken pugilist Jake Blount and black doctor Benedict Copeland are both committed to Marxism but argue about the relative importance of class and race in the struggle. And all-night-café proprietor Biff Brannon observes the town's inhabitants with a brooding, solitary detachment. McCullers's renowned GOTHICISM can here be seen to be rooted in a harsh yet poignant REALISM. Her androgynes, freaks and outsiders, and the barely contained violence of their existence, are observed with highly sensitive detail.

The 1968 film version was praised for its subtle adaptation of the novel's fugal structure.   MO'D

Heat and Dust (1975) RUTH PRAWER JHABVALA's Booker-Prize-winning novel is simultaneously set in the colonial British past and the post-colonial present. A young white British woman goes to India following a kind of detective trail of clues about her grandfather's first wife, whom he divorced amid great scandal. Slowly the two characters converge into near mirror images of each other; both are seduced by India and Indians: Olivia, a 1920s upper-middle-class colonial wife, shipped out to marry her local government administrator, proves unequal to the rigours of the British Way, and falls in love with and pregnant by, the local Nawab. In turn, the narrator falls in love with her Indian landlord, and also finds herself pregnant. Both characters are portrayed as moving between equally intractable cultural extremes, despite their separation and experience, marginalized in retreats of their own making.

Heat and Dust was adapted by Jhabvala and Merchant Ivory Productions for film.   STS

Heat of the Day, The (1949) The central plot of ELIZABETH BOWEN's novel of wartime London deals with the fate of a suspected pro-German traitor, Robert Kelway, whose bitterness about the Dunkirk retreat (in which he was wounded) seems to have turned him against his country. The bulk of the book, however, tells the story of his mistress, divorcee Stella Rodney. Stella is told of Robert's apparent crimes by a shady and predatory stranger named Harrison, whom she refuses either to believe or to placate with sexual favours. Meanwhile, her son Roderick, a soldier, inherits an estate in Ireland from an elder cousin and finds out the unexpectedly sad truth about his parents' divorce thanks to the dead cousin's wife, who has sought refuge from the world in a sanatorium. Amid eloquent meditations on the metaphysical and moral crises peculiar to wartime, Bowen weaves in a quirky sub-plot involving a slightly addled young woman named Louie Lewis, whose adultery produces a baby no doubt intended to represent post-war England and its infinite, if indelicate, possibilities. BWB

Heilbrun, Carolyn 1926– American academic and thriller writer, Avalon Foundation Professor of Humanities, Columbia University. Heilbrun has been on the editorial board of the feminist journal *Signs* and written *Towards Androgyny* (1973), *Reinventing Womanhood* (1979), *The Garnett Family* (1961) and *Representation of Women in Fiction* (1982). Well known as a theorist and liberal humanist feminist, she is probably better known under the pseudonym of DETECTIVE FICTION writer Amanda Cross, in which guise she develops heroine Kate Fansler, whose generation and identity Heilbrun herself says grows from her own 1960s middle-class American origins. Indeed, her analyses of difficulties of feminist scholarship in Harvard in *Death in a Tenured Position* (*Death in the Faculty* (1988) UK) draw on her faculty experience. Janet Mandelbaum believes her worth led to appointment as the English department's first woman professor. Her mysterious death, shrouded in possible lesbian activity, her corpse discovered in a male toilet, suggests a feminist onslaught and patriarchal repercussions. Ironically, her position's contradictory nature led to internal rifts and suicide. *Sweet Death, Kind Death* (1984) also concentrates on feminist studies. Kate Fansler represents a bourgeois, liberal, privileged feminism, more readily discoverable in the US than the UK, where feminism has more often involved arguments based on class and money. *No Word From Winifred* (1988) foregrounds women's literary history, whilst *The James Joyce Murders* (1967) and *The Theban Mysteries* (1972) feature literature. *The Last Analysis* (1981), *Poetic Justice* (1979) and *The Question of Max* (1976) concentrate on issues of class, and *A Trap for Fools* (1989) on race issues. Heilbrun acted as series editor for *Mothers in Law* (1995) and other works. In 1995 she published an admiring biography of Gloria Steinem: *Education as a Woman: The Life and Times of Gloria Steinem*. GW

Heir of Redclyffe, The (1853) Informed by the principles of the Oxford Movement, CHARLOTTE YONGE's popular ROMANCE debates the proposition that the sins of the fathers are necessarily visited upon their children. For the heir to the Redclyffe estate, Guy Morville, is also heir to 'a violent and fiery race'. Most sceptical about Guy's ability to transcend this latter inheritance is his cousin Philip, who is initially regarded as his intellectual and moral superior. Yet Guy's hasty temper is superficial; Philip's more serious vices – pride, deviousness and jealousy – are merely well hidden.

In spite of interference from the antagonistic Philip, Guy eventually marries another cousin, Amy. However, their ideal relationship, entailing perfect trust in both God and each other, is short-lived. Whilst nursing Philip through a deadly fever, Guy himself succumbs and dies. During the lengthy and religiously conceived death-bed scene, Philip asks, and receives, Guy's forgiveness. Subsequently, as Amy and Guy are without male issue, the repentant Philip himself becomes the heir of Redclyffe. However, full of remorse, he cannot enjoy his inheritance. EMH

Hellman, Lillian 1905–84 American writer best known as a playwright, screenwriter, memoirist and partner of Dashiell Hammet, also for her decisive stand against the McCarthyites on the House Un-American Activities Committee in the 1940s. Her first play, *The Children's Hour* (1934), with its highly charged lesbian subject matter, was a Broadway success and remained at the Maxine Elliott Theatre for a record 691 performances. She also adapted the work as a screenplay entitled *These Three* (1936) and it was remade as *The Children's Hour* in 1962, the script of which contained several comments by her with the note 'Awful – L.H.' The movie was a critical and financial failure. *Days to Come* (1936) followed, then *The Little Foxes* (1939), a melodrama, but with the accoutrements of craft, which she adapted to the screen in 1941. She also wrote the screenplays for *Watch on the Rhine* (1941, 1943), for which she won the Drama Critics' Circle Award, and *The Searching Wind* (1944) before she was blacklisted in 1948 and thereby banned from writing any more screenplays.

In her memoir, SCOUNDREL TIME (1976), she recounts with what she called 'understated fury' the degradation of that period of American history. *Another Part of the Forest* came out in 1947 followed by *The Autumn Garden* (1951). Between 1949 and 1956 she adapted Emmanuel Roblès's play *Montserrat*, Jean Anouilh's play, *L'Alouette* as *The Lark* and Voltaire's *Candide*, music by Leonard Bernstein, lyrics by Richard Wilbur. Her 1960 play *Toys in the Attic* also won a Drama Critics' Circle Award and in 1963 she adapted the Blechman novel *How Much?* as *My Mother, My Father and Me*. Her memoir, *An Unfinished Woman* (1969), won a National Book Award, and was followed by three other memoirs. She also wrote the screenplays for *The Chase* (1935), *The Dark Angel* (1935), *Dead End* (1937) and *The North Star* (1943). The 1977 film, *Julia*, based on her account of her life, created controversy, as she had so often done before: it won three Academy Awards, but doubts were raised about whether Hellman herself was truly Julia's original. MRA

Heloise *c.*1100–1 – *c.*1163–4 Noted scholar of Latin and Greek and a Benedictine abbess, perhaps best known

Felicia Dorothea Hemans.

to modern readers as the pupil, mistress and wife of the philosopher Peter Abelard. Having secretly married the reluctant Heloise, Abelard was castrated by her vengeful relations when he refused to acknowledge the marriage. Both partners then entered religion in 1119.

These events are recorded in Abelard's *Story of my Misfortunes* (c.1132) and the three letters which Heloise, by this time abbess of the Paraclete, wrote to Abelard in response. In the first two letters she analysed her despair with sharp intelligence. Adopting a position of aggressive humility, she defiantly named herself Abelard's 'whore' and refused to repent of their affair. In correct, formal Latin she wrote with painful honesty of her continuing love and desire for Abelard, her utter submission to his will, and of her sense of being unworthy of the praises she received for her pious demeanour: 'Men call me chaste; they do not know the hypocrite I am.'

The emotional appeal of the first two letters should not be allowed to overshadow the third, in which Heloise apparently obeyed Abelard's instruction to forget her bitterness, and embarked on a scholarly critique of the *Rule of St Benedict* and of contemporary monastic practices. She pointed out that Benedict's *Rule* was written for men, and demanded it be revised for nuns, taking into account matters such as menstruation and women's greater capacity for wine. Adhering to Abelard's concept of the 'ethic of inten-

tion', she argued that monastic life overvalued physical asceticism at the expense of inner spiritual development. Her enforced interest in monasticism evidently served her well, for under her leadership the Paraclete founded six daughter houses and received numerous grants.

Heloise had a strange literary afterlife. She was known to the later Middle Ages as an exotic combination of learned woman, faithful lover and anti-matrimonial thinker, in which guise she appears in Chaucer's *Wife of Bath's Tale* (c.1392–5). She later metamorphosed into a martyr of love in Pope's *Eloisa to Abelard* (1717). HELEN WADDELL's *Peter Abelard* (1933) also concentrates on her relations with Abelard. Although she spent only two years with Abelard, and more than forty in the cloister, it seems likely that Heloise will continue to be remembered, as she defined herself, as Abelard's lover. MSALS

Hemans, Felicia Dorothea 1793–1835 Poet of considerable popularity in Britain and in America. She was one of the six children of a Liverpool merchant who took his family to live in Wales when his business collapsed in 1800. Her mother undertook the education of her children and encouraged Felicia to write poetry. When she was 14 years old her parents published her 'Poems' in a quarto volume but it was not well received. About the same time her father left home for Quebec and never returned, leaving his wife and daughter to shoulder the responsibility of providing for the family.

In 1812 she married Captain Alfred Hemans and the couple moved to the family home in Wales in 1813, where over the next five years she gave birth to five sons. In 1818, when Felicia was awaiting the birth of her fifth son, Captain Hemans took a trip to Italy and never returned. Between 1818 and her death in 1835 she published fourteen volumes of verse and became one of the most popular poets of the early 19th century. Her mother died in 1827 and this death had a profound effect upon her poetry.

She found both her domestic responsibilities and her fame burdensome, and her poems explore the contradictions of her own and other women's lives: tensions between fame and domestic responsibility, love and creativity. She was drawn to and wrote about real and fictional women poets of the past whose lives mirrored the tensions of her own: the free-spirited heroine of MADAME DE STAËL's *Corinne: Or Italy* (1807), for instance, crowned at the Capitol at Rome; and SAPPHO, the lyric poet who lived apart from society on an island and reputedly committed suicide because of unrequited love.

Hemans's poetry was popular during the first half of the 19th century, particularly amongst women readers and in America, but by the end of the century her reputation had waned. The most famous of her poems, 'Casabianca' which begins with the lines 'The boy stood on the burning deck', appeared in 1829 and, like so much of her stirring writing, explored defiant and heroic death. RS

Henderson, Zenna 1917–83 American SF writer and schoolteacher, whose short stories are typical of the liberal strain in American science fiction. It is perhaps relevant to her subsequent career, and her interest in good intentions and false positions, that during the war she taught interned Japanese-Americans in a 'relocation camp'. Most of her stories belong to a linked series and are collected as such in the fixups *Pilgrimage: The Book of the People* (1961) and *The People: No Different Flesh* (1966). They feature crashlanded telepathic aliens, who pass as human over a period of many generations by living quiet rural lives; their moral superiority to humanity is constantly demonstrated and never over-stressed. It is not clear whether Henderson, writing shortly before the Women's Movement of the 1960s, consciously intended this as a feminist metaphor. Her sometimes sentimental work retains interest without relying on synthetic excitement; the stories can be somewhat repetitive. RK

Hendry, Joy (McLaggan) 1953– Scots writer, notably the editor of *Chapman*, one of the leading journals of the second Scottish literary renaissance. Joy Hendry was born in Perth and educated at the University of Edinburgh and the Moray House College of Education. She married Ian Montgomery in 1986, and has worked as a teacher, a freelance broadcaster and critic for the *Scotsman*. She is an active commentator on Scottish cultural affairs and lives in Edinburgh.

Hendry's activism on behalf of other Scots writers has overshadowed her own creative output. This includes two impressive plays, *The Waa' at the Warld's End,* broadcast on Radio 3 in 1993, and *Gang Doun Wi' a Sang* (1995), about the life and work of the Scottish poet William Soutar. Other books include a survey of literature and language, *Scots: The Way Forward* in 1981, and *The State of Scotland: A Predicament for the Scottish Writer* in 1990. She edited volumes of critical essays on Sorley Maclean in 1986 and Norman MacCaig in 1991. In addition she oversaw a *festschrift* for MacCaig's 85th birthday, and continues a busy, altruistic career in post-referendum Scotland. DM

Henning, Rachel 1826–1914 Born in Bristol, England, letter-writer Henning followed her brother Biddulph to Australia in 1854, went home in 1856, disappointed with colonial life, but returned to Australia in 1861. Henning's literary fame rests on the letters written to family and friends in Australia and England following Biddulph's emigration in 1853. They are most prolific after she joined Biddulph and her sister Annie on his sheep run, Exmoor, inland from Port Denison (Bowen) in northern Queensland. She married Deighton Taylor, an overseer on Biddulph's property, in 1866 and they eventually settled on a farming property near Wollongong, south of Sydney. The collected edited letters, from 12 August 1853 to 27 November 1882, show an intelligent, sensitive middle-class Englishwoman adapting with good humour and stoicism to isolated pioneering environments and sustaining adversity through family ties and friendship. Henning's letters were first published by the *Sydney Bulletin* in 1951–2. The edition by David Adams (1963) brought a wider audience and included a foreword and illustrations by the artist Lionel Lindsay. Anne Allingham's 'Challenging the Editing of the Rachel Henning Letters', *Australian Literary Studies*, May 1994, criticized the omission of interesting or controversial material deleted from Adams's edition. Another edition by Ada Veitch was published in 1979. Henning's letters illustrate the erosion of middle-class Victorian conventions in a colonial environment but also the preservation of the ethical values that underlay them. EPe

Her [HERmione, United States title] (written in 1927, published in 1981) H.D.'s autobiographical novel about her brief engagement to Ezra Pound (George Lowndes in the text) and her emotional relationship with another woman, Frances Gregg (Fayne Rabb). The novel's protagonist Hermione Gart ('Her') returns from college a failure, and is soon enmeshed in a network of relations and expectations which stifle her awakening to sexuality and creativity. She refuses to adopt the Bryn Mawr affectations of her peers or succumb to the heavy, patriarchal American-ness of her Philadelphia country home and family; even George Lowndes's 'harlequin' appropriation of European culture offers only false escape. Her finds self-recognition in Fayne Rabb, but the overwhelming mutuality and mesmeric mirroring that Fayne provides does not release Her from turmoil. Following a breakdown she sets her sights on independence, Europe and the future.

There are strong similarities in plot and tone between H.D.'s intense, rhythmic narrative of the emergence of a woman writer from depression, confusion and mental collapse, and SYLVIA PLATH's autobiographical novel *THE BELL JAR* (1963). AG

Herbert, Dorothea 1770–1829 Author of a JOURNAL which combines vivid description of Irish middle-class and gentry society with the record of her own psychological disintegration. Born in Kilkenny, Dorothea was the eldest child of Revd Nicholas Herbert, rector of Carrick-on-Suir, County Tipperary, and his wife,

Martha. When the family moved to Knockgrafton in 1789, Dorothea met John Roe, son of a neighbouring family, and developed a passionate attachment to him. She claimed to have contracted 'an eternal union sacred and sure' with him, and regarded his marriage to another woman as a betrayal, describing him as a 'perjured wretch', who had 'joined himself in execrable union with a common drab of the city'.

Retrospections of an Outcast ... the Life of Dorothea Herbert purports to be a true account of her life to 1806, and may indeed have been based on earlier notes, but the narrative also contains elements of GOTHIC and sentimental fiction. Dorothea became increasingly unstable and, according to her own account, was confined and abused by her mother and other relatives. The period since 1806, she wrote, 'I have pass'd in a bitter imprisonment and a total seclusion from life and all its cheerful joys – continually maltreated by a family in whom I once implicitly trusted.' She found her 'chief solace' in writing, producing four large volumes of 'poems, plays, novels and these retrospections'.

None of Dorothea's works were published during her lifetime. However, the manuscript of *Retrospections* was preserved by her family, and was published a century after her death, in 1929.   RR

Herbst, Josephine (Frey) 1892–1969 Josie Herbst was a leading proletarian novelist of the inter-war years. After graduating in 1919 from the University of California, Berkeley, Herbst worked as an editorial reader for H. L. Mencken. After several years travelling in Europe she married John Herrmann, a young writer in the *transition* group. Despairing of living on $600 per year in New York, they bought an old farmhouse in Bucks County, Pennsylvania. Her first novel, *Nothing is Sacred* (1928), carried jacket blurbs from Hemingway and Ring Lardner, and was favourably reviewed by Herbst's friend KATHERINE ANNE PORTER. A second novel, *Money for Love* (1929), established her reputation as an autobiographical writer, drawing upon events, dignified and otherwise, in her family's life in Sioux City. The first novel of Herbst's 'Trexler' trilogy, *Pity is Not Enough* (1933), was based upon the life of an uncle who went South after the Civil War as a carpetbagger. It was followed by *The Executioner Waits* (1934) and *Rope of Gold* (1939).

The trilogy was a rich panorama of American life over a century, and was compared to Dos Passos's *USA* (1930–6, collected 1938). The collapse of the Stock Market in 1929 radicalized the literary world. Herbst went to Spain and wrote powerful articles on strikes. She attended writers' congresses and was interviewed in the press. After the Stalin–Hitler pact in 1939, Herbst withdrew from literary politics. She divorced her husband; her books went out of print; and she was sacked from a wartime job in Washington through false allegations, made anonymously by Katherine Anne Porter, that she was a Soviet courier. Two novels appeared in the 1940s, and a book about John and William Bartram, *New Green World*, published to acclaim in 1954. Herbst's fragmentary memoirs, *The Starched Blue Sky of Spain*, appeared posthumously in 1991.   EH

Here Lies (1939) The first volume of DOROTHY PARKER's collected prose from the *New Yorker* is an ironic and perceptive social critique of shallow, heartless and parasitic behaviour. The twenty-five stories are more varied in tone than the melancholically self-centred verse of *ENOUGH ROPE* (1926): this is the recognizable Parker territory of the jazzy interwar metropolis of the Bright Young Things suffering from emotional and not-so-emotional hangovers, with snappy colloquial dialogue, one-sided conversation-as-diatribe pieces or interior monologue as her trademark. Her most sardonic portrayals travesty the 'American dream' in the glitzy yet dully repetitive nightlife of Broadway shows, celluloid dreams and cocktail parties, and reveal the excruciating boredom of stale middle-class marriages, precariously upheld by the civilities of laconic husbands and their wives' romantic expectations. There is, however, a sharp divide between the caustic wit reserved for the absurdities of the heartless, and the abruptly and frighteningly sober mode of the stories about the harsh reality of the Spanish Civil War, racism ('Clothe the Naked') or an orphan's misery ('Little Curtis').   PUR

Heron, Mary fl. 1786–92 British poet and novelist, about whom little is known except that she probably lived in the North of England. In 1786 she published *Miscellaneous Poems*, later followed by *Odes, etc., on Various Occasions* (1792). These works are a strange *mélange*, made up of occasional and nature poems, and faltering attempts to use the demanding form of the Pindaric ode. *The Conflict*, an EPISTOLARY NOVEL, appeared in 1790, and was reprinted in London three years later. There is some confusion as to whether it was the same author who wrote *The Mandan Chief: A Tale in Verse*. Appearing in 1791, this ambitious work celebrates the American Indians, comparing them to 'Homer's heroes', and seems to militate against the Christian viewpoint espoused in earlier works.   RDM

Hervey [née March], Elizabeth 1748?–1820 English novelist. Born into a family with strong but fading court connections, Elizabeth lost her father as a child. Her widowed mother married William Beckford, one of the era's wealthiest men, and Elizabeth grew up in his household along with her half-brother William, author of *Vathek* (1782) and builder of Fonthill Abbey. Her marriage to Col. Thomas Hervey ended tragically when he died in Liège in 1778, after his gambling debts forced the couple to flee abroad. Eventually returning to England, she began to write novels to support herself.

Her first work, *Melissa and Marcia, or The Sisters* (1788), follows a pair of twins, one wise and one vain. Similarly sentimental, her second novel, *Louisa* (1790), concerns a virtuous heroine bullied by a foolish mother. Other works include *The History of Ned Evans* (1796), a picaresque tale told in a naturalistic style; *The Church of St Siffrid* (1797), the story of a Welsh noblewoman forced to marry an adventurer; *The Mourtray Family* (1800), a moralistic treatment of characters representing different vices; and *Amabel: Or Memoirs of a Woman of Fashion* (1814), her last known work. Sadly, her wealthy, eccentric brother lampooned *Louisa* in print in 1796.　　　　　　　　　　　　　　　　　JHP

Hewett, Dorothy 1923–

Dorothy Hewett is Australia's most widely recognized woman playwright although her depictions of rebellious female characters, and their explicit sexual explorations, have made her and her plays controversial. Hewett grew up in rural Western Australia and completed her education in Perth where, in 1940, she was awarded the University of Perth's medal in English. She has worked as a university teacher, journalist, and activist for workers' rights, has five children and is married to the writer Merv Lilley. Hewett is extremely respected both for her dynamic contribution to Australia's intellectual and cultural life and for her writing. She won national drama awards (AWGIEs) in 1974 and 1982. The autobiographical significance of aspects of Hewett's drama has been criticized, but this view is dispelled by the widespread acknowledgement that her plays are outstanding nonpolemical depictions of how political and social circumstances impact on people's lives and subjective perceptions. Certainly, Hewett is concerned with serious themes but her drama is often comical and wonderfully imaginative.

THE CHAPEL PERILOUS (1971) is considered a feminist classic. The central character, Sally Banner, aspires to be a writer and undertakes a journey of self-discovery. She has numerous lovers including her schoolfriend Judith, and leaves her husband, Thomas, and their baby for her lover, Michael. Sally's parents try to control her unconventional behaviours, which include a suicide attempt, and the state later tries to forestall her political activism and communist sympathies.

The prodigious scope of Hewett's fourteen plays spans *Mrs Porter and the Angel* (1970), a proto-feminist, absurdist drama about the perils of suburban life for women, to the major undertaking of *The Jarrabin Trilogy*, completed in 1997, chronicling life in a West Australian country town from 1920 to 1970. Some of her best-known plays include the REALIST *This Old*

Man Comes Rolling Home (1964), about the working-class Dockerty family; *The Golden Oldies* (1976), about three generations of women; *The Tatty Hollow Story* (1976), about sexual freedom; and her popular children's dramas, *Golden Valley* (1982) and *Song of the Seals* (1983). Her eight music dramas and operas include *Bon-bons and Roses for Dolly* (1972) about an ageing female star, and the popular *The Man from Mukinupin* (1979) set in small-town white and Aboriginal Australia at the time of World War I. Hewett's drama is expressionist, episodic and nonlinear in structure. She creates richly layered and philosophically profound dialogue with quirky elements, integrating song and other references from popular culture and literature: these repetitious and poetic refrains overlay strongly visual texts.

In addition, Hewett has written two novels, BOBBIN UP (1959/1985) and *The Toucher* (1994); ten books of acclaimed, award-winning poetry, which include *Peninsular* (1994), winner of the 1994 National Book Council Poetry Award, and *Collected Poems* (1995), winner of the 1994 West Australian Premier's Prize; screen and radio plays; and an autobiography, *Wild Card* (1990), winner of the 1991 Victorian Premier's Prize for Nonfiction.　　　　　　　　　　　　PT

Heyer, Georgette 1902–74

Prolific British novelist, best known for her ability to serve up what she described as the 'Regency mixture' of historical ROMANCE fiction. Born in Wimbledon to middle-class parents, Heyer lived briefly in Tanganyika and Macedonia before settling in Sussex and London. She was educated informally and wrote her first book, *The Black Moth*, aged 17, to amuse her convalescent brother Boris and 'to relieve my own boredom'. Encouraged by her Anglo-Russian father, the book appeared in 1921 and was followed by over fifty novels (one under the pseudonym 'Stella Martin') before her death from lung cancer, aged 71.

Most famous for Regency romances such as *The Convenient Marriage* (1934), *Friday's Child* (1944) and *Frederica* (1965), Heyer also wrote HISTORICAL FICTION and, between 1932 and 1953, twelve DETECTIVE NOVELS (most notably *Death in the Stocks*, 1935) for which her barrister husband provided plot suggestions. Married in 1925, she had one son and lived privately as 'Mrs Rougier', refusing all interviews and publicity. Her romance fiction, although formulaic, is minutely researched and distinguished by its scholarly attention to the material details – especially the cant and slang vocabulary – of Regency life. An accomplished genre writer of what A.S. BYATT has called 'honourable escape', Heyer both recognizes and manipulates the conventions which shape her 'Heyer-Novel' and define the 'typical Heyer-hero' (whom she stereotypes as 'Model No. 1' and 'Model No. 2'). An intelligent and successful author, Heyer described her writing in historical terms as a 'mixture of Johnson and AUSTEN'. However, her work across genres and her unhappiness at having been 'born into this *filthy age*' also places her firmly within the 20th-century literary tradition exemplified by writers like AGATHA CHRISTIE and DAPHNE DU MAURIER. AS

Hidden Side of the Moon: Stories, The (1987)

This collection of feminist, SCIENCE-FICTION short stories by JOANNA RUSS was selected from twenty-five years of her work and comprises twenty-four short stories covering diverse topics with both humour and anger. She inverts the conventions of traditional science fiction, parodying images of monstrous aliens and submissive, swooning women, in an attempt to break the pattern of male myths and standards based on masculine experience and to engage the reader actively in her feminist polemic. Russ is concerned to retrieve positive images of female relationships, particularly those of mother/daughter, and several of these short stories are a tribute to the debt owed to other women. In order to free women from perceiving their female ancestors as co-conspirators under patriarchy, Russ shows the necessity to acknowledge them as victims of oppression. By stepping back through time or space the female protagonists are able to break through patriarchal taboos surrounding female friendship. JP

Higgins, Rita Ann 1955–

Irish poet and dramatist born in Galway, she was one of eleven children and left school at 14. Writing poetry in her late twenties, she joined a writer's workshop in 1982 and became Writer-in-Residence at University College Galway Library. Receiving the O'Donnell Award in 1989, she has read her poetry on Irish television, at festivals in Ireland and England, and at conferences in Germany and Hungary. She has been described as reinvigorating poetry in Ireland with writing that is promising, gutsy and anarchic. Her poetry and plays include: *Goddess on the Mervue Bus* (1986), *Witch in the Bushes* (1988), *Goddess and Witch* (1990), *Face Licker Come Home* (1991) and *Philomena's Revenge* (1992). Her new and selected poems, *Sunny Side Plucked* (1996), contains 'Higher Purchase' (1996) which is notable for the way in which she manages to capture a rich range of different poetic voices and through them depict with immediacy life amid a working-class community. Higgins is a powerful reader and has published a collection entitled *Hearsay: Performance Poems* (1994). Receiving varying reviews, she has been praised by Ailbhe Smyth, EILÉAN NÍ CHUILLEANÁIN and Paul Durcan for reflecting Ireland in the 1980s: 'exposing the lies, the posturing and petty cruelties of the powerful', and tearing away 'the shameful veils of hyprocrisy to bite deep into the very bones of Irish society' (Smyth). SFu

High Tide in the Garden (1971)

The collection that established New Zealand poet FLEUR ADCOCK's range of tone and style, from the BLUESTOCKING's surprisingly sensual praise of the colour of Latin words in 'Purple Shining Lilies' (*ferrugine, ostro, luteus, purpureus*) to the urban pastoral of the London garden she'd chosen over faraway New Zealand ('Saturday') and the eerily quiet apocalyptic world of 'Gas', where a universal accident deals out death in the form of duplication, cancelling individuality. In between there are lyrics of love and loss, and heretically anti-romantic verses like the notorious 'Against Coupling' or three stanzas on 'The Three-Toed Sloth', admired because it 'never cleans itself, but lets fungus grow/ on its fur', and 'doesn't care'. Adcock's work, prim and pungent at once, has an aura of self-sufficiency – not a legacy on which the poems rely, but something created afresh and with craft each time. Her style of feminism could not have been more at odds with the CONFESSIONAL POETRY many of her contemporaries were writing, and that contrast too underlines the value she puts on private space. LS

Highsmith, Patricia 1921–95

American Patricia Highsmith is crime fiction's supreme portraitist of obsession and anxiety. Described by Graham Greene as 'the poet of apprehension rather than fear', Highsmith populated her claustrophobic fictional worlds with edgy characters whose identities are unstable and whose behaviour is unpredictable – and often violent. She has enjoyed much attention from European critics over the years, and also from the film industry; her books have been made into movies by the likes of Claude Chabrol, Wim Wenders and Alfred Hitchcock (who filmed her first novel, *STRANGERS ON A TRAIN* (1950)). Oddly, Highsmith's work received little acclaim in her native United States until relatively recently, though her American reputation has been climbing since the 1980s. Born in Texas and educated in New York, Highsmith lived almost her entire adult life in Europe. She died in Switzerland at the age of 74.

Highsmith's most enduring creation is her one series character, Tom Ripley, the hero of five eponymous novels published between 1955 and 1991. Ripley is a genial psychopath, an American of malleable character whose unusual career begins in *The Talented Mr Ripley* when he murders another American in Europe and steals his identity. Such deadly duplicity and disguise are constant motifs in the series. Ripley kills people without remorse when they get in the way of things he wants to do, but he remains oddly likeable in spite of his amorality. Highsmith herself described Ripley as someone who 'just doesn't feel guilt in a normal way'. See *RIPLEY'S GAME* (1974).

The workings of guilt on the human psyche stands out as Highsmith's most consistent theme. This interplay is usually interwoven with violence, which reflects a freedom from social restraint. In *This Sweet Sickness* (1960), for example, the protagonist invents a fully documented *alter ego* for himself and then gradually slips into it – and into madness – after accidentally killing his romantic rival. The mystery, for Highsmith, lies not in whodunnit, but in how such metamorphoses happen. Accordingly, police and detectives figure only peripherally in her psychodramas – unless they are the ones who come unglued, as in *A Dog's Ransom* (1972). 'Emotion', she said, 'is worth more than intellect.'

In over twenty novels and six collections of short fiction (see LITTLE TALES OF MISOGYNY, 1975), Patricia Highsmith looked at her world almost exclusively through male protagonists. 'Women', she explained, 'are tied to the home … Men can jump over fences.' But Highsmith showed an interest in gender issues in various indirect and covert ways, including a notable preoccupation with homosexuality. *The Price of Salt* (1952), which Highsmith wrote pseudonymously as 'Claire Morgan', is a lesbian love-story written long before gay literature became a recognized genre. Elsie Tyler, the enigmatic object of desire – and obsession – of almost everyone in *Found in the Street* (1986), is gay. But most important, the relations among Highsmith's tense and frequently depraved male characters in so many of her novels have a distinctly homoerotic tension – as, for example, between the two principals in *Strangers on a Train*. Highsmith described sex as 'the motor' that frequently drives her fiction, but this erotic energy gains its strange potency through its links to violence and crime. Scholars have lately begun to appreciate the textured depth of Highsmith's creativity, but work on gender and psychology in her fiction remains an open and promising field.   LC

Hill [Leatham], Lorna 1902–91 British writer, best known for popular PONY and BALLET STORIES for girls. Her roots were in the North of England, where she grew up in a Durham ironmonger's family. After the local Girls' High School, and finishing school in Switzerland, she graduated in General Arts (1925) as a 'Home' student at Durham University. Marriage (1928) brought her the responsibilities of a vicar's wife, first in Newcastle-upon-Tyne, then in the remote Northumberland border country which provides a powerful background for her stories. Like many women, she moved gradually from private writing into publication, via home-produced stories for her small daughter, Vicki. Vicki's years at Sadler's Wells Ballet School inspired the material for the bestselling 'Wells' series (1950–64), whose determined heroines, with their passion for dance, their fierce opposition to cruelty to animals, and their love of the North country, offered girl readers strong role models as well as imag-

inative entry into the world of the burgeoning postwar British ballet.   PEK

Hill, Selima 1945– British poet whose work combines fierce engagement with metaphorical reach. Hill is prepared to take risks with her imagery, which can at first seem fantastic or absurd:

> because the last night I spent longing for you
> was like spending the night with no clothes on
> in a Daimler full of chows
> with the windows closed
> I have decided to calm myself down,
> and imagine my head as a tinkly moss-padded cavern
> where nothing happens.

Line by line Hill compresses desire into discomfort, indignity and then agony. We are concomitantly aroused, amused and disturbed only to be wrenched out of it into an inhuman serenity.

This ecstatic tension, the free exchange of the animate and inanimate, the conversational tone, are all characteristic of Hill's work. Her first two collections, *Saying Hello at the Station* (1984) and *My Darling Camel* (1988), showed her gift for eliding home and the world, the literal and the figurative, casual observation and the explosive force of buried emotion.

The Accumulation of Small Acts of Kindness (1989) is a woman's diary of a nervous breakdown, her fragmented state propelled and contained by an iambic pentameter which intensifies into couplets and then dissipates into broken lines and looser rhyme. The narrative is punctuated by another typical Hill device: unlikely trios of objects that become concrete expressions of abstract states. 'Chicory, cashew nuts, paper zebras', for instance, all share qualities of intricacy, strangeness, and of being somehow locked.

A Little Book of Meat (1993) is another sequence, written in the voice of a woman living on an isolated farm, one of the 'duck-feeding, stern-faced daughters, / their dresses smelling of church / and giant azaleas'. Her passion for a slaughterman is the subject of some of Hill's most visionary and sensual work. Hill's selected poems, *Trembling Hearts in the Bodies of Dogs*, appeared in 1994.   LG

Hill, Susan 1942– NATURALISTIC English writer whose best-known fictions have protagonists marked by isolation and grief. Born in Scarborough, she was educated there and in Coventry, before studying English at King's College London. She showed early ambition: her first novel, *The Enclosure* (1961), was written when she was 16; her second, *Do Me a Favour* (1963), while she was an undergraduate. After five years reviewing for the *Coventry Evening Telegraph*, she turned to writing full-time. *Gentleman and Ladies* (1968) and *A Change for the Better* (1969) were followed by *I'M THE*

KING OF THE CASTLE (1970), a study of one boy's cruelty to another, which won the Somerset Maugham Award. Both *Strange Meeting* (1971) and *THE BIRD OF NIGHT* (1972, Whitbread Prize) focused on close male relationships, while *In the Springtime of the Year* (1974) explored a young woman's recovery from her husband's death. Hill's short-story collections from this period include *The Albatross* (1971, John Llewellyn Rhys Prize) and *A Bit of Singing and Dancing* (1973); her radio work was collected in *The Cold Country* (1975).

After marrying Shakespeare scholar Stanley Wells in 1975, she said she would write no more novels and worked in other forms: the ghost story in *The Woman in Black* (1983); children's books, among them *One Night at a Time* (1984), *Mother's Magic* (1986) and *Can It Be True?* (1988); and non-fiction, notably the autobiographical *The Magic Apple Tree* (1982) and *Family* (1989), the latter a harrowing account of her longing for – and the eventual birth of – a second child. She did return to the novel with *Air and Angels* (1991), an anatomy of a Cambridge don's obsessive love for a young girl. It was followed by *The Mist in the Mirror* (1992) and *Mrs de Winter* (1993), a surprising sequel to DAPHNE DU MAURIER's classic *REBECCA* (1938).   MO'D

Hindmarch, Gladys (Maria) 1940– Canadian short-story writer and college instructor, born at Ladysmith on Vancouver Island to Taimi (Aho) and Robert Hindmarch. She earned her Bachelor of Arts and Master of Arts at the University of British Columbia, where she was a founding editor, in 1961, of the important newsletter *Tish*. Because Hindmarch wrote prose she did not publish in *Tish*, which focused exclusively on avant-garde poetry. She began teaching English at Capilano College in North Vancouver in 1973.

Her major works include *The Peter Stories* (1976), a series of five stories based on the Peter Pumpkineater nursery rhyme; *A Birth Account* (1976), which records the author's body sensations, thoughts and feelings during the course of a pregnancy, miscarriage, second pregnancy and birth; and *The Watery Part of the World* (1988), a collection of linked stories based on her experiences working as a mess girl (1962–3) and cook (summer of 1964–5 and one trip in 1968) on a small passenger freighter plying the British Columbia coast. Her writing is often described as 'proprioceptive' due to its attention to the position of her own body; Hindmarch has applied the terms 'improsement' and 'post prose'.   JBM

historical novel, The Women writers were active in the development of this genre, which evolved in close relations with GOTHIC and regional novels. The vaguely past setting of Gothic novels became specifically historical in SOPHIA LEE's very popular *The Recess* (1783–5), in which two fictional illegitimate daughters of Mary Stuart were victimized by a wide range of historical characters. Lee's mix of fictional and historical characters, her preoccupation with royalty and courts, and accompanying paradoxical emphasis on the pathos of women's lives written out of history, were all to be highly suggestive for the genre. MARIA EDGEWORTH's *CASTLE RACKRENT* (1800), the founding document of historical and regional fictions, as Scott's *Waverley* acknowledged, explored Irish historical development and national identity. The PORTER sisters, ANNA and JANE, responded to European revolutionary ferment with fictions of romantic revolt, including Jane's William Wallace novel, *The Scottish Chiefs* (1806). These early developments established enduring strands in the genre: the conservative romance, the regional chronicle, the history of the unrecorded and oppressed.

In the Victorian aftermath of Scott's dominance, most specialists in the genre were male, but Edgeworth's and Scott's most important influence in English writing was on the novels of leading women writers, on CHARLOTTE BRONTË's *SHIRLEY* (1849) and ELIZABETH GASKELL's *Sylvia's Lovers* (1863) – both myths of national development emphasising the pains of transition – and especially on GEORGE ELIOT. All Eliot's novels provoke Henry James's question of *MIDDLEMARCH* (1871): 'If we write Novels so, how shall we write History?' Her concept of 'society as incarnate history' informed all her novels, but *Romola* (1863), set in Renaissance Florence, required additional research to document her vision of society and women's relations to social development. Comparably, in the 20th century, WILLA CATHER transplanted the understanding of the development of pioneer society which informed all her novels to her novel of early Quebec, *SHADOWS ON THE ROCK* (1931).

In the earlier 20th century many of the new academic women historians specialized in women's and popular history, and their research informed historical novels, as in SYLVIA TOWNSEND WARNER's use of Eileen Power's *Medieval English Nunneries* (1922) in her chronicle of medieval convent life, *The Corner that Held Them* (1948). Such reconstruction of the life hidden from history, which early fascinated VIRGINIA WOOLF in her 'Journal of Mistress Joan Martyn', has been one major 20th-century emphasis in the historical novel. Another has been the challenge to the metropolitan centre. The question 'Whose history?' has been asked ever more sharply. HENRY HANDEL RICHARDSON's 'RICHARD MAHONY' trilogy (1917–29), drawing on family records to write the forgotten Australian pioneers back into history, was still clearly in the Edgeworth tradition, mediating between centre and periphery. JEAN RHYS's *WIDE SARGASSO SEA* (1966) represented the distinctively alienated creole woman's experience by exposing the history obliterated in a classic Victorian text. TONI MORRISON's *BELOVED* (1987) drew on intensive debates about the relations of gender and race to write the woman's experience of slavery back into history. Other novelists have sought the elusive actuality behind copious documentation, as in MARGARET ATWOOD's reconstruction of a Victorian Canadian murder case, *ALIAS GRACE* (1996). Some feminist writers have chosen to reject historical actuality altogether, turning to fantasy for a dynamic reimagining of alternative histories. Despite 'Joan Martyn', Woolf chose fantasy for *ORLANDO* (1928), freeing her heroine from the inexorable conventions of periodization. More recently fantasy has liberated the heroines of ANGELA CARTER, reimagining the utopian possibilities of 1900 in *NIGHTS AT THE CIRCUS* (1984), and JEANETTE WINTERSON, moving between past and modernity, history and FAIRY TALE, in *SEXING THE CHERRY* (1989).

Meanwhile Sophia Lee's recipe of victimized females in high life has been the staple of many bestselling novels with historical settings. Although Ethel Voynich revived the Porter tradition in her Risorgimento romance, *The Gadfly* (1897), which sold millions in Eastern Europe, the conservative model of BARONESS ORCZY's *The Scarlet Pimpernel* (1905) proved more influential in the West. Alongside the romance of court and royalty, the regional historical romance, from MARGARET MITCHELL's *GONE WITH THE WIND* (1936) to CATHERINE COOKSON's Tyneside novels, has also sold millions. Many novels at various levels of historical seriousness profited from the discovery, made by NAOMI MITCHISON with her ancient barbarian novels of the 1930s or MARY RENAULT with her ancient Greek romances of the 1950s, that historical fiction permits a more explicit sexuality than might be tolerated in works about contemporary life. One subgenre in which women writers have always been prominent is juvenile historical fiction, in which specialist writers, such as Anne Manning and EVELYN EVERETT-GREEN, emerged in the Victorian period. The robuster children's novels of this century evoked the continuity of past and present on the basis of more thorough research; ROSEMARY SUTCLIFF's romances of early Britain were a major postwar example. Fantasy, notably in the perennially popular device of time travel to the past, first popularized by E. NESBIT's Edwardian romances, has also been used to engage the child reader. Historical fiction in all its relations with other genres has proved flexible in allowing women writers to imagine unrecorded lives.   AT

Historical Trilogy, The (1941–53) *The Timeless Land* (1941), *Storm of Time* (1948) and *No Barrier* (1953) are commonly referred to as ELEANOR DARK's 'Historical Trilogy'. The novels cover the first twenty-five years of settlement history in the colony of New South Wales, commencing with the arrival of Governor Phillip in 1788 and finishing with the building of a road which crosses the Blue Mountains, in 1813. The trilogy is overtly traditional in form and structure but the novels interweave sub-texts which resist a conventional reading of social history. In *The Timeless Land*, the relationship between Governor Phillip and Bennelong is explored and embodies the irreconcilable differences between European and Aboriginal cultures. In *Storm of Time*, the governorships of Hunter, King and Bligh are described in meticulous detail, and in *No Barrier*, following the Bligh rebellion and the discovery of a route over the Blue Mountains, the settlement of Sydney is able to expand across the rich western country and begin to prosper. Throughout the novels, the saga of the fictitious Mannion and Prentice families is interwoven with the historical detail. Central to the trilogy is the Australian landscape and the opposing relationships the two cultures have with the land, an issue which has returned to dominate socio-political and cultural debates in Australia in the 1990s.   JN

History of England from the Accession of James I to that of the Brunswick Line, The (8 volumes published in irregular succession by different London printers 1763–83) CATHERINE MACAULAY's most substantial and acclaimed work and perhaps the first historical tract published in England by a woman, the *History* answers David Hume's *History of England from the Invasion of Julius Caesar to the revolution in 1688 in 8 volumes* (1754–62). In contrast to Hume's Tory interpretation, Macaulay intended her work as a defence against contemporary erosions of English 'constitutional rights'. Of the Glorious Revolution, Macaulay argues that England had not seized 'this fair opportunity to cut off all the prerogatives of the crown . . . which had ever prevented the democratical principles of the constitution from acting to the security of those liberties and privileges vainly set forth in the letter of the law'. Modern and innovative in her method, Macaulay read 17th-century pamphlets and manuscripts, quoting at length and sometimes publishing documents representing both sides of an issue. In comparing Macaulay's and Hume's works, NATALIE Z. DAVIS has argued that 'her footnotes contain references to manuscripts and tracts in the British Museum, to which Hume . . . came late, if at all'.   JHP

History of Lady Julia Mandeville, The (1763) FRANCES BROOKE's EPISTOLARY sentimental novel both typifies the genre and ironically deflates many of its more extravagant gestures, having as its chief correspondents the complementary figures of Harry, the apparently star-crossed sentimental lover, and Lady Anne Wilmot, a young widow of unashamedly unsentimental views, whose central function is to provide a wry commentary on the doings and demeanour of Harry and the woman he loves, Lady Julia Mandeville. Anne's letters are full of dry humour directed at both the conduct of the lovers and the broader social scene. The novel makes much of contemporary political divisions, its heroes (such as Julia's father, Lord Belmont) being landed and rural while its less desirable figures (such as the 'cit' Mr Westbrook and the nouveau-riche Viscount Fondville) are monied and urban. The apparent endorsement of a traditional patriarchal order is undermined, however, not only by Anne's commentary but also by the tragic yet wholly preventable deaths of the two lovers, which suggest how ludicrous sentimental extremes can be and simultaneously destroy the rural idyll Belmont wishes to maintain.   GS

History of Maria Kittle, The (1790–1) ANN ELIZA SCHUYLER BLEECKER blends the CAPTIVITY NARRATIVE with the sentimental, EPISTOLARY NOVEL in her fictional account of Maria Kittle, who is kidnapped during the French and Indian War. Native Americans, depicted as brutish demons, raid Maria's home and kill her children while her husband has travelled to town, ironically, to hire carriages to move his family to safety. This brief novel focuses on the sensational violence of Indian raids, detailing how Maria's child is dashed against stones and how the pregnant Comelia Kittle is tomahawked and has her foetus torn from her body. The narrative also emphasizes, however, that the sorrow aroused by tales of captivity is a beneficial emotion that creates sisterhood among women. Released in Montreal, Maria joins a community of French and British women who have overcome national prejudices through their shared sensibilities as mothers and victims of violence. Playing upon conventional ideals of female emotion versus male action, the sub-text of the novel suggests that European women can find safety only among themselves.   DKo

Hit-him-home, Joane Author of *The women's sharpe revenge: Or an answer to Sir Sel dome Sober that writ those railing Pamphlets called the Juniper and Crab-tree lecture, &c. Being a sound Reply and a full confutation of those Bookes: with an Apology in this case for the defence of us women*, written in response to John Taylor's two misogynist lectures of 1639. This reply is believed to have been written in collaboration with MARY TATTLEWELL. Other theories purport that Tattlewell was Hit-him-home's pseudonym (another possible pseudonym is 'Mary Make-Peace') or even that the text was written by Taylor himself in answer to his own work. The text relays the prevailing dialectical debate of the defences and praises of women complete with disparaging remarks and personal insults. One section in particular, however, is indicative of female authorship as it comments on the suppression of female growth through limited or denied education. The author laments that learning for women was limited to that which benefited her male counterparts rather than herself as she comments that reading was frowned upon for women whilst activities such as sewing were encouraged.   KTu

Hobbes, John Oliver (Pearl Mary-Teresa Richards Craigie) 1867–1906 American-born novelist, TRAVEL WRITER and dramatist. Daughter of a wealthy purveyor of patent medicines, she was born in Chelsea, Massachusetts, raised in London, and educated in private schools in London and Paris. At the age of nine she published her first stories in a Congregationalist newspaper. In 1887 she married Reginald Walpole Craigie, a wealthy but dissipated banker, whom she divorced soon after the birth of their child in 1895. She added Mary-Teresa to her name when she joined the Catholic Church in 1892. During her marriage she wrote criticism for periodicals, and afterwards she enrolled at University College London to study classical languages. She coined the pseudonym 'John Oliver Hobbes' (combining her father's first name with the names of Oliver Cromwell and the philosopher Hobbes) when her first novel, *Some Emotions and a Moral* (1891), was accepted for publication in Fisher Unwin's Pseudonym Library. The novel was quickly successful and she wrote nine others, including *The Gods, Some Mortals and Lord Wickenham* (1895, another popular success); *The School for Saints* (1897) and *Robert Orange* (1902), both with fictional portraits of Disraeli; *The Herb Moon* (1896); *The Vineyard* (1904); and *The Dream and the Business* (1906). Her first play was *Journeys End in Lovers Meeting* (1895); her best-known, *The Ambassador* (1898). She also wrote journalism and headed the Society of Women Journalists from 1895 to 1896. A series of her articles is collected in *Imperial India* (1903). Hobbes's caustic style lent itself to witty epigrams, for which she was much parodied. She was also a target of unflattering gossip, much of it spread by her one-time collaborator, George Moore, who based characters in his fiction on her. Opposed to women's political involvement, Hobbes joined the Anti-Suffrage League founded by MRS HUMPHRY WARD.   JSG

Hobomok (1824) Abolitionist, pioneering feminist, and Indian rights advocate LYDIA MARIA CHILD published this first novel anonymously. Set in 17th-century colonial Massachusetts, *Hobomok* is the story of Mary Conant, a rare Puritan woman who defies her orthodox father's wishes and betrothes herself to an Episcopalian, Charles Brown. When she believes him killed at sea, she takes her rebellion a giant step further by marrying an Indian, Hobomok, and moving to his wigwam. Child's daring depiction of interracial courtship and marriage reflects her early advocacy of women's rights and her prescient concern over the emerging American policy of Indian Removal from their native lands. Her title character is an early prototype of the 'noble savage' which would become prominent in the national imagination later in the century. In the end, Child backs away from the most radical possibilities of her story: Brown returns from the dead, and Hobomok renounces Mary and their child, leaving for the western frontier. But this retreat into a conventional marriage plot does not obscure Child's strong reformist impulse; *Hobomok* stands as a far more progressive novel than James Fenimore Cooper's *The Last of the Mohicans* (1826), to which it is often compared. LC

Hobson, Laura Z. 1900–86 American novelist, short-story writer. Known for her depictions of prejudice and her focus on liberal causes, Laura was the daughter of Adella Kean and Michael Zametkin, labour organizer and editor of a Yiddish newspaper. She graduated from Cornell University and worked for *Time* magazine until 1940, first as an advertising copywriter and later as promotions director, helping in 1936 to launch *Life* magazine.

In 1930 she had married publisher Thayer Hobson, with whom she wrote her first two books, both westerns. Divorced in 1935, she published her first novel, *The Trespassers,* in 1943. Her best-known novel, *Gentleman's Agreement* (1947), tells the story of magazine writer Phil Green, whose first assignment at a new job is to explore American anti-Semitism. Although a Gentile, Green introduces himself as a Jew, and learns first-hand of the bigotry practised by even his friends and family. Although some reviewers found the book heavy-handed, most responded favourably. *Gentleman's Agreement* was made into a film and won the 1948 Academy Award for Best Picture. Hobson's other novels, although less successful, covered a wide variety of themes, including Jewish assimilation, single motherhood and American asylum for Jews during World War II. In 1975, she published *Consenting Adult,* which explores the changing reaction of Tessa Lynn to her son Jeff's revelation that he is gay, and ends with her accepting and blessing him. At the age of 80, she began *Laura Z.: A Life* (1983–6), a two-volume autobiography. SP

Hoby [née Dakins], Margaret 1571–1633 British diarist and devout Puritan whose 1599–1605 record may provide the earliest extant British account of daily life. Her DIARY begins as a religious exercise to record her devotions and catch out her sins, but becomes in time a report instead on her busy days as a landed gentlewoman. An heiress married young and twice widowed, during the diary period she was wed to her final husband, Thomas Posthumous Hoby, second son of Sir Thomas Hoby, and living at Hackness in Yorkshire. The marriage was childless and, according to neighbourhood gossip, an unhappy one, though Lady Hoby never complains of it; all her entries are dispassionate records. Her manifold estate and domestic chores, from doctoring to paying wages to making jam and washing lace, form an important part of her record; she also received young gentlewomen in her home for domestic training and advised estate tenants. A frequent trait at the outset is attributing her illnesses and toothaches to punishment for her sins; a frequent refrain is ending the days with 'and so to bed'. Her diary breaks off abruptly in 1605, possibly because she realized that her record had become too worldly. HB

Hodge, Merle 1944– African-Caribbean writer, born in Cuepe, Trinidad. On a scholarship (1962) she gained BA and M.Phil. in French at London University, travelled widely in Europe and Africa, returning to Trinidad and Tobago in the early 1970s. Hodge taught French, English and West Indian Literature, lecturing at the University of the West Indies. In 1979 she worked in Grenada with Prime Minister Maurice Bishop, returning in 1983, after his assassination and the US invasion. Hodge writes CHILDREN'S STORIES, articles and reviews. Her seminal novel *Crick Crack Monkey* (1970), about a sensitive girl growing up in the difficult social context of Trinidad, broke new ground for the expression and publication of Caribbean women's writing. Hodge writes and lectures about women's oppression and misrepresentation in the Caribbean in essays like 'The Shadow of the Whip: A Comment on Male–Female Relations in the Caribbean' (1974). In 'Challenges of the Struggle for Sovereignty: Changing the World versus Writing Stories' (1990), she argues for political sovereignty, against 'admission into the world of *their* storybook': 'Caribbean literatures can contribute to the process of empowering Caribbean people.' Her *For the Life of Laetitia* (1995) is for children. GW

Hodgman, Helen 1945– Anglo-Australian lesbian writer who portrays the sexual, often sinister, underside of suburban domestic life. Born in Aberdeen, Scotland, in 1945, she lived in Essex until 1958 when her family emigrated to Tasmania. She left school at 15 and returned to London where, after a number of menial jobs, she began to write. Her first novel, *Blue Skies* (1976), is set in Tasmania and, in its tale of murder, duplicity and transvestism, it inhabits the 'unexplored places on this heart-shaped island'.

Winner of the Somerset Maugham Prize in 1979, *Jack and Jill* (1978) surveys similar themes in its depiction of a young girl growing up with her widowed father on a sheep farm in the New South Wales outback. With the arrival of farm hand, Jack, a diabolic *ménage à trois* pertains. The relationships which ensue reveal the crippling consequences of dependence and surreptitious desire.

Broken Words (1989) is Hodgman's London novel and focuses on the intricate Clapham Common lives of lesbian couple, Moss and Hazel, who are still trying to elude the designs of their ex-husbands.

She has also written a play, *Oh Mother, Is it Worth It?* (1982); a screenplay, *The Right-Hand Man* (1984); and a television mini-series, *The Silence of Dean Maitland* (1986).   JAH

Hoey [née Johnston], Frances Sarah 1830–1908
Respected Irish literary critic, translator, novelist and journalist. The eldest of eight children, she was born at Bushy Park, Dublin, and educated at home. In 1853 she began to contribute reviews to Dublin periodicals including the *Freeman's Journal* and the *Nation*. After her first husband's death in 1855, she moved to London where, with William Thackeray's patronage, she wrote for the *Morning Post* and the *Spectator*. She converted to Roman Catholicism in 1858 and married John Cashel Hoey, political essayist, member of the Young Ireland party, and one-time editor of the *Nation*.

While she shared her husband's nationalist sympathies and wrote several short 'tales' set in Ireland, her novels' settings tend toward more exotic locales such as Cuba and India, including her first full-length work, the SENSATION novel *A House of Cards* (1868). She wrote several more novels, including *A Golden Sorrow* (1872) and *The Blossoming of an Aloe* (1874), and is considered to have been largely responsible for five novels attributed to the journalist, Edmund Yates. She also translated works from French and Italian, wrote a fortnightly 'Lady's Letter' for an Australian newspaper for over twenty years, and was the first English journalist to report on the Paris Commune.   MO'C

Hoffman, Alice 1952–
American novelist whose humane fictions discover the submerged edges and mysteries of suburban life. Born and raised in New York, Hoffman received an MA from Stanford University before settling outside Boston with her husband and their two children. Her early novels – including *Property Of* (1977), *White Horses* and *Fortune's Daughter* – explored darker subjects such as incest, street gangs and drug dealing; in the late 80s with *Illumination Night* and *At Risk* her tone became gentler and more knowing. The latter, a story of an ordinary family whose daughter contracts AIDS through a blood transfusion, was a bestseller which some considered sentimental. Her incorporation of supernatural elements such as ghosts or mysterious vengeful creatures has invited the tag of 'magic realism', while her focus on local loves and rivalries suggests a comparison with ANNE TYLER. Her geographies – *Seventh Heaven*'s Long Island, *Turtle Moon*'s Florida – may vary, but her characters inhabit a familiar, near-mythic suburban America. She admits to a phobic nature herself, but believes her phobias have enriched her work: 'Writers and phobics have something in common . . . they see the dark possibilities'. Later novels include *Second Nature, Practical Magic* and 1997's *Here on Earth*. SB

Hoffman, Eva 1945–
Polish-American writer who deals with a range of cultural subjects. Hoffman was born into a Jewish family in Cracow, Poland, from where she emigrated to Canada at the age of 13. After graduating with a Ph.D. from Harvard, she turned to journalism, and worked as an editor of the *New York Times Book Review* for a number of years; she then moved to London. Her memories connected with the painful loss of her childhood paradise and immersion in a new language and culture were described in her first autobiographical book, *Lost in Translation* (1989): 'From now on, I'll be made, like a mosaic, of fragments.' *Exit into History: A Journey Through the New Europe* (1993) is an attempt to revisit Eastern Europe from the perspective of 'the Westerner', speculating on the possibilities of cross-cultural encounters. In *Shtetl* (1998), Hoffman presents the history of Polish–Jewish relations set in a European framework. Here, the author attempts to give testimony to two different historical truths, and thus negotiate her way between multiple – but not necessarily exclusive – identities: that of woman, writer, Westerner, Pole and Jew.   JZ

Holcroft, Frances 1778/83–1844
British novelist and poet. She was the daughter of the radical 'Jacobin' novelist Thomas Holcroft and his third wife. In 1797 she published a poem in support of the abolition of the slave trade in the *Monthly Magazine* and after a period travelling in Europe she produced translations of German, Spanish and Italian plays for the *Theatrical Recorder* edited by her father (1805). After her father's death in 1809, Holcroft applied to the Royal Literary Fund for financial assistance in order to start a school, and she also turned to novel writing. *The Wife and the Lover* was published in 1813 and *Fortitude and Frailty* in 1817. Holcroft's style combines the interest in radical politics that characterized the Jacobin novelists of the 1790s with the preoccupation with virtue, manners and female morality that was a feature of the fictional tradition of FANNY BURNEY, MARY BRUNTON and JANE AUSTEN. Her work can be compared with that of ELIZABETH INCHBALD and AMELIA OPIE, in that it exposes the tension between radical allegiance and an increasingly reactionary moral climate.   LBe

Holland, Cecelia 1943–
American writer of HISTORICAL NOVELS, distinguished for her capacity to

empathize with the fortitude of brutal men and women from warrior cultures.

Early novels like *The Firedrake* (1966), *Rakossy* (1967) and *Kings in Winter* (1967) dealt with extreme situations – a Hungarian provincial fortress besieged by victorious Turkish invaders, a dishonoured Irish noble caught up in the intrigues that will lead to the battle of Clontarf and the murder of Brain Boru. Holland reversed the cosy optimism of much historical fiction to show protagonists whose only consolation is a degree of grace in inevitable defeat.

Until the Sun Falls (1969) covers the Mongol invasion of Eastern Europe from the Mongol point of view. Holland's capacity for empathy is at its most remarkable here; she wears her research lightly yet manages to make the reader inhabit a mindset in which genocidal massacre is part of the day's work. In her one SF novel, *Floating Worlds* (1975), she adapts her usual techniques to a fluent sequence of space opera tropes. More recent novels deal with less harsh themes, but with the same terse bitterness; the principal benefit of civilization for Holland's characters is cynicism. Her deliberately terse and unemotional diction has led some critics to underrate her – she is an uncomfortable writer.   RK

Hollar, Constance 1880–1945 Jamaican poet who worked as a classics teacher. Her edited volume *Songs of Empire* (1932) was published to mark the visit of the Prince of Wales and Prince George to Jamaica in 1931. Although the allegiance of this work to colonial culture is obvious, her own poems often offer more complex representations of nationalist sentiment. 'Mangoes' and 'Cassia' in *Flaming June* (1941) join the nationalist project of naming the Caribbean landscape. Another volume, *The Silver Nutmeg*, may have been published in 1943. Hollar's poetry also appeared in local newspapers and anthologies, including the *Year Books of the Poetry League of Jamaica*, and was broadcast on the BBC *Caribbean Voices* programme, but a great deal of her writing remains uncollected and unpublished.   AD

Holme, Constance 1880–1955 English regional novelist who recorded 'the great slide' in traditional ways of life in early 20th-century Westmorland. Her family had been land agents in Milnthorpe for generations, and she spent her life in Westmorland, attending school there, and in 1916 marrying Frederick Punchard, land agent at Kirkby Lonsdale. Her earlier novels, most notably *The Lonely Plough* (1914), are panoramic accounts of farming communities; their detailed emphasis on working practices, rhetoric of loyalty and self-sacrifice, and stylistic dependence on Kipling evoke a hard-pressed border community. Her post-war novels, *Beautiful End* (1918), *The Splendid Fairing* (1919), *The Trumpet in the Dust* (1921) and *The Things which Belong*

(1925), each focus on the consciousness of an elderly working-class protagonist during one day. They are clearly responsive to developments in MODERNIST fiction; Holme also claimed the influence of Rabindranath Tagore and of Greek drama. She wrote several one-act dialect plays, including *The House of Vision* (1932), which was acted by EDY CRAIG's company. In the 1930s all her novels were published in World's Classics. Her novels are more attentive to rural work practices, and more responsive to contemporary developments in fiction, than most regional writing of the period.   AT

Holmes, Mary Jane Hawes 1825–1907 American author of more than thirty novels, primarily popular in the 1850s and 1860s. Born in rural New England, she began teaching at a district school at the age of 13 and married Daniel Holmes, a lawyer, of Brockport, New York, in 1849. The couple lived briefly in Kentucky, but eventually remained in Brockport; characters in Holmes's novels often divide their time between North and South. She was in financial terms extremely successful – her novels were serialized in the *New York Weekly* and distributed widely in paperback; circulation figures are estimated in the millions. Holmes's best-selling novels, including *Tempest and Sunshine* (1854), *The English Orphans* (1855), *Lena Rivers* (1856), *Dora Deane* (1858) and *Marian Grey* (1863), employ the formula for women's fiction typical of the period, in which a young woman negotiates the romantic and economic perils of the American marriage market. Like her contemporaries, Holmes addresses the effect on women of critical social issues such as poverty and alcoholism, but her approach to woman's moral development is distinctly more secular, marked by a wicked sense of humour that undoubtedly contributed to her extraordinary popularity.   VC

Holtby, Winifred 1898–1935 British novelist, playwright and journalist whose fiction and political polemics were defined by the joined commitments to social reform and to feminism. Born in Rudstone, in the East Riding of Yorkshire, she imaginatively portrayed her mother Alice, one of the first women aldermen in England, as Mrs Beddows in her popular novel *SOUTH RIDING* (1936). She was educated at Queen Margaret's School, Scarborough, and Somerville College, Oxford, where her studies were interrupted by World War I when she enlisted as a WAAC to serve in France. Upon her return to Somerville in 1919 to read History, she met VERA BRITTAIN, with whom she moved to London in 1921. Holtby remained a member of Brittain's household after the latter's marriage, and participated in raising Brittain's two children until her early death from renal failure.

Her fiction reflected the social and political causes

which she supported through her active participation in the 'equality' feminist Six Point Group, the League of Nations Union, the Labour Party, as director of *Time and Tide* (from 1926) and as an advocate for the unionization of black workers in South Africa. Her REALISTIC novels, *Anderby Wold* (1923), *The Crowded Street* (1924), *The Land of Green Ginger* (1927) and *South Riding*, explored feminist themes in provincial English settings. In *Mandoa, Mandoa!* (1933) and the anti-fascist dystopian play *Take Back Your Freedom* (published posthumously, 1939) she experimented with political satire. Her non-fiction included a perceptive study, VIRGINIA WOOLF (1932), and *Woman in a Changing Civilization* (1932) where she articulated a clear position of feminist anti-fascism. JVG

Home Truths: Selected Canadian Stories (1981)

This collection by MAVIS GALLANT brings together sixteen short stories, each connected – by setting or character – to the author's country of birth. One of her most popular collections, it won Canada's highest literary honour, the Governor General's Award. 'Bonaventure' and 'In the Tunnel', in the section entitled Canadians Abroad, both provide ironic glimpses of the effect of pitting alienated, but eloquently presumptuous, Canadian naivety against the weight of European experience. The six Linnet Muir stories in the final section are generally considered the author's most important achievement in this collection. Linnet's isolated remembrances are presented with authoritative clarity, embedded in unassuming – but terrifyingly precise – language. The linked narratives create a memory text made complicated by the dreamlike passage of time and the author's skilful deployment of the ambiguities associated with 'autobiography'. Readers should heed Gallant's own warning: 'Stories are not chapters of novels. They should not be read one after another . . . Read one. Shut the book. Read something else. Come back later. Stories can wait.' SLK

Hope, Laurence [Adela Florence Nicolson]

1865–1904 British poet. She was the daughter of an Irishwoman, Fanny Elizabeth (Griffin), and Arthur Cory, a colonel in the Indian Army. Born at Stoke Bishop, Gloucestershire, she was educated at a private school in Richmond before going out to India. In 1889 she married Colonel Malcolm Hassels Nicolson, who referred to her as 'Violet'. They settled in Madras and had one son, Malcolm Josceline.

Hope's first book, *The Garden of Kama and Other Love Lyrics from India* (1901), was thought to be a man's work. Critics have detected the influence of Swinburne and other English poets. The passionate poems were sometimes controversial, as were the novels of her sister, VICTORIA CROSS(E). Hope addressed racial issues, and admired the beauty of Indian men – occasionally she disguised herself as a Pathan boy, and there were rumours of an affair with an Indian prince. *Stars of the Desert* came out in 1903, but *Indian Love* (1905) was published posthumously. A number of her poems were given musical arrangements, and became popular.

Hope's husband died in 1904, because of a maladministered anaesthetic, and she committed suicide two months afterwards by taking perchloride of mercury. SF

Hope Leslie (1827)

CATHERINE MARIA SEDGWICK's third novel is set in 17th-century New England at a time of territorial conflict between Puritan settlers and the Indians of the region. These events of the historical past mirrored Sedgwick's own present, when the expansion of the United States led to the harsh policy of Indian Removal and the creation of numerous Indian reservations. *Hope Leslie* is a lively combination of frontier adventure story and ROMANCE, with an involved plot featuring villainous disguise and duplicity, and heroic virtue and valour. But instead of white men defending the national cause, Sedgwick recruits her heroes from groups on the traditional margins of such plots: women and Indians. The indefatigable Hope, a rebellious Puritan, is matched by Magawisca, the proud and severely dignified Pequod Indian who demands justice for her people, but who also sacrifices her arm to save Hope's captive brother from being summarily executed by her vengeful father. By juxtaposing these righteous rebels with the staid Massachusetts governor, John Winthrop, and his wife, Sedgwick endorses an alternative to the traditional Puritan patriarchy – and she underscores her commitment to this view by depicting Hope's sister as a voluntary outcast from Puritan society, the willing bride of Magawisca's brother. LC

Hopkins, Pauline Elizabeth

1859–1930 African-American novelist, short-story writer, playwright, BIOGRAPHER and journalist. Born in Boston, Massachusetts, Hopkins completed her first play, *The Slaves' Escape: Or The Underground Railroad*, at the age of 20. She performed the lead role a year later when the play was produced, initiating her twelve-year career on the stage. In 1900, she became a founding member of the *Colored American Magazine*, an African-American journal that sought to encourage African-Americans' interest in the humanities and social sciences. Her short stories were widely published in the magazine. In 1900, she published her first novel, *Contending Forces* (1900), a HISTORICAL romance that engages race, gender and cultural issues at the turn of the century. In the following year, Hopkins became editor of the Women's Department of *CAM*, and in 1903 she became the literary editor. Hopkins also published numerous biographical sketches of people of African descent and three serialized novels in *CAM*: *Hagar's Daughter: A Story of Southern Case Prejudice* (1901–2), *Winona: A Tale of Negro Life in the South and Southwest* (1902), *Of One Blood: Or, the Hidden Self* (1902–3). Her works often blend domestic and historical issues to address the personal significance of race and gender oppression.   CJ

Hopper, Nora [Chesson] 1871–1906 British 'Celtic Twilight' poet, novelist and literary journalist, born in Exeter in 1871. Her father was Irish and her mother Welsh, but she lived for most of her life in London, first with her widowed mother, and then with her husband, W. H. Chesson, whom she married in 1901. In 1894, she published *Ballads in Prose* which won admiration from W. B. Yeats, although he noticed that her style was perilously close to his own early manner. Her poetry is characterized by its lyricism and its allusions to Irish folklore, and many poems are set in a mythical Irish past. Yeats was less enthusiastic about her second volume, *Under Quicken Boughs* (1896), and he later remarked that 'our Irish fairyland came to spoil her work'. The poetry undoubtedly appealed to the late 19th-century taste for the sentimental – later volumes appeared with such titles as *A Dead Girl to her Lover* (1906) and *The Waiting Widow* (1906). Yet Hopper's professionalism and success as a writer should not be underestimated. She was widely published in popular journals, and became a very well-known poet among their readership. She died, aged 35, in London, and her husband published her novel *Father Felix's Chronicles* in 1907 posthumously.   CPe

Horowitz [née Hooker], Frances 1938–83 Poet and broadcaster. Horowitz was born in London, read English and Drama at Bristol University, then went on to train at the Royal Academy of Dramatic Art. Specializing in the art of poetry reading, she made many notable recordings and broadcasts for BBC Radio and the Open University. She began to publish her own work in the late 1960s.

Her poems are formally exquisite, delicate yet intense: critics have often commented on the influence of Japanese literary traditions, such as the haiku. Many explore English landscapes, from London streets to Cumbria to the Cotswolds. These landscapes are represented as historical and mythical texts – palimpsestic and enigmatic – marked by stone circles, ancient barrows and white horses cut into the hillsides. Natural features both invite and resist interpretation: 'Crow' is a 'hieroglyph between hills'; 'Winter Woods' are full of 'omens / we cannot decipher'; 'January' reveals 'the runes of trees'.

Horowitz died of cancer in her mid-forties. The poet and critic Roger Garfitt, whom she married shortly before her death, went on to edit and introduce her

Collected Poems, published in 1985. The haunting quality of many of these poems derives in part from the fact that they are not end-stopped: they do not reach comfortable conclusions or resolutions. 'Dream', for example, ends in an exhilarating defiance of closure: 'I have outrun darkness / do not stop me now – '.   AFT

Hosain, Attia 1913–98 Indian novelist and short-story writer, born in Lucknow. Attia Hosain's liberal English education was blended with home instruction in Urdu, Persian and Arabic. She graduated in 1933, the first woman to do so from a *Talugdari* family. Influenced by the nationalist movement and the progressive writers' group in India in the 1930s, she became a writer, journalist and broadcaster. In 1947 she settled in London with her husband and two children. Her collection of short stories *Phoenix Fled* (1953) and her novel *Sunlight on a Broken Column* (1961) have been recently reissued.

Sunlight on a Broken Column, described by Mulk Raj Anand as 'one of the few deeply sensitive novels in Indian English', has the partition of India as its background – a story enacted in the historic city of Lucknow, and commingled with the life of Leila, privileged by birth but orphaned at a tender age, educated but compelled by male-dominated social norms to observe polite silence at all times, though slowly but surely she succeeds in breaking these shackles. The novel is redolent of a historic time when graciousness was an end in itself and social hierarchy mattered. The author's grounding in the eastern classical languages is evident in her usage of English. Its descriptive passages are full of poetic charm.

Several of the short stories in *Phoenix Fled* present the reader with a close observation of the feudal society of Awadh earlier in the century, as seen in the trials and tribulations of both lord and servant. They also explore the repressed needs and faiths of women, and the lamentable replacement of person-to-person relationships by the impersonal and anonymous relationships of the modern age.   VQ

Hospital, Janette Turner 1942– Australian fiction writer, born in Melbourne into a Pentecostal family and brought up in Brisbane. Hospital's novels and stories are prime examples of 'Brisbane baroque' and her work shares with that of THEA ASTLEY a fascination with north-eastern Australia's landscape and society. Despite her transient existence – she has lived in the United States, India and Canada and is often considered to be a Canadian writer – she still considers Queensland home and that region plays an increasingly important role in her fiction.

Hospital's first novel, THE IVORY SWING (1982), is set in south India and establishes her preoccupation with portraits of women who have been oppressed, and often silenced, by male-dominated society. Her subsequent novels – *The Tiger in the Tiger Pit* (1983), *Borderline* (1985), CHARADES (1988), *The Last Magician* (1993) and OYSTER (1996) – are complex analyses of power relationships and of the corruption and danger that can exist under the veneer of polite society. The underground is a theme running throughout her work, from the world of illegal immigrants in *Borderline* to the more literally underground worlds of subterranean Sydney in *The Last Magician* and the opal mine in *Oyster*. The intellectually rigorous and densely intertextual nature of her work – quantum physics play an important part in *Charades* – is matched by her evocative and elaborate use of language. This is nowhere more apparent than in her powerful descriptions of the landscape of Queensland, from Brisbane rainforest to the parched inland heat of Outer Maroo, in *Oyster*. In that novel her portrait of rural Australian dystopia is combined with a very personal and disturbing exploration of religious fundamentalism and communal violence.

Hospital has published three collections of short stories: *Dislocations* (1986), *Isobars* (1990) and *Collected Stories 1970-1995* (1996). While her first collection reflects her itinerant lifestyle with stories emanating from many different locations and reflecting her diverse influences, in the last section of *Collected Stories* Hospital explores most clearly her relationship with her homeland. She concludes, 'Wherever I am, I live in Queensland. I know to what brown country and to what wet rainforests my homing thoughts will fly.' SS

Hossain, Rokeya Sakhawat 1880–1932 Bengali essayist, humourist, polemicist, best known for her 1905 story, 'Sultana's Dream', an irreverent critique of Indian patriarchy, and perhaps the first example of feminist SCIENCE FICTION worldwide. Though influential in her time, her writing lay 'forgotten' until the 1980s when it was 'rediscovered' by feminist scholars in both Bangla Desh and India.

Rokeya and her sister were tutored in Persian at home, but had to learn English and Bengali secretly at night. In 1898 she married Syed Sakhawat Hossain who, like her, believed in the education of women. After his death in 1909 she founded and built up a school for girls, in the face of calumny and even physical attack. Many of Rokeya's thoughtful and witty essays, collected in *Motichur* ('Pearl Dust', 1905; vol. II, 1921), *Pipasa* ('Thirst'; 1922) and *Avarodhbasini* ('Secluded Women'; 1931) were written to gather wider support for the cause of women. ST

Hotel du Lac (1984) ANITA BROOKNER's fourth and best-known, Booker-Prize-winning novel explores female responses to the illusory nature of romantic love. The deceptively simple plot hinges on the experiences of Edith Hope, a middle-aged writer of romantic fiction who has escaped to Switzerland in order to avoid social embarrassment after cancelling her wedding to a man she does not love. The book unfolds to provide an insight into the lives of the other residents of the hotel, amongst them a domineering, wealthy widow and her cosseted daughter, and Monica, the victim of an eating disorder. Brookner's shrewd exposition of character and her reconstruction of Edith's past through narrative flashback are suggestive of the complexities of female experience, whilst the critique of marriage which underpins all her writing is supplied through the ironic depiction of relationships between the sexes. With its ambiguous and unresolved ending, the novel self-consciously examines the conventions of ROMANTIC fiction but also suggests the difficulties women face in the quest for autonomy outside the traditional structures of marriage and the family. RCo

Hoult, Norah 1898–1984 Irish novelist and short-fiction writer. Born in Ireland but educated in England following the death of her parents, Hoult was a prolific and popular writer. Her first collection of short stories, *Poor Women* (1928), was remarkable for its bleak depiction of the lives of women constrained by want, loneliness and ageing. A later novel, *Holy Ireland* (1935, reprinted 1985), examines sectarian attitudes and prejudice through an account of a mixed marriage in Ireland and the pressures brought to bear on the young woman concerned. *Husband and Wife* (1959) extends this theme of marital struggle, this time within the narrow social conventions and poverty of rural Ireland. The ambitions and aspirations of the protagonist, Diana, as portrayed in Hoult's preceding novel, *Father and Daughter* (1957), are cruelly destroyed.

A Poet's Pilgrimage (1966) describes 'the long uphill road of being and becoming a writer' for a young man who begins life in an orphanage run by the Christian Brothers. The challenge is accepted 'as a young priest accepts once and for all the heavy but rich vestment laid upon his shoulders'. This novel is also notable for its rendition of the atmosphere of Dublin in the days of the Irish Literary Revival and the souring of idealism that comes with age.

Hoult's characters are often concerned with issues of autonomy and relationship. Many of her finer observations and characterizations, along with a ruthless insight into human motivation and vanity, anticipate William Trevor in their acuity. LM

House [née Pegram], Amelia (Blossom) 19?– South African short-story writer and poet. She was born and grew up in Wynberg, Cape Town. She trained as a teacher and in 1955 took up her first job as a teacher with Kensington Central School in Cape Town. While she was still teaching she studied part-time at the University of Cape Town and gained her BA in English and History in 1961. In 1963 she moved to England and continued her teaching career.

She began writing in response to increasing political oppression in South Africa. Her first published poems, 'You are Born in a Coffin' and 'Mark my Birth' appeared under the name of Blossom Pegram in the *Literary Review: South Africa* (1971). The following year she began writing under her married name, Amelia House. She and her husband moved to Kentucky in the United States and in 1977 she received her Master of Arts for several short pieces of fiction including the short story 'Conspiracy', later published in *Unwinding Threads* (1983). In 1980 she published the bibliographical text *Black South African Women Writers in English: A Preliminary Checklist*. Her first collection of poetry, *Deliverance: Poems for South Africa*, was published in 1986, followed by *Our Sun Will Rise* (1988) and *Echoes Across a Thousand Hills* (1994). She co-edited an anthology entitled *Nelson Mandelamandla* (1989). Her poems and short stories describe the suffering caused by racial oppression and demonstrate a commitment to the anti-apartheid struggles of South Africa.   GMS

House and Its Head, A

(1935) IVY COMPTON-BURNETT's fifth novel (discounting *Delores*) is regarded as having one of her best and most complex plots. It is certainly one of her most social novels, including the local villagers (particularly, the sanctimonious busybody Dulcia Bode) in withering satire that is usually aimed more narrowly at claustrophobic, dysfunctional families. Like all her novels, this one focuses on Victorian/Edwardian domestic arrangements and exposes the greed, hypocrisy and violence that lurks under the surface of a deceptively calm and well-ordered society. The 'head' of the title is the tyrannical Duncan Grant, who rules his house like a god and demands unswerving devotion from the members of his household. His lust for power blights the lives of all the characters and leads to classic Compton-Burnett scandals such as illegitimacy, possible incest, and murderous concerns with inheritance. Compton-Burnett's precise language and penetrating wit reveal the ways power corrupts both victimizers and victims and illuminate the complicity of society and religion in propping up domestic despots.   LCo

House is Built, A

(1929) Exemplifies the collaborative work of MARJORIE BARNARD and FLORA ELDERSHAW. Serialized as *The Quartermaster* in the *Bulletin* as joint winner of that journal's 1928 prize for fiction, it was published in book form in London in 1929. A carefully researched social REALIST novel of early urban Australia, it traces the fortunes of a Sydney merchant family from the 1830s to the 1880s, offering within this framework a critique both of the boom-and-bust pattern of Australian entrepreneurial activity and of the high cost imposed by bourgeois capitalism upon individuals inappropriately endowed (especially women and the artistic male). Fanny, failing in the female enterprise of marriage, succeeds as businesswoman during her brother's absence on the goldfields, but must dwindle to genteel charitable works when he reclaims his role as family and business head. Human wastefulness also shapes the fate of Fanny's nephews: when the capable older commits suicide, shamed by a passion-inspired betrayal of business secrets, the younger must sacrifice his natural artistic inclinations to ensure the continuity of the all-demanding 'House'.   JStr

House of All Nations

(1938) CHRISTINA STEAD's fourth novel has been described as a Balzacian satire of men and money. Teeming with characters, the narrative uses documentary REALISM, but in its excesses veers toward MODERNISM. The title refers at once to the shadowy Bank Mercure and an infamous Parisian brothel, and the novel equates money-dealing with flesh-trading. Its multitude of plots coalesce, finally, in the story of the bank's ruinous collapse. Counterpointing the machinations of cowboy capitalists – like the womanizing Léon, the mercurial Bertillon and the monstrous Raccamond – is the utopian world of the communist fraternity. Mediating both worlds is Michel Alphendéry, economic wizard, communist sympathizer and loyal confidant of the high-flying, capitalist Bertillon brothers. Containing some of Stead's most memorable writing, including the savagely funny dinner-party scene, 'A Stuffed Carp', *House of All Nations* also represents in microcosm the politics of 1930s Europe. As wives, mothers and prostitutes, women mostly function symbolically in this narrative, something which has presented problems for feminist readers. The novel's fascinated attention to 'masculine realms', however, suggests productive avenues for feminist reading.   BR

House of Mirth, The

(1905) EDITH WHARTON's first full-length novel and first bestseller secured her reputation as a writer. It turned her, she said, 'from a drifting amateur into a professional'. The novel charts the failure of the social ambitions of its heroine, Lily Bart, a beautiful but marginal and impoverished member of New York's social elite, who needs to marry money to secure her position in high society. The complex circumstances which frustrate Lily's plans and lead to her ultimate demise allow Wharton scope to display her characteristic interests in psychological, moral and social forces at work on the individual. One of the most Jamesian of Wharton's fictions, this novel also displays her close attention to women's economic status and to the historical shift in American social formations at the turn of the 19th into the 20th century. Despite the fact that this is an early novel, Wharton is already writing at the height of her powers to produce a classic both of American and of women's fiction.   KF

House on Mango Street, The (1985) SANDRA CISNEROS's stories, variously described as prose poems and a novel, were originally published by a small Texas press specializing in Mexican-American writing; the work was enthusiastically repackaged later by a New York publisher in a climate newly favourable to ethnic American fictions. Narrated in the lyrical voice of a child (one piece was illustrated and published separately as a children's book), the vignettes describe life on a delapidated Chicago street in a Latin community. Though there are painful episodes – a girl beaten by her father, a Mexican immigrant killed in a hit-and-run accident – the musical, poetic language and affectionate details give the work a basic optimism. The stories chronicle Esperanza Cordero's coming of age and her hope that writing will provide her an escape from Mango Street: her ambition is to live in a house 'quiet as snow, a space for myself to go, clean as paper before the poem', though she promises never to forget her origins. This, Cisneros's first work, was soon considered a modern classic of Hispanic-American fiction and was widely taught in American schools and colleges.   SB

Howard, Elizabeth Jane 1923– British novelist in the post-war REALIST tradition of women's fiction who writes of family life in a deceptively light and characteristically ironic register, bringing emotional and sexual candour to the study of complex relationships. Much of her fiction examines the ways in which individuals, couples and families are forced to reform after traumatic fractures. The quest for authenticity and the dangers of both honesty and deceit are major themes. *The Beautiful Visit* (1950), *The Long View* (1956) and *After Julius* (1965) explore attraction, loss and guilt in the context of marriage. *Something in Disguise* (1969) disturbingly centres around a woman's realization that her husband is a murderer. *The Odd Girl Out* (1972) is an astute tragi-comedy about a young woman's chaotic effect upon a happily married couple.

Howard elegantly updates the family saga in her series, 'The Cazelet Chronicles' (*The Light Years*, 1990; *Marking Time*, 1991; *Confusion*, 1993; *Casting Off*, 1995), interweaving the various perspectives of an extended middle-class family during World War II. The historical atmosphere is vividly realized through a meticulous recording of domestic and period detail, made interesting through its connection with the characters' inner lives. Here, as in general, Howard's characterizations of women and men are strong, if deliberately mannered; her considerable attention to children and young adults is unsentimental and perceptive.

Howard was educated at home and studied acting, performing at Stratford-upon-Avon and in repertory theatre. She worked for a time as a model before spending the war years in radio and television broadcasting. A move into book publishing inspired her to begin publishing her fiction in the 1950s. As well as novels, she has written short stories, screenplays and television scripts. She was married three times (in 1965 to writer Kingsley Amis; divorced 1983).   LDo

Howard, Maureen 1930– American fiction writer, autobiographer and literary critic. She was born in Bridgeport, Connecticut, daughter of an Irish Catholic police detective, and raised in a working-class neighbourhood. After graduating from Smith College in 1952, she worked in publishing and advertising, then married a professor, Daniel F. Howard, with whom she had one child. They divorced in 1967. A second marriage to Professor David J. Gordon also ended in divorce, and she later married stockbroker–novelist Mark Probst. She published her first novel, *Not A Word About Nightingales*, in 1961. Later she deprecated this story of a scholar's family, calling it a parody of the 'mannered academic novel'. *Bridgeport Bus* (1966) mixes omniscient narrative with first-person sketches to tell the story of a working woman's midlife sexual initiations – a 'heartfelt feminist novel . . . long before that genre appeared', according to Howard. In *Before My Time* (1974), a middle-aged journalist and housewife vicariously joins the youth rebellion through her teenage cousin, a would-be revolutionary. *Grace Abounding* (1982) follows several women characters through the challenges of personal and professional fulfilment. Among these are the colourful Le Doux sisters, spinsters famed for sexual promiscuity and poetry. Howard continued to experiment with form in *Expensive Habits* (1986), *Natural History* (1992) and *A Lover's Almanac* (1998) – a love story set on New Year's Eve 2000 and punctuated with entries of miscellaneous information. Critics have compared Howard to MARGARET ATWOOD and ANNE TYLER. She has taught at the University of California, Santa Barbara; the New School for Social Research; Columbia University; Amherst College; and Brooklyn College. Her autobiography, *Facts of Life* (1978), won a National Book Critics Circle prize for non-fiction.   JSG

Howarde, Kate [Catherine Clarissa Jones] 1869–1939 Australian playwright, actor, theatrical entrepreneur. In an industry almost universally dominated by men, Kate Howarde entertained urban and country Australians for over twenty years in the early decades of the 20th century, touring extensively with her own bush dramas and city tales along with the popular melodramas, musical comedies and pantomimes of the era. Born in England, she began writing as a child, received her first payment at the age of 9 and made the decision early in life 'to attain a self supporting position . . . No doubt, no hesitation. The stage!' At the age of 16 she moved to Australia from New Zealand where her parents had migrated, and at 17 established her own theatre company in Sydney.

Howarde left Australia while still in her teens and worked for five years as a theatre reviewer and journalist in New York. Following some time in England she returned to Australia and re-established her company there. Operating from the National Theatre in Balmain, Sydney, she again catered to popular tastes in which classic Australian types – squatters, selectors, struggling bush people – were represented in bush dramas and comedies liberally interspersed with slapstick routines and melodramatic plotlines. As a successful businesswoman Howarde produced theatre designed to make money. Her most popular play was 'Possum Paddock', a simple tale of a country family facing financial difficulties and the evil intent of a classic rogue. It made a profit of £5,000 in a single season in 1919, touring widely not only in Australia but also in New Zealand and South Africa. Howarde financed, directed and starred in the 1921 film adaptation of 'Possum Paddock', which became a box-office success in the then burgeoning Australian film industry. 'Gum Tree Gully' (1924) was another popular play set in the outback.

Howarde also explored more unusual themes. 'The White Slave Trade' (1914) reflects the contemporary xenophobic attitudes of Australians toward Asians, depicting an imagined trade in virginal white women. Highly melodramatic, it is set in Sydney and in an unidentified Asian country and tells the story of the kidnap and eventual rescue of Joy Arden, a 'typical' Australian girl who exhibits qualities of strength, resilience and inventiveness in the face of extreme peril. Other plays, such as 'Why Girls Leave Home' (1914), 'The Limit' (1923) and 'Common Humanity' (1927), are set in America and Europe but retain Howarde's popular character types. Although successful during her life, Kate Howarde's contribution to the Australian theatre and film industries has been ignored or obscured in written histories. Her plays remain unpublished, located in the Australian Archives, Canberra. She is buried in an unmarked grave in Sydney.   KK

Howe [Tute], Jemima Sartwell Phipps c. 1715–1805 New Hampshire woman, captured (like SUSANNAH WILLARD JOHNSON) in an Indian raid during the French and Indian War, purported author

of a narrative of her experience. Her husband Caleb was killed in the July 1755 attack; Howe and her children were marched to Quebec and she was sold to a French family named Saccappee. After both the elder Saccappee and his son became enamoured of her, Howe was rescued from the situation by a Dutch agent for the French governor and returned home. Howe's CAPTIVITY STORY first appeared in David Humphreys's *An Essay on the Life of the Honorable Major-General Israel Putnam* (1788). His third-person account, highly sentimentalized and somewhat eroticized, became the basis for the subsequent first-person versions published by a New Hampshire minister, Bunker Gay (1792), and by historian Jeremy Belknap (1791). Both Gay and Belknap name Jemima Howe 'the Fair Captive' after Humphreys's description of her as 'a fair captive, whose history would not be read without emotion if it could be written in the same affecting manner, in which I have often heard it told'. Gay's and Belknap's versions of Howe's captivity owe much to seduction novels and to their concern with historiographical 'authenticity'. Their use of her 'I' contributes to an emerging historiographical practice of authorial impersonation, one which often relied on recognizably 'female' rhetorics of seduction and emotionalism to construct a strongly nationalist (anti-British and anti-French) history for the new Republic.   LCa

Howe, Julia Ward 1819–1910 American poet and reformer. She was born in New York City, fourth of seven children in a Wall Street banker's family, and raised in Manhattan and Newport, Rhode Island. She was educated by governesses and tutors and sent to a young ladies' school. In 1843 she married social reformer Samuel Gridley Howe and moved to Boston. They had six children. She published her first collection of poems, *Passion Flowers* (1854), anonymously; *Words for the Home* (1857) followed. Her play *Leonora* (1857), about a woman who commits suicide after failing to kill her unfaithful lover, was condemned as immoral and closed after a week.

Converted to abolitionism in the mid-1850s, she became a lifelong campaigner for social reform despite her husband's opposition to her public life. She composed 'THE BATTLE HYMN OF THE REPUBLIC' in 1862 in the dark of early morning, having attended a review of Union troops the day before and determined to contribute to the Civil War effort despite her responsibilities as a mother of five. First published in *Atlantic Monthly*, 'The Battle Hymn' became an anthem of Union troops and one of the most frequently anthologized poems in English.

In 1870 she founded the weekly *Women's Journal*. After her husband's death in 1876, her literary and reform activities broadened and met with increasing success. She was a founding member of the American

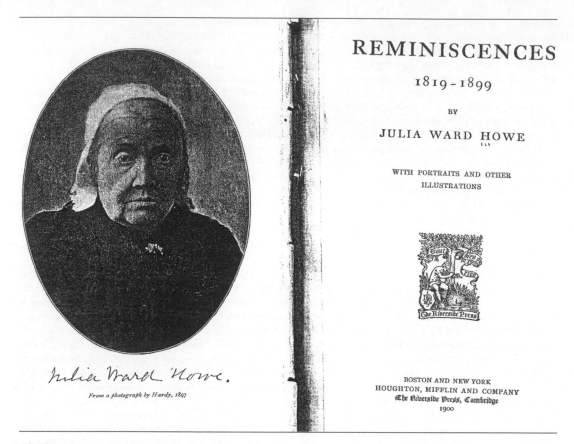

REMINISCENCES

1819–1899

BY

JULIA WARD HOWE

WITH PORTRAITS AND OTHER
ILLUSTRATIONS

BOSTON AND NEW YORK
HOUGHTON, MIFFLIN AND COMPANY
The Riverside Press, Cambridge
1900

Julia Ward Howe.

From a photograph by Hardy, 1897

Julia Ward Howe: portrait and title-page of
Reminiscences.

Woman Suffrage Association and the New England Woman's Club, preached in the Unitarian Church, served as president of Woman's International Peace Association (1871), and presided over the Association for the Advancement of Women (1878–88). In 1888 she closed her public career with a triumphant lecture tour of the West. Her poetry was collected in *Later Lyrics* (1866) and *From Sunset Ridge* (1899). Other writings include *Sex and Education* (1874), *Modern Society* (1881), *Margaret Fuller* (1883), and *Is Polite Society Polite?* (1895). Her memoirs, *Reminiscences* (1899) and *At Sunset* (1910), record links and conflicts among social change movements throughout the century. In 1908, she became the first woman elected to the American Academy of Arts and Letters.   JSG

Howe, Susan 1937– American poet and academic. Susan Howe is one of the most interesting practitioners of Language Poetry, a literary phenomenon originating in the States in the 1970s. Detractors have claimed that Language Poetry is virtually unreadable, having – in the words of critic Stuart Klawans – 'the

texture and allure of drying asphalt'. Enthusiasts, however, hold that it is a ground-breaking, shape-shifting and politically radical exploration of the power and strangeness of language. As Howe suggests, 'we are language Lost / in language'.

Howe's influences can be traced back through American MODERNISTS such as GERTRUDE STEIN and H.D. to EMILY DICKINSON, with whom she engages in her illuminating 1985 study, *My Emily Dickinson*. Here she argues that Dickinson 'exploded habits of standard human intercourse': the kinship with Howe's own project is clear.

Above all, Howe is interested in unmapped regions, exploration and frontiers. For example, *Articulation of Sound Forms in Time* (1987) deals with the wanderings of Hope Atherton, a 17th-century minister, in American frontier-country – and this preoccupation carries forward into her critical work, *The Birth-mark: Unsettling the Wilderness in American Literary History* (1993). Uncharted territory may be historical as well as geographical: her writing often aims to activate the faint traces of voices suppressed by official history.

Howe practises what might be called a politics of the signifier, interrogating the operations of power in language, and asking, 'Whose order is shut inside a sentence?'   AFT

Howitt [née Botham], Mary 1799–1888 British writer, best remembered today for her poem 'The Spider and the Fly' (1834). But during her long, highly successful literary career, she authored, co-authored, translated and edited over a hundred books. Howitt introduced humour into children's poetry, penned some of the most popular ballads of her time, and was the first English translator of Swedish feminist Frederika Bremer and Hans Christian Andersen. Her marriage to William Howitt endured for more than half a century, and American transcendentalist MARGARET FULLER cited the couple as an example of the union of intellectual companionship. The Howitts gathered around themselves an intellectual and artistic circle and began publishing books jointly and independently. From the 1830s to the 1850s, they published each year between one and four books of poetry, fiction and non-fiction prose, and worked for humanitarian and liberal political causes. LETITIA LANDON described Mary Howitt as one who 'gave me more the idea of poet than most of our modern votaries of the lute'. One of Howitt's tales for children inspired ELIZABETH GASKELL'S MARY BARTON (1848).   PRF

Hull, Eleanor c.1394–1460 English translator of French devotional works. Born into a well-connected gentry family from Somerset, she served in the household of Henry IV. After her husband's death, she retreated for a period to Sopwell Priory, and eventually retired permanently to a small Benedictine priory close to the place of her birth. Like other devout women of the period, she had a close relationship with her confessor (Roger Husswyf), who may well have encouraged her scholarship. Her translations reflect the interests of a wealthy and well-born woman dedicated to piety. One is a series of prose meditations on the days of the week, the second a commentary on the penitential psalms. Both are highly conventional texts, carefully rendered into readable English prose. Typical of the sort of pious writing in wide circulation in the later Middle Ages, they are of particular interest because they are part of a tradition of women's religious translations which included the works of figures like LADY MARGARET BEAUFORT and extended into the Renaissance and beyond.   DW

Hulme, Keri 1947– Author of *the bone people* (1983), the novel which gained a cult following in New Zealand after publication by The Spiral Collective, having been rejected by mainstream publishers. The only New Zealand novel to win the Booker Prize (1985), it is now a key text for people who seek an acquaintance with New Zealand literature. Hulme's impor-

Mary Howitt.

tance, as one-eighth Maori and a fluent speaker of the language, is in bringing Maori and Pakeha into new conjunction. *the bone people*'s hybrid blend of both cultures and languages in the problematic relationship between 'outsider' figures, projects New Zealand's bicultural complexities. But although to some readers her epic's concluding vision of unification signifies the dawn of a new consciousness, to others it merely reinscribes a colonized perspective. Hulme draws strongly on Maori myths and spirituality, but through the dominating presence of her heroine, Kerewin, comes a strong influence from European literature and literary stereotypes.

Hulme is comparable to ANNIE PROULX in her linguistic vitality and originality; but the novel's uniqueness also emerges out of a pathology in which sexual denial and violence co-exist. The inadequate symbiosis in adult relationships is compensated for by a third principle, the child Simon. His characterization is for many readers a tour de force: the most abject of all three, the oddly rich mixture of pain, violence and love which he endures leads to a form of communal self-empowerment. This focus on the consciousness of an *ingénue* is familiar in Hulme's mythology, emerging in the short story 'Hooks and Feelers'. Other stories in *Te Kaihau / The Windeater* (1986) show a vision strongly attuned to life's raw forces: her protagonists are the fringe dwellers of rural and urban New Zealand; she incessantly probes how we hurt yet redeem one another.

Hulme's poetry (*The Silences Between* (*Moeraki Conversations*), 1982; *Strands*, 1991) has an Anglo-Saxon flavour, blending forceful rhythms with linguistic density. All her writing conveys through her quirkily humorous persona a surging narrative power. She lives on the West Coast of New Zealand's South Island, surrounded by an extended *whanau* (family) of friends and neighbours.   JMW

Hundred and One Dalmatians, The (1956)

A friend's offhand remark, that an elegant coat could be fashioned from her beloved Dalmatian, inspired DODIE SMITH – primarily a playwright – to write an adventure for children. In the fabulously chic Cruella de Vil, Smith created a lasting contribution to fictional villainy; her diabolism countered only by the Dearly's benevolence – the dogs' human pets in the tale's inverted reality. Against a Christmas setting, Pongo and Missis, the anthropomorphized canine couple, rescue stolen Dalmatian puppies from under the noses of De Vil's half-witted assistants, the Badduns, whose devotion to a television quiz show, 'What's My Crime?', enables escape. Smith's endearing fable entertains adults with its wit, and charms children, all the while suggesting that the esteem and protection of animals and the vulnerable are essential Christian virtues.

Whilst the 1961 Disney animation of *The Hundred and One Dalmatians* – dir. Ken Anderson – surpassed even the novel's success, the 1996 film version – dir. Stephen Herek – was generally felt to have lost some of the original's charm.   TY

Hunt, Violet 1862–1942

NEW WOMAN novelist whose speciality, in life as in art, was the unconventional sexual relationship. Daughter of Margaret Hunt and painter Alfred Hunt, she always moved among stimulating people. 'One to whom sensation is the breath of life, and irregular situations are meat and drink', she was involved with (among others) Wilde, RADCLYFFE HALL, Maugham, Wells and, notoriously, Ford Madox Ford. Her 1890s experiments with dialogue, collected in *The Maiden's Progress* (1894), presage her later short-story successes such as the macabre *Tales of the Uneasy* (1911), and her translation of Casanova (1902) indicates her interest in sexual psychology. Her autobiographical novel, *Sooner or Later* (1904), slyly updates the cliché of *roué* and virgin, and her best, *White Rose of Weary Leaf* (1908), abrasively modernizes the double-standard theme. The passionate, erratic liaison with Ford (1909–15) had literary benefits for them both. She wrote for the *English Review*, *New Freewoman*, *Bystander* and *Pall Mall Gazette*, collaborated

on *Zeppelin Nights* (1916), and (afterwards) wrote the determinedly unromantic *Their Hearts* (1916). When Ford characterized her as promiscuous Florence Dowell in *The Good Soldier* (1915) and vindictive Sylvia Tietjens in *Parade's End* (1924–8), she retaliated with spirit in her memoir, *The Flurried Years* (1926). By her last book, *The Wife of Rossetti* (1932), syphilitic dementia was confusing her mind, but it remains a fervent reiteration of her favourite theme, 'the duel to the death' between women and men.   MSM

Hunt the Slipper (1937)

VIOLET TREFUSIS's fifth novel is a stylish comedy of love and manners. It is the story of Nigel Benson, a plump, bubble-curled, bespectacled 49-year-old sybarite who lives in comfort with his handsome sister Molly in their gracious country home near Bath. One day, he visits his neighbour and his new young wife, Caroline. She is a gauche and reluctant hostess and Nigel, used to more sophisticated responses from women, makes an effort at conversation for politeness's sake. When they meet later in Paris, however, and Caroline confides in the avuncular Nigel that her heart has been bruised by a young Chilean, Nigel sees her afresh and falls passionately in love. Now begins an exquisite, tantalizing game. Caroline returns to England; Nigel travels the flesh-pots of Europe, desperate for word from her which doesn't come. Meanwhile, Caroline realizes she is in love with Nigel, and back in England there is a brief spell of happiness, spoilt by his agony of doubt and torment over whether she can really love him. The 'slipper' of the title is the ever-elusive treasure of the childhood game – happiness forever just beyond reach.   JLB

Hunting the Wild Pineapple (1979)

THEA ASTLEY's acclaimed short-story collection is set in the mythic town of Mango in north-east Queensland, a place of 'limbo for those who've lost direction and have pitched a last-stand tent'. The stories are populated by a series of extravagantly grotesque characters: the competing clerics Canon Morrow and Father Rassini in 'The Curate Breaker', the pathetic Georgy in the title story, the repressed and hysterical virgin Clarice from 'A Northern Belle', Leo and Sadie who engage in a complex battle for dominance in the rainforest in 'Ladies Need Only Apply'. These stories articulate a number of Astley's primary thematic concerns: the hypocrisy of organized religion (particularly Catholicism), the opportunism and torpor of the southern hippies who colonize the north and the constant threat of societal humiliation and denigration. Astley's reiteration of the figure of a victimized woman enhances her identification of the Queensland landscape, in its fury and drama, with male violence and the oppression of women.   SS

Hurst, Fannie 1885–1968 American short-story writer and novelist. She reached the height of her immense popularity in the 1920s. Born in Hamilton, Ohio, at the childhood home of her mother, Rose Koppel Hurst, she was raised in St Louis, Missouri, where her father, Samuel, was president of a shoe factory.

After graduating from Washington University, Hurst moved to New York City in 1911 to pursue her writing. Her stories appeared mostly in the *Saturday Evening Post* and *Cosmopolitan* and eventually earned her as much as $5,000 each. She wrote her first novel, *Star-Dust*, in 1921. Hurst's publications include seventeen novels, eight short-story collections, an autobiography and several dozen uncollected stories and articles. Early in her career, critics considered Hurst a serious artist, admiring her sensitive portrayals of immigrant life and urban working girls.

A quartet of Hurst stories appeared as silent movies between 1920 and 1923. *Star-Dust* premièred on the silent screen the same year it was published. Her best-known novel, *Imitation of Life* (1933), has two sound film versions.

Hurst secretly wed musician Jacques Danielson in 1915. Hurst's German-Jewish family opposed her relationship with Danielson, a Russian Jew. Her personal friends included novelists Theodore Dreiser, Charles and Kathleen Norris, Carl Van Vechten and ZORA NEALE HURSTON, whom she employed as a secretary and chauffeur in 1925.   LMC

Hurston, Zora Neale 1891–1960 African-American novelist, folklorist and anthropologist, and prominent member of the 1920s 'Harlem Renaissance'. This 'Genius of the South', as ALICE WALKER wrote on the tombstone she erected over Hurston's neglected grave, was America's most prolific black woman writer, for three decades, and also one of its most controversial African-American writers.

For a woman of her race and generation, Hurston lived a privileged life. Born ten years earlier than she always claimed, Hurston grew up in an all-black town, Eatonville, Florida, where her father was mayor. She later won a scholarship to New York's Barnard College, where she studied Cultural Anthropology under the renowned Franz Boas. Graduating in 1928, she undertook field research on black folklore in Alabama, Florida, Louisiana and the Bahamas. *MULES AND MEN* (1935) and *Tell My Horse* (1938) record oral tales, religious practices and hoodoo rituals collected on those travels. Prestigious fellowships and white patronage enabled her to continue writing. Besides much journalism, she published four novels: *Jonah's Gourd Vine* (1934), *THEIR EYES WERE WATCHING GOD* (1937), *Moses, Man of the Mountain* (1939) and *Seraph on the Sewanee* (1948).

Dubbing herself 'Queen of the Niggerati' among Harlem intellectuals and artists, she refused to speak on behalf of her oppressed race and defended the South, and white culture, against charges of racism. In her much-criticized autobiography, *Dust Tracks on a Road* (1942), she noted that Africans had sold their own people to slave-traders, and appeared to defend the 'Jim Crow' system of race segregation: 'I do not belong to the sobbing school of Negrohood . . . I do not weep at the world – I am too busy sharpening my oyster knife.' In later years, her political and racial conservatism (including opposition to the landmark 1954 Supreme Court ruling on school desegregation) isolated her from other African-American intellectuals. Her final years were spent working as a maid in Miami. She died in poverty.

Her reputation was revived in the 1970s by the vigorous patronage and detective work of Alice Walker, who found her burial site and ensured the republication of her fiction. Since then, Hurston's work has become a transatlantic industry, with new editions, a place on many curricula, a biography by Robert Hemenway, seminars and critical articles galore. To critic Hazel Carby, this international enthusiasm for Hurston grew because the looming crisis of urban blacks condemned to poverty, violence and despair was too close for (critical) comfort. Her anthropological perspective on southern blacks produced a pastoral, romantic, colonial view of them as a form of folk culture, symbolizing positive, holistic blackness. Nevertheless, Hurston is rightly celebrated for her sensuous southern dialect and rhythms, vivid and exuberant characters and descriptions, and especially for her brilliant woman-centred 'prototypical Black novel of affirmation' (JUNE JORDAN) that has influenced generations of African-American women writers: *Their Eyes Were Watching God*.   HT

Hutchinson, Anne 1591–1643 Like the slave rebel Nat Turner, Anne Hutchinson is the author of a mediated text. Her actual words reach us only through the transcript of her trial for heresy, the culmination of the Antinomian Crisis that rocked the social and theological foundations of New England life in the late 1630s.

Hutchinson emigrated to Boston, Massachusetts, from England in 1634, motivated by her strong Puritan religious beliefs. Once there, she established herself as a spiritual counsellor to women in her community, and her growing popularity expanded her public. Her statements at religious meetings at her home kindled colonial New England's most dramatic religious controversy.

Hutchinson accused most of the Boston clergy of preaching salvation by works rather than through the covenant of grace, the latter being central to Puritan Calvinism. For Hutchinson and her allies to question the clergy – the source of governmental authority –

amounted to a threat to the social order, one whose gravity is clear from the journal entries that Governor John Winthrop wrote about her at the time. When she refused to back down, Hutchinson was arrested and tried, and she admitted during a gruelling examination that she believed that she received guidance directly from the Holy Spirit. For this heretical assertion, Hutchinson was convicted and exiled to Rhode Island in 1638. She died in New York in 1643, unrepentant to the end.   LC

Hutchinson [née Apsley], Lucy 1620–81 Civil War BIOGRAPHER, translator and poet. She grew up in the Tower of London where her father was Lieutenant. She could read at 4 and by the age of 7 had eight tutors in different subjects – she later wrote that 'my genius was quite averse from all but my book'. Some words by her to a song attracted Colonel John Hutchinson, 'fancying something of rationality in the sonnet, beyond the customary reach of a she-wit', and they were married in 1638.

She had eight surviving children; her translation of Lucretius's *De rerum natura* was carried out in their schoolroom during their lessons, predating the first published English Lucretius of 1682.

Her husband died in 1664, inspiring her *Memoirs of the Life of Colonel Hutchinson*, an account of his service to the Parliamentary cause during the Civil War, written for her children over the years 1664–71 and not published until 1806. Despite its partiality, its vivid insight into the life of the period gives it both historical importance and literary merit. It is prefaced by an autobiographical fragment.

She also wrote treatises *On the Principles of the Christian Religion* and *On Theology* (published together in 1817) and translated a Latin treatise by the congregationalist divine John Owen. Her Puritanism increased through her life. By 1675, when she complied with a request from the Earl of Anglesea for a manuscript of her Lucretius, she questioned the value of 'pagan' texts and expressed regret that 'I did attempt things out of my own sphere.'   HH

Hutton [née Mackay], Albinia Catherine 1894–? Jamaican poet born in Kingston to Scottish parents, Hutton published her first volume, *Poems by Albinia Catherine Mackay*, in 1912. Her 1930 sketch, *Life in Jamaica*, can be read as a piece of amateur, eurocentric ethnography. Hutton's most anthologized poem, the patriotic and colonial 'The Empire's Flag', appeared in *Hill Songs and Wayside Verses* (1932). She also published poems in the *Jamaica Times* and the *Year Books of the Poetry League of Jamaica*, and had works read on the BBC *Caribbean Voices* programme. A private collection of poems, *Sonnets of Sorrow*, was circulated in Kingston in 1939. In the early 1930s Hutton was the original editor

of *Singers Quarterly*, a 'scrap-book' publication circulated among and written by a small group of middle-class poets.   AD

Huxley [née Grant], Elspeth (Josceline) 1907–97 Prolific British novelist and writer. Huxley grew up in East Africa, where her parents owned a coffee farm, and was educated at the European school in Nairobi. She returned to England in 1925 to attend Reading University, receiving a degree in Agriculture, and then studied at Cornell University in New York. In 1931, she married Gervis Huxley, cousin of Aldous and Julian, and together they travelled extensively. After World War II, the couple settled on a farm in Wiltshire, England, cultivating pigs and roses. Huxley's childhood experiences in Kenya greatly influenced her writing. Her best-known work, a semi-autobiographical trilogy of novels, includes two volumes set in Africa, *The Flame Trees of Thika* (1959) and *The Mottled Lizard* (1962). The third work in the series, *Love Among the Daughters* (1968), captures the spirit of her youthful student days at Reading and Cornell. Huxley has been praised for her keen observation of English manners and morals, precise language and piercing wit, prompting comparisons to the MITFORD sisters and to JANE AUSTEN. These qualities also characterize her mystery novels, which she began writing while travelling, 'to pass the time on shipboard and avoid playing bridge'. *Murder at Government House* (1937), *Murder on Safari* (1938), *Death of an Aryan* (1939) and *The Merry Hippo* (1963) are all set in Africa and were praised both for rivalling the work of AGATHA CHRISTIE and for being a cross between P.G. Wodehouse and Evelyn Waugh. She wrote numerous non-fiction works about her experiences in Africa, most notably *The Challenge of Africa* (1971) and *Out in the Midday Sun* (1985), as well as studies of other travellers, such as David Livingstone and MARY KINGSLEY. She was awarded the CBE (Commander, Order of the British Empire) in 1962.

LCo

Huxley [née Heathorn], Henrietta A(nne) 1825–1914 Australian-born poet, who, after her marriage to the scientist T. H. Huxley, lived permanently in the UK. Much of her life was devoted to her family, but she published privately a volume of verse in 1899, republished with additions by Duckworth as *Poems of Henrietta A. Huxley with three of Thomas Henry Huxley* in 1913. It contains narrative poems for children, nonsense verse, domestic poems about home life and the family, a translation from Goethe, poems on the funerals of Tennyson and Browning, and many pieces on death more generally and the pain of bereavement. Although Huxley remained a churchgoer, much of her poetry expresses doubt about Christian doctrines, especially life after death. In 'The Quest', however, she presents a determined stoicism in the face of such uncertainties:

Accept things as they are:
Our tenure here is sure,
To work, to love, to grieve;
Reverently to endure.

Huxley also edited *Aphorisms and Reflections from the Works of T.H. Huxley* (1907), a volume which aimed to show her husband's moral teaching and the 'beauty of [his] English writing'.   FJO'G

Hyde, Robin [Iris Guiver Wilkinson] 1906–39 New

Zealand poet, novelist, journalist. Hyde was born in South Africa, but her family emigrated to New Zealand when she was one month old. Able to support herself in journalism from the age of 17, Hyde surmounted great personal trauma to achieve a prolific writing career. Despite the death of her first love, poor health, the death of her first baby son, attempted suicide and her consequent admission to a psychiatric ward, Hyde fought back. She is a crucial figure in New Zealand literary history.

Alongside numerous articles, Hyde wrote her professional memoirs, *Journalese* (1934); a novelized biography of Baron Charles de Thierry, *Check to Your King* (1936); and the social-REALIST novels *Passport to Hell* (1936) and *Nor the Years Condemn* (1938), which depict life in New Zealand in the 1910s–1930s, using historical 'everyman and outcast' figure, Douglas Stark. Hyde's fantasy *Wednesday's Children* (1937) presages the meta-fictional experimentation of JANET FRAME, while her impressionistic, fictionalized autobiography, *The Godwits Fly* (1938), recalls aspects of MANSFIELD. The posthumously published *A Home in This World* exposes the social conservatism which ostracized Hyde as a single mother upon her second son's birth.

Hyde's poetry begins in ROMANTIC and Georgian tones with *The Desolate Star* (1929) and *The Conquerors* (1935), using elaborate personifications, abstracts, archetypes and fable within strictly controlled forms and through rich, allusive language. *Persephone in Winter* (1937) is a transitional volume: the mythical abstracts persist, yet there is a nascent focus on New Zealand. The ecstatic exclamations of a poem like 'Red Berries' imitate Hyde's awakening to the potentials of the local landscape as literary material:

O, red berries, red berries!
Surprise in the wilderness,
Coral on dark green dress
Nay, don't tell me she's blank,
My own land, she makes things –

The posthumous *Houses By the Sea* incorporates freer forms, a sharpened pictorial sense and franker self-exposition. Hyde's meditations on the Sino-Japanese war exist alongside her prose account of her experiences as the first woman journalist at the Chinese front. *Dragon Rampant* (1939) is an eclectic documentation of history, customs and anecdote, its final chapters satirizing Hyde's role as reporter amidst the brutal, chaotic scenes which she became witness to and victim of.

Hyde survived assault from Japanese soldiers and reached England in 1938. There, experiencing financial difficulties, illness and anxiety over delays to a stage adaptation of *Wednesday's Children*, she died from a drug overdose.   EJN

I

I Know Why The Caged Bird Sings (1970) In the first of her serial autobiographies, MAYA ANGELOU recalls her growth from 3 to 16 years old in the face of abandonment, rape, racism and sexism. It begins with the image of frightened children of divorced parents, Marguerite Johnson (Maya) and her brother, travelling alone away from home (Long Beach, California) to live with their grandmother in Stamps, Arkansas. This sense of displacement is balanced somewhat in the end with the picture of Maya's mother offering comfort to her daughter, who is now the mother of a 3-week-old baby. Maya's account of her life in these early years indicates that hers is a spirit that will not be broken: the self-imposed silence for almost five years following the rape, for example, is also a period of careful listening, reading, and of a profound appreciation for the power of words. The voice that tells the story of adolescent pain and survival in *Caged Bird* is both the product of and a release from that period of recuperative silence.   KO

I Live Under a Black Sun (1937) For readers familiar with EDITH SITWELL's pioneering poetry, her first and only attempt to write a fictional work seems rather surprising. Written in 1937, the book was doubly layered with Sitwell's concern with the poverty and hopelessness that she witnessed following World War I, as well as with her personal experiences of unrequited love for the painter Pavel Tchelitchew. As a basis for the novel, Sitwell used the life story of Jonathan Swift and the characters surrounding him, and transposed them into World War I and its aftermath, offering an insightful critique of modern times. Written as an allegory of a modern world gone mad over power the novel evokes the despair of one's own powerlessness over one's life, but, more disturbingly, the absence of relief and resolution until one's grave. The result however is rather confusing. The novel's unimaginative prose, stale dialogues and misplaced lyrical passages fall a long way short of its visionary and powerful theme, leaving a lot to be desired.   MPe

I Passed This Way (1979) SYLVIA ASHTON-WARNER's prize-winning autobiography vindicated her claims to be a misunderstood genius by gaining her belated recognition as a writer and educationalist in her native New Zealand. Born into a large family with a dominating mother and a disabled father, Sylvia spent her early childhood at small country schools in Taranaki. At Auckland Teachers' Training College she met and married Keith Henderson and, following a severe breakdown after the birth of her first child, determined to live a creative life. While teaching Maori pupils from the 1930s to 1950s in back-block country schools (Pipiriki, Horoera, Fernhill) on the east coast of the North Island, she evolved the 'key vocabulary' reading system. But her revolutionary methods were treated with suspicion by the New Zealand educational authorities and recognition came at first only from overseas with the success of *Spinster* (1958) and the testing of her ideas in the UK and USA where she worked for years. Ashton-Warner fuelled her flamboyant artistic personality with passionate lesbian relationships and her autobiography, like her novels, gives public meaning and status to the alternative, private worlds that she inhabited.

I Passed This Way was the basis for the film, *Sylvia* (1985).   JMW

Illness as Metaphor (1978) SUSAN SONTAG later described as 'a polemic' her meticulously rational essay on the cultural and literary meanings of illness, which, along with *Against Interpretation*, was one of her most influential works of non-fiction. In it Sontag honed her critical technique of moving through a linguistic territory – in this case, descriptions of illness, primarily tuberculosis and cancer – to comment on a social phenomenon – here, western attitudes to death and disease. In writers from Kafka to Mann she examines the contrasting metaphors that have clustered around TB (a romantic affliction, a 'disease of the soul') and around cancer (a degrading affliction, emphatically a disease of the body). She critiques the use of cancer as a metaphor for moral decay, and the 'punitive' notion of cancer-prone psychologies. Her cool but palpable rage came from her own cancer treatment, which led to her determination to strip cancer, rhetorically, of its shame. In her later companion essay, *Aids and Its Metaphors* (1989), she rereads her original work with characteristic clarity and wit, explaining that her purpose had been 'to apply that quixotic, highly polemical strategy, "against interpretation" to the real world this time. To the body.'   SB

Illustrations of Political Economy (1832–4)

HARRIET MARTINEAU's nine-volume collection of stories depicting aspects of political economy was the publication which successfully established her writing career in the aftermath of her father's financial collapse. Frustrated by works of economics which were dry and dull, and convinced that until ordinary people learnt about the subject they would never be able to 'petition intelligently or effectively' about social conditions, she wrote a series of accessible, didactic stories 'picturing out' issues and themes, such as the advantages of the division of labour, the operation of taxation and the necessity of 'bringing no more children into the world than there is subsistence provided for'. The argument for population control prompted controversy from those who thought it an unsuitable subject for a woman (*Fraser's* called *Illustrations* a 'frightful delusion') but in general the work, coming at a time of some sympathy to liberal reform, was well received. It shows Martineau's confidence in society as progressive, concluding with a final moral that 'we must mend our ways and be hopeful', and also reveals her firm Utilitarian conviction that the aim of society is to secure 'the greatest happiness of the greatest number'.   FJO'G

I'm Dying Laughing (1986)

CHRISTINA STEAD's most important late novel, despite its difficult gestation (written over a quarter of a century, and abandoned before her death to 'the garbage can or the deep freeze'). It is a brilliant and unflinching portrait of a marriage between two American Reds, working-class writer Emily and patrician Stephen, beginning in 1935, and tracing their fall from ardent idealism to personal and political betrayal so venal that its consequences are suicide and madness. The first half is set in New York and in Hollywood where Emily becomes a screenwriter; there they are thrown out of the Communist party for individualism and deviancy, and – fearing persecution also from the Right, in the form of the House Un-American Activities Committee – they head for exile in post-World-War-II Paris, where they succumb to an expatriate life of gargantuan consumerism, debauchery and bad faith. Stephen betrays his friends and names names to keep his US citizenship, Emily prostitutes her talent. They descend, like so many Stead characters before them, into a nightmare Bohemia where they are unable to abide their self-inflicted alienation. *I'm Dying Laughing* was edited from different sets of manuscripts by Stead's literary executor R.G. Geering.   KWc

I'm the King of the Castle (1970)

An early novel by SUSAN HILL, for which she won the Somerset Maugham Award. It covers only a short period of time and has few characters, all affected in some way by iso-lation and loneliness; the chronological narration and terse style are reminiscent of Hill's short stories. It presents an uncompromising study of the dependency between schoolboy bully Hooper and his victim Kingshaw. Hooper's father and Kingshaw's mother complete this picture of dependency and selfishness, unwittingly contributing to the victim's suffering. When Fielding, another schoolboy, befriends Kingshaw, even he cannot defuse the dark atmosphere of hostility, misery and suffering; Kingshaw's sense of the inevitability of his fate is confirmed, and Hooper pushes him toward his eventual suicide.

The narrative is mostly advanced through dialogue, but also offers telling glimpses into Kingshaw's increasingly unstable state of mind. Although it makes sparing yet effective use of imagery, the novel contains GOTHIC elements. The setting is a remote Victorian house whose rooms contain a collection of dead moths, and Kingshaw is pursued by a giant crow, which becomes a haunting image of his fear.   MET

Images in Aspic (1965)

CHARMIAN CLIFT wrote these thirty-six short essays in 1965, after returning from nearly fifteen years in Europe, the last ten spent in romantic poverty in the Greek islands with her husband, novelist George Johnston, and three small children. The essays, published as a weekly column in the Women's pages of the *Herald*, Melbourne, and the *Sydney Morning Herald*, provide a worldly, sometimes arch, and extremely self-possessed vision of Australian life, defamiliarized by long exile. They describe and analyse an Australia 'desperate to be re-defined', and to emerge from its long period as a dreary provincial outpost of the British Empire, and join the global village. While Clift insists that there is a world elsewhere, of 'whitewashed Mediterranean towns', disreputable artists and 'aimless foreign wanderers', that Australia had better learn to take into account, she also celebrates the 'bizarre, original, strange, appealing' qualities of distinctively Australian life. Clift's essays take for granted that women may be highbrow, counter-culture, bohemian, and this sophisticated angle fascinated a middle-class female readership just beginning to feel the stirrings of second-wave feminism.   KTS

Imaginary Friends (1967)

The third novel by ALISON LURIE tells the story of two sociologists, Roger Zimmern and his academic hero Tom McMann, who set out to infiltrate a religious cult in order to undertake a unique group study. Their involvement with the Truth Seekers (who believe that they are subject to the laws of the planet Varna and its leader Ro, and that these laws are announced on Earth by the prophetess Verena) allows Lurie to explore many of the themes of group behaviour, closed communities and the power exerted over individuals by charismatic figures that run through the rest of her work. In *Imaginary Friends*, these delicate relationships are taken to extremes in a somewhat fantastical setting, and the bonds of intellectual and rational enquiry between Roger and Tom are broken, as Tom becomes subsumed by the group's desire to elect a new earthly leader. Lurie's satirical look at the emergence of sociology as a new form of religion appears partly as a *jeu d'ésprit*, but partly as a serious analysis of the dangers of making assumptions about academic objectivity.   AC

Imperialist, The (1904) SARA JEANNETTE DUNCAN's only novel set in Canada centres on the lives of Lorne and Advena Murchison in the fictitious community of Elgin, Ontario. The offspring of a self-styled nation-builder, Lorne and Advena betray their privileged upbringing by naively pursuing political and amorous ideals that small-town Elgin cannot fulfil. Lorne's promising bid as the Liberal candidate in a parliamentary election founders when he lectures the more pragmatic constituents of Fox County on the idea of Imperial Federation – including his hope that Canada would someday supplant England as 'the center of Empire'. Similarly, Advena fosters a rarefied love for the new local minister and declines to contravene her sense of social propriety when the shamed Scottish *émigré* reveals that he is already engaged to a woman he does not love. By tracing the parallel flight of idealism and subsequent disillusionment of the Murchison siblings, Duncan creates an intimate forum for elucidating key historical and political trends in the development of Canada. The novel's conclusion underscores – and gently satirizes – the Canadian predilection for compromise.   IR

In a Convex Mirror (1944) Poet ROSEMARY DOBSON's first collection of verse (aside from her juvenile *Poems* of 1937), published when Dobson was just 24 years old, established her as one of Australia's leading poets. A slim volume of only twenty-five poems, *Mirror* prefigures many of the concerns which still inform Dobson's poetics half a century later. Two of its most notable works, the title poem and 'In a Café', begin what will be a continuing preoccupation with the visual arts, especially the paintings of the Renaissance. In these and other poems, Dobson explores the role of the artist and of art, especially in relation to the exchanges made possible between past and present, between painter and viewer, and between life and art. Dobson has Botticelli 'In a Café' catching his Venus 'between the gesture and the motion', in that space hanging between movement and stillness, whilst in 'In a Convex Mirror', she wonders whether her subjects can make 'eloquent' the 'silence between tick and tock'. Art, for Dobson, is neither 'words' nor 'silence', but subverts dualities in allowing 'words to wiser silence pass'.   MLA

Elizabeth Inchbald.

In Search of April Raintree (1983) Revised for inclusion in high-school curricula (*April Raintree*,1984) this moving and suspenseful novel by BEATRICE MOSIONIER is about the life of two Métis sisters. As a work of 'autobiographical fiction' the simply told story re-presents native women's struggles in Canada. The novel is narrated in the first-person recollection of the elder sister April, but her sister Cheryl participates in the telling, not only through dialogue but also, quite effectively, through her writing. A pivotal scene of the novel in which light-skinned April, trying 'to pass' as white, is raped by two white men who 'mistake' her for her 'native sister' Cheryl, dark-skinned and identifying with Métis culture, not only exposes the double victimization of Native women, but also exemplifies how this text blurs the boundaries of identity construction. The novel conveys in its tightly structured plot the connectedness of stories and histories, and reveals in terse language a web of lies which makes it difficult for April to find her own truth.   REi

In Search of Our Mothers' Gardens (1983) ALICE WALKER's first volume of non-fiction, which she prefers to describe as 'womanist prose', includes the essay on female African-American cultural traditions which gives the volume its title. This volume spans the 1970s, ranging from radical protest and politics to personal reminiscence, and ends with a 1983 piece which confronts the effect of her brother's blinding her in one eye when she was 8. Although the collection is of occasional pieces, a coherence emerges as issues of civil rights, black women's identity and affiliations, and Walker's womanist cultural stance mutually relate. She refuses to be dogmatic; instead she draws on various sources to construct a style that allows individual experience and political discourse to cross-fertilize each other. The collection offers the reader of her fiction insight into the concerns which motivated her at the start of her writing career, valuable indications as to the authors she recognizes as influential and significant (including Albert Camus, MURIEL RUKEYSER and ZORA NEALE HURSTON), and a consistent expression of her own generosity of spirit and deeply felt emotionality and spirituality.   HMD

Inchbald [née Simpson], Elizabeth 1753–1821 Actress, novelist, major dramatist and theatre critic. She was born into a Catholic family at Standingfield near Bury St Edmunds in Suffolk, the youngest-but-one of nine children, to John Simpson – a farmer – and Mary Rushbrook. She was an early admirer of the theatre and it was her ambition to become an actress. At 18 she ran away to London to act and was pursued by a number of men enamoured by her beauty. She married Joseph Inchbald, a much older actor, in 1772 to gain both protection from other men and an introduction into the theatre. She managed to work regularly – despite a speech impediment – touring the provinces and often acting opposite her husband.

In 1779 her husband died unexpectedly, and, while continuing to act, the direction of her career changed and she became an established and popular writer. She began her most famous work, the novel *A SIMPLE STORY* (1791) in 1777, but when refused publication turned her mind to writing dramas. In 1784 *A Mogul Tale* was accepted and produced at the Haymarket. She went on to write over twenty other dramas, including *I'll Tell You What* (1785), *Everyone Has His Fault* (1793) and *Wives as They Were and Maids as They Are* (1797). Her most famous play is her adaptation of Kotzebue's *LOVERS' VOWS* (1798) which was performed in JANE AUSTEN's *MANSFIELD PARK* (1814). She was a friend of radicals Godwin and Holcroft, whose influence on her second novel, *Nature and Art* (1796), is clear. She also edited three collections of plays including *The Modern Theatre* (1806–9). She was persuaded to burn her memoirs. Always careful to live within her means, renting modest rooms, she died a rich woman, leaving £5,000.   PJW

Infernal Desire Machines of Doctor Hoffman, The (1972) This combination of SCIENCE FICTION, fabulation and erotic fantasy combines the passion of

THESE ARE FAIRIES, BUT WHAT ARE YOU?   p. 101

Jean Ingelow: 'These are fairies, but what are you?' – illustration from *Mopsa the Fairy*, 1869.

ANGELA CARTER's earlier work with the more thoughtful theorization of her later manner. Its use of cliché – the mad scientist who wants to change the world into his own image – has elements of the twice-told tale. The narrator Desiderio is an agent of a city assaulted from Hoffman's machines, which deconstruct causation and rationality. Carter takes Desiderio to strange places – a funfair whose peepshow machines are among Hoffman's weapons, a murderous and charming tribe of barge-dwellers, Hoffman's magic castle with its laboratory full of plugged-in lovers. Seduced by Hoffman's daughter Albertine, Desiderio has to choose and we know that his choice will be a tragic one; this is a powerful novel because it is one which refuses reconciliation and confronts us with his regret.   RK

Ingelow, Jean 1820–97 Poet and writer of CHILDREN'S STORIES, born in Boston, Lincolnshire. Her father had banking interests and when these collapsed the family moved several times in the south of

England before finally settling in London. She remained in the family home for the rest of her life. In 1860 she became a member of the Portfolio Society, established by BARBARA BODICHON and BESSIE RAYNER PARKES as a forum in which women might exchange and perform their own poetry or paintings. Her second volume of poetry, *Poems* (1863), was her most successful, particularly in the United States where it sold 200,000 copies and ran into 30 editions. Her most popular poem was 'High Tide on the Coast of Lincolnshire, 1571', and there is a strong sense of place throughout her poems which are often impersonal and high-minded.

In 1869 she published a children's fantasy story called MOPSA THE FAIRY that became something of a classic, influenced by the new developments in children's fantasy literature and punctuated by poems or songs. It describes the adventures of a boy who crosses into fairyland, meets a number of strange, melancholy and violent creatures and helps Mopsa the Fairy grow into a Fairy Queen.   RS

Inglis, Esther (later Kello) 1571–1624 Renowned early modern calligrapher. The daughter of Huguenot refugees who fled to Scotland after the Massacre of St Bartholomew's Day in Paris, her original surname may have been Langlois, Inglis being the corrupted or anglicized form. Her mother was also a distinguished calligrapher and trained her daughter in the art. Some of her volumes of writing include self-penned poetry (in her native French) and her exquisite miniature self-portrait is held in the National Library of Scotland.   JS

Inner Landscape: Poems 1936-1938 (1939) MAY SARTON's second volume of poems, published when she was 27, received the mixed reviews that would follow Sarton's writing throughout her long and prolific career, striking many readers as overly genteel, sentimental, simplistic, privileged, abstracted. The opening 'Prayer Before Work' invokes the qualities Sarton seeks: 'ease', 'precision' and 'form'. These formalist brief lyrics, invocations, sonnets and love poems demonstrate Sarton's quest for what she called 'deceptive clarity', or 'clarté'. Balanced, rhymed and metrically regular (only three of the fifty-four poems are in free verse), these poems explore, as their title suggests, Sarton's dual interests of self and space. Inner psychological landscapes confronting absolutes – love, death, silence, solitude – are depicted through images of outer landscapes – cities, buildings, fields, winds, countries, prisons, beaches, oceans, storms. The volume concludes defiantly, suggesting that 'if there are miracles we can record', they happen in personal closed spaces, in little wars and loves, in loneliness, in 'perishable songs for one', in building small poetic 'houses' where 'every man may take his ease'.   SC

Intimate Strangers (1937) KATHARINE SUSANNAH PRITCHARD's 'broken-backed' REALIST and feminist narrative revolves around Elodie and Greg Blackwood as they struggle with the *ennui* of married life. Elodie has sacrificed a promising career as a concert pianist to become a wife and mother and Greg is a returned serviceman who is retrenched in the early years of the Great Depression. Elodie embarks on an extra-marital affair with the dashing sea captain Jerome Hartog and is torn between her familial obligations and a desire to escape domestic incarceration. The narrative is interwoven with numerous musical motifs including Beethoven's F Minor Piano Sonata and Wagner's *Die Fliegende Hollander*, which point toward a tragic conclusion. This is never realized. The novel, completed in manuscript form in 1933, originally culminated in Greg's suicide. Following the death of her own husband in disturbingly similar circumstances, Prichard altered the final chapters. The ending of the published version in many ways denies the internal logic of the novel. Instead of the anticipated tragic conclusion, the resolution is awash with romantic sentiments framed by socialist realist ideology.   CE

Invitation to the Waltz (1932) ROSAMUND LEHMANN's third novel concerns the relationship between two sisters. The plot is slight – Olivia and Kate prepare for and attend their first dance – but the texture is rich in its evocation of rural middle-class life between the World Wars, evoking both a disappearing world and the young women's excitement at the prospect of change. Most of the novel is related from Olivia's more unconventional point of view, through which Kate appears as a highly capable and self-confident, if limited, young woman on her way to marriage. Olivia suffers more acute self-consciousness and is less certain of who she is, but she is also more aware of others and is empathetic to a disabling degree. Almost half the novel is taken up with the dance itself. The sisters experience various trials and triumphs through a series of encounters and exchanges, at the end of which Kate has embarked on her first relationship and Olivia runs to embrace the future. A sequel, *The Weather in the Streets*, was published in 1936.   SAS

Irby, Adeline Paulina 1831–1911 and **Mackenzie, Georgina Muir (Lady Sebright)** 1833–74 British TRAVEL WRITERS. Irby, the youngest daughter of an English rear admiral, and Mackenzie, the eldest child of a Scottish baronet, travelled together across Europe from the late 1850s, becoming particularly interested in the Balkans which they described in several works which appeared between 1861 and 1877. Their first book, *Across the Carpathians* (1862), was published anonymously. Their most important work, *Travels in the Slavonic Provinces of Turkey in Europe* (1867), is a 700-

page account of travel in Macedonia, Serbia, Albania and Montenegro. Its brief account of their journey along the borders of Bosnia-Herzegovina was considerably expanded with an account of Irby's visits to Bosnia in the revised second edition, published after Mackenzie's death, with a preface by W. E. Gladstone.

In 1871 Mackenzie, whose failing health made further travelling impossible, married Sir Charles Sebright, the British Consul General in the Ionian Islands and lived with him in Corfu until her death. Bosnia-Herzegovina became the focus of Irby's life and work. She travelled there with a new friend, Priscilla Johnston, and lived for many years in Sarajevo where she established a school for Serbian girls and a cultural–educational society, 'Prosvjeta'. (A street in Sarajevo – Mis Irbina Ulica – was named after her.) The two women were in Bosnia-Herzegovina during the rebellion against the Ottoman rule in 1875 and subsequently moved with the refugees across the border into Austria-Hungary where they worked for three years, establishing several schools for refugee children. After her death, Irby bequeathed all her property to her school and 'Prosvjeta'.   VG

Italian, The (1797) This vintage GOTHIC ROMANCE is ANN RADCLIFFE's best-known work after THE MYSTERIES OF UDOLPHO (1794). A reaction against Matthew Lewis's overtly demonic and sadistic *The Monk* (itself inspired by *Udolpho*), its imaginative power partly derives from a solemn and restrained tone. Set in Italy in 1758, the complex plot concerns the machinations of the aristocratic Marchesa di Vivaldi, in league with the villainous monk Schedoni, to prevent her son Vincentio from marrying the genteel but poor Ellena Rosalba. Shedoni owes much to Milton's Satan; his austere, melancholic character is invested with a tragic stature new to the genre. The main narrative is encased within a frame tale which enables the author to imply lack of knowledge or even unreliability concerning events or states of mind. Fear and unease often derive from what is not fully seen or understood, as in the scenes where the heroine is threatened at the convent of San Stefano, or the hero tortured by the Inquisition. This strategy of suggestion has served the fiction of terror well.   MO'D

Ivory Swing, The (1982) JANET TURNER HOSPITAL's first novel, written after her family's sabbatical in India, and recording her reading of the land and culture, was awarded the prestigious (and lucrative) Canadian Seal Award. It utilizes some of her own experience to tell the story of a Canadian family not unlike her own, sojourning in India for similar reasons. They are drawn into the affairs of the landlord's family, especially the tragedy of his beautiful widowed kinswoman. What transpires leaves none of them untouched. Poverty, politics, religion and the treatment of women are all part of the complex background texture. This novel established many of the themes, structural elements and stylistic flourishes that were to become endemic in Hospital's writing: her rich prose and pithy aphoristic style; feminist motifs; and religious or mythological symbolism. This was to be Hospital's first – but not her last – use of the Women's Quest genre, particularly popular in Canada, where she had been based for some years. While later works wittily subvert the genre, however, this is more conventional.   LB

J

Jabavu, Noni 1919– South African writer, and daughter of a prominent Xhosa-speaking South African family, whose lives are closely linked with the history of black education and with the University of Fort Hare. As a young girl of 13 she was sent to Mount School in York, and later studied at the Royal Academy of Music. In 1955, after having married an Englishman, she returned to South Africa for a three-month stay. During this time she visited her father and relatives in the Eastern Cape and Johannesburg. The first part of her autobiography appeared as *Drawn in Colour: African Contrasts* (1960) and the second as *The Ochre People: Scenes from a South African Life* (1963). In both texts her concern is with the return of a Xhosa woman, who has been living in England, to her family and to a world dominated by Xhosa customs. In an author's note in *Drawn in Colour* she writes: 'I belong to two worlds with two loyalties; South Africa where I was born and England where I was educated.' Throughout, she is concerned with questions of representativeness, voice and audience. Her primary audience is a British one, and she attempts to present Xhosa family and cultural life as equivalent to British practices and norms. At times the voice is doubled as she describes herself acting according to the unwritten rules of Xhosa tradition, but narrating these in the voice of the woman who stands separate from, and is at times critical of, aspects of a patriarchal and hierarchical system that often demands that a daughter and daughter-in-law remain quiet. Her work reveals an interest in questions of linguistic and cultural translation, what she calls 'refingering the fabric' of life. CCo

Jackowska [née Tester], Nicki 1942– British poet who has published several small-press collections of poetry and three novels. Her lyrical, political and passionate poems have won her a following and several awards; her musical work with the Irish folk band *Moving Clouds* is also noteworthy. Jackowska trained as an actor and for a number of years worked in theatre. During the late 1960s and early 1970s she lived and worked in Cornwall, writing, publishing *Poetry St Ives*, and performing with her own theatre company, 'Tower of Babel'. She acquired a reputation as 'the *enfant terrible* of the folk-poetry circuit', and directed a three-day festival in St Ives. The festival became locally famous for its strong ideological agenda, as well as a police presence at a supposed 'lewd' performance.

During the late 1970s she read Philosophy at Sussex University, and went on to work full-time as a writer, living in Brighton. She married the artist Andrezej Jackowska and has one daughter, Laura. Her first poetry appeared in pamphlet form – *The bone palaces* (1977) and *Incubus* (1981) are an attempt to look at nuclear holocaust unsparingly and relentlessly. She continued to explore the themes of violence and power in her first major collection, *The House that Manda Built* (1981). Other collections also investigate power, but are less prescriptive in tone, more personal and subtle in both their syntax and their stance. *News from the Brighton Front* (1993) contains thoughtful poems about marital separation, and ironic dissections of Thatcher's Britain and its protagonists. DM

Jackson [née Fiske], Helen Hunt 1830–85 American poet, novelist, essayist and crusader for native American rights. She was born in Amherst, Massachusetts, daughter of a professor. Her parents died when she was a child. She was raised thereafter by an aunt and educated at private schools. Her first husband, Edward Bissell Hunt, and her two sons all died within a short time. She began writing poetry to cope with these losses and became one of the foremost American poets, especially noted for her craft, which has been compared with that of CHRISTINA ROSSETTI because of lines such as these:

> I see thy tendrils drink by sips
> From grass and clover's smiling lips;
> I hear thy roots dig down for wells,
> Tapping the meadow's hidden cells
>
> ('My Strawberry').

Volumes of her poetry were published in 1870, 1873, 1886, 1892 and 1895. She also wrote CHILDREN's books, TRAVEL books and articles, using the pseudonyms 'H.H.', 'Saxe Holm', and 'Rip Van Winkle'. Jackson contracted her second marriage to William Sharpless Jackson on the understanding that he would allow her complete freedom for self-development. In 1860 she became acquainted with EMILY DICKINSON, whose poetry she greatly admired. The heroine of Jackson's novel *Mercy Philbrick's Choice* (1876) is a fictionalized impression of Dickinson.

Hearing Chief Standing Bear speak in 1879 on dispossession of the Plains Indians inspired Jackson to begin pioneering work for Indian rights. *A Century of Dishonor* (1881), the first of Jackson's works published with her name, exposed the repeated violation of treaties and massacre of tribes. The book led to the founding of the Indian Rights Association. Appointed by the government to investigate the provision of land to Mission Indians in California, she transformed her investigative material to fiction in *Ramona* (1884), hoping to replicate the political effectiveness of UNCLE TOM'S CABIN by HARRIET BEECHER STOWE.   JSG

Jackson, Rebecca Cox 1795–1871 American preacher, autobiographer and religious visionary who founded a community of African-American Shakers. She was born a free black in Philadelphia and experienced a dramatic conversion at the age of 35. Convinced that she was elected to follow God and that celibacy was necessary for a devout life, Jackson left her family and her African Methodist Episcopal community to follow her intuition of God's word. She travelled as an independent preacher, joined the Methodist Holiness movement, and finally united with the Shakers, a socialist sect, in Watervliet, New York. Attracted to the Shakers' celibacy, Jackson also appreciated their belief in a male and female Godhead. Jackson's sense of responsibility to her race, however, led her to leave Watervliet and form a community of African-American Shakers in Philadelphia. This group existed until thirty or forty years after her death.

Jackson's autobiography, first published in 1981, is particularly remarkable for the visions she recounts, in which she often transcends time and space and converses with spiritual figures. These detailed, spectacular visions gave Jackson an authority with which to defy convention and prejudice.   AE

Jackson, Shirley 1919–65 American writer of novels and short stories. Born in San Francisco, Jackson studied at Syracuse University. With the exception of two memoirs of family life, *Among the Savages* (1953) and *Raising Demons* (1957), written with her literary critic husband Stanley Hyman, most of the stories and novels can be characterized as psychological thrillers dealing with the destruction of women by domesticity and small communities. Her most famous short story, 'The Lottery' (1948), shows a small American town which, we gradually realize, has adopted the ritual murder of selected housewives as one of its unquestioned customs. Both *Hangsaman* (1951) and *The Bird's Nest* (1954) deal with women's mental collapse. In *The Haunting of Hill House* (1959) a house takes over and destroys a woman resident; in *We have always lived in the castle*

(1962), later dramatized, an adolescent girl becomes murderously protective of her sister. Her work is characterized by a quiet dignity of pace which makes her GOTHIC conclusions all the more shocking. She is highly regarded among connoisseurs of horror, but surprisingly little known as a proto-feminist writer whose use of ghost story tropes follows on from CHARLOTTE PERKINS GILMAN.   RK

Jacob, Rosamund 1888–1960 The daughter of a middle-class Irish Quaker family, Jacob was a prominent feminist republican who was a very significant figure in persuading insurgent nationalists to commit the independent Irish state they sought to women's suffrage. Her life was a catalogue of radical activity, including campaigns for women's employment, against vivisection and for prisoners' rights. Her fiction is sometimes overwhelmed by her political concerns and her attempts to reconcile the rival claims of feminism, nationalism and aesthetics. *Callaghan* (1920) contains probably the only account in Irish literature of the experience of selling suffrage newspapers on the streets of Dublin and features extended conversations about the relevance of such activities to the struggle for national liberation. In *The Troubled House* (1937), a family is torn apart by political differences during the War of Independence. Jacob's own difficulty in negotiating between her Quaker inheritance of pacifism and her support for armed insurrection is dramatized in the novel's conflict between one son's advocacy of passive resistance and another's participation in the war. Jacob's feminism, her attempts to link sexual and aesthetic freedom to national politics and her acquaintance with a broad circle of intellectual and artistic women uneasily attempting to adapt to the new conservatism of Ireland in the thirties fuel the novel's most vibrant and interesting character, a gifted young woman artist who tries to live free of convention and politics, but whose paintings are destroyed by the British Army when she shelters a wounded rebel. Jacob also wrote history and children's stories.   GM

Jacob [née Kennedy-Erskine], Violet 1863–1946 Scottish writer whose work explores boundaries of national identity, gender and class. She began writing seriously when she accompanied Arthur, her army officer husband, abroad. Unlike the archetypal 'memsahib', Jacob smoked and wore mannish clothes on solitary excursions into the Indian bush.

For many years, she was dismissed as a 'minor' poet; however a reappraisal of her output is underway. Her peripheral status as female Scottish expatriate fuelled her interest in marginalized characters and borderline places. She wrote vernacular poetry, drawing on the oral and folk traditions and often assuming the persona of an 'outsider' figure in order to express radical

INCIDENTS

IN THE

LIFE OF A SLAVE GIRL.

WRITTEN BY HERSELF.

~Linda Brent

"Northerners know nothing at all about Slavery. They think it is perpetual bondage only. They have no conception of the depth of *degradation* involved in that word, SLAVERY; if they had, they would never cease their efforts until so horrible a system was overthrown."

A WOMAN OF NORTH CAROLINA.

"Rise up, ye women that are at ease! Hear my voice, ye careless daughters! Give ear unto my speech."

ISAIAH xxxii. 9.

EDITED BY L. MARIA CHILD.

BOSTON:
PUBLISHED FOR THE AUTHOR.
1861.

Harriet Jacobs: title-page of *Incidents in the Life of a Slave Girl: Written by Herself*, Boston 1861.

sentiments. Sexual frankness characterizes her work. Many of her poems and stories implicitly question society's view of unconventional women.

The Sheep Stealers (1902) and *The Interloper* (1904) feature characters of different social backgrounds and inter-class relationships. Her most complex novel, *Flemington* (1911), concerns the 1745 rebellion. In a skilful re-working of the adventure-ROMANCE form, she explores 'borderlands': physical and metaphorical, moral and of gender. Although some of her work recalls older traditions, *Flemington* demonstrates that Jacob was capable of a dark modern vision.   JH

Jacobs, Harriet 1813–96 African-American writer who wrote *Linda, Incidents in the Life of a Slave Girl*, which was first published under the pseudonym 'Linda

Brent' in 1861. In this autobiography, Jacobs recounts how she hid for seven years in her grandmother's garret, a room 3 feet high, 9 feet long, and 7 feet wide, as part of her effort to elude the sexual demands of her owner and achieve freedom for herself and her children. After publishers told Jacobs that she needed a well-known abolitionist to verify her story, Jacobs contacted LYDIA MARIA CHILD, who then served as editor for *Incidents*.

Jacobs's narrative creatively fuses the genres of the slave narrative and the DOMESTIC novel, a rhetorical strategy that frames her experiences of agency and exploitation within a discourse of domesticity. Her approach allowed *Incidents* simultaneously to appeal to a white middle-class audience and to expose the moral contradictions inherent in a mid-Victorian culture that valorized women's roles as mothers but permitted the sexual and economic exploitation of bondswomen and the sale of their children. Jacobs's use of sentimental rhetoric is often ironic, and the sub-text of her narrative offers a critique of the values of true womanhood. She re-writes the paradigm of the slave narrative, which posited the male slave as the solitary Romantic hero and the female slave as a brutalized victim. In contrast, Jacobs depicts her *alter ego* Linda Brent as a strong-willed woman who achieves freedom through the help of her family and friends. *Incidents* also employs imagery from the Bible and the African-American folk tradition, especially the trickster figure. Indeed, the literariness of *Incidents* led historians to believe that Jacobs's narrative was fictional, until Jean Fagan Yellin in 1981 illustrated the authenticity of Jacobs's autobiography.   DKo

Jalna (1927) MAZO DE LA ROCHE's third novel, the first in her series of sixteen about the Whiteoak family, won the prestigious *Atlantic Monthly* Prize and propelled her overnight to world fame and fortune. The Whiteoaks are a landowning dynasty living on the banks of Lake Ontario, presided over by the old matriarch, Adeline. In her 90th year, she still exerts an iron control over her descendants, most of whom live under one roof – that of the ancestral home of Jalna. The plot of this first novel involves the marriages, one approved and one disapproved, of two of her grandsons. By the last chapter all conflicts are resolved and the family unites to celebrate Adeline's birthday. The popularity of the book was based largely on her lively cast of characters and particularly that of Adeline herself, a feisty, cranky old woman with a parrot on her shoulder. There are also fine descriptive passages invoking the landscape of Southern Ontario.

The play *Whiteoaks* by Nancy Price ran in London from 1936 to 1939. A film, *Jalna*, appeared in 1935. A CBC television production, the script written by Timothy Findley, appeared in 1972. A French television production, starring Danielle Darrieux as Adeline, appeared in 1994. JG

James, Alice 1848–92 American diarist, letter-writer. The only sister of novelist Henry and philosopher William, as well as two other brothers, Alice spent her childhood travelling throughout Europe with her nomadic family. Just before the Civil War, they settled in Newport, Rhode Island, where Alice, as a result of the James family's focus on its men, was educated sporadically at home and began developing symptoms diagnosed simply as 'neuralgia'. As Henry wrote later, 'in our family group, girls seem scarcely to have had a chance'. In 1873, Alice met Katharine Peabody Loring, who moved with her to England in 1884, and remained her close companion until her death. Although she is known primarily through her DIARY, Alice did not begin keeping it until 1889. Her focus, perhaps understandably, is on herself, although she brilliantly analyses the literature, society and politics of her time. Her relief and elation at being diagnosed, in May 1891, with breast cancer, are remarkable: 'My aspirations may not have been eccentric, but I cannot complain now, that they have not been brilliantly fulfilled. Ever since I have been ill, I have longed and longed for some palpable disease, no matter how conventionally dreadful a label it might have.' Despite having dictated most of her diary to Katharine or to a nurse, Alice managed to keep it a secret from the rest of her family. Nevertheless, she had it typed just before her death, and seems clearly to have wanted it published, although it did not appear until 1934. SP

James, P(hyllis) D(orothy) 1920– Author of classically structured English DETECTIVE FICTION with an emphasis on psychological intensity and moral ambivalence. Born in Oxford, P.D. James attended Cambridge Girls' High School, but left at 16 to work in a Tax Office (her father was an Inland Revenue official). She married in 1941, but was left as sole provider for their two daughters after her husband's death in 1964. From 1949 to 1968 she was a hospital administrator, and from 1968 until retirement in 1979 worked at the Home Office, first in the Police Department and then in the Criminal Policy Department. Her intimate experience of hospital and police procedures was to provide her with rich material. Her first novel, *Cover Her Face* (1962), introduces her major detective figure, Adam Dalgliesh, a cerebral, introverted police inspector and poet. Cordelia Gray – a young private eye – makes her first appearance in *An Unsuitable Job for a Woman* (1972). Her regular trio of detectives is completed by Dalgliesh's colleague, Kate Miskin, first seen in *A Taste for Death* (1986).

P.D. James's fiction follows conventional genre patterns in the tradition of AGATHA CHRISTIE and DOROTHY L. SAYERS, with pacy, thrillerish plotting, but her later work displays an increasing preoccupation with questions of morality, truth and justice, as well as a rigorous investigation of the criminal mind. Strongly praised for its atmospheric depictions of landscape and insular communities, her writing has, in its creation of an extensive fictional world, also been compared to Dickens. Many of her novels have been adapted for television and film, including *Devices and Desires* (1989; televised 1991).

P.D. James has served as a Middlesex and London magistrate, was a governor of the BBC from 1988 to 1993, and chairman of the Arts Council's Literary Advisory Board from 1988 to 1992. She was awarded the Crime Writers' Association Silver Dagger several times and in 1987 was presented with their Diamond Dagger for services to crime writing. In 1991, she was made a life peer. *Original Sin* (1994) and *A Certain Justice* (1997) once more have Dalgliesh as protagonist. CS

Jameson, Anna Brownell 1794–1860 Irish essayist, art critic, traveller and translator whose writing (like AGNES STRICKLAND's, MARY HOWITT's or MARY SHELLEY's) began in the *belles-lettres* tradition of the Keepsake market, and then matured and deepened into scholarly enterprises that were nonetheless accessible to a wider audience. At 16 she worked as a governess, and wrote professionally before and after her unsatisfactory marriage to a lawyer. Her most substantial books were thoroughly researched accounts of religious iconography: *The Poetry of Sacred and Legendary Art* (1848), *Legends of the Monastic Orders* (1850), *Legends of the Madonna* (1852). Like her earlier compendia, *Loves of the Poets* (1829), *Memoirs of . . . Female Sovereigns* (1831) and *Characteristics of Women* (1832) (actually on Shakespeare's heroines), she used investigations into visual or verbal representations of women as a vehicle for examining how stereotyping, hypocrisy and circumstance constrained women's potential. Concern for women's position was also reflected in her travel writing on Canada and Germany, but she avoided the language of women's rights, exploring and extending instead the traditional discourse of their 'influence' and distinct role. She insisted on women's need for better education, to equip them for work. In the 1850s she was a respected mentor to Langham Place feminists such as BARBARA BODICHON and BESSIE RAYNER PARKES. CCO

Jameson, Storm (Margaret) 1891–1986 British woman of letters, wrote forty-five novels, many of which centre on strong women characters and engage with the important political issues of her day. In her acclaimed autobiography, *JOURNEY FROM THE NORTH* (1969–70), Jameson provides her own epitaph, 'the greatest passion of her life, too little indulged, was for travel'. She was born into a seafaring family in Whitby, the daughter of Hannah Margaret and William Storm Jameson, and educated at Scarborough Municipal School. Jameson obtained a first-class degree in English from Leeds University in 1912, and an MA from London University. She married Charles Douglas Clarke in 1913, had a son, William, in 1915, divorced, and married the historian, Guy Chapman. In the 1920s she worked as an advertising copywriter and managed the English affairs of the publishing firm, Knopf. The first of her socially engaged trilogies, *The Triumph of Time* (1927–31), was followed by the well-known 'Mirror in Darkness' novel sequence; *Company Parade* (1934), *Love in Winter* (1935) and *None Turn Back* (1936) centred on the character of Hervey Russell. In the 1930s she joined the Peace Pledge Union, which she later left, and was active in Labour Party politics. As President of PEN, in 1939–45 Jameson visited Austria, Hungary and Czechoslovakia and raised funds to bring Jewish intellectuals and other writers to Britain. Her visit to Hungary is imaginatively evoked in *Europe to Let* (1940) and *The Journal of Mary Hervey Russell* (1945). Other political novels, *The Fort* (1941), *Cloudless May* (1944) and *The Other Side* (1946), are set in occupied France and concerned with separation, loss and the need for reconstruction. Her discursive writings include *Parthian Words* (1971) and *Speaking of Stendhal* (1979). She died in Cambridge.   MJ

Jamie, Kathleen 1962– Scottish poet who grew up in Midlothian, studied Philosophy at Edinburgh University and lives in Fife. Since her début at 20 – *Black Spiders* (1982) – Jamie has gone on refining and extending her style, one of unrhetorical language, supple lines and the restrained use of vivid imagery. She chases after the truth squeezed between expectation and appearance, as in the title poem of *The Way We Live* (1987):

> To the way it fits, the way it is, the way it seems
> to be: let me bash out the praises – pass the tambou-
> rine.

Many of Jamie's poems have this fissured quality (as well as this promise of violent music). They reflect social, gender or national constructs riven by change, individual assertion, economic reality or imaginative flight. Linebreaks add spin to meaning, as in the falter in 'it seems/ to be'.

Jamie has written about her extensive travels – *The Golden Peak* (1992) and *The Autonomous Region* (with photographer Sean Mayne Smith, 1993). Whether in Edinburgh or Pakistan, it is the female experience that interests her most, something she approaches with a fine balance of empathy and confrontation. She can be furiously funny or excoriating.

The enlarged themes and more spacious forms of *The Queen of Sheba* (1994) intensify Jamie's voice. These are clear, disciplined, risky poems that pull all ways without breaking:

> Breathe that steamy musk
> on the Curriehill Road, not mutton-shanks
> boiled for broth, nor the chlorine stink
> of the swimming pool where skinny girls
> accuse each other of verrucas.
> In her bathhouses women bear
> warm pot-bellied terracotta pitchers
> on their laughing hips.
>
>   ('The Queen of Sheba')
>   LG

Jane Eyre: An Autobiography (1847) CHARLOTTE BRONTË's first novel, published anonymously as 'Edited by Currer Bell', created a stir of notoriety; not only does it assert women's right to equal opportunity with men for self-development and expression, even proclaiming inherent equality before God; it also allows adult Jane a passionate attraction to her married employer. For 20th-century readers, these have instead become reasons for its popularity. This growth novel recalls both FAIRY TALES of the 'Ugly Duckling' type and moral quests such as *Pilgrim's Progress*. Plain Jane is an orphan who suffers for her rebellious, unfeminine nature in the cold household of her unloving Aunt Reed; learns to control her temper amidst the rigours of Lowood School; and, having become a governess, withstands the temptation of yielding to an affair with her employer, Mr Rochester, after the failure of his attempt to marry her although already secretly married to the madwoman incarcerated in his attic. Not only morally but also psychologically sound, Jane also refuses a loveless marriage with an ascetic newfound cousin and finally, in a triumph of female virtue, is reunited with widowed Rochester: he blind and with a crippled hand, she empowered by recently inherited wealth.   HB

Jasmine (1989) BHARATI MUKHERJEE's immigrant novel. The heroine Jasmine, born in a small village in India, emigrates to the States, under-age and widowed, to fulfil her husband's last wish. However, her fate is not that of a mourning widow, as her astrologer had foretold, but that of a reckless migrant. In the course of her many transactions she acquires new names, Jyoti, Jasmine, Jase, Jazzy, Jane, each indicative of a new phase in her Americanization. The initial 'J' represents the element of continuity within her transformations, but *Jasmine* is a celebration of multiple, fluid identities. The heroine's metamorphosis symbolizes a revenge upon the bleak destiny foretold by the astrologer, her way of resetting the stars, leaving behind her 'old world dutifulness' and embracing America's opportunities.

Mukherjee's bizarre fable of transformation has often been seen as unrealistic and superficial. However, the energetic and volatile depiction of her Indian female protagonist makes the experience of migration a rather rewarding adventure. SPo

Jellicoe, Ann (Patricia) 1927– Born and educated in Yorkshire, Jellicoe trained as an actress at the Central School of Speech and Drama where she later became a lecturer and director. She emerged as one of the new generation of playwrights in the late 1950s with *THE SPORT OF MY MAD MOTHER*, produced in 1958, and *THE KNACK* (1964). The first of these had only a short London run but remains an extraordinary play where the author radically experiments with theatrical space, improvisational structures, ritual and rhythm of language. The play provides an apocalyptic vision of London street life presided over by a mother-warrior figure who, at the end of the play, gives birth on stage while one of her aides holds an instruction manual. In *The Knack*, Jellicoe makes use of jazz structures as the architectural framework for dialogue. Although the play is very funny in parts there is a continual undercurrent of ritualistic violence as the battle of the sexes is played out. Other plays include *Shelley: Or, The Idealist* (1966) and *The Rising Generation* (produced in 1967). During the 1970s Jellicoe concentrated on directing work and on the development of community plays such as *The Reckoning* (1978) about the Monmouth Rebellion of 1685. Jellicoe worked with many of the next generation of playwrights, including David Edgar and Howard Barker, and her book *Community Plays: How to Put Them On* (1987) is an indispensable text on the subject. MBG

Jemmat, Catherine (Yeo) 1714–66 English autobiographer and poet whose assertion, in her *Memoirs* (1762), impertinently challenges Richardson and his fictions: 'Why may not the true story of Catherine Yeo, who absolutely does exist, divert as much ... as those of Miss Pamela Andrews and Miss Clarissa Harlowe?' Her mother dying early, she was left to the mercy of a tyrannical father, an admiral, who refused his consent to all her suitors, even locking her up. She finally married a mercer who, she discovered, had relied on her marriage settlement to pay his creditors, and was a drunkard and wife-beater. Her *Memoirs*, probably written to earn money, are lively and genuine, describing dreams, tragi-comic misadventures and romantic affairs. In 1766 she published *Miscellanies in Prose and Verse* with an 'Essay in Vindication of the Female Sex' which criticizes the double standard. LMT

Jennings, Elizabeth (Joan) 1926– British poet Jennings was born in Boston, Lincolnshire. Her father, a Catholic convert and a doctor, was much admired by his daughter for his intelligence and moral courage. The family moved to Oxford when Jennings was 6. She had two siblings, one a real older sister, the other an imaginary brother called Jack Baycock who lived in the greenhouse (Jennings is quoted as saying 'I abhor Freud and all he stands for'). She had a serious breakdown in her late teens before going to Oxford. She read English at St Anne's College and associated with Philip Larkin, Kingsley Amis and D. J. Enright. After a stint as a copywriter for a London advertising agency, Jennings returned to Oxford to work in the city library for eight years. She was a reader for Chatto and Windus from 1958 to 1960 before turning to writing full-time in 1961. She never married and despises domesticity – 'Boring, too much of it'.

Jennings began writing poetry as an Eliot-struck adolescent, but her style was chastened by reading the Metaphysicals, Graves and Auden at university. She was the only woman to be included in Robert Conquest's influential Movement anthology *New Lines* (1956). *A Way of Looking* (1955), her second collection, won the Somerset Maugham Award which enabled her to go to Rome; the Italian landscape and literature still hold a strong attraction for her. Early successes came to haunt Jennings, especially under the stress of mental illness: *The Mind has Mountains* (1966) is the culmination of her early style, concentrating on hospital experiences. Out of those a different poet emerged, whose formal style moved closer to an individual voice, and whose human insight was more penetrating. She began as a love poet, lyrical and not ironic (unlike the Movement poets with whom she associated), examining relationships between objects and between people. The theme of isolation is obsessive: the solitary person in an unstable environment is further removed by the mind's unpredictability.

In 1987 she won the W. H. Smith Literary Award for *Collected Poems* (1986). Since then she has published a number of volumes, notably *Tributes* (1989), *Times and Seasons* (1992), *Familiar Spirits* (1994) and *In the Meantime* (1996), and accepted one of the first Paul Hamlyn Foundation Individual Awards for Artists of £15,000 in 1998. The themes that have captivated her through a long and distinguished career are childhood, friendship, nature, time, travel and religion, but in particular, lack and loss. DM

Jennings, Gertrude (Eleanor) 1877–1958 The daughter of an American actress and an erstwhile editor for the *New York Times* who later became an MP for Stockport, Manchester, Jennings was a dramatist associated with the fight for women's SUFFRAGE. She established a reputation as an author of one-act plays before World War I, upgrading the form by using well-known performers such as Lilian Braithwaite, Athene Sayler and Irene Vanburgh. At one time known as our 'most acted woman playwright', Jennings was popular with amateur companies although, keen to protect authors' rights, she once fought a much-publicized copyright and licensing case with an amateur group. She found success in the West End theatres in the inter-war years with plays like *The Young Person in Pink* (1920), *Family Affairs* (1934) and *Our Own Lives* (1935). She foregrounded domestic issues and women's lives and always had an eye on current trends of thought which showed in such plays as *Husbands For All* (1920), a farce in which the government decrees that, due to shortages of marriageable men, all men under 40 must have two wives by 1925. A loosely autobiographical work, *Happy Memories*, was published in 1955.　　　MBG

Jensen, Laura 1948– American poet born in Tacoma, Washington, of Scandinavian origins. She studied at the University of Washington, then attended the Writers' Workshop at the University of Iowa. Author of three collections, including *Bad Boats* (1977) and *Shelter* (1985), Jensen writes most often of ordinary, domestic details and objects in their sometimes odd vestments; unusual images describe the most obvious particulars of life . . . an egg, a window, the wing of a bird. In addition, there is a slightly surreal quality to the poems, complemented by an energetic imagery which animates the work. This quality is often reflected in the poems' titles: 'The Red Dog', 'Talking to the Mule' and 'The Crow is Mischief', for example. Jensen turns the minutiae of life into illustrative wonders: 'Roses are red / because their ears are burning.' Her awards include a National Endowment for the Arts prize in 1972. In 1989 she won a second Guggenheim Fellowship and travelled to Scandinavia to write.　　　ACH

Jerusalem the Golden (1967) MARGARET DRABBLE's third novel describes, with echoes of Bunyan's *Pilgrim's Progress*, heroine Clara's infatuation with the cosmopolitan, stylish, civilized Denham family, who represent all that her own provincial lower-middle-class world, with its emotional penny-pinching, its inarticulacy and its puritanism, seems to deny. The writing is deliberately REALIST and traditional, defined by concrete social conditions, possessions and limitations. Indeed this book established most fully and elegantly Drabble's characteristic formula for fiction – the extended-family plot – which stood her in good stead throughout the 1960s and 1970s, only to be more or less abandoned in the fragmented and fissile 1980s. The main device is to entangle the protagonist in a 'constellation' of relationships, and to enforce the ironic moral that life proceeds by gradual accretion, not by violent dislocation. Clara's adulterous love-affair with Gabriel Denham is transposed into a new key as she remakes her connections

with her own dead and rejected mother, and settles for a tragi-comic vision of living as a matter of 'rearrangement'.　　　LS

Jesse, F[ryniwyd] Tennyson 1888–1958 English novelist with especial interest in crime. A Kent parson's daughter and Tennyson's great-niece, she studied art with the Newlyn School in Cornwall, but turned to writing. She lost the use of her right hand early in life. In 1912 she collaborated on a play, *The Mask*, with the dramatist, H. M. Harwood – whom she was to marry in 1918 – and in 1913 published her first novel, *The Milky Way*. During World War I she became one of the few women war correspondents. *The Sword of Deborah* (1919), about the British Women's Army in France, emphasized women's capacity for strength, as did the ROMANCE, *Moonraker* (1927), which juxtaposed its pirate captain heroine with Toussaint l'Ouverture. However, her two major novels employ self-centred fantasizing heroines participating centrally in large public events beyond their understanding. In *A Lacquer Lady* (1929) the jilted Eurasian heroine's revenge is the catalyst for the British annexation of Upper Burma. Based on research Jesse undertook in Burma, the novel is part of the inter-war reassessment of imperialism, foregrounding the British psychological and sexual fantasies realized on the road to Mandalay. *A PIN TO SEE THE PEEP-SHOW* (1935) fictionalizes the controversial Bywaters-Thompson trial of 1922. A novel which begins as a reconstruction of lower-middle-class life in the manner of Arnold Bennett becomes a savage indictment of the social and sexual prejudices which hanged Edith Thompson for, effectively, adultery. Jesse's 1924 treatise, *Murder and its Motives*, explored the idea of the 'born murderee'. She was the first woman to edit volumes in the 'Notable British Trials' series, including two on fantasizing women, *Madeleine Smith* (1927) and *Alma Rattenbury* (1935). Her best work is notable for its feminist exploration of women caught up in crime.　　　AT

Jewett, Sarah Orne 1849–1909 Like Capt. Sands in her first collection of stories, *Deephaven* (1877), the American writer Sarah Orne Jewett was 'a collector of odd memorable things'. The daughter of a doctor in South Berwick, Maine, Jewett accompanied her father on his rounds instead of attending school, and always felt she belonged to the world of her grandfathers, uncles and aunts. HARRIET BEECHER STOWE's *The Pearl of Orr's Island* (1862) inspired Jewett to write about New England, and Jewett's strengths as a writer were deeply rooted in the stability of the New England village, which she declined to romanticize.

In her time New England was in sharp decline. The railroad and industry had robbed it of autonomy. Migration from its harsh climate and stony soil, memorably the subject of EDITH WHARTON's ETHAN FROME (1911), left only the hardiest and most rooted. Jewett's characters, as F.O. Matthiessen put it, 'do not revolt; they do not try to escape'. They are often 'isolatoes' who have nothing to do with the hurry of modern life and lead narrow and pinched lives, yet strive to make out of narrow circumstances something fine. For most Americans, pioneers and rebels, not survivors, are the true culture heroes. Reserve, separateness, the 'sanctity of the front yard' were the values she admired. 'We Americans', Jewett wrote, 'had better build more fences than take any away from our lives.'

Deephaven was followed by five novels, nine further collections of stories, and four books for children. Her most important works are *A Country Doctor* (1884), *A White Heron* (1886) and her masterpiece, THE COUNTRY OF THE POINTED FIRS (1896). Jewett's natural *métier* was the linked short story or sketch, each aspiring to a Flaubertian finish. Critics have placed Jewett, as a regionalist or local-colourist, with a 'certain language of diminution'. The fineness of her work is fully acknowledged, but the restriction of its range remains a limiting judgement on Jewett's achievement.   EH

Jewsbury, Geraldine [Endsor] 1812–80 British novelist and woman of letters. She was born in Derbyshire; her father was an insurance agent and cotton merchant, and the family settled in Manchester in 1818. Her mother died soon after, and Geraldine was brought up by her sister, Maria, and became housekeeper to her father until he died in 1840, then to her brother, Frank. In 1841 she met Thomas Carlyle and his wife, Jane, and became intimate with the couple. In the 1940s, she wrote for Douglas Jerrold's *Shilling Magazine* and later said she would have liked to have been a journalist but her delicate health made the life too taxing for her. Nevertheless, she contributed tough-minded and astute reviews to the *Athenaeum*, and was a 'reader' for the publisher, Richard Bentley.

But her main effort was in fiction: she published her first novel, *Zoe: The History of Two Lives*, in 1845. In 1848 she visited revolutionary Paris with her friend W.E. Forster, and published *The Half Sisters*, and in 1851, her 'industrial' novel, *Marian Withers*, was serialized in the *Manchester Examiner and Times*. Released from her housekeeping duties by her brother's marriage in 1854, she moved to London to be closer to the Carlyles and kept up an intimate correspondence with JANE CARLYLE, most of which has since been destroyed. *Constance Herbert* came out in 1855 and was dedicated to Carlyle. *Sorrows of Gentility* (1856) and *Right or Wrong* (1859) followed – all displayed her particular interest in the 'woman question': the paucity of educational opportunity, the risks and wearisome obligations of marriage and the need for gainful occupations for women. She was considered a radical and a wit and,

although she never married, she was rumoured to have had love-affairs. Jewsbury also wrote books for children, such as *The History of an Adopted Child* (1852). After the death of her friend, Jane Carlyle, in 1866, she moved to Kent and remained there until her cancer advanced so far that she was obliged to move into a private hospital in London, where she died.   CPe

Jhabvala, Ruth Prawer 1927– British novelist, born in Cologne of Jewish parents and educated in Jewish schools in Germany until war forced the family to flee to England in 1939. Continuing her education in England she went to Queen Mary College, London, and became a British citizen in 1948. She married C.S. Jhabvala, an architect, in 1952 and then lived in India with him and their three daughters until 1975. Her novels are concerned with the ambiguous, often difficult relationship between India and the West, and her elegant, poised prose has won her much admiration. In 1975 she won the Booker Prize for her novel HEAT AND DUST which she adapted into a film in 1983 in collaboration with James Ivory. The novel, set in the 1920s and the 1970s, concerns the story of Olivia, the bored wife of an English civil servant who outrages the Indian society of Satipur by eloping with an Indian Prince (the Nawab). Their relationship is seen in a political as well as a romantic context, exposing the fissures between nationalities as well as personalities. Jhabvala has since also adapted several classic texts for Merchant/Ivory films including E.M. Forster's *A Room With a View* and *Howard's End*, for both of which she won Academy Awards for Best Adapted Screenplay. She was also nominated for her adaptation of Kazuo Ishiguro's *The Remains of the Day*. A frequent contributor to the *New Yorker*, Jhabvala has published collections of her short stories, *A Stronger Climate* (1968) and *How I Became A Holy Mother* (1976; originally published as *An Experience of India* in 1971). Among her other novels are *A New Dominion* (1973), *In Search of Love and Beauty* (1983) and *Three Continents* (1987). In 1984 she received a MacArthur Foundation Award and in 1994 she received the Writers Guild of America's Screen Laurel Award, which is their highest honour.   JHB

Jiles, Paulette 1943– Born in the Missouri Ozarks, Jiles emigrated to Canada in 1969, later working in the Arctic and teaching creative writing in British Columbia. Her collections of poetry include *Celestial Navigation* which won many awards (1984), *Waterloo Express* (1973) and *The Jesse James Poems* (1988). Jiles characterizes herself as a 'Third Force Feminist' and writes daring, unconventional, quirky works, playfully reworking narrative away from 'plain icky regular prose fiction'. Her novel *The Late Great Human Road Show* (1986) is an innovative post-apocalyptic fantasy, whilst *Sitting in the Club Car Drinking Rum and Karma-Kola* (1987), set on board a transcontinental train journeying across Canada, parodies DETECTIVE FICTION and the picaresque. Indeed, in her explorations of 'the problem of women taking action in a world which is hostile to action-taking females', Jiles has identified the picaresque 'of all the literary genres' as 'the most interesting area to look at since it's the absolute opposite of what we've been told is our "proper" sphere'.

CSt

Joan Makes History (1988) Published in the year of Australia's bi-centennial celebrations, Australian KATE GRENVILLE's novel is a clever, POST-COLONIAL revision of Australia's white history from a female perspective. Joan is a plain, ordinary wife and mother, but she also lives as an unobtrusive presence at all the defining moments of that history, from Captain Cook's first sighting of Australia, to the opening of the first Federal Parliament. Grandiose masculine claims which represent the triumphant climaxes of official histories are humorously deconstructed and undermined by shrewd female observation and pre-emptive interventions: convict Joan dives out of a porthole and swims ashore to place the first white foot on the shore of Botany Bay. The official, benign history of colonization is revealed to be a lying sham, as when the assigned servant Joan witnesses the effects of poisoned flour given to the Aboriginals. In the city, Joan becomes a man, and, as Jack, experiments with the freedom of a masculine identity. She finally becomes a wife and mother, but not before fulfilling her ambition of making a new history for Australia.

HTh

John Halifax, Gentleman (1856) Published three years before Samuel Smiles's *Self-Help*, DINAH MULLOCK CRAIK's novel charts the rise to prosperity of a penniless orphan, John Halifax, who knows nothing of his origins save what may be deduced from a family Bible bearing the legend 'Guy Halifax Gentleman', this being his father's name and station in life. Integrity, hard work and self-education gain him both material success and social acceptance. However, he also benefits from the good offices of his employer's invalid son, Phineas, who narrates the story. The novel pays particular attention to employer/employee and inter-class relations.

It also charts the eponymous hero's marriage with Ursula March, an heiress who chooses to marry for love rather than wealth and position, fashionable marriages being another theme in the novel. Rejecting the corrupt fashionable world into which they are ultimately invited, the couple live with their family in perfect domestic harmony for many years. They then die on the same day, Ursula being unable to continue living after the death of her husband.

EMH

Johnson, Amryl? – Caribbean-British writer, was born in Trinidad but has lived in Britain since she was 11. She is active in promoting African Caribbean poetry throughout Britain where she has travelled extensively, performing her own work and that of other Caribbean poets and running workshops. She has published a travelogue/novel, *Sequins For a Ragged Hem* (1988), three collections of poetry, and recorded a cassette of her poems, *Blood and Wine* (1992).

Johnson describes her writing as being profoundly shaped by the experience of migration to a hostile 'mother country' and many of her poems catalogue the personal cost of that journey, making use, particularly in *Long Road to Nowhere*, of an intensely focused poetic anger. Connections are often made between historical oppressions and the contemporary experiences of black British people. Other poems seek to retrieve the lost landscape of the Caribbean in evocative, painterly descriptions while, in her most recent collection, *Gorgons*, Johnson uses the Greek Medusa myth as a poetic vehicle to explore a range of female speakers and a range of linguistic registers (demotic, biblical, calypso, song). Johnson's commitment to a black womanist poetics remains powerfully inspirational in its insistence on a poetic voice which 'shouts' *and* 'sings'.

DdeCN

Johnson, Diane 1934– American novelist, biographer and critic, whose elegant REALIST fictions feature clever but insecure women in search of richer lives and identities. Born in Moline, Illinois, Johnson's was a 'bookish childhood': she reputedly wrote her first novel at the age of 10. Education, marriage, motherhood and writing were closely enmeshed in the fifties and sixties. She left Stephens College to marry Lamar Johnson, Jr; two of their four children were born shortly before she gained her BA at the University of Utah in 1957. After moving to California – of which she was a long-time resident – an MA at UCLA was followed by completion of her Ph.D. and marriage to her second husband, Professor of Medicine John Frederic Murray, in 1968.

Her first two novels, *Fair Game* (1965) and *Loving Hands at Home* (1968), both witty anatomies of young women seeking their place in life, date from this period. Her seventies work explored more extreme states: a Californian couple's secrets told after a concoction of drugs and sex in *Burning* (1971); the inner world of a rape victim in *THE SHADOW KNOWS* (1974); and the fragile lives of three women (one of them hiding out from student crimes committed in the 1960s) in *Lying Low* (1978). She also diversified into other genres, with BIOGRAPHIES – of Mary Ellen Meredith ('a new – a modern – Victorian heroine') in *Lesser Lives* (1972), and *Dashiel Hammett: A Life* (1983) – and collaboration with film director Stanley Kubrick on the screenplay for his family horror *The Shining* (1980). Her book reviews were collected in *Terrorists and Novelists* (1982). *Persian Nights* (1987) explores the leisured milieu of its American heroine in Iran on the eve of the 1979 revolution. Her 1990s works include *Health and Happiness* (1990), *Natural Opium* (1993), and *Le Divorce* (1996), set in Paris, where she now also lives. MO'D

Johnson, Emily Pauline (Tekahionwake) 1861–1913 Popular part-Mohawk Canadian author and performer, whose poetry and prose frequently advocate the rights and values of First Nations Canadians. The youngest of the four children of an English-born Quaker mother and a mostly Mohawk father, Johnson was born and raised in a comfortable, literate Victorian household on the Six Nations Reserve near Brantford, in what is now the Province of Ontario. After the death of her father in 1884 she turned to writing to support herself. Little of her early published work draws directly on her native heritage; however, after the highlight of her first significant staged reading (January 1892) proved to be her dramatic recitation of several of her Indian poems, Johnson gradually adopted a public persona emphasizing her Mohawk origins, as well as her great-grandfather's original name of 'Tekahionwake'.

Johnson's first book of poetry, *The White Wampum*, was published in London by John Lane at the Bodley Head in 1895, following a triumphant season of society performances in England during the summer of 1894. Until she retired to Vancouver in 1909 (where she died of breast cancer in 1913), Johnson pursued a successful touring career during the course of which she crossed Canada several times, occasionally appeared in the United States, and returned twice to England (1906, 1907). For half her programme she appeared in evening dress, and for the other half in native costume; in addition to her poetry and stories, her repertoire included satirical sketches that were never published. Her poems, some of which were collected in *Canadian Born* (1903) and *Flint and Feather* (1911, misleadingly subtitled 'Complete Poems'), circulated widely in the periodical press, along with articles and stories drawing on her expertise as a canoeist and on her knowledge of native culture. Over time, she developed a pan-Indian identity, speaking on behalf of various native cultures; her *Legends of Vancouver* (1911) retells stories of the Squamish people of coastal British Columbia. Dismissed as a popular 'poetess' during the modernist era in Canadian literature, Johnson is gaining recognition among current First Nations authors who claim her as an important foremother. CG

Johnson, Georgia Douglas 1880–1966 Poet, playwright and fiction writer who gave poetic expression to the difficulties, rather than the joys, of motherhood for African-American women. Born in Atlanta, Georgia, she studied music at Oberlin and Cleveland College of Music. She originally aspired to becoming a professional composer. Upon winning first prize in the *Opportunity* drama contest for her play *Plumes*, she wrote of her shift from music to literature in an essay for the journal: 'The words took fire and the music smouldered and so, following the lead of friends and critics, I turned my face toward poetry and put my songs away' ('The Contest Spotlight', July 1927).

She worked as a schoolteacher after moving to Washington, D.C., in 1910, with her husband, Henry Lincoln Johnson – a lawyer and politician – and their two sons. The demands of being a working mother and the wife of an ambitious politician hindered her writing. She was, however, encouraged by other African-American artists and published her first poem, 'Omnipresence', in *Voice of a Negro* in 1905, and her first of four volumes of poems, *The Heart of a Woman and Other Poems*, in 1918. In response to criticism that her poetry was not racially conscious, she composed *Bronze* (1922), a collection of race poetry. After her husband's death in 1925 she began hosting literary gatherings made famous by her eccentricity and by the attendance of such Harlem Renaissance writers as Gwendolyn Bennett, ALICE DUNBAR-NELSON, ANGELINA GRIMKÉ WELD, Langston Hughes, James Weldon Johnson, ANNE SPENCER and Jean Toomer.

She continued to explore 'the heart of a woman' in *An Autumn Love Cycle* (1928), a moderately well-received collection of love poems that expressed the desires of the older woman. She also freed herself from the restraints of writing as an African-American woman by publishing under at least two pseudonyms, 'Paul Tremaine' and 'John Temple'. She continued to write and apply (unsuccessfully) for fellowships and grants until her death at 85.

Much of her work, unpublished or published under unidentified pen names, is lost. VM

Johnson, Joyce 1935– American fiction writer and memoirist, born in New York. After graduation from Barnard College, she worked as an editor for various publishers while writing her first two novels – *Come Join the Dance* (1962), and *Bad Connections* (1978), a novel about a magazine editor who chooses an independent lifestyle instead of enduring destructive relationships. After evolving as a feminist in her early middle age, Johnson looked back at her life in her memoir *Minor Characters* (1983), the book for which she is best known. This is a candid account of her relationship with Jack Kerouac and other members of the group of Beat Generation writers in New York City, before they became famous in the late 1950s. Johnson described the lives of the women in the Beat group – herself, Elise Cowan, Hettie Jones, among others – as those of 'minor characters' in the lives of the men. Her portrayal of this bohemian, male-oriented group of friends was affectionate, but it included descriptions of their selfishness and self-destructiveness, and the risks for the women involved with them as lovers, wives and caretakers. *Minor Characters* won a National Book Critics' Circle Award in 1983. Five years later Johnson published *In the Night Café*. A chapter of this third novel originally appeared as the short story 'In the Children's Wing' and won the O. Henry Award for Best Short Story of 1987.   ACh

Johnson, Pamela Hansford 1912–81 English novelist known for her accounts of suburban life among the shabby genteel. She was the daughter of a civil servant whose early death left her without the means of getting a private or university education. After attending a state grammar school, she was trained as a stenographer and worked from 1930 until 1934, when she made her entrance into literary circles, winning a *Sunday Referee* prize for poetry. In the same year, she met the celebrated poet Dylan Thomas (to whom she was briefly engaged). He suggested the title for her surprisingly successful first novel, *This Bed Thy Centre* (1935), whose narrative style has been compared to the surrealist irreverence of Thomas's own stories. Unlike Thomas, Johnson grew into a politically committed and influential figure in English literary life: many of her fictional protagonists evince the socialist ideals current in the 1930s and she edited a leftist weekly publication called the *Chelsea Democrat*. In 1936, she married Gordon Stewart, an Australian with whom she co-wrote two murder mysteries (using the pseudonym Nap Lombard). This marriage ended in 1948, after an estrangement due to the war but also attributable to Johnson's close attachment to her mother, who had moved in with her daughter's family. Meanwhile Johnson's career as a novelist proceeded apace; her published titles include *World's End* (1937), *The Monument* (1938), *Girdle of Venus* (1939), *Too Dear for My Possessing* (1940),*The Family Pattern* (1942), *Winter Quarters* (1943) and *An Avenue of Stone* (1947). In 1950 she married the novelist C. P. Snow, with whom she once more collaborated lightheartedly. Among her later works are her first comic novel, *The Unspeakable Skipton* (1959), and a satirical account of her tenure as writer-in-residence at an American university, *Night and Silence, Who is Here?* (1963).   BWB

Johnson [Hastings], Susannah Willard 1730–1810 New Hampshire woman, purported author of *A Narrative of Mrs Johnson* (1796). In an attack on Charlestown, New Hampshire, in 1754, Susannah Johnson, her family and two neighbours were taken by Abenaki Indians and carried to Canada. The family was dispersed among various Indian families in Quebec until their sale to French families. Susannah Johnson and two of her children later joined her husband, James, who was imprisoned in Quebec City. In 1757, Susannah and the children sailed for England in a prisoner exchange. James was killed shortly after his release, but the rest of the family returned to Charlestown by 1759. The circumstances of publication and the style of the narrative itself suggest composition by someone other than Johnson. Prefatory material and interpolated EPISTOLARY passages rely extensively on a recognizably 'female' rhetoric of sentiment and emotionalism. As well, the text's strong anti-French stance and its recurrent references to its own utility as an authoritative historical work signify that the *Narrative*, although the story of an actual woman's experiences, represents an editor–composer's idea of how those experiences might be shaped to suit specific political and cultural agendas. (See CAPTIVITY NARRATIVE.)   LCa

Johnston, Dorothy Margaret 1948– Australian writer born in Geelong, Victoria, moved to Canberra in 1978. Johnston is known for applying a lyrical style to social themes not usually encountered in Australian fiction. Her first novel, *Tunnel Vision* (1984), was set in a Melbourne massage parlour; her second, *Ruth* (1986), shortlisted for the prestigious Miles Franklin Award, deals with the thwarted aspirations of a working-class housewife. In 1988 she published *Maralinga My Love*, a novel concerned with the testing of nuclear weapons in the South Australian desert. After a long break Johnston once again engaged with the moral dimensions of working life with the publication of *One for the Master* (1997), a novel set in the Geelong textile mills, many of which were closed in the 1980s. Because of her themes, Johnston has often been misrepresented as a social realist writer and has not achieved the fame of other writers of her generation, but has instead a strong and devoted critical following, particularly among other writers. HELEN GARNER, for example, has written that 'Johnston achieves the difficult double feat: she creates and maintains a convincing physical world, and yet transcends it through a lovely and original imagination.'   SDo

Johnston, Jennifer 1930– Irish novelist who is concerned mainly with cultural balance and social understanding in a divided Ireland. Her earlier novels address but are not exclusively concerned with the decline of the 'Big House' culture in Anglo-Irish society: she is always interested in the smaller details which reflect the wider issues and tensions in life. Born in Dublin, the daughter of actress Shelagh Richards and playwright Denis Johnston, she studied English at Trinity College Dublin where she met her first husband, with whom she had four children. After living in

England for twenty years they subsequently divorced and she moved to Derry with her second husband and five step-children.

As a writer, she reflects that it took time and courage to discover her woman's voice. In a 1996 interview with Roza Gonzales she said – 'when I started to write, when I was teaching myself to write, I didn't have the courage in a way to approach writing as a woman, and so I came at it obliquely through writing through the eyes of a man, and this was, I think, lack of courage. Because you can't jump in at the deep end of a swimming pool unless you can swim and I had to teach myself to swim before I really started to write about the things that I wanted to write about.' In 1979 she won the Whitbread Award for Fiction for her novel THE OLD JEST (made into a film in 1988), and in 1977 her novel *Shadows on our Skin*, which focuses on the life of a Catholic family in Derry, was shortlisted for the Booker Prize. Her earlier novels, *The Captains and the Kings* (1972), *The Gates* (1973) and *How Many Miles to Babylon?* (1974), draw heavily on friendships and class difference, while *The Christmas Tree* (1981), *The Railway Station Man* (1984; filmed in 1994), *The Illusionist* (1995) and *Two Moons* (1998) focus on women and independence. She contributed to *Finbar's Hotel* (1997), has published a collection of dramatic pieces, *The Nightingale Not the Lark* (1988), and the play *The Desert Lullaby* (1996).   EF

Jolley [née Knight], Elizabeth 1923– Australian writer with a national and international reputation. Jolley's comment in the preface to *Five Acre Virgin* (1976), her first published work – 'The characters appear to inhabit a crazy world. I think it is our world' – could stand as an epigraph to all her writing, with its ironic, darkly comic, poignant and compassionate representation of the lives of sad, lonely, often rather unlikeable characters. Jolley was born in Birmingham and brought up in the English Midlands. Her father was English and a pacifist; her mother Viennese and deeply disappointed in her exile. These parents, their ideologies and the tensions between them have provided Jolley with rich fictional material. She has written of her 'vicarious experience of homesickness and exile'. Educated by a series of governesses, then in a Quaker boarding school, Jolley trained and worked as a nurse. In 1959, she migrated to Perth, Western Australia, with her husband, Leonard (now deceased), a university librarian, and their three children, and has lived there since. German and English literatures, especially of the 18th and 19th centuries, are a major influence in her work; classical music is also important. Jolley's literary output includes novels, short-story collections, radio drama, poetry and a collection of autobiographical pieces, essays and speeches. Her work has won numerous awards, and among other honours she holds several honorary degrees from Australian universities.

Jolley's work finally gained recognition in the mid-1960s when both the BBC and the ABC began to broadcast radio plays and stories. This medium is still one to which her work translates successfully. At the same time, some stories were published in journals and anthologies. Jolley's writing process is layered, not linear, and the chronology of her publishing, which seemed unusually rapid once she achieved her first book publications, does not reflect a creative chronology, which stretches back over her lifetime. Her writing is characterized by repetition or recurrence, both internal and between works, of characters, situations, motifs, allusions, even phrases and stories. It is also notable for its exploration of relationships among women, including lesbian relationships. Another major preoccupation is the nature of the writing process and many of her characters are writers. Miss Halley in *Mr Scobie's Riddle* (1983) warns of the dangers of literal readings: 'Don't, but do not take everything I say *au pied de la lettre*.' At once REALIST and experimental, humanist and POSTMODERN, Jolley's writing mixes genres, uses multiple narrative voices, develops fragmented narratives, and is marked by unsettling tonal variations. Her characters are alienated and displaced individuals who inhabit often bizarre settings which relate to and comment on wider social environments. Jolley's interest is in the ways such people survive – how they retain hope and are able to love. See *WOMAN IN A LAMPSHADE* and *MISS PEABODY'S INHERITANCE* (both 1983), *THE WELL* (1986) and *MY FATHER'S MOON* (1994).   DB

Jones, Gwyneth 1952– British writer of SCIENCE FICTION and fantasy, whose novels for CHILDREN and young adults generally use the pseudonym 'Ann Hallam'. Jones studied the History of Ideas, and Latin, at Sussex University. The novels as Ann Hallam include a specifically feminist sequence – *The Daybreaker* (1987), *Transformations* (1988) and *The Skybreaker* (1990). Her widely admired first adult novel, *Divine Endurance* (1984), portrays a matriarchal society, set in a future South-East Asia, with considerable ambivalence and melancholy; her protagonists, a gynoid and a cat, disrupt the world merely by arriving in it. Her most accomplished, though, at times, deliberately difficult novels are the sequence *White Queen* (1991), *North Wind* (199?) and *Phoenix Cafe* (1997), which create, and then deconstruct, a future Earth in which the well-intentioned meddlings of somewhat superior aliens have made things worse rather than better. Jones's inventive portrayal of creatures whose nature is to assimilate rather than to confront, is attractively realist. A collection of revisionist FAIRY STORIES, *Seven Tales and a Fable* (1995), won the World Fantasy Award.

RK

Jones, Marion Patrick (O'Callaghan) 1934– Born in Trinidad, where she won the Girls' Open Island Scholarship of 1950 and was one of the first two girls admitted to the Imperial College of Agriculture, Jones is a qualified librarian and did post-graduate work in Social Anthropology at London University. She has published two novels, *Pan-Beat* (1973) and *J'Ouvert Morning* (1976). *Pan-Beat*, set in Trinidad in the mid-1960s, focuses on Earline Hill's need to recapture her West Indian roots after many years of promiscuous living in London and New York. Earline's personal crisis mirrors Trinidad's crisis of racial and national identity, seen most particularly through the ruling middle class's failure to address the impact of the island's economic underdevelopment on the poor. A crucial feature of *Pan Beat* is Jones's use of the rich symbolism of calypso, the steel band, and the pan and fête culture of Trinidad in her reconstruction of the harried lives of the men and women who live in Port of Spain's slums. *J'Ouvert Morning* focuses on the Grants, a disgruntled and abrasive family whose alienated members try to escape their failures through futile flights into alcoholism, religious fanaticism, womanizing, abortion and madness, and through which Jones seeks to portray the social stagnancy and superficiality that contributed to the Port of Spain riots of the 1970s. Although in *J'Ouvert Morning* Jones uses multiple points of view to construct a panoramic portrait of 20th-century Trinidadian history, her attempts at stream of consciousness, a technique she used very effectively in *Pan Beat*, here deteriorate into incoherence and careless composition. The novel's most successful chapters focus on Elizabeth, whose anguish and pain are rendered with remarkable dignity and pathos. Excerpts from Jones's third unfinished novel, 'Parang', have appeared in journals and anthologies. Her work has been praised for its disquieting exploration of post-independence Trinidad and for the 'startling lucidity' of its depiction of problems of race, class, gender and politics that afflict educated women in the Caribbean, but her novels, despite their acknowledged importance in Trinidadian literary history, have long been out of print. LP-G

Jones, Mary d.1778 English writer of light, humorous verse and member of the Oxford literary circle in the 18th century. Her origins were fairly humble. She wrote that her maternal grandfather 'was the first of his particular Branch that ever set up for a Gentleman', and Jones may have worked for a time as a governess or tutor. For most of her life she lived in Oxford with her brother, Revd Oliver Jones, and while she was intimate with many aristocratic families, she was constantly aware of the social and financial distance between herself and them. From the age of 15 she translated Italian songs into English, and wrote poetry as a way of expressing the trials and frustrations of her life. At first, her writing was carried out in secret, but some was printed, including the broadside ballad THE LASS OF THE HILL, which in 1742 became 'the Fashion of the Town'. In 1750 her *Miscellanies in Prose and Verse* was published by subscription. There were 1,400 subscribers, including the Princess Royal, and the volume was published commercially after the distribution of the subscription copies. The collection includes letters, translations and verse epistles but Jones is nowadays best known for her poems on domestic subjects such as her 'Soliloquy on an Empty Purse'. These have a wit, freshness and simplicity which appeals to the modern audience. The *Miscellanies* was well reviewed on publication and received the approbation of Samuel Johnson, who referred to Jones as 'The Chantress'. LBe

Jong [née Mann], Erica 1942– American writer best known for her uninhibited depictions of sex. One of three daughters, she was born in New York into a family of Jewish artists and intellectuals and educated at Barnard College and Columbia (MA in 18th-century English Literature, 1965). She married her second husband, Allan Jong, a child psychiatrist, in 1966: her fourth husband is a lawyer. She has one daughter, Molly, from her third marriage. She has published several volumes of poetry, beginning with *Fruits and Vegetables* (1971); *Becoming Light: Poems New and Selected* appeared in 1992.

Jong's first and finest novel, FEAR OF FLYING (1973), ensured her place in the history of women's erotic fiction. Through her *alter ego*, Isadora Wing, she introduced the concept of 'the zipless fuck': an ideal of casual, fulfilling, guilt-free sex which liberated the sexual expectations of a generation of women. Isadora Wing figures in the sequels *How to Save your own Life* (1980), *Parachutes and Kisses* (1984) and as the 'author' of *Any Woman's Blues* (1990). Jong has ventured into a variety of genres including 18th-century pastiche (*Fanny: Being The True History of the Adventures of Fanny Hackabout-Jones*, 1980), feminist mythological revision (*Witches*, 1981) and fantasy ROMANCE (*Serenissima, A Novel of Venice*, 1987). Her 1997 novel, *Of Blessed Memory*, attempts to tell the story of the 20th century through the lives of women. Committed to attacking the repression of female desire under patriarchy and celebrating the 'pagan force' of sex, Jong's best writing is energetic, funny and shrewd, but her later work often falls into cliché and easy sensationalism.

In *The Devil at Large: Erica Jong on Henry Miller* (1993) she defends Miller against the feminist critiques initiated by KATE MILLETT. Her *Fear of Fifty: A Midlife Memoir* (1994) relates a personal history of sexual exploits and celebrity encounters. Despite her writerly egotism and arrogant dismissal of critical reviews from other women, Jong does explore the complexity of living as a liberated, modern woman: as she confides in *Fear of Fifty*, 'I wish, above all, to be undivided, to be whole.' AG

Joolz [Julie Denby] 1955– British performance poet whose punk ethics and spoken word performances have a following on mainstream student and rock circuits. Julie Denby was born into an army family in Colchester, and grew up in Portsmouth and Harrogate where she received 'a private and somewhat unbalanced education'. Dropping out of art school at 19, Denby married a member of a motorcycle gang and moved to Bradford. After separating from her husband in 1979, she began promoting local poets and musicians before returning to her own performing career, reinventing herself as 'Joolz'.

Her first book, *Mad, Bad and Dangerous to Know*, was published by Virgin in 1986, and her collections *Emotional Terrorism* (1990) and *The Pride of Lions* (1994) by Bloodaxe Books. The latter shows a development of her narrative skills over and above the coat-trailing middle-class punkery of her early work. She has a persuasive literary design – the examination of character and motivation of ordinary people in extreme circumstances and the revivification of story-telling within poetry. But her adoption of shell-shocked personae – war veterans, bitter young mothers, drug addicts – is questionable in its indifference to emotional truth.

DM

Jordan [née Meyer], June 1936– American poet born in Harlem; educated at Barnard College, Jordan began writing at 7 years old. Her poems share a universal theme of concern: a voice for others as well as self. Her lines are simple and strong, if self-conscious in turn. Jordan also practises a variety of forms (as well as subject and tone); all of her collections contain elegies and ballads, 'raps' and rhymes. She is not afraid to challenge forms of violence – in politics and people – and while many of the poems read as straightforward polemic, they also tend to combine a lyrical and somewhat abstract imagery juxtaposed against the explicitly didactic line:

> sometimes thinking about the 12th House of the
>   Cosmos
> or the way your ear ensnares the tip
> of my tongue or signs I have never seen
> like DANGER WOMEN WORKING.
>   ('Poem about Police Violence')

and,

> I am raising my knife
> to carve out the heart
> of no shame.
>   ('Poem on the Road; for Alice Walker')

Jordan defines herself as a 'New World' poet, in the spirit of Walt Whitman and Pablo Neruda, though her work may be more closely identified with that of other contemporary black writers like NIKKI GIOVANNI and Amiri Baraka. In *Passion: New Poems*, published in 1980, she writes, 'Within the Whitman tradition, Black and Third World poets traceably transform, and further, the egalitarian sensibility.' The title of a selected poems, *Lyrical Campaigns* (1989), encapsulates well the sentiment and cadences of Jordan's writing. Her other collections include *New Days: Poems of Exile and Return* (1974), *Things That I do in the Dark* (1981), *Living Room: New Poems 1980-84* (1985) and *Naming Our Destiny: New and Selected Poems* (1989). Another selection is *Kissing God Goodbye: Poems 1991-1996*. Jordan also writes children's stories, essays and plays. She was appointed Professor of African-American Studies and Women's Studies at University of California, Berkeley in 1989. ACH

Joseph, Jenny (Jenefer Ruth) 1932– British poet born in Birmingham. Educated at Oxford, Jenny Joseph became a scholar at St Hilda's College. She worked as a newspaper reporter, an adult-education lecturer and a pub landlady, and has lived in South Africa. She is best known for writing 'Warning' ('When I am an old woman I shall wear purple') – polled as 'The Nation's Favourite Poem' in Britain in 1997 (just ahead of STEVIE SMITH'S NOT WAVING BUT DROWNING).

Her first book, *The Unlooked-for Season* (1960), won a Gregory Award, and she won a Cholmondeley Award for *Rose in the Afternoon* (1974). She has published several books for children, and a series of collections culminating in *Selected Poems* (1992) and *Ghosts* (1995). An experimental poem-novel *Persephone* (1992) incorporated fiction, letters and a teenage-style photo-story. Ambitious, Joseph has an exacting eye for human detail and her later poems – particularly in *Extended Similes* (1997) – demonstrate a highly intelligent and playful command of language that belies the reader-friendliness of 'Warning'. However, Joseph has commented, 'It seemed to me the absolute fame to be the "anon" whose garbled ballads are sung in the street. I have realised that with "Warning" I have had that luck.' DM

Joubert, Elsa 1922– South African writer publishing mainly in Afrikaans. She is one of the first Afrikaans authors to write sympathetically about Africa, in both travelogues and fiction, and her work is sometimes regarded as an example of the new journalism style. She has received numerous literary awards, including the WINIFRED HOLTBY Prize awarded by the British Royal Society, of which she is also a fellow. She is most famous for her novel *The Long Journey of Poppie Nongena* (1980), which was first published in Afrikaans as *Die*

Swerfjare van Poppie Nongena (1978). This novel is written as the autobiography of a black South African woman, and is based on the actual narrative told by a woman, for whom Joubert employs the pseudonym 'Poppie Nongena', who came to Joubert's house in Cape Town one day, to tell her life story to someone who would write it down. Critical reception of the novel has focused on the extent to which Joubert was merely an amanuensis; Joubert herself acknowledges that she reworked the narrative as a novelist. The debate surrounding the status of the text and its authorship is illustrative of a trend in South African writing, namely a concern with questions of ventriloquism and representativeness in art and public discourse.

Other fiction by Joubert that has been translated include her first novel, *Ons Wag op die Kaptein* (1963), published as *To Die at Sunset* (1982), and *The Last Sunday* (1983), a translation of *Die Laaste Sondag* (1983). In her recent fiction, Joubert – like many South African writers – has turned to topics from the history of South Africa. CCo

Journals see DIARIES

Journals 1916–1930 (1946) Lady AUGUSTA GREGORY's diverse interests, along with the sensitivity and acuteness of someone living through times of political and social upheaval, all come together in her *Journals*, which constitute a momentous and critical representation of the Irish people: '*Dec.3*. Whispers in the countryside tell of anxiety about the two Shanaglish boys who were taken away and have not been heard of . . . *Dec.6*. There was news brought last night that the bodies of those two boys were found in a pond . . . Friends had gone to the place where they were found and saw the bodies although they could not be sure what way they met their death. The flesh was as if torn off the bones. God help the poor mother! There is one sister but no boy left in the house.' Similar transcriptions of the Black-and-Tan terror years, full of stories of assault, torture and robbery, get blended and juxtaposed with domestic scenes of family life creating a collage-like quality where historical events interpenetrate everyday life. The *Journals* are an invaluable record of cultural history. MPe

Journals of Susanna Moodie, The (1970) MARGARET ATWOOD's third volume of poetry was inspired by MOODIE's ambivalence toward Canada, its landscape and its people, an ambivalence she saw as an enduring national obsession. She noted also 'the gaps between what was said and what hovered, just unsaid, between the lines, and the conflict between what Mrs Moodie felt she ought to think and feel and what she actually did think and feel'. Atwood fleshes out those gaps. She divides her eighteen poems into three

Journals. The first portrays the first years of Moodie's life in Upper Canada, from her arrival until she left the bush and moved to the town of Belleville. The second covers the same period from a different perspective, presenting dreams and reflections on those years in the bush. The first poem here is the powerful 'Death of a Young Son by Drowning'. In the third section Moodie is reincarnated in the present. The final poem shows her as an old woman riding a Toronto bus and having become 'the spirit of the land she once hated'. The first edition of the book was enhanced by cover art and collages by Atwood. JG

Journey From the North (2 vols.; 1969 and 1970) STORM JAMESON's classic memoir ranks high if autobiography is seen as a genre. An acute psychological self-portrait, it also offers a stringent analysis of 20th-century intellectual life. Jameson evokes her youth and university education in Yorkshire; her first, unhappy marriage; her son born in the terrible years of World War I; her self-making as a novelist; and her second, happy marriage. Between the World Wars, Jameson was a REALIST, 'documentarist', anti-Fascist, pacifist (friend of VERA BRITTAIN) and socialist. She was English President of the PEN Club in 1938–45 ('one of my more insane blunders', she quips with derisive hindsight). An impassioned and effective public intellectual, she worked with (and argued with) Wells, Forster, Priestley and Spender. However, the 'political' Jameson should not eclipse the writer of many fine novels, still found in public libraries. She herself viewed English Literature as a Mount Parnassus where she trod only the lower slopes, and, in *Journey*, she presents harsh judgement of her own work, and eschews all vainglory or sentimentality. JL

Joys of Motherhood, The (1979) Bitingly satirical, this novel continues BUCHI EMECHETA's preoccupation with traditional values and how they are impinged on by change in the colonial era. In *Joys*, Emecheta takes a cold look at the stasis in the definition of womanhood even as everything else is shown to be transient. People have migrated from villages to the urban areas and men now hold down jobs as washermen, cooks and railway workers, and still a woman is defined in terms of motherhood. Through the protagonist, Nnu Ego, Emecheta presents motherhood as smothering; quite the converse of what tradition upholds it to be. Although she bears many children and suffers a great deal to bring them up, Nnu Ego's status in Lagos is not enhanced. In fact, when she dies, she is all alone by the side of a road, a paradoxical symbol of fixity and transience. In a subtle way, Emecheta introduces in *Joys* another concern that she later explores in other novels, notably *Double Yoke*, that of fatherhood and manhood in the face of change. PMM

Judith (1978) ARITHA VAN HERK's award-winning first novel is the story of a secretary turned pig-farmer. Having grown up on a farm, Judith is disillusioned with city life and her city lover (her boss) and returns to the country to make her living from a rural rather than urban world. After her parents die in a car accident, Judith buys a pig farm and single-handedly runs it against all odds and in spite of the scepticism of most of her neighbours. In the beginning, Judith is deeply dissatisfied. The difficult relationship with her father looms over her. Tense and silent, she hardly gets along with either the pigs or her neighbours. Once she becomes friends with her much older neighbour Mina and takes Mina's son Jim as her lover, she becomes more relaxed and finally decides to make this new place her home. Van Herk was often criticized for having overdone the father-figure in *Judith*. Yet, this mixture of modern re-writing of old myths (Circe) and realistic descriptions of life in rural Alberta is an intelligent and amusing story about a woman finding and making her own way.   TP

Julian of Norwich 1342/3 – *c*.1416 In May 1373, at the age of 30, Julian of Norwich experienced the series of visions which gave rise to her book, *A REVELATION OF LOVE*. At that time she was presumably either a laywoman – possibly widowed – or a nun, and her subsequent vocation as an anchoress, or recluse, may have been stimulated by her visions. She is recorded as an anchoress in Norwich between 1394 and 1416, which was a time of increasingly strictly policed religious orthodoxy. Julian may have composed the long version of her text, at least, in the anchorhold.

Female and male recluses are recorded in Norwich from the early 13th century. They dedicated themselves to an austere life of prayer and meditation, and were confined to cells built against the walls of parish churches, with one window giving onto the chancel and another onto the street. Anchoritism was an increasingly urban and feminine calling in the later Middle Ages, when the earlier practice of groups of anchoresses living together seems to have given way to more solitary modes of living. Nevertheless we should not simply adopt the terms in which the reclusive life is defined in much anchoritic literature, where interchange with the world is represented as necessarily corrupting. Anchoresses seem often to have been the daughters of mercantile or artisan families, and were members of a spiritual elite. Sustained by charity, they represented an approved form of poverty which had a symbolic function in the urban world of money. Their position was not marginal: Julian was attached to the parish church of St Julian's Conesford, in a wealthy, residential area near the city's busy quays on the river. Recluses acted as spiritual counsellors, as Julian did for MARGERY KEMPE around 1413, while in the 1390s a Leicester anchoress was accused of holding Lollard meetings in her cell. Three York anchoresses are recorded as members of the city's prestigious Corpus Christi guild in the 15th century. Julian was not the only visionary recluse: others were the male Dominican anchorite of Lynn who was Margery Kempe's confessor, and Emma Rawton of York whose visions of the Blessed Virgin in the 1420s contained political messages supporting the powerful Beauchamp family. Julian differs from these in that she turned her visions into a book. Norwich was a centre of literacy, and several male clerical writers are also recorded from the period.

Although the isolated anchoress, voluntarily confined to her cell, seems to represent a paradigm of the autonomous author, Julian's authorial identity can also be seen as social. The process of composition would have entailed collaboration with a scribe and the support of her bishop, while the nature of her text – a bold piece of vernacular theology written in the 'everydaily' language of the town – was the product of an intimate and unpatronizing relation with her lay readership. There is only one surviving 15th-century manuscript of the short version, and three manuscripts of the long, copied in the 17th century by recusant nuns.   FJR

K

Kael, Pauline 1919– American film critic. Educated at the University of California at Berkeley, where she read Philosophy, Kael became interested in film and for some years wrote reviews for such magazines as the *New Republic*, while managing movie theatres. Her growing reputation took her to the *New Yorker* as one of their two regular movie critics from 1968; her books from *I Lost it at the Movies* (1968) to *Movie Love* (1992) are collections of reviews, most of which appeared there. Kael's emphasis was on the experience of watching film and on the collective work that goes into creating them; she was thus directly hostile to *auteur* theory, both as inaccurate and as tending to overvalue male directors at the expense of, for example, women screenwriters and stars. She was often epigrammatic and scathingly witty – her highly wrought polemical tone influenced some younger journalists, notably JULIE BURCHILL. Kael's fascination with the making of movies caused her to write an account of the making of *The Group* based on the novel by MARY MCCARTHY and, in *The Citizen Kane Book*, to look at the creative process whereby a group of people, rather than just Orson Welles, made *Citizen Kane*.   RK

Karma Cola (1979) GITA MEHTA's scintillating array of anecdotes about the East–West encounter in an era of global capitalism. With razor-sharp observation Mehta wittily dissects the adventures of those eager western travellers in search of eastern spirituality who do not find enlightenment in India but are instead ripped off. This mordant book reveals the casualties of spiritual tourism, by intersecting various stories of naive visitors and fraudulent gurus 'wearing Adidas running shoes', cultural misfits and mysticism on sale. While feeding the western travellers, ranging from wealthy businessmen to 1970s hippies to poor students, with wisdom, mantras and ashrams, India's yogis are revealed to prefer dollars to namastes. This clearly illustrates that within the East–West encounter the East is taking its subtle revenge by teaching the West a very precious lesson in materialism. This theme will return in Mehta's *A River Sutra* (1993) which narrates further disillusionment with Indian spirituality. An impoverished Indian college lecturer seeks a way out from his daily drudgery in his Urdu guru but finds only a seedy, dissolute and rambling old man.   SPo

Karodia, Farida 1942– South African short-story writer and novelist. She grew up in the largely Afrikaaner town of Sterkstroom where her parents ran a small general store. She attended a 'Coloured' primary school where she was taught Afrikaans. At home she spoke English. She went to high school in East London and attended Coronationville Teacher Training College in Johannesburg. In 1965, after the failure of a short marriage, she went to Zambia and the South African government promptly withdrew her passport. As a stateless person she was unable to return to South Africa for her father's funeral in 1966.

In 1969 Farida emigrated to Canada where she began writing radio plays. In 1980 she completed her first novel, *Daughters of the Twilight*, which was published in 1989 by The Women's Press. The novel tells of two sisters, Meena and Yasmin, who grow up in Sterkstroom and battle to survive dispossession, the destruction of moral codes, identity and female dignity under the harsh conditions of Apartheid. Nana tells Meena, 'What we're trying to do is make the best out of a bad situation.' Her short-story collection, *Coming Home and Other Stories* (1988), describes alienation and dislocation in South Africa's fractured society. In 1993 she published her second novel, *A Shattering of Silence*, about the 8-year-old daughter of Canadian missionaries who witnesses massacres and the death of her parents in her village in remote northern Mozambique.   GMS

Kavan, Anna [Helen Woods] 1901–68 Versatile, enigmatic English novelist acclaimed for her chilling insight into states of psychological disturbance. She was born in Cannes to a wealthy family and educated in California, Switzerland and England, but spent a good deal of time in South Africa. Introduced to drugs by a tennis coach, she began to use heroin in her mid-twenties and endured this addiction, as well as mental illness, for most of her adult life. Her second novel, *Let Me Alone* (1930), which shows some of the influence of D.H. Lawrence, draws on her experiences in Burma during an unhappy and short-lived marriage to Donald Ferguson. These experiences also inform her later, much more vividly impressionistic and experimental novel *Who Are You?* (1963), whose alternative endings and recurrent surrealistic touches earned the admiration of peers such as JEAN RHYS, with whose

360

work Kavan's has provoked comparisons. Kavan's most characteristic writing begins with *Asylum Piece and Other Stories* (1940), and includes the Kafkaesque *Sleep Has His House* (1948), a book of war-time stories based on her work with psychiatric patients; *I Am Lazarus* (1945); and an award-winning SCIENCE-FICTION novel, *Ice* (1967). Her relationship with the painter Stuart Edmonds brought Kavan temporary stability but, as her bitter novella *My Soul in China* (published posthumously in 1975) obliquely reveals, her antisocial habits and suicidal impulses gradually alienated him. Kavan's reclusive and eccentric life has attracted many interested scholars, but has also made it difficult for prospective biographers to uncover important events which might bear on her writing.   BWB

Kavanagh, Julia 1824–77 Irish novelist. Although not considered a 'political writer' she was astutely aware of patriarchal double standards and her novels and essays draw on the very core of sexual politics.

Born in Thurles, she later moved to London and then to Paris, settling finally with her invalid mother in Nice, where she herself died. Though she lived most of her life outside Ireland she was always conscious of her origins. In a letter to Charles Gavan Duffy, editor of the *Nation*, she states – 'I am Irish by origin, birth and feeling, though not by education, but if I have lived far from Ireland . . . I have ever been taught to love her with my whole soul.' A portrait of her by Henri Chanet was presented by her mother to the National Gallery of Ireland in 1884.

An only child, left to care for her mother after they were abandoned by her father, Morgan Peter Kavanagh, when she was a young woman, she turned to writing as a means of survival. By the age of 26 she was an established writer who met with commercial success in both Europe and America, producing seventeen novels, mainly patterned ROMANCES, some later translated into French, as well as stories for children. Her novel *Nathalie* (1850) influenced CHARLOTTE BRONTË'S *VILLETTE* (1853). Her non-fiction includes articles and reviews for English journals, a full-length study on women and Christianity, a two-volume account of travel in Sicily and three major studies: *Women in France During the Eighteenth Century* (1850), *French Women of Letters* (1862) and *English Women of Letters* (1862).   EF

Kay, Jackie 1961– Scottish poet whose work focuses on issues of identity. She was born in Edinburgh and brought up in Glasgow. In her late teens, she started writing: 'because there wasn't anybody else saying the things I wanted to say and because I felt quite isolated in Scotland and being black . . . I started out of that sense of wanting to create some images for myself.'

She studied English at university and worked as

tour co-ordinator for poets with the Arts Council of Great Britain. Although she has written drama, film and documentary, she is best known for the poetry in her collections *The Adoption Papers* (1991), *That Distance Apart* (1991), *Two's Company* (1992), *Other Lovers* (1993) and *Bessie Smith* (1997).

Often, her work is an exploration of race. The first part of the award-winning *The Adoption Papers* is a set of narrative poems about a black child's adoption by white parents, told through three voices: the girl, her birth mother and her adoptive mother. The sequence follows the adoption process, then the grown child's attempts to trace her birth mother. The use of different typefaces creates a sense that the women share a language and have related, yet different, voices.

Her work also foregrounds gay sexuality. Kay, who moved to live in London, said that this part of her work would be difficult to take to her native Scotland. 'I don't know if I could actually read lesbian poems there. I'm sure I will one day, but I don't know if I could at the moment.' In 1998 *Trumpet*, her first novel, won the *Guardian* fiction prize.   JH

Kaye-Smith, Sheila 1887–1956 British writer born in St Leonard's-on-Sea who excelled in depicting the idiom and countryside of her native Sussex in novels including *Sussex Gorse* (1916), *Tamarisk Town* (1919) and *The End of The House of Alard* (1923). Her father, Edward Kaye-Smith, was a physician. She converted from Methodism to Anglo-Catholicism and then to Roman Catholicism. She married Theodore Penrose Fry in 1924 and built a chapel on their farm, dedicated to St Thérèse de Lisieux about whom she wrote in *Quartet in Heaven* (1952). In her autobiography, *Three Ways Home* (1937), she wrote 'my happiness comes from three things – the country, my writing, and my religion'. Two novels with strong, assertive central women characters have attracted the attention of feminists: *Joanna Godden* (1922) which was filmed in 1946 starring Googie Withers, and *Susan Spray the Female Preacher* (1931), a study of self-deception. She wrote two books on JANE AUSTEN with G. B. Stern.   MJ

Kazantzis, Judith 1940– British poet who is noted for engaging the sensual and intellectual with acerbic wit and political bite. Born in London, Kazantzis studied Modern History at Somerville College, Oxford. She married in 1982 and has a daughter and a son. She has worked as a tutor for Inner London Education Authority, reviewed for *Spare Rib* and been poetry editor for the PEN Broadsheet. She is also known as an artist.

Kazantzis is a poet who speaks with an intensely personal, informal voice about matters of public concern. Her first collection, *Minefield* (1977), was sparked by painting, psychoanalysis and feminism.

Her experience of marriage and children underpinned her writing of *The Wicked Queen* (1980), in which her savage wit is deployed in the service of a rage at injustice. Her themes range from the stoning of an adulteress in Jeddah to a harsh retelling of *Little Red Riding Hood*. Her next major work, *A Poem for Guatemala* (1986), is a significant move forward, emerging from a 'wish to honour the life-force and courage of Guatemalans living and dying in the current unnatural conditions'. Harold Pinter celebrated her work as 'a major political poem . . . beautifully wrought, concrete, passionate'. Several collections followed, unified by linguistic confidence, mordant wit and taut control, notably *The Rabbit Magician's Plate* (1992) and *Selected Poems* (1992).

DM

Keane, Molly [Mary Nesta Skrine] 1905–96 Irish novelist and playwright. Born into the Ascendancy, a wealthy, landowning class in Ireland whose loyalties and affiliations were complicated and ambiguous and who were largely preoccupied with hunting, shooting and fishing. Because of this, Keane initially wrote under the pseudonym 'M.J. Farrell', claiming that writing was an unacceptable activity for members of her circle. Her mother, Agnes Nesta Skrine [née Higginson], was a poet, but she also used a pseudonym ('MOIRA O'NEILL'). Keane's early plays and novels were successful and popular but, despite her affection for the world she portrays in her fiction, she represents that world with devastating accuracy as farcically doomed, self-obsessed and barren, so her subterfuge may have been justified.

The 'Big House', home to the Ascendancy, is a major theme of Anglo-Irish fiction, and Molly Keane is one of its most skilled exponents (see also MARIA EDGEWORTH, SOMERVILLE and ROSS, ELIZABETH BOWEN). In her work, these houses are as meticulously evoked and as significant as the characters who inhabit them. Human relationships are explored with insight, intelligence and wit. *Full House* (1935) is an accomplished psychological study, while *Two Days in Aragon* (1941) is an ambitious attempt to address conflicts of class, religion and political loyalty in Ireland.

After a long period of silence, she re-emerged in 1981 with the triumphant black comedy *GOOD BEHAVIOUR*, this time under her real (married) name. This was followed in 1983 by *Time After Time*. These two novels stand as classic accounts of the decline of the Anglo-Irish as a class. They also caused a revival of interest in Keane's earlier work, leading to the re-publication of many of her novels in the 1980s as part of the Virago Modern Classics series. Keane continued to write. She published an anthology (with her daughter, Sally Phipps), *Molly Keane's Ireland* in 1993.

LM

Keese, Oline see LEAKEY, EVELINE

Kefala, Antigone 1935– Australian poet and novelist. Born in Rumania of Greek parents, Kefala migrated first to New Zealand in 1951, and then to Australia. She is better known today for her poetry than for her novels. Like ANIA WALWICZ, Kefala charts the dislocation of the migrant in the movement from the 'old' world of Europe to the 'new' world of Australia. She published her first volume of poetry, *The Alien*, in 1973, and a second volume, *Thirsty Weather*, in 1978. Her poetry constructs a writing subject for whom 'the use of words is not a reassuring entry into the social but, rather, a journey onto a tight-rope with no safety nets'. Kefala has also produced three short novels which further investigate the dynamics of the migrant experience. In 1975 a book collecting two of the novels – *The First Journey* and *The Boarding* – was published under the former title, and in 1984 a third novel, *The Island*, appeared, along with a CHILDREN'S STORY, *Alexia*. While the three novels have central narrators who are migrants, the effects of other acts of location and dislocation are at the centre of Kefala's concerns, namely the 'estrangements and dislocations' of sexuality and gender which inform the sexual identity of Alexi and Melina in *The First Journey* and *The Boarding*.

JAM

Keith, Sheridan 1942– New Zealand short-story writer and novelist whose first novel *Zoology* (1995), won the Montana Award for Fiction. Keith's stories are about the human zoo, for she perceives that the irrational impulses which drive our sex lives and our bafflement at them bring us closer to animals. This comical, sometimes threatening dimension to being alive underpins her ironic detachment; but she also approaches fiction writing scientifically, by 'stating a problem' through her stories. Her first collection, *Shallow are the Smiles at the Supermarket* (1991), exposes the thinness of society's rituals, but shows her embattled heroines as empowering themselves by their wit and economic independence. In *Animal Passions* (1992), 'a sonata in ennui', she combines surface humour with deeper unease to evoke spontaneous yet uncertain reactions. *Zoology*, expanded from one of these stories, investigates how people come to mean something to each other. It narrates an unequal encounter between a middle-aged, passionless man, exhausted by life, and a shimmering, flamboyantly clad art student who pursues him. The novel's zoologically naturalistic sex scenes are among its most memorable: 'She was a cave . . . a warm wet suede shoe . . . a moist chamois mitten'. Keith's sensuous style and striking images make her prose supple and poised: 'Her skin is like dried-out pale leather, cracked over by ravines, as if some ice-age has passed through.' A contemporary of MARILYN DUCKWORTH, FIONA KIDMAN and BARBARA ANDERSON, she has been acclaimed as a voice for women of the 'Forgotten Generation'.

JMW

Keller, Helen Adams 1880–1968 American essayist, memoirist. Rendered blind and deaf by an illness at 19 months of age, Helen grew up wild and unreachable until her parents appealed to the Perkins Institution for the Blind, and Anne Sullivan was sent to help them. Helen's famous breakthrough moment, the epiphany at the centre of William Gibson's play *The Miracle Worker* (1959), occurred when she could relate the water flowing out of the pump to the word Sullivan spelled into her hand. Accompanied by Sullivan, who remained her 'Teacher' and companion until Sullivan's death in 1936, she graduated magna cum laude from Radcliffe in 1904. Her first book, *The Story of My Life* (1902), appeared serially in the *Ladies' Home Journal*, and vividly describes her experience of education and of her world. An advocate for handicapped people her whole life, she travelled extensively throughout the United States and the world and received half a dozen honorary degrees as well. Among her numerous books are *The World I Live In* (1908), *Midstream: My Later Life* (1929) and *Teacher: Anne Sullivan Macy* (1955).   SP

Kelly [née Fordyce], Isabella *c.*1758–1857 Scottish novelist, poet and educational writer. Born to parents whose secret marriage had alienated their wealthy Scottish families, Isabella was raised in genteel, though financially uncertain, circumstances. Although he obtained a military commission and later a Court position, her father eventually fell from favour. In 1794, Isabella published her *Collection of Poems and Fables* (reissued 1807). Including verses written before she was 14, the volume focuses on domestic pathos and social satire:

> Be still, sweet babe, no harm shall reach thee,
> Nor hurt thy yet unfinished form;
> Thy mother's frame shall safely guard thee
> From this bleak, this beating storm.
>
> ('To an Unborn Infant')

The author's profligate first husband, Col. Robert Kelly, died abroad, leaving her with several children. Writing to support her family, Isabella published *Madeline: Or The Castle of Montgomery* (1794). A series of moderately successful novels, many modelled on ANN RADCLIFFE's GOTHIC style, quickly followed, including *The Abbey of St Asaph* (1795), *The Ruins of Avondale Priory* (1796) and *Jocelina* (1797). Published mainly by the Minerva Press, Isabella's numerous novels range in setting from London coffee houses to the plantations of Barbados and explore themes as diverse as sexual morality and agricultural labour unrest. *The Child's French Grammar* (1805) suggests Isabella may also have run or taught at a school.

A brief marriage to a wealthy merchant named Hedgland left Isabella widowed again after 'specula-tion lost his fortune and broke his heart'. Using this name, she published *Instructive Anecdotes for Youth* (1819), and her anonymous *Memoir of the Late Mrs Henrietta Fordyce* (1823) records many aspects of her own life.   JHP

Kelly, Maeve 1930– Irish fiction writer and poet who has described her writing as both a 'protest and a memorial' to the lives of women, written after search-ing 'fruitlessly for half a lifetime for women's words'. Her vast range of fictive subjects – Irish Travelling women, rural farming women, battered women, middle-class married women, artists, ageing single women, single mothers, feminist activists, nurses-in-training, feminist doctors, wealthy landed women – offers one of the richest and most humane oeuvres in Irish literature. Both a farmer and the creator/director of the Limerick women's shelter, her pioneering work has put her at the centre of the Irish Women's Movement since the early 1970s.

Her 1985 historiographic novel *Necessary Treasons* explores varieties of violence and resistance move-ments in the west of Ireland, drawing connections between the colonization of historical Ireland and of women in the late 17th and 20th centuries. This work and the novel *Florrie's Girls* (1989) were both published in England, while the playful *Alice in Thunderland* (1993) was one of Dublin's Attic Press feminist fairy-tale series. Her poems, *Resolutions* (1986), were Irish-pub-lished, but, although they were well received, it is her short stories, *A Life of Her Own* (1976) and *Orange Horses* (1990), that have earned her an international audience after being widely anthologized and translated into several languages.   CStP

Kemble, Fanny (Frances Ann) 1809–1903 British poet, essayist, autobiographer and leading lady of the Victorian theatre. Born into London's first family of the stage, Kemble was the niece of John Phillip Kemble and Sarah Siddons and the daughter of the actor-pro-prietor of Covent Garden and a Swiss-French actress. Despite achieving great fame acting Shakespeare, she longed for a literary career.

Her father opposed his spirited daughter's initial plan to become a governess and instead cast her in the role of Juliet in 1829. Her instant success helped offset some of the family's debts. By 1832, however, bank-ruptcy loomed and father and daughter embarked on a profitable two-year American theatrical tour, an expe-rience recounted in her JOURNAL *of Frances Ann Butler* (1835). In April 1834 she had happily traded theatrical success for marriage to wealthy American Pierce Butler. 'In leaving the stage', she wrote to a friend, 'I left nothing I regretted'.

Regret set in two years later when her husband inherited a Georgia plantation that made him one of the state's largest slaveholders. She recorded her horror at the conditions of slave life in her *Journal of a Residence on a Georgian Plantation 1838–1839*. The outbreak of the Civil War and Britain's apparent willingness to support the Confederate cause led her to publish this passionate attack on the slave-holding South in 1863.

Matrimonial difficulties culminated in divorce in 1849 at which point she lost custody of her two daughters. After briefly resuming her acting she abandoned it for a successful career doing staged readings of Shakespeare. In addition, she wrote and translated plays and poetry, and published her *Records of Girlhood: An Autobiography* (1878–9) and *Records of Later Life* (1882) which James called 'one of the most animated autobiographies in the language'. At 80 she published her first novel, *Far Away and Long Ago* (1889).   MAD

Kemp, Jan 1949– Cosmopolitan and experimental New Zealand writer living in Germany, known for her public performances, the powerful rhythms of her verse and its zestful celebratory mood. Kemp's first collections, *Against the Softness of Woman* (1976) and *Diamonds and Gravel* (1979), are dominated by love poetry; but in other, 'exotic' poems she is the exuberant traveller embracing the surge of life, recording snatches of foreign languages, strident street cries. The Canadian 'Paperboygirl' is pure verbal energy:

> *globe 'n mayall*
> zip zip zip zip
> here i come
> *globe 'n mayall* ... early sidewalks
> early dogs
> early skies
> early morning
> treeeeeeeeeeeeeeeeeeeeees.

In *The Other Hemisphere* (1991) the sounds of the Orient ring comically:

> ding dong deng (xiao ping)
> dong
> maggie thatcher in beijing.

Kemp can be fanciful:

> I want to be
> a Viennese lady
> eating up Art in a cloche

but she also excels at short poems with a prayer-like meditative quality.   JMW

Kempe, Margery *c.*1373 – after 1449 The English mystic who gave her name to THE BOOK OF MARGERY KEMPE was a historical figure, the daughter of John Brunham, a leading citizen of Bishop's (now King's) Lynn in Norfolk. As represented in the *Book*, Margery becomes demented after childbirth by a secret sin, which remains unconfessed, and is restored to health by a vision of Jesus. After failing in a number of business ventures and giving birth to fourteen children, she finally persuades her husband to let her live chastely and pursue her mystic marriage to Christ. The body of the text recounts this inner life, as a series of conversations and meditations, and the irregular outer life she leads in the world as she travels widely in England and on pilgrimage in Europe and the Holy Land, making her presence felt with her pious weeping and roaring. The major part of the book is set between 1413 and 1417, a period in which the Lollard heresy culminated in open rebellion and its fierce repression. A shorter second part, set in the 1430s, depicts the production of her book, dictated in Margery's old age to a male cleric. Like other women religious, Margery is represented as illiterate; less conventional is the degree of agency Margery retains, saving her book from the bad English of her first scribe and the failing eyesight of the second (he is cured by her prayer).

In all this, her *Book* foregrounds Margery's own voice as its dominant character and its subject. It is full of identifiable historical figures: prelates and influential religious characters of East Anglia such as Richard Caister and JULIAN OF NORWICH, whom Margery meets. Its local references are accurate. But this does not mean that her *Book* is necessarily an autobiography – nor that a 15th-century autobiography would set out to be factually accurate. There are other factors at work: the representation of Margery as a prospective saint, rivalling St. Bridget of Sweden (1313–73); the generic influence of Julian of Norwich; and the need to distinguish Margery from Lollards. Recent scholars (noting that her examinations of heresy do not appear in contemporary records) suggest that 'Margery Kempe' is partly a fictional character, and her life a parable of the interdependency of lay people (who need the Church even if they have unmediated access to Jesus) and priests (who need the laity for support and inspiration). Wynkyn de Worde published a brief pamphlet of Margery's holy sayings in *c.*1501, but the only surviving manuscript of her *Book* belonged in the 15th century to Carthusians at Mount Grace Priory in Yorkshire. Their annotations suggest that they acknowledged Margery's spiritual authority – a far cry from the response of religious critics after its rediscovery in 1934, who invoked the notion of hysteria to ridicule its lay woman's claim to be the wife of Christ.   DL

Kennedy, A.L. 1963– Novelist and short-story writer who portrays urban Scottishness with melancholy understatement and oddball humour: her characters lead flotsam, disembodied lives, caught between despair and the weirder byways of hope. Alison Kennedy was born in Dundee but read English at Warwick University where the other students were 'insanely patronising about Scotland'. She 'surrendered' and returned to Scotland, where she sold brushes door-to-door before finding a job as a community arts administrator. Her first story collection, *Night Geometry and the Garscadden Trains* (1990), was distinctively quirky and compassionate in its treatment of unglamorous lives. Her first novel, *Looking for the Possible Dance* (1993), featured a young woman oscillating between the emotional ties and narrow horizons of Glasgow and the alienness and freedom of England. Its subtly defiant refusal to make neat connections was echoed in her next novel, *So I Am Glad* (1995), about an emotionally cauterized heroine who falls in love with the ghost of Cyrano de Bergerac. Kennedy has also published other story collections – *Now That You're Back* (1994) and *Original Bliss* (1997) – as well as writing for the theatre. Selected as one of Granta's Twenty Best British Young Novelists in 1993, she is often cited as an example of the recent 'Renaissance' in Scots writing.

KE

Kennedy, Margaret Moore (Lady Davies)

1896–1967 English novelist, playwright and critic, Margaret Kennedy was born in London, the daughter of a barrister. Her first novel, *The Ladies of Lyndon* (1923), was followed by *The Constant Nymph* (1924), with which she achieved critical recognition and displayed her talent for social comedy. The 'Sanger's Circus' of this book was inspired by a painting which Kennedy had seen of Augustus John and his wives; the book examines the inherent tensions and tragic consequences of a marriage between a wild, free-thinking composer and a clever though conformist woman who believes she can domesticate him. The eponymous nymph is a 15-year-old girl for whom the husband has an enduring and reciprocated passion, and with whom he eventually elopes; she dies before their love can be consummated. Kennedy, with Basil Dean, re-wrote *The Constant Nymph* as a play (1926) and several film versions have been made.

Kennedy published in all some sixteen novels, the majority 'drawing room' novels: clever, erudite, but light. Of her post-World War II fiction, most noteworthy are *Lucy Carmichael* (1951), the story of a spirited girl, jilted on her wedding day, whose courage and integrity are eventually properly rewarded, and *Troy Chimneys* (1953) (awarded the James Tait Memorial Prize), a study set in Regency England, of inner conflict, lost opportunity and blighted lives.

In 1950 Kennedy published a short biography of JANE AUSTEN, and in 1958 *The Outlaws on Parnassus*, a study of the art of fiction and what she saw as its decline in public esteem in the 20th century. CT

Kesson, Jessie

1916–95 Scottish writer whose work foregrounds the struggle to achieve self-realization in the oppressive north-east of Scotland. She was born in the workhouse and raised in the deprived area of Elgin. Her mother was not the prostitute of popular myth but 'an enthusiastic amateur' who contracted syphilis. Kesson was subsequently put in an orphanage. Although she excelled at school, the Orphanage Trustees felt that university would be wasted on a girl. She later developed neurasthenia and spent a year in psychiatric care. While convalescing she met Johnnie, a farm labourer, and they married in 1936. Kesson wrote over forty radio-plays and worked as a cleaner, social worker and in Woolworths. In 1954, she moved to London in order to be taken seriously and shake off her status as 'cottar wife' who wrote.

Almost all her work, though not directly autobiographical, is informed by her background. She published three novels, *The White Bird Passes* (1958), *A Glitter of Mica* (1963) and *Another Time, Another Place* (1983); and a volume of shorter pieces, *Where the Apple Ripens* (1985). Her style is confident and precise. Kesson aimed for 'the sma' perfect', paring down the prose and using silence and understatement to hint at underlying emotions. In *The White Bird Passes* her vision is optimistic. The heroine Janie rejects the menial jobs she is offered because she wants to write poetry. However, the options for women in Kesson's later work are limited: madness, suicide or entrapment within an oppressive community.

Another Time, Another Place was released as a film in 1983. JH

Keynotes

(1893) GEORGE EGERTON's first volume of short stories, denounced for 'the hysterical frankness of its amatory abandonment', made a considerable contribution to women's literature of the FIN-DE-SIÈCLE and anticipated MODERNIST writing. Financial hardship induced Egerton to become an author. The stories swiftly gained notoriety, going into eight editions, and gave rise to John Lane's 'Keynote' series. *Punch* parodied the work as 'She-Notes' by 'Borgia Smudgiton', including 'Japanese Fan-de-Siecle' (*sic*) illustrations by 'Mortarthurio Whiskersly' to mock Aubrey Beardsley's cover design. Egerton was influenced by Scandinavian writers, especially Knut Hamsun. She captured specific moments in her characters' lives, experimenting with new modes of expression to describe innermost feelings and sexual desires: 'I realized that in literature, everything had been better done by man than woman could hope to emulate. There was only one small plot left for her to tell: the *terra incognita* of herself, as she knew herself to be, not as man liked to imagine her – in a word to give herself away, as man had given himself in his writings.' SF

Khalvati, Mimi

1944– Iranian poet writing in English. Khalvati was born in Tehran. Her mother-tongue was Farsi, a language she admits to quickly forgetting when she came to school in England at the age of 6. After further education in Switzerland, she returned to Iran when she was 17, and came to Britain at 25. Later she set about re-learning Farsi when she had to work with Iranian actors in her home country. She came to poetry late, and embarked upon a rapid course of self-education, co-winning the Poetry Business Competition in 1989 and publishing a pamphlet, *Persian Miniatures*. Carcanet published her substantial collections – *In White Ink* (1991), *Mirrorwork* (1995) and *Entries on Light* (1997).

Each book demonstrates a growing confidence in her voice, and the desire for extended sequences or long poems over and above the short lyrics of her earlier phase. Khalvati's linguistic background informs her subject matter, the very music of her syntax and choice of structures. She characterizes her work as 'melodic rather than contrapuntal' and has reinvigorated models from traditional Persian verse. Khalvati's distinctiveness is her ability to carry over the aesthetic of Persian prosody – its circularity, its symphonic structures – and hone it in contemporary English. DM

Khamadi Were, Miriam ?– Miriam Khamadi Were is known for the three novels for young readers (see CHILDREN'S BOOKS) that she published in Kenya: *The Eighth Wife* (1972), *Your Heart is my Altar* (1974), *The High School Gent* (1978). They are characterized by an unsentimental approach to the realities of life in a changing Africa, a no-nonsense message that young people must learn early to face things. Apparently circumstances did not encourage her to write for a wider public; nonetheless her original voice can be heard strongly, in particular in *The Eighth Wife*. The book seems at first to fit in the category of anthropological fiction, with a detailed account of life in a rural Luo community. Yet it examines squarely the oppression of young people, and of women, in a polygamous household. The contrived happy ending underlines how bleak, in real life, are the prospects for a young girl married against her will to an elderly patriarch. In an even voice, with subdued irony, the writer makes a forceful statement opposed to the idealization of rural modes and traditional wives as found in the widely acclaimed contemporary *Song of Lawino* (1966) by Okot p'Bitek. She goes against the prevailing mood of national culturalism by showing up rural order as brutal to the weak, the young and women. JB

Kidman [née Eakin], Fiona 1940– New Zealand fiction writer and poet, whose stories of women's rebellion against domestic and marital expectations has attracted a wide readership. Like KIM EGGLESTON's, her poetry shows affinities with the local REALIST tradition, and her flair for tracking uneasy undercurrents in adult relationships, especially in her short stories about Peter and Bethany Dixon, can be traced to this apprenticeship. Her third story collection, *The Foreign Woman* (1993), has been likened to the work of ALICE MUNRO.

Kidman's first novel, *A Breed of Women* (1979), was a runaway success: her heroine's trajectory exposed bourgeois New Zealand values, and provided a desirable paradigm for New Zealand women. She has subsequently developed other narrative models to represent women's states of self-entrapment: *Mandarin Summer* (1981), a confrontation between a wealthy, decadent European family and a naive New Zealand family, recalls scenes from JANE EYRE and owes something to the GOTHIC horror genre. *Paddy's Puzzle* (1983) extends the enquiry into marginality: its settings are Hamilton during the Depression, and Auckland's tenement slums for prostitutes during World War II. *The Book of Secrets* (1987), however, is a HISTORICAL fiction, based on the charismatic figure of Revd McLeod who led his followers from Scotland to Nova Scotia, and New Zealand. Through journals, letters and dreams, Kidman examines the lives of three generations of women. Most recently women appear within broader contemporary canvases: *True Stars* (1990), set in the last days of the Labour government under David Lange, traces the collapsing political dream against the tensions of small-town rivalries and the victimization of a middle-aged woman. In *Ricochet Baby* (1996), she magisterially entwines a melodramatic marriage collapse with narratives of two families, and with humour and compassion suggests a way forward for her heroine.

Although Kidman's attention to women's self-empowerment is comparable to MARILYN DUCKWORTH's, her social conscience is stronger: her vivid descriptions and sharply nuanced dialogues suggestively expose the Puritan, small-town mentality. She has written for radio and television, and published three volumes of poetry, including *Wakeful Nights. Poems Selected and New* (1991), and autobiographical essays in *Palm Prints* (1994). JMW

Killigrew, Anne 1660–85 Accomplished English poet and painter, whose untimely death from smallpox enabled her to be memorialized by Dryden as 'the much lamented Virgin' whose life and work could endure even the most minute moral scrutiny. The daughter of theologian and loyal Royalist Dr Henry Killigrew, she benefited from his teaching and the writerly bent of her dramatist uncles, Thomas and Sir William Killigrew. As maid of honour to Mary of Modena, the Catholic bride of James II, she met poet ANNE FINCH, COUNTESS OF WINCHELSEA, and composed a series of religiously fervent poems praising the royal couple. Despite a use of conventional stock phrases and epithets which invited an unfounded charge of plagiarism, her poetry contains startling images and grave insights into court life. 'The Discontent' reveals the cynicism of an experienced courtier: 'And for one Grain of Friendship that is Found, / Falsehood and Interest do the Mass Confound'. This and other later poems suggest a maturing style and a move away from strict moral invective that might have developed had she not died at 25. Her father published a volume of her poetry, for which he engaged Dryden to write the prefatory verse, three months after her death.   JRS

Kincaid, Jamaica [Elaine Potter Richardson] 1949– Antiguan-American writer, born in St John's, Antigua. Kincaid was an intelligent child with a love of books but found few avenues open to her in her teens. Leaving Antigua for New York in 1965, Kincaid took night classes while working as an au pair and then a secretary. She briefly attended college in New Hampshire before returning to New York. Kincaid began writing poetry in 1973 and then articles printed in *Ingenue* magazine. Her friendship with George Trow led to a piece on the West Indian carnival in Brooklyn for the *New Yorker*, where she has remained a staff writer since 1976. Much of Kincaid's early fictional work was published in the *New Yorker*, including extracts from *At The Bottom of the River* (1983). This collection of short poetic narratives describes the rituals of socialization of an Antiguan girlhood and begins Kincaid's extended exploration of the mother–daughter relationship. ANNIE JOHN (1985), also set in Antigua, focuses on adolescent female identity, with the rebellious and resistant Annie testing her mother's rules, as well as those laid down by a colonial education. A little-known publication, *Annie, Gwen, Lilly, Pam and Tulip* (1986), with paintings by Eric Fischl, was followed by *A Small Place* (1988). This complex essay departs from Kincaid's earlier writings, discussing the politics of tourism and other neo-colonial modes of foreign intervention, as well as the corruption of post-colonial leadership. *Lucy* (1990), a novel set in America, explores the life of an au pair 'from the islands' and the unravelling of her American Dream. The intense, ambivalent bond between mother and daughter in this work can be read as analogous to that between motherland and colony. *The Autobiography of My Mother* (1996) moves along the continuum between fiction and auto/biography in order to address the writing of a personal history alongside wider debates concerning the politics of identity. Kincaid, one of the Caribbean's most important women writers, lives in Vermont.   AD

King, Grace Elizabeth 1852–1932 American short-story writer, historian, novelist. Daughter of a loyal Confederate lawyer, Grace grew up in New Orleans and was formally educated in French at the Institut Saint-Louis. In 1885, when she openly criticized George Washington Cable's characterization of Creole society, the editor of *Century* magazine (and Cable's editor) challenged her to write her own version. In 1886, she published 'Monsieur Motte'; three other stories were included in the 1888 book *Monsieur Motte*. She followed this with the collection *Tales of a Time and Place* (1892) and her most popular book, *Balcony Stories* (1893). Her 'local colour' stories focus on issues of race and gender, usually set in antebellum upper-class Creole society. In 1887, King travelled to Connecticut, where she met Samuel and Olivia Clemens, the latter becoming a lifelong friend, as well as Isabella Beecher Hooker, who sparked in her a passion for women's writing. Throughout the 1890s, she wrote four histories, two specifically about New Orleans and Louisiana. Her 1916 novel, *The Pleasant Ways of St Médard*, addresses the problems of Reconstruction for New Orleans women. Her autobiography, *Memories of a Southern Woman of Letters*, was published only a few months after her death in 1932.   SP

King, Sophia *c.* 1781–? English novelist and poet. Beyond elements revealed in the prefaces to her novels, little is known of Sophia King, who apparently concluded her literary career by the age of 25. As a teen-ager, she collaborated with her sister Charlotte in publishing a volume of poems, *Trifles of Helicon* (1798), to mediocre reviews. She next wrote *Waldorf: Or, the Dangers of Philosophy* (1798), a blood-drenched chronicle of atheism and revenge, and *Cordelia, or, A Romance of Real-Life* (1799). Embracing GOTHIC fiction, Sophia prefaced her 12th-century ROMANCE *The Fatal Secret: Or, Unknown Warrior* (1801) with this invocation: 'Oh, welcome then ye little elves, ye ruined abbeys, and tranquil moonbeams: come all ye artillery of glorious Radcliffe.' (See ANN RADCLIFFE.) Unlike her model, though, she chose the fantastic over the 'explained supernatural': after ruining a damsel, the mysterious knight of the title reveals himself as the Devil. In 1801, Sophia published *The Victim of Friendship, A German Romance*, and married Charles Fortnum. She also apparently wrote newspaper verse as 'Sappho'. Reprinting much of her earlier verse, she published *Poems, Legendary, Pathetic, and Descriptive* (1804), and her last novel, *The Adventures of Victor Allen* (1805), traces an orphan character made ruthless by adversity.   JHP

Kingsley, Mary 1862–1900 British author and TRAVELLER, pioneer in the field of anthropology. Her father, the younger brother of the novelist, Charles Kingsley, was widely travelled: Africa was the only country unknown to him. When he died his daughter, 'gay, gallant and shockingly tough' and brought up an agnostic, determined to complete his anthropological studies. She travelled as a trader, carrying trading goods to the west coast of Africa, and some account of this first trip appears in *Travels in West Africa* (1897): her journeys were all accomplished between August 1892 and November 1895.

She wrote in a racy, colloquial style and the account of her second journey in 1894, which appeared as *West African Studies* in 1900, shows indomitable courage and humour in the face of great danger in hostile country. She brought the application of academic discipline to procuring rare specimens for the British Museum, which made her a much sought-after lecturer and her books bestsellers.

When the South African War broke out in 1899, she volunteered for duty and was sent to nurse Boer prisoners in appalling conditions. She continued, however, strongly to oppose causes such as women's suffrage and the riding of bicycles. Two months later she contracted enteric fever and died at the age of 38.

MEW

Kingston, Maxine Hong 1940– Chinese-American 'magical realist' who calls on the tradition of the Chinese 'talk-story', a mélange of gossip, legend and conversational dialogue. She is best known for her fictional autobiography, THE WOMAN WARRIOR: MEMOIRS OF A GIRLHOOD AMONG GHOSTS (1976), which garnered her a National Book Critics' Award. The novel coalesces the virtues of Cantonese peasant wisdom with lyrical and often surrealistic prose. Woven into the fabric of the fiction are characters of friends and family alike (not least her mother), characters at the same time founded on the stories, myths and legends of Chinese women she learned as a child. A stage version which attempted to capture the spectacle of the novel's prose was produced in 1995. *China Men* (1980) is, in its own way, a companion piece to *The Woman Warrior*. The latter was the memoir of the mothers and daughters of a magical time, the former a memoir of the fathers and brothers of that era. In *The Tripmaster Monkey: His Fake Book* (1989), she creates a unique character in playwright/poet Wittman Ah Sing, a Chinese American who inhabits the pre-hippie Haight district of San Francisco and whose most eccentric habit was reciting the poetry of Rilke to anyone who will listen. The title is fashioned after both the 'trip-master' (i.e. s/he who guides the 'pilgrim' on a drug-induced, hallucinogenic journey of the mind) and the 'monkey' (i.e. the Master of the Way of Chinese legend) and Wittman becomes the pilgrim who journeys through a rite of passage to self-discovery. When the entire manuscript of a new novel was destroyed, with her home, in the 1994 Oakland, California fire, Kingston set about rewriting it from memory. MRA

Kinnan, Mary 1763–1848 Writer of CAPTIVITY NARRATIVE. Kinnan's domestic life in Virginia was dis-

rupted in 1791 when her husband and one of her three children were killed during a Shawnee raid, at which time she was taken captive. She was sold to the Delaware, with whom she spent three years, finally escaping with the help of her brother by dressing as a man. She never returned to Virginia, but lived out her years with relatives in New Jersey.

The only piece of writing for which Kinnan is known is her 1795 captivity narrative, *A True Narrative of the Sufferings of Mary Kinnan*; her collaborator on this work was Shepard Kollock, who reportedly transcribed and 'improved' Kinnan's account of her experiences. The narrative portrays her captors as cruel, anonymous and interchangeable, and offers few details of her daily life during her three years of captivity. Literary scholars often cite Kinnan's narrative as an example of the captivity genre's shift in the late 18th century from emphasis on piety to emphasis on sentiment. The text provides ample evidence for this argument, detailing the pastoral ideal of her pre-captivity life and the depths of despair of her ordeal: 'The picture of my life was deeply, too deeply dashed with shade'. Appearing in the same decade as the first popular American novels, the narrative is also notable for its literary references: those to the Bible are outnumbered by those to Shakespeare. KMP

Kirkland, Caroline Matilda (Stansbury) 1801–64 Two years spent living on the American frontier in Michigan in the 1830s made Caroline Kirkland the foremost female interpreter of the West in antebellum America. Raised in Connecticut and New York, she received a superior education in Quaker schools. After marrying in 1828, she and her husband William assumed direction of a Female Seminary near Detroit. From her letters to friends describing this experience came *A New Home–Who'll Follow?* (1839, using the pseudonym 'Mrs Mary Clavers'), followed by *Forest Life* (1842) and a series of essays, *Western Clearings* (1846). The Kirklands returned to New York in 1843, and, after the death of her husband in 1847, she built a successful career writing about European TRAVEL (*Holidays Abroad: Or, Europe from the West*, 2 vols., 1849); she also published a novel (*A Search After Pleasure*, 1852). Kirkland was a devoted and energetic advocate of moral reform, and in *The Helping Hand* (1853) described her efforts to rehabilitate female convicts. Her guides to domestic management (for example, *The Book of Home Beauty*, 1852) were commercially successful. During the Civil War, Kirkland worked as a volunteer for the United States Sanitary Commission. EH

Kiss on the Lips and Other Stories (1932) KATHARINE SUSANNAH PRICHARD's first collection of short stories includes two of her most popular: the award-winning 'The Grey Horse' and 'The Cooboo'.

'The Grey Horse' juxtaposes the wildness and virility of a beautiful stallion with the ageing, ungenerous nature of its owner. The strength and prowess of the 'Grey Ganger' is the talk of the district but his inherent fine qualities have disrupted and imperilled the lives of his admirers. The Ganger becomes a symbol of male envy and of life lived to the full. 'The Cooboo' ('infant') describes the brutal slaying of a baby by his Aboriginal mother during mustering on a cattle station in the remote north-west of Western Australia. Thwarted from mustering effectively by her suckling child, this 'masterful' woman wrenches 'the cooboo from her breast' and dashes his brains out. Prichard stayed on Turee Station in 1926 to write this and other stories, including her play BRUMBY INNES and her novel COONARDOO. JN

Klee Wyck (1941) First published work by west-coast Canadian painter EMILY CARR, this collection records her courageous forays into remote and often deserted Indian villages to sketch the totem poles for which her paintings have become famous. Once, asked to justify her presence in a hostile village, she says she wants to paint the totems: 'Because they are beautiful. They are getting old now ... I want to make pictures of them, so that your young people as well as the white people will see.' Rarely does she need to argue, as the Indians grow to respect and love her – as she does them – christening her 'Klee Wyck' or 'laughing one'. She writes with openness and humour of the cultural differences between her very accommodating guides and herself, and records with painstaking exactitude the details of landscape, seascape, life habits and artistic creation. She is particularly open to the women and to the female imagery on totem poles: the essay 'D'Sonoqua' vibrates with the mythic power of the enormous goddess carved out of the cedar tree. She also writes with great compassion about the erosion of health, life and dignity of urban native people. She later wrote in her biography that she worked hard for 'plain, straight, simple prose'. She succeeded, but the prose is also dazzling and alive. FD

Klein, Melanie 1875–1960 Psychoanalyst, pioneer in the analysis of children and founder of 'object-relations' theory. Klein was the daughter of a Jewish doctor (Moriz Reizes) of Polish origin, and a strong and bookish mother. With her beloved brother, Emanuel, the young Klein enjoyed the intellectual and creative exuberance of *fin-de-siècle* Vienna. She wrote experimental short fiction in her thirties, but it was not until she began to read Freud's work in 1914, when she was already the mother of three children, that she found her intellectual milieu and a life-long vocation. She was analysed by two masters of psychoanalysis, Sándor Ferenczi and Karl Abraham, and quickly began to develop her own ideas about child analysis. Always controversial, Klein found it difficult to get her ideas accepted in Vienna and Berlin. In 1926 she moved to England where she found a new home in the thriving psychoanalytic community there, which had close links to the Bloomsbury group (Klein gave her first London lectures in 1925 in the house of Adrian Stephen, VIRGINIA WOOLF's brother). Klein's theoretical and clinical daring transformed child analysis. The same daring ensured that her work has remained controversial.

Freud had uncovered the unconscious through the hysteria of women, dreams and the melodramas of the Oedipal family. Klein shifted his patriarchal emphasis with her sustained focus on the child's fantasies about his or her mother. Through her 'play-technique', in which she interpreted children's play with toys, she opened up an entirely new psychic domain, first explored in *The Psychoanalysis of Children* (1932). Klein developed a detailed and vivid account of the infant's psychic life: our early lives, she insisted, start with anxiety, aggression and envy. The human capacity for love begins with a profoundly ambivalent relation to the world. Her most original contribution to psychoanalysis is her work on mourning. Prompted by her grief on the death of her own son, Klein showed how the death of a loved one reactivates those first loves and losses of childhood; as she put in a short story that predated her psychoanalytic career, it is 'as if something beautiful which I had lost and found again, was lost once more'.

LJS

Klein, Robin 1936– Australian CHILDREN's author. Best known for *Hating Alison Ashley* (1984), which has won many awards, has been translated into German, Danish, Spanish and Swedish, and has also become a highly successful stage play. Born in a New South Wales country town, Klein worked as a teacher, nurse and library assistant before becoming a full-time writer in 1981. Since then she has been extremely prolific, helped by the fact that she is able to appeal successfully to a wide range of age groups. Her works for younger readers range from the fantasy of *Thing* (1982) and *Thingnapped* (1984), which centre on a pet dinosaur, to the more realistic countrytown and inner-city settings of *Oodoolay* (1983) and *Junk Castle* (1983). A similar range can be seen in her books for older readers. A number combine the comic depiction of the outsider seen in *Hating Alison Ashley* with non-realistic settings: *Thalia the Failure* (1984) deals with a young witch who has trouble learning her craft; *Birk the Berserker* (1987) with a timid Viking; and *The Princess who Hated It* (1986) with a royal who would prefer to be anyone else. Other works, such as *Boss of the Pool* (1986), depict children who are mentally handicapped or have other disabilities.

Klein has also written successful SCIENCE FICTION: *Halfway Across the Galaxy and Turn Left* (1985) and *Turn Right for Zyrgon* (1994) depict an alien family's visit to Earth and the subsequent return to their planet. A more recent series of HISTORICAL NOVELS set in the 1940s chronicles the misadventures of a mother and four daughters, trying to survive in a country town and later in the city: *All in the Blue Unclouded Weather* (1991), *Dresses of Red and Gold* (1992) and *The Sky in Silver Lace* (1995). Klein's many other books include a comic series featuring Penny Pollard, and collections of stories and poems. In 1991 she was awarded the Dromkeen Medal.

EW

Knack, The (1961) ANN JELLICOE's play is now best known because in 1965 it provided the screenplay for a 'Swinging London' film in which, under Dick Lester's direction, a provocative drama became the excuse for teenage antics as four young people let urban detritus provide the décor for their playful life-style. Even so, remnants of Jellicoe's intellectual originality do remain: her updating of the picaresque pattern in which a provincial girl survives urban predators, and the notorious scene in which the *ingénue* frightens off her would-be seducer by screaming 'rape'. It's not only that by turning violence into comedy Jellicoe rescues her quick-witted heroine, the scene also builds up through verbal repetition to the point where, at the moment of release, the balance of sexual power can be felt to have fundamentally shifted. *The Knack* is innovative throughout, requiring a black and white set in which chairs are stuck to ceilings and shadows painted on walls, as if the stage space had been reconstructed as a surrealist painting. Performed in London at the Royal Court in 1962, it has rarely been revived, perhaps because of the continuing dominance of the film. JSto

Knight, Ellis Cornelia 1757–1837 Knight's connection with the BLUESTOCKINGS and with three generations of British royal women sheds interesting light on the moral and cultural interests of both groups. An admiral's daughter, she received a classical education. Her well-read mother knew Johnson, Burke and ELIZABETH CARTER; Joshua Reynolds's sister Frances taught her painting. Her debut, *Dinarbas*, (1790), dedicated at FANNY BURNEY's recommendation to Queen Charlotte, gave Johnson's *Rasselas* a happy outcome, and was imbued with sentimental neo-classicism, though not necessarily feminism. Some of her poems celebrating Nelson's victories were set to music by Haydn. After twenty-four years in Italy she became Lady Companion to Queen Charlotte, dedicatee of *Description of Latium* (1805); she also assisted Princess Elizabeth's historical summaries. Her year as Companion to heiress-apparent Princess Charlotte was less happy; she then returned to the continent. She published *Marcus Flaminius* (1792), *Sir Guy de Lusignan* (1833) and a discreet autobiography (1861). CCO

Knight, Sarah Kemble 1666–1727 Colonial American DIARIST. Married sometime around 1688 and widowed by 1706, Knight was a businesswoman who took the unusual measure of travelling alone in 1704–5 to help settle the estate of a relative. *The Journal of Madam Knight* recounts her travels, but in a unique style and voice.

Knight's *Journal* is often noted for its use of humour. Indeed, though the road presents inconvenience and danger, Knight often makes light of them. While travelling at night through Narragansett country, Knight's imagination transforms the vast and howling wilderness into a sumptuous city in which trees become steeples and castles; rather than calling on God for salvation, she praises the moon in neoclassical-style verse. The wit and lightheartedness of Knight's work is perhaps best seen in light of comparison to the narrative of another woman traveller, MARY ROWLANDSON. Both texts engage in the observation of the customs and daily life of strange people, but where Rowlandson's 1682 narrative focuses on physical and spiritual struggle, Knight's *Journal* pokes fun at others and herself through recounting her mishaps (among them bad roads and food and uncomfortable lodgings). Knight's *Journal* was most likely written to be shared with friends; it was finally published to a wider audience in 1825 by Theodore Dwight. Popular among 19th-century readers, the work depicted an American past which, though hardly distant, was indeed different. KMP

Knox, Elizabeth 1959– New Zealand novelist and writer of novellas about childhood. Knox made her debut with *After Z-Hour* (1987), a POSTMODERN ghost story which juxtaposes realism, fantasy and melodrama, and, in a narrative *tour de force*, switches between different voices. *Treasure* (1992) is an ambitious but incompletely integrated follow-up, blending realism, the supernatural and futurism. Its contrasting stories and settings – the charismatic Christians of South Dakota with a present-day Wellington romance – create a narrative potpourri which climaxes in a Miracle Healing Rally at Wellington Town Hall.

Knox's semi-autobiographical trilogy of novellas interleave her novels chronologically, providing naturalistic evocations of her family and early life. *Paremata* (1989) was acclaimed for its spicy, sensuous images. Brimming with incipient sexuality, it crisply narrates events in 1969 (the heroine, Lex, is 9) in the lives of the Keene family and their neighbours concentrating on the children's games: a pitched battle between boys and girls; Lex's chance discovery of orgasm in a game with her sister; their 12-year-old friend's romantic feelings for a mysterious stranger. *Pomare* (1994) set in 1966, is more restrained, and the theme of death overshadows the children's activities. The distant adult world again comes into view in moments of intimacy, the child's world is full of magic and discovery. Although closely identified with Lex's perceptions, it evokes the social, cultural climate of the 1960s. In *Tawa* (1998), set in the early 1970s, Lex attends Tawa College; through her dilemma about her younger sister's sexual abuse, Knox shows the teenager's horizons broadening into adulthood.

Glamour and the Sea (1996) is a rich biographical–fictional recreation of New Zealand during World War II and after. Based on Knox's father's youth, first at sea on a square-rigger, followed by romance, small-time intrigue and a case of mistaken identity, it is intricately focused. The plot keeps rolling through the narrator's personal involvement and a wealth of finely observed detail, while the atmosphere of Wellington adds flavour to the personal dramas: 'the wind dusted down the black boughs and pollen streamed, yellow veils . . . Pine cones complicated the brushstroke branches, clustered like barnacles.' Praised for her command of 'word, image and sensation', Knox's realism depends on her sharp observing eye.   JMW

Kogawa [née Nakayama], Joy 1935– Japanese-Canadian novelist, poet, essayist and activist, known for her precise, lyrical and often political writing. Born in Vancouver, Kogawa is a 'Nisei' or third-generation Japanese-Canadian, whose family was forcibly interned in Slocan, British Columbia, as a result of the resettlement of Japanese-Canadians from the West coast during World War II. Later her family moved to Coaldale, Alberta, where Kogawa continued her education before studying at the University of Alberta. She then taught in elementary school for a year before going to study music at the University of Toronto. In 1957 Kogawa married, divorcing eleven years later, and going on to work in Ottawa as a writer in the Prime Minister's Office (1974–6), and afterwards as writer-in-residence at the University of Ottawa (1978).

Among her collections of poetry are *A Choice of Dreams* (1974), which includes poems that recall her internment experience, and *Woman in the Woods* (1985). Both her poetry and her subsequent writing are influenced by Kogawa's desire 'to make sense of my life'. For much of her young life Kogawa admits that, 'I experienced myself as White'. However, personal change, politicization and acclaim came during the writing and after the publishing of OBASAN (1981), her autobiographically based novel dramatizing the wartime experiences of Japanese-Canadians. *Obasan* won several prizes and was followed by *Naomi's Road* (1986) – a children's novel – and *Itsuka* (1992), which continues the story of Naomi, *Obasan*'s child protagonist. Having

worked actively with the National Association of Japanese-Canadians, Kogawa acknowledges the difficulty of being a writer and political activist, especially when 'political realities' threaten to destroy her sense of other realities and their complexity: 'I've become so political, and in many ways very one-dimensional, that I'm afraid of destroying the poetry, the richness, of realities other than political realities. There are thousands of realities, but the political reality is so overwhelming in the world, I get drawn to it now.' It is these other realities, however, that she tries to explore in her writing, and by doing so, 'I keep breathing, I keep living, and it feels so good when I've got that right word out.'   SEP

Kotash, Myrna 1944– Canadian writer, born and raised in a Ukrainian family in Edmonton, she earned a BA (University of Alberta) and an MA (University of Toronto). She has written for magazines such as *Border Crossings* and *Châtelaine*, for theatre cabaret, radio drama and TV documentary. She describes herself as 'one of Canada's best-known writer-exponents of creative non-fiction', and she has lectured and been writer-in-residence in Canada and the USA. Her work is anthologized in collections such as *Still Ain't Satisfied* (1982), *Women Against Censorship* (1995), *Ethnicity in a Technological Age* (1988), *The Thinking Heart: Best Canadian Essays* (1991), *Pens of Many Colours: A Canadian Reader* (1993) and *Eating Apples: Knowing Women's Lives* (1994).

Her book *All of Baba's Children* (1977) explores the lives of Ukrainian immigrants in Two Hills, Alberta; in *Long Way From Home* (1980), she wrote about the 1960s and the students' movement in Canada; in *No Kidding* (1987), she explored the lives and values of teenage girls in a search for positive changes resulting from the Women's Movement of the 1970s. *Bloodlines: A Journey Into Eastern Europe* (1993), identified by *MacLean's Magazine* as one of the Ten Best Books of 1993, is based on her TRAVELS in Slavic countries in the final days of Communist rule just before the collapse of the Soviet Union. She based her book on interviews with relatives and other people she met along the way.   GHN

Kroll, Jeri 1946– Australian poet and short-story writer, was born and grew up in New York. Since 1978 she has lived in Australia, where she works as an academic. Kroll's writing considers woman's experience – the gap between prescribed definitions of female social roles and responsibilities and the multiple, concrete identity of woman as mother, daughter, wife and creative artist. Her first book of poems, *Death as Mr Right* (1982), won second prize in the Anne Elder Award. This was followed by *Indian Movies* (1984) and a short-story collection, *The Electrolux Man and Other Stories* (1987). A third book of poems, *Monster Love* (1990), defines, against patriarchal idealization and with direct

honesty, the ambiguities of female love in its maternal, relational and creative capacities. *House Arrest* (1993) continues the theme of women as mothers and daughters, their relationships with society and their artistic work. Active in the Friendly Street Poetry readings begun in Adelaide in 1975, which are still running, Kroll edited the *No 8 Friendly Street Reader* (1984, with R. Clarke) and *Tuesday Night Live: Fifteen Years of Friendly Street* (1993, with B. Westburg). MF

Kulyk Keefer, Janice 1952– Canadian writer and critic born in Toronto. Although she grew up in a WASP neighbourhood, the fact that Kulyk Keefer attended Ukrainian school and summer camp, led her to situate herself on the margins of both communities, 'English' and ethnic. After gaining her BA at the University of Toronto, Kulyk Keefer won a Commonwealth Scholarship to pursue graduate work at the University of Sussex, focusing on Henry James, Joseph Conrad and VIRGINIA WOOLF (who becomes a subject of obsession in Kulyk Keefer's second novel, *Rest Harrow*, set in Thatcher's Britain). On her return to Canada, as part of a rediscovery of her identity as a Canadian Ukrainian woman, she became an avid reader and teacher of Canadian literature.

Kulyk Keefer's writing demonstrates a sustained interest in the lived realities of gender and multicultural politics: 'the focus of my work has been on transcultural experience, and women's experience, and my own experience of hybridity (growing up in an Eastern European immigrant family in pre-multicultural Canada) has been crucially formative'. She has written short stories, novels, poetry, non-fiction and criticism, including a study of the Canadian writer MAVIS GALLANT, and *Under Eastern Eyes: A Critical Reading of Canadian Maritime Fiction* (1987) which was nominated for the Governor General's Award, as was her third novel, *The Green Library* (1996). *White of the Lesser Angels* (1986) was the regional winner of the Commonwealth Poetry Prize. Kulyk Keefer is a professor at the University of Guelph, Ontario, and she is actively involved in the Canadian literary community. See TRAVELLING LADIES (1990). DF

Kumin [née Winokur], Maxine 1925– American poet born in Philadelphia, educated at Radcliffe College. She is a popular poet whose work addresses with intelligence and sensitivity such familiar themes as relationships, place, continuity and nature. Most often she uses formal lines to spin out her linguistic skills; the poems are stable, under control but not inhibited:

> Now I lie under the grasses
> they crop, my own swift horses
> who start up and spook in the rain
> without me, the warm summer rain.
>
> ('Gus Speaks').

She is a domestic poet, yet not limited by the familiar; a voice honest and independent. Her early poetry collections include: *Halfway* (1961), *The Privilege* (1965), *The Nightmare Factory* (1970) and the Pulitzer-Prize-winning UP COUNTRY: POEMS OF NEW ENGLAND in 1972. Since then she has published many other books of poems and also fiction, essays and children's stories. Her other collections include *The Retrieval System* (1978), *Our Ground Time Here will be Brief* (1982), *Nurture* (1988) and *Looking for Luck* (1992).

While not directly linked to the CONFESSIONAL poets of the 1960s, Kumin was close in spirit and correspondence with some of them, particularly ANNE SEXTON, with whom she wrote two children's books. Like Sexton, Kumin shares a concern for the art of survivals through loss and the human/natural bonds which dictate these losses and loves. Other more recent poems focus on larger survival, human fate and our implicit responsibilities to the world, as well as the role of the poet in all this:

> Tonight again they walk up to
> the hills, they walk on canes
> or crutches or in ancient overshoes
> to wait for food to fall from planes.
>
> ('After the Cleansing of Bosnia').

Connecting the Dots was published in 1996 and *Selected Poems: 1960-1990* in 1997. Kumin holds more than fifteen national poetry awards which include the American Academy and Institute of Arts and Letters Award, an Academy of American Poets Fellowship and, in 1989, she was appointed Poet Laureate of the State of New Hampshire. She has taught as writer-in-residence at several American universities and in 1997 was appointed McGee Professor of Writing at Davidson College in North Carolina. ACH

Kuzwayo, Ellen 1914– Kuzwayo's *Call Me Woman* (1985) is probably the best-known of the autobiographies of black South African women published in the 1980s. The purpose of these life-narratives, to mobilize support against the Apartheid regime, influences the shape of the texts with interesting implications for autobiographical conventions. The genre has come to be regarded as promising a single self's exploration of interiority, a confessional mode inviting the reader into an intimate retrospection which lays bare the psychological building blocks of the narrating 'I'. Written in a mode of appeal, black South African women's autobiographies of this period negotiate, often uneasily, distinctions between a life as representative of a common history, and the singularity of personal experience. Kuzwayo's wish to detail a hidden history of the landed black middle class through reminiscences of her own family collides with her need to present a unified black community. Unity across class lines is preserved through distinctly class-bound notions of respectability: Shebeen Queens are acceptable where they meet Kuzwayo's standards of cleanliness, hospitality and motherliness. For Kuzwayo, motherhood functions as a unifying trope signifying black South African women's resistance to a political system which destroys families. Motherhood, invoked as a universal experience, serves also as an invitation to identification and empathy to the reader. At the same time, Kuzwayo insists upon boundaries of privacy (around marital problems, for example), which clearly mark a distinction between autobiography written as political appeal and that of the confessional mode.

C-AM

L

La Fayette, Madame de (Marie-Madeleine Pioche de la Vergne) 1634–93 French writer famous for *La Princesse de Clèves*, the first modern French novel, which she published anonymously in 1678. It is in four parts, which critic Michel Butor describes as 'scenes like a pattern generating one another and responding to each other perfectly'. The novel's story was taken from the *Memoirs* of Brantôme. La Fayette's first novel, *La Princesse de Montpensier*, was published anonymously in 1662, and her second, *Zayde*, under the name of 'J. Regnault de Segrais' in 1670. She lived in the Paris family home in Rue de Vaugirard, except for one period of five years at her husband's country property, and attended the salons of the Marquise de Rambouillet and Madeleine de Scudéry (where she met La Rochefoucauld). She became the friend of Henriette d'Angleterre, who married Louis XIV's younger brother, Philippe, in 1661. Her writings, which include *Histoire de Madame Henriette d'Angleterre* (1723; *The Secret History of Henrietta, Princess of England*), in collaboration with Henriette herself, are mainly concerned with the Court and intellectual life of her times. Her major works were translated into English soon after their original publication. In one of her many letters, La Fayette memorably wrote, 'Il nous coute cher pour devenir raisonable, il ne coute la jeunesse.'   SD

Ladder of Years, The (1995) In the story of the defection of 40-year-old Delia Grinstead, wife and mother of three, ANNE TYLER uses her familiar leitmotivs of running away and returning home to turn a potential tragedy into a farcical comedy of manners. Tyler's voyage-out is always a return ticket, too. The narrative reflects on appreciation and awareness, on time and (second) chances: Delia almost casually recreates her old environment; her aromatherapist spinster sister attempts to finally bewitch the left-over husband; a perky septuagenarian fathers a child. The BILDUNGSROMAN element can be taken very literally as the heroine discards trash romances in favour of the great writers of the American South in whose tradition Tyler herself writes; motifs from *King Lear* mingle with fairy lore. Yet despite the witty dialogues and the well-paced (though not always plausible) plot, the characters lack some of the depth and darkness of *DINNER AT THE HOMESICK RESTAURANT* (1982) or the sparkling

eccentricity of *The Accidental Tourist* (1985). Occasionally Tyler's generous compassion – sad but never tragic, comical yet never caustic – slips over into sentimental optimism.   PUR

Ladies Almanack (1928) DJUNA BARNES wrote the *Almanack* as a high MODERNIST satire on NATALIE BARNEY's bohemian lesbian circle in Paris in the 1920s. While Barnes dismissed her comic text as a 'piece of fluff', the book is a great deal more serious than this comment suggests. A palimpsest composed of pseudo-archaic drawings, poems, anecdotes and prayers, it revises the notion of the ladies' conduct book by focusing itself on the adventures of Dame Evangeline Musset, the forceful patron saint of the lesbian calendar. Mixing the sacred with the bawdy profane, the *Almanack* celebrates women who love women while satirizing the inanities and exploitative practices which even women who have declared their sexual emancipation from men can impose on each other. The text, written for an American expatriate coterie which recognized itself easily in its characters, constructs a new religion for women, populated by its own saints and goddesses, and delights in the varied possibilities of women's bodies, minds and spirits.   KF

Lady Audley's Secret (1862) MARY ELIZABETH BRADDON's bestselling satiric answer to Wilkie Collins's SENSATION NOVEL, *The Woman in White* (1860), has all the ingredients of the genre: a woman with a secret, bigamy, fraud, attempted murder, madness. The novel's heroine–monstrosity re-invents herself as the unmarried governess Lucy Graham following her husband's departure to seek his fortune in Australia, successfully impersonates the compliant feminine ideal, and captivates the wealthy Sir Michael Audley. Lucy's Cinderella story is disrupted by her first husband's return, and the suspicions of his friend (Sir Michael's nephew) Robert Audley. The narrative becomes a contest between Lucy and Robert: she, ever more scheming, devious and, ultimately, violent; he, developing the forensic and evidential skills hitherto avoided in his desultory reading for the Bar. The novel ends with the apparent containment of transgressive femininity, the reinscription of normative gender roles, and the transfer of power from the aristocracy to the professional class: Lucy is confined to an asylum (a reference to contemporary debates about the scandalous ease with which the stigma of madness was attached to women's refusal to conform to gender roles); Robert, a rising barrister, reigns over a parodically perfect Victorian family.   LP

Lamb, Lady Caroline 1785–1828 British novelist and poet, she was the wild and wilful daughter of Frederick Ponsonby, 3rd Earl of Bessborough, and his wife, Henrietta Frances. Brought up in a sophisticated, cosmopolitan atmosphere and educated by the poet Frances Rowden, Lamb refused to live conventionally and eschewed traditional standards of feminine behaviour, stating that she 'ought to have been a soldier'. She married William Lamb in 1805; he later became Lord Melbourne, Prime Minister of England. Their one surviving child was retarded. Her passionate nine-month affair with Lord Byron between 1812 and 1813 was a *cause célèbre*, fictionalized in her extremely popular novel *Glenarvon* (1816); this was posthumously reprinted as *The Fatal Passion* in 1865. Other novels of greater merit followed, including *Graham Hamilton* (1822) and *Ada Reis* (1823), as well as her *New Canto* to Byron's *Don Juan* (1819), and lyrics published with the poet's *Fugitive Pieces* (1829).   RDM

Lamb, Mary Ann 1764–1847 English CHILDREN's writer and poet. Raised in the Inner Temple, she was the daughter of a servant to Samuel Salt, an MP and director of the East India Company. Through Salt's patronage, Mary read widely and trained in dressmaking, while her brothers received scholarships to attend Christ's Hospital. After Salt's death, Mary nursed her invalid parents, but exhaustion eventually broke her mind. Within the family's history of mental illness, Mary's hysteria was the most pronounced and violent – during a domestic argument, she fatally stabbed her mother. Placed under her brother Charles's guardianship, Mary avoided incarceration in an asylum, and the siblings established their own household, frequently changing lodgings after outbreaks of Mary's illness. Eventually they adopted, raised and educated an orphan, Emma Isola.

The Lambs had many literary friends, including Coleridge, the Wordsworths, the Hazlitts and Leigh Hunt. Encouraged by William Godwin, Charles and Mary published *Tales from Shakespeare* (1807), an immensely popular prose collection for children. Although Mary adapted fourteen comedies and histories and Charles only six tragedies, he appeared alone on the work's title-page. Similarly, Mary remained anonymous though largely responsible for their next work, *Mrs Leicester's School* (1809), a collection of instructive 'autobiographies' told by fictive school girls. The Lambs also collaborated on *Poetry for Children* (1809),

with Mary writing most of the verses. In her essay 'On Needlework' in the *British Lady's Magazine* (April, 1815), Mary argued for women's employment. After Charles died in 1834, Mary survived, though rarely lucid, for another thirteen years.   JHP

Lambert, Mary Eliza (Perine) Tucker 1838–? American poet and journalist, born in Cahawba, Alabama, daughter of a wealthy slaveowner. Her mother died at her birth. She went to live with a grandmother in Milledgeville, Georgia, at the age of 8. After being educated at a New York finishing school, she married John M. Tucker, with whom she had two children. She published her first book, *Confessions of a Flirt* (1863), under the pseudonym 'Mrs Edward Leigh'. Her father and husband both lost their property in the Civil War, and she returned to New York to earn money with her writing. In 1871 she married James H. Lambert and moved to Philadelphia. Her rediscovered *Poems* (dedicated to an anti-Reconstructionist governor of Georgia) and *Loew's Bridge: A Broadway Idyll*, a long poem about street scenes in postbellum New York (both 1867), were mistakenly identified as African-American (see LAMBERT, MOLLIE E.) by 1970s researchers.   JSG

Lambert, Mollie E. 1842–1904 American poet, editor and fiction writer. She was born in Cincinnati, Ohio, and, when a child, moved with her parents to Toronto, where she received a college education. In 1867 she married Toussaint L'Ouverture Lambert, member of a prominent African-American family of Detroit, Michigan. She founded a school for black children and worked to integrate the public schools. She led in the charitable work of St Matthew's Episcopal Church, was highly praised as an elocutionist, and edited *St Matthew's Lyceum Journal*. Her poems were published in *Christian Recorder*, *A.M.E. Church Review* and the Detroit *Plaindealer*. She also contributed to *New National Era* and the *Monitor* and was literary editor of *Ringwood's Afro-American Journal of Fashion*. No surviving copies of her fiction on 'the vicissitudes of the colored people' in the North or her *Child's Book of Stories* have been found.   JSG

Land of Spices, The (1941) Widely considered her best work, KATE O'BRIEN's novel of convent life in early 20th-century Ireland was condemned – on the strength of a single sentence – for immorality by the Irish Censorship Board. The novel begins by detailing the self-doubts that vex English-born Helen Archer, Reverend Mother of the Sainte Famille convent. About to request a transfer from the Irish convent that she feels unable to lead effectively – because she is regarded as a cold and alien 'Sassenach' – she abandons the plan when struck by the beguiling openness and

Letitia Elizabeth Landon.

brilliant potential of the convent's youngest student, Anna Murphy. The small girl recalls Helen to her own promising childhood and the shattering loss of innocence that compelled her to circumscribe that promise within cloister walls. A distant but enduring connection is established between Helen and Anna, and, through flashbacks, their stories unfold as parallel narratives. Facing inexorable forces of modernization, ranging from women's suffrage to World War I, these exemplary Kate O'Brien heroines struggle to reconcile the demands of the soul and the world.   MO'C

Landon, Letitia Elizabeth [later Maclean] 1802–38 English writer – a popular icon of her age as well as an accomplished poet, fiction writer and editor. As a teenager, she published poetry in the *Literary Gazette* where, in 1821, a series of 'Poetical Sketches', signed 'L.E.L.', quickly became the rage. These were collected under the title *The Improvisatrice and Other Poems* (1824), which had impressive sales and established Landon's poetic reputation. *The Troubadour, Catalogue of Pictures, and Historical Sketches* (1825) was so successful that Landon wrote a sequel *The Golden Violet* (1826). By this time, Landon was her family's sole support. She read and composed with unusual rapidity, and was so prolific that her work became ubiquitous in the literary annuals. From 1831 to 1838, she edited *Fisher's Drawing-room Scrap-book*. Two novels, *Romance and Reality* (1831) and *Francesca Carrara* (1834), also belong to this period.

The Vow of the Peacock and Other Poems (1835) included an engraved portrait of L.E.L., the first visual image her readers had ever seen. *Traits and Trials of Early Life* (1836), prose tales for children, includes an autobiography. *Ethel Churchill: Or, The Two Brides* (1837) was her last but most accomplished novel. Landon's literary success and her open way with men inspired rumours of sexual indiscretion. Secretly, in 1838, she married George Maclean, Governor of Cape Coast, and departed shortly thereafter for Africa. Two months after arriving, she was dead. The question of whether she committed suicide, suffered an accidental drug overdose or was murdered added to the mystique of her posthumous reputation.   PRF

Langer, Susanne Katharine (Knauth) 1895–1985 American philosopher. She was born in New York City, daughter of a lawyer, and educated at Radcliffe, earning a Ph.D. in 1926. In 1921 she married William L. Langer, with whom she had two sons; they eventually divorced. She taught at Radcliffe from 1927 to 1942, then at other universities, and received several honorary degrees. Her first book was a collection of FAIRY TALES, *Cruise of the Little Dipper* (1923). After *The Practice of Philosophy* (1930), she began ground-breaking work which established her as a precursor to semiotics. Her contribution included her translation of Ernst Cassirer, *Language and Myth* (1946), as well as her own *Introduction to Symbolic Logic* (1937), *Philosophy in a New Key, a Study in the Symbolism of Reason, Rite, and Art* (1942), *Feeling and Form, a Theory of Art* (1953), *Problems of Art* (1957), *Philosophical Sketches* (1962) and *Mind: An Essay on Human Feeling* (3 vols., 1967–82). Langer stressed the importance of emotion, abstraction, and art in shaping individuality.   JSG

Langford Ginibi, Ruby 1934– Aboriginal Australian writer, educator and political activist, a member of the Bundjalung group whose land is in the area now known as New England in New South Wales. Ginibi was born on Box Ridge Mission at Coraki in New South Wales and was brought up there, then with relatives at Bonalbo. She trained as a clothing machinist in Sydney after her education ended early, because of Aborigines' lack of opportunity and access to education, and has worked in clothing factories, as a domestic and as an itinerant country labourer.

Her first novel, DON'T TAKE YOUR LOVE TO TOWN (1988), winner of a Human Rights Award for Literature (1988) and the Pandora Women's Writing Award (1989), is autobiographical (see AUSTRALIAN ABORIGINAL LIFE-WRITING). It tells a story of the hardship, deprivation and cultural dispossession suffered by an Aboriginal woman and her family, with great passion and good humour, and ends with a statement of its intention: to 'give some idea of the difficulty we have of surviving between two cultures, that we are here and always will be'. Enormously successful, the work aroused some controversy when questions were asked about the extent of the intervention of Ginibi's white editor, SUSAN HAMPTON, into her text. Ginibi then determined to write using her own Aboriginal English, rather than conform to white language and textual structures. *Real Deadly* (1992), its title a reference to the way her people praise her work as 'real deadly Ruby', a collection of stories and poems, and *My Bundjalung People* (1994) have followed. *Haunted by the Past* will be published in 1999. Ginibi is dedicated to educating non-Aboriginal Australians in Aboriginal cultural life, and delivers numerous lectures in Aboriginal history, culture and politics at high schools, universities, colleges and conferences.   DB

Langley, Eve 1904–1974 Australian poet and novelist whose prolific published verse and Prior-Prize-winning novel THE PEA PICKERS (1942) received wide critical acclaim. As in its sequel, *White Topee* (1954), Langley engaged in subversive gender and textual games and resignifications in *The Pea Pickers*, although these were accommodated within relatively conventional narrative. Her parodic and ironic juxtapositions, iconoclasm, intertextualities and destabilizations reflect pervasive Menippean influences. The manuscripts of her ten subsequent 400-page unpublished 'novels' are based on her journals and DIARIES – lifewriting that is an extraordinary exploration and redefinition of textual, psychic, personal and political spaces.

Whilst living and writing in New Zealand, she had three children to Hilary Clark, in an otherwise impoverished and unsuccessful marriage. In 1954 Langley changed her name by deed poll to 'Oscar Wilde', thereby adopting a celebrated male as *alter ego*, and wittily and subversively redeploying the latter as her reincarnated Other/Self in the manuscript of her potentially finest, and still unpublished, 'novel', 'Wild Australia', to create identity inversions and temporal, spatial and textual dislocations that make the gender politics of ORLANDO pale by comparison.

Langley's radical and arcane disruptions of normative textual and gender boundaries presented the 1950s editors of the mainstream publishing house of Angus and Robertson with lifewriting/novels which were designated as 'brilliant', but 'scarcely publishable', in that conservative contemporaneous Australian scene. In the 1990s there were moves to edit at least some of these manuscripts in a more congenial critical climate.   RJC

Lanyer [née Bassano], Aemilia 1569–1645 Author of one of the earliest original works of verse published in English by a woman, *Salve Deus Rex Judaeorum* (1611);

"They bear me down to yon abysmal deep."   Page 301.

Lucy Larcom: 'They bear me down to yon abysmal deep', illustration from *The Poetical Works*, 1884.

her coda to this volume, 'The Description of Cookeham', may also be the first English estate or country-house poem. Lanyer's father, Baptista Bassano, an Italian of Jewish origin, was one of QUEEN ELIZABETH's musicians. Lanyer spent part of her youth in the pious Protestant household of Susan Bertie, Dowager Countess of Kent. According to Simon Forman, whom she visited in 1597, Lanyer later became the mistress of Henry Carey, first Lord Hunsdon and Lord Chamberlain; in 1592, after she became pregnant, she was hastily married to a Captain Alphonso Lanyer, one of a French family of royal musicians, with a dowry of £40. In *Salve Deus*, Lanyer attributes her conversion to a true Christian faith, as well as her poetic work, to Margaret, Dowager Countess of Cumberland, and her daughter, ANNE CLIFFORD, Countess of Dorset, whom she visited at the country house of Cookham in Bedfordshire some time before 1607. After her husband's death in 1613, Lanyer briefly established a school in St Giles' Field; in later life she was supported by her son Henry, a flautist at court.   PJB

Larcom, Lucy 1824–93 American poet, critic, editor and chronicler of mill life. She was born in Beverly, Massachusetts. An idyllic rural childhood ended when her sea-captain father died. His widow moved their ten children to Lowell, Massachusetts, where she ran a dormitory for young female millworkers. Lucy and her sisters went to work in the mills. Already a lover of poetry by the age of 11, she made her bench into a library (books were forbidden in the factory) by papering it with poems clipped from newspapers. In 1846 she went to Illinois to teach. From 1849 to 1852 she attended Monticello Seminary in Godfrey, Illinois. In 1854 she returned to Massachusetts to teach at Wheaton Seminary. Having refused a suitor who did not share her abolitionist views, Larcom embraced unmarried life. She edited the children's magazine *Our Young Folks* from 1865 to 1873, collaborated with John Greenleaf Whittier in compiling anthologies for children, and frequently contributed poems to *St Nicholas* and other children's periodicals. She described her mill experiences in *An Idyl of Work* (1875) and *A New England Girlhood* (1889). Beginning in 1867 she published four volumes of her poetry. She also edited anthologies of verse and wrote a book of criticism, *Landscape in American Poetry* (1879). JSG

Larsen, Nella 1891–1964 Harlem Renaissance writer whose fiction chronicles the figure of the educated, urban woman of mixed race. Herself the daughter of a Danish mother and West Indian father, Larsen was raised in Chicago and lived her adult life in New York City. From 1916 to 1926 she worked as a nurse and a librarian, marrying Elmer S. Imes, a prominent black physicist, in 1919. Encouraged and aided by her social contacts (which included Carl van Vechten, the white supporter of many Harlem Renaissance figures), she began writing in 1925 and published the novel QUICKSAND in 1928. An autobiographical BILDUNGSROMAN, *Quicksand* explores the cultural displacement of the mulatta Helga Crane, whose repeated self-reinventions – she becomes (among other things) a teacher at a black college, the exoticized pet of Danish relatives, a member of Harlem's ruling class, and the suffering wife of a poor Southern minister – ultimately fail to give her the socially integrated identity for which she yearns. The following year, Larsen published PASSING, a novella exploring the tension between two African-American women friends, one of whom has long presented herself as white. In 1930 Larsen capped this period of literary success by becoming the first black woman to receive a Guggenheim Foundation Fellowship. That same year, however, she was publicly accused of having committed plagiarism with one of her short stories. Though she and her editors adamantly denied the charge, it seems to have shattered her confidence and abruptly ended her short-lived literary career: she published nothing more, fled her social milieu and resumed work as a nurse until her death. RE

Last Man, The (1826) MARY SHELLEY's apocalyptic *roman à clef* is her most highly regarded work after the mythopoeic FRANKENSTEIN. One of the earliest secular fictions on the theme of the end of the world, it draws in particular on Count Volney's anti-despotic *Ruins of Empire* to fashion Lionel Verney's first-person narration of humanity's gradual destruction by plague late in the 21st century. The narrative encases a multi-layered allegory critiquing the failure of the (masculine) ROMANTIC aesthetic, of the bourgeois nuclear family and of early 19th-century systems of government. Writing *The Last Man* in 1824–5 helped Mary Shelley in coming to terms with the deaths of loved ones: for all its apparently global reach, its central concern is with England and with the tragedy of a small elect group, among whom the angelic Adrian and the fiery Raymond are clearly portraits of Percy Shelley and Lord Byron. Its haunting entropic vision resonates throughout the 'female GOTHIC' tradition, from EMILY BRONTË to ANGELA CARTER, as well as SCIENCE-FICTION and POSTMODERN writing. MO'D

Latourette, Aileen 1946– American writer resident in the UK since 1968; she holds an MA in poetry from Huddersfield University. Her first novel, *Nuns and Mothers* (1984), is a heady brew in which a bisexual woman ultimately rejects her lesbian lover, less for her husband than for closeness to her mother; convent school days and a highly eroticized religiosity are passionately evoked. *Cry Wolf* (1986) is a mythicized novel of atomic holocaust and its aftermath; the earlier highly charged REALISM of *Nuns and Mothers* and of *Weddings and Funerals* (1984) – a collection of stories by Latourette and SARA MAITLAND – is replaced by a more poetic language. Several of Latourette's radio plays have been performed by the BBC. She was one of *Poetry Review*'s New Poets in 1992, writer-in-residence at Ford Prison from 1992 to 1995 and lecturer in Imaginative Literature at John Moores University Liverpool from 1998. She has worked as creative writing tutor to the *Big Issue*'s pool of homeless writers. RK

Latter, Mary 1722?–77 English poet, dramatist and essayist. Latter's first published volume, *The Miscellaneous Works, in Prose and Verse, of Mrs Mary Latter* (1759), proved to be her most successful work. Having developed a local reputation as writer and wit in her home of Reading, Latter had turned to publishing by subscription after her mother's millinery business began to fail. Her lively collection contains a satiric EPISTOLARY NOVEL, pastoral dialogues, moralizing Soliloquies and such playful moments as, 'To Capt. – of Ld. A – 's Dragoons; On his falling from his Horse, and breaking his Nose'. This success notwithstanding, Latter fell into debt and moved to London where she spent years trying to produce her tragedy *The Siege of Jerusalem* (1761). She finally published it, along with 'An Essay on the Mystery and Mischief of Stage-Craft' (1763). Her later writing reflects a sense of desperation and despair, although the subject and style of her satiric poem 'Liberty and Interest' (1764) was favourably compared to Swift. Her perseverance as a writer in the face of economic hardship bears out her promise never to 'TREMBLE at [the] uncouth and vociferous Rage' of her male critics or give in to the limits of her 'common Female Education'.   JRS

Laurence, Margaret 1926–87 Leading Canadian novelist who writes about marginalized people struggling to attain freedom under harsh circumstances: or, as she has written, 'the needs of fledgeling pharoahs in an uncertain land'. She was born in Neepawa, Manitoba, which inspired 'Manawaka', the prairie town in her novel cycle about Canada. At the age of 13 she first used the invented name, Manawaka, in a story: orphaned when young and brought up by an aunt, she had decided as a child to be a writer. After graduating in English at the United College of Winnipeg, she became a reporter in 1947, when she married. Between 1950 and 1957 she lived with her husband in Africa. *A Tree for Poverty* (1954), her first published book, was a translation and retelling of Somali poetry and stories. In paying attention to the oral tradition which fostered this material, Laurence wrote a landmark study. Subsequently she gave rein to her anti-colonial, anti-imperialist views in her African novel *This Side Jordan* (1960) and short-story collection *The Tomorrow Tamer* (1963). She is attuned to the plight of those, both African and European, who no longer belong anywhere. Laurence's greatest achievement, the four interconnected novels dominated by Manawaka (see the fourth, A BIRD IN THE HOUSE (1970)), offsets the narrow respectability of the prairie community with dissenting, dissatisfied voices: a proud, embittered old woman, Hagar, in THE STONE ANGEL (1964); an ossified and introverted schoolteacher, Rachel, in *A Jest of God* (1966); an isolated wife and mother in *Firedwellers* (1969); and a writer, Morag, in THE DIVINERS (1974). The sequence explores time, memory and understanding by evoking a rich common life connected with the prairie town, making allusion to the Bible and the natural world as well as to the four elements. After finishing the last novel in the epic sequence in 1973, Laurence settled in Lakefield, Ontario, and thenceforward published only childrens' books and essays.   KE

Lavin, Mary 1912–96 Story writer and novelist born in Walpole, Massachusetts, who emigrated to Ireland in 1921, where she lived the rest of her life. While still studying for her Master's degree from the National University of Ireland she published her first story; her first collection, *Tales from the Bective Bridge* (1942), won the James Tait Black Memorial Prize. She married the same year and raised three daughters, living in the tra-

ditional, provincial Ireland evoked in her fictions. Widowed in 1954, she remarried in 1969. Though in the course of her career she published a couple of books for children as well as two novels – *The House in Clewe Street* (1945) and *Mary O'Grady* (1950) – and a novella – THE BECKER WIVES (1946), she herself believed short stories were her strength, and she came to be considered one of the masters of the form. Her volume *The Great Wave* won the Katherine Mansfield Prize in 1962. In 1971 a collection was published with an introduction by V.S. Pritchett who wrote of her stories: 'They make the novel form irrelevant.' Often likened to her compatriot Sean O'Faolain, she wrote with an understated empathy and subtle humour of loneliness and the difficulties of love; her narratives were spare, yet in the manner of the Russian writers she admired (particularly Turgenev) she brought her humble characters richly to life, chronicling with acuteness their disappointments and veiled emotions. She once wrote, 'Short story writing – for me – is only looking closer than normal into the human heart', and in over a dozen collections – including *A Memory, and Other Stories* (1972) whose title story is one of her masterpieces – she showed the great gift she had for that close and careful looking.   SB

Lawless, Emily 1845–1913 Irish poet and novelist. A daughter of the third Lord Cloncurry, her family history was one of changing religious and political affiliations, a legacy not without repercussions in the Ireland of her time.

As a young woman, Lawless aspired to be an explorer and a naturalist. However, she learned 'to grow down gracefully, as the sedums and pennyworts do'. Her works include a history, *Ireland* for 'The Story of the Nations' series (1884) and a biography, MARIA EDGEWORTH, for the 'English Men of Letters' series (1904). In her biography of Edgeworth, Lawless argued that, contrary to the accepted opinion of the time, Edgeworth's Irishness was a crucial and formative dimension of her writing, rather than a handicap. This reading is significant in light of Lawless's own complex position in Irish letters. (Ironically, however, she did not challenge the gender issues implicit in the series title.)

Initially she found favour among the key participants in the Irish Literary Revival for her poetry which expresses a deep physical love for the land of Ireland. But her anti-Land-League novel, *Hurrish* (1886), angered many. Here, the Irish people are characterized as mindless, primitive and violent. While she remained popular abroad, particularly in England where her supporters famously included Gladstone, in Ireland she was viewed with suspicion. She eventually moved to England and died in Surrey. Lawless's work is strongest and most authentic when she represents the

Emma Lazarus's words from 'The New Colossus' adorn the Statue of Liberty, New York.

perspective of the outsider, someone whose position in a community/society is tenuous and suspect, as in *Grania: The Story of an Island* (1892), *With Essex in Ireland* (1890) and *Maelcho* (1894). In *Grania*, she was the first writer to take life on the Aran Islands as a subject. She was also one of the first Anglo-Irish writers to acknowledge publicly the ethical and technical difficulties of representing the speech of ordinary Irish people in the English language without caricature. LM

Lawson [née Albury], Louisa ['Dora Falconer']

1848–1920 Australian feminist and journalist, and mother of Henry Lawson. Born in New South Wales, the second of a station-hand's twelve children, and educated at Mudgee National School, she had to refuse an opportunity to become pupil-teacher, being required to help at home. Following her marriage to 'Peter' Larsen (later Lawson) in 1866, they joined the gold rush and set up home in Eurunderee. By 1883 they were living apart, ostensibly because of his work, and she subsisted by running a boarding house in Sydney. After publishing and editing the *Republican* for a time in 1887, she founded the *Dawn* in 1888, which she ran until 1905, writing much of the copy herself, and employing female printers in the face of union opposi-

tion. A spirited amalgam of household advice, feminist polemic, short stories and poetry, the *Dawn* campaigned for female suffrage, employment for women, for improved female access to education, and temperance, attracting subscribers across the world at the height of its popularity. Her later years were clouded by concern for Henry, her son, renowned for his bush stories and verse. Some of her work is collected in *Dert and Do* (c.1904) and *The Lonely Crossing and Other Verse* (1905).
JSte

Lazarus, Emma

1849–87 The New York Jewish poet whose 'The New Colossus' was chosen to adorn the Statue of Liberty. Emma's father, the industrialist Moses Lazarus, belonged to the small, exclusive Sephardic Jewish community of New York. The Lazarus family were no longer observant Jews. Moses was a founder-member of the Knickerbocker Club; they took their summers at Newport.

From the beginning of her career as a poet, Emma Lazarus turned to Jewish history for her subject matter (*Songs of a Semite*, 1882) and was deeply immersed in German culture. She wrote a novel, *Alide* (1874), based on the autobiography of Goethe, and translated the poems of Heine in 1881. Lazarus sought the endorsement of Emerson, and was invited in 1876 to visit the poet in Concord. A portrait of Emerson had a revered place on Lazarus's mantelpiece. During the 1880s she was active in assisting the newly arrived Russian Jewish immigrants, and included a poetic drama, 'The Dance of Death', in *Songs of a Semite*, portraying the plight of 12th-century Thuringian Jews. It was written as an impassioned answer to the anti-Semitic pogroms in Russia. There was about Lazarus a distinctly aristocratic aura. Though barriers of social exclusion were heightening in New York, both German and Russian Jews were quick to take as a slur the reference to 'wretched refuse' in 'The New Colossus'. They failed to rally behind the appeal to build a base for Bartholdi's statue on Bedloe's Island, leaving the initiative to wealthy Sephardim, and the Society leaders of the appeal.
EH

Lazy Thoughts of a Lazy Woman

(1989) GRACE NICHOLS's third collection of poems, continues her poetic project of asserting the sensual presence and power of black women at home in the Caribbean and in their newer diasporic locations. Nichols uses an irreverent humour to expose restrictive (Western) definitions of femininity and to insist instead on representing black female subjectivity as diverse, sensuous and bold. Many of the poems celebrate the erotic power of female sexuality, both thematically (by assertion) and aesthetically in the sustained metaphoric use of the sexualized female body. This emphasis on the personal/sexual domain is given political 'bite' in many of the poems which chart the particularly destructive effects of patriarchal power structures on Third World women. DdeCN

Le Guin, Ursula K[roeber] 1929– American writer of SCIENCE FICTION and fantasy whose work is notable for its feminist, environmentalist and philosophical concerns, and for her fascination with the theory, as well as the practice, of fiction. She studied Medieval and Renaissance Romance Literature at Radcliffe, with a Master's from Columbia, before marrying and bringing up children, and writing in her spare time.

Her earliest novels were conventional except for their fascination with anthropology – her parents were distinguished anthropologists. The background of these and later novels – a species of humanoids, the Hainish, has planted habitable worlds with variations on their own genotype, Earth being one such world – make them a sequence of thought experiments in anthropology and politics.

A Wizard of Earthsea (1968), first of the 'Earthsea' fantasy trilogy, brought her to rather greater prominence, as did THE LEFT HAND OF DARKNESS, a Hainish novel (1969). The Earthsea sequence is characterized by an inventive approach to magic which owes much to Taoism's sense of balance; they are written in a fluent yet austere style which at once makes them accessible to a younger audience and offers adult readers a serious corrective to much other fantasy. The Taoism implicit in these tales is intrinsic to Le Guin's versions of feminism and environmentalism.

THE DISPOSSESSED (1974), also set in the Hainish universe, opposes an anarchist utopia to a capitalist dystopia creating an ethical dilemma for a scientist whose work one will ignore, and the other abuse. *Malafrena* (1979) shares this interest in the historical process, dealing as it does with the revolutions of 1848 from the perspective of an imaginary Central European country, also featured in *Orsinian Tales* (1976).

Always Coming Home (1985) portrays a future Californian society living in harmony with nature and itself with a non-linear mode of narrative which refuses story in favour of songs, recipes, descriptions and fragments of legend; Le Guin sees this as an attempt to find a narrative mode that mirrors women's gathering rather than men's hunting. She returned to more conventional narrative modes and the Hainish universe for *Four Kinds of Forgiveness* (1996), a set of four linked novellas on the theme of revolution and reconciliation, prompted by the overthrow of Apartheid.

Le Guin has been a major influence on science fiction and fantasy from the late sixties onwards, both through emulation of her practice and because of a few important essays. Her 'Science Fiction and Mrs Brown' echoes VIRGINIA WOOLF's 'Mr Bennett and Mrs

Brown' in its polemical call for a greater interest in characters as opposed to ideas. As an anthropologist and as a short-story writer, she has made fabulation acceptable alongside more 'realistic' modes of SF and fantasy.

Her attempt to bring SF close to the concerns of the literary mainstream has made her a controversial figure inside the genre; it has also made her one of the most studied of SF writers in academic circles. RK

Le Marquand Hartigan, Anne 1937– Painter, poet, playwright, writer of short fiction and actress. She was born in England, grew up in the Channel Islands and moved to Ireland in 1962 where she now lives in Dublin with six children. *Long Tongue* was published in 1982, followed by *Return Single* (1986), *Now is a Moveable Feast* (1991) and *Immortal Sins* (1993). Her plays are *Beds* (1982) and *La Corbière* (1989), which were both performed at Dublin Theatre Festivals in 1982. In 1995 she won the Mobil (Ireland) competition for playwriting for *The Secret Game*. Her trilogy, *Jersey Lilies* (1996), set during World War II was performed at the Samuel Beckett Theatre and hints at the influence of her father. Her essay 'Clearing the Space: A Why Of Writing' (1996) was delivered as a paper at a 1995 conference on Violence and Reconciliation, and mixes the different genres of poetry and prose, dealing with varying subject matter and sources from Plato to VIRGINIA WOOLF, as she explores the issues of gendered spaces, national identity, the need for imaginative freedom and her position as a woman artist in Ireland. SFu

Le Sueur, Meridel 1900–96 Poet, fiction writer, journalist and political activist of the American Midwest, considered the most important woman proletarian writer of the 1930s. She was born in Iowa to a white, middle-class family of radical socialists and feminists. A high-school drop-out, she lived in an anarchist commune with EMMA GOLDMAN, worked as a Hollywood stuntwoman and was jailed for protesting against Sacco's and Vanzetti's executions. She was blacklisted for being a communist writer during the McCarthy era.

In the 1930s, the great decade of proletarian writing, she left her husband and took her children to live with a group of women and their children in an abandoned warehouse in St Paul, Minnesota. Her novel, *The Girl* (1978), was written from the women's shared stories, a process she described as 'a communal creation'.

Much of her writing attempted to forge a new language out of feminine, working-class and Native American perspectives. This attempt has sometimes been criticized as an appropriation by an 'outsider'. In response she argued that writers, in this case middle-class writers, could effectively change their group affiliation by participating in a 'communal sensibility' that 'reverses the feeling of a bourgeois writer'.

Often considered too feminist for the Communist party and too communist for the mainstream press, most of her fiction remained unpublished until it was discovered by the Feminist movement in the 1970s. VM

Lead[e] [née Ward], Jane 1623–1704 British religious mystic and writer. Anglican by birth, she had mystical experiences from a young age. These increased in regularity until they were an almost daily occurrence by the time she was in her late forties. She had married William Lead, a distant relative, in about 1644. Following his death in February 1670 she devoted her life to God, adopting the Oxford scholar Francis Lee, who later married her daughter.

Lead's religious life was given direction by a 1663 meeting with John Pordage, follower of German mystic Jacob Boehme, and the first of her fifteen publications appeared in 1681. This was the controversial *Heavenly Cloud Now Breaking*. The second book, *The Revelation of Revelations* (1683), was translated into both German and Dutch. Her writings included her JOURNAL, *A Fountain of Gardens*, in which she recorded many of her mystical experiences, and which she published in four volumes from 1696. Other works include *The Enochian Walks with God* (1694), published in the year in which she established the Behmenist Philadelphian Society with the assistance of Lee. The Society gave rise to a monthly journal, *Theosophical Transactions*; she continued as its leader, aided, she claimed, by divine inspiration. She died in London at the age of 81 having been blind for some time, dictating to Lee the last of her works, *The First Resurrection in Christ*. This was published four years after her death. Lee's *Last Hours of Jane Lead* (1704) provides much information about her life and philosophy. ELER

Leadbeater [née Shackleton], Mary 1758–1826 Irish Quaker author and DIARIST. Although she spent all her life in the small County Kildare village of Ballitore, Mary received a good education from her mother and schoolmaster father, and had access to the wider Quaker community and to intellectual circles in Ireland and England. Her correspondents included Edmund Burke – a family friend – and the poet Crabbe. She maintained a long friendship with MELESINA TRENCH, with whom she shared an interest in literature, in education and in the condition of the Irish poor.

Her first work, *Extracts and Original Anecdotes for the Improvement of Youth*, appeared anonymously in 1794, and in 1808 she published *Poems*. Her *Cottage Dialogues* (1811) were intended as a means of instructing and improving the living conditions of the poor. Subsequent publications included a sequel, *The Landlord's Friend* (1813), which was directed at the prop-

ertied classes, *Cottage Biography* and a memoir of her parents (both 1822).

Leadbeater's writings offer an invaluable insight into domestic and communal life in rural Ireland. However, her most important work is the journal which she began at the age of 11, and which describes her development in adolescence and adulthood, and daily life in Ballitore from 1766 to 1823, including a graphic first-hand account of the impact of the 1798 rebellion in the neighbourhood. Extracts from this journal and from her correspondence were published as *The Leadbeater Papers* in 1862. RR

Leakey, Caroline 1827–81 Australian writer, author (as 'Oline Keese') of the much-reprinted convict novel, THE BROAD ARROW (1859). She had spent the years from 1848 to 1853 in Tasmania, staying with her sister's family and other members of the clergy. Her literary apprenticeship was in writing moral tales, and strong traces of this tradition can be seen in her narrative of Maida Gwynnham, a beautiful middle-class girl, seduced and abandoned and then wrongly convicted and sentenced to transportation 'for the term of her natural life'. Yet Leakey transforms the moral tale through the well-developed characterization of the heroine and her spiritual conflicts, the dramatization in dialogue form of encounters between a variety of characters, bonded and free, and the vivid account of the female convict system. SMS

Leapor, Mary 1722–46 British poet, born into a working-class family at Marston St Lawrence, Northants., where she received only a rudimentary education. Writing verses based upon Pope from a very early age, Leapor produced a large body of work, even whilst working as a kitchen maid, keeping house after the death of her mother and suffering constant bouts of ill health. Her local fame came to the attention of a rector's daughter, Bridget Freemantle, 'Artemesia' in Leapor's verses. Freemantle tried to raise a subscription to enable the poet to continue work but Leapor died of measles before this could be achieved. *Poems upon Several Occasions* was published in 1748, and a second volume appeared three years later. Celebrated as a 'natural', uneducated poet, Leapor's work was frequently reprinted during the 18th century, appearing in such prominent works as *Poems by Eminent Ladies* (1755) and Duncombe's *Feminead* (1754). She also wrote a blank-verse tragedy, *The Unhappy Father*, and left an unfinished play. RDM

Learner, Tobsha 1959– Tobsha Learner was born in England, but left for Australia when she was 20. There she completed art school and was a participant in the 1986 Playwright's Studio at the National Institute of Drama Art, before she moved again to America. She is the author of *Witchplay* (1987), *Wolf* (1992), *The Glass Mermaid* (1994), about a sexual encounter between an older widow and a younger man, and an erotic novel, *Quiver* (1996). Like HANNIE RAYSON, Learner exemplifies the 1990s practice of depicting socially successful women characters facing dilemmas in their personal lives while having the male characters debate feminist ideas. The most successful example of this is her widely performed *S.N.A.G.* (1992), for a solo male performer.   PT

Leduc, Violette 1907–72 French writer of autobiographical fictions, born in Arras. Violette Leduc's autobiography, *La Bâtarde,* was first published in 1964 with a preface by Simone de Beauvoir. It became an immediate literary sensation: the story of a woman who aggressively proclaimed her illegitimate birth, her ugliness, her bisexuality, her poverty and her failures. It brought Leduc to international attention although she had already been writing for more than twenty years. Much admired by the Paris intellectual set of the forties and fifties (Sartre, DE BEAUVOIR, Cocteau, Camus and Genet) and featured in *Les Temps Modernes* in which extracts appeared prior to publication, Leduc's work was seen as a 'poignant cry of painful feminine sensitivity' and much admired for its mixture of biography, autobiography and fiction. Her other books, *Ravages* (1955, *Devastation*), *L'Asphyxie* (1946, *In The Prison of Her Skin*) and *L'Affame* (1948, *Ravenous*) are similarly autobiographical, dealing with female sexuality with a frankness that often led to censorship or private publication. Paradoxically she did not become successful and then write her autobiography, but became successful though recounting her failures. Perhaps her most interesting work historically is the second volume of her autobiography, *La Folie en tête* (1970, *Mad in Pursuit*) in which she recounts her first meetings with De Beauvoir and Sartre.   JHB

Lee, Harper 1926– Southern American writer; author of *To Kill a Mockingbird* (1960). She was born in Monroeville, Alabama, to Amasa Coleman Lee, a lawyer, and his wife, Frances Finch Lee. As a young girl, Lee became friends with the boy living next door, Truman Capote. At the University of Alabama she wrote plays and parodies and edited the campus humour magazine. In 1950 she moved to New York, and worked in the reservations departments of two airlines while beginning her first novel. Against the background of her girlhood in Alabama, and the racial divisions and conflict she had seen – from the Scottsboro Incident of 1931, in which nine young black men, later proved innocent, were accused of raping two white women on a train, to Rosa Parks's arrest in Montgomery in 1955 for refusing to move to the back of a city bus – Lee created *To Kill a Mockingbird*.

Her novel is widely read, and assigned in schools, nearly forty years after its publication. Its characters are familiar people to American readers: Atticus Finch, the white lawyer defending a black man charged with raping a poor white girl; Tom Robinson, the defendant fighting for his life; Boo Radley, the terrifying presence who haunts the novel but appears, only once, to save his young neighbours in the end; the children, Jem and Dill and the narrator, Jean Louise 'Scout' Finch, through whose eyes the story unfolds. The book won the Pulitzer Prize for Literature in 1961, and within two years *To Kill a Mockingbird* had sold over 4 million copies worldwide. Lee was a consultant on the well-known 1962 film, starring Gregory Peck as Atticus Finch.

Although she assisted Truman Capote with *In Cold Blood*, which he dedicated to her in 1965, Harper Lee has not, to date, published another novel. She lives, quietly, in Alabama.   AMD

Lee, Jarena 1783–? African-American autobiographer and the first female preacher of the African Methodist Episcopal Church. Born in New Jersey, Lee became a servant at the age of 7 and moved to Philadelphia as a young woman, where she converted to Methodism. Around 1811, Lee requested the right to preach from A.M.E. leader Richard Allen, who denied it because of her sex. Lee then married a preacher but felt stifled and unsatisfied. After her husband's death, she returned to Philadelphia. Her preaching career began when she interrupted an uninspired preacher during a service and exhorted on the text he had chosen. Impressed with her eloquence, Bishop Allen authorized her to preach. Although never ordained, Lee travelled thousands of miles on the Methodist circuit, from Canada to Maryland and from the middle Atlantic states to Ohio. She became involved in antislavery societies and argued for the right of women to preach God's word. Lee also flouted conventional women's roles, often leaving her son with relatives in order to follow her religious mission.

Lee records her conversion and call to preach in *The Life and Religious Experience of Jarena Lee*, which she published herself in 1836. In 1849, she published *Religious Experience and Journal of Mrs Jarena Lee*, which contains the first autobiography plus a travel journal that expresses her opinions on African-American education, slavery and women's rights. The second autobiography provides the last known information about Lee's life.   AE

Lee, Sophia 1750–1824 One of two literary sisters, had great early success with a comedy, *A Chapter of Accidents*, in 1780 at London's Haymarket Theatre. She went on to write the GOTHIC ROMANCE for which she is famous, *The Recess*, in 1785. This energetic historical fantasy ran through several editions, and was translated immediately into French, with cuts designed to appease a Catholic audience; the plot concerns the fortunes of two sisters, Matilda and Ellinor, who are the secret offspring of MARY, QUEEN OF SCOTS and the Duke of Norfolk, brought up in an underground apartment beneath the ruins of St Vincent's Abbey on the estate of Lord Scroope by his sister Gertrude Marlow – one of QUEEN ELIZABETH's ladies-in-waiting – and good Father Anthony. Gertrude describes on her deathbed how Mary, carried away by the noble Norfolk's campaign to free her, 'thought it but generous to let the recompense rather precede the service than follow it'. While Mary's sexual generosity marks her good old Catholic spirit, and the author's romantic Jacobitism, Elizabeth is portrayed as a deformed and jealous shrew ('the defect in her shape, taking off all real Majesty, she supplied that deficiency by an extreme haughtiness'). Matilda and Ellinor fall passionately in love with, and yield to, her favourites, Leicester and Essex, respectively. The narrative passes from sister to beautiful sister, as their mutually corroborating stories turn history into a fictional vortex of sexual intrigue (Matilda secretly marries Leicester and Sydney falls in love with her for good measure, while Essex 'really' dies for Ellinor . . .), urgently, but knowingly, transposing the main events of Elizabeth's reign into a secret undergound world of female desire.   VS

Lee, Tanith 1947– British fantasy writer, whose work spills into SCIENCE FICTION or horror. Lee's novels vary from bloodthirsty dynastic fantasies to dark sardonic CHILDREN'S BOOKS, from *The Silver Metal Lover* (1981) with its robot stud to a sequence of GOTHICS, starting with *Dark Dance* (1992) in which the heroine gradually becomes monstrous. Lee's tone is always intense, and her style decadently luscious. Perhaps her most interesting work is her short stories, particularly those in which, under the influence of ANGELA CARTER's THE BLOODY CHAMBER, she revisits FAIRY STORIES; her Snow White in *Red as Blood* (1983) is a vampire, whose redeeming Prince turns out to be a Wildean Christ. Many of her short stories fit into loose sequences, notably the 'Tales from the Flat Earth' sequence which commenced with *Night's Master* (1978): the eponymous demon king, Azharn, dies and is resurrected to save the beauty of the world, whereas the gods sit uncaring in Paradise. The moral and aesthetic framework of Lee's work is often perverse, but rarely routinely so.   RK

Lee, Vernon (Violet Paget) 1856–1935 English expatriate woman of letters of exceptional range and (for some) exceptionable manner. She was born to TRAVEL WRITING, as it were, near Boulogne, to parents changing French and German lodgings twice-yearly – 'this

was *moving*, not travelling' she would reminisce. Her father had tutored her widowed mother's first child, Eugene Lee-Hamilton, who became a minor 'Aesthetic' poet. Violet in turn was intensively educated by Eugene and her unconventional mother, and, more informally, by intimates on the continental circuits, John Singer Sargant and family. In 1889 she settled at the Villa del Palmerino in Florence, where she held court until her death.

Over forty volumes followed her ground-breaking first book, *Studies of the Eighteenth Century* (1880), well-received under the male pseudonym she would always use: travel writing, short stories, plays, essays and books on aesthetics, history, social psychology, ethics and pacifism besides novels. Relations between art and life, and the difficulty of human contact, are recurrent themes. Her first novel, *Miss Brown* (1884), satirized Aestheticism; its florid aspects elicited a protest ('art is icy') from its embarrassed dedicatee, Henry James. Along with her original intelligence and acuity, critics noted lack of restraint and even 'dangerous' tendencies, as with the sensuous effects and unorthodox sexual undercurrents in the *Yellow Book* tale, 'Prince Alberic and the Snake Lady'. *Gospels of Anarchy* (1908) articulates her opposition to REALISM; *Satan the Waster: A Philosophical War Trilogy* (1920), her deeply held pacifism. Her writings on psychological aesthetics foregrounded empathy and influenced T.E. Hulme; another essay (1897), written with her friend Kit Anstruther-Thomson, sparked a long-standing dispute with her Italian neighbour, Bernard Berenson, over plagiarism. The neglected *The Handling of Words* (1923) emphasizes the relational components of meaning and anticipates I.A. Richards's *Practical Criticism*.   KC

Left Hand of Darkness, The (1969) This SCIENCE-FICTION novel by URSULA K. LE GUIN embodies her concern with sexual politics, spirituality and anthropology. An envoy from a confederation of humanoid worlds finds himself caught up in the politics of the Gethenians, neuters who develop the sexual characteristics of either gender during periodic oestrus. His flight, along with a disgraced local politician, across an icy continent in deep winter becomes a metaphor for a spiritual journeying out of emotional bleakness. The tragic love story of the (heterosexual) diplomat and someone he perforce sees as male was a challenge to the conventional sexual mores of much SF; the book nonetheless won awards for the Best Novel of its year. The novel is studded with fragments of Gethenian folklore and literature; Le Guin's enthusiasm for Taoism interests her in the very different possible dualism of humans without gender.   RK

Lehmann, Rosamond (Nina) 1901–90 British author, born into a gifted, cultured family, the daughter of Rudolph Lehmann, the Liberal MP, and his wife, Alice. Her sister was the Shakespearean actress Beatrix Lehmann, and her brother, the writer John Lehmann. She was educated privately and then at Girton College, Cambridge. Her first novel, *Dusty Answer* (1927), describes the sexual and emotional awakening of a fictional avatar, Judith Earle, and her relationships in a Cambridge women's college. Lehmann married Leslie Runciman in 1922 and Wogan Phillips, later Lord Milford, in 1928, by whom she had two children. After he left her to fight in the Spanish Civil War she began an important nine-year love-affair with the poet Cecil Day Lewis.

Rosamond Lehmann is an accomplished stylist who excels at depicting feminine sensibility and evokes the inner turmoil caused by romantic love in her sensitive, intelligent heroines with unusual honesty and perceptiveness. THE WEATHER IN THE STREETS (1936), her best-known work, was a 'bench-mark' book for many women readers who wrote to Lehmann telling her that they identified with the romantic predicament of its central protagonist. Lehmann's work is strongly influenced by 19th-century women writers, especially by JANE AUSTEN and ELIZABETH GASKELL, and she eschews MODERNIST experimentation in favour of traditional narratives, albeit informed by a 20th-century consciousness. Her fiction is characterized by its skilful observation of the social life of the privileged sector of society to which she belonged. *A Note in Music* (1930) evokes the frustration of a woman trapped in a provincial city and a loveless marriage. *The Weather in the Streets* describes the passionate intensity of a love-affair with a married aristocrat from the viewpoint of 'the other woman', a divorcee, Olivia Curtis, a character to whom readers had been introduced as she prepared to go to her first ball in AN INVITATION TO THE WALTZ (1932). In *The Ballad and the Source* (1944), the 10-year-old Rebecca Landon becomes party to the scandalous family history of an enigmatic old woman, Sibyl Jardine. Lehmann contributed several short stories including 'The Red-Haired Miss Daintreys' (1941) and 'Wonderful Holidays' (1944) to the war-time editions of *Penguin New Writing*. These were published as *The Gipsy's Baby and Other Stories* (1946). Her next novel, THE ECHOING GROVE (1953), is about the love of two sisters for the husband of one of them.

A cause of great personal anguish was the unexpected death of her daughter, Sally, of poliomyelitis in Indonesia in 1958. Lehmann came to believe that it was possible to communicate with the dead and was vice-president of the College of Psychic Studies from 1971 until her death. *A Sea Grape Tree* (1976), in which Lehmann returns to an older Rebecca Landon, who is in contact with the spirit of the deceased Sibyl Jardine, appeared after a long interval in which she had ceased to publish new fiction. *The Swan in the Evening* (1967) is an autobiographical fragment. Lehmann was awarded a CBE in 1982. *Rosamond Lehmann's Album* of photographs was published in 1985. MJ

Leigh, Dorothy ?–1616 Writer of a popular 'mother's advice' book, *The Mothers Blessing* (1616), published posthumously. The 'mother's advice' book usually justified its existence on the grounds both of the necessity of passing on maternal wisdom to a child and of the imminent death of the author. Leigh utilizes the rhetoric of this genre, but carefully markets her work for posterity; and it begins with her own dedicatory epistle to Princess Elizabeth, rather than the more common preface by a male printer lamenting the author's death. She defends her writing on the grounds that 'the love of a mother to her children is hardly contained within the bounds of reason', but the identification of her sons as the recipients of her wisdom becomes overshadowed by her references to 'women' as her addressees.

Leigh argues for the equality of women, for their right to be loved by their husbands and to be free from rape and seduction. She advocates female education on the basis of its religious content, and identifies it as a defence against seduction, by closing the woman's ears to the 'vain words of men'. In a lengthy discussion of rape, she engages with the long-standing controversy over the suicide of rape victims, condemning suicide not because of its sinful nature, but because rape does not render a woman impure. JC

L.E.L. see LANDON, LETITIA ELIZABETH

Leland, Mary 1941– Irish author who was born in Cork: the history, landscape and society of this part of Ireland is at the centre of her fiction. A successful journalist and a mother of three children, she began writing prize-winning short fiction in her late thirties. In 1985 she published *The Killeen*, a historical novel set in the 1930s when die-hard republicans were still attempting to subvert Eamon de Valera's government. Centring two stories – one of a rich widow of a dead diehard hunger striker, the other of a country girl seduced by a republican on the run – the novel traces their resistance to violent versions of Irish nationalist heroism. When the maid's baby is spirited off to the countryside where her family still lives, it ends up abused and finally buried in the Killeen, a site in traditional Ireland where unbaptized babies were buried after being denied the church's blessing. This bleak and savage place serves as metaphor for the killing politics of post-civil-war Ireland, and the harshness of the land which can brutalize those who work it.

Her novel *Approaching Priests* (1991) creates a central character who is searching for spiritual health and meaning in pre-Vatican-II Catholicism, but within the contradictory context of a sophisticated journalistic career and the sexually liberated life of a thoroughly modern woman. The unusual moral and ethical problems explored here, like those of *The Killeen*, make these works distinctively and uniquely Irish.   CStP

L'Engle [née Camp], Madeleine 1918– American

writer whose influential SCIENCE-FICTION novels for young adults explore moral issues through fantastical adventure stories combining scientific fact and Christian theology. Born to Charles Wadsworth Camp, a music and theatre critic, and Madeleine Bennett, a talented pianist, she was exposed to Manhattan's artistic circles as a child and attended boarding schools in Europe and America, and Smith College (BA 1941). Settling in New York, she produced her first novel, *The Small Rain* (1945), receiving critical approval for her portrait of a young pianist. Over the next fifteen years she married, raised three children and continued to write. L'Engle again won critical praise with the publication of *Meet the Austins* (1960), her first book in this series for young adults being named the American Library Association Book of the Year. L'Engle's next series remains her best known, combining as she says 'good, solid science with good, solid theology'. Initiated with the Newberry-Award-winning *A Wrinkle in Time* (1962) and followed by *A Wind in the Door* (1973) and *A Swiftly Tilting Planet* (1978), the 'Time Fantasies' series follows the Murry children who travel through a *tesseract*, the mathematical concept of a 'wrinkle' in time and space. Author of over forty published titles, including a trilogy of reflections on the Book of Genesis, and volumes of memoirs and poetry, L'Engle has also actively dedicated herself to churchwork, most notably at the Cathedral of St John the Divine in New York.   RL

Lennox [née Ramsay], Charlotte 1729/30–1804

The daughter of an army officer, Lennox spent her earliest years in the colony of New York, an experience she used in her first and last novels, *The Life of Harriot Stuart* (1750) and *Euphemia* (1790), which both include scenes involving native Indians.

A precocious child, she was sent to England in 1742, where she soon published *Poems on Several Occasions 'By a Young Lady'* (1747). Her marriage to Alexander Lennox, who worked for the publisher William Strahan, provided access to London's literary market. Her husband's inability to earn any money turned Charlotte into a determined professional. Samuel Johnson became a lifelong friend and mentor, citing her under 'Talent' in his dictionary. Both Johnson and Richardson strongly encouraged Lennox in writing her second and most celebrated novel, THE FEMALE QUIXOTE (1752). Arabella, the novel's heroine, is an avid reader of ROMANCES, the contents of which she

embraces rather too literally. While the novel acts as a satirical warning against the immoral effects of romance, it also reveals the paradoxical effects of reading in a subtle and sophisticated light. *Shakespeare Illustrated* (1753–4), the first compilation and translation of the sources for his plays, highlights the important role of romances in the construction of Shakespeare's plots. Important translations include *The Greek Theatre, Translated from the French of Pierre Brumoy* (1759) and the *Memoirs for the History of Mme de Maintenon* (1757). As editor of the conduct periodical, the *Lady's Museum* (1760–1), Lennox included a revised version of *The History of Harriot and Sophia*. Toward the end of her life she separated from her husband and lived with Frances Reynolds (sister of Joshua), surviving on a small grant from the Royal Literary Fund. ESE

Lenski, Lois Lenore 1893–1974 Author, illustrator,

artist, specializing in juvenile fiction. One of the most prolific children's writers (see CHILDREN'S BOOKS) of the 20th century, she published more than ninety books between 1927 and 1974, many of which are self-illustrated. She was particularly acclaimed for her historical and regional series. She spent her childhood in Anna, Ohio, and subsequently attended the celebrated Art Students League in New York City during the momentous years of 1915–20, and the Westminster School of Art in London in 1920–1. Exhibitions of her oil paintings were held in New York in 1927, her watercolours five years later, but as she noted in her autobiography, *Journey into Childhood* (1972), her professional career moved gradually, and almost imperceptibly to her, from artist to author.

Nonetheless, her immersion in the New York art world in the effervescent years of the late 1910s into the 1930s is expressed in her writing in choice of subject matter – the variegated American land and its good, common people – and in style – a vigorous, plain style grounded in REALISM. Both the HISTORICAL NOVELS – including *Ocean-Born Mary* (1939), *Indian Captive: The Story of Mary Jemison* (1941) and *Phebe Fairchild: Her Book* (1942) – with their vivid depiction of life before mechanization, and the regional novels, including *Bayou Suzette* (1944), and their celebration of the rural, the local, the commonplace, the ordinary, express the same preoccupation with cultural nationalism as depicted on canvas by such artists as Thomas Hart Benton and the Regionalist school of American painting. Like reporters, photographers, artists and folklorists of the period, Lenski travelled the country in a documentary quest of American scenes, peoples, stories, songs, dialects and habits. Her specificity of detail and straightforward veracity brought to life for her young audience the hitherto hidden world of the poorer segments of American society, from the mountain peoples of Appalachia – *Blue Ridge Billy* (1942) – to the Florida 'crackers' – *Strawberry Girl* (1945) – to share-croppers in the South – *Cotton in My Sack* (1949). Lenski wanted her young public to know their country better, 'to know and understand people different from ourselves'. For through understanding would come admiration for such virtues as thrift, hard work, truthfulness and education.   EDG

Lentin, Ronit 1944– Journalist, novelist and feminist sociologist. Born in Israel, Lentin has lived in Ireland since 1969. Initially her work was published in Hebrew in Tel Aviv: two novellas and a collection of conversations with Palestinian women (1982), which explores the link between the personal and the political. Since then she has written in English.

Lentin's fiction explores the tensions of displacement and a legacy of catastrophe, as well as ethnic conflict. Her novella, *Tea with Mrs Klein* (1985), explores the tentative friendship between a lonely, ageing Jewish woman and a Catholic priest in Ireland. *Night Train to Mother* (1989) represents a more personal quest for identity through a woman's journey back to Romania, to the town from which her family were expelled during World War II, and thereby destroyed – and her subsequent reclamation of a lost culture and a strong female lineage. Her 1996 novel *Songs on the Death of Children* also tells the story of a quest. Here the protagonist is a journalist, born in Ireland, who travels to Israel in search of a sister lost during World War II.

Lentin's academic work focuses on issues of gender and racism. She has edited a collection of essays, *Gender and Catastrophe* (1997), and co-ordinated work on Ethnic and Racial Studies at Trinity College, Dublin. Active in the Platform against Racism, she is an outspoken critic of racism and exclusion in Irish society.
                    LM

Leslie, Eliza 1787–1858 American COOKERY writer. Born in Philadelphia, where her father was a friend of Thomas Jefferson and Benjamin Franklin, Leslie was well educated at home and in London before the family fell on hard times. Writing always as 'Miss Leslie', she published verses, stories, essays and even a novel in periodicals such as *Godey's Lady's Book*, but she was best known and best paid for her COOK BOOKS. Her first one, *Seventy-Five Receipts for Pastry, Cakes, and Sweetmeats* (1828), went through twenty editions. Far more original and comprehensive was her *Directions for Cookery: Being a System of the Art, in its Various Branches*, which she copyrighted in 1837 but continued to enlarge, and revised in fifty-six editions over the next twenty years. In *New Receipts for Cooking* (1854), she added 'One Thousand and Eleven new Receipts', including a large section on 'Indian Meal Preparations', along with such ancillary concerns as a lady's conduct while 'Crossing the Sea'. Following the

Illustrated frontispiece by Lois Lenski from *Strawberry Girl*, 1945.

lead of Mary Randolph's *The Virginia House-wife* (1824) in adapting to the American hearth popular manuals of English housewifery by Susannah Carter and MARIA ELIZA RUNDELL, Leslie was the first to delineate in minute detail and encyclopaedic scope 'a manual of American housewifery'. With admirable clarity and precision, whether describing basics like butter making or luxuries like lobster fricassees, Leslie reveals not only the sophisticated taste of Philadelphia society but that of other major eastern cities in mid 19th-century America.   BF

Lessing [née Tayler], Doris (May) 1919– British novelist and short-story writer whose work spans the imploded empire of English. She was born in Kermanshah, where her father worked for the Imperial Bank of Persia (now Iran), and grew up in Zimbabwe (then Southern Rhodesia) where he became a farmer in the 1920s. In 1968 she wrote (about another white African writer, OLIVE SCHREINER, but describing her own background): 'To the creation of a woman novelist seem to go certain psychological ingredients . . . a balance between father and mother where the practicality, the ordinary sense, cleverness, and worldly ambition is on the side of the mother, and the father's life is . . . weighted with dreams and ideas and imaginings'. Not until her autobiographical fantasy

THE MEMOIRS OF A SURVIVOR (1974) did she imagine her mother Emily as once a dreamer too.

Lessing herself left school at 14, married for the first time in 1939, and divorced in 1943: her two children stayed with her civil servant ex-husband. By now she was fired with political passion, a member of a Communist group in Salisbury whose leader, Gottfried Lessing, she married in 1945. In 1949 they divorced, and she left for London with their small son Peter and the manuscript of her first novel, THE GRASS IS SINGING (1950). Her African life would supply the material for stories and the first three novels of 'CHILDREN OF VIOLENCE', a serial BILDUNGSROMAN which established her 1950s reputation as a social-REALIST writer. She was, however, growing radically disillusioned with the political culture – and the practice of writing – she had espoused, and in THE GOLDEN NOTEBOOK (1962) she broke ranks to explore 'breakdown' as the truly representative experience for a woman of her generation. Relations between men and women, between races, between generations, between present and past selves, were all at once in question. 'The novels as they proceed', wrote NICOLE WARD JOUVE, 'become aware of something false, a vacuity, which is the falsity of their own fictional mode.' Lessing completed 'Children of Violence' as speculative psycho-history, drawing (particularly in The Four-Gated City, 1969) on Sufi teachings, mystical writings, anti-psychiatry.

Middle age became her second great formative period. Leaving behind her 'progressive' self, she experimented with many different genres, notably SCIENCE-FICTION in the 'Canopus in Argos' series, exploring post-imperial politics in mythic style. Characters in SHIKASTA (1979) 'repose in their imaginations on chaos, making strength from the possibilities of a creative destruction'. She broke off this series too, to invent a fake authorial identity, 'Jane Somers', under which she published two documentary fictions in the mid 1980s. THE GOOD TERRORIST (1985) describes a new generation of violent children torn apart by contradictory desires to play house, and confront authority, acting out one of their author's worst nightmares – the same mistakes again, repetition masquerading as radical sentiment. 'What Lessing shows', novelist JEANETTE WINTERSON wrote, 'is that no one knows what evolutions are necessary ... we only know that movement is the key.'

Her inventiveness rests on a readiness to jettison possessions and positions. In AFRICAN LAUGHTER: Four Visits to Zimbabwe (1992) she wrote, 'There are more and more people who have had to leave, been driven from a country, the valley, the city they call home.' London is her city because it's here the colonies have 'come home to roost'. Her autobiographies UNDER MY SKIN (1994) and Walking in the Shade (1997), lay claim to continuity –

'the sense of yourself ... is the same ... in a small child's body, the sexual girl, or the old woman' – while demonstrating her formidable gift for cutting her losses, living with change.   LS

Lette, Kathy 19??– Popular Australian satirist who explores the sticky pragmatics of being a woman in a cross-cultural 'age of options' still regulated by men. Born in Sydney and once a columnist for the Sydney Morning Herald, she wrote her first novel, Puberty Blues (1979), when she was only 17. A bestseller, it was adapted for the cinema. Her fiercely demotic style of furious punning and ribald one-liners continues in her collection of stories lampooning eighties life, Girls' Night Out (1989).

Drawing on her experiences as a comedy writer for Columbia Pictures in California, her second novel, The Llama Parlour (1991), also a bestseller, follows a young Australian woman's attempts to cope with brazen American excess. With a mixture of bravura and vulnerability typical of Lette's heroines, Kat remains bemused ('I can't merge'). She survives instead on her forthright Antipodean wit.

Lette moved to London (where she married the barrister Geoffrey Robertson, with whom she has two children) in 1989, and became a media personality with a reputation for witty and outspoken views on social mores. Her next novel, Foetal Attraction (1993), 'about a man's obligation to an egg', ridicules irresponsible fathers and seeks to 'debunk the myth of the joy of natural childbirth' whilst its post-natal follow-up, Mad Cows (1996), traces the antics of a recent mother who behaves 'like some escapee from The Exorcist'. Altar Ego (1999) continues this irreverent series by following a woman's life after she has jilted her husband-to-be at the church. Her plays include: Grommit, Wet Dream and Perfect Mismatch.

A passionate Republican, Lette sees Australia as 'the most multi-cultural nation in the world – a human minestrone' and considers the Queen an 'overpaid model for a postage stamp'.   JAH

Letters From Orinda to Poliarchus (1705) This posthumously published volume of letters between 'The Matchless Orinda' (KATHERINE PHILIPS), and Sir Charles Cotterell, follows the unsuccessful suit of the widow Calanthe by Poliarchus. Several interwoven narratives recount the story of Orinda's distress when her friend Calanthe (Anne Owen), also known as Lucasia in Philips's friendship poetry, decides to marry Memnon (Marcus Trevor, later Lord Dungannon) instead of Poliarchus (Sir Charles Cotterell). These narratives are complemented by detailed comments on the royal family, contemporary poets and writers. The book reports Philips's translation of Corneille's La Mort de Pompée (1663) and its successful performance in

Dublin's Smock Alley Theatre in the same year and gives her own comments about the disputed publication of *Poems. By the Incomparable Mrs K.P.* in 1664. The correspondence ends on 17 May 1664, a few weeks before Philips's death and culminates in an enthusiastic tribute to friendship 'between Persons of different Sexes . . . with Delight and Innocence'. The second edition of the *Letters* (1729) includes one additional letter.

NBP

Levant Trilogy, The OLIVIA MANNING's sequel to 'THE BALKAN TRILOGY' with which it forms the 'Fortunes of War' hexalogy. It comprises *The Danger Tree* (1977), *The Battle Lost and Won* (1978) and *The Sum of Things* (1980). Set in the Middle East around the time of the battle of El Alamein, the novels continue the story of Guy – an English lecturer – and Harriet Pringle, as told in 'The Balkan Trilogy'. They closely follow the war-time paths of Manning and her husband, R.D. Smith, both of whom were evacuated to Egypt in 1941 after the fall of Greece. 'The Levant Trilogy' consists of two interwoven narrative strands: the story of Simon Boulderstone, a young British Army officer; and the lives of Harriet and Guy, amid their expatriate circle. Boulderstone's experience of the desert war includes coming to terms with his brother's death and being seriously wounded himself. At the same time Harriet and Guy drift further apart. Harriet leaves Egypt and is believed to have been killed at sea until they are finally reunited in Cairo.

VG

Leverson [née Beddington], Ada 1862–1933 English novelist and parodist. To Oscar Wilde, who nicknamed her 'Sphinx', she was 'the wittiest woman in the world'; to her publisher Grant Richards she was 'the Egeria of the whole Nineties movement'. Born to a wealthy Jewish family and educated at home, she married Ernest Leverson, a diamond merchant and gambler, in 1881, without her parents' consent. The couple had two children before separating in 1902 when Ernest, almost bankrupt, emigrated to Canada without her.

Today she is best remembered for having sheltered Wilde between his trials when no hotel would admit him, but in her own era she was hailed as a talented writer and wit. Throughout the 1890s she published clever sketches, in *Punch* and other periodicals, that parody Wilde as well as other male aesthete friends including Aubrey Beardsley ('Weirdsley'), Max Beerbohm ('Mereboom') and Henry James. In one of her best, 'An Afternoon Tea Party', Salome gets into a scuffle with Charley's Aunt over a tartan shawl left in the cloakroom. In 1895–6 she published two short stories in the *Yellow Book*, but it wasn't until 1907 that her first novel, *The Twelfth Hour*, appeared. This was followed by five more comedies of manners (all written in

bed and dictated to a stenographer) that chronicle marriage among the upper-middle class in the Edwardian era: *Love's Shadow* (1908), *The Limit* (1911), *Tenterhooks* (1912), *Birds of Paradise* (1914) and *Love at Second Sight* (1916). After finishing her novels she produced a recollection of the first night of *The Importance of Being Earnest* ('The Last First Night') published by T.S. Eliot in the *New Criterion* in 1926 and reprinted in *Letters to the Sphinx from Oscar Wilde, with Reminiscences of the Author* (1930).

MAD

Levertov, Denise 1923–1998 Poet who was born in England and emigrated to the United States in 1948. Levertov was a prominent figure in American poetry from the 1960s and her voice and preoccupations have much about them that is of that time. Since *The Double Image* in 1946, she published more than twenty books of poems as well as essays and translations. Levertov also held professorships at a number of American colleges.

Levertov's poems often take place at moments of connection between different worlds or times or states of being. Several of her collections make this sort of mystical bridging their central image: *The Jacob's Ladder* (1961), *Breathing the Water* (1987), *A Door in the Hive* (1989) and *Overland to the Islands* (1958), the title poem of which begins:

> Let's go – much as that dog goes,
> intently haphazard. The
> Mexican light on a day that
> 'Smells like autumn in Connecticut'
> makes iris ripples on his
> black gleaming fur – and that too
> is as one would desire – a radiance
> consorting with the dance.

A Levertov poem is an enactment of intellectual release; the consciousness becomes more receptive, instincts sharpen. There is a desire in this for a primitive, unlearned state of innocence, for the ancient and mythical world to reassert itself. 'The World Outside' may be tenements, chimneys and soot but

> The goatherd upstairs! Music
> from his sweet flute
> roves from summer to summer.

However vague their direction, Levertov's poems often culminate in (or cohere as) a moment of epiphany or transformation. The dog may be 'intently haphazard' but the light endows it with exaggerated beauty. Her conclusions are persistently reassuring:

> Our eyes smart from the smoke but
> we laugh and
> warm ourselves.

What might seem naive or hortative is complicated by tension between this affirmation and a suggestion of ephemerality. In the same way, Levertov's urge to escape is grounded in the immediacy of her imagery – wherever the poem is going, it usually starts right where she is. Her associative leaps are shaped by hard line breaks that split noun from adjective, verb or pronoun.

Critics have aligned Levertov with the Black Mountain poets, an American movement of the 1950s that prized pure observation, fluid association and natural diction. While these qualities are all apparent in her work, and are amplified by her empathy for nature, her gentle and oblique approach is of her own making.

Levertov's *Sands of the Well* was published in 1996, and a book of memoirs, *Tesserae: Memories and Suppositions*, in 1997. (See THE SORROW DANCE (1967) and TO STAY ALIVE (1971)).   LG

Levy, Amy 1861–89 Anglo-Jewish poet, novelist and essayist of the 1880s who earned praise from the literati of her day. She grew up in London's middle-class Jewish community, and was the first Jewish woman to matriculate at Cambridge. There she published her first book of poetry, *Xantippe and Other Verse* (1881), which displays a strong feminist sensibility, particularly in the title poem, a dramatic monologue from the viewpoint of Socrates' wife. Levy became friends with several contemporary feminist writers, including CLEMENTINA BLACK and OLIVE SCHREINER. Her second volume, *A Minor Poet and Other Poems* (1884), was followed by short novels: *The Romance of a Shop* (1888) and her best-known work, *Reuben Sachs* (1888), a critical portrait of London's Jewish community. That community largely rejected the novel (Levy depicted London Jews largely as narrow-minded philistines), but it received favourable notices from many reviewers, including Oscar Wilde. She contributed to his magazine *Women's World* and other periodicals. Her final work, *A London Plane-Tree and Other Verse*, appeared posthumously in 1889. Levy apparently suffered from depression for much of her life, which undoubtedly led to her suicide at the age of 27.   KW

Levy, Andrea 1956– British novelist, born in England to Jamaican parents, whose work focuses on the experiences and culture-clashes of Caribbean immigrants and their British-born children. Levy grew up on a council estate in Highbury, north London, an area which combines large, racially mixed estates with leafy enclaves full of writers and intellectuals. Its rougher corners feature heavily in both her novels. A graphic designer, she wrote *Every Light in the House Burnin'* (1994), after attending a creative writing course at the City Lit, London's biggest centre for adult education. It is an affectionate, moving and funny portrayal of a family coping with poverty, racism and, finally,

bereavement. The characterization is sharp, the style punchy and direct, full of warmth and humour and dialogue that echoes Levy's cockney-Caribbean legacy.

In her second novel, *Never Far From Nowhere* (1996), the gentle humour gives way to something much harsher. The characters are less sympathetic and the narrating voices angry and raw. The tale is told by two sisters who have responded to the challenges of their background in different ways. Their interweaving narratives and wildly differing accounts of the same episodes throw up unexpected subtleties and nuances, revealing as much about the painful, messy reality of family life as about the troubling complexities of identity and race.   CP

Levy, Deborah 1959– British writer, widely regarded as one of the country's leading experimental voices. She studied Theatre at Dartington College of Arts and has written two plays, *Pax* (1984) and *Heresies* (1987), praised for their intellectual rigour and poetic fantasy. Her cross-arts background is reflected in the range of her work, which includes opera libretti, film scripts and the poetry collection, *An Amorous Discourse in the Suburbs of Hell* (1990). She was Fellow in Creative Arts at Trinity College Cambridge from 1989 to 1991.

In her collection of short stories, *Ophelia and the Great Idea* (1988), Levy reveals the surrealism, lyric intensity and poetic compression that have become her trademark. Drawing on the textures of contemporary life, it explores different types of border-lines and the collision of diverse worlds. Her preoccupation with the nature of desire and identity continues in her novels *Beautiful Mutants* (1989) and *Swallowing Geography* (1993), which both use fractured narratives and a range of voices to reflect contemporary disintegration. Her fourth novel, *The Unloved* (1994), is more accessible, a disturbing examination of violence and emotional pain in the guise of a highly subversive country-house murder mystery. This theme continues in *Billy and Girl* (1996), which grapples with the universality of pain in a suburban consumer paradise.   CP

Leyel [née Waunton], Hilda (Winifred) 1880–1957 The daughter of a housemaster at Uppingham, Hilda left school early to work in the theatre, where she met and married Carl Frederick Leyel, a Swedish theatrical manager. In the 1920s she began to study the practice of herbal medicine, in particular the work of Nicholas Culpeper, a 17th-century English herbalist. In 1925 she published her first book, *The Gentle Art of Cookery*, written in conjunction with Miss Olga Hartley. Later, she wrote seven books about herbs, which included recipes for such things as vine leaf fritters, green almond tarts and rose petal sandwiches.

The Gentle Art of Cookery is a direct descendant of 17th-century books like *The Closet of the Eminently Learned Sir*

PARTED BY FATE.

A Novel.

BY

LAURA JEAN LIBBEY,

AUTHOR OF "IONE," "A MAD BETROTHAL," "MISS MIDDLE-
TON'S LOVER," ETC.

ILLUSTRATED BY HARRY C. EDWARDS.

NEW YORK:
ROBERT BONNER'S SONS,
PUBLISHERS.

"OH, ULDENE!" SHE CRIED, "HE'S ACTUALLY FOLLOWING US!"
See Page 153.

Laura Jean Libbey: frontispiece ('"Oh, Uldene!" she cried, "He's actually following us!"') and title-page of *Parted by Fate*, 1887.

Kenelme Digby, Knight, Opened. Yet it is at the same time unusually sophisticated with its use of cosmopolitan ingredients like saffron and chick peas, anchovies and rosewater, pistachios and pine kernels, Parmesan and Smyrna figs.

Ever since Stuart times, COOKERY BOOKS had been firmly grounded in common sense and thrifty housekeeping. Suddenly the horizons broadened as Mrs Leyel stimulated and enthused her readers with descriptions of dishes like green pea soufflé, Dover sole sandwiches, nasturtium salad, geranium jelly, damson cheese and ice cream of roses.

She went on to found the Culpeper Shops and the Society of Herbalists, which still exists today as The Herb Society. Her herbals are out of print, alas, but *The Gentle Art of Cookery* has become a classic, thanks in part to ELIZABETH DAVID who wrote the introduction to the 1983 paperback edition. Mrs David had found a kindred spirit, and could not resist an author who wrote, *à propos* cooking fish: 'Life at the bottom of a muddy pond must be dull, yet who would not like to chat with the enormous carp in the pond at Versailles? The famous carp who is older than the French Revolution and comes to the surface . . . only when there is political trouble in Paris'.   AB

Libbey, Laura Jean 1826–1925 American popular novelist. Although close to 15 million of her books sold during her lifetime, little is known about her life. She was born in Brooklyn, New York, and educated privately. When she submitted a short piece to the New York *Ledger* at the age of 14, the editor published it and told her to return when she reached 18. She did, and began regularly contributing serialized stories to the *Ledger* as well as such popular magazines as *Fireside Companion* and *Family Story Paper*. Her serials were collected in inexpensive paperbound editions. In all she wrote over sixty novels, which brought her as much as $50,000 a year. Libbey's specialty was the 'working-girl novel', ROMANCES addressed to an urban and immigrant female readership, with titles like *Leonie Locke: The Romance of a Beautiful New York Working Girl* (1889), *Willful Graynell: Or, The Little Beauty of the Passaic Cotton Mills* (1890) and *Little Leafy, the Cloakmaker's Beautiful Daughter: A Romantic Story of a Lovely Working Girl in the City of New York* (1891). Typically a virtuous young heroine overcomes a genteel seducer and finds deliverance from the daily grind of work by marrying into wealth and respectability. Some novels end with the revelation that the working-class heroine is actually an heiress. Libbey edited *Fashion Bazaar* from 1891 to 1894. She married a lawyer, Van Mater Stillwell, late in her life (1898) and stopped writing. JSG

Life and Death of Harriet Frean, The (1922) In

this tragic tale of denial and self-repression, MAY SINCLAIR finds the space to rework the question of women's subjection that she had previously explored in *Mary Olivier: A Life* (1919). As a woman writer breaking away from the thematic and stylistic conventions of Edwardian fiction and an active suffragette, Sinclair was more than sensitive to women's social realities during the Victorian period. The character of Harriet Frean embodies centuries of female sexual oppression under the weight of provincial morality and Victorian decorum. At a time when to 'behave beautifully' seemed all that was required of women, Sinclair offers her sharp critique of social mores and values by having her protagonist destroyed by her own unfulfilled desires. Short, succinct and intense, the novel sketches effortlessly the suffocating years of Harriet's life. In its final pages, Harriet's realization and final breakdown evoke sympathy as well as terror for the destructive powers of unsatisfied longings. MPe

Life and Loves of a She-Devil, The (1983) FAY

WELDON's savage fantasy was a bruising fictional contribution to the ongoing war of the sexes. Its fiendish picaresque plot charts suburban housewife Ruth Patchett's revenge on her accountant husband, Bobbo, and his lover, romantic novelist Mary Fisher. Hate transforms Ruth from large, clumsy victim to ingenious criminal subversive. Weldon's brisk, didactic NATURALISM here cleverly underpins the overthrow of women's ROMANCE conventions, embodied in Mary Fisher's work and life, by those of demonic GOTHIC, vested in Ruth. The ideology of romantic love is attacked as the thinnest of veils for the subordination and pacification of women. Ruth's entrepreneurial skills and her Frankenstein-ish cosmetic metamorphosis into the image of her female rival (the image of Bobbo's desire) arguably perpetuate capitalist and masculine notions of success and beauty; but if that is the game, the novel proposes, better by far to be a winner than a loser.

Eminently filmable, it was successfully adapted for BBC television in 1986; the 1989 Hollywood version, *She-Devil*, however, lacked the genuine nastiness which distinguishes Weldon's original. MO'D

Life in the Iron-Mills (1861) In this astonishing first

work, REBECCA Harding (later DAVIS) published one of the most challenging stories by any mid 19th-century American writer. Though influenced by STOWE, GASKELL and Dickens, among others, Harding Davis was working out her own innovative mode of apocalyptic REALISM to raise strong feelings about the iniquities of the industrial United States. In a sequence of sketches, a present-day narrator evokes the lives of the factory-hands who used to live in a former tenement house. Having introduced Wolfe, the furnace-tender, and his devoted cousin, Deborah, the embedded story moves to an encounter across the manufacturer/worker divide. During a tour of the iron-mills, a group of variously hard-bitten capitalists and patronizing liberals pause at the fires at the heart of the inferno. In this enigmatic crisis, these gentlemen, and the *Atlantic Monthly*'s genteel readers, are faced by Wolfe's extraordinarily powerful statue of a woman, sculpted from korl, an iron-ore refuse. This haunting image of 'soul-starvation', and the tragedy that ensues from the meeting, encodes reproach and warning. Thirty years on, the statue, now curtained in the narrator's study, still asks desperate questions about the darkness, deformities, and waste of prosperous America. PEK

Lilian's Story (1985) Australian novelist KATE

GRENVILLE's best-known work. Loosely based on the life of Sydney eccentric Bea Miles, the story of Lilian Singer's triumph over stifling bourgeois respectability, sexual stereotyping, paternal bullying, failed romance and committal to an insane asylum is as vivid as its heroine's character. Lilian employs fatness and eccentricity to prevent conscription into a married life as pitiful and empty as her mother's. Her father's extreme attempts to control her through paternal rape and incarceration only confirm Lilian's rebelliousness. Refusing the role of victim, she happily comes to identify with society's outcasts, finding happiness in the arms of an old university flame, F.J. Stroud, wrapped in newspapers in a stormwater drain. Born on 'a wild night in the year of Federation', with a father called Albion (subject of Grenville's 1994 novel *Dark Places*), Lilian's story also invites a metaphorical and POST-COLONIAL reading of Australia's resistance to patriarchal, colonial power. At the individual and national level, here is a rebellious daughter who triumphs over corrupt, bullying age. HTh

Lili'uokalani ('lily of the heavens') (Lydia Kamakaeha) 1838–1917 Last Hawaiian monarch, poet

and DIARIST. She was born in Honolulu, third of four children of the royal couple, and educated by European-American missionaries. In 1862 she married John Owen Dominis, who became governor of Oahu and Maui. She succeeded to the throne in 1891, but when she tried to restore powers to the monarchy in 1893, American businessmen organized to overthrow her. She spent eight months under house arrest in 1894 and in 1896 travelled to Washington, D.C., pursuing

Hawaiian sovereignty. While there she published *Hawaii's Story by Hawaii's Queen* and assembled a song book. She composed over 400 *mele* (songs or poems), including the still-popular 'Aloha'oe,' many for competitions held by singing clubs of the Hawaiian court. She kept extensive diaries in English mixed with Hawaiian poetic allusions, both recording and concealing her thoughts and experiences.   JSG

Lingard, Joan [Amelia] 1933– Scottish novelist whose writing is informed by her passionate belief in tolerance and social justice. She was born in Edinburgh, moved to Belfast at the age of 2, and returned to Edinburgh when she was 18. From 1953 to 1961, she worked as a teacher.

Her early adult fiction (Lingard has also written many novels for younger readers) depicts modern Scottish society and the way in which women are hemmed in by austere conventionality. The female characters in *The Prevailing Wind* (1964), *A Sort of Freedom* (1969) and *The Second Flowering of Emily Mountjoy* (1979) are disappointed by life's limitations, but *The Women's House* (1989) presents a more affirmative view of women's potential.

Lingard writes about displacement and resettlement: 'uprooted people trying to come to terms with their new environment and in so doing they … have to face up to different aspects of themselves … Another theme which fascinates me is the way patterns tend to repeat themselves in life. People usually take the obvious path, do what is expected of them, repeat their mistakes; but some – and these are the ones I am interested in – struggle to break what at times seems to be almost a pre-ordained pattern.'

Both *After Colette* (1993) and *Dreams of Love and Glory* (1995), and her young adult novels *Tug of War* (1990) and *Between Two Worlds* (1991), show Lingard operating on a grander scale. These later novels re-inforce the connection between history and its effects on individuals, and elevate Lingard's work into a broader, international sphere.   JH

Linton, Eliza Lynn 1822–98 A pioneering female journalist who paradoxically became a leading opponent of women's emancipation. Self-educated, she rebelled against her conservative background and moved to London in 1845, becoming one of the earliest women to support herself as a journalist and publishing carefully-researched HISTORICAL ROMANCES, *Azeth the Egyptian* (1847) and *Amymone* (1848). In her radical and agnostic *Realities* (1851), she attacks the sexual double standard. At this time she and poet Walter Savage Landor developed a very close father–daughter friendship. In 1858 she married William James Linton, a writer and Chartist republican with seven children, but the marriage ended amicably in 1867. Linton is most famous for her articles in the *Saturday Review* in 1868, which lambasted 'The Girl of the Period' and 'The Shrieking Sisterhood' for their unwomanly athletic and professional aspirations. These vitriolic depictions cased a great furore and were later republished in THE GIRL OF THE PERIOD (1883). In *The Autobiography of Christopher Kirkland* (1885) Linton wrote a thinly disguised autobiography with a male persona. Many of her later novels work through her conflicted religious feelings. *The True History of Joshua Davidson, Christian and Communist* (1872) is a biography of a Christlike figure. Other novels include *Patricia Kemball* (1874), *The Atonement of Leam Dundas* (1876), *Under Which Lord?* (1879). While her novels are largely propagandistic outlets for her religious or gender beliefs, her journalism is still powerful. Linton remains a fascinating figure, a woman whose furiously reactionary politics contradict the ground-breaking achievements of her career.   TS

Lion's Bride, The (1981) GWEN HARWOOD's third collection of verse is her most significant single volume. As early as 1964, soon after the publication of her first book, she wrote to her friend Tony Riddell about her pressing need to find new ways of writing. She was dissatisfied with the elaborate metaphorical and syntactic textures of her published work to date; partly influenced by the new directions in Australian musical composition, she began to experiment with simpler language and freer metrical and syntactical structures. Some familiar Harwood themes are here – the pain of absence, the restorative power of memory and music, the indivisibility of matter and spirit, the power of language to create at least the semblance of order; but there is a new voice to be heard, one characterized by dazzlingly witty juxtapositions of thought and feeling within individual poems. There is a new personal note, a confidence in drawing upon her own experience of the dailiness of life; several of the poems are addressed to particular friends. Here, too, are some of Harwood's finest celebrations of sexual love. She was fond of quoting Vincent Buckley's 'The personal word must speak or sing for all'; in this volume it does.   GKr

Lions in the Way (1956) By Canadian ANNE WILKINSON, this is a history of her mother's family, from early 19th-century Cornwall to 1933. It is assembled from letters and journals and from published accounts of Featherstone Osler, lawyer and judge; Britton Bath Osler, lawyer; Sir William Osler, physician and professor of medicine; and Sir Edmund Boyd Osler, financier and member of parliament. The narrative contains a vivid account of pioneer hardships as Featherstone Osler Senior served the church as pastor for 200 miles of Ontario bush, and saw not only to the building of his own house, but also to the establishment of a number of churches and church schools. In the letters of Ellen Free Picton Osler, wife to Featherstone, mother of nine, and grandmother and great-grandmother to more than forty others, details of domestic life are interwoven with vignettes of religious and political tension in colonial Ontario. Wilkinson obviously delights in the development of the Oslers from 'Tecumseh Cabbages' to courtly, erudite and cultivated family men. She concludes with a personal memoir of the last days of Sir Edmund, her grandfather, who called Winston Churchill 'that young pup' for his bad manners as house guest.   FD

Lisle [Grenville Basset], Honor, Viscountess

*c.*1493–5 – 1566 Letter-writer Honor Lisle was the second wife of Viscount Lisle, who was Lord Deputy of Calais from 1533 to 1540. Although Honor is at the hub of the mass of correspondence edited as the *Lisle Letters* (1981), only forty-one of her own letters, all dictated, survive.

Nevertheless, the correspondence gives a detailed picture of the activities of a Tudor noblewoman. The letters show Honor screening petitioners to her husband, managing her own West Country estates, prescribing medicine, exchanging gifts and arranging the education of her many children and stepchildren. Personal, political and business matters are not readily separable: Honor called on an extensive network of relatives and allies in her successful campaign to get her daughter an advantageous place in the Queen's household.

Honor's style as a writer was direct and flexible. She was businesslike to Thomas Cromwell, flirtatious to Archdeacon Thirlby, and courteous to those whose help she needed. Letters to the children tend to be limited to admonitions to be good, and the supply of smocks and hose, but her letters to Lord Lisle, her 'sweet heart', are tender and trusting: 'my heart is so heavy . . . which I know well will never be lightened till I be with you'.   MSALS

Lispector, Clarice

1920–77 Brazilian writer, best known in Europe for HÉLÈNE CIXOUS's assimilation of her writing to 'écriture feminine'. The elder of her two sisters also became a well-known novelist. Her Jewish parents emigrated in her infancy from the Ukraine to north-eastern Brazil, where her father worked as a farm labourer, then as a sales representative. The family, now motherless, moved south to Rio de Janeiro in 1937. By 1944 she graduated in legal studies, married and published her first novel, NEAR TO THE WILD HEART (1944). After years in Europe and the USA with her diplomat husband and two sons, she divorced and returned to live in Rio from 1959, latterly under the military dictatorship (1964–79). She wrote novels, stories, translations and a newspaper column.

Clarice (as she was known in Brazil) attempted to write encounters with the flesh and fabric of the world. *The Passion According to G.H.* (1964) and *Agua Viva* (1973) explore experiences of a sculptor and painter, who turn to writing. Translators confess to turning her experiments with the limits of Portuguese into exposition. She wrote in fragments and disliked structuring them. Writing to the moment, she also had a strong sense of evolution, and sacrifices made between human and animal, even inorganic, being. She shares with VIRGINIA WOOLF an image of fishing for reality, between the lines: 'The word fishes for something that is not a word. And when that non-word takes the bait, something has been written' (*Agua Viva*).

Encountering 'Clarice' could begin with short stories (*Family Ties*, 1960, *The Foreign Legion*, 1964). Associations are often made with existentialism or Catholic mysticism. Until *The Hour of the Star* (1977) she avoided the socio-political explicitness of other Brazilian fiction, mainly addressing the alienation of middle-class women, but then, dying of cancer, unfolds 'in a state of emergency and public calamity' the story of an immigrant to Rio from the north-east, whose consciousness she can barely imagine, employing a male narrator because as a woman she would weep. 'She Doesn't Know How To Protest' was one of thirteen possible titles. Lispector envisioned transformations between delight and disgust, terror and quietness; and what it might be like to be the smallest woman or the strangest man.   EJ

Little Disturbances of Man, The

(1959) One of the main threads running through GRACE PALEY's collection of short stories is the celebration of the everyday lives of ordinary people. Paley's women are independent, often having been abandoned by their husbands after, if not because of, childbearing. Nevertheless, these women accept the challenge of their difficult situations and, like the strong-minded single women in these stories, actively explore their sexuality and willingly surrender themselves to new relationships. Paley dons a male voice for three stories in this collection in which she addresses the crisis of social and personal relationships through a masculine point of view. Paley's unaffected, pacifist men are ideally suited to exploitation, either by a relentlessly unforgiving society or by selfish and determined women. The tragic situations in the lives of the characters become tragi-comic through Paley's skilful manipulation of perspective. While her style exemplifies typical, wry Jewish humour, her eclectic fusion of the extraordinary with the conventional allows her to explore human relationships at their most vulnerable moments.   JAHa

Little Tales of Misogyny

(1975) PATRICIA HIGHSMITH's second collection of short stories exploits stereotypes of femininity for a malevolently clever portrayal of human nature. In these seventeen stories Highsmith shrugs off feminist expectations as well as a more literal misogynist intent: in this respect the title is mischievously misleading and confirms in the reader the kind of guilty, manipulated sympathy that made her Ripley novels so disturbing. Although some tales specifically ridicule the absurdities of clichés ('The Hand' or 'The Fully-Licenced Whore, or, The Wife'), we recognize these types as disconcertingly real. But, as usual, Highsmith is not interested in any moralistic or ideologically tinged stance: she kills off guiltlessly where others theorize. Her murdered women and victimized men (and vice versa) are less the result of the incompatibility of males and females than of a beguiling consequentiality of injustice. Highsmith's style is most sardonic in the introductory vignettes; the later tales lead on to the acrimonious picture of parochial American neuroses and Reaganite paranoia she would draw in the eighties.   PUR

Little Women (1868) LOUISA MAY ALCOTT's best-known work for children is a highly autobiographical exploration of the coming-of-age of a family of sisters during the American Civil War. The March girls – Meg, Jo (the feisty stand-in for the author), Beth and Amy – face poverty, illness and their own failings; Alcott works out their trials, Jo's in particular, through a parallel with Bunyan's *Pilgrim's Progress*. Although the Alcotts' reformist political bent and their frequently turbulent home life are downplayed in the novel, *Little Women* scorns social conformity and encourages independence and self-reliance for women, showing Jo's often-thwarted attempts to earn money through her 'scribbling'. Alcott's writing was also directed at supporting her family, and *Little Women* brought financial comfort. The novel was immediately followed by a sequel, GOOD WIVES, which is now frequently appended to *Little Women* as a second volume. The novel has retained its popularity, and has been made into successful films, notably in 1933 with the young Katharine Hepburn as Jo, and in 1995 by director Gillian Armstrong with a strong feminist slant.   KW

Lively, Penelope 1933– English writer of precisely observed, quietly witty social fictions about middle-class characters struggling to integrate memory and the past into their lives. She keeps the brash materialism of modern-day Britain at arm's length. Her nostalgic vision of life was shaped by growing up in a war-time Cairo of 'pink gins and . . . white-gowned servants'. After going to boarding school in Sussex and taking a degree in Modern History at Oxford in 1956, she married in 1957 and had two children. Between 1970 and 1976 she published eleven highly acclaimed NOVELS FOR CHILDREN – some of which were also

published on adult lists – and presented a BBC radio programme on children's literature. In 1977 *The Road to Lichfield*, her first novel for adults, was shortlisted for the Booker Prize. Like Lively's children's fiction, it addresses the disruptive and ultimately renewing effect of memory and history on the present. She makes sly observations of class, manners and social environment, capturing the nuances of Englishness. Her backward-looking characters are treated with mild irony. As the narrator of *Going Back* (1975) says, 'What you know happened isn't always what you remember.' In her Booker-Prize-winning MOON TIGER (1987), a subtle dissonance is created between the story a dying historian tells herself about the past and the story the reader perceives. *Treasures of Time* (1979) and *According to Mark* (1984) are about an archaeologist and a biographer respectively, whose researches make them re-evaluate the present, but for whom personal change is tinged with resignation. Her characters' behaviour in crisis is either moderately nasty or modestly brave. Her understated view of life is shown in her novel about a middle-aged widow painfully coming to terms with life after her husband's death, wryly entitled *Perfect Happiness* (1983). Thoughtful, well-made and well-mannered, Lively's work is in the tradition of the English social novel she so admires.   KE

Lives of Girls and Women (1971) ALICE MUNRO's first novel has also been considered a series of interrelated stories. It is a female BILDUNGSROMAN which tells the story of Del Jordan, a girl desperate to escape from Jubilee, her small hometown, and its stifling, conservative sense of femininity. The novel explores the mother–daughter relationship, sexuality and growing up in a style that reflects optimism as much as disappointment. Munro's working title was *Real Life*, but her final title, taken from a chapter heading, reflects more accurately the novel's emphasis on the ways that femaleness and identity entwine in different ways for different women. Del's quest for freedom is juxtaposed with tales of women who willingly chose captivity in the domestic space, or who find that despite their best efforts, the domestic space consumes them. Del's escape is effected through education and sexuality, and through her struggles, she comes to understand, if not always accept, the forces that shape the lives of the women around her.   HSM

Livesay, Dorothy (Kathleen May) 1909–96 Canadian poet, political activist and feminist. She was born in Winnipeg, the older daughter of Florence (Randal) Livesay, a poet and journalist, and John Frederick Bligh Livesay, a journalist who became the general manager of the Canadian Press. The family moved to Toronto in 1920 and she attended Toronto schools, the University of Toronto and the Sorbonne.

During the Depression she was active in the Communist party and did social work. In 1936 she moved to Vancouver, married and raised two children. Widowed in 1960, she did a three-year teaching stint in Zambia.

Encouraged by her mother, Livesay published poetry as a teenager and brought out her first collection, *Green Pitcher*, when she was 19. She continued to publish over the years, winning a Governor General's Award in 1940 for *Day and Night*, and another in 1947 for *Poems for People*. Her return from Africa in 1963 coincided with an outburst of poetic activity in Vancouver. Energized by that and by the growing Women's Movement, she was able to unite her political and personal concerns to produce her strongest poetry. She wrote frankly about her sexuality as an older woman, her relationship with a young lover and about the same-sex relationships she had experienced in her youth and returned to later. *The Unquiet Bed* (1967) and five later collections consolidated her reputation as 'the uninhibited champion of female sexual experience'. *Collected Poems: The Two Seasons* appeared in 1972 and *Selected Poems: The Self-Completing Tree* in 1986. She also wrote a three-part autobiography. This consisted of *Beginnings* (1986), a short-story collection designated as 'essentially autobiographical'; RIGHT HAND, LEFT HAND (1977), a memoir of the 1930s; and *Journey With My Selves* (1991).

When she died in Victoria at 87 she was mourned as a revered foremother and hero to a younger generation of women poets, many of whom she had mentored and encouraged.   JG

Living in the Maniototo (1979) JANET FRAME's most self-consciously POSTMODERN fiction playfully thematizes the writer who seeks renewed communion with her imaginative powers, figured as Living in the Maniototo – a little-known plain in the South Island. In a 'replicating' and triangular infrastructure of doubles and triples (mad twins; four guests; three narrative 'voices'; three settings in Baltimore, Berkeley and Blenheim in New Zealand), Frame exploits a postmodern aesthetic in order to satirize commodity fetishism. As her literary heroine, Mavis Barwell Halleton, transforms her guests into 'characters' in a 'fiction', she turns an autobiographical TRAVEL NARRATIVE into a depiction of the erased creator, who becomes a reflex of her fictional world. But this metafictional bubble in turn collapses toward realism, as the internal struggle to discover an original in a world of replicas subsides. This complex parody of the art of writing – Frame's manifesto about the prerogatives of the imagination – progressively enlarges the powers of the author, while distancing them from the site of her own subjectivity.
                                                JMW

Living My Life (1931) EMMA GOLDMAN's autobiography describes her struggles and triumphs as a Russian Jew who emigrated to the USA, becoming the most prominent speaker in the anarchist movement of the early 20th century. Goldman's narrative opens with her arrival in New York City at the age of 20, having escaped first the violent, impoverished life of her parents in Russia, and second the confinement of her life in Rochester, New York where she had worked in a clothing factory, and had been briefly married. Once involved in the anarchist movement, she travelled through America and Europe, advocating economic and sexual equality. Told with the passion and vivid detail that characterized her public speaking, her book recounts her involvement in the central political events of her day, including the assassination attempts on industrialist Henry Clay Frick and President McKinley, the Haymarket riots and the London general strike, as well as her personal struggle to establish an intimate partnership with men, free from the constraints of marriage and motherhood.   RL

Livingstone, Dinah 1940– British poet, novelist and translator, born in Tokyo where her father worked in the British Embassy. Livingstone was 2 when her family moved to Britain following the Japanese attack on Pearl Harbour. She was brought up in Somerset and lives in Camden Town where she runs a poetry performance group. Livingstone is a prolific poet, her reputation linked to London poetry circles. Her début came in 1969 with *Tohu Bohu*. Between that and the publication of *May Day* in 1997 she published numerous collections, novels and translations. A selected poems, *Keeping Heart*, came out in 1989. This edition makes a useful digest of what Livingstone does well – anatomization of marriage, love-affairs, children, Camden Town and the poet's eccentricities. It avoids the uneven quality of her individual collections in which her verbal liveliness is undermined by political didacticism.   DM

Llewellyn, Kate 1940– Poet and novelist born and educated in South Australia, and has lived in adult life in Adelaide, Sydney, the Blue Mountains and the South Coast of New South Wales. Llewellyn's literary output has been prodigious: *Trader Kate and the Elephants* (1982), which won the Anne Elder Award, was followed by *Luxury* (1985), *Honey* (1988), *Figs* (1990), *Selected Poems* (1992) and *Crosshatched* (1994). She has also published a number of prose volumes, including *The Waterlily* (1987), *Dear You* (1988) and *The Mountain* (1989), which together make up the 'Blue Mountains Trilogy', an extended DIARY- and letter-based autobiographical work which, like all Llewellyn's writing, is rich in its treatment of the difficulties and complexities of love – for both families and lovers – and of the pleasures of the body and domestic life, with GARDENING a particular focus. Llewellyn has also produced an extensive body of TRAVEL WRITING, including two full-length volumes, *Lilies, Feathers and Frangipani* (1993, on New Zealand) and *Angels and Dark Madonnas* (1991, on India and Italy); a large number of essays, some collected into *The Floral Mother and Other Essays* (1995); and has made a very significant contribution to the documentation of Australian women's writing through her involvement in the 'Sisters Poets' series, and her collaboration with SUSAN HAMPTON to produce the *Penguin Book of Australian Women Poets* (1986). MLA

Lochhead, Liz (Elizabeth Anne) 1947– Scottish

poet, playwright and performer. She was born in Motherwell – and has described her upbringing as 'sort of Protestant ... posh working class'. Having studied at the Glasgow School of Art, she worked as a teacher for eight years. During this time, however, she was producing increasingly successful poetry – and became a full-time writer in 1978.

While often textually complex and subtle, her work is not intended to sit sedately on the page. It is not just her plays that are written for performance: her poems also have a striking dramatic quality. In fact, this poetry often pushes at the limits of genre, presenting as recitations, songs or cabaret acts. Lochhead asserts that her inspiration derives less from 'serious Literature' than from '"blood and guts" ballads ... vernacular narratives ... rude and unrespectable rhymes, the "oral tradition"'. This is a far cry from traditionally 'poetic' and 'personal' first-person lyricism. As a versatile performer with many different voices, she cautions, 'I'm not nearly as autobiographical as people think. It's a lot of fiction, personae, personifying.'

A great deal of her work is concerned with reinterpreting familiar narratives from feminist and Scottish perspectives. Her work includes a Scots version of Molière's *Tartuffe* (1986) and volumes entitled *The Grimm Sisters* (1981) and *Dreaming Frankenstein* (1984). As one of her speakers declares:

I am (beauty and the beast) at my business
of putting new twists
to old stories. AFT

Locke [Lok, née Vaughan], Anne 1533?–95? Likely

author of the first English sonnet sequence, also the first in any language by a woman. A Calvinist, she left England for Geneva with her two small children in 1557. She translated *Sermons of John Calvin upon the Song that Ezechias made after he was sick* in 1559 (published 1560). The dedicatory epistle to Katharine Bertie, Duchess of Suffolk, is an accomplished piece of devotional prose. The volume ends with twenty-six sonnets entitled *A Meditation of a Penitent Sinner*.

The first five sonnets are headed 'The preface'; the ensuing twenty-one are meditations on the 51st Psalm, with translated psalm verses printed alongside. The poems show knowledge of Sir Thomas Wyatt's Penitential Psalms, while using the sonnet form of the Earl of Surrey. They show remarkable technical skill: the first two sonnets are one continuous sentence.

Locke corresponded with John Knox, to whom the sonnets have sometimes been attributed. She translated John Taffin's *Of the Marks of the Children of God* (1590), and wrote Italian verses alongside some in Greek by her second husband, Sir Edward Dering. Her son Henry Lok wrote poetry including devotional sonnets. The philosopher John Locke descended from the same family. HH

Locke [née Farrelly], Elsie (Violet) 1912– Editor,

author, activist. A third-generation New Zealander, the youngest of six children, who worked her way through the University of Auckland, gaining a BA in 1933 and a Distinguished Alumna Award in 1997. In her *Student at the Gates* (1981) she records her personal reminiscences of the turbulent years of the 1930s. As the slump deepened, she joined the New Zealand Communist party, becoming editor of the *Working Woman* in Wellington. Her severance from the party is explained in her essay 'Looking for Answers' (published in *Landfall* in 1958), which won the Katherine Mansfield Award.

In 1941 she married fellow activist Jack Locke and moved to Christchurch, looking after their four children until they were independent enough for her to put time aside for writing. Unashamedly regionalist, she appreciates both the privilege and the responsibility of being able to write for children, publishing junior fiction and non-fiction stories in the New Zealand *School Journal* from 1959 and producing her first book, *The Runaway Settlers*, in 1965. Set in the mid 19th century, it conjures up vivid pictures of life in those isolated colonies. The book is now considered a New Zealand children's classic; it was translated into four languages and re-issued in 1971. Since that first success she has published some thirty CHILDREN'S BOOKS noted for their strong New Zealand tone, fine characterization, authenticity of detail, scrupulousness of research and strong sympathy for the underdog.

A passionate moral concern for justice and peace informs her life and work. A member of the New Zealand Campaign for Nuclear Disarmament, she published *Peace People: A History of Peace Activities in New Zealand* in 1992. In 1995 she presented the Margaret Mahy Award Lecture. In 1987, the University of Canterbury (New Zealand) conferred on her an Honorary Doctorate of Literature in recognition of her work as a writer and historian. REn

Logan, Deborah [Norris] 1761–1839 American diarist. Daughter of Charles Logan and Mary Parker Norris, Deborah was born into one of the foremost Quaker families of Philadelphia. By her marriage to Dr George Logan, she became a member of a second prominent Quaker family. Formally educated by the noted Quaker teacher, Anthony Benezet, she also had an extended family who taught her the classics and the art of conversation. After her marriage, Deborah Norris Logan and her husband attracted some of the best minds of the new republic to their home at 'Stenton'. Conscious that some of these people and conversations ought to be remembered and that her family and friends had many historical documents in their private libraries, Deborah Logan began her diary in 1815 and continued it until her death in 1839. In the beginning, she included anecdotes about famous people whom she knew and copied many letters of historical significance. As her love of 'scribbling' took over, she added her own memories of her relatives and friends and the domestic events of her daily life, so that the accumulated diary reveals a picture of elite society in Philadelphia when that city was a significant hub of political and literary activity. She did not publish the diary, which came to seventeen volumes, but gave it to the Historical Society of Pennsylvania. Besides the DIARIES, Deborah Logan wrote a memoir of her husband, which was not published in her lifetime.   CLB

Lohrey, Amanda 1947– Australian novelist, born in Hobart, Tasmania, where she lives with her politician husband; Lohrey grew up near the waterfront where her father, uncle and grandfather were waterside workers. The family's strong union affiliation and working-class Labour politics are a major influence in Lohrey's life and fiction. Her second novel, *The Reading Group* (1988), presents a dystopian vision of a bleak political state in which Australian pragmatism has led to insidious authoritarianism and a social structure sharply divided between those with power and privilege and those with none. It was the subject of a libel action by a Tasmanian senator on publication.

Lohrey's sophisticated understanding of the ineradicable correspondence between personal and public politics is central to all her work. Reminiscent of Huxley's or Orwell's political satires, *The Reading Group* is more menacing for being set in the present. Her first novel, *The Morality of Gentlemen* (1984), is a fictionalized account of an actual industrial waterfront dispute of the 1950s. In it, Lohrey conveys a sense of a range of social and political positions through her use of rapidly switching narrative perspectives and voices. Lohrey is always preoccupied by the question of how to find a fictional form to express the intersecting political structures that construct social, personal and psychic lives. Her award-winning novel, *Camille's Bread*

(1996), presents its exploration of family relationships and power structures using dual, feminine and masculine, narrative voices.   DB

Lolly Willowes: Or The Loving Huntsman (1926) SYLVIA TOWNSEND WARNER's first novel is an alternative 'fantastic' female BILDUNGSROMAN that celebrates individuality and independence. Her middle-aged spinster-heroine Laura Willowes follows a mysterious longing: she settles in a village in the Chilterns to enter a pact with a very sympathetic devil and becomes a witch. The issues of contemporary female life Warner explores (the necessity of economic independence, the burden of familial demands, or the anxiety about female education) link this narrative to VIRGINIA WOOLF's *A ROOM OF ONE'S OWN* (1929). Warner's narratological trademark is already fully developed in *Lolly Willowes*: the novel touches upon an array of potential leitmotivs and genres without settling for any. It lampoons urban modernity with a more traditional pastoral, but it also links the medieval trope of the witch to the post-war spectre of the surplus woman, and reinterprets the myth of 'feminine evil'. The supernatural motifs could be uncanny but in fact make for a wicked whimsical humour characteristic of most of Warner's prose.

John Ireland composed a sonatina based on the witches' Sabbath in *Lolly Willowes* in 1928.   PUR

Lonely Girl, The (1962) This second novel of EDNA O'BRIEN's 'COUNTRY GIRLS' trilogy follows the progress of Caithleen, who having moved from the sodden dark of the Irish countryside to Dublin, has the ill-luck to meet the man of her dreams – an Englishman, a film maker, an atheist, whom she hopes will provide the rarefied protected life which will save her from the drunken violence of her father's house. The book's gloom is relieved initially by some humorous anecdotes of batchelor-girl life, but slides inexorably through the idyllic beginnings of her relationship toward the long and intractable end. O'Brien describes Caithleen as the victim of two patriarchal systems, one home-grown and Catholic, another 'foreign' and godless, and slowly unravels the painful process whereby a young woman becomes less appealing to her older lover. When she finally loses her will to please, she is shut out entirely, and loses everything, even her son. The message seems not 'stick to your own kind' but rather 'you may not have a kind'.   STS

Loos, Anita 1893–1981 American novelist, screenwriter. Born in Mount Shasta, California, Anita was a child actress in her father's amateur stock company, when, bored with the shows, she drafted a script for D.W. Griffith's company, Biograph. *The New York Hat* starred Lillian and Dorothy Gish, Mary Pickford and

Lionel Barrymore. In the years from 1912 to 1915, she wrote over 100 scripts for Griffith, most of them either romantic melodramas or slapstick comedies. In 1919, she married the producer–director John Emerson, with whom she collaborated on scripts for several more years. In 1925, she published her best-known work, GENTLEMEN PREFER BLONDES, sub-titled 'The Illuminating Diary of a Professional Lady'. The novel, conceived to caricature a blonde with whom H.L. Mencken was infatuated, so entertained the editor of *Harper's Bazaar* that the book was serialized there, and praised by James Joyce, William Faulkner and EDITH WHARTON, who called it '*the* great American novel'. Its gold-digging heroine, Lorelei Lee, exemplifies the excesses of the Jazz Age as well as the rags-to-riches story, perhaps most famously in her claim 'Kissing your hand may make you feel very good but a diamond bracelet lasts forever.' Loos followed with the sequel *But Gentlemen Marry Brunettes* (1928). She went on to make *Blondes* into a musical (1949) and a film (1953). When she and her husband lost their money in the 1929 stock market crash, she returned to Hollywood to write for MGM. Among her other works are the scripts *Red-Headed Woman* (1932), *San Francisco* (1936) and *The Women* (1939), and the plays *Happy Birthday* (1946) and *Gigi* (1951). In her later life, she wrote two memoirs, *A Girl Like I* (1972) and *Kiss Hollywood Good-bye* (1974), full of gossipy details about her meteoric rise in Hollywood and the antics of the celebrities she knew.

SP

Lord, Gabrielle 1946– One of Australia's most successful writers of crime and psychological thrillers, and film and television scripts in the same genre. Born and educated in Sydney, Lord began writing full-time in the late seventies. *Fortress* (1980) was based on a real-life hostage incident, and was followed by *Tooth and Claw* (1983), *Jumbo* (1986), *Salt* (1990), *Whipping Boy* (1992), *Bones* (1995) and *The Sharp End* (1998). Though she has written a number of short stories and essays, these remain uncollected, and her reputation is based firmly on her fast-paced and well-plotted novels. *Whipping Boy*, a shocking and violent tale of paedophilia and power, was made into a successful television drama in 1996. The vulnerability of children to the cruelties of the adult world is a continuing theme in her novels, with several of her memorable characters – including the tenuously married Harry and Meg Doyle of *The Sharp End* – responsible both for allowing their own absorption with adult concerns to blind them to the dangers their children face, and for the ultimate salvation of those children through determined parental love.

MLA

Lorde, Audre 1934–92 Black American lesbian feminist poet and theorist whose influence reaches far beyond the contexts in which she lived and worked. Her parents were from Grenada, but she was born in Harlem and spent much of her life in New York working as an academic and writer-in-residence, only moving to the Virgin Islands to renew her fight against the cancers that eventually caused her death. Her reflections on the early stages of that struggle are recorded in THE CANCER JOURNALS (1980).

Much of her polemical writing was concerned with the vexed and vexing nexus of black/white/lesbian/straight/feminist writing and politics. Her most well-known essays are published in the collection *Sister/Outsider* (1984), including the famous 'Poetry is Not a Luxury', in which she stated that poetry, for women 'is a vital necessity of our existence. It forms the quality of the light within which we predicate our hopes and dreams toward survival and change first made into language, then into idea, then into more tangible action.' She both supported and challenged other feminist writers: in 1974 she accepted the American National Book Award with ADRIENNE RICH and ALICE WALKER, and in *Sister/Outsider* she addressed an open letter to MARY DALY, critiquing the Eurocentric perspective of Daly's *Gyn/Ecology*.

She published an autobiographical – or 'biomythographical' – novel, *Zami: A New Spelling of My Name* (1982), which details her experience of coming out and living as a lesbian in 1950s New York, while confronting central questions regarding black lesbian identity and the reclamation of black histories and mythologies.

Her early poetry appeared under the pseudonym 'Rey Domini', but the collections were published in her own name. From *First Cities* (1968) through *Cables to Rage* (1970), *Coal* (1976), *Between Our Selves* (1976) and *The Black Unicorn* (1978), Lorde wrote passionately about sexuality and race. In the title poem from *Coal* she wrote 'I am Black because I come from the earth's inside / now take my word for jewel in the open light', and this sense of discovery and recovery may be seen in her most tender work, such as 'Hanging Fire' from *The Black Unicorn* where a 14-year-old girl wonders 'will I live long enough / to grow up' while 'momma's in the bedroom / with the door closed'. *Chosen Poems* (1982), *Our Dead Behind Us: Poems* (1986) and her last collection, *Undersong: Chosen Poems Old and New* (1992), became more elegiac, not because she mourned her own death but rather expressing the sorrows and strength of her African and Caribbean heritage.

RW

Lost Father, The (1988) In her third novel, which follows three generations of one Italian family, recreating early 20th-century Italy in all its political turmoil, MARINA WARNER mythologizes Davide, a figure from the family history of her narrator Anna. Warner presents material from Anna's 1980s manuscript about her grandfather Davide's life, called 'The Duel', entries from Davide's diaries, and contemporary newspaper articles. The narrative follows his family's optimistic emigration to America and disillusioned return to Italy. Warner gradually reveals the circumstances of the mysterious Duel, encouraging the reader to accept Anna's version of events. Her writing almost complete, Anna discovers evidence which casts doubt on the accepted family interpretation of the most significant event in their lost father's life; it may change their view of him. The family, Anna and the reader must decide whether Davide was wounded by his best friend in a duel about his sister's honour, or injured in a revolutionary skirmish. When Anna's mother says she no longer knows where Anna's book ends and her life begins, she voices Warner's questions about myth, interpretation and reality.   MET

Lothrop, Harriet 1844–1924 American author of CHILDREN'S BOOKS. Born in New Haven, Connecticut, to a wealthy family, Harriet was educated at private schools and raised with a strict religious ethos. In 1878, writing under the pseudonym 'Margaret Sidney', she published her first story in *Wide Awake*. The story was immediately popular and she was commissioned to write twelve more instalments. In 1881, these stories became the bestseller, *Five Little Peppers and How They Grew*. Set in a little brown cottage which it was always Harriet's fantasy to occupy, the book follows the adventures of the impoverished Pepper children and their overworked mother. The tone is decidedly earnest and moralistic, with the children cheerfully facing constant hardship, helping each other and their mother, and showing satisfaction with the little they have. Harriet's work attracted the attention of publisher Daniel Lothrop, whom she married in 1881. The following year, Lothrop bought her the Concord, Massachusetts, house 'Wayside', which had previously been owned by Hawthorne and also by the Alcotts. Their daughter Margaret was born in 1885. Although Harriet wrote ten additional 'Pepper' books, as well as several HISTORICAL NOVELS, none attained the success of the first book, which had sold over 2 million copies at her death.   SP

Love in a Cold Climate (1949) NANCY MITFORD's fifth novel, like those which precede it, perversely derives some of its extravagantly comic caricatures from real-life models. Based on gossip passed on to Mitford by her friend Christopher Sykes, the novel recounts the love-affair between a beautiful aristocrat and her mother's lover, who, in turn, runs off with the mother's heir. The mother in question is based on Mitford's mother-in-law, Lady Rennell, while narcissistic, homosexual Stephen Tennant provides the original for Cedric Hampton. Like *The Pursuit of Love* (1945),

the story is narrated by Fanny Logan, whose own colourlessness throws these caricatures into relief, just as her conventional marriage foregrounds far less orthodox couplings in the unexpectedly conducive 'cold climate' of England. Camp intertextuality pervades: 'highbrow' VIRGINIA WOOLF becomes a society writer, headlines from the *Daily Express* ('Man's long agony in a lift-shaft') provide 'shame-making' hilarity for both characters and readers, and the tone and subject matter of the novel clearly owe much to the Oxford comedies of Evelyn Waugh and Max Beerbohm.   MM

Love Letters between a Nobleman and his Sister (1684–7) APHRA BEHN's first work of fiction depicts the real story of Lord Grey of Werke, a member of the Whig nobility who had married one of Lord Berkeley's daughters, but eloped with another, Lady Henrietta Berkeley. Although this EPISTOLARY NOVEL embraces romance and pastoral conventions, it clearly precedes 18th-century 'histories' and presents an intricate narrative structure and complex characterization of the protagonists. Philander (Lord Grey) seduces the innocent Sylvia (Lady Henrietta) and abducts her to France. Ruined and expelled from polite society, forcibly married to another man, Sylvia turns into a pugnacious and materialistic woman whose behaviour challenges the authority of the men who surround her. Despite the displacement of the plot to France, Behn weaves real-life events, people and issues into the story and overtly comments on contemporary English political life. Her main reference is the unsuccessful attempt by the Duke of Monmouth (Cesario in the novel) to overthrow James II, in which Lord Grey of Werke was actively involved.   NBP

Love Poems and Revolutionary Actions (1988) With this book BOBBI SYKES announced that she was not only an Aboriginal activist, but also a poet. The book was first published in 1979 by a collective before being taken up by University of Queensland Press. Sykes's poetry is clear and straightforward, often rhyming or breaking into chants. But, as Mudrooroo commented in his foreword to her second book of poetry, *Eclipse* (1996), it is 'mercifully free from the reliance on the ballad structure we find in other black poetry'. Sykes writes about black deaths in custody and the continuing poverty of Aboriginal families, but she also addresses the more divisive issues in the black community – such as the mistreatment of Aboriginal women by black men, and the ongoing disputes about who has the right to speak on behalf of the black community. Her poetry appears to come from personal experiences, such as those she has documented in two volumes of autobiography, *Snake Dreaming: Autobiography of a Black Woman* (1997) and *Snake Dancing* (1998).   SPL

Lovers' Vows (1798) MRS [ELIZABETH] INCHBALD adapted and translated this ripe melodrama for the Covent Garden Theatre (with many refinements and alterations) from the German text by Kotzebue, originally entitled *Das Kind der Liebe*. The story concerns the emotional reunion of Frederick (the 'love-child' of the original title) with his wronged mother, Agatha, and eventually with his natural father, the Baron Wildenhaim, and ends happily. After much tearful overflowing, the parents are reunited with each other and their son, and the legitimate sister, Amelia, is paired at last with the chaplain, Anhalt, whom she loves, and released from her arranged engagement to Count Cassel. The play is chiefly remembered for its importance to the story of JANE AUSTEN's novel *MANSFIELD PARK* (1814), where it becomes the controversial focus for some highly charged erotic exchanges between members of the Bertram family and their friends. Frequently reprinted, the play had great vogue in its day and Austen assumes a familiarity with it on the part of her readers, who would have appreciated the irony of the inverted parallels between the *Lovers' Vows* plot and that of *Mansfield Park*.   JLB

Lowell, Amy Lawrence 1874–1925 American poet, critic and BIOGRAPHER. She was born in Brookline, Massachusetts, to a prominent New England family, and raised on a large estate. She had eight years of education in private schools, then occupied herself with society life, travel and volunteer work. She wrote her first book, a collection of FAIRY STORIES, with her mother at the age of 13 to raise money for charity. In 1902, inspired by seeing a performance by Eleonora Duse, she began writing poetry; her first publications appeared in *Atlantic Monthly* in 1910. In 1912 she met actress Ada Dwyer Russell, with whom she formed a literary and domestic partnership that lasted until Lowell's death. Her first book of poems, *A Dome of Many-Coloured Glass* (1912), was derivative of Keats, but reading H. D.'s imagist work in HARRIET MONROE's *Poetry: A Magazine of Verse* inspired her to experiment. During trips to England in 1913 and 1914, she met H.D., Ezra Pound, J.G. Fletcher, and other literary figures who helped induct her into the Imagist movement. Lowell defined the poetics of imagism as 'precision of language, clearness of vision, concentration of thought' expressed through a 'dominant image'. Although Pound later broke from the movement and disparaged Lowell's popularizations of imagism, he at first embraced her work, publishing a poem of hers in *Des Imagistes* (1914). Fletcher praised her work in a special issue of the *Egoist* on imagism (1915). Lowell edited three imagist anthologies (1915–17). She published regularly in *Poetry* and other periodicals. Her later poems are collected in *Sword Blades and Poppy Seed* (1914), *Men, Women and Ghosts* (1916), *Can*

Grande's Castle (1918), *Pictures of the Floating World* (1919), *Legends* (1921) and *What's O Clock* (1925) which won a Pulitzer Prize, and posthumous collections, *East Wind* (1926), *Ballads for Sale* (1927) and *Complete Poetical Works* (1955). She also wrote influential books of criticism, *Six French Poets: Studies in Contemporary Literature* (1915) and *Tendencies in Modern American Poetry* (1917), and a biography of Keats (1925).   JSG

Lowther, Pat 1935–75 Author of four volumes of poetry and active promoter of poetry in Canada. The child of working-class, socialist activist parents, she lived all her life in Vancouver, British Columbia, reading and writing poetry from the age of 4 and winning a poetry competition at 10. By the age of 16, she had left school for a job as a keypunch operator, and began a lifetime concern with poetry and its connection with politics. She was divorced from her first husband and lived as a single mother in her parents' basement; she remarried, had two further children, and lived in poverty with her second husband (a teacher, fired for radical politics) until he murdered her. At the time of her death she was co-chair of The League of Canadian Poets which commemorates her with an annual prize. Her poetry breaks taboos ('How can I begin? / So many skins / of silence upon me'), gives stark definition to experience ('Thirty summers rock me / on my knees / blinded with migraine'), and confronts humdrum suffering ('I dream / of being stoned to death / and am resurrected / pulling thistles'). In the seventies, it was her frank treatment of sexuality that captured the critics' attention. She is now remembered more for her personal courage and dedication. A last collection, *A STONE DIARY*, was published posthumously in 1977.   FD

Loy, Mina [Mina Gertrude Lowy] 1882–1966 British poet and painter who experimented with poetic structure under the influences of futurist painting and literature. Born into a conservative middle-class family, Loy rebelled against their Victorian values and social prejudices, a struggle recorded in the long poem, *Anglo-Mongrels and the Rose* (1923–5). She studied in Munich, London and Paris while pursuing a career as a painter and began writing and publishing free-verse poetry after meeting with Italian futurists in Florence. Embracing their vitality and experimentation but rejecting their misogyny, Loy's early work is characterized by verbal compression, use of collage and montage techniques, typographical fragmentation, and frank treatment of female sexuality and oppression. Her later work, although less experimental in form and diction, continued these themes and explored the lives of the destitute.

Often grouped with American MODERNISTS, Loy published her work in American little magazines alongside that of Eliot, Moore, Williams and Stevens in the years 1914–25. *LUNAR BAEDECKER* (*sic*) (1923) selects the poetry she wrote as a member of the New York avant-garde. Although she was highly praised by Pound and Williams, her work fell into obscurity after 1925, due, in part, to her own indifference to publication; it was 're-discovered' in the 1940s by Kenneth Rexroth. His enthusiasm led to the publication of *Lunar Baedeker and Time Tables* (1958) by Jonathan Williams, to whom Loy wrote, 'Why do you waste your time on these thoughts of mine – I was never a poet?': a statement subsequently refuted by poets and literary scholars. *The Last Lunar Baedeker* (1982) and *The Lost Lunar Baedeker* (1996) collect the bulk of Loy's published and unpublished work.   MCJ

Lucky Chance, The (1686) This play by APHRA BEHN centres on sexual property relations and female subjectivity, and combines a number of complicated plots. Two of these centre on young men whose mistresses have fallen into the clutches of wealthy dotards, displaying the common Restoration concern of the differences between old lovers and young husbands. In the first plot, Bellmour has been forced to flee the country after killing a man in a duel, leaving behind his betrothed, Leticia. Gulled by Sir Feeble Fainwou'd into believing Bellmour is dead, Leticia consents to marry him, but is saved on her wedding day by the arrival of a disguised Bellmour. The second plot concerns the rake, Gayman, who loves Lady Julia Fulbank, but in pursuit of her has wasted his estates and become heavily indebted to her husband, Sir Cautious. At the end of the play, the old men lose out to the younger generation as Fainwou'd has to give up Leticia to Bellmour and Sir Cautious, having lost heavily at cards, consents to compound his losses by resigning Julia to Gayman.   RDM

Lucy (1991) A semi-autobiographical novel, this 'portrait of an artist as a young woman' both simplifies and complicates JAMAICA KINCAID's earlier works. The protagonist, Lucy (named after Lucifer and only revealed in full – Lucy Josephine Potter – at the end of the book), leaves her Caribbean home to work as a nanny in New York, only to discover that the imperial centre is not the new and exciting Eden she had hoped. A stranger in a strange land, she is caught between two 'worlds': her island home governed by a mother she wishes to forget, and her employer's family whose own collapse symbolizes a contemporary decline of the West. This is a novel which politicizes the many complexities of the POST-COLONIAL encounter from the position of the West Indian woman. Constantly aware of the difficulties of leaving the past behind, Kincaid offers a new model of female migrancy which begins to 'see the sameness in things that appeared to be different'.   MRE

Luhan, Mabel (Ganson) Dodge 1879–1962 Luhan, whose *Intimate Memories* (1933–7) constitute one of the key documents in the history of American women, was no feminist nor an advocate of causes. She was an aesthete, a society lady who believed in the perfection of the life, and her considerable skills in self-analysis were aimed toward an ideal of aesthetic fulfilment summed up in a phrase given to her by a schoolgirl friend: 'la grande vie intérieure.' All else – from an unhappy childhood in a wealthy 'society' family in Buffalo, a marriage to a dilettante architect, an affair with the radical writer John Reed, her famous salon at her home at 23 Fifth Avenue, and then escape from New York to Taos, New Mexico, in 1918 – meant little, save what each contributed to the making of a rich, cultivated inner life. *Movers and Shakers* (1936), the third volume of her memoirs, is the best of the many accounts of the Armory Show and the Paterson Strike Pageant of 1913. 'I was going to dynamite New York and nothing would stop me', she wrote. Her salon, created with the help of Lincoln Steffens, brought high art, radical politics and money together. Nonetheless, for a woman of her class to live openly with Reed while still married to Edwin Dodge was a shocking break with Victorian codes of behaviour. After Luhan, New York was never quite so conventional a city. *Lorenzo in Taos* (1932) was an account of D.H. Lawrence's final days in Taos.   EH

Lumley [née Fitzalan], Lady Jane 1535/7–76 Author of the first known translation of a Greek play into English. Daughter of Henry Fitzalan, twelfth Earl of Arundel, and cousin to LADY JANE GREY, she was educated in Greek and Latin, and had recourse to her father's extensive library, later inherited by her husband, John, Baron Lumley, whom she married in 1549 or 1550. A manuscript in her autograph in the British Library contains her translations of Isocrates from Greek into Latin, along with Latin epistles to her father, and *The Tragedie of Euripides called Iphigeneia*, probably written some time after 1553. Lady Lumley may have used Erasmus's Latin translation, which was certainly in her library, as a guide. Her *Iphigeneia*, however, is an adaptation rather than a literal translation, in which she methodically abridges the original, omitting the choral odes, and focuses on the themes of female knowledge and heroism.

Euripides' tragedy concerns the sacrifice of Iphigeneia by her father, Agamemnon, to raise a wind to sail to Troy; this plot Agamemnon covers with the story of an arranged marriage between Iphigeneia and Achilles. The text Lumley chooses is thus one in which the equation of arranged marriage with sacrificial murder is implicit, and in which the denial of knowledge to its female characters is prominent. The story of a father's exploitation of his daughter to further his own political agenda also finds a resonance in Lumley's background – her own father was involved in the rise and fall of Lady Jane Grey in 1553–4 and, later, in the Ridolfi plot to marry MARY, QUEEN OF SCOTS to Norfolk – although the precise date of her translation is unknown. Lumley's rendition focuses on Iphigeneia's intelligence as central to her heroism, adding references to her delighting her father with her 'wit' and to the 'stoutness of her mind'. By emphasizing the gender-specificity of the predicaments of her female characters, she underlines the social circumscriptions governing what women may say, do and know.   JC

Lunar Baedecker (sic) (1923) The first of only two collections of MINA LOY's poetry published in her lifetime. Issued by Robert McAlmon's Contact Press along with GERTRUDE STEIN's *THE MAKING OF AMERICANS*, this collection consolidated Loy's position as a MODERNIST poetic innovator. Divided into two sections, the poems (as the title poem 'Lunar Baedecker' exemplifies) chart Loy's ambivalent participation in the avant-garde – as woman and mother, and as a modernist writer. 'Poems 1921–1922' includes considerations of her contemporaries ('Joyce's Ulysses', 'Brancusi's Golden Bird', '"The Starry Sky" of Wyndham Lewis'), while 'Crab Angel' and an early version of 'English Rose', the second poem in her major sequence *Anglo-Mongrels and the Rose* (1923–5), confront simplistic notions of gender identity. 'Poems 1914–1915' presents versions of thirteen of her *Love Songs to Joannes* and other futurist/feminist poetry such as the satirical portrait of F.T. Marinetti ('Sketch of a Man on a Platform'), and the ground-breaking representation of childbirth, 'Parturition'. All these poems demonstrate the linguistic, typographical and thematic challenge that Loy's work poses to mainstream literary history.   AG

Lunn [née Swoboda], Janet 1928– Canadian author of children's and young adults' literature. Born in Dallas, Lunn grew up in New England and has lived in Canada since 1946. Her fiction is characterized by her interest in Canadian and American history, particularly during the 19th century, and by her skill in weaving past and present into a compelling narrative. Her first novel *Double Spell* (published in the United States as *Twin Spell*) uses the discovery of an antique doll as a means of transporting twin girls back into an earlier era of Toronto. *The Root Cellar* moves from the present to the period just after the American Civil War in Washington, D.C., and *Shadow in Hawthorn Bay* describes a woman's journey in the early 19th century from Scotland to Canada. She has also written short stories, stories for picture books and, in collaboration with Christopher Moore, the text for an illustrated history of Canada. Lunn's work has received numerous awards. She is regarded as a leading authority on CHILDREN'S LITERATURE and has written and lectured extensively on the subject.   JG

Lurie, Alison 1926– American novelist, born in Illinois but brought up in New York and educated at Radcliffe College. She has received Guggenheim and Rockefeller Awards and taught Children's Literature at Cornell University since 1968. As well as several non-fiction books, including *The Language of Clothes* (1982) and *Clever Gretchen and other Forgotten Folktales* (1991), she has published eight novels, serious comedies or satires on contemporary American life, which often combine an exaggerated description and elaborate metaphor – and sometimes magic – with close observation and shrewd social analysis. Her books often make use of representative dichotomies: a marriage and a love-affair in *Love and Friendship* (1962); East Coast and West Coast in *Nowhere City* (1965); sociology and religion in *IMAGINARY FRIENDS* (1967); male and female views of society in *THE WAR BETWEEN THE TATES* (1974), which presents a cleverly worked out, large-scale analogy between the war in Vietnam, campus disturbances and the battle of the sexes. *Foreign Affairs*, which won the Pulitzer Prize in 1985 and which contains portraits of figures in literary London, some of whom appear as themselves, some as fictitious characters, looks at the differences between Britain and the United States. In addition to panoramic views, her work features a number of characters who go from novel to novel to give an impression of development – and for her comic version of Yaddo Writers' Colony, *REAL PEOPLE* (1970), she provides a sumptuous afterlife for Undine Moffat, a character from EDITH WHARTON. Her mockery of feminism in her novel about a woman painter and her biographer, *The Truth about Lorin Jones* (1988), meant that, although the book was well received in England, it attracted hostile criticism in the United States.

Lurie is a dry and sophisticated writer and a self-consciously worldly person who spends much of her time exploring the different atmospheres of London, where she has many friends, New York and Key West.   LD

Lyall, Edna (Ellen Ada Bayly) 1857–1903 British novelist and feminist. Born in Brighton the daughter of a barrister, she wrote under the pseudonym of 'Edna Lyall', a partial anagram of her real name. In 1886 she announced her identity in response to a claim by an impostor to be Edna Lyall, and a rumour that the novelist was in a lunatic asylum: she later published an account of the incident, *The Autobiography of a Slander*, in 1887.

Her first story, called *Won by Waiting*, the story of a girl's life, was written in 1879 when she was 22: it was poorly received, but her subsequent stories went into many editions. *Donovan*, a three-volume novel written in 1882, was admired by W. E. Gladstone, but it was *We Two* which established her reputation as an author.

She was a woman of determined character and a strong supporter of political causes, such as women's emancipation. She also supported the radical politician and atheist, Charles Bradlaugh, although she herself was deeply religious. Her writing was clear and constructive, her characterization dextrous. She championed the cause of Home Rule for Ireland, and in her last novel, *The Hinderers* of 1902, she expressed her opposition to the Boer War.   MEW

Lyndsay, David see DODS, MARY DIANA

Lyssiotis, Tes ?– Tes Lyssiotis is the most prolific bilingual Australian dramatist. While her plays are predominantly in English, her use of Greek in the text contributes to the poetic and lyrical sound of the beautifully written dialogue. Lyssiotis is a Melbourne-born Greek-Australian who, like Aboriginal playwrights – such as Eva Johnson, author of *Murras* (1988) – and other Australian writers from a wide range of cultural backgrounds, writes about characters who identify with and/or inhabit more than one culture. Lyssiotis's work is both contributing to the recognition of bilingual drama and creating precedents for this emerging genre.

Her first play, *I'll Go To Australia and Wear A Hat* (1982), was followed by nine more including the monodrama, *A White Sports Coat* (1988). *The Forty Lounge Café* (1990) charts Eleftheria's experience from her childhood years when her widowed mother sends her to a Greek orphanage, to an arranged marriage and life as a Greek migrant wife and mother in small-town Australia working in the family café. The all-female cast of characters depict both the pain and the fun of Eleftheria's life. This play, like its sequel *Blood Moon* (1993), depicting four sisters who meet in Greece to divide up their dead mother's property, raises questions about how gender identity and cultural geographies disengage from place and a sense of belonging.   PT

Lytton, Constance 1869–1923 British suffragette, autobiographer, and daughter of the viceroy of India,

the Earl of Lytton, whose family seat was Knebworth House, Hertfordshire, Lady Constance rebelled against the privileges of her class by identifying with the poor and oppressed. In 1908, a chance meeting with Annie Kenney persuaded her to join the Women's Social and Political Union.

Her militancy, imprisonment and hunger striking is recorded in her autobiography *Prisons and Prisoners* (1914), where she describes how the prison authorities refused to force-feed her, knowing that she was a member of the aristocracy. Later, while at Walton Prison, she disguised herself as a working woman using the alias 'Jane Warton', which ensured that she was treated like any other suffragette prisoner. The ordeal ruined her health and contributed towards her subsequent partial paralysis. As part of her campaign for women's suffrage (see SUFFRAGETTE LITERATURE), she published the pamphlet 'No Votes for Women' in 1909, wrote newspaper articles and delivered impassioned speeches.   MM-R

Lytton, Rosina Bulwer, Baroness 1802–82 English novelist whose spirited *romans à clef* excoriated Victorian double standards. Daughter of feminist ANNA WHEELER, she grew up in Ireland, Guernsey, and a London circle which included CAROLINE LAMB and LETITIA LANDON. She wrote her first novel, *Cheveley* (1839), after separating from her abusive husband, Edward Bulwer [Lytton]; fierce and funny, it protests against the powerlessness of women and mercilessly lampoons Bulwer and his set. *Budget of the Bubble [sc. Bulwer] Family* (1840), dedicated to FRANCES TROLLOPE, established a life-long pattern of accusation followed by Bulwer's retaliation. She survived poverty, ostracism, threats and separation from her children, to publish a dozen similar novels, including the autobiographical *Miriam Sedley* (1851) and *Very Successful!* (1856), subverting the image of the famous man. FLORA TRISTAN and GEORGE SAND admired her writing, and Anthony Trollope put her situation into *He Knew He Was Right* (1869). After 1858, when Lytton temporarily committed her to a lunatic asylum, she published little under her own name. Her autobiography, *A Blighted Life* (1880), is detailed, indignant and convincing.   MSM

M

Macardle, Dorothy 1899–1958 Irish historian, novelist and dramatist, a prominent activist in the struggle for independence and an initially influential member of Fianna Fáil, the political party which dominated southern Irish politics for much of the 20th century. Macardle was typical of the middle-class intellectual women who were important organizers and publicists in nationalist movements before and during the Irish War of Independence, but who turned their energies to cultural production when the independent state proved inimical to political women. Her first collection of short stories, *Earthbound* (1924), was written in prison. A powerful propagandist against the 1922 treaty, her best-known work, *The Irish Republic* (1937), was one of the most influential 20th-century works of Irish history. Her fiction tends to be set outside Ireland and to deal, often through the medium of sensational or supernatural tales, with issues suppressed in her public support for the southern Irish state. *Uneasy Freehold* (1942, published in the USA and filmed as *The Uninvited*) is a ghost story – a young woman is haunted by the evil, cold spirit of the conventionally 'good' woman who raised her, and protected by the nurturing spirit of her wild and socially ostracized natural mother. *Fantastic Summer* (1946) examines the way in which an Italian woman who fought alongside local partisans during World War II becomes feared and hated as a witch thereafter. A number of Macardle's plays were performed in the Abbey Theatre, most notably *Ann Kavanagh* (1937). GMe

Macarthur [née Veale], Elizabeth 1766–1850 Australia's First Lady, Elizabeth emigrated from rural Devon to the British penal colony at Sydney Cove, aged 22, on board the *Neptune*, part of the notorious Second Fleet. Her voyage-journal recounts the horrors experienced during her confinement alongside her co-passengers, those 'monstrous' female convicts, whilst her letters, covering a sixty-year period, mainly to friends and family 'back home', offer a unique insight into colonial culture from the perspective of an educated woman. In 1794, her husband, John Macarthur (empire-builder and colonial 'perturbator'), established his pastoralist power-base at 'Elizabeth Farm', Parramatta, only to be (twice) exiled for twelve years. During this time Elizabeth successfully managed the family's extensive farming and business affairs, including John's merino wool industry. Ever the capable pioneering wife and mother, Elizabeth's social responsibilities included the preservation of her family's exclusive status, particularly during the pro-Emancipist period of her later years, and the successful integration of her children into Australian society. She was never seriously tempted to return to England. Her remarkable life marks the formation of a 'transplanted' Anglo-Australian lady, from the close of the Enlightenment period to the end of the transportation era. MRE

Macaulay Graham [née Sawbridge], Catherine 1731–91 Whig historian, political theorist and educationalist. She was born in Olantigh, a parish of Wye near Kent, the second daughter and youngest of four children, to John Sawbridge, a Kentish landowner, and Elizabeth Wanley, heiress of a London banker, and educated privately at home by a governess. In 1760 she married Dr George Macaulay, a Scottish physician who was in charge of a London lying-in hospital. He died in 1766 leaving her one daughter, Catherine Sophia. Prior to his death, she began writing her most famous work, *The History of England from the Accession of James I to that of the Brunswick Line* (1763–83), a political history of the 17th century which came out in eight volumes over a period of twenty years. It was the first republican history based on an exclusive knowledge of hitherto unused tracts from the 1640s and 1650s and provided an alternative to Hume's Tory *History of England*. While many commentators such as Horace Walpole and Thomas Gray praised her history, her reputation was marred by rumours about her private life. Forced by ill health to leave London in 1774, she had moved to Bath, where the Revd Thomas Wilson, an admirer of her work, invited her to share his residence, Alfred House. He adopted her daughter and made extravagant preparations for her 46th birthday celebrations in 1777. The following year she married 21-year-old William Graham, younger brother of the well-known 'quack-doctor' Dr James Graham, and was publicly ridiculed in the popular press. Yet she continued to write, publishing works on Hobbes, copyright, another history, and theology and ethics (*A Treatise on the Immutability of Moral Truth*, 1783). She wrote replies to Burke on two occasions. In *Letters on Education with Observations on*

Religious and Metaphysical Subjects (1790) she covered issues such as capital punishment, prison reform, slavery and the treatment of animals as well as educational matters, and greatly influenced MARY WOLLSTONECRAFT. She won great acclaim in both France and America for her contribution to republican politics, but in England her reputation was more controversial. PJW

Macaulay, (Emilie) Rose, Dame 1881–1958 English novelist, travel writer and essayist. Born in Rugby the daughter of Anglo-Catholic parents, Macaulay spent part of her childhood in Italy, which began a life-long love of travel and of Mediterranean societies. On her return to England, she was educated at Oxford High School for Girls and Somerville College, Oxford. A highly prolific writer, Macaulay worked in several different genres and styles. Her first novel, *Abbot's Verney*, appeared in 1906, but it was with her witty and satirical novels of the 1920s that she really began to earn widespread recognition. In particular, *Potterism* (1920), which satirized popular culture and thought, as represented by a press magnate and his novelist wife, *Dangerous Ages* (1921), which targeted psychoanalysis, and the Utopian saga *Orphan Island* (1924), drew praise.

During a period in which her novels were less well received, Macaulay turned to journalism and, in particular, TRAVEL WRITING, at which she was highly successful. Her travel books include *They Went to Portugal* (1946), *Fabled Shore* (1949) and *Pleasures of Ruins* (1953). After a ten-year break from fiction writing, Macaulay returned triumphantly with two final novels, the texture of her writing deeply altered by personal loss – the bombing of her London flat, and the death in 1942 of her long-term lover, the married former priest Gerald O'Donovan: the end of a relationship which caused her estrangement from the Church. *The World My Wilderness* (1950), the story of a rebellious adolescent girl who has been involved with the French *maquis*, is a compelling exploration of civilization and chaos. THE TOWERS OF TREBIZOND (1956), a mixture of the high comedy revolving around an Anglo-Catholic missionary party and the pain and guilt of religious commitment, is probably Macaulay's finest novel. She was made a Dame in 1958, shortly before her death. AC

McBreen, Joan 1946– Irish poet, born in Sligo, who lives in Tuam, County Galway, where she has raised a family of six children. She worked as a teacher for many years and was slow to look for publication for her work. Her first collection, *The Wind Beyond the Wall* (1990) was simultaneously published in Ireland and in America where it won the Nicholas Roerich Poetry Prize. Her second collection, *A Walled Garden in Moylough* (1995), was also well received. These two collections represent an exploration of the inner and emotional life of an individual, a strong sense of place and a heightened sense of the ordinary. Together they record a journey of discovery. McBreen uses vivid, evocative imagery and a strong lyric voice in representations of epiphanic moments and the complexities of human existence. In 'Christmas Eve', McBreen writes of how, even in the most heightened moments of communal and social activity, the poet is apart:

> I will still be searching
> for new words
> to believe again in
> the reason for it all.

An active member of the Galway Writers' Workshop, McBreen has compiled a bibliographical dictionary of the work of contemporary Irish women poets. LM

McCafferty, Nell 1944– Irish feminist journalist and campaigner, well known for her wit and passion. She was born in Derry and gained a BA from Queen's University, Belfast, before travelling in Europe and the Middle East. Returning to Derry in 1968 she was involved in the Civil Rights movement but moved to Dublin to work on the *Irish Times* in 1970. Her journalism is collected in *The Best of Nell: A Selection of Writings over 14 Years* (1983) and *Goodnight Sisters: Selected Writings Volume Two* (1987), gathered from Irish newspapers including the *Sunday News* and *Irish Press*, together with magazines such as *In Dublin*, *Kerry's Eye* and *Magill*. *The Best of Nell* was a bestseller in Ireland, as was *A Woman to Blame: The Kerry Babies Case* (1985).

Much of her writing reflects on 'the gulf between the lip service – paid by priest, politician and lay fundamentalist to their own notion of womanhood – and the reality of women's lives'. More recent elements of her work touch a lighter vein; she reported from Italy on the 1990 World Cup for the Pat Kenny Show on Radio Telefis Eireann Radio 1, memorably articulating Ireland's love-affair with its football team. RW

McCaffrey, Anne (Inez) 1926– American writer of SCIENCE-FICTION heavily incorporating fantasy elements. McCaffrey trained as an operatic singer, but abandoned her career on discovering that her voice was a character soprano rather than a lyric one; this is perhaps relevant to the constant presence in her work of Ugly Duckling figures. Her best-known work is the 'Pern' series of novels, starting with *Dragonflight* in 1968. They deal with a lost colony of human beings who have reverted to a medieval culture, and with a caste who ride and bond with semi-intelligent dragons; the purpose of this caste has been forgotten and is crucial to continued survival. The popularity of the early books in this series has proliferated endless sequels and prequels; many of these have lost the toughness of the first stories and replaced it with sentimentality and repetitive plot devices like abduction and misunderstanding. The same is true of the collaborative sequels to McCaffrey's tales of a cyborg spaceship *The Ship Who Sang* (1969). She is, however, one of the most popular writers in the field.   RK

McCarthy, Charlotte fl. 1745–67 Irish poet and religious controversialist. Nothing is known of McCarthy's background, except that she described her father as a gentleman, and spent several years in London, before publishing *The Fair Moralist, or Love and Virtue* in 1745. This was a prose account of Melissa's progress toward 'the welcome chains of matrimony', and also included a number of poems. The first edition, by 'a gentlewoman' was followed by a second edition under her own name in the following year, with added poems and an essay of moral and social advice to women.

McCarthy's *News from Parnassus, or Political Advice from the Nine Muses* made her a target of criticism and even, she claimed, of a Jesuit assassination plot. She described these trials in *The Author and Bookseller* (1765). In 1767 she published *Justice and Reason, Faithful Guides to Truth*, which she dedicated to George III, and in which she showed sympathy toward Catholics, but hostility to Methodists. The volume also includes anecdotes, letters and poems. Under the pseudonym 'Prudentia Homespun', she also produced a *Letter to the Bishop of London* (c.1767), in which she discussed women's poverty, morality and religion.   RR

McCarthy, Mary (Therese) 1912–89 North American journalist and novelist, active in the Left-wing politics of a loosely-affiliated group of 1930s New York writers and intellectuals whose public voice was *Partisan Review*. Born in Seattle, she was at Vassar with MURIEL RUKEYSER and ELIZABETH BISHOP, graduated in 1933 and married an actor, who introduced her to New York communist social circles. In 1938 she married Edmund Wilson, another member of the group. Her first novel, *The Company She Keeps* (1942), is a series of semi-autobiographical portraits, satirizing the mores of a young woman and the New York communist circles in which she moves. Her second novel, *The Oasis* (1949), was published in Britain as *Source of Embarrassment* (1950), and details the trials of a group of utopian socialists who are divided between idealism and realism, representing the split in American Marxism over America's entry into World War II. Unlike many of her peers she resisted the deradicalizing effects of the Cold War and McCarthyism on the American Left and her political writings reflect her continuing engagement with contemporary issues: these include *On The Contrary: Articles of Belief 1946–1961* (1961), *Vietnam* (1967), *Hanoi* (1968) and *The Mask of State: Watergate Portraits* (1975).

MEMORIES OF A CATHOLIC GIRLHOOD (1957) is explicitly autobiographical, detailing her childhood and adolescence, but as with her novels the narrative works to problematize the clear division between history and fiction, self-consciously examining the unreliability of memory as a documentary source. In the foreword to her first novel she noted that, regarding the identity of the narrative voice, 'the search is not conclusive: there is no deciding which of these personalities is the "real" one; the home address of the self, like that of the soul, is not to be found in the book'.

Her most celebrated work is undoubtedly THE GROUP (1963), a bestselling novel in which she returned to Vassar, following a group of female friends from their graduation in 1933, through subsequent confrontations with motherhood, psychoanalysis and Left-wing politics in New York. As in *The Oasis*, the tension between idealism and material reality is a central theme. In its concern with politics and femininity *The Group* may be read as a precursor to MARILYN FRENCH's THE WOMEN'S ROOM (1977) and was made into a film directed by Sidney Lumet in 1966.

Her fictional oeuvre also includes *The Groves of Academe* (1952), *A Charmed Life* (1955), BIRDS OF AMERICA (1971), CANNIBALS AND MISSIONARIES (1980) and the collection of short stories, *Cast a Cold Eye* (1952). She continued to write for *Partisan Review* through to the 1980s, having been nominally appointed editor of the drama review section at the magazine's relaunch in 1937.   RW

McCracken, Esther (née Esther Helen Armstrong) 1902–71 English dramatist educated at Central Newcastle High School, McCracken began her working life as an actress for the Newcastle-upon-Tyne Repertory Company, later playing roles in London productions of her own plays. Her second play, *Quiet Wedding* (1938), ran for over 200 performances, and brought her to London; her fifth, *Quiet Week-end* (1941), ran for more than 1,000 performances. A number of her plays were made into films, the best-known being *No Medals* (1944), given the ironic film title of *The Weaker Sex* (1948), which dealt with the 'unsung heroines of the home' during war time. Here McCracken explored once more the domestic environment and focused specifically on the relationship between women and the social structure. Accused of being an amateur because she talked about writing with a note pad on her knee in the kitchen while everyday life went on around her, McCracken had a flair for kindly caricatures of middle-class life, showing the absurdity beneath the seeming cosy normality. She succeeded DODIE SMITH as the leading commercial woman playwright of the late 1930s and 1940s.   MBG

McCrae, Georgiana 1804–90 Australian DIARIST and artist best known for *Georgiana's Journal* (1934), a selection of her journals from 1838 to 1865, edited by her grandson, the poet Hugh McCrae. Born in London, the natural daughter of George, fifth Duke of Gordon, she was trained as a portrait painter. In 1830 she married lawyer Andrew McCrae and followed him to Victoria in 1841, where they lived in Melbourne and later on various country properties. Though her husband refused to allow her to pursue her profession, she found an outlet for some of her creativity in her journals which give a lively, insider's account of life in early Melbourne's highest social circles. On 2 March 1843, for example, she recorded seeing a Mr and Mrs Pohlman riding by: 'Mr Pohlman, well-macassared, managing a leather hat-box (perhaps the receptacle of madame's best *cheveux*!). Mr McLure amused us by remarking: "What an attentive *son* she has!"' Her journals are currently being re-edited to restore much material omitted or rewritten by Hugh McCrae. EW

McCullers, Carson [Lula Carson Smith] 1917–67

American writer whose lyrical, evocatively titled fictions, set in imaginative versions of her native South, explore dreaming, wandering, isolation and love. Aspiring to be a concert pianist, and encouraged by her mother, she left Georgia for New York City in 1934 to study music – always important in her writings. Without money, taking casual jobs, she joined writing classes, publishing 'Wunderkind' in 1936. Concentrating on a young girl's feelings for music she cannot perform, this powerful story of frustrated expression set the note for Carson's subsequent writings.

Having married Reeves McCullers in 1937, she immersed herself in THE HEART IS A LONELY HUNTER (1940), published when she was 23. A formal *tour de force,* this narrative of solitary souls, desperate to communicate, aimed, Carson wrote, at 'a feeling of balanced completion' and won appreciative reviews. The violence and sexual intensities of REFLECTIONS IN A GOLDEN EYE (1941) were felt unacceptably disturbing, but the controlled unfolding of the tragic love-triangle in 'The Ballad of the Sad Café' (1943), and of Frankie's dreams in THE MEMBER OF THE WEDDING (novel, 1946; play, 1951) earned Carson lasting critical regard. Her innovative forms, her haunting prose, her reconfigurations of gender and sexuality, her focus on the intense inner lives of the odd and lonely, continue to fascinate readers.

Her work articulated Americans' 'longing and unrest' ('Look Homeward, Americans', 1940), a need to lose a 'sense of separateness' ('Loneliness . . . An American Malady', 1949). Divorcing and remarrying McCullers (who committed suicide in 1953), she was involved in complicated emotional and sexual liaisons with men and women, and in friendships with MURIEL RUKEYSER, Tennessee Williams,

ELIZABETH BOWEN and others, moving frequently between writers' colonies and temporary homes in the USA and Europe. Suffering various maladies from childhood, after 1941 her illnesses intensified, and though she completed *Clock Without Hands* (1960), her last years were devastated by pain. She died in 1967 in a coma following a brain haemorrhage. PEK

McCullough, Colleen 1937–

Born in Wellington, New South Wales, and later a resident of Norfolk Island, she is generally regarded as Australia's most respected ROMANCE writer, although she herself disputes this categorization of her work. Her second novel, *The Thorn Birds* (1977), established McCullough's reputation and became an international bestseller. This historical fiction focuses on the Clearys, a family of Irish Catholics who languish in poverty in New Zealand but then become neo-colonial aristocrats on a property in western New South Wales. The popularity of the novel is in part due to its sensationalist plot, which focuses on an affair between a young woman and a Catholic priest, and also due to the ways it draws on the classic tradition of Australian outback or bush literature and realizes immigrant fantasies about fabulous prosperity achieved through hard work on the land. The novel, in its celebration of Irish Catholic settlement in Australia, allows no place for the Aboriginal inhabitants nor the diverse origins of Australian immigration. Critics have observed that other Australian family sagas by RUTH PARK and NANCY CATO are more aware of these social and political complexities.

A later novel, *The Ladies of Missalonghi* (1987), became notorious through allegations of plagiarism based on striking textual similarities to L. M. MONTGOMERY's *The Blue Castle* (1926). Canadian readers and critics in particular have resented what they see as the recycling of Montgomery's romance. But the resemblances may well be due to generic similarities arising from the master plot of popular romance.

More recently McCullough has been absorbed in producing a series of HISTORICAL NOVELS based on the Roman empire, beginning with *The First Man in Rome*. For her research on these fictions, McCullough has been recognized as a scholar of antiquity. GWh

McDermid, Val 1955–

British crime writer whose stylish and shocking thrillers are characterized by realism of setting. McDermid grew up in a Scottish mining community and read English at Oxford University. From 1975 she worked for regional south-eastern newspapers, the *Scottish Daily Record* and Manchester *People*, and held several posts in the National Union of Journalists. She achieved a certain notoriety by introducing Lindsay Gordon, arguably the first lesbian private eye, in *Report for Murder* (1987). A second series, starring private investigator Kate Brannigan, began with *Dead Beat* (1992), while *The Mermaids Singing* (1995) won the Crime Writers' Association Gold Dagger for its serial-killer plot featuring clinical psychologist Tony Hill. In her depiction of the male-dominated worlds of the police, journalism and private investigation, McDermid highlights the impediments prejudice presents to the truth. Also the author of a study of female private detectives, *A Suitable Job for a Woman* (1995), McDermid is based in Manchester. *The Wire in the Blood* (1997) again places Tony Hill and the new techniques of criminal profiling to the fore, taking her brand of DETECTIVE FICTION far from the gentle traditions of classic crime, and into the problematic realm of urban violence.   CS

MacDonald, Ann-Marie 1959– Canadian actor, playwright, television writer and novelist, whose family roots are in Cape Breton Island, Nova Scotia, MacDonald was born on a Canadian Air Force base in West Germany, has lived in Ottawa and Montreal, and currently lives in Toronto. She graduated from the National Theatre School of Canada (1980) and has performed in various films: *Island Love Song* (CBC, 1987), *I Heard the Mermaids Singing* (1987) and *Where the Spirit Lives* (CBC-TV, 1990, Gemini Award), as well as in Toronto theatre. Involved in feminist fringe theatre, she worked on collective creations such as *Smoke Damage* (1985), *This is for you, Anna* (1985) – which won the Dora nomination for theatrical innovation – and *Clue in the Fast Lane*, co-written and co-performed with Beverly Cooper. Her play, *Goodnight Desdemona (Good Morning, Juliet)* (1990) written in blank verse, toured Canada the same year and has had over fifty productions worldwide. It won the Chalmers Canadian Play Award, a Governor General's Award and the Canadian Authors' Association Award, all in 1990. In 1995 she wrote the play, *The Arab's Mouth*, which won the Dora nomination for best new play. Her first novel, *Fall on your Knees*, won her the Giller Prize and the Commonwealth Writers Best First Book Prize in 1997. The novel traces the lives of four generations of a half-Lebanese half-Scottish family in New Waterford, Cape Breton Island. It has a compelling plot, its characterization and sense of place are riveting, and the narrative voice is fresh and clear.   GHN

McDowell, Katherine Sherwood Bonner 1849–83 American novelist and short-story writer. Born in Holly Springs, Mississippi, to an Irish immigrant doctor and a southern society belle, Katherine was educated at a private school in Alabama. During the Civil War, she saw the deaths of her mother and sister, and lived through the occupation of her town and her own house by Union soldiers. Editor Nahum Capen published her first story in 1864, written under her pseudonym 'Sherwood Bonner', and was enthusiastic about her depictions of local characters and vernacular. In 1871, she married Edward McDowell and had a child, but two years later she separated from McDowell, left her daughter with relatives, and moved to Boston. Capen introduced her to Longfellow, for whom she worked as a secretary. During her travels around Europe, she wrote several articles for American journals, and her only novel, *Like Unto Like*, was published in 1878. Soon after the deaths of her father and brother from yellow fever, Katherine herself fell ill with breast cancer. She died in Holly Springs at the age of 34. Two books of short stories, *Dialect Tales* (1883) and *Suwanee River Tales* (1884), published immediately after her death, are her best work, and are considered excellent examples of the 'local-color' movement. She is also often said to have created the Mammy character in her 'Gran'Mammy' tales.   SP

MacEwen, Gwendolyn 1941–87 Anglophone Canadian poet, novelist and playwright who created an eloquent exotic universe of intense imagery, weaving together modern and mythic ambivalences of existence, merging archetypal patterns with mythic and present times. Her expertise in re-connecting opposites, in re-uniting dualities, into enigmatic poetic realities is legendary. Born in Toronto, Ontario, of Scottish and English parents, she was raised there and in Winnipeg, Manitoba. MacEwen left school at 18, taught herself French, Hebrew, Arabic and Greek and travelled in the Mediterranean, preferring life as such, and travelling, to a university education, as shapers of her personal imagination.

MacEwen published over twenty books in various genres. Together with her first husband, Milton Acorn, and Al Purdy she edited the journal *Moment* (1960–2) and for a year (1972) she ran the Toronto coffee house 'The Trojan Horse' together with her second husband, the Greek singer Nikos Tsingos (they were divorced in 1978). She wrote two novels: *Julian the Magician* (1963), a hybrid fantasy/history connecting Christianity and philosophy, and a reconstruction of ancient Egypt, *King of Egypt, King of Dreams* (1971). Her second collection of short stories, *Noman's Land* (1985), describes a mythical 'Kanada' perceived by a stranger, Noman. MacEwen published eleven volumes of poetry and scripted several docudramas for the Canadian Broadcasting Corporation. Her elusive and introspective early selected poetry of *Magic Animals* (1974) developed with *The T. E. Lawrence Poems* and *Earthlight* (both 1982) into oracular, emphatic verse. *The Armies of the Moon* (1972) won the A. J. M. Smith Poetry Award and both *The Shadowmaker* (1969) and *Afterworlds* (1987), the latter being inspired by modern physics and nuclear politics, won Governor General's Awards. Two poetry collections have been posthumously published (1993–

4) edited by MARGARET ATWOOD and Barry Callaghan. DMM

McGuckian, Medbh 1950– Northern Irish poet, born in Belfast where she still lives. In 1986, McGuckian became the first woman writer-in-residence at Queen's University. She has also been Visiting Fellow at Berkeley.

The Flower Master (1982) established the heightened, averted, meditative style for which McGuckian is known. Criticized at times for being difficult or obscure, she is rightly confident of her voice: 'This oblique trance is my natural / Way of speaking.' Her work rewards close reading with its revelatory and detailed observations.

In *Venus and the Rain* (1994) McGuckian consolidated her handling of traditional lyric themes. She writes of love, landscape, home and family but charges her poems with a disorientating percipience and erotic tension. Her metaphors are tightly packed but they work to open and expand their subject, as in these lines from 'My Brown Guest' (*On Ballycastle Beach*, 1988):

> I brushed
> His faults away, as in my mind I threw away
> The truthfulness of the room – it was like
> Trying to shovel away the sky, or the smell
> Of snow, as meaningless and recognizable
> As that of roses.

The dismissive brushing gains weight in the similes that follow. Throwing away and then shovelling are increasingly physical and desperate acts. The repetition of 'away' is a kind of hopeless shovelling in itself, subsiding into the abstract flatness of 'meaningless and recognizable'.

McGuckian's resistance to conclusive meaning can seem like an evasion. It has more to do, perhaps, with an awareness that the experience she articulates is not only specifically female but, within that, interior and individual. She is ambitious and exact in her explanations but wryly acknowledges the limited possibilities of being understood.

In *Marconi's Cottage* (1991) and *Captain Lavender* (1994) McGuckian continues her investigation into disjunctive states: gender opposition, the political divide and the conflicting demands of domesticity and art. LG

Mack [née Hamilton], Mary Louise 1870–1935 Australian journalist, novelist and poet. Mack was born in Hobart to an Irish Wesleyan minister and attended Sydney Girls' High School where she wrote poetry and edited the *Girls' High School Gazette*. In the early 1890s her first piece of writing was accepted by the *Bulletin*, and over the following years her short stories and poetry were published in nearly all the Sydney papers. In 1895 her first novel, *The World is Round*, was published, followed by *Teens and Girls Together*, based on her school experiences. *Teens* became the 'Bible of all the bright young things who did not know they were "flappers"'. In 1898 she took over as the writer of the *Bulletin*'s 'Women's Letter' under the pen-name 'Gouli Gouli' and became a well-known bohemian figure. She departed for England in 1901, wrote her third novel, *An Australian Girl in London*, and contributed to W.T. Stead's *Reviews of Reviews*. From 1904 to 1907 she lived in Florence where she edited the *Italiano Gazette*, but by 1913 she was back in London writing popular serials for the *Daily Mail* and *Daily Mirror*. Her unrelenting energy and enthusiasm were described as gaining 'force under pressure ... the heavier the work the more capable she is of expressing herself'. During World War I she became the first female war correspondent; her adventures were published in *A Woman's Experiences in the Great War* (1915). MRE

Mackay, Shena 1944– Scots writer, educated at Tunbridge Girls School and Kidbrook Comprehensive. Mackay's career falls into two sections, punctuated by a period when she wrote little and was bringing up her daughters; her earlier novels were as sensational in subject matter and as full of bleak comedy as her later ones, if somewhat quieter in tone. She achieved a measure of instant recognition with the two novellas *Dust Falls on Eugene Schlumberger* and *Toddler on the Run* (published together in 1964); these and their immediate successors, *Music Upstairs* (1965) and *Old Crow* (1967), were misunderstood at the time as urban realism – Mackay's eye for the details of life in bedsitter land was impeccable – and their moments of the macabre accordingly as excessive.

Her return to fiction was gradual; she started publishing short stories and developed through them her later, more intense manner. *Babies in Rhinestones* (1983) and *Dreams of Bad Women's Handbags* (1987) established this manner even in their titles; in these, and such novels as *A Bowl of Cherries* (1984) and *Redhill Rococo* (1986), Mackay developed a vein of surreal, synaesthetic imagery which, along with her superficially affectless plots, dramatized tellingly the escape and freedom of the victimized. *Dunedin* (1992) was less successful in its more ambitious attempt to contextualize a feckless suburban family through its past as failed emigrants to New Zealand and in its satirical picture of a near-future Britain where street people are sent to extermination camps. Perhaps her finest novel, *The Orchard on Fire* (1996), realistically evoked a 1950s childhood as a lost domain of innocence and friendship; two young girls, one brutalized by a violent father, the other inconclusively pursued by a potential seducer, invent their friendship through children's fiction and a willed misunderstanding of the realities of their situation.

RK

Mackellar, Dorothea 1885–1968 Australian poet (and minor novelist) known to generations of Australian schoolchildren and choristers for the patriotic manifesto:

> I love a sunburnt country,
> A land of sweeping plains,
> Of ragged mountain ranges,
> Of droughts and flooding rains.

This actually begins the second stanza of 'My Country', originally published as 'Core of My Heart' in the London *Spectator* (1908). The usually forgotten first stanza, addressed to an English audience identified as loving mistiness and greenery, places the poem among those positive assertions of colonial difference (see COLONIAL WRITING) found in the 1890s and early 1900s. Mackellar was, however, not only a bush patriot, but an enthusiastic traveller who enjoyed the sophistication of living abroad as well as life on her family's substantial property near Gunnedah in New South Wales. There are interesting, sometimes witty, poems about contemporary sexual mores and accomplished translations as well as 'nature poems', in the four volumes published between 1911 and 1926, after which date she gave up writing because of ill health. *The Poems of Dorothea Mackellar* (1971), re-issued as *My Country and other Poems* (1982), show her reputation as a one-poem writer to be less than just. JStr

McKemmish, Jan(ette Anne) 1950– Australian novelist. Born in Tongala, Victoria, and educated at La Trobe University, Melbourne. First came to prominence with her experimental feminist spy thriller, *A Gap in the Records* (1985), which concerns a supposed global network of women whose aim is the subversion of male power structures. *Only Lawyers Dancing* (1992) performs a similar feminist rewriting of the detective story, dealing with the forces of crime and corruption in contemporary Sydney. These first two novels also reflected McKemmish's interest in contemporary literary and feminist theory, especially as they related to such issues as the representation of women, power, crime and genre. Her third novel *Common Knowledge* (1996), was markedly different in style and content; set in Corella, a small farming community in Victoria during the 1930s and 1940s, it more obviously draws on McKemmish's family background in its investigation of the impact of war and modernity on ordinary lives. Together with other women, she has also written performance pieces which question mainstream understandings of form, narrative and politics. These include 'As Much Trouble as Talking' (1988), 'Women Behind Barthes' (1986) and 'The Return of the Dead' (1986). McKemmish is also a very experienced teacher of creative writing and established the MA programme in Creative Writing at the University of Queensland, where she is a Senior Lecturer in English. EW

McKenzie, Alecia 1960– Jamaican writer who first came to the notice of the Caribbean reading public in 1993 when she won the regional (Canada and the Caribbean) Commonwealth Writers' Prize for Best First Book with the collection *Satellite City*. The stories in that collection are graphic and humorous but hard-hitting, laying bare the Jamaican political and cultural experience in uncompromising words. The volume has been translated into Dutch, Italian and Polish with selected stories translated into Spanish. She has also published poems and short stories in international journals on both sides of the Atlantic, as well as a novella, *When The Rain Stopped Falling in Natland*, in 1995.

A journalist, she has written articles on a wide range of subjects for prestigious publications all over Europe and America. She has worked for media organizations including the Wall Street Journal/Europe (1986–8) and InterPress Service (1992–5). She also teaches creative writing and writing for the media at Vrije Universiteit, in Brussels where she went to live with her husband and son in 1985.

Alecia McKenzie was born and grew up in Kingston, capital city of Jamaica. Her stories are close-up shots of different (sometimes unpleasant) aspects of the urban experience. She published poetry even while still in high school. She also enjoyed painting, and her university studies were in Art and Journalism. She still paints but prefers to write. The eye of the artist, however, is always with her, as the clear, precise descriptions in her stories attest. VEP

Mackenzie [née Wight], Anna Maria before 1783– after 1816 English novelist and essayist. The daughter of an Essex coal merchant, Anna Maria received the 'confined education' available to most middle-class women. After her first husband, Mr Cox, died in financial ruin, Anna Marie turned to her 'ardent love of writing' to support her four children. She appears to have written magazine essays, and she published her first novel, the EPISTOLARY *Burton Wood* (1783) anonymously. Anna Maria used her second husband's name, Johnson, in publishing *Calista* (1789); *Monmouth* (1790), a HISTORICAL ROMANCE set in the Restoration; and *Slavery: Or The Times* (1792), the tale of an OROONOKO-style half-African Prince educated in England. By 1795, Anna Maria published under 'Mackenzie', the name of her third husband. One work, *The Neapolitan: Or The Test of Integrity* (1796), bears the pseudonym 'Ellen of Exeter'. Anna Maria produced at least sixteen novels in various genres. Although her lengthy volumes and multiple sub-plots may appear stilted to modern readers, her popular novels often received appreciative reviews from contemporary critics. JHP

411

McKittrick Ros, Amanda 1860–1939 Irish novelist and poet. Born Anna Margaret McKittrick in County Down, she trained as a teacher. Her first husband, Andrew Ross, arranged to have her first novel, *Irene Iddesleigh* (1897), published privately as an anniversary present. Deeply hurt by derisive criticism of the novel, McKittrick Ros (*sic*) subsequently devoted as much energy to maligning her detractors (frequently in verse, as in *Poems of Puncture* (1912)) as she did to writing fiction. She quickly became a cult figure and a number of Amanda McKittrick Ros clubs met regularly to read her work in order to laugh at it. There was a brief craze for themed dinners based principally on *Irene Iddesleigh* and *Delina Delaney* (1898) where passages from the novels were read and 'Amanda' questionnaires circulated. Some of her contemporaries acknowledged her originality, her energy and a passion for language which yield moments of brilliance but more often explain why she was once called the worst novelist in the world. She favours romantic plots, constructed on a flow of alliteration and extravagant language, startling metaphor and bizarre grammatical constructions. Some of her peculiarities are inspired, for example her use of the word 'sister' as a verb.

She once described herself as 'the personality who has disturbed the bowels of millions' and wrote to a friend speculating that 'I expect I will be talked about at the end of 1,000 years'. LM

McMaster, Rhyll 1947– A relatively unprolific Australian poet whose work has nonetheless been highly regarded by critics, judges of literary awards and anthologists ever since her first volume, *The Brineshrimp* (1972), published in the 'Paperback Poets' series initiated by University of Queensland Press, won the Harri Jones Memorial Prize. In subsequent volumes, *Washing the Money* (1986), *On My Empty Feet* (1993) and *Chemical Bodies* (1997), she has maintained a distinctive voice. Whether she is writing about her Brisbane childhood, family relations (both loving and difficult), or the natural world, the combination of sharply literal observation and imaginative evocations of the oddity and mystery of people and things produces an effect both lucid and luminous. She has said that she thinks of a poem as 'a freeze-frame for some definitive moment' or as a 'short short-story'. Both are apt descriptions of aspects of her work, but they do not entirely convey the engaging play of speculative intelligence with which she addresses her material. Apart from such other literary activities as short-story writing, fiction reviewing and being poetry editor of the *Canberra Times* (1994), she manages a small sheep property near Braidwood, New South Wales. JStr

Macmillan, Terry 19?– American writer who holds a BA in Journalism from the University of California at Berkeley. Her novels of black urban life are popular and vigorous, with strong characterization that owes much to the populist psychology of talk shows and self-help manuals. *Mama* (1987) shows patterns of drug and alcohol dependency, and a preparedness to tolerate physical abuse, transmitted from generation to generation, but also shows the characters' steady self-improvement in spite of these disadvantages: strong black women are capable of surviving even their own weakness. The less satisfying *Disappearing Acts* (1990) tackles some of these issues again, along with the issue of class within the American black community; the relationship between Franklin and Zora is complicated by drugs, epilepsy and rape, but class status is the issue that breaks them apart. *Waiting to Exhale* (1992) explores female solidarity and its limits and *How Stella Got Her Groove Back* (1996) shows a middle-class black woman professional regaining access to lost sensuality while vacationing. She was an Associate Professor in English at Arizona and a Visiting Professor in Creative Writing at Wyoming and Stanford. In 1990 she edited *Breaking the Ice*, an anthology of new black American writing. RK

Macnaughtan, Sarah Broom 1864–1916 Scottish writer, war-time volunteer, diarist. A successful popular novelist (thirteen novels between 1898 and 1915, the most skilful being the genial satire *The Fortune of Chistina M'Nab* (1901)), she kept a detailed DIARY of her experiences during World War I. A Red Cross volunteer during the Boer War, in 1914 she served with Mrs St Clair Stobart's women's hospital unit during the siege of Antwerp. When Antwerp fell, she joined Dr Hector Munro's ambulance unit at Ostend, and, helped by three Belgian Sisters, instituted a soup kitchen at the railway in Furnes to succour the wounded with food and dry socks; shelled out, she established another kitchen near La Panne. At her own expense, though disillusioned with war, in 1915 she gave thirty-five lectures throughout Britain to encourage munitions workers. Unfortunately she became fatally ill while attempting to serve with the Red Cross in Persia. HB

McNeill, F(lorence) Marian 1885–1973 Born in Orkney and educated in Glasgow and Paris, McNeill was a historian, primarily interested in Highland folklore, and in Scottish food and drink. She moved to Edinburgh as a young girl, but remained close to her island childhood. Her *magnum opus* was *The Silver Bough* (1957–68), a study of Scottish folklore in four volumes. Still widely read today is *The Scots Kitchen* (1929). Other books followed, notably *The Scots Cellar* (1956).

McNeill would have welcomed devolution. In 1929 she wrote: 'From a purely cultural point of view, Scotland lost more than she gained by the Union of the Crowns (1603). She lost the old, close contact with the most highly civilised nation in the world (France), and established a new close contact with a nation for whom efficiency, not culture; comfort, not elegance; manufacture, not art; were paramount things. She lost her reigning family . . . her nobility . . . her Parliament; and finally she lost her intelligentsia.' AB

Macpherson, Jay 1931– Poet and critic, winner of the Governor General's Award. She was born in England and moved with her family to Canada in 1940. She grew up in Ottawa (her mother Dorothy closely associated with the National Film Board), took her BA at Carleton and MA and Ph.D. at Toronto, where she has been a Professor of English for more than forty years. Her first three books were published in rapid succession (1952, 1954, 1957); the third, THE BOATMAN, attracted the greatest attention and was reprinted five times. *Welcoming Disaster* (1974) contains more recent work, and *Poems Twice Told* (1981) contains all the poems of both third and fourth collections. Her work is mythic and spare, influenced by William Blake, Robert Graves and Northrop Frye. She sees her role as poet as 'To convert the gentle reader to an Ark', to persuade him 'To admit both gnat and camel', and then, as poet and guide, to 'pull him through his navel inside out / . . . to get his beasts outside him'. This process is most clear as social/cultural mission in *The Boatman*, whereas more recent poems chart her own descent into a personal 'dark well', or Hades, with an old teddy-bear as 'Tammuz' or sacrificial and resurrection figure. FD

McQueen, Cilla 1949– New Zealand poet. Well known for her witty, colloquial and satirical performance poetry, McQueen has won the New Zealand Book Award for poetry for three of her collections – *Homing In* (1983), *Benzina* (1988) and *Berlin Diary* (1990). Born in Birmingham, England, she came to New Zealand as a child and took an MA in French at Otago University. She taught French full-time in Dunedin secondary schools before being awarded a Writer's Fellowship (1985 and 1986) and becoming a full-time poet. She married the well-known Maori artist Ralph Hotere (since divorced) who has used her poems in his art. Her poetry aims at being surprising, amusing and fast-moving: 'poetry is a shock / it wide eyes & spreadeagles you'. It's also clever, technically skilful and playful and positions itself on the boundary between fantasy and reality to give insights into daily life, the here and now of New Zealand: '3 million people with / a little flock of sheep each so we're all sort of / shepherds' ('Living Here'). In 1994 she published *Crik'ey: New and Selected Poems 1978-1994*. AM

McWilliam, Candia (Frances Juliet) 1955– Scottish novelist and short-story writer. She was born in Edinburgh, educated at Sherbourne School for Girls

and Girton College, Cambridge. She married the Earl of Portsmouth in 1981 and, following divorce, F.E. Dinshaw in 1986. She has three children. She was affiliated to British *Vogue* from 1976 to 1979 and the fascinatingly named advertising agency, Slade, Bluff and Bigg, from 1979 to 1981.

Her first novel, *A Case of Knives*, was published by Morrow in 1988 and demonstrated a highly complex literary style – concise poetic prose hallmarked by beautifully dense imagery and elaborate metaphor. However, McWilliam never relaxes into any settled style. *A Little Stranger* (1989), *Debatable Land* (1994) and *Wait Till I Tell You* (1997) each break new ground for her voice, and represent a substantial re-invention of the authorial self, one rendered even more attentive to a personal language of redemption following the tests of experience. McWilliam has won the Betty Trask Award from The Society of Authors for a romantic novel as well as the *Guardian* Fiction Prize. DM

Madan [née Cowper], Judith 1702–81 Although Madan was an accomplished poet and prolific letter-writer, only 5 of her 45 poems have ever been published. Her best known, *Abelard to Eloisa* (1720), which responds to Pope's *Eloisa to Abelard*, may have inspired the year-long correspondence between the two poets. Called 'no mean companion to Pope's Eloisa', Madan's Abelard explores the terrible conflict of his desires – 'A thousand jarring Thoughts my Bosom Tear, / For thou, not God, O Eloise, art there.' Niece of the first Earl Cowper and aunt to the poet William Cowper, Madan benefited materially and educationally from both the aristocratic and the literary pretensions of her family. Before her marriage in 1723, Madan composed her most ambitious piece, 'The Progress of Poetry', first published in 1731. These 264 lines of heroic couplets celebrate a pantheon of poets from Homer and SAPPHO to Granville and Rowe, ending in her elegant confession: 'Unnumber'd Bards distract my dazzled sight, / And my first choice grows faint with rival light.' While her husband, a military officer, was frequently away, Madan raised nine children and carried on a vast correspondence, of which nearly 500 letters still exist.

JRS

Magic Toyshop, The (1967) ANGELA CARTER's accomplished and exuberant second novel won the John Llewellyn Rhys Prize for 1967. It provided the reading public with a taste of the mixture of sensuously inflected REALISM and FAIRY TALE which Carter made distinctively her own. Like so many of Carter's fictions, this is a fiction of the faux-uncanny which is particularly alive to the fabrications generated by the imagination working under pressure. The imagination, in this text, is primarily that of the pubescent girl, Melanie, who is looking for ways to structure her urgent, newly felt sexual desires. After a breakdown following her parents' deaths, Melanie goes to London, to live with her sinister Uncle Philip in his toyshop. Evading violation by Philip and finding her first love in her contemporary and equal, the red-haired, elfin, Finn, Melanie's adventures partake of the GOTHIC, the mythic surreal, and the utterly ordinary. A compellingly readable text, *The Magic Toyshop* is one of the most striking in Carter's always scintillating oeuvre. KF

Magona, Sindiwe 1943– South African writer living in New York, who has published in English and whose most recent novel has been translated into Xhosa, her mother tongue. She was born in the Transkei, from where she moved to Cape Town and later went to Columbia University in New York. Her first work, *To My Children's Children*, was published in 1990, and is described by the author as a letter from a Xhosa grandmother addressed to her grandchildren. The narrative is an account of the first twenty-one years of her life; it was later reworked by the author, and published in Xhosa as *Kubantwana Babantwana Bam* (1995). In 1992 she published the second part of her life story as *Forced to Grow*, which traces the development of her life during the turbulent mid-seventies in South Africa, and her departure to study at Columbia. *Living, Loving and Lying Awake at Night* (1991) is an exploration of the lives and circumstances of African women in South Africa, which includes a unique set of stories told from the perspective of black domestic workers. *Push-Push, and Other Stories* was published in 1996. CCo

Mahy, Margaret 1936– Prolific New Zealand CHILDREN's writer whose work ranges from humorous and lively picture books to psychological thrillers for teenagers. Born in Whakatane and educated at the Universities of Auckland and Canterbury, she worked for many years in Christchurch as a librarian. Having written since childhood, her work began to appear in New Zealand school journals in 1961, and in 1969 her award-winning picture book *The Lion in the Meadow* was published. Her work characteristically blends exaggeration, humour, realism and fantasy. She favours unusual or comic names for her characters and delights in the humorous eccentricities of language and situation seen in *Mrs Discombobulous* (1969) or *The Great Piratical Rumbustification* (1978). A versatile and original author, Mahy's work for children includes picture books, poetry, stories, school readers, novels, television scripts and plays. Her full-length novels for older children and teenagers, such as the *The Haunting* (1982) and *The Changeover* (1984), which both won the Carnegie Medal, blend the supernatural with subtle examination of family dynamics and emotional

undercurrents. *The Catalogue of the Universe* (1985) is a realist teenage novel and *Memory* (1987), which won the *Observer* Teenage Fiction Award, deals with Alzheimer's disease. AEG

Maitland, Sara 1950– Raised in Scotland, and settled in the south of England, Maitland has created multiple, writerly roles for herself, as feminist, theologian and story-teller. Her career in fiction began in a feminist collective, with work jointly published as *Tales I Tell My Mother* (1978). Her first novel, *Daughter of Jerusalem* (1978), explored infertility and appended rewritten Old Testament tales as ironic counterpoint to the anchor narrative. Maitland went on to reinterpret tales and myths of numerous other cultures in *Virgin Territory* (1984), *Arky Types* (1987 – with MICHELENE WANDOR), *Three Times Table* (1989). The latter saw her stocktaking what feminism had done for contemporary women, in its examination of three generations living under one roof. It was also her first fully fledged magic realist novel, leading to *Home Truths* (1992) and *Hagiographies* (1998). In her short stories, collected primarily in *A Book of Spells* (1987) and *Women Fly When Men Aren't Watching* (1992), the heterogeneously complex voices are allowed to run off and forge their own, brief forms, and the ideas are less jammed together than in the novels. There is a sense of fierce, intellectual play in stories such as 'Seal Self', 'A Fall From Grace' and 'Fag Hags: A Field Guide'. PM

Makin [née Pell], Bathsua 1608? – *c*.1680 Author of a significant pamphlet on women's education in 1673 (*An Essay to Revive the Antient Education of Gentlewomen*), a Civil War pamphlet and several extant poems. Makin had been tutor to Charles I's daughter, Princess Elizabeth, and her brother-in-law was a noted mathematician. By the 1640s she was one of the most learned women of her day and acquainted with many others, including Anna Maria van Schurman who preserved Makin's letters to her (written in Greek) in her own *Opuscula*. The *Essay*, an anonymously published pamphlet, written, perhaps as self-protection, in the form of letters by male personae, is in part an advertisement for Makin's own school for young gentlewomen. In it she argues that women's education has ancient precedent and that only contemporary patriarchal society has restricted it. She names role-models such as van Schurman and ANNE BRADSTREET in her support. Makin was no strident feminist, however: her own politics were largely conservative and the text is at pains to stress that she does not intend to hinder good housewifery, nor to equalize men and women. Because of the emphasis placed by the *Essay* on poetry it is likely she wrote far more verse than has survived. What is extant includes elegies and poems addressed to female patrons. JS

Making of Americans, The (1925) GERTRUDE STEIN's monumental account of a middle-class, West-coast American family, the Herslands, distinctively Steinian in its repetition and syntactic idiosyncrasy. Written between 1902 and 1911, this enormous (925-page) text evokes a 'continuous present' in which to express, in the simplest and commonest language, the essential being in people; it is almost completely descriptive and the few events related appear non-sequentially. There is no real plot, although the three Hersland siblings – Martha, the eldest; Alfred (with his first wife, Julia Dehning); and the youngest son, David – are each central figures in the middle three books. The first book introduces the Hersland and Dehning families whose older generations are emigrants from Europe. The voice of the ever-present, self-reflective narrator dominates the final, brief book.

The method of this universal history of personality closely relates to Stein's later verbal portraits while its abstractionism gestures toward the achievements of TENDER BUTTONS (1914). She explores the workings of this text in *Composition as Explanation* (1926) and 'The Gradual Making of the Making of Americans' (1935).

AG

Malange, Nise (Bulelwa Margaret) 1960– South African resistance poet. She grew up in Guguletu, Cape Town. Her mother, Grace Ngesi, was a midwife, and her father, Sam Malange, was a farmer. As a teenager she attended secondary school in Whittlesea and in 1981, after completing Matriculation, she moved to Durban. She completed a diploma in Adult Education at the University of Natal and in 1982 began work with the Federation of South African Trade Unions. She became involved with the Durban Worker's Cultural Local which encouraged workers to respond creatively to major political and industrial events. She believes everyone has a story to tell and culture must be taken out of the framework of leisure time and put back into the working lives of people.

In 1985, a selection of her poetry was published in *Black Mamba Rising*. The poems, including, 'Poem Dedicated to Brother Andries Raditsela' and 'First of May', condemn death in detention and salute workers' struggles. In 1990 her poems, 'Long Live Women' and 'Nightshift Mother', were published in *Breaking the Silence*, and 'I Cry Sing for Peace' and 'Listening is Healing' were published in *Poetry for Peace* (1994) which she co-edited.

GMS

Malet, Lucas [Mary St Leger Kingsley Harrison] 1852–1931 One of the most important British women writers of the turn of the century. The daughter of Charles Kingsley, Malet grew up in an atmosphere of intellectual ferment. She attended the Slade School but left in 1876 to marry her father's curate, William

Harrison (they later separated). *A Counsel of Perfection* (1888) and *Colonel Enderby's Wife* (1885) describe ordinary people transfigured by great love; both explore the glory of martyrdom, here given an ironic twist by the unworthiness of the beloved. Malet became famous for her next novel, *The Wages of Sin* (1890), about a radical artist torn between his adoration for a pure lady and his duty to his slovenly mistress (this novel inspired much of *Jude the Obscure*). *The Gateless Barrier* (1900) is a parable about a female ghost who terrorizes her male decadent heirs. A year later, she published the celebrated and controversial *The History of Sir Richard Calmady* (1901), a detailed psychological case-study of a physically deformed man's maturing sense of his body, self and sexuality. In the 20th century, Malet continued to experiment with unusual narrative perspectives: madness, clairvoyance and multiple unreliable narrators characterize *Adrian Savage* (1911). Her novels explore marginalized sexualities, lonely and inarticulate subjects, and surreal encounters. However, Malet's reputation deteriorated, partly because of her conversion to Catholicism (apparent in *The Far Horizon* (1907)) and partly because her long novels looked old-fashioned to modernist readers. Malet's life ended in obscurity, poverty and illness, and today her radical expansion of the late-Victorian novel has been largely forgotten.

TS

Man Lay Dead, A (1934) NGAIO MARSH's first DETECTIVE NOVEL. Sir Hubert Handesley arranges a weekend party at his country house, to which he invites an assortment of society types, with the intention of playing the game 'Murder'. When the abrasive, philandering Charles Rankin is found stabbed with a ceremonial Russian dagger, Inspector Roderick Alleyn is called in. Is it the sinister Russian Tokareff, the scorned Mrs Wilde, her husband the archaeologist, the tempestuous Rosamund Grant, the ingénus Nigel and Angela, or perhaps the butler? Classic detection relying on the layout of the house, the timing of each guest's movements, and the discovery of physical evidence is complicated by a Buchanesque sub-plot of Russian secret societies, treason and torture. Marsh enjoys the artificiality of her genre which she enriches with Wodehouse social comedy and a dash of lightly borne erudition (Conrad, Chaliapin and Hamlet all feature). Alleyn describes the image of the 'mysterious, omnipotent detective' as 'impossibly vulgar' and confesses, 'My only information is based on detective fiction.'

JSt

Man Who Loved Children, The (1940) CHRISTINA STEAD's disturbing and intense novel of the horrors of family life is told from the perspective of Louie, the eldest child of the sanctimonious naturalist Sam Pollit. Though set in Washington it draws heavily on

Christina Stead's Australian childhood. As Louie enters adolescence her father's childishness and his psychological cruelty become more apparent to her, and not only because she is increasingly his victim. She feels some sympathy for her selfish but embattled, formerly genteel stepmother, Henny, but ultimately Louie is most motivated by her concern for the brood of children to whom she is half-sister. Sam's fun games, private family languages and jokes are inextricable from his monstrous and undermining surveillance and control of his family. Henny, frustrated by poverty, debt, the demands of children, and the inescapable bonds of her marriage is violent and suicidal. Louie finds some solace in an intense relationship with her schoolfriend Clare, and in her imaginative life. Her writing and story-telling suggest her future career. She is finally reduced to drastic measures, and the novel ends with her running away.   SKM

Mandava, Bhargavi C. 1966– Indian writer and music critic resident in Los Angeles. Born in Hyderabad, South India, Mandava emigrated with her family to New York in 1971. She graduated in Journalism at New York University in 1988, and moved to California in 1993.

As well as music criticism Mandava has written fiction and poetry which have appeared in anthologies and literary reviews. Her first novel, *Where the Oceans Meet*, appeared in 1996 and was short-listed for the Small Press Book Award. Constructed with several plots which intersect and diverge, this unconventional novel sketches, in compelling but sober prose, a myriad of finely interwoven stories. For example, we encounter Navina, a bride-to-be, at her first meeting with the tailor of her wedding sari, then in a flashback chapter we see her family arranging her marriage to Ajay, and in another more distressing chapter the lower-caste tailor splashes Navina's face with acid in a rage at her indifference to his love. Central to the chain of loosely related events are the destinies of women, some of them emigrants to the United States, and the cacophony of contemporary India.   SPo

Mandelbaum Gate, The (1965) MURIEL SPARK's eighth novel is set in the partitioned Jerusalem of 1961, the time of the Eichmann trial. Barbara Vaughan, like Spark a half-Jewish Catholic convert, is also divided. She comes to Israel intending to make a pilgrimage to the Christian shrines, then mostly in Jordan, where her divorced archaeologist fiancé is working. Both countries are internally further divided by the variety and complexity of Judaism, Islam, Christianity, Zionism and Arab nationalism: most of the characters have to negotiate incompatible personal, political, sexual and religious identities. The Arab Ramdez family is uncommitted but involved, in both countries, in everything – travel, insurance, smuggling, prostitution, espionage – and the attractive younger members, Abdul and Suzi, find evidence of Christian baptism convenient. Freddy Hamilton, working in the British consulate in Israel and allowed to walk through the Mandelbaum Gate into Jordan, eschews commitment and also values 'diplomatic immunity' in his private life. However, in an experience of 'transfiguration' he joins Abdul and Suzi in aiding Barbara's pilgrimage, dangerous for a Jew, which leads to escape from a convent, disappearance, disguise, discoveries, border shootings and amnesia. The story resembles a thriller but continual prolepsis defuses suspense and suggests the providence of God or author and a teleology of which the characters are unaware.   PMar

Mander, (Mary) Jane ['Manda Lloyd'] 1877–1949 New Zealand journalist and novelist whose fiction confronts the psychosexual wilderness of her homeland. Her father was involved in the bush clearance and milling in kauri forest – an environment which was later to provide the background to her novels – and during her early years the family moved from place to place. She worked as a schoolteacher from the age of 15, but gave this up to help run the family home for a time when they moved to Whangerei. In 1902 her father was elected as MP for Marsden and in the same year he bought the *Northern Advocate* newspaper, where she gained her first experience of journalism by running the editorial department. Although he sold the paper in 1906 she continued in journalism, working as editor of the *North Auckland Times* before taking a place at the School of Journalism at Columbia University, New York, in 1912, at the age of 35.

Like fellow New Zealanders, KATHERINE MANSFIELD and ROBIN HYDE, she required to escape the confines of her homeland to be able to write. Her first novel, *The Story of a New Zealand River* (1920), explores female sexuality and the implications of marriage against the puritanical backdrop of New Zealand society. Her title's resemblance to that of OLIVE SCHREINER's *THE STORY OF AN AFRICAN FARM* (1883) is no coincidence, for she acknowledged her wish to emulate Schreiner. However, she was castigated for her continued focus on 'the sex question' in this and two subsequent novels, *The Passionate Puritan* (1921) and *The Strange Attraction* (1923). She lived in London from 1923 and published *Allen Adair* (1925), *The Besieging City* (1926) and *Pins and Pinnacles* (1928) before returning to New Zealand in 1932, but although contracted to write her reminiscences, published nothing further.   JSte

Manley, Delarivière 1663–1724 The potency of her scandal writing (see SCANDALOUS MEMOIRS), combining political acumen with erotically charged fiction and an insider's knowledge, boosted Tory fortunes in

1710. Her career began inauspiciously with a bigamous marriage to her cousin, appointed guardian by her father (Royalist Army officer, historian and Lieutenant-Governor of Jersey) on his death in 1687. Outcast from respectability after her son's birth in 1691, Manley was offered protection, in 1694, by the Duchess of Cleveland (long-term mistress of Charles II). In this establishment she gained an extensive knowledge of scandal, which she later employed to great effect in her *romans à clef, Queen Zarah* (1705) and *THE NEW ATALANTIS* (1709) which attacked Whig corruption. Arrested for libel but disingenuously claiming she wrote merely 'for her own Amusement and Diversion', Manley, undeterred, published *Memoirs of Europe* (1710) and *Court Intrigues* (1711) in the same vein. She took over editorship of the *Examiner* from Jonathan Swift in 1711, but after the Tory decline in 1714 she turned to autobiographical fiction with *The Adventures of Rivella* (1714), while her last publication *The Power of Love: In Seven Novels* (1720), eschewed politics.

Her first play, *The Lost Lover*, was unsuccessful but *The Royal Mischief* achieved critical acclaim, while she herself was satirized, also in 1696, in *THE FEMALE WITS*. Later plays *Almyna* (1707), and *Lucius* (1717) for which she received 600 guineas from her erstwhile friend and foe Richard Steele, consolidated her popular success. Involved in liaisons with several prominent men – Sir Thomas Skipworth (manager of Drury Lane), John Tilly (Governor of the Fleet Prison) and John Barber (printer and later Lord Mayor of London) – she was later discredited as degenerate. Recent scholarship, however, has recognized the originality and effectiveness of her integration of autobiography, fiction, scandal and politics.   LMT

Mannin, Ethel 1900–84 British popular novelist, journalist, TRAVEL WRITER, and political activist, the daughter of Robert Mannin, a postal worker, and his wife, Edith. She was born in Clapham, London, and worked as a shorthand typist in Higham's advertising agency. She married Jack Porteus, an advertising copywriter by whom she had a daughter, in 1919, divorcing him in 1927. She was married for a second time to Reginald Reynolds, a friend of Ghandi, in 1938 and became a pacifist.

Her ninety-five works include several novels about working-class women: *Children of the Earth* (1930), *Linda Shawn* (1932) and *Venetian Blinds* (1934). Mannin admired ETHEL M. DELL and wrote popular romantic fiction including *Martha* (1923), *Hunger of the Sea* (1924), *Sounding Brass* (1925) and *The Pure Flame* (1936).

Common Sense and the Child (1931) was influenced by the progressive educator, A.S. Neill. In 1933 she joined the Independent Labour party and wrote energetically for their organ, the *New Leader*. *Women and the Revolution* (1938) argues that feminism must be subsumed in the struggle against capitalism. *Comrade O Comrade* (1947) is a satire on the literary Left in the 1930s. Her travel books record her journeys across the world, including Europe (*Forever Wandering*, 1934), Russia (*South to Samarkand*, 1936), Asia (*A Journey to Burma*, 1955) and America (*An American Journey*, 1967). She wrote books espousing the rights of the Palestinians: *Aspects of Egypt* (1954), *A Lance for the Arabs* (1963) and *The Lovely Land* (1965).

Mannin's autobiographical works include *Confessions and Impressions* (1930), *Privileged Spectator* (1939) and *Young in the Twenties* (1971).   MJ

Manning, Mary 1906– Irish playwright, novelist and journalist. She was born in Dublin, where, as a young woman, her *ésprit* was renowned in a city which prides itself on the keen wit of its writers. She was a pupil of DOROTHY MACARDLE's at Alexandra College. Her training as an actress and artist was put aside in favour of playwriting, and she established herself with *Youth's the Season – ?* (1931) at the Gate Theatre. It is a sparkling tragi-comedy of young Dublin manners and starred Michael MacLiammoir as 'a youthful invert in a cyclamen polo jumper'. Also featured is Egosmith, a silent character based on Manning's childhood friend Samuel Beckett. The play was highly successful and two more comedies for the Gate followed, *Storm Over Wicklow* and *Happy Family*. Manning edited the Gate Theatre house journal, *Motley* (1932–4), before settling in Boston, Mass., where she married and had three daughters. Her first novel was *Mount Venus* (1938), a highly entertaining and acute portrait of upper-middle-class Dublin manners after Independence. In Boston she founded the Cambridge Poets' Theatre in 1950. The company produced many poetic plays, including Manning's adaptation of Joyce's *Finnegans Wake*. Her 'brilliant condensation', entitled *The Voice of Shem*, wowed the Dublin Theatre Festival in 1961 and was acclaimed by critics. In Dublin once more after the death of her husband, she worked as a journalist and reviewer. She married again in 1980 and returned to Boston.   CL

Manning, Olivia 1908–80 British novelist. Olivia Manning was born in Portsmouth of Anglo-Irish parentage which, in her own words, gave her 'a sense of belonging nowhere'. That feeling of dislocation, heightened by her father's naval career, contributed to her readiness to travel widely and to act as an observer of the meeting points between British and other cultures. In 1939, she married the British Council lecturer R.D. Smith, and the couple travelled to Bucharest, where he was posted. During the course of World War II, they lived in Greece, Egypt and Jerusalem, before returning to London in 1946.

Manning's wartime experiences inspired and informed her best-known work: two sequences entitled 'THE BALKAN TRILOGY' (*The Great Fortune*, 1960, *The Spoilt City*, 1962, and *Friends and Heroes*, 1965) and 'THE LEVANT TRILOGY' (*The Danger Tree*, 1977, *The Battle Lost and Won*, 1978, and *The Sum of Things*, 1980). Both trilogies were dramatized by the BBC under the title *Fortunes of War* in 1987. The novels focus on Guy and Harriet Pringle and, at least on a surface level, mirror Manning's and Smith's circumstances very closely. The range and scope of the work is immense, involving a huge cast of characters – among them a Russian *émigré*, an alcoholic poet and a young army officer – and undertaking a close study of the effects of the war in Europe and North Africa. However, at the heart of the novels is the skilful depiction of the marital tensions between Guy, an endlessly gregarious and dynamic man, and Harriet, a more troubled and introspective character.

Manning's other novels are *The Wind Changes* (1938), *Artist Among the Missing* (1949), *School for Love* (1951), *A Different Face* (1953), *The Doves of Venus* (1955), *The Play Room* (1969) and *The Rain Forest* (1974). She also published two volumes of short stories, *Growing Up* (1948) and *A Romantic Hero* (1967). She was a frequent contributor to the *Spectator*, the *Sunday Times*, *Vogue* and *Punch*; a collection of sketches from *Punch* were published as *My Husband Cartwright* (1956). Olivia Manning was created a CBE in 1976.   AC

Mansell, Chris 1953– Australian writer whose poetry and prose fiction have been widely published and anthologized. She has given many live and recorded readings of her work and is active in performance, print production, editing and lecturing about writing. Her poetry aims to destabilize expectations of rhythm and meaning, using techniques which include the exploitation of clichés (images of society in which the writer can find 'an archaeological wonder'), using the 'productive ambiguity' of language, and challenging the function of line breaks and breath breaks ('not the same thing'). Her first book of poems, *Delta* (1978), appeared the year she founded the literary magazine *Compass Poetry and Prose*, which she edited until 1987. Her second book, *Head, Heart and Stone* (1982), was followed by *Redshift/Blueshift* (1988). The following year saw the release of *Raptors Blue* (1989), an audio cassette with music by Rob Cousins. Her collection of poems, *Day Easy Sunlight Fine in Hot Collation* (1994), was shortlisted for the National Book Council's Banjo Awards. *Little Wombat*, a children's book, was published in 1996. In 1993 she won the Queensland Premier's Award for Poetry.   MF

Mansfield, Katherine [Kathleen Mansfield Beauchamp] 1888–1923 Short-story writer from New Zealand, a major force in the construction of MODERNIST short fiction. After a childhood spent in and near Wellington, Katherine Mansfield, along with two older sisters, was sent by her banker father to finish her education at Queen's College, London, in 1903. There she met Ida Baker (called LM), who remained her close and loyal friend for life. Although her parents demanded her return to New Zealand in 1906, she left again for London in 1908, funded by them, hoping to establish herself as a writer and relishing the prospect of personal freedom. By March 1909 she was pregnant after a love-affair with a young violinist, and precipitately married George Bowden, a singing instructor eleven years older than she. She left him the next day. She then went to Germany, accompanied by her mother, miscarried her baby, and wrote the stories for her first book.

Back in London in 1910, these stories appeared in A.R. Orage's influential experimental magazine, the *New Age*. They were published as the successful collection, *In a German Pension*, in 1911. After a number of love-affairs and a serious bout of venereal disease, which probably left her both sterile and addicted to painkillers, Katherine Mansfield met the writer and editor, John Middleton Murry, then an Oxford undergraduate, late in 1911, and invited him to live with her in April of 1912. They married in 1918. Together they edited the avant-garde publication, *Rhythm*, whose publisher went bankrupt, leaving Murry responsible for his debts. The couple, in financial difficulties and trying to establish themselves as writers, shared a stormy friendship with D.H. and Frieda Lawrence. Katherine Mansfield's brother, Leslie, was killed in France, at the Front, in 1915, to her great grief. The war years saw other developments: an affair with the writer Frances Carco; a significant personal and professional friendship with VIRGINIA WOOLF (the two writers alternately saw each other as allies and rivals); the development of an illness which was diagnosed as tuberculosis in 1917. The Woolfs' Hogarth Press published Katherine Mansfield's longest, and most accomplished, story, *Prelude*, in 1918. Often separated from Murry and from all friends except for LM, Katherine Mansfield spent her last years in a pathetic and often irritable search for health in Italy and the South of France. Two more collections of her work, BLISS AND OTHER STORIES (1920) and THE GARDEN PARTY AND OTHER STORIES (1922), appeared in London during her lifetime. She died at the Gurdjieff Institute at Fontainebleau in January 1923.

Murry published additional collections of her stories, and her letters and journals after her death. His carefully cultivated legend of his wife as a fey creature, writing elfin stories, has given way to a view of Mansfield as a strong and subtle modernist writer, with a highly developed sense of the tragic and stoic dimensions underpinning the most ordinary lives, and a grasp of her craft which allowed her to work with extreme economy of expression. Her letters and journals are now as highly valued as her fiction, and, in all her writing, she can be seen as working closely on the characteristic modernist obsession with the fractured and disordered self.   KF

Mansfield Park (1814) This stoical REALIST novel offers JANE AUSTEN's richest exploration of the values informing her fiction. Concerned with 'ordination' (her word), it narrates the breakdown and restoration of the established order enshrined in a rural Northamptonshire estate. The property of the benign but cold Tory baronet Sir Thomas Bertram, its model of stable propriety is threatened when he leaves to attend to his Caribbean plantation. His children are led astray by the attractive but selfish Henry and Mary Crawford, representatives of Regency wit and emergent urban capitalist market relations. Only the novel's sentient centre, the quiet, passive Fanny Price, a poor cousin who has lived with the Bertrams since she was a child, refuses to join in with the tragi-comedy of errors enacted as the youngsters rehearse Kotzebue's *LOVERS' VOWS* and engage in a round of mismatched relationships. Austen's most virtuous and least ironized heroine is rewarded with marriage to the younger clergyman son, Edmund; their inheritance rests on Fanny's spiritual goodness and, in the margins of the plot, wealth derived from colonizing capitalism. MO'D

Mantel, Hilary 1952– English novelist, reviewer and travel writer. She studied Law at LSE without finishing a degree and then did social work, before spending eight years teaching in Africa and the Middle East. Her social-work background was the subject of caustic and attractively tasteless satire in her first two novels, *Every Day is Mother's Day* (1985) and its sequel, *Vacant Possession* (1986). *Eight Months on Ghazzah Street* (1988) was a psychological thriller about the status of expatriate women in the Arab world; *Fludd* (1989) was an apocalyptic comedy about evangelical preachers; *A Place of Greater Safety* (1992) was a richly drawn account of the Jacobins' mutual betrayal during the French Revolution; *An Experiment in Love* (1995) was an account of intense relationships among students that paid overt homage to MURIEL SPARK's *The Girls of Slender Means* (1963).

Mantel wrote several extremely accomplished books which had in common intelligence and fluency; the protean quality of her subject matter and choices of an appropriate style for each book made her a somewhat difficult writer to pin down. It is clear, for example, from several of the books, that the experience of having had religious belief was important to her and crucial to various of her characters; it was ambiguous

whether it was legitimate to describe her as a religious writer. She was a very funny writer who, in some of her books, notably *A Change of Climate* (1994), abandoned comedy almost entirely, relegating it to sly observations on the innerness of tragic and pathetic characters. She received the Shiva Naipaul Memorial Prize in 1987 for her uncollected travel writing.   RK

Manvill, Mrs P.D. ?–? American memoirist or novelist. Nothing is known of the life of this author other than what is related in her one book, *Lucinda, or the Mountain Mourner* (Johnstown, N.Y., 1807; five subsequent editions), which may be EPISTOLARY FICTION although the author claims it is made up of authentic letters to her sister and relates actual events that occurred in a rural community of New York state. The writer, a widow with one child, marries Elias F. Manvill, a poor widower with six grown children. She supports the family by sewing. When her stepdaughter Lucinda becomes pregnant as a result of being raped by a suitor, the writer supports and cares for her, tells her story and urges her to read *The Coquette*, a seduction novel by HANNAH FOSTER. The local magistrates, following Puritan customs, try to jail Lucinda or expel her from the community. When her health fails, they become ashamed of their verdict and rescind it. Lucinda dies after childbirth. The second edition includes a letter of sympathy from the magistrates and a letter from Mrs Manvill about Lucinda's growing child.   JSG

Maracle, Lee 1950– West-Coast-born First Nations writer who interweaves oratory, life-writing and Aboriginal myth to articulate the complex legacy of colonialism (see POST-COLONIAL WRITING) in Canada. Her autobiographical novel, *Bobbi Lee: Indian Rebel*, was printed in 1973 by a small Aboriginal press, but did not have mass market circulation until its reprinting in 1990. The novel details Maracle's experiences as a child, growing up on the mudflats of Vancouver, and her burgeoning political and social awareness as a First Nations woman. In 1988 Maracle produced *I Am Woman* as an independent publishing venture. This enabled her to resist the editorial constraints placed on oral-based cultures, and to question the tragic stereotypes imputed to First Nations people, in favour of a more personal narrative that is grounded in the everyday. Her collection of short stories, *Sojourner's Truth* (1991), combines the generic conventions of the European short story and First Nations oratory to create open-ended stories that demand the engaged participation of the reader/audience, where 'you become the trickster'. Her 1993 novel, *RAVENSONG*, employs the figure of the raven as a textual device to address the tensions between white Canadian society and a First Nations community gripped by a flu epidemic. Maracle has been a writer-in-residence at the Enowkin International School of Writing and has worked on cultural healing with First Nations communities.   SCM

Marchessault, Jovette 1938–
Francophone artist, novelist and playwright, born in Montreal, Quebec, of partially Aboriginal heritage, she left school at the age of 13 to work in a textile factory. She is a lesbian feminist whose work focuses mainly on women and on the profound bonds between women. Her early work describes matrilinear bonds and women's culture and spirituality; her later writing focuses on a more global cultural and spiritual vision. Her work is eclectic in its imagery, experimental in its form, and rich in its language.

Marchessault's autobiographical novel is a trilogy entitled *Comme une enfant de la terre* – known in English as *Like a Child of the Earth* (1988) – of which the first part is entitled *Le Crachat solaire* (1975), the second *La Mère des herbes* (1980), and the third *Les Cailloux blancs pour les forêts obscures* (1987). It explores human relationships with one another and with the spiritual, animal, vegetable and mineral worlds, and describes many facets of women's experience. The third part of the trilogy addresses the question of the unbridgeable gulf between women and men. *Comme une enfant de la terre* won the Prix France-Québec in 1976. *Tryptique lesbien* (1980) – translated into English as *Lesbian Triptych* (1985) – celebrates the strength of women and their need to have control of their bodies. One part of it, 'Les Vaches de nuit' – 'Night Cows' in English – written in rich and evocative language, has been successfully turned into a dramatic monologue and performed throughout Canada in both English and French.

Marchessault introduces historical characters into some of her theatrical work. In *La Saga des poules mouillées* (1981), four Quebec women writers from various eras meet and their works are reinterpreted from a feminist standpoint. *La Terre est trop courte, Violette Leduc* (1982) celebrates the turbulent life and the work of the French author. *Alice & Gertrude, Natalie & Renée et ce cher Ernest* (1984) presents a moment in lesbian history by dramatizing an imagined meeting of ALICE B. TOKLAS, GERTRUDE STEIN, Renée Viven and Ernest Hemingway in NATALIE BARNEY's salon. *Le Voyage magnifique d'Emily Carr*, which won the Governor General's Award in 1990, celebrates the life of the Canadian artist, her struggle against Victorian conformity, and her attraction to an Aboriginal goddess which leads her to her appreciation of cosmic forces within nature. A section of the National Film Board of Canada film, *Firewords – Les Terribles Vivantes* (1986) by Dorothy Todd Hénaut, is devoted to Jovette Marchessault.   GHN

Marian, or the Light of Someone's Home (1859)
MATILDA EVANS's first novel tells the story of a young governess, Marian Herbert, newly arrived in the South Australian colony. Loved by Allen, the son of her employer, she refuses to marry him until he becomes a Christian. Clutching her Bible she tells him, 'Those that marry let them marry in the Lord.' Evans re-works the young woman's quest novel to make Marian a powerful figure, who helps bring true religion, ordered domesticity and civilization to the Australian settlers.

Marian first appeared in parts, published by an evangelical printer in a small South Australian town. Evans explained her intention: 'a sincere desire to exhibit the beauty of true *Religion* as exemplified in the daily walk of life'.

The novel was taken up by a British publisher, appeared in six separate editions and was re-issued some twenty times.   MA

Markandeya, Kamala (Purnaiah Taylor) 1924–
Indian novelist who lives in England. Born in a Brahmin family in Bangalore, educated at the University of Madras, she worked as a journalist in India and the UK, where she married an Englishman. Most of her novels deal with the impact of modernization on a traditional society. She made a mark with her first novel, *Nectar in a Sieve* (1954), a bleak, neo-realistic (see REALISM) account of how a poor rural family is dislocated and destroyed by industrialization. Translated into seventeen languages, the book drew comparisons with THE GOOD EARTH by PEARL S. BUCK. *Some Inner Fury* (1955) and *Possession* (1963), both depict fruitless Indo-British encounters. In the first, the freedom movement drives apart an Indian woman, Mira, from her British lover, Richard. In *Possession* (1963), a wealthy British aristocrat, Lady Caroline, takes a fancy to a rustic prodigy, Valmiki, hoping to turn him into an international art celebrity. *A Silence of Desire* (1960) shows a conflict between modern rationality and traditional faith: Sarojini, the heroine, goes to a faith healer instead of a hospital to get her tumour cured. In *A Handful of Rice*, the scene shifts to the city, where Ravi, an urban vagabond, marries the daughter of a poor tailor and is forced into lower middle-class respectability. *The Coffer Dams* (1969) has a POST-COLONIAL setting and theme; a team of engineers, British and Indian, have uncomfortably close encounters at a dam site in the interior of tribal India. *The Nowhere Man* (1972), certainly one of Markandaya's most moving, if pessimistic, novels, shows the increasing alienation, and, finally, death of Srinivas, an Indian widower settled in London. *Two Virgins* (1973) is about two sisters, Lalita and Saroja, the first of whom is lost to the big, bad city, where she is lured by the prospect of becoming a film star. *The Golden Honeycomb* (1977) is a much more ambitious novel about three generations of a

princely family, from the 1850s to India's independence. In *Pleasure City* (1982), a multi-national hotel company spoils an idyllic coastal village in rural South India. Despite the fact that some of her novels seem unconvincing and contrived, Markandaya has shown enduring compassion for the victims of history, and has tried to depict a society in transition, suffering from the ravages of modernity, colonialism, racism and 'development'. MP

Marked Man, A (1891) This was ADA CAMBRIDGE's most successful novel, in both critical and commercial terms. It was first published in the Melbourne *Age* as a serial, *A Black Sheep*, a title which gives a more accurate sense of the comic elements in this narrative of a young man's elopement from his family's seat in England to make a career in Sydney, Australia. Cambridge openly rewrites George Meredith's *The Ordeal of Richard Feverel* and delineates the class and religious prejudices of the Old Country in the first half of the novel, before moving to describe those of the new. Her characters find life on Sydney Harbour more conducive to the discussion, if not the active pursuit, of their liberal ideals. In the first part of the novel, based on Cambridge's memories of Hunstanton, an ironic narrative voice offers sympathy and shrewd judgement on Richard Delavel's foolish marriage. The second part wavers in tone from comic to tragic moments, as Richard fails to fulfil J.S. Mill's liberal principles and the responsibility falls to his daughter. SPL

Markham, Beryl 1902–86 English aviator, race-horse trainer and writer. In 1906 Beryl left for Kenya with her father, an impoverished younger son hoping to make his fortune in farming. She would remain in Kenya for most of her life. She obtained a pilot's licence in 1930, and in 1936 became the first woman to fly solo across the Atlantic from east to west, crash-landing in Newfoundland. She was famously beautiful, and attracted a string of aristocratic lovers in Kenya on safari. She married three times, retaining the name of her second husband, Mansfield Markham, the father of her only child, Gervase, born in 1929. Her third husband, American writer Raoul Schumacher, almost certainly helped Markham write her poetic memoir, *West with the Night* (1942). Its style serves to conceal the real hardships she had experienced living in the bush. Indeed throughout her life she struggled to make ends meet. *West with the Night*, republished by the feminist press Virago to great acclaim in 1983, finally helped her financially. In the introduction MARTHA GELLHORN wrote, 'Beryl Markham was a woman of action, the way men are; her book is a freak event in her career.' RH

Markham, Violet Rosa (Mrs James Carruthers) 1872–1959 English public servant, committee woman, pioneer social worker, campaigner and writer, Markham was the daughter of a prosperous industrialist. Financially independent from early adulthood, she founded the Chesterfield Settlement, offering recreational and educational facilities to the poor. She viewed unemployment with deep horror, but clung to a simplistic belief in the efficacy of domestic service as the means of increasing female employment and freeing more prosperous women to attain excellence in art, literature and the professions. Staunchly but idiosyncratically liberal, she was ambivalent about universal suffrage, and for many years prominent in the campaign against women's suffrage.

Markham's writings were primarily vehicles for her political and philosophical beliefs. Before 1914 she published three books about South Africa, written from the vantage point of a Liberal Imperialist with strong views on the need to educate the black population. Her residence in Germany in the aftermath of World War I led to the publication in 1921 of *A Woman's Watch on the Rhine*, in which she expressed her pro-German sentiments; and in 1935, as a work of filial piety, she published a biography of her maternal grandfather and his work at Chatsworth, *Paxton and the Bachelor Duke*. War work interrupted her writing: her autobiography, *Return Passage*, was published in 1953. CT

Markyate, Christina of c.1096–98 – c.1155–66 Recluse, visionary, and monastic founder. That she can also be described as a writer testifies to the difference between medieval and modern understandings of authorship. Her Latin *Life* (c.1142) was written by a monk of St Albans, but is so plainly based on extensive interviews with Christina herself that it is arguably best described as a third-person auto-hagiography, a genre peculiar to medieval holy women.

The *Life* inserts the tropes of the virgin martyr legend into the daily life of the 12th-century gentry. It is interested in the inner life, describing Christina's spiritual development in terms of her visions of Christ, the Virgin, saints, and demonic apparitions in the forms of toads and bulls.

The *Life* tells how Christina, born Theodora to a noble English family, privately dedicated herself to virginity in her teens, and how she resisted family pressure, even to the extent of violence and attempted rape, to make her marry. She was forced to flee her family home 'with manly courage' and in male disguise and to live concealed in great discomfort for six years until her vow was recognized. Christina became a recluse, her reputation for sanctity attracting so many women to join her that the community was formalized as the Benedictine priory of Markyate in 1145, with Christina as the first prioress. Although never formally canonized, she was revered as a saint and her advice sought by many. MSALS

Marlatt, Daphne 1942– Born Daphne Buckle in Melbourne, Australia, to British parents, she grew up in Penang before immigrating to Vancouver, Canada, in 1951. Marlatt's writing in the early sixties was associated with the TISH group, poets who explored ideas of a West-Coast identity and the edges of language through their writing. Her early career, then, is closely associated with this largely male coterie which included George Bowering, Fred Wah, and Nichol and Frank Davey. Marlatt moved with her husband, Alan, to Bloomington, Indiana, in 1964, where she received an MA in Comparative Literature from the University of Indiana. She published *Frames of a Story* (1968) and *leaf leaf/s* (1969), both experimenting with poetic style, before returning to Vancouver when her marriage ended. Her next two works, experimental long poems, grow closely from her sense of place in the local and the immediate: *Vancouver Poems* (1972) and STEVESTON (1974), a documentary collaboration with photographer Robert Minden, which began in an oral history project. *Zocalo* (1977), is a journal-novel, which Marlatt describes as 'a travel book about getting lost'.

Marlatt's work in the 1980s surges with the energy of feminist writing and criticism in Canada. She helped to organize the germinal Women and Words / Les Femmes et Les Mots conference in 1983 and edited the feminist Anglo-Quebecois journal *Tessera*, which has produced ground-breaking innovative feminist writing in both languages. Alongside JANE RULE, NICOLE BROSSARD, Barbara Godard, Kathy Mezei and GAIL SCOTT, among others, Marlatt became part of a series of brilliant 'collaborations in the feminine', including the poems/essays/photographs of *Touch to My Tongue* (1984) (with Cheryl Sourkes) and *Double Negative* (1988), a long poem co-written with her lover, Betsy Warland. Two autobiographical fictions continue the interest in women's history and women's language and the ways that lesbian relationships cast new moulds for both language and history. In ANA HISTORIC (1988), the story of Mrs Richards, a woman of no history who appears briefly in the civic archives of Vancouver in 1873, Marlatt explores the possibilities of decolonizing settler histories by refiguring the past. In *Taken* (1997), the narrative shuttles between a woman's meditation on her mother's life in Australia and Malaya during World War II, the Gulf War and the loss of her lover. Here, as always, Marlatt returns to place and belonging, identity and migration, and the subversive potential of female body and language.   GWh

Marryat, Florence 1838–99 Popular and prolific British author, who wrote over seventy novels, and was also a dramatist, actress, singer, editor and manager of a school of journalism. She was the tenth daughter of Captain Frederick Marryat, writer of sea stories. Florence married T. Ross Church at the age of 16, had eight children, and then married Col. Francis Lean in 1890. Her most powerful work is *The Nobler Sex* (188–), a semi-autobiographical account of two abusive marriages, which powerfully details the Victorian woman's physical, emotional and legal helplessness in such situations. She began writing novels to distract herself while nursing her children through scarlet fever. Marryat is best known for her spiritualist novels, including *The Risen Dead* (1893), and an intriguing variation on the vampire myth, *Blood of the Vampire*, written from the perspective of the unhappy vampiric woman involuntarily condemned to destroy the men she loves. Marryat was a wide-ranging writer with an uneven output, but produced some original occult/SENSATIONALIST romances, and an important, courageous social document in *The Nobler Sex*.   TS

Marsden, Dora 1882–1960 English renegade suffragette who fuelled feminist debate in the 1910s through her editorship of the controversial magazine, the *Freewoman* (1911), which became the *New Freewoman* in 1913 and then the *Egoist* in 1914.

Marsden was born in Yorkshire of a lower-middle-class family and she became a brave activist for the Women's Social and Political Union. After clashing with the Pankhursts in 1910, however, she left the WSPU and founded the *Freewoman*. In its frank discussion of women's sexuality, morality and marital relations, it was condemned both by the WSPU and by the police, who threatened to prosecute Marsden for indecency. In addition to advocating a politics of consciousness-raising, she developed an anarchist feminism which championed the freedom of individual women. Dogged by ill health, Marsden stopped writing for the *Egoist* and developed an increasingly abstract and esoteric philosophy in her work of the 1920s and 1930s. RP

Marsh, Ngaio 1892–1982 New Zealand DETECTIVE writer and theatre director. Born in genteel circumstances in Christchurch, that most English of New Zealand cities, she trained as a painter and worked as an actor before writing her first detective story, *A MAN LAY DEAD*, in 1934. Between 1934 and 1982 Marsh wrote thirty-two detective stories, becoming, along with AGATHA CHRISTIE, one of the acknowledged 'Queens of Crime'.

The detective story was already a genre with pretensions above its populist audience, and Marsh develops this high tone, with complex plots, careful characterization and a range of erudite references flattering to the reader. Several of her works use a theatrical context, and, while she makes frequent use of the conventional country-house, English-village milieu, four novels have New Zealand settings, and several more have New Zealand characters. Her detective, Roderick Alleyn, is acute, empirical rather than intuitive, and pessimistic about human nature. He is less eccentric than Christie's detective, Hercule Poirot, or SAYERS's Lord Peter Wimsey. Alleyn's wife, Agatha Troy, is a painter, and there is perhaps a certain amount of autobiographical parallel, actual or wishful, in her character.

Marsh divided her time between England and Christchurch, where she became involved in the nascent, still-amateur theatre scene. She directed a number of productions, most memorably of Shakespeare, for the Canterbury University Drama Club. They established a high standard and an enthusiastic audience, despite what now seems her somewhat dated adherence to Eurocentric imperatives.

Marsh's autobiography, *Black Beech and Honey Dew*, was first published in 1966, and revised in 1981. She never married and, after the death of her parents, lived alone. A 1997 New Zealand novel, *Blue Blood* by Stevan Eldred-Grigg, which portrays her as a lesbian, has drawn heated denials from her friends. Her appearance – she was tall, deep-voiced and theatrical in her dress – her independent life and professional self-sufficiency cut across traditional stereotypes, as does the peculiar and largely unexamined place her writing has in the context of New Zealand literary nationalism.   JSt

Marshall, Paule 1929– Caribbean-US writer. Her parents emigrated from Barbados, which is where her second novel, *The Chosen Place, The Timeless People* (1969), is based. Her first novel, BROWN GIRL, BROWNSTONES (1959), however, is set in New York, where she grew up, and is a feisty account of a young girl, Selina, and how she forges her own life and independent relations with the powerful forces in her world, forces like her domineering mother and a racist society.

The Chosen Place, Praisesong for the Widow (1983) and *Daughters* (1991) move to the Caribbean to recreate a sense of roots and belonging, principally through a restoration of spiritual health and a sentiment of community. The 'place of origin' is romanticized and its culture dehistoricized and wrapped in mysticism. Rituals, dream visions, healing sessions, clairvoyant sages become the staples of her fiction. *The Chosen Place* uses as its point of departure two slave rebellions in the Caribbean in the 17th century and their continued celebration as myth on the island of Bournehills. The pageant recreating the rebellion is not examined in all its post-colonial ironies. Instead, it is used as a motif to give meaning to the life of deracinated Merle, almost destroyed by her time in Britain, her relationship with a white lesbian, and her antagonism with a white American woman, with whose husband she has an affair. Merle's return to her own husband and child marks the return to her community. Black roots are counterposed to the money-crazy, spiritually barren,

white USA. Marshall's overall critique is of a spiritually dead materialism and her middle-aged women characters return to themselves in powerful acts of restoration. Her short-story collections include *Soul Clap Hands and Sing* (1961) and *Merle and Other Stories* (1983). She has been a strong influence on subsequent generations of black women writers in the United States.   ATe

Marson, Una 1905–1965 Jamaican poet and playwright, often described as the first Caribbean woman poet. Marson published her first volume of poetry, *Tropic Reveries*, in 1930 and her second volume, *Heights and Depths*, in 1931. She had won a scholarship to Hampton High School, an unusual achievement for a black girl, but left when her parents died, to work as a secretary and later a reporter for the *Gleaner* newspaper. Marson visited England in 1932 and it was while working as assistant editor on the League of Coloured Peoples' magazine, the *Keys*, that she published her most powerful poem on racism, 'Nigger' (1933). In 1935 she was the only black woman to address the first International Women's Congress in Turkey, and in 1936 she travelled to Geneva as secretary to HIM Haile Selassie. Back in Jamaica, Marson founded the Kingston Drama Club in 1937 and saw two of her plays staged: *London Calling* (1937) and *Pocomania* (1938). Her third volume of poetry, *The Moth and the Star* (1937), reveals a striking awareness of race and gender politics. Returning to London in 1938, Marson presented *Calling the West Indies* for the BBC. Despite fragile health, she published *Towards the Stars*, mostly from collected poems, in 1945 and left for Jamaica where she worked for the nationalist publisher, Pioneer Press. She moved to the USA in 1960 but after a failed marriage returned to Jamaica. She continued to travel in connection with her charity work and began an autobiography but died in Kingston, at 60.   AD

Martin [née Mackay], Catherine Edith MacAuley *c.*1847–1937 Poet and fiction writer, born to a Skye crofting family which emigrated to South Australia in 1855, she grew up in a rural area at the end of the frontier era. She published short stories, verse and translations widely in the local press from her youth, and her writing career spanned some fifty-eight years. She also worked as a teacher and a clerk. Her first book, *The Explorers and Other Poems* (1874), contained translations from French and German, as well as a long poem on the ill-fated exploring expedition of Burke and Wills. A friend of CATHERINE HELEN SPENCE, she was influenced by GEORGE ELIOT. Her work draws upon wide intellectual roots, including German ROMANTICISM and the 19th-century debates about religion, and explores moral questions and questions of Australian identity. Her best-known novel, *An Australian Girl* (1890), was republished twice in London

Harriet Martineau.

1833.

John Howard, the prison reformer, for the Society for the Diffusion of Useful Knowledge (unpublished). In 1829, a bank failure ruined her family and she struggled to earn money by needlework and writing. In 1830, she won all three essay prizes in a Unitarian competition, but her real success came in 1832 with a series of stories, ILLUSTRATIONS OF POLITICAL ECONOMY which ran until 1834 and rapidly made her a literary celebrity.

Among her literary friends were Hallam, Sydney Smith, Malthus, Monckton Milnes, Bulwer, and she later knew Carlyle. After a trip to America, she published *Society in America* (1837) and her novel DEERBROOK, which she considered her best work, appeared in 1839. By now, she had repudiated Unitarianism and espoused rationalism, although she dabbled in mesmerism in the 1840s. After a visit to Egypt and Palestine, she published *Eastern Life, Past and Present* in 1848. In the 1850s, Martineau was much influenced by the French philosopher, August Comte, and condensed and translated his work in 1853. The following year she was told she had a fatal disease of the heart, and hastily wrote her *Autobiography*, in which she assesses her own talents as 'earnestness and intellectual clearness within a certain range' and claims 'she could popularise, though she could neither discover or invent'. This is a modest underestimation of a woman who was one of the most radical and intelligent thinkers of her day. The disease did not, in fact, prove immediately fatal, and she continued to write for another twenty years. CPe

in the 1890s. It was followed by *The Silent Sea* (1892). Her *Incredible Journey* (1923) was the first work with Aboriginal people as sympathetically drawn protagonists. Her work, which appeared under a number of pseudonyms such as 'M.C.' and 'Mrs Alick McLeod', is little known. MA

Martineau, Harriet 1802–76 British woman of letters – novelist, economist and essayist. The sixth of eight children of a Norwich textile manufacturer, Harriet was a 'gloomy, jealous and morbid' child (*Dictionary of National Biography*) who had read Milton by the time she was 7. She was educated at home and then from 1813 to 1815 at school. By 1816 Harriet had almost entirely lost her hearing and much of her later life was to be blighted by illness. Her family was Unitarian, and her brother, James, became a well-known theologian. In her youth, Harriet was also a devout Unitarian: her first article was published in the Unitarian *Monthly Repository* in 1821, and in 1823 she published *Devotional Exercises*. She became engaged, but her fiancé went insane and died in 1826. Despite illness, Martineau wrote steadily, working on a life of

Marx (Aveling), Eleanor (Eleanor Marx Aveling) 1855–98 The youngest of Karl Marx's three daughters, Eleanor was at the heart of the international socialist movement. She travelled widely in Europe and America, disseminating her father's ideas, but lived in London. She was a gifted polemicist, linguist, editor, teacher and public speaker; she also introduced translated fiction, drama and political tracts to an English readership. With her friends William Archer, Havelock Ellis and George Bernard Shaw, she was at the forefront of the Ibsen debate, championing his work for its endorsement of women's emancipation and its exposure of the hypocrisy of family life. She translated *An Enemy of Society* (1888) (later *An Enemy of the People*) and *Lady from the Sea* (1890), and co-wrote, with Israel Zangwill, an ironical sequel to *A Doll's House* called *A Doll's House Repaired*, in which Nora becomes a repentant wife. Hers was the first, for many years the only, translation of Gustave Flaubert's *Madame Bovary* (1886). She worked tirelessly for the early trades unions, teaching some of the working-class socialists to read and write. Much of her political writing was done in collaboration with her partner, the free-thinker Edward Aveling, notably 'The Factory Hell'

(1885), 'The Woman Question' (1886) and 'The Working-Class Movement in America' (1888), but many in the Marx–Engels circle blamed Aveling for her suicide. FE

Mary: A Fiction (1788) MARY WOLLSTONECRAFT'S autobiographical first novel investigates the social and economic causes of women's subjection in the track of her later pivotal text, A VINDICATION OF THE RIGHTS OF WOMAN (1792). At the same time, *Mary* ingeniously subverts the conventional genre of the sentimental novel. The book portrays in the life of its protagonist Wollstonecraft's archetypal marginalized 'genius' that 'will educate itself'. The highly sensitive, charitable and introspective Mary finds herself imprisoned in an arranged marriage when only 17. In the course of trying to evade her fate and follow her own inclinations, she loses not only her beloved friend Ann (based on Fanny Blood, Wollstonecraft's long-term friend) but later also Henry, her true soul mate. Unable to escape her social and economic disenfranchisement, Mary retreats into sentimental self-absorption and melancholy. Wollstonecraft later distanced herself from this short novel, considering it a 'crude production'. NBP

Mary Barton (1848) For her first novel (published anonymously), ELIZABETH GASKELL drew on her pastoral experience as the wife of a Unitarian minister to depict the grim social and domestic realities of industrial Manchester during the 'hungry forties'. John Barton is 'a thorough specimen of a Manchester man' whose 'extreme earnestness; resolute either for good or evil' is turned bad by personal deprivation and economic down-turn, culminating in his murder of the local mill-owner's son. Mary is his daughter, an apprentice dressmaker caught between her father and her future husband, Jem Wilson, when the latter is accused of the former's crime. Gaskell originally called the book 'John Barton' claiming that, despite his 'widely-erring judgment', he was the character 'with whom all my sympathies went'. She blamed the 'London thought' of her publishers for recasting it as *Mary Barton: A Tale of Manchester Life*, but by invoking the formula of the 'social problem' novel (pioneered by Disraeli in *Sybil: Or The Two Nations* (1845)), this title successfully characterized the most political of Gaskell's fictions. AS

Mary [Stuart], Queen of Scots 1542–87 Object of scandal and sanctification, and poet. Crowned when one week old, she was raised at the Catholic French court. After the early death of her husband, the Dauphin, in 1560, she returned to Protestant Scotland. Marriage to Lord Robert Darnley produced a son, James, later King of Scotland and England. Suspicions of Mary's involvement in Darnley's murder in 1567 were heightened by her hasty marriage to the disreputable Earl of Bothwell. Mary fled to England, only to be imprisoned. After inspiring several Catholic plots against ELIZABETH I, she was executed in 1587.

Mary wrote mainly in French. The notorious 'Casket letters' implicated her in Darnley's murder at her first trial in 1568; the accompanying sonnets to Bothwell are of more probable authenticity. These express intense passion and insecurity:

> You promised that we two should taste the pleasure
> Of planning the fair future at our leisure;
> Yet all night long I lie and languish here.

Mary's other poetry includes verses to, and in the style of, Ronsard; a sonnet to Elizabeth I, craving a meeting, which uses Petrarchan imagery of desire (1568); and meditations written during her long imprisonment. She also wrote an essay on adversity (1580) and numerous eloquent letters. HH

Mary I [Mary Tudor] 1516–58 First Queen Regnant of England since the 12th century; Henry VIII's eldest child. Her mother, CATHERINE OF ARAGON, employed distinguished tutors for her, including the Spanish humanist Juan Luis Vives. Her legitimacy and status became uncertain after the King's repudiation of Catherine, and because of her rigid adherence to the Church of Rome. She was kindly treated by Henry's last queen, CATHERINE PARR, who urged her to publish her translation of Erasmus's *Paraphrase of the Gospel of St John* under her own name. When it appeared in 1548 a preface by Nicholas Udall eulogized the erudition of the young women of Henry's court.

Mary followed her brother, Edward VI, to the throne in 1553. Her marriage to Philip II of Spain and her persecution of Protestants were unpopular. Her desperate wish to conceive a Catholic heir was unfulfilled, despite an imagined pregnancy which went as far as public bell-ringing for the reported birth. On Mary's death her half-sister, ELIZABETH I, restored the Protestant Church of England. HH

Mashinini, Emma 1929– Mashinini's autobiography, STRIKES HAVE FOLLOWED ME ALL MY LIFE (1989), offers an insight into the political struggles of black South Africans. The life, as signalled in the title, is shaped primarily by the socio-political context of Apartheid South Africa. Like KUZWAYO, Mashinini maintains a distinction between private life and the recounting of personal experience toward a political end. Her second marriage does not feature as an event in her narrative, and the circumstances surrounding the death of her daughter are left deliberately vague. This insistence on privacy might be read in terms of her 'fight for the dignity of individuals' in a context where such rights are denied to black people.

The distinction between documenting personal involvement in political struggle and the exploration of the self breaks down in the writing of the traumas of detention and of the period spent at a clinic for victims of detention. Here Mashinini speaks of the autobiographical enterprise as therapeutic. The process of the writing of the autobiography itself raises interesting questions around issues of agency, collaboration, and marketing imperatives as they influence the shape of the text. Mashinini began by recording aspects of her life on tape prompted by questions from Elizabeth Wolpert who was instrumental in persuading The Women's Press to publish the autobiography. The transcribed notes were then reworked by Mashinini together with her editor. To consider how 'the personal' is defined in such contexts is of significance to the study of autobiography as a genre.   C-AM

Mason, Bobbie Ann 1940– Though this American story-teller settled with her writer husband in Pennsylvania, the rural Kentucky she was born and raised in has been the primary home of her fictions. Early academic writings included two works on authors who intrigued her: Nabokov and Nancy Drew. With her first prize-winning collection *Shiloh and Other Stories* (1982), she mapped out a distinctive territory stylistically and culturally: in direct, affectless prose the stories describe a world of misplaced people drifting through an alcohol- and television-numbed present, in places where tobacco fields are yielding to strip malls, subdivisions and uncertainty. Her authenticity of details such as brand names marked her as one of the 'K-Mart REALISTS', as Tom Wolfe dubbed those 1980s writers of spare social realism that included Raymond Carver; but her work had more warmth and humour than Carver's. Her novel *In Country* (1985) was a layered work, politically and historically: it's the story of a teenage girl living with her uncle, a veteran whose damaging war experience sets the girl searching after the hidden meanings of the country's encounter with Vietnam. Bruce Springsteen is one of the girl's primary consolations – pop music is always an important presence in Mason's work. *In Country* was filmed by Norman Jewison in 1989. The novel *Spence + Lila* and a further volume of stories, *Love Life* (1989), followed, mining much the same material as the first two. *Feather Crowns* (1993) was a slight shift – a novel about a Kentucky mother who gave birth to quintuplets in 1900.   SB

Masters [née Lawler], Olga 1919–86 Australian novelist, short-story writer and journalist. She grew up on the far south coast of New South Wales, and devoted most of her adult life to domestic duties as the wife of an itinerant schoolteacher and mother to seven children. In her fifties she began part-time work as a jour-

nalist in the Sydney suburb of Manly, publishing occasional short stories, but her first book of stories, *The Home Girls*, was not published until 1982. In the four years before her death from a brain tumour, she published a further novel, *Loving Daughters* (1984), and a collection of related stories, *A Long Time Dying* (1985). Another novel (*Amy's Children*, 1987), a book of stories (*The Rose Fancier*, 1988), and a collection of her newspaper journalism were published posthumously.

In her short publishing career, Masters gained a strong critical following which encouraged her to work furiously, as if she were making up for lost time. She claimed to have 'mini nightmares about the time I have left, whether there is enough of it to write down all I want to'. Her fiction was almost exclusively about life in Australian country towns during the 1930s, a time of financial and cultural poverty. She had a remarkable eye for the details which gave women's lives meaning – for the sewing and embroidery, the cooking and careful husbanding of resources. Yet, a dark humour and sharp ironic tone pervades all her writing: the two sisters in *Loving Daughters* repress their sexual longings through their different domestic obsessions; Amy of *Amy's Children* survives in the city by developing a shield of selfishness. *A Long Time Dying*, though, probably shows Masters's talents at their most developed, as she carefully delineates the daily nature of poverty.   SPL

Materfamilias (1898) In this novel ADA CAMBRIDGE experimented with an unreliable, and unsympathetic, narrator – one of her selfish Victorian mothers. Mary describes her career as a vain, wilful and manipulating woman, from her teenage abandonment of her father, to the birth of her first grandchildren. She matures into a matriarch who interferes in the marriages and family life of her children, while remaining oblivious to their responses to her meddling. The novel has often been read as an unironic celebration of domesticity and motherhood, though from its first pages Mary declares her wilfulness and, from time to time, suspects that she may 'have a tendency to be inconsiderate'. It may be that Cambridge has made her narrator too lifelike for her satirical purposes, for even Mary has lyrical moments describing Cambridge's own loves – the Australian bush and the sea, and she falls silent when her beloved son, Harry, dies. Indeed, the *materfamilias*'s narration reads at times like a parodic version of Cambridge's own autobiographies, *Thirty Years in Australia* (1903) and *The Retrospect* (*c*.1912).   SPL

Mathers, Helen 1853–1920 British novelist whose best-known books (with titles frequently drawn from popular songs) tended to focus on the sexual and emotional maturation of young women. Her father, Thomas Mathers, was a country gentleman with twelve children (Helen was the third), whom he disciplined sternly. When young, the children were educated by a governess; Helen was sent away to school at 13, and became partially deaf there after an illness brought on by overwork. D.G. Rossetti encouraged her early attempts at writing (she sent him a poem when she was 16), as did George Augustus Sala, who helped her publish one of her stories in *Belgravia*, the magazine run by MARY ELIZABETH BRADDON. She turned to longer fiction in 1875 with *Comin' thro' the Rye*, a secretly written and anonymously published autobiographical novel influenced by the work of RHODA BROUGHTON. The story of a sexually maturing young girl attempting to escape from a tyrannical father, it was daring at the time, and was highly successful. Among her numerous books are *Cherry Ripe!* (1878), *My Lady Greensleeves* (1879) and SENSATION novels such as *Murder or Manslaughter* (1885). She married Henry Albert Reeves, an orthopaedic surgeon, in 1876, and had one son.   KW

Maurice Guest (1908) HENRY HANDEL RICHARDSON's first novel, depicts in lush detail the intrigues and love-affairs preoccupying a set of music students in Leipzig. Naturalistic in form but MODERNIST in its thematisation of art and desire, *Maurice Guest* draws partly on Richardson's life and rehearses intellectual debates of the period. A 1998 scholarly edition (Probyn and Steele) restores to the text material considered, by its first publishers, too controversial. The product of a provincial English family, Maurice Guest arrives in Leipzig to further his piano studies. At first 'full to the brim of ambitious intentions', he is soon distracted from his music on becoming infatuated with Louise Dufrayer, an enigmatic Australian beauty. Louise is involved, however, with Schilsky, a brilliant student who treats her with insolent Nietzschean misogyny. Schilsky's seduction of the pretty young American, Ephie Cayhill, precipitates Louise's doomed liaison with Maurice. Both Maurice and Louise occupy the role of outsiders, as desire draws each beyond the realms of conventional bourgeois morality. Rich with vignettes and vividly drawn characters, including the sexually ambiguous Krafft and the practical Madeleine, *Maurice Guest* is structured by the changing seasons which parallel its cycle of promise, fulfilment, doubt and departure.   BR

Mayor, F.M. 1872–1932 British author Flora Macdonald Mayor, daughter of the Revd Joseph Mayor, Professor of Classics and of Moral Philosophy at King's College London, grew up in a distinguished and scholarly family. Although the clergyman's daughter, unmarried and restricted to a life of good works in the parish, recurs in her writing, Flora herself seized the growing opportunities and freedom for middle-class women. She read History at Newnham College, Cambridge, then wrote *Mrs Hammond's Children* (1901) and embarked on a (very unsuccessful) acting career which she gave up on her engagement.

After the sudden death of her fiancé, despite years of mourning and ill health she produced three sad and striking novels, *The Third Miss Symons* (1913), *The Rector's Daughter* (1924), *The Squire's Daughter* (1929), and a posthumously published collection, *The Room Opposite and Other Stories* (1935). As the titles suggest, her main themes are family relationships and marginal women. *Mrs Hammond's Children*, a book about children for adults, rejects idealization of childhood and foregrounds quarrels, persecution, disappointment and guilt. *The Third Miss Symons* and *The Rector's Daughter* have now won classic status as portrayals of the disappointed spinster: dull and disagreeable Henrietta Symons is portrayed as compassionately as intelligent and altruistic Mary Jocelyn, the rector's daughter. The Victorian and 'pre-war' societies of these novels were already in the past. *The Squire's Daughter*, much less sympathetic and successful, reflects Mayor's later conservatism in the face of post-war change. The tales of the supernatural in *The Room Opposite* perhaps spring from her need to believe in personal immortality and reunion after death.   PMar

Mead, Margaret 1901–78 American anthropologist whose world-renowned studies of Samoa and New Guinea both advanced theories of cultural determinism and opened the study of anthropology to a popular readership. Born in Philadelphia, Pennsylvania, to academic parents, Mead attended Barnard College and received her Ph.D. from Columbia University. She studied under the eminent anthropologist Frank Boas, whose influence is seen in her first book, *Coming of Age in Samoa* (1928), in which she insists that nurture, rather than nature, proves the central force shaping human life. Produced out of field work conducted in 1925 on adolescent girls in Samoa, *Coming of Age* has become the world's bestselling anthropological book, challenging western conceptions of adolescence by arguing that this period of maturation was culturally, rather than biologically, determined. Her second book, *Growing Up in New Guinea* (1930), also proved a bestseller, furthering her theories on childhood.

Mead's subsequent studies continued her pioneering work on the social basis of behaviour, emphasizing in particular the behavioural differences between men and women in her studies *Sex and Temperament in Three Primitive Societies* (1935) and *Male and Female* (1949). One of the first anthropologists to use the mediums of photography and film, as in *Balinese Character* (1942) and *Growth and Culture* (1951), she also originated the concept of national character, a branch of anthropology which analyses culture through nationality. In addition to her anthropological work, Mead actively participated in social debates in America, often taking a radical stand on such issues as ecology, education, feminism, atomic power and legalization of marijuana. The author of more than 40 books, and over 1,000 monographs and articles, Mead also received numerous awards and honorary degrees. The director of Columbia University Research in Contemporary Cultures after 1948, Mead also became Curator Emeritus of Ethnology at the Museum of Natural History in 1965 and served as president of the American Association for the Advancement of Science in 1976. RL

Mears, Gillian (Debra) 1964– Australian novelist and short-story writer. Grew up in various northern New South Wales river towns, an area which features in much of her work, and where she still lives. After completing a BA in Communications at the University of Technology, Sydney, she published her first collection, *Ride a Cock Horse* (1988), eighteen stories which combine to tell the life story of a jockey, Albert Ertle. This was followed by another collection of interlinked stories, *Fineflour* (1990), set in the country town of the title. Her first novel, *The Mint Lawn* (1991), won the 1990 Vogel Award for an unpublished novel by a young writer. Its heroine, Clementine, still lives in the northern New South Wales town of her childhood, where she is haunted by memories of her dead mother. With *The Grass Sister* (1995), Mears attempted to move away from the more directly autobiographical material of her earlier work, setting part of this novel in Africa. Its central character is a lesbian on the edge of middle age, obsessed by memories of her younger sister, who it appears has committed suicide in Africa many years before. The sensual lyricism which is a feature of all Mears's work is strongly apparent here. Recent publications include a *Collected Stories* (1997), an excellent showcase for her talented use of language and construction of character, and *Paradise is a Place* (1997), a collection of photographs and essays. EW

Meehan, Paula 1955– One of Ireland's leading young poets. Born in the tenement area of inner-city Dublin, she grew up in a working-class environment. Educated at Trinity College Dublin, she was later to return as Writer Fellow-in-Residence of the English Department. Meehan also completed a Master's degree in Fine Arts from Eastern Washington University. Demonstrating a zest for performance, she has read poetry in Ireland and America. Working with musicians, visual artists and contemporary dance companies in Dublin, she has written for community and political theatre such as TEAM, Ireland's theatre-in-education company. Awarded several Arts Council bursaries, she has taught workshops as a community

activist and in prisons. *The Man Who Was Marked By Winter* (1991) and *Pillow Talk* (1994) were both shortlisted for the *Irish Times* / Aer Lingus Irish Literature Prize. Her other work includes *Return and No Blame* (1984), *Reading the Sky* (1986) and *Mysteries of the Home* (1996). Receiving praise from fellow poets EAVAN BOLAND and Paul Durcan, her poetry has attracted critical attention, and she has been discussed alongside the Galway poet and dramatist RITA ANN HIGGINS. Like Higgins, she writes of patriarchal violence as in 'Woman Found Dead behind Salvation Army Hostel', to indicate how Irish experience is fractured by gender and class, as well as religion and race. In 1992, Theo Dorgan recorded a lively interview with her where she describes her first encounter with poetry: 'we had to learn a verse of English and Irish poetry every day, off by heart. And I remember the sensation of trancing off on the rhythms. Even though we hadn't a clue what half the words meant, or what the poems "meant". But I found the rocking immensely comforting.' SFu

Meeke, Mary d.1816? English author of large quantities of popular GOTHIC novels in the late 18th and early 19th centuries. She may have been the wife of Revd Francis Meeke, who died in 1801 and whose widow died at Johnson Hall, Staffordshire, in 1816. She published various translations and seventeen novels under her own name, two of them (*The Veiled Protectress, or The Mysterious Mother* (1818) and *What Shall Be, Shall Be* (1823)) appearing posthumously. In addition, she seems to have used a number of pseudonyms, including 'Gabrielli', under which she produced another eight novels, including *The Mysterious Wife* (1797), *Harcourt* (1799) and *Something Strange* (1806). Most of Meeke's works were published by William Lane's Minerva Press, ensuring wide distribution and a reasonable rate of pay for their author. The novels tend to follow an established formula combining Gothic setting, sentimental philosophy and an inheritance plot. They enforce passive obedience and assert the values of the aristocracy, and can be connected with the increasing dominance of conservative values in the fiction of the early 19th century. Their popularity indicates the desire amongst the reading public for works which combine the *frisson* of the exotic location with a reassuring moral message. LBe

Mehta, Gita 1943– Indian writer born in Delhi into a well-known political family. Her father, Ajai Singh Mehta, was a famous freedom-fighter and, until his death in 1997, a major political leader of the eastern state of Orissa. Gita Mehta was educated in India and at Cambridge (UK) where she met her husband, president of the publishing house Knopf. She lives in New York, London and Delhi.

Her first book, *A River Sutra* (1993), explores a philosophical quest and narrates the disillusion in the Indian spirituality. An old man goes to Benares, the holy city, to purify his soul, only to find noisy crowds, dirt and depravity. The several stories are embroidered in a precious tapestry. *KARMA COLA* (1994) is an enjoyable satire on western travellers escaping from the boredom of an increasingly materialist world and in search of Indian spirituality. However, they often find out from fraudulent gurus, that the 'mystic East, given half a chance, could teach the West a thing or two about materialism'. *Raj* (1989) is a highly successful HISTORICAL NOVEL, a bestseller about the maharajahs and the early phase of India's independence struggle. The story is told through the life of a Princess who slowly breaks free from patriarchal and colonial bondage. She will mature from the role of an *ancien-régime* oppressed Princess to that of a politically enlightened freedom-fighter. *Snakes and Ladders: Glimpses of India* (1997) is a set of wide-ranging essays about India since independence. A witty story-teller and part of the international literary jet set, Gita Mehta combines a sharp interest in Indian history and culture with a teasing view of western myths of the Orient.   SPo

Melville, Jenny see BUTLER, GWENDOLINE

Melville, Pauline ?– Caribbean writer, born in Guyana of European and Amerindian parents. She has worked in Britain as an actress and has published two collections of short stories and a novel. Her first collection of stories, *Shape-Shifter*, won the *Guardian* Fiction Prize, the Macmillan Silver Pen Award, and the Commonwealth Writers' Prize and her novel, *The Ventriloquist's Tale*, won the Whitbread First Novel Award and was shortlisted for the Orange Prize.

Melville's short stories shift effortlessly between a broad range of geographical and cultural locations – in Europe, South and North America – to explore the ways in which a very diverse range of characters survives the trials, and joys, of daily life. Melville combines Amerindian myths and legends with a variety of playful literary strategies with dexterity and ease. This narrative 'shape-shifting' – the collection is entitled *Shape-Shifter* – is combined with an irreverence and wit which allows Melville to interrogate the connections and clashes between – and within – cultures, with a distinctive lack of piousness. In the title story of *The Migration of Ghosts*, Melville offers incisive insights into European and Amerinidan culture and history when a Macusi woman visits Prague and London with her European husband.

In *The Ventriloquist's Tale*, Melville provides a detailed representation of a Wapisiana community living in the hinterland of Guyana. Remarkable for being one of the very few representations of the 'original inhabitants' of the Caribbean, the novel manages both to lovingly document this endangered culture *and* to critique it.

DdeCN

Member of the Wedding, The (1946) A motherless 12-year-old is caught at the terrifying and mundane point of metamorphosis from child to adolescent, in a sensitive, powerful novel by CARSON McCULLERS. The three stages of the child's crisis are reflected in her three names: Frankie is her childish, tomboy self; F. Jasmine is the persona she adopts while preparing for her future, projecting her lonely fantasies onto her brother's wedding and rehearsing a variety of self-flattering outcomes; and Frances is the adolescent identity she assumes at the end of the novel. Set in a stifling late-summer Southern town with World War II in the background, the narrative is focused entirely through Frankie's consciousness and flavoured with her particular voice as she struggles to understand her own fears and desires, her society's constrictions, the wider world, and many of the big ontological and epistemological concerns of adolescence. McCullers's observations are acute; her prose highly physical, poetic and economical; her writing suffused with the GOTHIC: the novel encompasses freaks and freakishness, drugs, drink, violence and death.   SAS

Memento Mori (1959) MURIEL SPARK's first novel both celebrates and denigrates the literary world which she knew in the early part of her London career. A group of elderly literary folk start to receive calls from a hoaxer, or, more probably, Death himself, reminding them that they must die. Instead, they continue old feuds and lusts; some fall prey to a blackmailing housekeeper. They are explicitly contrasted with an idealized group of elderly working-class women who share a hospital ward with the book's moral centre, Jean Taylor, former maid and confidante of novelist Charmian. A Catholic, Taylor knows that the humiliations of old age can be offered up as penance. This is Spark at her most moralistic – a novel which appears REALISTIC and which tantalizes us with rational solutions, but is actually a fable; however, as often in her work, Spark is more interested in bad characters than in the saintly Taylor.   RK

Memoirs of a Survivor, The (1974) This dystopian fable by DORIS LESSING, set in a collapsing future society, treats with a combination of fantasy and psychological realism several of her major recurring preoccupations. The novel explores the development of self-knowledge, the 'nightmare of repetition' (of both parental deficiencies and hierarchical social structures), the consequences of political irresponsibility and the need to break down old ways of thinking and allow new modes of being and communication. Adolescent Emily grows up between the narrator's flat and the disintegrating world outside, where unofficial and alternative strategies provide the only means of coping with social breakdown. Here in the streets child gangs enact a reversion to savage tribalism and animality in sharp contrast to the humane efforts of the protagonists and the delicate loyalty of Emily's cat–dog Hugo. The narrator meanwhile explores a mystical realm beyond the flat's internal wall, a place where she discovers the impossibility of repairing what has occurred and witnesses scenes of past emotional damage and of potential co-operative harmony. The transcendent, hopeful ending looks forward to both *The Marriages of Zones Three, Four and Five* and *The Making of the Representative for Planet 8*.   SAS

Memoirs of Emma Courtney (1796)

Adopting the first-person confessional mode of romantic–revolutionary writers wishing to harness fiction to radical political purpose, MARY HAYS explores woman's equal right to expression of passionate feeling and intellectual ardour. She scandalized contemporaries who detected autobiographical influences: Emma's fervent pursuit of Augustus Harley echoed Hays's own unrequited love for William Frend, while the philosopher/mentor Francis (one of Emma's male educators) mirrors her friendship with William Godwin. In fact Hays assumes a cautionary stance toward Emma's amorous avowals, severely questioning women's lack of education and opportunity for work and independence which contributed toward such overwrought sensibility. Hays's EPISTOLARY format, and her intricate unpicking of psychological nuances, recalls Samuel Richardson's *Clarissa*, while Emma's complaints about women's lack of emancipation prefigure the frustrations of CHARLOTTE BRONTË's *JANE EYRE*. Her sympathy for a 'fallen' heroine (a theme Hays developed further in *The Victim of Prejudice* (1799)), provided ample ammunition for a critical backlash. After this women's fiction would turn toward authorial authority based more on moralizing and less on radicalism and self-exposure.   LMT

Memoirs of Miss Sidney Bidulph (1761)

FRANCES SHERIDAN's novel of sentiment, which was dedicated to Richardson, tackles complex moral issues, exploring the tragic consequences of women's solidarity in challenging the sexual double standard. Sidney is persuaded by her mother to give up the prospect of a happy marriage to Faulkland because another woman is expecting his child. She marries Mr Arnold who is adulterous, just as it transpires that Faulkland was deliberately trapped into marriage, and his wife also proves unfaithful. When Sidney is widowed and Faulkland believes his wife dead, they finally marry. Noble gestures based on moral principle end disastrously, and

Sidney's obedience to parental authority and fortitude in the face of suffering earn her no reward. However Sheridan's social satire is incisive and her characters' dilemmas convincing. Despite her pessimistic conclusions, the book was critically acclaimed and popular at home and, in translation, abroad, and she published a sequel, *Conclusion of the Memoirs*, in 1767.   LMT

Memories of a Catholic Girlhood (1957)

A classic of American autobiography, this *tour de force* combines eight essays, originally written for magazines (primarily the *New Yorker*). Spanning the years from MARY MCCARTHY's birth in 1912 to her departure for Vassar, these roughly chronological memoirs range through family history to examine the reconstruction of memory and are linked by commentaries that attempt to distinguish fact from fiction, knowledge from conjecture, truth from honesty. McCarthy depicts her Dickensian early years with abusive relatives with outrage for injustice, but without self-pity.

Eventually rescued by her maternal grandfather, McCarthy devotes most of the book to her school years, and her gradual, difficult, acknowledgement of the distinction between morality and religion, between the real and the ideal. Vivid, dramatic, detailed, these memoirs are coolly honest, analytical and forthright as they explore power and powerlessness, rejection and inclusion, the privileged and the underprivileged. Inviting allegorical readings in her commentaries, McCarthy turns her appraising eye onto herself as often as onto those around her. With superb prose, rich portraits of character and place, and a critical but understanding tone, this book is often judged McCarthy's finest work.   SC

Memory Board (1987)

JANE RULE's sixth novel is a REALIST vision of how old age can help people reconsider the opposition between the heterosexual genders which is created between boys and girls and affirmed throughout their adult lives. It is a rare example of an unsentimental yet hopeful novel about the limitations and possibilities of old age. This reconsideration is embedded in the interactive re-telling and writing of past and present by a woman for a woman, symbolized by the memory board.

Set in Vancouver, the story focuses on the twins David and Diana, and Diana's lover, Constance. Diana's relationship was disapproved of by David's wife, which is why David kept silent about his twin's existence, until at 65 he begins to question his conformity. Diana is reluctant to have him back, but Constance's loss of memory and her own arthritis create a new need and place for him.   CES

Menken, Adah Isaacs (Theodore) 1839?–68

American actress, journalist and poet. Her early life is

obscured in conflicting accounts, but she was probably born in New Orleans. She married at least four times, had and lost two children, had affairs with Swinburne and Alexander Dumas *père*, and counted GEORGE SAND and literary men of both American coasts among her friends. She married her first husband, a Jewish businessman, at 15, studied Judaism, and wrote for the *Israelite*. Beginning her acting career in 1856, she became famous in the United States, England and France. Her consummate role was the lead in *Mazeppa* (based on Byron's poem) which she played in a body stocking, riding across the stage chained to a horse. As a journalist, she championed Whitman's poetry. In 1867, she prepared *Infelicia*, a collection of 31 free-verse poems on Jewish and women's themes. She died in Paris a week before the book's publication.   JSG

Menzies [née Calvert], Trixie Te Arama 1936–
New Zealand poet born in Wellington, of Scottish and Tainui descent, who performs her poetry in Auckland pubs, at local festivals and national huis. Her poetry collections, *Uenuku* (1986) – which won the PEN Best First Book Award – *Papakainga* (1988) and *Rerenga* (1992), were published by Waiata Koa, an Auckland-based collective of Maori women and artists. Deeply steeped in Maoritanga, Menzies acclaims flax-making and weaving as 'Our work [which] will fashion the nets to catch the star', and celebrates the earth's nourishing provender of puha (sow thistle) and watercress. Like KERI HULME'S her hybridized poetry reconciles ancient Polynesian legends with contemporary themes and she transforms Western cultural icons with Maori myths: Stephen Hawking, for example, becomes a present-day Maui: 'keyboard happy / Plucking the fiery fingernails of Time'. Menzies has published critical articles and edited *He Wai: A Song: First Nations Women's Writing* (1996).   JMW

Meredith, Louisa 1812–95 Australian writer and illustrator who had already established her reputation in England before emigrating to Tasmania as a bride of 26 in 1839. She began writing observations of colonial life and local flora and fauna from the point of view of a short-term settler, but fluctuations in the family's fortunes meant that she remained in Australia for nearly fifty years. She became famous in Australia and Britain for her beautifully illustrated descriptive books such as *Notes and Sketches of New South Wales* (1844), which went into many editions, *My Home in Tasmania* (1853) and *Our Island Home: A Tasmanian Sketch Book* (1879). She also turned her hand to novels and children's fiction and poetry. Four novels were published in book form, one of them set and published in Hobart (*A Tasmanian Memory of 1834. In Five Scenes*, 1869).   SMS

Mernissi, Fatima 1941– Moroccan feminist and sociologist who was born in Fez and studied Political Science at the University of Rabat, and Sociology in Boston, Massachusetts. Since 1980 she has been a member of the Research Institute of Mohammed V University, Rabat, where she is currently Professor ofOciology. She recalls how she began her writing career with 'vitriolic' and controversial articles for the now-defunct magazine, *Lamatif*, but changed to a more constructive approach, joining a writers' collective in Rabat in 1984 'to meet to spell out our vision of change together, to show how Morocco could be transformed, to offer alternatives'. She has published widely in French and Arabic, and many of her books have been translated into English; these include *Beyond the Veil* (1975), *Women and Islam* (1991), *The Forgotten Queens of Islam* (1993), *The Harem Within* (1996), *Women's Rebellion and Islamic Memory* (1996). Her work combines historical research into Islamic tradition with sociological analyses that draw on demographic surveys, interviews and questionnaires. At once scholarly, lively and polemical, her writing is inspired by a mission to change the negative stereotypes of women widespread in modern Arabic states by finding in Islamic tradition a more positive feminine ideal – one suited to the needs of a progressive, modernizing democracy. She argues that through a selective reading of Islamic tradition, political power and social order have come to be identified with the control of women in modern Arab states.   WJB

Mew, Charlotte 1869–1928 British poet who also wrote essays and short stories. Mew's themes of renunciation, isolation and loss reflect a troubled private life. A noted member of the London literary scene, one of her stories appeared in the second issue of the notorious *Yellow Book* in 1894. Mew's friend MAY SINCLAIR later showed her work to Ezra Pound who published it in the *Egoist*.

THE FARMER'S BRIDE (1916), just sixteen poems, attracted the support of such figures as Siegfried Sassoon, Thomas Hardy (whom Mew revered) and VIRGINIA WOOLF, who described her as being 'unlike anyone else'. An expanded edition was published in England and America in 1921, but she wrote little after this. A book of uncollected early poems, *The Rambling Sailor*, appeared a year after her death.

Mew negotiated private agony through lyric convention as can be seen in the title poem of *The Farmer's Bride* – a ballad that bursts its seams. The girl who 'turned afraid / Of love and me and all things human' is held captive:

> She sleeps up in the attic there
>   Alone, poor maid. 'Tis but a stair
> Betwixt us. Oh! my God! the down,
> The soft young down of her, the brown,
> The brown of her – her eyes, her hair, her hair!

431

While the language is romantic, this crescendo of exclamatory bursts is forcefully erotic. The farmer cannot suppress his desire and there is sympathy for him in this. Mew frequently adopted a male persona and addressed many of her poems to women. Disguised or not, her own presence in her work is a troubling, demanding and desirous one.

Two of Mew's siblings died in asylums and she gave her fear of inherited insanity as her reason for renouncing marriage and motherhood. The death of the sister with whom she lived did in fact lead to a breakdown and her eventual suicide.

In her poems, you can sense Mew looking both forwards and back. There are the heightened, elaborate rhythms of Tennyson and the imaginative force of her beloved EMILY BRONTË; but also the fractured imagery and associative freedoms of H.D. or WOOLF. Writing at the crux of MODERNISM, Mew was a pivotal figure whose work has the force and urgency not to suffer from this. LG

Meynell [née Thompson], Alice Christiana Gertrude 1847–1922

Prolific poet, essayist and journalist, the younger of the two daughters of Thomas and Christiana Thompson. Her sister, Elizabeth (later Butler), was well known as a painter of battle-scenes. The family lived in Italy and France before settling in England in 1864, and the girls were educated by her father who was a friend of Charles Dickens. Her mother, a concert pianist, converted to Catholicism in the late 1860s and her daughters followed her example. Her first volume of poems, *Preludes*, appeared in 1875, when she was 28, and was much praised by Tennyson and Ruskin.

In 1877 Alice married Wilfrid Meynell, a Catholic journalist and began a career in journalism. Between 1879 and 1891 she bore eight children (one of whom died). Her close friends included Francis Thompson (who wrote poems to her), Coventry Patmore and George Meredith. Her numerous essays, published in the *Pall Mall Gazette*, the *National Observer* and other periodicals, were collected under various titles including *The Rhythm of Life* (1893), *The Colour of Life* (1896) and *The Spirit of Place* (1899). In her later years she became a staunch supporter of non-militant suffragism, marching alongside Ethyl Smyth, CICELY HAMILTON and MAY SINCLAIR in the demonstrations of 1910–12, and she travelled widely in France, Germany, Italy and the United States.

Her poetry, much of which deals with the theme of religious mystery, is largely personal and lyrical. She was one of the first Victorian women poets to acknowledge the ambivalent feelings of motherhood and to engage with the social and political pressures upon mothers. Her poems were published in *Poems* (1893), *Other Poems* (privately printed, 1896), *Later Poems* (1902),

A Father of Women and other Poems (1917) and, posthumously, *Last Poems* (1923). Her volumes of prose include a book on John Ruskin (1900), and *Mary, The Mother of Jesus* (1912). She also edited three anthologies of poetry and wrote prefaces to over a dozen volumes of selections of poetry. She died in London on 27 November 1922. A nearly full-length pencil-drawing of her by John Sargent (1895) is in the National Portrait Gallery. RS

Mhlophe, Gcina 1958–

South African writer and story-teller. Mhlophe was born in Hammarsdale, near Durban, and went to school in the Transkei, moving to Johannesburg in 1979. In the play *Have you Seen Zandile?* (1989) some autobiographical elements can be identified. Mhlophe's contribution to the revival of traditional story-telling in South Africa is significant. She has written a number of books for children, and appears on children's television where she has found a new medium through which to continue the story-telling tradition of Zulu mothers and grandmothers. She is the leader of the Zanendaba story-tellers who have travelled in Africa and America, and whose work consists of dramatizing African folktales. She collaborated on a book called *African Story Theatre* (1996), which contains a collection of plays based on African folktales, and which includes notes giving guidance on staging these dramatized tales. As resident director of the Market Theatre in Johannesburg, she instituted an annual short-story festival, designed to recreate the oral story-telling tradition. CCo

Michaels, Anne 1958–

Canadian poet, novelist and teacher of creative writing whose two collections of poetry, *The Weight of Oranges* (1986) and *Miner's Pond* (1991), each won awards. International stature, however, and a string of major prizes followed the publication of FUGITIVE PIECES (1997), her first novel, which saw editions in twenty-two countries. Ten years in the writing, this meditation on the Holocaust resembles a narrative poem more than simple prose. Its uniqueness derives in part from Michaels's musical experience, writing theatrical scores, but is most noticeable in her imagery and pin-point sharp imaginative intensity. Silent on the relevance of the book's content to her own family, she admits to motivations driven by conscience and moral concerns. The novel's focus is less the charted monstrosities of Nazi extermination, more the unforgettable details of lives marked by grief, heroism and the legacy of past crimes: an honouring of the memory of those who died and an illumination of the pain of those who survived. She has been compared with fellow Toronto-dweller Michael Ondaatje, another poet–novelist, but in a single work of fiction has established the distinction of her voice: 'I did not witness the most important events of my life. My deepest story must be told by a blind man, a prisoner of sound. From behind a wall, from underground. From the corner of a small house on a small island that juts like a bone from the skin of sea.' ELi

Middlemarch (1872) The scope of GEORGE ELIOT's sixth novel is evident in the subtitle, 'A Study of Provincial Life', and encompasses this life as it appears from the perspectives of the gentry, the business classes and the poor. Set in the tumultuous period forty years prior to the time of its writing, the novel combines this social panorama with analysis of the impact of historical events on individual lives. The intersection of the public and private is nowhere clearer than in Eliot's treatment of marriage and its effects on both social structures and the self. The idealistic heroine, Dorothea, finds her noble expectations of heroic self-sacrifice fail to match the petty realities of marriage to an elderly scholar, while a young doctor has his public-spirited ambitions thwarted by the limited vision of his profoundly conventional wife. These marriages, founded on a 'total missing of each other's mental track', illustrate the necessity of recognizing an 'equivalent centre of self' in the other. This parallels the demands placed on the reader by an ever-present narrator who, by also implicating us in the human failings of the characters, denies facile judgements and demonstrates a liberalism which seeks to explain the motivations of moral agents whose lives are inextricably linked. MM

Mildmay [née Sherington], Lady Grace c.1552–1620 Autobiographer and medical and devotional writer. At her father's seat of Lacock Abbey in Wiltshire she received a strict Puritan education. In 1567 she married Anthony Mildmay, later a knight, and moved to Apethorpe, Northamptonshire, the estate of her father-in-law, Sir Walter Mildmay, a prominent courtier and Puritan.

She had one child, Mary, for whom she wrote a volume of reminiscences. This passes on her views on education, and records her occupations during her husband's frequent absences at court or on embassies. Her chief pursuits were reading the Bible, singing psalms, playing her lute, and medicine. She relates that 'every day I spent some time in the Herbal and books of physic'. She made and administered cures and corresponded with male practitioners. She also managed the Apethorpe estate after her husband inherited it.

A portrait of Lady Mildmay in later life shows her with books and medical flasks. Her remedies were posthumously assembled by her daughter into a volume entitled 'For the Workhouse'. The full text of her autobiography was published in 1993, with parts of her extensive religious meditations and medical records. HH

Mill on the Floss, The (1860) GEORGE ELIOT described this, her second novel, as a 'companion picture of provincial life' to the pastoral REALISM of *ADAM BEDE* (1859). As brother and sister Tom and Maggie Tulliver grow up, their family fortunes decline, changing the shape of their adult lives. Eliot recognized that the extended (and semi-autobiographical) treatment of Tom's and Maggie's childhood – 'my love of my subject in the first two volumes' – confers a skewed emphasis on the book. As a result, she acknowledged, the concluding 'tragedy' in which the river floods and Tom and Maggie drown together, 'is not adequately prepared'. Critics have also argued that in renouncing her love for Stephen Guest, her cousin's admirer, Maggie makes the conventional choice between the twin injunctions of 'passion and duty' which Eliot herself did not. Overall, however, these flaws do not negate but rather enhance the book's effect. They show the disintegration and renewal of sibling relationships to be its dominant theme as well as its defining motif: by repeating the words of the epigraph in the closing sentence, Eliot marks both boundaries of the text with her insistence that '"in their death"' Maggie and Tom '"were not divided"'. AS

Millay, Edna St Vincent 1892–1950 American poet, playwright and fiction writer. She was born in Rockland, Maine, to a nurse and a schoolteacher, and raised by her mother after the age of 8 when her parents divorced. She published her first poems in her teens and, at 20, attracted national attention with her long poem 'Renascence', which led to a scholarship at Vassar. In 1917, the year she graduated from Vassar, she published *Renascence and Other Poems* and starred in a production of her play, *The Princess Marries the Page*. After graduating she moved to Greenwich Village where she joined a group of socialist feminists and earned a living writing magazine sketches under the pseudonym 'Nancy Boyd'; these sketches are collected in *Distressing Dialogues* (1924). The Provincetown Players in Greenwich Village staged three of her plays: *The Princess Marries the Page* (1918), *Aria da Capo* (1919) and *Two Slatterns and a King* (1921). With the publication of *A Few Figs from Thistles* (1920) and *Second April* (1921), she was hailed as the poetic voice of NEW WOMANHOOD because of her sexual frankness and unconventionality. From 1921 to 1923 she worked as European correspondent for *Vanity Fair*. In 1923 she married Eugen Jan Boissevain, widower of suffragist Inez Milholland, whom she idolized. They settled on a farm in Austerlitz, New York.

In all Millay published seventeen books of poems, four plays, an opera libretto and a translation of Baudelaire (*Flowers of Evil*, 1936). *The Ballad of the Harp-Weaver* (1923) earned her the first Pulitzer Prize for Poetry ever awarded to a woman. In 1927 she joined the crusade on behalf of condemned anarchists Sacco and Vanzetti, about whom she wrote five poems after their execution (in *The Buck in the Snow*, 1928). She wrote socially conscious poetry during the Depression and, during World War II, contributed verse propaganda to the war effort with *Make Bright the Arrows: 1940 Notebook* and *The Murder of Lidice* (1942), a radio play written for the Writers' War Board. Later collections are *Lyrics* (1939), *Sonnets* (1941) and *Poems* (1956); her letters were published in 1952.   JSG

Millett [née Murray], Kate 1934– American feminist, political activist, sculptor, artist and writer, whose social commentaries played a prominent role in defining first-wave feminism. Born in St Paul, Minnesota, she graduated from the University of Minnesota in 1956 and received a first class degree in Literature from St Hilda's College, Oxford, in 1958. After studying for a Ph.D. at Columbia, Millett pursued a career in sculpture and married the artist Fumio Yashima in 1965, writing about these experiences in *Flying* (1974). She held posts at Barnard and Bryn Mawr Colleges and Sacramento State and founded the Women's Art Colony Farm in Poughkeepsie, New York. She was active in the Civil Rights movement and an original committee member of the National Organization for Women (NOW) founded in 1966.

In 1970 she published her immediate bestseller, *Sexual Politics*, based on her thesis, which undertakes a radical analysis of patriarchy as it operates in history, culture, religion, psychoanalysis and, most centrally, literature. Providing witty and innovative readings of Freud, D.H. Lawrence, Henry Miller, Norman Mailer and Jean Genet, the book's polemic urges a cultural revolution headed by the oppressed and alienated minorities, predominantly women. Millett argues that humanity will be freed from the constrictions of sex, race and class, by exposing and eliminating the grounds on which oppression operates. During the 1970s and after she put her theory into practice, demonstrating for the Equal Rights Amendment and as a member of the Congress of Racial Equality. She visited Iran in 1979 to advocate women's rights after the revolution, but was expelled by Khomeini's government for her efforts. Millett's other projects largely explore the meaning of liberation in her own life and others', including a film about women, *Three Lives* (1971), and her books *The Prostitution Papers* (1973), an account of her love-affair with a woman; *Sita* (1977), an inquiry into an actual case of sadism; *The Basement* (1979); *Going to Iran* (1982); *The Loony Bin Trip* (1990), describing her own manic-depressive history; and *The Politics of Cruelty* (1994).   EM

Milligan, Alice 1866–1953 Irish poet, playwright and journalist. Alice Milligan was born into a prosperous Presbyterian family in Omagh, County Tyrone. The family moved to Belfast in 1878. Milligan studied in London and Dublin before returning to Belfast in 1891. Her political, historical and cultural education was steeped in the ideas of the emerging Irish Literary Revival and she became increasingly republican in her politics. In 1895 she co-edited the first issue of the *Northern Patriot* with ETHNA CARBERY (ANNA JOHNSTON). But the political thrust of the paper was too radical for the Henry Joy M'Cracken Society who had initiated it, and Milligan and Johnston established their own magazine, *The Shan Van Vocht* (*An tSean Bhean Bhocht* / The Poor Old Woman) which ran from 1896 to 1899. The entire focus and motivation of the magazine was political, its ultimate goal to promote an Irish national consciousness and culture.

A popular lecturer and prominent member of the Gaelic League, Milligan was well known as a journalist, poet and dramatist, but she also wrote fiction (sometimes under the pseudonym 'Iris Olkyrn'). Her one-act play *The Last Feast of the Fianna*, staged in 1900, was the first to dramatize Irish legend, an example soon followed by other dramatists of the Irish Literary Theatre and later the Irish National Theatre. Although Thomas MacDonagh had once referred to her as 'the greatest living Irish poet', she ended her life in obscurity and poverty. Works include *A Royal Democrat* (novel, 1892), *Hero Lays* (poetry, 1908) and, with Seamus MacManus and Ethna Carbery, *We Sang for Ireland* (poetry, 1950).   LM

Millin, Sarah Gertrude 1888–1968 South African novelist, short-story writer and non-fiction writer. She was born in Lithuania into a Russian Jewish family, who emigrated to South Africa when she was a baby. The themes on which Millin's reputation rests, and which have made her unfashionable in modern-day South Africa, are racial purity and racial identity. She was a prolific writer, whose most influential work is the novel *God's Step-children* (1924), which deals with the theme of miscegenation. Her novels, seventeen in all, return obsessively to the question of racial purity. Among her many works of non-fiction is her *The People of South Africa* (1951), in which she divides South Africans into the Afrikaners, the English, the Jews, the Indians, the Half-castes and the Africans. Apart from the addition of the Jews as a special category, her chapter division follows the Apartheid racial classification system. She also published two autobiographies, *The Night is Long* (1941) and *The Measure of my Days* (1955), as well as biographies of Cecil John Rhodes and General J.C. Smuts. Her journals kept during World War II were later published as *War Diaries, 1944–1948*.   CCo

Milner, Marion [Joanna Field] 1900–98 British writer and psychoanalyst. She read Psychology and

Physiology at London University, and in the 1930s did research in girls' schools and began to train as a psychoanalyst. From World War II on, she practised and wrote as a psychoanalyst.

Milner thus began her career as a thoroughly modern woman, armed with a strong grasp of one of the most important new sciences of modern times, psychology. But she is perhaps best described as a modern romantic. In her thirties she wrote *A Life of One's Own* (1934) and *An Experiment in Leisure* (1937) under the pseudonym of 'Joanna Field'. Her subject was the self and its potential creativity in the modern world. Her quest for a way of living that lies beyond the suffocating constraints of modern individualism made Milner a romantic as much as a modernist; Keats and Blake are her constant references. Her third book, *On Not Being Able to Paint* (1950), is a study and a demonstration of the unconscious and conscious dramas of the creativity of the amateur painter and is an educational and psychological classic. Psychoanalysis, for her, was much more than a systematic scientific approach to human misery; like a painting, a day-dream or a myth, the analytic session was a place for self-discovery and creative adventure.   LJS

Miner, Valerie 1947– American feminist whose writings testify to a life of political engagement. Born in New York, after university she went to London, where in the 1970s she contributed to feminist publications and wrote stories that appeared in *Tales I Tell My Mother*, a book whose contributors included MICHÈLE ROBERTS. She set an early novel in London: the controversial tale of women in the IRA, *Blood Sisters: An Examination of Conscience* (1981). Like her other novels – including *Murder in the English Department* (1982) and *Winter's Edge* (1984) – *Blood Sisters* explores the lives of women shaped by their political situations. Her prose is conventional, her style documentary rather than lyrical, but she experimented moderately with form in *Movement* (1982), a novel about a married woman who eventually comes out as a lesbian, that interspersed episodes from its heroine's life with vignettes about other unrelated characters. The novel is set largely in Berkeley, where she has lived and taught. Other works include *All Good Women* (1987) and *Competition, a Feminist Taboo?*, as well as *Trespassing*, a volume of stories published in 1989. In the 1990s new work appeared in the USA: a non-fiction collection, *Rumors from the Cauldron*, and the novel *A Walking Fire* (1994).   SB

Mirrlees, Hope 1887?–1978 British author and scholar, primarily of interest for her third novel, *Lud-in-the-Mist* (1926). She studied Classics at Newnham College, Cambridge, where she became a favourite student of Jane Ellen Harrison; family money enabled her to pursue her intellectual and literary interests.

Mirrlees's poem *Paris* (1919) published by the Hogarth Press, is an interesting exercise in imagist travelogue, which uses a full battery of expressionist shock tactics – interjected advertising slogans, cinematic cuts from one sequence to another, lines laid out in imitation of their subject matter. Her other poetry, most of it occasional, is elegant and fluent but not remarkable.

Of her three novels, *Madeleine – One of Love's Jansenists* (1919), is a historical study in which an intense young woman attempts to befriend Madame de Scudery and other BLUESTOCKINGS of her circle and is cruelly rebuffed, going mad as a result. This possibly reflects Mirrlees's close relationship with the much older and better-known Harrison, with whom she began to live and collaborate (on translations from the Russian) at about this time. *The Counterplot* (1924) follows up the secondary religious themes of *Madeleine*, as a young woman tries and fails to win her lover back from his aspiration to the Catholic priesthood.

Lud-in-the-Mist is a far more solid achievement, a fantasy which sets up an opposition between the stodgy bourgeois world of Nathanael Chanticleer and the menacing incursions from Fairyland which steal his children and cause his disgrace. The plot offers compromise and reconciliation; the world of Fairy needs Law if it is to avoid cruelty, just as the mundane world needs the Magical to avoid stupidity (perhaps a comment on Harrison's work on cthonic religion). The tone is assured and urbane, with a real sense of the menacing and the bizarre. Its elegant wit has influenced genre fantasy since its republication in the late 1960s.

Harrison died in 1928 and Mirrlees fell silent for most of the rest of her life, emerging only in 1962 with the first volume of her projected biography of Cotton the Antiquary *A Fly in Amber*. T. S. Eliot called this project her 'Penelope's Web'; it is digressive and arch, but not unappealing.   RK

Miss Peabody's Inheritance (1983) ELIZABETH JOLLEY's most positive and perplexing novel is told through parallel narratives. The primary narrative revolves around an Australian novelist, Diana Hopewell, and her devoted English fan, Miss Dorothy Peabody, who strike up a prolonged correspondence. In her letters, Diana describes herself as a horseback-riding *ingénue* who navigates through the Australian outback guided by a harbour of sky between the foliage of gum trees. In response, Miss Peabody records the minutiae of her day-to-day, sexless life of administrative and domestic servitude. Her only source of entertainment comes in the form of a new novel, composed by Diana in her epistles. Set in the confines of a rural girl's boarding school this 'novel-within-a-novel' contributes another narrative level. The regulated and routine term-time lives of the Headmistress, Miss Thorne, and her staff, Miss Edgely and Miss Snowdon, contrast with the debauched expeditions and lesbian sexual intrigues on which they embark with their students and with each other. Both narrative levels are carefully interwoven as the novel approaches its unexpected conclusion, which exposes yet another level of 'reality' in this intricately constructed work.   CE

Mister Sandman (1995) Canadian novelist BARBARA GOWDY's third novel, a succinct and darkly comic dysfunctional family saga: an 'X'-rated sit-com narrative occasionally marred by a jumbled time sequence. Chapters are discrete revelations, of characters who continually startle themselves, and each other, with their candour. Both parents have their respective homosexual affairs discovered and become queer grandparents to their blimpish daughter's love-child. Their other daughter Marcia meanwhile takes boyfriends off to hotels where vibrating beds give her shocks. The family's youngest member, mutely and weirdly privy to their secrets, is genius dwarf Joan, the love-child in the closet, recording their confessions and compiling an avant-garde sound-collage. When Joan lies in a coma this recording unites them in a marvellously funny, polyphonic climax. Like John Irving's *The Hotel New Hampshire* in that it has the smallest, most articulate daughter as the family saviour, Gowdy's *Mister Sandman* reinvents the DOMESTIC NOVEL along queer, vaguely magical realist lines.   PM

Mitchell, Elma [Elizabeth Manuel] 1919–

Scottish poet, born in Airdrie, Lanarkshire, and educated at Somerville College, Oxford. Mitchell took a diploma in librarianship at University College, London, and worked for the BBC and as information officer for various organizations, including the British Employee's Confederation. On retirement she went to live in Chard, Somerset. Mitchell won the Cheltenham Festival Poetry Competition in 1977.

Elma Mitchell's poetry is championed by the energetic small press, Peterloo Poets. Her humanist plain-style is charged by an alert intelligence, a focus on the quotidian:

> He was always first at everything
> And now
> The first man ever to be dead. Perhaps, as gardeners,
> We should have learned from the leaves
> What it means to be deciduous.

The lack of pose or pretension draws on the very English 'Movement' tradition represented by the poetry of Philip Larkin. She published *People Etcetera: New and Selected Poems* in 1987, drawing judiciously on two earlier collections. Of these, her first book, *The Poor Man in the Flesh* (1976), is very strong – the poems had

been stored up for some time. It contains the poems that rightly underpin her reputation, 'A Very Cold Winter' and 'Thoughts after Ruskin'. An excellent introduction of her work is available in *Penguin Modern Poets* (1976).   DM

Mitchell, Gladys 1901–83 One of the most assiduous

and idiosyncratic DETECTIVE writers of all time, Gladys Mitchell (born in Cowley, Oxfordshire) began her working life as a mistress in a girls' school, and continued in this profession even while producing her extraordinary series of crime novels (one a year for over fifty years) featuring the psychoanalyst and pterodactyl-like investigator Mrs Bradley (later Dame Beatrice). First appearing in *Speedy Death* (1929), Mrs Bradley soon endeared herself to aficionados of the wayward and untoward. There's an element of spoof or satire in many of the Mitchell novels, particularly the early ones, and always something unexpected, even subversive in a good-humoured way, in the style or outcome. Quite often Mrs Bradley exonerates from blame the person who has struck the fatal blow, and takes steps to save him (or her) from arrest. She operates within a moral framework not restricted by the usual assumptions of popular fiction.

Just occasionally, the plot complications result in something of a snarl-up, causing sheer bewilderment for the reader; more often, though, Gladys Mitchell is in complete control of her intriguing material, which may include murder and apparent resurrection, high jinks at school or college, stone circles infested by wraiths, social gatherings at castles and other urbane occasions. From the early tongue-in-cheek *The Mystery of a Butcher's Shop* (1930), through the 1945 *tour de force The Rising of the Moon* (wonderfully lucid and sinister), to the last dashing novel *The Crozier Pharaohs*, posthumously published in 1984 and centred on the world's oldest breed of domestic dog, Gladys Mitchell has repeatedly extended, enlivened and taken the most rewarding liberties with the conventions of the detective genre.   PC

Mitchell, Margaret ('Peggy') Munnerlyn 1900–49

American journalist and novelist, who gained lasting fame as 'the woman who wrote GONE WITH THE WIND'. Her image as popular romantic myth-maker and professional white Southerner has been complicated by more recent reappraisals of the social critiques, alternative histories and strong feminist cross-currents in all her writing. Born to a dour Atlanta lawyer and an energetic suffragist mother, she grew up ambiguous about her mother's politics, but as daughter, debutante and wife she was always markedly unconventional. Her mother's death (1919) broke off Peggy's freshman year at Smith. Back home, she found the demands of her father's household and the Atlanta social season less than fulfilling. On marrying Berrien ['Red'] Upshaw in 1922 (they formally separated in 1923), she joined the *Atlanta Journal*, becoming one of its liveliest writers. Keeping her own name after marriage to John Marsh (1925), a *Journal* colleague, she continued working, but ill and increasingly frustrated at lack of time for her fiction (she had produced stories and plays from girlhood), she left the newspaper in 1926.

Reading, fiction and illness, with commitments to friends and family, occupied the next decade, though, always underplaying her identity as writer, she kept her main project private. *Gone With the Wind*'s astonishing impact as epic book (1936), movie (1939) and cultural phenomenon overwhelmed the rest of her life. (Her letters alone – over 10,000 to fans and critics – consumed endless time.) She died in 1949, fatally injured in a street accident.   PEK

Mitchell, Susan Langstaff 1866–1926 Irish poet, critic and editor. As assistant editor of the *Irish Homestead* under A. E. (George Russell), and later editor of its successor, the *Irish Statesman*, she wrote articles and literary and dramatic reviews. Her most enduring contribution to the Irish Literary Revival is as its satirist. She was a lively and popular figure in the vibrant atmosphere of Dublin of the period, a noted hostess with a distinctive singing voice, given to singing her satires in a manner reminiscent of the traditional court poet in Gaelic Society. It is a testament both to her skill and to the objects of her wit that she remained friends with most of them throughout her life. Her skits and satirical verse offer a corrective to the solemn and somewhat self-important note often struck in accounts of the Revival and its participants by her contemporaries, a note which was precisely her target. *Aids to the Immortality of Certain Persons Living in Ireland (Charitably Administered)* appeared in 1908 and an irreverent biography of *George Moore* in 1916. Her religious poetry (*The Living Chalice*, 1908/1913; *Frankincense and Myrrh*, 1912), which is reflective and lyrical in quality, is less well known than her humorous verse. She contributed a poem on the Playboy Riots to *The Abbey Row, Not Edited by W. B. Yeats* (1907).   LM

Mitchison, Naomi (Mary Margaret) 1897–1999 British historical novelist, writer for children, woman of letters, born in Edinburgh, the daughter of Louisa and John Scott Haldane. She was educated at the Dragon School in Oxford and St Anne's College, Oxford, interrupting her studies to volunteer as a Voluntary Aid Detachment nurse in St Thomas's Hospital in World War I. In 1916 she married Dick Mitchison, later Labour MP for Kettering, by whom she had five children. In 1937 the family went to live in Scotland, and Mitchison, who had a strong interest in

Scottish politics and culture, served on the Argyll County Council for twenty years. Her best-known HISTORICAL NOVELS, which often use settings in ancient Greece and Rome, include *Cloud Cuckoo Land* (1925), *The Corn King and the Spring Queen* (1931), *The Delicate Fire* (1933) and *The Bull Calves* (1947). A lifelong feminist and socialist, Mitchison was active in anti-Fascist activities in the 1930s. Her most controversial novel, *We Have Been Warned* (1935), imaginatively evokes the dangers of Fascists coming to power in England and contains explicit sex scenes and abortion scenes set in the Soviet Union, which were daring for their time. Mitchison wrote speculative fiction including *Memories of a Spacewoman* (1962). She travelled extensively and was made tribal mother to the Bakgatla in Botswana. In her seventies and eighties she wrote lively autobiographies – *Small Talk* (1973), *All Change Here* (1975), *You May Well Ask* (1979) – which are illuminating about the culture and values of the radical and artistic circles in which she moved.   MJ

Mitford, Jessica 1915–96 Anglo-American writer of polemic and memoirs. Educated privately at home as one of five remarkable sisters, including the novelist NANCY MITFORD, she rejected, more decisively than Nancy, the ultra-Right politics of her family – her sister Diana married Oswald Mosley and, with another sister Unity, was part of Hitler's circle – to help Spanish refugees from the Civil War. A second marriage to Robert Truehaft involved her in Communist, anti-racist and anti-war politics in the USA. *Hons and Rebels* (1960) was an entertaining account of her childhood, counterpointing the account in Nancy's early novels. *A Fine Old Conflict* (1977) was a memoir of her later life as a political activist, and was equally, though more caustically, witty. Mitford also wrote a series of exposés of American business – *The American Way of Death* (1963), *Kind and Usual Punishment – The American Prison Business* (1974) and *The American Way of Birth* (1992); *The Making of a Muckraker* (1980) was a collection of pieces linked to these studies with a commentary on research techniques. These books were characterized by incisive analysis of advertising copy, a keen sense of the movement of money and a capacity for deriving the most scathing condemnations of her subjects from their own mouths.   RK

Mitford, Mary (Russell) 1787–1866 British poet, essayist and dramatist. The only child of rich parents, she was sent to a good school in London. In 1810, she published *Miscellaneous Poems*, which ran into a second edition, and became very popular in America. She published three more volumes of poetry between 1811 and 1813. By 1820, her father's extravagance had reduced the family to poverty and they moved to a small cottage at Three Miles Cross, a village between Reading

Mary Russell Mitford.

and Basingstoke. Mitford now faced an economic imperative to write, and she turned to writing verse tragedies for the stage.

Her achievements in the male-dominated business of commercial theatre were extraordinary. Talfourd accepted her *Julian* and the famous actor, Macready, performed the title role at Covent Garden in 1823. *Foscari* followed in 1826, and *Rienzi* was produced in 1828. Mitford records that *Rienzi* 'passed the twentieth night which . . . insures the payment of 400 pounds from the theatre (the largest price any play can gain)'. More plays followed, but much of the money she earned was squandered by her father.

It was initially for financial reasons that she, as she said, stooped 'from the lofty steep of tragic poetry to the every-day path of village stories'. 'Our Village' began as a series of articles in the *Lady's Magazine* in 1819 and became immediately immensely popular: it has since been judged to mark a new style of pastoral. The essays were based on Mitford's own experiences at Three Mile Cross, as she explains in the preface: '[the] descriptions have always been written on the spot and to the moment, and in nearly every instance with the closest and most resolute fidelity to the place and the people'. ELIZABETH BARRETT BROWNING, who became a friend, called her 'a sort of prose Crabbe in

the sun'. She published a novel, *Belford Regis, or Sketches of a Country Town*, in 1837. In 1842 her father died, and in 1851 she moved to Swallowfield, near Reading. In 1852 she wrote the autobiographical *Recollections of a Literary Life: Or Books, Places and People*. Ruskin praised her last work, *Atherton and Other Tales* (1854).　　　CPe

Mitford, Nancy 1904–73 English novelist and BIOGRAPHER. Aristocratic daughter of the second Baron Redesdale, Nancy was the eldest of seven children, several of whom (notably JESSICA, Diana and Unity) achieved equal personal notoriety. Educated at home in the Cotswolds, Nancy immortalized the 'eccentricity and restlessness of our upbringing' in her semiautobiographical bestseller *The Pursuit of Love* (1945). Her eight novels, published between 1931 and 1960, are written with a characteristic frivolity and hyperbole which reflects both the unique Mitford humour and vitality (most notably, Nancy's love of elaborate 'teases') and the arcane language and mannerisms of upper-class inter-war society. Married in 1933 but later divorced, Nancy moved to Paris in 1945 and expressed her innate Francophilia in her novels LOVE IN A COLD CLIMATE (1949), *The Blessing* (1951) and *Don't Tell Alfred* (1960). Other writing included two collections of family letters, a series of historical biographies and *Noblesse Oblige* (1956), an infamous satire on English class-consciousness. Shortly before her death, aged 68, from Hodgkin's disease she was awarded both the Légion d'honneur and the CBE, provoking the characteristically Francophile and Mitfordesque tease: 'I've never heard of the CBE but of course I'm delighted to have it . . . I hear it ranks above a knight's widow, oh, good.'　　　AS

modernist women Modernism, the early 20th-century movement in the arts dedicated to 'making it new' in form and consciousness, to use Ezra Pound's famous phrase, was inspired by the belief that art could have a transformative impact, redeeming a deadened commercial society from its bourgeois philistinism. This transformative agenda was part of the sense of revolutionary possibility, including upheavals in gender relations, pervading turn-of-the-century politics and culture.

The period from 1880 to 1920, within which modernism emerged and rose to preeminence as the dominant art form in the West (it remained dominant until the end of World War II), was also the heyday of the first wave of feminism, consolidated in the Woman Suffrage movement. The protagonist of this movement was known as the NEW WOMAN: independent, educated, (relatively) sexually liberated, oriented more toward productive life in the public sphere than toward reproductive life in the home. The New Woman was dedicated, as VIRGINIA WOOLF passionately explained in 'Professions for Women', to the murder of the 'Angel in the House', Coventry Patmore's notorious poetic idealization of Victorian nurturant–domestic femininity. This New Woman inspired a great deal of ambivalent modernist characterization, from Hardy's Sue Bridehead (*Jude the Obscure*, 1896) and Ibsen's eponymous Hedda Gabler to CHOPIN's Edna Pontellier (*THE AWAKENING*, 1899) and Woolf's Lily Briscoe (*TO THE LIGHTHOUSE*, 1927).

What had been the exclusively male Anglo-American high modernist canon (James, Conrad, Yeats, Pound, Eliot, Lawrence, Joyce) constructed by mid-century New Criticism has been entirely reconceived during the past twenty-five years of feminist criticism to incorporate the crucial role of modernist women writers. Modernism had mothers as well as fathers. In texts such as CHARLOTTE PERKINS GILMAN's 'THE YELLOW WALLPAPER' (1892), Kate Chopin's *The Awakening*, GERTRUDE STEIN's *Three Lives* (1903–6), and Virginia Woolf's *THE VOYAGE OUT* (1915), we can see that women writers produced modernist formal innovation concomitantly with the men generally credited with inventing modernism (modernist forms are generally seen to encompass aesthetic self-consciousness or self-reflexiveness; abstraction, artifice, rupture of REALIST convention; simultaneity, juxtaposition, montage, fragmentation; paradox, ambiguity and uncertainty; dehumanization and the demise of subjectivity conceived as unified and self-consistent).

Three Lives was composed at the same time as early versions of Joyce's *A Portrait of the Artist as a Young Man* (*Stephen Hero*). With its fluid, obtuse narration, detached, ironic tone, impressionist as well as spatial or synchronic temporal structures, and disruptions of conventional diction and syntax, *Three Lives* has just as valid a claim to modernist origination as Joyce's *Portrait*. Though Virginia Woolf's first novel, *The Voyage Out*, was not published until 1915, she began working on it about the same time Stein was writing *Three Lives*. *The Voyage Out* initiates a number of modernist formal practices, particularly the predominance of symbolism as conveyer of the novel's central meanings, along with a pervasive sense of dreamlike irreality.

A decade earlier, 'The Yellow Wallpaper' prefigures Kafka and the surrealists, with its progressively deranged first-person narration and its use of dream structure as an ordering principle. *The Awakening* develops several modernist formal strategies, such as ambiguous, shifting narrative stance, density and foregrounding of imagery, and passages of repetitive, incantatory, poetic prose. Though Chopin and Gilman did not continue as modernist writers – Chopin died and Gilman turned almost exclusively to politics – Stein and Woolf must be central to any account of modernism. Women writers continued, throughout

the decades of modernism's dominance of Anglo-American high literary art, to produce a large quantity of its most important writing.

Gertrude Stein's revolutionary 'Melanctha', the centrepiece of *Three Lives*, goes well beyond earlier fiction's development of modernist forms, initiating an unprecedented stylization of the prose surface through reduction and simplification of the prose 'palette' comparable to that of the cubists with whom Stein shared such a powerful co-influence. Jefferson Campbell, male protagonist of 'Melanctha', is a transformation of the autobiographical protagonist of Stein's earlier, formally conventional, lesbian novel, *Q.E.D.* (1903). Like his prototype, he is bourgeois, restrained, 'regular' in his habits, whereas Melanctha, based on Stein's first lover, is 'reckless' and irregular, given to 'wandering' in search of 'wisdom' (central keywords in the text). Melanctha's subversive femininity enables Stein simultaneously to undo her own NATURALIST narrative (Melanctha as hapless victim of cruel societal circumstances beyond her control) and to explore dangerous thematic possibilities. The conflation of non-white and working-class origins in Melanctha, embodied in the undecidable (dangerous, fascinating) feminine, produces a quintessential modernist locus of formal and thematic disruption and innovation. It is in following Melanctha's sexual and intellectual 'wandering' that Stein is able to take her text out into its formal *terra incognita*.

Once there, Stein, for the next three decades, went further than any other 20th-century writer in English (perhaps in any language) in reinventing literary language and form. She was one of the most prolific, important and influential writers of this century, with twenty-five books published in her lifetime and approximately the same number, including anthologies, published posthumously. However, until, in the 1970s, feminist and POSTMODERNIST criticism began to take Stein's writing seriously, most studies of her were biographical, focusing on her influence on other writers and her life in the Parisian bohemian modernist art world rather than on this remarkable productivity, or on the revolutionary impact of her work.

Fortunately, that is not the case for Virginia Woolf. Partly because of her key position in the Bloomsbury group, the nodal centre of British modernism, and partly because her fiction is at least superficially closer to recognizable convention than Stein's genre-bending experimentalism, her four great high modernist novels – *Jacob's Room* (1922), *MRS DALLOWAY* (1925), *To the Lighthouse* and *THE WAVES* (1931) – have long been readily available and widely read. Her other five novels, her two great works of feminist theory – *A ROOM OF ONE'S OWN* (1929) and *THREE GUINEAS* (1938) – and, more recently, her multi-volume stories, essays, DIARIES and letters, have subsequently become almost as well known, and, in the case of ORLANDO (1928), better known. No writer, perhaps not even CHARLOTTE BRONTË, has benefited more from feminist criticism than Virginia Woolf. She has become, with solid justification, one of the great literary 'mothers' we 'think back through if we are women', as she herself said in *A Room of One's Own*.

Woolf's arguments for the subversiveness of modernist form gendered feminine its representations of the underlying, multiplicitous truths of consciousness and psyche excavated from beneath the outward, unitary, coherent appearances of social, and realist fictional, convention, most notably in 'Modern Fiction' (1919), and in 'Mr Bennett and Mrs Brown' (1924), as well as in *A Room of One's Own*. Beginning with her first novel, *A Voyage Out*, with its New-Woman-inspired heroine Rachel Vinrace attempting (unsuccessfully) to 'voyage out' of Europe and thereby of its patriarchal-imperialist gender relations, and throughout her career, Woolf used literary form to explore the possibility of releasing into representation the subversiveness of a culturally suppressed and repressed femininity. Writing for Woolf could embody a subversive feminine consciousness by penetrating the mind of 'Mrs Brown', the anonymous, humble, marginal everywoman, and showing how different the world looks when viewed through her eyes.

Woolf was not alone in these ambitions. She was joined by a wide range of other women modernists, many of whose works and even names have only recently been revived, made available and studied by feminist criticism. A 1990 volume entitled *The Gender of Modernism*, edited by Bonnie Kime Scott, has chapters on experimental novelist DJUNA BARNES, prolific novelist WILLA CATHER; NANCY CUNARD, editor of *Negro: An Anthology* (1934); Poundian imagist and later epic poet H.D. (HILDA DOOLITTLE); Harlem Renaissance novelists JESSIE REDMON FAUSET, ZORA NEALE HURSTON and NELLA LARSEN; experimental poet MINA LOY and unique modernist poet MARIANNE MOORE; KATHERINE MANSFIELD, CHARLOTTE MEW, JEAN RHYS, DOROTHY RICHARDSON (inventor of 'stream of consciousness'), MAY SINCLAIR, SYLVIA TOWNSEND WARNER, REBECCA WEST, ANTONIA WHITE, ANNA WICKHAM – all of whom made vital contributions to the rich legacy of modernism.   MDeK

Modjeska, Drusilla 1946– Born in England, migrated to Australia in 1971 via Papua New Guinea, lives and works in Sydney – originally as an academic and critic, later as a writer, critic and editor. Her status as one of the most innovative contemporary Australian writers was established with her book POPPY (1990), which began as a biography of her mother and became in the process of writing a mixture of fact and fiction,

biography and novel. Modjeska acknowledges the writing of CHRISTA WOLF, in particular the pursuit of different possibilities of form and voice, as a precursor of *Poppy*. The development of a kind of matrilineal 'autobiology' is given a distinctively Antipodean twist here, as Modjeska is concerned to pursue the interconnections of personal, imperial, indigenous and colonial histories. Although *Poppy* is the most celebrated of her works, Modjeska's perceptiveness and eloquence was evident in her first book, *Exiles at Home. Australian Women Writers 1925–1945* (1981), where she uses letters, DIARIES, notebooks and journals to uncover a rich and supportive network amongst women writers who had hitherto not been linked in this way. In *The Orchard* (1993), Modjeska continues the shape-shifting of generic forms. Described as essays, the pieces are part fiction, autobiography and myth. As an editor, Modjeska has produced *Inner Cities* (1989), which explores women's experiences of urban space in Australia, and *Sisters* (1993), a very successful collection in which women write about childhood with a particular focus on sisterhood. In 1997 Modjeska contributed, with AMANDA LOHREY and Robert Dessaix, to a *troika* of very different stories and essays on the theme of *Secrets*.   GWh

Moers, Ellen 1928–1979 American feminist literary historian who redrew the literary map in the wake of the Women's Liberation movement which, she wrote, 'pulled me out of the [library] stacks' into the open air. Contemporary poems and polemics and 'ribald and outrageous fictions' by women were transforming the literary scene. Moers's *Literary Women* (1976) celebrated the work of the Libbers' forerunners in 18th- and 19th-century America and Europe. For her there was something 'distinctive of modernity itself' in the way 'the written word ... became increasingly and steadily the work of women'.

She published her first book, *The Dandy: Brummel to Beerbohm*, in 1960. From the mid 1970s she taught at Brooklyn College and in the Graduate School of the City University of New York. Visiting England in the course of her research for *Literary Women*, she encountered GERMAINE GREER at Warwick, in the guise of 'a superbly scholarly heckler'. Moers was thoroughly 'bookish', but she also relished panache, and her interpretation of women's work was resolutely opposed to the view of them as victims: 'My tale is one of triumph ... literary women provide no evidence of female passivity, for if there is one ruthless activity that seeks to dominate and shape life itself, it is writing.' Her tragically early death, and the late 1970s / early 1980s feminist focus on marginalization and fragmented, fugitive texts, combined to mute her influence. However, more recent critical alertness to performance on the page recalls her style.   LS

Moggach, Deborah 1948– English novelist and short-story writer, a number of whose novels have been adapted for television. Their popular appeal owes much to traditional narrative values of strong story lines (child abduction, incest, surrogate motherhood) and casts of clearly delineated and sympathetic characters, often centred around an extended family. These dangerously dramatic themes are, however, not treated in simple terms: pain and despair are shown to be caused not by evil doing but by fallible people who are, at worst, self-absorbed, and outcomes are messy and provisional. The tone is usually wry, and Moggach has comic potential always clearly in her sights. The comedy can be satirical: she has a sharp eye for the particulars of modern mores in therapies and kitchen fittings. Her characters are often people modest in expectation and in social position. While this allows them an innocent ability to deflate pretension, the techniques most characteristic of these novels – first person narration or extended free speech – mean that the characters' necessarily limited linguistic patterns result in a certain flatness of style.   EA

Moise, Penina 1797–1880 American poet, educator and hymnist. She was born in Charleston, South Carolina. Her parents had lost their wealth in the Haitian slave revolution (1791). She left school to work at the age of 12 when her father died. Refusing offers of marriage, she devoted her life to writing and service. *Fancy's Sketch Book* (1833) includes satiric as well as religious verse. She wrote for Jewish journals as well as the Charleston *Courier* and *Godey's Lady's Book*, and composed instructional songs and recitations. Her most lasting accomplishment was to write nearly all of *Hymns Written for the Use of Hebrew Congregations* (1856), the first American Reform Jewish hymnal. In 1842 she became superintendent of Beth Elohim school. During the Civil War she founded a school with her sister and niece. Nearly blind, she wrote on a chalk slate, which her niece transcribed. A literary salon attended by the Charleston intelligentsia met at her house.   JSG

Molesworth [née Stewart], Louisa (Mary) 1839–1921 British novelist and writer for children. Though born in Holland, she grew up in Manchester where her father had become a senior partner in a firm of merchants and shippers. She attended a Swiss boarding school and was also privately tutored by the novelist ELIZABETH GASKELL and her husband, William, neighbours and friends of the Stewarts. But it was her maternal grandmother in Scotland whose storytelling stimulated her imagination and guided her toward a literary career.

In 1861 she married Major Richard Molesworth; they had seven children, two of whom died young. Wounded in the Crimean War, her husband was short-tempered and financially irresponsible, which made their union an unhappy one. Her earliest novels, written for adults under the pseudonym 'Ennis Graham' (the name of a friend who had disappeared in Central Africa with her father), revolve around Victorian marriages.

It was as a writer of CHILDREN'S BOOKS that she became famous. Her first volume for children, *Tell Me a Story* (1875), was dedicated to the 7-year-old daughter she lost and whose death is recounted, from a child's perspective, in one of the tales. Separated from her husband in 1879 and no longer able to count on parental assistance after the death of her father, Molesworth wrote story after story to support her surviving five children. Her last published work, *Fairies Afield* (1911), is said to be her hundredth book. Her best-known works, *The Cuckoo Clock* (1876) and *The Tapestry Room* (1877), artfully blend realism and fantasy.   MAD

Mollineux, Mary 1651–95 British poet, who possibly lived in Liverpool, but about whom little was known until she was identified seven years after her death as the author of *Fruits of Retirement: Or Miscellaneous Poems, Moral and Divine* (1702). From the preface, written by her cousin Frances Owen, we learn that she was an only child, 'who, in her Childhood was much afflicted by weak eyes, which made her unfit for the usual Imployment of Girls'. Instead, her father taught her Latin, Greek, arithmetic, science and medicine, and later she was to claim to have 'so much Learning, it makes her mad'. From the age of 12 she began to write verses to family members; later followed letters, heroic couplets, and stanzas which cover various subjects, including the importance of modesty, friendship, marriage and the potency of language. In 1684 she was imprisoned in Lancaster Castle with Quaker writer Henry Mollineux; on their release they married and had two sons.   RDM

Molloy, Frances 1947–91 In *No Mate for the Magpie* (1985), Irish writer Frances Molloy produced one of the finest satirical dialect novels written in English since MARIA EDGEWORTH'S *CASTLE RACKRENT* created the genre in Ireland in 1800. Like Ann Elizabeth McGlone, the first-person narrator of *No Mate*, Molloy was born in Derry into a poor working-class Catholic family, left school to work in a factory at the age of 15, and died tragically young (1991) after publishing one novel and several stories in English magazines. She characteristically uses the limited perspectives of first-person narration to stage situations of social injustice, her speakers both victims and perpetuators of discrimination. The opening of *No Mate* reveals and subverts the inherited enmities of Northern Ireland that plague the lives of the heroine Ann McGlone, her creator, and the North generally: 'Way a wee screwed up protestant face an' a head of black hair a was born, in a state of original sin. Me ma didn't like me, but who's te blame the poor woman, sure a didn't look like a catholic wain atall.' The novel follows Ann through the northern Civil Rights movement of 1968–9 and right 'outa Ireland' in search for a place where 'life resembled life more than it did here'. A posthumous collection of stories, *Women are the Scourge of the Earth*, was published in 1998. CStP

Monck [née Molesworth], Mary 1678?–1715 Irish poet. Born in Dublin, Mary was the daughter of Laetitia (née Coote) and Robert, first Viscount Molesworth. Although her father disapproved of education for women, she somehow acquired a knowledge of several languages and of the classics. Her marriage to George Monck, a member of the Irish parliament, was unhappy. He was subject to bouts of insanity, and by 1714 the couple were probably living apart.

Mary died of a 'languishing sickness' in Bath. Her poems were discovered after her death, and published by her father in *Marinda: Poems and Translations on Several Occasions* (1716), a collection which included translations from Italian and Spanish, as well as odes, eclogues, songs and epigrams. In his preface, Molesworth declared that the contents were the work of 'a young gentlewoman lately dead', written 'in a remote country retirement, without any assistance but that of a good library, and without omitting the daily care due to a large family . . . little expecting, and as little desiring the publick shou'd have any opportunity of applauding or condemning them'. Monck's 'Verses from a Lady at Bath Dying with a Consumption, to her Husband' was published in the *Gentleman's Magazine* in 1750 and in *Poems by Eminent Ladies* (1755). RR

Monkey Grip (1977) HELEN GARNER's gritty and powerful novel focuses on the desperation of addiction. Set in suburban 1970s Melbourne, the narrative explores the intricate and delicate web of free love, feminism and infatuation. Javo is addicted to heroin and Nora is addicted to romantic love. Together they struggle in a wretched relationship, locked together in a 'monkey grip' of sexual urgency and chemical reliance. Regardless of their efforts to disengage from each other or remain true to their beliefs, the intensity of their habits forms a pattern of disappointment, desertion and dependency. The myth of free love and emotional detachment is shattered as the impact of their troubled and overwhelming passion is felt by family, friends and housemates in an ever widening circle of disturbance. Separated by metaphorical as well as physical barriers, Javo and Nora are forced to question and contest their concepts of love and devotion. Friendships, loyalties and convictions are tried and tested as the narrative struggles to its inconclusive yet profoundly satisfying resolution. CE

Monkey's Mask, The (1994) Frequently described as a detective novel in verse form, DOROTHY PORTER's narrative deploys elements of ROMANCE, DETECTIVE FICTION, MODERNIST poetry and popular song lyric. Unfolding with the pace and tension of a thriller, Porter's narrative also converses with feminist theories of gender, sexuality and textuality. The narrator, Jill Fitzpatrick, a hard-bitten free-lance detective and 'out-of-the-closet' lesbian, is hired by a conservative suburban couple to find their missing daughter. Mickey's body is soon discovered, but the intrigue increases as Jill finds corruption rife in Sydney's academic and bohemian circles. The stock *femme fatale* of detective fiction is embodied in the dangerous feminist academic, Diana, whose self-serving seduction of Jill temporarily threatens to derail the murder hunt. Porter's poetry is spare, taut and lucid, always advancing the narrative while employing sharply dramatic and colloquial dialogue, as well as strikingly sensual images of the body. The metafictional device of embedding the victim's poetry within Jill's narrative presents reading as detection, but a detection always waylaid by textual pleasure. BR

Monroe, Harriet 1860–1936 American poet and critic. As the indefatigable editor of *Poetry*, Monroe laboured mightily in Chicago, the very home-town of Mammon, to hold high the banner of art and culture. The daughter of a lawyer, she suffered from neurasthenia and at the age of 16 was sent to a convent boarding school in Washington, D.C., where verse writing was a regular exercise in English classes. Monroe returned home, fended off several suitors, and became a critic on the *Chicago Tribune*. Monroe's sister had married the architect John Wellborn Root, and she had a close-up view of the architectural debates preceding the opening of the Columbian Exposition in 1892. (Monroe published a memoir of Root in 1896.) Her literary career began when she wrote an ode to celebrate the opening of the Exposition. Her effort was read and sung with orchestral accompaniment. Monroe published *Valeria and other Poems* (1891) and *The Passing Show* (verse plays, 1903), and founded *Poetry: A Magazine of Verse* in 1912. She proved to be a broad-minded editor, but was altogether too broad-minded in the eyes of her London editor, Ezra Pound, who berated Monroe for the many failings of American provincialism. Pound saw Monroe as a kind of schoolmarm, when she was actually writing in praise of cubism in the Chicago press. Her literary criticism was collected in *Poets and Their Art* (1926). Monroe edited a generous anthology, *The New Poetry* (1917), and published *Chosen Poems* in 1935. Her informative and lucid autobiography, *A Poet's Life: Seventy Years in a Changing World*, appeared in 1938. EH

Montagu [née Robinson], Elizabeth 1720–1800 British critic, letter-writer, hostess and literary patron. Sister of the novelist SARAH SCOTT, she was born in York and educated in Cambridge. She married the much older Edward Montagu in 1742; their only child died in infancy. Edward died in 1775 and she continued to channel her energies into holding resplendent literary and artistic gatherings at her homes, or 'salons' – as they became – in London and at Sandleford Priory in Berkshire. Dubbed 'Queen of the Blues' by Samuel Johnson because of her patronage of learned women BLUESTOCKINGS, in 1776 she visited French salons, returning to England to continue in her philanthropic works and to enlarge her reputation as a sophisticated and eloquent hostess whose parties were frequented by royalty.

Visitors to her salons included the writers Edmund Burke, FANNY BURNEY, ELIZABETH CARTER, Samuel Johnson and HANNAH MORE. In 1760 she wrote three dialogues published anonymously as part of her friend George Lyttelton's *Dialogues of the Dead*, a witty contribution to the ongoing 'Battle of the Books'. This was followed, in part due to the influence and encouragement of her close friend Elizabeth Carter, by *An Essay on the Writings and Genius of Shakespeare* (1769), in which she argued against Voltaire in defending Shakespeare's 'uncommon felicity in painting manners, and developing characters'. In this essay, published anonymously but with the author's identity the subject of wide public knowledge, she persuasively and learnedly argued for Shakespeare as 'certainly one of the greatest moral philosophers that ever lived'. The volume met with disapproval from Johnson, but proved extremely popular. It was reprinted several times and was translated into several European languages.

Her spirited and amusing letters were published as *The Letters of Mrs Elizabeth Montagu* (1809 and 1813), edited by her nephew and adopted heir Matthew Montagu, and as *Letters of Mrs Elizabeth Carter to Mrs Montagu* (1817). The letters traverse much of the 18th century and disclose a great deal about the activities and affections consequential to her life. She died in London and was buried alongside Edward in Winchester Cathedral. ELER

Montagu, Mary Wortley, Lady 1689–1762 English poet, essayist and letter-writer. Her mother, Lady Mary Fielding, died when Mary was only 4, and she grew up in London and Nottinghamshire, overseen by her somewhat neglectful father, Evelyn Pierrepont, first Duke of Kingston, and, for a time, by her paternal grandparents near Salisbury. Reading widely in the family library, Mary taught herself Latin as a girl and, through her father's influence, discovered both Whig politics and fashionable literature. As her topical poems circulated among the era's smart set, Mary's reputation as a wit and beauty grew. A lengthy, turbulent courtship ended when Mary defied her father and eloped with Edward Wortley in 1712. Her son Edward was born a year later.

Acquainted with Congreve, Arbuthnot and Addison, Mary also developed strong friendships with Gay and Pope. In this circle, she wrote town eclogues and a description of court life. In 1715, smallpox left Mary with a ravaged complexion and no eyelashes, and, a year later, Wortley's appointment as ambassador took the family to Constantinople. In Turkey, she wrote her *TURKISH EMBASSY LETTERS* (published posthumously to immediate acclaim in 1763). Breaking with the conventions of TRAVEL literature, the *Letters* describe overlooked elements of everyday life, particularly the situation and habits of women, and openly depict scenes of horror and oppression. Before her husband's recall from Constantinople in 1718, Mary gave birth to a daughter, also named Mary, and innoculated her son against smallpox. Despite violent resistance in England, she became an early evangelist of innoculation.

Resettling in Twickenham, she befriended MARY ASTELL and Lord Hervey and extended patronage to Edward Young and to her cousin Henry Fielding. Her friendship with Pope became strained, according to later accounts, after she rejected his romantic advances. More likely, their political differences and opposing views of Hervey drove them apart. Pope attacked Mary in the *Dunciad* (1728) and in subsequent satires as 'Sappho'. Joining with Hervey, another victim of Pope's pen, she responded in 'Verses Address'd to the Imitator of the First Satire of the Second Book of Horace' (1733): 'You strike unwounding, we unhurt can laugh.' In the anonymous 'Reasons that Induced Dr. S[wift] to write a Poem call'd the Lady's Dressing Room' (1734), Mary similarly attacked Swift as impotent and miserly.

Mary also wrote essays on manners, morals and politics, anonymously publishing her own journal, *The Nonsense of Common-Sense* (1737–8), as a retort to the Opposition paper *Common Sense*. Estranged from her profligate son and living apart from her husband for many years, Mary broke with many of her closest friends, living in relative isolation and genteel poverty. In 1736, she fell in love with Francesco Algarotti, a 24-year-old bisexual Italian writer also desired by Hervey. Although she pursued Algarotti to Italy, their alliance ended unhappily. For the next twenty years, she lived abroad. After Wortley's death in 1762, she returned to England but soon died of breast cancer. While her social position encouraged only anonymous publication, Mary covertly arranged for some of her writing to reach print after her death. JHP

Montgomery, L(ucy) M(aud) 1874–1942 Canadian novelist and diarist best known for her fiction concerning gifted adolescent girls. She was born in the Canadian province of Prince Edward Island, whose eccentric pioneer world is reconstructed in her books. Her first novel, ANNE OF GREEN GABLES (1908), written in Cavendish, Prince Edward Island, was a spontaneous best-seller, and was translated into numerous languages, garnering its author international fame. In 1911 Montgomery married the Revd Ewan Macdonald and moved with him to Ontario where she struggled to reconcile her need to write with the demands placed on her by the roles of minister's wife and mother of two boys.

Concerned with the plight of imaginative adolescent girls who possess a pantheist's love of their native landscape on the one hand, and a desire for independence and self-realization on the other, Montgomery's novels are most often written in the form of a series. The most autobiographical of these, *Emily of New Moon* (1923), *Emily Climbs* (1925) and *Emily's Quest* (1927), chronicle the coming-of-age of a young author much given to spiritual 'flashes' during which the importance of her vocation as a writer is impressed upon her. Repeatedly thwarted, by first the adults and then the men in her life, Emily's ambitions are, nevertheless, realized when her benign, 'simple' Cousin Jimmy sends one of her manuscripts to an American firm where it is accepted for publication. As the narrative unfolds, the turmoil of Emily's inner life is expressed in frequent journal entries which resemble Montgomery's own DIARIES. Several volumes of the latter have been published in recent years, revealing Montgomery to have been as adept at social commentary as she was at reflective lyricism, but also exposing her increasing unhappiness.

Her books remain in print in various countries, including Japan where *Anne* has developed a cult following. In Canada, *Anne of Green Gables* has been made into a musical comedy, a film, and various characters from the 'Anne' books people a television series entitled 'The Road to Avonlea'. Most recently, *Emily of New Moon* became a CBC television mini-series.

Montgomery died in Toronto and is buried in Cavendish, Prince Edward Island.　　　　JU

Monument of Matrones, The (1582) A collection of prayers and meditations by and for women compiled by a student of Gray's Inn, Thomas Bentley. The volume is divided into seven books or 'lampes of virginitie'; its emphasis on virginity was intended to compliment QUEEN ELIZABETH I, to whom the work is dedicated. But although it is addressed especially to virgins, the book aims to provide virtuous examples and precepts for all women, whatever their condition; thus, while the third 'lampe' or book contains prayers

and meditations to be used by the Queen on the anniversary of her accession, later books include prayers for silence, chastity, and use by women after childbirth. But it is in the second 'lampe', which begins with Marguerite de Navarre's *Mirror of a Sinful Soul*, translated by the young Princess Elizabeth, that Bentley has gathered several significant texts by Renaissance women; those whose prayers and meditations are printed here include ANNE ASKEW, Queen CATHERINE PARR and LADY JANE GREY.　　　　PJB

Monuments and Maidens (1985) MARINA WARNER's wide-ranging, erudite examination of female imagery in western iconography over 2,000 years. Sub-titled 'The Allegory of the Female Form', the study takes on a swathe of material from antiquity to the present, deconstructing the myriad and sometimes paradoxical uses to which the female body is put. Opening with lucid critiques of the Statue of Liberty, the Parisian street and the construction of the persona of Margaret Thatcher by the British media, Warner then encompasses a range of sources from art to advertising, myth to magazines. With the premise that the ubiquitous female form is universalized much more readily than the male, the very basis upon which femininity is founded is interrogated. As the conflicting forces of culture and nature, and order and disorder come into play, so the female is coerced into representation. Ending with a rallying cry to the female subject to become a sentient being, and for the iconographers to respect the individuality of women, *Monuments and Maidens* is a major work of feminist cultural history. CS

Moodie, Susanna 1803–85 Born in Suffolk in 1806, she was one of the STRICKLAND sisters who set out to establish themselves as writers, inspired by the popularity of authors such as MARIA EDGEWORTH, MRS FELICIA HEMENS and LETITIA LANDON (L.E.L.). A prolific contributor of lyrical poetry, tragic drama and romantic tales of history to literary annuals and magazines, Susanna produced *Enthusiasm and Other Poems* in 1831. In that year, in the house of Thomas Pringle, secretary to the Anti-Slavery League, she was the amanuensis for the autobiographies of two ex-slaves, MARY PRINCE and Ashton Warner. There too she met J.W. Dunbar Moodie, recently returned from South Africa in search of a wife. They were married in the spring of 1831; a year later Susanna emigrated to Canada as a wife and mother.

Like other middle-class, ex-military folk, the Moodies did not prosper in the backwoods. Writing was an important financial resource and personal outlet, and from the early 1830s Susanna sent poems and fiction to provincial newspapers and magazines in Canada and the United States. Her reputation rests on a series of autobiographical sketches, ROUGHING IT IN

THE BUSH: OR, LIFE IN CANADA (1852), a classic in Canadian writing and literature of emigration and settlement more generally. Here she makes their failure as settlers, and her own fallibility as the young Mrs Moodie, the centre of a series of humorous and satirical sketches. They are an interesting counterpoint to her sister Catharine's book, THE BACKWOODS OF CANADA, and the publication recently of letters written by John and Susanna Moodie and CATHARINE PARR TRAILL amplifies the complex ways that literary writings were used by the sisters to produce a sense of place and identity following emigration.

After *Roughing It*, Susanna, eager to capitalize on her success, published a series of fictions, including *Mark Hurdlestone: Or, The Gold Worshipper* (1853), and *Matrimonial Speculations* (1854). Moodie herself has become a significant historical figure, who intrigues contemporary Canadian feminist critics and writers in particular. She is a character or voice in a number of contemporary literary works, including MARGARET ATWOOD's *THE JOURNALS OF SUSANNA MOODIE* (1970) and *ALIAS GRACE* (1996), CAROL SHIELDS's *Small Ceremonies* (1976) and Elizabeth Hopkins's play *Susanna*.

GWh

Moon Tiger (1987) PENELOPE LIVELY's Booker-McConnell-Prize-winning novel is obsessed with memory and history. Respected historian Claudia Hampton is dying of cancer, and, in a complex pattern of flashbacks ('chronology irritates me', asserts Claudia), she reflects upon her personal history and the transitoriness of human life and happiness. Lively explores how conceptions of the past, both personal and historical, create who we are and who we have been. Denied the opportunity to create who she will be because she is dying, Claudia realizes that when she is gone, her story is gone, and she becomes part of other people's memory and past. Her flashbacks reveal a period of brief happiness with a tank commander she met in Egypt in World War II, who is later killed in action: 'picked off by history' but alive in her memory. The central image is the moon tiger, a spiral coil used to repel mosquitos. It burns slowly through the night by their bed in the Winter Palace at Luxor and leaves only ash in the morning.

LCo

Moore, Julia A. 1847–1920 American poet. Born in rural Michigan, Moore was the eldest of four children, and grew up taking care of her ailing mother while also attending school. In 1876, she was married to a farmer and published her first book of poems, *The Sweet Singer of Michigan*. Critical response was divided between humorous rants about how bad the writing was and sarcastic praise of its brilliance. Moore's verse, some of which was intended to be sung, covered topics such as children's deaths, casualties of war, the need to

be kind to orphans, and yellow fever ('The yellow fever was raging / Down in the sunny south / And in many cities, / There was a death at every house'). Even her publisher took an amused position, writing that its style would 'prove a healthy lift to the overtaxed brain'. The critical response was so great, ironically, that it enabled Moore to publish a revised edition in 1878, with seventy-five pages of critics' reviews at the front, and in its third edition, *The Sentimental Song Book*, as it came to be known, became one of America's best selling books of poetry.

SP

Moore, Lorrie 1957– Witty, poignant and unobtrusively surrealistic American fiction writer. Moore has a jauntily inconsequential way of evoking everyday suffering; for instance, a woman's face, 'like an open bird-feeder where every year of her, the past and the future, had come to feed'. Born in Glen Falls, New York, she studied for her undergraduate degree in New York from 1974 to 1978 and her Master's at Cornell. The stylistic experiment and wordplay in her first two books testify to her academic training. She has lectured in English at the University of Wisconsin since 1984. Her first book, *Self-Help* (1985), was a collection of stories which teetered with comic pathos between the bossiness of self-help manuals and the suicidal uncertainty of their readers. In *Anagrams* (1986), Moore expanded her whimsical style to novel-length. The narrator shifts identity from chapter to chapter and her most important relationships are with a best friend and a daughter who don't exist. Moore's second book of short stories was *Like Life* (1988), and her second novel, *Who Will Run the Frog Hospital?* (1994). The latter was not as disjointed as her first novel and was consequently more moving, retaining Moore's distinctive blend of bleakness, charm and eccentricity.

KE

Moore, Marianne 1887–1972 American poet who was a powerful and admired presence among such contemporaries as T.S. Eliot, Wallace Stevens and Ezra Pound. She worked as a teacher and librarian and, after publishing *Poems* (1921) and *Observations* (1924), became editor of the influential magazine, the *Dial*, for three years from 1926. Born in Missouri, she spent most of her life in New York and lived to edit her own *Complete Poems*, first published in 1967. Her rigour and modesty are evident in this book's epigraph: 'Omissions are not accidents.'

Moore was famous not least for her subjects. She had a predilection for exotic creatures – the pangolin, jerboa or unicorn – and handled them like artifacts, leading Randall Jarrell to comment that 'All her zoos are Egyptian.' This enthusiasm for research continues in her extensive footnotes as well as her acknowledgement of odd facts gleaned from journals and used as sources. Moore absorbed the world with avid curiosity but at a distance, through archives, museums and books, and she gives it back to us in a similarly mediated way. When she writes of Sweden it is through 'A Carriage from Sweden'. The opening lines of 'The Steeple-Jack' show her to be highly conscious of the process of creating imagery:

Dürer would have seen a reason for living
   in a town like this, with eight stranded whales
to look at; with the sweet sea air coming into your
    house
on a fine day, from water etched
   with waves as formal as the scales
on a fish.

Such discrete, precise detailing suggests the influence of imagists such as H. D. What with her complex syllabic schemes and pedantic tone, it is surprising how well Moore's poems read aloud, and how funny and no-nonsense she can be.

Dwarfs here and there, lent
to an evident
    poetry of frog grays,
      duck-egg greens, and egg-plant blues, a fantasy
      and a verisimilitude that were
       right to those with, everywhere,
power over the poor.   (from 'The Jerboa')

She was stringently thorough. ELIZABETH BISHOP, upon whom Moore was a profound influence, said 'If she speaks of a chair you can practically sit on it when she has finished.' Bishop learned a great deal from Moore's patient curiosity and fixed gaze, as well as from her startling but exact imagery. Moore had no time for 'unimaginative analyses'. While her fish 'wade / through black jade', she also called for 'imaginary gardens with real toads in them' and was not above writing about the weasel or snail. The lines above – the frogs, ducks and dwarfs – show her unafraid of indelicacy or bathos, another aspect of Moore to surface in Bishop, along with the device of linking compound-adjectives through the repetition of a word, here 'egg', used in entirely different ways.

Moore's crystalline style and distance from her subjects would make for brittle poetry without her warmth, self-effacement and playfulness. She understood, even enjoyed the limitations of her art and warned against over-sophistication:

these things are rich instruments with which to experiment.
   But why dissect destiny with instruments
      more highly specialized than components of
destiny itself?

                    'Those Various Scalpels'
                              LG

Moore, Milcah Martha [Hill] 1740–1829

Transcriber and compiler of manuscript commonplace books and a printed miscellany. Moore belonged to an elite network of Quaker families, descendants of Thomas and Mary Lloyd, who arrived in Philadelphia from Wales in 1683. When she married her first cousin, Dr George Moore, she was disowned by the Quakers, but she returned to official membership after the death of her husband in 1801. Throughout her life, Moore exchanged letters and poetry with her family and friends and transcribed many of them into commonplace books, which are a type of 'literary' miscellany or collection of poems, letters or other types of prose writing. The commonplace book that she compiled in the 1770s is notable for documenting the rich literary and intellectual life among educated women in early America and for the way the manuscript as a whole reflects the debate on the American Revolutionary War. Included in this manuscript are twenty-four poems by SUSANNA WRIGHT and a previously lost portion of the JOURNAL kept by ELIZABETH GRAEME FERGUSSON during her trip to England in 1764. The largest selection of poetry and prose is by her cousin HANNAH GRIFFITTS, whose elegies and satires give an insight into the tensions within the Quaker community during the Revolutionary War. This commonplace book was not published but circulated informally among family and friends. After the Revolutionary War, Moore published *Miscellanies, Moral and Instructive* (1787–1829) for use as a textbook in schools, which went through many editions. A dramatic departure from the manuscript commonplace book, the majority of the selections are from British male authors, some reflecting patriarchal attitudes toward women. In part *Miscellanies* followed a post-Revolutionary trend that emphasized education for women but placed the intelligent woman at the service of the new Republic. Moore, who did not have children of her own, used the royalties from the book to endow her school for indigent girls.   CLB

Moorhead, Finola 1947–

Australian writer born in Victoria, Finola Moorhead worked as a teacher before becoming a full-time writer in 1973. She has published a number of short stories in periodicals and anthologies; a collection of prose, *Quilt* (1985); and two novels, *Remember the Tarantella* (1987) and *Still Murder* (1991), the latter winning the 1991 Victorian Premier's Award for fiction. She has also written and directed plays.

Quilt is a feminist mixture of writings that celebrate women and their strengths. *Remember the Tarantella* gives notice of her interest in complex form, the reader having to work to piece together a puzzle of narrative threads. The employment of a number of female protagonists (and no male ones) was intended to give the broadest possible vision of the female condition. Also harnessing a self-conscious postmodernity in its aim of portraying the female plight in a violent and often misogynist society, *Still Murder* is a feminist crime thriller of considerable originality. Employing a variety of modes of expression, from a madwoman's diary to a floppy disk, the novel is radical in its suggestion that women's best hope is not only in self-help, but in lesbianism. It also explores the personal and social destructiveness of Australia's involvement in the Vietnam War and its brutalizing effect on the prized mateship of Australian men.   HTh

Mopsa the Fairy (1869) JEAN INGELOW's best-known CHILDREN'S STORY has echoes of *Alice in Wonderland* (1865) but is also an almost Keatsian evocation of faery landscapes, with some very physical, unsentimental Victorian fairies (one of whom is beheaded and eaten by a raven) and a telling gender reversal. Jack leaves his nurse and enters Fairyland through a hole in a hedge, pockets a nestful of baby fairies, wakes one – Mopsa – with a kiss, then nurtures her through many adventures until she grows to his own (10-year-old) size and must become a Fairy Queen, complete with wand. Unsettlingly, he is forced to leave her with his shadowy double so that she will not miss him when he returns home (an opposition between 'real' and 'imaginary' anticipating that developed by French psychoanalyst Jacques Lacan). Ingelow sets lyrics into the narrative (as in *The Princess*, 1847, by her friend, Alfred Tennyson). The final chapter, 'Failure', begins with a sonnet about Orpheus; through this, and the character of the old apple-woman who is trapped in Fairyland, Ingelow seems to address not simply the issue of growing up, but the business of artistic creation itself. It is not whimsical, not in the least moralistic ('what you can do, you may do' is the rule) and is splendidly unfussy. The final words are simply 'And that's it.'   VP

Moraga, Cherrie 1952– Native of California, daughter of an Anglo- and a Mexican-American, Cherrie Moraga writes self-consciously as a feminist, lesbian and Chicana. She is best known for *This Bridge Called My Back: Writings by Radical Women of Color* (1981), which she co-edited with GLORIA ANZALDÚA. The anthology received the Before Columbus Foundation's American Book Award in 1986 and consolidated the importance of women of colour in the feminist movement. Equally radical, *Loving in the War Years: Lo que nunca paso por sus labios* (1983), a pastiche of prose and poetry, struggles explicitly with Moraga's difficult coming-of-age as half-white and lesbian in a Catholic, Mexican-American culture. *The Last Generation: Prose and Poetry* (1993) continues to explore these themes of gender, race and identity, arguing at last for a politics of survival. As a playwright, she is widely recognized as having been crucial in strengthening Chicano theatre, broadening its scope to include issues of gender and sexuality. She has been awarded a National Endowment for

the Arts Theatre Playwrights' Fellowship for her plays, which include *La Extranjera* (1985), *Giving up the Ghost: Teatro in 2 Acts* (1986), *Shadow of a Man* (1988), and *Heroes and Saints* (1989). Moraga has also co-edited *Cuentos: Stories by Latinas* (1983) and *The Sexuality of Latinas* (1989). More recently, she has written *Waiting in the Wings: Portrait of a Queer Motherhood* (1997), a memoir of lesbian motherhood.   SMSt

Morante, Elsa 1912–85 Italian novelist and poet, natural daughter of a Jewish Italian mother and a Sicilian. She became known to a wide public in 1974, with the publication of *La Storia* (*History: A Novel*, 1978), which at her behest was published directly into paperback, becoming the first Italian literary bestseller. Morante described the book as 'a political action' rather than a novel. Her earlier work had been more complex and enigmatic in style. *Menzogna e sortilegio* (1948; *House of Liars*), *L'isola di Arturo* (1957; *Arturo's Island*, 1988) and *Aracoeli* (1982) are narratives from memory of unrequited love, often for a parent. She had no formal education after school, and suffered great poverty until her marriage to Alberto Moravia in 1941, finally achieving financial independence with the success of *La Storia*. During the war she and Moravia were forced into hiding due to their part-Jewish descent and Moravia's anti-Fascist writings.   SD

Mordecai, Pamela 1942– African-Caribbean writer, born in Jamaica and educated in Jamaica and the USA, she taught English in schools and at Mico Teacher's College. She has been a journalist and radio and television broadcaster, the publications officer for the School Of Education at the University of the West Indies, and editor of the *Caribbean Journal of Education*. She is concerned with women's issues and the development of curriculum materials for language arts in the Caribbean. Her poems have appeared in journals and anthologies and the book, co-edited with Mervyn Morris, *Jamaican Women: An Anthology of Poems* (1980). Her work looks at relationships of power and love, and women's roles, so in 'For Eyes to Bless you' she talks of ownership and identity in a relationship:

you don't know
and even now you can't find out
that masquerade, that play
it's old as woman, old as birth
that's joy and riddance both at once.

Mordecai published *Her True, True Name: An Anthology of Women's Writing from the Caribbean* (1989) with Betty Wilson, and *From Our Yard: Jamaican Poetry Since Independence* (1987).   GW

More, Hannah 1745–1833 BLUESTOCKING writer in many genres including tracts, dramas, educational and pious works, she has been called the most influential woman writer of her period. She was born in Stapleton, Gloucestershire, the fourth of five daughters of Jacob More, a learned headmaster of a free-school in Gloucestershire, and Mary Grace, a farmer's daughter. She and her sisters were educated so that they could support themselves by setting up a school. She began her literary career by writing *The Search after Happiness* (1762) to be performed by the young ladies in her sisters' school. More plays followed, with *The Inflexible Captive* (1774), *Percy* (1778) and *The Fatal Falsehood* (1779). She was a close friend of David Garrick and his wife, and Dr Johnson, and she knew Burke, Horace Walpole and Joshua Reynolds. She also socialized in bluestocking circles, visiting frequently at ELIZABETH MONTAGU's and at MRS BOSCAWEN's; she wrote *The Bas Bleu* (1786), a poem which celebrated their civilized salon community. After Garrick's death, she lived with Mrs Garrick briefly in London, and then moved to Cowslip Green, a cottage she had built near Bristol. She made friends with the Clapham set of evangelicals, and with William Wilberforce. She wrote tracts, (including *Village Politics* (1792), which criticized Tom Paine by dramatizing a dialogue between a blacksmith and a mason). A series of moral tales and Bible stories, later published as 'Cheap Repository Tracts' (1795–8), sold for a penny or a halfpenny each to an audience of 2 million. She set up Sunday schools, friendly societies and weekly classes with her sisters, acted as patron to ANN YEARSLEY (the milkmaid poet), and campaigned against slavery. She also wrote extremely popular educational works (including her *Strictures on the Modern System of Female Education* (1799) which went into thirteen editions). Toward the end of her life, she produced pious and devotional works such as *Practical Piety* and *Moral Sketches* (1818).   PJW

Morgan, Lady see OWENSON, SYDNEY

Morgan [née Milroy], Sally 1951– Australian writer, painter, printmaker whose colourful blocked prints and drawings are instantly recognizable and internationally known. The eldest of five children of an Aboriginal mother and a non-Aboriginal father, Morgan grew up in Perth, Western Australia, where she lives now. She has a BA with a Psychology major and in 1996 was appointed inaugural director of the new Centre for Aboriginal Culture and History at the University of Western Australia. Early artistic inspiration came from a distant relative, Solomon Cocky, who drew his dreaming stories incessantly on paper. Knowledge of their Aboriginal heritage was kept from Morgan and her siblings by her mother and grandmother, for fear that if it were known the children would be removed from the family.

Morgan began writing her celebrated autobiograph-ical work, *MY PLACE* (1987), to find answers to the questions she had been asking since childhood about her family background. Hugely successful, *My Place* has won several awards and sold over half a million copies. Through the voices of her mother, Glad, her grandmother, Nan, and her Uncle Arthur, who all tell their own stories in the book, Morgan finds and acknowledges her 'place'. At once humorous and enormously sad, *My Place* has its own place in the disturbing and painful history of white racism in Australia, telling a story which was repeated countless times in the lives of Aboriginal people in this century. Always divided between her desire to write and to paint, Morgan's preferred literary genre is drama and she has said that painting is her primary vocation. One of her plays, *Sistergirl* (1992), has been widely and successfully performed. She has also published three children's books and collaborated with Jack McPhee, her tribal grandfather, to write his story, *Wanamurraganya* (1989).   DB

Morrell [neé Bentinck], Lady Ottoline (Violet Anne Cavendish) 1873–1938 British memoirist and artistic patron. Ottoline was the only daughter of her father's second marriage. Upon the deaths of her father, Lt-General Arthur Bentinck, in 1877, and his second cousin John Bentinck, fifth Duke of Portland, in 1879, Ottoline's step-brother Arthur became the sixth Duke of Portland, and her mother, Augusta Browne Bentinck, was created Baroness Bolsover. Having grown up privileged but lonely, Ottoline found her purpose in life in helping people. After her marriage to Phillip Morrell in 1902, this purpose changed from spiritual instruction of the lower classes to artistic patronage, which reached its peak with the purchase of Garsington Manor in Oxfordshire in 1913. Here the Morrells entertained many of the leading writers and thinkers of the 20th century. Visitors to Garsington included VIRGINIA WOOLF, Bertrand Russell, DORA CARRINGTON, Siegfried Sassoon, KATHERINE MANSFIELD, T.S. Eliot and Lytton Strachey. Ottoline and Garsington society are parodied in novels by two frequent guests, Aldous Huxley's *Crome Yellow* (1921) and D.H. Lawrence's *Women in Love* (1921). Her memoirs were published posthumously: *Memoirs of Lady Ottoline Morrell: A Study in Friendship, 1873–1915* (1963) and *Ottoline at Garsington: Memoirs of Lady Ottoline Morrell, 1915–1918* (1974).   MCJ

Morris, Margaret [Hill] 1737–1816 American diarist and letter-writer. Daughter of Dr Richard Hill and his wife, Deborah Moore, Margaret Morris was born into an educated and well-connected Quaker family, who enjoyed corresponding with each other. Married in 1758 to William Morris, a merchant, she was widowed with five children after only eight years of marriage. During a portion of the Revolutionary War, Morris

kept a private JOURNAL 'for the amusement of her sister', MILCAH MARTHA Hill (later, MOORE). Morris's narrative gives a vivid picture of the anxiety and suffering of families living in New Jersey during 1777–8, when British and American troops fought their early battles. In one memorable anecdote, she recounts the way she delayed a patrol who wanted to search her house by pretending to be confused about their allegiance. This ruse gave time for a prominent loyalist to hide in her attic. Morris also had a gift for healing the sick and wounded; this became her vocation for the rest of her life.   CLB

Morrison, Toni [née Chloe Anthony Wofford]

1931– A native of Northern Ohio, she did not begin her writing career until she was 40 when, after working for two decades as editor for Random House, she came to realize her invisibility in the Western literary canon. As she put it: 'I didn't exist in all the literature I had read.' Her first novel, THE BLUEST EYE (1970), is a rewriting of the 'Dick and Jane' elementary primer, the classic American school-child's text, and an exploration of the damaging effects of an aesthetics based on the negation of the non-white other. This novel was followed by SULA, where, in the investigation of the life-sustaining qualities of a tightly-knit community, Morrison pursued her interest in writing 'fiction that is really for the village, for the tribe'.

Song of Solomon (1977), followed by *Tar Baby* (1981), established Morrison's reputation as one of the most successful writers in North America. However, both the award of the Pulitzer Prize for Fiction to BELOVED (1987), and of the Nobel Prize to Morrison in 1993, were controversial and spurred a debate on the question of canonicity. While she responded to her detractors with the often-quoted phrase, 'Canon building is empire building, canon defense is natural defense', she was no more pleased with those critics who praised her by comparing her to William Faulkner and VIRGINIA WOOLF, protesting against what she considered an attempt to place her fiction into an established literary tradition.

Although Morrison claims the slave narrative as literary precursor for *Beloved*, rather than confronting the physical brutality of slavery as this genre does, she puts 'the heart of the story within the minds of the slaves themselves'. Moreover, she eschews the chronological movement characteristic of the slave narrative to focus on the imaginative capacity of memory to construct the significance of the past. Over the individual experience of remembering she privileges the act of 'rememorying', which belongs to the community, and is passed on orally, in defiance of the 'deliberate survivalist's intention to forget' an unspeakable past. Morrison has spoken of using language to struggle against the final devastation of having no voice, to tell 'how offended the tongue is, held down by iron'. All of her works, down to *PARADISE* (1998), the third volume of the trilogy begun with *Beloved* and continued in *Jazz* (1992), are about language as well as about silence, whether that silence is metaphorical or literally enforced by the 'bit', the instrument employed by slave owners.

For Morrison, the best art is 'unquestionably political and irrevocably beautiful at the same time'. Her political engagement involves an effort both to force a recognition of the plight of the black subject, and to ask herself, 'other than melanin and subject matter, what, in fact, may make me a black writer?' To create a form that embodies the tension between the victims' need to record and reluctance to remember, Morrison claims the freedom to move beyond language that is associated with music. If *Beloved* is heavily influenced by the blues, the claim to the freedom to render experience and emotions as musicians do is made explicit in *Jazz*, where, as always in her fiction, it is women who are the primary tale-tellers and the transmitters of history.   CBr

Mortimer [née Fletcher], Penelope (Ruth) 1918–

British novelist whose ironic, unsettling, occasionally humorous treatment of female experience in the 1950s, 1960s and 1970s advanced the development of women's writing and (due to recognition in mainstream literary circles) its status. She deflated the post-war romantic myth through detailed examinations of the emotional lives of a familiar (and it was presumed, complacent) class of women: middle-class mothers and housewives who hopefully embraced the domestic ideal only to find it cheated them of the very intimacy and purposefulness they were seeking. *The Pumpkin Eater* (1962), her best-known novel (adapted for film in 1964 by Harold Pinter), chronicles the disintegration of its unnamed narrator, a mother of countless children who undergoes an abortion and sterilization to save her fourth marriage, already shattered by her husband's infidelity. *The Bright Prison* (1956), *Daddy's Gone a Hunting* (1958), *The Home* (1971), *Long Distance* (1974) and *The Handyman* (1983) scrutinize female characters whose identities are tragically constructed upon the false security of the home. *My Friend Says It's Bullet-Proof* (1967) depicts with pathos and black humour the struggles of a fashion correspondent who is forced to revalue the female body following a mastectomy. Mortimer has also written short stories, reviews, screenplays and a royal biography, *Queen Elizabeth: A Life of the Queen Mother* (1986).

She attended London University for one year and briefly worked as a secretary. She has six children and was married twice (for over twenty years to writer John Mortimer). In *About Time: An Aspect of Autobiography* (1979), she writes with characteristic directness of her migratory childhood (in North Wales, Oxfordshire, London and Derbyshire) and sexually complicated relationship with her clergyman father. She has taught in New York and at Boston University and is a Fellow of the Royal Society of Literature.   LDo

Mosionier, Beatrice 1949– Métis novelist, CHIL-DREN's story writer, publisher, playwright and script-writer, formerly known by her married name 'Beatrice Culleton', whose publications make powerful social and political statements about the treatment of native and Métis communities in Canada. Born in St Boniface, Manitoba, into a Métis family of four children, Mosionier and her siblings were removed from their alcoholic parents and placed in separate foster homes, much like the fictional Métis sisters April and Cheryl Raintree in her REALIST novel, *IN SEARCH OF APRIL RAINTREE* (1983). Years later, after both of Mosionier's sisters had taken their own lives, she decided to write the novel to try and 'find answers as to why our family seemed to come up against all these things'. A year after its publication the novel re-appeared as *April Raintree* (1984) in a revised edition for schools. Since then Mosionier has also written the children's books, *Spirit of the White Bison* (1985/1993) and *Christopher's Folly* (1997), a forthcoming play, *Night of the Trickster*, and a film-script, *Walker*, which was one in a series of four called 'Playing Fair' produced by the National Film Board. Alongside her writing activities, she has also worked as manager for the only Métis publishing house in Canada, Pemmican Publications. The mother of two adult children, Mosionier writes for the purpose of getting published and finds the labour involved pleasurable: 'It's like seeing a movie in my mind and telling you what I see.'   SEP

Moths (1880) Following the career of the ingenuous Vere, who is tricked into marriage with a wealthy but dissolute Russian duke, OUIDA's novel provides a damning commentary on the vices and follies of the upper classes. Vere's life is shaped by a meeting with the famous singer, Correze, who tells her: 'Th[e fashionable] world . . . does no woman good. It is a world of moths. Half the moths are burning themselves in feverish frailty, the other half are corroding and consuming all that they touch. You are made for something better than a moth.' Vere strives to avoid mothdom. Consequently, her marriage is a failure and she is unpopular in society. Finally, when gossip magnifies Vere's innocent friendship with Correze into a sordid affair, her husband challenges Correze to a duel and divorces her. Vere and Correze eventually marry but this is no happy ending. Known to be innocent, Vere is cut socially by the voluptuaries who have falsely accused her: 'So the moths eat the ermine; and the world kisses the leper on both cheeks.'   EMH

Mott, Lucretia Coffin 1793–1880 American Quaker minister and reformer. Born in Nantucket, Massachusetts, Mott grew up in a Quaker family, who later moved to Philadelphia. She became a Quaker minister in 1821. She challenged authority within Quakerism, believing that spiritual truth lies within each individual instead of in Church authority or doctrine. This belief inspired her to fight social injustice. Mott founded the Philadelphia Female Antislavery Society in 1833. She attended the 1840 London Antislavery Convention, but the convention's male delegates refused to let women speak. At the convention, she met ELIZABETH CADY STANTON, with whom she organized the Seneca Falls convention on women's rights in 1848. She helped lead the Women's Rights movement until 1869. In addition, Mott participated in the non-violence movement and, with her husband, hosted escaping slaves and numerous reformers. After the Civil War, Mott continued to work for peace and the rights of blacks and women; she also became involved in the Free Religious Association.

Believing that she should speak only as the Spirit instructed her, Mott did not write her sermons and speeches; however, many were transcribed by Quakers or newspaper reporters. She also kept a JOURNAL of her trip to London and wrote numerous letters.   AE

Mouré, Erin 1955– Canadian poet and essayist whose work combines an interest in feminist and related political issues with attention to language. Born in Calgary to English-speaking parents, Mouré spent two years at university before getting a job with Canadian National Railway and then VIA Rail, living for a while in Vancouver before moving to Montreal. In 1979 she published *Empire, York Street*, which was followed by *The Whisky Vigil* (1981) and *Wanted Alive* (1983). Her fourth book, *Domestic Fuel* (1985), won the League of Canadian Poets' Pat Lowther Award, after which she published *Furious*, which won the 1988 Governor General's Award for poetry. Since then she has published several more collections, including *WSW (West South West)* (1989), *Sheepish Beauty, Civilian Love* (1992) and *Search Procedures* (1996). Central to Mouré's poetics is her attempt to heighten awareness of the paradigms we learn to see through, by writing poems that are not easily absorbed by the 'status quo', and by re-writing or reconsidering already-written poems from a different perspective, a strategy foregrounded in the prose poems in *Furious*. This is because, in Mouré's view, 'language never seems transparent . . . Remember, it is a surface; it lies, it reduces some of us to absence!'. As part of this process Mouré stresses the importance of her friendship with GAIL SCOTT and the feminist community to which she belonged, which challenged Mouré's and other women's theoretical thinking. Mouré and the English Canadian writer, BRONWEN

WALLACE, pursued a two-year discussion of feminist theory that was published as *Two Women Talking: Correspondence 1985-87 Erin Mouré and Bronwen Wallace*.

SEP

Mourning Dove (Humishuma, Christine Haines Quintasket Galler) 1888?–1936 Native American

writer. An Okanogan who both lived on the Colville reservation and was educated briefly at several schools run by whites, Mourning Dove – also known by several English names – simultaneously assimilated to white ways and valued Native American traditions. Her novel, *Cogewea: The Half-Blood* (1927), reflects this combination of two seemingly incompatible ways of life, teaching her audience about Okanogan culture through the popular (white) genre of Western romance. The product of Mourning Dove's collaboration with Lucullus Virgil McWhorter, the novel presents the dilemma of a young woman faced with choosing between white and Native American worlds. Unfortunately, some of McWhorter's changes to the novel were unknown to Mourning Dove and are generally seen as weakening the text.

Mourning Dove's second literary work, also written in collaboration with McWhorter, is a collection of Salishan tales. The stories required that she approach native languages from an ethnographer's point of view as well as occasionally 'sanitize' myths told by elders. They appear in three different published configurations: *Coyote Stories* (1933), *Tales of the Okanogans* (1976) and *Mourning Dove's Stories* (1991).

Mourning Dove's personal life was marked by loss, illness, and financial and physical hardship: she often wrote only after a full day's work as a migrant worker. By all accounts, her two marriages were difficult ones. Nevertheless, she persisted in writing a second novel (now lost) and became an activist in local tribal issues. After her death, Jay Miller edited and published *Mourning Dove: A Salishan Autobiography* (1990), a work noted for its importance in recording the role of women in her culture.

KMP

Moving Image, The (1946) JUDITH WRIGHT's first

collection of poetry was enthusiastically received, its sensuous imagery and confident rhetorical voice praised as lending new energy to prevailing Australian poetic preoccupations, notably a long-standing concern with writing the landscape, and a more recent one with Time (her remarkable poems of sexuality and motherhood would follow in *Woman to Man* in 1949). The tragic sense of the destructiveness of Time and darkness marking *The Moving Image* would be gradually transformed by a Jungian view of wholeness as residing in reconciled oppositions, but Wright's response to a loved land would become increasingly troubled. The particularity of her evocations of the

Coyote Stories

By Mourning Dove *(Hu-mis'-hu-ma)*

Edited and illustrated by Heister Dean Guie with notes by L. V. McWhorter *(Old Wolf)* and a foreword by Chief Standing Bear, Oglala Sioux

The CAXTON PRINTERS, Ltd.
CALDWELL, IDAHO
1934

Mourning Dove: title-page of *Coyote Stories*, republished in 1934.

New England region was welcomed as breaking with nationalistic and totalizing attempts to define 'Australia'. Yet latent in these celebratory and loving poems were anxieties explicit in Wright's later work as both poet and activist – anxieties about the adequacy of language, love's endurance, and the legitimacy of any at-homeness for white Australians haunted by the dispossessed Aboriginal ghosts of the 'Bora Ring' or the accusing 'Dust' of an eroded environment. JStr

Mowatt (Ritchie), Anna Cora (Ogden) [Helen Berkley] 1819–70 American playwright, novelist,

journalist and actress. The ninth of fourteen children, she was born to an American family in Bordeaux, France, but her family soon returned to New York. Educated at home, she began acting at the age of 5. At fifteen she eloped with lawyer James Mowatt, with whom she adopted three orphans. He died in 1851; in

1854 she married William Ritchie, a journalist. Her first play, *Gulzara* (1840), was privately produced, but the following year, as ill health impeded her husband's ability to support them, she began writing professionally. Her New York acting début and the début of her first play, *Fashion: Or Life in New York*, both in 1845, launched a brilliant career in the USA and abroad, through which Mowatt overcame rebuffs of her forwardness and widespread scepticism about the reputability of public employment for women. *Autobiography of an Actress* (1854) recounts her remarkable career. *Fashion*, a satire of corrupt New York society after the manner of R. B. Sheridan, has been acclaimed as the first truly American drama and revived in the 20th century. She also wrote articles under the pseudonym 'Helen Berkley' and novels about New York society (*The Fortune Hunter*, 1844, and *Evelyn*, 1845). In two novels about the theatre, *Mimic Life* (1856) and *Twin Roses* (1857), she promotes women's developing their talents and earning their living. *Fairy Fingers* (1865) and *The Mute Singer* (1866) reflect her Swedenborgian ideals through devout but professionally tenacious heroines.

JSG

Mrs Dalloway (1925), VIRGINIA WOOLF's fourth novel, takes place in London on one day in 1923, when Clarissa Dalloway, the wife of a Conservative MP, gives a party and Septimus Smith, a shell-shocked veteran of World War I, commits suicide. It continues both chronologically and experimentally from *Jacob's Room* (1922), portraying post-war society and eroding the boundaries of time, place, gender and personal identity in its exploration of consciousness. It is a radiant and pessimistic novel, opposing only moments of joy and the transient harmony of the party to the immutable facts of solitude and death. Since the sixties its feminism and critique of 'masculine' public life and military values have been increasingly understood. PMar

Mugo, Micere (M.) Githae 1942– Kenyan poet, dramatist and literary critic, whose work addresses the possibility of a meaningful liberation for Africa after independence. Her parents were teachers in Baricho, in the Kirinyaga district of Kenya. She showed an early interest in, and talent for, drama, winning the Best Actress Award at the Uganda Drama Festival while an undergraduate at Makerere University, where she gained a BA (Hons) in English in 1966. She published poetry and a short story in *Penpoint*, a literary magazine based at Makerere, being encouraged in her writing by Chinua Achebe and Eldred Jones. As part of her Master's thesis for the University of New Brunswick, Canada, she presented two plays, *Disillusioned* (a play for radio), and *The Long Illness of Chief Kiti* (published 1971) which depicts the 'ugly scars' left by 'the experience of colonization and the war for liberation', while

women are made key figures of national regeneration. In her collected poems, *Daughters of My People, Sing!* (1976), pessimism at the competitiveness and materialism dividing Kenyan society is balanced by a celebration of the strength of women. In 1976, she collaborated with Ngugi wa Thiong'o on *The Trial of Dedan Kimathi* in an epic dramatization of the life of the Kenyan freedom-fighter, which also sought to recognize the important role of women in the Mau Mau war. She has published a number of critical studies and monographs. As a Marxist she believes 'the role of the progressive writer' is to 'create a consciousness for the people, workers and peasants, old women and men, and children'. She taught in the English Department at the University of Nairobi, as Senior Lecturer, then Dean, from the mid 1970s to 1982, when she went into exile to preserve her right to political and social comment. In 1982 she took up a teaching post at the University of Zimbabwe. WJB

Muir, Willa (Wilhelmina Johnstone) 1890–1969 Scottish poet, essayist and translator. Raised in Montrose by parents recently arrived from the Shetland Islands, she called herself a 'Displaced Person' for most of her life. Hence the poignant title of her memoir *Belonging*, which revisits her marriage to the poet Edwin Muir, with whom she travelled and collaborated for nearly fifty years (their numerous translations include major works by Franz Kafka, Hermann Broch and Gerhard Hauptmann). Her own career began in earnest with her essay *Women: An Inquiry* (1925). Its feminist concerns resurface more substantially in her later book *Mrs Grundy in Scotland* (1936) and her article 'Moving in Circles' (1938). Her published novels include *Imagined Corners* (1931) and *Mrs Ritchie* (1933), but her most ambitious work, 'The Usurpers' (finished in 1952), was never published. Her husband's death in 1959 prompted a final burst of creativity, manifested in a book of poems, *Laconics, Jingles and Other Verses* (1969). BWB

Mukherjee, Bharati 1940– Indian novelist and short-story writer. Born in Calcutta into a wealthy Brahmin family, she attended the Loreto Convent school for girls. After finishing her Master's degree in English and Ancient Indian Culture she went to the University of Iowa to attend the Writers' Workshop, where she also earned her Ph.D. In 1963 she married the Canadian author Clark Blaise and moved to Canada where she became a naturalized citizen in 1972. She taught English at McGill University in Montreal. After enduring several racial attacks for being 'dark-skinned', she moved to the United States in 1980. She taught creative writing at Columbia University, New York University and Queens College, before becoming a Distinguished Professor at Berkeley University.

Mukherjee's first novel, *The Tiger's Daughter* (1972), is her only fictional backward look at India. The following novel, *Wife* (1975), deals with an immigrant Indian woman, the first of a long series of uprooted heroines. These recurrent female models will offer Mukherjee the possibility of exploring the issues of fluid identities and of diasporic imagination. In 1977 she published *Darkness: Days and Nights in Calcutta*, co-authored with her husband. In these stories she undergoes the transition from the 'aloofness of expatriation' to the 'exuberance of immigration'. Her collection, *The Middleman and Other Stories* (1988), won the National Book Critics' Circle Award for best fiction, and with the novel *Jasmine* (1990) Mukherjee establishes herself as a major American writer. It is about the real transformation of a village girl from Punjab into an emancipated self-assured American woman at ease with her sexuality and 'shuttling between identities'. Her more accomplished book, *The Holder of the World* (1994), is a historical novel with a tinge of SCIENCE-FICTION. With this work, Mukherjee attempts to reinscribe the making of America by stretching the myth of its ancestors back to the glorious past of Moghul India. In *Leave It To Me* (1997), the issues of gender, migration and Americanization are approached from the perspective of an Indian girl adopted into a middle-class Italo-American family. Mukherjee is sometimes criticized for creating fables rather than realistic depictions and for using orientalizing icons to market her books in the West. However credit must be given to her original use of American slang and her unusual representation of peripatetic female characters.   SPo

Mules and Men (1935) A collection of African-American folklore gathered by ZORA NEALE HURSTON during four years' research in the South (including Eatonville, Florida, her home-town). The book includes tales, sayings, songs, games, sermons and hoodoo (voodoo) practices, held together by Hurston's narrative presence which moves between literate narrator and idiomatic black voice. Part 1 contains seventy 'Folk Tales' detailing the exploits of Jack (or John) and Ole Massa, the Devil and God, and the natural history of man and creation. The tales are framed by the everyday voices and lives of the black communities who offer up these 'big old lies', and by Hurston's confident participation in them. The second part on 'Hoodoo' relates Hurston's experiences in the New Orleans world of spells, conjures, hexes and divination, including her own initiation with several prominent 'two-headed doctors' (voodoo practitioners).

The collection has scholarly shortcomings, but Hurston's concern is less with analytical anthropology than with revealing and celebrating the humour and wisdom and the rich oral heritage of black Americans.   AG

Mule's Foal, The (1993) FONTINI EPANOMITIS draws on her Greek background for this collection of linked fables, woven into a larger pattern perceivable in its entirety only at the end. The 'illusory security of village life' is destroyed by the villagers' responses to a series of remarkable figures. There is Vaia, from the house of saints and strong women, and mother of the remarkable gorilla child who brings vitality to the sleepy village. There is Meta, a woman of extraordinary powers whom the villagers tried to contain. And there is the narrator, Mirella, who keeps the whorehouse and everyone's secrets. Written in classically simple prose, this tale is both timeless and timely. Though set in a tiny Greek village in the mythical past, it is really about the limits of community and the acceptance of difference. The alienation and dislocation it explores cut to the heart of the migrant experience. Published when the author was only 22, this novel is a remarkably assured accomplishment for one so young, and won both the Australian/Vogel award and the Victorian Premier's Prize.   LBer

Mulford, Wendy 1941– Avant-garde, venturesome British poet whose output appears to be a project for measuring just how much syntax can take. Mulford grew up in Wales, took degrees at the universities of Cambridge and London, and married the poet and editor John James. She lives and teaches in Cambridge and has a daughter. She ran the small press, Street Editions (founded in 1972), and published several of the British avant-garde associated with J.H. Prynne, the 'Cambridge School' and writers associated with the anthology *A Various Art* (1987). She was one of the first to recognize the talent of VERONICA FORREST-THOMPSON, requesting a collection days before Forrest-Thompson's tragic death in 1975.

Mulford has a considerable reputation among non-mainstream poets on both sides of the Atlantic. During her career she has chosen to have her poetry appear in a range of small-press, limited-run editions or magazines such as the *English Intelligencer*. Her poetry is elliptical but her stance is far from elitist despite charges of her syntax being 'so ragged as to be almost missing' (Peter Porter). Mulford has published eleven collections, including the striking *Lusus Naturae* (1990), illustrated by Liz Rideal. *The Bay of Naples* (1992) is a sequence of twenty-six poems inspired by paintings shown in Howard Hodgkin's 1985 Whitechapel Gallery Exhibition. The poems, like the paintings, have a jewel-like intensity: 'rust tawny flaming', 'red glowing/green' and 'aquamarine bleeding' are juxtaposed 'in violent proximity'. Her collaborative work with artists is both noteworthy and accessible. Her work was anthologized in *The New British Poetry* (1988) and she edited *The Virago Book of Love Poetry* in 1990.   DM

Munda, Constantia [pseud.] fl.1617 Writer of a polemical pamphlet, *The Worming of a Mad Dogge: Or, A Soppe for Cerberus the Jaylor of Hell* (1617). Munda's pamphlet participates in the 'woman controversy' of 1615-20, which began with Joseph Swetnam's *The arraignment of lewde, idle, froward, and unconstant women* (1615): it is the third proto-feminist response to this work, following pamphlets by SPEGHT and SOWERNAM, to whom she refers. Like the earlier polemicist ANGER, she is aware of the threat to women posed by male writing; 'woman' is a book 'most shamefully blurred, and derogatively razed by scribbling pens of savage . . . monsters'. She offers no defence of women, instead ridiculing Swetnam, and using the 'woman question' as the vehicle for her wit. The pamphlet, which quotes extensively in Latin and Greek, is noteworthy for challenging stereotypical sex roles, in particular the association of men with war and women with peace.   JC

Munro, Alice 1931– Novelist whose REALISTIC 'snapshots' of small-town Canadian life, particularly the life of women, are deftly ironic. In Munro, photography stands for the elusiveness of truth, as does the short-story structure, which forms the basis of her novels. She was born in Western Ontario and her work identifies her with this region. She married at 20, and moved with her husband to British Columbia, where they established a bookstore and raised three daughters. She wrote short stories for magazines and radio, in 1968 publishing her first story collection, *Dance of the Happy Shades*, and in 1971 her most celebrated work, THE LIVES OF GIRLS AND WOMEN. Munro's vision is filtered through the consciousness of an imaginative girl who feels 'different' from those around her. Del Jordan's present-time relations and adolescent sexuality are offset by the histories of her female contemporaries and older relatives. In her third book of stories, *Who Do You Think You Are?* (1978), Munro achieved her distinctive mode. The tales are held together by a single character, offering a variety of perspectives on her life and that of her community. Munro is a consummate artist of shame and social unease, revealing the complex depth of ordinary folk, making bold, quasi-cinematic cuts between present and past. Her achievement is to subtly intimate the anarchy that underlies sedate appearances: 'Now I no longer believe that peoples' secrets are defined and communicable, or their feelings full-blown and easy to recognize.' The short story, with its mix of economy and elusiveness, remains her preferred form. See also THE PROGRESS OF LOVE (1986).   KE

Murder at the Vicarage (1930) AGATHA CHRISTIE's novel marks the official début of Miss Marple, the elderly and ostensibly retiring resident of the cosy English village of St Mary Mead, whose denizens have a surprising predilection for murder, adultery and burglary. The mystery concerns the death of Colonel Protheroe, the universally disliked warden of the Church of St Mary. He is found dead in the study of the church's saintly vicar, Len Clement. Clement tells the story, and Christie charmingly reveals his character through her adroit handling of the first-person narrative, but it is the unique character of Jane Marple that makes the novel memorable. Unlike any DETECTIVE before or since, the amateur Miss Marple challenges assumptions about gender and age. Unsentimentally aware of the evil lurking under the surface of respectability, she is a keen listener and a shrewd observer, skills for which her love of gossip and bird-watching are eminently well suited. Faced with a tangle of clues and the dismissiveness of professionals, Miss Marple, in the end, is 'right on every count'.   LCo

Murder of Roger Ackroyd, The (1926) Generally held to be one of AGATHA CHRISTIE's best DETECTIVE THRILLERS. Always a master of misdirection, in this book she has the criminal, Dr Sheppard, as the largely sympathetic narrator apparently investigating a murder that he himself has perpetrated, pretending to the role of 'Watson' to the 'Holmes' of her famous Hercule Poirot. The 'unreliable' narration is a triumph of disingenuous fact-veiling: we are only allowed to perceive how much Sheppard has left out of his account of events when the game is up and he reveals all to Poirot at the end. The reader has, of course, been fooled far more than the redoubtable Poirot, who has inveigled his chief suspect into a position of supposed trust. The 'high-tec' of the 1920s figures largely in the plot in the form of a dictaphone and a timing-device. Probably, the most memorable chapter is the one entitled 'An Evening At Mah Jong', in which the calls of this absorbing game intersperse the atmospheric speculation and village gossip between the players.   JLB

Murdoch, Iris 1919–99 Iris Murdoch was one of the most distinguished of British post-war women writers. She achieved both popular and critical success, won the Booker Prize with *The Sea, the Sea* (1978) and was awarded the DBE in 1987. A professional philosopher as well as a novelist, she read Greats (Latin, Greek, ancient history and philosophy) at Oxford. After a wartime position in the Treasury (1942–4), work for refugees in Belgium and Austria (1944–6) and a research studentship at Cambridge (1948), she returned to Oxford as Fellow in Philosophy at St Anne's College. *Sartre: Romantic Rationalist* (1953), her first critique of existentialism, was followed by her first novel, the picaresque *Under the Net* (1954). In 1956 she married John Bayley, later Warton Professor of English Literature at Oxford. She wrote twenty-six novels, several philo-

Magpie Players
The Cotswolds,   Keep the card!

POSTCARD PICTURE
BY JUDGES' LTD., HASTINGS
ENGLAND

Had a superb audience at Bicester yesterday, & Lady Bicester gave us lunch (off silver plate!) & was particularly taken with my acting. Have had a quiet afternoon here – a beautiful little place. Bibury has unexpectedly cancelled our performance – Crisis, I suppose. We are most wonderfully oblivious of the international situation. love I.

Mr & Mrs Murdoch
4 Eastbourne Rd.
Chiswick
London
W.4.

Iris Murdoch: postcard written to her parents on 30 August 1939, the eve of World War II.

sophical works, a collection of poems, some short plays and 'Platonic Dialogues'.

Murdoch's major fictional subject is love. Her characters fall in love, sometimes repeatedly, forming new combinations and permutations with an almost patterned inventiveness. The effect is intensely romantic, comic and quizzical. Like Shakespearean comedy (a major influence), the novels acknowledge and question the power of love. They suggest several answers. Bradley Pearson, the narrator of *The Black Prince* (1973), proposes a Freudian view: 'the unconscious delights in identifying people with each other. It has only a few characters to play with.' In *A FAIRLY HONOURABLE DEFEAT* (1970), Julius claims that 'Anyone will do to play the roles' and his partial success in making people fall in and out of love (as in *Much Ado* and *Othello*) partially bears him out. The unconscious resembles the cave in Plato's *Republic*, where prisoners with their backs to the distant sun see only shadows of fire-lit images. But in his *Symposium* human love begins the ascent of the soul and Murdoch locates in the fire of Eros the genesis of creativity and unselfing.

In *The Fire and the Sun* (1977) and *Art and Eros* (1980) Murdoch engages with Plato's hostility to art. She both suspects and reveres art. Art offers the consolations of fantasy. Yet art may illuminate and in her novels inspires epiphanies which, like 'genuine' mystical experience, make the characters (if only temporarily) more virtuous.

Murdoch, an atheist, is preoccupied by the definition of virtue in a world without God. *The Sovereignty of Good* (1970) debates the problem in philosophical, the novels in imaginative, terms. Murdoch's novels are full of characters who have or had religious vocations. *The Time of the Angels* (1966) depicts our post-religious age as haunted and demonic. Hugo in *Under the Net* is the first of the psychopomps and gurus placed in dialogic relation to an artist and, like many of them, he disowns and dismantles his unsought authority. In the later novels Buddhism is more potent than Christianity, as less dogmatic and less flattering to the ego. Despite Murdoch's expertise in theorizing, her most virtuous characters distrust theory and accept the muddle and contingency of life. As conceptual constructions her novels are both elegant and provisional. Absolutism, moral and erotic, is subjected to the particularity of experience, in social comedy, sexual peripeteia, chilling scenes of terror and powerfully vivid evocation of place and time. See also *THE BELL* (1958) and *A SEVERED HEAD* (1961).   PMar

Murphree, Mary Noailles [Charles Egbert Craddock]
1850–1922 American regionalist, novelist and short-story writer. She was born in Murfreesboro, Tennessee, daughter of a wealthy plantation-owner, and educated at private schools in Nashville and Philadelphia. An illness at the age of 4 left her

permanently lame. Spending summers with her family in the Cumberland Mountains, she became acquainted with the local residents. The Civil War impoverished her family and she contributed to their support with her writing. Her fiction, which she wrote under a male pseudonym, beginning in the 1870s, was the earliest to depict mountain life in the South and earned her a reputation as a 'local-colourist'. Her most acclaimed work was a collection of stories, *In the Tennessee Mountains* (1884). Readers widely believed she was a man, since her themes and style were 'unfeminine', until she disclosed her identity to the editor of *Atlantic Monthly* during a visit to Boston in 1885, causing a sensation that increased her literary success. Like MARY WILKINS FREEMAN and SARAH ORNE JEWETT, she portrayed her characters sympathetically. She showed acute awareness of class differences between the local people and genteel outsiders, and gave the mountaineers' viewpoint on the visitors as well as the genteel view of local life. Murfree also wrote novels about Tennessee mountaineers, including *The Prophet of the Great Smoky Mountains* (1885) and *The 'Stranger People's' Country* (1891), as well as historical fiction.

JSG

Murphy, Dervla 1931– Irish TRAVEL writer and social commentator with a high international profile. Murphy was born and raised in County Waterford. A graduate of Trinity College Dublin, her writing career took off, when, after the death of her parents, she documented her travels through Afghanistan to India in the popular *Full Tilt* (1965). Murphy's books have enjoyed critical as well as commercial success, and she has been the recipient of many prizes including the Irish-American Literary Award in 1975, the Christopher Ewart-Biggs Memorial Prize in 1978 and the Irish American Cultural Institute Literary Award in 1985. Respected for her unpatronizing and incisive observations of other cultures, Murphy has published profusely and her books include accounts of travels to Ethiopia, Latin America, Madagascar, South Africa, Tibet and Transylvania. Her lack of fear in tackling contentious social and political issues is evidenced in her study of Northern Ireland, *A Place Apart* (1978), while *Tales from Two Cities* (1987) looks at different racial groups in British cities, and *The Ukimwi Road* (1993) documents the spread of AIDS in Africa. She has one daughter, Rachel, who has accompanied her on a number of her journeys.

MSu

Murphy [née Ferguson], Emily (Janey Canuck) 1868–1933 Canadian social and feminist activist, also a writer, she was born to a well-connected Ontario Conservative family. After graduating from Bishop Strachan school in Toronto, she married Arthur Murphy, an Anglican minister, in 1887. From 1898 to 1900, the family lived in England where the pervasiveness of poverty inspired her first book, *The Impressions of Janey Canuck Abroad* (1901). Using the persona of a somewhat naive narrator, she described her observations of England.

When the family returned to Toronto in 1900, Murphy wrote book reviews and articles on housekeeping and fashion for small magazines under the pseudonyms of 'Lady Jane', 'the Duchess', 'Earlie York'. Because her writing was accessible, enjoyable and inspired by situations and issues around her, she had a loyal audience. In 1908 the family moved to Manitoba, where Emily travelled with her husband, always conversing with people about their lives. These informal 'interviews' inspired more 'Janey Canuck' books: *Janey Canuck in the West* (1910) defends immigrant cultures; *Open Trails* (1912) compares Canadian and American life; and *Seeds of Pine* (1914) is about Indian legends.

In 1907, the family moved to Edmonton where Emily Murphy became involved in feminist and other social justice issues and local and national politics. She was a founding member of the Equal Franchise League (1913) which petitioned for and won women's suffrage in Alberta (1916) and was active in winning women's suffrage nationally (1918): 'the distinguishing mark of a really fine woman', she said, 'is loyalty to her sex'. As a magistrate she became aware of trafficking and drug addiction, and initiated the Patent Medicine Act of 1919. In 1922 she published *The Black Candle*, the first comprehensive book on drug addiction in North America.

When the Montreal Women's Club proposed Emily Murphy for an appointment to the Senate in 1921, the Prime Minister refused, claiming that women lacked qualification for appointment: they were not 'persons'. With four other women, Emily Murphy took the 'Person's Case' – to establish whether or not the word 'persons' included women – to the Supreme Court of Canada which upheld the Prime Minister's interpretation (1928). The highest court of appeal, the Judicial Committee of the Privy Council in England, ruled that women were persons (1929) and therefore eligible for appointment. However, Mrs Murphy, a Conservative, was not named to the Senate; Cairine Wilson, a prominent Liberal, was named by the Liberal government. In honour of the achievements of Emily Murphy and her four partners in the Person's Case, the Government of Canada has instituted a 'Person's Prize', awarded every October to five Canadian women who have contributed significantly to the lives of women in Canada.

GHN

Murray, Judith Sargent 1751–1820 American essayist, poet and playwright, best known for her essays on women's equality. Born into a socially and politically prominent Massachusetts family, she lamented the formal education withheld from her sex but read widely of European fiction, history and philosophy, as well as American literature of the period. She withdrew from the Calvinist Church in 1776 and joined the Universalists, early establishing herself in opposition to dominant cultural models. The egalitarian nature of Universalist doctrine, her anger at being denied a formal education, the Revolutionary climate of dissent, and her misgivings on the morality of war came together in Murray to create a profound commitment to gender equality. She married Universalist minister John Murray in 1788 and gave birth to a daughter, Julia, in 1791.

She began publishing poetry and essays in New England journals in 1784. Her essays, including 'Desultory thoughts upon the utility of encouraging a degree of self-complacency, especially in female bosoms' (1784) and 'On the equality of the sexes' (1790), appeared under the pen name 'Constantia'. She also wrote in the male voice of 'The Gleaner', a move calculated to give her work credibility. The collected and expanded 'Gleaner' essays were published in a three-volume work of the same name in 1798; they address character, politics, economy, law, education and the status of women. Influenced by the intellectual currents of the Enlightenment and firmly rooted in her Federalist heritage, the essays display a rationalism characteristic of the era, alongside a poetic taste for the sublime and the use of exemplary characters that suggests her interest in the potential influence of fiction. Her plays, *The Medium* (1795) and *The Traveller Returned* (1796), were performed at the Federal Street Theatre in Boston to mixed reviews.   VC

Murray, Louisa 1818–94 Canadian novelist and critic who turned her experience of immigrant culture-shock into an insistence on Old World standards for New World writing. Self-educated in a literate military family in England and Ireland, she spunkily countered her isolation as a settler's daughter on Wolfe Island, Ontario (1844), by opening a school and writing. But, as she remarked of CHARLOTTE BRONTË, 'genius craves recognition', and helped by SUSANNA MOODIE she published her first novels, *Fauna* (1851) and *Settlers of Long Arrow* (1861), as magazine serials. Melodramatic but perceptive, they centre on the exotic and savage in the COLONIAL experience, especially its impact on women and native peoples. Other novels include *The Cited Curate* (1863) and *Little Dorinn* (1873), on Irish 'troubles', and *Marguerite Kneller* (1872), on the problems of the woman artist, a recurring topic in her vigorous literary criticism for the new magazines of the 1870s–80s. The intellectual calibre of her work drew comparisons with GEORGE ELIOT, but the uncertainties of 19th-century Canadian publishing prevented any from appearing in its planned book form.   MSM

Murray, Sarah (later Aust) 1744–1811 British TRAVEL and educational writer whose intrepid journeys through Scotland are detailed in her *Companion and Useful Guide to Scotland* (1799). She combines practical details (distances, costs, state of roads and inns) with folklore and history, description of 'romantic' scenery and acerbic comment. Noblemen who open their houses to travellers, she complains, expect them 'to pay their servants' wages' with exorbitant tips. Travelling with a man, maid and carriage (which she often abandoned to walk), she observed Highlanders staring at 'a fearless female stranger, scrambling alone amongst the crags' – and clearly enjoying herself – even if, at the King's House Inn, she sat writing with 'my petticoats tucked to my knees for fear of the dirt'. She established successful schools at Bath and Kensington, writing *The School* (1766-72) in the form of letters about school life from a girl to her mother. After her second marriage, she journeyed to the Hebrides and published volume II (1805 and 1810) of her 'unique' *Guide* for travellers who will 'follow my steps'.   LMT

Murry, Ann Before 1778–after 1818 English poet and children's educational writer. Ann Murry turned to private tutoring after her father's London wine business failed. She dedicated her first work, *Mentoria, or, The Young Ladies Instructor* (1778), to the Princess Royal, and, by 1791, she had become preceptress in the royal nursery. A dialogue between a governess and her aristocratic charges, *Mentoria* explicates grammar, conduct, geography, arithmetic, religion and history. The text includes anecdotes, classical and scriptural tales, and verse – often Murry's own but also that of Milton, Thomson and Pope. Essentially conservative, *Mentoria* urges female virtue and religious devotion, condemns Roman Catholicism, excoriates slavery and supports the American rebellion. The work's immense popularity led to frequent reprintings well into the 19th century.

The *Sequel to Mentoria* (1799) offers lessons in geology, physics and astronomy. Murry's other educational works include *A Concise History of the Kingdoms of Israel and Judah* (1783), the eight-volume *Mentorian Lectures* (1809) and an abridged *History of France* (1818). Beyond her writing for children, Murry published *Poems on Various Subjects* (1779) with a list of famous and aristocratic subscribers. Somewhat dated, her verse recalls Augustan models, particularly the works of Swift and Pope, in its heroic couplets and social satire.   JHP

My Ántonia (1918) WILLA CATHER's Nebraskan epic finds the American novelist wrapping a wistful lyricism around the cherished character of Ántonia Shimerda. The novel, one of Cather's most autobiographical in the Western series that includes *O Pioneers!* and *Song of the Lark*, is narrated by decent lawyer Jim

Burden, who as a child moves to the prairie town of Black Hawk (Cather's Red Cloud). There he tutors and befriends Ántonia, eldest daughter of a Bohemian family. The tale is a love story, not between Jim and Ántonia – whose bond is deep but oddly platonic – but between the two of them and the awesome prairie landscape, for which they share an entranced passion and in whose presence they experience a wordless joy. 'That is happiness, to be dissolved into something complete and great', is Jim's description of the feeling. Ántonia's vivacity and hard work make her a classic Cather heroine: she embodies the light and liveliness of what Cather saw as the genuine pioneer spirit – for which Cather, settled in New York by the time of writing, was already nostalgic. H. L. Mencken's assessment was: 'No romantic novel ever written in America, by man or woman, is one half so beautiful as *My Ántonia*.'

SB

My Brilliant Career (1901) Written by Australian MILES FRANKLIN when she was 16. Its playful tone is indicated by its chapter headings, which swing in register between 'Was e'er a rose without its thorn?' through 'Ta-ta to Barney's Gap' to 'Yah!' The narrator, Sybylla, perversely assures the reader that the novel is 'a *real* yarn', with no 'such trash as descriptions of beautiful sunsets' yet the last page of the book describes a spectacular sunset. Sybylla despises female wiles yet is a determined flirt; she attacks her suitor with a whip but wants to be dominated; she is both egalitarian and snobbish, both a child and a woman, a tomboy and an artist, a feminist and a traditionalist. European FAIRY TALES are subverted. Sybylla undergoes a classic 'Ugly Duckling into swan' transformation, but when Prince Charming appears to rescue Cinderella/Sybylla, who is back in her rags, she turns down his proposal of marriage. The social range of life in the Australian bush and in rural towns, and the lure of grog, are sketched with vivid complexity.

ASm

My Father's Moon (1989) By way of random imagery and constantly altering time frames, ELIZABETH JOLLEY's narrator, Vera Wright, recounts the early part of her life: her complex relationships with parents and friends; her time at boarding school; her nursing training in an army hospital during World War II; her seduction by the charming, but faithless, Dr Metcalf; and her experience of the loneliness and social stigma associated with unmarried motherhood in the years following the war. The first part of a trilogy, *My Father's Moon* is succeeded by *Cabin Fever* (1990) and *The Georges' Wife* (1993), subsequent novels which continue Vera's story. Although *My Father's Moon* stands as a novel in its own right, strands of recollection run through all three works, the persistent and almost obsessive surfacing of familiar material giving them a strange,

dream-like quality that evokes a sense of disorientation and psychological uncertainty. Although it is generally read as autobiographical fiction, *My Father's Moon* has been described by Jolley as an 'episodic novel . . . set in an environment which had an overwhelming effect on the author'. Vera's narration stands as a poignant representation of one woman's anguished quest for identity, depicted through the distorting mirror of memory.

DT

My Place (1987) SALLY MORGAN's autobiography/novel has been a deeply influential text within Australia. Morgan is one of the country's best-known Aboriginal writers and artists, and this book was at the centre of the flowering of autobiographical texts by Aboriginal women in the 1980s (see AUSTRALIAN ABORIGINAL LIFE-WRITING). *My Place* describes Morgan's discovery and exploration of her Aboriginal identity after being brought up by her mother and grandmother to believe she was Indian. Included within her own story are the transcribed oral narratives of her great-uncle, her grandmother and her mother, and her text is very much an attempt to rewrite Australian history and culture to include the Aboriginal voice. The multiple autobiographical stories that Morgan includes are a process of retrieval and reclamation of the past, and of a reality that has been systematically denied by white authorities.

SS

Mysteries of Udolpho, The (1794) ANN RADCLIFFE's fourth and most famous novel popularized the GOTHIC form and gave it a distinctive new tone by skilfully blending GOTHIC sensationalism with sentimental fiction. The psychological effects of incidents here take precedence over thrills, and all mysteries prove rationally explicable in the end. Versed in contemporary aesthetic theories, to expand the soul toward the sublime Radcliffe also combines terror with beauty achieved through extensive scene painting. Her orphaned, virtuous young heroine, Emily St Aubert, undergoes suspenseful ordeals after being imprisoned in the picturesquely gloomy castle of Udolpho in Italy by a villainous uncle, but, though constantly fearing for her life and honour, Emily is never injured and even escapes with two servants for another round of adventures in France, after which she is reunited with the lover from whom she had been torn away. Amid its gothic trappings *Udolpho* is a growth novel in which Emily progresses from Edenic innocence to knowledge of the evil and self-interest in the world without losing her ideals, but tempering them to reality; she learns also not to succumb to an overactive imagination that creates supernatural mysteries but to relegate evil to its ordinary human manifestations.

HB

Mysteries of Winterthurn (1984) JOYCE CAROL OATES's multi-layered novel is part DETECTIVE FICTION, part GOTHIC ROMANCE, and was apparently inspired by real-life events. Set in the 19th century and supposedly edited by an 'amateur "collector" of Murder', the three stories follow the career of detective Xavier Kilgarvan, whose faith in pragmatic investigative strategies is progressively shaken by cases that refuse to yield a rational solution. Half-eaten corpses and other grisly discoveries; incest, madness and a trompe-l'oeil painting of demonic cherubs that comes to life: in the first mystery the supernatural interferes with any realist explanation. In the second, a tale of misogyny and anti-Semitism, young women are allegedly murdered by the forces of demonic possession, and in the third, Xavier's sanity is jeopardized by the involvement of his beloved cousin Perdita in an apparent crime of passion; despite a pat solution, subtle ambiguities remain. Such ambivalences pervade the novel, in which dark intricacies of plot and constant shifts of genre encourage multiple interpretations. Playful and parodic, it also raises unsettling questions about attitudes toward women and about the nature of guilt.

KSi

N

Naidu [née Chattopadhyay], Sarojini 1879–1948 Indian English poet, national leader, activist and orator, was one of India's best-known women of this century. Her father, Aghorenath Chattopadhyay, a D.Sc. from Edinburgh, was a social reformer, alchemist, savant and founder of the modern education system in Hyderabad state. Her mother, Varada Sundari, raised in a Brahmo home for girls, held liberal views. The Hyderabad that she grew up in and romanticized in her poetry was a dreamy, feudal principality ruled by the benevolent, but eccentric, Nizam of Hyderabad, Mir Mahbub Ali Khan. The eldest of eight children of a rather unconventional, transplanted Bengali household, Sarojini was something of a prodigy. At 12 she passed the Madras matriculation examination and was composing 1,300-lined poems at 13. The next year, she fell in love with Govindarajulu Naidu, a medical officer in the Nizam's army, nine years her senior. It was a passionate, if precocious, romance, which culminated in an inter-caste marriage in 1898. But, prior to that, in 1895, at the age of 15, she was sent to England with the Nizam's help. After a stint in London where, thanks to Edmund Gosse's patronage, she made her acquaintance with the leading poets of the time, she spent nearly three years at Girton College, Cambridge.

By then, she had begun writing pleasant, musical songs, in the style of the Decadents. Gosse proved to be her literary godfather, advising her not to offer her readers 'a réchauffé of Anglo-Saxon sentiment in an Anglo-Saxon setting but some revelation of the heart of India'. Sarojini made this advice her watchword and published, after her return, three collections of verse – *The Golden Threshold* (1905), *The Bird of Time* (1911) and *The Broken Wing* (1917). All of them show a marked romanticism in content and an excessive ornamentation in style; these she used, along with her considerable metrical dexterity, to paint pretty portraits shoring up native self-respect in a colonized country. By the time her last collection was published, however, poetic taste in Europe underwent a sea-change and Sarojini's poetry gradually went out of favour.

She herself moved on from literature, eventually gaining wider recognition as a leading light of the freedom movement and a close associate of Mahatma Gandhi. In 1925 she became the President of the Indian National Congress, the first Indian woman to do so. She was jailed four times and often suffered ill health, but did not let that deter her from travelling extensively both inside and outside India as a spokesperson of the Congress. She did write another sheaf of poems in July–August 1927, published posthumously to hostile reviews. During the rest of her life, she had an active political career, which culminated in her being made the Governor of United Province, the largest state in independent India.   MP

Nairne [née Oliphant], Carolina, Baroness 1766–1845 Lyricist born in the Scottish Highlands to Jacobite, aristocratic parents. Early in life, she learned the manners, customs and speech patterns of the common people and used this knowledge as she rewrote the earthy words to traditional Scottish songs to make them more suitable for the drawing room. In the 1790s her revision of 'The Ploughman' became a hit, although she remained anonymous. At this period she also penned the heart-wrenching 'Land o' the Leal', comic songs such as 'John Tod' and 'The Laird o' Cockpen' and many Jacobite songs. In 1806, when she was 41, she married her second cousin.

In 1821 Nairne joined a group of women committed to sanitizing the national minstrelsy for polite company and revised many songs published pseudonymously in the *Scottish Minstrel*. At the age of 76, she wrote 'Would you be Young Again? So Would Not I'. She died in 1845 having guarded her literary anonymity to the grave. Shortly after she died, though, her songs were collected and published as *Lays from Strathearn* (1846), with her authorship finally acknowledged. Many of these songs are still sung, including especially her humorous satire of the pompous, self-important Laird of Cockpen.   PRF

Nambisan, Kavery 1949– Indian English novelist who with good humour and surgical precision, dissects and delineates personae from various strata of society from around the country and especially the feudal gentry of Coorg, Karnataka, her birthplace. Kavery Nambisan learnt English only when she was 12, after her father was elected to the national parliament and the family moved to Delhi. A doctor, she obtained the Fellowship of the Royal College of Surgeons in London at the age of 24. She has worked in various rural hospi-

LIFE AND SONGS

OF THE

BARONESS NAIRNE

WITH A

MEMOIR AND POEMS

OF

CAROLINE OLIPHANT THE YOUNGER

EDITED BY THE

REV. CHARLES ROGERS, LL.D., F.S.A. Scot.

HISTORIOGRAPHER TO THE HISTORICAL SOCIETY

WITH A PORTRAIT AND OTHER ILLUSTRATIONS

Edinburgh

JOHN GRANT

31 GEORGE IV. BRIDGE

1896

THE BARONESS NAIRNE.

Carolina Nairne: frontispiece and title-page of *Life and Songs of the Baroness Nairne*, 1896.

tals in India since her return. She has published books for children, and novels: the picaresque *The Truth (almost) About Bharat* (1991) which was under her earlier name of Kavery Bhatt, and *The Scent of Pepper* (1997) which is an ambitious tale of three generations of a family in Coorg, spanning sixty years, and explores the quiet heroism of ordinary people in the face of change.

GJVP

Nannestad, Elizabeth 1956– New Zealand poet. Her collection *Jump* was published in 1986 and *If he's a good dog he'll swim*, which she describes in the final poem as a 'small / self-possessed / and apprehensive book of poetry', in 1996. This diffidence and cautious precision is characteristic of her writing. Many of her poems consist of carefully described images – of places and people, of emotions – all expressed in a reserved voice, with clarity and exactness, and an arresting use of metaphor: 'The fear that last night licked on my ankle', she writes, 'now stands beside me like a man'. While her subject matter is usually the personal, her stance eschews sentiment. There is a sense of the awk-

wardness of communication and the dangers of linguistic excess. Nannestad's second collection is more self-conscious about its literary status, exploring, often with a certain amount of amused despair, the problems of creativity and textual production, possibly reflecting the ten years between her two books: 'The empty page / looks all innocence', she warns, 'but has its own sense of humour'.

JSt

Napier, Elma [Elizabeth Garner] 1892–1973 Born in England to an aristocratic family, Napier was already an established writer before she settled in the West Indian island of Dominica in 1932. Her travel narratives, many of them previously published in the *Manchester Guardian*, had been collected in her first book, *Nothing So Blue* (1928). In Dominica she quickly established herself in politics, becoming an elected member of the local legislature in 1940, thus beginning a long career in island government during which she focused on the improvement of the Dominican infrastructure. Her first novel, *Duet in Discord*, an autobiographical narrative set in Dominica, was published in 1936 under a pseudonym. A second novel, *A Flying Fish Whispered*, also set in Dominica, appeared in 1938. During the 1940s Napier turned to autobiography, publishing two volumes, *Youth Is a Blunder* (1944) and *Winter Is in July* (1948). She is also the author of a number of short stories about Dominica published in the *Manchester Guardian*, *Blackwood's Magazine*, the *West Indian Review* and *Bim*. The best and most often anthologized of these, 'Carnival in Martinique', interweaves the daydreams of a servant girl with the story of the Martinican young woman who a century before had become Napoleon Bonaparte's Empress Josephine.   LP-G

naturalism Naturalism was a late 19th-century outgrowth of REALISM in art and literature that features a harsher, more fatalistic world-view. Most notable for a rigorous narrative determinism, naturalism began in France, but reached its height of influence in the United States around the turn of the 20th century. Because of its frequent focus on criminals and criminality, naturalism has always been a deeply moral genre. Paradoxically, naturalists spotlight such issues through their absence from the lives of characters pursuing their desires in an apparently amoral world. Naturalism has always lent itself easily to the expression of social causes because the typical naturalistic narrative depicts outmatched individuals fighting against an oppressive world order of some kind. In the hands of women writers, this basic plot became a lens through which to focus on the ruthless workings of a male-dominated world.

For male writers, naturalism was a seemingly objective enterprise whose central precepts are traceable to the influence of evolutionary thinking at the time – drawn from the science of Charles Darwin and the philosophy of Herbert Spencer (and the followers of both). Literary naturalism was first advanced as a concept by the French novelist Emile Zola, who began experimenting with scientific ideas early in his writing career. Zola created a world where, as Spencer put it, 'events are the proper products of the characters living under given conditions'. Zola insisted that he was writing about people 'without free will'; in the preface to *Thérèse Raquin* (1868), a lurid tale of greed and murder, he made the first explicit attempt to define what he was doing, declaring his goal to be the 'scientific' study of human behaviour. The 'scientific' approach he brought to his naturalist story-telling, Zola insisted, amply defended the books against charges of indecency and 'putridity' that were levelled against them.

Zola's work influenced English novelists such as George Moore and George Gissing, but it had its most significant effect on a group of FIN-DE-SIÈCLE American writers who were seeking to take realism in less genteel directions. Supporting each other's ideas, and, in some cases, each other's careers, Frank Norris, Jack London, Theodore Dreiser and other early American naturalists helped to resituate literary realism in a less refined, often dirtier world where people struggled – often unsuccessfully – against the shaping forces brought to bear on their existences. The common threads of hereditary and environmental determinism run through the varied work of the male American naturalists, featuring a continuing tension among inherited ability, external forces and wilful human enterprise.

Female naturalists emphasized the social order, and consequently used the naturalist form differently. American women naturalists depicted male-dominated society as the most powerful of many environmental forces acting on the world. The scrutiny of this social environment in the work of American women naturalists created a different kind of naturalist tragedy that shifted the emphasis on heredity that is so much a part of male naturalist writing. Naturalism by American women writers thus owes less to Darwin's *Descent of Man* (1877) and its ilk than to books like CHARLOTTE PERKINS GILMAN's *Women and Economics* (1898), in which the author elaborated a theory of economic determinism that highlighted women's lack of choices.

American women wrote naturalistic books from the beginning of the movement in the United States, and even before: REBECCA HARDING DAVIS's novella, *LIFE IN THE IRON-MILLS* (1861), stands as an important proto-naturalistic text. For American women writers, naturalism was one of the logical sequels to sentimentalism, which was itself an early (and largely underappreciated) crucible for realistic writing in the United States. Naturalism followed sentimental literature in portraying women fighting to survive in a world largely indifferent (and often hostile) to their needs and desires. While sentimentalist writers commonly sought solutions in religion and domesticity, female naturalists saw no refuge in these values – and usually not in any others, either. KATE CHOPIN's *THE AWAKENING* (1899) is a touchstone of American literary feminism, for instance, but it is also a naturalistic tale of a woman crushed by the social forces of her environment. EDITH WHARTON's first masterpiece, *THE HOUSE OF MIRTH* (1905), was the first of many books in which she represented high society as a pressure chamber where forces interacted to determine the fates of relatively powerless individuals. Her account of the downfall of Lily Bart is self-consciously naturalistic, replete with Darwinian analogies. Issues of race and gender blend readily in the crucible of ANN PETRY's naturalistic fiction. Inspired by Richard Wright's *Native Son* (1940), Petry's *THE STREET* (1946), to name just one example from among her works, binds race and sex discrimination together into a socioeconomic juggernaut that overwhelms the considerable will and skills of a young black single mother who wants only to escape from her neighbourhood with her son.

The fusion of feminist issues with traditional determinism in the work of American women writers has provided new possibilities for critical inquiry into naturalism. Meanwhile, insights from new historicism and cultural studies have done much to bring naturalism as a whole back from the critical margins. An important consequence of this welcome new attention has been the construction of more nuanced ways of looking at gender issues in texts that were once thought to treat these issues rather simply. Gender-oriented critics have, for example, lately begun to examine the tensions that underlie the construction of masculinity and femininity in naturalist literature – most of which was written at a time when these ideas (and the roles attached to them) were significantly evolving in industrializing western society. The work of this new generation of critics thus interrogates not only naturalist assumptions and *fin-de-siècle* gender roles, but also the web of social relations that is implicated with them. Thanks to such research, the intersection of gender studies and naturalism has in a short time become a burgeoning critical field.   LC

Naylor, Gloria 1950–
African-American novelist born in New York to working-class, Southern migrant parents, she worked as a telephone operator (1968–75), gained a BA in English at Brooklyn College (1981) and an MA in Afro-American Studies at Yale (1983). Naylor has been writer-in-residence and lecturer and won a National Endowment for the Arts grant. Three novels explore the harsh everyday experience of African-American urban ghetto women. The most famous, *The Women of Brewster Place: A Novel in Seven Stories* (1982), received an American Book Award for Best First Novel. Her novels explore black women's lives, and opportunities for sisterhood and support. However, the sixth tale explores heterosexual women's fears about, and rejection of, lesbians. 'The Two', Lorraine and Theresa, lesbian professionals in a loving but claustrophobic relationship, attempt to camouflage their sexuality by moving to the end of a slum block but incur prejudice: 'The quiet that rested around their door on the weekends hinted of all sorts of secret rituals, and their friendly indifference to the men on the street was an insult to the women as a brazen flaunting of unnatural ways.' The two women's responses to discovery divide them – one responds by wishing to fit in, the other hopes to remain defiantly an outsider: 'Why should she feel different from the people she lived around? Black people were all in the same boat – she'd come to realise this even more since they had moved to Brewster – and if they didn't grow together, they would sink together.' As a story of homophobia, leading to violent rape and near-murder, it has shocked many lesbians, black and white, representing, perhaps, a terrifyingly realistic version of potential vulnerability. *Mama Day* (1988) concentrates on the powers

of maternal heritage: a matriarch explores her psychic powers against responses of the younger generation. *Linden Hills* (1985) focuses on problems African-Americans inherit when buying into the American Dream's materialistic offer, including a black homosexual's response – leaving his lover for an arranged marriage. Naylor's treatment of African-American gay and lesbian lives is at once cautionary, pessimistic and an enlightened critique of homophobia.   GW

Near to the Wild Heart (1944; UK 1990)
CLARICE LISPECTOR's first novel prepares the ground for what HÉLÈNE CIXOUS would later call the 'écriture féminine', a perfect combination of female and feminine writing. On the surface, the novel tells a commonplace story of Joana, a precocious child who grows up to become an independent-thinking woman, trapped in a love triangle and looking for fulfilment outside her marriage. However, life for Joana is lived through intensity rather than fact or detail, and thus events in the novel are superseded by states of feeling and instances of thought. Taking delight in 'happiness close to horror', Joana greedily imbibes sensations coming from the outside world, always craving more pleasure and pain. The desire for excess, summed up in her dramatic question, 'Who could prevent someone from living expansively?', is manifested on the level of both plot and language. Lispector's narrative fluctuates between the alternating states of now/then, day/night, she/I, and life/death. The novel combines prose with poetry to produce a fascinating genre of confession–philosophy, in which thought and feeling meet in a sensual embrace.   JZ

Nelson, Dorothy 1952–
Irish novelist born in Bray, County Wicklow. Nelson's first novel, *In Night's City* (1982), won the Rooney Prize. The novel is a powerful exploration of the experience and dynamics of sexual abuse, told from three different perspectives: that of Sara, her *alter ego* Maggie – who experiences her father's violent abuse on her behalf – and Sara's mother Esther. The novel is both lyrical and horrifying and contains a climactic, orgasmic fantasy of destruction toward its close. However, there is no easy redemption here . . . as Sara leaves her parents' house she still tries to convince herself that her parents have loved her, that her childhood was normal.

A later novel, *Tar and Feathers* (1987), returns to the theme of poisonous family dynamics. Here the narrative again shifts perspective among the characters, in this case a violent and abusive man, his alcoholic wife and their teenage son, Ben. Nelson has a distinctive voice, simultaneously lyrical, shocking and exuberant. Her use of form is experimental. Her female characters often express anger and disgust with the institutions which perpetuate the nightmarish quality of their lives. They are also reluctant participants in the sexual activities demanded of them within families. In *Tar and Feathers*, Ben says 'It was against Ma's principles to have sex so the memory of being raped by Da was as common as combing her hair to her. It was a bad habit he couldn't get out of and she couldn't stop him, like wanting death very bad and not being able to stick a knife in your own back.'   LM

Nervous Conditions (1989) As its epigraph suggests, TSITSI DANGAREMBGA's remarkable first novel writes back to Frantz Fanon's diagnosis of colonial psychiatric disorder, showing neurosis to be the product not just of colonial but of patriarchal domination and the insidious interaction between the two. Set in 1969, the novel describes how a Rhodesian headmaster tries to bring the benefits of western economic and cultural capital to his extended Shona family. The pressures of negotiating English and African identities manifest themselves in a range of neurotic symptoms: his own 'bad nerves', the self-effacing infantilism of his wife and the life-threatening bulimia of his daughter. All this is observed by his niece, the narrator, whose own determination to escape the oppressed femininity represented by her traditional Shona mother leads to an enthusiasm for English culture, and her own 'reincarnation', first at a missionary school and then at a European convent. Only gradually does she recognize the alienation implicit in her own re-culturation and the justice of her mother's reflection: 'It's the Englishness . . . It'll kill them all if they are not careful.'   WJB

Nesbit, E(dith) 1858–1924 English children's writer, novelist and poet whose works for children influenced later children's writers by mixing realism with fantasy. Born in London and educated at boarding schools in Britain and on the continent, her teen and adult years were spent in Kent and London. In 1880 she married Hubert Bland, later a well-known columnist, with whom she had three children. They lived a bohemian life at the heart of a literary salon and were founder members of the Fabian Society. For years their household included Alice Hoatson and her two children by Bland whom Nesbit raised as her own. Nesbit unconventionally cut her hair short, wore comfortable aesthetic clothes and smoked, yet she opposed women's suffrage.

Early in the marriage she supported the family through writing. She published as 'E. Nesbit' but also used 'E. Bland' or, for collaborations with her husband, 'Fabian Bland'. She wrote prolifically: stories, sketches, Pre-Raphaelite-influenced poetry and novels such as *The Red House* (1902). However, her reputation rests on the CHILDREN'S LITERATURE written in her forties. She achieved fame in 1899 with *The Story of the Treasure*

Seekers, a series about the Bastable children who also appeared in *The Wouldbegoods* (1901) and *New Treasure Seekers* (1904). These stories mixed the family story with adventure, comedy and parody while avoiding moral didacticism. Her more sentimental *The Railway Children* (1906) is a children's classic. Most influential are books such as *Five Children and It* (1902), *The Phoenix and the Carpet* (1904), *The Story of the Amulet* (1906) and *The House of Arden* (1908), in which fantasy elements such as time travel or wish fulfilment are introduced into otherwise realist texts. Having remarried in 1917 after Bland's death, Nesbit died, probably from lung cancer, at 65.   AEG

Nestle, Joan 1940– Lesbian historian and self-described 'Jewish femme from the Bronx', Nestle records the histories of US lesbians of this century, especially working-class lesbians and lesbians of colour. Raised in New York by her widowed mother, Regina, Joan came out as a lesbian at 18, left home and embarked on a decade of activism which saw her protesting against the McCarthy hearings, marching in the Civil Rights movement and helping to sow the seeds of post-Stonewall gay liberation.

In her work as a writer and editor, Nestle has insisted that the personal be seen not only as political, but as historical. A collection of autobiographical essays, *A Restricted Country* (1978), is exemplary of this method, part theory, part erotica, part memoir. In 1982, she edited *The Persistent Desire*, the first collections of writings by and about 'butch-femmes' and their identity, and since then has co-edited three volumes of *Women on Women* (1990, 1993, 1996), an award-winning anthology of lesbian short fiction.

In 1973, Nestle co-founded New York's Lesbian Herstory Archives, the only library in the world dedicated entirely to the preservation of lesbian materials and lesbian culture.   JGr

New England Nun, A (1891) In this collection of stories, MARY WILKINS (later FREEMAN) calibrates the strength of emotion, and potential for revolt, which reverberates in the smallest details of restrained and uneventful lives. The title story, recording Louisa Ellis's tactful dissolution of her fourteen-year-long engagement, is a wonderfully gauged balance between images of loss and new power, of repression and fulfilment. Many of the stories bring to the centre women, like Louisa, who go unnoticed in the dominant family-focused dramas of 19th-century fiction, exposing the limits of the society which discounts them. Wilkins's spinsters, like Betsey Dole in 'A Poetess', old women like Candace Whitcomb, the superseded church soprano in 'A Village Singer', paupers or eccentrics like 'Christmas Jenny', all emerge from these narratives vindicated as supreme artists or psychologists, firm in their own identity. Even where stories end with a death, they give significance to the lives of those with little or nothing. Most allow their characters to shape that significance themselves: Polly Moss in 'Sister Liddy' suddenly pours out a story, Sarah Penn in 'The Revolt of "Mother"' hijacks herself a new home, and Hetty Fifield outfaces the church committee to become 'A Church Mouse' who wakes up the entire community.   PEK

New Woman A fictional archetype of the late 19th century, appearing in novels by overtly feminist writers such as OLIVE SCHREINER, SARAH GRAND, MONA CAIRD, MENIE MURIEL DOWIE and ELLA HEPWORTH DIXON, as well as infiltrating fiction by male writers who weren't necessarily wholeheartedly committed to women's emancipation (Thomas Hardy, George Gissing, Grant Allen, Henry James, Bram Stoker). The New Woman also frequently took centre stage in short stories of the period, with GEORGE EGERTON most memorably articulating a definitively 'feminine' consciousness using the short-story form. The term 'New Woman' was coined in 1894 in a pair of articles by OUIDA and SARAH GRAND in the *North American Review*, and quickly became a familiar phrase in the journalistic vernacular of the day. The feminist as a literary type pre-dated these articles by more than two decades, though: the New Woman's predecessors include ELIZA LYNN LINTON's *GIRL OF THE PERIOD* (1868) and, later, the 'Glorified Spinster' (named in an anonymous article from 1888). The New Woman, like her forebears, was a cultural phenomenon made possible by the burgeoning Women's Movement of the late Victorian years. Critics have identified a 'second generation' of New Woman writers in the 1920s and 1930s, including VIRGINIA WOOLF, DJUNA BARNES and RADCLYFFE HALL – but her heyday was undoubtedly the 1880s and 1890s.

The identity of the fictional New Woman was by no means homogeneous. Her opponents represented her as, variously, a 'mannish', overeducated bore (frequently a 'Girton Girl'), a bad mother (if not an embittered spinster), and as lacking in all the attributes usually associated with ideal Victorian womanhood (a penchant for self-sacrifice, a talent for home-making, a willingness to defer to men). She was also sometimes configured as an oversexed vamp (Bram Stoker's Lucy Westenra in *Dracula* (1897), and MARIE CORELLI's Sybil Elton in *The Sorrows of Satan* (1895)). The New Woman was frequently lampooned in *Punch*, which printed a plethora of articles and cartoons ridiculing and condemning her throughout the mid 1890s.

Those writers (always female) who were keen to promote the New Woman and her cause represented her as an intelligent, sensitive and sexually healthy woman, who often had ambitions beyond mother-hood. The most important 1880s prototype of the New Woman was Olive Schreiner's Lyndall, in *THE STORY OF AN AFRICAN FARM* (1883), whose ambition is to be an actress, regretting the decorative and domestic education she has received at a girls' boarding school. She is wary of the claims of motherhood – 'I do not so greatly admire the crying of babies', she remarks at one point in the novel – and yet acknowledges the significance of women's maternal role, describing the bringing-up of children as 'The mightiest and noblest of human work'. A conflictual attitude toward motherhood is typical of a good deal of New Woman writing by women: Sarah Grand regarded it as central to women's self-identity, as did George Egerton, whereas Mona Caird was vehement in her opposition to the binding ties of maternity. Hadria Fullerton, the heroine of Caird's *THE DAUGHTERS OF DANAUS* (1894), is filled with a 'sensation of disgust' at the sight of a woman 'with her new born child, full of pride and exultation'. The promotion of motherhood as part of women's 'mission' by some New Woman writers meant that their fiction sometimes became entangled with the discursive currencies of that other great 'mission' of the late 19th century: imperialism. Olive Schreiner's fiction in particular is marked by what can be described as a 'missionary maternalism' as well as, at times, by the racist hierarchies typical of late 19th-century imperialist writing.

Whilst the female New Woman writers did not always agree on the value of motherhood, what they did agree on was the necessity of a broader education for women as well as access to a wider cultural world than that deemed suitable for the bulk of middle-class Victorian women. The need for a proper education for women is one of the main themes of Sarah Grand's *The Heavenly Twins* (1893), and was the subject of a good deal of feminist journalism of the period. Women's non-domestic roles are similarly emphasized in New Woman writing, and a particular interest is shown in the more bohemian types of employment. Women writers, journalists, artists and musicians people the pages of a good many New Woman novels: Sarah Grand's *THE BETH BOOK* (1897) and *Ideala* (1888), Ella Hepworth Dixon's *THE STORY OF A MODERN WOMAN* (1894), MARY CHOLMONDELEY's *RED POTTAGE* (1899) and Isabella Ford's *On the Threshold* (1895).

The fictional New Woman was emphatically of the middle and upper classes. None the less, a number of New Woman writers explored the possible connections between feminism and socialism, most notably Jane Hume Clapperton in *Margaret Dunmore, or A Socialist Home* (1888), Isabella Ford in *On the Threshold*, Gertrude Dix in *The Image Breakers* (1900) and LADY FLORENCE DIXIE in *Gloriana, or the Revolution of 1900* (1890). The New Woman phenomenon was also frequently aligned with Decadence. Just as Decadents and

DONNA QUIXOTE.

[" A world of disorderly notions *picked out of books*, crowded into his (her) imagination."—*Don Quixote*.

New Woman: 'Donna Quixote ["A world of disorderly notions picked out of books, crowded into his (her) imagination" – Don Quixote]', *Punch, or the London Charivari*, 28 April 1894.

Aesthetes were regarded as a threat to Victorian masculinity (Oscar Wilde being the most obvious example), so the New Woman challenged the dominant gender codes governing Victorian femininity. Some writers characterized the New Woman as an incipient lesbian: George Moore's Cecilia Cullen, in *A Drama in Muslin* (1886), and Henry James's Olive Chancellor, in *The*

Bostonians (1886), are pathologized as predatory, man-hating lesbians, whilst Edith Arnold, in *Platonics* (1894), and Isabella Ford, in *On the Threshold*, explore same-sex friendship between women much more sympathetically.

New Woman novels often entered the 'bestsellers' lists, and owed a large debt to 19th-century literary realism. In retrospect, though, some of the New Woman fiction has been rightly claimed as contributing toward the formation of a proto-MODERNIST aesthetic at the FIN DE SIÈCLE. The elliptical, impressionistic short stories of George Egerton in particular closely approximate to a modernist literary aesthetic, as do Olive Schreiner's non-realist 'Dreams' and allegories.   SL

Newcastle [née Lucas], Margaret Cavendish, Duchess of 1623–73 British prose fiction writer, poet, natural philosopher, dramatist and proto-feminist. Born into a wealthy family in Colchester, Cavendish served as a maid of honour to Queen Henrietta Maria in Oxford and, with the outbreak of the Civil War, in her exile in France. In 1645, she married the former commander of the King's Northern army, William Cavendish, the later Duke of Newcastle. During the Interregnum, the Cavendishes spent their time in Paris and Antwerp and finally returned to England in 1660. Whilst her exceedingly prolific oeuvre, ranging from natural philosophy, drama, prose fiction and poetry to biography, was given only mixed reception, she was notorious for her eccentricity and her desire for fame. Despite her political conservatism, Cavendish was committed to an extensive critique of contemporary gender politics. Her scientific works such as *Philosophical Fancies* (1653) and *Observations upon Experimental Philosophy* (1666), engage critically with Baconian 'New Science' and develop a different scientific epistemology. Her prose, such as the SCIENCE-FICTION tale *The Description of a New World Called The Blazing World* (1666), experiments subversively with generic conventions. Her unconventional dramatic works, including THE CONVENT OF PLEASURE (1662), and *Bell in Campo* (1662), investigate issues of women's identity and self-determination.   NBP

Newman, Frances 1883–1928 Combined a career as librarian with journalism, literary scholarship, reviewing and translating, eventually publishing two devastatingly original novels that take apart the embedded assumptions of Southern society in the United States where she grew up. Born in Atlanta, in a traditional family, she extended her formal schooling and college library studies through a personal programme of reading, music, languages and, when possible, travelling, that separated her further from Southern culture. From 1913, she worked in libraries, including almost a decade (1914–22) as head of the Lending Department in the Carnegie Library in Atlanta, later satirically refracted in her second novel. Meanwhile, her column for the *Atlanta Journal Sunday Magazine*, called, after JANE AUSTEN, 'Elizabeth Bennet's [*sic*] Gossip' (eventually taken over by MARGARET MITCHELL), and her sharp reviews for various journals began to gain her a reputation for critical ferocity. (F. Scott Fitzgerald was deeply stung by her views on *This Side of Paradise*.)

Following a study visit to Paris in 1923, she published a prize-winning story, 'Rachel and Her Children', and an anthology, *The Short Story's Mutations:*

From Petronius to Paul Morand (1924), including her own translations from classical and European languages. She pursued her interest in form into her novels: *The Hard-Boiled Virgin* (1926; William Faulkner had a copy in his library) and *Dead Lovers Are Faithful Lovers* (1928). Intense, stylistically oblique, experiments in representing the real inner life of conventional Southern women, these made her permanent name, as sensationalist and eccentric, and as a MODERNIST artist. The projected sequels never followed. Suffering a debilitating eye affliction, Newman struggled with her final translations, but died suddenly, possibly of cerebral haemorrhage (suicide was rumoured), in a hotel room in New York.   PEK

Ngcobo, Lauretta 1931– South African novelist, who was born in Natal, South Africa, and left the country after the political upheavals of the 1960s. Settling in London in 1969, she wrote her first novel, *Cross of Gold* (1981), which has a male protagonist. She edited an important collection of essays by black women writers in 1988, *Let It be Told*, which explores the perceptions, memories and critical viewpoints of a minority of black women writers in Britain. Her most important publication to date is her fine portrait of rural black South African women's lives in *And They Didn't Die* (1991), which tells the story of South African life from the point of view of the impoverished rural proletariat who were only very sporadically politicized over the decades of the fifties and sixties. Her heroine, Jezile, struggles to find a place for herself and her family between the strictures of customary African law and the myriad of Apartheid laws, especially the pass laws which attempted to control the migration of Africans to the urban areas. The story spans a few generations, reveals the pressures of poverty and the emotional distress of families sundered by the migrant labour system, the politicization of schoolchildren after the Soweto upheavals of 1976, and especially the plight of generations of women under the multiple pressures of sex–gender systems and reinforced forms of colonialism and racism in South Africa.   CC

Ní Chuilleanáin, Eiléan 1942– Poet and academic born in Cork, daughter of Cormac Ó Chuilleanáin – a Professor of Irish – and Eilis Dillon, a children's writer and novelist. She is married to the poet Macdara Woods, and they have one son. Ní Chuilleanáin was educated at Cork and Oxford, and in 1966 became a lecturer in Medieval and Renaissance English at Trinity College Dublin. Her first collection, *Acts and Monuments* (1972) won the Patrick Kavanagh Award. She has since won the *Irish Times* / Aer Lingus Award and the O'Shaughnessy Prize for poetry. Other work includes: *The Site of Ambush* (1975), *The Second Voyage* (1977), *The Rose Geranium* (1981), *The Magdalene Sermon* (1989) and

The Brazen Serpent (1994). She has been selected for many anthologies of Irish writing including one of Cork graduates writing in Irish and English, entitled *'Jumping off Shadows': Selected Contemporary Irish Poets.* She is editor of *Cyphers* and has edited *Irish Women: Image and Achievement* (1985). The imagery of her poetry is precise and striking as she invokes seascapes and water to 'Wash the man out of the woman'. Her poems have provoked discussion regarding the position of the contemporary Irish woman poet within a predominantly male literary tradition, which has also been taken up in the Republic of Ireland by the poets EAVAN BOLAND and NUALA NÍ DHOMHNAILL.   SFu

Ní Dhomhnaill, Nuala (Maire) 1952– Irish-language poet born in St Helens, Lancashire, who grew up in the West Kerry and Tipperary Gaeltachts (Irish-speaking area). She studied English and Irish at University College, Cork, taught English at the Middle East Technical University in Ankara, before settling in Dublin with her Turkish husband and four children. She is a member of Aosdana and was artist-in-residence for Cork University in 1991–2. Dublin City University awarded her an honorary degree in 1995.

Nuala Ní Dhomhnaill is the most prominent poet writing in the Irish language. The cultural politics that inform her poetry also explain her decision not to write in English. She was one of the generation of young poets associated with the radical periodical *Innti* who emerged in the 1970s and who, after initial wariness on both sides, were finally admitted into the canon of Irish-language poetry. Her reputation was firmly established by her first two books, *An Dealg Droighin* (1981) and *Féar Suaithinseach* (1984). International recognition followed when her new and selected poems, *Pharaoh's Daughter*, appeared in 1990 with translations by some of the finest Irish contemporary poets, including Paul Muldoon, Seamus Heaney and MEDBH MCGUCKIAN. Her three following collections, *Feis* (1991), *The Astrakhan Cloak* (1992), with translations by Paul Muldoon, and *Cead Aighnis* (1998), develop her earlier themes of locale and naming, of the universal stories of the small life and rooted community. She is also a fine story-teller – her Ireland not only has music, priests and 'miraculous grass', but is modern and European.

Her poetic power comes from the level of commitment to the Kerry Gaeltacht, known both through her sojourns there, talking and listening, and through time spent reading in the archives of the Department of Irish Folklore at University College, Dublin: 'Labhrann gach cúinne den leathinis seo liom / ina teanga féinig, teanga a thuigim' ('Every nook of this Peninsula [west Kerry] can speak to me in its own tongue, in words I understand'). Nuala Ní Dhomhnaill 'reads to and is read by audiences from Poland to California: interest in her work is enormous', Angela Bourke acknowledges in her 1992 essay 'Change of Style: The Male and Female of Writing in English'. Her example, like Heaney's, is regarded as central to public perception of contemporary poetry in Ireland.   DM

Ní Dhuibhne, Eilís 1954– Irish novelist, short-story writer and playwright, born in Dublin, who writes fiction in English, and writes plays in both languages. Her early stories were encouraged and published by David Marcus in the influential 'New Irish Writing' pages of the *Irish Press*. Ní Dhuibhne has a deep and enduring interest in issues of language, identity and sexual politics. She explores these themes from a strong narrative base, and her stories and plays often draw on folklore, juxtaposing tradition and modernity in an inventive manner. Collections of fiction include *Blood and Water* (1988), *Eating Women is not Recommended* (1991) and *The Inland Ice* (1997).

Her novel *The Bray House* (1990) is set in the future and describes an archaeological expedition to a devastated, post-nuclear Ireland. Here, a single house and its contents are used to construct an understanding of the fabric of daily life in a world that has vanished forever.

Under the pseudonym 'Elizabeth O'Hara', Ní Dhuibhne has written many prize-winning books for children. Her 1997 play *Milseog an tSamhraidh* won the Stewart Parker Award.   LM

Nichols, Grace 1950– African-Caribbean poet, born in Guyana, who has lived in Britain since 1977. She began her writing career as a journalist in Guyana but has since written children's books, short stories, a novel and several collections of poetry. The pre- and post-COLONIAL turbulence of Guyana (the focus of her novel, *Whole of a Morning Sky*) subtly informs Nichols's work, though she is perhaps most well known for her poetic evocations of feisty women.

Her first collection of poetry, *i is a long memoried woman*, won the Commonwealth Poetry Prize in 1983. In these poems, Nichols charts the history of the slave woman in the New World, outlining the particular cruelties faced by women on the plantation as they laboured in the canefields, produced children to swell the labour force and were forced to service *Massa's* sexual appetites. Nichols uses a spare and elegiac poetic tone to frame this catalogue of brutality and often the possibility of *resisting* fractures the monolithic narrative of victim/oppressor to foreground the s/heroic articulations of subjectivity which emerged *despite* the horrors of plantation slavery:

> I have crossed an ocean
> I have lost my tongue
> from the roots of the old
> one
> a new one has sprung

Nichols's second and third volumes of poetry continued to keep the black woman's body centre-stage. *The Fat Black Woman's Poems* provides a series of sassy and sumptuous images of black female beauty to counter the facile reductiveness of the 'black mammie' stereotype and, simultaneously, to dramatize the ridiculousness of dominant notions of female beauty (symbolized by the slim, white, mannequin). In LAZY THOUGHTS OF A LAZY WOMAN (1989), Nichols continues this recuperative project in poems which harness the power of the erotic and insist on the black woman's body as a site and source of possibility rather than limitation:

My black triangle
is so rich
that it flows over
on to the dry crotch
of the world

In *Sunris*, Nichols spreads her poetic net wider to encompass a broader range of speaking voices and cultural contexts but her strongly feminist orientation remains central to her work.   DdeCN

Night in Acadie, A (1897) A collection of twenty-one stories set in Louisiana, KATE CHOPIN's book was praised for its psychological insight and delicacy. The pastoral overtones of the title, playing on the 'Acadia' of French Louisiana, belied the more complex operations of the writing. Unfulfilled, even unacknowledged, desires lie at the heart of a number of stories. Some, like 'After the Winter' and 'A Matter of Prejudice', work in the sentimental tradition of restoring what has been lost; others, like 'A Respectable Woman' or 'A Sentimental Soul', hint at a woman breaking conventions 'to take her conscience into her own keeping'. But elsewhere, Chopin ends the story with the sense of abandonment. In 'Regret', a self-sufficient fifty-year old farmer recognizes what she has sacrificed by choosing an independent, childless, orderly life; in 'Caline', a city man permanently disrupts the life of a country girl. 'Athénaïse', the longest story, ends with a young woman's joyous discovery of her pregnancy, but for modern readers, Athénaïse's prospective motherhood is probably less interesting than Chopin's suggestions of her peculiarly disturbing relationships with her brother and husband, and the atmospheric, meditative, unfolding of her retreat to a room of her own, a boarding-house in New Orleans. PEK

Nightingale, Florence 1820–1910 English nurse and hospital reformer whose writings reveal her reforming aims, spiritual thought, and frustrations at the enforced idleness of upper-class women. Born in Florence into a wealthy family, she was raised in Derbyshire and educated by her father. In her teens she experienced a call to God's service which she sought to fulfil by becoming a nurse. Family objections meant that she only realized her ambition in her thirties. Famous as superintendent of nurses during the Crimean War, the founder of modern nursing and active in reforming military hospitals, Nightingale, for many years an invalid, also wrote widely: letters, DIARIES, articles, spiritual explorations, government reports, books on nursing.

Her writing shows her strong belief in work and action for women. *Notes on Nursing* (1860), a textbook for nurses, was her most successful book. *Suggestions for Thought to the Searchers after Truth Among the Artizans of England* (privately printed, 1860) reveals her unorthodox religious beliefs and justifies her role in public service. The autobiographical fragment 'Cassandra' included in *Suggestions* attacks the Victorian family and deplores the wasted lives of upper-class women trapped in a world of inaction and dreaming.   AEG

Nights at the Circus (1984) In ANGELA CARTER's eighth novel, the sceptical American journalist, Jack Walser, interviews Fevvers, the winged *aerialiste*, who, aided and abetted by her foster parent, Lizzie, regales him with her flamboyant and improbable life-story. Emblazoned on the wall of her turn-of-the-century London dressing room, her slogan – 'Is she fact or is she fiction?' – sets up the central enigma of the novel for both Walser and the reader. Hoping to debunk her for his article on the Great Humbugs of the World, Walser, disguised as a clown, follows her on a Grand Imperial Tour to St Petersburg where he himself begins to undergo a personal transformation. Carter's textual strategy oscillates between fantasy and reality, combining a utopian feminist politics with a committed materialist critique of patriarchal institutions, such as the Madame Schreck's GOTHIC Museum of Woman Monsters and Colonel Kearney's Carnivalesque circus. The multiplication of narrative points of view – cross-cutting between metafictional argument, elaborate set pieces and the subjective voices of Fevvers, Lizzie and Walser – is reminiscent of the shifting narrative perspectives in THE BLOODY CHAMBER (1979).   CCr

Nightwood (1936) This doom-laden vision of bohemian life in inter-war Europe is American MODERNIST DJUNA BARNES's major prose work. A Baudelairean poetics of evil informs her symbolist and surrealist method but *Nightwood*, with its beautiful/ugly language, is more than a triumph of style. As lesbian critics especially have argued, it is equally an experimental attempt to create a record of those excluded by official history, notably Jews and gay men and lesbians. Thus the destiny of Austrian Jew Baron

Felix Volkbein (his barony is bogus), obsessed by his race's treatment by Christians, folds into that of young, promiscuous Robin Vote, who marries him and bears his child, only to leave him for successive affairs with Nora Flood and Jenny Petherbridge. All take their troubles to Dr Matthew O'Connor (his credentials, too, are fake), a transvestite and inveterate monologuer, who mixes with Frau Mann and her circus performer friends. Carnivalesque and human-into-beast imagery presides over the text's horrible nightmare of 'bowing down' to damnation, which both addresses and sublimates its (still) transgressive subject.   MO'D

Nimbkar, Jai 1932– A bilingual Indian writer, like her sister GAURI DESHPANDE. Daughter of a well-known anthropologist mother (Irawati Karve) she was born and brought up in Pune from where she took her BA before going to the University of Arizona for an MA in Sociology and Psychology. Between her first book of short stories in English (*Lotus Leaves and Other Stories*, 1971) and the most recent one (*The Phantom Bird and Other Stories*, 1993), Nimbkar has published three novels – *Temporary Answers* (1974), *A Joint Venture* (1988), *Come Rain* (1993) – all characterized by her understated, ironic and nuanced representation of middle-class family life in India. She has written three books in Marathi and is also an accomplished translator. She has not received her fair share of literary fame, perhaps because she shies away from publicity, living quietly in the Nimbkar family farm in Phaltan, which she and her husband have developed into a model autonomous rural unit.   MMu

Nin, Anais 1903–77 Self-mythologizing American writer whose erotica and autobiography made her a cult figure. Born in Paris of artist parents, aged 11 she began her lifelong DIARY (it numbered 35,000 pages at her death) when her composer father, Joaquin, abandoned the family. Her teenage years were spent in New York with her mother and brothers. She married artist and banker Hugo Guiler, whose income was to support her bohemian lifestyle, in 1923. In the thirties she met and had affairs with June and Henry Miller, the psychoanalysts Rene Allendy and Otto Rank, the Peruvian Marxist Gonzalo More and, most contentiously, her father.

Her earliest published fictions, the surrealist prose poem *House of Incest* (1936) and the linked novelettes of *Winter of Artifice* (1939), date from this period. In the 1940s her own Gemor Press brought out handcrafted editions of her works, including *Under a Glass Bell* (1944). At this time, too, she wrote the (in)famous sexual fantasies later collected in *Delta of Venus* (1977) and *Little Birds* (1979), and began work on the ambitious novel sequence which became *Cities of the Interior* (1959). After falling in love with aspiring actor Rupert Pole,

for twenty years she led a bigamous double life, dividing her time (allegedly unbeknownst to them) between her two husbands. Late in life she became a feminist *cause célèbre* – her followers dubbing themselves 'Ninettes' – with the publication of the diary (seven volumes, 1966–81). The posthumous 'unexpurgated' version, *A Journal of Love* (first volume 1986), further reveals her experimental life and writing as interweaving self-conscious performances. She died of cancer at the height of her fame.   MO'D

No Fixed Address (1988) ARITHA VAN HERK's third novel is the story of Arachne Manteia, a travelling saleswoman. Arachne successfully sells underwear although she does not wear any herself. Returning from her trips, she tells her best friend and confidante, Thena, the stories of all her adventures. Spidering her way through rural Alberta, Arachne picks up more than the occasional man, has lunch-breaks in some of her favourite cemeteries and openly misbehaves.

After Arachne helps Joseph, her 90-year-old lover, to escape from an old-people's home, she leads the life of a runaway, losing touch with reality and driving her black vintage Mercedes into unmapped northern territories, thus disappearing from the realm of REALISM and the reach of anyone trying to trace her.

Written in the picaresque mode, a 'feminist' travesty and parody of 'on the road' novels and movies, the travelling-salesman tradition and the GOTHIC, *No Fixed Address* is a book about disguise and disappearance. It is a wild and unconventional book daring to let the main character be an unrepentant sinner.   TP

No Place on Earth (1979; UK 1982) CHRISTA WOLF's novel describes a fictitious encounter between two prominent writers of German Romanticism, who both committed suicide in real life: the poet Karoline von Günderrode and the writer Heinrich von Kleist. The meeting takes place at a tea-party, where the wit and politeness of the social exchange serve as a façade concealing the inner dramas of the two main characters. Kleist suffers for his inability to find his 'place on earth' and to resolve the conflict between social responsibility and personal satisfaction. This prototypical ROMANTIC hero, unable to overcome his malaise, is confronted by the woman poet Günderrode, who challenges Kleist's spirit of resignation. Günderrode's authentic verse, skilfully interwoven into the novel, is her declaration of uncompromising passion: 'Everything, my whole being, will be fulfilled to the brim by the object to which I yield myself in the bonds of love.' Exploring Günderrode's 'exaggerated inclination to autonomy', Wolf seems to accuse Romanticism of legitimizing male suffering, while confining women to the realm of silence, passivity and madness.   JZ

None to Accompany Me (1994) NADINE GORDIMER's first novel after the democratic elections of 1994 in South Africa marks a new phase in her work. Expanding the range of her themes away from the racial preoccupations of her anti-Apartheid texts, Gordimer homes in on her female protagonists. Set in Johannesburg with the exiles from Apartheid returning, this novel of home-coming, though characteristically REALIST, uses a fragmentary technique to explore the multi-faceted nature of South African life, and what it terms 'the real POSTMODERNISM' produced by its contrasts of wealth, poverty and culture. Crossing threads through this cityscape are the lives of Vera Stark and Sally Maqona, old friends from the sixties, coming from very different backgrounds. Sally, just returned from England, is now an up-and-coming politician on the ANC Executive. Vera, consolidating her career as a legal-aid lawyer, works over her past again in this novel. She will eventually leave home and husband in mid-life to cut a path toward a new and 'unaccompanied' identity rooted in the shifting geographies of Johannesburg.   HLR

North and South (1854–5) ELIZABETH GASKELL's engagement with raw topical themes – an extension of her role as minister's wife – develops in this third novel into a rich, original recipe for REALISM. At first named for its heroine Margaret Hale, the narrative transforms a young lady's entrance into the world into a metaphor for the 'marriage' of industrial north with rural south, of 'masculine' aggression and nurturing 'feminine' family feeling. Margaret, from the genteel home counties, moves to Milton Northern, where she meets mill-owner John Thornton, a heroic, uncultured bully who owes something to BRONTË heroes. Their passion is played out against intimately observed social settings. The formula sounds familiar because GEORGE ELIOT, E.M. Forster and D.H. Lawrence all used it. Gaskell eroticized class relations, so that social inequality, like sexual difference, became a source of creative tension. *North and South* invented new cultural common ground for Victorian England. It acquired its oppositional title for serialization in Dickens's magazine *Household Words*. Dickens and Gaskell discovered their own (utterly unerotic) mutual dislike in the process.   LS

Northanger Abbey (1818) Generally thought to be JANE AUSTEN's earliest major work, this novel dates from the 1790s, but first received publication posthumously. A female BILDUNGSROMAN, *Northanger Abbey* describes Catherine Morland's growth into maturity and marriage with Henry Tilney, but combines this with a strong attack on the absurdities and unrealities of the GOTHIC novel. A keen reader (including the works of ANN RADCLIFFE), Catherine visits the Abbey with 'an imagination resolved on alarm' and 'a

Caroline Norton.

mind . . . craving to be frightened'. Whilst there, she discovers a mysterious manuscript (in reality, a laundry-list) and wrongly suspects Henry's father of killing his wife. These mistaken assumptions cure Catherine of her 'self-created delusion' but also ironize Gothic convention by hinting at the far greater horrors of domestic entrapment. Like its contemporaries, PRIDE AND PREJUDICE (1813) and SENSE AND SENSIBILITY (1811), *Northanger Abbey* is structured around the conflict between good sense and excessive SENSIBILITY, and although it lacks the sophistication which Austen's later revisions brought to these two texts, all of her characteristic ambivalence and playfulness are here.   AS

Norton [Stirling-Maxwell], Caroline 1808–77 English poet and novelist. Her ranking as 'the Byron of Modern Poetesses' for romantic lyrics and sentimental ballads such as 'The Arab's Farewell to His Steed' and 'Not Lost But Gone Before' annoyed ELIZABETH BARRETT BROWNING, but she also wrote condition-of-England poems (ELIZABETH GASKELL quoted *A Voice From the Factories* (1836), in MARY BARTON (1848)) and vehement pamphlets which inspired BARBARA BODICHON and helped change legal discriminations against women. Witty granddaughter of Richard Sheridan and great-granddaughter of FRANCES SHERIDAN, she turned to writing in her unhappy marriage to George Norton (m.1827). Her autobiographical *Sorrows of Rosalie* (1829) paid for her first confinement, while more poetry, fiction and editing financed her sometimes indiscreet social life. Her surprising story 'The Coquette' (1834) deals harshly with her beauty and impulsiveness; George Meredith's more sympathetic portrait of her after her death in *Diana of the Crossways* (1885) includes her husband's abuse, removal of their children and unsuccessful adultery case (1836) against her friend the Prime Minister, Lord Melbourne.

Her public airing of her marital battles scandalized society, but she thought it 'of more importance that the law should be altered, than that I should be approved'. Her pamphlets *Observations on . . . the Custody of . . . Children* (1837), *Separation of Mother and Child* (1838) and *Plain Letter* (1839) strongly influenced the Infant Custody Act (1839); *English Laws for Women* (1854) argued a wife's right to her own property; *Letter to the Queen* (1855) and *Review of the Divorce Bill* (1857) helped to word the Marriage and Divorce Act (1857). *Letters to the Mob* (1848) and her novel *Lost and Saved* (1863) reflect her relationship with reformer Sidney Herbert, which ended after suspicions that she had leaked political information to *The Times* (1845). After her husband's death (1875), she married her old friend, Sir William Stirling-Maxwell (1877), but died only three months later.   MSM

Norton [née Pearson], Mary 1903–92 Popular British children's writer (see CHILDREN'S BOOKS) of the post-war period best known for her delightfully detailed series introduced with *The Borrowers* (1952), about a resourceful and wary Lilliputian race of people who live in unseen spaces, making ingenious use of what they can scavenge from Brobdingnagian humans. The first tale was followed by *The Borrowers Afield* (1955), *The Borrowers Afloat* (1959), *The Borrowers Aloft* (1961) and, later, *The Borrowers Avenged* (1982). Written mostly through the viewpoint of Arriety, a young girl Borrower who longs to escape her carefully concealed life for a bigger world, the books offer moral commentary on myopic self-delusion, balanced by comic touches and the charm of the miniature.

The daughter of a doctor, Norton was convent-educated and spent much of her childhood at the family's Bedfordshire estate, which inspired the setting for many of her stories. She acted with the Old Vic Company, worked for the BBC, married and had four children before writing her first book, *The Magic Bed Knob* (1943), which, combined with its sequel, *Bonfires and Broomsticks* (1947), made the successful *Bed Knobs and Broomsticks* (1957), filmed by Disney. *The Borrowers* has been televised and was filmed in 1997.   LDo

Not Waving But Drowning (1957) The title poem of this collection by STEVIE SMITH is probably also her best-known, illustrating the preoccupation with death and the pain of everyday living which is inherent in almost all of her work. Smith's apparently jocular and flippant tone often masks her interrogation of more serious topics. Poems such as 'The English', 'Parents' and 'The English Visitor', for instance, explore class structures and issues of national identity, whereas her ambivalence toward organized religion is implicit in 'Why are the Clergy?' and 'God the Eater'. Eclectic in her sources, she draws on material from limericks, fairy tale and Arthurian legend and this accounts for the consciously constructed, multiple voices at work in the collection. *Not Waving But Drowning* suggests Smith's resistance to society's impulse to judge on surface appearance, whilst also articulating a craving for independence, even isolation. Ultimately, the poetry in this volume is testament to her shrewd observation of human nature, always expressed with a strong sense of irony, and conveys her opposition to institutionalized systems of power.   RCo

Nothing Natural (1986) JENNY DISKI's first novel explores the exploitative yet collusive nature of a sado-masochistic relationship from the point of view of the compliant mortified victim. The narrator is Rachel, damaged survivor of a traumatic childhood, divorced, with a young daughter, cynical and prone to depression. Rachel is horrified to find how easily she falls into the role of verbally challenging but fundamentally undemanding participant in Joshua's acted-out fantasies of control and abuse, a role to which she quickly becomes addicted. Explicit scenes of sexual arousal, spanking and buggery verge on the pornographic, a daring strategy to bring into full focus the dangerous appeal of such a relationship. The odds are nevertheless quite heavily weighted against Johsua: although intelligent and attractive he is shown to have no empathy, to resist all feeling for Rachel in his efforts to isolate, 'punish' and defeat her for his own satisfaction. The sub-plot concerning the degeneration and suicide of Rachel's adolescent tutee Pete and her own wretched and life-denying depression emphasize the deathly aspects of degradation.   SAS

Nourbese-Philip, Marlene 1947– Caribbean writer, she was born in Tobago and studied at the University of the West Indies before moving to Canada in 1968 where she studied Law. She is now a full-time writer and has published several essays, novels and short stories, though she is best known as a poet.

Nourbese-Philip's essays reflect her commitment to revealing and challenging the racism which she sees as endemic to Canadian culture. Describing herself as an 'Afrosporic' writer, Philip makes the experience of the black diaspora central to her writing agenda and focuses on the issue of language and the way in which colonially inherited European languages have exiled the Caribbean speaker/writer, reducing them to 'linguistic squatters'.

Making use of the kind of formal experimentation often associated with 'écriture féminine', Nourbese-Philip's poetry interrogates 'raced' *and* gendered discursive structures: 'I want to write about kinky hair and flat noses – maybe I should be writing about the language that *kinked* the hair and *flattened* noses'. In her third collection of poetry (which won the Casas de las Americas Prize), *She Tries Her Tongue, Her Silence Softly Breaks* (1989), Philip powerfully exposes the processes through which words derive their meanings in the New World context and offers her own, stuttering and fragile, linguistic alternative to the 'anguish of english'. In *Looking For Livingstone* (1991), she dramatizes the way in which Livingstone's printed word is predicated upon, and obliterates, the silences and realities of 'the dark continent', symbolized here by an African woman traveller.   DdeCN

Novel on Yellow Paper (1936) STEVIE SMITH's first novel, written because she could not get her poems published, and consequently filled with her poems. Influenced by DOROTHY PARKER, by turns whimsical and melancholy, aptly described as 'the talking voice that runs on', it reads like an internal monologue addressed to the reader. The jaunty narrator, named Pompey Casmilus, sees herself as 'just one of those Romans that have lost their investments and are living on their wits and on their friends'.

Like Stevie Smith, Pompey works in publishing and lives with a beloved aunt in a suburb of London (Bottle Green, which reflects the author's home of Palmer's Green); like Stevie, she lampoons pomposity and pretension. Pompey charts the daily round of her life at the outbreak of World War II. She is in the throes of deciding not to marry her boyfriend, is scathing about the social obligations of the marriage market, devoted to her friends, eloquently opinionated on such subjects as classical drama, the Catholic Church and Nazi

Germany, and poignantly humorous about loneliness, love and death. Although its whimsy now seems coy, *Novel on Yellow Paper* is one of the most distinctive works in modern fiction.   KE

Nwapa, Flora 1931–93 Nigerian novelist, short-story writer, children's writer. Born in Eastern Nigeria, Flora Nwapa was educated in Lagos, gained her BA at University College, Ibadan, and a Diploma in Education at the University of Edinburgh. She was also a teacher, an education officer, an assistant registrar at the University of Lagos, and a Commissioner for Anambra State, Nigeria. During the Civil War in Nigeria she travelled as a spokeswoman for the Biafran cause.

With the publication of *Efuru* in 1966, Flora Nwapa became Nigeria's first woman novelist. Like her second novel, *Idu* (1970), *Efuru* is set in a traditional rural community in Eastern Nigeria similar to the community portrayed in Chinua Achebe's *Things Fall Apart*. But whereas Achebe gives women a minor role, mainly as wives and mothers, Nwapa focuses on strong, independent, often exceptional women. Her innovative use of dialogue and anecdote (dismissed by several male critics as mere 'gossip') allows a whole community of women to speak their own stories. Her later novels and stories, *This is Lagos and Other Stories* (1971), *Never Again* (1975), *One Is Enough* (1981), *Wives at War and Other Stories* (1981) and *Women Are Different* (1986), portray women caught up in the Civil War and urban life, being forced to survive independently, and then choosing to continue doing so as they reject attempts to coerce them into polygamous or even monogamous marriages. Published by her own press, Tana Press, in Enugu, and distributed by Nwapa in Nigeria and in London and the United States when she was invited to international conferences and events, these later works combine the styles and values of popular ROMANCE and traditional oral tales. Tana Press has also published a number of books for children written by Nwapa.   CLI

O

O Pioneers! (1913) This was WILLA CATHER's first novel to open up, through stories of her native Nebraska, the force of 'human strivings' in shaping out the American land. Beginning in her characters' youth, she interweaves two main narratives, one following the successful career of Alexandra, an innovative farmer, and the other the fatal love-affair of her brother, Emil, fusing their destinies into a picture of the emerging 20th-century United States. In the details of Alexandra's cultivation of the discouraging prairie, the novel celebrates the breaking of the wild land, but only by those who, like her, remain in touch with its spirit. Elements of myth and FAIRY TALE underpin Cather's history, and images of death, sacrifice, fertility and rebirth suggest that the pioneers are playing out older rituals on the vast arena of the land. Alexandra enters the new world as goddess of the wheat, as well as a shrewd agricultural speculator; Emil and Marie, perhaps as the necessary blood-sacrifice of 'the best we have'. Her readers may inhabit the flatter, homogeneous, reality of the modern age at the end of the novel, but Cather restores to them a haunting myth of their own past. PEK

Oakes-Smith, Elizabeth 1806–93 American poet, prose writer and feminist activist, born in North Yarmouth, Maine. Her father, a ship's captain, died when she was 2 and the family moved to Portland, Maine. In 1823 she married Seba Smith, editor of a Portland newspaper. She assisted him and, in the 1830s, published her essays, stories and sketches of historical women in his newspaper. When he went bankrupt in 1837, she began writing professionally. Her first novel was *Riches Without Wings* (1838). In 1839 they moved to New York, where Oakes-Smith wrote poetry, fiction, criticism and children's literature for prominent journals, including *Godey's Lady's Book* and *Southern Literary Messenger*. Later novels include *The Salamander* (1848), a transcendentalist meditation; *The Newsboy* (1854), a reform novel; and *Bertha and Lily* (1854), the story of an intellectual woman who bears an illegitimate child. A leader at the Seneca Falls conference for women's rights in 1848, Oakes-Smith was the first woman to lecture on the lyceum circuit beginning in 1851 and a founding member of the first women's club in New York (1868). She became pastor of a church in Canastoga, New York, in 1877. Her feminist articles for the New York *Tribune* were collected in *Woman and Her Needs* (1851). JSG

Oates, Joyce Carol 1938– American fiction writer who chronicles the violence of contemporary life. Oates earned a BA from Syracuse University, an MA from the University of Wisconsin, and has pursued a teaching career at the University of Detroit, the University of Windsor, and finally at Princeton, where she holds a prestigious endowed chair. Since the 1970s with her husband (scholar and academic Raymond Smith), she has published the *Ontario Review*, a journal devoted to nurturing new talent. She is a hugely prolific novelist and has also written hundreds of short stories, several books of poetry, plays, reviews and essays. Under the pseudonym 'Rosamond Smith' she has published several mystery stories. Her well-received book, *On Boxing* (1987), has made her an unlikely authority on the sport.

Oates has said that her exposure to violence began when she was growing up during the Depression in a poverty-stricken rural area of upstate New York. There intermarriage caused mental retardation and the retarded grew nasty and menacing. An incident in which she was molested by a group of boys is a recurring motif in her fiction. There was also violence in her own family. Her forebears – Irish Catholic on one side and Hungarian immigrants on the other, with one German-Jewish great-grandfather – included a wife-beater who shot himself and a murder victim. Her father was a boxing enthusiast who encouraged her interest in the sport. A life-long sufferer from anorexia, depression, insomnia and tachycardia, she developed an early habit of counteracting those problems with her amazing literary productivity.

Her work is characterized by an unremitting bleakness of vision and a fascination with the brutal aspects of 20th-century urban and rural life. Her characters are often psychopaths – sadists, murderous children, girl gangs and serial killers. Some of them are inspired by famous people and incidents – *Zombie* (1995) on the Milwaukee cannibalistic killer, and the novella *Black Water* (1992) on the Chappaquiddick accident involving Senator Edward Kennedy. She has also turned to the 19th century for the settings of *Bellefleur* (1980), *A*

Bloodsmoor Romance (1982) and *MYSTERIES OF WINTERTHURN* (1984). While her powerful evocation of the atmosphere of her times and her technical expertise are widely praised, she is only grudgingly acknowledged as one of the pre-eminent novelists of her generation. The sensational subject matter, the plot-driven novels, the unrelieved drabness of tone and lack of a leavening sense of humour are often criticized. It is more often her short stories, such as those in *Where Are You Going, Where Have You Been?* (1970) and *THE ASSIGNATION* (1988), that are universally acclaimed, anthologized and achieve the status of classics. See, however, *DO WITH ME WHAT YOU WILL* (1973) and *CHILDWOLD* (1976). JG

Obasan (1981) Based on JOY KOGAWA's own experiences, her first novel describes the treatment of Japanese-Canadians in Canada in the 1940s. The narrator, Megumi Naomi Nakane, remembers and tries to come to terms with her childhood, which was shaped by internment during World War II and policies of repatriation and dispersal after the war. While her aunt and guardian, Obasan, reacts with silent submission and acceptance, her aunt Emily becomes a 'word warrior'. Naomi's memories surface when reading Emily's collection of historical documents which also, finally, explains the absence of her mother. Naomi's narrative is the thread which links journal entries, letters, newspaper clippings, as well as other public documents weaving the fabric of her personal history, while also placing it within the larger context of the history of the Japanese-Canadian community. Through metaphors and images of silence and voice, of pain and hope, Kogawa creates fiction of great poetic beauty that not only presents an individual's quest for knowledge and healing but also demands the public acknowledgement of the injustices suffered by three generations of Japanese-Canadians. An official apology and redress was offered by the Canadian government in 1988. NR

O'Brien, Edna 1932– Irish novelist and short-story writer whose frank treatment of female sexuality and male treachery earned her the opprobrium of Irish censors. Born in the west of Ireland to Michael and Lena Cleary O'Brien, she was educated at the Convent of Mercy at Loughrea, County Galway, and later attended pharmaceutical college in Dublin. In 1951 she married Ernest Gebler. The couple had two sons and divorced in 1964. Like many Irish writers before her, O'Brien felt the need to leave Ireland in order to write about it, and in 1959 she moved to London.

The youthful experiences of her convent days and the excitement of moving to the city are vividly captured in her first and most famous novel, *THE COUNTRY GIRLS* (1960), which traces the lives of two West Country girls, Kate and Baba, as they search for love and experience amid the crowds and clamour of Dublin. This was followed by *THE LONELY GIRL* (1962) and *Girls in Their Married Bliss* (1964), which form a trilogy, charting the disillusionment and failed romances of the two women. Through confessional first-person narratives, O'Brien reveals the intense and often brutal transition from innocence to experience and explores the emotional and sexual frustrations of women raised on false romantic expectations of love and marriage. O'Brien highlights the sexual desire and attitudes of the women in her novels, and there is a wantonness in her heroines' search for lovers and husbands which led Stanley Kauffman to describe her novels as 'lyrics of the loins'. However, O'Brien's emphasis is on how women's lives are blighted by their dependence on men, and her next two novels, *August is a Wicked Month* (1965) and *Casualties of Peace* (1967), also deal with women who are victims of failed marriages.

By 1969 all five of O'Brien's novels were banned in Ireland, her uninhibited treatment of sex deemed pornographic and obscene. Her later fiction includes *A Pagan Place* (1970), which won the *Yorkshire Post* Book Award, *Night* (1972), and *Johnny I Hardly Knew You* (1972) which met with generally unfavourable reviews. O'Brien's numerous short stories have appeared in a variety of periodicals and are collected in *The Love Object* (1969); *A Scandalous Woman and Other Stories* (1974); *Mrs Reinhart and Other Stories* (1978); and *RETURNING* (1982). O'Brien has also written for stage and screen, and in 1981 penned *Virginia*, a play based on the DIARIES of VIRGINIA WOOLF. She adapted screenplays of her own works: *The Girl with Green Eyes* (1964) from *The Lonely Girl*; *Time Lost and Time Remembered* (1966) from the short story 'A Woman at the Seaside'; and *X Y and Zee* (1971), starring Elizabeth Taylor, from *Zee & Co.* (1971). LCo

O'Brien, Kate 1897–1974 Irish novelist, born into a prosperous middle-class Catholic family in Limerick. After her mother's death when she was 5, she spent most of her childhood in a convent boarding school. Graduating from University College Dublin, in 1919, she moved to England as a freelance journalist and teacher, with a year as an au pair in Spain. A play was followed by a successful first novel, *Without My Cloak* (1931), set in 'Mellick', Ireland, and by, among others, *The Ante-Room* (1934), *Mary Lavelle* (1936), *THE LAND OF SPICES* (1941) and *That Lady* (1946). Her fiction fuses the conventions of REALISM (through a 19th-century Catholic middle-class milieu) and ROMANCE (internalized as the discourse of desire). A 'Catholic agnostic', O'Brien illuminates a highly charged struggle between her protagonists' moral values, shared with their society, and a more inexorable integrity which requires them to risk (in their terms) their own souls.

Kate O'Brien: portrait by Jill Teck.

However, they eventually resist the temptations of both love and faith in a bid for autonomy.

Ireland's Censorship of Publications Board baulked at such scandal, banning *Mary Lavelle* and also the convent-set *Land of Spices*, in which Helen Archer (later Reverend Mother) witnesses her father in a homosexual embrace. O'Brien condemned the self-righteous judgementalism of De Valera's Ireland indirectly, generally by displacing the chronology of her plots to the 19th century. Her final novel, *As Music and Splendour* (1958), confronts the lesbian taboo, denying, as do the other texts, the right of any outsider, including parents and lovers, to judge another's motives and actions, while insisting on the individual's moral responsibility to judge herself.

From 1950 to 1960 she lived in Ireland, dying in Kent in 1974. Republished by the Irish feminist publishing company, Arlen House, in the 1980s, O'Brien's novels have begun to attract feminist, lesbian, psychoanalytic and POST-COLONIAL readings, along with belated recognition of her status as one of Ireland's major women novelists.   JFG

O'Brien, Mary fl.1783–90 Irish poet, novelist and playwright. Little is known of Mary O'Brien's life, but her work shows her to have been a supporter of the 'patriot' movement within Irish politics, which demanded political reform and opposed British interference in Irish affairs. A collection of poems, *The Pious Incendiaries, or Fanaticism Display'd* (1785), dealt with the anti-Catholic Gordon riots, and *The Political Monitor: Or Regent's Friend* (1790) was prompted by the Regency crisis of 1788. It included, in 'The Freedom of John Bull', an attack on the administration of William Pitt ('Billy'), and on England ('Jacky Bull'):

> As Bacchus on a barrel rides
> So he on liberty bestrides,
> Trotting with hobby horse's motion

> To mount the cliffs of mother ocean.
> Firm on a rock, a Briton born,
> A foreign coast he views with scorn.

'Paddy's Opinion', an Irishman's complaint about taxation, concludes with a hint that dissatisfaction might turn to more active protest:

> Arrah, then, my dear Billy
> It might prove in the pull,
> Paddy's not quite so silly
> As your Jacky Bull.

O'Brien also produced a play, *The Fallen Patriot*, published in 1790; a novel *Charles Henley*, now lost; and possibly an opera, *The Temple of Virtue*.   RR

O'Connor, (Mary) Flannery 1925–64 American novelist, short-story writer and essayist celebrated for her 'Southern GOTHIC' allegories of rural backwoods Georgia. Her mother's family were prominent Georgia Catholics, and Catholicism was central to her life and writing. Born in Savannah, she grew up in Milledgeville, and attended the Georgia State College for Women where she began to write and draw cartoons, practising the caricatures that would emerge in her fiction. She took her MA at the Writers' Workshop, Iowa, spending time at Yaddo artists' colony, New York. The early 1950s saw her most creative period, with a novel, *WISE BLOOD* (1952), and short fiction, first in leading journals, then as *A GOOD MAN IS HARD TO FIND, AND OTHER STORIES* (1955). This period also saw the severe onset of lupus, a hereditary disease of the immune system that had killed her father in 1951; cortisone injections helped arrest it, but caused crumbling bones and severe disablement. O'Connor continued to write, travel and lecture, giving talks to university, Catholic and writers' groups on subjects from raising peacocks to regional writing, religion and teaching literature. These were collected by her lifelong friends, Sally and Robert Fitzgerald, as *Mystery and Manners: Occasional Prose* (1969). The second novel, *The Violent Bear It Away* (1960), was the last publication before her death in 1964, at the age of 39. A collection of stories, *EVERYTHING THAT RISES MUST CONVERGE*, appeared posthumously in 1965, as did *The Complete Stories* (1971) and *The Habit of Being: Letters of Flannery O'Connor* (1979). In 1979, a film version of *Wise Blood* was made by John Huston.

In 1960 O'Connor said, 'While the South is hardly Christ-centered, it is most certainly Christ-haunted.' Her main subject was the region's (predominantly Protestant) fundamentalism and the spiritually sterile, fallen modern world. The work is imbued with Catholic allusions and parody, most obviously in her fictional titles and concern with problems of good and evil. Her spiritual vision has been described as that of an Old Testament prophet or an irascible Christian saint. Associated with the Southern Gothic of William Faulkner, CARSON MCCULLERS and Tennessee Williams, Flannery O'Connor focused on grotesque and violent characters and situations with a merciless eye for individual gesture and ear for dialogue. The richly comic writing evoked the banal and cliché-ridden expression of rural white Southerners. O'Connor has been compared with writers as disparate as JANE AUSTEN, Dostoevsky and William Faulkner. She captured a variety of poor white Southern women through their struggles with problematic definitions of modern Southern femininity. Despite her mainly white subject matter, ALICE WALKER admired her, visited her Milledgeville home and claimed her as an influence. HT

Odaga, Asenath Bole 19??–

Kenyan author and publisher, she has written children's stories and plays, novels for adults, collections of folktales, an English-Dholuo dictionary, and is an important figure in the development of an indigenous Kenyan and African literature. She was born in western Kenya, and studied History, Literature and Education at the University of Nairobi, where she also did postgraduate work in the university's Institute of African Studies. Since 1967, she has written over fifty CHILDREN'S BOOKS in English and Luo. Her aim with these, as with her two works on oral literature, was to counter colonial cultural domination – 'for us to be really free, children must read about their own background'. *Oral Literature: A School Certificate Course* was written with K. Akivaga in 1982, followed in 1984 by *Yesterday's Today: The Study of Oral Literature*. Her first adult novel, *The Shade Changes* (1984), questioned the relevance of traditional parental control to the modern university-educated Kenyan woman. She caused controversy in Kenya with a research paper attacking the negative stereotypes of women in popular fiction by male Kenyan authors. In the mid 1980s, she decided to establish her own publishing house to resist the influence of foreign multi-nationals responsible for such profit-driven projects as the Macmillan Pacesetter series. She is married with children and has combined family life with a hectic schedule of reading manuscripts, managing a publishing company, writing on her own projects and supporting several Kenyan women's groups. WJB

O'Donnell, Mary 1954–

Irish poet, novelist and short-story writer. She was born in Monaghan and was educated at St Patrick's College, Maynooth. She has taught at a secondary school in Dublin and worked as a translator, library assistant and drama critic for the *Sunday Tribune*. Her first volume, *Reading the Sunflowers in September* (1992), received favourable reviews. Other collections of poetry are: *Spiderwoman's Third Avenue*

Rhapsody (1993) and *Unlegendary Heroes* (1998). Her poems have appeared in American and in Irish publications such as *Poetry Ireland*, *New Irish Writing*, *Cyphers*, the *Honest Ulsterman*, *Tracks*, the *Salmon* and *Krino*, while her stories have been published in the *Irish Press*. Her prose includes *Strong Pagans and Other Stories* (1991), *The Light Makers* (1993) and *Virgin and the Boy* (1996). During the Autumn of 1987, she broadcast on Irish television a series entitled 'The Poet's Eye'. At its best, her poetry is daring, intense and recognizable for its sensual language and surprising imagery. SFu

Of Woman Born: Motherhood as Experience and Institution (1976)

ADRIENNE RICH's text is an extended meditation on motherhood, both as personal experience and as patriarchal institution. Rich's reflections on her own experience of mothering in post World War II, Boston, Brahmin culture form the core of her analysis. She ponders the dilemmas and contradictions she felt two decades previously as a young mother, with a sense of urgency which renders her prose powerful and compelling.

Rich draws on studies in anthropology, history, literature, mythology and sociology; but her method of selection and organization is that of 'poetic knowledge' (her term) rather than that of scientific rationalism. The book is structured around major themes, including: female anger and maternal tenderness, power – both male power over women and maternal power over children – and the predominance of patriarchy as opposed to myths of matriarchy.

This is a classic enunciation of US radical lesbian feminism, especially in its belief that the primary oppression is the patriarchy's oppression of women. It remains an influential yet problematic text, not least because a subjective, lesbian position is articulated in a prophetic and universalizing mode. HMD

O'Faolain, Julia 1932–

Irish novelist and short-story writer who has a more cosmopolitan and varied range than many of her contemporaries. She comes from a literary family: her mother Eileen was a children's writer and her father Sean was a major dissident writer and intellectual in post-Civil-War Ireland. She was educated at University College Dublin, the University of Rome, and the Sorbonne. While living in Florence she married the American historian Lauro Martines, with whom she edited the documentary history *Not in God's Image: Women in History from the Greeks to the Victorians* (1973); she has also published translations from the Italian. She lives in London and Los Angeles.

While the short stories in *We Might See Sights!* (1968) and *Man in the Cellar* (1974), and the novel *Godded and Codded* (1970; as *Three Lovers* in USA, 1971), are stylishly satirical, their critique of Irish sexual repression and hypocrisy is conventional and unambiguous. As a writer impelled to dismantle myths because of her background in a country where myth ran rampant, O'Faolain is aware that myths are grander when intact; it is this ambivalence which marks her best work.

In the fascinating and accomplished novel WOMEN IN THE WALL (1975), which mixes history and fiction in the story of a group of nuns in 6th-century Gaul, rather than satirizing religiosity, O'Faolain treats it as a form of human passion; in this and its examination of the intersection of religious and secular politics the novel establishes important themes. *No Country for Young Men* (1980) again has a nun as a central figure in its story of an Irish political family, with a dangerous secret, from the Civil War to the present. Another collection of short stories, *Daughters of Passion* (1982), which ranges across clerical politics, feminist FAIRY TALES and unwitting involvement in terrorism, was followed by three novels. *The Obedient Wife* (1982), set in modern California, relates the Italian Carla's involvement with a priest, and her reasons for eventually returning to her husband. *The Irish Signorina* (1984) is a tale about a young Irishwoman being drawn into her mother's past on a visit to Italy. *The Judas Cloth* (1992) is a long and not wholly controlled novel about the intermeshing politics of a declining church and a burgeoning state in Rome during Pius IX's papacy.   EHu

Offshore (1979) PENELOPE FITZGERALD won the Booker Prize in 1980 for this, her second novel, which focuses on a community of houseboat dwellers whose lives are as precariously moored as their ramshackle vessels. On Battersea Reach the Thames is tidal, and the characters spend half their lives on land and half on water, reflecting the uncertainties and drift of their lives. Combining a hard edged realism with a lyrical prose style, the novel precisely and factually evokes the specific requirements of houseboat life at the same time it metaphorically captures the lives of 'tideline creatures', who have not found stability and who do not quite fit in anywhere. Depicted with sensitivity and depth, the characters are all unique but not presented as a gallery of clichéd eccentrics. Drawn together by their love of the river and the irregularity of houseboat life, the characters, like the boats, bump up against each other, connect and drift apart, and Fitzgerald moves between their stories with a carefully crafted narrative style that perfectly captures the movement of the river.   LCo

Ogot, Grace Akinyi 1930– Kenyan writer who trained as a nurse in St Thomas's Hospital, London. She married in 1959, and studied at Makeree University in 1963-4, before becoming an announcer for BBC Radio and principal of the women's training centre, Kisumu Kenyashe. Ogot has been a UN delegate, member of UNESCO, member of parliament and founding chair-person of the Writer's Association of Kenya. Her first novel, *The Promised Land* (1966), the first imaginative book in English by a Luo writer, concentrates on her concern for women's roles and fascination with the supernatural and mystery. A young couple move to farm in Tanzania, despite the wife's misgivings, and discover that witchcraft has given the husband an illness which can only be relieved by leaving. The short stories in *Land Without Thunder* (1968) are folktales of fantasy and magic, mixing travel stories with examples of conflicts between western and African tribal healing practices. In 'The Rain Came', traditions and myths are questioned. Oganda, the chief's daughter, due for traditional sacrifice to the lake monster to provoke much-needed rain, is rescued by the love and cunning of her betrothed, Osinda. The rain falls anyway. *The Other Woman* (1976) mixes magic and REALISM, while her later work, *The Island of Tears* (1980) and *The Graduate*, a novelette (1980), focus on tensions and benefits created when women travel, become educated, return as an educated elite and participate in social change. Her work mixes traditional medicine and magic with a feminist agenda for political change.   GW

O'Keeffe, Adelaide 1776–1855 Irish poet and romantic novelist, born in Dublin, her parents were Mary Heaphy and the popular Irish dramatist John O'Keeffe (1747–1833). Her parents separated in 1780, by which time her father was in London, writing for the Covent Garden and Haymarket Theatres. Due to blindness, her father retired in 1799. She maintained a close relationship with him and, acting as his amanuensis, collaborated in the writing of his *Recollections* (1826). Following his death and after unsuccessful attempts to sell his unpublished dramatic works, she published a collection of his poems in *A Father's Legacy to his Daughter* (1834). In addition to her literary projects with her father, thirty-four of her own poems were published in Taylor's *Original Poems for Infant Minds by Several Young Persons* (1804). She was also the author of *National Character* (1808) and *Patriarchal Times* (1811). In 1814, she published a ROMANCE, *Zenobia, Queen of Palmyra*. In 1819, she released a collection of poems, *A Trip to the Coast*, and another novel, *Dudley*. A further collection of poems came out in 1849, while her final published work was the romantic tale, *The Broken Sword* (1854).   BTF

Okoye, Ifeoma 19??– Nigerian novelist and writer of CHILDREN'S STORIES and textbooks, her adult fiction deals with marital conflict and corruption in the affluent Nigerian business classes. Born in Umanachi, Nigeria – she is unwilling to give her birth date – she was educated at St Monica's Training College at Ogbunike and the University of Nigeria, Nsukka, where she took her BA in English in 1977. She is married with four daughters and a son and lectures at the Institute of Management and

Technology in Enugu. In 1978, she received the Macmillan Children's Literature Prize for *Village Boy*. In her first novel for adults, *Behind the Clouds* (1982), she examines the pressures that childlessness places on a middle-class Nigerian couple. Her second novel, *Men Without Ears* (1984), satirizes the corruption generated in a society where 'without money you are nothing . . . and business is the quickest way of making money'. It won the Association of Nigerian Authors Award.　　WJB

Old English Baron, The (1777)

Originally published as *The Champion of Virtue* and reissued in 1778 under its present title, this was the first novel by CLARA REEVE. In the preface to the second edition Reeve explains that her purpose was to graft didacticism onto the GOTHIC form, providing a tale that was exciting but also probable. Her work therefore represents a transition between the extravagance of Horace Walpole and the rationalized Gothic of ANN RADCLIFFE. The novel is set in the 15th century and has a rather predictable inheritance plot. The supposedly humble hero, Edmund, is ultimately revealed to be the son of a great landed family, deprived of his inheritance by evil relatives. His true status is part-exposed by the interventions of the supernatural, although Reeve limits these to a few bumps, bangs and ghastly groans. Thus the forces of the paranormal are portrayed as mechanisms which further the interests of truth, justice and the Christian way, instead of being in opposition to them.　　LBe

Old Jest, The (1979)

Won JENNIFER JOHNSTON the Whitbread Award for Fiction and was made into a film in 1988.

Set in 1920, the period in which the 'Big House' of the Anglo-Irish Ascendancy was on the decline and its inhabitants a dying breed, the novel juxtaposes the reality of terrorism and death and the brutal progress of commercialism as agents of change. Events are seen primarily through the eyes of 18-year-old Nancy Gulliver, the youngest member of the Protestant Dwyer household, whose world of cushioned innocence is challenged by the reality of the wider world around her. Johnston's narrative is a compelling series of events which focuses on the inevitable, and painful, necessity of change from a heritage of stifling 'accepted' privilege which, paradoxically, offers no real choice, to a life which forces Nancy to make choices. In the end it is the old jester, Death, that wins.　　EF

Olds, Sharon 1942–

Contemporary American poet who writes with a frank and tender sensuality of the varied experiences of womanhood. Born in San Francisco, Olds was educated at Stanford University and Columbia, where she received a Ph.D. in 1972. She has taught at New York University and at Goldwater

Hospital in New York, and is married with two children, a son and a daughter, who figure in her work. Her first collection, *Satan Says*, appeared in 1980, followed by *The Dead and the Living* (1984) in which photographs and poems of political atrocities are juxtaposed to poems of childhood abuse, burgeoning sexuality and physical mother-love. *The Gold Cell* (1987) continues the dominant themes and tone of Olds's poetry, telling stories of birth, sex and death using autobiographical material with an unflinching, unsentimental honesty. She celebrates especially the erotic mother–child relationship and the valour of the female body. *The Sign of Saturn: Poems 1980-1987* (1991) collects poems from the previous books.

Olds's father died of throat cancer. Her collection *The Father* (1993) deals with the complex emotions and physical sensations of a daughter experiencing the slow, unlovely death of an abusive, alcoholic father.　　AG

Oliphant, Margaret 1828–97

A prolific novelist and reviewer, Oliphant grew up in Scotland and maintained life-long links with the Edinburgh publishing world, but settled in the south of England after marrying an unsuccessful stained-glass designer who died young, leaving her in debt. Oliphant published nearly a hundred novels to support a succession of parasitic male relatives (husband, brother, sons, nephews). Her posthumously published *Autobiography* (1899) movingly describes her ambivalence about sacrificing 'the higher objects of art' to the hurried hackwork needed to earn money for her family. In part because her productivity always threatened to glut the market, Oliphant worked in nearly every genre of prose, from history (*The Makers of Florence*, 1876) to biography (*Edward Irving*, 1862), to tales of the afterlife (*A Beleaguered City*, 1880), to literary history, to historical fiction, to children's books. Her 'CHRONICLES OF CARLINGFORD', a cycle of novels and short stories set in a small English town, mixed domestic comedy with sensation plots (*Salem Chapel*, 1863), mock epic (in *Miss Marjoribanks*, 1866) and church politics. Unlike Trollope's 'Barsetshire Chronicles', with which they were immediately compared, the Carlingford novels dealt with Dissenting congregations as well as Anglican clergy, sometimes (as in *Phoebe, Junior*, 1876) focusing on the relations between them. Oliphant's essays polemicize against women's rights, but her novels and reviews attack traditional courtship plots and much of her fiction deals with women's work (notably *Hester*, 1883). *Blackwood's Magazine* serialized many of her novels and published even more of her reviews, often running several pieces by her in a single issue. Oliphant described herself as Blackwood's 'general utility woman'; she died while at work on an official but opinionated history of the firm.　　LPr

Oliver, Mary 1935– A much-admired American poet, born in Ohio, her awards include the Pulitzer Prize for *American Primitive* in 1983. She attended Ohio State University and Vassar College. Oliver writes lyric poetry that observes the natural world with a careful eye, one acutely tuned to the rhythms of nature and its often powerful forces. Her language lends a tactile beauty to her observations; in 'Black Oaks' she writes: 'After a while I'm pale with longing / for their thick bodies ruckled with lichen'. Although her writing appears quite formal in approach, Oliver does not shun free-verse forms: 'You can't keep me from the woods, from the tonnage / of their shoulders, and their shining green hair'. Following a series of awards, including the Shelley Memorial Award and an Achievement Award from the American Academy and Institute of Arts and Letters, in 1992 she was awarded the National Book Award for *New and Selected Poems*. Her other publications include: *No Voyage and Other Poems* (1965), *The River Styx and Other Poems* (1972), *The Night Traveler* (1978), *Dream Work* (1986), *A Poetry Handbook* (1994) and *West Wind* (1997). In 1996 she was appointed as the Catherine Osborn Foster Professor at Bennington College in Vermont.   ACH

Olsen, Tillie Lerner 1913– American fiction writer who began writing in the early 1930s, but then for 22 years published nothing, and was a forgotten, minor casualty of the Depression hard times. Politics, war, economics, to say nothing of family life, exacted a heavy toll in broken and interrupted careers. Henry Roth and George Oppen were similarly 'forgotten', and rediscovered in the 1960s.

Olsen, whose Russian Jewish immigrant father was an official in the Nebraska Socialist Party, joined the Young Communist League when she was 17. Her brief career as a political activist and author ended when she was 21. Olsen subsequently lived in California, had four children, and worked at miscellaneous jobs. In 1955 she won a Creative Writing Fellowship at Stanford University, and published 'I Stand Here Ironing', a short story which announced the resurrection of her writing career. The title story of Olsen's *Tell Me a Riddle* (1961) won an O. Henry Award; it was followed by fellowships, teaching appointments and stays at the MacDowell Colony. In 1972 she published an edition of REBECCA HARDING DAVIS'S LIFE IN THE IRON-MILLS which restored that story to the canon. In the next year she found the manuscript of her novel about a migrant family, begun in 1934, which was completed and published as YONNONDIO: FROM THE THIRTIES (1974). The final text was described by Olsen as 'the work of this older writer in arduous partnership with that long-ago younger one'. SILENCES (1979), a fragmentary meditation upon the causes of broken and interrupted literary careers, was followed by *Mother to Daughter, Daughter to Mother: A Day Book and Reader* (1984). Olsen's interrupted career has come to be a measure of the obstacles which women over many centuries have encountered in the pursuit of their creativity.   EH

Oman, Carola (Mary Anima), afterwards Lady Lenanton

1897–1978 British writer and historian. Daughter of Sir Charles Oman, the distinguished scholar and Fellow of All Souls, Oxford, she was brought up in an academic atmosphere and displayed not surprisingly an intense love of history, publishing novels, children's books and biographies.

Her first book was published in 1919, *The Menin Road and Other Poems*, followed in 1924 by two HISTORICAL NOVELS, *Princess Amelia* and *The Road Royal*. Contemporary novels followed, in particular *Mrs Newdigate's Window* (1927), and several children's books, the most popular of which were *Ferry the Fearless* (1936) and *Robin Hood* (1937). The historical biographies were the works for which she was most noted, most particularly *Prince Charles Edward* (1935), *Henrietta Maria* (1936) and *Elizabeth of Bohemia* (1938).

The outstanding work of her lifetime of writing was her biography of Nelson, reprinted several times. Meticulously written and researched, this book gives a picture of the whole man and his naval activities: she took a heroic subject and dealt with it superbly. She worked with the British Red Cross during World War I and maintained this connection throughout her life.   MEW

On Lies, Secrets and Silence, Selected Prose 1966-1978

(1979) ADRIENNE RICH'S complex and influential collection of essays could be called 'seminal' if that weren't disrespectful to its author's uncompromising feminism, and to a poet with a meticulous eye on the meanings of words. 'As long as our language is inadequate, our vision remains formless', Rich writes, and here she creates a fluid, politicized prose to complement the anger and passion voiced in her poetry. Throughout, her concern is to champion women writers, especially poets, whether in scholarly readings of ANNE BRADSTREET or EMILY DICKINSON, or in appreciations of peers such as Judy Grahn. As the pieces, arranged chronologically, progress, she becomes more radical in her lesbian feminism, which she calls 'a wholly new force in history'. Such idealistic commentary seems more specifically of its time than her personal and historical exploration of white feminists' relation to issues of race – discussions which make reference to friends such as AUDRE LORDE and Rich's partner, Michelle Cliff. Rich's fiercely intelligent vision was inspirational to a generation of American feminists and gay women, and opened the way for later essayists such as KATHA POLLITT, who employed more irony in their analyses.   SB

O'Neill, Moira [Agnes Nesta Shakespeare Higginson] 1863–1955 Ulster dialectical poet. Born in County Antrim in 1863 into a relatively privileged lifestyle, she married Walter Clement Skrine and became the mother of five children, one of whom is the novelist and playwright known as MOLLY KEANE and M.J. FARRELL. She lived for some time in Canada before returning to County Antrim, a sojourn which she remembered with 'Songs from North-west Canada', part of her *Songs of the Glens of Antrim*. She was a humorous woman and her wit is reflected in much of her poetry. Her subject matter was primarily that of the lives of ordinary country workers. Her poetry was often romantic and was very popular. She described her poems as 'written by a glenswoman in the dialect of the glens and chiefly for the pleasure of other glens-people'. She also wrote poems and songs for children as well as translating Italian poetry. Her collected poems were published in 1933. She lived for some time on country estates in Counties Kildare and Wexford and died in Wicklow at the good age of 92.

MSu

Onwueme, Tess 1955– Like ZULU SOFOLA, Nigeria's pioneer woman dramatist, Onwueme was born into an Igbo community in Nigeria's mid-west. Pursuing a career in theatre studies, in 1990 she left Nigeria to take up a series of academic appointments in the United States. Widely admired as a theatre practitioner and producer, she is a prolific dramatist. Many of her plays are large-scale works that explore the intersection of class, race and gender, sometimes from a world-historical or intercontinental perspective. Notable, too, is the explosive energy of Onwueme's stagecraft, which both explores and extends earlier African developments in total theatre.

Onwueme's early plays, such as *A Hen Too Soon* (1983) and *The Broken Calabash* (1984), problematize traditional value systems, especially in respect of their bearing on women's rights. In *The Reign of Wazobia* (1988) Onwueme turns her attention to women's role in pre-colonial systems of government. While these three plays have relatively monolinear (though powerful) dramatic structures, in *The Desert Encroaches* (1985) and *Ban Empty Barn* (1989) – two of the most innovative plays in the Nigerian English-language theatre – Onwueme employs fabular elements, a vehemently caustic vaudeville-type satire, and striking disjunctions between contrasting plot elements, to dramatize Africa's position within the world order. *Tell It To Women* (revised edition 1997) is a massive work that once again combines contrasting dramatic materials to explore the exploitation of rural African women and the – for Onwueme, problematic – role of feminist movements in transforming women's rights.

CD

Oodgeroo [Kath Walker] 1920–93 Highly respected Aboriginal poet, commentator and campaigner for Aboriginal rights. Oodgeroo was also the first published Aboriginal poet in Australia with *We Are Going* (1964). Her work is still widely read, admired and anthologized.

A member of the Noonuccal tribe, Oodgeroo was born on Stradbroke Island, off the Queensland coast. She worked in domestic service, and in the Australian Women's Army Service during World War II. In 1960 she joined the Federal Council for the Advancement of Aboriginal and Torres Strait Islanders (FCAATSI), a peak Aboriginal organization in 1958–72, and served as its state secretary for Queensland in 1960–70. Her political work continued in many fields, including education and the arts.

Oodgeroo always insisted on the political nature and value of her work, describing her own poetry as 'sloganistic, civil rightish, plain and simple'. White critics have tended to overlook the claims implicit in this often-quoted statement, choosing to insist, patronizingly, that her work is 'more and better than that'. It is more useful to compare her work to poetry by white writers about Aborigines, in order to note the ways she avoids a tone of lament for 'a dying race', insisting rather on the vitality and continuity of Aboriginal voices, and on the political nature of poetic language: 'They came here to the place of their old bora ground / Where now the many white men hurry about like ants . . . / They sit and are confused, they cannot say their thoughts' ('We Are Going').

In addition to her collections *The Dawn is at Hand* (1966), and *My People* (1970), Oodgeroo published a short-story collection, *Stradbroke Dreamtime* (1972), and a children's book *Father Sky and Mother Earth* (illustrated with her own paintings; 1981).

Oodgeroo won a number of literary awards including the Jessie Litchfield Award (1975) and the Mary Gilmore Medal (1970). She was made MBE in 1970, but returned the award as a protest against the Australian government's preparations to celebrate the bicentenary in 1988.

BO

Opie [née Alderson], Amelia 1769–1853 English novelist and poet whose work is characterized by a strong moral tone. Born and brought up in Norwich, she was the only child of Amelia and James Alderson, her father being a respected physician and strong Unitarian. She began her literary career by contributing articles to periodicals, including *London Magazine*, and published her first novel, *The Dangers of Coquetry*, anonymously in 1790. On trips to London she became acquainted with the radicals William Godwin, MARY WOLLSTONECRAFT and ELIZABETH INCHBALD, but she withdrew from this circle when she married the successful portrait painter John Opie in 1798. (Her

Amelia Opie: 'Lady Pemberton instructs her sons in the duties of charity', illustration from *Tales of the Pemberton Family*, 1825.

novel ADELINE MOWBRAY (1804) was based upon Wollstonecraft's life.) Her most successful work was *The Father and Daughter* (1801), 'a simple moral tale' as she described it, which went through ten editions by 1844 and brought her wide renown. It was greatly admired by Scott. She also wrote some poetry, including *Poems* (1802) and *The Warrior's Return* (1808). In 1825 she converted to Quakerism, abandoning novel-writing for the Bible Society and charitable works. Her support for the anti-slavery movement is reflected in *The Black Man's Lament* (1826). Her later writings, including *Illustrations of Lying* (1825) and *Lays for the Dead* (1833), were increasingly religious in tone.   SA

Optimist's Daughter, The (1972) The most autobiographical of EUDORA WELTY's novels. Laurel McKelva, a woman who lives in the past and whose emotions are controlled by painful memories, travels home in a journey that proves to be a psychological one of self-reflexivity. Her father, Judge Clinton McKelva, is taken to New Orleans for eye surgery, where his optimism fades during the long, slow recovery. He dies on the last day of the Mardi Gras festival and his body is brought home to Mount Salus, Mississippi. As the story unfolds in this small community, Laurel confronts her emotional ghosts, the memories of her father, her husband and particularly her

mother. She endures simultaneously an embittered confrontation with Wanda Fay Chisolm, her father's much younger second wife, a woman with neither passion nor imagination. Liberated by her ability to gain control of her memories, Laurel is enabled to confront Fay and thus enter a new phase of her life with confidence.

The Optimist's Daughter appeared in shorter form in the *New Yorker* in 1969. It won for Welty the 1973 Pulitzer Prize.   JAHa

Oranges are not the Only Fruit (1985) JEANETTE WINTERSON's first novel is a largely autobiographical account of a girl's upbringing by an Evangelical adopted mother. The mother's desire to make the child into a missionary cultivates in her a supreme self-assuredness which makes it possible for her to withstand rejection, exorcism and moral blackmail when, in her teens, she comes out as a lesbian. Both daughter and mother are monsters of ego; the relationship is seen with surprising objectivity. Where most memoirs of religious upbringing talk of aesthetic deprivation, Winterson shows faith and the faithful as a rich collection of eccentric types and passions. The story of mother and daughter is interleaved, not wholly successfully, with episodes of a sardonic FAIRY STORY which offers a metaphoric commentary. *Oranges are not the Only Fruit* won the Whitbread Prize for Best First Novel and was successfully adapted by the author for television.   RK

Orczy, Emma Magdalena Rosalia Marie Josepha Barbara, Baroness 1865–1947 Novelist and story writer, Baroness Orczy was born in Hungary but led a peripatetic early life following her musician-father around Europe. The family finally settled in London where Emma attended art school and met Montagu Barstow. They were married in 1894 (their son was born in 1899) and lived together in London and Monte Carlo.

Early experiments in writing brought mixed results. A series of DETECTIVE stories ('The Old Man in the Corner') was popular but Orczy's first novel, *The Emperor's Candlesticks* (1899), was not. When her second, *The Scarlet Pimpernel*, was rejected by publishers, Orczy rewrote it successfully for the stage, thus transforming its fortunes: after this, publication as a novel (1905) was followed by numerous sequels and adaptations for film and television. The story blends adventure and ROMANCE in its eponymous hero, Sir Percy Blakeney, who rescues aristocrats from the guillotine in Revolutionary France. He is a formulaic man-of-action, concealing his 'indomitable energy' beneath a foppish, indolent exterior. The setting is likewise stereotypical and fervently patriotic: the 'shores of protecting England' offer beleaguered exiles a 'safe retreat' and hint perhaps at Orczy's own sense of geographical displacement, as well as the turmoil then bubbling under in continental Europe. But in the end what endures is the Scarlet Pimpernel's derring-do, echoing in his famous lyric:

> We seek him here, we seek him there,
> Those Frenchies seek him everywhere.
> Is he in heaven? – Is he in hell?
> That demmed, elusive Pimpernel.   AS

Orlando (1928) By VIRGINIA WOOLF, this purports to be the biography of a blue-blooded, sex-changing English (wo)man who lived from the Elizabethan age to the time of the novel's writing. It is really an arch, airy, fantastical romp through English history, an extended flirtation dedicated to VITA SACKVILLE-WEST. Its impressionistic style sends up BIOGRAPHY's plodding factualism. Lavishly descriptive, its jokily familiar attitude to history gives it an effect of endless, mildly parodic quotation. Orlando has a series of typically upper-class careers, mutating from courtier to poet to squire to diplomat, at which point, at the dawn of the 18th century, he becomes a woman. Woolf sends up the constraints of petticoats and modesty, while satirically acknowledging the seductions of male gallantry. Orlando's one consistent trait throughout the book is that s/he is a writer, which gives rise to some wonderful evocations of characters from literary history. The centuries for Woolf are sexed differently, for while Orlando gets away with having male and female lovers in the 18th century, as a Victorian she is implacably feminine and feels compelled to get married. With the 20th century returns a sense of liberation, and the book ends with 'the present moment'.   KE

Oroonoko (1688) For this novella APHRA BEHN returned to the events of a quarter of a century before, basing it on the 'journal observations' she had made during her stay in Surinam before her marriage. The eponymous hero, a black prince of great beauty and accomplishment, has been sold into slavery by his uncle, the King of Coramantien, and arrives in the colony a little after the author, to find his wife, Imoinda (the cause of his enslavement), is already there and herself a slave. When she becomes pregnant he resolves to escape, rather than allow their child to be born into captivity, and he leads a rebellion of the other slaves. They are persuaded to surrender but imprisoned as soon as they do and savagely whipped and tortured. When Oroonoko (or Caesar, his slave name) recovers, he takes to the woods with Imoinda and kills her before attempting to kill himself. Recaptured, he is tortured again and executed in the most brutal fashion. The story is remarkable for its sympathy with the black slaves and the Amerindian natives, as well as for the pace and economy of its writing. Rousseau acknowledged his debt to *Oroonoko* and Thomas Southerne adapted it successfully for the stage.   MD

Ortiz-Taylor, Sheila 1939– Lesbian Chicana poet and novelist. She was born in Los Angeles to a mother from a large Mexican-American family and a father of German-American descent. In her memoir, *Imaginary Parents* (1996), Sheila Ortiz-Taylor recreates this childhood as the daughter of a Hollywood beauty and a 'vaudevillian-lawyer'. Brief vivid vignettes are refracted by 3-D collages contributed by her elder sister Sandra Ortiz Taylor, a visual artist. From different perspectives both assemble *ofrendas* on an altar to remember and celebrate their family.

Ortiz-Taylor has two daughters from a marriage that ended in divorce and a struggle for custody. She studied for her degrees while raising her children, graduating with a Ph.D. in English. Some of these autobiographical experiences, including falling in love with a woman, are fictionalized in the first lesbian Chicana novel, *Faultline* (1982). The protagonist, Arden Benbow, is a survivor helped by her wise Mexican-American aunts, her six children, her numerous friends and her belief in non-linear possibilities. A sequel, *Southbound* (1990), takes Arden to Florida where Ortiz-Taylor herself teaches 18th-century Literature and creative writing at Florida State University.

Other work includes a book of poems, *Slow Dancing at Miss Polly's* (1989); *Spring Forward, Fall Back* (1985), a novel about relationships between and among women (and men); and *Coachella* (1998), a mystery about AIDS in which the gardener is the murderer. Her writing is characterized by rich imagery, empathy for diverse characters, irresistible humour and an outstanding story-telling talent.   CES

Osborn, Sarah 1714–96 American autobiographer and letter-writer, Osborn's writing confronts the loneliness of widowhood and the desolation of America's 'howling wilderness' with the conviction and hope of a pious devotion to God. Osborn married Samuel Wheaton in 1731 after moving with her parents, British-born Benjamin and Susannah Haggar, from Boston to Newport, Rhode Island. Two years later her husband was lost at sea, and she soon suffered the additional loss of their only child. Her autobiography, 'The Nature, Certainty, and Evidence of True Christianity' (1755), chronicles ten years spent as a member of the Congregational Church in Newport and her friendship with Susanna Anthony with whom she engaged in a lifetime correspondence. In 1799 with the help of the minister Samuel Hopkins, she revised and published her manuscript as the *Memoirs of the Life of Sarah Osborn*. A posthumous edition of her correspondence with Anthony, *Familiar Letters Written by Mrs Sarah Osborn and Miss Susanna Anthony* (1807), contains ample evidence of a vital, highly valued friendship and a deep engagement with ethical and religious questions of her day. Like her literary foremother, ANNE BRADSTREET, Osborn's strong belief in 'this good, and faithful God', and devotion to others competes in her writing with the hardship and material deprivations of a woman's life in the New World. Sentiment and extreme piety often belie personal fears of abandonment and the violent legacy of the Revolutionary War.   JRS

Osborne [Temple], Dorothy 1627–95 Letter writer, ROMANCE reader, and statesman's wife. She was the youngest child of an eminent Royalist family. In 1648, when she was 21 and he 20, she met William Temple (later knighted), son of a Parliamentarian. Their courtship, opposed by their families, was conducted mainly by letter for seven years until their marriage in 1655. For the next forty years Lady Temple shared in her husband's achievements, accompanying him on diplomatic postings to Brussels, the Hague and Ireland, and participating in the crucial negotiations for the marriage of William of Orange to Princess Mary, who became her friend.

Some of her courtship letters were published in a biography of her husband in 1836, where they drew an enthusiastic response from Thomas Babington Macaulay. Fuller editions followed, including one in 1928 of which VIRGINIA WOOLF commented, 'Had she been born in 1827, Dorothy Osborne would have written novels.' The letters are remarkable for their verve and for the insight they offer into the life of a young 17th-century gentlewoman. Osborne believed that letter-writing should be 'as free as one's discourse', and wittily satirized her acquaintances, relatives and suitors. Topical comments on public events were interspersed with vivid recreations of domestic scenes.

Osborne was a keen reader of the fashionable multi-volume French romances of De la Calprenède and Madame de Scudéry. She lent volumes to Temple and discussed their plots and characters in her letters with both energy and discrimination. She asked him, 'can there be a more romance story than ours would make if the conclusion should prove happy?' She mocked the literary efforts of her contemporary Margaret Cavendish, DUCHESS OF NEWCASTLE: 'Sure the poor woman is a little distracted, she could never be so ridiculous else as to venture at writing books and in verse too. If I should not sleep this fortnight I should not come to that.'   HH

Ostriker, Alicia (Suskin) 1937– American feminist poet and critic. She was born in New York and received a Ph.D. from the University of Wisconsin in 1964. In 1965 she began teaching at Rutgers University where she became a Professor of English. She married Astrophysics professor Jeremiah Ostriker in 1958 and

has three children. Her critical work can be divided into three stages. Initial formal studies of male writers (notably William Blake) were followed by an exploration of a female poetic tradition with *Writing Like a Woman* (1983), a study of individual poets (H.D., SYLVIA PLATH, ANNE SEXTON, ADRIENNE RICH) and her own poetic practice. The next study, *Stealing the Language: The Emergence of Women's Poetry in America* (1986), excavates a literary movement of (especially) women's revisionary mythmaking. In her third stage as a feminist and critic she draws on her Jewish heritage to write about Judaism and Jewish culture in *Feminist Revision and the Bible* (1993) and *The Nakedness of the Fathers: Biblical Visions and Revisions* (1994) in which she produces critical rewritings of biblical narratives. She has published eight books of poetry, beginning with *Songs* (1969) and including *The Mother/Child Papers* (1980) and *Crack in Everything* (1996).   AG

Ouida (Marie Louise de la Ramée) 1839–1908 Writer of 'fast', sensational ROMANCES. Brought up in Bury St Edmunds, Suffolk, and educated by her father, Louise later moved to London with her mother. Harrison Ainsworth published 'Dashwood's Drag, Or The Derby and What Came Of It' (*Bentley's Miscellany*, 1859) and her first novel, *Granville De Vigne* (serialized in the *New Monthly Magazine*). Published in three volumes (as *Held in Bondage*, 1863), this novel had all the Ouida hallmarks: set in London high society, Cambridge, India and the Crimea, it is a tale of the mis-spent youths and military, sexual and marital adventures (including bigamy) of a pair of wealthy, athletic, public-school friends. This successful formula was repeated in *Strathmore* (1865), *Chandos* (1866) and *Under Two Flags* (1867), Ouida's best-known novel (later a Hollywood film), whose womanizing, gambling, aristocratic hero, fleeing disgrace at home, becomes a *chasseur d'Afrique*; he inspires the fierce devotion of the exotic, epicene, Cigarette, who sacrifices her life so that he survives to marry the mysterious Princess Corona (actually the aristocratic English sister of his best friend, who improbably turns up in the African desert). Ouida's forty-four novels also included sharp social satires of aristocratic mores, such as MOTHS (1880) and *The Massarenes* (1897). Her periodical articles on such subjects as the Boer's predicament, anti-vivisectionism, the NEW WOMAN, and female suffrage were reprinted in *Views and Opinions* (1895) and *Critical Studies* (1900).   LP

Our Nig (1859) The first novel written by an African-American woman, *Our Nig: Or, Sketches from the Life of a Free Black* was rediscovered in 1983 and remains one of the most important finds of the ongoing archival excavation of America's literary past. The few known facts about HARRIET WILSON suggest that *Our Nig* is an autobiographical tale, one which dissolves the already

porous boundary between fact and fiction. Inspired in large measure by the popular genres of slave narrative and sentimental fiction, it is the story of Frado, a young woman of mixed race who is born free and subsequently abandoned to the care of a Northern family that virtually enslaves her. Particularly resented by the women of the home, Frado is tortured and cruelly overworked before she rises up to claim her freedom. In an unusual final chapter, the author steps free of the tale to appeal directly for help from her readers. With its graphic depictions of Northern prejudice and indifference to the plight of free blacks, it is perhaps no wonder that *Our Nig* sank without a trace (there are no known reviews) upon its initial publication in Massachusetts. Its recovery has stimulated much contemporary scholarship.   LC

Our Sister Killjoy (1977) In AMA ATA AIDOO's first novel, a trip to Austria on a cultural programme enables the Ghanaian narrator to re-assess the relation between Europe and Africa – no longer based on the direct domination of colonial times, but on assimilation into global capitalism's cult of modernity and technological advance. The subtitle, 'Reflections of a Black-eyed Squint', points up the novel's marginal, resistant, female voice, which satirizes the betrayal of independence by a predominantly male neo-colonial elite, whose investment in Western images of consumption and status has alienated it from traditional family networks and communal values. The central relationship between the narrator and a Bavarian *hausfrau* – who compensates for the sterility of her own home life by an intense pursuit of her Ghanaian friend, plying her with plums – is a bitter parody of the colonial relation itself. Disrupting linear monologic narrative with rapid shifts of time and genre – prose, poetry, dialogue, epistle – the novel subverts hegemonic form with a more fluid mode, closer to the collective aesthetic of the African oral tradition.   WJB

Out of Africa (1937) ISAK DINESEN / Karen Blixen's loving and nostalgic account of her life on the coffee farm she had owned in Kenya, at the foot of the Ngong Hills, from 1913 until 1931, when she was forced to sell it and return to Denmark. Part of her yearning is for lost colonial status, freedom and power; part is an orientalist construction of Africa: 'The dhows of the traders knew all the African fairways, and trod the blue paths to the central marketplace of Zanzibar.' However, Blixen's in-between position makes her an astute observer of the British settlers, for instance the doctor who refused to treat Blixen's servants because 'he had, before now, practised to the elite of Bournemouth'. The unselfconscious racism of her use of animal imagery to describe Africans is juxtaposed against a fascination with difference, expressed in memorable sketches of such people as Farah, her Somali servant, and her joy in the landscape and seasons of the African highlands, their colours 'dry and burnt, like the colours in pottery'.

ASm

Ovbiagele, Helen 19??– Nigerian writer of popular fictions whose fast-moving plots combine romance and adventure to chart the impact of urban life on traditional family relationships and values. Born in Benin City, Nigeria, she attended the College of Education of the University of Lagos and the Institut du Royaume Uni in South Kensington, London. After periods of teaching and working for a motor company, she joined the staff of a Lagos newspaper. She has written several novels for the Macmillan Pacesetter series. Her third, *You Never Know* (1982), deals with a couple from the Lagos professional and business class, whose relationship is undermined by the seductive, hedonistic lifestyle offered by male and female peer groups. Hints of urban violence are developed in her fifth novel, *Who Really Cares* (1986), which depicts an underclass of petty criminals and semi-employed labourers in a picaresque tale of upward mobility that mirrors a competitive society with no place for loyalty or deep emotional attachment.   WJB

Over the Frontier (1938) STEVIE SMITH's second novel continues the soliloquy of her *alter ego*, Pompey Casmilus, transforming it into a meditation upon power and cruelty. Pompey's melancholy at her failed reunion with Freddy is expressed against a background of international menace. Whilst the droll humour and conversational tone initially recall NOVEL ON YELLOW PAPER (1936), the second half has a nightmarish quality, as the threat of imminent war permeates the quotidian and Pompey becomes engaged in espionage. In a chilling exploration of Smith's fear that the 'cruelty in the air now' arouses individuals to exchange 'death-in-life' for a dehumanized authority, Pompey abandons her sociable life, takes a uniform and – with a punning allusion to nightmare – rides on horseback through the night. Like THREE GUINEAS (1938), *Over the Frontier* is punctuated by images of uniforms and haunted by their power to 'harden . . . emotional arteries.' Smith fiercely resists allegiance to 'any groupismus whatever' but recognizes instead the ease with which uniforms can be donned, believing 'power and cruelty' to form the core of every life.   TY

Owens, Agnes 1926– Scottish writer notable for her bleak vision of life at the margins of contemporary Scottish society. She was born on the outskirts of Glasgow and has worked variously as a typist, a cleaner, a factory worker and a shop assistant. She began writing after joining a writing group.

Her fiction first appeared in the episodic novel *Gentlemen of the West* (1984), and then in *Lean Tales* (1985) where nine of her stories are sandwiched between the work of James Kelman and Alasdair Gray. Her second novel, *Like Birds in the Wilderness* (1987), features the same protagonist as the first: Mac, a young bricklayer, who comes to represent the archetypal feckless, drunken Scot. *A Working Mother* (1994) – a sharp novella of nasty surprises which is reminiscent of MURIEL SPARK's work from the early 1960s – marks a development in Owens's confidence.

Owens's vision is relentlessly bleak. Her characters endure lives without a shred of dignity. Often, they are outsiders who have difficulty articulating their needs, like the alcoholics and down-and-outs of *People Like That* (1996). The language she uses is aggressively non-literary. Her purpose is similar to that of fellow Glaswegian, James Kelman – to represent political and social marginalization on a massive scale in contemporary Scotland. By showing the monotony and futility of her characters' lives, she illuminates the indifference of the system which allows such injustice to continue. She refuses to compromise this grim vision by allowing her characters redemption of any kind.   JH

Owenson, Sydney (Lady Morgan) 1776–1859 Novelist, biographer, poet and travel writer whose birth, reputedly on-board ship, crossing the Irish Sea, symbolized her parentage (Irish father, English mother) and literary ambition to inveigle the English into understanding Irish politics. Her first ROMANCES, *St Clair* (1803) and *The Novice of St Dominick* (1805), were written while she was a governess, but *THE WILD IRISH GIRL* (1806) brought fame and popularity. Passionately espousing Irish nationalism and despite savage personal criticism, particularly in the Tory press, she continued to make explicit use of fiction for political ends in *O'Donnel* (1811), *Florence Macarthy* (1811), and *The O'Briens and the O'Flahertys* (1827) which advocated Irish emancipation.

Owenson travelled extensively with her husband, physician Sir Charles Morgan, and wrote books on France (1817) and Italy (1821) which Byron praised as 'fearless and excellent'. Works expressing her feminist views are *Ida of Athens* (1809) and *Woman and her Master* (1840). She also wrote an opera, poetry and adaptations of Irish songs (learnt backstage in her father's theatre). Charismatic and controversial, her salons attracted diverse literary figures, while she was the first woman to receive a pension for 'services to the world of letters'.   LMT

Owls Do Cry (1957) JANET FRAME's first novel, about the Withers family, is psychologically close to events in her early life. Set in provincial, pre-1940 New Zealand's South Island it concerns a close-knit family beset by tragedy and loss – the death of Daphne's sister; her brother, Toby's epilepsy. But the controlling theme is the loss of childhood and the inevitable entry into an adult world contaminated by 'false' values. The conflict is symbolized by the death of Francie on the verge of maturity, at the rubbish dump where the children search for treasure. Daphne's other sister, Chicks, marries and acquires pretensions to social status, while Daphne, becoming mad, is sent to a mental asylum where she receives shock treatment. Represented in italics her voice from 'the Dead Room' haunts the novel with its poetic insights. At one level an attack on middle-class New Zealand, the novel also affirms the marginal individual's creative potential. Frame's complex of emotions toward the social outcast – the deprived and the mute–is inextricable from her artistic subjectivity.   JMW

Oyster (1996) The opal-mining town of Outer Maroo, in Queensland's outback ('lawless, dangerous') provides the setting for JANETTE TURNER HOSPITAL's dystopian novel, a millennium tale of religious fanaticism inspired by the Waco massacre. The arrival of strangers (first Susannah Rover the schoolmistress, then Oyster the cult messiah, finally two parents searching for their 'kidnapped' children) precipitates a spiral of social collapse which ends in catastrophe and eventual freedom. The mysterious nature of desert landscapes, the search for lost children, the guilty silence of past secrets, the desire to escape to the real world (Maroo and Oyster's Reef are literally off the map), the patience of the Aboriginal inhabitants, all reveal a new POSTMODERN preoccupation with an old question, 'What is Australia?' Hospital's tried and tested formulae – the female 'detective' figure, the dangerous fascinations of sex, the literary intertextual references – find new expression in this, her most thoroughly researched modern 'fable': 'I didn't set out to write a book with a moral but I would like to think it can act as a warning'.   MRE

Ozick, Cynthia 1928– American novelist, essayist, literary critic, translator. Among her themes are the Jewish past, the tragedy and the burden of the Holocaust.

Educated at New York University, from which she graduated in 1949, and at Ohio State University, where she received a Master's degree in 1950, Ozick started her literary career in the fifties writing poetry, but soon devoted herself to fiction; at first under the influence of Henry James. Her intensive and extensive reading of the literature, history and philosophy of Judaism – her translations of Yiddish poetry appeared in a well-known anthology in 1969 – strongly influenced her writing: as she says 'I began as an American novelist and ended as a Jewish novelist.'

From her first novel, *Trust* (1966), in her short stories – collected in *The Pagan Rabbi and Other Stories* (1971) – in *Bloodshed and Three Novellas* (1976) and in *Levitation: Five Fictions* (1982), and in her later books, particularly her essays *Art and Ardor: Essays* and her novel THE CANNIBAL GALAXY, both published in 1983, she explores the tragedy of the Holocaust and its meaning in history in connection with the relationship, or, more often, the conflict, between nature and art, the holy and the pagan.

In her writings, she addresses a wide range of literary and political subjects, including gender-politics. In her story 'Virility', from *The Pagan Rabbi*, essay and tale typically interact in expressing the refusal of what Ozick calls 'The Ovarian Theory of Literature' – and, equally, of its complement, 'The Testicular Theory' – the idea of 'literature as physiology' which denies women creativity as it considers it opposed and irreconcilable to childbearing. 'It is insulting', she writes, 'to a poet to compare titanic and agonized strivings with the so-called "creativity" of childbearing, where-consciously-nothing happens.'

The theme of childbearing and motherhood often recurs in Ozick's writings, connected with the artistic process and creativity, and the treatment of female identity. She expresses what has been defined as 'classical feminism', i.e. 'feminism at its origins, when it saw itself as justice and aspiration made universal, as mankind widened to humankind'. Female characters in her novels and stories, particularly the unforgettable protagonists of *The Shawl* (1989) and Ruth Puttermesser in *Levitation* and *The Puttermesser Papers* (1997), are impressive, and it is through them that she endeavours to penetrate the multiple significations inhering in human experience. MB

P

Page, Gertrude 1873–1922 British writer and rancher. Born in Bedford, she married Captain Alexander Dobbin at the beginning of the century and left England for Rhodesia, where they bought a ranch and kept cattle. Her novels are notable for creating an entirely new genre, set in the Rhodesian bush, and they were bestsellers: they included *The Silent Rancher* (1909), *Love in the Wilderness*, *The Edge of Beyond*, *The Veldt Trail*, *Where the Strange Roads Go Down*, *Paddy-the Next-Best-Thing*, and *Jill's Rhodesian Philosophy* (1910).

There was a long pause in her writing during which she and her husband volunteered for war service in England during World War I. After the war they returned to Rhodesia, and in 1920 she wrote a partly autobiographical story, *Jill on a Ranch*, which was published as a serial in the *Quiver* during 1921. She had a deep love of Rhodesia and 'The Old Country' which was very apparent in her books: they give a lively and frequently humorous picture of a hard, often dangerous life. She died a wealthy woman in her beloved Rhodesia, at the age of 49.   MEW

Paget, Violet see LEE, VERNON

Paisley, Mary [Neale] 1717–57 Irish Quaker minister and religious writer. Born near Mountrath in County Laois, Mary was the daughter of poor cottagers, and was brought up as a member of the Society of Friends. For many years, she records, she lived 'in disobedience' but following a riding accident resolved to devote herself to a life of spirituality. In 1744 she became a minister, her decision to do so coinciding with 'unexpected domestic trials, which brought her very low in mind, from a sense of the singularity of her situation'. Despite this, and 'much bodily weakness and indisposition', she embarked on a preaching career, first in Ireland, and later in England and America.

In 1754 Paisley wrote a letter to Virginia Quakers which expressed dismay 'on account of the state of the Church in your colony'. In an account of her American tour, she noted that 'one thing which friends here . . . were in the practice of, gave us considerable pain, and we apprehended was the cause of truths not prospering amongst them . . . that is, buying and keeping of slaves, which we could not reconcile with the golden rule of doing unto all men as we would they should do unto us'.

In 1756 Paisley returned from America and in the following year married Samuel Neale, whom she had converted seven years previously. On the evening of her wedding she preached 'clear and sweet' and with 'the usual zeal', but two days later she was taken violently ill, and died within a short time. *Some Account of the Life and Religious Exercises of Mary Neale . . . principally compiled from her own writings*, edited by her widower, appeared in 1795.   RR

Pale Horse, Pale Rider (1939) KATHERINE ANNE PORTER's fine collection brought together 'Old Mortality', 'Noon Wine' and the title story. 'Noon Wine' is a simply told, but highly enigmatic, quasi-murder story, involving three men and a woman on a small Texas farm. The others, two self-contained narratives of rites of passage, feature 'Miranda', a semi-autobiographical figure who appears in stories elsewhere. The first follows her entanglement in family histories, myths and memories from 1885 to 1912, leaving her at 18, trying to find her own path out of the labyrinth. The second takes place at the start of World War I, refracting Miranda's career as a newspaper woman, and her romance with Adam, through hallucinatory episodes during the devastating epidemic of Spanish flu. In both stories, Porter's narrative shifts and surprises, and startling images, question conventional women's plots and cultural ideals of femininity, and vividly represent the structures that trap her heroine and confuse her sense of self.   PEK

Paley [née Goodside], Grace 1922– Poet, essayist – and one of the great American story-tellers. The daughter of Russian immigrants, she was raised in the vibrant multi-lingual Jewish community of the Bronx, which she richly evoked in the stories in her first collection, *THE LITTLE DISTURBANCES OF MAN: STORIES OF MEN AND WOMEN AT LOVE* (1959). ('They debated a little in Yiddish, then fell in a puddle of Russian and Polish', is a description of two arguing fathers from that book.) She wrote poetry before turning to stories, and while a love of talk is the hallmark of her work, a poet's feel for rhythm shapes her prose. Philip Roth praised the collection's 'deep feelings and wild imagination', and it had an unprecedented republication in hardback in 1968. By this time she had divorced her first husband, with whom she had two children. She remarried in 1972.

Politics has been central to her life and work, in her belief inseparable from it: 'Art makes justice in the world.' A self-described 'combative pacifist and cooperative anarchist', her committed opposition to war took her to Vietnam, to Moscow, and to jail, briefly. The stories of ENORMOUS CHANGES AT THE LAST MINUTE (1974) are full of activist mothers and 'revolutionists' and in their frank, comic explorations of the dilemmas and despairs of women, are a testament to her committed feminism. Her *365 Reasons Not to Have Another War* was published in 1989.

She never wrote a novel because 'Art is too long and life is too short.' But *Enormous Changes*, while broadening her range of voices, features several recurrent characters including her *alter ego*, the wise-cracking, resilient Faith. 'A Conversation with My Father' is simultaneously a poignant testament to her father's humane intelligence and a portrayal of their aesthetic differences – he wants from her well-crafted works like Chekhov's, while she explains her contempt for plot: 'It takes all hope away. Everyone, real or invented, deserves the open destiny of life.' By *Later the Same Day* (1985) she was drawing occasional criticism for the open-endedness of her work: some pieces are fragments, some in her words 'are just like arguments and discussions'. Though she never received a college degree, she taught writing at colleges in and around New York, where she continues to make a home (as well as in Vermont). *Begin Again: New and Collected Poems* was published in 1991; essays, *Long Walks and Intimate Talks*, the same year. Her stories were collected in one volume in 1994. A. S. BYATT has written of her 'cocky, deployed intelligence, the civilized wit, juxtaposed with the neatly located grotesque'; and in the busy arena of American storywriters, her unique voice – warm, wry, odd, loud – continues to rise above the crowd.   SB

Palmer [née Higgins], Nettie 1885–1964 Australian critic, autobiographer, poet.

Palmer was born in Bendigo, Victoria and educated at the University of Melbourne and in Europe where she travelled and studied modern languages. Following her marriage to Vance Palmer in 1914 she returned to Victoria, writing for the *Argus*. As a couple, the Palmers publicly promoted their shared interests in socialism, anti-Facism, national Australian culture and European literature. Two major publications – *Modern Australian Literature 1900-1923* (1924) and her (edited) *An Australian Story Book* (1928) – created fresh standards of criticism and a new Australian literary canon. Her widespread correspondence with female writers, including MILES FRANKLIN, ELEANOR DARK, HENRY HANDEL RICHARDSON, MARY GILMORE and KATHARINE SUSANNAH PRICHARD, placed her at the centre of an expanding literary network, what MARJORIE BARNARD called 'the first literary club'. As well as being an enthusiastic and pro-Australian literary diplomat, Palmer contributed to a wide range of journals and newspaper columns, including *All About Books* and the *Illustrated Tasmanian Mail*. It has been said that 'no important English and American writer and certainly no significant Australian writer between 1927 and 1933 failed to get a mention in her columns'. Palmer's critical biography *Henry Handel Richardson: A Study* (1950) – based on a 25-year friendship – served to popularize her work. Her other biographies include *Henry Bourne Higgins: A Memoir* (1931) and *Bernard O'Dowd* (1954). Whilst her poetry remains largely forgotten – *In the South Wind* (1914), *Shadowy Paths* (1915) – her *Fourteen Years, Extracts from a Private Journal 1925-1939* (1948) reflects her pioneering contribution to Australian literature.   MRE

Paradise

(1997) 'Paradise' in TONI MORRISON's seventh novel is Ruby, Oklahoma, and we see it being built from scratch by blacks whose ancestors were enslaved by whites and then rebuffed by light-skinned blacks. Ruby would actualize the wish of these blacks for freedom, home and happiness. The Founding Fathers of Ruby come to define this heaven on earth by the absence of the 'unsaved', the 'unworthy' and the 'strange'. The threat to paradise thus defined is located seventeen miles north in a house full of women who have no need for men or God, the Father. The chilling instances of abuse they have escaped from rival anybody's in Ruby; but, in the house (built by an embezzler) that used to be a School for Native Girls, these women have found 'the most peaceful place on earth' to create and celebrate templates of their undiminished selves. Here too is paradise. The planned massacre of these women, deemed strange, unworthy, and unsaved by the Fathers of Ruby is the action that begins and ends this novel.   KO

Paretsky, Sara 1947–

Chicago-based writer of DETECTIVE FICTION featuring female private investigator V.I. Warshawski. Born in Ames, Iowa, into a middle-class family, Paretsky moved to Chicago in the late 1960s, earning both a Ph.D. in History and an MBA from the University of Chicago (1977). While working as an insurance executive, Paretsky began writing detective fiction, with her début novel, *Indemnity Only*, appearing in 1982. In 1985, Paretsky left the corporate world to pursue writing full-time.

Indemnity Only was the first of ten works featuring hard-boiled, tough-gal protagonist V.I. Warshawski, including *Deadlock* (1984), *Killing Orders* (1985), *Bitter*

Medicine (1987), *Guardian Angel* (1992) and *V.I. For Short* (1995). Warshawski, half-Polish and half-Italian, is a street-smart, sexually independent, ruthlessly rational heroine who specializes in cases involving white-collar and organized crime: insurance fraud, medical malpractice, industrial poisoning and pension scams. Triumphing in the name of individual – frequently women's – rights against corrupt institutional power, Warshawski champions the weak against the abuses of big business or the state. Like her protagonist, Paretsky sees herself as 'trying to make a success in a field traditionally dominated by men'. In 1986, she founded 'Sisters in Crime', a group devoted to advancing the careers of women mystery-writers and to counteracting the ever-worsening image of women in detective fiction. To this end, she has also edited two collections of short fiction by female detective writers, *A Woman's Eye* (1991), and the more recent, international anthology, *Women on the Case* (1996).   JGr

Park, Ruth 1923– One of Australia's best-loved and most versatile writers, she was born in Auckland, New Zealand. After travelling around rural Australia with her husband, D'Arcy Niland, she settled in Surry Hills in Sydney in 1943, providing the location for her first novel. *The Harp in the South* (1948) concerns the Darcy family's attempts to overcome poverty and tragedy. That novel was followed by the sequel, *Poor Man's Orange* (1949), and the prequel, *Missus* (1985). In addition to her novels for adults and young adults, such as *The Witch's Thorn* (1951), *A Power of Roses* (1953) and *Come Danger, Come Darkness* (1978), Park has written a number of picture-books (many illustrated by her twin daughters, Deborah and Kilmeny Niland) and a series of books for young children about the Muddle-Headed Wombat. She is also an accomplished scriptwriter and has written between 30 and 40 adult plays and 5,000 children's scripts.

Ruth Park was awarded the Miles Franklin Award for her adult novel *Swords and Crowns and Rings* in 1977, and the Children's Book of the Year Award for *Playing Beatie Bow* in 1981. That novel – in which the protagonist, Abigail Kirk, slips between modern Sydney and the Sydney of the 19th century – has been made into a film. The televised treatments of the 'Harp in the South' trilogy have also served to cement Park's popularity. In 1987 Ruth Park was awarded a Medal of Australia for services to Australian Literature.   SS

Parker [née Rothschild], Dorothy 1893–1967 American poet, story writer and critic, in danger of being remembered chiefly for her prodigious gift for one-liners. Born in New Jersey, she married stockbroker Edwin Pond Parker II and happily traded her Jewish surname for his, which she kept in spite of their early divorce.

She achieved journalistic success quickly, writing copy for *Vogue* in the 1910s ('Brevity is the soul of lingerie'), then razor-sharp reviews for *Vanity Fair* and later the *New Yorker* (see HERE LIES, 1939). While notorious for her quotable putdowns she could also be a sensitive and discerning critic. In 1926 she published ENOUGH ROPE, a volume of the bitter pills of poems that became her trademark – it was a surprise bestseller, and became required reading among a smart set that thrilled to her work's brittle frankness and acid humour, qualities shared by her masterful monologues and short stories. Edmund Wilson praised her for having 'the wit of her particular time and place'. She published several other volumes of verse and stories, which she eventually collected in 1944.

With her second husband, actor and writer Alan Campbell, she went to Hollywood in the 1930s to write scripts. In spite of many Hollywood years – during which she befriended LILLIAN HELLMAN and became active on the Left – she will always be associated with New York, specifically the Algonquin Hotel. The Round Table, a group of writers that included her good friends Robert Benchley and Robert Sherwood, lunched there in the 1910s and 1920s and became synonymous with a hard-drinking, wise-cracking urbanity; they were the subject of Alan Rudolph's 1994 film *Mrs Parker and the Vicious Circle*. In later years she would deprecate the group as a 'not especially brave little band that hid its nakedness of heart and mind under the out-of-date garment of a sense of humour'. In 1952 she co-wrote a play, *The Ladies of the Corridor*; she was proud of it, but it was not a success. 'People ought to be one of two things', she once wrote, 'young or dead', but in spite of several suicide attempts in early life she was 73 when she died in New York, still associated above all with the brusque-talking speakeasy 1920s she'd so raucously lived and written.   SB

Parkes, Bessie Rayner 1829–1925 Mid-Victorian feminist activist and writer. The daughter of Joseph Parkes and Elizabeth Priestley (granddaughter of Joseph Priestley), Parkes grew up in the heart of English radicalism. In 1854 Parkes published *Remarks on the Education of Girls*, a protest against the restrictions of women's education. Two years later, Parkes was one of 26,000 women to sign a petition which resulted in the introduction of the Married Woman's Property bill in Parliament. In 1858 Parkes took over the *English Woman's Journal* with her friend BARBARA Leigh Smith (later BODICHON). The revamped *Journal* focused on women's work, and soon Langham Place, site of the *Journal*'s offices, had attracted a number of young women inspired by Parkes and Bodichon. Before long the *Journal* had spawned a women's employment bureau, reading room and clerical school, as well as the Victoria Press.

In 1864 Parkes converted to Catholicism, and in 1867 she married Louis Belloc, son of a French painter, and had two children, Marie, and Hilaire, who went on to become a well-known writer. In the years following her religious conversion and her marriage, Bessie Parkes Belloc retired from active involvement in the Women's movement.   EC

Parr, Katherine, later Borough, Neville, Queen (Tudor), Seymour 1512–48 Writer of conventional courtly poetry but best known as sixth wife of Henry VIII. Parr had been raised at court and was an intimate friend of Princess Mary. Both were educated by the Spanish humanist scholar Juan Luis Vives. Her first marriage, aged 12, to an elderly widower, Lord Borough, lasted only three years before his death. Her second husband, John Neville, Lord Latimer, was involved in a rebellion against the English Reformation and Katherine was forced to plead with Henry VIII for his life. Latimer died in 1542, the same year that Henry executed his fifth wife Katherine Howard. Katherine's poetry is written in the courtly language of French and seems mostly to derive from her youth, a common feature of courtly women's literary productions and no doubt connected with the demands of their education.   JS

Parry, Lorae 1955– New Zealand lesbian playwright. Parry was born in working-class Sydney and came to New Zealand for the first time at the age of 15. She trained at Toi Whakaari – the New Zealand Drama School – and then spent time in Europe, performing with other New Zealanders in London and at the Edinburgh Festival. She is best known for *Frontwomen* (1988), a lesbian coming-out story about a TV presenter and a suburban school-teacher and the first text to be published (1993) by The Women's Play Press, which Parry co-founded. While *Frontwomen* is REALIST in style, Parry's earliest writing for the theatre, *Strip*, initially performed in London and rewritten for New Zealand in 1982, offers the metatheatricality of a text that doubles from backstage to downstage in a strip-joint setting. *Cracks* (1994) also uses a non-realist dramatic style, including a convict-pirate ancestress. Parry's most significant and sophisticated play to date is *Eugenia* (1996), with a basis in Australasian history, about an Italian woman migrant who cross-dressed successfully and married a wife in the 1910s, a play with a double time-frame set (as well) in a high school where it deals with present-day lesbian and feminist issues. Parry is actor, director and theatre entrepreneur as well as playwright, held the Victoria University of Wellington's Writing Fellowship in 1998 and continues to create dramatic works that unite writerliness and theatricality.   JD

Passing (1929) NELLA LARSEN's challenging exploration of racial passing articulated through the consciousness of the central protagonist, Irene Redfield. The novel juxtaposes Clare Kendry – seductive and dangerous, living a duplicitous life hiding her black ancestry – to the light-skinned black Irene, self-sacrificing wife, mother and hostess. Clare, taunted by her racist husband (although he is unaware of her actual heredity), turns to the community and familiarity of Irene's middle-class life in Harlem with tragic results. Larsen's use of a stream-of-consciousness technique places this novel alongside the experimentalism of major MODERNIST writers, and her evocation of feminine psychology parallels that of VIRGINIA WOOLF's writing. *Passing* also offers a sublimated evocation of a feminine erotic – the desire of one woman for another – which connects Larsen to later writers such as ALICE WALKER and NTOZAKE SHANGE. Irene finds a self-reflective fulfilment in the contraries of her psychological double, which is ultimately betrayed by Clare's involvement with Irene's husband. The narrative culminates in Irene's violent rejection of her transgressive Other and the disruptive desire she embodies.   AG

Passionate Heart, The (1918) MARY GILMORE's second collection of poetry opened with a number of elegies for the dead of World War I, including the extended and rhapsodic 'These Fellowing Men' and the brief, poignant 'Gallipoli', demonstrative of competing formal impulses in Gilmore's work. These poems celebrate the courage of the Australian soldier, lament the wasteful shedding of young blood, and seek consolation in the continuing vitality of nature, while her more politicized anti-war poems, published mainly in the *Worker* on the Women's Page of which she was editor, are omitted, perhaps in deference to the very recent ending of the war. The *Worker* tradition is present, however, in her ballad-style depictions, indignant or comic and affectionate, of the life of the urban poor or of the rural pioneers. The love poems generally affirm both passion and commitment, but recent feminist readers have responded more strongly to poems (such as 'Eve-Song' or 'The Woman') with a perceptible undertow of disillusionment about women's experience of love and marriage.   JStr

Paston, Margaret *c.*1421–2 – 1484 The heiress Margaret Mautby made herself known to posterity when in 1440 she married into the letter-writing Paston family of Norfolk. More than 100 of Margaret's letters, all dictated, survive, along with her will and a few business documents. The letters show her managing estates, ordering cloth and spices from relatives in London and discussing local and national politics insofar as they affect the Paston interests. She was no

mere housewife: her duties as a Paston wife on one occasion included defending a besieged manor in person. Personal matters tended to be relegated to post-scripts, except in times of crisis, such as the discovery of her daughter's secret marriage to the family steward, of which Margaret wrote, 'remember . . . we have lost of her but a brethele, and set it the less to heart'.

Her style was plain and precise, especially when dealing with financial matters. When she recounted dramatic events, such as an attack on her chaplain or her daughter's rebellion, indignation gave a vivid immediacy to her narrative. She was capable of pithy or proverbial phrases, dismissing a timeserving opponent as 'a flickering fellow'. The hierarchy of her personal relationships is apparent in her modes of address: her children are (usually) offered her blessing, but John Paston I is always 'my right worshipful husband'.   MSALS

Pastors and Masters (1925) IVY COMPTON-BURNETT considered this wickedly funny satire to be her first novel (she rejected *Delores* as a 'piece of juvenilia'), and it can be regarded as one of the first 'campus novels', a genre popularized by later novelists such as Kingsley Amis and David Lodge. The plot concerns Nicholas Herrick and his sister Emily, the *fainéant* owners of a boys' preparatory school, whose cultured leisure is maintained at the expense of the couple who actually run the establishment, the overworked and singularly underqualified Mr and Mrs Merry. The other two masters are Richard Bumpus and William Masson, dons at the local university. All are gossips and given to fervent speculation about one another's private lives, when not amusing themselves with discussions of equality for women and the changing nature of God or plotting to pass off other people's work as their own. Injustices are never revealed, and the novel's wry attitude toward the mingled thread of human nature is summed up by Emily, the philosopher of the status quo: 'good' is merely 'bad condensed'.   LCo

Patchwork Screen for the Ladies, A (1723) JANE BARKER's series of narratives contributed to the development of the novel in the 18th century, and provides a telling comment on how women justify their writing. Ostensibly a novel of decorum which instructs 'the ladies' to ignore the 'high' world of politics, religion and art for a domestic world, Barker encourages women to reject 'pernicious' embroidery in favour of patch-work, which allows readers to preserve their 'Posterity' by congregating and piecing together the 'patches' of their lives. These 'patches' correspond to words, so that when Galesia is asked to contribute to the making of a screen, she finds 'Pieces of *Romances, Poems, Love-Letters*, and the like' in her work basket, instead of the usual silks and brocades. These, however, are acceptable to the other ladies, and the screen thus becomes a metaphor for women's ability to construct experience through writing. *A Patchwork Screen* was followed up in 1726 by a sequel, *The Lining of the Patch-Work Screen*.   RDM

Patriarchal Attitudes: Women in Society (1970) EVA FIGES's witty tract on patriarchy's construction of woman remains a classic feminist text. Conceived (in the spirit of Havelock Ellis) as an exercise to clear away the 'undergrowth of prepossession and superstition' informing man-made images of women, *Patriarchal Attitudes* reveals the ideology of subjugation at work in a tradition stretching from the Old Testament to Freud, via the standard-bearers of capitalism, romanticism and idealism. In line with second-wave feminist thinking, Figes constantly seeks to demonstrate that women's oppression is social in origin and, therefore, amenable to change. As a German Jew intensely aware of the Holocaust, some of her most powerful insights occur in her critique of German idealist philosophy, most notably the conflation of misogynist and racist imagery in the work of Otto Weininger. Less loud and militant than GERMAINE GREER in *The Female Eunuch* (1970) – a product of the same moment – Figes aligns herself with the 'better feminine minds' of history, attempting to undo gender stereotypes which are, she argues, just as damaging for men as they are for women.   MO'D

Patrick, F.C. fl. 1797–9 Novelist and biographer. Patrick's background is obscure, but she is said to have been the wife of an officer. She was clearly a critic of British policy in Ireland, and a defender of the interests of Irish Catholics at a time when they were still subject to legal and social discrimination.

Patrick was the author of three novels, all of them published by the Minerva Press. *The Irish Heiress* (1797) is a first-person account of the Catholic daughter of an Irish squire and English mother. The spirited heroine lives through the Revolutionary Terror in Paris, an attempt at seduction, imprisonment and escape, and her husband's murder, surviving all her trials to become an improving proprietor of her Irish estates. The author's political stance is evident in her contemptuous and hostile depiction of the English in Ireland.

More Ghosts! (1798) is a burlesque, which in its treatment of military families probably reflects Patrick's own experience, and *The Jesuit, or The History of Anthony Babington Esquire* (1799) is a biography of the 16th-century Catholic martyr.   RR

Patronage (1814) This ambitious novel by MARIA EDGEWORTH explores the evils of both financial and sexual patronage. The plot revolves around two families, the Percys and the Falconers whose destinies reflect and contrast with each other. Whilst Mr Percy's

sons succeed by their own merit and prosper in medicine, the law and the army, the Falconers are initially successfully promoted into the army, the church and diplomatic service. However, since they depend solely on devious personal connections and the favours of the great, the Falconers ultimately fail in the world. The novel also criticizes the conventions and degradations of the marriage market and advances the single life for women. Edgeworth's inspiration lay in a similar story, 'The Freeman Family', which her father created. *Patronage* clearly tells a moralistic tale. However, it is also a humorous comedy of manners which portrays the workings of intrigue and ambition in contemporary society. NBP

Peabody, Elizabeth Palmer 1804–94 American educator. Born near Boston, Elizabeth had an extraordinary career. As a teenager, she taught in her mother's private school. In 1822, she opened her own school and was tutored in Greek by Emerson. When her school failed, she became secretary to William Ellery Channing, and in 1834 taught for two years with the brilliant but difficult Bronson Alcott. Although she did not marry, Peabody introduced her sister Sophia to her future husband Nathaniel Hawthorne. In 1839, she opened a bookstore in Boston, which became the central meeting place for liberal clergymen, Harvard professors, and writers and thinkers in the Transcendentalist movement. MARGARET FULLER held her conversations there, plans for Brook Farm were made there, and the *Dial* was printed there. In 1860 Peabody established the first kindergarten in the United States. Although not known for her writing style, she wrote several books about her educational experiences, including *A Record of a School* (1835) and *Lectures in the Training Schools for Kindergartens* (1888). She was considered an inspired educational reformer as well as an accomplished speaker, and she lectured at Alcott's School of Philosophy from 1879 to 1884. Henry James is said to have modelled Miss Birdseye in *The Bostonians* (1886) after her. SP

Pea-Pickers, The (1942) EVE LANGLEY's first published novel, based on the author's own youth, details the picaresque adventures of two young Australian women. Adopting male names and dress, narrator Steve – a poet – and her sister, Blue, travel throughout rural Victoria and New South Wales as itinerant workers, picking peas and beans, and packing apples. Embracing an attitude as much as a disguise, the women crave mobility more than masculinity, wanting to see some of their beloved country before settling down to marriage and domesticity – described by Steve as 'the sexual mould from which I had fled, but which I secretly desired with all its concomitants, love, marriage and children'. Yet the highly emotional Steve is at war with herself. Her longing to fulfil the strictures of womanhood conflicts with her avowed desire to be a man. Her bodily desires are countered with her yearning for a pure, virginal romance. *The Pea-Pickers* ends with Blue returning home to Melbourne to marry, while Steve resolves to remain alone on the land, determined to wait forever for ideal love. AL

Pearce, Philippa (Ann) 1920– British CHILDREN'S NOVELIST, daughter of a flour miller and corn merchant, she was educated at Perse Girls' School and Girton College, Cambridge, and worked as a civil servant, scriptwriter, producer and publisher's editor up to 1967. Three of her books use the idyllic setting of her riverside childhood home in a Cambridge village: *Minnow on the Say* about two boys' adventures with a canoe, *A Dog So Small* about the intensity and dangers of desire and *Tom's Midnight Garden* (1958, Carnegie Medal) in which a lonely boy makes friends with a Victorian girl in a wholly believable night-time landscape that no longer exists by day. The themes of friendship and loneliness are strongly developed, with a satisfying *dénouement* to the plot, but the novel is also remarkable for its evocation of the world Tom and Hattie inhabit, and the description of their skating on the frozen river to Ely is unforgettable. Pearce's writing is generally marked by acute psychological perception and sensitive but robust handling of important and delicate issues and the strong feelings these provoke. Other novels include *The Elm Street Lot* (1969), *The Battle of Bubble and Squeak* (1978, Whitbread Award) and *The Way to Sattin Shore* (1983). SAS

Pencarrow (1932) The first of NELLIE SCANLAN's sequence of historical novels about Wellington, New Zealand, the others being *Tides of Youth* (1933), *Winds of Heaven* (1934) and *Kelly Pencarrow* (1939). The book begins with the arrival of Matthew and Bessie Pencarrow in the new settlement in the 1840s. Attention quickly moves to the next generation, Michael, Hester, Kitty, and especially Miles who becomes a lawyer. The relationship and interdependence between the land and the emerging culture of the city is one of the novel's themes: 'Town life's all right for those that have money to spend', says Matthew, 'But the country's the place to make it.' However, the main focus is relentlessly domestic. The historical and local setting is only superficially rendered, and while the sequence progresses to take in World War I, the Depression and the social changes of the 1930s, its characters – especially Miles and his wife, Norah, and their grandchildren, Kelly and Genevieve – are the primary concern. This gives the books a conservative and somewhat escapist tone, which no doubt contributed to their huge readership in Depression New Zealand. JSt

Penn, Hannah 1671–1726 British letter-writer, who was born in Bristol to a Quaker family where she was taught accounting, business and merchandizing. Eventually she married William Penn, the recently widowed Proprietor of Pennsylvania in 1696. Three years later, she moved with him to America, but returned in 1701 after problems which resulted in her husband being unfairly imprisoned for debt. Made executrix of her husband's affairs, Penn continued a lengthy correspondence with the councilmen in Philadelphia; although her letters remain uncollected, those that have been published reveal the extent to which she helped to govern the Province and her refusal to surrender it to the Crown. After her husband died in 1718, she successfully won a legal battle against his son, and continued to look after the Province. Her descendants continued in this role until the Revolution.   RDM

Pennington, Elizabeth 1734–59 English poet and member of Samuel Richardson's literary circle. During her short life she wrote a number of poems which were widely anthologized. Her most famous piece is *The Copper Farthing* which appeared in the 1763 *Poetical Calendar*. In the style of earlier works, such as John Phillips's *Splendid Shilling*, Pennington's poem celebrates the ease and carelessness of youth:

> Happy the boy, who dwells remote from school,
> Whose pocket or whose rattling box contains
> The copper farthing!

Her other works include *Ode to Morning* and *Ode To a Thrush*, both of which continued to appear in collections of occasional verse through the early 19th century. The close friend of FRANCES SHERIDAN, Pennington receives a mention in John Duncombe's poetic catalogue of Britain's eminent and learned women, *The Feminiad* (1754).   KD

Pennington, Lady Sarah fl. *c*.1746–83 British author of a widely read conduct book. Pennington received no formal education, married Sir Joseph Pennington around 1746 and lived in Yorkshire. Twelve years later, after a series of private disagreements which rapidly escalated into a public scandal, they separated. Pennington moved to Bath, leaving her children with their father and it was there that she wrote *An Unfortunate Mother's Advice to her Absent Daughters; in a Letter to Miss Pennington* (1761). In this hugely popular work, Pennington integrated a public defence of her own virtue into the traditional conduct-book account of feminine propriety. This exercise in self-vindication was largely successful. Unlike other 18th-century women whose accounts of marital discord and private unhappiness made them the subject of public censure (CHARLOTTE SMITH, for example), Pennington's

book rapidly made her the focus of sympathetic and even eulogistic attention. *An Unfortunate Mother's Advice* was widely read, often reprinted and continued to appear in educational anthologies throughout the 19th century. Pennington also wrote *Letters on Different Subjects . . .* (1766), which included a piece of EPISTOLARY FICTION, and *The Child's Conductor* (1777).   KD

Perera [née Hejmadi], Padma 1939– Indian citizen, US resident, short-story writer and photographer. Born in Madras, educated there and in Delhi, she began writing while still a student. Perera's first collection of short stories, *Coigns of Vantage* (1972), was quickly followed by regular publication in the *New Yorker*, and marked her (along with Ved Mehta, KAMALA MARKANDEYA and others) as a highly accomplished exponent of what used to be called 'Indo-Anglian' writing. *Dr Salaam and Other Stories of India* (1978) and *Birthday, Deathday* (1985, 1992) established her as a writer who excelled in interpreting her culture with rare sensitivity. A profound and passionate belief in the underlying kinship of all peoples informs both her fiction and her photography, and is highlighted in *Sumi Spaces* (1998) and *Views From a Portable Tradition* (1999). Living and working in the US for over a quarter-century, married first to a Guatemalan, now to a North American, Perera's writing demonstrates an acute awareness of the interleaving of cultures and the relationship between fiction and social history; and these are features that characterize her own situation as a writer, as well.   RM

Perkins, Emily 1970– Born in Christchurch, studied at New Zealand Drama School before attending Bill Manhire's acclaimed Creative Writing Course at Victoria University of Wellington. Her short stories, *Not her Real Name* (1996), set mainly in Wellington, were published to wide and international acclaim. Striking the chord of the present 'Generation X', they recycle many 1960s delinquencies with a POSTMODERN fracture. Set mainly in Wellington they're a far cry from Maurice Shadbolt's similar début, *The New Zealanders* (1959), which put his generation on the map. Perkins's fascination is with the alternating panic, boredom and helplessness (no job, flat, friends, lovers) of her characters who, whether indolent or distressed, are searching desperately for identity. The title story is about the excruciating self-consciousness of falling in love and trying to keep cool. Cody meets Francis in a restaurant. Thrown together again by chance, the agonies of enforced intimacy become farcical: 'Bummer says Francis. – Bummer? Look at this. Bummer? It's fucked. It's soaked . . . My bed – he goes to his bed and wrings out a corner of the sheet, – my bed is fucking soaking. Where am I going to sleep?' Other melodramas expose characters grappling with what they consider intolerable adult good-will, seemingly talking themselves into hangups; the guy who drops out of drama class and becomes obsessed with a stranger; the unemployed anorexic, who makes it to the dole office naked with the door bell round her neck. Risk-taking, despairing, they gesture idealistically, even self-destructively, at society's rituals in their bid to get a life at any cost.   JMW

Persuasion (1818) Published posthumously and written when JANE AUSTEN was in failing health, this novel recounts, in a graver mood than previously, the fulfilment of a love-affair. Exploiting the convention of the obstacles in love's crooked path, the eventual reunion of Anne Eliot and Captain Wentworth occurs only after the bloom of youth has faded, their initial parting the result of well-intentioned advice. The novel stands on a significant cultural threshold in its treatment of marriage: to marry for money, or to marry for love; a conflict, in short, between Enlightenment sense and Romantic SENSIBILITY. Resolution is finally attained between the two, for romantic love is now legitimized by Wentworth's material success, and he has no longer 'nothing but himself to recommend him'. Gentility of origin is shown to be a fake front, by the impecunious Sir Walter's misplaced snobbery, and the ethic of self-improvement is endorsed in its place. Alongside this readjustment is proposed another, as Anne remarks, 'Men have had every advantage of us in telling their own story . . . the pen has been in their hands'.   MM

Petry, Ann 1908/11– Born into relative poverty in one of the few African-American families in Old Saybrook, Connecticut, Petry studied Pharmacy, received her degree in 1931, and worked in the family drugstore. She married in 1938, moved to New York and combined newspaper-reporting for the Harlem paper, the *People's Voice*, with social agency work in slum areas, then studied creative writing at Columbia University (1946), out of which mixed experience came her first stories, published in *Crisis* and *Phylon*, including 'Like a Winding Sheet' (1945) and her famous novel, the first by a black woman to sell over a million copies, *The Street* (1946), followed by *Country Place* (1947). Her other work concentrates on the lives of poor urban black women – such as *The Drugstore* (1949), *The Drugstore Cat* (1949), *The Narrows* (1954) and *Miss Muriel and Other Stories* (1971) – or on recuperating important women in black history, such as *Harriet Tubman, Conductor on the Underground Railroad* (1955).

Gritty in its historical REALISM, Petry's work testifies to the struggles of black women's lives. *The Street* looks at the harsh realities of urban African-American women's lives by concentrating on how Lutie Johnson survives in Harlem with her young son, although crippled, exploited and driven to murder by her experiences of racism and misogyny. Lutie circles round the street, hot – 'the dark passages were like ovens' – in summer, with its bar, the 'Junto', offering the lure of muted lights, music and companionship (and danger) from 'sleek, well dressed men who earned their living as tipsters', pimps and hustlers. Petry lectured at Berkeley, Miami and Suffolk Universities, and was Visiting Professor at Hawaii University.   GW

Pfeiffer [née Davis], Emily (Jane) 1827–90 British poet and writer on women's issues, grew up in a family troubled by financial problems. She did not receive a formal education but she was encouraged to write from an early stage. In 1853 she married J.E. Pfeiffer, a German businessman working in London. Her first significant publication was *Valisneria* (1857), a prose tale, followed by the poem *Margaret: Or, The Motherless* (1861). For some years afterwards, she devoted herself to making up lost ground in her education. In 1873, however, she published *Gerard's Monument and Other Poems*, the title work of which is a long, melancholy narrative poem based on a Sussex legend. Other pieces express a generally gloomy outlook: the last presents Love contemplating the dismal state of human life and anticipating a time when 'the weird world [is] wreck'd upon the sun'. Many other volumes followed, including *Poems* (1876); *Glan-Alarch: His Silence and Song* (1877), a substantial narrative poem in which Pfeiffer tried, she said, 'to penetrate beneath the veil of chivalry . . . to the homelier life which it in part conceals from us'; *Quarterman's Grace and Other Poems* (1879); and *Sonnets and Songs* (1880), of which the *Sunday Times* said 'These sonnets are poetic gems of which any writer might be proud.' The death of Pfeiffer's husband in 1889 prompted the publication of the 'sad-coloured rhymes' of *Flowers of the Night* (1889), expressing her grief but concluding with a measure of acceptance in 'A Hymn of Praise to Death' in which Death is addressed as the 'Angel of change and of progress, Angel of peace,/Who bringest God's order in time for the soul's release'. In prose, Pfeiffer wrote *Women and Work* (1888), defending the 'enlarged sphere of action' of the modern woman, and the largely descriptive travel book, *Flying Leaves from East and West* (1885).   FJO'G

Phelps (Ward), Elizabeth Stuart 1844–1911 Popular fiction writer of late 19th-century USA, whose lifelong credo was 'art for truth's sake'. Born in Boston, Massachusetts, to ELIZABETH STUART PHELPS and Austin Phelps (eventual president of Andover Theological Seminary), christened Mary Gray, at 8 years of age she adopted her mother's name, upon the latter's death. She helped raise two brothers and two stepbrothers. She was educated at Mrs Edwards' School for Young Ladies in Andover from 1860, when she was inspired by ELIZABETH BARRETT BROWNING's verse novel about a woman poet, *AURORA LEIGH* (1857). Her first critically noticed work, 'The Tenth of January' (*Atlantic Monthly*, 1868), concerns a mill disaster. Her career was established by *The Gates Ajar* (1868), utopian fiction, offering not theological explanation but empathic consolation for life's losses, as did *Beyond the Gates* (1883) and *The Gates Between* (1887). Today we admire her critique of industrialization, *The Silent Partner* (1871); her artist novel, *The Story of Avis* (1877); and her physician novel, *Doctor Zay* (1882) – all feminist in attitude. She acknowledged in her autobiography, *Chapters from a Life* (1896), the influence of REBECCA HARDING DAVIS's *LIFE IN THE IRON-MILLS* (1861) and HARRIET PRESCOTT SPOFFORD's 'The Amber Gods' (1860). Other titles include *Old Maid's Paradise* (1879), a comic denial of male protecting female; *A Singular Life* (1895), about a temperance-mission pastor; and five collections of short stories. She co-authored four unremarkable books with her husband, Herbert Dickinson Ward, whom she married in 1888. CFK

Phelps, Elizabeth (Wooster) Stuart [H. Trusta]

1815–52 Popular fiction writer for children and adults of mid 19th-century USA. Born in Andover, Massachusetts, to Moses Stuart and Abigail Clark, fifth of nine children, she attended Abbot Academy in Andover, then Mount Vernon in Boston. In 1842 she married Austin Phelps, bore him three children, and died in Andover after a decade. Upon her husband's acceptance of a faculty position at the Theological Seminary, she had returned to Andover in 1848 with foreboding, her health never again reliable. Nonetheless, she proceeded to write Sunday-school stories, as well as the internationally popular *The Sunny Side: Or, the Country Minister's Wife* (1851), deriving from her mother's life; *A Peep at 'Number Five': Or, a Chapter in the Life of a City Pastor* (1852), deriving from her own; the much-anthologized New Year's story, *The Angel Over the Right Shoulder* (1852); and two short-story collections, *The Last Leaf from Sunny Side* and *The Tell-Tale: Or, Home Secrets Told by Old Travellers* (both 1853). Her daughter ELIZABETH STUART PHELPS considered her mother a victim of her father's 'feudal view' – appreciating his wife's 'fireside graces' at the expense of her creativity. CFK

Philips [née Fowler], Katherine, 'The Matchless Orinda'

1632–64 Poet, translator and dramatist. After the death of her father, a London merchant, her mother remarried and Katherine moved with her to Wales. In 1648, aged 16, she married her stepfather's 54-year-old kinsman James Philips. He was a prominent Parliamentarian while she held strong Royalist views. A daughter, Katherine, survived infancy.

Philips addressed poems to a coterie known as the Society of Friendship, whose members were assigned classical pseudonyms. They included her schoolfriend Mary Aubrey ('Rosania'); her closest friend after Aubrey's marriage, Anne Owen ('Lucasia'); Sir Charles Cotterell ('Poliarchus'); Sir Edward Dering ('Silvander'); and Dr Jeremy Taylor ('Palemon'). Philips herself was 'Orinda' and her husband was 'Antenor'. Her poems to female friends were especially intimate, using neo-platonic terms, pastoral settings and echoes of John Donne to express fervent affection. She also wrote panegyric of court figures, and poetry on themes of solitude and melancholy which implies a desire for more access to metropolitan society.

Some of her poems were published with Henry Vaughan's poems and William Cartwright's plays in 1651, and in Henry Lawes's *Second Book of Ayres* (1655). Meanwhile manuscript circulation spread her fame. In 1662 she accompanied Anne Owen, who had married an Irishman of whom Philips disapproved, to Dublin, where her translation of Corneille's *Pompey* was produced to acclaim in 1663. It was published with her initials on the title-page. In 1664 she travelled to London to suppress a pirated edition of her poems: she claimed that she had 'never writ a line in my life with the intention to have it printed', and that she feared that verse-writing was unfeminine. While there, she died suddenly of smallpox.

A volume containing Philips's collected poems, *Pompey*, and an unfinished translation of Corneille's *Horace* was published in 1667. *Horace* was completed by Denham and performed in 1668. Her letters to Cotterell (*LETTERS FROM ORINDA TO POLIARCHUS*) were published in 1705 and 1709. She was regarded as a model of propriety for female poets, in opposition to the libertine APHRA BEHN. In recent years, however, the intensity of her poems to female friends has interested students of homoerotic writing. HH

Phillips [née Payton], Catharine

1727–94 English Quaker, traveller, autobiographer, pamphleteer and campaigner. Born in Dudley (Worcestershire), she was the youngest daughter of devout Quakers, Henry Payton and Ann (née Fowler). Her skill as an orator was apparent from an early age and, after being sent to boarding school in London at the age of 16, she became convinced that she was called to the Quaker ministry, which she entered in 1748. Her preaching tours took her to Wales, Cornwall and Ireland in 1751, and Scotland in 1752. Between 1753 and 1756 she visited America, preaching to Friends across New England. Even after her marriage to William Phillips in 1772 she continued travelling in Britain. During her lifetime she published pamphlets on political and social concerns reflecting her Quaker conscience. Her 'sacred poem' *The Happy King* (1794) describes the obligations of the monarch from the Quaker perspective, attacking war and the slave trade. After her death, the *Memoirs of the Life of Catharine Phillips* were published (1797) describing her travels and reflections and showing her belief that every aspect of her life was subject to the guiding hand of God. LBe

Phillips, Jayne Anne 1952– Fiction writer who, in stories and novels, has made a particular American darkness vividly her own. The daughter of a construction worker and a teacher, Phillips worked her way through the University of West Virginia, then drifted for a couple of years, as her characters often do. Her literary success came when she was just 26 with her short-story collection BLACK TICKETS (1979; some pieces had already been published in small-press editions, *Sweethearts* and *Counting*). These edgy, often brief fictions – of life in El Paso, of keen adolescent lust, of night roads and rituals – won accolades from writers ranging from Raymond Carver to NADINE GORDIMER and earned her a range of prizes and honours. The later stories of *Fast Lanes* (1987), while still written in the dense, lyrical prose she had become known for, did not live up to the sharpness of the first. Her first novel, *Machine Dreams* (1984), was a complex epic of a family in 'Bellington' West Virginia (modelled on Phillips's own home-town, Buckhannon) – its struggles through the Depression years, World War II, and on through Vietnam. In the 1980s Phillips married and settled in Boston where she raised her sons and also taught, at Harvard and elsewhere. In 1994 she emerged with her second novel, *Shelter*. It creates the ominous, claustrophobic world of Camp Shelter, a girl-guide camp governed by stern rules and anti-communist lectures. Set in 1963, the novel vibrates with political resonances in its tale of the girls' loss of innocence – prefiguring the imminent national shock of Kennedy's assassination. As with all of Phillips's work, the eery thrills of sex and violence move starkly through this book; a powerful, ambitious story, it nonetheless seemed to lack the raw immediacy of her earliest work. SB

Phillips, Teresia Constantia 1709–65 Bankrupt after a lawsuit to prove the validity of her marriage to wealthy Henry Muilman, Phillips detailed the corruption and obfuscation of the law in her *Apology of the Conduct* (1748). Already well known as the mistress of politicians and derided for her promiscuity in the press and in Pope's *Sermon on Adultery* (1735), she accused a 'noble Lord' of raping her when she was 13 years old. Historians assumed she meant Lord Chesterfield, to whom she wrote an arch but playful *Letter humbly address'd* (1751), but recent research suggests her real target was Lord Scarborough to whom she sarcastically dedicates her *Apology*.

An anonymous *Defence by a noble Lord* (1749) hastened to deny her allegations, while a poem, *The Happy Courtezan* (1735), and *A Counter-Apology* (1749, both falsely attributed to Phillips), were published to discredit her. Phillips's brazen self-exposure scandalized Samuel Richardson's circle, but her memoirs were promoted in the Opposition press, contributed to Hardwicke's Marriage Act (1753) and inspired Jeremy Bentham's later legal reforms. LMT

Philo-Philippa fl. 1667 An anonymous Irish poet, her poem 'To the Excellent Orinda', appeared in the posthumous 1667 edition of KATHERINE PHILIPS's works. Inspired by Philips's translation of Corneille's *Mort de Pompée* and perhaps by its performance in Dublin's Smock Alley in February 1663, the poet simultaneously praised Philips's excellency and challenged male, poetic authority, asserting that poetic 'Wit's now Feminine'. Philips made a probable reference to Philo-Philippa in a letter, dated 8 April 1663, to Sir Charles Cotterell. Following the *Pompey* performance, Philips noted receiving a complimentary poem from an unknown person 'who pretends to be a Woman, [who] writes very well'. Philips's unwillingness to concede female authorship may reflect a reaction to Philo-Philippa's disturbing conceits. The thrust of Philo-Philippa's poem is sexually charged by subversive images of role reversals and mythic sexual transformations. The poem's allusions to Philips's dislike for sea travel and to 'Lucasia' (Philips's coterie name for her friend, Ann Owen) indicate that Philo-Philippa had personal knowledge of Philips, while the poem's reference 'to our coast' implies that the anonymous poet's home was Ireland. Although anonymously written, Philo-Philippa's poem remains as a dynamic testimony of women's poetic voices. BTF

Piercy, Marge 1936– American novelist and poet educated at Northwestern University. Piercy's work was consistently informed by agendas that derive from the radical movement of the late 1960s and by feminism. There was accordingly a vein of populism in her work which rendered the criticism that her work was stylistically limited and structurally unsophisticated rather beside the point. Several of the novels – *Small Changes* (1973), *Braided Lives* (1982) – chronicled aspects of the Women's movement, while the more powerful *Vida* (1980) looked at the predicament of 1960s activists obliged by past actions to remain underground; these novels combined, successfully, their radicalism with the structure of middle-brow blockbusters. The utopian novels *Woman on the Edge of Time* (1976) and *He, She and It* (1991; UK title *Body of Glass*) handled genre SCIENCE FICTION material with sophistication, flair and a vein of mythicism; the latter counterpointed conscious homage to the cyberpunk fiction of William

Gibson with evocations of the medieval Prague ghetto and Rabbi Loewe's Golem. The HISTORICAL NOVEL *City of Darkness, City of Light* (1996) combined a well-researched portrait of some of the women involved in making the French Revolution with a weary sense of the ultimate futility of violence. Her poetry, in collections like *The Moon is Always Female* (1980), reflected similar preoccupations in simple passionate utterances that some critics found banal, but others saw as an authentic female voice unbothered with the merely literary.   RK

Piers, Sarah [Royden], Lady

Piers, Sarah [Royden], Lady fl.1690s–1714 English poet, noted primarily for her verses in praise of playwright CATHERINE (TROTTER) Cockburn and John Dryden. Three of Trotter's five plays were published with commendatory verse by her intimate older friend, Sarah, Lady Piers, who praised the teenaged prodigy's 'judicious rules' and 'chaste . . . thoughts', comparing her to APHRA BEHN and KATHERINE PHILIPS. Along with Trotter, SARAH FYGE EGERTON, MARY PIX, DELARIVIÈRE MANLEY and SUSANNAH CENTLIVRE, Piers contributed to *The Nine Muses* (1700), a collection of elegies on Dryden's death. Writing as 'Urania', she mourned the passing of the 'glorious Bard' and posited Samuel Garth as Dryden's successor. The daughter of Matthew Royden of Yorkshire and wife of Sir George Piers of Kent, an officer under Marlborough and Clerk of the Privy Seal, Piers was vilified in Manley's *The New Atalantis* (1709) as a member of a lesbian 'cabal', whose friendship with Trotter was 'beyond what Nature design'd'. The British Library holds Piers's correspondence to Trotter, dating from 1697, wherein can be found a 1708 untitled, printed poem by Piers paying homage to the beauties who frequented Tunbridge Wells. Her only other known work is the panegyric *George for Britain* (1714).   JSM

Pilgrimage

Pilgrimage (1915–38) DOROTHY RICHARDSON'S massive literary project, and the major feminist epic of the MODERNIST period. A twelve-volume series of novels (one of which was published every few years), *Pilgrimage* offers a bold rendering of a happily self-supporting, single and adventurous woman by chronicling the development of its protagonist, Miriam Henderson, from the ages of 17 to 40. In a chain of events modelled closely on Richardson's own life, Miriam works (first as a teacher at a school in Germany and then, for the bulk of the text, as a secretary in a London dental office), has friendships and romances (most notably with the character Hypo Wilson – a fictional portrayal of H.G. Wells, with whom Richardson had an affair), and matures politically (by honing a sophisticated feminist perspective). The first modernist work to be labelled 'stream of consciousness' (by MAY SINCLAIR), *Pilgrimage* is remarkable for its complex depiction of states of mind: underlying (and often overshadowing) its plot is the intricacy of its narration, which captures in joyous and rigorous detail Miriam's continuous, small epiphanies – the intellectual, emotional and sensory discoveries that shape her daily life. Often compared to the work of Joyce and Proust, *Pilgrimage* was Richardson's deliberate, gendered attempt to intervene in literary history – to produce what she called the 'feminine equivalent of the current masculine REALISM'.   RE

Pilkington, Letitia

Pilkington, Letitia 1712–50 Outraged contemporaries by lambasting public figures and revealing intimate anecdotes from her friendship with Jonathan Swift in her *Memoirs* (1749). Defying feminine decorum, she also documented her own unconventional behaviour, and in language which veers from witty to vituperative or melancholic, she blamed her clergyman husband (who divorced her for adultery in 1738) for her subsequent struggle to earn her living by writing.

Born in Dublin, Pilkington became an intimate of Swift and was renowned for her wit and levity. Ostracized after her divorce, she sold her poem *The Statues* (1739) in London, wrote dedications and commissions, and was befriended by Colley Cibber and Samuel Richardson. Booksellers initially rejected her *Memoirs* which she subsequently published by subscription after returning to Ireland in 1747. The *Memoirs* enjoyed some success (instalments appeared in the *Gentleman's Magazine*) and precipitated a pamphlet war with her husband, and were unfinished when she died, still destitute, aged 39. Her son attempted to vindicate her reputation in *The Real Story of John Cartaret Pilkington* (1760), and *The Celebrated Mrs Pilkington's Jests* (1764) was published posthumously. Meanwhile Swift's biographers have gladly utilized her insight while denigrating her.   LMT

Pilkington [née Hopkins], Mary

Pilkington [née Hopkins], Mary 1766–1839 English children's educational writer, poet and novelist. Daughter of a Cambridge surgeon, Mary lost an anticipated income to a male heir at 15, driving her mother mad. Her husband, the successor to her father's practice, abandoned her to become a naval surgeon, and she was forced to find work as a governess. This profession prepared her to write CHILDREN'S LITERATURE and educational tracts. Translating Madame de Genlis and Marmontel, Mary also published many very popular works of her own, including *A Mirror for the Female Sex* (1798), *Biography for Boys* (1799), *Biography for Girls* (1799), and *The Sorrows of Caesar: Or Adventures of a Foundling Dog* (1813). Favouring stern didactic tales, Mary stressed Christian virtues and the importance of obedience, studiousness and decorum.

She appears also to have published *Miscellaneous Poems* (1796), containing wry, mock-humble addresses to harsh husbands, male critics, Apollo and Hymen. Her volume *Original Poems* (1811) concerns children, female friendship and aspects of etiquette. Her works for adults include novels and *Memoirs of Celebrated Female Characters* (1811), which mixes disapproval and admiration for CHARLOTTE CHARKE, APHRA BEHN and MARY WOLLSTONECRAFT, among others.   JHP

Pin to See the Peepshow, A (1934) F. TENNYSON JESSE's novel was primarily based on the trial of Mrs Thomson (she had her younger lover murder her husband), which had shaken British courts and public alike. Having an already-established career as a journalist and playwright, Jesse was also a brilliant criminologist, an ability which she fully employed in this novel by seamlessly weaving the facts of the trial into her larger feminist concerns. A genuine believer in a woman's right to independence, Jesse was also wary of the dangers that loom behind a liberation at any cost. In the same way that Julia Almond gets caught in the 'mad but glamorous world of the peepshow', she also gets trapped in her fantasies of romantic love. The only difference is that her illusions and ignorance of the conventions of 20th-century life cost her more than a pin. In the novel's *dénouement*, Jesse's powerful psychological insight into Julia's last hours before execution remains unsurpassed.   MPe

Pinckney, Eliza (Elizabeth Lucas) 1723–93
American letter-writer unknown beyond her native South Carolina until the publication of her selected correspondence in 1896. The series in which it appeared, 'Women of Colonial and Revolutionary Times in America', scarcely affords a better example of an intelligent, resourceful woman adapting courageously to events which altered the shape of her world for ever. Daughter of a colonial governor, Eliza, at the age of 16, was left in charge of her father's plantation. Five years afterwards she married Charles Cotesworth Pinckney, a middle-aged widower whose first wife had apparently recommended the match on her deathbed. Having pioneered the cultivation of indigo as a profitable cash crop on her husband's estate, Eliza accompanied him to England, where the pair spent five years. When Charles died, following their return in 1758, she found herself becoming more deeply involved in political issues leading to the War of Independence, in which two of her sons played an important part. Besides documenting her inevitable shift from colonial loyalism to patriotic fervour, her letters, with their abundant details of Southern plantation life, reveal Eliza Pinckney as a woman whose practicality and business acumen was balanced by a continuing interest in contemporary theological and philosophical debate. Decorum in tone and style is offset by touches of acerbic humour and a sense of the ridiculous.   JK

Piozzi, Hester Lynch (Salusbury, also Thrale)
1741–1821 Diarist, poet, letter- and TRAVEL-WRITER whose intellectual verve magnetized eminent contemporaries. Her early education was haphazard until her precocity was cultivated by Dr Collier (also SARAH FIELDING's tutor). She published poems anonymously in the *St James's Chronicle* (1762) before being persuaded to marry (for convenience, she claimed, not love) the brewer Henry Thrale. Having charmed Dr Johnson with her fearless repartee and her playful translation of Boethius (he became a virtual member of their household), she drew Edmund Burke, David Garrick, Oliver Goldsmith and Sir Joshua Reynolds to the Thrales' bountiful dinner parties. She also mixed in BLUESTOCKING circles, counting ELIZABETH MONTAGU and FANNY BURNEY as intimate friends.

Her DIARY, *Thraliana* (1776–1809), records her active involvement in her husband's business and political affairs, her children's education and illnesses (out of thirteen pregnancies, only four children survived to adulthood) and her social milieu. Widowed in 1781, she was thrown into confusion by her love for the talented Italian musician Gabriel Piozzi, and by the shocked disapproval of Johnson (who never forgave her), her eldest daughter 'Queeney', and her friends Montagu and Burney. Deciding to marry (this time for love) she left England with Piozzi in 1784 and settled happily in Italy. Her literary career flourished: *Anecdotes of the Late Samuel Johnson* (1786), which rivalled Boswell's biography, was followed by her correspondence with Johnson (1788) and *Observations and Reflections made in a Journey through France, Italy and Germany* (1789). However, her poems for the 'Della Cruscans's' *Florence Miscellany* (1785), a political pamphlet (*Three Warnings to John Bull before he Dies*, 1798) and *Retrospection* (1801), a popularized world history, were less successful. Back in London in 1787, and later in Wales where she retired with Piozzi in 1795, she again became a renowned hostess. While some have ridiculed her presumption and indiscretion, her diaries and correspondence are vivid testimonies to her gusto, courage and perceptiveness.   LMT

Pitt [née McKeown], Marie E(lizabeth) J(osephine) 1869–1948 Australian poet and socialist, born in the Gippsland region of Victoria. She had little formal education and spent her childhood doing the drudging work of a poor selector's eldest daughter. At 23 she married William Pitt and began life as a miner's wife in the newly opened minefields on the west coast of Tasmania. Her experiences there inspired her to become a socialist and a political campaigner. When her husband's health declined, she took the family to

Melbourne where she helped support them by a variety of clerical jobs, and occasional journalism.

Though poetry was one among many commitments, she was a fine poet – and a political one, who claimed that 'without the capacity to hate and to sing of hate, the power to love, the song of love would be a lesser thing'. She began publishing poetry while in Tasmania, and was encouraged by literary friends in Melbourne, including Bernard O'Dowd with whom she lived from the 1920s. Her poetry is traditional in form, based on a Celtic heritage of Scots border ballads and Irish lyric poetry. She wrote nature lyrics, rousing ballads and several bush ballads worthy to be compared with those of 'Banjo' Paterson. But most of her poetry addresses social and political issues – the evils of capitalism, the future of Australia and the place of women. Her work was published in two books, *Horses of the Hills* (1911) and *Selected Poems* (1944).   SPL

Pitt-Kethley, Fiona 1954– Uninhibited British feminist poet. She studied to be a painter before switching to poetry and publishing an irreverent set of poems called *London* (1984, privately published after publishers Bloodaxe withdrew), about the city from the Middle Ages to the 19th century. However, she really came into her own with her extremely funny and scatalogical collections, *Sky Ray Lolly* (1986), *Private Parts* (1987) and *The Perfect Man* (1989), which were candid about sex, men, fucking and all its attendant mishaps. Banned from the Poetry Society for her too-frequent use of four-letter words, she also published a hilarious travelogue, *Journey to the Underworld* (1989), about a search for Sibyls in Italy, involving sexual escapades and ruins in equal measure. She also published a collection of her wry and rambunctious journalism, *Too Hot to Handle* (1992); and another book of poetry, *A School for Life* (1993), showed why she chose poetry, and why the body and sexuality interest her. She edited *The Literary Companion to Sex* (1992) and, in 1995, *The Literary Companion to Low Life*. Both are full of rare and unusual pieces, showing her as a non-canonical and original anthologist.

Pitt-Kethley is unsparingly acerbic about the people she encounters, but also about herself, and this humility and inability to take herself too seriously make hers an unusual feminist voice. She writes about sex in a way that few people can: her style is conversational, her iambs effortless, her perspective down-to-earth and her libido generous and wholly (and refreshingly) unqueasy about itself. A mistress of the send-up and the one-liner, Pitt-Kethley is a true sexual radical, a voice of female autonomy.   ATe

Pitter, Ruth 1897–1992 English poet who embraced the term 'poetess' as expressive of women's characteristic privacy and homeliness. The daughter of elemen-

tary-school teachers in East London, she attended school in Bow, worked as clerk in the War Office in World War I, and for a Suffolk arts and crafts firm. Hilaire Belloc funded her *First Poems* (1920). In the 1930s, with her partner Kathleen O'Hara, she established a crafts business in Chelsea, making furniture to traditional models. Her poetry also specialized in modelling older forms. In *A Mad Lady's Garland* (1934), creatures pursue their destinies in comic pastiche; the spider in 'Maternal Love Triumphant' is an Augustan. *A Trophy of Arms* (1936) used serious pastiche, especially of Metaphysical poetry, to explore the spiritual in mundane appearances. *The Rude Potato* (1941) continued this juxtaposition of Spiritual and mundane, drawing on Pitter's gardening interests in poems about potatoes, rhubarb and potting-sheds. *The Ermine* (1953) explored her sympathy with non-human creation. Pitter saw poetry as essentially private, 'that secret movement of the poet's being in response to the secret dynamism of life'; her few public poems such as '1938' or 'The Great Winter 1946–47' escape from public to private. She was, however, committed to making poetry more accessible, gave many radio talks and appeared on BBC Television's *Brains Trust* as part of that commitment. Her popular, traditionalist poetry is best understood as a protest against the elitism of MODERNISM.   AT

Pix, Mary 1666–1709 British playwright and novelist, born in Oxfordshire, who turned to writing after the death of her husband. She produced two novels, *The Inhuman Cardinal* (1696) and *Violenta* (1704), as well as six tragedies and six comedies. Although *Ibrahim* (1696), *Queen Catharine* (1698) and *The Czar of Muscovy* (1701) were poor imitations of the unfashionable Beaumont and Fletcher tradition, they were well received. Equally successful were *The Innocent Mistress* (1697), *The Deceiver Deceived* (1697) and *The Beau Defeated* (1700). These were skilfully written intrigue comedies, with forced or unhappy marriages as a major theme. Mary Pix's practice of writing commendatory verses for other female dramatists, including CATHERINE TROTTER and DELARIVIÈRE MANLEY, was mocked in THE FEMALE WITS (1696), where she appeared as Mrs Wellfed. Successful during her lifetime, Pix appears to have made little money from her writing, and a benefit performance of SUSANNAH CENTLIVRE's popular THE BUSY BODY (1709) was held on behalf of her estate after her death.   RDM

Places Far From Ellesmere (1990) ARITHA VAN HERK's fourth book gives critics a hard time defining its genre. The book, called a 'geograficction' by its author, is a collection of long poems with a strong autobiographical focus combined with traces of travel writing and literary criticism.

There are four sections, called 'exploration sites', the first three of which explore the author's/narrator's relationship to Edberg, her first home; Edmonton, the place where she studied; and Calgary, her present place of residence. Van Herk describes how these places shaped her but also how she shaped and created the places through her writing. The last section, 'Ellesmere, woman as island', is an account of a hiking trip through Ellesmere Island but it is also a re-reading and re-writing of Tolstoy's *Anna Karenina*. Anna is the archetypal victim of the 19th-century realist tradition, a woman who had to commit suicide in Tolstoy's novel because circumstances inevitably led her to it. Van Herk creates Ellesmere as 'a place of mind', an alternative realm for women, both real and fictional, where they can escape the grasp of REALISM and patriarchy.

TP

Plath, Sylvia 1932–63 American poet, novelist and short-story writer. Since her death in 1963, her controversial life story and writings have become battlegrounds on which biographers, critics, feminists, anti-feminists, psychoanalysts and others have all fought to stake their differing claims.

She was born in Boston, Massachusetts, to parents of German and Austrian extraction. With precocious talents and ambition, she excelled academically and published early. In 1955 she graduated *summa cum laude* from Smith and won a Fulbright scholarship to study at Cambridge University, where she was to meet and marry British poet Ted Hughes. The couple spent time in both America and England, and raised two children.

Plath placed work in publications as diverse as *Seventeen*, *Ladies Home Journal* and the *New Yorker*, cheerfully subverting conventional distinctions between 'high' and 'popular' culture. She wrote the continuously bestselling novel *THE BELL JAR* (1963), which is a mordantly witty and satirical BILDUNGSROMAN exploring the traumas of becoming a woman in 1950s America. In her lifetime she saw one volume of poetry into print, *The Colossus* (1960); *ARIEL* (1965), *Crossing the Water* (1971), *Winter Trees* (1971) and finally the *Collected Poems* were all assembled and published posthumously.

Her achievements were shadowed by spells of sometimes suicidal depression. She and Hughes separated in 1962, and there followed for Plath a brief period of feverish and furious productivity, during which she lived in a house once occupied by W.B.Yeats and wrote what is now considered to be her most powerful work. Then, during the bitterly cold London winter of 1963, in the early hours of the morning while her two young children slept, she took her own life.

Because Plath's work tends to be viewed retrospectively through the dark lens of the author's suicide, it is sometimes read as little more than a negative and personal expression of depression and despair, representing a vector toward death. However, such crudely reductive biographical approaches occlude the wit, energy and intelligence of Plath's work, down-playing its stylistic inventiveness and its semantic subtlety.

Undeniably much of this work still makes grim reading: as Hughes puts it, Plath was determined to confront 'central, unacceptable things'. However, as a poetry of crisis it has an uncanny power to undermine the seeming stability of conventional meanings, positions and relationships, prompting the reader into a series of double-takes and rethinks. Well-travelled and well-read, Plath was alert to contemporary political issues, appalled by the Cold War and McCarthyism, haunted by the atrocities of World War II and visions of nuclear apocalypse. 'Does this influence the kind of poetry I write?' she asked – responding, 'Yes, but in a sidelong fashion'. Some of her best work interrogates the power relationships and 'violent hierarchies' which make up our personal and public lives, revealing both their destructive potential and their inherent instability. Particularly interested in the politics of gender, she has been claimed as a kind of maverick vanguard to the second wave of Anglo-American feminism, which was just beginning to gather force at the time of her death.

AFT

Plato, Ann 1820?–? American poet and essayist, born and raised in Hartford, Connecticut. She attended school and, while still in her teens, became a teacher of young children. At the age of 13 she joined the Colored Congregational Church of Hartford, whose pastor was abolitionist W.C. Pennington. She contributed poetry to the periodical *Colored American* and, with Pennington's encouragement, published a book, *Essays; Including Biographies and Miscellaneous Pieces, in Prose and Poetry* (1841), for which he wrote an introduction. The book is notable for being the only known book by an African-American published between 1840 and 1865. Little is known of Plato's life. Her poem 'The Natives of America' implies that her paternal ancestors were native American; 'I Have No Brother' mourns the death of a brother, Henry. Her essays, in the pious Puritan tradition, cover such topics as 'Education', 'Religion', 'Benevolence', and 'Employment', and reflect a knowledge of classical and modern history. Also included are four eulogies for young women, which provide glimpses of the lives of middle-class black women of antebellum New England.

JSG

Play It As It Lays (1970) JOAN DIDION wrote of her first novel that she intended it to be 'so elliptical and fast that it would be over before you noticed . . . a book in which anything that happened would happen off the page'. A collage of narrative fragments, cinematically juxtaposed in montage, the novel reconstructs the year leading up to Maria Wyeth's institutionalization for complicity in a producer's suicide. As Maria, an actress married to a film director, suffers an extended breakdown, Didion's journalistic eye and mordant wit record scenes of 'the unspeakable peril in the everyday', encapsulated in the adultery, promiscuity, sadomasochism, drugs and self-indulgence which characterize this microcosm. Maria's coerced back-alley abortion and divorce are the central events of a novel structured by metaphors of film, gambling and driving. Maria's pain is absorbed into the blank spaces throughout the novel, 'snapshots' that end and jump-cut without 'close-up' or 'reaction shot'. Didion's black comedy undercuts Maria's self-absorbed nihilism in a tone reminiscent of SYLVIA PLATH's THE BELL JAR; Maria's culminating 'Why not?' in answer to an existential 'why?' concludes the novel's satiric blend of passivity with impassivity.   SC

Plum Bun (1929) The second novel by Harlem Renaissance novelist and editor JESSIE REDMON FAUSET manipulates the conventions of the marriage plot and the novel of manners. Angela Murray, the daughter of a light-skinned mother who 'passes for play' to enjoy whites-only department stores and tearooms, moves to the bohemian Greenwich Village of the 1920s and lives as a white woman to attend a segregated art school. The pleasures of access to the white world, however, are not without their risks: the 'plum bun' of the novel's title is Angela herself, who in her establishment of herself as a NEW (white) WOMAN, has ultimately commodified herself for white male consumption. Only when she is abandoned by a white lover who learns of her racial identity, does Angela begin to question the validity of passing as a means of self-making. Finally, Angela finds happiness with a fellow passer; until the dénouement of the novel, each believes the other to be white. Despite its conventionality, *Plum Bun* remains interesting in its refusal to resolve its own ambiguities, for, despite her ultimate acceptance of her blackness, Angela refuses to regard race as a primary determinant of her identity.   MG

Plumptre, Anne 1760–1818 English translator, novelist and miscellaneous writer, her father was Dr Robert Plumptre, president of Queens' College, Cambridge. Well-educated, particularly in languages, Plumptre translated the plays of August von Kotzebue. Her novels included *The Rector's Son: A Novel* (1798), a sentimental precursor of the modern thriller; the EPISTOLARY *Something New: Or, Adventures at Campbell House* (1801); and *The History of Myself and a Friend* (1813). Friendships with those sympathetic toward Revolutionary France, such as HELEN MARIA WILLIAMS, and a sojourn in France with AMELIA OPIE from 1802 to 1805 led to the publication of *Narrative of a Three Years' Residence in France* in 1810, a work which strongly defends Napoleon: 'In all the governments where Bonaparte has any influence, he has uniformly been the means of procuring relief to the people from some of the most grievous of their oppressions.' Later travels in Ireland led to *Narrative of a Residence in Ireland* (1817), which was badly received. Along with her author-sister, Annabella, she also wrote *Tales of Wonder, of Honour and of Sentiment, Original and Translated* (1818).   RDM

Plunkett [née Gunning], Elizabeth 1769–1823 Prolific English novelist and translator. The daughter of SUSANNA GUNNING, the sentimental novelist, she began writing in 1794, following her involvement in the infamous family scandal which Horace Walpole called the 'Gunningiad'. According to her accusers, she had forged a letter from one suitor in order to heighten her chances of marriage with another. In her mother's sensationalist version of events (published in 1791), authorship of the mysterious letter was attributed to her cousins, the Bowens. In 1803, she married John Plunkett and produced two collections of children's stories and a number of novels and translations. Her numerous works include *The Packet* (1794); *The Gypsy Countess* (1799); a translation of Fontanelle's *Plurality of Worlds* (1803); and *Exile of Erin* (1808). The plots of Plunkett's novels are routinely sentimental, and her language tends toward the hyperbolic style popularized by her mother. However, her later work shows her attempt to integrate political commentary into the sentimental formula.   KD

Poems, North & South – A Cold Spring (1955) ELIZABETH BISHOP's second book of poetry to be published in the United States. To make up the volume, she agreed, reluctantly, with her publishers, Houghton Mifflin, to re-publish her first book, *North and South*, which had come out in 1946, and to add to it, under the title *A Cold Spring*, most of the poems she had written between 1946 and 1954. The collection is obliquely autobiographical, a discontinuous narrative referring to the different versions of North and South that Bishop had travelled between, from Newfoundland to New England, from New York to Florida and finally from the United States to Brazil, where Bishop had settled with her lover, Lota Soares, in 1951. Many of the poems show Bishop's celebrated attentiveness to the changing surfaces of the world. But the poems are always more than just descriptions. Bishop watches the world to transform or defy it by the work of imagination. The tone of the poetry is fastidious, measured, deliberately un-confessional. What might look like modesty in Bishop's work is in fact the starting point for a poetry of exceptional imaginative power and technical accomplishment.   JCo

Pogson [née Godsell], Patricia 1944– Scottish-born poet Patricia Pogson trained at art colleges in Preston and Oxford. With her husband she lived on a narrowboat for two years, and travelled to Australia, India and Canada. She has two children. She later married the poet Geoffrey Holloway (d.1997) and settled with him in the Lake District. In 1989 she won second prize in the National Poetry Competition (UK). Her early pamphlet collections *Before the Road Show* (1983) and *Snakeskin Belladonna* (1986), signalled her attraction to the subjects of physicality and mental illness. These themes, among others including abuse and natural history, are developed in three exceptionally powerful full-length volumes – *Rattling the Handle* (1990), *A Crackle from the Larder* (1991) and *The Tides in the Basin* (1994), the latter containing controlled, apparently formal, poems which challenge poetic decorum with their combination of shocking subject matter and a wry, generous humour. Pogson is a confrontational writer whose predilection is to transform the mundane and domestic into something menacing and disturbing. Her writing can also be appreciated for its virtues of wit and empathy, and the physical power of her imagery.   DM

Policy and Passion: A Novel of Australian Life
(1881) (Also published as *Longleat of Kooralbyn*.) In her second novel, ROSA PRAED tells the complicated story of Honoria Longleat, stuck in the Australian bush at Kooralbyn, longing for European culture. Her father is the Premier of Leichardt's Land (*sic*; Queensland) and is hiding a secret even darker than his affair with Mrs Vallancy, wife of an opposition minister. Honoria refuses a proposal of marriage from Australian Dyson Maddox, and becomes fascinated with the English nobleman Barrington, thus introducing a common Praed theme in which women's national affiliation is decided through a choice of European or Australian partners. Longleat refuses to let his daughter marry into the English upper classes. It turns out that he is being blackmailed over his concealed convict past. Brokenhearted by the likely effects of such information on the proud Honoria, the collapse of his career, and his betrayal by Mrs Vallancy, he kills himself. Honoria, outraged by the indecent proposals of Barrington, refuses his marriage proposal and ultimately marries Maddox.   SKM

Pollitt, Katha 1949– American poet and essayist who survived the 1980s backlash to sustain a clear, witty feminist voice in the noisy territory of America's cultural conversations. Pollitt initially made her mark as a poet; her 1982 volume *Antarctic Traveller* – a collection of warm, conversational poems with a supple intelligence – won the National Book Critics Circle Award. She began a long association with the Leftist

weekly, the *Nation* in the early 1980s, first as its literary editor and later as a columnist. At the *Nation*, Pollitt honed her skills as a political and cultural commentator, developing an incisive, sharp-humoured style. Like fellow-feminist Barbara Ehrenreich, Pollitt has a layered awareness of class issues rare in American political essayists. Subjects she tackled in her influential collection *Reasonable Creatures: Essays on Women and Feminism* (1994) include surrogate mothers, media handling of prominent rape cases, and battles over the literary canon. The book's opening sally: 'Like Broadway, the novel, and God, feminism has been declared dead many times.' Pollitt's important writings prove the reports of such a death to be greatly exaggerated.   SB

Polwhele, Elizabeth fl. *c*.1670–91? British playwright about whom little is known, although she may have been the daughter of a nonconformist minister. Married, with five children, Polwhele is credited with having written *The Faithful Virgins*, a recently discovered manuscript in the Bodleian Library. Composed in about 1670 and probably performed by the Duke's Company, this rhymed tragedy is written in an old-fashioned Jacobean style, incorporating a masque, ghosts and violent deaths. Polwhele's next work, *The Frolicks: Or The Lawyer Cheated*, appeared in print a year later, although there is no conclusive evidence that it was staged. The play contains stock characters and situations, and concerns Clarabell's attempts to marry the rakish but impoverished Rightwit, and Meanwell's suspicions that he is being cuckolded by his easily impressionable young wife. Its light comic touch shows a vast improvement in confidence and awareness of current dramatic techniques, particularly in its use of song and dance. Polwhele also refers in the dedication to another work by her, *Elysium*, which may be a religious masque.   RDM

Ponder Heart, The (1954) In this humorous masterpiece set in Clay, Mississippi, EUDORA WELTY employs dialogue which reflects the oral tradition of the South. Edna Earl Ponder, niece and childhood companion of her uncle, Daniel Ponder, narrates the contemporary history of the Ponder family, which is effectively the history of Uncle Daniel. The altruistic simple man, who has spent time in a nearby mental asylum, is addicted to giving things away. Accused of the murder of his second wife, Bonnie Dee Peacock, he is tried in the Clay Courthouse. The trial becomes a spectacle in which many of the local citizens perform; the most spectacular performance, however, is by Uncle Daniel himself. Although Edna Earl significantly contributes to his defence by refusing to let him tell his version of the story, it is his own altruistic final act, distributing the Ponder wealth among the courtroom audience at the moment of crisis, which ultimately saves him from conviction.

Ponder Heart was originally published in the *New Yorker* (1953) and was dramatized in 1956 on Broadway, where it was received with moderate success.   JAHa

Ponsonby, Sarah 1755–1831 Irish diarist, letter-writer and one of the 'Ladies of Llangollen'. Having lost both parents by the time she was 7, Sarah remembered her childhood as one of 'silence and solitude'. At boarding school in Kilkenny, she met the 29-year-old LADY ELEANOR BUTLER. Their friendship developed into a secret correspondence, and in 1778 the two friends eloped together.

After touring Wales, the Ladies settled at Llangollen, where they lived together for over fifty years, their partnership becoming the epitome of the contemporary concept of 'romantic friendship'. Despite their expressed desire for 'retirement', they received a constant stream of visitors. Friends included Edmund Burke, the Duke of Wellington and William Wordsworth, as well as BLUESTOCKINGS such as Harriet Bowdler, ANNA SEWARD and HESTER PIOZZI.

More practical and less high-handed than her partner, Sarah was often called upon to conciliate those whom Lady Eleanor had offended, and during the final years of their lives she impressed observers by the tenderness with which she cared for her 'beloved companion'. She survived her older friend by two years, dying in 1831, and the two were buried side by side in Llangollen churchyard.   RR

pony stories Pony books began in the late 1920s when the automobile had largely replaced the horse as a means of transport, and children started to ride ponies for pleasure. They can be grouped into three main categories: those narrated by the pony itself, and clearly influenced by ANNA SEWELL's classic *BLACK BEAUTY* (1877); books narrated from the point of view of the young rider but offering little instruction on riding techniques; and those whose aim is clearly that of instructing the reader in horsemanship.

It is generally acknowledged that the author who started it all was Golden Gorse (Muriel Wace, née Maude), whose classic *Moorland Mousie* appeared in 1929. Another pioneer was M(arjorie) M(ary) Oliver, who, together with Eva Ducat, wrote *The Ponies of Bunts* (1933) and several other titles. Primrose Cumming's 'Silver Eagle' series, begun in 1938, sparked a trend for heroines who ran riding schools, often against their parents' wishes and always successfully. After World War II, it was the Pullein-Thompson sisters, twins Christine and Diana, and Josephine, who *did* run a successful riding school and wrote the sort of stories that were full of instruction to young riders – increasingly

popular due to the development of International Horse Shows, and the heroic status of British team champions. This link was strengthened with the publication of the first of Pat Smythe's seven 'Three Jay' titles, *Jacqueline Rides for a Fall* (1957), in which the reader learns not only about riding, but also about the demanding life of a professional showjumper and eventer.

Similarly instructive – as well as highly readable – are Ruby Ferguson's 'Jill' books (1949–62), which have never been out of print. The pony book's heyday was over by the 1970s, although they now enjoy a considerable revival, both here and in the USA.   JLB

Poor Cow (1967) Adapted for film in the same year, the script was co-written by its author NELL DUNN, and Ken Loach, who directed it. The book is intensely visual and translates easily into film, but is too poetic and lyrical for social REALISM. Dunn handles the irony of 'Joy' – 'Poor Cow' – with subtle delicacy. The 22-year-old Joy is adrift with her new baby in the slum-clearance landscape of south London, daydreaming of a Home all pastel shades and lacey curtains. When her husband is sent down for robbery, she falls in love with his mate, Dave. They share a brief idyll in the countryside before life and the 'flying squad' intervene. Joy writes to Dave in prison – miserable misspelt letters – and, like a perverse version of Dorothy from *The Wizard of Oz*, she moves in with her Auntie Emm. She and little Johnny live in a slum version of her dream-home. She tries to lose herself in sex with strangers, whilst heading inevitably toward her husband's release from prison. Life backs her into a desolate corner, but she emerges bravely as no-one's creature.   STS

Poppy (1990) DRUSILLA MODJESKA's first piece of 'faction' or fictionalized biography, recounts the story of Poppy, the narrator's mother, and of her family. The narrator is called 'Lalage' and her own life, as an eldest daughter, a sister, a friend, an emigrant and a feminist, is central to the narrative. Central also is the very process of writing biography and history, of trying to encapsulate lives – her own, her mother's, her family's – and to divine motivations. The story follows the narrator's journey through Poppy's rather unhappy childhood with her rich, cold, parents, China and Jack, through her conventional marriage in wartime Britain to the rather ordinary Richard. Present throughout the book is the puzzle and trauma of Poppy's mental breakdown at the end of the 1950s, which left her young daughters and husband bewildered and the family fragmented. Richard leaves, and Poppy remakes her life apart, going through analysis, doing a degree, starting a day centre for young offenders, finding new, if somewhat difficult, romantic love with Marcus, a priest.   SKM

Porter, Anna Maria 1780–1832 British writer of eighteen novels including sentimental comedies of manners and HISTORICAL FICTION, published during and after the Napoleonic Wars. Porter, sister of JANE PORTER, made her début in her teens with *Artless Tales* (1793). *The Lake of Killarney* (1804) and *A Sailor's Friendship and a Soldier's Love* (1805) reflect debates on the equality of the sexes and women's ability to effect a 'reformation of manners' in the spirit of HANNAH MORE. Male heroes are men of SENSIBILITY concerned with honourable conduct, in love and war, most obviously in *The Hungarian Brothers* (1807). Later novels project these themes in various historical settings (e.g. *The Village of Mariendorpt* (1821), set during the Thirty Years War), portraying epic events from the standpoint of a small, private circle. This reflects Porter's restricted female situation as Surrey-based sister of cosmopolitan Robert Ker Porter, the much-decorated author, diplomat, soldier and artist.　　　　　　CCO

Porter, Dorothy (Featherstone) 1954– Australian poet and novelist who is probably the only writer to have written a lesbian DETECTIVE NOVEL in verse. Porter was born in Sydney, and has lived and worked (as a creative writing teacher) for extended periods in both Sydney and Melbourne, with both cities figuring strongly in her work. She has published eight volumes of poetry, with the first, *Hoodlum*, appearing in 1975, and the most recent, *Crete*, published in 1996. She has also written two novels for adolescents. THE MONKEY'S MASK (1994), her audacious, riveting and page-turning verse novel won several major awards, and has attracted a very wide readership in Australia and overseas, selling many thousands of copies in a milieu in which even the best poetry sales often only number in the few hundreds. *Akhenaten* (1992), similarly if not so spectacularly ground-breaking, was conceived as a fictionalized autobiography of the Egyptian king, complete with sensuous and disturbing accounts of incest among the royal family. All of Porter's works are much concerned with the sensual world and with the complexities of human sexuality, often reading these concerns against a background of history and legend, but, while her earlier works are almost baroque in their accumulation of detail, her more mature work is one of refined and often chillingly apposite images.　　MLA

Porter, Jane 1776–1850 British HISTORICAL NOVELIST whose main works, *Thaddeus of Warsaw* (1804) and *The Scottish Chiefs* (1810), influenced her childhood friend Walter Scott, and were frequently reissued. *Thaddeus*, set after the recent partition of Poland, drew on knowledge of Polish exiles in her brother's circle. She was proud of descent from the Elizabethan poet Endymion Porter, and admired Philip Sidney, whose aphorisms she edited, as a model hero relevant to the

Jane Porter.

19th century. *The Scottish Chiefs* celebrated Wallace and his contemporaries as chivalrous heroes whose descendants, united with their English counterparts, fought against Napoleon in Spain. Residing near Windsor, she cherished contacts with royalty, and at George IV's request fashioned *Christian of Luneburg* (1824) around his 17th-century Brunswick ancestor. She co-published novellas with ANNA MARIA PORTER, and an 18th-century COLONIAL NARRATIVE of Sir Edward Seaward's journal, mistakenly believed authentic. CCO

Porter, Katherine Anne 1890–1980 American short-story writer and novelist acclaimed as one of the preeminent stylists of the 20th century. Born Callie Russell Porter in Indian Creek, Texas, she was raised, following her mother's death in 1892, by her paternal grandmother, Catherine Anne Porter. In 1906, barely 16, she entered the first of her four marriages, converting a few years later to her husband's Catholic faith but eventually leaving him and their unhappy union; upon their divorce in 1915 she took the name Katherine Anne Porter. A nearly lethal bout of tuberculosis that same year helped redirect her aspirations from the stage to the pen when in her sanitorium she became close to several women journalists, and, after working on newspapers in Fort Worth and Denver, she moved in 1919 to Greenwich Village, determined to be a writer. She published a series of children's stories and ghost-wrote a novel, but it was her extended trips to Mexico, beginning in 1920, that gave her material for her first serious fictions.

Her first collection, *Flowering Judas* (1930), which included several stories set in Mexico, brought critical recognition and a Guggenheim Fellowship that she used to travel to Europe. Though deeply ambivalent about her Texas childhood – in fact in public she invented an aristocratic Southern past to replace her pinched upbringing – in Europe she transformed her memories into psychologically penetrating stories of her youth, often told through her narrative *alter ego*, Miranda. Three of these novellas were collected in *PALE HORSE, PALE RIDER* (1939), her last major work until the 1962 publication of her long-awaited first (and only) novel, *SHIP OF FOOLS*. A bestseller, *Ship of Fools* gave Porter, for the first time, financial independence and literary fame, and perhaps eased the frustration that so many years of uncompleted work often brought (she was a notorious procrastinator, diverting her energy into voluminous correspondence and tumultuous affairs). Despite her modest output she was highly praised for her irony, economy and symbolism and was a favourite of the New Critics; EUDORA WELTY, one of many writers influenced by Porter (others include FLANNERY O'CONNOR, TILLIE OLSEN and CARSON McCULLERS) called her writing 'distilled'. What Porter gave crystallizing focus to were the experiences of women struggling against their prescribed roles in a patriarchal society, the importance of both freedom and form, and the power – and terror – of memory. 'The real end of art,' she once wrote, 'is to create order and harmony and form out of [the artist's] share of Universal chaos.' In 1964 her *Collected Stories*, just over two dozen in all, received the Pulitzer Prize. She died at 90 in Maryland but had her ashes returned to Texas, where they were buried at Indian Creek. WG

Possessing the Secret of Joy (1992) Just as ALICE WALKER'S *THE COLOR PURPLE* (1982) 'signifies' upon HURSTON'S *THEIR EYES WERE WATCHING GOD* (1937), so *Possessing the Secret of Joy* 'signifies' upon Camus's *L'Etranger*. The novel is the third part of the trilogy, *The Color Purple* and *The Temple of My Familiar* constituting the first two parts. Walker adopts the tactic of continuing the story of one of *The Color Purple*'s minor characters, who becomes the main protagonist, namely the Olinka, Tashi, who marries Adam Johnson and returns to the USA.

Walker uses the novel to investigate the issue of female circumcision, also known as female genital mutilation, and makes a passionate case against this widespread African practice. She portrays Tashi-Evelyn as both physically and emotionally traumatized by the mutilation which she chose to undergo. Through her protagonist's experiences she explores the history and justification of the practice, drawing on social and cultural anthropology and Jungian

psychoanalysis. The novel ends with Tashi's execution, but simultaneously proclaims the importance of resistance to injustice and oppression. In conjunction with the novel, Walker made a television documentary, entitled *Warrior Marks*. HMD

Possession: A Romance (1990) A. S. BYATT's multi-layered narrative explores the powerful desire for ownership in human relationships and in the pursuit of knowledge. The chance discovery by an unknown researcher of some hundred-year-old love letters from a respectable Victorian poet to his mistress culminates in a race between several eccentric present-day literary scholars to uncover the truth about their clandestine affair. Drawing parallels between the love stories of the past and present, Byatt combines elements of medieval quest and the contemporary DETECTIVE story and produces a strongly plot-driven novel which perhaps owes something to the influence of IRIS MURDOCH. Written in the form of the 19th-century 'triple-decker', *Possession* can be read as an analysis of the dynamics of gender in Victorian society as well as a critique of its poetic tradition, whilst the conscious use of character stereotyping provides a satirical view of faculty life and the cut-and-thrust of academic publishing. The novel was awarded both the Booker Prize for Fiction and the *Irish Times* / Aer Lingus International Fiction Prize in 1990. RCo

Post, Lydia Minturn A 19th-century American editor of documents from the American Revolution and Civil War, born in New York; little else is known about her life.

In 1859, she published *Personal Recollections of the American Revolution: A Private Journal*. The narrative is about Mary, a colonial woman married to a revolutionary officer who, in her husband's absence, had to live with her Loyalist father and care for a wounded enemy officer during the British occupation of Long Island. Although the book was typically accepted as Lydia's non-fiction JOURNAL, various records indicate that the subject of *Personal Recollections . . .* could only have been Lydia's grandmother, Mary Titus Post. However, because of the book's anachronistic language many believe that Mary could not have written the journal. One argument asserts that the journal is Lydia's fictional account of her grandmother's life while another claims that Lydia pieced together her grandmother's biography from diaries, letters, family recollections and Quaker church records.

The journal's editor was listed as Sidney Barclay, Lydia's pseudonym. Inexplicably, a second edition was published in 1866 as *Grace Barclay's Diary*. In 1862, this time under her own name, Lydia edited and published *Soldiers' Letters, From Camp, Battle-field and Prison* in order to raise money for the Sanitary Commission – an agency that cared for sick, wounded or destitute soldiers. VM

Postcards from Surfers (1985) In this collection of eleven short stories, HELEN GARNER uses a variety of narrative styles and voices to 'bend the bars a little'. She writes of the problems of being a female artist in a world dominated by the male aesthetic, the egotisms and betrayals of love, the struggles involved in attempting to live the 'alternative' life outside conventional family structures, the glimpses of the bizarre and horrific which wrench a child from the world of innocence, the loneliness that can swoop in the world 'after feminism' and the consolations of female friendship. The geography of space and place is central to these stories; physical and psychic dislocation mirror each other. The title story's crassly materialistic Surfers' Paradise is a metaphor for the emptiness and inhibitions of the interior life; but elsewhere, a weighty atlas in London can comfort with the familiar shape of Australia. Central too, is the female body, represented as both the object of male fear and derision and the powerful site of maternity and creativity. CM

post-colonial writing The term post-colonial writing generally refers to that literature emerging from once-colonized (for those working in English, usually 'Commonwealth') countries since the 1940s, the time of independence from European empire. It can also be used to denote pre-independence writers who overtly or otherwise subverted colonial distinctions and definitions in their work (see COLONIAL WRITING). Though there are crucial differences between their approaches, post-colonial writing by both men and women is typically marked by a stylistic impurity or hybridity – a mingling of voices, dialects, cultural traditions and forms of English – which wilfully disregards the social divisions and racial distinctions which characterized colonial rule at all levels.

The constraints under which women writers have generally laboured, have been for post-colonial women writers exacerbated not only by the legacy of colonialism but also by the masculine identifications of nationalist movements and their vocabularies of self-expression in the post-independence period. This situation of overlapping forms of marginalization, captured in the phrase 'double' or 'triple colonization', has formed and continues to form one of the central preoccupations of post-colonial women's writing.

It was a notable paradox of the post-independence period that forms of exclusion based on gender, as well as on class, caste, race and ethnic identity, established during the colonial period, were in many cases reinforced by the demands of national liberation. The stereotyping of the native male as passive and effeminate produced, as a direct reaction, movements of aggressive self-assertion led and dominated by men. Literature, always a crucial vehicle of nationalist self-imagining, reflected this predominance, both in the subjectivities projected in texts, in who was writing, and in plots and symbolism – for example, quest motifs featuring a male hero (the nationalist everyman) and in the familiar iconography of women as custodians and nurturers, if not embodiments, of national integrity and purity.

From the early 1970s, however, this situation began inexorably to change as Indian, African and West Indian women, and black women in the West, sought to define their own positions, not only vis-à-vis the nationalist movements which had elevated their male counterparts, but also in relation to middle-class Western feminism. Up till (and even beyond) this period, the critical appreciation of post-colonial women's literatures had been inhibited, even as it had been facilitated, by, on the one hand, Europe-centred readings of post-colonial male writing as individualistic self-representation, and on the other, by Anglo-American and French feminist criticism which laid particular emphasis once again on selfhood and the individual body, and on the subversion of masculine narrative and conceptual patterns.

From the first, post-colonial women writers found in autobiography and biography, including family and communal stories, a key vehicle of oppositional and celebratory self-expression. As we see in the work of the West Indian writers OLIVE SENIOR or JOAN RILEY, or in the writing of BAPSI SIDHWA, NAYANTARA SAHGAL or ARUNDHATI ROY in South Asia, or in the South African situation in the 1980s and 1990s, in telling their own stories women writers tested their voices as well as uncovering their often obscured or buried histories. To speak of themselves, to articulate themselves, was to give shape to the localities and actualities of their lives, and in so doing to bring into being empowering images of identity and community. Such issues – of story-telling as identity making, of the importance of a woman-centred history as well as of the need to historicize the body, to speak the body's historical griefs and pain – have remained central in post-colonial women's writing. However, post-colonial writers do not only excavate the past in order to account for the losses and frustrations of the present. They are also in quest of hidden resources, of tales of survival and unsung strength, including the private languages or habits through which women in the past might have protected and sustained themselves under difficult circumstances. Some post-colonial women writers' explorations of and experimentations with such secret, arcane or deliberately convoluted languages aim, as in the past, at forestalling appropriative readings from without, as is evidenced in the complex, allusive writing of the

Jamaican ERNA BRODBER or the Canadian lesbian poet DAPHNE MARLATT.

In response to the biases of Western feminism, writers have also laid stress on their differential experiences of exclusion, hardship and endurance, at the same time as underlining the importance of communal bonding and solidarity between women. While post-colonial novelists, playwrights and poets have been comparatively less concerned than their Western counterparts to safeguard or create women-only spaces and practices, at the same time they have been involved in celebrating women's creativity, as well as in recognizing the processes, rituals and rites of passage particular to women's lives. This focus often leads them to foreground the compounds, side-rooms, marketplaces and firesides where women tend to predominate in their societies, as well as the more problematically secluded or veiled spaces of the *zenana* and the *burkha*.

The stress on the specific multiple textures of their own lives is clearly manifested in the forms taken by post-colonial women's writing. Inevitably influenced by contemporary POSTMODERN trends, but also, crucially, by the writers' often mixed cultural backgrounds and layered identities, a prominent feature of their writing is its mosaic or composite quality, in particular the interleaving of forms derived from indigenous, nationalist and European literary traditions. Themselves often straddling different cross-fertilized cultural contexts, writers emphasize the need for an inventive 'impurity' of styles and speaking positions in their work, and favour hybrid, translated, interconnected and choric forms. Story-telling can be self-consciously many-voiced, or interrupted and expansive, as is an oral tale. Poetry, such as that of the pioneering Jamaican Creole poet LOUISE BENNETT, taps into kitchen chat and street natter, and picks up on the rhythms and vocabulary of everyday speech. This attention to voice, specifically the spoken voice, relates not only to post-colonial women writers' interest in articulating silence, or conversely in privileging women's talk. It also connects with the writers' proximity to different oral traditions: African folktales and praise-singing, public narrations of traditional epics in India, and song- and story-based traditions in the Caribbean. The work of such diverse writers as AMA ATA AIDOO, Michelle Cliff, BESSIE HEAD, KERI HULME, GRACE NICHOLS and Rebekah Njau, among many others, embraces incantation and song, word games, dream-sequences and dramatic interchanges, all of which techniques work against the unifying viewpoint more typical of European REALISM, and of nationalist novels by male post-colonial writers.

The inclusion of white women writers from such countries as Australia, New Zealand, Canada and South Africa under the title 'post-colonial' continues to be controversial. However, the writers' preoccupation with aesthetic and political issues grounded upon the unearthing and representation of women's voices connects them with post-colonial writers based elsewhere in the world. Writers ranging from the now well-established MARGARET ATWOOD, CAROL SHIELDS or JANET FRAME to the less widely known Australian HELEN GARNER or the Canadian ANNE MARIE MacDONALD, are similarly concerned with women's history as encoding forgotten or neglected suppressions and subversions, and with the related themes of women's madness, work, pleasure, motherhood and daughterhood, self-making and endurance.

One of the greatest riches of post-colonial women's writing, which after all embraces the inhabited continents of the world, is its immense versatility and variety. It is this heterogeneity that West-based post-colonial criticism is seeking to find ways of recognizing, while also allowing for points of convergence and connection between the different regional and national literatures.   EBo

postmodernism The term 'postmodernism' was initially used in the sixties, mostly in relation to architecture and the visual arts, gradually gaining currency in the seventies and eighties. By the nineties, it is used to describe not only aesthetic forms, but a broader cultural and historical period. Defining what postmodernism actually is presents certain difficulties, since to represent it as a coherent and stable poetics is to deny its project from the outset. Postmodernism describes a set of aesthetic practices that destabilize the truths or paradigms – of history, of ethics – by which Western culture represents a unified, perceptible reality whose concepts have a continuous meaning for everyone.

Postmodernism necessarily suggests an engagement with the modern by its incorporation of the term. The parameters of this engagement are contradictory – postmodernism is articulated as both a break from the modern and a continuation of it, depending on how the term 'modern' is understood. While many theorists and practitioners understand postmodernism in relation to the periodising or epochal condition of modernity, others view it as either a break with – or, alternatively, an extension of – the aesthetic and stylistic practices of MODERNISM.

Modernity is commonly associated with the post-Enlightenment age; and the Enlightenment with visions of a social order based on the principles of reason, rationality and progress. The modern attempt to systematically ground truth and knowledge, to legitimate dominant discourses of reason and REALISM, inevitably excluded dissenting voices and repressed difference. Privileging order over chaos, reason over madness, and rational masculinity over hysterical femininity, these legitimating discourses served to construct a fabric of social coherence and an ordered society. In contesting the repressive discourses of modernity, postmodernism and feminism share a similar impetus, along with post-colonialism and other discourses from the margins.

The postmodern celebration of the heterogeneous, plural, antihierarchical and fragmentary narrative calls into question the validity and authority of a single unified discourse. The idea of a representative voice which can speak for everyone – regardless of gender, sexual orientation, class, ethnicity and other identities than those considered to be the norm – is exposed as a fabrication. Using postmodern forms, many women writers work against the grain of these dominant narratives of history, subjectivity and femininity.

History has long been represented from universalizing viewpoints. To counter this, much postmodern writing is engaged in highlighting the difficulties of representing the past in the present. Many works question the assumption that history is objectively knowable, instead positing knowledge and truth as culturally situated rather than able to be viewed objectively from outside the text – to postmodernism, there is no outside. Narratives usually construct a position of authority, often founded on qualities like consistency and logic; ambiguities and contradictions are dissolved and resolved. But the postmodern text takes a different approach. Inconsistencies, gaps and speculations are foregrounded to draw attention to the plurality of voices previously subjugated. This can be seen in the work of writers like KERI HULME, MAXINE HONG KINGSTON and TONI MORRISON, all of whom draw on the knowledge of marginalized social groups and oral cultures to add a multitude of layers to official history, interrogating and challenging its authority.

Postmodernism exposes and interrogates a text's implicit claims to represent a transparent view of an externally verifiable reality. Representation, as the production of meaning, gives truth and significance to paradigms of patriarchy and models of femininity that particular societies produce and reify; the narrative strategies of postmodernism are used by women writers to explore and reveal the fallibility of traditional systems of representation. With the destabilization of narrative authority, texts are seen as spaces in which different discourses, voices and experiences can mix and compete. The narrative is no longer stable, transparent and seamless. Instead, it is often self-reflexive, drawing attention to its own constructedness and, in the process, nudging readers to query the stability and authority of other texts and discourses.

Of course, self-reflexivity in aesthetic practice is nothing new. Modernism, like postmodernism, has been variously described as self-conscious, playful, non-representational, non-realist, ironic and ambiguous. Where postmodernism parts company from modernism, though, is over the high modernist impulse to develop aesthetic practices – the arts – as an exclusive realm, quite separate from everyday life. This impulse was set against the backdrop of a mass culture burgeoning under monopoly capitalism, new means of communication, and the advent of mechanical reproduction which threatened the notion of originality and authenticity in artistic practice. Modernists, with their principle of 'art pour l'art', and their focus on style and form, proclaimed the autonomy of art, separating it from other spheres of society. The artwork was privileged as unique, and modernism became valorized in museums and the academic canon as 'high art', in opposition to mass culture. It is this institutionalized distinction between 'high' and 'low' culture, and allied class, ethnic and gender distinctions, that postmodernism works to efface. Postmodernism, exploring the interaction between high and popular culture, becomes an examination of how meaning and value are ascribed in a society. Women writers formerly relegated to the margins of literature as writers and readers of 'lowbrow' genres are now using these genres to interrogate the very images of femininity genre fiction is supposed to perpetuate. JOYCE CAROL OATES, MARGARET ATWOOD and the Australian poet DOROTHY PORTER have deployed genres as diverse as GOTHIC, ROMANCE, SCIENCE-FICTION and DETECTIVE novels to self-consciously denaturalize the codes and signs of femininity. In postmodernist writing, such self-reflexivity about literary practice no longer emphasizes the separation between art and life, but blurs this border, underlining the fictiveness of texts through pastiche, parody and appropriation from other texts, as well as a bricolage of styles, forms and genres. Postmodern practice includes revising the fictions and myths that underpin Western culture, and this is a strategy utilized by many women writers. Rewriting the received collective wisdom of one's culture, particularly by parodying its representations of women, enables women writers to problematize and subvert the representation of femininity. Postmodern women writers are engaging their readers' knowledge of well-known cultural texts and drawing attention to their hitherto implicit assumptions about the role of women and ideals of femininity. Parodic revisions of this type can be found in the works of writers such as ANGELA CARTER, JEANETTE WINTERSON, FAY WELDON and KATHY ACKER.

The benefits of a postmodern poetics which throws into question totalizing discourses which perpetuate stereotypes of women are manifold for feminism. This non-hierarchical approach, favouring a multiplicity of voices and decentring the knowing masculine subject, can be positively employed by women writers concerned with dismantling a system of representation that has long essentialized sexual difference, fixing 'woman' as the passive object of discourse.

But the feminist intersection with postmodernism is not without vicissitudes. Postmodernism valorizes a fragmented subject with no authoritative speaking position, the deferral of meaning and the constructedness of all discourses. However, women who have struggled for a voice and political agency cannot uncritically embrace a discourse which eschews coherent positions. This is why many women writers do not consider themselves to be postmodern, but choose to use the tools of postmodernism strategically to serve their political ends.   AL

Potiki (1986) PATRICIA GRACE inscribes her second novel firmly within Maori history and the importance of story-telling: the 'carvers' fashion the passing generations in wood, the family narrators outline the struggle to maintain their ancestral land in the face of commercial pressures. 'Everything we need is here, Hemi said. It's true, and he's always known it. What Toko said was also true – the stories had changed.' Hemi and his family attempt to reclaim the family land of the Tamihanas, become self-sufficient and pass on a different non-Pakeha history – 'It is rare for us to find ourselves in books ... but our main book was the *wharenui* which is itself a story, a history, a gallery, a study, a design structure and a *taonga*' – whilst Toko, the disabled Christ-like child, foresees the dangers which threaten the community through his gift of 'eversight'. The figure of Dollarman, his idea of progress and the various attempts at destroying the Maori community are successfully imagined from within, and Grace's simple yet complex (spiral) narrative structure provides the necessary unity, poetry and passion.   MRE

Potiki, Roma 1958– Maori New Zealand poet. Her tribal affiliations are Te Aupouri, Te Arawa, Ngati Rangitihi. She is a visual artist, academic, theatre director and writer, and is best known for her poetry which is direct, strong and both feminist and Maori. *Stones in Her Mouth* (1992) has attacks on transnational companies and their effect on New Zealand, some of which declare:

> some men are bastards
> they just want women they can put down
> to make themselves feel better
> they call it 'fucking that bitch'.

But through them all is an awareness of the power of being a Maori woman – 'i am Papatuanuku / giving completely i hold strength in its upright form – i am papatuanuku, the land.'   AM

Potter (later Heelis), (Helen) Beatrix 1866–1943 English writer and illustrator whose distinctive miniature animal books have become CHILDREN's classics.

Born in Kensington, London, into a wealthy family with domineering parents, she led an isolated childhood and was educated privately by governesses. At 15 she began keeping a diary in code which was not deciphered until after her death. She showed an early talent for natural history illustration, dissected dead animals, collected botanical specimens and kept a variety of pets. She worked on watercolour studies of fungi which she was unable to publish, before writing *The Tale of Peter Rabbit* in 1893 as an illustrated letter to a child, publishing it privately in 1901. Picked up by publishers, *Peter Rabbit* quickly became popular and Potter wrote and illustrated many other small-sized animal books for young children, including *The Tale of Squirrel Nutkin* (1903), *The Tale of Mrs Tiggy-Winkle* (1905) and *The Tale of Jemima Puddle-Duck* (1908). Her work is marked by humour, awareness of physical danger and JANE AUSTEN-like social observation. Her precise and detailed watercolour illustrations depicting her animal characters in human dress and domestic scenes are integral to her art. Most of her children's books appeared before her marriage in 1913 to solicitor William Heelis, after which she settled in Sawrey in the Lake District and largely devoted herself to farming, sheep breeding and the land preservation aims of the National Trust. Almost from the time of publication, her work has been merchandized as part of traditional English heritage.   AEG

Pound, Louise 1872–1958 American scholar, athlete, linguist and folklorist. She was born in Lincoln, Nebraska. Her father was a judge and senator, her mother a botanist who identified new wildflower species. Educated by her mother in early childhood, she entered Latin School in 1886, then attended the University of Nebraska, where she became the orator and poet of her class and earned varsity letters in tennis competing against men. Also renowned as a long-distance bicycler and basketball player, Pound lectured throughout Nebraska on the need to extend opportunities for women in sports. She was the first woman inducted into the Nebraska Sports Hall of Fame. She taught at the University of Nebraska from 1894 to 1945, taking a year off to complete a Ph.D. at the University of Heidelberg in 1900 and teaching summer sessions at Berkeley, Yale and the University of Chicago. As a scholar, she pioneered in the study of American literature, language and folkways. She published hundreds of articles on regional American language and wrote two ground-breaking books on the folk ballad, *Poetic Origins and the Ballad* (1921) and *American Ballads and Songs* (1922). In 1954 she was elected the first woman president of the Modern Language Association. She also served as president of the American Folklore Society and co-founded and edited *American Speech*.   JSG

Powell, Dawn 1897–1965 American satirist whose novels richly capture the glitter of New York City in the 1930s and 1940s. Born in Ohio, she moved to New York in 1918, married advertising man Joseph Gousha in 1920, with whom she had a son, and lived in Manhattan the rest of her life. Her early novels *She Walks in Beauty* (1928) and *Dance Night* (1930) are set in the Mid-West, but with *Turn, Magic Wheel* (1936) she turned to the Greenwich Village café society which became her own. Often likened to DOROTHY PARKER because of her keen wit, she never attained Parker's success, and in the comic slant of her fictions was closer to MURIEL SPARK. Mercilessly adept at capturing people's ambitions, social and artistic, she wrote nonetheless with genuine sympathy. She rejected the term 'satire' to describe her work, claiming she was simply a REALIST; though she admitted of her flawed characters: 'I give them their heads. They furnish their own nooses.' By the 1940s her talent had matured: her best work includes her autobiography of childhood *My Home Is Far Away* (1944); and *The Locusts Have No King* (1948) and *The Wicked Pavilion* (1954), two gleefully sharp, complex novels which take on literary and bohemian pretensions. Her own life had its unconventional dimensions: she carried on an open affair, and there were suspicions that the two made up a *ménage à trois* with Gousha. In addition to fifteen novels, she wrote plays, scripts and a volume of stories, *Sunday, Monday and Always* (1952). Her last novel was *The Golden Spur* (1962). After her death, her friend and fan Gore Vidal worked to ensure her name didn't disappear; in the 1990s her diaries were published and her reputation as one of America's superb comic novelists was belatedly established.   SB

Praed, Rosa Campbell 1851–1935 Australian-born novelist, brought up in Queensland. She went to live in England with her husband in 1876 and there wrote her forty-plus novels. After separating from her husband she lived for many years with Nancy Harward, a spiritual medium. Her fiction demonstrates a fascination with women's states of mind, their desires and dissatisfactions, their often heightened capacity for occult spirituality.

Her first novel, *An Australian Heroine* (1880), was published by Chapman and Hall, where novelist George Meredith was publisher's reader and encouraged her. Its success launched her into literary London, where she already had connections through Praed's family. This, and her prolific talent, made her the first Australian-born woman to gain an international literary reputation. POLICY AND PASSION (1881), her second novel, was a romance in which Honoria, the headstrong heroine, has to choose between two suitors, an attractive but caddish Englishman and a dull, reliable Australian. This dramatization of the colonial dilemma of identification set the pattern for several novels with Australian settings where the romance narrative plays on the question of colonial origins. Although tales such as *Affinities* (1886), *Mrs Tregaskiss* (1895) and *Some Loves and a Life* (1904) have tragic outcomes for their heroines, two novels set in the Australian bush, *Fugitive Anne* (1903) and *Lady Bridget in the Never-Never Land* (1915), portray the reconciliation of passion and commitment. The first of these is primarily an adventure story in which the heroine successfully escapes her abusive husband and falls in love with her rescuer. *Lady Bridget*, on the other hand, makes the accommodation to marriage its central theme. In these Australian settings, the recognition of female desire is linked to the heroine's relationship to the 'Never-Never', a mythical construction of the Bush.

SMS

Prelude to Christopher (1934) ELEANOR DARK's second novel intersects the subjects of motherhood, eugenics and feminism in a work she considered one of her best because it contained 'a sort of spontaneity' and intensity which made it unique. Dark structures the novel using a condensed time-frame, interior monologue and stream of consciousness technique. She concentrates twenty-four years of Linda and Nigel Hendon's married life into four days. Linda is a scientist, and her husband is a medical doctor and a passionate eugenicist. Nigel forbids Linda to have children because of hereditary madness in her family. Linda's accelerating insanity, culminating in her suicide, raises the question: is she mad or has society sent her mad? The novel spans the years when the eugenics movement was most active in Australia (*c.*1910–30) and continues to raise issues concerning the ethics of genetic engineering, the subject of motherhood and the interrogation of gender identity. Dark, however, refuses to respond or assign meaning to the issues surfacing in the novel, leaving them open to readers' own judgements.

JN

Press, Karen ?– South African poet, CHILDREN'S BOOK author and cultural commentator. Her poems are strongly influenced by the political situation in South Africa. For children she has written two books on significant South African women whose lives are not generally included in the old history books. The first is called *Nongqawuse's Prophecy* (1990), and is a sympathetic account of the life of the young prophetess of the Xhosa cattle killings. The second, *Krotoä* (1990), narrates the life of a Khoikhoi woman who acted as interpreter in the household of the first Dutch commander to the Cape in the 17th century. This material is reworked in her important poem cycle, 'Krotoä's Story', included in a poetry collection called *Bird Heart Stoning the Sea* (1990). Her second volume of poetry, *The*

Katharine Susannah Prichard's signature.

Coffee Shop Poems (1993), is a playful collection of rewritings of poems by, amongst others, Keats, Yeats, Lawrence and PLATH. Together with INGRID DE KOK she edited a collection of responses to Albie Sachs's paper on culture, 'Preparing Ourselves for Freedom', called *Spring is Rebellious: Arguments about Cultural Freedom* (1990). CCo

Price, K(athleen) Arnold 1893–1989 Irish poet, novelist and short-story writer. Born into a Church of Ireland family, Price spent most of her childhood in County Limerick. Her maternal family, the Arnolds, were distinguished educationalists, her grandfather Thomas Arnold, was Professor of English at University College Dublin; and her great-grandfather, Thomas Arnold, was the reforming headmaster at Rugby School in England. In 1927 she graduated in English and French from Trinity College Dublin, then spent time at King's College London and the University of Lyons. A keen traveller, she lived in Athens, Crete, the Basque country and England, pursuing her interests in local architecture and furniture. On her return to Ireland she lived first in County Wicklow, then in Ballsbridge in Dublin. Price was not overly fond of company and published only occasionally in journals and magazines when she was alive. Her poetry was first published in the *Dublin Magazine* in 1925 and she didn't publish again until 1943. The *Irish Press*, The *Kerryman*, *Dublin Magazine*, *Envoy* and *Irish Writing* all published her work. She died in 1989 not long after having published her novel, *The New Perspective* (1980), and her collection of short stories, *The Captain's Paramours* (1985). MSu

Prichard, Katharine Susannah 1883–1969 Australian novelist, short-story writer, poet, dramatist, political pamphleteer and activist. She was born in Fiji where her father was the editor of the *Fiji Times*, grew up in Tasmania and Melbourne, and settled in Western Australia with her husband and son. Denied a university education, she worked as a governess before travelling to London as a freelance journalist in 1915. There she investigated alternative philosophies including socialism, syndicalism, anarchism, theosophy and mysticism. Appalled by slum conditions, she adopted communism after reading Marx and Engels. Returning to Australia she became a founding (and life-long) member of the Communist party – supporting the Spanish Civil War, campaigns for universal suffrage and anti-conscription before devoting her political activities to the Peace movement and nuclear disarmament. In 1959 she won the World Peace Council Medal.

Fiercely committed to the common people and their struggle against capitalist exploitation, her novels, all with memorable female characters, portray the outback life of early settlers (*The Pioneers*, 1915), opal miners (*BLACK OPAL*, 1921), timber workers (*Working Bullocks*, 1926) and prospectors (the social-REALIST gold-fields trilogy: *Roaring Nineties*, 1946, *Golden Miles*, 1948, and *Winged Seeds*, 1950). Her prize-winning novel, *COONARDOO* (1928), and play, *BRUMBY INNES* (1927), initiated a frank exploration of the sexual exploitation of Aboriginal women by white men. Like the indomitable Sally of the trilogy, she lived by the belief that 'life could not defeat her if she were working for something bigger than herself'. See also *KISS ON THE LIPS AND OTHER STORIES* (1932) and *INTIMATE STRANGERS* (1937). KS

Pride and Prejudice (1813) A novel by JANE AUSTEN first published in 1813, some sixteen years after an early version with the title 'First Impressions' was rejected by a London publisher.

This is an elaborate and romantic comedy of manners, central to which is Elizabeth Bennet's prejudice against the proud but eligible Mr Darcy and his own attempts to suppress his involuntary attraction to her. Her relations are a handicap: her younger sisters are notorious for their pursuit of uniformed officers, her mother is vulgar and voluble, and her clever acerbic father an indifferent and irresponsible parent. Elizabeth gives too credulous a hearing to the superficially charming Mr Wickham, who traduces Darcy, and when she discovers that Darcy has worked to dampen the romance between her decorous sister Jane and his friend Mr Bingley, ironically because Jane's discreet behaviour leads Darcy to doubt the strength of her feelings, Elizabeth's prejudices are confirmed. Darcy's first proposal of marriage is rejected with contumely, but he learns to distinguish her from her embarrassing relations, and his subsequently heroic and disinterested behaviour teaches Elizabeth his true worth. The novel ends happily with all the main protagonists worthily married. CT

Prime of Miss Jean Brodie, The (1961) This most famous of MURIEL SPARK's novels, adapted for stage and screen, is her most successful portrait of a *monstre sacrée*, the eponymous Edinburgh schoolteacher, who forces her obsessions on to a group of schoolgirls, manipulating them into acting out her romantic and political fantasies. Structurally, it is flashily non-linear, playing games with time that endlessly circle round the riddle of which of her *protégées* betrayed her and got her dismissed; it constantly flashes forward from the 1930s to their adulthood, notably to the later fame of Sandy, subsequently an enclosed nun and famous mystic. The conscious affectlessness of Spark's style is here less sardonic and more a touching correlative for the inexperience of the girls and the delusions of their teacher; it is technically one of her most accomplished books, but also one of her warmest.   RK

Primrose, Diana fl. 1630 'Noble Lady' and author of *A Chaine of Pearle. Or a memoriall of the peerles Graces, and Heroick Vertues of Queene Elizabeth of Glorious Memory* (1630), dedicated to 'All Noble Ladies and Gentlewomen'. These ten couplet poems itemize Elizabeth's 'true Religion' ('Shee ban'g the Pope'), Chastity, Prudence (a gift 'rarely incident / To our weake Sex'), Temperance, Clemency, Justice and Fortitude. This praise of Elizabeth twenty-seven years after her death accentuates virtues which may have been considered lacking in Charles I (during this period faith in Charles was seriously diminishing due to his Papist interests and imprudence in trusting Buckingham). The source of *A Chaine of Pearle* is Camden's *Annals of Queen Elizabeth* (published in Latin (1615) and French (1624)). The political dimension of the poetry suggests a link between Diana and Gilbert Primrose (*c*.1580–1641), a minister of the French Protestant church and author of a 'Panegyric' to the King. Diana's work contains commendatory verse by the otherwise unknown Dorothy Berry. In 1823 John Nichols ascribes Diana Primrose's work to ANNE CLIFFORD. The enigmatic nature of her identity is deepened by Robert Herrick's poem 'To His Booke', which concludes: 'Blush not at all for that; since we have set / Some *Pearles on Queens*, that have been counterfeit'.   KTu

Prince, Mary *c*.1788–? Bermudan writer and anti-slavery campaigner. Born into slavery in Bermuda, Prince resisted her condition from an early age and travelled to Turks Island in 1805 to escape a brutal owner. Having discovered that vicious beatings were not to be escaped, she began saving for her manumission on return to Bermuda in 1810. In 1814 she travelled to Antigua to work for John Wood, a sadistic owner who refused all requests to buy her freedom, even after her marriage to Daniel James in 1826. Prince came to England with the Woods in 1827 and managed to remain in London when they returned to Antigua. She worked as a domestic servant for Thomas Pringle, secretary of the Anti-Slavery Society. With the support of the Society, *The History of Mary Prince, A West Indian Slave,*

Related by Herself (1831) was published in London and Edinburgh, with three editions in the first year. Prince's association with the Anti-Slavery Society almost certainly shaped her narrative, which was transcribed by Susanna Strickland and edited by Pringle. As the first black woman to publish her life history in Britain, Mary Prince wrote in a way that would most effectively challenge the institution of slavery and thus excluded material which might have been regarded offensive. Although detailed in its descriptions of physical abuse, the narrative is clearly censored in relation to sexual abuse.   AD

Prince, Nancy (Gardner) 1799–? American TRAVEL WRITER. She was born in Newburyport, Massachusetts, to parents of African and native American ancestry. Her father died when she was young. At the age of 8 she became a servant, though she had early aspirations of becoming a teacher, writer and humanitarian. Her mother suffered an emotional breakdown after her stepfather's death, and Gardner helped to support her siblings, resisting the fate of her older sister, who was 'deluded away' into prostitution. She took a position in Salem, Massachusetts, at the age of 14. In 1824 she escaped servitude by marrying Nero Prince, a prominent widower who had been a footman in the court of the Russian Tsar. They moved to St Petersburg, where she established a successful business making baby linens and learned Greek, French and literary English. Nine years later, her health weakening in the Russian winters, she returned alone to the United States; her husband died before he could join her. After meeting LUCRETIA MOTT, she became active in the abolitionist and women's rights movements, where she earned a reputation as a powerful speaker. In 1850 she visited Jamaica, a trip recounted, together with her Russian experiences, in her *A Narrative of the Life and Travels of Mrs Nancy Prince* (1850).   JSG

Procter, Adelaide Ann 1825–64 Author of popular sentimental verse. Adelaide grew up in London, in a literary and intellectual environment, educated by both parents. Her father was a poet and lawyer and was the friend of Charles Dickens and Robert Browning.

About 1851 she and two of her sisters became Roman Catholics. She began to publish poetry in Dickens's periodicals, *Household Words* and *All the Year Round*, in 1853 under the name 'Mary Berwick'. Her collected poems in two volumes, *Legends and Lyrics* (1858–61), ran into ten editions by 1866. She campaigned for the education of the poor, housing for the homeless and the employment of women and published *A Chaplet of Verses* in 1861 for the benefit of a Catholic refuge.

She died of consumption on 2 February 1864. Her complete works were issued in 1905 with a foreword by

Dickens. Her most well-known poems are 'The Angel's Story', 'A Legend of Provence' and 'The Story of a Faithful Soul'. Her songs, 'Cleansing Fires', 'The Message' and 'The Lost Chord', are well known, and many of her hymns are in common use. In 1877 her poems were more popular in England than those of Tennyson.   RS

Progress of Love, The (1986) ALICE MUNRO's fifth

collection of short stories explores love and loss through a series of poignant stories, each of which, through extended flashbacks, spans time periods longer than most novels. The collection received the Governor General's Award and the Marian Engel Prize and confirms Munro's place as one of the foremost short-story writers of her generation. REALISTIC in mode, yet able to incorporate the inexplicable fluidly, the individual stories provide snapshots of moments spliced together from a variety of narrators' perspectives in order to form a collage-like picture in which 'truth' and 'reality' are questioned and recreated. The unreliability of memory is foregrounded, as characters deliberately compose their memories, sometimes in direct opposition to the 'facts' of events. This transformation of the past is accepted as valid; as one narrator reports, 'It seems so much the truth it is the truth.' Munro's eleven stories focus on family fragmentation, the loss of partners through death or divorce, adolescent titillation and middle-aged resignation; the ageing female body is the most frequently repeated image.   HSM

Progress of Romance, The (1785) In one of the first

works of modern literary history and criticism, CLARA REEVE traces the novel's roots to early ROMANCE, citing illustrious originators – Homer, Chaucer, Spenser, Sidney and Milton – and thus elevating its status. Structured as a dialogue, or verbal duel, between friends (and the sexes), Hortensius (male) initially resists Euphrasia's (female) arguments. Speaking through Euphrasia, Reeve praises novelists, many of them women, who have incorporated the 'moral tendency' of romance, which speaks to the 'noblest feelings', with the novel's ability to deceive us 'into a persuasion . . . that all is real', so that we lose 'sight of the author'. Reeve's judgement of novelists is based on this integration, which leads her to favour Daniel Defoe, Samuel Richardson, SARAH FIELDING, FRANCES SHERIDAN, CHARLOTTE LENNOX and FRANCES BROOKE, while Hortensius champions Henry Fielding and Laurence Sterne. Warnings that the novel is dangerous to youth when it 'awakens those passions which should be regulated' mean amorous novelists like APHRA BEHN and ELIZA HAYWOOD are criticized, although allowances are made for their historical context.   LMT

Promised Land, The (1996) GRACE OGOT's first

novel is a cautionary tale about ethnic tension caused by economic migration from Kenya to Tanganyika. The young hero, frustrated by land disputes and impoverished soil in his native Kenya, persuades his reluctant wife to emigrate. Greeted with hospitality by earlier Kenyan settlers in Tanganyika, Ochola and his wife Nyapol enjoy a period of prosperity until their rapid material and social success offends a medicine man from another ethnic group, who uses his preparations to drive Ochola into the forest in a wild frenzy. Reduced to bestial status, he is only cured on condition he returns to his homeland, which he does in Nyapol's care. The novel relates issues of emigration to those of gender, so that the hero's stereotyped masculinity, combining economic ambition, physical prowess and adventure, is contrasted with his wife's loyalty to the feminized communal ethos of her motherland. The ending subverts the hero's masculine project (associated – through the title's biblical allusion – with colonialism itself), and privileges the female voice and power.   WJB

prophecy Together with SPIRITUAL AUTOBIOGRAPHY, prophecy constituted one of the major generic sites for the proliferation of women's published writing in the 17th century. Produced predominantly (though not exclusively) within the radical Puritan sects such as the Quakers, Baptists and Independents, prophecy was particularly abundant during the years of the Civil Wars, Commonwealth and Protectorate. It was thought that women's humoral composition, which resulted in an irrational and emotional nature, made them particularly suited to be the conduits of God's word, and this capacity had a brief moment of more widespread acceptance under conditions of uncertainty and upheaval.

At its broadest, prophecy was taken to be *any* utterance resulting from divine inspiration; more narrowly, it indicated a concern with predicting or delineating future events. Whether addressing an individual (such as Cromwell) or a community (such as the inhabitants of Oxford or Aylesbury), this was usually a warning to turn from sin and cleave to the godly way. Rather than these predictions being random prognostications, however, they were rooted in scriptural interpretation, which was then related to contemporary people and events. This relationship to the Bible was sometimes systematic and exhaustive – as in MARY CARY's *The Little Horns Doom and Downfall* (1651), which is constructed around a reading of Daniel 7.24–7.27, or Cotton and Cole's TO THE PRIESTS AND PEOPLE OF ENGLAND (1655), which engages with St Paul's proscriptions against women speaking in church – and sometimes more general and allusive – as in Anne Audland's *A True Declaration* (1655) or ANNE

WENTWORTH's *Revelation of Jesus Christ* (1679). The register of the prophecy also varied: it might be ecstatic and extemporary, such as ANNA TRAPNEL's *THE CRY OF A STONE* (1654), transcribed whilst Trapnel lay in a trance, and comprising verse as well as prose, and readings of her own prophetic dreams as well as of the Bible, all addressed, with characteristic panache, to 'the Governors, Army, Churches, Ministry, Universities, and the whole Nation'. Other prophecies, however, were less rhapsodic in tone: Cary's, for example, despite sharing Trapnel's millenarian beliefs, are more measured, practical and programmatic. Whatever the register, the tone is, more often than not, admonitory, the political uncertainty of these years, not to mention the plethora of competing and constantly realigning religious groupings, generating a sense of urgency in the prophets.

Although their style and tone might at first seem alienating to the modern reader, these prophecies constitute the first large-scale engagement in public affairs by English women writers. Since politics and religion were inseparable at this time, each concerned with the working-through of God's plan for his people in this world (and beyond), these writings demonstrate the extent of women's engagement in the struggle over the spiritual/social/political dimensions and interpretations of the divine plan. The radical sectarian moment was relatively shortlived, but the space it had opened up for women within published public debate was never again closed, as the work of women essayists and polemicists in the later 17th and 18th centuries testifies.   HAH

Proulx, E. Annie 1935– American novelist whose monumental evocations of life in rurally remote parts of North America have won many awards and a loyal readership. After many years as a freelance journalist writing about 'weather, apples, canoeing and mice, cuisine, beadwork, libraries and lettuce', she published her first novel, *Postcards* (1992), when she was 52 and became the first woman to win the PEN/Faulkner Prize. In taut, muscular prose, full of tragic resonances, it tells the tale of Loyal Blood, a man escaping from a terrible, accidental crime. Like its protagonist, the book is imbued with a sense that 'Life cripples us up in different ways but it gets everybody.'

Less bleak, but also set in a harsh landscape – the rocky coast of Newfoundland – her second novel, *The Shipping News* (1993), won international acclaim, together with the Pulitzer Prize, the National Book Award and the *Irish Times* International Fiction Prize. Bringing warmth and wit to a world still full of pain and disaster, it presents, in its inarticulate and gawky hero Quoyle, one of the most sympathetic characters of recent fiction.

Proulx's preoccupation with violence continues in her short stories, *Heart Songs* (1994), compressed poetic narratives depicting the bitter feuds and harsh realities of life for farming families struggling in the backwoods. Her catalogue of disasters reaches epidemic proportions in her third novel, *Accordion Crimes* (1996), which follows the fate of a green accordion and the pursuit of the American Dream through generations of immigrants.   CP

Pugh, Sheenagh 1950– English poet. Born in Birmingham, she studied Russian and German at the University of Bristol before going on to lecture in Creative Writing at the University of Glamorgan. With subject matter ranging from car-boot sales and Buffalo Bill to 'Voices in Mousa Brach', a paean to the Shetland Isles, Pugh merges humorous observations about the quotidian world with the grander themes of a mythical aspiration. She has published several collections, including *Crowded by Shadows* (1977), *Beware Falling Tortoises* (1987) and *Sing for the Taxman* (1993). Her *Selected Poems* (1990) won the Welsh Arts Council Prize for poetry. She also translates German poetry and has work by Andreas Gryphius and Friedrich von Logau included in her own collections. *Id's Hospit* (1997) – its title taken from a broken sign outside a closed hospital – exemplifies her playful pitting of levity against gravity, and in the poem, 'Booklifting', she mischievously informs the reader that she once 'half-inched a Martin Amis'.   JAH

Pye [née Mendez], Jael 1737?–82 Occasional poet and author, born the daughter of a rich Jewish merchant. Little is known of her early life. She married first in 1762 and again in 1766, and after quickly spending her fortune, she was left alone with her young daughter in near-poverty. Pye's first publication was the pamphlet, *A Short Account of the Principal Seats and Gardens in and about Richmond and Kew in 1760*, reprinted with her *Poems* (1767) and as *A Peep into the Principal Seats and Gardens in and about Twickenham* (1775). She was a good friend of David Garrick who produced her farce 'The Capricious Lady' at Drury Lane in 1771; it had only one performance and was not published. In the same year Pye published *Poems. By a Lady*, which included a modernized version of 'Childe Waters', a poem addressed to Garrick and an epistle, 'On the Report of Dr Sterne's Death, in the Year 1760'. A melodramatic novel, *Theodosius and Arabella*, appeared in 1786, centring on two lovers who wrongly believe their relationship is incestuous.   RDM

Pym, Barbara 1913–80 Postwar English comic novelist who details the habits and perceptions of middle-class spinsters. Born in Oswestry, Shropshire, as a child she was strongly involved with the Church of England – her mother was the local organist and the clergy often visited for tea – a preoccupation which surfaces, tinged with quizzical scepticism, throughout her work. She was educated at Liverpool College, Huyton, and at St Hilda's College, Oxford, where, despite a series of romantic attachments (notably with Henry Harvey), she remained single. The quiet village existence of the middle-aged, spinster Bede sisters, in her first novel, *Some Tame Gazelle* (begun 1934, published 1950), is strangely proleptic of her own later life, shared with her younger sister Hilary. She may have chosen to remain single in order to pursue her vocation as a writer.

After WRNS service during World War II, she worked at the International African Institute in London until her retirement in 1974. Here she interacted with anthropologists, whose professional rituals resembled her narrative technique: 'remembering her role as an anthropologist and observer – the necessity of being on the outside looking in – she crept away', muses one of her narrators. Between 1950 and 1961 she published six novels; *Excellent Women* (1952), *Less Than Angels* (1955) and *A GLASS OF BLESSINGS* (1958) were the most highly regarded. Concerned with the lives of women drawn to but disappointed by men, she is frequently compared to JANE AUSTEN, with whom she shares wit, irony and a subtle malice in reinforcing or undermining social distinctions. Pym is camper than Austen, though: witness *The Barbara Pym Cookbook* (1988), based on recipes in her fiction. The sixties and seventies saw her out of vogue (though she continued writing) but her reputation has grown steadily since her 'rediscovery' in 1977 by Lord David Cecil and Philip Larkin. *QUARTET IN AUTUMN* (1977), *The Sweet Dove Died* (1978) and *A Few Green Leaves* (1980) – the latter self-consciously revisiting her oeuvre – were published before her death from ovarian cancer in 1980. Earlier novels and fragments have appeared posthumously, along with *A Very Private Eye: An Autobiography in Letters and Diaries* (1984), which confirms the close connections between the life and the fiction.   MO'D

Q

Quartet (1928) In JEAN RHYS's first novel, the heroine Marya marries Stephan Zelli, who takes her from cold, gloomy London to inter-war Paris, where *déclassé* exiles flourish in a manic-depressive fever. Marya is a *tabula-rasa*, but doesn't acquire an identity: instead, she is in flux, embodying the textual experiments of the MODERNISTS. Rhys's cool, lucid prose represents the quiet passion lying underneath frivolity, recording the fate of Marya's body, trapped in the treacherous duality of the world. After Stephan is arrested, she becomes a dependant of the Heidlers. Mr Heidler, modelled on Ford Madox Ford, who encouraged Rhys to write fiction, is attracted to Marya, and they fall into an adulterous father–daughter affair. Marya visits Stephan in the gaol regularly, and helps him when he is released, which touches Heidler's male-egotistic nerve. The 'posture' (the title at the first publication) of Marya abandoned by Stephan and Heidler concludes the scene. Deprived of her male props, who are themselves never stable, she is lost in a masochistic, existential void, where her language of self-representation is conceived.   CY

Quartet in Autumn (1977) 'The position of an unmarried, unattached, ageing woman is of no interest whatever to the writer of modern fiction', is Letty's belief, to which this, BARBARA PYM's seventh novel – which appeared after a gap of sixteen years, when no-one would publish her – is an elegant rebuttal. The story features two such women, Letty and Marcia, as well as bachelor Norman and widower Edwin, all of whom have worked for years in the same dreary office, returning each evening to their lonely bedsits or houses. Pym delicately interweaves the four's experiences of 'the strangeness of life, slipping away like this', and their separate attempts to fight it, whether in church involvement, excursions to the country, or a submerged passion. Reminiscent of MURIEL SPARK's *MEMENTO MORI*, and considered by many Pym's best novel (its publication sparked a renewed appreciation of her work), it is in some ways atypical of her fiction: though the comedy of manners is characteristically observant and light-handed, the tale is more melancholy than the vicarage- or university-based comedies which came before.   SB

Question of Power, A (1973) BESSIE HEAD's third novel after leaving South Africa is a powerful, fragmentary and autobiographical text. It represents a series of breakdowns induced in its refugee protagonist, Elizabeth, by racist and sexist abuse experienced in South Africa and Botswana, and by her anxieties about burgeoning post-colonial corruption in independent Africa. These are focused through two symbolic and visionary figures around which the novel is constructed – the people's leader, Sello, and dictator, Dan. Interspersed with the surreal visionary world and characters of Elizabeth's breakdowns, the reassuring REALISM of the development garden in which Elizabeth works suggests the potential of the 'African' village philosophy of 'man's humanity to man'. Often read as a life tale depicting the psychic trauma induced by Apartheid, the novel is also a highly literary, allusive and symbolic critique. Its MODERNIST fragmentation produces a jazz-like counter-history of Elizabeth's life, bringing together voices from the past, symbolic figures and suppressed histories in a way that found an echo in the symbolism and fragmentation of the Soweto poets of the seventies.   HLR

Quicksand (1928) The first novella by Harlem Renaissance novelist NELLA LARSEN, *Quicksand* was hailed in its moment for its psychologically rich portrayal of its mixed-race middle-class heroine, Helga Crane, who struggles to negotiate a morass of racial and sexual anxieties. Although written in a psychoanalytically inflected style, *Quicksand* simultaneously draws upon the novels of manners of Henry James and EDITH WHARTON in its depiction of the African-American elite, which led W. E. B. DuBois to praise the novel for its depiction of 'the better class of Negroes'. Beginning with Helga's renunciation of her career as a teacher at a Tuskegee-inspired black college, the novel charts her picaresque journey from Chicago to Harlem to Denmark and finally to the rural South, where Helga marries a Southern preacher and enters an endless cycle of reproduction and childbearing. Despite the novel's grim conclusion, however, Larsen transcends the trope of the tragic mulatto/a in American fiction, casting Helga not only as a victim in her fate, but as an active agent in it.   MG

R

Radcliffe [née Ward], Ann 1764–1823 The most famous, influential, and highly paid, of 18th-century GOTHIC ROMANCE writers. She was born of a Holborn haberdasher and his wife; the Ward family was a striking mixture of the humble and the illustrious: the paternal line containing both bishops and surgeons, while the maternal branch included plumbers and glaziers from Chesterfield. The posthumous memoir of the author by Thomas Talfourd, jealously supervised by her husband William, was careful to emphasize the illustrious.

A key figure in Ann's early life was her uncle, Thomas Bentley, a genial, enlightened entrepreneur who was the business partner of Josiah Wedgwood. At his house in Chelsea and later at the mansion in Turnham Green, the 'little sprightly Neece of Bentley' (as Wedgwood called her) met many important people, including Joseph Priestley. Bentley also had connections on the *Gentleman's Magazine* and the *Monthly Review*. In 1772, the Wards moved to Bath, where Ann's father was to manage the Wedgwood and Bentley showrooms. Ann Ward spent the next fifteen years in Bath, where she knew the literary LEE sisters, Harriet and SOPHIA, who ran a school there. In 1786, she married William Radcliffe, an ambitious journalist and lawyer who seems to have encouraged her writing. Shy and asthmatic, though rapidly becoming one of the most internationally famous novelists of the century, she shunned all publicity.

Radcliffe's first novel, *The Castles of Athlin and Dunbayne*, came out in 1789, the year of the French Revolution, when she was 26. It is a pastiche of *Macbeth*, which the critic of the *Monthly Review* took to task for an excess of dungeons and passages, spotting her hallmark. The more powerful *Sicilian Romance* (1790), which foreshadows much of her mature manner, was better received. THE ROMANCE OF THE FOREST (1791) was universally declared a success by the reviewers and the way was open for one of the triumphs of the European 18th century, THE MYSTERIES OF UDOLPHO (1794). After *Udolpho* came THE ITALIAN (1797), her riposte to M.G. Lewis's *The Monk* (1796) and the climax of her career. After that, she retired into travel and silence; after her death her husband brought out poems, a dialogue and a historical romance.

The unique edginess of Radcliffe's writing is insepa-rable from its prolixity and awkwardness; its ambiguity has proved fertile for generations of readers and critics. Her novels combine the obscurity of the Burkean Sublime with a Rousseauistic strain of SEN-SIBILITY that gives the reassuring effect of a female BILDUNGSROMAN to most of her plots. Sir Walter Scott, having credited Radcliffe with inventing the 'explained supernatural' – a mechanism which rationalized away all supernatural effects – claimed that she was the victim of her own invention, dissipating 'romance' into fantasy in the process. He thus made her seem a crude forerunner of his own (balanced, more sophisticatedly rational) 'historical romance'. But 'explanation' in Radcliffe never seems to explain: the very prolixity of the reading process guarantees a rigorous separation of the reader from the object of knowledge: the central symbol is 'veiling', which mixes Romantic aesthetics, anti-Catholic propaganda and epistemological doubt. Her wicked uncles/fathers, orphaned and abducted daughters/nieces, gloomy fortresses and forbidden rooms, reenact Bluebeard in *sadique* slow motion, edging constantly into the threat of rape and transgression of the incest taboo. VS

Radcliffe, Mary Ann 1746?–1810? An English radical who wrote the spirited *The Female Advocate: Or An attempt to Recover the Rights of Women from Male Usurpation* (1799), Radcliffe's wish to remain anonymous was thwarted by her publisher, who wanted her to capitalize on the success of the famous GOTHIC novelist, ANN RADCLIFFE.

Since the fortune-hunter she married whittled away her family estate, Radcliffe had difficulty supporting their eight children. As a result, she was forced to provide for her family by working as a milliner, seamstress, pedlar of patent medicines, and seller of pastries. Her treatise gives practical guidelines on how a woman can earn a living. For instance, she advocates protectionist strategies so as to guard against men, who exclude women particularly from female professions like millinery. The second edition was published in 1810, with her *Memoirs* which are written in the form of letters to a female friend. MM-R

Radiant Way, The (1987) MARGARET DRABBLE'S tenth novel records the United Kingdom in the 1980s through the lives of three women. The tone is set as Liz, one of the three, prepares for a party on the last day of 1979 – a party which will see in a new political era. In the ensuing years the women's relationships and opinions are intimately depicted against a background of political and social upheaval: the miners' strike, the Falklands' War, AIDS. Drabble's proclaimed vision is of 'a vast web, a vast network . . . humanity itself', of people's place within their social context, but with the constant intervention of the self. With the fictional northern town of Northam as a foil to the metropolitan habitat of the protagonists, the habitual themes of London and the provinces, ambition and domesticity, and the fate of intelligent women are revisited. Written predominantly as social REALISM, but with moments of telling coincidence, *The Radiant Way*, along with its sequels *A Natural Curiosity* (1989) and *The Gates of Ivory* (1991), documents a decade and its individuals.

CS

Raffald, Elizabeth

Raffald, Elizabeth 1733–81 A singularly talented woman – during her short life she started a catering business and shop, wrote a successful COOKERY BOOK, ran two inns, founded an employment agency, and compiled Manchester's first business register.

Her enlightened parents, Joshua and Elizabeth Whitaker, ensured that their daughter could read and write, and even speak French, before leaving home in Doncaster to go into service. From the age of 15, Elizabeth worked in some of Yorkshire's great country houses, gradually improving herself until in 1760 she became housekeeper to Lady Elizabeth Warburton at Ardley Hall in Cheshire. Her employer was a strong influence and *The Experienced English Housekeeper* (1769) is dedicated to her.

Elizabeth describes her recipes as 'written purely from practice', to distinguish them from the work of those authors who never ventured into the kitchen and whose recipes are perforce copied or paraphrased from other books; and in the book's introductory letter she apologizes for 'the plainness of the style'. Yet this is the essence of her lasting appeal, and her clarity and economy with words find an echo in the work of ELIZA ACTON a century later.

GH

Raine, Kathleen (Jessie)

Raine, Kathleen (Jessie) 1908– British poet, co-founder of the journal *Temenos*, and notable scholar of Blake, Yeats and Hopkins. She practises an overtly philosophical poetry that has considerable depth and power, particularly in her first three books, *Stone and Flower* (1943), *Living in Time* (1946) and *The Pythoness* (1949). She was born in London and educated at the County High School in Ilford and at Girton College, Cambridge, where she took an MA in Natural Sciences and associated with a number of poets who were making their mark, including Charles Madge. Cambridge

Elizabeth Raffald: title-page of *The Experienced English House-keeper*, 1769.

was not a formative influence on her work, and she felt she required to escape its analytic and scientific ethos before finding her own poetic voice.

She has been married twice – to the writer Hugh Sykes Davies, and the poet Madge by whom she had a daughter and a son. Kathleen Raine was already established as a poet when she met Gavin Maxwell in the late 1940s. She became convinced of a spiritual affinity between Maxwell and herself, despite his misogyny and his neglect of her. Maxwell's famous account of his life at Sandaig, where Raine was a frequent visitor, took its title from a poem by Raine: 'He has married me with a ring, with a ring of bright water / Whose ripples travel from the heart to the sea'. Maxwell never acknowledged the source. Their relationship became increasingly turbulent – during one of Raine's jealous tempers, she laid her hands on a rowan tree outside their cottage and prayed aloud to 'let Gavin suffer as I am suffering now'. Maxwell died in 1969 – Raine blamed herself despite trying later to retract her curse on the same spot. Her biographies of this and other periods of her life and spiritual development include

Farewell, Happy Fields (1978), an account of a pastoral childhood; *The Land Unknown* (1975); and *The Lion's Mouth* (1977). A remarkable and intense book of psycho-poetics, *The Inner Journey of the Poet* (1976), assists an appreciation of her poetic achievement.

She has received numerous awards, notably the Queen's Gold Medal for Poetry in 1993. *Selected Poems* (1988) covers her work well if less completely than *Collected Poems* (1981). She co-edited *Temenos* in 1981–92 and founded the Temenos Academy in 1982. The journal and academy sought to reaffirm values Raine regards as essential, namely the imaginative vision – the sacred dimension – in an increasingly secular society. See DEFENDING ANCIENT SPRINGS (1967).   DM

Raisin in the Sun, A (1959) LORRAINE HANSBERRY turns the raw material of family history (her father's decision in 1938 to defy Chicago's restrictive real-estate covenants) into a play whose appeal derives in part from the specificity of its focus (on the Younger family) and the universality of its main concern (dreams deferred). The simmering tensions generated by competing dreams are brought to a climactic boiling point before the play's focus shifts – from limited funds gained the hard way by the late Big Walter and lost carelessly by his son, Walter, to priceless family treasure in the form of values preserved over five generations. The living embodiment of these values is Mama, and, through her prodding, Walter turns the search for his elusive 'manhood' inward and ends up saving himself and his family. The values that hold families together are shown to be priceless and timeless. The play, the first by a black woman to be produced on Broadway, won the New York Drama Critics Circle Award as Best Play of the Year.   KO

Rand, Ayn (Alyssa Rosenbaum) 1905–82 Russian-born American novelist, playwright and philosopher. Daughter of a chemist, she was born in St Petersburg. As the Russian revolution intensified, the family moved to Crimea, where she completed high school. They returned to St Petersburg (now Petrograd) after the Bolshevik victory and Rand enrolled in a university programme in Social Pedagogy, from which she graduated in 1924. Her studies of Dostoevsky and Nietzsche had a lasting influence on her thought and writing. She took the name 'Ayn Rand' when she immigrated to the United States in 1926. She worked in Cecil B. DeMille's studio from 1926 to 1929, married an actor, Frank O'Connor, in 1929, and became a US citizen in 1931. Repelled by the Leftism of American writers and intellectuals in the 1930s, she made it her mission to combat this trend. Her first novel, *We the Living* (1936), places its young Russian heroine in a tragic love triangle, blaming the tragedy on the totalitarian system which makes honest relationships impossible. Rand revised the book and downplayed its Nietzschean themes after her later novels captured a popular audience for her early work. In the futuristic world of *Anthem* (1938), a member of a dystopian collective rediscovers the word 'I'.

Rand approached the novel as a philosophical forum, embodying basic principles in her characters. In *The Fountainhead* (1943), Howard Roark, an original and daring architect (modelled on Frank Lloyd Wright), signifies integrity as he struggles to resist mediocrity. Another architect, Peter Keating, whose success depends on his ability to manipulate people and conform to convention, has Roark design a public housing project, to which he agrees on the condition that his plans will be realized to the letter. The project is altered in construction and Roark dynamites the buildings. Placed on trial, Roark presents the principles of ethical egoism in his defence, claiming he had a right to destroy his own creation since it was altered without his permission. In *Atlas Shrugged* (1957), her last work of fiction, Rand followed up a question Roark asks: 'What would happen to the world without those who do, think, work, produce?' She presents a world in which government regulations strangle entrepreneurship. Amid the ensuing social chaos, the hero, John Galt, thinker, scientist and engineer, articulates Rand's philosophy of rational self-interest in lengthy monologues. Despite a hostile reception from critics who found it mean-spirited and offensive, *Atlas Shrugged* became a long-term bestseller. A Library of Congress survey in 1991 showed that its influence on American readers was second only to the Bible. *Atlas Shrugged* became the scripture for a philosophical movement which Rand called objectivism and inspired the Libertarian movement (which Rand repudiated).

In the 1960s Rand lectured widely and published in *The Objectivist Newsletter*. From 1969 to 1976 she irregularly published the *Ayn Rand Letter*. Her later books include *The Virtue of Selfishness* (1964), *Capitalism: The Unknown Ideal* (1966), *The Romantic Manifesto* (1969), *Introduction to Objectivist Epistemology* (1979) and the posthumously published *Philosophy: Who Needs It* (1982).   JSG

Randall, Deborah 1957– British poet, born in Gosport, Hampshire. She worked in hotels, a plastics factory and a children's home before enrolling at Sheffield University to study English. She began writing in 1986, won the first and only Bloodaxe Competition in 1987, an Eric Gregory Award and the Bridport Prize. Bloodaxe published *The Sin Eater* in 1989 and *White Eyes, Dark Ages* in 1993. She moved first to Kirkwall in the Orkneys, then to Ullapool in 1992.

The Sin Eater is a charged collection full of sexual gusto. Her second collection impresses even more. It is an imaginative exploration of the life and mind of

John Ruskin through his relationships with women. Randall is clearly fascinated by the disparities between Ruskin's emotional petrification and his deeply felt responses to art. Her poems set up some significant inner debates and offer a striking revaluation. *White Eyes, Dark Ages* proved Randall capable of producing an outstanding work of synthesis and psychological insight. DM

Rapoport, Janis 1946– Canadian poet and playwright, born in Toronto, who attended the University of Toronto (BA in Philosophy, 1967). Rapoport has been an editor at the *Tamarack Review* (1970–82) and *Ethos* (1983–7). She has also been writer-in-residence at several Ontario libraries and playwright-in-residence at the Tarragon Theatre in Toronto (1974–6) where her plays *Gilgamesh* (1976) and *Dreamgirls* (1979) were produced. *Dreamgirls* is about a halfway home for women, and has a cast of six female characters.

Rapoport has published several books of lyric poetry: *Within the Whirling Moment* (1967), *Jeremy's Dream* (1974), *Winter Flowers* (1979), *Upon Her Fluent Route* (1991) and *After Paradise* (1996). Her early poetry focuses on emotional experiences such as love, motherhood, family and scenes from Jewish life. Her later work focuses specifically on women, especially the magical power of witches, goddesses and mothers. GHN

Rau, Santa Rama 1923– Indian writer in English. Born in Madras into a diplomatic family, she has travelled extensively. She wrote that during the few years she spent in her mother country she really made an effort to learn 'to be an Indian' and she remains attached to this identity despite being a citizen of the world. In her writings she has a predilection for the investigation of her own identity. She has written several travelogues praised for their vividness and sensitivity – among the best coming from Indian writers in English: *East of Home* (1950), *View of the Southeast* (1957), *My Russian Journey* (1959) and *The Cooking of India* (1970). She is also the author of two novels, *Remember the House* (1956) and *The Adventuress* (1970), and of two autobiographical works, *Home to India* (1945) and *Gifts of Passage* (1961) which also have a travelogue character since Rau's life has always been on the move. She has also written a play, *A Passage to India* (1960), an adaptation of E. M. Forster's novel for the stage. SPo

Ravensong (1993) This novel by LEE MARACLE, set along the Pacific northwest coast of Canada in the early 1950s, unfolds in a native urban community near Vancouver, which has been devastated by a flu epidemic. Stacy, the 17-year-old protagonist, aware that her future lies in both worlds, balances her family's traditional ways against the intrusive new values of white society. Her sister Celia imparts visions from the past

while the voice of Raven crows: 'Great storms alter earth, mature life, rid the world of the old, ushering in the new. Humans call it catastrophe. Just birth'. The song of Raven is a beginning in conquering the gulf between the different worlds of natives and whites, human beings and nature, young and old, men and women, Christian belief and native belief. Maracle's directness and humour present a clear picture of the gulf between two cultures. She shows, through this novel, that bridges need to be built so that reconciliation between all peoples can occur, thus securing not only the survival of native peoples but also meaningful survival for all humanity. SM/PRH

Rawlings, Marjorie Kinnan 1896–1953 American essayist, novelist and short-story writer. She was born in Washington, D.C., daughter of a patent attorney, and educated at the University of Wisconsin, from which she graduated in 1918. In 1919 she married newspaperman Charles A. Rawlings; they divorced in 1933 and she married hotel-owner Norton Sandford Baskin in 1941. Her earliest publications were newspaper columns for the Louisville *Courier-Journal* and the Rochester *Journal-American*. She was unsuccessful in finding publishers for her stories until she began writing about north central Florida, where, in 1928, she bought a farm which she later immortalized in her autobiographical *Cross Creek* (1942). In 1930, Scribners accepted 'Cracker Chidlings' and 'Jacob's Ladder,' sketches of Florida folklore and country people; and a selection of her stories, *When a Whippoorwill*, was published in that same year. 'Gal Young Un', a story about an exploited older woman, won the O. Henry Award in 1933. In her first novel, *South Moon Under* (1933), a Book of the Month Club selection, she described country activities occurring during the dark of the moon. *The Yearling* (1938), a coming-of-age story about a boy raising a fawn, won a Pulitzer Prize and was filmed in 1946. *Golden Apples* (1935), which she called 'interesting trash', depicts sex and cruelty between an ignorant country woman and an Englishman. She followed the success of *Cross Creek* with *The Cross Creek Cookery* (1942), which sparked a precedent-setting lawsuit when Zelma Cason sued Rawlings for using her name without permission and won nominal damages. Rawlings eventually repudiated regionalism because she felt it exploited quaintness while diminishing the humanity of its characters. Her last novel, *The Sojourner* (1953), is set in the Hudson Valley after the Civil War. JSG

Rawlinson, Gloria (Jasmine) 1918–95 Poet, novelist, short-story writer and editor; born in Tonga, she settled in New Zealand in 1924 and recorded its exotic sights and fragrances in her much-anthologized long poem 'The Islands Where I Was Born' (1955). As a child she fell victim to the 1925 poliomyelitis epidemic and was confined permanently to a wheelchair, nonetheless leading an active life and travelling extensively, particularly in the 1950s.

Her first significant publication was *Gloria's Book* (1933). The poems, with their romantic, whimsical and often fantastical themes, were welcomed by readers enduring the harsh realities of economic depression. She was acclaimed as a child prodigy and her weekly mail averaged 300 letters 'from all over the world'. Her second book of poems, *The Perfume Vendor* (1935), was equally successful. Sales exceeded 7,000 copies, the work was translated into Dutch and Japanese and she enjoyed celebrity status in New Zealand. Her success as a poet was followed with the publication of her first and only novel, *Music in the Listening Place* (1938). Writer JANE MANDER called it 'a triumph for a young writer nurtured in a materialistic country where delicacy and exquisite fancy is increasingly in danger of being smothered'. As a story writer, Rawlinson contributed frequently to the Australian *Bulletin* and from 1947 to 1954 her work appeared regularly in the Australian anthology *Coast to Coast*. Her last volume of poetry, *Of Clouds and Pebbles*, was published in 1963.

A close friend of novelist, poet and journalist ROBIN HYDE (Iris Wilkinson) who committed suicide in 1939, Rawlinson edited and introduced a painstakingly researched collection of Robin Hyde's poems, *Houses by the Sea*, and in 1970 Hyde's novel *The Godwits Fly*. Her extensive biography of her friend's life remained unpublished.

In 1957 she received a PEN Award for her writing achievements but ironically, Rawlinson's involvement with and promotion of Robin Hyde's work perhaps curtailed her own development and accomplishments as a poet.

REn

Rayson, Hannie 1957– Australian playwright Hannie Rayson is a graduate of Melbourne University and the Victorian College of Arts, and has worked as a performer. Her multi-award-winning *Hotel Sorrento* (1990) was one of the most successful realist Australian theatre productions of the early 1990s. It has been made into a film and translated into French and Japanese. *Hotel Sorrento* concerns the reunion of the three Moynihan sisters, as Meg, who is nominated for the Booker Prize, is living in England and Pippa is a New York advertising executive. Despite its Chekhovian echoes, only the widow, Hilary, has stayed to raise her son, Troy, and look after their father, Wal. Wal disappears at sea and this precipitates revelations of betrayal between the sisters.

While the woman writer in DOROTHY HEWETT's *THE CHAPEL PERILOUS* (1971) is a controversial figure, in *Hotel Sorrento*, written twenty years later, it is Meg's novel which is the source of controversy. As well as discussing Australia's continuing cultural cringe in relation to Europe, a legacy of its colonial past, the characters reject the accusation that if women's literature is autobiographical, it is less valuable as art. Hannie Rayson's recent plays include: *Room to Move* (1985), *Falling From Grace* (1994) and *Competitive Tenderness* (1996).

PT

Read Franklin, Deborah 1708–74 Pennsylvania businesswoman and correspondent. Deborah Read met Benjamin Franklin while Franklin boarded at her parents' house. Their plans to marry were aborted when he left for England in 1724; Read married John Rogers after Franklin broke the engagement. When the marriage failed, Rogers left Philadelphia. Because no one knew if Rogers was alive, Deborah Read and Benjamin Franklin married without legal proceedings in 1730. Over time, Franklin's business and political activities took him away from home for long periods, and Read Franklin was left to tend the home and the family business. Read Franklin's letters record the effects of Franklin's public life on the family: 'We have nothing stiring amoungst us but phamlits and Scurrilitey but I have never sed or dun aney thing or aney of our famely you may depend on it nor shall we.' Although the long separations, especially in the last years of the marriage, seemed to indicate that Read Franklin and her husband had grown apart, the salutation on the letters to him – 'My Dear Child' – and her valediction – 'I am your afeckshenit wife' – diverge from the often formal mode of husband–wife correspondence in the period. Her letters provide a fuller understanding of the seldom-mentioned frugal housewife in Franklin's *Autobiography*.

LCa

readers The history of women as readers presents several challenges. There have been many notions expressed about what women read, how women read, how and what they should read, and the most appropriate times and places and methods of reading. Indeed, the very privacy and subjectivity of the silent, absorbed reader has made her a particularly vulnerable subject onto whom has been projected a succession of cultural and sexual anxieties. From the 16th century onwards, it has been argued both that certain texts might corrupt woman's naturally innocent mind, hence diminishing her value as a woman, and, paradoxically, that as a woman, she was peculiarly susceptible to emotionally provocative material.

Throughout Europe, the ROMANCE became a matter for conspicuous concern, its subject matter and narrative dynamics stimulating, it was believed, a range of emotions from dissatisfaction with one's daily life to the extremes of sexual desire. Dante's tale of Paolo and Francesca, in which reading the romance inflamed passion between the young couple and precipitated them toward hell, was frequently rehearsed as a warning. The Renaissance educator Juan Luis Vives marvelled in the mid 16th century 'that wise fathers will suffer their daughters, or husbands their wives, or that the manners and customs of people will dissemble and overlook, that women shall use to read wantonness'; the 18th-century Swiss physician Samuel Tissot warned that 'if your daughter reads novels at age fifteen, she will be hysterical at age twenty'. MARY WOLLSTONECRAFT criticized sentimental fiction for encouraging 'a romantic twist of the mind' and a false view of human nature; much more recently, in the late 1980s, Helen Taylor attacked romances as being a means 'of keeping women quiet, compliasant, heterosexual and home-and-family oriented'. Reading for escape, in other words, has always been treated with more suspicion than reading which leads to spiritual development or inculcates desirable social skills: it has been accused of damaging the health, of detracting from family responsibilities, and creating unrealistic ambitions and desires. Some critics, however, such as Janice Radway, have argued that the mere act of reading offers a necessary suspension of the quotidien, and that to read of a context – any context – in which a woman's concerns are presented as being of paramount importance has enabling possibilities.

Even in didactic contexts, the history of women readers is full of paradoxes. Luther's conscious wish that women and girls should read canonical and confessional material certainly helped to extend female literacy, but restricted the scope of what was considered desirable reading. In the second half of the 17th century, there was a notable increase in books purposefully directed toward a women's readership, but their nature – conversational guides, codes of proper conduct, manuals teaching particular skills – mean that they are more valuable for what they reveal about expectations concerning women's roles than about women's reading practices. There is no guarantee that a woman will internalize and absorb what is intended for her consumption, or that she will not develop the skills of what Judith Fetterley has termed the 'resisting reader'. Such resistance may be toward misogynistic or stereotyping attitudes, or toward other forms of domination: in JAMAICA KINCAID's post-colonial fiction, for example, books both inspire girls' imaginations, and represent a colonial educational legacy against which they must write themselves.

It is far easier to recover ideas concerning women as readers than it is to access the experience itself. From medieval times onwards, women appear as readers in illustrations, but we are left in ignorance, very often, as to how they responded. We can reconstitute the contents of certain women's libraries, whether these were within institutions, or individual homes, and, from the mid 19th century, consider the evidence of surveys and borrowing records. But possession, unless accompanied by further evidence in the form of DIARIES, letters, or marginalia, indicates availability rather than consumption. Written evidence brings the challenge of its own textuality. It may usefully serve as a record of what has been read, but the effects of that reading – the impact of the pious, the shock of the improper, the spur to suffrage or anti-slavery action – are framed and composed with further readers in mind, a qualification which must be extended to the ideal self constructed in journal composition.

What is certain is that in the latter part of the 18th century, and during the 19th century, increased literacy among women, and a growing middle class, ensured the development of books marketed expressly with women in mind, whether these were novels (often, themselves, like the fiction of RHODA BROUGHTON or MARY BRADDON, full of references to women as readers which served to underline both the dangers and the legitimacy of this leisure activity), annuals, or even books which offered guidance on reading. In the Victorian period, reading was seen, variously, as a means to self-improvement, a tool for developing sympathy, a way of informing oneself about the world in order to be a more knowledgeable and entertaining companion to one's suitor or husband, and a way to extend one's experience vicariously through reading of other countries, other cultures. Reading, then as now, could be a means both of a woman developing her individual subjectivity, and of consolidating social relations, whether in the conservative sense envisaged by advice manuals, or through bonding in oppression or anger or shared forms of desire. Reading, in other words, encourages recognition of both difference and similarity within communities of women. Necessarily, differences between women, whether of class, age, race, religion or nationality, are always going to complicate any attempt to generalize about 'women readers'.

A sense of solidarity among women readers has been consolidated since the 1970s by the growth of women's publishing houses, such as Virago, the Women's Press, Kitchen Table Books or Aunt Lute, and by women's bookshops. Certain genres, such as DETECTIVE NOVELS with strong female protagonists, or the new brand of women's romance (*Bridget Jones's Diary, Jemima J*) have been deliberately promoted by mainstream publishers with women audiences as their targets, premised on the enduring belief that women are far more prone than men to identify with the subjects of their reading.

KFl

Real Charlotte, The (1894) A novel by E. Œ. SOMERVILLE and MARTIN ROSS set in the latter days of the Anglo-Irish Ascendancy, this tragi-comedy describes the career of ruthless Charlotte Mullen – plain, unmarried and 40 – who combines an unrequited love for married Roderick Lambert, agent of the Dysart estates, with the Irish peasant's greed for land. Charlotte takes charge of her cousin, Francie Fitzpatrick, for whom she schemes a brilliant marriage with the Dysart heir. Francie, who is as artless, lovable and truthful as Charlotte is not, beguiles Christopher Dysart despite himself, but falls in love with the worthless Lt Gerald Hawkins. When she realizes that Hawkins does not intend to marry her, Francie marries on the rebound the newly widowed Lambert, who has always loved her, and thus precipitates the final tragedy. Charlotte, mad with jealousy and bent on revenge, seeks to destroy Lambert, whom she had hoped to marry herself. She tacitly encourages Francie to elope with Hawkins, and reveals to Christopher Dysart evidence of Lambert's embezzlement, but the book's *dénouement* shows the futility of her scheming: news of Francie's tragic death arrives as Charlotte confesses to Lambert her part in his downfall.   CT

Real People (1970) The fourth novel by ALISON LURIE is set in Illyria, a New England writers' colony that is a thinly disguised version of its real-life counterpart, Yaddo. Herself the recipient of three Yaddo grants, Lurie could be said to be biting the hand that feeds her in this satirical look at the creative and pastoral idyll, suggesting that while it intends to nurture new talent, it also prizes celebrity and often ends by pandering to already-inflated egos. Yet through her heroine Janet, who decides that 'you can't write well with only the nice parts of your character, and only about nice things' and that writing must also consist of 'hate and envy and lust and fear', Lurie also explores the nature of the creative impulse and the sacrifices that must be made in order to write. In addition, the novel reprises many of Lurie's abiding interests in the behaviour of individuals in closed communities, cut off from the rest of the world, where their motivation and action becomes both intensified and more easily observable.   AC

realism When cultural critic Raymond Williams wrote that 'the centenary of "realism" as an English critical term occurred but was not celebrated in 1956', he was distinguishing the literary realism which emerged in the mid 19th century from much older traditions of mimetic or representational fiction and hinting at realism's doubtful reputation.

In the 18th century, novel-writing had emerged, at least in part, as a rationalist, Enlightenment reaction against the fantasy and unrealities of the ROMANCE tradition. In *Tom Jones* (1749), Henry Fielding exhorted writers to keep 'within the bounds of possibility' and remember 'that what it is not possible for man to perform, it is scarce possible for man to believe he did perform'. When in 1816 JANE AUSTEN described 'a lit-

tle bit of ivory, two inches wide, on which I work with a brush so fine as to produce little effect after much labour', she gestured, with her usual self-deprecating irony, toward a type of faithful attention to detail which became characteristic of realist writing.

Up until the 1840s, however, these experiments in believable and probable fiction writing existed as only part of a literary culture which was dominated by the poetic voices of Romanticism, and remained in love with fantastical prose (the GOTHIC, 'silver fork' and 'Newgate' novels). What shifted the balance decisively in favour of realism was a combination of cultural, social and political circumstances which focused attention on the everyday, ordinary and material circumstances of life, and the attempts of writers to capture these faithfully and accurately in words. HARRIET MARTINEAU complained that 'youths and maidens looked for lords and ladies on every page of a new novel', but in this altered climate she found a publisher for the more realistic DEERBROOK (1839).

In the 1830s, railways improved communications and revolutionized transport. The Reform Act of 1832 enfranchised many of the English middle classes, whose lives were also being transformed by industry and commerce. Rapid advances in science and technology provided empirical beliefs in the place of old religious certainties, whilst the invention of Daguerreotype photography (1839) promised a new era of visual verisimilitude. The renewed threat of social upheaval also clarified minds. In England a series of economic depressions culminated in the 'hungry forties' and increased working-class militancy. Thomas Carlyle meditated on the 'Condition of England' question (*Past and Present*,1843) and so gave a name to a certain type of realist 'social problem' novel (Disraeli's *Sybil: Or The Two Nations*, 1845; ELIZABETH GASKELL's *MARY BARTON*, 1848). In France, the events of 1830 and 1848 created a similar intellectual climate. Balzac declared 'this drama is not fiction or romance. All is true' in his opening to *Le Père Goriot* (1834–5). The terms 'réaliste' and 'réalisme' entered the French language, then crossed the Channel: in 1851 *Fraser's Magazine* described Thackeray as 'chief of the Realist school'. The *Westminster Review* first used 'realism' as a critical term in 1853.

The centenary to which Raymond Williams refers is that of the publication in 1856 of volume III of Ruskin's *Modern Painters*. GEORGE ELIOT reviewed it with high praise: 'The truth of infinite value that he teaches is realism – the doctrine that all truth and beauty are to be attained by a humble and faithful study of nature, and not by substituting vague forms, bred by imagination on the mists of feeling, in place of definite, substantial reality.' Shortly afterwards Eliot began to write fiction, putting into practice her own version of this doctrine and transforming herself into the foremost realist writer in English.

Eliot's work is exemplary of realist ideology – her plots and characters typify the democratization of art as well as society, valuing the poor and ordinary equally with, if not more than, the great and good. The sophistication of her practice dispels one of the commonest myths associated with realism: the idea that realists were simply naive transcribers, holding up language as a flat mirror in which to reflect life. Eliot and her contemporaries knew that the act of writing was a distorting intervention: in *ADAM BEDE* (1859) she qualified her ambition 'to give no more than a faithful account of men and things as they have mirrored themselves in my mind' with the concession that 'the mirror is doubtless defective; the outlines will sometimes be disturbed; the reflection faint or confused'. But George Eliot was an exemplary realist in other ways also: her occasional excess of high moral seriousness – almost humbuggery – makes plain the homelier attractions of the DOMESTIC NOVEL or the excitement of SENSATION FICTION (most popular, uncoincidentally, in the 1860s).

Feminist critics have struggled to rationalize the role of women realists. Unlike later women writers of NATURALISM, novelists like Eliot and Gaskell do not appear to be subverting or questioning the inbuilt sexual and political bias of their writing. And as MODERNISTS and POSTMODERNISTS have questioned the bourgeois and masculinist assumptions which held together the idea of a single, unified reality, the place of these women in literary history is problematized further. VIRGINIA WOOLF was one of the first to attack the legacy of realism, asking 'what is reality? And who are the judges of reality?' For Woolf, the 'tools' and 'conventions' of realist writing 'are not our tools ... For us those conventions are ruin, those tools are death' because they cause the writer to pile up material, descriptive detail at the expense of never really looking at 'human nature' ('Mr Bennett and Mrs Brown', 1924). And yet Woolf herself wrote like a realist at various times, not just at the beginning of her career (*THE YEARS* in 1937 is a portrait of a family across generations), and in this creative inconsistency she anticipates the complexity of 20th-century developments in representational writing. Realism survived modernist experiments. As French New Novelist NATHALIE SARRAUTE ruefully complained, in the 1940s, Balzac's characters were alive and well, and critics too continued to look for lifelikeness in the novel. Novel theory was mostly theory about realism: critical accounts of the canon focused on moral vision and continuity. There were neo-realist revivals in the period post World War II, including socialist-realist and 'committed' work in the visual arts, in fiction, in theatre and in film.

Nonetheless, by the 1960s it was generally agreed that realist traditions no longer had their old power to create the sense of cultural common ground. MARY MCCARTHY wrote in 1960 that 'the novel, with its common sense, is of all forms the least adapted to encompass the modern world, whose leading characteristic is irreality. And that ... is why the novel is dying'. DORIS LESSING's *THE GOLDEN NOTEBOOK* (1962) acts out the disintegration of the realist conventions she'd used until then in the BILDUNGSROMAN structure of her 'CHILDREN OF VIOLENCE' series. But this was not the death of the novel, nor of realist writing. It was part of a process by which the novel would recognize itself once more as many genres, reincorporating ROMANCE, SCIENCE-FICTION and FAIRY TALE. Latin American magic (or magical) realism, widely disseminated during the 1970s, was one revitalizing mutation of realism, which became now only part of the picture, one mode among many. British novelist IRIS MURDOCH described her fiction as exploring the relations between real people and images; in the United States JOYCE CAROL OATES writes in a stunning variety of styles, from documentary realism to parodic Gothic. The recognition of the limits and partiality of realism also works positively in many autobiographical works and revisionist chronicles by feminist women – KATE MILLETT's *Flying* (1974), MARILYN FRENCH's *THE WOMEN'S ROOM* (1977) – and by POST-COLONIAL writers unrepresented or misrepresented until now, like AUSTRALIAN ABORIGINALS. Many of these works are written in a realist mode, though their message is that there is no single, unified reality – and the same is true of other genres flourishing on the boundaries of fiction, like TRAVEL WRITING and BIOGRAPHY. AS/LS

Rebecca (1938) DAPHNE DU MAURIER's fifth and most popular novel describes in retrospect the struggle of the nameless *ingénue* narrator with the overpowering heritage of her husband's deceased first wife Rebecca. Though significantly indebted to BRONTË's *JANE EYRE* (especially in its GOTHIC elements), the novel is more conservative in tone and does not carry a similar feminist appeal. Du Maurier's narrative, like her other novels clearly intended as a conventional heterosexual ROMANCE (it is still widely read as such), also challenges the demands of 'romantic' fiction by internalizing its clichés almost to absurdity: the fatherly husband, the voracious 'phallic' first wife, the devoted servants, culminating ultimately in the nonperson of the female narrator. The homoerotic *frissons* between the nymphomaniac Rebecca, the sinister housekeeper Mrs Danvers and the intimidated narrator raise questions of female and sexual identity that are mirrored in the author's own ambivalences. *Rebecca* just about manages a precarious balance between a conventional representation of feminine evil and a transgressive fascination with its liberating potential.

Rebecca has been filmed twice, most atmospherically in 1940 by Alfred Hitchcock.   PUR

Red Pottage

Red Pottage (1899) MARY CHOLMONDELEY's best-selling satirical novel reflects the author's own repressed longings: indeed the stifling of female creativity is a theme in a number of notable contemporary novels such as MONA CAIRD's THE DAUGHTERS OF DANAUS and ELLA HEPWORTH DIXON's THE STORY OF A MODERN WOMAN (1894). The text is a searing indictment of the priggishness and false values of society, especially the Church; nevertheless the Bishop of Stepney referred to it approvingly in a sermon, and Queen Victoria reputedly enjoyed the book. *Red Pottage* highlights the sisterhood between Rachel West and Hester Gresley: a 'very deep, very tender' friendship which sustains them through their tribulations. Rachel, a NEW WOMAN figure, has to support herself by typewriting, until she inherits money. Hester aspires to change the world through her fiction, but finds that her duties deprive her of precious time. She is distraught when her clergyman brother burns the manuscript of her novel, *Husks*, denouncing it as profane and immoral. She accuses him of killing her 'child'.   SF

Reef, The (1911) Considered by critics the most Jamesian of EDITH WHARTON's novels, and considered 'Racinian' by James in its incestuous pairings and tragic irony, Wharton's fourth novel is distinctly her own. Written shortly after her affair with Morton Fullerton, *The Reef* draws upon Wharton's sexual awakening but emphasizes the tragic possibilities of such an awakening for young, unattached women. Sophy Viner, a young American off to Europe to work as a governess, enjoys a brief fling with George Darrow, an older American awaiting a response from his fiancée, the widow Anna Leath. After the affair, Darrow arrives at Anna's home to find that Sophy is Anna's employee, soon to become engaged to her son. Sexual knowledge and paranoia soon contaminate the relationship between the members of this quartet, and each potential marriage is poisoned. Recalling Wharton's earlier novels in its depiction of the grim consequences of transgression of feminine norms, *The Reef* is hauntingly beautiful despite its chillingly pessimistic vision.   MG

Reeve, Clara 1729–1807 British novelist and critic who recommends domestic virtues, upholds social subordination and judges literature on moral grounds. A rector's daughter whose maternal grandfather was a successful goldsmith, Reeve lived a genteel, retired life in Ipswich and Colchester. Her early publications were poetry and translation, but she made her name in 1777 with *The Champion of Virtue*, later renamed THE OLD ENGLISH BARON, an early GOTHIC novel imitating Horace Walpole's *Castle of Otranto* but avoiding what she saw as his excessive use of the supernatural. Another Gothic novel, *Memoirs of Sir Roger de Clarendon* (1793), followed the statesman Edmund Burke by favourably comparing medieval chivalry to modern revolutionism, and in *The Exiles* (1788) she tried a French-influenced tragic narrative of bigamy and highly charged emotion. Her other novels, *The Two Mentors* (1783), *The School for Widows* (1791), *Plans of Education* (1792) and *Destination* (1799), are didactic DOMESTIC stories with a contemporary setting. In THE PROGRESS OF ROMANCE (1785), a pioneering work of novel criticism, she distinguishes between the ROMANCE and the novel, praises the former for its morality and proper respect for women, and recommends the latter in the hands of Samuel Richardson, SARAH FIELDING, CHARLOTTE LENNOX and other writers of a moral tendency. This is one of her liveliest works, couched in a spirited exchange between Hortensius, Sophronia and Euphrasia, who, as Reeve's spokeswoman, defends romance and female authority against her initially sceptical male friend. Reeve was a widely respected writer, and her domesticated, moralized Gothic had some influence on ANN RADCLIFFE's more exciting creations.   JSp

Reflections in a Golden Eye (1941) CARSON MCCULLERS's second novel abandons psychological realism in order to create a brooding vision of evil and cruelty in the narrowly circumscribed environment of a Southern army base. McCullers describes the crippled emotional lives of six characters; undeveloped figures, incapable of forming relationships with each other and further distanced from the reader by a dispassionate narrative voice which, by combining the horrific with the inconsequential, gives the violence a shockingly casual quality. Four of the characters are married unhappily to each other, watched over by the sexless dwarf, Anacleto, and Ellgee Williams, a near-voiceless 'natural'. However, the issue of spectatorship is complicated by the recurrent images of sightless eyes, distorting patterns of light and shadow and a landscape which shifts and alters with the seasons. The natural is stylized or, in the case of Ellgee and Firebird, the spirited horse, destroyed. Replacing the bonds of affection with obsessive behavioural tics, McCullers paints a comic, chaotic and frightening macabre picture of human isolation.   MM

Remember Me (1976) FAY WELDON's fourth novel uses the author's familiar devices of black comedy and the supernatural to propel its plot of revenge and reconciliation. Weldon's mature narrative voice, ironic and detached, reaches full development in this novel in which passages of dialogue are 'translated' to reveal

when I ~~told her~~ *said* that, I was telling her Edith
Webster had died in the night and left
cupboardsful of clothes behind her, and she laughed & said,
'I've never come across anyone as superstitious as you'
~~Susan,' she said~~
' You' see if I'm not right,' I said. 'Her daughter's
here now, handing her things out to all & sundry but
~~They'll rot on their backs.~~' You know what they say,
"as the body rots the clothes rot."
'Is that what they say, Susan? Who are they?'
I didn't answer. She was teasing me and didn't

Ruth Rendell: an extract from the manuscript of *The Brimstone Wedding*, 1996.

characters' hypocrisies and insecurities. The tension between scruffy Madeleine and her ex-husband Jarvis's sleek wife Lily – who schemes to captivate Madeleine's daughter Hilary, though she feels no tenderness for the recalcitrant adolescent – is not relieved by Madeleine's death. She continues to haunt Jarvis and Lily through Jarvis's office assistant, Margot. Margot's susceptibility to this possession rises from her lingering guilt over a long-ago sexual indiscretion with Jarvis and from a new questioning of her identity as wife and mother. It is Margot's motherliness, however, on which Madeleine relies to ensure that Hilary remembers her own mother and resists Lily's glamour. The bond between mother and child, emblematic of the vital 'linkages' between generations, finally subdues the sexual competition driving women apart and provides a closing note of optimism.   MO'C

Renault [Challans], Mary 1905–83 English HISTORICAL NOVELIST with a strong interest in bisexuality and homosexuality. She grew up in a medical household and, though she took a degree in English Literature at Oxford (1928), she later trained as a nurse (1936). Her first published novel, *Purposes of Love* (1939), is a variation on the familiar hospital romance, introducing sexual ambiguity in a sympathetic and unsensational way. *The Friendly Young Ladies* (1944) was written partly as a corrective to the 'earnest humourlessness' of RADCLYFFE HALL's THE WELL OF LONELINESS (1928) and stresses tolerance and understanding in a lesbian relationship (while fudging the ending). *Return to Night* (1947) won a £40,000 MGM prize which allowed her to write full-time, and she emigrated with her friend Julie Mullard to South Africa. *The Last of the Wine* (1956) draws implicit parallels between the repressive regime at Athens in the time of Socrates and 20th-century South Africa. Her last contemporary novel, *The Charioteer* (1953), openly portrays homosexual love (notably male, rather than female) as positive and fulfilling. Her greatest achievement is in her novels about Theseus, *The King Must Die* (1958) and *The Bull from the Sea* (1962), remarkable for their total immersion in the moral and spiritual universe of their period, unmediated by anachronistic modern perspectives. Set in Bronze Age Greece and Crete as matriarchal culture gives way to patriarchy, they combine meticulous research and powerful imaginative reconstruction, which she sustained in her trilogy about Alexander the Great: *Fire from Heaven* (1969), *The Persian Boy* (1972, movingly narrated by the slave Bagoas) and *Funeral Games* (1981). She also wrote a biography, *The Nature of Alexander* (1975), and two other Greek novels, *The Mask of Apollo* (1966) and *The Praise Singer* (1979).   MSM

Rendell, Ruth / Barbara Vine 1930– Ruth Rendell was born Ruth Grasemann in London, and worked as a newspaper reporter between 1948 and 1952. She married Donald Rendell, a fellow journalist, in 1950. Her first novel, *From Doon With Death*, featuring Inspector Wexford of the 'Kingsmarkham' Police Force, was published in 1964. This marked the start of a long (and continuing), more-or-less orthodox DETECTIVE series – though composed with unusual style and pungency. Interspersed with the Wexford mysteries, from 1965 on, came a series of somewhat more unsettling suspense novels, in which criminal maladjustment is shown in action. With both types of novel, you find converging strands of plot first held in equilibrium, and then brought together with breathtaking impact. Outstanding examples of this technique are *The Lake of Darkness* (1980) and *The Tree of Hands* (1984).

In 1986 came a new departure, the start of yet a further series of novels, written under the name of 'Barbara Vine' and moving in the direction of mainstream fiction – though still containing a strong element of intrigue. These are both more elaborate and glossy, and more openly romantic in tone, than the non-Wexford Rendells – down to the fairy-tale motifs they often accommodate. There's a *bois dormant* feel about *Gallowglass* (1990), for example, and a touch of Hans Andersen in *Asta's Book* (1993). Ruth Rendell's (and her *alter ego*'s) literary impetus is tied up with exorbitance of all kinds; her practice is to delineate an obsession on the part of some prominent character in each of her narratives, and push its consequences to an extreme. It may be a sexual obsession – as in *The Bridesmaid* (1989) – or an obsession with the London Underground, or with 'desert island' literature; but it's always linked to some lethal turn of events, or colourful derangement. Whatever it is, it rivets the attention. This author's skill is such, indeed, that she can even place a rapist at the centre of a full-length plot without sacrificing the reader's assent.

With the Wexford novels, as a general rule, the horrors are toned down, though the narrative expertise remains mightily on display. Detective Chief Inspector Reginald Wexford is a well-read policeman, middle-aged, a bit overweight, amiable but implacable, and furnished with an unexceptional home life. The last acts as a counterpart to all the murk, violence and disorder which are rife in Kingsmarkham, as elsewhere. Children go missing or are threatened with molestation, illicit passions flare, blood is spilt all over the place, not excluding the dinner table. Ruth Rendell, with her endless inventiveness, is as much of a literary phenomenon as AGATHA CHRISTIE; and all three strands in her output, in their slightly differing ways, bring a unique richness, complexity and magnitude to the traditional novel of detection or suspense.   PC

Renée 1929– New Zealand lesbian feminist playwright, novelist and activist. Renée left school at 12 to go to work, faking her age. At nearly 50, a cleaner in a city theatre while also teaching English and drama in a secondary school, she wrote her first theatre play because she 'began to get more and more angry about the fact that there were no really good parts for women' even though 'every woman you meet has a story'. Her best work is a dramatic trilogy dealing with the forgotten lives of ordinary women. *Jeannie Once* (1991) is set in Dunedin, 'the Edinburgh of the south', in 1879 and moves from workshop, manse, prison-cell and boarding house to a music hall, with a cast of British regional migrant women and men. *Wednesday to Come* (1985) occurs during the Depression as an unemployment march to Parliament passes a household of four generations of women, where one awaits the body of her husband who has committed suicide in a 'relief camp'; like all of Renée's work it offers a clear analysis of the drudgery experienced by working women. The third play of the trilogy *Pass It On* (1986), is set during the 1951 waterfront lockout-alias-strike, rejecting the REALISM of *Wednesday to Come* for a more didactic style and equally Left-wing politics.

Renée's ancestry is both Maori and British and there are other plays on themes of racial prejudice and shame, mothers and daughters, gender issues, sexual abuse and similar *Secrets* (1982). She has written seventeen plays and four novels and was awarded the Robert Burns (Writing) Fellowship at the University of Otago in Dunedin in 1989. The novels are vividly funny and at the same time schematically issue-driven. *Willy Nilly* (1990) and *Daisy and Lily* (1993) have present-day plots peopled with multitudinous characters, with an important emphasis on age. *Does This Make Sense to You?* (1995) is about a woman whose baby was adopted out in the early 1960s; *The Snowball Waltz* (1997) is a grim, funny story that explores small-town small-mindedness.

Renée's most recent writing sublimates these concerns under a wash of humour, in a collection of short pieces called *Yin and Tonic* (1998).   JD

Return of the Soldier, The (1918) REBECCA WEST's first novel, dramatized in 1928 and filmed in 1981, is a MODERNIST fusion of war, Freudian psychology, and the decline of England's class system, besides being an intriguing tale about love. When Captain Baldry returns to his country home from the 'Great War', shell-shock has caused his memory to fail. He has forgotten the last fifteen years, his marriage to Society beauty Kitty, and their son who died in infancy. Baldry has himself reverted to a youthful, happy mental state and thinks himself still in love with a local girl, now grown up into a drab suburban housewife. Yet she, Margaret, has a nobler character than furious, seigneurial Kitty. Kitty summons a specialist mind-doctor to assist, yet wise Margaret is the first to realize that the key to Baldry's psychosis is to 'remind him of the boy'. Thus triggered, Baldry returns to 'normality', though West implies that delusion is preferable; the 'cure' which makes him 'every inch a soldier' also heralds his return to 'the hell of War'.   JL

Returning: A Collection of Tales (1982) In this short-story collection EDNA O'BRIEN returns to themes and subject matter familiar from her early fiction. Chronicling the hardscrabble village life of mid-century Ireland, these mostly first-person tales of 'returning' all tell of its ultimate impossibility. The land of childhood, both geographical and emotional, is lost forever; marooned in a desolate adulthood, characters wander and stumble, as does Mabel in the story 'Savages'. An emigrant returned from Australia, Mabel tries to overcome her estrangement via a desperate strategy of sexual intrigue. As in many of the stories, adult sexuality means unassailable loneliness. The narrator of the collection's first story, 'The Connor Girls', leaves home, marries against her parents' wishes, and has a son. With her new family she returns to her native village, finding its inhabitants familiar yet utterly alien. The bitterness of her closing insight resounds throughout these tales: 'I realised that by choosing his world I had said goodbye to my own and to those in it. By such choices we gradually become exiles, until we are quite alone.'   MO'C

Revelation of Love, A (Short Text completed *c*.1388; Long Text *c*.1395–1415) The short version of JULIAN OF NORWICH's first-person account of the 'visions' that make up the single 'revelation' which accompanied her near-death illness in 1373 is the earliest surviving text in English known to be written by a woman. Revised and expanded over a period of perhaps forty years, it is a work of serious speculative theology. Desiring identification with Christ's passion, Julian describes a series of visions, including startling and homely images of Christ's bleeding head and body, a hazelnut, and Jesus as Mother, all of which are concerned with sin and salvation, and especially with Christ's reassurance that – in the work's most famous phrase – 'all shall be well'. Its primary argument – a daring one for the time – is that God's anger at sinners (a cornerstone of the Church's teaching), though true in a relative sense, is 'absolutely impossible'. Unlike most women mystics, Julian does not represent herself as being instructed to write by God. Confounding tidy oppositions between experience/authority, literate (able to read Latin)/illiterate, masculine/feminine, and homeliness/strangeness, the treatise is simultaneously a personal meditation and an ambitious theological work, deeply informed by orthodox clerical and scholastic Latin traditions yet also decentred from them.   REV

Rhys, Jean 1890–1979 Anglo-Caribbean novelist and short-story writer. Rhys was educated privately in Dominica, at the Perse School for Girls, Cambridge, and at RADA. An inability to speak verse without an accent barred her from the mainstream theatre and she accordingly spent years as a chorus-girl. The jailing of her first husband for embezzlement caused her to move to Paris, where she had an affair with Ford Madox Ford. He mistreated her, but also recognized and encouraged her talent, writing an introduction to her first collection of sketches and stories, *The Left Bank* (1927). Ford is caricatured in the novel *QUARTET* (originally entitled *Postures*; 1928); Ford, his other lover Stella Bowen and Rhys's husband also published novels about the relationship. Rhys's work fitted the agenda of Ford's MODERNISM since she applied psychological realism, including mild forms of stream of consciousness, and a sense of the telling image, to the rackety life she had been leading; part of her importance, and much of her popularity since her death, has to do with the extent to which her fiction aggressively celebrates sorts of women excluded from literature except as minor characters, and, specifically, their sense of their identities as inauthentic: 'Something happens and you stop being yourself; you become what others force you to be. You lose your wisdom and your soul'. *After Leaving Mr Mackenzie* (1931), *Voyage in the Dark* (1934) and *GOOD MORNING, MIDNIGHT* (1939), and the short-story collection *Tigers are Better Looking* (1937), all utilize her background in a way that transforms both picaresque and confessional elements by grim precision; her doomed heroines are never too depressed to notice brand names and smart furnishings. It is worth noting, however, that Rhys was rarely as entirely alone as her heroines and that the confessional elements include, productively, a degree of self-pitying fantasy and paranoia about money which re-anchors all this to reality. Some mild success did not provide Rhys with an income that would support her life-style and drinking, and she retreated to the countryside; her working method included endless obsessive rewriting. In old age, after a radio broadcast of *Good Morning, Midnight* in 1959, she was encouraged by friends to finish the short stories collected in *Sleep It Off, Lady* (1971) and the novel *WIDE SARGASSO SEA* (1966), in which she uses her wide and undisciplined reading and West Indian upbringing to recreate the early life of CHARLOTTE BRONTË's Mrs Rochester in *JANE EYRE*. This has been adopted as a feminist text for its handling of colonialism and sanity, but Rhys herself had no conscious agendas except personal ones – she saw this as the book she was born to write. The intense realism, and self-pity, of Rhys's earlier books is transfigured into a hallucinatory vividness that dramatizes the heroine's exile from her Caribbean home and her earlier illusions. The autobiographical fragment *Smile Please* (1979) deals with her childhood and early life; this and her *Collected Letters* (1990) reveal a sense of herself as being as doomed as, but less naive than, the characters of her fiction.   RK

Rhythm of Life, The (1893) ALICE MEYNELL was the major woman practitioner of the late Victorian belletrist essay. In this first collection of essays, mostly reprinted from the *National Observer*, the running theme is the restraint involved in recognizing the first-rate. She remembers her 'subtle education' by her non-writing father: 'he had an exquisite style from which to refrain'. She compares luxuriant English parkland scenery unfavourably with the austere classicism of Italian agricultural landscapes. She regrets the parasitism which great art inevitably encourages: 'trash . . . is impossible without a beautiful past'. Meynell's emphasis on perceptual and stylistic scrupulosity was widely admired. Arnold Bennett's *Journalism for Women* recommended her as the only safe model for women writers. Max Beerbohm complained that her admirers treated her prose as 'substitute for the English Sabbath'. In this collection a caustic analysis of the sexism of mid-Victorian caricature represents Meynell's life-long feminism; there are no essays on women writers, a later speciality. WOOLF criticized Meynell's 'airless' 'word-paring' approach, but her own essays, especially in authorial persona, are clearly influenced by Meynell's.   AT

Rice [née O'Brien], Anne 1941– American novelist, the second daughter of a New Orleans Irish Catholic family. In childhood, she was steeped in the baroque symbolism of the church. In the early 1960s, she married Stan Rice, a poet and university professor at Berkeley, and she moved to San Francisco. Their first child, a daughter, died from leukaemia at the age of 6. After this tragedy, the family moved back to her native New Orleans, where Anne Rice wrote *Interview with the Vampire* (1976), a narrative replete with yearning for a lost child: as Louis, the 'young' Vampire, goes for his first 'kill', he hears the 'rapid, tenacious heart of the child . . . beating like a tiny fist on a door, crying, "I will not die . . ."'. The book's originality lies in the way it transfers the traditional vampire story into the vampire's point of view, providing desire with a hellish image of its own tormenting, ambiguous freedom from history: '*Again* . . . is a human word'. The vampire looks at loss, and tragedy, and even change, with a decadent nostalgia that struck a chord with the AIDS generation of the 1980s.

The sequels to *Interview*, *The Vampire Lestat* (1985) and *The Tale of the Body Thief* (1992) tend to dilute the extraordinary vision of the first book, but Anne Rice regained her power with CRY TO HEAVEN (1990), a remarkable piece of literal baroque, set in early 18th-century imperial Venice, a sublimely dark tale of revenge between castrato, Tonio, who becomes the sexual icon of his age, and his brother, Carlo, who caused him to be 'cut'. Anne Rice is also the author of *The Sleeping Beauty Trilogy*, under name of A. D. Roquelaure.   VS

Rich, Adrienne 1929– American poet and essayist. She was born in Baltimore, into a well-to-do white Jewish family, and educated at Radcliffe College. In her twenties she married a Harvard economist and bore three sons. However, she later commented that 'marriage and motherhood, experiences which were supposed to be truly womanly, often left me feeling unfit, disempowered, adrift'. She has since chosen to live and write as a lesbian, diagnosing her own identity as 'split at the root', a 'Jewish lesbian raised to be a heterosexual gentile'.

She has had a long and distinguished career, about which it is unwise to make generalizations. However, her work has been of immense importance to the Anglo-American feminist movement, which, in the words of critic Barbara Charlesworth Gelpi, she has served as a 'pioneer, witness and prophet'. As well as writing poetry of great beauty and power, she is author of many influential essays, focusing on feminist literary criticism, the role of the poet, education, motherhood, Jewish identity, racism and heterosexism. See ON LIES, SECRETS AND SILENCE (1978) and OF WOMAN BORN (1976).

Her poetry achieved relatively early recognition, when *A Change of World* won the Yale Series Younger Poets Award in 1951, the year of Rich's graduation. This first volume was much influenced by Yeats, Stevens, Eliot and Frost – and W.H. Auden commented, 'The poems . . . are neatly and modestly dressed, speak quietly but do not mumble, respect their elders but are not cowed by them'. This was the work of what Rich herself has called a 'middle-class white girl taught to trade obedience for privilege'. However, there is a certain irony to Auden's review in the light of the outspoken and polemical nature of much of her later work – work which manifests an increasingly politicized commitment to transformation of the social and linguistic arrangements of patriarchy. In the 1960s she discarded her white literary 'fathers', and turned to writers like James Baldwin, SIMONE DE BEAUVOIR and EMILY DICKINSON for alternative inspiration. See THE DREAM OF A COMMON LANGUAGE: POEMS 1974–1977 (1978).

In the sixties and seventies she became a resourceful explorer of the political nature of the personal, and the unconscious processes at work in both of these interdependent realms. In 1973, on the jacket of *Diving into the Wreck*, she defines this project: 'I feel this book continues the work I've been trying to do – breaking down the artificial barriers between private and public, between Vietnam and the lovers' bed, between the deepest images we carry out of our dreams and the most daylight events "out in the world". This is the intention and longing behind everything I write.'

A selection of Rich's poetry, *The Fact of a Doorframe*,

was published in 1985 – while *An Atlas of the Difficult World* (1991) assembles poems written between 1988 and 1991. *Blood, Bread and Poetry* (1986) brings together the most influential of her essays. However, none of these can be taken as definitive summaries of her writing career. As Rich writes in this latter volume, 'there is … in our lifetimes, no end to the process'. AFT

Rich [née Boyle], Mary, Countess of Warwick

1624–78 Irish diarist, autobiographer and patron of Puritanism. At 15, 'unruly Mary' defied the wishes of her father, the Earl of Cork, in order to marry Charles Rich. As a young wife, she supervised the running of a large household at Leighs Priory in Essex, and engaged in charitable works in the neighbourhood. These responsibilities increased after her husband became Earl of Warwick in 1658.

In about 1647 Mary underwent a religious conversion, resolving to 'become a new creature'. Strongly influenced by the Puritan emphasis on self-examination, she kept a journal (1666–77) in which she recorded her daily routine and spiritual progress (see SPIRITUAL AUTOBIOGRAPHY), lamented her faults and expressed remorse at her failure to control her temper in arguments with her husband. She also wrote a short autobiography as a record of the 'providences' which had resulted from her conversion.

After her husband's death in 1673 Mary was free to devote her income to charitable causes, and when she herself died, her spiritual advisor, Dr Walker, remarked that her sole 'fault' had been an excess of charity, arising from her 'credulous easiness to believe most people good, or at least better than they were'. Walker's funeral sermon, *The Virtuous Woman Found*, was published in 1686, together with some of her own devotional writings. Extracts from her diary were published in 1847 and her autobiography in 1848. RR

Rich Like Us

(1983) NAYANTARA SAHGAL's political novel was awarded the Sinclair Prize for Fiction. It investigates the condition of India shortly after Indira Gandhi's declaration of the state of Emergency. The novel has two narratives. First, Sonali's account: she is a civil servant who believes in the democratic progress of her country until she is arbitrarily dismissed from her post in July 1975. She is one of the many victims of Indira Gandhi's authoritarian rule and increased paranoia about betrayal. Sonali's reflection on her life, on her profession and on the nation makes her realize her privileged position as part of a 'powerful minority' against many appalling realities within India, such as dowry murders, child brides and the existence of the practice of sati. In the middle of the novel is a text provided by Sonali's grandfather's manuscript written in 1915, at the time of the Raj, an era which saw the making of British India. This literary device sheds light on the legacy of colonialism within India's contemporary political and social turmoil. SPo

Richardson, Dorothy (Miller)

1873–1957 English author of a sequence of thirteen novels called PILGRIMAGE – the first volume of which, *Pointed Roofs*, was published in 1913, the year when Lawrence's *The White Peacock* and the first volume of Proust's *Du Côté de chez Swann* came out and a year before Joyce's *Dubliners*. She has been thought of as a feminist and a MODERNIST writer, credited by VIRGINIA WOOLF with inventing the woman's sentence but also criticized for letting 'the damned egotistical self' get in the way, as it had with Joyce. An interest in the techniques of early filmmaking – she reviewed films for *Close-Up* between 1927 and 1933 – influenced her writing.

Born in Abingdon, the third of the four daughters of a prosperous grocer, whose aspirations to leave trade and live on his investments as a gentleman ended in bankruptcy in 1893, Richardson always needed to earn her living. She did so as a governess, a secretary and then later as a translator and journalist. She lived in Bloomsbury, London, for most of her life. In 1917 at 44, she married Alan Odle, a painter sixteen years younger than she, with whom she was happy and whom she outlived.

Pilgrimage – published as separate novels, the final one in 1938 – draws on the events and relationships of Richardson's life. Its central character, Miriam Henderson, is watched and heard between the ages of 17 and nearly 40 as she develops from a serious, watchful young woman to someone who might write the novel she occupies. Miriam becomes an argumentative intellectual, caught up in contemporary debates, a friend of writers (H.G. Wells was famously Richardson's friend and briefly her lover), but her own intention as a writer is to include what is 'left out of' the heroic, REALIST novels of writers like Tolstoy, James and Conrad. In attempting to break with 'man's hilarious expostulating narrative voice' Miriam is shown working for a language of impression and thought – dense, flexible, playful, open: the 'years falling into words, dropping like fruit' – a language, she hoped, that would convey consciousness rather than mediate it. Her sexual ambivalence is a matter of language, but also how she experienced herself in her family and in her adult life. A characteristic allusion to this is 'how utterly detestable mannishness is; so mighty and strong and comforting when you have been mewed up with women all your life'.

Pilgrimage prefigures DORIS LESSING's *THE GOLDEN NOTEBOOK* both as a novel about a woman intellectual and writer and in its struggle to find a new and appropriate form. There have been studies of Richardson and her work by Gloria Fromm and Gillian E. Hanscombe, amongst others. John Cowper Powys's effusive 1931 essay became an embarrassment to Richardson, and Leslie Fiedler's charge of '*avant-garde* dullness' may have helped to put off readers. Her reputation has persisted despite this, and new editions of *Pilgrimage* were published in 1967 and 1979.   JM

Richardson, Henry Handel [Ethel Florence Lindesay Richardson] 1870–1946 Australian novelist whose interest in character led her to pursue NATURALIST approaches to the novel. In 1929 she wrote to Nettie Palmer, 'I never cease to believe that character drawing is [the novel's] main end and object, the conflict of personalities its drama.' While her trilogy, THE FORTUNES OF RICHARD MAHONY, with its Australian setting, has been most honoured in Australia, her three other novels and her short stories together demonstrate Richardson's original and various talent.

She was born in Melbourne, to an immigrant doctor and his wife – who, in order to support the family, became a postmistress after her husband's mental breakdown in the mid 1870s. From the age of 13, Richardson boarded at the Presbyterian Ladies' College in Melbourne, which became the basis for her second novel, THE GETTING OF WISDOM (1910). In 1888, she left Australia with her mother and sister to study piano and composition at the Conservatorium of Music in Leipzig. There she met her husband, J.G. Robertson, who encouraged her literary talent after she abandoned her aspirations as a performer. They married in 1895 and returned to England in 1903 where Robertson became Professor of German Literature at London University.

Richardson's first novel, MAURICE GUEST (1908), drew on her experiences as a student in Leipzig and her reading of European naturalist literature. It may be read as a conscious inversion of the conventional naturalist pairing of doomed woman and misguided man as it details the slow decline of a young man in love with an older and more experienced woman. The novel refuses to moralize about adulterous sexual love (or homosexuality) and insists that the sexual woman can survive. It also explores the conflict between the aspiration and idealism which make life meaningful, and the material conditions in which idealists must live.

The Getting of Wisdom conveys a more optimistic and comic mood. Yet, as Richardson remarked, the novel also examines 'crime and punishment; the workings of sex; passionate love' within its story of a teenage schoolgirl at odds with convention. Her short stories, too, concentrate mainly on the lives of girls and women. Her last novel, *The Young Cosima* – a fictional account of the life of Cosima Wagner – returns to many of these concerns.

But *The Fortunes of Richard Mahony* (*Australia Felix*, 1917, *The Way Home*, 1925, and *Ultima Thule*, 1929) shows Richardson at her most ambitious and compelling. Based on her parents' life together, it begins on the Ballarat goldfields just before the Eureka Stockade, and follows her characters to Melbourne, back 'Home' to England and back again to more straitened circumstances in Australia. In its concentration on the financial successes and failures of Richard Mahony and his eventual decline into mental illness, the novel is DOMESTIC and personal; yet Mahony's experience of Australia, and his vacillation between the colony and 'Home', reflects the divided heritage of a generation of migrants. For this novel alone, Richardson has been accorded an unchallenged place in the canon of Australian literature.   SPL

Riddell [née Cowan], Charlotte Eliza Lawson 1832–1906 Irish-born novelist whose work focusing on businessmen and the City of London made her a popular success. Her father, the sheriff of County Antrim, died when Charlotte was young. After some years of nursing her chronically ill mother in Ireland, in 1856 Charlotte moved to London, where, to support herself, she began writing. She married Joseph Hadley Riddell in 1857, but her early novels appeared under the name 'F.G. Trafford', including her third novel (and first success), *The Moors and the Fens* (1858). After this book, she turned to the stories of London business for which she was best known, including *City and Suburb* (1861), and *George Geith of Fen Court* (1864), the tragic, enormously successful (and complicated) story of a country curate who flees from a disastrous marriage, becoming a City accountant and ultimately an inadvertent bigamist. In the novel, Riddell defended her discussions of the financial world: 'Every other class has found some writer to tell its tale; but I can remember no book which has ever described a shopkeeper as a man … no one who does not jeer at business and treat with contempt that which is holy in God's sight'. Other novels describing the business world were *Mitre Court* (1885) and *The Head of the Firm* (1892). Riddell wrote more than thirty books, most published under the name 'Mrs J.H. Riddell', in a variety of genres, among them many ghost stories and SENSATION NOVELS. She also edited *St James's Magazine*, beginning in 1867.   KW

Riddell, Elizabeth 1910– Australian poet and distinguished journalist, winner of a prestigious Walkley Award. She came from her native New Zealand in 1928 to work on the Sydney *Truth*, but left for England in 1935 and spent the war years as a journalist in New York, England and Europe. On returning to Australia she continued to work as a journalist, a freelance reviewer and feature writer. There is a lengthy break between her first three poetry collections – *The Untrammelled* (1940), *Poems* (1948) and *Forebears* (1961) – and the later work that began with *An Occasion of Birds*

(1987). It is in this later period that she has received most critical recognition, with *Selected Poems* (1992) winning both the New South Wales Book of the Year Award and the Gold Medal of the Association for the Study of Australian Literature. *The Difficult Island*, a collection of new work, followed in 1994. A worldly poet (in the best sense of that word), Riddell moves with confident intelligence between sensuous celebratory lyrics, sardonic observations of human behaviour (especially of the lies people tell), and poems with an intense but controlled sense of what Peter Porter has called 'the sadness of the creatures'. JStr

Riding [née Reichenthal], Laura 1901–91 American MODERNIST poet who attempts to move beyond what she calls the 'abnormal cultivation of the classics' in the work of Pound and Eliot by creating intellectual, witty and metaphysical modernist poems. Riding was the child of working-class New York Jews; her father was active in the American Labour movement and hoped that she would become 'America's Rosa Luxembourg'. She began sending her precociously brilliant poems to little magazines in the early 1920s and when 'The Quids', her most successful early poem, caught the attention of Robert Graves, he asked her to collaborate on a book on modernist poetry in 1926. During their subsequent fifteen-year intellectual partnership they published a number of collaborative critical works, including *A Survey of Modernist Poetry* (1927), the first book to develop the techniques of close-reading.

In her own critical works *Contemporaries and Snobs* (1928) and *Anarchism Is Not Enough* (1928), and her early poetry collections, *The Close Chaplet* (1926), *Love as Love, Death as Death* (1928) and *Twenty Poems Less* (1930), Riding is stunningly pertinent but at times impenetrable, and her work often met with hostile responses. (See EXPERTS ARE PUZZLED, 1930). In 1929, she threw herself out of a fourth-floor window and, miraculously, broke her back but not her spinal cord. Dogged by scandal she moved to Majorca with Graves that year. In *Poet: A Joking Word* (1930), *Poems: A Lying Word* (1933) and in articles published in *Epilogue*, the journal she edited from 1935 to 1938, she focused on the consequences of what she saw as her physical and spiritual rebirth and began to create increasingly authoritarian and woman-focused essays and poems. Her *Collected Poems* (1938) is one of the most important poetry collections of the 1930s, a kind of 'principia' for truth-telling in poetry, as Fitzgerald called it. When the Spanish Civil War broke out in 1936, Riding and Graves were forced to leave Majorca and Riding returned to America in 1939. By 1941 she had married Schuyler Jackson, severed her ties to Robert Graves, stopped writing poetry and dedicated her life to the language project, *Rational Meaning* (1997), which occupied her until just before her death. RP

Right Hand, Left Hand (1977) DOROTHY LIVESAY's collage of essays, newspaper clippings, diary entries, reviews, poems, personal letters and reminiscences bears the cumbersome sub-title: 'A True Life of the Thirties: Paris, Toronto, Montreal, the West and Vancouver. Love, Politics, the Depression and Feminism'. Nevertheless this retrospective assembly of pieces written by herself and others is a very effective construct for weaving together the personal experiences of Livesay (she designates it as the second volume of her autobiography) and an overview of larger social events. During the decade she was a student in Toronto and Paris, an activist in the Communist party and a social worker in Montreal and New Jersey. She finally moved west to Vancouver, married and started a family. Her travels afforded many vantage points and changing perspectives for her obervations. What she saw determined the direction of her future life and work. Throughout the decade she wrote poems and stored away material for future writing. *Right Hand, Left Hand*, therefore, not only documents the turmoils of the times but provides essential background material for her poetry and fiction. JG

Riis, Sharon 1947– Canadian novelist, short-story and script-writer. Born in High River, Alberta, she received a BA in History from Simon Fraser University in Burnaby, British Columbia, in 1969. She has lived in Longview, Vancouver, London, Paris, Edmonton, Lac La Biche and Saskatoon.

Her first novel, *The True Story of Ida Johnson*, published in 1976, is a Canadian classic. It is still considered to be her most important work. Set in Longview, Alberta, the oral story of a waitress who deliberately murdered and burned her husband and children unravels through a double narrative that questions its authenticity. Ida Johnson is finishing the night shift when Luke, a goodlooking stranger, offers her twenty 'bucks' for the story of her life. Ida tells Luke her story until by the end of the narrative, she recognizes Luke as Lucy, her childhood friend. The filmic novel's brief scenes are witty and amusing. It is a story of survival and friendship and it is about shaping and creating your own life as much as it is a treatise on truth and fiction. *Midnight Twilight Tourist Zone* (1989) is Riis's second novel. Set in a cabin in a storm, it is a story about empathy and the merging and re-separating of identities.

This novel developed out of the film script for *Latitude 55* (1982). Riis's first two feature films, *Latitude 55* and *Loyalties* (1986), were both Genie Award finalists for the Best Original Script. *Loyalties*, directed by Anne Wheeler, is about a dark secret and two women from different cultures becoming friends. Other important productions are *The Wake* (1986) and *Change of Heart* (1993).

Riis's art is concerned with the notion of 'lebensraum', with 'knowing when you can recreate yourself and your circumstances, give shape to your life'. TP

Riley, Denise 1948– British poet and critic, born in Carlisle and educated at Oxford, Cambridge and Sussex, where she completed a doctorate in Philosophy. She has worked as a researcher at numerous universities in the UK, USA and Australia, including Brown University, The Institute for Advanced Studies Princetown, Griffith University Brisbane and the University of East Anglia, as well as being writer-in-residence at the Tate Gallery in 1996.

Riley has published widely in the field of feminist theory and social history. Her most challenging work, *Am I That Name?* (1988), is an investigation of the category of 'women', setting it in a historical context and arguing that the term comes to us out of a historical and philosophical ambiguity. She sees a recognition of the indeterminacy of 'women' as essential to an effective feminist political philosophy, arguing that from the late 17th century gender has become increasingly polarized in the face of changing ideas of the human. Much like SIMONE DE BEAUVOIR, she argues that 'women' are made and not born and asks 'Is "women", then an eternally compromised noun?' Her other work includes *War In the Nursery: Theories of The Child and Mother* (1983), and her poetry collections include *Dry Air* (1985) and *Mop Mop Georgette, New and Selected Poems 1986-1993* published in 1993. JHB

Riley, Joan 1950– Novelist born in St Mary, Jamaica, who migrated to England as an adolescent. She received a BA from the University of Sussex (1979) and an MA from the University of London (1984). Her work – *The Unbelonging* (1985), *Waiting in the Twilight* (1987) and *Romance* (1988) – is associated with graphic portraits of immigrant life in England. Riley has published three novels to date: *The Unbelonging* narrates the experiences of an 11-year-old girl summoned from Kingston to London by a father she has never known. In her new world she encounters alienation, hostility from her classmates, violence from her father, an uneasy relationship with her step-mother and step-siblings, and retreat into a world of dreams of her lost homeland. *Waiting in the Twilight* is the story, told in flashbacks, of Adela, a woman who joins her husband in England after World War II, leaving several children behind in Jamaica. *Romance* tells of how the lives of two West Indian sisters – fat Verona, prone to escape into romantic dreams, and Desirée, dissatisfied with her life as a wife and mother – are shaken up by the arrival of the children's grandparents from Jamaica, bringing with them the forgotten stories of home and the needed impulse for change.

One of the salient elements of Riley's fiction is her use of the female body as the site of oppression; her heroines' powerlessness, from Hyacinth's inability to control her bladder in *The Unbelonging* to Verona's inability to manage her weight in *Romance*, embodies the effect of sexism, racism and child abuse on their ability to triumph over their circumstances. Riley's interest in the problems brought about by migration and exile is evident in her 1996 edited collection, *Leave to Stay: Stories of Exile and Belonging*. Riley is also the author of two unpublished SCIENCE-FICTION projects: *The Waiting Room* (a collection of stories) and *Diaspora Under Twin Suns* (a novel). A collection of short fiction, *A Kindness to the Children*, was published in 1992. LP-G

Rinehart, Mary (Roberts) 1876–1958 American novelist, short-story writer, journalist and dramatist. She was born in Allegheny, Pennsylvania, daughter of a sewing-machine salesman. Trained as a nurse in Pittsburgh, she married Dr Stanley Marshall Rinehart in 1896. They had three sons. By 1904, their financial difficulties led to her selling poems and sensational fiction to magazines. By 1910, she had published three mysteries and a romance, and a play she co-wrote with Avery Hopwood – *Seven Days* – had been successfully produced on Broadway. She continued to write in all three genres and, through the 1940s, was a leading American popular writer, earning as much as $65,000 for a serialized novel. At least twenty of her works were filmed. Her most memorable character, an adventurous spinster named Tish, appeared in a series of stories in the *Saturday Evening Post* from 1910 to 1940. During World War I, Rinehart spent three months in France reporting from the front lines for the *Post*. She drew on this experience to write war fiction as well (*The Amazing Interlude,* 1918). In 1920 she collaborated with Hopwood on two more successful plays, *Spanish Love* and *The Bat.* Her serious fiction (*Lost Ecstasy,* 1927; *This Strange Adventure,* 1929), giving grim views of women's experiences in love and marriage, was poorly received. Rinehart's husband died in 1932. She wrote an autobiography, *My Story* (1931, expanded 1948), and created fictionalized self-portraits in her mysteries (including *The Swimming Pool,* 1952). JSG

Ripley's Game (1974) The third in psychological thriller writer PATRICIA HIGHSMITH's renowned 'Ripley' series – which numbered five at her death – shows the (conventionally) innocent suffering more than the guilty. Her favoured character, American expatriate Tom Ripley, is a thoroughly modern psychopath. At once a likeable charmer and a habitual criminal, he schemes and murders to support a life of leisure with his beautiful wife, Heloise. On a whim to help out an underworld friend, he involves timid family man Jonathan Trevanny, who may be dying of

"I AM A WRITER," I SAID IN A LOW, EARNEST TONE.
"NO! HOW—HOW AMAZING!"

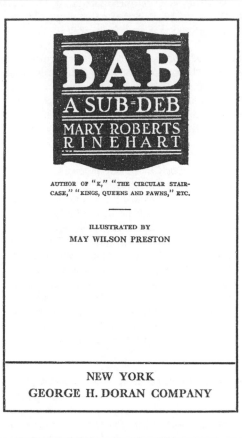

Mary Rinehart: frontispiece ('"I am a writer", I said in a low, earnest tone. "No! How – How amazing!"') and title-page of *Bab: A Sub-Deb*, 1917.

an incurable disease, in a scam to incite Mafia rivalries. With her customary slow yet inevitable plotting and startling insight into the disarmingly flawless logic of the criminal mind, Highsmith gradually unfolds the tragic cost of a moment of moral vulnerability. The intrusion of horrible violence into bland domesticity is a cruel reminder of the author's dictum that 'neither life nor nature cares if justice is ever done or not'.

Wim Wenders re-inflected Highsmith's preoccupation with the unstable male in a distinguished film version of the novel, entitled *The American Friend* (1977).

MO'D

Ritchie, Anne, Lady Thackeray 1837–1919 British writer and eldest daughter of William Makepeace Thackeray. Ritchie's sister Minnie's marriage to Leslie Stephen and subsequent death involved Ritchie with the Stephen family, an involvement which extended to the children of Leslie Stephen's second marriage –

among them VIRGINIA WOOLF. Woolf memorialized her 'Aunt Anny' in the character of Mrs Hilbery of *Night and Day* (1919).

At 14 Anne began working as her father's secretary. She published her first novel, *The Story of Elizabeth* (1862), in Thackeray's magazine *Cornhill*, and went on to publish several other novels, the most well-known of which are two DOMESTIC fictions, *The Village on the Green* (1867) and *Old Kensington* (1873).

When Anne Thackeray was 40 she and her cousin, Richmond Ritchie, fell in love and married despite the fact that he was seventeen years her junior. Following her marriage, Ritchie's literary efforts shifted from novels to memoir, biography and essay writing. Her biographical work includes *Madame de Sevigne* (1881), and the introductions to her father's collected works.

Woolf's obituary of her 'aunt' (*Times Literary Supplement*, March 1919) portrays Ritchie as a gifted writer of memoir. Even when Ritchie's description wanders from the 'great man' who is her subject, Woolf assures us, 'never mind – there was an ink-pot, perhaps a chair, he stood this way, he held his hat just so, and miraculously and indubitably there he is before our eyes'. From such 'slight materials', Woolf claims, Ritchie makes us 'feel that we have been in the same room with the people she describes'.   EC

Rivers of China, The (1987) First performed by the Sydney Theatre Company in 1987, this is Australian playwright ALMA DE GROEN's most ambitious and critically acclaimed play to date. A complex, challenging dual narrative puts feminist theory to the test and profoundly explores the dilemmas of the female artist. The first plot concerns the New-Zealand-born writer KATHERINE MANSFIELD in 1923 when, seriously ill with tuberculosis, in the last weeks of her life, she joins the Gurdjieff Institute for the Harmonious Development of Man at Fontainebleau in France. There, under the influence of Gurdjieff, she finds peace despite his philosophy limiting women's spiritual and artistic agency. The other narrative, set in the present in a Sydney hospital, is a feminist dystopia, where sexual roles have been reversed when women acquired the power of the Medusa Look. The Man, recovering after a suicide attempt, is hypnotized and reconstructed by female surgeon Rahel, recreating in him the spirit, but also the disease, of Katherine Mansfield. He chooses to die rather than lose his female spirit and creativity.

HTh

Robert Elsmere (1888) MRS HUMPHRY WARD's account of the religious journey of her eponymous hero, in which she examines the problem of declining Christian belief and spiritual poverty in a democratic, rational age. She used this novel to advance her own beliefs, and argued for a new and revitalized religion of good works, in which Christianity is stripped of its miraculous content.

The novel traces the career of an earnest young man through Oxford, too-easy ordination and appointment to a family living. He marries an austerely Evangelical wife, and together they lead virtuous useful lives in a rural parish. But Elsmere's faith is shallowly rooted; he falls under the influence of the Squire, a dry rationalist whose work on historical testimony undermines Elsmere's belief in the divinity of Christ. Catherine Elsmere's temperament and instinctive, child-like faith make her view her husband's spiritual crisis with uncomprehending horror, and their marriage becomes unhappy. Elsmere's conscience leads him to resign his orders, and he devotes the remainder of his short life to the New Brotherhood, an educational settlement he helps to found in the London slums.   CT

Roberts, Elizabeth Madox 1881–1941 American novelist, poet, short-story writer. Born and raised in Springfield, Kentucky, where she spent most of her life, Elizabeth was raised on her father recounting leg-

ends and family pioneer histories in the evenings. She attended local high schools and went to the State College of Kentucky for one year in 1900. She taught for several years, and published her first book of poems, *In the Great Steep's Garden*, in 1915. Matriculating at the University of Chicago in 1917, she graduated with honours in 1921, at the age of 39. Returning to Springfield, she published a second poetry volume the following year. Using her native Kentucky as the setting for her work, she often created in her novels a female consciousness grappling with the contrast between the natural order and the difficulty of country life. Her first novel, *The Time of Man* (1926), was a critical success and portrays the hardships of Ellen Chesser, daughter of a Kentucky farmer, whose ancestors were pioneers. Her 1930 novel, *The Great Meadow*, is set during the Revolutionary era and depicts the trials of early Kentucky pioneers in the hostile wilderness. Although Roberts's work is generally considered to be uneven, she has been praised by critics for the strong lyric voice in her novels. Critics have variously characterized her as a feminist, comparing her to DICKINSON and WOOLF, or a Southern regional writer, in the tradition of Faulkner.   SP

Roberts, Michèle (Brigitte) 1949– Feminist poet and novelist, educated at a convent school and Somerville College, Oxford. Influences she cites include the language, rhythms and rituals of the Catholic church; French (she was brought up bilingual); Shakespeare; Chaucer; and her English grandmother's 'rude rhyming epics'. Her work is characterized by preoccupations with love, death and religion, food, female sexuality, the body and the unconscious. Both poetry and prose are strong and lyrical, involving layers of meaning. The writing is highly sensuous, sometimes erotic, often witty, combining acute evocations of the material world with strong emotional responses. She makes use of biblical, classical and Anglo-French reference, together with numerous female images – sibyls, mother goddesses, nuns, priestesses, housewives, mothers, midwives – claiming that although writing is a 'bisexual practice . . . it's inseparable that I'm a woman, a poet, and writer. Feminism is part of my bones and my blood.' Her first two novels draw on her French and English childhoods: *A Piece of the Night* (1978; *Gay News* Literary Award) and *The Visitation* (1983). *The Wild Girl* (1984) tells an alternative, feminized, version of Christ's life and death from the perspective of Mary Magdalene. *The Book of Mrs Noah* (1987) contains a kaleidoscope of female narratives. *In the Red Kitchen* (1990), centring on a young 19th-century medium, presents the intercommunicating narratives of four women, from ancient Egypt to the present. Her most profound, funny and moving novel, *DAUGHTERS OF THE HOUSE* (1992, WHS

Literary Award 1993), focuses on two cousins (one half-English) growing up in a secret-ridden house in post-war Normandy. Concerned with betrayal, it blends issues of universal importance with fierce private emotions, stressing the need to bear honest witness. *FLESH AND BLOOD* (1994) is an ingeniously constructed exploration of memory and history. She has published one collection of short stories, *During Mother's Absence* (1993), and three of poetry: *The Mirror of the Mother* (1986), *Psyche and the Hurricane* (1991), *All the Selves I was* (1995).   SAS

Robertson [née Swan], Hannah 1724–1800?

British autobiographer and writer of popular guides to cookery, sewing and crafts, Robertson's active life of labour and travel reflects an indomitable spirit and talent for survival. Robertson turned first to tavern-keeping and then to teaching in order to pay off debts and support herself following her husband's death in 1771. Living in Edinburgh, York, London and Birmingham, she instructed girls in needlework and embroidery and published two volumes entitled *The Young Ladies School of Arts*. In them she presents 'practical receipts, in cookery', directions for 'gum-flowers, filigree, japanning, shell-work, [and] gilding' and shrewd tips for marketing the resulting food or wares. While impecunious and ill, Robertson wrote her autobiography in 1791. Claiming to be a granddaughter to Charles II and the 'miserable inheritor of his misfortunes', she presents her sad tale in a confident and engaging style. Written to an unknown benefactress, this account chronicles a woman's struggle to make her wits, needle and pen the means of survival for herself and her children. Its publication, which one hopes brought its author some material relief, marks the end of our knowledge of this remarkable woman.   JRS

Robertson, Heather Margaret 1942–

Canadian journalist and fiction writer, born in Winnipeg, who graduated from the University of Manitoba (BA, 1963) and from Columbia University (MA, 1965). She currently lives in Toronto.

She started her writing career as a reporter and critic for the *Winnipeg Tribune* (1964–6) and in 1971 became a feature freelance writer for *MacLean's* and for the Canadian Broadcasting Corporation (CBC). She was a radio producer for CBC-Winnipeg and a TV story educator for public affairs programmes (1968–71). Some of her non-fiction publications are: *Reservations are for Indians* (1970), *Grass Roots* (1973), *Salt of the Earth* (1974), *A Terrible Beauty: The Art of Canada at War* (1977). Her published fiction includes *The Flying Bandit* (1981), *Willie: A Romance* (1983), *Lily: A Rhapsody in Red* (1986) and *Igor: A Novel of Intrigue* (1989). She has also written two books on Canadian political life: *More than a Rose: Prime Ministers, Wives and Other Women* (1991) and *On the Hill: A*

People's Guide to Canada's Parliament (1992). She is especially interested in exploring the boundaries between journalism and fiction, preferring to write about real people and events in order to capture the truth and to reveal its meaning.

She has received ACTRA Awards, the Canadian Authors' Association Fiction Prize (1984) and the Books in Canada Best First Novel Award (1983).   GHN

Robins [Parks], Elizabeth 1862–1952

American-born actress–manageress who established Ibsen on the English stage and enjoyed success as a journalist, playwright, short-story writer, novelist ('C.E. Raimond') and suffragette propagandist (see SUFFRAGETTE LITERATURE). Robins launched her acting career in 1881, and left for Europe in 1888 after her husband's suicide. In London her breakthrough came with *Hedda Gabler* in 1891. Celebrated as the Ibsenite NEW WOMAN *par excellence* (*Ibsen and the Actress*, 1928), she was close to William Archer, Henry James (*Theatre and Friendship*, 1932), and GERTRUDE BELL, and knew Wilde, the WOOLFS, and Shaw (*Both Sides of the Curtain*, 1940). Retiring from the stage in 1902 to become a publicist for the Women's Social and Political Union (*Way Stations*, 1913), she made her mark with *Votes for Women!* and *The Convert* (both 1907), and acted as president of the Women Writers' Enfranchisement League. As a writer she was drawn to social problems, engaging with class (*Alan's Wife*, with Florence Bell, 1893; *Below the Salt*, 1896), race (*The Secret That Was Kept*, 1926), marital oppression (*George Mandeville's Husband*, 1894) and prostitution (*Where Are You Going To?*, 1913; American title: *My Little Sister*). *The Open Question* (1898) and *The Magnetic North* (1904) draw on her childhood and Alaskan travels. Later she was involved with *Time and Tide* (*Prudence and Peter*, 1928, with Octavia Wilberforce), and wrote the feminist polemic *Ancilla's Share* (1924). *My Little Sister* and *A Dark Lantern* (her 1905 novel about the rest cure) were filmed by Fox Film Corporation (1919) and Realart Picture Corporation (1920).   AH

Robinson, Marilynne 1943–

North American writer of fiction and non-fiction. Her exceptional only novel, *Housekeeping* (1980), was made into a film starring Christine Lahti in 1987. The story concerns two sisters, Ruthie and Lucille, who are orphaned by their mother's suicide and brought up by their grandmother. When the grandmother dies two elderly sisters-in-law take her place until the girls' aunt Sylvie arrives to 'housekeep' in her own fashion. Ultimately Ruthie and Lucille are divided by the former's decision to follow Sylvie's itinerant lifestyle and the latter's desire for a more conventionally feminine role. Around this simple plot the novel weaves a lyrical account of sibling rivalry and love in the bleakly beautiful Northwest, ending ambiguously with alternative possible futures for the two sisters. Her work of non-fiction, *Mother Country* (1989), expands on a controversial article published in *Harper's* (February 1985), dealing 'with Sellafield and the peculiarities of British culture which allow it to flourish' in an attempt to raise North American consciousness of the nuclear industries across the Atlantic.   RW

Robinson, Mary 1758–1800 An English novelist and poet, she also had a career as an actress and the mistress of the Prince of Wales. When the affair ended, she ended up with an annuity of £500 a year for life, which barely kept her out of debt. It had been in order to alleviate the financial hardship of her marriage to Thomas Robinson, gambler and profligate, that she had first turned to writing. Her poems were published in 1775 and earned her the title of the 'English SAPPHO', which had been taken from her cycle of love sonnets called *Sappho and Phaon: In a series of Legitimate Sonnets* (1796). After a disastrous love affair with Colonel Banastre Tarleton and the onset of a paralysis, she started writing novels: *Vancenza: The Dangers of Credulity* (1792), *Walsingham: Or, The Pupil of Nature* (1797) and *Angelina: A Novel* (1796). Sentimental melodrama was the hall-mark of her fiction, but underneath was a core of social protest at the way in which women were misused by men. In the treatise *Thoughts on the Condition of Women, and on the Injustice of Mental Subordination* (1798), she confronts these issues directly, drawing attention to the hypocrisy of men who, in spite of professing to be the protectors of woman, are, in fact, 'the most subtle and unrelenting enemy she has to encounter'. MM-R

Roche [née Dalton], Regina Maria 1764–1845 Irish novelist. Born in County Waterford and brought up in Dublin, Regina began to write at an early age. Her first novel, *The Vicar of Lansdowne*, appeared in 1789, and she went on to publish fifteen more, many of which were translated into French. Most of her novels were published by the Minerva Press, whose popular tales of ROMANCE and horror were dismissed by Charles Lamb as 'these scanty intellectual viands of the . . . female reading public'.

Roche herself is best known for the immensely successful *The Children of the Abbey* (1796). The novel, whose orphaned heroine undergoes a series of privations at the hands of a wicked aunt and a villainous suitor, appeared in ten editions before 1825 and remained in print until 1882. JANE AUSTEN cites it as one of Harriet Smith's favourite books in *EMMA*, and another of Roche's novels, *Clermont* (1798), is mentioned in *NORTHANGER ABBEY* as a delightfully 'horrid' example of GOTHIC fiction.

Roche's subsequent novels failed to repeat the success of *The Children of the Abbey*. After living for some years in London, she returned to Waterford, where she

died at the age of 81, having published her last novel, *The Nun's Picture*, in 1836.   RR

Roden [née Douek], Claudia 1936– FOOD WRITER who became a British citizen in 1959, Claudia Douek was born and brought up in Cairo, in a Sephardi Jewish family whose forebears had settled in Egypt centuries earlier. She was sent to school in Paris, then moved to London in 1954 to study painting at St Martin's School of Art. Two years later, after the Suez crisis, she was joined by her parents who, having lost all their possessions, settled in London with Claudia and her two brothers. In the introduction to her most recent work, *The Book of Jewish Food – An Odyssey from Samarkand and Vilna to the Present Day* (1997), she wrote: 'At 16 Woodstock Road it seemed we had never left Cairo. The smell of sizzling garlic and coriander seeds in the kitchen, or of rose water in a pudding, and my mother's daily meals, reinforced the feeling.'

In 1959 she married Englishman Paul Roden, with whom she had three children. They were divorced in 1974. In the 1960s, overcome with a sense of loss, she began to write about the foods of her childhood in *A Book of Middle Eastern Food* (1968). Other books followed, among them *Mediterranean Cookery* (1987) and *The Food of Italy* (1989).

Her books share with ELIZABETH DAVID's early books a depth of feeling that transcends their subject. Both women spent the war years in Cairo, and missed the food of the Eastern Mediterranean deeply in later years.

She combines emotional depth with the accuracy of the scholar, conveying in her prose the symbolic importance of a specific dish and precise directions for making it. She describes the rituals associated with the making of Turkish coffee: sugary sweet for weddings and birthdays, bitter at funerals, regardless of personal taste. She writes with ease and inborn authority, familiar since early childhood with such exotic ingredients as sumac and zahtar, rose buds and pomegranate seeds, mastic and *citrons confits*.   AB

Rodriguez [née Green], Judith 1936– Australian Judith Rodriguez, born in Perth, has published a number of volumes of poetry since her first appearance, under her maiden name of Green, in *Four Poets* (1962: with David Malouf, Rodney Hall and Donald Maynard). Also a teacher of creative writing, she has anthologized and edited several poetry collections, was poetry editor of the periodical *Meanjin* from 1979 to 1982, and has edited the Penguin Australian Poetry series since 1989. Her own vivid and energetic poetry is characterized by its forthright charting of personal experience as well as broader political subjects. Its concerns are also those of women in general, the life happenings such as divorce and subsequent dislocation giving form to the female predicament in these circumstances. She has also illustrated many of her volumes of poetry with lino- and woodcuts. The poem 'Witch heart (going to ROBYN ARCHER's "A Star is Torn")' from her 1982 volume of the same name, records –

we go to see a red bitch raise
eleven nobles from the grave
... raped and bent and drunk and broke
and jailed and dead and young that ache

in empathetic tribute to both feminist performer and the 'eleven dead whores' who constitute her subject. *Mud Crab at Gambaros's* (1980) contains a series of poems celebrating the unlikely subject of the Queensland mud-crab, hedonistic symbol and frequent occasion of uninhibited feasting. Her other books include *Nu-Plastik Fanfare Red* (1973), *Water Life* (1976), *Shadow on Glass* (1978), *Floridian Poems* (1986), *New and Selected Poems: The House by Water* (1988) and *The Cold* (1992). Judith Rodriguez's poems are enjoyed for their wit and intelligence, their clear-sighted analysis of women's positions in the contemporary world and a never-flagging energy of expression. HTh

Roe, Sue 1956– English writer, whose work in women's fiction and feminist theory was particularly important in the 1980s and early 1990s. Her novel, *Estella* (1982), employs sensuous and fetishistic imagery to investigate the neurotic obsession of the main heroine, for whom 'Writing's far too complicated. You can only tell stories, that's the problem, if you want any-one to read it.' The question of the difficulty of writing as such, combined with the unexpected bliss it may offer, can be traced throughout most of her work. The collection of essays she edited on women writers, *Women Reading Women's Writing*, in 1987, explores the possibility of 'the gendered theory of pleasure'. Author of *Writing and Gender* (1990), a critical study of VIRGINIA WOOLF's writing practice, and editor of Virginia Woolf's *Jacob's Room* (1992), Roe seems to have adopted Woolf's desire 'to use writing as an art, not as a mode of self-expression' as a motto for her multiple artistic practices (novels, criticism, short stories, drawing, publishing). JZ

Rogers, Jane 1952– British novelist whose fictions consistently explore the inequalities engendered by hierarchies of power and represent marginalized voices. She was born in London and grew up in Birmingham, New York state and Oxford. After reading English at Cambridge, she became a teacher but has also worked as a writer-in-residence at the Northern College, Barnsley, and has held Writing Fellowships at Cambridge University and Sheffield Hallam University where she has taught on the MA in Creative Writing. Her first novel, *Separate Tracks*, came out in 1983 and was followed by *Her Living Image* (1984), winner of the 1985 Somerset Maugham Award, and *The Ice is Singing* (1987). *Mr Wroe's Virgins* (1991), which she adapted as a screenplay for the BBC and which won a Bafta nomination for Best Drama Serial, is set in Lancashire in 1830–1 and relates the events in the lives of seven women when they enter a community of Christian Israelites. *Promised Lands* (1995) juxtaposes the lives of Stephen and his Polish wife, Olla, in present-day Britain with that of William Dawes, a lieutenant sent to work in a penal colony in Australia in 1788. It won the 1996 Writers Guild Best Fiction Award. She has written other screenplays – *Dawn and the Candidate*, which won a Samuel Beckett Award (1989), and *The Vice*.

While her writing is woman-centred, Rogers is not afraid to point out the narrowness of a feminism that is predominantly middle-class or the limitations of liberal notions of freedom. Her fictions, which often interweave multiple narratives, explore themes such as the function of story-telling, gaps in official history, and the relationship between past and present. EP

Roland, Betty [née Elizabeth Maclean] 1903–96 Australian playwright, novelist and children's writer. Betty Roland wanted to be Australia's Eugene O'Neill and, although she became a successful ROMANCE novelist and CHILDREN'S WRITER, drama was her first and abiding love. Like most Australian playwrights of her generation, Roland suffered from the lack of public and institutional support for serious drama apparent until the 1960s. *The Touch of Silk* (1928), the play for which she is best known, was lauded as hailing a new era for Australian drama; hopeful words which did not bear fruit. Written during a period of intense debate about an Australian identity, *The Touch of Silk* is representative of the shift toward a self-conscious examination of Australian culture. Set in a drought-stricken country town following World War I, it traces the story of Jeanne, a young French woman married to an Australian veteran. The play sensitively explores the dual alienation of the 'other' in the environment of the bigoted town and harsh physical landscape. The aridity of the land is matched by the mean-spiritedness of the small-minded townsfolk and represents Australian characters who are very different from the bumptious hayseed types commonly portrayed on the commercial stage then. Produced numerous times in amateur theatres during the 1930s and broadcast on radio, it received its first professional production in 1976.

Roland's other plays include: *Granite Peak* (1952) which, similar to *The Touch of Silk*, deals with racism and loneliness in outback Australia; *Morning* (1937), a powerful short play concerning the murder of an interloper in the lives of an escaped convict and his wife; *Feet of Clay* (1928), a comedy based on the Pygmalion and Galatea legend (first produced and published in 1995). She also wrote the script for the first sound film made in Australia, *Spur of the Moment* (1931). For the Communist party in the 1930s she wrote numerous agitational-propaganda plays depicting the classic capitalist/worker divide.

Roland left an unhappy marriage in 1933, travelled to Russia with Guido Baracchi, a prominent Communist, and lived there for two years. She continued to write throughout her life, working as a journalist, radio script-writer and playwright during the 1930s and 1940s while being involved in amateur theatre. Radio drama provided employment for many Australian writers when there was little support for local theatre and with Catherine Shepherd (1902–76), Catherine Duncan (1915–), Gwen Meredith (1907–) and others, Roland became known for her radio plays and serials. She moved to London in 1952, with her daughter, Gilda Baracchi. There Roland wrote a series of adventure stories based on her childhood but was required by the publisher to change the gender of the main protagonist because male characters were regarded as more saleable. After her return to Australia in 1961 she wrote four volumes of autobiography.   KK

romance The label 'romance' has been attached to an extraordinarily divergent body of texts, from the Arthurian romance *Gawain and the Green Knight* (*c*.1400) to Shakespeare's so-called late romances, Keats's *Endymion: A Poetic Romance* (1818) and 'trashy' romances like Miranda Lee's *An Obsessive Desire* (Mills and Boon, 1989). A deeply troubled and contradictory term, romance can't be boiled down to a single definition. No single text instantiates romance: mass-market love-stories with titles like *Pagan Enchantment* or *Stranger From the Past* are not versions of the Elizabethan romance (Spenser's *The Faerie Queene*, 1590s) or of Walter Scott's *Ivanhoe* (1819/20). Romance pops up in all historical periods. It crosses the boundaries between high and low culture, and invades texts that would not otherwise be considered romance, such as CHARLOTTE BRONTË'S *JANE EYRE* (1847) or the novels of JANE AUSTEN. Romance is truly an errant form.

A European phenomenon, romance emerges as a recognizable literary genre in late 12th-century France (key texts are Chrétien de Troyes's dream-like *The Knight of the Cart* (*Lancelot*) and *Yvain* (*c*.1170–82), and the allegorical quest-poem *The Romance of the Rose* (1225–75)). Chaucer hints that women form romance's natural reading constituency (*Nun's Priest's Tale*, 1386). Yet the ideological function of the earliest chivalric quest romances, of which about sixty Middle English examples survive, appears to have been to consolidate positions of privilege for the male aristocracy and to console younger sons for the economic loss entailed by primogeniture. And for Caxton, romance-reading is essential in forming both gentlewomen *and* gentlemen (*Blanchardyn and Eglantine*, 1489) but he directs them to read for different things: identification with acts of valour for the men, constancy in loving men for the women. And although romance mutated into the novel (*roman*), a form often associated with women, there is plenty of male investment in the mode. Masculine quest-romances – sometimes labelled 'Westerns' or 'adventures' – include texts as heterogeneous as Bunyan's Christian allegory *Pilgrim's Progress* (1678), William Gibson's cyberpunk *Neuromancer* (1989) and Umberto Eco's *The Name of the Rose* (1983). This suggests the complexity of gendering issues at work throughout the history of romance.

Yet romance is a woman's genre in several senses. In the traditional generic hierarchy romance is secondary to epic, and hence, through the association of the secondary and inferior with the feminine, identified with women. CLARA REEVE'S *THE PROGRESS OF ROMANCE* (1785) defends romance from accusations that it is a despised feminine genre. Romance is also associated with the (secondary, feminine) vernacular: *enromancier* means 'to translate (from Latin) into the vernacular'. And it is still the genre of and for women in mass culture. Under the Harlequin Mills and Boon imprint six mass-market romances are sold globally every four seconds.

Romance has had a bad feminist press. The highly formulaic plots of 'trashy' romances – coldly phallic heroes, heroines living in a constant state of semi-arousal – have provoked feminist outrage for their view that pleasure for women equals men. But the negative view of popular romances has given way to the acknowledgement that their narratives, despite deploying retrogressive stereotypes, can also challenge traditional identities for women. DAPHNE DU MAURIER'S inter-war *REBECCA* (1938) offers women the romance of a full and unified subjectivity, transcending gender and class. And the self-indulgence of romance reading may be at odds with the patriarchal ideology of submissiveness contained within it. Romance's encouragement of 'naive identification' with a passive heroine can be politicized in psychoanalytic terms via the Freudian scene of fantasy. Identification is never a simple matter. It can entail occupying a plurality of subject positions, plunging us into fantasies – of the origins of sexual difference and of seduction – that are crucial to our constitution as subjects. 'Trashy' romance's delicious foreplay may be 'pornography for women', but this pleasure can be theorized as a fantasy of total immersion in sense experience that evokes babylike omnipotence. Romance elements in otherwise REALIST novels can disrupt the boundaries between fantasy and realism to raise questions about history and novelistic truth.

Romance is often considered not to be a genre at all unless paired with other categories: historical romance (the novels of GEORGETTE HEYER and CATHERINE COOKSON), GOTHIC romance (WUTHERING HEIGHTS, 1847), Arthurian romance, family-saga romance (COLLEEN MCCULLOUGH's *The Thorn Birds*, 1977). Attempts to define romance in formalist terms have foundered. Propp's structuralist analysis remains too much on the surface of the text. However, Northrop Frye (1957) reads romance as a kind of free-floating 'mode' of wish-fulfilment that is at the structural core of all fiction. Historicizing Frye, Fredric Jameson (1975) argues that romance 'expresses a transitional moment', one in which its contemporaries 'must feel their society torn between past and future in such a way that the alternatives are grasped as hostile but somehow unrelated worlds'.

Therefore, given the welter of contradictory definitions, it may after all be more satisfactory to locate romance's major dynamic not in its form or content but in its mode of address, focusing – as outlined above – on the reader's investment and acquiescence in its seductive pleasures. Roland Barthes's account of reading as a site of erotic pleasure (*The Pleasure of the Text*, 1975) explains why lack of fulfilment paradoxically satisfies: 'you can never have too much romance'.

Romance may be archetypally about true love but is always available for parody and interrogation. ANGELA CARTER's bleak *Love* (1971) and KATHY ACKER's pornographic-picaresque *Kathy Goes to Haiti* (1978) register sophisticated forms of enchantment and disenchantment. A.S. BYATT's POSSESSION: A ROMANCE (1990) offers a knowing deconstruction of the romantic myth of reciprocal passion. Nor is romance all compulsory heterosexuality: RADCLYFFE HALL's THE WELL OF LONELINESS (1928), while relying heavily on the forms of popular heterosexual romance, does not speak only for the desire of the individual traditionally celebrated in romance but for the suffering millions of 'inverts', opening up the mode to unexpected political uses.

Because it represents forms of desire, romance can bring together issues of sexual difference and nationalism. This can be politically conservative: the masculine imperial quest-romances (Rider Haggard's *She*, 1886; Conrad's *Heart of Darkness*, 1899), rife with racial and sexual anxieties and almost totally devoid of women, lay claim to a homosocial world of English masculinity by opposing it to an effete and feminized otherness; and MARGARET MITCHELL's GONE WITH THE WIND (1936) offers an unreconstructed racial and sexual politics. However, romance's long history includes examples that play self-reflexively with the possibilities of the form: CHARLOTTE LENNOX's THE FEMALE

QUIXOTE (1752) gently lampoons its English heroine's taste for French romances, understanding romance-reading as a form of complex self-fashioning in which both national and gendered identities are at stake.

So, no overall purchase on the term 'romance' is possible. Romance has a complex history but is not itself synonymous with the past, although there have been several attempts to align romance with the past and to claim realism for the present, most famously in Bishop Richard Hurd's *Letters on Chivalry and Romance* (1762) which both repudiates and mourns a lost world of 'fine fabling'. On the contrary, romance as a mode endures in a huge range of cultural texts, from psychoanalysis (Freud's 'family romance', 1909) to accounts of the search for scientific discoveries, and from classical Hollywood cinema (both straight – *Casablanca*, *Brief Encounter*, *Pretty Woman* – and ironic: *True Romance*) to popular culture (Valentine's Day, the media romance with Princess Diana, and movements such as the New Romantics). Romance, it seems, is something we can't do without.

REu

Romance of the Forest, The (1791) ANN RADCLIFFE's third ROMANCE is set in mid 17th-century France, where the Marquis de Montalt, an avaricious Gothic villain puts virtuous *ingénue* Adeline 'in distress'. Her misfortunes bring her to a Mediterranean site of sublime scenery. The chevalier, M. Verneuil, criticizes the 'wretched policy' of the French, while praising their animated air. In an uncharacteristic note to the text, Radcliffe reminds us that this applies to the 17th century, subtly satirizing reactionary discourse against Revolutionary France. Adeline maintains her liberal, bourgeois SENSIBILITY, resisting the oppression of feudal patriarchy and finally achieves the kind of pastoral harmony depicted in Rousseau's *Emile*. The picturesque scenery reflects contemporary accounts of the Grand Tour. Radcliffe's political intent is ambiguously woven in the design of the novel, defined by the coexistence of the picturesque and the sublime, and reflecting the tension between 'the proper lady' and 'the woman writer'. Her discourse flows between the vicious oppressor in the GOTHIC castle and the virtuous monarch in a Rousseauesque utopia, without overtly asserting the radical cause.

CY

Rombauer, Irma von Starkloff 1877–1962 American COOKERY WRITER. Born in St Louis, Missouri, to a physician and diplomat, Rombauer was educated in Europe before studying at Washington University's School of Fine Arts. Marrying a lawyer in 1899, she became a mother of three and a civic and cultural leader. Widowed at 43, she alleviated her grief by privately printing a small volume based on notes she had kept to instruct her cooks. She enlisted the help of her daughter, Marion Rombauer Becker, to expand this initial *The Joy of Cooking* (1931) into an encyclopaedic work published by Bobbs-Merrill in 1936. Revised editions in 1943, 1946, and 1951 sold 6 million copies and proved the success of combining witty anecdotal chat with practical step-by-step recipes. Becker revised the work alone in 1978, but the Bible of American cookery had lost its charmingly idiosyncratic voice with the death of Irma Rombauer. BF

Room of One's Own, A (1929) VIRGINIA WOOLF's elegant book is a classic of feminist criticism. Part essay, part fiction, it argues for the importance of economic and artistic autonomy for women's literary production, and puts the case for a specifically female aesthetics. Its author's self-fashioning as a feminine stereotype ('Lies will flow from my lips') is deployed as an artful means of destabilizing the truth-claims made about women by men. Touring the fictional worlds of Oxbridge and the British Museum Library, the work vividly realizes the relationship between male privilege and the cramping of female potential but resists delivering a transparent truth about women's situation. Its disarming tactics are thus integral to its unsentimental dissection of the reasons for women's exclusion from history and the house of fiction. Putting style firmly on the agenda for feminists, Woolf opens up a gap between referents and representations that exposes the arbitrariness of sexist judgements. The address to the reader is fundamental to the reception of the text, for to resist its style is to subscribe to the very desire for truth that Woolf critiques so brilliantly. The text's utopian imaginings (including its twin ideals of the private room and androgyny) continue to make it productive for a feminist politics. REv

Roosevelt, (Anna) Eleanor 1884–1962 Eleanor Roosevelt's long dedication to reform causes earned her a place in the affections of the Democratic party in America which has never been surpassed. Her uncle Theodore had been governor of New York, vice-president and then president when she was a teenager. Her husband also was governor of New York, and served for four terms as president. If there was an American political elite in this century, it revolved around Eleanor Roosevelt. She wrote a regular column for the American press, and was a prolific and controversial author. Her *Autobiography* (1958) was abridged from three earlier books, *This Is My Story* (1937), *This I Remember* (1949) and *On My Own* (1958): 'About the only value the story of my life may have is to show that . . . in spite of a lack of special talents, one can find a way to live widely and fully'. EH

Roper [née More], Margaret 1505–44 Scholar, translator and letter-writer. She was the eldest child of Sir Thomas More, who held the progressive view that, although women's primary role was to serve the family and household, it was of general benefit to give them a humanist education. Margaret and her sisters, Elizabeth Dancy and Cecilia Heron, were renowned for their learning and corresponded in Latin with Erasmus. Margaret was also fluent in Greek and had an extensive knowledge of philosophy, theology and astronomy. Her English translation of Erasmus's *Devout Treatise upon the Pater Noster* (completed 1524, published 1526) went into four editions in her lifetime. She also wrote Latin poems, a treatise on the Four Last Things, and a translation of Eusebius from Greek to Latin, all now lost.

She married William Roper in 1521, and had five children. Her husband's biography of Sir Thomas More shows 'Meg' as her father's confidante, especially in his last days. Her surviving letters to him in the Tower strenuously and eloquently debate his acceptance of his fate. Margaret's daughter MARY BASSETT carried on the family tradition of female scholarship. HH

Ross, Martin [Violet Martin] see SOMERVILLE and ROSS

Rossetti, Christina (Georgina) 1830–94 Victorian poet, whose compact, cryptic lyrics and experimental narrative poems explore religious, social and sexual issues of her time with an unconventionality often disguised by the obliquity and reticence of her poetic style. Her Italian émigré family was distinguished for its literary interests. Like her elder brothers – William Michael, later a critic and editor, and Dante Gabriel, the Pre-Raphaelite painter and poet – and her sister Maria, who became an impressive devotional writer and Dante scholar, she was encouraged to read widely in Italian, continental and English literature. Famously, they engaged in the games of *bouts rimés* (writing poems starting from the rhymes and working backwards) which clearly shaped the economy and exactitude of her poetic style. Her early poems were privately published in 1847, and she contributed, as 'Ellen Alleyne', to the Pre-Raphaelite journal, the *Germ* (writing however, a brief, irreverent satire on the Brotherhood, 'The P.R.B.'), but her first and best-known collection, GOBLIN MARKET AND OTHER POEMS, only appeared in 1862.

Goblin Market, an enigmatic FAIRY TALE written as if from an oral tradition, narrates the story of two sisters. One is seduced by the voluptuous fruit offered by goblins, pines when deprived of it, and is rescued by the other, who risks assault from the goblins. Enigmatic because it appears both scandalously sensuous and didactic, the poem has provoked inexhaustible discussion, not only of its cultural and sexual meanings but also of its biographical significance. Rossetti lived in

London with her mother almost all her life, refusing, it seems, two offers of marriage (from James Collinson and Charles Cayley), and the incest, abuse and illicit love extrapolated from the poem are hard to reconcile with known facts. Other riddle-like poems of desire, exclusion and painful lack – poems structured through subtle negative particles and subjunctives which disclose haunting hypothetical worlds – do indeed explore deprivation of many kinds. But the wit and political sharpness of the title poem of *The Prince's Progress and Other Poems* (1866), the metaphysical playfulness of her poems for children (*Sing-Song*, 1879), the revisionary devotional sonnet sequence, 'Monna Innominata' (*A Pageant and Other Poems*, 1881) and the rapture of late poems in *Verses* (1893) also indicate the speculative power and variousness of her work.

Rossetti wrote two volumes of short stories, *Commonplace* (1870) and *Speaking Likenesses* (1874), and, as an Anglican, six volumes of searching, often unorthodox religious prose, of which *Seek and Find: A Double Series of Short Studies of the Benedicte* (1879) and *Time Flies: A Reading Diary* (1885) are most discussed. After Graves disease transformed her appearance in 1871, she became reclusive, but she had worked with unmarried mothers in the Highgate Penitentiary and campaigned against child prostitution. She corresponded with the socialist and poet AUGUSTA WEBSTER, and was acquainted with other women poets – DORA GREENWELL, ADELAIDE ANNE PROCTER, JEAN INGELOW, KATHARINE TYNAN. She described EMILY DICKINSON as 'reckless', perhaps recognizing aspects of herself. VIRGINIA WOOLF wrote perceptively of her, and she was 'rediscovered' by feminists in the 1970s.   IA

Roughing It in the Bush, Or Life in Canada

(1852) SUSANNA MOODIE's lively retrospective account of her pioneering life in Canada covers the years 1832–40 and moves with broad sweeps of her pen from her first landing, through the uncleared forests and the vicissitudes of a basic life in log cabins, to her eventual settlement with her husband in the town of Belleville, Ontario. Written chiefly for the British market as an emigration handbook, its enduring appeal comes from Moodie's centrality to the text as heroine and her use of episodic 'sketches' of the inhabitants of the forests – humans and animals – to illustrate her confrontation with both the physical and psychic wilderness. The chief threats come not only from starvation, fire, cold, illness and wild bears, but also from her lawless fellow immigrants and the simmering ever-present threat of insurrection.

Early editions include stanzas of poetry and some chapters which have been omitted from at least one recent reprint where the chapter on First Nation People, whom she calls Indians, is a particular loss. JSte

Rover, The

Rover, The (1677) Based on an earlier play, *Thomaso* by Thomas Killigrew, this was APHRA BEHN's most popular work for the theatre and is set in the period before the restoration of Charles II when the Cavaliers were forced to lead a wandering, impoverished life of exile. Wilmore, the Rover, is a drunken, witty womanizer whose rude, macho behaviour makes him irresistible to women. Hellena, 'destined for a nun', and the courtesan Angellica Bianca, both fall hopelessly in love with him in the course of the action. Angellica foolishly gives him not only her heart but her body while Hellena holds out for marriage. The interwoven sub-plots of the love-affair between Belvile and Florinda and the cozening of the Essex bumpkin, Ned Blunt, ensure a constant flow of action with frequent shifts of mood from broad comedy, through witty social comment to frustrated sexual violence. The stars of the Duke's Company excelled in their roles: the rising Elisabeth Barry as Hellena; Thomas Betterton himself as Belvile; Will Smith, who made the part his own, was Wilmore, a character thought to be based on Rochester; and the comedian Cave Underhill played Blunt.   MD

Rowe [née Singer], Elizabeth

Rowe [née Singer], Elizabeth 1674–1737 British poet, religious and prose fiction writer. Born into a Dissenting Presbyterian family of Ilchester, Somerset, Rowe received a broad academic and religious education. After the sudden death of her husband, Thomas Rowe, in 1715, she moved to Frome, Somerset, where she spent the rest of her life in seclusion. Her literary works celebrate the simplicity and piety of rural life, honour true friendship and aim to instil 'the Notion of the Soul's Immortality' in the reader. Her acclaimed poetry, partially published in *Poems on Several Occasions, by Philomela* (1696), appeared regularly in journals by the Athenian Society. Her renowned *Friendship in Death, or Letters from the Dead to the Living* (1728) and the sequel *Letters Moral and Entertaining* (1728–32), adeptly fuse ROMANCE fiction and religious doctrine. She continued this popularization of religious themes in her verse epic, *History of Joseph* (1736). Rowe left numerous letters and manuscripts which were published posthumously in 1737 as *Devout Exercises of the Heart*.   NBP

Rowe, Jennifer

Rowe, Jennifer 1948– Australian publisher and writer who has had several successful and simultaneous literary careers. Born and educated in Sydney, Rowe has extensive experience in the Australian publishing world, working as an editor for Angus and Robertson, and as long-time editor of Australia's leading women's magazine, the *Australian Women's Weekly*. She has also established herself as a leading proponent of two genres: CHILDREN'S NOVELS and DETECTIVE FICTION. As 'Emily Rodda', she has written a string of popular and well-loved novels for younger readers, including *Pigs Might Fly* (1986) and *Finders Keepers*

(1990). At the same time, she has produced a steady stream of novels featuring her unassuming detective, Verity Birdwood, who investigates a series of situational murders in books including *Grim Pickings* (1987), *Murder by the Book* (1989, set in a publishing house), *The Makeover Murders* (1992), *Stranglehold* (1993) and *Lamb to the Slaughter* (1995). Her latest crime novel, *Deadline* (1997), features a female police detective, Tessa Vance, and is the basis for the successful television series, *Murder Call*. She has also written a number of short crime fictions, collected in *Death in Store* (1991), and edited *Love Lies Bleeding* (1994), a light anthology of short stories and verse in the crime genre. MLA

Rowlandson [later Talcott, née White], Mary

c.1637–1711 Mary Rowlandson was America's first bestselling writer, the founder of a long-running American literary genre, and one of the most important authors of the American COLONIAL period. She wrote one book, a harrowing personal narrative of captivity, suffering and deliverance that was born of her experience as a prisoner of war in 1676. Taken captive by the Wampanoag Indians in their raid on Rowlandson's frontier home-town of Lancaster, Massachusetts, during King Philip's War, Mary White Rowlandson and her children were held for several months under harsh nomadic conditions. Redeemed in May 1676, she wrote a narrative of her ordeal that was published in 1682. *The Sovereignty & Goodness of God, Together, with the Faithfulness of His Promises Displayed: Being a Narrative of the Captivity and Restauration of Mrs Mary Rowlandson* was an immediate and unprecedented publishing success. No first editions of the work survive, in fact, as they were read until they literally fell apart. The book remained in print until well into the 19th century, and became the template for scores of other CAPTIVITY NARRATIVES, creating a genre which persists in American literature to this day. Today Rowlandson's narrative stands as a landmark early American text, receiving much attention from contemporary critics who study, among other things, Rowlandson's open treatment of issues of race and gender. The preface to the narrative – which may have been written by the powerful cleric Increase Mather – has drawn attention to questions of authorship and authority.

Though recent discoveries have brought certain new facts to light, little is known of Rowlandson's life before or after her captivity. Born around 1637 in England, she travelled to the New World with her family in 1639. Married to the Revd Joseph Rowlandson around 1656, she gave birth to four children during the next thirteen years. The oldest, Mary, died in 1661, while the youngest, Sarah, was wounded and taken captive along with her mother, and died soon afterwards. Her death is the subject of a moving passage in Rowlandson's narrative.

The Rowlandsons moved to Wethersfield, Connecticut, soon after Mary's release. Joseph Rowlandson died in 1678, and Mary Rowlandson remarried the next year. Her second husband, Samuel Talcott, died in 1691. Mary White Rowlandson Talcott died in 1711, aged about 73. LC

Rowson [née Haswell], Susanna 1762–1824

Susanna Rowson has been waggishly described as 'the father of American literature', a reference to her extraordinary productivity and influence during a period when the American literati were self-consciously searching for a national literature for the newly formed republic. Rowson played little direct role in such debates – which were primarily conducted among men – but her work spoke loudly for her.

Born in England, Susanna Haswell was brought to America as a child and stayed until the Revolution forced the family to return to England. She married William Rowson in 1786 and returned to America with her husband in 1793, this time for good. Rowson's husband was an indifferent actor and a worse businessman, and his continual indebtedness drove his wife to make a living. She did so mainly by her pen. Between 1786 and 1822 Susanna Rowson wrote eight novels, seven plays, two books of sketches, two collections of poetry, six instructional books and numerous song lyrics and occasional prose pieces. Her topics ranged from biblical dialogues to female etiquette to white slavery in the Orient. Rowson was also known in her own time as an actress (in her own plays and others'), and as the founder and head of a school for young ladies.

One novel, CHARLOTTE TEMPLE, stands out from Rowson's substantial body of work. The book was first published in England, where it was popular – but in America it became a sensation when it was issued in 1794. Essentially adopted by the new nation as an American novel, *Charlotte Temple* became one of the most widely read works of fiction in American history. A tale of a young English girl's seduction by an army officer and subsequent abandonment and death in the New World, the story went through nearly 200 editions and strongly influenced the development of the American sentimental tradition. So powerful was its hold on its readers that many ventured to New York to visit the cemetery where Charlotte was supposedly buried. Today Rowson's life and work invite consideration of gender issues in a transatlantic context. Her last novel, published posthumously in 1828, is a sequel, *Lucy Temple*, that follows the adventures of Charlotte's daughter. LC

Roy, Arundhati 1960–

Maverick architect and filmmaker, now a dazzlingly original writer whose début novel, *The God of Small Things* (1997), took the literary world by storm. She was the first Indian woman writer to win the Booker Prize, but the award was accompanied by cheers and jeers, charges of 'vulgarity' and some barely concealed ill-will on the part of assorted literary stalwarts.

Daughter of Mary Roy, an iconoclastic educationist and crusader for women's rights, Arundhati acknowledges her mother's fierce independence and free thinking as powerful influences on her own life and work. Roy's privileged yet splintered Kerala childhood and her Syrian Christian background form the core of her novel, remarkable for its razor-sharp observation of social and political mores, and its evocation of a fragile world under threat. Bohemian in sensibility, life-style and creative expression, Roy defies any literary stereotyping – 'I don't know the rules, so I can't say I've broken them' – and forges a unique idiom for her idiosyncratic vision.

Something of a crusader herself, she took up the cause of nuclear disarmament in the wake of India's nuclear testing in 1998, using her pen effectively to expose the hypocrisy of both the nuclear haves and the have-nots.   RM

Rubens, Bernice 1923– British novelist. Rubens was born into a highly musical Jewish family in Cardiff and attended Cardiff High School for Girls and University College of South Wales and Monmouthshire. She taught English for two years and then became a documentary film-maker, working on several United Nations projects and an award-winning film about mentally handicapped children, *Stress* (1968).

A prolific novelist, her work is frequently informed by her interest in families, particularly Jewish ones, and associated themes of duty, guilt, maternal oppression, religion, personal fulfilment and frustration. *Madame Sousatzka* (1962), which was filmed by John Schlesinger, explores the relationship between a music teacher and a young Jewish prodigy, while *The Elected Member* (1969) tells the story of a rabbi's son who becomes a drug addict; it won the Booker Prize in 1970. Pessimistic though Rubens's outlook often is, her delicate sense of irony and capacity for sophisticated black comedy transform the bleakness of her stories. A taste for the bizarre and the macabre distinguishes some more fantastic novels, including *Spring Sonata* (1979), which features a foetus who refuses to be born and plays the violin in the womb, and *Autobiopsy* (1993), the story of a frustrated writer who literally siphons the brain of his dead mentor for inspiration. Other novels include *The Ponsonby Post* (1977); *A Five Year Sentence* (1978) which was short-listed for the Booker Prize; the historical novels *Brothers* (1983) and *Kingdom Come* (1990); *Mr Wakefield's Crusade* (1985); and *The Waiting Game* (1997). In 1999 she published *I, Dreyfus*, a reworked and updated version of the *cause célèbre* in

which she examined the prevalence of anti-Semitism in contemporary society.   AC

Rubinstein, Gillian 1942– Australian CHILDREN'S AUTHOR. Born in England, she completed a BA at Oxford University before moving to Australia in 1973. Achieved an immediate success with her first novel, *Space Demons* (1986) which won several awards. Like its sequel, *Skymaze* (1989), it centres on children who are drawn into a computer game. Several later novels adopt a more specifically SCIENCE-FICTION mode, either involving aliens coming to earth, as in *Beyond the Labyrinth* (1988), or children going to another planet, as in *Galax-Arena* (1992). In the more traditional fantasy vein, *Foxspell* (1994) concerns a young boy with rapport with foxes, and *Under the Cat's Eye* (1997) is a time-travel story, involving a villainous headmaster who attempts to capture children's souls. Rubinstein's other novels include the more comic *Flashback: The Amazing Adventures of a Film Horse* (1990). She has also written collections of stories for both older and young readers as well as several picture books. *Squawk and Screech* (1991) features the adventures of two lorikeets who manage to capture a burglar; *Jake and Pete* (1995) centres on two abandoned kittens hunting for a home. Her versatility, and skill in capturing the interests and reflecting the feelings of her readers, have rapidly established Rubinstein as one of Australia's leading writers for children.   EW

Rubyfruit Jungle (1973) RITA MAE BROWN's gutsy first novel is a classic of lesbian feminist fiction. Working with the conventions of the picaresque BILDUNGSROMAN, its episodic first-person narrative recounts the tragi-comic odyssey of upwardly mobile Molly Bolt (a molly-bolt is a fastener that's meant to stick to anything), from her bastard working-class Southern childhood to new-found if painful freedom as an adult in New York. Brown's simple and didactic tale-telling sees her semi-autobiographical heroine encountering all the economic and ideological strategies which patriarchal capitalism uses to keep lesbians, women and the poor in their place. If she doesn't exactly grow as a result of her experiences – she acts as a positive role model for lesbians throughout – the novel nevertheless successfully stages the contradictions of the sexual outsider determined to succeed at the American way of life.

Rubyfruit Jungle was originally published by the small feminist press Daughters Inc. It gained a mainstream readership with its 1977 Bantam House reissue, replacing THE WELL OF LONELINESS as *the* lesbian novel non-lesbians might encounter.   MO'D

Ruck, [Amy Ro]Berta 1878–1978 Prolific British romantic novelist, established through long

545

apprenticeship in women's magazines. Born in India, she was brought up by her grandmother in Aberdovey until her army officer father returned in 1888 to become Chief Constable of Caernarvonshire, attended boarding-school in Bangor, and studied art at the Slade and in Paris. She began as a magazine illustrator, but in 1901 turned to writing fiction for women's magazines. In 1909 she married the novelist Oliver Onions; they had two sons. A successful *Home Chat* serial became her first novel, *His Official Fiancée* (1914). A series of novels addressing war-time ROMANCE problems followed, including *The Lad with Wings* (1916), *The Girls at His Billet* (1917), *The Land Girl's Love Story* and *Sweethearts Unmet* (both 1918). After the war she wrote at least two novels a year, and undertook many lecture tours in Britain and America, seeing her role, in agony-aunt fashion, as alleviating contemporary love problems. A self-proclaimed lowbrow, she relished encounters with highbrows such as WOOLF and REBECCA WEST, and describes many in her entertaining autobiography, *A Storyteller Tells the Truth* (1935). She returned to Aberdovey in later years and continued to write into her nineties. AT

Rukeyser, Muriel 1913–80 Poet, scholar, translator, political activist: a major 20th-century American writer, whose range of subjects and interests embraced history, anthropology, popular culture, the history of science, poetics, politics, psychology and religion. Her feminism and her politics, committed and complex, worked in and through all these concerns. In the thirties she came of age politically in the Spanish Civil War and fought for exploited American workers, whether Pennsylvania miners or immigrant Mexican grape-pickers. She was jailed for protesting against the Vietnam War, and used her position as president of PEN to assist persecuted writers the world over. She was under FBI surveillance for forty years. Her translations of Brecht, Ekelöf and Paz among others bear witness to her internationalism.

But in the thirties fellow-Americans like her friend Lewis Mumford were discovering the unacknowledged richness of past and contemporary American writers, architects, painters, sculptors, craftsmen and women and designers, a movement to which she contributed her biographies of the 'unknown' Yale mathematician, Willard Gibbs (1942) and the fitfully historically visible English Renaissance mathematician, Thomas Hariot (1971), who accompanied Raleigh to the New World. These works were not so much biographies as great experimental and imaginative analyses of moments of cultural, economic, scientific and historical change. Her theories of poetry were articulated in an extraordinary short work, *The Life of Poetry* (1949) which emphasized, as did all her work, her belief in the 'American imagination'; a com-

prehensive term for a wished-for synthesis in American life and writing, for creative axiom-breaking and personal emotional courage, both of which were born in truthful disclosures of a type of speech which achieved its most articulate form in poetry. Poetry itself guaranteed the possibility of true speech and was placed centrally as the art most useful and necessary to the aspirations of a free society. She wrote some fourteen books of poetry, including *Theory of Flight* (1939), *A Turning Wind* (1939), *Beast in View* (1944), *Waterlily Fire* (1962), *The Green Wave* (1948), *One Life* (1957), *The Speed of Darkness* (1968), *Breaking Open* (1973) and *The Gates* (1976). Like her contemporaries Kenneth Rexroth and Hugh MacDarmaid she worked with the contraries of mysticism and radical politics, national voice and discourses which engaged a range of world poetries and poetic forms. Her *Elegies* (1939–48) is her most brilliant long sequence of poems. But she was equally at home in the short lyric and the last poems show an extraordinary intensity of language and rhythm which not only articulated her love of the world in the face of death but spoke the unsayable to the last for the poetry she wanted: 'I'd rather be Muriel / than be dead and be Ariel.' CBu

Rule, Jane 1931– Lesbian Canadian fiction writer and activist, whose writings explore possibilities for human community across such conventional divides as orientation, ethnicity, race, age and health. Raised in the United States, Rule received a BA in English from Mills College and then studied for a year at University College London. In 1954, while teaching at Concord Academy in Massachusetts, she met her life partner, Helen Sonthoff. Shortly thereafter the couple moved to Canada. Since 1976 they have lived on Galiano Island, British Columbia.

Rule is best known for her first published novel, *DESERT OF THE HEART* (1964), which provides one of the few positive portrayals of lesbian love in pre-Stonewall (pre-gay-liberation) fiction. Drawing on such crucial source texts for English fiction as the Bible and *The Pilgrim's Progress*, *Desert* recounts the love-story of Professor Evelyn Hall and cartoonist Ann Childs. The two women fall in love amidst the divorce courts and casinos of Reno, Nevada, an allegorical setting for Rule's ironic commentary on moral and literary conventions' incapacity to mirror lesbian love. The popular 1985 film *Desert Hearts*, directed by Donna Deitch, is based on the novel.

Like the first, Rule's second novel, *This is Not For You* (1970), examines the homophobic plots to which conventional Christian beliefs relegate lesbian heroines. Rule's interest in exploring narrative and social patterns of community that include lesbian or gay characters in turn directs her subsequent five novels. Among them, *Against the Season* (1971), *The Young in One Another's*

Arms (1977), MEMORY BOARD (1987) and *After the Fire* (1989) focus on several characters; these works reflect Rule's REALIST commitment to telling truths about a world that she defines as 'whole', 'real' and 'mixed'.

In addition to her seven novels, Rule has published numerous short stories and essays. She has also actively protested against government censorship of lesbian and gay work.   MBr

Rumens [née Lumley], Carol (-Ann) 1944–
British poet, novelist and editor whose synthesis of the personal and political, and activism as anthologist of women poets has earned her many admirers and readers. Rumens was born in London and attended a convent school and the University of London. She married David Rumens in 1965 and has two daughters. The implications and exactions of marital break-up, love and parentage subsequently enter her poetry. She went on to become a publicity assistant and advertising copywriter, after which she became a freelance writer and poetry editor for *Quarto*, in 1981–2, and the *Literary Review* where her inclusive but quality-driven policy became a byword among poets for meaningful editing.

Rumens has travelled in many directions – geographical and poetic. She has held residencies in a number of British universities and written well of her experiences in eastern Europe and Russia. Rumens's particular gift is to combine serious reasoning in poems with emotion not seldom passionate, whether on the current human scene or more personal events and situations. She is never dogmatic and has become formally venturesome in several genres. Her novel *Plato Park* (1987) explored themes of power and affection; a play, *Almost Siberia*, was staged at Newcastle Gulbenkian Theatre and Soho Polytechnic in 1989–90. Her newer poems have become ever more syntactically inventive and insightful. A new collection, *Best China Sky* (1995), sets exacting and formally energetic standards way beyond *Thinking of Skins: New and Selected Poems* (1993), which sampled her excellent previous collections. Rumens also edited *Making for the Open: The Chatto Book of Postfeminist Poetry* in 1988 and *New Women Poets* in 1990.   DM

Rundell, Maria 1745–1829
When Maria Rundell wrote her only work, first published as *Domestic Happiness* in 1808, she used the conventional *nom de plume*, 'A Lady'. Payment of royalties was also regarded as unseemly in some circles at the time, hence the 'Advertisement' states 'she will receive for it NO EMOLUMENT'. A second edition was entitled *The Family Recipe Book* (1809). But it was the 1810 edition, *A New System of Domestic Economy*, that became a notable bestseller, with almost half a million copies sold by the time of Mrs Rundell's death and remaining in print until 1886. (See COOKERY BOOKS.)

Born in Shropshire in 1745, the only child of Abel Johnstone Ketelby, Maria married Thomas Rundell, a well-known jeweller of Ludgate Hill. The couple lived in London and then Bath but by the time her book appeared Maria was widowed and living with a married daughter in Swansea.

After a decade of commercial success for which she had received £150, an acrimonious correspondence developed between the author and her publisher, John Murray. Eventually Mrs Rundell was paid 2,000 guineas for her work though this represented only a fraction of the monies earned, and in subsequent editions her authorship of this strikingly practical and charmingly unpretentious work is acknowledged on the title-page.   GH

Rush, Rebecca
fl. 1779–1812 Rebecca Rush wrote one novel, *Kelroy* (1812), a work whose significance lies almost entirely beyond its time. *Kelroy* is a novel of the Philadelphia mannered society that Rush herself was born into. The book never found an audience, probably because the war with Great Britain distracted the American reading public at the time that it was published. The novel quickly disappeared from view, and for more than a century it has been noticed only by literary historians. It was reprinted for the first time in 1992.

As the story of a secretly poor mother's schemes to marry off two daughters of contrasting temperaments to wealthy gentlemen, *Kelroy* presumably owes a good deal to AUSTEN'S *SENSE AND SENSIBILITY* (1811), but Rush's novel is more unrelenting in its social criticism. The title character is the suitor of one of the two daughters, and he too is seeking to camouflage his own penury and marry into financial security; the girl's mother knows better and works to prevent the match. Subsequent plot machinations lead not to the sort of balanced happy ending that Austen provided for her social satires, but instead to a harsher outcome, as Rush kills off many of her main characters.

It is not known how long Rush lived, or whether she wrote anything else. Her one novel offers an interesting example of mercenary social climbing in a young country, with suggestive links to developing ideas of liberalism, capitalism and republicanism.   LC

Russ, Joanna
1937– American feminist polemicist, critic and SCIENCE FICTION novelist. Joanna Russ read SF as a child and started to publish in the field from 1959. Her discovery of her mature voice coincided with her coming out as a lesbian, her involvement in feminism and the development of SF's New Wave, so that her experimental use of standard SF narrative modes to declare war on the unthinking sexism of much previous SF reached an audience prepared for it. Educated at Cornell and Yale, she was for many years

Maria Rundell: frontispiece and title-page of *A New System of Domestic Cookery by a Lady*, retitled in this *c.* 1835 edition.

Associate Professor of English at Washington State University and currently teaches at the University of Arizona.

Her most important novel is THE FEMALE MAN (1975) which sets various versions of reality, each containing a different state of play in the conflict between the sexes, in direct apposition and opposition to each other. It is a novel about the struggle between texts for authenticity, about how to read, and how to listen to, the stories that the culture tells us about ourselves.

The novel is closely linked to her award-winning short story 'When It Changed' (1972), which depicts a women-only utopia not at all grateful for being 'rescued' by male visitors, and to her earlier 'Alyx' stories, which subjected the clichés of heroic fantasy to friendly subversion. Russ's non-SF novel, *On strike against God* (1979), punctuates an autobiographical coming-out narrative with witty diatribes about the sexism of the SF community.

Russ's playful POSTMODERNISM is worn lightly — what is said is always more urgent than the mode of expression; her work exists fruitfully at the interface between artifice, witness-bearing confessional and feminist propaganda.

As critic, Russ is important for the theory of 'the wearing out of genre materials'; her own work embodies the assumed corollary that genre work must always end up choosing between cliché and self-subversion. The sense of who is taking advantage of whom and the abhorrence of highflown cant are, for Russ, an important part of feminist consciousness, and are also polemical engagements with the tropes and assumptions of genres to which Russ remains committed. *How to Suppress Women's Writing* (1983) dissects the pressures militating against the growth of a full tradition of women's literature, while her polemical and critical essays are collected in *Magic Mommas, Trembling Sisters, Puritans and Perverts* (1985) and *To Write as a Woman* (1995).   RK

Ruth (1853) The popular Victorian theme of the 'fallen woman' is taken up in ELIZABETH GASKELL's novel, where the heroine is seduced and then abandoned by the wealthy Mr Wellingham. The novel is partially based on fact and recounts the mortifying fate of a girl named Pasley whom Gaskell met at the New Bayley Prison in 1850. Whilst it ends with the tragic but, according to literary convention, typical death of the protagonist Ruth Hilton, it does not surrender to the orthodoxy of mid-Victorian England. Gaskell openly addresses the social problem of unmarried mothers from a woman's point of view. She opposes their denunciation and exclusion from society and emphasizes the social and economic causes of their afflictions. Whilst *Ruth* was heavily criticized by contemporaries because of its candid and forcible portrayal of women's lives, it had an impact on activists such as JOSEPHINE BUTLER whose work with destitute women and prostitutes culminated in the repeal of the discriminatory Contagious Disease Act in 1886.　　　　NBP

Ryan, Gig (Elizabeth) 1956– Australian poet, singer and song writer, perhaps best known for her much-anthologized 'If I Had a Gun' which begins:

I'd shoot the man who pulled up slowly in his hot car
　　this morning
I'd shoot the man who whistled from his balcony
I'd shoot the man with things dangling over his creepy
　　chest

As this extract suggests, many of Ryan's poems are strongly feminist, and from 1975 to 1978 she worked on the Melbourne women's literary magazine *Luna*. Her poetry is also distinguished by its use of contemporary urban settings and a concentration on the difficulties of sustaining personal and sexual relationships in this milieu. Tonally, it ranges from anger to a resigned fatalism, from wry humour to an unexpected pure lyricism. Her collections include *The Division of Anger* (1980), *Manners of an Astronaut* (1984), *The Last Interior* (1986) and *Excavation* (1990), the latter being subtitled 'Arguments and Monologues', a further indication of the style of much of her work. Ryan has lived at various times in both Sydney and Melbourne and has also performed with Disband, releasing the album *Six Goodbyes* in 1988. Her most recent collection is *Pure and Applied* (1998)　　　　EW

Ryder (1928) An eclectic, bawdy chronicle in which DJUNA BARNES, with minimum plot and maximum linguistic flourish, explores the events and family situation that is revisited in *The Antiphon* (1958). The text mimics and parodies a range of genres and styles including: Chaucer, Shakespeare, the Bible, Sterne and 19th-century sentimentalism. The prose is interspersed with songs, illustrations, parables and soliloquy as the narrator describes the history of Wendell Ryder, idle agrarian polygamist; his forbearing English wife, Amelia; his resourceful, cosmopolitan mother, Sophia; his blowsy mistress, Kate Careless; and his brood of eight children. *Ryder* also contains an early, sympathetic version of Dr Matthew O'Connor, the transvestite doctor of *Nightwood*. The novel subverts the patriarchal domination embodied by Wendell Ryder, deriding masculinity and domesticity alike. Although the book is far from autobiographical, the Ryder family do bear a resemblance with Barnes's own – her experiences parallel those of Julie Ryder, the resentful daughter of Amelia and Wendell.

Briefly a bestseller in America, *Ryder* was subject to censorship on its publication, with drawings of, and references to, bodily functions and fluids excised from the text.　　　　AG

Ryves, Eliza 1750?–97 Irish author, journalist and translator. Born 'of a good family', Ryves was swindled out of her inheritance following the death of her father. She left Ireland for London, where she earned a meagre living as a writer and translator.

In her search for livelihood, Ryves turned her hand to a variety of literary forms. She produced articles, plays, a novel (*The Hermit of Snowden* (1789), which describes the tribulations and poverty-stricken death of a female author) and seven volumes of poetry, among them *Poems on Several Occasions* (1777), which incorporated a comic opera as well as elegies and odes. Her translations from French included Rousseau's *Social Contract* (1791) and other political works.

In her 'Ode to Sensibility', Ryves disdained heartless serenity in favour of 'a generous soul' which

bravely bears the galling yoke,
And smiles superior to the stroke
With spirits free and mind unbroke.

This self-portrait was confirmed by Isaac Disraeli, who recorded that she possessed 'a mind of fortitude . . . virtuous amid her despair', and that 'even in her poverty Ryves's native benevolence could make her generous'. Dogged by illness, misfortune and neglect, Ryves died destitute in London.　　　　RR

S

Sackville-West, Hon. Victoria ('Vita') 1892–1962
British woman of letters who is as well remembered
for her turbulent affairs with VIOLET TREFUSIS and
VIRGINIA WOOLF as for her lively but traditionalist
poetry and fiction. Born at Knole, Kent, she was the
only child of the third Baron Sackville and Victoria,
the illegitimate daughter of Pepita de Oliva, the
Spanish Flamenco dancer. Already in youth the twin
impulses that would define her adult life were in evidence: she began writing and discovered her emotional bisexuality. Her conviction that her 'maternal
ancestry [was] hard to beat for sheer picturesqueness',
inspired her to fill the role of family historian, writing
Knole and the Sackvilles (1922) and the biography of
Pepita (1937). This love for Knole and its legends accentuated her sense of loss when she was prevented from
inheriting the family seat by the 'technical fault' of
sex; with *The Heir* (1922) she bade farewell to the
Elizabethan palace, but with the setting of her bestselling THE EDWARDIANS (1930) she reclaimed imaginative proprietorship. Sackville-West's attachment to
the family estate was complemented by her rustic
patriotism to which she gave expression both in her
poetry – *Collected Poems* (1923), *The Land* (1926), *The
Garden* (1946) – and in the famous garden she designed
at Sissinghurst Castle.

In 1913 Sackville-West married the young diplomat
Harold Nicolson, with whom she had two sons. In 1918
she began her three-year-long affair with Violet
Trefusis, her school friend, but returned to Nicolson
('the only person of whom I think with consistent tenderness'). Sackville-West fictionalized the intense liaison in *The Challenge* (1922), but withdrew it from her
English publisher, and her autobiography chronicling
these traumatic years was only published posthumously by her son Nigel Nicolson in *Portrait of a
Marriage* (1973). She began her 'Sapphist' affair with
Virginia Woolf in 1926, and was the inspiration for
Woolf's ORLANDO (1929). While both were openly
bisexual, she and Nicolson maintained traditional
views on marriage, exemplified by their comments on
the subject on BBC Radio in 1929. Sackville-West rarely
swerved from an aristocratic conservatism, and only
with ALL PASSION SPENT (1931), a tale of an elderly
widow seeking freedom from societal constraints, did
she explore feminist themes.   JVG

Sacrifice, The (1956) The extraordinary first novel by
28-year-old Canadian ADELE WISEMAN won the
Governor General's Medal for Fiction and established
this writer's reputation as an important scribe of
Jewish immigrant experience. In the tragic story of
Abraham, Sarah and their three sons, Wiseman captures the disastrous effects of too much loss and suffering on the mind of a man who 'wanted only to build, to
grow, to understand'. Like his biblical ancestor,
Abraham has to deal not only with the violence and
hatred of Gentiles, but with the tensions, conflicts and
betrayals within his own community. He is obsessed
with sacrifice, with the memory of being forced to perform ritualistic slaughter of animals, with the deaths
by hanging of his two eldest sons in an Easter pogrom,
with his youngest son's rescue of the Torah from a
burning synagogue. Finally, maddened by grief and
loss and self-disgust, he performs a ritual slaughter of
a woman who attempts to seduce him. The author has
a fine ear for the idiom of the immigrant Jews and a
sharp eye for details of character that bring three generations alive. The title carries multiple nuances,
including the extent to which the immigrant generation has sacrificed everything to make a dignified
homeland for their descendants.   FD

Sagan, Françoise [Quoirez] 1935– French novelist. Sagan excited considerable media attention with
the precocious publication of her first fashionably
existentialist novel, *Bonjour Tristesse* (1954), which she
wrote after failing the entrance exam to the Sorbonne.
Her success was confirmed with the publication of *Un
certain sourire* in 1956, and after that her conviction for
possession of cocaine and her gambling debts kept her
in the public eye. Sagan's support for the Algerian
Independence movement and state-funded abortions,
along with her contribution to the metamorphosis of
Saint-Tropez from a fishing village into a glamorous
Riviera resort, established her as an intellectual activist
of the European jet set.

Her novels are set within a morally ambivalent,
bohemian and wealthy milieu, in which women do not
conform to bourgeois convention, often embarking on
illicit love-affairs – as, for example, in the short history
'L'Echange' in *Musiques de scènes* (1981; *Incidental Music*).
Her work was best known during the 1950s and 1960s

(her novel *Aimez-vous Brahms?* (1959) was made into a film entitled *Goodbye Again* in 1961). Her most characteristic novels are brief and bitter-sweet, dedicated to the study of the psychology of love in contemporary life. Her collected works, *Oeuvres*, were published in 1993.   SD

Sahgal, Nayantara 1927– Indian novelist and political columnist from a leading political family. Daughter of Vijaylaxmi and Ranjit Pandit, Sahgal grew up in Gandhian India and is the niece of India's first Prime Minister, Jawaharlal Nehru. All her work reflects a pre-occupation with things political, and an ongoing analysis of power structures, whether religious, familial or political. Translated into several languages, Sahgal has won many awards for her literary and political work.

Her autobiographical writing falls into two phases. Two early volumes, *Prison and Chocolate Cake* (1954) and *From Fear Set Free* (1962) are youthful records of the 1940s and 1950s. After stating in an interview in 1990 that she would 'never write another autobiography', she has published a volume of correspondence, *Relationship* (1994), and also *Point of View: A Personal Response to Life* (1997).

Her fictional work so far falls clearly into two phases, the early semi-autobiographical, feminist novels reflecting contemporary politics, and the post-divorce, post-Emergency novels which focus more sharply on historical re-evaluation of the political happenings, where she moves into fantasy and myth-making in order to project cultural nuances.

A Time To Be Happy (1958) reflects the upswing mood of its period, while with *This Time of Morning* (1965), she enters the corridors of bureaucracy and introduces feminist issues. The next two novels, *Storm in Chandigarh* (1969) and *The Day in Shadow* (1972), are emotional autobiographies which juxtapose political and personal value structures.

Sahgal's next novel, *A Situation in New Delhi* (1977), is an uncanny prediction of the Emergency (1975), the publication of the novel having been delayed until 1977 for political reasons. This novel marks a transition between the first and the second phase. To this period also belongs a great deal of political journalism, highly critical of India's inability to transcend narrow religious structures and the style of functioning of her cousin, Indira Gandhi, the then Prime Minister of India. Sahgal published a lengthy article 'Indira Gandhi's Emergence and Style' (1978) later expanded as *Indira Gandhi: Her Road to Power* (1982).

In the mid-eighties three novels followed in quick succession: *RICH LIKE US* (1985), *Plans for Departure* (1986) and *Mistaken Identity* (1988). These three novels connect history and culture with political trends and are a questioning of the past. Her work reflects both an ironic distance and an intense involvement with India. To her goes the credit for establishing the political novel as a legitimate form and for highlighting feminist concerns which deconstruct a whole society. Speaking about her later work, Sahgal is conscious of having abandoned authorial intervention and submitting to the requirements of the form. Like Faulkner, she says, she has a hard time 'keeping up' with her characters. A novel ends when it ends: 'Only then will I know what the ending is'.   JJ

St Aubin de Teran, Lisa 1953– English novelist, poet and TRAVEL writer. Born in London, Teran married an exiled Venezuelan farmer, Jaime Teran, when she was 17, and they returned to his native country and ancestral home. For several years during the 1970s, Teran farmed sugar cane, avocados, pears and sheep in Venezuela, an experience which provided the inspiration for her first novel, *Keepers of the House* (1982; published in the USA as *The Long Way Home*), which won a Somerset Maugham Award. The novel tells of an Englishwoman's attempt to record her husband's rich family history; its emphasis on oral history, elements of magic realism and the intensity of its Latin American setting invited comparisons with writers such as Carlos Fuentes, Cabrera Infante and Gabriel García Márquez. Teran explored this territory further in her novels *The Slow Train to Milan* (1983) and *The Tiger* (1984), and in her memoir, *The Hacienda: My Venezuelan Years* (1997). Her other novels include *The Bay of Silence* (1986); *Black Idol* (1987), based on the life and dramatic death of the American poet Harry Crosby; *Joanna* (1990); *Nocturne* (1992); and *The Palace* (1997). Her second husband was the poet George MacBeth.   AC

Saint Maybe (1992) One of ANNE TYLER's later multi-generational Baltimore-set tales of invented families, disappointment and brief moments of optimism. Ian believes his one-time desire for his sister-in-law killed both her and his brother. Born again and a member of the shabby Church of the Second Chance, he atones by adopting their three young, awkward children. He forgoes his own life and ambles haphazardly into middle age. The novel is Tyler's best demonstration of a nuclear family eroded and replaced by one cobbled together. Three generations disharmonize and everyone is viewed with the same lucid tenderness. From befuddled matriarch Bee to combat-booted granddaughter Daphne, no single character has any more idea of the wider picture; just that you have to make space for the new, and you still have to try for second chances.   PM

Salkeld, Blanaid 1880–1959 Irish poet, essayist, dramatist, translator, actress and publisher. She was an enterprising and resourceful woman, born to Irish parents in

Chittagong (now Pakistan), who spent most of her childhood in Ireland. Married to Henry Lyde Salkeld, with whom she lived in Bombay and Decca, she was widowed at 28. She returned to Ireland where she joined the second company of the Abbey Theatre as Nell Byrne. 'Scarecrow over the Corn' was the only one of her fourteen unpublished verse plays performed in her lifetime. Her poetry was regularly published in the *Dublin Magazine*, *Ireland Today*, *Irish Writing*, *Poetry Ireland* and the *Bell*. Salkeld wrote many prose pieces, book reviews and essays which were published in other Irish journals. She also translated Akhmatova, Bruisov and Pushkin from the Russian, as well as Hindustani folk songs and works from Irish to English. In 1937 she founded Gayfield Press with her elder son, Cecil Ffrench Salkeld, an important Irish artist, who also illustrated her first volume of poetry, *The Engine is Left Running* (1937). Her granddaughter Beatrice married Brendan Behan. Salkeld died at 79 years of age in Dublin.   MSu

Sam, Agnes 1942–

South African poet and short-story writer. Sam is the great-granddaughter of indentured labourers from India who were shipped to South Africa in 1860. She has lived and worked in South Africa, Lesotho, Zimbabwe and Zambia, and in 1973 chose to live in exile in Britain, undertaking a degree in English Literature at the University of York. Sam returned to South Africa in 1991. She has published poetry and short stories in journals and anthologies such as *The Story Must Be Told* (1986), *Let It Be Told* (1987) and *Charting the Journey* (1988). Her collection of short stories, *Jesus is Indian* (1989), explores her concerns with diasporic histories and cultures. She is particularly concerned with the figure of the migrant woman, celebrating the modern woman's claim to choice and agency in her migrations, in stark contrast to the past where 'migration emphasised the chattel nature of a woman's existence'. The stories explore the making of hybrid identities, the attempts to stave off the loss of language, culture and religion through fusions with dominant cultural forms. The complexities of such negotiations are considered in 'High Heels' where the child narrator, Ruthie, recognizes the mixture of shame and a pragmatics of survival and covert resistance which prompts her Catholic family to keep a secret Hindu prayer room. That such fusions often threaten the stability of dominant cultures is a central preoccupation of the collection.   C-AM

Sand, George [Amandine Aurore Lucile Dupin]

1804–76 The parents of French novelist, playwright, journalist and social reformer Sand were the ill-assorted Franco-Polish aristocrat Maurice Dupin and Sophie Victoire Delaborde, the daughter of a Paris bird-seller. Sand was 4 when her father died, and her paternal grandmother became responsible for her edu-cation. In 1817, she was sent to the convent of the English Augustinians in Paris; in 1820 she returned to her grandmother's country estate at Nohant, where she rode, and read widely in French and English. Following her grandmother's death in 1821 she married a young Berrichon squire, Casimir Dudevant, and their son Maurice was born in 1823. Tiring of her marriage, she embarked on a passionate affair with Stéphane de Grandsagne, a free-thinking neighbour who did much to transform her into 'George Sand', a character who had shed both moral inhibitions and religious belief. In 1831 she separated from her husband and left Nohant to live with the poet Jules Sandeau.

This marked the beginning of a long and fruitful literary career (Sand produced over seventy novels, as well as plays, autobiographical works and journalism); it also marked the beginning of life with a series of lovers – among them poet Alfred de Musset (this relationship was explored in her novel, *Elle et lui* (1857)) and composer Frédéric Chopin, with whom she had an affair that lasted from 1838 to 1847. She later wrote to Flaubert that 'a union in which there is neither liberty nor reciprocity is an offence against the sanctity of nature'. She had her first newspaper column in *Le Figaro*, in 1831, and was obliged to dress in men's clothes in order to get cheap tickets for the plays that she was reviewing (women were not allowed in the orchestra seats). In 1832 she produced her first novel, *Indiana*, signed 'Georges Sand' (the 's' was later dropped). This novel foreshadows several themes in her work; the hypocrisy inherent in the institution of marriage, (impossible) love across social classes and an active desire for social reform. *Lélia* (1833) explores the difficulties of finding an equal partner: the young poet Sténio is passionately in love with the eponymous heroine, who leaves to live in a convent of which she becomes the abbess, creating an environment where a 'new kind of woman can become into being'. These early novels are overtly feminist; in the later 1830s her writing took on a more Christian and socialist cast (*Spiridion* (1838), *Consuelo* (1842–3) and the play, *Les Sept Cordes de la lyre* (1840), a re-working of Goethe's *Faust*). The French remember her best for her last works, which include *La Petite Fadette* (1849), versions of pastoral concerned with the fate of foundlings and other marginalized members of society, idealized visions of rural life. Among her 19th-century English admirers were George Eliot, John Stuart Mill and Elizabeth Barrett Browning.   SD

Sandes, Flora 1876–1956

An officer in the Serbian Army, decorated with the Order of Karageorge for bravery, and the author of *An English Woman-Sergeant in the Serbian Army* (1916) and *The Autobiography of a Woman Soldier* (1927). Born in Yorkshire as the youngest daugh-

OLD JULES

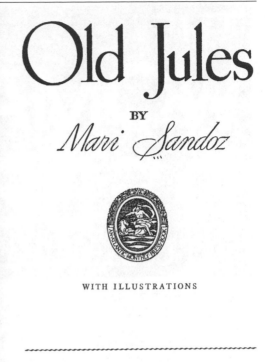

Old Jules

BY

Mari Sandoz

WITH ILLUSTRATIONS

BOSTON
LITTLE, BROWN, AND COMPANY
1935

Mari Sandoz: frontispiece (Sandoz's father) and title-page of *Old Jules*, 1935.

ter of a retired rector, by the time of World War I she was living with her father, working as a secretary and, at weekends, touring in a French racing car. In 1914 she joined the Serbian Red Cross as a nurse. As a reward for courageous work in a typhus hospital, she was posted to a Serbian Army ambulance unit, a position usually barred to women. When visiting England on her second fund-raising trip in 1916, Sandes was hailed as the 'Serbian Joan of Arc'. Her first book, describing her army experience and the retreat of the Serb forces through the Albanian mountains, contributed to the success of her mission. Her autobiography describes her promotion to lieutenant in 1919, and to captain in 1926. In 1927, Sandes married Yurie Yudenich, a White Russian officer who joined the Serbian Army and was, for a time, her sergeant. The couple lived briefly in Paris before returning to Belgrade. At the outbreak of World War II, Flora Sandes was interned by the Germans and forced to report to the Gestapo. Her husband died in 1941. After returning to Britain in 1946 she lived in Suffolk.   VG

Sanditon (1817) An unfinished novel by JANE AUSTEN, written shortly before her death. The title refers to a small village on the Sussex coast, which the endlessly enthusiastic and entrepreneurial Mr Parker hopes to see develop into a fashionable resort. His efforts in that direction form a significant part of the story, with Austen satirizing the spirit of novelty and change which characterized the time, and the hypochondria and vogue for new cures involved in resort life. The other strand of the novel describes the social and romantic entanglements of Charlotte Heywood, a sensible and level-headed young woman; the local great lady, the avaricious Lady Denham; and another young woman, Clara Brereton, who is being courted, not entirely honourably, by Lady Denham's nephew Edward. The arrival of a West Indian heiress toward the end of the story, whom Lady Denham plans to pair with Edward, complicates the scene even further. Commentators, including MARGARET DRABBLE, have remarked on Austen's ability to poke fun at the health-obsessed whilst herself fatally ill, and on the difficulty of predicting entirely confidently how the novel would have progressed.   AC

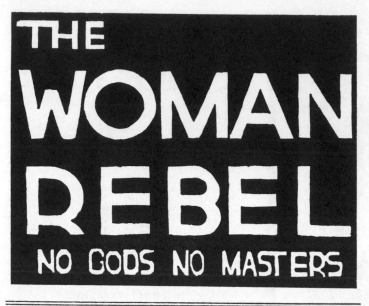

THE WOMAN REBEL

NO GODS NO MASTERS

VOL I.   MARCH 1914   NO. 1.

THE AIM

This paper will not be the champion of any "ism."

All rebel women are invited to contribute to its columns.

The majority of papers usually adjust themselves to the ideas of their readers but the WOMAN REBEL will obstinately refuse to be adjusted.

The aim of this paper will be to stimulate working women to think for themselves and to build up a conscious fighting character.

was with a sweetheart or through the desire for a sweetheart or something impelling within themselves, the nature of which they knew not, neither could they control. Society does not forgive this act when it is based upon the natural impulses and feelings of a young girl. It prefers the other story of the grape juice procurer which makes it easy to shift the blame from its own shoulders, to cast the stone and to evade the unpleasant facts that it

lows." His sole aim is to throw off responsibility. The same uncertainty in these emotions is experienced by girls in marriage in as great a proportion as in the unmarried. After the first experience the life of a girl varies. All these girls do not necessarily go into prostitution. They have had an experience which has not "ruined" them, but rather given them a larger vision of life, stronger feelings and a broader understanding of human nature. The adolescent girl does not understand herself. She is full of contradictions, whims, emotions. For her emotional nature longs for caresses, to touch, to kiss. She is often as well satisfied to hold hands or to go arm in arm with a girl as in the companionship of a boy.

It is these and kindred facts upon which the WOMAN REBEL will dwell from time to time and from which it is hoped the young girl will derive some knowledge of her nature, and conduct her life upon such knowledge.

It will also be the aim of the WOMAN REBEL to advocate the prevention of conception and to impart such knowledge in the columns of this paper.

Other subjects, including the slavery through motherhood; through things, the home, public opinion and so forth, will be dealt with.

It is also the aim of this paper to circulate among those women who work in prostitution; to voice their wrongs; to expose the police persecution which hovers over them and to give free expression to their thoughts, hopes and opinions.

And at all times the WOMAN REBEL will strenuously advocate economic emancipation.

Margaret Sanger: front page of *Woman Rebel*, no. 1, vol. 1, March 1914.

Sandoz, Mari (Marie) Susette 1896–1966 American historian, biographer and novelist. Daughter of Swiss German homesteaders, she was born and raised in Sheridan County, Nebraska, where her early contacts were with other settlers and the Lakota Sioux. She did not learn English until the age of 9, when local officials forced her parents to send their children to school. She became a teacher herself at the age of 16. After a brief marriage to Wray Macumber (1914–19), she studied intermittently at the University of Nebraska (1922–33), where LOUISE POUND inspired and encouraged her. Extensive, careful research characterizes Sandoz's most significant work, a series of books on the Great Plains: *Old Jules* (1935), a biography of her violent, visionary father;

Crazy Horse (1942), a biography of the legendary Sioux chief; and *Cheyenne Autumn* (1953), an account of government brutality toward the Cheyennes. With *The Buffalo-Hunters* (1954), *The Cattlemen* (1958) and *The Beaver Men* (1964), she fulfilled a long-standing plan to write about the Trans-Missouri area. Other nonfiction includes *Love Song to the Plains* (1961), *The Battle of the Little Bighorn* (1966) and *These were the Sioux* (1961). Two novellas for young readers, *The Horse-catcher* (1957) and *The Story Catcher* (1963), describe Cheyenne and Lakota life before whites settled in the Great Plains. Of her novels, *Slogum House* (1937), an anti-Fascist allegory set in the Nebraska sandhills, is considered the best.   JSG

Sanger, Margaret [Higgins] 1879–1966 The most influential leader of the American birth-control movement, and the founder of Planned Parenthood. She was the sixth of eleven children born in Corning, New York, to the devout Catholic Anne Higgins and the free-thinking Irish immigrant Michael Higgins. Seven of Anne Higgins's eighteen pregnancies ended in miscarriage.

Margaret was married to William Sanger from 1902 to 1921; they had three children. Her unconventional activities began in 1912 when she authored a column for women in the *Call*, a socialist newspaper. In 1914 Sanger started her own paper, the *Woman Rebel*.

Sanger was a trained nurse; she claimed her crusade was in response to the death by self-induced abortion of a young mother who had begged her for the contraception information Sanger was prohibited by law from disclosing. Sanger established birth-control clinics, prepared pamphlets explaining different contraceptive methods used around the world, published a periodical entitled the *Birth Control Review* and wrote a number of books, including two autobiographical works, and a collection of letters from women all over America soliciting her help in obtaining reliable methods of contraception.   LMC

Sansom, Hannah [Callender] 1727–1801 American diarist. Daughter of Quakers William Callender and Katherine Smith, Hannah was educated in Quaker schools in Philadelphia. With some gaps in time, her DIARY (1758–88) covers a thirty-year period, which includes her marriage to Samuel Sansom in 1762 and the birth of five children. The diary begins with an account of her journey from Philadelphia to New York City. She travelled with a diverse company: fellow Quakers, 'some sailors shipwrecked in the "King of Prussia", a humorous old Dutchman, and an officer of the Jersey Blue'. Once in New York, she was a curious and observant visitor, reporting on the people she met in mansions and huts, on the architecture of English and Dutch churches, and on a family of Indians living in a wigwam. The rest of the diary primarily concerns her life in Philadelphia, particularly her friendships with ELIZABETH and Sarah DRINKER. Throughout her diary, she comments on her reading, from Benjamin Franklin's 'drolleries' to Samuel Richardson's *Clarissa*.   CLB

Sappho Sappho is thought by classical scholars to have been an actual woman who lived and wrote on the Aeolian island of Lesbos in the 7th century BC. The earliest copy of a Sappho poem appears on a potsherd of the 3rd century BC on which can be deciphered lines that appear to be substantially the same as some quoted as by Sappho by both the grammarian Hermogenes in the 2nd century AD, and contemporaneously, by the miscellany writer Athenaios. The text we now attribute to Sappho consists of quotations from metricians and grammarians and fragments gleaned from papyri of the 2nd and 3rd centuries AD; together with the 'Hymn to Aphrodite' quoted by Dionysius of Harlicarnassus in about 20 BC; and the four stanzas beginning 'fainetai moi', given by Longinus in the 1st century AD as an example of the sublime and imitated by Catullus, whose version has ever since been better known than its Aeolian Greek model and has influenced the reading of it. Though Sappho was active in various genres, all the known poems are lyrics; as she was a woman and therefore to be sexualized by masculinist culture, all those lyrics are assumed to be both about love and autobiographical.

The disappearance of Sappho's work is thought by some to have been engineered by malevolent Christian church authorities, but it seems as likely that, as Attic Greek became the language of the international elite, the Aeolian idiom she used became first unfashionable, then archaic and ultimately incomprehensible. As the hard evidence for Sappho's achievement as a poet decayed, Sappho became a legendary figure, either a squat and swarthy lover of women to be caricatured at will, or the rejected lover of Phaon who committed suicide by leaping off the Leucadian rock. As Phaon himself is supposed to have been a ferryman who was rewarded by Aphrodite, for his kindness in ferrying her in the figure of an old woman, free of charge, with a miraculous ointment that conferred perfect beauty, we may assume that Sappho's suicide is equally improbable.

By the 12th century AD Sappho had ceased to be read; in the 13th century she became the heroine of someone else's poem, the Latin 'Epistula Sapphus', written in the person of Sappho who pleads with Phaon in the manner of Ovid's Heroides. The 'Epistula' remained the principal source of information about Sappho until Renaissance humanists began investigating the Greek past; in the mid 16th century Sappho's two poems began appearing in print. Continental poets were no sooner able to read 'fainetai moi' in Greek or in Latin than they began translating and imitating it. English poets were slow to follow the example of Belleau, De Baif and Ronsard; the first English versions of 'fainetai moi' appeared a hundred years later, but from then on every poetic schoolboy who knew Greek tried his hand at an imitation of it, making it the most influential short lyric ever written. An absolutely literal translation would go something like this:

Appears to me that one equal to the gods
to be who face to face with you
sits and your beautiful voice
    listens to

and laughter charming. True that my
heart in breast shakes

for when I look at you at once speech
  deserts me

certainly my tongue unstrings, a subtle
under my skin fire slips
my eyes are darkened, hum
  my ears

down from me water oozes, trembling
all over grips me, greener am I made
than grass. Of death little short
  to myself I seem

While male scholars were aware of Sappho's reputation for excessive and disorderly sexual desire, CHRISTINE DE PIZAN in the 16th century, and Madame Dacier and Madeleine de Scudery in the 17th, refashioned Sappho as an acceptable heroine, exemplary in her delicate sensibility and her capacity for sentimental friendship. As Plato had dubbed Sappho the Tenth Muse, women poets who achieved a measure of success were sure to incur the title of Tenth Muse, so unseating Sappho and all other claimants. APHRA BEHN and LADY MARY WORTLEY MONTAGU, both dubbed 'Sappho', were well aware that the apparently flattering name bore the imputation of all Sappho's more questionable attributes. Less audacious women poets could expect themselves to be praised for their sexlessness in contrast to immodest Sappho.

Though Sappho is in some sense a creation of masculinist culture, women writers have devised their own versions of her. In the 19th century, MARY 'PERDITA' ROBINSON, FELICIA HEMANS, L.E.L. and CAROLINE NORTON espoused the persona of Sappho. At 16 CHRISTINA ROSSETTI wrote a poem in the persona of Sappho, and at 18 another, which was never printed in her lifetime. Some years before, Baudelaire is credited with reviving Sappho as an incarnation of decadence, valued even more for her suicide than for her transgressive sexuality. 'MICHAEL FIELD', Bliss Carman, AMY LOWELL and SARA TEASDALE, EDNA ST VINCENT MILLAY, and Carolyn Kizer have all treated the Sappho theme. The rehabilitation of Sappho as a self-regulating artist has been furthered also by new translations such as that of Mary Barnard (b.1909), first published in 1958.   GG

Sarraute [née Tchernaik], Nathalie 1900–

French novelist and theorist, most well known for *Le Planétarium* (*The Planetarium*, 1959), and *Les Fruits d'or* (*The Golden Fruits*, 1963) which won the Prix International de la Littérature – an impeccably metafictional text all about the dissolution of the traditional novel, and its mainstay, the character: 'I the centre, I the axis around which everything gathered, revolved . . . I am displaced, deported.' Born in Russia of Jewish parents who divorced when she was 2, she joined her father and stepmother to live in Paris, learning to speak French, Russian, English and German. She read English at the Sorbonne, studied in Oxford and Berlin, and returned to Paris to complete a degree in Law, which she practised for twelve years. Her first book, *Tropismes* (1939), received only one review. At the beginning of World War II, she worked for the Resistance before being forced into hiding. Jean-Paul Sartre wrote the preface to *Portrait d'un inconnu* (1948; *Portrait of a Man Unknown*), and with the 1953 collection of essays, *L'Ere du soupçon* (*The Age of Suspicion*), she came to be identified as a leading theoretician and author of the *nouveau roman*.   SD

Sarton, May 1912–

Prolific American novelist and poet whose work examines the struggles of women for courageous, honest self-expression, addressing such fundamental issues as loneliness, depression, inspiration and sexuality. Born in Belgium, she has resided in New England for most of her life, living as both a citizen and an exile, a position held by most of her novels' heroines, who chart their paths amidst new and often hostile environments. As heroine Hilary Stevens claims in Sarton's now classic novel of lesbian love and artistic inspiration, *Mrs Stevens Hears the Mermaids Singing* (1961), 'we have to dare to be ourselves, however frightening or strange that self may prove to be'. The theme of self-expression, central to this novel, also characterizes her poetry and popular memoirs, entitled *Plant Dreaming Deep* (1968), *Journal of a Solitude* (1973) and *The House by the Sea* (1975), in which she explores the writer's inner life, inspired by muses and wrestling with critics. Incisive in her portrayal of female artistry, she is also one of the most sympathetic writers on women and ageing, addressing the courage of women confronting both old age and illness in *As We Are Now* (1973), *A Reckoning* (1978), *The Magnificent Spinster* (1985) and *After the Stroke* (1988). While much admired and widely read, Sarton has only just begun to receive the critical recognition due to a writer who so tenderly and observantly charts the challenges of the individual quest for fulfilment. As Sarton herself has claimed, 'it has been a rather long struggle in the wilderness . . . It is the young who are persuading their professors that it is time I was recognized.' The author of more than forty books, Sarton is a member of the American Academy of Arts and Sciences and the Poetry Society of America; she has also received honorary degrees and numerous awards.   RL

Sassafrass, Cypress and Indigo (1982)

In her first novel NTOZAKE SHANGE relates the story of three sisters from the American South as they strive to establish a sense of identity, and learn to define and express themselves on their own terms in a predominantly white, patriarchal world. Mother–daughter relations are a major theme and, while each of the characters rejects her mother in some way, the novel points to the special sustenance that can be drawn from the mother–daughter bond. Through its portrayal of the lives of the three main protagonists – one a weaver, one a dancer and one a conjure woman – *Sassafrass, Cypress and Indigo* celebrates womanist principles and stresses the importance of the spiritual and creative aspects of an African cultural heritage. The innovative narrative form incorporates spells, recipes, poems, letters and journal entries which, together with her evocation of African-American speech rhythms, conveys Shange's distinctive and intensely lyrical voice.   EP

Sattianadan, Krupa (Krupabai Satthianadhan)

1862–94 The first Indian English novelist. An intense and precocious child, she was educated partially at home, partially at a mission school for girls in Bombay. When she joined the Madras Medical College in 1878, she became the first woman to do so. Though she was registered alongside the men for a formal degree, and by the end of the year had stood first in every subject except Chemistry, she discontinued her studies because 'her nerve forsook her and her health broke down completely'.

She met and married Samuel Sattianadan, who had in 1881 just returned from Cambridge. It may have cost Krupabai an effort to 'give up the freer life of intellectual pursuits that she had sketched out for herself', her husband acknowledges in a biographical note. During the next four years the couple moved several times as Samuel took up various jobs. Only after moving back to Madras in 1886 did Krupa begin writing the autobiographical novel *Saguna: The Story of a Native Christian Life*. This appeared serially in the *Christian College Magazine* in 1889–90 and was widely and enthusiastically reviewed. She began work the very next year on *Kamala: A Story of Hindu Life* (1892–4), the later episodes of which were written as she hung, fevered, between life and death.

In contrast to the good and bad women of the tracts invoked by her sub-titles, Krupa's protagonists are individuated figures; their lives movingly – rather than didactically – presented. Her much-acclaimed settings strain against the traveller's-eye logic of colonial landscapes and initiate a celebratory, Romantic-nationalist realism.   ST

Saxton, Josephine

1935– British writer of short stories and novels, most of them categorizable as SCIENCE FICTION, fantasy or fabulation, and characterized by a tough-minded but charming surrealism. She was one of the few British women writers associated with the so-called New Wave; many of these early stories are included in *The Power of Time* (1985). In the late 1960s and early 1970s, a number of her novels, including *The Hieros Gamos of Sam and An Smith* and *Vector for Seven: The Weltanschauung of Mrs Amelia Mortimer and Friends*, were published in the USA; these are semi-comic quests through inner space. After a period of neglect, she produced two further novels *The Travails of Jane Saint* (1980) and *The Queen of the States* (1986) and a collection, *Jane Saint and the Backlash*. This later work is informed by Saxton's intense, though quirky, feminism.   RK

Sayers, Dorothy L(eigh)

1893–1957 British author of the Lord Peter Wimsey mysteries, stylish classics of character-based DETECTIVE FICTION; and essayist, dramatist, translator and formidable Christian polemicist whose plays for radio were popular innovations in religious broadcasting. Only child of an Anglican clergyman in the remote Fens, she was a gifted linguist and received a First (Medieval French) from Somerville College, Oxford. From 1921, she spent ten years as an advertising copy-writer in London. In 1924 she secretly bore a son, whom she supported from a distance. She married Oswold Arthur Fleming in 1926.

Her first novel, *Whose Body* (1923), introduces Wimsey and his manservant, Bunter. *Strong Poison* (1930) features Harriet Vane, with whom Wimsey conducts a chivalrous courtship consummated in the final Wimsey mystery (initially written as a stage-play), BUSMAN'S HONEYMOON (1938). *Murder Must Advertise* (1933) reflects with satiric humour Sayers's years in advertising. *The Nine Tailors* (1934) is a highlight of the genre, its evocative Fenland atmosphere inspired by her childhood home. (See also GAUDY NIGHT, 1935). War prompted a permanent transition to essays and religious plays, especially *The Man Born to be King* (1943), a series of twelve BBC productions on the life of Christ. Also of interest is the feminist essay, 'The Human-Not-Quite-Human', in *Unpopular Opinions* (1946). Outspoken and sometimes outlandish, sharp-witted and witty, she thrived on intellectual combat. She received an honorary doctorate of letters from Durham University in 1953 and was president of the Modern Languages Association from 1939 to 1945. From 1949 until her death she was president of the Detection Club. Her final work was a translation of Dante's *Divine Comedy*. *Hell* was published in 1949; *Purgatory* in 1955. She died from coronary thrombosis before completing *Paradiso*, which was finished by Barbara Reynolds and published posthumously in 1962.   LDo

Sayers, Peig

1873–1958 Gaelic autobiographer and story-teller. Born in County Kerry, Ireland, she moved to the Blasket Islands following an arranged, yet very successful, marriage. Of ten children born to her, five survived to adulthood. An exceptional story-teller, her lyrical, idiomatic mastery of her native Gaelic attracted students, scholars and folklorists to whom she

THE

WOMAN OF THE TOWN;

OR,

AUTHENTIC MEMOIRS

OF

MARIA MAITLAND;

WELL KNOWN IN THE VICINITY OF

COVENT GARDEN.

WRITTEN BY HERSELF.

We beg mirth will spare one moment to pity. Let not delicacy be offended, if we pay a short tribute of compassion to those unhappy examples of misconduct. How much, therefore, ought common opinion to be despised, which supposes the same fact that betrays female honour can add to that of a gentleman! When a beauty is robbed of her virtue, the hue and cry which is raised, is never raised in her favour. Deceived by ingratitude, necessity forces her to continue criminal. She is ruined by our sex, and prevented reformation by the reproaches of her own.

LECTURE ON HEADS.

London:

Printed by T. Maiden, Sherbourne-Lane,

For J. ROE, No. 38, Chiswell Street, Finsbury Square,

And ANN LEMOINE, White-Rose-Court,

Coleman-Street.

Sold by all the Booksellers in the United Kingdom.

[*Price Sixpence.*]

Scandalous memoirs: title-page of Phebe Phillips's *The Woman of the Town: Or Authentic Memoirs of Maria Maitland*, 1799.

recounted the myths and legends that were her inheritance. Her anecdotal autobiographies, *Peig* (1936), *Machtnamh Seana-Mhna* (1939) and *Beatha Pheig Sayers* (1970), dictated to her son, record communal festivals and tragedies and the isolated loneliness of personal suffering. Taken from school at 14 and sent into service, she welcomed the personal freedom that marriage and her own home promised; at the same time she acknowledged: 'The days of my youth were certainly gone forever and I had to spend the balance of my life in ease or in hardship according as they came my road.' Despite the difficulty of capturing her eloquent, witty phraseology and haunting imagery in translation, English versions of her works were attempted by Seamus Ennis (*An Old Woman's Reflections,*

1962) and Bryan MacMahon (*Peig,* 1973). Folklorists Robin Flower and Kenneth Jackson have published some of her stories in the journal *Bealoideas* while Seosamh O'Daligh has made tape-recordings of hundreds more. She has been revered as a national icon and included for many years in the Irish school curriculum, but serious studies of her critical attitude to her patriarchal society are only now beginning.   BHu

scandalous memoirs By the early 18th century APHRA BEHN's scandal writing, particularly LOVE-LETTERS BETWEEN A NOBLEMAN AND HIS SISTER (1684–7), had set a precedent for the association of scandal, and the propagation of rumour and gossip, with women's writing. DELARIVIÈRE MANLEY further invested in the association, collaborating with Swift who employed her as a disguise for his own political pamphleteering. Manley's *The Secret History* (1704) and *The New Atalantis* (1709), both provocative satires concerning Whig politicians, were hugely successful; but when arrested for seditious libel she made fiction her alibi, thus indicating the future direction of women's writing. ELIZA HAYWOOD tended toward fiction mixed with scandalous allusion, although in *The Adventures of Eovaai* (1736) she explicitly attacked Robert Walpole. However, scandal writing by women was increasingly censured, by Pope amongst others, who referred in *The Dunciad* (1729) to scandalous exposures by 'shameless [female] Scriblers' in 'libellous Memoirs and Novels'.

Going against the shift toward respectability, the already infamous 'scandalous memoirists' CONSTANTIA PHILLIPS (*Apology for the Conduct,* 1748), LETITIA PILKINGTON (*Memoirs of Mrs Letitia Pilkington,* 1749), LADY FRANCES VANE (*Memoirs of a Lady of Quality* (inserted in Smollett's *Peregrine Pickle,* 1751)) and CHARLOTTE CHARKE (*Narrative of the Life of Mrs Charlotte Charke,* 1755) briefly revived the association of women's writing and scandal. With nothing to lose in terms of reputation, they exposed their own and others' 'frailties' and were pilloried in the *Gentleman's Magazine* (1751) for advertising their 'shame' and making themselves heroines of their own 'romances'. They were also credited with veracity and their originality lay in their integration of the exposure of public figures with an intensified confessional and autobiographical mode, which arguably contributed to greater depth and complexity in representations of subjectivity in the novel.

First-person accounts by unconventional (or immoral) women continued to be popular, for instance: the soldier-in-disguise Mrs Christian Davies's *Life and Adventures* (1740), CATHERINE JEMMAT's *Memoirs* (1762), ELIZABETH GOOCH's *Life* (1792), actresses George Anne Bellamy's *An Apology* (1785), Ann Archer's *Memoirs* (1787) and Phebe Phillips's *Authentic Memoirs*

Olive Schreiner: facsimile of her 'small upright' handwriting, *The Letters of Olive Schreiner*, edited by S.C. Cronwright Schreiner, 1924.

(1799), amongst others. However, MARY WOLL-STONECRAFT's 'scandalous' life, revealed in William Godwin's *Memoirs* (1798) of his wife and the posthumous publication of her semi-autobiographical fiction, was used to tarnish her intellectual status. Writers like CHARLOTTE LENNOX, FANNY BURNEY and MARIA EDGEWORTH, who sought serious approbation, tended increasingly toward the relative safety of fiction, insisting on the apolitical non-referentiality and 'innocence' of their texts.   LMT

Scanlan, Nellie 1882–1968 New Zealand novelist whose family saga – PENCARROW (1932), *Tides of Youth* (1933), *Winds of Heaven* (1934) and *Kelly Pencarrow* (1939) – gained a large popular readership in New Zealand. Scanlan spent her early career working as a journalist in Britain and the United States, specializing in social news and, in particular, royal occasions. Her autobiography, *The Road to Pencarrow* (1963), deals with this period of her life in some detail. She came to fiction late. Her first novel, *Primrose Hill*, appeared in 1931 when she was nearly 50. That was followed in quick succession by fifteen novels, nine of which have New Zealand settings.

The Pencarrow novels deal with three generations of the Pencarrow family and its offshoots. Money, marriage and business, from farming to politics, are the staples. Scanlan's plots are domestic in their orienta-tion, romantic, conservative and may now seem limited in their treatment of class and race. Despite their New Zealand context, they conform to many of the conventions of popular British fiction of their period. And yet critics have described her as laying down the basis of a national literature by making New Zealand settings and characters normal and acceptable to the local middle-brow reading public whose reading experience would hitherto have been almost entirely British. By the early 1960s, 80,000 copies of the Pencarrow saga had been sold.   JSt

Schreiner, Olive 1855–1920 South African novelist, short-story writer, feminist, political commentator, celebrated in her lifetime, often attacked and neglected later. Born to a severe Evangelical Englishwoman and a German missionary, she was brought up on South African mission-stations, and was sufficiently independent at 9 – steeped in the Bible and acutely conscientious – to reject organized Christianity, against formidable odds, for a more mystical faith. At 15 she started teaching, and encountered Herbert Spencer's *First Principles*. This validated her religious doubts and provided systematic recompense in scientific naturalism.

Between 1874 and 1881 she was a 'governess' – really a 'higher servant' – which meant domestic chores and low pay. Such experiences heightened her identification with the disadvantaged and her tendency to seek them out – later she would bring prostitutes home. The year 1881 brought 'England at last!'; she was fêted for THE STORY OF AN AFRICAN FARM (1883). Back in South Africa (1889) she championed labour and opposed the country's racist and imperialist policies. In 1894 she married Samuel Cronwright, who entered politics. Twenty years later she returned to English life.

She had begun writing seriously in the South African diamond fields in 1873, producing short stories and the characters and themes of novels which would foreground African landscapes to powerful effect alongside women's subordination and constructions of femininity: the posthumously published FROM MAN TO MAN (1926) and *Undine* (1929), besides *The Story of an African Farm* (which appeared under the pseudonym 'Ralph Iron'). Its restless heroine echoes Schreiner's own early views – 'I regard marriage as other people regard death' – and prefigures with striking directness and intensity the NEW WOMAN fiction of the 1890s. The later collection, *Dreams* (1891), pursues sexual equality with a range of allegories, fantasies and maxims typical of her writing's variability and unsettled identity. Marked by progressive faith, sexual anxieties and passion, topical debates and personal dilemmas, her work occasioned and reflected the friendship of 'advanced' thinkers – Havelock Ellis, Karl Pearson, Edward Carpenter, ELEANOR MARX – and membership of the Men and Women's Club. Social Darwinism qualified her egalitarianism, and though she championed Africans – as in *Trooper Peter Halket of Mashonaland* (1897) – her *Woman and Labour* (1911), the 'Bible of the Women's Movement', draws on racist attitudes. It remains remarkable in grasping interconnections of sex and class, technological change, range of argumentation – reaching an un-modernist star-fish – and its sustained case against 'sex-parasitism'.   KC

Schulman, Sarah 1958–

Schulman, Sarah 1958– American writer and activist who studied Modern Languages at the University of Chicago, Hunter College and Empire State; she took menial jobs in order to fund her writing, which often draws on these early experiences. She was always involved in feminist and AIDS activism and in lesbian and gay politics, co-convening the Lesbian Avengers protest group; *My American History* (1974) is a collection of political writings. Her fourth novel, *People in Trouble* (1990), is a deliberately propagandist work in which estranged lovers find a *modus vivendi* in activism and political art.

Her third, most individual novel, *After Dolores* (1988), draws on her earlier books – a thriller, *The Sophie Horowitz Story* (1984), and *Girls Visions and Everything* (1986) – using thriller material to explore jealousy and revenge, and the Kerouac-inspired bohemianism of the latter to paint a night-journey. Later novels are concerned with psychoanalytic exploration of gender and with the AIDS crisis.   RK

science fiction

science fiction The separation of a tradition which can usefully be termed 'science fiction' from the broad sweep of fantasy in general and GOTHIC fantasy in particular is generally dated from the publication of FRANKENSTEIN by MARY SHELLEY in 1818. Sf can usefully be defined as that branch of fantasy which takes both plot material and concretized metaphorical structure either directly from scientific and sociological speculation, or at second-hand from other sf.

Frankenstein is a good starting point because it combines an interest in concepts from the popular science of the time – galvanic experiments with dead animals, polar exploration – with an evocative use of them as metaphors for a general human estrangement (also, of course, for the particular concern of women in an age before childbirth anaesthesia, with 'creation' as a task involving squalor and pain). *Frankenstein* is also a useful starting point because the general effect of all this is to start an argument, an argument about ethical responsibility in science with which we are not yet done.

However, the direction that the evolving genre took in the late 19th century was, in general, away from women's concerns and from women writers; the utopian tradition, which gradually amalgamated with science fiction in the work of Wells, was generally more congenial and suited better with the pressures on educated women to remain lady-like. It is not particularly helpful to regard the work of women utopian writers such as CHARLOTTE PERKINS GILMAN as science fiction, though their work was, when reissued, to become a significant influence on later feminist sf.

When women writers of sf did emerge in the 1930s and 1940s, it was into, quite specifically, a magazine sf culture, 'pulps' in which neither literary quality nor production values were at a premium and which recruited new authors from their readership. Two women sf magazine writers from this period are of particular interest: C.L. (Catherine Lucille) Moore (1911–87) who produced feverish Freudian nightmares set on alien worlds or in legendary pasts, and LEIGH BRACKETT. Both women were accepted in this heavily masculine world partly because they used male versions of their names.

The misogyny of the 1950s made sf even less congenial to women who were not prepared to play the game. The standard woman sf writer of the 1950s was either sentimental and concerned with eternal emotional verities, like Judith Merril and ZENNA HENDERSON, or acidly and surreally amusing, like Evelyn E. Smith. They were, in any case, marginalized. The genre as a whole was divided between a technophile, Right-wing adventure fiction which ignored women and a liberal satirical or sociological sf that was often actively hostile.

The women writers who began commercially

successful careers in the late 1950s and early 1960s did so by publishing planetary ROMANCES with a strong vein of fantasy, of a sort that was at the time regarded as old-fashioned. The subsequent popularity of MARION ZIMMER BRADLEY and ANNE MCCAFFREY was by no means predictable.

When the new sf wave came along in the 1960s, its artistic values were still often those of a boy's clubhouse, but the political radicalism that went along with the naturalization into sf of avant-garde literary techniques ensured that a generation of women sf writers who had been radicalized into a nascent feminism had a place to go. Writers like URSULA K. LE GUIN, ALICE SHELDON/JAMES TIPTREE and JOANNA RUSS were not feminists who saw in sf a useful set of techniques to colonize; they were aspiring sf writers who became feminists at a point when they already had careers.

Science fiction became part of the décor of the 1960s and its gaudy tropes were there to be picked up by any who fancied them as material for fabulations and other experimentalist modes. The British magazine *New Worlds* and various occasional American anthologies offered a home to work of this kind which was neither wholly sf nor wholly separate from it, and various women writers like Carol Emshwiller (b.1921), Pamela Lifton-Zoline (b.1941) and JOSEPHINE SAXTON became more or less associated with the genre as a result. Other writers, whose work tended in this direction, such as EMMA TENNANT or ANGELA CARTER, were not so directly associated with sf, though both women contributed to *Bananas* which, like *New Worlds* in its later phase, was co-edited by HILARY BAILEY.

Gradually the commercial sf market was opened up to women writers in a way that it had not been before. Much of the sf published by women in the 1970s and 1980s was fairly standard adventure story fare, though feminist sub-texts were increasingly common elements in this; many new writers were heavily influenced by Le Guin, at least in the early stages of their careers. C.J. CHERRYH and the early work of MARY GENTLE are typical here, not least in the alternation of sf and fantasy in their work. TANITH LEE by contrast was a genre fantasy writer who regularly wrote sf and introduced sf tropes into her fantasies.

Specifically feminist sf and fantasy was less common; the British publishing company Women's Press made a particular point of reprinting Joanna Russ's work, the short fiction of LISA TUTTLE and Gilman's *Herland*, and of commissioning novels by new writers. Of a generation of women writers that emerged in the late 1980s and 1990s, NICOLA GRIFFITHS, GWYNETH JONES and ELIZABETH HAND were perhaps those most directly intellectually involved in feminism.

In the mid-1980s cyberpunk emerged as a significant movement and sub-genre within sf, a technophiliac sf obsessed with the possibilities of virtual reality and artificial intelligence. The manifestos of this movement were often carping about 'personal politics', and cyberpunk was usually very male. However, women writers like PAT CADIGAN and CANDAS JANE DORSEY successfully colonized this material, exploring the same quasi-feminist concerns displayed by theoreticians interested in cyberpunk, like Sherry Turkle and Sandy Stone. Cyberpunk's rival movement, the so-called New Humanism of writers like Kim Stanley Robinson was equally dominated by men, but included women writers like KAREN JOY FOWLER.

Science fiction has always been a genre dominated by men, but has been a congenial home for many women writers who liked its flashy backdrops. Its rarely fulfilled promise of showing how the future might be different has more often been honoured by women writers.   RK

Scott, Evelyn [Elsie Dunn]

Scott, Evelyn [Elsie Dunn] 1893–1963 Avant-garde American novelist and poet. Born in Clarksville, Tennessee, to an aristocratic family, Elsie Dunn early rejected the conventional paths for beautiful Southern girls of her class. Highly intelligent, attempting controversial writing even in her teens, she was admitted young to Tulane University, but cast off social respectability when she abandoned her art course to elope to Brazil with Dr Frederick Creighton Wellman, an older, married, professor. (Both changed their names to 'Scott'.) *Escapade* (1923) fictionalized her South American years in precise, impressionistic prose, detailing the passion and pain of her own experiences (including the course of her pregnancy) and reflecting on the lives of Brazilian women. She maintained a writing career throughout her nomadic and complex life – which included spells in the Algerian desert, the Pyrenees, Bermuda and England; marriage to British author, John Metcalfe; affairs; mentorship of writers such as JEAN STAFFORD and JEAN RHYS; and challenges to collective socialism.

Her experimentally exciting novels included ambitious histories: of families ('The Narrow House' trilogy, 1921–5); of 19th-century America (*Migrations*, *The Wave*, *A Calendar of Sin*, 1927–31); of writing and creativity (*Eva Gay*, 1933). In these and others, she enters the labyrinths of the self, and ranges panoramically across the broadest canvases of American culture in war and peace. In later years, poor, ill and forgotten, she was unable to complete her work. 'It is terrible to have such a living mind', she once wrote (*Escapade*), but all her writing remains remarkable for that mind's intrepid exploration of new materials, new forms, new visions.   PEK

Scott, Gail

Scott, Gail ?– Canadian novelist, short-story writer, essayist, teacher, translator, living in

Montreal, who participated with Québécois feminist writers NICOLE BROSSARD, FRANCE THÉORET and others in the La Théorie, un Dimanche group, addressing questions of POSTMODERNISM and feminism and developing the notion of 'fiction-theory'. She has also had a long friendship with the poet ERIN MOURÉ. Scott grew up in an English-speaking family, observing the different relationship the neighbouring French Catholic women seemed to have to their bodies, and realizing that 'culture is not only an intellectual process, but is experienced as a whole physical being'. It is the implications of this for women, as well as her early experiences as an anglophone journalist sympathetic to the Québécois Independence movement that provided Scott with some of the questions she has asked in her experimental writing. Since the late 1980s Scott has been exploring how fiction written on the cusp of sometimes antagonistic language systems encourages exploration of genre and syntax. Her work includes the short stories *Spare Parts* (1982), and the novels *Heroine* (1987) and *Main Brides: Against Ochre Pediment and Aztec Sky* (1993). In addition, Scott has also published a collection of essays, *Spaces like Stairs* (1989), and co-edited the French-language critical journal *Spirale* (1980–3) as well as co-founding *Tessera*, a feminist journal which she co-edited from 1984 to 1989. Throughout her work evidence of Scott's interest in trying to trace the sounds of minor voices, notably female, means that listening is crucial. After all, 'writing starts in trying to create a text that listens'.   SEP

Scott, Mary Edith 1888–1979 New Zealand novelist who wrote twenty-six popular ROMANCES set on New Zealand farms and co-authored five 'thrillers'. Brought up in Napier, New Zealand, she went to Auckland University College where she got a first-class degree, and became a teacher. In 1913 she was the first woman to climb the Remarkables and in 1914 she married Walter Scott, farming in a remote area of the North Island and bringing up four children. Her autobiography, *Days That have Been* (1966), tells how she began writing to supplement the family income during the Depression years, when she wrote sketches and stories about farm life for newspapers. In 1953 she became a bestseller with the publication of *Breakfast at Six*. Based on her experience, it tells of the marriage of Susan and Paul, their life on a back-blocks farm and the problems and pleasures of a rural community. Subsequent novels continued their story, and that of Susan's friendship with Larry, wife of a neighbouring farmer – 'everything was fun with Larry'. Other novels about other families – humorous, pragmatic and, at times, ironic accounts of everyday life in rural New Zealand, together with a romantic story line – remained the basis of her popularity.   AM

Scott, Mary (Taylor) 1751–93 English poet who is best known for writing 'The Female Advocate; a poem occasioned by reading Mr Duncombe's Feminiad' (1774). She married John Taylor, a Dissenting minister between 1787 and early 1789; their son, John Edward Taylor, eventually founded the *Manchester Guardian*. After her marriage, Scott lived in the house previously owned by an earlier Dissenting poet, ELIZABETH ROWE. She was a friend of ANNA STEELE, HELEN MARIA WILLIAMS, and carried on a long correspondence with ANNA SEWARD. 'The Female Advocate' is unusual in following earlier male writers such as George Ballard and John Duncombe by listing exemplary women of the past, including the DUCHESS OF NEWCASTLE, ANNE KILLIGREW, LADY CHUDLEIGH, SARAH FIELDING, CHARLOTTE LENNOX, CATHERINE TALBOT and MRS BARBAULD. Scott's main argument is expressed in her preface, when she asks that women make good use of their abilities and that there should be equal education for both sexes. She died at Bristol during her third pregnancy.   RDM

Scott, Rosie (Judy Rosemary) 1948– Australian/New Zealand novelist. Born in Wellington, New Zealand, where she attended university, studying English and Drama. She later worked as a counsellor, and in publishing and films. Her own publishing career began with a collection of poems, *Flesh and Blood* (1984), and a prize-winning play, *Say Thank You to the Lady* (1985), later filmed as *Redheads*. She is, however, best known for her novels, beginning with GLORY DAYS (1988), whose eponymous central character is a remarkable painter, as well as a singer in seedy clubs, who lives on the fringes of Auckland society. *Nights with Grace* (1990), a love-story set on the island of Roratonga, was followed by the futuristic *Feral City* (1992), set in a now-decayed Auckland, an urban nightmare inhabited by society's outcasts. The novel focuses on two sisters, Faith and Violet, who reopen their parents' bookshop as a token of the continued power of the word and the imagination. *Lives on Fire* (1993), set in Brisbane, also takes a sympathetic view of the urban poor and of those who attempt to improve their lot through art. *Movie Dreams* (1995), also set in Queensland, breaks with Scott's earlier novels in focusing not on a woman but on a young boy who runs away from home after the suicide of his best friend; a particular concern here is the influence of popular movies on the imaginative life of a troubled adolescent. Scott lives in Sydney where she has been an active committee member of the Australian Society of Authors for several years: in 1998 she was elected as its Chair.   EW

Scott [née Robinson], Sarah 1723–95 British novelist, philanthropist and sister of BLUESTOCKING patron ELIZABETH MONTAGU. In 1748 Scott met

Lady Barbara Montagu with whom she subsequently shared her life, her literary vocation and her charitable projects. Their relationship continued during her brief marriage to George Lewis Scott in 1751, which ended in a sudden and secretive separation. Scott's novels divide into exemplary historical biographies, such as *The History of Gustavus Ericson, King of Sweden* (1761), *The History of Mecklenburgh* (1762) and *The Life of Theodore Agrippa D'Aubigné* (1772), and didactic novels, like *A Journal Through Every Stage of Life* (1754) and *A Test of Filial Duty* (1772). Her most acclaimed work, *Millenium Hall* (1762), depicts the establishment of a female utopian community and offers a radical critique of contemporary materialism and political economy. It also reflects Scott's own attempts to establish philanthropic female communities in Bath and, after the death of Lady Barbara, in Hitcham, Suffolk. In 1785, Scott died in Catton, Norwich, ordering all her papers to be destroyed. NBP

Scoundrel Time (1976) The third and final volume of LILLIAN HELLMAN's autobiography. It is a personal account of her tangled and triumphant involvement in the 1950s American witch-hunt known as McCarthyism, which had begun with the House Un-American Activities Committee. It was before this Committee that Hellman was subpoenaed to testify in 1952, and although the letter she addressed to the Chairman was refused, copies were circulated to the press and inserted in the Congressional Record, and it became a manifesto of protest, a battle cry: 'I cannot and will not cut my conscience to fit this year's fashion.' *Scoundrel Time* is filled with intimate, amusing detail – her purchase of a Balmain dress for her appearance before the Committee; her confession, on a visit to the zoo, 'I always wanted to go to bed with an orang outan'; her nicknames for McCarthy and his pretty assistants (Roy Cohn and David Schine), 'Bonnie, Bonnie and Clyde'. If it is sometimes self-serving and questionable on matters of fact, it is nonetheless a book that jolts a disgraceful time vividly into memory. TC

Scovell, Edith (Joy) 1907– British poet Edith Scovell was born in Sheffield and educated at Casterton School, Westmoreland, and Somerville College, Oxford. She then worked in London as a secretary and in journalism. In 1937 she married the distinguished ecologist Charles Elton and had two children. She travelled in later years in the rain forests of northern Brazil and Panama, working as field assistant to her husband, and has several times visited the West Indies. Of a generation of fine poets which includes KATHLEEN RAINE and SHEILA WINGFIELD – and Auden and MacNeice (both b.1907) – Scovell has emerged in high regard as a poet relatively late in life.

Favourable notice was given to earlier work – she was regarded by Geoffrey Grigson as 'the purest of women poets of our time', and *The River Steamer* (1956) was a Poetry Book Society Recommendation. But the passing of time between that volume and her next, *The Space Between* (1982), slowed her reputation. Simply, Scovell had made her own terms with poetry. She has published only four collections, her first in 1944 though she started writing in the 1920s. Her talent was neither for sophisticated fireworks nor for the prevailing neo-Romantic verse of the 1940s. She is a reflective poet, sometimes metaphysical, always with a deft sense of how rhythm carries imagery and argument. Scovell has written of her poems: 'I should like the surface to be entirely clear, and the meaning to be entirely implicit.' A pamphlet-length volume, *Listening to Collared Doves*, appeared in 1986.

She received a Cholmondeley Award in 1989 for her *Collected Poems* (1988). DM

Sea, The Sea, The (1978) IRIS MURDOCH's Booker-Prize-winning novel uses one of her favourite devices – the unreliable male narrator – to construct the voluble monologue of 60-year-old theatrical man Charles Arrowby. At its centre are the events and emotions sparked off when he re-encounters his adolescent love, Hartley, now living with her husband in the coastal village where he has, at the outset, retired to write his memoirs. Aesthete, game-player, tyrant and misogynist, Arrowby struggles to overcome his narcissism and connect meaningfully with the lives of others, whose wishes may not be the same as his. The novel adeptly mixes styles and concerns: messy, comic and, at times, camp REALISM (he lives at 'Shruff End', she at 'Nibletts', pages are spent detailing his favourite recipes); melodramatic plotting; eruptions of the unconscious, as when he sees monsters rising from the sea; and Murdoch's ongoing philosophical concerns with the meaning of the good life and the (limited) power of art to bring order to existence. Her aesthetic of imperfection is here beautifully realized, since little or nothing is actually resolved. MO'D

Seacole, Mary (Mary Jane Grant) 1805–81 Born in Kingston, Jamaica, to a Scottish army officer and a free black business-woman, Seacole gained widespread fame in her lifetime for her humanitarian and medical services to the British Army in the Crimean War (1854–6). Her efforts, for which she is often compared to FLORENCE NIGHTINGALE, earned her the titles of 'Mother Seacole' and 'the Creole Doctress'. The autobiographical account of her extensive travels through the Caribbean, Latin America, the United States and Europe, and of her medical work during the Crimean War, *The Wonderful Adventures of Mrs Seacole in Many Lands* (1857), was an instant success, going into multiple printings in the year following its publication. The main thrust of her autobiographical narrative is her celebration of a freedom to travel – and to define herself professionally as a skilled practitioner of medical arts combining European, African and West Indian healing practices – that moves her away from her marginal status as a mulatto woman from the colonized periphery of Jamaica toward fame and celebrity at the very centre of British imperial government and power. The text – despite its acceptance of the superiority of British values, its occasional snobbery, its prejudices against native Americans and other marginalized groups, and its glorification of war – remains one of the most important personal accounts written by a West Indian woman in the 19th century.   LP-G

Second Sex, The (1949) SIMONE DE BEAUVOIR's ambitious work of philosophical and literary imagination uses an existentialist framework (somewhat obscured in the English translation) to argue that women have as much right as men to 'freedom'. What prevents them is internalization: 'bad faith'. The book's mode is transformative, aimed at the demystification of internalization so that women can act to confer meaning upon their existence. Beauvoir splits the analysis into two. Book 1, surveying biology, history, economics, psychoanalysis and literature, is concerned with the self–other hierarchy: with Woman as the 'other' that sustains the fiction of male superiority. Book 2 is concerned with the 'becoming' of woman in her individual life-cycle from childhood to maturity. Using a *bricolage* of case-studies, historical narrative, literary examples and personal anecdotes – and wonderfully incisive on the murder-inducing frustrations of housework and stifling pieties of bourgeois marriage – Beauvoir radically claims that the philosophical is inescapably social, political, embodied. Although embodiment is more problematic for women than for men, Beauvoir insists that what woman *might* become can never be known in advance. Hence her refusal to name – let alone glorify – a prior female specificity. Her horrifying descriptions of female sexuality can be read against the grain as citational: ironic repetitions that demystify the myths that have kept women in their place.   REv

Secret Garden, The (1911) FRANCES HODGSON BURNETT's novel for children focuses on Mary Lennox, a disagreeable and neglected Anglo-Indian orphan who is sent to Yorkshire to live with her reclusive widowed uncle. There she meets her spoiled invalid cousin, Colin, and the children, despite (well-founded) initial mutual dislike, become friends. Burnett's use of uncongenial children as protagonists broke with the conventions of CHILDREN'S LITERATURE; though both children eventually become more

likeable, the novel escapes the worst excesses of Victorian and Edwardian sentimentality. This is not to say, however, that Burnett eschews all sentiment. Mary and Colin cultivate a garden that seems to them magical, and in so doing cure themselves: Colin learns to walk, Mary becomes pleasant, and between them they help Colin's father to recover from the long-ago death of his beloved wife. Burnett's prescription for children – plenty of fresh air, a 'bit of earth' to till, and no pampering – was perhaps ahead of its time, but it is probably the combination of such commonsense with whimsy that accounts for the book's continuing popularity.   KW

Secret Memoirs and Manners of Several Persons of Quality, of Both Sexes from the New Atalantis, an Island in the Mediterranean (2 parts, 1709) This controversial *roman à clef* and fierce Tory satire caused its author, DELARIVIÈRE MANLEY, to be briefly imprisoned. It tells the story of two goddesses, Virtue and Astrea, who, guided by Lady Intelligence, are initiated into the Atalantian aristocratic society and manners. Astrea seeks to improve her knowledge of humankind in all its virtues and vices in order to be a better instructor to the Prince of the Moon. The two goddesses encounter a society which is dominated by personal and public corruption, orgies, seductions, rapes and deceit. Whilst Manley employed pseudonyms and sold the book as a mere translation, contemporaries, aided by separately published keys, quickly identified the members of the Whig establishment. The book was so popular that Manley published a sequel, *Memoirs of Europe, Towards the Close of the Eighth Century* in 1710 and inspired other writers such as ELIZA HAYWOOD and Daniel Defoe to produce other 'secret histories'.   NBP

Sedgwick, Catharine Maria 1789–1867 American novelist. One of thirteen children, born in Stockbridge, Massachusetts, to a prominent Federalist family, Sedgwick was educated and lived in Boston, Albany and New York City. She remained single, devoted to her four brothers, who encouraged and promoted her literary career. From her first ROMANCE, *A New England Tale: Sketches of New-England Character and Manners* (1822), in which she hoped to 'add something to the scanty stock of native American literature', and which features a sympathetic Quaker family, Sedgwick became a pivotal figure in the formation of an American national literature and one of the most renowned writers of her day. In HOPE LESLIE: OR, EARLY TIMES IN MASSACHUSETTS (1827) and *The Linwoods: Or, Sixty Years Since in America* (1835), she adapted the HISTORICAL and regional NOVEL of Sir Walter Scott to the American scene. But in the figure of Hope Leslie's powerful Pequod woman, Magawisca, and in the Indian–white marriage of two central characters in that novel, Sedgwick expresses racial views radically at odds with the prevailing white fantasy of the 'Vanishing American'. Breaking with the elitism of her childhood, Sedgwick devoted several books to 'farmers and mechanics', promoting democratic virtues and homely morality. Generically hybrid, such works as *Home* (1835), *The Poor Rich Man, and the Rich Poor Man* (1836) and *Live and Let Live: Or, Domestic Service Illustrated* (1837), are grown-up versions of the children's stories she admired by ANNA LAETITIA BARBAULD and MARIA EDGEWORTH: characters given ethical challenges to prove their mettle and display moral lessons. A straightforward conduct manual, *Means and Ends, or Self-Training* (1839), is often cited by her contemporaries as a guide for girls. While no activist for women's rights, neither is she a conventional ideologue of domesticity. Her somewhat paradoxical position is that rights will arrive when women become qualified for them by education: then 'they cannot long be withheld from you'. Though her last novel, *Married or Single?* (1857), resolves in a conventional marriage plot, Sedgwick herself remained single, and independent, strong-willed women recur throughout her work.   PCr

Catharine Maria Sedgwick.

Seduction and Betrayal (1974)

Seduction and Betrayal (1974) A collection of essays by ELIZABETH HARDWICK, whose common subject is indicated by the book's sub-title, 'Women and Literature'. Hardwick's critical style is anecdotal, cultured and sustained by perceptive acts of reading. Her method is eclectic, ranging from a family biography of the BRONTËS to studies of Ibsen's women, the poetry of SYLVIA PLATH, and the passions of DOROTHY WORDSWORTH and JANE CARLYLE. She provides a prescient and acerbic critique of the English fascination with the Bloomsbury group in an essay which brings out Hardwick's own ambivalent relation to VIRGINIA WOOLF's fiction. The concluding essay, which gives the book its title, is a brilliant meditation on one of the central plots of the novel. Hardwick writes with equal fascination about the psychology of the seducer and that of the seduced woman. She shows how stories about seduction are the strange meeting point for imagining women as victims and as heroines, for understanding their power as well as their oppression. Her tone in dealing with this vexed cultural material is at once elegiac and ironic. Hardwick knows how much suffering can get into literature and how much can get left out.   JCo

Selden, Catherine

Selden, Catherine fl. 1797–1817 Irish novelist. Selden was the author of seven novels, most of which were published by Minerva Press. Her first work was *The English Nun* (1797). This related the story of Lady Louisa Percy, a beautiful and aristocratic Catholic, who renounces her Protestant lover in order to enter a Portuguese convent. Hearing of her lover's death, she declares her wish to join him, and shortly afterwards 'breathed her last, displaying even in the moment of closing life, the same sweet and placid composure of soul, and pious resignation, which she had ever shown in the midst of all her calamities'.

Selden's other novels included *Serena* (1800), which exposed women's vulnerability to exploitation inside and outside marriage but feared that education would make them less 'docile and agreeable', and *German Letters* (1804), which describes in EPISTOLARY form the trials and ultimate triumph of the saintly Adelheide, who leaves her home and child to nurse her disgraced sister, Camilla, pregnant by Adelheide's own husband: 'At length, this horrible scene terminated in the birth of her child, but her frame was so exhausted by her sufferings, that she only survived long enough to know me, and to receive from me, not only the most solemn assurance of my perfect forgiveness, but my promise to befriend the infant she left behind her.' Adelheide subsequently returns to her husband, together with 'the orphan child of Camilla, which she has named after herself'. Selden's other works included *Villa Nova* (1805) and *Villa Santelle: Or The Curious Impertinent* (1817), a GOTHIC novel with elements of comedy.   RR

Self-Control (1811)

Self-Control (1811) MARY BRUNTON's first novel centres on the relentless pursuit of the virtuous Laura by the superficially attractive but morally reprobate Hargrave. Although Laura bears many hallmarks of the sentimental heroine, the novel (like many at the time) explicitly ridicules affected SENSIBILITY and dissociates itself from the increasingly unfashionable cult. Laura's idolization of Hargrave ends when he attempts to seduce her and, although he subsequently proposes marriage, she wishes to wait until time proves his amendment. Time, however, proves Hargrave irredeemable and Laura's Christian conscience revolts against marriage with him, her determination in rejecting all persuasion from either Hargrave himself or her aunt, Lady Pelham, showing an independence of purpose that at times seems almost liberated. Yet the novel also acquiesces in conservative views on female conduct, advocating modesty, domestic virtue and selflessness as the *desiderata* of female existence. In an irresistibly far-fetched *dénouement*, Hargrave has Laura abducted and taken to the Canadian wilderness, from where she makes a heroic escape downriver in a canoe, returning to her native Scotland and marriage with the virtuous De Courcy.

GS

Senior, Olive 1941– Anna Rutherford, reviewing Olive Senior's SUMMER LIGHTNING AND OTHER STORIES in 1986 wrote: 'This is the most exciting collection of short stories to come out of the Caribbean for a very long time'. That collection was to win the first Commonwealth Writers Prize and has been read all over the English-speaking world. It has been translated into Dutch with selected stories translated into Spanish, German and Russian.

Senior's second collection, *Arrival of the Snake Woman and Other Stories* (1989), and her third, *Discerner of Hearts And Other Stories* (1995), have lived up to the promise of the first and have kept readers alternately laughing and crying as she continues to look at universal features of life illustrated by the Jamaican experience – frequently from a child's point of view, always with an honesty of vision and precision of word that are hallmarks of the style of both her prose and her poetry. There are two collections of poems: *Talking of Trees* (1986) and *Gardening in the Tropics* (1994).

Olive Senior was born and grew up in rural Jamaica and her stories and poems reflect her great love for, and appreciation of, the Jamaican countryside and her concern for the life of the people.

She studied Journalism at Carleton University, Ottawa, realizing a dream she had always had. 'At a very early age for some strange reason, I decided I was going to be a journalist. I am not sure I knew what a journalist was but I knew that writing was somewhere in my future.' Her life as a journalist began when as a high school student she worked part-time for the *Daily Gleaner*. She joined the staff when she left school; after university she worked as a freelance journalist and researcher and later as editor of prestigious academic and cultural journals in Jamaica. In 1990 she went to live in Toronto, Canada. VEP

sensation novel This was a fictional sub-genre which flourished in the 1860s. Seen by many contemporary commentators as a symptom of cultural degeneracy, sensation fiction drew its plots from the real-life dramas played out in the Divorce Courts following the passing of the Matrimonial Causes Act (1857) – e.g. the Yelverton bigamy–divorce case – and from trials concerning crimes of passion and domestic violence – e.g. the Madeline Smith and Constance Kent murder trials – which were reported in the highly sensationalized journalism popular in the 1860s. Another contemporary press sensation which was reproduced in sensation novels was a series of investigative pieces in *Household Words* on the ease with which men could effect the incarceration in lunatic asylums of their 'disturbed' or 'difficult' female relatives.

Bestselling sensation novels, such as Wilkie Collins's *The Woman in White* (1860), MARY ELIZABETH BRADDON'S *LADY AUDLEY'S SECRET* (1862) and MRS HENRY WOOD'S *EAST LYNNE* (1861), caused a sensation with reviewers as well as readers. Unknown as a generic term until the early 1860s, 'sensation' (or 'sensational') became an established part of the reviewer's vocabulary during the 1860s and into the 1870s. Wilkie Collins, Charles Dickens, Charles Reade, Mary Elizabeth Braddon, Mrs Henry Wood, OUIDA (Marie Louise de la Ramée), RHODA BROUGHTON, CHARLOTTE ELIZA RIDDELL, AMELIA EDWARDS, FLORENCE MARRYAT, Helen Reeves, and Sheridan Le Fanu were all discussed (and often dismissed) as sensation novelists. For contemporaries, 'sensation' designates an affective mode of address and reading experience: the sensation novel was said to 'preach to the nerves' and to produce effects in the body. 'Sensation' also denotes a particular fictional content – murder, adultery, bigamy, blackmail, false imprisonment, deception, duplicity and fraud – and a range of special structural and formal devices or effects: the subordination of character to plot; the prolongation of suspense and narrative secrecy; a generic hybridity which mixes DOMESTIC realism with the fantastic, the journalistic with the exotic and/or with the GOTHIC horror or ROMANCE.

The sensation novel has a complex genealogy (and legacy). Its progenitors were (variously) the 'silver fork' novel of fashionable high life, the 'Newgate novel' of criminal low life, the Gothic romance, and the stage melodrama. The Gothic, with its characteristic focus on the domestic imprisonment of women, and melodrama – with its intensification of the emotions, moral polarization, and focus on female vulnerability – are among the dominant modes of the female sensationalists. Several sensation novels were adapted for the stage, and *Lady Audley's Secret* and *East Lynne* have remained part of the repertoire of the stage melodrama.

Dismissed by many contemporary critics as a feminized popular culture form, the sensation novel has gained a greater critical prominence since the late 1970s. Recent debates on the sensation novel have focused on its relationship to REALISM (whether it constitutes a challenge to realism, or is merely symptomatic of a crisis within realism), and on the degree to which it can be appropriated for feminism. Focusing on the women sensationalists' display of female sexuality, and of assertive or transgressive behaviour in their heroines or villainesses, some critics have sought to argue that the women's sensation novel is a subversive form which expresses women's covert anger at the injustices of their lot. Others have focused on the way in which the women's sensation novel manages and contains its transgressive heroines and dangerous feminine feeling.   LP

Sense and Sensibility (1811) JANE AUSTEN's first published novel, originally conceived as *Elinor and Marianne* in 1795, opposes the Romantic notion that powerful feelings are the best guide to behaviour to an Augustan endorsement of thought and judgement as pre-eminent virtues. This opposition is embodied in practical, sensible and prudent Elinor Dashwood and her sister Marianne, who is romantic, headstrong and disposed to exhibit all her feelings in public. The two girls and their widowed mother live in reduced circumstances in Devonshire, after their selfish stepbrother John Dashwood (with the support of his grasping and contemptuous wife) reneges on his promise to provide for them. The plot turns on the unexpressed admiration of Elinor for John Dashwood's subdued and initially unavailable brother, Edward Ferrars, and Marianne's passion for the dashing but ultimately calculating Willoughby who throws her over in favour of a legacy. In the end Elinor's lack of display reveals her to feel all the more deeply, while Marianne's self-indulgence proves a burden to her family and a wholly unreliable guide to conduct.   SAS

sensibility A complex interrelationship of physiological and mental qualities, of central importance within 18th-century culture. Rooted in the sensational psychology of John Locke and in medical discourse about the nervous system, the notion of sensibility centred on susceptibility to stimuli. Unlike the rival discourse of reason, which was based on the idea of strong minds in strong bodies, both considered masculine, that of sensibility associated quick intelligence, emotional sensitivity and physical vulnerability, encouraging a new emphasis on the value of feminine qualities. The growth of sensibility was a feature of the increasing refinement of middle- and upper-class life in the period, and its influence can be seen in the rising public value attached to domesticity, childhood and a compassionate interest in human and animal life. It provided a rationale for the softening of male manners that attended the growth of bourgeois society.

Influential throughout the 18th century, sensibility was most fashionable during the latter half, when it pervaded literature. HANNAH MORE addressed a poem to 'Sweet Sensibility', while in *The Man of Feeling* (1771), a novel whose fragmented structure mimetically conveys the disordered nature of emotion, Henry Mackenzie created a hero too sensitive for earthly existence. In Sterne's *A Sentimental Journey* (1768), Yorick's sensibility is a self-indulgent search for erotic and emotional stimulation, mocked yet shared by the author. The ambiguous mingling of physical and spiritual feelings is caught in Yorick's mourning for Father Lorenzo: 'upon pulling out his little horn box, as I sat by his grave, and plucking up a nettle or two at the head of it . . . they all struck together so forcibly upon my affections, that I burst into a flood of tears'.

The social and political significance of sensibility has been much debated. It is viewed as socially conservative because it institutes an aristocracy of feeling that mirrors the social hierarchy – peasants being considered immune to the delicate distresses that afflict their superiors; or democratic because of its emphasis on the ties of sympathy binding all humanity. Anti-authoritarian when it puts individual feeling above social convention as a behavioural guide, it is quietist in its glamorization of passive suffering. Allied to an optimistic sentimentalism, it promotes a view of humanity as naturally benevolent and gregarious; but the feeling individual is typically isolated and vulnerable in a hostile world. Its particular significance for women is similarly multiple. Sensibility's affinities with the developing ideology of femininity promoted female social authority on limiting terms of delicacy and propriety, and feminine sensibility was arguably most valued when displayed by men. Sensibility encouraged women writers, authorizing them as experts on the finer feelings. At the same time it reinforced the idea that women lacked reason. In *A VINDICATION OF THE RIGHTS OF WOMAN* (1792) MARY WOLLSTONECRAFT pointed out that to define women by a quality belonging to the animal body, not the rational mind, ultimately denied them the immortal souls of full human beings: 'And what is sensibility? "Quickness of sensation, quickness of perception, delicacy." Thus is it defined by Dr Johnson; and the definition gives me no other idea than of the most exquisitely polished instinct. I discern not a trace of the image of God in either sensation or matter.' The high value placed on sensibility was always qualified by an awareness of its links with weakness, and excessive sensibility was seen as physically and morally debilitating. By the end of the 18th century, sensibility had been mocked out of fashion; but many of its elements continued into Romanticism, which gave a more masculine image, and more valued cultural place, to what Keats called 'a life of sensations rather than of thoughts'.   JSp

Serious Money (1987) CARYL CHURCHILL prefaces her 'City Comedy' (the ironic sub-title) with an excerpt from Thomas Shadwell's *The Volunteers or the Stockjobbers* (1692), establishing that the 'main end' of the fledgling share market is 'to turn the penny', irrespective of all other considerations. In the post-Big-Bang dealing rooms, billions in every form of currency and commodity are 'turned' legally and illegally, during the breakneck action of Churchill's play, by rapacious traders fuelled by champagne and cocaine. Gender and class distinctions become irrelevant; success is the only criterion, the crudest sexual language the universal form of expression. The state of the British economy is symbolized by a take-over bid by an international cartel for the deliberately unsubtly named Albion Products, a company hampered by 'old-fashioned and paternal management'. To the Brechtian model of dialectical theatre, Churchill adds the further alienation effect of rhyming dialogue, highlighting the artificiality of the world due to collapse, as she foresees, on 'Black Monday' seven months after the play's first performance.

Serious Money won the 1987 Laurence Olivier Award for Best New Play.   WAP

Serious Proposal to the Ladies: Parts I and II, A (1694 and 1697) The first part of MARY ASTELL's anonymously published tract, *For the Advancement of their True and Greatest Interest*, proposes the foundation of a 'monastery' or 'religious retirement' for the education of gentlewomen. The most famous of the numerous contemporaneous proposals for women's education in England, the work outlined both the reasons such instruction was required, including the faults it should correct, and many of the general particulars of the proposed school.

The second part of the proposal, *Wherein a Method is offer'd for the Improvement of their Minds*, was written when the first resulted in discussion and debate, but not the proposed academy; Astell reiterates her arguments about the faults of uneducated women and offers instruction – heavily influenced by Descartes – in rhetoric and logic. The main focus of the work, however, is to argue, through means of Cartesian epistemology, for women's intellectual capacity, and to outline the moral and Christian philosophy upon which such an academy should be based.   MCJ

Seton, Elizabeth Ann Bayley 1775–1821 American religious writer, founder of the Catholic Order of the Sisters of Charity, and first American-born Catholic saint. Elizabeth Ann Bayley was born into a well-to-do Anglican family in New York and in 1794 married William Seton. In 1803, the Setons travelled to Italy in order to relieve William's tuberculosis; there, Elizabeth Seton wrote letters and JOURNAL entries revealing her deeply held religious convictions. After his death, she remained in Italy with the devoutly Catholic Filicchi family, who encouraged Elizabeth to convert to Catholicism. Her spiritual struggles before her 1805 conversion, described in letters to Bishop John Carroll of Baltimore and to Antonio Filicchi, reveal her desire for instruction: 'rather pray for me than reproach me – for indeed I make every endeavour to think as you wish me to, and it is only the obstinate resistance of my mind that prevents my immediately doing also as you wish me to'. In 1808, with the support of Baltimore clergy, she opened a school for girls and subsequently established the motherhouse for the Order of the Sisters of Charity in Emmitsburg, Pennsylvania. Her writings from this later period include letters, journals, 'Reflections' and instructions for meditation and service for the women of her order.   LCa

Seven Gothic Tales (1934) ISAK DINESEN is one of the author identities of Karen Blixen, created for this début collection of tales. Dinesen – writing during the inter-war Depression – sets her characters at the dawning of the modern age, the period of original GOTHIC and of the French Revolution. There are no supernatural horrors, we are on the stage of the *Theatro Mundi* where externalized selves ('the dandy') celebrate the gaiety of vision. Moments of sublimity arrive when melancholic reality is banished by kaleidoscopic changes of identity in a *fantaisie macabre*: transvestites, female impersonators and Donna Quixottas burst out in a carnivalesque laughter. The Cardinal in 'The Deluge at Norderney' declares what is fallen is not man but the divinity: this is where the bodies of flamboyant super-women come in, to give us a relief from the stale, depressive habits of representation.   CY

Seven Little Australians (1894) ETHEL TURNER's first and best-known novel is this still popular CHILDREN'S STORY, which recounts the adventures of the children of the authoritarian Captain Woolcot. Only the baby, called 'the General', is the son of the Captain's 20-year-old wife, Esther. With an ineffectual stepmother, absent father and seven lively children, their rambling old Sydney house is aptly nicknamed 'Misrule'. Adventures range from the romantic awakenings of the eldest, 16-year-old Meg, through the antics of gentle Baby, greedy Bunty, pretty Nellie, and eldest brother, Pip. The liveliest, smartest, funniest and most disobedient of the family is 13-year-old Judy, who is sent to boarding school for her misdemeanours, runs away, walks seventy-seven miles home, contracts a serious respiratory ailment, and is thus allowed to stay. To the outrage of generations of Australian children, during Christmas holidays in the bush the rebellious Judy is crushed when she rescues the General from a falling tree. The closing chapters describe her death and the sad aftermath. The novel has three sequels.   SKM

Seven Poor Men of Sydney (1934) CHRISTINA STEAD's first novel, published in London soon after her début with *The Salzburg Tales*, was the only book of hers to be set entirely in Australia. It proved unpopular with some critics, including MILES FRANKLIN: 'Miss Stead has selected a gallery of ne'er-do-wells, with failure inherent in each for lack of inborn grit'. This radical novel was, in Stead's words, an attempt to relate the complexities of ordinary life against a backdrop of economic and spiritual depression: '[It] is not so much a novel, I suppose, as a cast of characters battling through daily life, as much passion being expelled on the small accidents of daily life as on any one of the great tragic themes'. It reveals concerns which would reappear throughout her writing-life: characters – inward-looking, intense, steeped in fantasy – rooted firmly in their social realities; experimentation with new narrative forms and highly poetic monologues. The seven poor men of the title – three printers, their press-owner, plus three other friends – are given to detailed philosophical arguments concerning their (thwarted) personal condition. Yet there is much wit and humour – traces of Dickens – and a dark almost Lawrentian sensuality.   MRE

Severed Head, A (1961) IRIS MURDOCH's fifth novel is a witty study of the emergence of psychoanalysis as one of the dominant belief systems of the 20th century. It tells the story of Martin Lynch-Gibbon, a wealthy middle-aged wine merchant who is married to a beautiful, accomplished and slightly older woman, Antonia, but also engaged in an affair with Georgie Hands, a 26-year-old economist. As the novel opens, Antonia announces that she has fallen in love with her psychoanalyst, the charismatic Palmer Anderson. In a parody of the therapeutic process, Martin is encouraged by Antonia and Palmer to work through his feelings of betrayal, jealousy and revenge by becoming part of a bizarre *ménage à trois* with them. Over against them, however, stands Palmer's half-sister, Honor Klein, an anthropologist who constantly urges Martin to give vent to his feelings of anger and abandonment, and with whom he eventually falls in love. The narrative fuses Freudian themes with the imagery of myth and war, as the characters play out Murdoch's ever-present concern with self-knowledge and self-deception, truth and falsehood and, ultimately, good and evil.   AC

Seward, Anna 1742–1809 Poet and letter-writer, she spent most of her life caring for her father, Thomas, Canon of Lichfield Cathedral and minor poet. His epistolary poem, 'The Female Right to Literature', advocated the education of women and was anthologized by Dodsley in 1748. Her maternal grandfather taught Samuel Johnson at Lichfield Grammar School. Anna later accused Johnson of misogyny in the *Gentleman's Magazine*, under the pseudonym 'Benvolio'. Anna's early literary efforts impressed Erasmus Darwin, influential member of the Lunar Society, who encouraged her to develop her skill. 'Colebrook Dale' (*Poetical Works*, 1810) reveals her interest in industrial and scientific change. Her style was melancholic, elaborate and, according to some contemporary critics, artificial.

Seward honed her craft at the provincial salon of Anne, Lady Miller, who held regular 'poetical assemblies' at Batheaston. Professional success began with her *Elegy on Captain Cook* (1780), which went into four editions in as many years. She regarded *Louisa, a Poetical Novel* (1784) as 'the best and ablest of my productions'. While experimental in structure, its plot is typical of the literature of SENSIBILITY, privileging passion over the power of 'attractive commerce'. *Llangollen Vale* (1796) describes a visit to the two Ladies of Llangollen, and *Original Sonnets on Various Subjects* (1799) asserts her role in the revival of the form, in which her chief rival was CHARLOTTE SMITH. Her *Memoirs of the Life of Dr Darwin* (1804) provide an important record of the cultural life of the Midlands Enlightenment, in which she played a central role encouraging young writers. Admirers of Seward, 'the Swan of Lichfield', included Wordsworth and Sir Walter Scott, who edited her *Poetical Works* in 1810.   ESE

Sewell, Anna 1820–78 English writer whose only book, *BLACK BEAUTY*, is one of the most enduring of CHILDREN'S CLASSICS. Born in Great Yarmouth, Norfolk, into a Quaker family, Sewell was largely educated at home. A brief period at school was ended in her early teens when she injured her ankles in a fall, leaving her permanently lame and dependent upon horses for transport. She also suffered from a debilitating semi-invalidism, perhaps depressive illness, which induced periods of 'enforced idleness'. Apart from visits to spas in England and abroad to improve her health, or holidays with Norfolk relatives, she lived her entire life with her parents in various English towns including Brighton, Bath and Old Catton near Norwich. She was very close to her mother, MARY SEWELL, who in her sixties became known as a writer of didactic verse for workers and children. Anna worked as her mother's unofficial editor. Both women were involved in the temperance movement and in setting up a Working Men's Evening Institute at which Anna taught. She was deeply religious and struggled through periods of religious doubt. She retained Quaker habits and beliefs throughout her life but, like her mother, experimented with other Protestant denominations. Her religious beliefs are evident in *Black Beauty* which contains a strong anti-cruelty message. Sewell wrote the novel during her final six years when she was suffering further illness which largely confined her to her sofa. In part the novel was dictated to her mother and in part written in pencil on slips of paper which her mother transcribed. Sold outright for £20, *Black Beauty* was published in 1877 just a few months before Sewell's death and quickly became popular.   AEG

Sewell, Elizabeth Missing 1815–1906 British children's writer (see CHILDREN'S BOOKS). The third daughter of a solicitor, Elizabeth was sent to school in Bath. The Sewell family was religious and strict. In 1840, her brother William introduced her to the leaders of the Oxford Movement: Keble, Henry Wilberforce and Newman. William later converted to Catholicism, but Elizabeth remained a committed High Church Anglican, and her beliefs clearly underpin her writing. The family fell into debt and, after her father's death in 1842, Sewell used her rapidly increasing literary earnings to pay off creditors. Her 1844 *Amy Herbert* was a great success, and she followed it with *Laneton Parsonage* in 1846 and *Margaret Perceval* in 1847. Her most popular book, T*he Experience of Life*, came out in 1852, and *Ursula, A Tale of Country Life*, proved another success in 1868. Most of her stories follow the development of female protagonists, and, unusually, celebrate female experience other than the romantic, although they tend toward pious and conventional endings. A great champion of women's education, she and her sister Ellen took in female pupils and she also published didactic works such as *Preparation for Holy Communion* (1864) and *Historical Selections*, the latter with her friend, CHARLOTTE YONGE.   CPe

Sewell [née Wright], Mary 1797–1884 British author of moral ballads and didactic fiction. She was born in Suffolk to a Quaker family, and became a schoolteacher before marrying Isaac Sewell when she was 22. By this marriage she became the sister-in-law and friend of SARAH STICKNEY ELLIS [Mrs. Ellis], and the mother of ANNA SEWELL who wrote *Black Beauty*. Sewell's early married life was spent in straitened circumstances, which perhaps influenced the empathy her ballads show with poverty. She left the Quakers but retained her simple Christian faith which formed the basis for all her writing. Her interest in liberal education for young children can be seen in *The Life and Letters of Mrs Sewell*, by Mrs Bayly (1889). In her sixtieth year Sewell began to write the 'Homely Ballads' for which she became celebrated, and which sold in con-

siderable numbers. These poems, written in simple language, convey moral messages with singular sweetness.   HST-M

Sexing the Cherry (1989) Far from conventional HISTORICAL FICTION, JEANETTE WINTERSON's experimental fourth novel calls into question concepts of history, narrative and time. Principally set in 17th-century London, at the height of the Civil War, the novel is narrated by Dog Woman – an immense Rabelaisian figure with a commensurate lust for life – and her adopted son, Jordan. Dog Woman's allegiances are firmly with the King, and she is an outspoken advocate of the 'sins of excess [rather] than sins of denial', violently and comically exposing the snivelling hypocrisies of Preacher Scroggs. Jordan's encounter with John Tradescant, gardener to the King and bearer of exotic fruit, leads him to voyage far afield, both on ship and in his mind. With pithily subversive retellings of FAIRY TALE interwoven along the way, the characters rupture the fabric of time, discovering their 20th-century selves: a boy obsessed with boats and an environmental campaigner. A POSTMODERN *tour de force*, *Sexing the Cherry* juggles alternative ideologies and identities in an extravagantly daring style.   CS

Sexton, Anne 1928–74 American poet. Anne Gray Harvey was born in Newton, Massachusetts, to R.C. Harvey, who owned a wool manufacturing company, and his wife, Mary Gray Harvey. Stunning in high school and thereafter, with the large blue eyes, dark hair and long-legged slimness noted by everyone who knew and has written about her, Anne fled a Boston finishing school and another fiancé to elope, at 19, with Alfred 'Kayo' Sexton. For the first years of their marriage the Sextons were separated: Kayo went to war in Korea, and Anne worked as a lingerie saleswoman and sometime model until the birth of their first child, Linda, in 1953. A second daughter, Joyce (Joy), was born in 1955. Following Joy's birth, Sexton went into a deep postpartum depression that led to her spending much of the late 1950s in hospitals or in treatment. Her children were raised by family members; when left alone by her husband, on one of his many long business trips, Sexton took an overdose of Nembutal on her 28th birthday, in 1956. In May 1957, Sexton again attempted suicide, but began writing poetry as she recovered.

Sexton's style was, from the beginning and through the majority of her work, 'CONFESSIONAL'. Other major American poets of the 1950s and 1960s, most notably John Berryman, Robert Lowell and SYLVIA PLATH, shared this uncensored, image-laden, tell-all style. By 1959, Sexton had begun to study with Lowell at Boston University – Plath was also in his class, and the two women became friends – and was publishing in *Harper's*, the *Hudson Review* and the *New Yorker*. Her first collection of poems, *To Bedlam and Part Way Back*, came out in 1960, followed in 1962 by *All My Pretty Ones*.

Poets who criticized her, as dissimilar as James Dickey and ELIZABETH BISHOP, objected to Sexton's poems about her literal, physical self ('Menstruation at Forty', for example, upset Dickey), and to their general egocentricity. These opinions were in a minority. Her collections sold extremely well, and her public readings were standing-room only. Sexton's own performance of her poems swiftly became legendary: the A-line dresses in vibrant colours and patterns; the perpetual cigarette; the voice, rising and sinking through the chronicling of the poet's own life, body and experiences. In 1966 Sexton completed *Live or Die* for which she won the Pulitzer Prize for Poetry the following year.

New works flowed; Sexton published a volume every two years. The sarcastic revisions of fables and FAIRY TALES in *Transformations*, and the feminist poems ('The Wifebeater') and religious visions and critiques ('The Jesus Papers') of *The Book of Folly* moved beyond Sexton's earlier confessional work. Her last volume, *The Awful Rowing Toward God* (1975), is full of poems in a new style for Sexton: shorter lines, hard images of the real and impersonal, a sense of the miraculous instead of personal mortality. See also *The Death Notebooks* (1974).

Living alone in her Massachusetts home, Sexton completed the poems in *The Awful Rowing Toward God* at an amazing speed, writing, on some days, more than three. She corrected the galley proofs of the book on 4 October 1974. Late that afternoon, Sexton took her own life.   AMD

Shadow Knows, The (1975) Set in Sacramento, California, DIANE JOHNSON's novel poses as a DETECTIVE STORY, but is written, oddly, from the point of view of the victim, Mrs Hexam ('hex'em'), who is also a witch, conjuring her assailant from the shadows in order to prove his existence; claustrophobically set in 'the units', the book is at once an acutely observed social novel about class relationships between white middle- and black working-class women, in a world where 'men are loyal to each other and women will do each other in', and an ironic metafictional revisiting of the occult connection between the murderer and the murderee. The price Mrs Hexam pays for being right is to become a 'shadow' herself; a running twist which parodies the Platonic theory of knowledge (the substance that lies beyond the shadows). Expecting murder, Mrs H is raped and, although she greets the event with ironical satisfaction as a final 'proof' that her innermost fearful projections are real, the reader is also allowed, in a worse paradox, to believe the event is merely a statistical occurrence outside the middle-class pale.   VS

Shadows on the Rock (1931) WILLA CATHER wrote that she intended in this novel the effect of 'a series of pictures remembered rather than experienced'. Following a cycle of seasons in late 17th-century Quebec, Cather unfolds a new way of telling COLONIAL history. Much of the narrative reaches us through 12-year old Cécile, the apothecary's daughter, evoking the secular and spiritual adventures of early French-Canadian pioneers, through stories Cécile loves and objects she cherishes. In some ways, the novel presents a conservative version of civilization, where Roman Catholic patriarchs and martyrs, and heroic European traders, struggle with the darkness of the strange continent; and where Cécile will grow up to be the mother of sons, safely preserving the old values in the New World. But this reading is off-set by the focus on strongly individual women, and particularly by the story at the novel's heart, of the anchorite, Jeanne le Ber, who rejects marriage, but is visited by the angels. Cécile hates stories with clear explanations, and Cather keeps her own narrative inconclusive and dream-like, leaving readers with memories of miracles that cut across conventional views of time and progress, and of the vivid details of lives that flicker only briefly on the grey rock.   PEK

Shane, Elizabeth [Gertrude Elizabeth Heron Hine] 1887–1951 Ulster poet, dramatist and musician, who was widely read and, along with MOIRA O'NEILL, considered one of the most important woman dialectical poets of Northern Ireland. Born in Belfast, she lived most of her life in Carrickfergus, County Antrim. Her most well-known play is *The Warming Pan*. Shane's poetry, which was largely about the everyday lives of Ulster people, was very popular in its time. In the introduction to *Tales of the Donegal Coast and Islands* (1921), she explains that her lyrical verses were 'begun without any idea of publication. They were simply written for my own and my "mate's" pleasure.' Certainly her work gives ample evidence of what she described as the 'simple everyday doings of a warm hearted people'. She wrote particularly about the islands and islanders off the Donegal coast and portrayed their lives and the countryside in a somewhat idealized manner. She was interested in Donegal folklore and wove aspects of local tales into her work. Her collected poems were published in 1945. She played first violin for the Belfast Philharmonic Orchestra until her death in 1951.   MSu

Shange, Ntozake 1948– An uncompromising, lyrical American writer whose explosive début in 1976 was *for coloured girls who have considered suicide / when the*

rainbow is enuf, a work of poetry, music and dance which Shange termed a 'choreopoem'. The award-winning piece, a powerful interweaving of the pained and joyful voices of a group of women, had its New York premiére in a Joseph Papp production and became a seminal piece of African-American feminist writing. Her 1978 volume of poems, *Nappy Edges*, was, according to one writer 'as de rigueur for artistically inclined young black girls as SYLVIA PLATH was for white ones'. Shange preferred the word 'coloured' as she felt it more inclusive: in her politics and especially in her aesthetic she aimed to be as broad as possible, considering her multi-disciplinary, collaborative approach to be characteristically African-American. The violent edges of her work earned her criticism, like that directed at ALICE WALKER, for her 'anti-male bias'; while white audiences sometimes resented her black nationalism.

Her two 1980s novels *SASSAFRASS, CYPRESS AND INDIGO* (1982) and *Betsey Brown* (1985) share the multilayered structure and vivid voices of her dramatic work. Other publications include the plays *Three Pieces* (1981) and volumes of poetry *A Daughter's Geography* and *Ridin' the Moon in Texas*. In any medium her work is recognizable for its fierce lyricism, its easy eroticism and her distinctive experiments with the language. She has said, 'I have spent my life undoing the language until it works for me.' She grew up in an artistic household in Trenton, New Jersey (visited by Dizzy Gillespie, among others), and lived and taught on the East coast, in California and in Texas. She has a daughter. In 1994 she published a newly adventurous novel, *Liliane*.   SB

Shapcott, Jo 1953–

British poet who studied at Trinity College Dublin, Oxford and Harvard. She has worked as an English lecturer and education officer and is now a freelance writer, living in London. Shapcott's poise grounds all kinds of disturbance, be it freak weather on the other side of the world or a child wetting herself at her birthday tea. Her cool surrealism is that of imaginative leaps that are also intellectual, presented without fanfare or self-consciousness.

The title poem of *Electroplating the Baby* (1988) is a characteristic combination of the academic and the bizarre, quiet horror and farce, and a restraining touch of homeliness. Like SELIMA HILL, Shapcott has an affinity with the animal world and manages zoomorphism without mawkishness. *Phrasebook* (1992) includes a sequence of poems about a 'Mad Cow', both the disease-struck animal and a disturbing female figure. These ambiguous scenes of comedy and terror, 'I love the staggers', make grim observations about misogyny and female constraint.

Transgression and subversion figure repeatedly. Borders between public and private are as fragile as the body's own bounds. This mess-making is vital, not least as part of the creative process: 'Cuckoo Spit or Ars Poetica' contrasts 'each perfect globe' of froth with the 'lumping larval life' from which it issues.

For Shapcott, the restrictions and potency of language are both subject and technique. Scientists indulge in an orgy of removing labels from bottles in 'Love in the Lab'; 'Phrase Book' interweaves military neologisms and acronyms with the archaisms of a guide for the Englishwoman abroad. She has a gift for dramatic monologues and uses it to iconoclastic effect: 'Superman Sounds Depressed' or 'Brando on Commuting'.

Jo Shapcott is a playful and, at times, intimate presence within her own work. Her light touch is all the more striking for the depth and complexity of the ideas it conveys. Her most recent collection is *My Life Asleep* (1998).   LG

Sheldon, Alice Hastings Bradley [Racoona] see TIPTREE, JAMES

Shelley, Mary (Wollstonecraft) 1797–1851

Daughter of William Godwin and MARY WOLLSTONE-CRAFT, first became a published writer (anonymously) at the age of 20. (The 'Mounseer Nongtongpaw' (1808) published by Godwin is not, except tangentially, her work.) She co-authored *History of a Six Weeks Tour* (1817), based on the journal kept on her elopement to the continent with P.B. Shelley in 1814, and achieved fame with her 'hideous progeny', *FRANKENSTEIN* (1818), offshoot of Byron's proposed 1816 ghost-story writing project. In 1818 the Shelleys (who in 1816 had reluctantly accepted conventional marriage after the suicide of P.B. Shelley's first wife) migrated to Italy. There Mary Shelley experienced the death of their two children, wrote a novella, *Matilda* (first published 1959), and the historical novel, *Valperga* (1823). After P.B. Shelley's drowning, she returned to England (1823) with her surviving son to an uncertain social position and relative poverty, exacerbated by her father-in-law's ban (lifted in 1838) on publishing her late husband's work.

Between 1824 and 1840 Mary Shelley published journal articles, tales for literary annuals, five volumes of well-researched, elegantly written literary biography (1835–9), essential editions of P.B. Shelley's works (1824 and 1839) and four novels: the vituperated, futuristic *THE LAST MAN* (1826) and the better-received *Perkin Warbeck* (1830), *Lodore* (1835) and *Falkner* (1837). Her later literary friendships included Washington Irving, Thomas Moore, Prosper Mérimée, SYDNEY OWENSON, CAROLINE NORTON and Charles Dickens. Her charming, politically engaged travelbook *Rambles in Germany and Italy* (1844) was written partly to benefit an exiled Italian revolutionary. Her last years were rendered painful by illness (probably a brain tumour), happy by her affectionate son and daughter-in-law.

Considered remarkable by contemporaries, Mary Shelley was posthumously interred under the reputation of one-book novelist and devoted widow. Pioneers of her rehabilitation as a complete woman of letters include MURIEL SPARK (1951); Brian Aldiss (1973), who hailed her as founding-mother of SCIENCE FICTION; and ELLEN MOERS (1976), who offered an influential female-centred reading of *Frankenstein*. Her *Letters* (1980–8) and complete *Journals* (1987) revealed both her professionalism and her covert unconventionality (for the latter see MARY DIANA DODS).

Frankenstein, in continuous print since the 1880s, continues to prove infinitely re-interpretable. Her other novels lack its page-turning, mythic qualities, but are intelligent, powerfully conceived fictions; the *British Magazine*'s 1823 characterization of *Valperga* applies to them all: 'energetic language, landscapes worthy of a poet or a painter, feelings strong in their truth'. *The Last Man* speaks tellingly to millenarian anxieties and *Valperga* to sexual-political issues. Recurrent motifs of the dead mother, father–daughter incest, androgyny, Byronic figures and doubles attract psychobiographical interpretations; for some the novels evidence unconsciously self-conflicted attitudes toward bourgeois values and female authorship. Others see in them individual, even subversive, variants on the travel-book, the Godwinian history, the silver-fork novel and the GOTHIC tale. Recent studies attend to their intertextuality, irony, political content, craftedness and centrality as Later Romantic texts. NC

Sheridan, Frances 1724–66 Novelist and playwright, educated in secret by her brothers because her father opposed women's learning, she wrote a first ROMANCE *Eugenia and Adelaide* (1791), in her teens. After publishing a verse fable, *The Owls* (1746), and a pamphlet defending the beleaguered actor/manager of the Dublin Theatre, Thomas Sheridan, she later met and married him in 1747. Moving from Dublin to London, her friend Richardson encouraged her to write THE MEMOIRS OF MISS SIDNEY BIDULPH (1761), which met with immediate critical and popular success (translations in French and German followed). Although the tragic consequences of the heroine's moral virtue caused Dr Johnson to complain that Sheridan made her readers suffer, the novel also provides penetrating and ironic social commentary.

Sheridan's comedy *The Discovery* (1763) was an immediate success, with her husband and Garrick playing leading roles, but *The Dupe* (1763) and *A Journey to Bath* (1902) were unsuccessful although they influenced the plays of her famous son, Richard Brinsley Sheridan. Settling in France, Sheridan wrote a sequel to *Sidney Bidulph* and *The History of Nourjahad* (1767), an oriental

Rom ℥ *9 - 55*

THE LAST MAN.

BY

THE AUTHOR OF FRANKENSTEIN.

IN THREE VOLUMES.

Let no man seek
Henceforth to be foretold what shall befall
Him or his children.
MILTON.

VOL. III.

LONDON:

HENRY COLBURN, NEW BURLINGTON STREET.

1826.

Mary Shelley: title-page of *The Last Man*, 1826.

fable popular when published posthumously. In her biography, Alicia Lefanu represents her mother as delightful company, but stresses the equal balance of her domestic and literary accomplishments. LMT

Sherwood, Mary Martha 1775–1851 English DIARIST, autobiographer and children's writer who travelled to India on her marriage to an army captain and there wrote immensely popular CHILDREN'S BOOKS, which incorporate expert story-telling with evangelism, knowledge of Indian culture and tragic personal experience. *The Indian Pilgrim* (1818) adapts Bunyan, while *Little Henry and his Bearer* (1814) features an

English orphan lovingly reared by an Indian servant, whom he converts to Christianity before his premature death (reminiscent of Sherwood's own son's death). Back in England, she published *The History of the Fairchild Family* (1818–47), again well-written and a bestseller, but later unacceptable due to its doctrinaire harshness. Her diaries give spirited descriptions of a cultured childhood, travels, establishment of schools, adoption of children and a prolific output (over 350 titles). They formed the basis of her autobiography, *The Life and Times of Mrs Sherwood* (eventually published in 1910) and her daughter's adaptation, *Mrs Kelly's Life of Mrs. Sherwood* (1854).   LMT

Shields, Carol 1933– American novelist and short-story writer, born in Chicago and educated at Hanover College, Indiana, spending some of her student and early married life in England. After writing the occasional short story and poem and a thesis on SUSANNA MOODIE, the 19th-century Canadian writer, she published her first novel, SMALL CEREMONIES (1976), about a biographer of Moodie, and concerned with the complex interrelations between fiction and biography – in her forties. *Mary Swann* (1990), the story of the 'construction' of an obscure 19th-century American woman poet by friends, feminists and academe, played with some of the ideas of POSTMODERNIST readings of literature which were later made popular by A.S. BYATT in POSSESSION. *Happenstance* (1991) used two earlier stories of the adventures of a husband and wife apart for a few days to make one novel, in which the two tales are printed back to back. THE STONE DIARIES (1993), again drew on her fascination with the paradoxes of life-writing for a fictitious autobiography published complete with family photographs. This novel which won the Pulitzer Prize for Fiction in 1995, consolidated Shields's international popularity. She now lives in Winnipeg, and has five grown-up sons.   LD

Shikasta (1979) The first in the 'Canopus in Argos: Archives' quintet, this 'space fiction' was seen as a major departure for the previously REALIST DORIS LESSING. Utilizing the traditional SCIENCE FICTION topos of inter-galactic conflict, it concerns the intervention of the benign Canopean emissary Johor (who assumes the human name 'George Sherban') in the destiny of the colony which gives the fiction its title. Shikasta, the 'broken or damaged place', is a fallen Earth deteriorating under the malign influence of Shammat. Eschewing dialogue or conventional characterization in favour of report, record and journal forms (archives), Lessing constructs a mystical apocalyptic allegory informed by sacred texts and myths, most notably those of the Old Testament. This sober jeremiad on humanity's 'last days' was not uniformly

well received, partly on account of its strongly didactic tone; it was, however, critically re-evaluated as each new work in the series appeared. Despite the surprising shift in generic architecture, *Shikasta* clearly contributes much to Lessing's ongoing serious and prophetic concerns, above all with the multi-faceted nature of colonization in the 20th century.   MO'D

Shikibu, Murasaki see THE TALE OF GENJI

Shinebourne, Jan(ice) [Lo] 1947– Guyanese novelist Shinebourne was born in Canje, a plantation village in Berbice, and spent her first twenty years in Guyana before moving to England in 1970. Here she obtained her BA in English and started teaching at various colleges in the London area. She was also co-editor of the *Southall Review* and has contributed literary and journalistic pieces to Caribbean and London-based newspapers.

The tumultuous political, social and cultural climate dominating her country in the 1950s and 1960s has strongly affected her writing and has provided the background to her two novels, *Timepiece* (1986) and *The Last English Plantation* (1988). Shinebourne is one of the first women writers to give voice to Indo-Caribbean women in her works. As she explained, 'the two novels are an exploration of experiences within my own lifetime, of lived experience in fictional form'. The tensions of the period are reflected in her heroines' arduous journey from the country to the town – in search of work or a better education – in the racial and sexual discrimination they face and the corruption of the political elite.

Timepiece won the Guyana Literary Prize for a first work of fiction.   PMa

Ship of Fools (1962) KATHERINE ANNE PORTER's long-awaited only novel began as a letter she wrote in 1931 when she travelled on the SS *Werra*, a German freighter, from Vera Cruz in Mexico to the German port of Bremerhaven. Over the next thirty years she shaped her account of the voyage into a novel. She saw the ship, with its polyglot passenger list, including many Germans heading home as to the promised land, as a microcosm of pre-war Europe. The novel was her attempt to understand 'the logic of this majestic and terrible failure of the life of man in the Western World'. When it finally appeared, critical reaction was mixed. Some hailed it as a second MIDDLEMARCH (1871–2), others questioned Porter's moral attitudes, detected anti-Semitism and found it over-schematized. Its chief virtues are the lyrical writing style and the exploration of women's lives through a series of subtly delineated female characters.

Ship of Fools was made into a film (directed by Stanley Kramer, screenplay by Abby Mann) in 1964; its dazzling cast included Vivien Leigh, Simone Signoret, Jose Ferrer and Lee Marvin.   JG

Shipley, Mary Elizabeth 1842–1914 English author of over twenty novels of religious and moral improvement, but also a fine topographical writer. Her celebrated Lincolnshire novel, *Like a Rasen Fiddler: A Tale of the Pilgrimage of Grace*, was published by the Society for Promoting Christian Knowledge (SPCK) in 1900. She moved from the south in early adulthood and ran a small school in Market Rasen. She portrays provincial society minutely in novels such as *Gabrielle Vaughan* (1876), *Looking Back* (1878), *Cousin Deborah's Whim* (1878 – her only three-decker novel) and *Bernard Hamilton, Curate of Stowe* (1880). Though her plots are slight, she has a keen eye for social change, writing of relations between servants and gentry and of the impact of economic development on village life. Shipley always conveys a vivid sense of place (inventing such Betjemanesque names as 'Moorby-cum-Straggleton'), and consistently champions the provincial against the metropolitan.   VP

Shirley (1849) Among the most ambitious Victorian fictions, CHARLOTTE BRONTË's third novel (second published) constructs a myth of national reconciliation for the 1840s. The story, set in an 1812 Britain in acute crisis in war, and in industrial and gender relations, ends with news of the Duke of Wellington's victory at Salamanca. Wellington's fictional counterparts are manufacturer Robert Moore, ROMANCE hero of industry, and landowner Shirley Keeldar, mediator between industry's necessary aggressions and its casualties. The book's principal relationship, between Shirley – Brontë's exploration of a new, active heroine – and Robert's eventual partner, the more conventional, gently enduring Caroline Helstone, allows debates about women's possible destinies in marriage, work and public life. This feminist story sometimes interacts uncomfortably with the class allegory, notably in the episode in which the heroines, partisan for Robert, watch the Luddite attack on his mill. The myth's triumphant incorporation of all national elements, including a reluctant working-class, is, however, questioned by the novel's readiness throughout to leave contradictions exposed, and by the final lament for the world obliterated by industrial advance.   AT

Shotlander, Sandra 1941– Sandra Shotlander is a graduate of Melbourne University and has studied writing in both Australia and the USA. She is one of the large group of Australian women dramatists who are orientated to community and minority groups and political activism about social issues. These women came to comprise 50 per cent of writers for smaller theatres by the early 1990s, and in many ways Shotlander is a representative figure. Less than 20 per cent of plays on the main stages are by women, but only a handful of writers (like KATHERINE THOMSON) are identified with both arenas. Shotlander's published plays include *Angels of Power* (1991), about women in politics, and *Blind Salome* (1985), but her plays about lesbian relationships – *Framework* (1983), co-winner of the inaugural (North American) 1984 Jane Chambers Award, about two women who meet in an art gallery, and *Is That You Nancy? – Collected Phonecalls of Gertrude Stein and Others* (1991), a comedy about lesbian lifestyles set in New York – are distinctive because they are produced and academically critiqued in both Australia and the USA. During the 1980s Australian women playwrights became better known overseas – for example, ROBYN ARCHER first performed *Pack of Women* in London in the early 1980s, plays by playwrights such as Thérèse Radic have been toured to non-English-speaking countries and, recently, there have been main stage productions: Mary Morris's *Two Weeks with the Queen*, in London in 1994, Jill Shearer's *Shimada* for Broadway in 1995, and Peta Murray's *Wallflowering* in San Jose, USA, in 1996. PT

Showalter, Elaine 1941– American literary critic, feminist and writer on cultural and social issues. Born in Boston, Showalter studied at Bryn Mawr, Brandeis and the University of California at Davis. Since 1984, she has taught at Princeton, where she is now a Professor of English and Avalon Professor of the Humanities. Showalter is a specialist in Victorian literature and the FIN-DE-SIÈCLE, and her most innovative and interesting work has been in the field of madness and hysteria in literature, and specifically in women's writing and the portrayal of female characters. Her critical works include *A Literature of Their Own: British Women Novelists from Brontë to Lessing* (1978), which contained a lengthy and much-discussed chapter on VIRGINIA WOOLF; *The Female Malady: Women, Madness and English Culture 1830–1980* (1985); and *Sexual Anarchy: Gender and Culture at the Fin-de-Siècle* (1991). She also edited *The New Feminist Criticism* (1985) and *Speaking of Gender* (1989).

Throughout her work, Showalter has sought to ground literary criticism in an understanding of the historical specificity of women's writing, coining for this approach the term 'gynocriticism'. Latterly, she has sought a wider audience. *Hystories: Hysterical Epidemics and Modern Culture* in 1997 explored six contemporary afflictions: Chronic Fatigue Syndrome, Gulf War Syndrome, recovered memories of sexual abuse, alien abduction, multiple personality disorder and Satanic ritual abuse. Although Showalter insisted that she was primarily interested in the interaction between the media and the public in propagating these conditions, she ran into a storm of controversy from those who suffer, or believe that they suffer, from the syndromes under discussion.   AC

Shuttle, Penelope 1947– English poet and novelist.
Rich in archetypally feminine images such as the moon, water and gardens, Shuttle's work nevertheless deals frankly and humorously with sexuality. A near-surrealist sensibility lends unembittered assertiveness to her statements about female erotic power. Her poetry revolves around the pleasures of the quotidian and the elemental; animals and children figure both as recurrent objects of contemplation and as surrogates for the poetic self. Her delight in 'delicious babies' she describes as 'manna, confiture, my sweet groceries' mirrors her enjoyment of her own physical existence, and she celebrates the 'magic of the amphibian' through which she suggests the human capacity to lose and find individual identity in others' bodies. *The Hermaphrodite Album* (1973), written with her husband, the poet and scientist Peter Redgrove, also testifies to this preoccupation. She and Redgrove (whom she met while undergoing psychiatric treatment for depression) also collaborated on an acclaimed study of the mythology and physiology of menstruation, *The Wise Wound* (1978), and on two novels: *The Terrors of Dr Treviles* (1974) and *The Glass Cottage* (1976). While their mutual influence has been considerable and their shared sympathy with Jungian psychology is evident, Shuttle's preoccupation with the difficulties and opacities of language makes her work recognizably distinct from Redgrove's. Her books of poetry include *The Orchard Upstairs* (1980), *Adventures with my Horse* (1988), *Taxing the Rain* (1992) and *Building a City for Jamie* (1996).
                                                                BWB

Sidhwa, Bapsi 1936– Pakistani writer of Parsi origin known for her humorous and compassionate novels about the Parsi, and the subcontinental diaspora.
Born in Karachi, and brought up in Lahore, she divides her time between the USA and Pakistan. A childhood bout of polio meant that she was educated privately at home till she went to college. She represented Pakistan in the Asian Women's Congress in 1975.

Her first published novel, *The Crow Eaters* (1978), established her reputation as a Parsi chronicler, a satirist with an unerring eye for the comic detail. *The Crow Eaters* is set in pre-Independence undivided India and introduces into the literature of the subcontinent a different perspective to the construction of the nations that constitute it. This is more acutely felt in her third novel, *Ice-candy Man* (1988), known as *Cracking India* in the USA, where the freedom struggle and the partition are seen from the perspective of a community which didn't belong to the conflict. Set in Lahore, the novel captures with great power and wit the turmoil of the partition from the point of view of a child-heroine

awakening to sexuality and the adult world as well as to the overwhelming historical disaster.

Her second novel, *The Bride* (1983), also known as *The Pakistani Bride*, chronologically her first since she wrote it earlier, was an attempt at serious social fiction, narrating the travails of a girl whose life is changed by events occasioned by the partition of India and later by her marriage and dislocation to the North-West Frontier. This novel also shows Sidhwa looking beyond the Parsi community in her sympathy for a fellow woman. Her fourth and latest novel, *The American Brat* (1993), sees her again in familiar territory – the comic world of diasporic dislocation, now in the new promised land of material benefit and liberation. Sidhwa's use of language, refreshingly free among the subcontinental women novelists of her generation in English, manages to capture the flavour of Parsi speech as well as to express her essentially comic vision of life. Bapsi Sidhwa's is a potent mix of laughter, ribaldry, honesty, story-telling ability, and sense of history. GJVP

Sidney, Mary, Countess of Pembroke 1561–1621
Devotional poet, translator and patroness who became the most influential literary woman in Elizabethan England. Born into the powerful Protestant Dudley and Sidney family alliance, she was presented at court at 13 and married at 15 to Henry Herbert, Earl of Pembroke. As sister to Sir Philip Sidney, she was instrumental in making him a Protestant martyr after his death. As Countess of Pembroke she used her money and influence to encourage writers such as Edmund Spenser, Samuel Daniel and Abraham Fraunce. Mary's own literary career only began after her brother's death in 1586. Determined to build up Sidney's reputation for posterity, she edited his *Arcadia* for publication (1593). She made her great house at Wilton into a high-minded literary centre that mingled Protestant piety with continental courtliness and learning. She furthered Sidney's mission to redeem English writing from provincialism by encouraging the composition of neo-classical drama, and Thomas Churchyard said 'She sets to schoole our poets ev'rywhere'.

In 1592 she published her translation of Robert Garnier's neo-Senecan drama *Antonie*; a highly assertive act for an Elizabethan Englishwoman. She also translated Philippe du Plessis-Mornay's *Discours de la Vie et de la Mort* (1592) and Petrarch's *A Discourse of Life and Death* and *The Triumph of Death*. Her miscellaneous collection of lyrics and poems includes three elegiac poems to her brother. However, her claim to literary significance lies in her continuation of Philip Sidney's translation of the Psalms of David, which were dedicated to ELIZABETH I. She humbly downplayed her own achievement in her dedication to her brother: 'So dard my Muse with thine itself combine, / As mortal stuff with that which is divine'. But her psalms' delicate formal experiment and luminous inwardness look forward to the 17th-century devotional lyric.

When her husband died in 1601, Mary Sidney's prestige lessened and she retreated to the fashionable continental town of Spa, where she founded another literary salon. She eventually returned to build her own estate in England.   KE

Sigourney, Lydia Huntley 1791–1865 American poet and essayist. Known and loved as the 'American HEMENS' and the 'sweet singer of Hartford', she wrote fifteen volumes of poetry, a novel, works of history, children's books, a memoir, conduct manuals and hundreds of magazine articles. The precocious daughter of a gardener, she found favour with her father's employer in Norwich, Connecticut, and acquired a good education. As a young schoolteacher, she wrote her first book, *Moral Pieces in Prose and Verse* (1815), for the classroom. Her writing often spoke for the powerless; her second book was a poem-cycle, *Traits of the Aborigines of America* (1822). Throughout her life she supported abolition and native American rights, and worked for the deaf and dumb. Though unhappily married herself, Lydia Sigourney promoted the values of domestic ideology in such influential conduct manuals as *Letters to Young Ladies* (1833) and *Letters to Mothers* (1838). Her own losses (including the deaths of several children), as well as the sentimental style of the day, account for the elegiac nature of much of her verse, which led to the eclipse of her reputation for much of the 20th century. She is now recognized for her wide cultural influence and for expanding the possibilities of professional authorship for women.   PCr

Silas Marner (1861) GEORGE ELIOT intended that this short novel should 'set in a strong light the remedial influences of pure, natural human relations'. Having rejected Evangelical Christianity she placed her faith in a religion of humanity, and stated: 'If art does not enlarge men's sympathies it does nothing morally.' Eliot described *Silas Marner* as 'a sort of legendary tale' given 'a more REALISTIC treatment'. The setting is her native Midlands region, and she was influenced by William Wordsworth's *Michael: A Pastoral Poem*. After being falsely accused of theft, the weaver Silas Marner moves to Raveloe. He lives as a recluse for fifteen years, working incessantly and taking miserly delight in hoarding his gold. When it is stolen he discovers an abandoned child with golden hair, and regards her as a replacement for his money. Silas determines to keep Eppie, and is transformed: 'as her life unfolded, his soul, long stupefied in a cold narrow prison, was unfolding too, and trembling into full consciousness'. Good triumphs over evil, and Silas is restored to the community.   SF

Lydia Huntley Sigourney.

Silences (1979) TILLIE OLSEN's book addresses the issue of unnatural silences and hiatuses in literary production. She experienced this in her own career with the loss and subsequent recovery of YONNONDIO: FROM THE THIRTIES (1974); thus the motivation for this study is not only political but also personal. Her thesis is that the social and economic circumstances surrounding class, colour and gender have affected adversely the potential to create literature. Her method is not that of academic scholarship, rather an accumulation of extracts from 19th- and 20th-century writers and associated sources, concerning the emotional and physical circumstances of literary production, with her own commentary interspersed throughout. In effect she lets the evidence speak for itself and much of it is tellingly eloquent.

She selects and organizes her materials to reinforce her main argument: that writers could have produced less flawed texts, written more consistently throughout their lives and indeed generated texts totally lost to the world, if their circumstances had been different. She writes in a passionate and inspirational style. Yet one might question whether the very circumstances and conditions, which made writing so very difficult for the authors she studies, did not also contribute to the eventual quality and maturity of their vision. HMD

Silko, Leslie Marmon 1948– Mixed-ancestry Southwestern USA writer (Laguna Indian, Mexican,

Posy Simmonds: cartoon from *Mustn't Grumble*, 1993.

European) of essays, poetry, and fiction. She was born at Laguna Pueblo, New Mexico, to Mary Virginia Leslie and Lee Howard Marmon, the first of three sisters. While their parents worked, they were cared for by their grandmother, Lillie Stagner, and great-grandmother, Helen Romero, both story-tellers. Silko's education included preschool Head Start, through fourth grade at Laguna BIA (Bureau of Indian Affairs) School, and then Albuquerque Indian School (a private day school), her father driving her 100 miles daily to avoid the boarding-school experience he had detested. After graduating from the University of New Mexico, she attended law school. She has two adult sons and is divorced from attorney John Silko.

Her first published short story 'The Man to Send Rain Clouds' appeared in *New Mexico Quarterly* (1969). While teaching for two years in Ketchikan, Alaska, she published *Laguna Woman* (1974), receiving a poetry award from the *Chicago Review*. Both 'Lullaby' (1975) and 'Yellow Woman' (1976) were included in Martha Foley's *Best Short Stories* collections. In 1977, she received a Pushcart Prize for poetry and published CEREMONY, her first novel, about a Laguna soldier on the Pacific front during World War II, who believes he has murdered his relatives as he confronts a Japanese enemy, and who reconfirms his life through the Thought Woman 'ceremony' of his culture. This novel established Silko as an important artist in the American Indian community.

In 1981, *Storyteller* (a multi-genre volume of stories, poems, essays, photos and autobiography) appeared, its powerful title story about Eskimo concepts of truth and honour set atypically in Alaska. A prestigious John D. and Catherine T. MacArthur Foundation 'genius' grant in 1983 supported her for five years. Silko credits the Foundation grant with making possible *Almanac of the Dead* (1991), her '763-page indictment' of European imperialism, covering five centuries of North American history and concluding with a vision of indi-

vidual 'self-improvement'. Her collected essays in *Yellow Woman and a Beauty of the Spirit* (1996) comment upon the current native American scene.   CFK

Simcox, Edith Jemima 1844–1901 English writer, linguist, political activist and trade unionist. Talented product of a middle-class mercantile background, Simcox is best known as a friend and passionate admirer (self-defined 'lover') of GEORGE ELIOT, whom she met in 1872. This unrequited passion, and the tensions implicit in her unresolved sexual orientation, are recorded in her unpublished JOURNAL 'Autobiography of a Shirtmaker'. Accounts of this relationship tend, however, to overshadow the life of committed public activity which Simcox also led. Elected to the London School Board in 1879, Simcox was an active figure in British and European socialism and trade unionism, and co-founder, in 1875, of 'Hamilton's', a women's shirtmaking co-operative. Her written work comprises the widely acclaimed *Natural Law: An Essay in Ethics* (1877), *Episodes in the Lives of Men, Women and Lovers* (1882) and *Primitive Civilisations* (1894), as well as regular contributions to periodicals and newspapers including, as a founding contributor, the *Academy*.   AS

Simmonds, Posy 1945– British cartoonist, known particularly for her *Guardian* comic-strip cartoon in which readers of that (liberal) newspaper saw themselves gently satirized every Monday from 1977 to 1987, and intermittently thereafter. Simmonds was born into a large middle-class family in Cookham Dene, Berkshire, began making comics at the age of 9 to amuse her family, was educated at boarding school, at the Sorbonne and at the Central School of Art and Design. She is married to Richard Harris, a graphic designer, and lives in Bloomsbury, central London.

Amongst the large cast of characters who inhabit Simmonds's cartoon world are the Webers – sensible, bespectacled, housebound Wendy and earnest, polytechnic lecturer George. The Webers aspire to live a wholesome, principled life in best liberal tradition but their many children (not least, the rebellious Belinda), friends, seductive students, neighbours and colleagues get in the way and the pretensions and neuroses are exposed. Simmonds's ear for the particular lingo of each of her characters – whether it be George's compulsive intellectualizing, the saloon-bar clichés of the dreadful Edmund Heep or the smooth talk of the philandering advertising executive Stanhope Wright – is as sharp as her eye for capturing visual detail in her characters' expressions, clothing, stance and setting.

Many of Simmonds's cartoons have been collected into books, including *Mrs Weber's Diary* (1979), *Pick of Posy* (1982), *Pure Posy* (1987) and *Mustn't Grumble* (1993). She has also created very successful and original, comic-strip CHILDREN'S BOOKS, the first of which was *Fred* (1987), a tale of the secret life of a recently perished cat. She has exhibited frequently in The Cartoon Gallery, been the subject of a TV documentary, *Tresoddit for Easter* (1991), and was Cartoonist of the Year (Granada TV / *What the Papers Say*) in 1980.   JAG

Simple Story, A (1791) ELIZABETH INCHBALD's first novel bridges contrasting fictional modes, exploring women's struggle with a repressive and imprisoning patriarchy (reworking it through two generations like EMILY BRONTË's later *WUTHERING HEIGHTS*), while also probing religious conflicts. Protestant, coquettish Miss Milner's passion for her guardian – Catholic, chaste Dorriforth – engages them in an erotically charged contest, which daringly harks back to Restoration comedy; but turns to tragedy after their marriage when she commits adultery and dies, defeated. Their daughter Matilda, educated in sober isolation and adversity, and banned from her father's presence, finally achieves a limited rapprochement with patriarchal power, with a more equal marriage to her father's inheritor Rushbrook. Woman's 'proper education' is the connecting theme, with Matilda's stoicism succeeding where her mother's erratic assertiveness failed, but the personal cost is high. Inchbald's use of dialogue and oblique authorial presence rather than didacticism drew high praise from MARIA EDGEWORTH: 'I never once recollected the author while I was reading it ... I believed all to be real'; while Inchbald's attention to her characters' psychological complexities presages 19th-century REALISM.   LMT

Simpson, Helen 1959– A confident and stylish writer, believed by many to be one of the great hopes of contemporary English writing. She was born in Bristol and was educated in London and at Oxford. After working in magazine journalism, she published her first collection of short stories, *Four Bare Legs in a Bed* (1990), to widespread enthusiasm, being heralded in enthusiastic terms by JULIE BURCHILL, RUTH RENDELL, Nick Hornby and FAY WELDON and being awarded the Somerset Maugham Prize. Simpson's second book of stories, *Dear George and Other Stories* (1994), in which the emphasis is on motherhood rather than, as in the first collection, sex, was also praised for its wit, its empathy and its literary, even baroque, imagination. One story in *Dear George*, 'Heavy Weather', weaves a critique of *Jude the Obscure* into a deeply felt account of coping with very young children; in the earlier volume, 'Good Friday, 1663' presents a 17th-century meditation on the extinction of hope and fear of death by a young pregnant wife: brilliant on the surface, both stories are lit by gleams of hope and sympathy. Simpson has also written opera libretti. She lives in South London with her husband and three young children.   LD

Simpson, Helen (de Guerry) 1897–1940 Australian novelist, poet, playwright, historical biographer and musician. The granddaughter of a French marquis who had settled at Goulburn, Simpson was educated at Rose Bay Convent. Following her migration to England at 16 she worked for the Admiralty during World War I, before studying music at Oxford. Her two most famous novels are *Boomerang* (1932), which was awarded the James Tait Memorial Prize, and *Under Capricorn* (1937), later filmed by Alfred Hitchcock (1949). Her collection of short stories, *The Woman on the Beast* (1933), contains some of her most imaginative and fantastical writing; the title story is set in the year 1999 and follows the prophecies of a female Antichrist, Emma Jordan Sopwith, and the eventual destruction of the Australian Annual Bridge Festival. She has been compared to CHRISTINA STEAD both in terms of her expatriate status and her extravagant, sophisticated and humorous disregard of literary conventions. She wrote nine other novels, including *Cups, Wands and Swords* (1927); a collection of poems, *Philosophies in Little* (1921); three collaborative novels (with CLEMENCE DANE); and four plays, including *A Man of His Time* (1923), an interpretation of Benvenuto Cellini.   MRE

Simpson, Mona (Elizabeth) 1957– American novelist and short-story writer whose scattered, detailed fictions chronicle the fray of the family and the restlessness at the heart of so many quests. Her first novel, *Anywhere But Here* (1986), is both a powerful portrait of mother–daughter compulsions and a vivid road story about the pair's effort to leave small-town disappointments behind and find a better life for themselves out West. Its central character, the charismatic, demanding, self-deceiving mother Adele is an unforgettable creation, and a compelling example of the corrosiveness of American ambition and optimism. Simpson called Adele 'unstable, but troubled by American troubles: by striving for gentility, the striving for a higher station'. At a time when other American fictions were exposing the underside of the American family in nihilistic explorations of drugs and violence, Simpson stood out as a writer interested in giving her brittle characters their difficulties and her sympathy. She was also a maximalist in an era of minimalists, and her novel became a defining classic of the late 1980s. In 1991 she published *The Lost Father* which examined a similarly displaced daughter seeking out her wandering and neglectful father. Having married Richard Appel, a writer for television's *The Simpsons*, Simpson herself moved back west, where her third novel is set. *A Regular Guy* (1996) again mined autobiographical material, with its portrayal of an ambitious founder of a high-tech company who seemed to be modelled on Simpson's own brother, Apple founder Steve Jobs. Like Jobs, the novel's Tom Owens has an illegitimate daughter who comes to reclaim him, bringing the themes of the novel back to familiar Simpson territory – a daughter's grappling with self and family.   SB

Sin Eater, The (1977) First novel of ALICE THOMAS ELLIS, an obliquely feminist, slightly fey, Anglo-Welsh moral comedy of manners, centres on two female protagonists: the dying Captain Ellis's witty, cynical and proactive daughter-in-law Rose, and his fatally passive youngest child Ermyn, who watches perceptively but helplessly as Rose engages in skilful, covert battle with the family and local retainers. The point of view moves between Rose, who through words and actions comments on those around her, and Ermyn who comments to herself on Rose. Rose's skills as stage manager and manipulator – through taunting, discomforting, confounding expectations and especially through the medium of her cooking – expose the faults of others while encouraging her own. Ultimately, she overestimates her power and this elegantly plotted novel comes to a disastrous climax. The novel establishes elements – such as the implacable primitiveness of Wales, the importance of death and the power of the cook – which Ellis returns to in subsequent novels, along with numerous targets, especially the stultifying conformity of middle England and woolly-minded, self-justifying liberalism.   SAS

Sinclair, Jo 1913– Ruth Seid, born in New York City into a Russian-Jewish immigrant family, claimed the name of Jo Sinclair when she began to publish in the Left-wing magazine *New Masses* in 1936; as she began to sell short stories to *Esquire*, known in the era for its quality fiction, she kept the name because the magazine published male authors only. Sinclair's intellectual development caused her to see parallels between her various identities as a woman, lesbian and Jew. Her political education began when she took a job with the Works Project Administration in the 1930s with the sole aim of keeping her parents off relief. Her job was to edit translated articles for the many ethnic newspapers of Cleveland, Ohio, to which her family had moved, and in doing so, she saw the connections, and the differences, between her Jewish background and other outsiders to the American dream. Sinclair's two major novels, *Wasteland* (1946) and *The Changelings* (1951), were dedicated to exposing the continuities between marginalized communities: homosexuals, African-Americans and Jews. In a significant difference from the major male Jewish writers of her day, Sinclair does not take the urban East as her text, but brings to light the lives of suburban, assimilated Jews in the heartland. Sinclair's work received much positive critical attention in the post-war years: *Wasteland*, with its frank representation of psychoanalysis, sexuality and Jewish self-hatred, won the prestigious Harper Prize. While Sinclair's style did not adapt well to the trends of POSTMODERN fiction, causing publishing silences of long duration, most of her novels are once more widely available, suggesting that the problems she grappled with are far from resolved.   MG

Sinclair, May 1863–1946 Early British modern novelist who coined the phrase 'stream of consciousness' (in a 1918 review of DOROTHY RICHARDSON's *PILGRIMAGE*) and who was one of the first writers of fiction to use the new psychology in her work. Born Mary Amelia St Clair Sinclair, she was the youngest of five surviving children and the only girl. She was largely self-educated, except for a year at Cheltenham Ladies' College, where Dorothea Beale recognized and encouraged her talent for philosophy. May Sinclair taught herself German, Greek and Sanskrit and, like her heroine Mary Olivier, read Hegel and Kant as relief from dull household tasks. She began to publish while still living with her mother. After her mother's death in 1901, she became enormously more prolific. In all, she published twenty-four novels, two books of poetry, six collections of stories, a 'novel in verse', a biography of the BRONTËS, two books of philosophy, a book on feminism, a book based on her experiences in Belgium during World War I, reviews of the work of Pound, Eliot, Richard Aldington and H. D., and translations.

Her first novel, *Audry Craven* (1897), is about a heroine who is overwhelmed by love, art, nature, religion. Her third novel, *The Divine Fire* (1904), about a poet who lives a principled life of self-sacrifice (which leads to self-fulfilment), became a bestseller and established May Sinclair as one of the leading writers of her time.

Three of her novels have been reprinted by Virago: *The Three Sisters* (1914), written just after Sinclair's work on the Brontës and evocative of them in the response of the heroine, Gwenda, to isolation, confinement and liberating nature; the autobiographical *Mary Olivier: A Life* (1919), a portrait of the artist as a young and middle-aged woman; and LIFE AND DEATH OF HARRIET FREAN (1922), a depiction of a woman who never questions her parents' ideas and never claims her own life. All three novels suggest that self-denial imposed from without (rather than authorized by conscience) can be destructive. May Sinclair's successful characters must fight to develop their minds and selves, while still accepting the duties their lives impose on them. Being able to bear confinement and tedium are threshold tests, but so is being able to respond to nature, art, love and religion. Her story, 'The Flaw in the Crystal' (1912), is an astonishing account of psychic healing; 'Where Their Fire is Not Quenched' (1923) is a memorable persuasion against sex without love.

May Sinclair developed Parkinson's disease in the 1920s and died of it in 1946.   EG

Singh, Rajkumari 1923–79 Guyanese poet and dramatist.

Despite the fact that polio in infancy caused physical disablement and continued health problems for Singh, her range of cultural activities and achievements was immense. A member of the British Guiana Dramatic Society in the 1940s, Singh was eager to promote the cultural distinctiveness of Indians in Guyana. The mother of eight children, she wrote for some time before publishing the collection A Garland of Stories (1960). As a founder member of the Messenger Group, she was committed to bringing Indo-Caribbean cultural forms to wider public attention. Her poetry, including Days of the Sahib Are Over (1971), addresses the Indian presence in Guyana, particularly the female presence. In addition to her work as a dramatist and organizer of cultural events and groups, Singh was politically active and involved in welfare and social work. She also played an important role in encouraging younger writers and artists in Guyana.

AD

Sitwell, Edith [Louisa] 1887–1964 Controversial

English poet, prominent in many earlier 20th-century fights for poetic hegemony. Born into a Derbyshire landowning family, she had an unhappy childhood, except for her close relations with her brothers, Osbert and Sacheverell, and with her governess, Helen Rootham, who introduced her to French poetry. From 1919 she lived in Bayswater with Rootham. From 1916 to 1921, with her brothers and NANCY CUNARD, she produced the annual anthology, Wheels, which opposed to the Englishness of the dominant Georgian school of poetry an emphasis on rococo artifice and eclectic internationalism. The first public performance in 1923 of Facade, her experimental collaboration with teenage composer William Walton, was a much-publicized cultural event. The lyrics mimicked dance forms, and engaged in nostalgic pastiche of Victorian poetry,

including Lear's nonsense verse. Other 1920s poems included 'Aubade' (1920), The Sleeping Beauty (1924) and 'Colonel Fantock' (1927). The satirical Gold Coast Customs (1929) used jazz rhythms in juxtaposing Mayfair and Ashanti rituals.

Yeats praised the childlike and primitivist qualities of her verses but in the 1930s she became, especially in the pages of New Verse, a convenient aristocratic epitome of everything younger poets sought to abolish. Dylan Thomas, however, was a close friend. The decade was also marked by her unrequited passion for the gay Russian painter, Pavel Tchetlichev. For financial reasons she turned to prose, including the controversial Aspects of Modern Poetry (1934); the bestselling biography, VICTORIA OF ENGLAND (1936); and I LIVE UNDER A BLACK SUN (1937), a novel about Swift. Her return to poetry with Street Songs (1942) matched the war-time mood: 'Still Falls the Rain' and 'The Weeping Babe' were set to music by Britten and Tippett.

In her last two decades, especially after her first lecture tour of America in 1948, she enjoyed a high media profile as an icon of poetry; this included a much-hyped friendship with Marilyn Monroe. She was made a Dame in 1954 and converted to Roman Catholicism in 1955. Her reputation as a serious poet deteriorated sharply, and her flair for publicity still makes judgement of her work difficult.   AT

Skene, Felicia [Mary Frances] 1821–99 British novelist,

essayist and charitable worker who was inspired by her Christian faith and sense of social duty. Skene was the youngest daughter of a Scottish country gentry family. Her father was a close friend of Sir Walter Scott. The family moved to Greece in 1838, where Felicia learned modern Greek, rode frequently and began writing poetry, which she later called 'simply worthless'. She did, however, publish Wayfaring Sketches among the Greeks and Turks (1847). The Skenes returned to Britain in the mid 1840s, settling at Oxford. Felicia's volunteer activities there included nursing cholera victims, visiting prisoners and working to 'rescue' prostitutes. Skene published a religious novel, Use and Abuse (1849), and Hidden Depths (1866), which concerned fallen women and social hypocrisy. She discussed her spiritual life in The Divine Master (1852), and wrote many essays on social issues, as well as an autobiographical sketch for Blackwood's, 'Some Episodes in a Long Life' (1896).   KW

Sleath, Eleanor fl.1798–1810 British novelist, about

whom little is known except that she wrote several GOTHIC romances. Her first book, The Orphan of the Rhine, was published in 1798 and severely criticized, by JANE AUSTEN amongst others, for its confusing plot and 'vapid and servile' imitation of ANN RADCLIFFE's style. Set in the 17th century, the novel contained all the usual elements of Gothic fiction: deserted castles, mistaken identities and imagined ghosts. Its overriding message is of the triumph of good over evil. *Who's the Murderer? or The Mysteries of the Forest* followed in 1802 and contained many of the same ingredients, as did *The Bristol Heiress, or The Errors in Education* (1809). *The Nocturnal Minstrel: Or, The Spirit of the Wood* (1810), sets its Gothic plot against a 15th-century background and, although both implausible and lurid, its treatment of such issues as enforced marriage and harsh property laws is of particular relevance to women. RDM

Sleeping with Lambs (1980) Canadian MARILYN BOWERING's fifth book of poems has been regarded as her richest and most representative collection, containing her most frequently anthologized poems. Her imagery is often startling, sometimes bordering on the horrible, as she explores a world in which:

No matter how you call,
there is death and violence, just out of sight,
in the hall.

The title poem typically sets conventional expectations on their ears, as it has nothing whatever to do with lions lying down with lambs, but with the shocking reality of the still-bloodied new-born lamb, 'its cord swinging and wet', stumbling away from crows swooping in 'their thick shadows', and with the old farm woman who sleeps with her chickens and lambs. There is some sense in which the poet is grappling with her own demons ('Oh, it's harrowing this – going under, going down, / writing out love like this'), but she never personalizes the struggle, often casting it in some universalizing story or image, whether the contextualizing imagery comes from a house of horrors, from the natural world, or from current events such as the discovery of the grave of Inuit shaman Oloalok. FD

Slesinger, Tess 1905–45 American novelist and author, Slesinger turned her back upon the most brilliant circle of New York intellectuals and became a $1,000-per-week writer in Hollywood. This apostasy was never quite forgiven. The daughter of prosperous Jewish immigrants, Slesinger was educated at the Ethical Culture School in New York, Swarthmore College and Columbia University. Her first story was published in the Menorah *Journal* in 1928. Herbert Solow, the *Journal*'s assistant editor, became Slesinger's first husband. His fiercely intellectual and anti-Stalinist friends, including Eliott Cohen and Lionel Trilling, warily welcomed the ironic Slesinger. She found them crushingly hostile to her creative impulses. After divorcing Solow in 1932, she published a novel, *The Unpossessed* (1934), which marked a final break with the New York intellectual Left. Cohen and Solow appeared in the novel as querulous, self-preoc-

cupied intellectuals searching for a cause. A collection of stories, *Time: The Present*, appeared in 1935. Slesinger went to Hollywood to write screenplays for MGM. She married the producer Frank Davis, had two children, and wrote six screenplays, four with her husband. Briefly a member of the Communist party, Slesinger was an activist in the Screen Writers Guild. Her New York work was forgotten for decades. EH

Slipperjack, Ruby (Farrell) 1952– An Ojibwa (native Canadian) novelist and painter from the Fort Hope Indian Band, she was born and raised in a traditional cultural setting with its teachings and discipline, passed down for generations, at Whitewater Lake, Ontario. Oral story-telling, an integral part of her formative years, is incorporated into her work as a teacher and author. Her novels convey the intimate knowledge and understanding that she learned from the wisdom of the old stories she heard as a child. *Honour the Sun* (1987) and *Silent Words* (1992) give a voice to those who, in the past, have been silenced. The construction of a native 'I' in these novels performs a shift from that which has always been constituted as Other to one of Self. Thus, the narrative perspective may be considered as a device for a Self that is communal and includes a society, a past and a place, and a sense of relatedness. Additionally, Slipperjack reclaims a native voice by representing the experience of people in REALISTIC detail, thus resisting the structure of internal colonialism in Canada. By reclaiming the oral tradition, largely through the entry of old stories into a print culture as well as through thematic use of the trope in texts such as *Honour the Sun* and *Silent Words*, Slipperjack stands firmly beside other First Nations Canadians engaged in giving voice to their past, present and future through the medium of the printed word. SM/PRH

Slouching Towards Bethlehem (1968) A collection of essays written from 1961 to 1967 that helped establish JOAN DIDION as a premier example of the 'New Journalism'. Didion combined the personal essay with reportage and dramatic narration to locate the shredded remains of the American dream in the 1960s. Elegiac and acidic, trenchant and compassionate, these essays contend with America's new myths of the west, myths Didion locates primarily around California. The title essay, the collection's centrepiece and masterpiece, describes Haight-Ashbury during the summer of 1967; Didion is characteristically caustic and mournful as she dramatizes 'atomization' and discontinuity, calling for a return to personal and social responsibility. She offers 'a reality which still eluded the press: we were seeing something important. We were seeing the desperate attempt of a handful of children to create a community in a social vacuum.' Essays on Hollywood, heroes, and personal reminiscences and meditations ('On Morality', 'On Self-Respect') are all rendered through Didion's diamond-hard, brilliantly controlled rhetoric as she manoeuvres through past and present, the individual and the community, to understand the gradual disintegration of human connectedness.   SC

Slovo, Gillian 1952– British-based South African novelist who uses popular forms to write feminist DETECTIVE NOVELS set in London, and more recently a South African family saga and two political thrillers. Slovo went into exile in Britain with her parents Ruth First and Joe Slovo, two of South Africa's most persecuted anti-Apartheid activists, in 1964, at the age of 12. She has said that growing in up South Africa taught her all about 'fear and secrets', and about 'what it feels like to be in a detective novel'. Thus she chooses fictional forms which reflect the apocalyptic dimensions of political struggle. Trying to adapt popular formulae with a feminist and anti-racist slant, her work has received mixed responses.

Her most interesting and controversial work to date is her memoir, *Every Secret Thing: My Family, My Country* (1997). Querying the implications for individual lives of a political culture based on clandestine activity, heroism and self-sacrifice, she uncovers the tensions under which her parents lived, and which charged her own childhood. Many have seen the book as a timely exposure of old narratives; others criticize it for having been written from outside the pressures of political activism itself.   SN

Small Ceremonies (1976) CAROL SHIELDS's first novel appeared soon after she finished a Master's thesis on the life and work of the Canadian pioneer and author, SUSANNA MOODIE. Judith Gill, the protagonist of her novel, is a biographer who, after an unsuccessful foray into writing fiction, completes a biography of Susanna Moodie. Gill is the wife of an English professor and several of her friends are or become writers. Before voice appropriation became a political issue, she was concerned with the morality of using other people's lives and other writers' plots. While Judith Gill reconstructs the life of Moodie, her Creative Writing professor uses the plot of her abandoned novel, and the owner of a flat she rented spins his gleanings about her family life into a successful novel. *Small Ceremonies* ends with Judith Gill in a restaurant enthralled by a table of deaf-mutes and recognizing that her destiny is to be an outsider and a watcher. For her husband and others she will act as a translator, a 'reporter of visions he can't see for himself'. The scene serves as a manifesto for Shields who henceforth takes the novel as her genre of choice.
                                                          JG

Smart, Elizabeth 1913–86 Canadian-born prose poet whose most imaginative and distinguished work, BY GRAND CENTRAL STATION I SAT DOWN AND WEPT (1945), a fictional autobiography based on her love-affair with the English poet George Barker, with whom she had four children, was considered by BRIGID BROPHY to be 'one of the half-dozen masterpieces of poetic prose in the world'. It is a novel mixture of melodious lyricism, mythology and romance which echoes the tenor and balance of Baudelaire. For over thirty years Smart was unacknowledged by Canadian critics and the novel itself was ignored, though Smart's family tried to suppress it. What Smart has done in *By Grand Central Station I Sat Down and Wept* is to expand the situational, episodic nature of the lyric text into a unified novella. As Brophy says, 'the story goes scarcely beyond the bare three lines of a love triangle, and even those have to be inferred from the narrator's rhapsodising or lamentation over them'. So the events and the action within the novel are peripheral to the poetic quality of the prose, and time and place are only important in relation to the narrator's feelings. Extending the notion of the *flâneur* (as one who walks in and observes the daily machinations of city life), Smart moves her autobiographical protagonist from the paradisical nature of California to the urban squalor of New York where her personal pain can best express itself.

Though *By Grand Central Station I Sat Down and Wept* stands out as her major work, it is anticipated in her earlier novella 'Let Us Dig a Grave and Bury Our Mother' (collected in *In the Meantime*, 1985), and followed much later by the short novel entitled *The Assumption of the Rogues and Rascals* (1978), another fictional autobiography which – while lacking in youthful passion – makes up something in maturity and humour. She also published two volumes of poems, *A Bonus* (1977) and *Eleven Poems* (1982), and two volumes of her journals, *Necessary Secrets* and *On the Side of the Angels*, edited by Alice van Wert, were published posthumously in 1992 and 1994 respectively. All of her work testifies to her love-affair with the English language, and the singularity of her feminist vision.   MRA

Smedley, Agnes 1892–1950 The flamboyant Agnes Smedley, an American Left-wing writer, appeared in September 1937 before a rally in China wearing a Red Army uniform. She scandalized her puritanical Chinese friends, and the event, captured in a photograph, was later used against her in America. In 1949 General MacArthur's staff produced a report on Sorge's spy ring in Japan which named Smedley as a spy. She forced an Army retraction, but the accusation, in the darkest days of the Cold War, ended a literary career which began in the 1920s. A posthumous FBI investigation exonerated Smedley, but it was not until the 1970s that feminist scholars rediscovered her as an exemplary activist and feminist. She was one of the most striking casualties of post-war anti-Communism.

Smedley was a novelist and journalist whose early years of poverty and hardship in Colorado stamped her with a fervent passion for a better life for women everywhere. She attended Tempe Normal School in 1911–12, where she met Ernest Brundin, her first husband. Dismissed from a job at San Diego Normal School in 1916 for political activism, Smedley moved to New York, wrote for the socialist papers, and got involved in Indian nationalist activity. She identified passionately with the suffering of wives, mothers and children, and found in the Indian and Chinese revolutionary struggles a broad canvas for her free-wheeling yearnings. *Daughter of Earth* (1929) was a thinly disguised autobiographical novel of Smedley's early years, and of the many obstacles facing a poor young woman. After a brief period in jail, Smedley went to Berlin in 1920, where she joined the Indian Revolutionary Committee. Sent to China in 1928 as a correspondent, Smedley's articles, broadly sympathetic with the Communists, were collected in *Chinese Destinies* (1933). It was followed by *China's Red Army Marches* (1934) based on first-hand accounts of Mao and General Chu Teh. *Battle Hymn of China* (1943), an autobiographical account of what she had seen and heard in China, was an influential and popular contribution to the wartime enthusiasm for the Chinese patriotic struggle against the Japanese occupiers. Smedley's biography of Chu Teh (1955) and *Portraits of Chinese Women in Revolution* (1976) appeared posthumously.   EH

Smiley, Jane 1949– American novelist specializing in sagas of family life in rural locations, usually the Mid-West. Born in St Louis, she took her Bachelor's degree at Vassar and her Ph.D. at the University of Iowa. She went on to lecture at Iowa, where the greater part of her fiction is set. Her first novel, *Barn Blind* (1980), takes place on a family farm which is a world unto itself, where a single parent's dominance over her children has tragic consequences. Her short-story and novella sequences, *The Age of Grief* (1988) and *Ordinary Love* (1990), also probed the perils of domestic life. *The Greenlanders* (1988) evoked the tradition from which the family saga derives: it was about a medieval Viking colony in crisis. Her Pulitzer-Prize-winning novel, *A Thousand Acres* (1991), gave epic scope to her familial themes by using the *King Lear* story. Told from the perspective of the eldest daughter (Shakespeare's Goneril), it made her a victim of parental abuse. Smiley linked landscape to the personality, and territorial aggrandizement to the family network, but retained her understated manner of dealing with weighty subjects. Her subsequent novel, *Moo* (1995), was a gentle

satire on a Mid-Western university: a good-humoured and entertaining soap opera.   KE

Smith [née Young], Anna 1756–80? After the death of their mother, Anna Young and her brother were raised by their aunt, the poet ELIZABETH GRAEME FERGUSSON, at Graeme Park near Philadelphia. One of Anna Young's early poems, 'An Ode to Gratitude', is dedicated to her aunt. Like Fergusson, she adopted a pseudonym when she wrote; Anna Young's was 'Sylvia'. She read widely and intelligently. Her poem, 'On Reading Swift's Works', reveals her deft handling of the couplet as she praises Swift's wit and 'perfect style', but charges him for castigating 'helpless woman', with: 'thy harsh satire, rude, severe, unjust, / Awakes too oft our anger or disgust'. Young supported the patriot side of the Revolutionary War, writing an 'Elegy to the Memory of the American Volunteers'. In 1775, Anna Young married William Smith; she died in childbirth at the age of 24. Several poems were published in literary magazines; others are in manuscript.   CLB

Smith, Charlotte 1749–1806 Poet and novelist, born in London. Her mother died when she was 3 and she was raised by an aunt, who arranged for her schooling and, when she was 14, her marriage to Benjamin Smith, son of a West India merchant, and director of the East India Company. He was 21 and the couple lived over her father-in-law's offices. Charlotte was required to take care of a difficult invalid mother-in-law. The marriage was not happy – her husband was extravagant, violent and had numerous affairs and in 1783 he was imprisoned for debt. Charlotte shared his sentence which lasted for seven months.

Charlotte began to look for ways of supporting herself and her eight children. She published a collection of sonnets, *Elegiac Sonnets and other Essays* (1784), at her own expense, which ran into several editions, and published a second collection of sonnets in 1787 which ran into eleven editions. She was one of the first 18th-century poets to popularize the sonnet form. For a while she lived with her children in a semi-derelict chateau near Dieppe in France, where she undertook translation work. Then the family moved to Sussex where she separated formally from her husband although she continued to send him money.

From the late 1780s she had considerable success as a novelist, publishing *Emmeline, or the Orphan of the Castle* (1788), which was admired by Sir Walter Scott; *Ethelinde* (1789); *Celestina* (1791); *Desmond* (1792); and *The Old Manor House* (1793); which was considered her best novel. Her novels are fast-paced, full of adventure and intrigue and are at best witty and occasionally ironic. She published a novel every year until 1799 and also wrote children's stories, sketches and several long poems.   RS

Smith, Dodie (Dorothy Gladys Smith) ['C.L. Anthony'] 1896–1990 Famed as the author of ONE HUNDRED AND ONE DALMATIANS (1956), and often accused of being merely a writer of romantic comedies, Dodie Smith was born in Lancashire and moved in with her extended family in Manchester after her bank-manager father died when she was a baby. Moving to London in her early teens, she attended St Paul's School and then RADA. Unable to find enough acting work in theatre, Smith became a buyer for Heals department store and whilst working there wrote her first hit play, *Autumn Crocus* (1931) – later made into a film starring Ivor Novello. This was followed by *Service* (1932), *Touchwood* (1934), *Call it a Day* (1935) and *Bonnet Over the Windmill* (1937). Her best-known dramatic text, *Dear Octopus* (1938), an insightful play which looks at the family as an emblem of newly threatened Nationhood, gave Smith her sixth West End hit in a row, a record rarely surpassed. Her marriage to a conscientious objector and her popularity in the United States precipitated her move to America in the late 1930s where she wrote film scripts, became a close friend of Christopher Isherwood and John van Druten, and wrote her first novel, *I Capture the Castle* (1949) which sold over a million copies and remains for many the seminal novel of their youth. Smith was unable to reclaim her popularity with London audiences on returning from America, although her novels were well received. She wrote four volumes of autobiography which include *Look Back with Mixed Feelings* (1978), was a voracious reader, letter-, journal- and DIARY-writer (her archives are held by Boston University). Known as generous and vivacious, she once claimed that she spent most of her money on books, gramophone records and Dalmatians.   MBG

Smith, Pauline ['Janet Tamson', 'Janet Urmson'] 1882–1959 South African novelist and short-story writer. Born in Oudtshoorn, daughter of the local doctor, she had a happy childhood but in adolescence received a double blow which was to colour the rest of her life when her father died unexpectedly not long after she had been sent 'home' to boarding school in Britain, and the family left South Africa never to live there permanently again. Writing about Oudtshoorn – as the fictionalized 'Platkops' – became a form of consolation and some of her early stories were published in Scottish newspapers. Following a chance meeting in Switzerland in 1909, Arnold Bennett adopted her as his *protégée*. Painfully shy and often suffering from ill health, she worked hard to meet her own – and Bennett's – high standards. Success came with the publication of several of her stories in John Middleton Murry's *The Adelphi* (1923–4) and the collection of these and others in *The Little Karoo* (1925). In 1926 she published her only novel, *The Beadle*. A successor to OLIVE

Illustration by Stevie Smith from *Me Again: Uncollected Writings of Stevie Smith*, 1981.

SCHREINER'S STORY OF AN AFRICAN FARM (1883), it moves beyond Schreiner's pessimism to suggest regeneration and hope under beneficent matriarchy. Further works include *Platkops Children* (1935), and a radio play, *The Last Voyage*, which was broadcast by the BBC in 1929.   JSte

Smith, Stevie (Florence Margaret) 1902–71 British poet and novelist whose eccentric tone and combination of humour with gloom made her a cult figure toward the end of her life. She was born in Hull, second of two daughters, to a mother in poor health who died in 1919, and a largely absent father, but grew up in Palmer's Green, a north London suburb, where the mainstay of the household was Madge Spear, her 'Lion Aunt'. Here aunt and niece spent the rest of their lives together. Until 1953, when an episode of suicidal depression caused her to resign, Stevie worked for the publishers George Newnes Ltd as secretary to the two baronets who appear, lightly disguised, in her novels. Afterwards she supplemented her pension by reviewing. She never married, and although she had a large circle of friends – reduced from time to time when those she wrote about dropped her – she seems not to have been greatly interested in sexual relationships. It has been suggested that living with her stalwart and supportive aunt, who died only in 1968, had the effect of infantilizing her personality, but probably her childlike mannerisms were only on the surface; she was not as naive as the persona of her poems.

She published three novels, all with strongly autobiographical content and marked by long digressions on art, literature, philosophy and religion. (She had a running battle with Christianity, whose cruelty angered her.) She came to dislike NOVEL ON YELLOW PAPER (1936) for its dated, American-influenced 'brassy' tone, but it made her name. OVER THE FRONTIER (1938), continuing the adventures of the Stevie-persona Pompey, sends her on a bizarre military mission in Germany, a premonitory vision of the coming war. The Holiday, a lachrymose if intermittently humorous tale of frustrated love, was written during the war and, after its initial rejection, imperfectly revised to set it in the period of its publication (1949).

Her lasting achievement is her poetry, which does not date. (See NOT WAVING BUT DROWNING, 1952). It has affinities with hymns, ballads, FAIRY TALES, Blake and Edward Lear. With its flatly presented anecdotes about lonely, deluded or ridiculous characters, its abrupt changes of mood and style, its idiosyncratic metres, its fond preoccupation with death, and its awareness of what she called 'the ticklish comic element in human suffering', it fits no categories. Editors found it disconcerting, and were reluctant to publish it until after the success of her first novel – particularly as she often insisted on the use of her brilliantly odd drawings to accompany the texts. Her reputation blossomed in the 1960s with her public performances of her poems, some recited in her rather drawling, semi-genteel voice, others chanted to slightly off-key tunes. Her little-girl pinafore dresses and solemn delivery of sometimes hilarious material made her a 'character'. But although frequently witty company she had always been in love with death and, like Scorpion in her poem, 'wishing to be gone'. She died of a brain tumour.   FA

Smither, Elizabeth 1941– New Zealand poet and prose writer noted for her elegance and wit, effects achieved partly by surprising similes, literary allusions and sudden leaps of thought. She has said that her writing is 'like someone juggling a lot of things together, and slightly out of control because they haven't rehearsed enough'. She has spent most of her life in New Plymouth and works as a librarian. Her first collection of poetry, Here Come the Clouds (1975), was followed by several more collections, including A Pattern of Marching (1989), winner of the poetry section of the New Zealand Book Awards in 1990. The mercurial agility of her poems also characterizes her prose writing.

In Nights at the Embassy (1990) and another short-story collection, Mr Fish and Other Stories (1993), plot and theme matter less than an embellished stylistic surface which renders the familiar surprising, but not unrecognizable. The outlook is generally cosmopolitan with no particular New Zealand or indigenous flavour: a novel, First Blood (1983), based on a real-life 19th-century murder in New Plymouth, is a vehicle for an exploration of a network of relationships rather than a historical novel. The Journal Box (1996) is an autobiographical piece in which she comments on her life and writing with the same fine style, perfected aphorisms and penchant for the bizarre noted in her poetry and prose fiction.   RB

Smyth, Donna E. 1943– Canadian writer and critic. Smyth grew up in a working-class family in Kimberley, British Columbia – sites which she explores in work that charts her home-town's histories in poetry and prose form. She has lived and worked on the West coast, in Britain, Saskatchewan and Ontario, and has degrees from the Universities of Victoria, Toronto and London (UK). Since 1973 Smyth has made her home in rural Nova Scotia and, until 1998, she was a professor at Acadia University in Wolfville where she taught creative writing, English and Women's Studies. The founding editor of Atlantis: A Woman's Studies Journal, Smyth was also a co-author of the bestselling No Place Like Home: Diaries and Letters of Nova Scotia Women 1771-1938 (1988). Much of her work engages with feminist theories of power, language and gender while challenging traditional generic boundaries: 'my writing is always crossing genres, slipping and sliding around definitions of what is "supposed to be"'.

Smyth's first play, Susanna Moodie (1976), dramatizes episodes from MOODIE's ROUGHING IT IN THE BUSH (1856) and incorporates fragments of MARGARET ATWOOD's JOURNALS OF SUSANNA MOODIE (1970), creating an intertextual dialogue between two of Canada's most influential literary figures. Quilt (novel, 1982) concerns a group of women in rural Nova Scotia whose work on a quilt for a local raffle also pieces together stories of domestic violence and community struggle. Subversive Elements (1986), a formally innovative novel, combines a love-story with an account of the controversy surrounding uranium mining in Nova Scotia, in a POSTMODERN text which integrates Smyth's own role as an environmental and peace activist into its narrative. Smyth's other works include a play (Giant Anna, 1993), a HISTORICAL NOVEL for young adults (Loyalist Runaway,1991) and a theatrical adaptation of Through the Looking Glass.   DF

Snell, Hannah 1723–92 Transvestite heroine of the anonymous and massively popular work, The Female Soldier (1750), which appeared in numerous reprints and abridgements until 1800. Daughter of a Worcester hosier, Snell was orphaned in 1740, and moved to London to live with a sister, Susannah, and brother-in-law, James Gray. In 1743, Snell married an adulterous and profligate Dutch seaman, who left her pregnant and penniless and returned to sea. Determined to follow him, Snell borrowed the clothing and name of her brother-in-law and enlisted as a foot soldier. From 1745 to 1750, passing as a boy, she pursued a varied military career, including service as a sailor and cook in the East Indies, where she was wounded at the siege of Pondicherry. In 1750, upon learning that her husband had been executed, Snell returned to London to capitalize on her exploits. In addition to participating in the publication of her biography, Snell appeared on the London stage, performed military exercises in full regalia at Sadler's Wells, and opened a public house under the sign of the 'Female Warrior'. She died at Bethlehem Hospital in 1792. Her story remains one of the most vivid, influential, and popular accounts of cross-dressed military heroines to emerge from the 18th century.   JGr

So Big (1924) The theme of this Pulitzer Prize-winning novel by EDNA FERBER, published in arguably the most opportunistic period in United States economic history, is anti-materialism. With echoes of *JANE EYRE*, the recently orphaned 19-year-old Selina Peake is forced in the 1880s to seek employment as a schoolteacher in a community of immigrant Dutch truck farmers, geographically near, but culturally far distant from, her former Chicago home. An imprudent marriage commits Selina to a life of gruelling labour, but she triumphs over adversity after her husband's early death. Denied the fulfilled life of beauty she recognizes as being pre-eminently important, she tries to transmit her values to her son, Dirk – fondly, but ultimately ironically, nicknamed 'So Big' as a baby. Ferber dared to challenge contemporary American concepts of success when Dirk, turning from architecture to a high-flying Wall Street career, becomes diminished in his mother's eyes, and is rejected by the artist he loves.

So Big was filmed three times: 1924 (silent version), 1932 (with Barbara Stanwyck, Bette Davis) and 1953 (with Jane Wyman).   WAP

Sobott-Mogwe, Gaele 1956– Born in Australia, fiction writer Sobott-Mogwe emigrated with her family to Botswana in 1978. She currently lives and works in Britain where she completed a doctoral thesis on black South African women writers at the University of Hull. Sobott-Mogwe has published CHILDREN'S FICTION and a number of short stories in magazines and anthologies such as *Fishwives and Fabulists* (1995). Her children's fiction explores the fear of, and fascination with, the unknown, the outsider, exemplified in *Weird*

Wambo (1994). Her first collection of short stories, *Colour Me Blue* (1995), continues these preoccupations, exploring the collisions and meeting points of internal and external constructions of identity. Through the medium of first-person narration, subtleties of gender, generation, 'race' and culture refuse the fixing of identity, revealing a complex shifting play. In *Revenge is Sweet* the narrator defeats an invasive Tokoloshe (destructive demon) by making common (female) cause with his mate. Distinctions of time, of myth, fable and 'reality' are collapsed as her protagonists draw upon rich internal resources to meet or defy situational demands.   C-AM

Sofola, Zulu 1935–95 The first Nigerian woman to achieve success as a dramatist. Born into an Igbo community in Nigeria's mid-west, as a postgraduate student Sofola researched traditional Igbo religious and ritual practice. The exploration of the norms of pre-colonial social organization provides a recurrent theme for her drama, especially when traditional structures are seen to come into conflict with modernizing trends. Sofola pursued a career in Nigeria as an academic in Theatre Studies, while writing plays for television and the stage (some of which remain unpublished). While her sense of stagecraft was widely admired, those of her plays focusing on women's rights were criticized for a conservative approach to issues of class, gender and culture.

Wedlock of the Gods (1972) is Sofola's most widely performed play, dramatizing a young rural widow's attempted rebellion against her society's religious beliefs and marital customs. The play's strong theatrical appeal is, arguably, compromised by an unreflective approach to motifs such as the supernatural and the community's understanding of the role of the gods. *King Emene* (1974) draws upon Sofola's knowledge of the history and cultural practice of her own community, exploring a political crisis within the traditional ruling elite. *The Sweet Trap* (1977) and *Old Wines Are Tasty* (1981) are both large-scale plays, the former dealing with an attempt by a group of university wives to assert their rights, the latter with the responsibilities of traditional and modernizing elites. *The Wizard of Law* (1975) is unusual amongst Sofola's published plays, an energetic and sharply funny adaptation of the medieval French comedy *Maistre Pierre Pathelin*. While Sofola's work increasingly provoked controversy in the 1980s and 1990s, her sudden death prompted a reappraisal of her achievement and warm tributes to the boldness of her initiative in the Nigerian English-language theatre.   CD

Some Experiences of an Irish RM (1899) This novel by SOMERVILLE AND ROSS is a skilful, affectionate and frequently hilarious series of glimpses into another world as experienced by the English foreigner. Described with droll self-effacement by the long-suffering, reluctantly adventurous Major Sinclair Yeates, RM, Skebawn and its inhabitants come to vivid life, as does the wild beauty of the surrounding landscape. This is no mere artistic flourish; in the form of weather, stray animals and stray people, 'landscape' is frequently indivisible from the Major's hearth and home, and it is clear from the outset that the 'law' as represented by Major Yeates is bound to be thwarted at every turn by the traditional and wholly unassailable 'lore' as practised by those under his jurisdiction. This book and its sequels are enhanced by Somerville's delightful illustrations in early editions. During the early 1980s, many of the episodes were dramatized for British television with Peter Bowles in the title role.   JLB

Somers, Jane see LESSING, DORIS

Somerville and Ross (Edith Œnone Somerville 1858–1949 and **Martin Ross [Violet Martin]** 1862–1915) Anglo-Irish novel-writing cousins. Edith Œnone Somerville was born in Corfu but lived most of her life at Drishane House, Castletownshend, County Cork, as part of a large, vibrant and demanding extended family network. As a young woman she studied painting in Paris, Düsseldorf and London. In 1886 she met her cousin, Violet Martin. Martin also came from an Ascendancy background, although her family was latterly more impoverished than Somerville's. Once they discovered a shared interest in language (particularly in the nuances of Hiberno-English) and in literature, the two women embarked on a literary partnership which contributed significantly to the financial support of their families.

Their first novel, *An Irish Cousin*, appeared in 1889, followed by a series of travel sketches (illustrated by Somerville) and THE REAL CHARLOTTE (1894), their major novel and one of the finest to emerge from the confusions of 19th-century Ireland. A REALIST novel, it exposes the limitations and pretensions of an entire society, and its ultimate and inevitable sterility and destructive tendencies, notably for women.

Despite its success, *The Real Charlotte* was not as lucrative as the subsequent 'Irish R.M.' series, which won them popular acclaim (SOME EXPERIENCES OF AN IRISH RM, 1899; *Further Experiences of an Irish RM*, 1908; *In Mr Knox's Country*, 1915). These sketches describe the attempt of Major Yeates, an English Resident Magistrate, to live something approaching a rational life in the chaos and subversive hilarity of Ireland. His major antagonist is his landlord, Flurry Knox. Misunderstandings, naivety and conflicting expectations create the comic situations described, usually in encounters between landlords and tenants, masters and servants.

There was much speculation among their contemporaries as to whether Somerville or Martin was the dominant or more creative partner, speculation which infuriated them. They described their methods as completely collaborative, many ideas and characters being talked through to outline form and then 'written down by the (wholly fortuitous) holder of the pen'. It was not until the death of her mother in 1906 that Violet Martin was able to come and live at Drishane until her own death in 1915. Prior to that time, the cousins were often separated and much of their work was developed through correspondence, with manuscripts travelling backwards and forwards between Ross and Drishane through the postal service, accompanied by vivid and amusing letters full of anecdotes which contain the seeds of future fiction.

Following the death of Martin, Somerville continued to use their joint pseudonym, asserting that their partnership continued beyond the grave. More novels emerged in this period, of which the most interesting is the *Big House of Inver* (1925), which explores themes of inheritance and dispossession and illustrates the plight of the daughters of decaying families.   LM

Something to Someone (1983) DOROTHY AUCHTERLONIE GREEN's third and final volume of poetry was produced in a limited edition by fine printer A.T. Bolton (1926–96), at the Brindabella Press in Canberra. Her poetry in this volume reflects a mature and distilled sense of the fine balance between fall and grace, and continues her meditations on loss and grief. Reflecting Auchterlonie's passionately professed Christianity, many of the poems are invested with a rich liturgical quality. They are not, however, simplistic in their concerns, and indeed often betray a profound disjunction between Green's publicly held Christian humanist position, and a distrust of and bitterness toward the masculinist world railed against in some of her most successful poems, including 'The Hollow Years' in which she laments her rejection as a woman poet, and 'Farewell Message', in which children, women and the natural world are portrayed as subjugated to a harsh and dominating masculinity, waiting 'always for the next blow'.   MLA

Sonnets from the Portuguese (1850) The most famous English sonnet sequence by a woman was not originally intended for publication, hence the title's pretence of being translation. In ELIZABETH BARRETT BROWNING's earlier poem, 'Catarina to Camoens', the Portuguese poet's muse addresses him. Here Browning plays with the gender reversals involved in her treatment of the traditional relations of sonneteer and addressee, imagining herself (Sonnet III) as a weary troubadour beneath her male muse's window. The sequence records the poet's rebirth

through the Beloved's cherishing into the strength of love and creativity. Despite much self-deprecation as an 'out of tune worn viol' (XXXII), the speaker learns to imagine a love of equal strength, notably in 'When our two souls stand up erect and strong' (XXII), and the penultimate, most famous, sonnet 'How do I love thee?' (XLIII). The treatment of the Petrarchan form is fluent and monotonous, the imagined situations more inventive, the emotional confidences engagingly direct. Sonnet XXXVII's description of the sequence as a commemorative 'sculptured porpoise' seems about right.   AT

Sontag, Susan 1933– American cultural critic, novelist and film-maker, a cool yet passionate anatomist of art and life in the (POST)MODERN era. Born in New York (where she lives today), she grew up in Tucson, Arizona, and Los Angeles. A precocious child and adolescent, she was writing essays and stories by the age of 8 and entered the University of California aged 15, transferring to Chicago and graduating in Philosophy in 1951. In the same year she married social psychologist Philip Rieff. Their son David was born in 1952; they divorced in 1959. She continued her academic studies throughout the fifties gaining MAs in English *and* Philosophy at Harvard and undertaking graduate study in Oxford and Paris.

Thereafter she lectured at colleges in New York and at Columbia University and was writer-in-residence at Rutgers. She has always wanted to be – and be known as – a creative writer; her early novels, though, the self-consciously effete *THE BENEFACTOR* (1963) and *Death Kit* (1967), received mixed notices, as did her later short-story collection, *I, etcetera* (1978). Instead she became a *cause célèbre* with her book of essays, *Against Interpretation* (1966), many of which were first published in the *New York Review of Books* (including the famous 'Notes on Camp' (1964), the source of her reputation as a stylish intellectual dandy). Alongside pieces on the European avant-garde, she championed a democratic POSTMODERN aesthetic privileging novelty, style and pleasure in a wide variety of arts: 'If art is understood as a form of discipline of the feelings and a programming of sensations, then the feeling (or sensation) given off by a Rauschenberg painting might be that of a song by the Supremes'.

In *Styles of Radical Will* (1969) and the later *Under the Sign of Saturn* (1981), Sontag's role as an interpreter of difficult European artists and intellectuals for an American readership blossomed in essays on Artaud, Beckett, Godard, Benjamin and Roland Barthes, to whose aphoristic and outrageous style her own is often compared. *On Photography* (1977) – for which she won the National Book Critics' Circle Award for Best Work of Criticism – along with her screenplays for the films *Duet for Cannibals* (1968) and *Brother Carl* (1969), and her

documentary on the Yom Kippur War (*Promised Lands*, 1974), reflected her growing interest in visual media (her advocacy of cinema, in particular, has since waned somewhat). After recovering from breast cancer in the seventies she wrote *ILLNESS AS METAPHOR* (1978), contending that our images of tuberculosis and cancer punish sufferers and block scientific understanding of real causes; *AIDs and its Metaphors* brought the argument up to date in the eighties.

The publication in 1982 of *A Susan Sontag Reader* saw her provisionally canonized while emphasizing the restless, unfinished quality of her work. She returned to fiction with *THE VOLCANO LOVER* (1992), a sprawling, inventive HISTORICAL ROMANCE based on the lives of Sir William and Lady Emma Hamilton, which combined her talents as a formalist connoisseur with surprising new emphasis on deep-felt emotion.   MO'D

'Sophia' fl. 1739–40 Pseudonymous feminist pamphleteer. Responding to a piece in *Common Sense*, 'Sophia' published *Woman Not Inferior to Man: Or A Short and Modest Vindication of the Natural Right of the Fair-Sex to a Perfect Equality of Power, Dignity, and Esteem, with the Men* (1739). She explained, 'I only mean to show my sex that they are not so despicable as the *Men* would have them believe themselves, and that we are capable of as much greatness of soul as the best of that haughty sex.' Immediately, an ironic and windy response by a 'gentleman' appeared, entitled *Man Superior to Woman* . . . In 1740's *Woman's Superior Excellence over Men* . . ., 'Sophia' countered that women's 'minds [are] as much more beautiful than the men's as their bodies are, and that, had they the same advantages of education, they would excel them as much in sense as they do in virtue'. All three tracts rely on 17th-century European feminist writers, including Poullain de la Barre. Speculation over the spirited, articulate 'Sophia' began immediately but has never yielded firm attribution. Proposed candidates include LADY MARY WORTLEY MONTAGU; Sophia Fermor, later Lady Granville; and an unknown male author of all three pieces.   JHP

Sorabji, Cornelia 1866–1954 Indian lawyer, publicist, women's rights activist. Cornelia was the first woman to graduate from Bombay University (the next did so only twenty-four years later), the first woman to study Law at Oxford (though debarred from practice for thirty years since women were called to the Bar only in 1923). On her return to India in 1894, she was engaged as legal advisor to widows in purdah whose estates had been brought under the guardianship of the colonial government. Her racy memoir, *India Calling* (1934), describes her experiences with these women who resented the forcible take-over of their property, and years spent fighting for a place for women in public life. Her personal life, however, was bitterly lonely; her only friend the English social activist, Eleanor Rathbone. Cornelia was a conservative, in feminism as in politics. She contemptuously dismissed the 'NEW' WOMAN, and felt that India 'was not ready' for independence, and that Gandhi might be genuine, but was 'exploited by his disciples'.   ST

Sorrow Dance, The (1967) This collection of poems inaugurated DENISE LEVERTOV's transition from meditative lyrics to poems of political protest. The book's three sections enact that shift, opening with lyrics of self, hymns to Eros, and personal narratives of discovery. The second section provides the centrepiece for the book in the 'Olga poems', an elegiac sequence for Levertov's sister. The 'Olga poems' provide a thematic and sensory bridge to the collection's final section, a series of jeremiads protesting the Vietnam War. Moving in a trajectory from celebration through sorrow to anger and protest, from the private to the public, from the personal to the sociopolitical, from lyricism to didactic exclamations against outrage and horror, these poems are bound together by the struggle to survive. Levertov's free verse is musical, breath-spaced, playing with silences as well as with words, non-metrical but rhythmically and melodically complex, examples of the kind of poem Levertov has called 'a sonic, sensuous event'. Here the poems' individual structural movements are echoed in the larger teleologies of the collection itself. These poems are 'faithful to / ebb and flow', both in prosody and in theme.   SC

Sorrows of Satan, The (1895) This extraordinary bestseller, for which no review copies were released, consolidated the success of the new single-volume, 6-shilling, novel format, and of MARIE CORELLI as the most popular English novelist. Satan, incarnate as an 1890s plutocrat, conversing in would-be Wildean epigrams, confronts his principal opponent on earth, popular novelist Mavis Clare. His *protégé*, the Faustian narrator Geoffrey Tempest, failed novelist turned millionaire, even sinks to writing hostile reviews of Mavis, whose genius he secretly envies. This shocks Satan, who recognizes Mavis as 'personified truth', despises modern materialism, and yearns for humanity to reject him. Geoffrey's self-consciously vicious bride, Lady Sybil, corrupted by reading Swinburne, NEW WOMAN and decadent writings, becomes infatuated with Satan and poisons herself. Geoffrey, comforted by Mavis, rejects Satan and embraces bankruptcy. Corelli alternates heavy satires of contemporary society, and of a literary world of venal reviewers and decadent writers, with delirious orientalizing visions of hell. These and her vengeful self-portrait as redemptive Mavis, bestselling novelist as 'guardian of men's souls', impressed a mass audience.   AT

Soueif, Ahdaf 1950– Egyptian fiction writer born in Cairo. Soueif was educated in Egypt and England and received her Ph.D. at Lancaster University. She has lectured on English Literature at the University of Cairo and of Riyadh.

Her first collection of short stories, *Aisha*, was published in 1983 and was received as a very promising début. Her first novel, *In The Eye of the Sun*, appeared in 1992 and was described as 'The Great English Novel about Egypt' which is also 'The Great Egyptian Novel About England'. The novel focuses on Asya Uluma, the daughter of two Cairo professors, who is forced to postpone her marriage to the handsome and westernized Saif for four years, a wait that, according to her, will ruin their sex life for good. After her marriage she decides to do her Ph.D. in a bleak northern English university. She lives apart from her curt husband who visits her infrequently. Time passes slowly, Asya starts an affair with the uncouth Englishman, Gerald, while her marriage slowly disintegrates. Asya goes back to Cairo to teach, alone but more in control of herself. In the background of this female path to self-awareness the book offers a great family saga of the Egyptian élite, a HISTORICAL NOVEL in which Soueif superbly interweaves the British culture with the turmoil of Middle East politics. The plot of *In the Eye of the Sun* is in part further explored by the author in *Sandpiper*, published in 1996. It is a collection of short stories about women in the wrong place, who have reached a crucial phase in their lives. Critic Edward Said describes Ahdaf Soueif as one 'of the most extraordinary chroniclers of sexual politics now writing'.   SPo

South Riding (1936) WINIFRED HOLTBY's last novel combines her strong, yet complex, moral sense with an intense political commitment. In a semi-imaginary south-east Yorkshire, leading county councillors intrigue against each other for what each sees as the common good, while a new headmistress, Sarah, fights for a better school and women's education. Ordinary people, meanwhile, get on with their lives. All this is complicated by Sarah's inconclusive love-affair with Carne, the doomed Tory farmer, whose accidental death marks the destruction of an old England of deference in favour of a managerial paternalism which may be no better. The novel's core theme, however, is more complex than its portrayal of love or politics: the reader is led to see that there are two sides to each question. In spite of occasional sentimentality and overwriting, this is one of the most politically and morally intelligent books of its period.   RK

Southcott, Joanna 1750–1814 British visionary and PROPHET, who was born in east Devon, the daughter of a poor farmer. She started work as a domestic servant, spending much of her free time studying the

Bible. In 1791 Southcott joined the Wesleyans. The following year she had several visions and began to prophesy in 'a mixture of doggerel verse and rambling prose', which led to charges of witchcraft being levelled against her. She identified herself with the woman in *Revelations*, and later foretold that she would give birth to 'the second Christ'. In 1801 Southcott found £100 to print *The Strange Effects of Faith*. Numerous printed works and manuscripts followed in which she relayed the messages of the 'Spirit', or reworked hymns and ballads. Eventually she was persuaded to move to London where her millenarian movement attracted large numbers of disciples, the Southcottians; many of these were women or poor people, on whose behalf she particularly claimed to speak. Although Southcott's verse was often dismissed as either unintelligible or fraudulent, her influence was felt throughout the 19th century and her work known by such poets as Blake, Byron and Keats.   RDM

Southwell [née Howard], Frances, Lady

fl.1598–1615 Courtier and satirical writer. Her parents were Charles Howard, ELIZABETH I's Lord High Admiral, and the Queen's cousin and friend, Catherine [née Carey]. Her husband, Sir Robert Southwell, a naval officer, died in 1598. She became chief lady-in-waiting to Anne of Denmark, James I's Queen, and her friends included CECILIA BULSTRODE and LADY ANNE CLIFFORD.

The 1615 edition of *New and Choice Characters . . . Together with . . . The Wife*, a collection of satirical writings by Sir Thomas Overbury and others, included both Bulstrode's 'News' and Southwell's 'Certain Edicts from a Parliament in Eutopia'. This is a list of witty aphorisms or 'edicts' concerning the social and sexual conduct of men and women, such as: '*Item*, no lady that silently simpereth for want of wit shall be called modest . . . *Item*, no woman that remaineth constant for want of assault shall be called chaste.' The tone is one of risqué and flirtatious raillery.   HH

Southworth, E(mma) D(orothy) E(liza) N(evitte)

1819–99 The most widely read of all the American DOMESTIC-sentimental novelists, Southworth published some sixty novels following the appearance of *Retribution* (1849). After her father, a merchant named Charles Nevitte, died in poverty in 1824, his widow and children were plunged into hardship. Until marrying Frederic Hamilton Southworth, Emma Nevitte experienced neglect and unhappiness. The Southworths lived briefly and unsuccessfully in Wisconsin, before settling in Washington, D.C., where she remained. Mr Southworth, repenting of marriage, headed for South America. Mrs Southworth turned to writing to support her family. It was on signing an exclusive contract in 1857 with Robert Bonner, proprietor of the *New York Ledger*, that Southworth became one of the best-paid writers in America, earning as much as $10,000 in her peak years. A Southworth novel featured stirring heroines, often mistreated, whose ultimate triumph is due to their faith, purity and commitment to domesticity. Among her successes were *The Missing Bride* (1855), *The Hidden Hand* (serialized in the *Ledger*, 1859; book form, 1880), *The Fatal Marriage* (1863), *The Maiden Widow* (1870) and *Self-Raised* (serialized in the *Ledger*, 1863–4; book form, 1876).   EH

Sowernam, Ester

The pseudonym given for the English writer of a tract entitled *Ester Hath Hanged Haman*, published in 1617. Sowernam's pamphlet was one of three responses by women writers to Joseph Swetnam's misogynist tirade, *The Arraignment of Women*.

Her tract participates in a generic tradition scholars call 'the controversy over women'. For decades, pamphlet writers had used attacks on women to demonstrate rhetorical skills and provide an excuse for telling ribald stories about cuckolded husbands. But Swetnam's tract made such outrageous claims, and became so popular, that Sowernam felt compelled to respond.

Sowernam's pamphlet brims with wit and rhetorical sophistication. Punning on names, she provides the 'sour' antidote to 'sweet' Joseph and 'hangs a man' in the title. She extends the trope of the trial which Swetnam introduced, staging his arraignment before the 'Judgesses' Reason and Experience. In the end Swetnam pleads for mercy, the trial is postponed and Sowernam gives a speech publishing the wrongs Swetnam has done to women.   GG-R

Soweto Stories

(1989) MIRIAM TLALI's second short-story collection appeared in South Africa in the same year as *Footprints in the Quag*. Tlali's earlier short stories had focused on the violent aftermath of the Soweto Uprising in the seventies. Here, her third-person narration details the difficulties, humanity and vigour of life in the Johannesburg ghetto, Sophiatown, and the township of Soweto from the thirties on, spanning the period in which Sophiatown's residents were evicted to Soweto. As backdrops to the individuals and episodes these stories depict, the diverse characters and geographies of the two townships emerge, with their different relationships to white Johannesburg. As a whole this collection still registers the increasingly violent impact of Apartheid on the African community. LAURETTA NGCOBO's valuable introduction rightly identifies Tlali's challenge, as South Africa's first home-based black woman writer, to the established patriarchalism of black South African literature. Here she focuses controversially on the sexism directed toward many township women by their men, acknowledging their strength, resourcefulness and suffering in urban environments where traditions and values are in constant jeopardy.   HLR

Spark, Muriel 1918– Scottish-born novelist, poet, biographer and short-story writer. Born in Edinburgh, she left Scotland at 19 and has lived in Africa, in London and New York, and in Italy, though the one book which exploits her Edinburgh childhood, THE PRIME OF MISS JEAN BRODIE (1961), is still her most famous. After intelligence work during World War II, she was a journalist and the editor of *Poetry*; she published books on MARY SHELLEY, EMILY BRONTË and John Masefield, and her own poems, before her first novel, *The Comforters*, appeared in 1957. In 1954 she had converted to Catholicism and had received the support of Graham Greene in turning to the novel, which she did reluctantly, thinking it 'an inferior way of writing'. It is a *métier* in which she has distinguished herself for over forty years and, though her quirky, lapidary technique and sometimes Olympian attitude toward her own characters have assured that she is not without detractors, she is by common consent one of the finest novelists writing in English.

Muriel Spark's religion – she maintains that 'I'm a Catholic writer, whether I like it or not' – is manifested less in any concern with doctrine or salvation than in a continuing exploration of issues of freedom and necessity (in her books the issue is the freedom of her characters within the world of a godlike novelist) and a readiness to incorporate the supernatural, the occult and the radically allegorical in her novels.

Spark's 1965 book THE MANDELBAUM GATE is her longest novel; based on her own experience covering the trial of Adolf Eichmann in Jerusalem, it is also her most social-REALISTIC. Her best work is briefer, more suggestive, more 'poetic'. Her early works focus on small groups of people, usually in urban settings, who encounter sinister, even demonic figures. *The Ballad of Peckham Rye* (1960) includes a man who seems to be the devil. In MEMENTO MORI (1959) the characters, all old, receive unexplained anonymous telephone calls saying 'Remember you must die.'

After *The Mandelbaum Gate* and her *Collected Stories I* (1967) Spark's novels changed noticeably: the narration is often in the present tense and the narrator regularly tells the reader what is to happen in the near or distant future. It would be wrong to suggest that this practice breaks the illusion, or spoils the suspense, since ordinary suspense and the illusion of reality are hardly the effect of a Muriel Spark novel; and, as early as *The Prime of Miss Jean Brodie*, she had begun to intercut her 'present' narrative with lucid explanations of her characters' futures.

Usually featuring characters who may be involved in intrigue and deception (as in *The Abbess of Crewe* (1974), a parody of the Watergate affair set in a nunnery, or

Reality and Dreams (1997), about an unsavoury crew making a film), the later novels are subject to the objection that the comedy is excessively brittle. Admirers stress the author's wit, her playful ambiguity and the economy with which she creates her strong but delicate fictions.

She continues to be an artist in the shorter forms: *Open to the Public: New and Collected Stories* was published in 1997. Her autobiography, *Curriculum Vitae* (1993), relates her life story up to 1957 when she published *The Comforters*. She has won numerous awards and was made a Dame of the Order of the British Empire in 1997.   MMos

Speght, Rachel *c.*1597–? Poet and polemicist, daughter of a London minister, James Speght, and the first woman to publish a rejoinder to Joseph Swetnam's scurrilous, misogynist and very popular *The araignment of lewde, idle, froward, and unconstant women* (1615), which was one of the best-known contributions to the contemporary 'controversy over women'. In her answer, *A Mouzell for Melastomus* (1617; i.e., a muzzle for Blackmouth), Speght has two main aims. First, she criticizes both the argument and the style of Swetnam's text, dismantling it on the grounds of logic, biblical precedent, ignorance and inelegance, calling his writing 'altogether without method, irregular, without grammatical concordance and a promiscuous minglemangle'. Secondly, she seeks to 'put forth the excellency of women', principally through specific readings of biblical narratives such as the creation story. Speght's text was swiftly followed by others seeking to rebuff Swetnam: those by the pseudonymous ESTER SOWERNAM (1617) and CONSTANTIA MUNDA (1617) are the best-known. In 1621, Speght published a second work, *Mortalities Memorandum*, a verse meditation on death dedicated to her godmother.   HAH

Spence, Catherine Helen 1825–1910 Australian novelist, journalist and social commentator. She was born into the family of a Scottish lawyer and emigrated with her family to Adelaide in 1839 when her father's speculation in foreign wheat left them 'hopelessly ruined'. Initially a governess, she wrote CLARA MORISON (1854), a novel depicting female independence and resourcefulness during the goldrush, to rebut a *Punch* article by Thackeray (1850). Further novels include *Tender and True* (1856), *Mr Hogarth's Will* (1865), and the novel which she considered her finest, *Gathered In* (1881–2). She greatly admired GEORGE ELIOT whom she visited at her home in 1865, but the meeting was not a success and Eliot later wrote her a letter of apology.

For Spence, the new colony offered boundless opportunities for social reform and she wrote two utopian novels – HANDFASTED (1984) which remained unpublished during her lifetime as it advocated trial marriage, and *A Week in the Future* (1889) about Britain – as well as promoting electoral reform in an earlier work, *A Plea for Pure Democracy* (1861). She helped found the Boarding-Out Society to rehouse children from orphanages to family homes, and wrote *State Children in Australia* (1907). Her book, *The Laws We Live Under* (1880), was the first social-science text to be used in Australian schools. Apparently indefatigable, she joined the campaign for women's suffrage in 1891, and later undertook a world tour to coincide with the Chicago World Fair (1893), lecturing and preaching across the United States.   JSte

Spencer, Anne [Annie Bethel Scales Bannister]

1882–1975 American poet and civil rights worker. She was born on a rural Virginia plantation and remained illiterate until the age of 11. At 17 she was valedictorian of her graduating class at Virginia Seminary and Normal School. She married and resided in Lynchburg, Virginia, but maintained friendships with major figures of the Harlem Renaissance. Georgina Douglas Johnson, Langston Hughes and W.E.B. Du Bois were among the guests the Spencers received at home.

James Weldon Johnson launched Spencer's literary career following a visit in 1919; he was impressed by samples of her poetry strewn about the house. Spencer's first published poem, 'Before the Feast at Shushan', appeared in the National Association for the Advancement of Colored People (NAACP) *Crisis* magazine in February 1920. Novelist JESSIE FAUSET admired her work.

Though Spencer never produced a volume of her own, her poems were collected in respectable anthologies, including Alain Locke's *The New Negro*, and Johnson's *The Book of American Negro Poetry*. Less than thirty of Spencer's poems appeared in print; tragically, thousands of her unpublished poems were mistakenly thrown away by hired housecleaners.

Spencer's celebrity as a poet was eclipsed by her local fame as a civil rights activist and horticulturist. The Spencer home and garden at 1313 Pierce Street was declared a historic landmark in 1977.   LMC

spiritual autobiography

Although the genre has its origins in the *Confessions* of St Augustine (345–430), it was not until the 17th century that spiritual autobiographies were produced in any number in England. However, with the Puritan insistence on the individual's duty of spiritual self-examination in order to determine and monitor his or her relationship to divine grace, published accounts detailing the experience of God within individual lives increased. These ranged from the collections of short 'conversion narratives' published by ministers of Independent congregations, such as Henry Walker's *Spirituall Experiences* (1653) or John Rogers's *Ohel or Beth-shemesh* (1653) – where such an (oral) account was required for a believer to be accepted into the congregation – to longer, individually published, spiritual autobiographies, such as JANE TURNER's *Choice Experiences* (1653) or Joan Vokins's *God's Mighty Power Magnified* (1691). Although many of these were produced within the radical Puritan sects, such as the Quakers and Baptists, there are also examples from more conservative Anglicans and Presbyterians, such as Mary Simpson's *Faith and Experience* (1649). Whatever the length or origin of the account, the structure of the narrative was in general highly conventionalized, charting retrospectively the progress of the subject from childhood onwards, through sin and ignorance of God, false confidence in salvation, despair and doubt, to genuine conviction, continuing temptation, and assurance. This common framework is important, testifying to and guaranteeing, for both writer and reader, the genuineness of the process being described, rather than the story of a sinner caught in a condition of hypocrisy and false conviction. Whilst a modern reader might expect an autobiography to serve to individuate its subject, these accounts serve, on the contrary, to tie the author closely into the spiritual community. Emotionally highly charged, but often offering scant detail of the material or familial circumstance of the subject, these narratives underline precisely how culturally and historically specific the constituents of a 'life' and 'self' are.

Like PROPHECY, spiritual autobiography proved to be significant in the history of women's published writing, as many 17th-century women published texts falling broadly within this genre. It is possible to see this work as 'conservative' in comparison with the more 'radical' prophecy: private and individual as opposed to public and political, dealing with the work of God in relation to a single believer instead of relating to broader social groupings and issues, and often prefaced and authorized by dedicatory epistles from husbands and ministers. However, the autobiographies themselves confound such binary distinctions: some texts, such as ANNA TRAPNEL's THE CRY OF A STONE (1654) and ANNE WENTWORTH's *The Revelation of Jesus Christ* (1679), combine autobiography and prophecy; Anne Wentworth argued in her *Vindication* (1677) that her personal experiences had a 'public ministry and meaning wrapped up in them'; and Jane Turner, urging meditation and self-examination, suggests that these 'private duties' are not above public ones, but instead *prepare* for them; moreover, her autobiography is concerned, prophecy-like, to explicate biblical texts as well as to delineate her spiritual experiences. Whilst, then, we might be tempted to make

Harriet Prescott Spofford: 'A number of the girls came dancing down, and happened to stop where Hester sat on the grass under the great beech-tree', illustration from *Hester Stanley at St Marks,* 1882.

sense of the increased number of women's spiritual autobiographies as the kind of 'public' utterance most easily recast as appropriately 'private' and therefore feminine, the texts themselves tell a more complicated, and interesting, story.   HAH

Spivak, Chakravorty Gayatri 1942– One of the foremost feminist critics on the Anglo-American academic scene, Avalon Professor in the Humanities at Columbia University. Born and educated in India, she is often used as the representative voice of 'Third World' feminism, though she is cited just as frequently in psychoanalytic and deconstructionist criticism, and this is symptomatic of the dual intellectual formation of many non-Western critics based in the Western academy. She is the translator both of Jacques Derrida's *Of Grammatology* from French (1976) and the Indian feminist Mahasweta Devi's novel *Imaginary Maps* (1995) from Bengali.

Spivak's work ranges across languages and disciplines and has a provisional, intellectually relentless quality to it. Her first book is the little-known *Myself I Must Remake: The Life and Poetry of W.B. Yeats* (1974) and her first collection of essays appeared over ten years

later: *In Other Worlds* (1987). A collection of interviews, *The Postcolonial Critic* (1990), was followed by *Outside in the Teaching Machine* (1993). Interspersed are essays, reviews, reports and debates showing a mind at the cutting edge of intellectual production. She is also involved with the Subaltern Studies history group in India and maintains ties with the Indian feminist movement and various 'Third World' movements. While her prose style is tortuous, her interventions in areas like POST-COLONIAL studies, psychoanalytic theory, poststructuralist writing and cultural studies are invaluable.   ATe

Spofford, Harriet (Elizabeth) Prescott 1835–1921 American novelist, poet and short-story writer. She was born in Calais, Maine, and educated at Pinkerton Academy in New Hampshire. Her father was a lawyer and lumber merchant. She began writing for Boston newspapers in her twenties to support her invalid parents. In 1858 she sent Thomas Wentworth Higginson, editor of *Atlantic Monthly*, a story that so impressed him he suspected it was plagiarized. Thereafter Spofford achieved critical and popular success with short stories and GOTHIC romances (*Sir Rohan's Ghost*, 1860; *The Amber Gods*, 1863; *Azarian*, 1864). In 1865 she married lawyer Richard Spofford, who was also a poet. They moved to Washington, D.C., then to Newburyport, Massachusetts, in 1874. Their home became a gathering place for literary friends (among them SARAH ORNE JEWETT, Louise Chandler Moulton, and Rose Terry Cooke), the topic of Spofford's *A Little Book of Friends* (1916). In her fiction Spofford championed sexual freedom for women ('An Ideal' in *Scarlet Poppy*, 1894; 'Wages of Sin' in *Old Madame and Other Tragedies*, 1900) and treated domestic culture as a scene of sisterhood (*Three Heroines of New England Romance*, 1894; *A Master Spirit*, 1896; and *An Inheritance*, 1897). Her poems are collected in *Titian's Garden* (1897).   JSG

Sport of My Mad Mother, The (1958) ANN JELLICOE's first full-length play came out of improvization groups organized at the Royal Court Theatre by the actor Keith Johnstone, where the aim was to release the revolutionary energy in archetypal situations. Signs of its origin are apparent in word-games, eruptions of physical activity, and headlong monologues. Their actions – accompanied by bursts from an on-stage drum kit, five London teenagers, an American and an Australian – kill time with horse-play and political banter, events reaching a climax when one of the girls, in imitation of Kali, the 'mad mother' of the title, gives symbolic birth. With its deliberate blurrings between art and life (heralding 'performance art'), its fascination with female myths (foreshadowing ANGELA CARTER) and its use of demotic slang and syncopated rhythm (like verbal acappella or rap poetry), this is one of the most uncompromisingly experimental plays ever written by an English playwright. In a lecture in 1967 Jellicoe was to speak of the role of the unconscious in theatre, the ways in which art is 'less a process of creation than a process of discovery'. This unique play is formal exemplification of that radical principle.   JSto

Spry [née Fletcher], Constance 1886–1960 A remarkable woman who revolutionized the art of flower arrangement and co-authored *The Constance Spry Cookery Book* (1956). This stood alone as champion of British food when the passion for Mediterranean food was at its height.

Constance Spry combined the gifts of teacher, lecturer, administrator and writer with an artistic talent shown in her original and decorative use of flowers, leaves and vegetables. She wrote twelve books on flower arrangement and COOKERY.

She was born in Derby, but the family moved to Dublin in 1901. On leaving school, she was employed by Lady Aberdeen, wife of the Lord-Lieutenant, as lecturer on hygiene, in her charity work.

Her love of gardening and old roses grew while living in Kilkenny, during her first marriage. In 1914 she became secretary of the Dublin Red Cross, later moving to Barrow-in-Furness as welfare supervisor for Vickers. From there she moved to London to run the Womens' Staff Welfare for the Ministry of Munitions.

In 1919 she divorced her first husband and took over the Womens' Staff Welfare at the Inland Revenue. Two years later she married again and became headmistress of a school in the East End, but in 1928 she abandoned both education and welfare to work with flowers.

Her first shop, in Belgrave Road, was an instant success. Fashionable painters, decorators and society women united in their acclaim, and she was invited to 'do the flowers' for every smart occasion from the Windsors' wedding to the marriage of Princess Elizabeth. (For the latter, she was awarded the OBE.)

In 1934 she opened a flower-arranging school in South Audley Street. During the war years she foresaw the post-war need for the middle classes to manage without staff, and in 1946 she opened a residential school for the domestic arts. Rosemary Hume, a professional chef, was joint principal, and the two went on to write *The Constance Spry Cookery Book*, and to found the Cordon Bleu School in London.

In *Come Into The Garden, Cook* (1942), Mrs Spry demonstrates her expertise in cultivating and cooking such unusual vegetables as seakale and kohlrabi, Himalayan black potatoes and sweetcorn, dandelions and mache. Here too, she formulates her belief that 'a working knowledge of both gardening and cooking would tend to give a young woman ... an added confi-

COME INTO THE GARDEN, COOK

BY

CONSTANCE SPRY

LONDON

J. M. DENT AND SONS LIMITED

Title-page illustration by Lesley Blanch for Constance Spry's *Come into the Garden*, 1942.

dence about living, a talisman in time of stress, and a reassuring sense of independence and power'.   AB

Staël, Madame de [Anne-Louise-Germaine Necker] 1766–1817 French novelist, literary theorist and celebrated wit, Staël was born into a Swiss Protestant family. Her father, Jacques, was the Finance Minister to Louis XVI and her mother held a salon which was frequented by the Encyclopaedists Diderot and D'Alembert and other cosmopolitan intellectuals, including Voltaire. Madame Necker was in charge of her daughter's education from an early age: she was influenced, too, by her father's writings on finance and economics. Married at 20 to Baron Eric-Magnus de Staël-Holstein, the Swedish ambassador to France, she embarked on an affair with

595

Talleyrand, bore illegitimate children to Louis de Narbonne, and had a long and intellectually fruitful love-affair with the novelist Benjamin Constant.

She began writing early, composing the *Lettres sur les ouvrages et le caractère de J.J. Rousseau* (1788), which contain themes she was to remain interested in, particularly the idea of a cultural enrichment that would come from both northern and southern Europe. In her enormously influential *Corinne, ou l'Italie* (1807), these ideas became explicitly bound to the belief in the education of women. Under Napoleon she was exiled several times for her veiled criticisms of the Republic, and obliged to return to the family home in Coppet, near Geneva, which became a refuge for other exiles from France. Her exile also took her to Russia and Sweden, and to England where she lived at Juniper Hall, near Dorking in Surrey, a house that had been rented since 1792 by French émigrés. During this period, although her politics and morals were considered undesirable by good society in England, she became a close friend of FANNY BURNEY. Madame de Staël's purely literary importance was far exceeded by her importance in the history of ideas, and her brilliant personality epitomized European culture of her time, marking the transition from the 18th to the 19th century. Her most important work, *De l'Allemagne*, was published in London in 1813. SD

Stafford, Jean 1915–79 American novelist and short-story writer. She grew up in California and Colorado and, because much of her best work is set there, is sometimes classified as a western regional writer. A precocious student at the University of Colorado, she earned simultaneous BA and MA degrees and constantly wrote fiction. She spent a year in Heidelberg during the rise of Nazism, and later used the experience as the basis for several short stories and a novella, as well as for various fictions which were never completed. An eight-year marriage to poet Robert Lowell replicated her abusive relationship with her father and left her severely injured in an accident caused by his bad driving. After she divorced Lowell, she married Oliver Jensen, a *Life* magazine editor, and later A.J. Liebling, a *New Yorker* writer.

She wrote three novels – *Boston Adventure* (1944), *The Mountain Lion* (1947), and *The Catherine Wheel* (1952) – and two highly praised volumes of short stories – *Children are Bored on Sunday* (1953) and *Bad Characters* (1964). Although in her last decade, as her life-long problems with physical ailments and alcoholism mounted, she stopped writing fiction, her *Collected Stories*, published in 1970, won the Pulitzer Prize. During her lifetime she was undervalued as a somewhat old-fashioned writer of fine prose who resisted MODERNIST techniques. Soon after her death, however, she was rediscovered by younger critics, the re-emergence of her works coincid-

ing with the growing interest in women writers. Her fiction, along with a collection of her essays and reviews published in 1989, remains in print and continues to attract scholarly interest. JG

Stainer, Pauline 1941– British poet, born in Burslem. Stainer read English at St Anne's College, Oxford. Before taking an M.Phil. at Southampton University, she worked in a mental hospital, a pub and a library. After many years in rural Essex, she went to live on the island of Rousay in the Orkneys, and published her first book, a pamphlet called *Little Egypt*. It was followed by a number of impressive collections: *The Honeycomb* (1989), *Sighting the Slave Ship* (1992), *The Ice-Pilot Speaks* (1994) and *The Wound-dresser's Dream* (1996). In 1993 her work was foregrounded in Bloodaxe's influential anthology *The New Poetry*.

Stainer focuses on a metaphysical synthesis of the scientific and the sacred. She investigates natural and historical phenomena with a language 'cold and passionate as the dawn', and derives her thought from compendious sources and subject matter. Her poetry is sometimes thought 'difficult' but this is a surface perception. It is an elegant, academic and challenging poetry, as sensuous as it is astringent. Her purpose is transformative, using the language of poetry as a scientific *and* alchemical catalyst. She attempts to evaluate the irrational, the purposelessness of the natural world, without taking away its mythic quality. DM

Stand in the Rain (1965) New Zealand writer JEAN WATSON's first novel deals with 'the innocence of first loving and the hesitance of first knowing'. Uncertain as to whether to go back to university and not having much motivation for anything, Sarah falls in love with Abungus – married, itinerant, emotionally complex – when he, observing the inadequacies of her relationship with Paul, says 'If he don't want you, I'll have you.' Abungus works variously as a possum-trapper, scrubcutter, truck driver, labourer and rabbiter, while Sarah, besotted in a fashion the reader may find hard to comprehend, follows him round the country. 'While a person is going somewhere, the destination takes the empty place in their mind which should be filled by "an aim in life"' she explains. Watson's analysis of the relationship is said to be based on her own marriage to the writer Barry Crump. The character of Sarah, purposeless, vulnerable yet resisting conformity, is reminiscent of Salinger and PLATH, and anticipates the more explicitly feminist novels of a decade later. JSt

Stanhope [née Peters], Eugenia *c.*1730–86 Editor and author. As the illegitimate daughter of a rich Irishman, Eugenia was poor but well-educated. In Rome in 1750, she met Philip Stanhope, the illegitimate son of Lord Chesterfield, whom she married *c*.1759, and by whom she had two sons. The marriage remained a secret, and Chesterfield discovered his daughter-in-law's existence only with the news of his son's death in 1768. He did, however, offer her financial assistance and corresponded with her on reasonably amicable terms.

Following Chesterfield's death in 1773, Eugenia sold the manuscript of his letters to Philip for £1,575. Although the Stanhope family tried to stop publication, the collection appeared in 1774 as *Letters written by the Earl of Chesterfield to his Son, Philip Stanhope, together with several other pieces on various subjects, published by Mrs Eugenia Stanhope*, with Eugenia providing a preface. She was accused of greed in selling for publication letters which were intended to be private, and the work itself was attacked for its worldliness and alleged immorality.

Eugenia may also have been the author of *The Deportment of a Married Life*, letters supposedly to a niece, which argued that the conventional ordinances on marriage and relations between the sexes should be respected. While severely condemning female infidelity, which it described as 'monstrous', it also denounced male inconstancy, and extolled freedom of choice and companionate marriage.   RR

Stanhope, Hester (Lucy) 1776–1839 English adventurer and EPISTOLARY writer, one of the first western women to travel extensively in the East. The daughter of 'citizen' Stanhope, the eccentric radical, and niece of William Pitt, she grew up in Kent and received no formal education. After a series of family disagreements, Stanhope left home in 1802 to become Pitt's companion. She revelled in the role of society hostess, gaining notoriety for her barbed retorts, outspoken manner and influence over her ageing uncle. After Pitt's death, Stanhope found her social standing diminished and in 1806 decided to travel. While in Europe she met Michael Bruce with whom she toured Egypt and Turkey. The pair became lovers, though, as she wrote to Bruce's father, they never intended to marry. After her possessions were lost in a shipwreck, Stanhope adopted the masculine Turkish dress she was to wear for the rest of her life and, with an expanding entourage, travelled further east. She met tribal leaders and journeyed to Palmyra, the first western woman to do so. Stanhope settled at Djouni, in an abandoned monastery on the slopes of Mount Lebanon where she provided shelter for refugees and entertained emirs and western tourists alike. Stanhope and her coterie developed their own brand of religious mysticism. She became renowned for her belief that she was one of a spiritual elect and for her ability to talk for hours without ceasing.

The tenor of her letters veers between the egotistical and the maudlin, the self-aggrandizing and the perse-

cuted. During her later years she became increasingly bitter about the neglect of the fashionable friends who had once lauded her. In 1838 after a disagreement with the British government regarding the state bequest she had received annually since Pitt's death, she dismissed her entourage and walled herself into the monastery, 'there remaining', she wrote to Palmerston, 'as if I were in a tomb, till my character has been done justice to, and a public acknowledgement written'. She died less than a year later. Stanhope's letters were collected by her niece, and a number of sensational accounts of her life were published in the late 19th and early 20th centuries.   KD

Stanley, Mary 1919–80 New Zealand poet, whose single collection, *Starveling Year*, was first published in 1953, and reappeared in an expanded edition in 1994. Stanley was not published in any major New Zealand literary journal (such as *Landfall*), or in any of the canon-making anthologies which appeared in New Zealand between the 1940s and the 1970s. She seems to have written little after 1958.

Stanley was married twice. Her second husband was the poet Kendrick Smithyman (1922–95) who edited the revised edition of her poems, contributing a somewhat defensive introduction.

Her poetry is rhetorically formal and cerebral, replete with literary and classical allusion. Her subject matter is often an intensely realized and intellectualized sensuality 'The body of my love is a familiar country / read at the fingertip, as all children learn / their first landscape'. Her articulation of a specifically female experience of love and sexuality is self-conscious and innovative: 'Being a woman', she writes, 'I am / not more than a man nor less / but answer imperatives / of shape and growth'. Unlike her contemporaries, she reflects very little sense of place in her writing, and no commitment to either the nationalist or MODERNIST projects of her period.

Contemporary criticism has rightly rediscovered and reinstated Stanley's work, seeing her as one of the chief victims of the literary masculinism of the 1940s and 1950s. But such accounts have not necessarily been accurate in their placement of her. To describe her neglect as resulting from her interest in the domestic or a stereotypically female focus on family and emotion fails to take account of the density, intelligence and structured formality of her work.   JSt

Stanton, Elizabeth Cady 1815–1902 American suffragist, writer, editor. Born into a family of six children, Elizabeth was only admitted into school to take her brother's place when he died. She excelled in Greek and Latin, and graduated from Emma Willard's Female Seminary in 1832. After her 1841 marriage to Henry B. Stanton, an anti-slavery lecturer, they took

their honeymoon in London for an anti-slavery convention, where Stanton was outraged to witness delegate LUCRETIA MOTT's dismissal from the floor because of her gender. In 1848, she and Mott organized the first women's rights convention in Seneca Falls, New York, for which she wrote the *Declaration of Rights and Sentiments*. Modelled on the Declaration of Independence, it argues for equality in education, employment, marriage and property for women. Stanton also set a precedent by including a then-controversial clause for women's suffrage. In 1851, she met her lifelong colleague and friend SUSAN B. ANTHONY. In 1868, she and Anthony published the journal *Revolution*. The next year, she and Anthony founded the National Woman Suffrage Association, of which Stanton served as president for twenty-one years. By 1868, she had seven children, and was touring the country eight months a year to support their education. She was enormously popular, despite her increasing radicalism – including arguments for unions, divorce, equal pay and birth control. In 1895, she even alienated the National American Woman Suffrage Association with her publication of *The Woman's Bible*. Less controversial was her three-volume *History of Woman Suffrage* (1881–6), written with Anthony, and her wonderfully rich and detailed autobiography, *Eighty Years and More* (1898).   SP

Stanwell-Fletcher, Theodora (Morris Cope)

1906– American botanist and nature writer, born in Dimock, Pennsylvania, to Evelyn (née Flower) and Francis R. Cope, Jr. She attended college at Holyoke and pursued graduate work at Cornell. After travelling to New Zealand, the Dutch East Indies, Asia and the British Isles, she visited subarctic Canada in 1930, where she met the English naturalist John Stanwell-Fletcher, whom she subsequently married. She later separated from Stanwell-Fletcher and in 1954 married Lowell Sumner, a biologist for the US National Park Service in the Pacific coast states and Alaska; in 1967 she married Dr Philip Gray of Scripps College, Claremont, California. She resides in Dimock, Pennsylvania.

Her most important publication is *Driftwood Valley* (1946), which recounts her experiences collecting flora and fauna specimens in northern British Columbia (1937–41). It features drawings by John Stanwell-Fletcher depicting their experiences travelling to the area, building their cabin, interacting with natives and observing birds and animals. *Driftwood Valley* earned the John Burroughs Medal, 1947. Other works include: 'Naturalists in the Wilds of British Columbia' (1940); *Some Accounts of the Flora and Fauna of the Driftwood Valley Region of Central British Columbia* (1943); *Tundra World* (1952), about flora and fauna on the edge of the Barrens; and *Clear and Icy Seas: A Voyage to the Eastern*

Arctic (1958), about a summer voyage aboard a Hudson's Bay Company supply ship around the coasts of Ungava, southern Baffin Island, and eastern Hudson's Bay.   JBM

Stark, Freya Madeline

1893–1993 British traveller, writer and photographer, best-known for TRAVEL BOOKS set in the Middle East, and memoirs. Born in Paris, Freya travelled from an early age. She and her younger sister were carried over the Dolomites in baskets, both under 4. At 5, she spoke English, German and Italian. Her parents were first cousins, and her childhood was spent between Genoa, Asolo near Venice, and Dartmoor, in Devon. When Freya was 6, her parents separated, and her mother became involved with a young Italian with a textile business in Dronero, in Piedmont. Mother and daughters moved to Dronero; five years later Freya lost half her scalp in an accident in the textile mill.

Life in Dronero was hard; at 13 Freya was set in charge of the housekeeping, with £10 a month to cover food and wages. World War I freed her from domestic chores, and she trained as a nurse, then as a censor. After a broken engagement and four years of illness, Freya and her mother left Dronero and settled in Asolo.

Between the wars Freya grew increasingly despondent. 'To be just middle-aged with no particular charm or beauty and no position is a dreary business', she wrote to her mother. But success as traveller and writer restored her self-esteem. She made her first trip to the Middle East in 1927, and published her first book, *VALLEYS OF THE ASSASSINS AND OTHER PERSIAN TRAVELS* (1936). Her publisher, Jock Murray, became one of her closest friends and advisers; he published all her (twenty-two) books. Her first is generally considered her best: an immensely readable account of a solitary journey in northern and western Persia. Having learnt Arabic while still living in Italy, she was an unusually independent traveller in an age when few women travelled alone outside Europe.

She spent World War II in Aden, Yemen and Cairo, organizing anti-Fascist propaganda. Her fourth book of memoirs, *Dust in the Lion's Paw* (1961), gives a fascinating account of her war experiences, including a month-long siege in Baghdad and showing propaganda films in the harems. In 1943 she went to the USA to rally support for the Arab cause, to counter the powerful Zionist lobby, and in 1947 she made an ill-fated marriage to Stewart Perowne, a former colleague. They divorced in 1952. Her last years were based in Asolo, travelling frequently with younger male companions – women were not acceptable – and enjoying her celebrity. In 1972 she was made DBE.

Her writing is unique, as she was herself: moving ('In the Alamut valley we met huge bunches of wild roses everywhere against the grey boulders: white ones with very large petals, or pink like English roses: the scent came in whiffs as we went by'), also honest, funny and unpredictable. *A propos* a planned meeting with orientalists, she writes: 'I shall be so plain that I will merely be taken as a warning NOT to go to the East.' And on camels: 'When another caravan comes by, you will hear a vague, individual rumble from a male as he passes, while the lady whom he will never meet again turns to look distantly at him, as if through invisible lorgnettes.'   AB

Stead, Christina 1902–83 Australian novelist and short-story writer whose fourteen books reflect her nomadic history and a temperament intellectually, sexually and politically passionate. Her life was one of contradictions and extremes: from grinding poverty in Sydney to Parisian elegance; from literary lion in New York in the late 1930s to impoverished translator and hack in London in the 1950s and 1960s; from being banned and attacked in her own country to receiving the 1974 Patrick White Prize for 'a lifetime's significant contribution to Australian Literature'. In the late 1970s, there were rumours of a possible Nobel Prize, yet during most of her lifetime her work was out of print.

By instinct left-wing and feminist, she was also a perpetual dissenter. Too critically aware to toe any party line, she nevertheless remained stubbornly pro-Stalinist long after the awful truth about Stalin was known (partly out of a dogged refusal to be a rat leaving the sinking ship in McCarthyite America). While few writers have mapped as trenchantly the sexual and intellectual double-binds of women's lives, she objected to being labelled 'feminist' and extolled passionate heterosexual love as the real goal of a woman's life.

The childhood years of poverty and domestic drudgery in Sydney, and the subsequent escape to university and Europe, provide the material so brilliantly transformed in THE MAN WHO LOVED CHILDREN (1940) and FOR LOVE ALONE (1944). In London, she met William Blake, American Jew, Marxist economist and banker, true believer in Stead's genius. He became employer, lover, husband. They lived in Paris (1929–35), London (1936), New York (1937–47; with a spell as MGM script-writers in Hollywood in 1943); in various European cities (1949–52); in furnished rooms in England (1953–68). After Blake's death in 1968, Stead was Distinguished Writing Fellow at the Australian National University in 1969; she returned to her native country in 1974, for her final years.

SEVEN POOR MEN OF SYDNEY and *The Salzburg Tales* (both 1934), already exhibit her dense, lyrical style and relentless analysis of character and of power structures. *The Beauties and Furies* (1936) and HOUSE OF ALL NATIONS (1938), a satire on high finance and the bank as whorehouse, are both set in Paris. *The Man Who Loved Children* transposed her childhood to Chesapeake Bay and Baltimore. Rescued from oblivion by a 1965 reprint, the novel is 'one of those books that their own age neither reads nor praises, but that the next age thinks a masterpiece', wrote Randall Jarrell in the introduction. *For Love Alone* moves from Sydney to London. *Letty Fox, Her Luck* (1946), *A Little Tea, a Little Chat* (1948), *The People with the Dogs* (1952) all have American settings, while COTTER'S ENGLAND (1966; pub. in New York as *Dark Places of the Heart*), *The Little Hotel* (1973) and *Miss Herbert* (1976) return to Europe. *I'm Dying Laughing* (pub. posthumously, 1986) is a grim satire on Hollywood in the McCarthy years.

The long-overdue appreciation of Stead's work has begun, but much remains to be said of her role as a definitive breaker of the mould of 'women's novels'. In thumbing her nose at the DOMESTIC formula of JANE AUSTEN (that 'tiresome chronicler of the country marriage-hunt' in Stead's own words), Stead has given wings (literally, in the case of ANGELA CARTER's wonderfully raucous Fevvers in NIGHTS AT THE CIRCUS (1984)) to a wide range of free-flying successors.   JTH

Steaming (1981) NELL DUNN's play is set in a Public Baths in London's East End, and was, appropriately enough, first performed at the Theatre Royal in Stratford East. Funny and touching, with an uninhibited dialogue and an all-female cast, it concerns the struggle of six women, who meet regularly to bathe, relax and share their troubles, to save the Baths from closure. The struggle unites the very different characters in a common cause, and each undergoes a personal transformation in the process: the long-serving attendant, Violet, takes on the council bullies with indignant confidence; with Nancy's help, outspoken Josie finds a 'voice' for public speaking and sheds her dependence on her violent boyfriend, while jilted solicitor's wife Nancy learns to acknowledge her desire for sex. For Mrs Meadow and her 'simple' daughter, Dawn, the roles reverse with Mrs Meadow's ill health; and Dawn's curiosity, encouraged by the others, prompts her to slip her mother's custody. A crowning moment is when Dawn, divested of her obligatory plastic mac, appears triumphantly naked with her nipples painted with red lipstick.   JLB

Steedman [née Pilling], Carolyn (Kay) 1947–
Social and cultural historian, born and brought up in London. In 1995 she became Professor of Social History at the University of Warwick. Her pioneering historical work has been illuminated by her wide reading in literature, her complex sense of class and gender and her earlier work as a primary-school teacher. Childhood has been a theme or trace in almost all her

work, but she has transcended and complicated it in a number of ways. *The Tidy House* (1982) put a story about their futures, written by three 8-year-old working-class girls, in a historical context which allowed adult perceptions of childhood to confront the accounts children have given of themselves. This initiated a concern with the lives and autobiographies of marginalized groups in society, and led to *Policing the Victorian Community: The Formation of English Provincial Police Forces, 1856–1880* (1984) and to work on teachers, soldiers and now servants, work which makes central the rare testimony of the individuals involved. Steedman has been especially interested in those groups of workers recruited from the working class in order to supervise class boundaries while upholding the values of property owners and professionals. *The Radical Soldier's Tale: John Pearman, 1819–1908*, an exemplary case of this, was published in 1988.

Steedman has also worked in the history and literature of the self, and this inspired her best-known book, *Landscape for a Good Woman* (1986), an autobiography that is also a critique of a genre that has thrived on the absence of working-class girls and women. Her *Childhood, Culture and Class in Britain: Margaret McMillan, 1860–1931* (1990) was a wide-ranging study of the history and politics of early state schooling for young children. Her most recent book, *Strange Dislocations. Childhood and the Idea of Human Interiority, 1780–1980* (1995) is an intellectual history encompassing traditions of study and preoccupations in romantic literature, in which the infinitely resonant figure of Goethe's Mignon has been revisited and reworked. A selection of her essays, called *Past Tenses: Essays on Writing, History and Autobiography, 1980–1990*, was published in 1992.   JM

Steel, Danielle (Fernande Schüelein-Steel)

1950– Prolific and internationally best-selling American author whose many publications, including novels, CHILDREN'S BOOKS and a volume of poetry, have sold over 360 million copies world-wide. A descendant of the Löwenbräu beer barons, Steel is part-Portuguese and part-German, and spent her childhood in Paris where she attended the Lycée Français. She later studied at the Parsons School of Design in New York and the University of New York, going on to work as an advertising executive in the Manhattan-based 'Supergirls', a public relations firm run by women. Steel published her first novel, *Going Home*, in 1973 and continued to write advertising copy and poems for women's magazines until 1979, when she wrote her first bestseller, *The Promise*. Her variously historical, romantic and GOTHIC novels are set within both the 19th and the 20th centuries, presenting the reader with familiar tropes, such as fame, love, friendship and marriage, alongside betrayal and adultery, in often glamor-

ous and dazzling settings. At least half of her novels, including *Palomino* (1981), *Crossings* (1982), *Changes* (1983), *Full Circle* (1984), *Star* (1989) and *Message from Nam* (1991) have been adapted for television and cinema. Their vivid characters – displaying easily recognizable emotion in enviable environments – are ideal for visual interpretation. Steel's work, as titles like *Secrets* (1985), *Daddy* (1989) and *Jewels* (1992) suggest, offer some social commentary on the workings of power, money and gender in contemporary culture to a vast audience, exploring a fantastical world where conventional sexual roles are exaggerated and subverted.   EM

Steel [née Webster], Flora Annie 1847–1929

British novelist and campaigner for women's rights in Britain and India. Born in England, the granddaughter of a Jamaican sugar planter, her marriage in 1867 to a British official in the Indian Civil Service took her to remote locations in India where she campaigned for the education of Indian women and became a member of the provincial education board (1885–8) alongside Rudyard Kipling's father. Her carefully researched novel, *On the Face of the Waters* (1896), attempts a balanced account of both sides of the 1857 Indian Mutiny, but is unable to free itself of 19th-century stereotypes. Further novels include *Miss Stuart's Legacy* (1893), *The Potter's Thumb* (1894) and *Red Rowans* (1895); in 1884 she published a collection of Indian folklore, *Wide Awake Stories*, republished as *Tales of the Punjab* (1894). In her autobiography, *The Garden of Fidelity* (1929), she discloses her life-long sexual frigidity.   JSte

Steele, Anna ['Theodosia'] 1717–78? American poet

of deep religious conviction and philanthropic beliefs, Steele spent a quiet life of writing, prayer and contemplation. Although she never left her New Hampshire home, her many hymns and devotional verse appeared in several editions and circulated widely. Aside from the fact that she was the sickly daughter of a Dissenting minister, little is known of Steele's life. Her work, including a version of the Psalms in which she regularizes the verse into hymn metre, deals invariably with religious themes: the promise of heaven, the ephemeral nature of earthly happiness, our ongoing responsibilities to God. Her 'Imitation of Mr Pope's *Ode on Solitude*' replaces Pope's secular and sensual concerns with a passion for heaven that diminishes the draw of worldly delights. This view was undoubtedly strengthened by her constant illnesses, often addressed in her poetry as a 'trial' she must endure to become closer to God. In 1760, the two-volume *Poems on Subjects Chiefly Devotional* appeared; a third volume was added just before her death and editions appeared well into the 19th century. For unknown reasons, her remaining works weren't published until 1841, in a volume entitled *A Summer Journey into the West*.   JRS

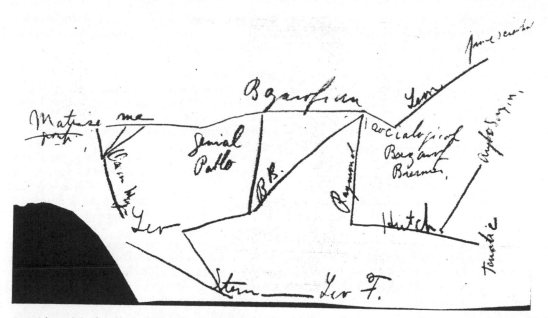

Gertrude Stein's sketch of relationships in the form of a sentence diagram, used for her 'Portraits' of Matisse, 'genial Pablo' (Picasso) and others.

Stein, Gertrude 1874–1946 American novelist, autobiographer, essayist, poet. Stein invented herself from promising materials: birth in Pennsylvania to wealthy, progressive German-Jewish parents who took her first to Vienna, then California, and education at the Radcliffe Annex (later Radcliffe College) of Harvard University, where she studied with philosophers William James and George Santayana. Both parents died early: 'Then our life without a father began a very pleasant one' (*Everybody's Autobiography*, 1937). Influenced by James's *Principles of Psychology*, Stein planned a career in experimental psychology and studied for two years at Johns Hopkins medical school before leaving for Europe in 1902 with favourite brother, Leo. Except for a lecture tour in 1934–5, she never returned, driving an ambulance for France in World War I, helping GIs in World War II, always remaining pragmatic, materialist and American. Leo and Gertrude were among the first collectors of emergent cubism: Pablo Picasso, a long-term friend, painted an important portrait of Stein, and they were patrons to Juan Gris, Georges Braque, Henri Matisse and Paul Cézanne. After an earlier lesbian relationship (described in the novel *Q.E.D.*), Stein met fellow-American ALICE B. TOKLAS in 1907; from 1909 to the end of Stein's life they lived together in Paris and then in the south of France. Their Paris salon was famous for warm hospitality to artists, writers and fellow expatriates, and for stylistic advice, notably to Ernest Hemingway, whom she advised to cut description and 'concentrate'.

Stein's earlier work maintains NATURALISM's 'scientific' objectivity without its determinism. In *Three Lives* (1909) small shifts in the consciousness of the black heroine, Melanctha, are presented through present-tense syntactic shifts with minimal authorial intervention. Character becomes a phenomenon of style, as in Stein's model, Flaubert's *Trois Contes*, but all parts of the portrait are equally valued, as in cubism and Cézanne's *Portrait of Mme Cézanne*. Despite Stein's lingering racism, the complex modern figure of Melanctha was a revelation to the young Richard Wright. At the same time Stein wrote the epically accumulating family beginnings of THE MAKING OF AMERICANS (1906–11, pub. 1925).

In middle-period works, from TENDER BUTTONS (1914) onwards, Stein redefined description and portraiture, evoking entity through 'cubist' metonymic groupings of objects and phrases, combined with figurative word-play. The works in *Geography and Plays* (1922) redefine the spatial and dramatic, as does the comic sublime of her 1927 opera *Four Saints in Three Acts* (composer Virgil Thompson). The erotic linguistics of the poem 'Lifting Belly' (1915–17) verbally enact lesbian lovemaking without representation. Stein's theoretical essays of the 1920s/1930s argue for a literature of presentness, divested of memory, externalized identity and stultifying 'patriarchal poetry'. THE AUTOBIOGRAPHY OF ALICE B. TOKLAS (1933), which created popular 'late' Stein, aggressively desubjectivizes autobiography, making Stein a character in a *faux-naif* memoir of the avant-garde purportedly written by Toklas as 'wife' of the 'genius'. A radical MODERNIST experimenter (influencing Hemingway,

Sherwood Anderson, EDITH SITWELL, William Carlos Williams and Thornton Wilder, among others), Stein developed concrete poetry, lyrical parody, erasure of the subject, deferral of meaning, presentation of surface as abstraction – 'POSTMODERNIST' issues which readers are still unpacking from her huge, not always available, oeuvre.   HM

Stephens, Ann Sophia 1813–86 American sentimental novelist and the first author to appear in Beadle's dime-novel format. A native of Connecticut, Stephens settled in Portland, Maine, after marrying, but was drawn to New York where the emergence in the 1840s of publishers specializing in cheap SENSATIONAL fiction created a new market for popular fiction. She had an editorial position on *Graham's Magazine*, and wrote flamboyant novels which were serialized in periodicals, issued in 'shilling' (12½ cents) parts, and eventually published in hardback. She was of the 'intense school' of popular writing, and her work 'contains many scenes of questionable taste and probability'. Stephens specialized in the fictionalizing of historical romances and adventures, such as *Alice Copley: A Tale of Queen Mary's Time* (1844). Her novels about America, including *High Life in New York* (1843, written under the pseudonym 'Jonathan Slick'), exhibited a vein of satire and varied humour which maintained her varied readership. *Fashion and Famine* (1854), and *Phemie Frost's Experiences* (1874) with its descriptions of opera in New York and use of actual personages such as Horace Greeley and Jim Fisk, brought Stephens into the vanguard of the 'Sunshine and Shadow' school of journalistic portraits of urban vice and virtue in mid-century.

EH

Stern, G(ladys) B(ronwen) 1890–1973 British writer who felt ambivalent toward the Jewish culture she helped to immortalize. In 1919 she married Geoffrey Lisle Holdsworth, but soon divorced. She wrote about forty novels, as well as short stories, plays and non-fiction, including a many-volume autobiography and studies of JANE AUSTEN and Robert Louis Stevenson, but she is best remembered for her famous series about the Rakonitz family, based on her own family: *Children of No Man's Land* (also published as *The Matriarch*; 1919), *Tents of Israel* (1923), *A Deputy Was King* (1926), *Mosaic* (1930) and *The Young Matriarch* (1942). These novels depict a prototypical Jewish family (based on her own) as cosmopolitan, generous, successful and kindly, but also as unbearably despotic. Stern's pride in her family is visibly mingled with resentment, and she converted to Catholicism after World War II. The 'Matriarch Chronicles' documents the vibrancy of pre-war Jewish European life, offering an intimate and unconsciously poignant view of a culture that would soon be destroyed.   TS

Stevenson, Anne 1933– Poet, critic and biographer. Stevenson was born into a middle-class American family, the product of what she has described as 'a protected academic environment [and] a liberal-arts education [which] appeared to guarantee . . . a future of bustling personal happiness and usefulness to society'. She attended the University of Michigan then, in the mid 1950s, married an Englishman and was transplanted 'from open-minded, prosperous America to class-ridden, war-depleted England'. In spite of this culture shock, Stevenson has carved out a successful and multi-faceted career. She has worked not only as a poet but also in higher education, publishing and bookselling, and is the author of *Bitter Fame* (1990), a notoriously controversial biography of her close contemporary, SYLVIA PLATH.

Stevenson's critical works include an illuminating essay entitled 'Writing as a Woman' (1979), a semi-autobiographical and double-edged argument which explores the dilemmas encountered by women who attempt to combine artistic creativity with socially acceptable patterns of femininity, yet goes on: 'I have never considered myself to be a specifically feminist poet'. In her poetry, attitudes to marriage and domesticity are also tantalizingly ambivalent. The final stanza of 'The Price' (1977) epitomizes this:

> My dear, the ropes that bind us
> are safe to hold;
> the walls that crush us keep us
> from the cold.
> I know the price and still I pay it, pay it –
> words, their furtive kiss,
> illicit gold.

Stevenson's *Selected Poems 1956-1986* was published in the Oxford Poets series in 1987.   AFT

Steveston (1974) This book combines DAPHNE MARLATT's poetic prose and Robert Minden's black-and-white photography to explore the small fishing town of the same name, located near the mouth of the Fraser River in British Columbia. Steveston then had a largely Japanese-Canadian population living with the memory of World War II, during which the Canadian government declared them 'enemy aliens', seized their homes and property, and interned them in the interior of the province. Marlatt and Minden focus on the divisions between the interpenetrating worlds of worker, capital, regulator and writer. Marlatt's MODERNIST poetics tease out the transactions and transitions which define regions of ethnicity, race, gender, economics, orientalism and exoticism.

In *Steveston*, Marlatt prefers reflexive language to referential language, so that the text's referents become less significant than its words. Yet Marlatt's experiences of the town and its people occur linguistically, so she must move from direct or raw experience (the phenomenological) toward engagement in a textual world. The 1984 expanded edition of *Steveston* includes five more photographs, and one additional essay, 'On Distance and Identity: Ten Years Later'. *Steveston* continues to attract ecological, ecofeminist and feminist attention.   JBM

Stillborn, The (1984) ZAYNAB ALKALI's first novel explores the impact of modernization and migration to the city on gender roles in northern Nigeria. Through the contrasting careers of two sisters, it assesses the adequacy of traditional conformism or a modern spirit of independence in adapting to social change. The more adventurous Li's move to the city brings exposure to urban alienation and abuse by a callous husband, while her sister's aim of becoming a traditional wife also proves illusory, since modern socio-economic trends encroach on the village itself and undermine her husband's masculine identity, transforming the exemplary 'man of the soil' into an alcoholic. The ending shows Li as a successful, home-owning teacher, empowered by her education to assume the role of 'man of the house', yet the novel's vivid evocation of the texture of village life shows how important traditional cultural references continue to be to her sense of identity. The novel's ambivalence toward tradition and modernity is reflected in its formal modes which combine a secular REALISM with mystical elements from a folkloric culture.   WJB

Stockenström, Wilma 1933– South African writer and actor. Arguably South Africa's foremost Afrikaans-language poet, Stockenström is also a novelist and translator. She was born in Napier, Cape Province, and lives in Cape Town. To English-speaking readers she is most famous for her novel, *The Expedition to the Baobab Tree* (1983), originally published as *Die Kremetartekspedisie* in 1981. Stockenström has been awarded numerous prizes, both in South Africa and internationally. In her work she returns to the themes of landscape and nature. Her interpretations of these themes include a rewriting of the Afrikaans farm novel, with its obsession with the natural bond between the white farmer and the land. The poet figure is often metaphorically represented as an intruder and destroyer; someone whose desire to acquire knowledge and express a relation with nature destroys that which it probes. So in *The Expedition to the Baobab Tree* Stockenström is less concerned with writing about the political significance of land than to find a radically new way in which her narrator can relate to nature. Her work is concerned with the signification of land and nature, and returns obsessively to a consideration of forms of power, of which language – European and African languages alike – is the prime example.
                                                        CCo

Stockton, Annis [Boudinot] 1736–1801 American poet, who wrote under the pseudonym 'Emelia' (spelled variously). Daughter of a tradesman of French Huguenot descent, and Catherine Williams, Annis Boudinot Stockton was raised in Philadelphia where she formed a life-long friendship with the poet ELIZABETH GRAEME FERGUSSON, with whom she exchanged letters and poetry. In 1752/53, the Boudinot family moved to New Jersey, finally settling in Princeton, the centre of social and intellectual activity. Boudinot tried her hand at various poetic invitations, satires and hymns, and wrote a series of pastoral letters with Benjamin Young Price. Late in 1757 or early 1758, she married Richard Stockton, a lawyer and future signer of the Declaration of Independence. They settled on the Stockton estate, which they eventually named 'Morven', after the kingdom of Fingal from the poem by James Macpherson. Their garden followed the published plan of Pope's Twickenham garden. Thus Stockton's poetry and home both reflected her preference for fashionable British modes of literature.

Morven became a well-known literary salon for women. After her marriage, she wrote many poems reflecting her domestic life, including incidents in the lives of her six children and her husband's last illness. Her political poems follow the fortunes of patriot soldiers in the battles of the Revolutionary War. After the war, she reflected on the transformative experience of the Revolution which she hoped would lead to a new golden age. Her position as a proto-feminist is ambivalent: her early poems attacked men's condescending attitudes toward women, but in post-Revolutionary America, she wrote a prenuptial poem to her niece advising her to submit to men. Stockton published many poems in newspapers and magazines; others circulated informally among her friends and family.   CLB

Stoddard, Elizabeth Drew Barstow 1823–1902 American poet and fiction writer. She was born in Mattapoisset, Massachusetts, daughter of a prosperous shipbuilder. She was educated at Wheaton Female Seminary. In 1851 she married poet Richard Stoddard, with whom she had three children; two died while young. The Stoddards' home in New York City became a meeting place for his circle of genteel minor poets. Elizabeth wrote poems, stories and sketches for periodicals, contributing the 'Lady Correspondent' column of the San Francisco *Alta* from 1854 to 1858. She commented irreverently on the temperance movement, women writers, gender relations and other topics. Her early fiction, notably *The Morgesons* (1862), mixes literary modes while challenging repressive gender conventions. Neither her nor her husband's writing was commercially successful. Stoddard suppressed her unconventionality in later writings (*Two Men*, 1865; *Temple House*, 1867), but she still failed to capture a popular market and became increasingly bitter over the success of others whom she regarded as less talented. Like her fiction, her poems (collected in 1895) show the influence of such GOTHIC authors as EMILY BRONTË in depicting family tensions, incest and decaying households. Her unflattering portrayals of New England life anticipate the 'local-color' realism of SARAH ORNE JEWETT and MARY WILKINS FREEMAN. JSG

Stone, Lucy 1818–93 American feminist, abolitionist and editor. She was born in West Brookfield, Massachusetts, to an old settler family. Largely self-educated, she became a schoolteacher at 16, later taught at Mt Holyoke Female Seminary, and in 1843 enrolled in Oberlin College, where she was inspired by the radical abolitionist Abby Kelley, who created a sensation when she visited the campus in 1846. After graduating in 1847, Stone joined the abolitionist and women's rights movements; she became one of the first female public speakers for abolitionism in 1854. She married reformer Henry Brown Blackwell in 1855 but retained her birth name. Together they issued a public statement on the disadvantages of marriage for women. After the Civil War, with other veterans of the abolitionist movement, she joined the new Universal Peace Union, an organization committed to non-violence in domestic and international affairs. In 1870 she led the American Women's Suffrage Association in its break from the more radical National Women's Suffrage Association led by SUSAN B. ANTHONY and ELIZABETH CADY STANTON. Beginning in 1872 she financed and edited the suffrage movement's organ, *Woman's Journal*. Her daughter, ALICE STONE BLACKWELL, wrote her biography in 1930. JSG

Stone Angel, The (1964) is MARGARET LAURENCE's first full-length novel about the fictional town of Manawaka which gave birth to so much of her work and which was based upon the town of her own birth: Neepawa, Manitoba. The title of the novel refers to a large imposing gravestone erected by Hagar's father over his wife's grave. During the lifetime of the heroine, Hagar, the monument leans, falls, is covered with graffiti, and generally charts not only the social decline of the Currie family, but the erosion of the notion of woman as angel: Hagar is no angel in any man's house, but she does, for most of her life, suffer from false pride and many other small-town pretensions which hinder her, like FLORENCE NIGHTINGALE's angel in *Cassandra*, from acting with agency on her own or anyone else's behalf. The novel is centred on the final weeks of Hagar's life, though her mind takes us back over the whole story. She tries 'to recall something truly free that I've done in ninety

years'. She becomes aware of how, till old age and imminent death release her, she has always been 'forced to a standstill by some brake of proper appearances'. This portrait of an old woman as 'a holy terror' is a unique creation. FD

Stone Diaries, The (1993) This is the third novel in which CAROL SHIELDS draws on the fascination with biography which was a legacy of her MA thesis on the Canadian author SUSANNA MOODIE. *The Stone Diaries* is more ambitious than *SMALL CEREMONIES* (1976) and *Swann* (1987) – Shields produces a fictional biography complete with a diagrammatic family tree and the hodge-podge of snapshots, portraits and sketches that generally accompany the biographical text. VIRGINIA WOOLF is a major influence on Shields and there are echoes of *ORLANDO* in her use of photographs and in her playful treatment of the conventions of biography. Conscious of the artificial divisions that biographers impose on lives, she divides the life of her fictional character, Daisy Goodwill, into ten equal chapters entitled Birth, Childhood, Marriage, and so on. There are frequent references to lost documents and gaps in the narrative. Since recognition of Shields's subtle art came slowly, it was generally (not altogether correctly) judged to be her crowning achievement. It was shortlisted for the Booker Prize, won the Governor General's Award in Canada and the Pulitzer Prize in the United States. JG

Stone Diary, A (1977) This posthumously published collection of poetry reveals the full flowering of PAT LOWTHER's poetic gift in the years preceding her murder in 1975. Through spare – but highly precise – images, *A Stone Diary* records Lowther's vivid psychological response to the natural and urban spaces in which she lived. In the stones, rainforests and aquatic life of the British Columbia coast, Lowther finds metaphors for endurance, sexuality and rejuvenation. Similarly, in her 'City Slide' series, Lowther connects the speaker's emotional complex to the 'spaces / within / spaces' of downtown Vancouver. The opening of 'City Slide / 6', for example, crystallizes the lurking presence of male violence that permeates much of Lowther's poetry with the words:

> Love is an intersection
> where I have chosen
> unwittingly to die

A passionate humanitarian, Lowther used poetry and politics to challenge the suppression of women and the poor. This commitment finds its clearest expression in a series of 'letters' to Pablo Neruda, who figures as a kind of South American, male counterpart in a shared lyrical and political project. IR

Story of a Modern Woman, The (1894) REALIST
BILDUNGSROMAN by ELLA HEPWORTH DIXON
about the moral and intellectual development of a
young woman struggling to achieve professional independence and emotional fulfilment in *fin-de-siècle*
London without compromising her principles. The
text interweaves the feminist themes of NEW WOMAN
fiction with autobiographical elements, offering ironic
insights into the cultural market-place of the time. In
this female version of George Gissing's *New Grub Street*
(1891), middle-class Mary Erle moves from painting
into journalism. Her professional life and friendship
with upper-class philanthropist Alison Ives provide a
satirical vignette of contemporary culture: fashionable
society (with its Oscar Wilde figure), populist art (a Pre-
Raphaelite painter), patriarchal authority figures (a
nerve specialist and a Conservative politician) and the
yellow press. Dixon engages with the debate on the
morality of literature, contrasting male opportunism
and corruption with the principle of feminist solidarity. The novel, whose open-endedness signals a resistance to conventional resolutions, was intended,
Dixon said, as 'a plea for a kind of moral and social
trades-unionism among women'. AH

Story of an African Farm, The (1883) The preface to
OLIVE SCHREINER's novel, which was first published
under a male pseudonym, challenges conventional
narrative expectations. As it claims, the book will be
untidy and leave loose ends; although it is set in southern Africa, it lacks lions and hairbreadth escapes, but
includes a cross-dressing farmer and a feminist bush
girl. The novel focuses on three orphans who are tyran-
nized by a predatory Boer woman and a brutal
European who claims kinship with both Wellington
and Napoleon. The Dickensian comedy of the first part
culminates abruptly; the mode changes to an extended
allegory, 'Waldo's Stranger', which predicts what will
follow. Waldo dies of fighting a hierarchical system
and Lyndall of attempting to contest the imperative of
women to 'fit our sphere as a Chinese woman's foot fits
her shoe, exactly'. Her obedient cousin is left to marry
Gregory, who is 'a true woman', most fulfilled when
wearing a frilled bonnet and gown. What survives
unaltered is the featureless Karroo. ASm

Stowe, Harriet (Elizabeth) Beecher 1811–96
Popular US novelist and essayist, whose Western
humour and colloquial language – assumed to have
been the innovations of Samuel L. Clemens – began to
appear in 1833, two years before his birth. Stowe was
born, the seventh of thirteen children, into a distinguished Evangelical New England family, the daughter of Lyman Beecher and Roxana Foote, and counted
among her siblings educator Catharine Beecher, popular preacher Henry Ward Beecher, and feminist

135,000 SETS, 270,000 VOLUMES SOLD.

UNCLE TOM'S CABIN

FOR SALE HERE.

AN EDITION FOR THE MILLION, COMPLETE IN 1 Vol, PRICE 37 1-2 CENTS.
"   "   IN GERMAN, IN 1 Vol, PRICE 50 CENTS.
"   "   IN 2 Vols,. CLOTH, 6 PLATES, PRICE $1.50.
SUPERB ILLUSTRATED EDITION, IN 1 Vol, WITH 153 ENGRAVINGS,
PRICES FROM $2.50 TO $5.00.

The Greatest Book of the Age.

Harriet Beecher Stowe: this advertisement for *Uncle
Tom's Cabin* appeared shortly after publication, indicating the popularity of her novel.

Isabella Beecher Hooker, the last being the daughter of
Lyman's second wife, Harriet Porter. CHARLOTTE
PERKINS GILMAN was the granddaughter of Stowe's
sister Mary.

Residing in Litchfield, Connecticut, Stowe was educated at the Litchfield Female Academy from 1819 to
1822 and then at the Hartford Female Seminary
(founded in 1823 by her sister Catharine) from 1824 to
1827, when Stowe became a teacher. One of her students was Sara Willis, later known as author FANNY
FERN. With the Beecher family, Stowe moved to
Cincinnati, Ohio, in 1832, where she joined the Semi-
Colon Club, a mixed-sex literary society, fostering the
1833 initiation of her writing career with the publication in the *Western Monthly Magazine* of 'Uncle Lot'
(reprinted in *The May Flower*, 1855). In 1836, she married
Calvin Ellis Stowe, a biblical scholar at Lane
Theological Seminary, then headed by her father. The
couple's seven children were born between 1836 and
1850. They moved to Brunswick, Maine, in 1850, then
moved again in 1852 to Andover, Massachusetts
(where neighbours were the ELIZABETH STUART
PHELPSES), and again in 1864 to Hartford,
Connecticut, the locale with which Stowe is primarily
associated.

The work for which she is best known is, of course,
the immensely popular and influential novel, UNCLE

TOM'S CABIN, serialized in the *National Era*, from 1850 to 1851, and published as a book in 1852. American novelist Ernest Hemingway might more accurately have named this, rather than Clemens's *Huck Finn* (1885), as the beginning of American Literature, for its use of dialect, dialogue, humour and irony. Stowe effectively blended literary realism, social satire and jeremiad in a work that continues to receive international recognition. Her *A Key to Uncle Tom's Cabin* (1853) provides a plethora of sources and documentation vindicating her presentation of the institution of slavery. (See also DRED, 1856). Other topics treated in her novels include anticlerical critique of patriarchal theology in *A Minister's Wooing* (1896), psychic dislocations of growing up female in *The Pearl of Orr's Island* (1862), and nostalgic recollections of a former New England in *Oldtown Folks* (1869) and *Poganuc People* (1878). In *My Wife and I* and *Pink and White Tyranny* (both 1870), she satirizes Gilded Age, USA, while developing her own moderate feminism. Stowe considered herself a literary moral guardian, performing the cultural work of educating and shaping bourgeois public opinion. All her work, her European travel essays, magazine contributions on social reforms – abolition, temperance, suffrage, education, religion – as well as her short and long fiction reveal her writing is shaped by cultural concepts of republican motherhood and true womanhood. CFK

Strangers on a Train

Strangers on a Train (1950) Her abiding concerns with the perfect murder and the notion that anyone can be a murderer motivate crime-writer PATRICIA HIGHSMITH's first novel. An ingenious psychological thriller, its plot utilizes another of her favourite devices, the one-on-one relationship in which characters are bound together by a guilty nexus of shared (here, exchanged) crime. The chance meeting of mother-fixated Charles Anthony Bruno and nervous architect Guy Haines sparks off Bruno's seemingly mad proposition: 'Hey! Cheeses, what an idea! I kill your wife and you kill my father!' Highsmith's taut and brooding prose casually but inexorably builds suspense and a mood of impending doom. Her depiction of the protagonists, cleverly reworking the GOTHIC idea of the double, probes the interpenetration of hunter and hunted, activity and passivity, and love and hate (Bruno's homoerotic attraction to Guy is barely concealed).

Alfred Hitchcock directed the famous adaptation of *Strangers on a Train* (1951) almost immediately after its publication. Punctuated by a series of brilliant set pieces, it, like its source, is regarded as a classic. MO'D

Stratton-Porter, Geneva Grace [Gene]

Stratton-Porter, Geneva Grace [Gene] 1863–1924 American writer, photographer and early conservationist, whose novels were prominent in the bestseller lists from 1911 to the mid-1920s. The youngest of many children, Gene enjoyed a childhood of unusual freedom on the family farm in Indiana, an idyll lost on a move to the city when she was 11. Admiring her father, a Methodist preacher as well as farmer, she developed her own strong messages of natural piety in her writings. The Indiana countryside, especially the Limberlost swamp, where she eventually set up home with her husband and daughter, gave her unique material. Becoming fascinated by the birds and moths, she memorialized the vanishing life of the swamp in her photographs and drawings, distancing herself from male 'Naturalists', whose arid dissection of dead creatures missed the living spirit, caught by the true 'Nature Lover'. 'When it came to books, all they had to teach me were the names', she wrote in *Moths of the Limberlost* (1912). Her own books offer her readers powerfully vivid representations of natural life, above all through her sympathetic fictional heroes and heroines (among them, *Freckles* (1904), *The Harvester* (1911), *The Girl of the Limberlost* (1908), *A Daughter of the Land* (1918)), all close observers of the land, natural healers, artists and early ecologists.

Famous and wealthy, becoming involved with screen productions of her books, she ended her days in Los Angeles, where she developed scare stories about the 'yellow peril', and was killed in a limousine crash in 1924. PEK

Strauss, Jennifer

Strauss, Jennifer 1933– Australian poet and critic, born in rural Victoria, she has had a distinguished career as an academic, her scholarly publications including *Boundary Conditions: The Poetry of Gwen Harwood* (1992) and her edited edition of *The Oxford Book of Australian Love Poetry* (1993). Her own poetry has been published in several collections: *Children and Other Strangers* (1975), *Winter Driving* (1981), *Labour Ward* (1988) and *Tierra del Fuego: New and Selected Poems* (1997). She has been an influential critic, editor and anthologizer, particularly of women's poetry, as well as developing her own distinctive poetic voice in her own poems. In the poem 'Guenevere Dying' this voice becomes that of a Queen betrayed by both husband and lover:

Men slaughter men with sword and lance
'Honourably': trees and women they burn
Always afraid of female blood.

Women, their lives as lovers and mothers, are the subject of many of her poems, characteristically speaking in voices of clear intelligence, often inflected with potentially tragic irony. The politics of feminism is rarely separated in her poems from the politics of other marginalized groups: powerless individuals from the Third World, or the hapless victims of historical oppressions, puzzled children and victimized women, whether that be Horatio's wife or an obscure migrant woman seen on a tram. The universality of the predicaments expressed with both passion and wit is partly conveyed in the wide range of settings all over the world, sharply observed and memorably rendered.

HTh

Streatfeild, (Mary) Noel 1895–1986 British actress, novelist, ROMANCE-writer ('Susan Scarlett'), speaker and broadcaster, best remembered for her books for CHILDREN. Her fictionalized autobiography (1960s–1970s) vividly evokes the constraints of middle-class girlhood in a southern English vicarage. Disaffected at school (and expelled from St Leonard's Ladies' College), she enjoyed family story-telling and amateur dramatics, discovering an enthusiasm for the stage that later inspired many of her novels. After wartime voluntary work in a munitions factory, and training at the Academy of Dramatic Art, she spent ten years as an actress ('Noelle Sonning'), chorus girl and model, but, increasingly disillusioned, resolved to turn to writing.

In *The Whicharts* (1931), the first of her sixteen adult novels, Noel drew on her theatrical experiences to raise questions about women's lives, family roles, sexual dependency and chances for economic freedom. At her publisher's suggestion, she purged its more overtly sordid elements, to transform it into a book for girls. Illustrated by Ruth Gervis (Noel's sister), *Ballet Shoes* (1936) rapidly became a classic. (See BALLET STORIES.) The adopted Fossil sisters, launching their professional ambitions from the strong base of an all-female household, set the tone for her subsequent children's narratives (1936–79). Featuring independent-minded children, full of drive and (often frustrated) creativity, these novels – though warm and humorous – remain psychologically acute explorations of children negotiating the complexities of gender, class and family.

PEK

Street, The (1946) ANN PETRY's bestselling first novel, with its NATURALISTIC depiction of life in contemporary Harlem, has drawn comparisons with Richard Wright's *Native Son*. When Petry's heroine, Lutie Johnson, moves with her young son to an apartment, the bleak, windswept world of the street becomes a microcosm of the life of violence, poverty and despair which threatens its black inhabitants. Petry's story of a black woman's rebellion against the cruelty and oppression imposed on her by both black and white men inevitably ends in murder. Racism and unemployment have driven the black community into a world of servitude, alcoholism and prostitution. The lonely mother, Lutie, is driven by neglect and frustration to turn on her abuser and, in fleeing the consequences of his death, is separated from her son. The haunting and evocative message that Petry conveys in *The Street* is as relevant to 1990s urban America as when it was written fifty-two years ago.

JP

Stretton, Hesba [Sarah Smith] 1832–1911 Writer of popular evangelical tales, primarily for children, this English author's bestselling work was *Jessica's First Prayer* (1866). Pleased with its reception, her principal publisher, The Religious Tract Society, translated the story into numerous languages for sales overseas. So successful were sales of this and her other works that by 1869 they accounted for more than one fifth of all RTS books sold.

Stretton's fundamental message may be summed up by quoting from one of her books for older readers, *Bede's Charity* (1882): 'all things . . . most surely work together for good for anyone, however poor and unlearned, who loves God'. Many of her books appear to be addressed to the poorer sectors of society, in whom she took a personal interest. She is known to have helped to found the London Society for Prevention of Cruelty to Children in 1884 and it is notable that the main protagonists in her tale *Lost Gip* (1879) both have dealings with a children's refuge and speak positively of child-emigration schemes. In all, Stretton wrote over fifty books. However, she also published in Dickens's periodicals *Household Words* and *All the Year Round* between 1859 and 1866.

EMH

Strickland, Agnes 1796–1874 Historian, received a gentlewoman's education in Southwold, Suffolk, and alongside her broad horizons maintained a life-long attachment to these roots, emphasizing, whenever appropriate, episodes of historical significance with an East Anglian setting. Her childhood with five sisters, four of whom eventually wrote professionally, and several brothers, was full of enthusiastic reading and shared composition, influenced by Shakespeare and tales of chivalry by the PORTER sisters and Walter Scott. The sisters wrote for the market after their father's business failure and death. Strickland is best known for the *Lives of the Queens of England* (1840–8, 12 vols.) and *Lives of the Queens of Scotland* (1850, 8 vols.), written in collaboration with her sister Eliza, who refused public acknowledgement. Editions of the former, repeated throughout the century, included runs of 50,000; a facsimile library edition in the 1970s was introduced by Antonia Fraser. Other joint series included Tudor and Stuart Princesses, while Agnes specialized in MARY QUEEN OF SCOTS, editing her papers and writing her biography. This success as historians followed twenty years of literary apprenticeship writing poetry and novels, and editing children's annuals. The compulsively readable biographies also broke new ground in using public and private documentary sources, in England and the continent, surpassing predecessors like Lucy Aikin, Elizabeth Benger and ANNA JAMESON. Though not overtly feminist the biographies consider women a powerful civilizing influence in history and quietly celebrate consorts like Anne of Cleves or Catherine of Braganza, who preserve their dignity as wives of churlish men.   CCO

Strikes Have Followed Me All My Life (1989)

EMMA MASHININI's autobiography offers an insight into the political struggles of black South Africans. The life, as signalled in the title, is shaped primarily by the sociopolitical context of Apartheid South Africa. Mashinini distinguishes between private life and the recounting of personal experience toward a political end. Her second marriage does not feature as an event in her narrative, and the circumstances surrounding the death of her daughter are left deliberately vague. This insistence on privacy might be read in terms of her 'fight for the dignity of individuals' in a context where such rights are denied to black people.

The distinction between documenting personal involvement in political struggle and the exploration of the self breaks down in the writing of the traumas of detention and of the period spent at a clinic for victims of detention. The process of the writing of the autobiography itself raises interesting questions around issues of agency, collaboration, and marketing imperatives as they influence the shape of the text. Mashinini began by recording aspects of her life on tape, prompted by questions from Elizabeth Wolpert who was instrumental in persuading The Women's Press to publish the autobiography. The transcribed notes were then reworked by Mashinini together with her editor.
                                                            C-AM

Strong, Eithne 1923– Irish novelist, short-story writer and poet in both Irish and English. Born in Limerick, Eithne Strong grew up in a *breach-ghaeltacht*, a region where many words in the vernacular are in Irish. She developed a keen and enduring love for the language and for traditional Gaelic poetry. As a young woman she was an active member of the Irish Language movement and her early published work appeared in Irish in *An Glór* and in *Comhar*. She and her husband, Rupert Strong, were founder members of the Runa Press and active in psychoanalytic circles in Dublin before such interest was fashionable or even altogether acceptable: 'We were quite brave, I think. Pioneering and liberal. We lived experimentally . . . so much so that the 60s left me quite cold. We had explored and experienced a great deal throughout the 40s and 50s.' She has nine children, the youngest of whom has a mental handicap. Her life within a large and loving family is 'integral' to her writing and to her re-interpretations of traditional images and forms in her poetry in both languages. Her first collection in English, *Songs of Living*, was published in 1961.

Subsequently, she returned to college as a mature student and obtained a degree in Irish and English and worked as a teacher and as a journalist. Love, relationships and responsibility are foregrounded in her work, notably in *Degrees of Kindred* (novel, 1979), *Patterns* (short stories, 1981) and *Spatial Nosing* (poems, 1993). She also offers a critique of oppressive social systems and their conventions, evasions and snobberies. *The Love Riddle* (1993) is dedicated 'To Life'.   LM

Stuart, Arbella Lady 1575–1615 Author of a remarkable body of letters, over 100, written to a variety of friends, relatives, court officials and the royal family. As a claimant to the royal throne, her marriageable status was a focus for anxiety during the Elizabethan and Jacobean reigns. She spent her early years in Derbyshire under the guard of her grandmother, Bess of Hardwick, who was also watching over MARY, QUEEN OF SCOTS.

Stuart attempted two clandestine marriages against the monarch's wishes: first a failed betrothal in 1603 to Edward Seymour, and in 1610 a marriage to his younger brother William, which led to their joint arrest. Stuart was exiled to the north but managed to escape to France in a famous cross-dressing incident. Captured at Calais, she was sent to the Tower of London where she died in 1615. There were rumours she went insane but she more likely died of malnutrition following self-starvation – a form of resistance she had used previously. Her story has been the subject of literature throughout the centuries.

Another of the Stuart Court's exceptionally learned women (she was multi-lingual), her letters display considerable rhetorical skill and are an astonishing record of their times. In those addressed to the Court she plays the part of humble servant; in those to her relatives, her genuine anger and frustration at her condition shine through.   JS

Stuart, Elizabeth, Queen of Bohemia 1596–1660

Significant figure at the Early Stuart Court who, like many elite women, wrote verse. Eldest daughter of James VI and I, and sister of Charles I. Separated from her mother at a very young age due to a power struggle between her parents, she was raised by Lord Harington (father of Lucy Russell, Countess of Bedford) at Coombe Abbey. Many of her letters from this time survive. Like other court women she was educated in French, Italian, music and dancing, although her father opposed her learning Latin or Greek. In 1613 she was married to Frederick V, Elector Palatine. When in 1619 he was elected as King of Bohemia she became Queen in a political manoeuvre which led to the so-called Palatinate Crisis and the Thirty Years War. She and her husband were forced to flee and spent the rest of their life in exile and she was accorded the romantic titles of 'Winter Queen' and 'Queen of Hearts' during that time by English sympathizers. She had thirteen children. Her verse is fairly conventional court poetry in terms of content, although its form ('This is joye, this is true pleasure' is written in rhyming quatrains) is sometimes unusual. Some important letters written by her also survive. JS

Stuart, Louisa, Lady 1757–1851 English memoirist and letter-writer. Child of despised former Prime Minister, the Earl of Bute, and granddaughter of the controversial BLUESTOCKING LADY MARY WORTLEY MONTAGU, Louisa educated herself by reading widely, despite her family's harsh censure. Honouring the restrictions placed upon women of her class, she remained in the background of political and literary circles, corresponding on cultural and social topics with leading figures and friends. Her political inclinations were decidedly Tory but tempered by sympathy for less fortunate individuals. Financially secure, she never married, concentrating instead on her profound gift for friendship. She is most famous for her fond correspondence with, and insightful pre-publication advice to, Sir Walter Scott. Published only after her death, her works include collections of correspondence to Scott, her favourite sister, a young *protégée* Miss Louisa Clinton, and others. She contributed introductory notes to *The Correspondence of Lady Mary Wortley Montagu* (1837) and to J. H. Jesse's *George Selwyn and His Contemporaries* (1843). For circulation among her friends, she wrote reverential but wry and candid memoirs of her relations and their circle, including *Memoir of John, Duke of Argyll* (1837, pub. 1899). Her greatest strengths were literary criticism and social satire. JHP

Studies of the Eighteenth Century in Italy (1880) The unpromising title conceals a lively and even absorbing appreciation written by the youthful Vernon Lee, which has none of the mealy-mouthed, genteel tone so frequent at the time. With perceptive yet affectionate irony she resuscitated the dusty, neglected writers and composers of Italy's Enlightenment, at the same time providing a panorama of the cultural life of the age. Beginning at the end of the 17th century with the Arcadian Academy in Rome, which spawned similar associations for would-be literati throughout the Italian peninsula, Lee produces a gallery of writers, poets and dramatists, some remembered but unloved, many 'extremely forgotten', without regret. While her occasionally hilarious descriptions bring foppish and desperate intellectuals alike to life, her masterly erudition places them firmly in context. This skilful evocation of the characters of a rather pompous period enjoyed much success, perhaps the more so when it was discovered that Vernon Lee

was Violet Paget, though the playful humour and insight might have suggested a feminine hand. EL

suffragette literature This gynocentric genre, which developed alongside the Edwardian Women's movement under the auspices of the Women Writers' Suffrage League, founded by CICELY HAMILTON and Bessie Hatton, and the Actresses' Franchise League (both 1908), served to publicize suffragist arguments and celebrate feminist heroism while indicting the violence with which the demand for equal civil rights was met. Typically reflecting the perspective of the militants – the Pankhursts' Women's Social and Political Union (1903) and CHARLOTTE DESPARD's Women's Freedom League (1907) – playwrights like Elizabeth Baker (*Miss Tassey*, 1910) also addressed the concerns of Millicent Garrett Fawcett's constitutionalist National Union of Women's Suffrage Societies (1892). ELIZABETH ROBINS, WSPU propagandist and first president of the WWSL, inaugurated the genre with her three-act *Votes for Women!* (1907) and subsequent novel, *The Convert* (1907). Heterogeneous in form, suffragette literature blurred the boundaries between fiction and factual writing, aesthetics and polemics, by incorporating reportage, the political tract and the memoir into its narrative or dramatic framework. The novel and play were complemented by the short story (Evelyn Sharp, *Rebel Women*, 1910), poetry (Elizabeth Gibson, *From the Wilderness*, 1910), and autobiography (Emmeline Pankhurst, *My Own Story*, 1914). As the cultural expression of first-wave feminism, suffragette literature was closely related to its predecessor, FIN-DE-SIÈCLE NEW WOMAN writing.

Foregrounding the political awakening (conversion), courage, self-sacrifice and suffering of individual women uniting across class barriers, and presenting their characters as survivors of personal abuse and systematic state torture (police assault, forcible feeding), writers drew attention to the close link between personal and political oppression, commemorating suffragettes as quasi-religious martyrs. In Gertrude Colmore's *Suffragette Sally* (1911), forcible feeding is associated with crucifixion in a scene which recreates LADY CONSTANCE LYTTON's personal experience (*Prisons and Prisoners*, 1914). Other key texts are *Outlawed* (1908) by Charlotte Despard and Mabel Collins, *Elisabeth Davenay* (1909) by Claire de Pratz, *No Surrender* (1911) by Constance Elizabeth Maud, and *The Poodle Woman* (1913) by Annesley Kenealy. To counter anti-suffrage propaganda by writers like H.G. Wells (*Ann Veronica*, 1909) and MRS HUMPHRY WARD (*Delia Blanchflower*, 1914), the femininity of suffragettes was thrown into relief.

In great demand at political events, the suffragette play proved of even more immediate appeal. Mostly one-acters, plays were based on monologues (L.S. Phibbs, *Jim's Leg*, 1911) or duologues (Graham Moffat, *The Maid and the Magistrate*, 1911), though larger casts were used in Hamilton's *How the Vote Was Won* and BEATRICE HARRADEN's *Lady Geraldine's Speech* (both 1909). Pageants and allegories celebrated female role models (Hamilton, *Pageant of Great Women*, 1909; Vera Wentworth, *Allegory*, 1911), while farces like Shaw's *Press Cuttings* (1909) and Joan Dugdale's *10 Clowning Street* (1913) poured scorn on the 'antis', or taught feminists how to fight back – Cecil Armstrong's *Physical Force* (1911) actually provided lessons in self-defence. Offering socialist feminist analyses of patriarchal capitalism (Gita Sowerby, *Rutherford and Son*, 1912) and adopting working-class perspectives (Evelyn Glover, *Chat with Mrs Chicky*, 1911), grimly REALIST plays demonstrated how important it was for women to gain the franchise in the face of legal, economic and sexual exploitation (Inez Bensusan, *The Apple*, 1910; Gertrude Vaughan, *Woman with the Pack*, 1911). Edy Craig's feminist Pioneer Players contributed to the genre by drawing analogies between women's private and public subjection (Margaret Wynne Nevinson, *In the Workhouse*, 1911) and by exposing prostitution (Antonia Williams, *The Street*, 1913). Suffragette literature was brought to a close by the outbreak of World War I and the conferral of the limited franchise in 1918.   AH

Sugar Heaven (1936) JEAN DEVANNY described her work, set in the canefields of North Queensland during the great Depression, as 'the first really proletarian novel in Australia'. Her lengthy involvement with the Communist party of Australia was troubled but her contribution to Left-wing cultural production was considerable. Indeed, this is Devanny's first novel to espouse an overt political agenda. The narrative traces the events of the cane-cutters' strike in northern Queensland. The workers agitate against dangerous conditions, specifically Weil's Disease (the plague) spread by rats through the sugar cane. In her dedication to the novel, Devanny suggests that this was a struggle not for wages 'but for life'. She dedicates the novel not to the workers, but to their wives 'who stood shoulder to shoulder with their men'. Indeed, the politicization and involvement of the wives in the strike is the central concern of the narrative. Cast in a socialist REALIST formula, the novel operates within the mode of 'revolutionary romanticism', reminiscent of Soviet literature of the time, also touching on issues of racism, particularly that directed at migrant and *kanaka* labour in North Queensland.   CE

Sula (1974) TONI MORRISON's second novel sees her in full command of her powers. A story centred on the friendship between two African-American women, Sula and Nel, the novel interrogates the ethical dimensions of love, friendship, community and responsibility against the background of American racial injustice. The novel is set in the small town of Medallion, where the black population have been displaced repeatedly at the whim of the white townsfolk. The return of the magnificent, independent and dangerous Sula to her home-town is presaged by evil omens which foreshadow both her own and the mass deaths which complete the fiction, and which are emblematic of the black community's need to revise its view of itself. This process of revision is enacted in the attitude of Nel toward Sula. Though they are inseparable as young girls, Nel opts for a life of conformity while Sula goes her own way. The breach between the two women, following Sula's seduction of Nel's husband, is healed only after Sula's death when Nel realizes that her link with her friend was the most important thing in her life.   KF

Sulter, Maud 1960– British journalist, poet and fiction writer, born in Glasgow. Her prize-winning first work was *As a Black Woman* (1985). Sulter takes an explicitly political stance, campaigning for civil rights, gender and racial equality: 'as a black woman creativity is central to my existence. It is a means of survival, covering a spectrum as diverse as singing, sculpture, hair braiding and childbearing. Our art demands participation.'

> Daughters, she cries
> learn the tongues
> of this world voices
> teach the children
> of their wonder
> love as only a woman can
> take up the pen, the brush
> explosive,
> and name
> yes name
> yourself
> black
> women
> zami
> proud
> name yourself
> never forget
> our herstory.   ('Full Cycle')

Her political work appears in several anthologies. She was active with London's Women's Resource Centre, in editing *Spare Rib*'s black women's edition and *Feminist Art News*. Maud Sulter has actively supported and encouraged black women's writing, films and artwork, and has herself received support from older writers such as GRACE NICHOLS. Her other books include *Passion: Discourses on Black Women's Creativity* (1990) with Ingrid Pollard, and *Echo: Works by Women Artists 1850–1940* (1991) for Liverpool Tate.   GW

Summer Bird-Cage, A (1963) MARGARET DRABBLE's first novel, a deceptively slight tale of two sisters, introduces many of the concerns of her later work. Narrated by the younger sister, Sarah, the story opens after her graduation from Oxford. Through a series of dramatic vignettes, it depicts the sisters' shifting relationship following Louise's loveless marriage to a wealthy novelist, setting in action a chain of events that leads to an eventual, wry reconciliation between the women. The marriages of various other couples are dissected and condemned for their depredation of the female partner. Sarah's 'bachelor girl' lifestyle in a squalid North London flat is no more attractive, and the ending of the novel proffers no resolution, leaving Sarah awaiting her lover's return from America, an uncertain future before her. Drabble's presentation of an emerging generation – literate, liberated young women confused by the conflicting pressures of economic insecurity, domesticity and maternity, the aimlessness of working life, and unsatiated intellect – is a bleak BILDUNGSROMAN far removed from those of the E.M. Forster novels to which her heroines glibly refer.
CS

Summer Lightning (1986) OLIVE SENIOR's first volume of short stories won the 1987 Commonwealth Writers Prize. Written and narrated entirely in a literary rendition of Jamaican nation language, it explores with humour and sparkle the multi-layered texture of rural life. Children, outsiders interloping on the sometimes incomprehensible dramas of the adult world, tell nearly all the stories in this volume. The naive candour of the child's perspective makes author and reader complicit in the critique they offer, negotiating between past and present, progress and tradition, race and class differences, the need for acceptance and the snobbery encouraged by finely tuned colour distinctions. Senior draws out the tensions and securities of her own childhood roots in rural Jamaica, lived between two homes of comparative wealth and poverty. Focusing on the domestic sphere, and anticipating her social study on Caribbean women, *Working Miracles*, she also concentrates on the contradictory status-empowerment and economic disenfranchisement Jamaican women experience as heads of households and mothers struggling to raise families, either with their men or alone.
HLR

Summer Will Show (1936) SYLVIA TOWNSEND WARNER's fourth novel merges ideas of political, sexual and racial otherness in the story of Sophia Willoughby who, after the death of her two children, leaves her Dorset estate for Paris to retrieve her estranged husband (and his procreative potential). However, she falls in love with his mistress, a Jewish story-teller, and becomes inadvertently involved in the 1848 revolution. Like LOLLY WILLOWES (1926), the narrative starts as a REALIST fiction with a more conventional portrayal of woman as a relational creature (wife, mother, mistress), but abandons this mode in favour of a more disorderly 'revolutionary' existence. Less whimsical in tone than the earlier novels, but equally utopian, *Summer Will Show* employs various narratological strands – historical novel, subtle lesbian fantasy, colonial critique and Marxist fiction – without necessarily attempting to reconcile the contradictions and implausibilities arising from this conflation. A continual experiment with different styles and genres, Warner's fiction rejects catch-all categorizations, and Sophia's rival-turned-lover Minna Lemuel, a professional story-teller, aptly represents Warner's tricky way of telling tall tales.
PUR

Summers, Essie (Ethel) 1912–98 New Zealand's bestselling ROMANCE novelist. Born in Christchurch of English parents, she worked in Christchurch drapery stores before marrying a Baptist minister. She wrote stories and poems for local papers and, for six years, a column in the Women's Page of the Timaru *Herald*, in the form of the humorous diary of a minister's wife. Her first novel, *New Zealand Inheritance*, was published by Mills and Boon in 1957, and was followed by many others in the same format. An autobiography, *The Essie Summers Story*, was published in 1974, and her last novel appeared in 1987. Many of her novels are set in New Zealand, typically on a South Island sheep station. The heroine, in her mid-20s and usually a nurse, teacher or secretary, 'good with children, animals and scones', comes from the town to the country and, after misunderstandings, marries the well-off rural hero. Summers said, 'I write for people to get enjoyment and pleasure and relaxation', and her works have been very popular. In 1981 she claimed her novels had sold 17 million copies and been translated into 12 languages.
AM

Surfacing (1972) MARGARET ATWOOD's second novel secured her reputation as a novelist whose fiction matched the excellence of her already widely praised poetry. Set in the Canadian forests the text registers the feminist impulses of its day, while also marking Atwood's strong engagement with issues of nationalism, consumerism, ecology, art, history and politics, which have continued to characterize her work. The unnamed narrator of *Surfacing* is a young woman who returns to her family's simple home on a forest lake along with her boyfriend and two new friends. Deeply disturbed by her parents' death and by the abortion for which she will admit no responsibility, the narrator drives back through memory and madness until she reaches a point of nullity from which she can begin to reconstruct her identity. Linking questions of personal and communal responsibility with the need for women to refuse the status of victim, Atwood's novel, with its deep sense of fear and mystery, offers a psycho-social analysis of the roots of power. KF

Survival (1972) MARGARET ATWOOD's first book of non-fiction, sub-titled 'A Thematic Guide to Canadian Literature', aims to answer the questions, 'What's Canadian about Canadian literature?' and 'Why should we be bothered?' Written partially in response to the encroachments of American and British cultures, Atwood's personable, concise, non-academic and accessible 'book of patterns', based on a reading of literature published mostly between the 1930s and 1960s, provides answers polemical and wry. Though Atwood's approach (based on that of Northrop Frye) attracted some criticism, her contention that the Canadian master metaphor is Survival (analogous to Island in England and Frontier in the United States) and that victimhood is a national literary pastime gathered considerably more. Atwood speculates that Canadians are an 'oppressed minority' whose literature reflects four Basic Victim Positions; and since literature is both a mirror and a map, understanding its literature is tantamount to knowing Canada's national consciousness. After outlining the modalities of Canadian victimhood, Atwood traces literary treatments of land, animals, ancestral figures, nature, artists and women, indicating how each falls within one victim category or another. Two concluding chapters – 'rays of light' – sample some new, positive developments in Canadian literature. BJG

Sutcliff, Rosemary 1920–92 British novelist who wrote mainly for CHILDREN. Her work offers a vivid example of a writer compensating for her own severe physical handicap through an imagined world of vigorous action and adventure. The daughter of a naval officer, she fell victim, as a baby, to chronic arthritis which confined her to a wheelchair and blighted her hopes of becoming a painter. Turning to fiction, she began at once to map out a distinctive personal territory, concentrating initially on the Tudor period in *Brother Dusty Feet*, a tale of strolling players, and *The Queen Elizabeth Story*, one of whose characters, the lonely lame boy Adam, is clearly intended as a self-portrait. Her interests soon shifted to the Britain of the Roman invasion and the Dark Ages, and, in *The Eagle of the Ninth* (1954), the tale of a young Roman officer, physically and emotionally maimed, who recovers the standard of his father's lost legion after a thrilling chase beyond Hadrian's Wall, she recast her narrative style, producing a classic in the process. History provides Sutcliff's backdrop, but the *dramatis personae* are her own invention. The atmosphere is predominantly male and military, dwelling on warrior comradeship,

survival against overwhelming odds and vindication of personal honour. Though interested in Arthurian legend, Irish folktales and the Old English epic, she returned continually to the world of Roman imperial frontiers, whose guardians become absorbed by this pagan freedom of the tribes who menace them. She received the Carnegie Medal in 1975. An account of her childhood, *Blue Remembered Hills*, was published in 1983. JK

Sutcliffe, Alice [Woodhouse] fl. 1633 English author of *Meditations of Man's Mortalitie: Or, A Way to True Blessednesse* (1633; second edn, 1634). She was the daughter of Luke Woodhouse of Kimberly, Norfolk, related to Sir Thomas Woodhouse, an attendant to Prince Henry in the court of James I. By 1624 she was married to John Sutcliffe, 'esquire to the body of James I' and later groom of the privy chamber to Charles I. Sutcliffe was apparently well connected at court, as evidenced by the second edition of *Meditations*. (The first edition is not extant.) Ben Jonson, George Withers and other prominent Caroline court poets contributed testimonial poems. The dedication implies intimate relationships with Catherine Villiers, widow of the first Duke of Buckingham, and Villiers's sister-in-law, the Countess of Denbigh; a flattering acrostic addresses Philip, Earl of Pembroke and Montgomery, joint dedicatee of Shakespeare's first folio. Consisting of six prose meditations and a poem of eighty-eight six-line stanzas that quote extensively from the Geneva Bible, the *Meditations* has been compared to AEMELIA LANYER's *Salve Deus Rex Judaeorum* for its profuse encomia and obvious self-promotion, but the text differs distinctively from Lanier's, particularly in its traditional treatment of Eve as a 'wicked woman'. JSM

Svendsen, Linda (Jane) 1954– Canadian short-story writer and Creative Writing professor, born in Vancouver to Hazel (née Sumner) and Robin Svendsen. She earned her Bachelor of Arts from the University of British Columbia in 1977, and moved to New York, where she completed a Masters in Fine Arts at Columbia in 1980. Svendsen won first prize in the 1980 American Short Story Contest sponsored by the *Atlantic*. She returned to Vancouver in 1989, where she now lives with spouse Brian McKeown and their children. She teaches Creative Writing at UBC.

Marine Life (1992) is a collection of connected stories set in Vancouver and New York, about a lower-middle-class family. It was selected to the Best Books List (1992) by the *Toronto Globe & Mail* and the *New York Times*. Alice Munro wrote of *Marine Life*, 'Linda Svendsen's stories are stunning – so easily embodying such terrific power. The last story, "White Shoulders", left me shaking.' Svendsen's screen adaptation of MARGARET LAURENCE's THE DIVINERS (1993) earned several awards. Svendsen also edited *Words We Call Home: Celebrating Creative Writing at UBC* (1990).   JBM

Swan, Susan 1945– Ontario-born Canadian novelist who questions and parodies conventional assumptions about gender, sexuality and nationhood. She took a BA at McGill University in 1967 and has published poems and plays, as well as contributing work to an anthology of women's erotic fiction. In 1983 Swan published *The Biggest Modern Woman of the World*, an allegory of American imperialism, which documents the life of Anna Haining Swan, the 19th-century Canadian giantess. This novel sparked a controversy within the family of Anna Swan, who objected to the sexually explicit portrayal of the giantess. *The Last of the Golden Girls* (1989), a novel that challenges the myth of female friendship, was followed by *The Wives of Bath* (1993), a carnivalesque presentation of a repressive girls' boarding school set in the suburbs of 1960s Toronto. Swan's disjunctive narrative incorporates scenes of sadomasochism, passing, and lesbian sexual encounters that question natural gender categories. *Stupid Boys Are Good to Relax With* (1996), a collection of short stories, celebrates women's sexual pleasure and empowerment in short-term relationships.   SCM

Swarton, Hannah ?–? Puritan captive. Most details known of Swarton's life come from her account of her five-and-a-half-year captivity with Indians and Canadians, which was published in Cotton Mather's *Humiliations Followed with Deliverances* (1697) and most likely written by him. During the 1690 raid which initiated her captivity as well as that of her four children, Swarton's husband was killed; one of her children was killed shortly thereafter. She was ransomed by French Catholics near Quebec, spending more time with them than with her original Indian captors. In 1695 she and her son Jasper were redeemed and returned to Boston.

Expanded and republished by Mather in *Magnalia Christi Americana* (1702), Swarton's narrative serves as one of the early examples of the popular CAPTIVITY genre – one which proved useful to Puritan ideology. Swarton's text supports the importance of law and church attendance in its clear explanation for her punishment by God: she and her family had moved away from the Puritan community for rich farmland, turning 'our backs on God's ordinances to get this world's goods'. It also presents a temptation common to many captives – namely, that of converting to Catholicism while awaiting their return home. Swarton's own daughter Mary was unable to resist this temptation; she remained in Canada after converting to Catholicism and marrying.   KMP

Swisshelm, Jane Grey Cannon 1815–84 American journalist and one of the leading writers on women's rights in the United States though one of the least well known. In the late 1830s she began writing for the Pittsburgh newspapers on literary subjects, as well as social issues such as the abolition of slavery and the procuring for women of their legal, personal and property rights. In the late 1850s she moved to St Cloud, Minnesota, where she became the proprietor of the *Minnesota Advertiser* which subsequently became the *St Cloud Visitor*. In 1863, she moved to Washington, D.C., to serve in the government and later sold her paper. She is best known for the collection *Crusader and Feminist: The Letters of Jane Grey Cannon Swisshelm 1815–1884* (1934), and for the book *Half a Century* (1880) which deals incisively with the issue of slavery and civil rights in the United States.   MRA

Syal, Meera 1960 – British-born Indian writer and actress whose spiky and insightful renderings of Asian life in Britain have won her a popular following. Syal came under the influence of Hanif Kureishi while living in the Midlands; it was he who encouraged her to write plays.

In 1994 she scripted *Bhaji on the Beach* for Channel 4 before publishing her first novel, *Anita and Me* (1996). Meera Syal's *alter ego* in her fiction is Meena, the feisty 9-year-old who is the only daughter of the only Punjabi family in the mining village of Tollington. Her ambitious parents and aunties prod her toward the path of good girldom; she wants to stray down the dangerous paths of western popular culture. *Anita and Me* was short-listed for the Orange Prize for Women's Fiction in 1996.

Meera Syal also writes well for radio, as well as having a number of radio and TV acting credits. She featured opposite the comedian and writer Sean Hughes in *Sean's Show*, playing a strong wife to the postmodern 'new man' husband of Hughes himself.   DM

Sykes, Roberta 1943– Prominent Australian poet, essayist and black rights activist, Sykes was born in Townsville, left school at 14, and has worked in many occupations. She returned to study after a period of political work, receiving a doctorate from Harvard in 1984. Sykes was the first executive secretary of the Aboriginal Embassy ('the tent embassy'), erected on the lawn in front of Parliament House in Canberra, in 1972. In addition to her collection of poetry, LOVE POEMS AND OTHER REVOLUTIONARY ACTIONS (1979), she has worked on a number of significant collaborations, notably with Colleen Shirl Perry on her autobiography, *Mum Shirl* (1981), and with Neville Bonner on *Black Power in Australia*. The first two volumes of her own autobiography, *Snake Dreaming*, have been published: *Snake Cradle* (1997) and *Snake Dancing* (1998).

Sykes received the Patricia Weickhardt Award in 1981, and the Australian Human Rights Commission

Human Rights Medal in 1995. In 1997 *Snake Cradle* won the Age Book of the Year Award and the Nita B. Kibble Award for Women's Writing. BO

Syrett, Netta 1865?–1943 Janet Syrett, known as Netta, was a prolific British writer of novels, stories and children's plays. Her family was artistic: of the ten children who lived to adulthood, two became writers and three were painters. At 11 Syrett boarded at the North London Collegiate School, established by the formidable Frances Mary Buss. In her late teens she studied at the Training College for Women Teachers at Cambridge, before finding employment as an English mistress at the High School in Swansea. Syrett's father then permitted her to live in a flat in London with four of her sisters, unchaperoned. She taught at the Polytechnic School for Girls alongside Aubrey Beardsley's sister, Mabel, and became acquainted with 'The *Yellow Book* set'.

Some of Syrett's short stories appeared in the *Yellow Book*, and her first novel, *Nobody's Fault* (1896), was published by John Lane in his 'Keynote' series. Like many female novelists of that time, she explored the subject of marriage and analysed the relationship between mother and daughter. The unhappily married heroine, Bridget Ruan, refuses to live with her lover because the inevitable scandal would devastate her mother.

Syrett's literary output was prodigious. Apart from novels, short stories and historical works, she had a special interest in writing and producing drama for children. The young Noel Coward participated in her variety entertainment at the Court Theatre. Her autobiography, *The Sheltering Tree* (1939), provides fascinating glimpses of many of her contemporaries, for example ELLA D'ARCY and MAY SINCLAIR. SF

T

Talbot, Catherine 1721–70 English EPISTOLARY writer and author of one of the most frequently read collections of essays of the later 18th century. Talbot was educated by Thomas Secker, a family friend and later Archbishop of Canterbury, who instructed her in scripture, Latin and modern languages. During the mid 18th century, Talbot was celebrated in London's social and literary circles for her learning. She discussed the progress of Richardson's *Sir Charles Grandison* with its author and in 1741 met ELIZABETH CARTER, with whom she was to maintain a close friendship and a voluminous correspondence for the next thirty years. Talbot was encouraged to publish the private writings which she kept in her 'green book', but the only publication which appeared during her lifetime was an essay which she contributed to Johnson's *Rambler* in 1750. When she died of cancer her private papers were entrusted to Carter, who published posthumous editions of Talbot's immensely popular *Reflections on the Seven Days of the Week* (1770) and *Essays on Various Subjects* (1772), which included a number of poems. The popularity of these works, with their conventional and occasionally didactic style may appear mystifying to the modern reader, though in their day they were seen as essentials of polite reading. Talbot's *Seven Days of the Week* was translated into French and appeared in nineteen different British editions between 1770 and 1798. Her *Collected Works* and her correspondence with Carter were published in 1809.   KD

Tale of Genji, The Composed during the early decades of the 11th century. Its author, known as Murasaki Shikibu, belonged to the middling aristocracy of Japan's Heian period, a diverse class who depended upon provincial posts for their men and, within the capital, positions for their women as literary tutors and scribes. The *Tale* is a long, multi-layered narrative interwoven with poetry, one that moves gradually from a traditional repertoire of motifs to an increasing focus on the psychological damage of passion and jealousy. It follows the young Genji, born to a serving woman and a reigning emperor, from the poisonous atmosphere of the central court through his early love-affairs, most notably with a consort of his own father and with Murasaki, the adolescent who eventually becomes his closest companion. Her death,

childless and alienated yet again from Genji's affections, is for many readers the most moving passage in all classical literature. (It is no surprise that the author, whose personal name remains unknown, comes down to us honoured with the name of her own creation.) After the death of Murasaki, the middle-aged Genji retreats from the world, and disappears from the *Tale*. The story leaves no doubt that the subsequent generation of Genji's grandsons is a lesser world; in this later world women characters may even choose death over the emotional and moral turmoil of life with men.

The *Tale* was read, studied and revered for centuries by a small, cultivated elite – male scholars could always point to it as a repository of courtly and poetic wisdom, educated women seemed to yearn for even its darker aspects, which they faithfully rehearsed in their own narrative attempts. In this century, *The Tale of Genji* has been appropriated as an exemplar of Japanese refinement and sensitivity toward nature; it has also been a key locus for the activity of female writers and intellectuals. Until 1945 Japanese women may not have had the vote, but they had their Judith Shakespeare and her work. Outside Japan, VIRGINIA WOOLF was the first important writer –female or male – to call attention to *The Tale*. In her 1925 review of the translation by fellow-Bloomsburyite Arthur Waley, she praised the sophistication of the work and its culture yet declared that the character Genji 'never passes the bounds of decorum'. Accordingly, she denied Murasaki equality with 'Tolstoi and Cervantes'. Forty years later, on a lecture tour of Japan, SIMONE DE BEAUVOIR used the examples of both Woolf and Murasaki to discuss the topic 'women and creativity'. For all her achievement (Beauvoir said) Murasaki was ultimately 'on the sidelines of society', trapped like other women in a spectator's role far from men's direct commitment 'to contest the world in its entirety'. Such Western condescension toward *The Tale of Genji* as inferior to European literary classics, or toward Murasaki Shikibu as a passive, merely female writer has, not surprisingly, been replaced in recent decades by detailed interpretations and imaginative re-readings by scholars and critics around the world.   MMo

Tales of Burning Love (1996) Jack Mauser's first wife dies the night they meet, get drunk and marry; she walks out into a blizzard and freezes as LOUISE ERDRICH's novel opens. Four wives later, Jack is thought dead after his house burns down; his four ex-wives are trapped in a blizzard after his funeral and, to survive, keep each other awake by telling stories of their lives and their relationships with Jack, who becomes increasingly peripheral to their interconnectedness. One wife still loves him, one loves her own first husband, and two of the wives have fallen in love with each other. The stories fuse images of fire, cold, falling and loss; the burning love that incinerates a nun, burns Jack's house down, and leads one grieving husband/mortician to cremate himself with his dead wife, contends against the blizzards in which wives are trapped, Jack's infant son is lost, and first wife June froze. A compassionate, humorous, quirky, ironic and occasionally surreal work that focuses less on Native American identity than Erdrich's previous novels. Here elusive, dangerous love determines identity.   SC

Tan, Amy (Ruth) 1952– Novelist who, like MAXINE HONG KINGSTON, has with great invention brought Chinese-American characters – especially women – into the mainstream of American fiction. Born in Oakland, she married and settled in San Francisco. She received a Master's degree in Linguistics and was a technical writer before turning to story-telling; she developed her first novel, *The Joy Luck Club* (1989), out of interwoven vignettes, taking LOUISE ERDRICH's *Love Medicine* as a model. A popular and critical success, the novel tells the stories of four Chinese women and their American daughters: with intelligence and a dry humour, it probes the many meanings of the generational and cultural gap in emigrant families. One daughter eventually travels to China to meet her Chinese half-sisters – an episode taken from the author's own life. Oliver Stone produced a film version in 1993. *The Kitchen God's Wife* (1991) is another intergenerational story, which also explores China's history in the 1920s and 1930s. She has written a book for children, *The Moon Lady* (1992), and in 1995 published *The Hundred Secret Senses*, a tale of two half-sisters – one Chinese, the other Chinese-American. As in all her work, the characters harbour secrets and mysteries, whose revelations finally enrich and deepen each other's lives.   SB

Taste for Death, A (1986) One of P.D. JAMES's bleaker novels, a substantial tale of the dark secrets of an aristocratic family. Following the traditional pattern of police DETECTION, the action starts with the discovery of two bodies, throats cut, in the vestry of a London church. The two victims are startling in their dissimilitude: an alcoholic tramp and a baronet recently resigned from government. As Adam Dalgliesh investigates the murders in a series of set-piece interviews, the passions and hatreds of the Berowne family are gradually revealed before the *dénouement* and tense capture of the murderer. With a strong sense of the importance (but also failings) of the establishment, and a carefully controlled cast of suspects, *A Taste for Death*, in its focus on Sir Paul's religious experience in the Church, centres on the 'personal load of guilt' of all concerned: murderer, victims and police. Introducing the ambitious Inspector Kate Miskin as Dalgliesh's junior colleague, James also portrays the uneasy position of women within the Force, and sharply foregrounds class issues.   CS

Taste of Honey, A (1958) Written when she was 18, SHELAGH DELANEY's first play is a grimly humorous account of life amid the 'tenements, cemetery, slaughterhouse' of 1950s working-class Manchester. At a time when the 'Angry Young Men' were taking over the theatre, Delaney was less concerned with anti-establishment posturing than with the plight of the individual trying to make the most of the little they have.

Jo, a disillusioned but perceptive school-leaver, seeks to escape the parochial, nostalgic world of her sharp-witted mother, Helen, a 'semi-whore', who tells her daughter, 'There's two w's in your future. Work or want.' Despite her keen intelligence and vitality, and her many sweet moments of happiness, Jo's life comes close to mirroring her mother's. However, the play is by no means bleak. It's a story of survival, drawing on the trenchant Northern spirit of sardonic humour and song.

The 1962 film of *A Taste of Honey*, for which Delaney wrote the screenplay, was directed by Tony Richardson and starred Rita Tushingham as Jo. It won the British Film Academy Award the same year.   JAH

'Tattle-well, Mary' Pseudonymous co-author with JOAN HIT-HIM-HOME, of *The Women's sharp revenge: or, an answer to sir Seldome Sober that writ those railing pamphelets called the Juniper and Crabtree lectures* (1640), a satirical response to the misogynist tracts by John Taylor (the 'water poet') printed in 1639. It has been suggested that there is strong evidence that John Taylor is the author of both sides of this apparently dramatic dialogue. The argument echoes the *querelle des femmes* debates of the late Renaissance. Taylor's *Juniper Lecture* 'light-heartedly' presents women as jealous, waspish and scolds. Mary Tattle-well's satire takes a similar frivolous tone, and at times defends some women at the expense of others. The satire takes the form of a lecture, delivered to a jury of twelve 'good women', which maintains that women are still the 'weaker vessells'. However, biblical female exemplars of chastity and piety are used, and Tattle-well takes formal issue with women's lack of education. *The Women's sharp revenge* is partially reprinted in *Half Humankind: Contexts and Texts of the*

Controversy about Women in England 1540-1640, edited by Katherine Henderson and Barbara McManus.　SMcK

Taylor, Elizabeth (later Lady Wythens, then Colepepper) fl.1680s English author of odes and songs widely circulated in Restoration miscellanies. The daughter of Sir Thomas Taylor of Maidstone, Kent, and Lady Elizabeth, she was married off in 1685 to a much older, 'infirm' judge, Sir Francis Wythens, despite her love for the 'young Chevalier' Sir Thomas Colepepper. Running up large debts, Taylor soon abandoned her husband, took up residence with Colepepper (who successfully sued for financial support for the Wythens children) and married her lover upon Wythens's death in 1704. This story of 'Olinda', a name under which Taylor's poems occasionally appear, was published along with an ode in DELARIVIÈRE MANLEY's *The New Atalantis* (1709), where she is deemed 'the wittiest [*sic*] lady of the [previous] Age'. APHRA BEHN, apparently a personal friend, published three of Taylor's songs in her 1685 *Miscellany*. Taylor's work appears in many other manuscript and print collections of the period, and at least one drinking song, declaring 'Tis safer for Ladies to Drink than to Love', was published as late as 1720. More than one contemporary account described her as 'sprightly'. JSM

Taylor, Elizabeth 1912–75 The author of eleven novels and five volumes of short stories; published her first novel, *At Mrs Lippincote's*, in 1945, while *Blaming* appeared posthumously in 1976. After a period of neglect occasioned by her unfashionable subject matter, the English middle-classes, her virtues have been recognized: *Angel* was selected by a Book Council promotion as one of the best British novels since 1945 and the majority of her works have recently been reprinted. Stylistically these virtues are those of elegance and subtlety, while her themes are treated with intelligence and an ironic wit: both the restricted field of her material and her treatment of it lead irresistibly to comparisons with AUSTEN. Her novels demonstrate an awareness of their vulnerability to a particular kind of criticism: in *A Wreath of Roses* (1949) a painter worries about the 'Englishness' of her work and its exclusion of 'turmoil, pain and chaos'. Taylor, however, while participating in certain features of 'Englishness' – a sharp eye for human frailty, a weakness for literary jokes and precocious children – also resists the genre's characteristic easy sentimentality. Death and despair stalk her pages with any emotional highs achieved against the odds.　EA

Taylor [née Hardy, later Mill], Harriet 1807–58 English feminist thinker and writer whose influence on the work of her long-time friend and second husband, John Stuart Mill, has sometimes been a source of critical controversy. Her father, a London surgeon, was rather tyrannical, and at 18 Harriet married John Taylor, a Unitarian druggist who associated with a group of radicals, including preacher W. J. Fox, SARAH FLOWER ADAMS and HARRIET MARTINEAU. They had two sons and a daughter, but the marriage broke down after Harriet met John Stuart Mill in 1830: the pair's intellectual relationship became the centre of both their lives. Harriet Taylor's influence on Mill (particularly on his thinking on women's rights) began early in their relationship, when they exchanged essays about marriage in 1831–2. Taylor's essay asks: '[W]hat evil could be caused by, first placing women on the most entire equality with men, as to all rights and privileges, civil and political, and then doing away with all laws whatever relating to marriage?' Unlike Mill's, her essay also advocated loosening the divorce laws. Harriet eventually left her husband's home for a separate residence, where Mill visited frequently. The Taylors, however, remained friendly and kept up some appearances; Harriet visited home for special occasions, for instance, and returned to nurse her husband in his final illness. He died in 1849, and Harriet married Mill two years later. She devoted much of her time and energy to helping Mill write and revise his work; he credited her with inspiring much of his thought, particularly *The Subjection of Women* (1869). In 1851, Harriet wrote an article, 'The Enfranchisement of Women', for the *Westminster Review*, and she and Mill wrote an article on domestic violence together in 1853. Taylor died seven years after their marriage, while the pair were travelling in the south of France.　KW

Taylor, Jane 1783–1824 English poet and essayist best known as a highly successful writer of CHILDREN'S LITERATURE. Born in London, she was the daughter of Isaac, an engraver and Dissenting minister, and Ann, also a Non-conformist and writer of didactic works. Jane trained as an engraver but also wrote poems, stories and plays from childhood, often in collaboration with her sister Ann (1782–1866). In 1805 the sisters published their highly acclaimed *Original Poems for Infant Minds*, a collection of lively moral verses which went through fifty editions and was translated into several European languages. Other works include *Rhymes for the Nursery* (1806) with Jane's famous 'Twinkle, twinkle, little star'; *Hymns for Infant Minds* (1810) which went through forty-eight editions; and *Original Hymns for Sunday School* (1812). Jane also wrote evangelical essays for *Youth's Magazine* under the pseudonym 'Q.Q.', which were edited by her brother Isaac in 1824.　SA

Te Arawa see POTIKI, ROMA

Teasdale, Sara 1884–1933 American poet. Born to a wealthy family in St Louis, Sara found her passion for poetry at an early age, publishing her first poems in 1902 in the *Potter's Wheel*, a journal she edited with several friends. She financed the publication of *Sonnets to Duse and Other Poems* (1917), which was a critical, although not commercial, success. Driven to dedicate herself to poetry, she nevertheless felt societal pressure to marry well. In 1912, the year HARRIET MONROE started *Poetry* magazine, Teasdale met John Hall Wheelock, the unrequited love of her life, while travelling to Europe. The following year, while completing her third manuscript, she had an affair with the eccentric Vachel Lindsay but chose to marry Ernst Filsinger, a St Louis businessman. These years were the most productive of her career, but also the most tumultuous. Modelling herself on SAPPHO and CHRISTINA ROSSETTI, she developed her lyric voice, but also the unswerving belief that great poetry was born of conflict and that happy marriages blunted creativity. *Rivers to the Sea* (1915) sold out in three months, contributed to her tremendous popularity through the 1920s, and earned her the praise of poets like Frost and Yeats. Her 1917 *Love Songs* won the Columbia Literary Prize (the Pulitzer forerunner), and her edited volumes, *The Answering Voice* (love poems by women poets) and *Rainbow Gold* (poems chosen for children), were reprinted for many years. By the end of the 1920s, she was seriously depressed and estranged from her husband when she met Margaret Conklin, her companion for the next six years. Fears about her health and grief over Lindsay's suicide drove Teasdale to overdose on sleeping pills in 1933. Conklin had *Strange Victory* (1933) published posthumously. Although New Criticism was hostile to Teasdale's poetry, because of its apparently simple themes and style, her work is enjoying a renaissance from current interest in the experiences and literature of women.   SP

Tenant of Wildfell Hall, The (1848) ANNE BRONTË's second novel defends the right of Helen Huntingdon to leave her brutal husband, taking her young son with her. She sets up as an artist in a remote part of the country, and her neighbour Gilbert Markham falls in love with the mysterious newcomer. It is only on reading the diary in which Helen has recounted the whole of her married life that he realizes she is still married, but, after the lingering death of her husband, Helen is finally set free to marry happily.

As with her first novel, *AGNES GREY* (1847), Anne drew her inspiration from the short and brutal life of her brother, Branwell, and the unhappiness of her governess years. Outspoken, particularly in its portrayal of a woman fighting for financial and social independence at a time when wives were considered the property of men, the novel was an immediate popular success. However, whilst the book contains some disturbingly violent scenes, it is also concerned with what

Anne called 'the doctrine of Universal Salvation' and the aim in writing the book was 'to tell the truth, for the truth always conveys its own moral'.   RDM

Tender Buttons (1914) Written by GERTRUDE STEIN as she later explained in 'Poetry and Grammar', to 'avoid nouns'. It is one of the funniest, and most delightful, of the canonical texts of high MODERNISM, and one of the stricter literary equivalents to the painterly cubism and surrealism of the period. The text is organized like an anarchic, hallucinated encyclopaedia, in which (often simple, domestic) 'objects' are specified by their names, and then, supposedly, pictured or defined. These glosses defeat all the expectations such a rationalist format gives rise to, varying between chortlingly 'cubist' parodies of practical or scientific manuals ('A BOX: A large box is handily made of what is necessary to replace any substance') and an alienation based on the careful derangement of sensory association ('EYE GLASSES: A colour in shaving, a saloon is well placed in the centre of an alley'). Every 'entry' is a poem and (still) heralds an epistemological crisis for the reader in which even the basic operations of language (singular and plural, repetition, time markers and so on) behave in a rigorously unreliable fashion.   VS

Tennant, Emma 1937– Comes from an upper-middle-class Scottish family, replete with estates in Trinidad (acquired in the mid 19th century) and a fake-baronial Gothic mansion, 'Glen', in Peeblesshire, where she spent parts of her childhood and adolescence; a house whose gargoyles become, in her 1979 pastiche of magic realism, *WILD NIGHTS*, 'mid-nineteenth-century replicas of forgotten fears'. The high point of the family fortunes was the Liberal ascendancy of the Edwardian period (Margot Asquith was her father's aunt). She remembered her father, Charles Tennant, as a combination of 'frightful rages and paternalistic benevolence'.

Deeply involved in the contradictions of revolution in the 1960s, Tennant came to prominence in Britain in the early 1970s, founding the periodical *Bananas*, which was an important outlet for young writers at the time. Her trademarks are an angular manipulation of literary pastiche and a persistent strain of female GOTHIC; an ironic juxtaposition of the inner world of 'bad sisterhood' (a mix of adolescence, witchcraft, vampirism, matriarchy and female terrorism) and the outer world of official post-war history. The classic early text is *THE BAD SISTER* (1978), an appropriation of Hogg's *Confessions of a Justified Sinner*, set partly in the old Ettrick forest: this is a schizophrenic text, the outer husk of which is the documentary 'case' of the murder of a Scottish Borders laird, Michael Dalzell, and his daughter, by a violent group of radical female terrorists. The inner narrative (positioned as an explanation but also denied) is a hallucinated account of the domestic madness of 'Jane', the apparent murderer and illegitimate daughter of Dalzell, who comes under the hypnotic influence of the ringleader, 'Meg', a magnificent Red Queen and lesbian vampire. *Queen of Stones* (1982), presented also as a documentary case, turns on a structural analogy between the behaviour of a party of female adolescent schoolgirls, lost one weekend in the fog of Chesil Beach, and the conflict between MARY, QUEEN OF SCOTS and ELIZABETH I.

The micro-struggles of female adolescence, conditioned by patriarchy and the historical mythology of popular ROMANCE, yield a macro-struggle to the death between the White and Red Queens. The different worlds of Tennant's novels map the (often POST-COLONIAL) geography of this occult narrative. *Black Marina* (1985) transfers the 'riddle where the answer is always incest, ruin, death' to the Eastern Caribbean and the fall of Grenada's Maurice Bishop. *Tess* (1993) returns to Wessex (another childhood world), the territory of Hardy, and 'unpicks', by a sinister, fanatical reintegration of the Master's biography into his own fiction, the determinism of female tragedy. (See also TWO WOMEN OF LONDON (1989).) vs

Tennant, Kylie 1912–88 Australian novelist probably best known for a trio of novels depicting the Depression of the 1930s. They are set in a country town (*Tiburon*, 1935), a Sydney slum suburb (*Foveaux*, 1938) and on the roads tramped by the 'travellers', men who, in order to receive the 'dole' (unemployment benefit), must prove that they are seeking work by 'moving on' from jobless town to town. These, with a ragtag company of the homeless and dispossessed, constitute 'the battlers' of the title of her 1941 novel, which won both the *Bulletin*'s S.H. Prior Prize and the Gold Medal of the Australian Literature Society and was later made into a television mini-series, as was *Ride on Stranger* (1943). Tennant actually joined those 'on the road' as preparation for *The Battlers*, later travelling with itinerant bee-keepers before writing *The Honey Flow* (1956) and living in Aboriginal communities before writing *Speak You So Gently* (1959), a documentary account of the first Aboriginal pastoral co-operatives. A social REALIST of staunch Left-wing sympathies, Tennant was too pragmatic – and had too highly developed a sense of the absurd – to idealize either the proletariat or ideologues of any kind. *Ride on Stranger* has attracted recent readers by its lively satirical depiction of the unworthy causes to which its enthusiastic heroine attempts to commit herself, a process that ends with her refusal to see the war that claims her newly acquired husband as anything but a triumph of folly. Shannon is one of Tennant's more fully developed characters (other novels tending toward group portraiture), and the novel

pre-empts many feminist criticisms of the social roles allocated to women. Some appreciation of the diversity of Tennant's own roles in life and in literature can be gained from her autobiography *The Missing Heir* (1986).

JStr

Tenney, Tabitha Gilman 1762–1837 Native of Exeter, New Hampshire, Tenney published *The Pleasing Instructor* (1799), an anthology for women, the objective of which was 'to blend instruction with rational amusement'. She is better known for *Female Quixotism: Exhibited in the Romantic Opinions and Extravagant Adventures of Dorcasina Sheldon* (1801), a comic, picaresque novel which parodies the sentimental literature of its period. *Female Quixotism* critiques the frivolous education of women, romantic notions of courtship and marriage, and the bourgeois pretensions and venality of virtually every segment of American society. Tenney's thoroughly unsentimental heroine is described as a 'middling kind of person, like the greater part of her countrywomen' whose pathetic adventures and final disillusionment serve as warning to early 19th-century Americans, eager to create political and social heroes and heroines for the new nation and to share in the wealth of republican America. While *Female Quixotism* reveals Tenney's insight regarding the anxieties of constructing a national identity, it also exhibits her sophisticated reading of Cervantes's *Don Quixote*, as well as of Samuel Richardson's *Sir Charles Grandison* and Tobias Smollett's *Roderick Random*. Wife of Dr Samuel Tenney, Revolutionary war surgeon and, later, judge, she spent several winters in Washington, D.C., while he served as US congressman (1800–7). DZB

Tenth Muse Lately Sprung Up in America: By a Gentlewoman of Those Parts, The (1650) ANN BRADSTREET's first volume of verse was published anonymously and without her consent, after her brother-in-law took the manuscript with him to England. Written between 1632 and 1643, the poems were one of the first accounts of life in the New World, a factor which contributed to their popularity in Europe. They reflected both Bradstreet's Puritan background and her literary fascination with the works of Spenser, Sidney, Donne and Herbert. However, 'to sing of wars, of captains, and of kings' was not her literary ambition. Instead, Bradstreet attempted to make her voice distinct by adopting a minimal perspective in her depiction of everyday, domestic life and personal religious experience. Defending her newly established position of a woman poet, Bradstreet proudly declared in the prologue: 'I am obnoxious to each carping tongue / Who says my hand a needle better fits'. Wittily asserting that she was writing 'for thyme and parsley wreath', the poet abandoned any pretence to the elevated, hermetic tradition of male decorum, and opted for a more modest approach. JZ

Terhune, Mary Virginia Hawes 1830–1922 Better known as 'Marion Harland', Terhune was one of the top-selling writers of popular American women's fiction in the 1850s and 1860s, but is remembered primarily as a domestic authority; her *Common Sense in the Household* (1871) was a bible in American kitchens well into the 20th century. (See COOKERY BOOKS.) A regular contributor to *Godey's Ladies' Book* and other magazines, she produced in her long career a staggering number of essays, stories, novels, cookbooks, domestic advice manuals, travel books, histories and biographies. Born and raised in upper-middle-class Virginia, she married Presbyterian minister Edward Payson Terhune in 1856 and subsequently moved with him to New Jersey. She remained in the North for the rest of her life, and her mixed feelings on the issue of slavery are evident in her personal and published writing. Her most popular novels, among them *The Hidden Path* (1855), *Moss-Side* (1857), *Sunnybank* (1866) and *Phemie's Temptation* (1869), reflect the profound conflicts over woman's cultural role that occupied the nation. Just as Terhune's own professional life was at odds with the traditional domestic role she advocated for women in her advice manuals, her novels are conflicted in their presentation of women's issues, characterized by textual ambiguities that contradict their conservative narrators. VC

Terrell, Mary [Eliza] Church 1863–1954 American social activist and writer. She was born in Memphis, Tennessee, to former slaves; nevertheless, her father Robert Church is reputed to have been America's first black millionaire. Mary was sent to Ohio at the age of 6 to begin her education, and remained there until her 1884 graduation from Oberlin College. ANNA JULIA COOPER was her classmate.

Terrell travelled extensively throughout Europe and spoke fluent French and German. She became a political activist and civil rights pioneer after marrying and settling in Washington, D.C. She was the first black woman appointed to the School Board of the District of Columbia, and the first president of the National Association of Colored Women. She lectured professionally, and addressed suffrage meetings alongside SUSAN B. ANTHONY.

Terrell wrote articles on race and gender issues for many prominent publications including the *Colored American* and the *Chicago Defender*. The *Washington Post* accepted her only published work of fiction, a short story called 'Venus and the Night Doctors'. Terrell regretted that her demanding public career left little time to devote to her literary ambitions.

Terrell's longtime friend H. G. Wells wrote the preface to her autobiography, *A Colored Woman in a White World* (1940). Her closest associates included Frederick Douglass, poet Paul Laurence Dunbar, and his wife, ALICE DUNBAR-NELSON. LMC

Testament of Youth (1933) The first volume of VERA BRITTAIN's autobiography covers the years from 1900 to 1925 and particularly World War I. Brittain, a pacifist by the time she wrote the book, evokes impressively the blinkered middle-class optimism and idealistic patriotism that led her brother and male friends to fight and die; she does not condescend either to them or to her younger self that nursed on the Western Front. The book is a feminist response to the war memoirs that appeared in the 1920s; Brittain was anxious to portray the ways in which the war affected women, not least through having to mourn the men who fell in battle. Later passages describe her university education, her friendship with WINIFRED HOLTBY and her eventual marriage. *Testament* was memorably dramatized by the BBC in the mid 1970s, and its reissue at that time helped Virago Books achieve financial stability. RK

Textermination (1991) CHRISTINE BROOKE-ROSE's novel features characters from world literature coming to life and attending the convention of the Modern Languages Association, where they learn that not only are they fictitious but the whole structure of subjectivity upon which they depend has been voided. JANE AUSTEN's Emma Woodhouse, GEORGE ELIOT's Dorothea Brooke and many others must listen to modern academics 'texterminate' them, while these academics are themselves threatened by violent religious extremists and disgruntled popular-culture icons. The novel is noticeably less experimental in form than other works by Brooke-Rose like *THRU* (1975), and it reads like an elaborate but respectful joke played on novelistic conventions as well as on its own likeliest readers, literary scholars. Perhaps the most interesting difference between Brooke-Rose's parodies of literary styles and most other authors' lies in the characters' ability to comment on their own (meta)fictional status in sophisticated yet plausible terms (Philip Roth's autobiographical protagonist Nathan Zuckerman and Salman Rushdie's Gibreel Farishta, both of whom show up in the novel, are cases in point). BWB

That Long Silence (1988) SHASHI DESHPANDE's fifth novel chronicles a watershed moment in the life of its protagonist Jaya, which radically changes her perception of it. Jaya is a typical middle-class, Indian housewife, with two children and a materially successful husband. However, he is accused of fraud and their lives are ruptured forever. Relentless in its exposé of middle-class hypocrisy and male double standards,

Deshpande's is a bleak and searing vision, capturing, without any sentimentality or recourse to spiritualist mumbo-jumbo, the disempowering and seemingly irreversible positions into which Indian women especially are forced.

However, Deshpande is not nihilist and through the act of writing her life, narrativizing it, the central character regains her sense of individuality and dignity, enabling her to end this revisionist process with the assurance that, from now on, she will not remain silent or the passive recipient of orders and changes, but that she will lead a life based on choices that take her into account equally, making her own dreams and desires possible. ATe

Their Eyes Were Watching God (1937) ZORA NEALE HURSTON's second novel traces Janie Crawford's growth from a symbolic mule into a mature woman in control of her life. Three marriages mark significant stages in her growth. When she leaves her first husband, she simultaneously frees herself from the slave mentality of her grandmother and refuses to become the husband's slave. Janie demonstrates her inner strength when she outlives Jody, her second husband, whose promise of freedom is devalued in time. It is from Tea Cake that Janie gets the respect and the commitment to reciprocity that have been missing in her previous relationships. The placid love games of Janie and Tea Cake are, however, overwhelmed by a hurricane. Nature's fury compels defenceless victims to pray for divine intervention, but things only get worse. A rabid dog bites Tea Cake, and Janie is forced to shoot and kill her sick lover. 'It was the meanest moment of eternity', notes the third-person narrator whose observations in standard English complement Janie's first-person narrative rendered in the black vernacular. KO

Théoret, France 1942– Francophone Canadian writer of poetry, 'prose poetry', short stories, novels, theatrical pieces and literary criticism. She holds a BA and MA from the Université de Montréal and a Ph.D. (1982) from the Université de Sherbrooke. She also pursued studies in semiology and psychoanalysis in Paris, and has taught literature at Collège Ahuntsic. Théoret writes about women's search for a symbology and language of their own, as opposed to what they must borrow from a patriarchal society which excludes them. She invents new forms of expression which she considers appropriate to women's voices: the prose poem, and the sometimes disembodied female voice. Her work is sometimes elusive and its subject is often woman's alienation from society and effort to find voice. Théoret contributed a piece, 'L'Échantillon', to *La Nef des sorcières* (1976), a collective play and one of the first feminist dramatizations of women's situation in Quebec. Here

Théoret develops the theme of women's alienation and necessary revolt, which she carries further in *Bloody Mary* (1977), *Vertiges* (1979), and *Nécessairement putain* (1980) where she develops the analogy of the woman writer with the prostitute. In 1978, Théoret got generally positive critical attention for *Une voix pour Odile*, a group of twelve monologues, and in 1982 she published her novel, *Nous parlerons comme on écrit*, which is a hybrid of several forms: the novel, the essay, the travel journal and an autobiography. While there is a narrative line to the work, it is interspersed with numerous fragments and sketches which lend an additional dimension to its unity. Théoret has participated in numerous collaborations with other women artists: she wrote the text for the musical, *Transit* (1984), with Micheline Coulome Saint-Marcoux; contributed to the collective work initiated by NICOLE BROSSARD, *La Théorie, un dimanche* (1992); and she wrote the poetic texts for *La Fiction de l'ange* (1992), illustrated by Francine Simonin. Her work has been critically acclaimed by both mainstream and feminist critics. Her writing reveals a constant search for new forms and ways of expressing women's hopes, thoughts and lives, or of 'Writing in the Feminine'. Her prevalent themes are women's oppression, their search for emancipation and happiness, and the transformation of society. GHN

Thicknesse [née Ford], Ann 1737–1824 English performer and occasional writer. She was a skilled viol player and an acclaimed singer, though the details of her education and early musical training remain unclear. The toast of fashionable society during the 1750s and 1760s, Thicknesse organized, played and sang at a series of concerts whose sensational success was heightened by her shrewd management of subscriptions and her father's attempts to stop the performances. She published a treatise on the instruction of the 'musical glasses' in 1761, and in 1763 became the third wife of Philip Thicknesse, the travel writer. While journeying in France during the tumultuous year of 1792, Thicknesse's husband died. She was arrested, confined to a convent, and released two years later upon the death of Robespierre.

Her *Sketches of the Lives and Writings of the Ladies of France* (1778) is a three-volume biographical dictionary which follows the conventions of the popular mid 18th-century genre of the catalogue of learned or 'celebrated' women. During the 1780s Thicknesse contributed a number of pieces to the *London Magazine* and in 1800 published *The School For Fashion*, a name-dropping novel which fictionalizes the lives of many notorious society figures and in which she herself appears as Euterpe, the muse of song. KD

Thimelby, Katherine, later Aston c.1620s–1650s Occasional poet and part of the remarkable Tixall circle in Staffordshire, which included several poets and letter-writers of historical note. Katherine married Herbert Aston in 1638. Their courtship had been the vivid subject of CONSTANCE ASTON FOWLER's letters written to her brother throughout the early part of the 1630s. Katherine, whose brothers also dabbled in poetry, wrote several poems which Constance, who became her firm friend during that time, collated in her commonplace book. One striking poem to her daughter Catherine urges her not to fast for Lent but to allow her mother to assume any sense of guilt or need for penance she might have. Also a collator of poems by others, Katherine, who died young through illness in the 1650s, is the subject of several family elegies and is a fine example of the typical pursuit of poetry by educated aristocratic families in the early modern period. Family precedent seems to have inspired a greater sense of vocation – as exemplified by the ASTON-Thimelbys, the Sidney-WROTHS, and the Cavendish-BRACKLEYS.   JS

Thimelby, Winefrid 1618 – c.1690s Author of a significant body of letters written between the 1630s and 1660s. Catholic, abbess of a convent in Louvain, France, and sister to KATHERINE THIMELBY (LATER ASTON), occasional poet and part of the so-called Tixall circle of poets. GERTRUDE ASTON-Thimelby joined Winefrid's convent following her husband's death, as did several of Katherine's children after hers. Much is known of the family during this period due to Winefrid's frequent letters home, mostly to Herbert Aston (Katherine's husband). Her letters register anxiety about the political and religious situation in England in the mid 17th century, particularly pressing for Winefrid as a Catholic. In one written in 1656 during the Cromwellian Protectorate, she reflects: 'As for the present, we are frightened with some feares of new troubles with you: if the tempest blow over, you may expect to see me this summer.' Interesting both as a recorder of family events and as an observer of the wider European political context.   JS

Thirkell [née Mackail], Angela 1890–1961 Social novelist who satirized English village life. She was the granddaughter of the painter Edward Burne-Jones and cousin of the writer Rudyard Kipling. She began writing to support herself and her sons after two failed marriages, and, after publishing a memoir of her Victorian childhood (*Three Houses*, 1931), she developed her famous series of Barsetshire novels, inspired by Trollope's 'Barsetshire Chronicles'. These describe the comic but poignant lives of ordinary people, including the benign, mildly disorganized writer Laura Morland and her atrociously precocious son, Tony. Barsetshire novels include: *Wild Strawberries* (1934), *August Folly* (1936), *Coronation Summer* (1937), *Summer Half* (1937),

Pomfret Towers (1938); *The Brandons* (1939); *Before Lunch* (1939), *Cheerfulness Breaks In* (1940). Thirkell's very popular yearly novels provided a welcome escape from war-time stress, though the novels after 1945 turned increasingly bitter. She was often compared to JANE AUSTEN for her use of intimate social groups, and Charles Dickens for her characters' humorous catchphrases, but can also be seen as a peer of E.F. Benson, DOROTHY L. SAYERS, and P.G. Wodehouse, a humorist who took refuge in chronicling the eccentric gentility of pre-war England.   TS

This is a short Relation of some of the Cruel Sufferings (1662) Written by English Quaker PROPHETS Katharine Evans and Sarah Chevers during their three-year imprisonment by the Italian Inquisition in Malta, this text comprises both poignant accounts of their experiences in prison and the ecstatic rendition of their prophetic visions whilst incarcerated. Evans and Chevers describe being kept in a small, hot room until 'our skin was like sheep's leather and the hair did fall off our heads'. The narrative testifies to their courage and tenacity in the face of incessant harassment and cruelty from the friars who sought their conversion to Catholicism, detailing their debates with them (in which, they suggest, they invariably had the upper hand). Their strength seems to have come in equal measure from their devotion to each other and from their passionate adherence to their Quaker beliefs, the latter resulting, on occasion, in prophetic visions, the most striking of which is Evans's own (she insists) personal experience of the prophecies set out in Revelation.   HAH

Thomas [née Callahan], Audrey (Grace) 1935– Canadian novelist and short-story writer. She was born in Binghamton, New York, and emigrated to Canada in 1959 after living in England and Scotland. She spent 1964–6 in Ghana. She became a Canadian citizen in 1979 and in 1972 went to live on Galiano Island off the West coast. She completed the Ph.D. course at the University of British Columbia but her dissertation on Beowulf was deemed unacceptable because it was more creative than scholarly. Her fiction, on the other hand, is characterized by her academic interest in the nature and history of language and by her literary allusions. Her work lends itself to serious scholarly analysis, including the application of current literary theory. Because of her literary sophistication and fondness for experimentation she is perceived as a demanding writer. Perhaps for that reason the general response to her work has been uneven and major awards have eluded her, although she is considered among the first rank of Canadian writers.

The settings of her fiction reflect her love of

travel, her astute, critical observation of her surroundings and her ability to use those surroundings metaphorically. Her feminist subject matter deals with mother–daughter relationships, the psychic damage resulting from a miscarriage, marriage break-down, and woman's unease within a patriarchal society. Her critically acclaimed novel *Intertidal Life* (1984) is her most popular work. This was followed by the short-story collections, *Goodbye Harold, Good Luck* (1986) and *The Wild Blue Yonder* (1990). *Graven Images* (1993) and *Coming down from Wa* (1995) repeat the earlier themes of a woman's coming to terms with her past through journeys into foreign countries.   JG

Thomas, Edith M. 1854–1925 American poet. She was born on a farm in Chatham, Ohio, and attended Geneva Normal School and Oberlin College. Visiting New York in 1881, she met HELEN HUNT JACKSON, who read and praised her poems. Her first publication in *Scribner's Monthly* led to a demand for her work in literary periodicals. After her mother's death in 1887, she moved to New York, where Dr and Mrs Samuel Elliot became her patrons, introducing her to leading artists and intellectuals. After Dr Elliot's death, she became increasingly reclusive. She worked as an editor on *Century Dictionary* and *Harper's*. Her poems, some well regarded by MODERNIST poets such as SARA TEASDALE, appeared in both adults' and children's periodicals, including *Atlantic* and *St Nicholas*, and in *Lyrics and Sonnets* (1887), *The Inverted Torch* (1890), *Fair Shadow Land* (1893), *A Winter Swallow* (1896), *The Flower from the Ashes* (1915) and *Selected Poems* (1926). Her nature poems and poems of inward life are comparable to EMILY DICKINSON's, though more conventional in form; e.g.

I am an ingrate in their eyes –
(Oh, when shall I be fed?)
From their best feasts I famished rise,
I dream of tables ampler spread.'
                    ('The Etherial Hunger').
                                        JSG

Thomas, Elizabeth 1675–1731 Poet, satirist and letter-writer. After the death of her father, Emmanuel Thomas, in 1677, Thomas moved to London with her mother, educated herself, and began to write poetry. In 1699, she sent two poems to the ageing John Dryden, who responded enthusiastically, dubbing her 'Corinna' and pronouncing her verses 'too good to be a Woman's'. Soon after, Thomas began a courtship with Richard Gwinnet, to whom she was engaged until his death in 1717. Their correspondence was published posthumously, along with her unfinished autobiography, under the title *Pylades and Corinna* (1731–2). After publishing her first volume, *Miscellany Poems on Various*

Subjects, in 1722, Thomas endured perpetual financial hardship: from 1727 to 1730 she was imprisoned for debt, during which time she resorted to unfortunate means to support herself. In 1727, she sold some of Alexander Pope's letters, given to her by Henry Cromwell, to Edmund Curll, who promptly published them in his *Miscellania* (1726). For this invasion of his privacy, Pope memorialized her in the *Dunciad* (1728) as 'Curll's Corinna'. Her revenge came in a literary form: the anti-Pope pamphlet *Codrus: Or, The Dunciad Dissected* (1729) has frequently been attributed to Thomas and Curll. *The Metamorphosis of the Town* (1730), a satire on London fashions, was the last work published in her lifetime.   JGr

Thomas, Gladys 1935– South African poet, playwright and short-story writer who is known for her angry depictions of the harsh realities of Apartheid. She was born in Salt River, Cape Town. Her mother, Dorothy O'Riodan, was the daughter of Irish settlers, and her father, John Adams, was from the Coloured community of Cape Town. At 18, Gladys married Albert Thomas and settled in Simonstown.

It was in response to the pain and humiliation caused by the forced removal of her community from Simonstown to Oceanview that she wrote her first poems, published in *Cry Rage* (1972). She warns: 'Don't sow the seed, Don't paint a wall, / Tomorrow it will have to fall'. She gave voice to the dispossessed children of the township in *Children of the Crossroads* (1986) and campaigned for the release of children from prison with the publication of *The Wynberg Seven* (1987). In 1989 she published a collection of stories called *The Spotty Dog*, for and about the children of Oceanview.

Her play, *Avalon Court,* comments on poverty, sexual exploitation and racism. The characters display a dogged determination to survive and laugh despite oppressive conditions. Her poetry and short stories have been widely anthologized.   GMS

Thompson [née Timms], Flora 1876–1947 British writer best known for sensitive and largely autobiographical chronicles of humble life in an Oxfordshire village in the 1880s and 1890s. Eldest child of a large and poor family, Thompson grew up in an atmosphere of discipline and tough practicality mingled with a romantic attachment to the intimate life of farmers and labourers and a deep love of nature. She married John Thompson in 1900, and in 1916 moved to Liphook, Hampshire. For the next fifteen years she published essays about nature and village life in small women's magazines. In 1939, *Lark Rise*, a book based on her early life in Oxfordshire, received warm praise. *Over to Candleford* appeared the following year and, despite failing health and the privations of war, she wrote *Candleford Green* in nine months. By 1945, when they were published as a trilogy called *Lark Rise to Candleford*, Flora Thompson's reputation was established. She combines the observations of a social historian with the sensitivity of a memoirist, and her descriptions of rural poverty are blended with sympathetic humour. She had just completed a novel, *Still Glides the Stream*, when she died suddenly of heart failure in 1947. ARF

Thomson, Katherine 1955– Australian dramatist, began her career in the theatre as an actor and was a founding member of Wollongong's Theatre South, where she performed in fifteen productions. Much of her earlier work was community and historically based, including such unpublished plays as 'Tonight We Anchor in Twofold Bay' (1986), set in the New South Wales coastal town of Eden, and 'Darlinghurst Nights' (1988), set in the Kings Cross area of Sydney and based on the poems of Kenneth Slessor. Her first play, 'A Change in the Weather' (1982), had drawn on the life stories of Wollongong women and many of Thomson's later plays have centred on older female characters. *Barmaids* (1992), while involving much comic by-play with the audience, presents sympathetic portraits of two ageing barmaids, facing competition from the rival attractions offered by topless bars and younger women. *Diving for Pearls* (1992) movingly depicts some of the effects on working-class lives of the job cuts and unemployment caused by economic rationalism, while *Navigating* (1998), set in a small town, focuses on an older, unmarried woman who is ostracized when she attempts to question the corrupt dealings of local businessmen. Thomson has also written many scripts for radio and television. EW

Thornton [née Wandesford], Alice 1627–1707 British autobiographer. Her Royalist father died when she was young and so she and her siblings received a pious upbringing – the family congregated three times a day for devotion – from her mother. She married William Thornton in 1651 and gave birth to eight children of whom three survived infancy. Her husband died in 1668 and she lived alone until her death. Thornton's writings are a curious and compelling blend of the domestic and the political and constitute a deeply personal response to many of the most consequential events in 17th-century English history. In her autobiography she repeatedly thanks God for saving her from life's hardships and delivering her from the worst excesses of the slander and poverty she suffered because of her brother and her husband. She ended her memoirs in 1669, but her son-in-law kept an account of the last years of her life and a transcript of her will. These were first published in 1875 as *The Autobiography of Mrs. Alice Thornton, of East Newton, Co. York.* ELER

Thorpe, Rose Hartwick 1850–1939 American poet, born in Mishawaka, Indiana. In 1860 her family moved to Litchfield, Michigan, where she attended public schools. When a teenager, she wrote 'Curfew Must Not Ring To-Night'. The title repeats as the refrain in a suspenseful ballad about Bessie, who saves her condemned lover by climbing a tower and clinging to the bell's clapper so that the bell cannot sound the time of his execution. 'Curfew' became a popular recitation piece following its publication in a Detroit newspaper in 1870. She married Edmund C. Thorpe, a carriage-maker who wrote German dialect verse, in 1871. They had two daughters. When her husband's business failed in 1881, she provided income by editing Sunday school publications. They moved to San Antonio, Texas, then to Pacific Beach, California. Thorpe published regularly in children's periodicals such as *St Nicholas*. Her verse was collected in *The Yule Log* (1881), *Temperance Poems* (1887), *Ringing Ballads* (1887) and *The Poetical Works of Rose Hartwick Thorpe* (1912); she also published children's books. After her husband's death in 1916, she worked for women's suffrage and with the YWCA and San Diego Women's Club. JSG

Thousand Faces of Night, The GITHA HARIHARAN's début novel won her the Commonwealth Writers' Prize for the Best First Novel in the Eurasia region in 1992. It is the story of Devi, a young Indian woman who has to come to terms with the stifling codes of Indian womanhood that are thrust upon her. She returns from having done a degree in the USA, and from a complex relationship with the Afro-American Dan, to her widowed mother in Madras and an extended family pressurizing her to get married. Her arranged marriage to the insensitive and typically Indian chauvinist Mahesh leaves her miserable, her misery only exacerbated by her inability to produce a child, like a good, breeding Indian woman. Her life is counterposed with that of Mayamma, her maidservant, who is also unable to have a child and suffers. But the central dynamic is between mother and daughter. The mother – whose sacrifice of her individual talents, dreams and desires to be a good Indian housewife have come to nought – is increasingly bitter about the stunting of her own life and is stifling her daughter in an act of subconscious revenge on the matrix that trapped her. ATe

Three Fates, The (1984) Poet ROSEMARY DOBSON's seventh major volume of poems was published in the same year in which she was awarded the prestigious Patrick White Literary Award. The volume includes four poem sequences – 'Daily Living', 'The Continuance of Poetry', 'Three Poems from America' and 'On Museums' – in addition to a number of individual poems, and continues Dobson's sustained meditations on the natures of art and poetry. Rather than considering the European Renaissance traditions as she does in earlier volumes, Dobson turns to Chinese models, including Li Po and Wang Wei, as she strives to relate the sacredness and mysteries of everyday life to the practice of art. Death is a major concern in the volume, with many poems written in memory of her friend and fellow-poet, David Campbell. Poems become talismans against grief and emptiness, possessing a sort of corporeality with which to recall what has been loved and is now lost, both at an individual level – 'Here are poems: stones, shells, water. / This one weighs in the hand. This one is shining. / This one is yellow' – and at the level of communities striving to remember collective pasts: 'Choose, use, create, / Put past to present purpose. Make.' MLA

Three Guineas (1938) VIRGINIA WOOLF's second political essay – *A ROOM OF ONE'S OWN* (1929) was her first – is a pioneering contribution to pacifist feminism. The book is an open letter to a concerned Englishman, who has asked her how to prevent war (a writer's engagement with politics was a matter of urgent debate in 1930s Britain). Although militarism is essentially alien to her because it is and has always been the product of male psychology, Woolf argues, the misery of the Spanish Civil War (1936–9) indeed demands action. She calls into question the foundations of civilization – education, the professions, culture, intellectual liberty, religion and even feminism – and uncovers connections between war and everyday violence. Furthermore, she invites us to reconsider the life histories of Englishwomen such as Mary Kingsley, JOSEPHINE BUTLER and FLORENCE NIGHTINGALE, for their self-made ethics of living can be made into ours, too (a theme Woolf used in THE YEARS, 1937). As an 'outsider' who writes outside parties and institutions, she finally proposes an 'Outsiders' Society', a society of anonymous experimentalists. AK

Thru (1975) Written 'tongue-in-cheek for a handful of narratologist friends', CHRISTINE BROOKE-ROSE's radical metafiction is a self-reflexive dialogue with the dominant novel tradition. Brazenly locating itself at the limit of readability – taking Joyce's *Finnegan's Wake* as its measure – it teasingly calls into question the habitual codes of REALISM. A bilingual critic and theorist (working at the time at the University of Paris), Brooke-Rose as fiction-maker here displays her familiarity with a bewildering array of avant-garde trends, from concrete typographical experiments through to the radical objectivity of the *nouveau romanciers* (in particular NATHALIE SARRAUTE) and the Tel Quel group's ideas on the death of the author and the primacy of (inter-)textuality. Paradoxically, undermining the ontological status of narration, text and reality foregrounds the real (!) author's role as a parodic manipulator of languages and fabricator of stories. Though its challenge to the reader means that it is still more known about than read, *Thru* remains an energetic experiment in playful philosophical fiction.

MO'D

Thurston [Madden], Katherine Cecil 1875–1911 Irish novelist. Born in County Cork and privately educated, she moved to England following her marriage to E. Temple Thurston in 1901. Her second novel, *John Chilcote MP* (1904), was an enormous popular success and was adapted twice for the screen (1922 and 1933). Although her novels can be categorized as popular and romantic, they are more complex than such a definition allows. Thurston's characters frequently face challenging moral problems. In *Max* (1910), published in the year of her divorce, the protagonist assumes the identity of a man in order to pursue her artistic ambitions. While the resolution of this novel is conventional, the representation of the problem is intriguing at many levels. *The Fly on The Wheel* (1908) is an accomplished, polished study of the prejudices and mores of provincial life, the restrictions and prejudices of a newly emerging Catholic Irish middle class. Thurston died in Cork shortly before her second marriage. LM

Tighe [née Blanchford], Mary 1772–1810 Irish poet whose work was virtually unknown until after her death. She was born in Dublin, the daughter of Theodosia, a Methodist leader, and William, a clergyman and librarian who died while Mary was still a baby. Educated by her mother in the classics as well as European languages, she married her cousin Henry Tighe, a member of the Irish parliament, in 1793. The couple moved to London but their marriage was an unhappy one. Mary's most well known work is a six-canto allegory of Love and the Soul written in Spenserian stanzas and privately printed (fifty copies) as *Psyche, or the Legend of Love* (1805). By this time, however, Mary was already suffering from the consumption which would kill her. Her final years were spent at Dublin and Roseanna, County Wicklow. *Psyche* was republished posthumously with a selection of Mary's other poems by her brother-in-law William Tighe in 1811, and went through many editions. Its sensuous writing was greatly admired by Keats. William also published *Mary, a Series of Reflections During Twenty Years* (1811). Mary was the subject of FELICIA HEMAN's poem 'Grave of a Poetess', where she is described as having 'A voice not loud but deep'. SA

Tillypronie, Lady Clark of 1824–97 A great collector of the Victorian age who amassed, not artifacts, but evidence of the important yet ephemeral activity of cooking. From 1841 onwards, she recorded the culinary details and COOKING instructions of dishes and meals that she enjoyed. Her legacy was 16 manuscript books containing more than 3,000 pages of recipes.

She was the daughter of a Scottish judge, Sir John Coltman. Following her marriage in 1851 to Sir John Clark, a career diplomat, she lived in Paris, Brussels and Turin, where she collected many recipes unknown in Britain at the time. Her work prefigures the great interest in foreign cooking that did not develop fully in Britain until after World War II, exemplified by the early writing of ELIZABETH DAVID.

Although it is unlikely that Lady Clark actually prepared her recipes, she places them in context – usually with a named source – and she observed the process and understood the purpose of cooking so completely that her book bears the warm and unmistakeable hallmark of authenticity. *The Cookery Book of Lady Clark of Tillypronie*, edited and prefaced by Catherine Frere (1909), was her only work; it is both valuable social history and a useful compendium of recipes.   GH

Tiptree, James, Jr. 1915–87 Principal pseudonym of Alice Hastings Bradley Sheldon, US writer known also as Racoona Sheldon. She spent her childhood in Africa and India – her mother, Mary Hastings Bradley, was a travel writer. After attending Sarah Lawrence, and a brief marriage, Sheldon worked as an artist, joining the Army in 1942, as a Pentagon analyst of aerial photographs. She left government work in 1955 and finished a Ph.D. in Experimental Psychology at the National Institute of Health in 1967. From 1968 onwards, she sold SCIENCE FICTION short stories to magazines under her male pseudonym. Most of her books are collections of these short stories; *Her Smoke Rose Up Forever* (1990) is the best selection. Sheldon's best stories combine radical feminism with a tough-minded tragic view of life; even virtuous characters are exposed as unwitting beneficiaries of disgusting socio-economic systems. Even good men are complicit in women's oppression – as in her most famous story, 'The Women Men Don't See' – or in ecocide. Her pseudonym started as a way of preserving privacy, but became a polemical issue when Tiptree was praised as a quintessentially masculine writer and felt obliged to reveal her identity. When both she and her husband became debilitatingly ill, she shot him and killed herself.   RK

Tirra Lirra by the River (1978) JESSICA ANDERSON's fourth, and best-known, novel, which was first a short story and then a radio play, tells how Nora Porteous, in her seventies, returns from years in London to her empty family home in Queensland. She is a woman artist who never fulfils her capacities. Possessed when young by daydreams of Camelot and ideal beauty, she waits to escape from provincial life,

and then from an unhappy marriage. Anderson makes Nora a convincing image of a woman with a gift for design who never even sees herself as an artist. After the war Nora finds happiness in friendship, and in making theatrical costumes. The novel's brief interwoven sections gradually piece together her life, reveal her neighbours' secrets, and explore through Nora's recollections the complex workings of memory, evasion and repression. Nora's loyalty to her half-grasped ambitions, her wry observations and her courage make her an attractive and even consoling figure of the older woman.   ABl

Tlali, Miriam 1933– The first black woman in South Africa to publish a novel, *Muriel at Metropolitan* (1975), which records the life of an urban black woman working in the mercantile Johannesburg world. The novel blends autobiography, social document and the typical conventions of REALIST fiction to show how Apartheid works on an everyday level, in the trivial but humiliating details of spatial arrangements, office power distribution, and separate and unequal facilities. The frameworks of class, race and gender are juggled in the novel to expose the uneven workings of diverse forms of inequity which have nevertheless always disadvantaged black South Africans and have often led to new forms of discrimination between an urban black *petit bourgeoisie* and the oppressed urban majority.

Tlali's next novel, *Amandla* (1981), was one of a number of works (other examples were provided by Mongane Serote and Sipho Sepamla) reacting to the new emergency conditions and the straitened police state which developed in the wake of Soweto 1976. (See also SOWETO STORIES.) Tlali's fictional method is to show people relating to one another in the mixed culture of the townships, where older customary tribal structures jostle with the ugly realities of arrests, violence, political and common crime, and the militarization of a younger generation. Tlali has also published *Footprints in the Quag: Stories and Dialogues* (1989), where she draws on journalism, sketches and short stories to express the stronger feminist awareness that developed as it became clear that the anti-Apartheid struggle might be won but it would take much longer to improve the inequities women suffered from under the complex forms of patriarchal power that had been established in the Apartheid form of colonialism in South Africa.   CC

To Bedlam and Part Way Back (1960) ANNE SEXTON's first volume of poetry presents the reader with asylum-scenes using the daring interior perspective of the CONFESSIONAL poet. The epigraph is from an 1815 letter from Schopenhauer to Goethe, stating that the philosopher must seek enlightenment despite the 'appalling horror' that awaits. Sexton's poetry inquires into the terrible truths of insanity with an 'inward look that society scorns' ('Kind Sir: These Woods'). The psychiatrist who directed Sexton to write as a therapeutic measure acts as a frontispiece for this theme in the opening poem of Part I, 'You, Dr Martin'. The senseless rhythm of institutional life is reflected in the patients' enforced bell-ringing practices ('Ringing the Bells'), endless doses of sleeping pills ('Lullaby') and electric-shock treatment. Part II's 'The Double Image' is a seven-section autobiographical piece portraying the speaker's struggle with her own suicidal illness as a 'graduate of the mental cases' and with her mother's cancer. The volume also includes 'Unknown Girl in the Maternity Ward', the poem that provoked Robert Lowell to incite the personal voice for which Sexton is remembered.   EM

To Stay Alive (1971) DENISE LEVERTOV's most explicitly political collection of poetry, including work from *The Sorrow Dance* (1967) and *Relearning the Alphabet* (1970). The first section, 'Preludes', provides a memorial to her sister Olga, whose death is verbally transformed into a powerfully inspirational force in Levertov's political life. The second part, 'Staying Alive', historically documents her personal and political activities, creating a 'record of one person's inner/outer experience in America' during the 1960s and 1970s. Levertov's aesthetic mix of politics and poetry blends with journal entries, letters, newspaper reports, manifestos, song lyrics and references to Keats, Rilke, Hopkins, Swinburne, Brecht, Camus and Gandhi. She imagines 'poets and dreamers studying / joy together' to achieve 'what could be our / New World even now, our revolution'. Alerting the reader to the dangers of nuclear power, environmental ruin and the prevailing horror of the world's inhumanity toward its people, the collection attempts to reconcile language – Levertov's 'Jerusalem' – and revolution, ultimately holding that 'when their rhythms / mesh … the singing begins'.   EM

To the Lighthouse (1927) VIRGINIA WOOLF's fifth novel remains her most celebrated. A key MODERNIST text, which simultaneously maps new gender roles for the 20th century and represents the culmination of the early phase of Woolf's development of new formalist techniques for the representation of consciousness, *To the Lighthouse* is one of the handful of novels which best encapsulate the characteristics of high modernism in English. The text is divided into three unequal parts, with the first and third directly concerned with the activities of the Ramsays and their family and friends at their holiday home in the Hebrides before and after World War I. The middle section, 'Time Passes', consists of an exercise in experimental prose which focuses on nature, time and death; it obliquely registers the divide marked by the war. The central character in the novel, Lily Briscoe, a young woman painter, must find a way to pursue her art in the face of the crippling gender stereotypes represented by Mrs and Mr Ramsay, who both stand in the way of Lily's self-fulfilment and inspire a great deal of affection in her. By the end of the text, the old gender order has been irrevocably altered, and Lily's 'vision' which closes the novel suggests the depth of the historical shifts which the text records.   KF

To the Priests and People of England (1655) One of the earliest known defences of women's preaching, written by English Quakers Priscilla Cotton and Mary Cole whilst imprisoned in Exeter Gaol. Throughout, their argument about who has or has not the spiritual authority to 'PROPHESY' engages with questions of gender (because of St Paul's proscriptions against women speaking in church) and with the spiritual authority (though for Quakers not necessarily the *literal* truth) of the Bible. In an extraordinarily bold move, they counter Paul's apparently unequivocal statements by ungendering the category 'woman', arguing that it is used metaphorically by Paul to signify 'weakness' – and they quote verses from St Paul himself to prove it. Their conclusion is that it is not 'females' who should not speak, but that 'it's weakness that is the woman by the Scriptures forbidden'. Thereby, they resolve the discrepancy between the Pauline proscriptions; they justify women's preaching; and, in a striking *coup de grâce*, they condemn to silence the priests who persecute them, telling them that 'you yourselves are the women, that are forbidden to speak in the church'.   HAH

Toklas, Alice Babette 1877–1967 American COOKERY writer and memoirist. Best known as the companion and lover of GERTRUDE STEIN, Toklas was born in San Francisco, California, to a wealthy Polish-Jewish family who had emigrated from Germany. Toklas travelled extensively in Europe with her family before training to be a concert pianist. After the San Francisco earthquake of 1906, she visited Paris, met Stein, and lived with her at 27 Rue de Fleurus for the next four decades. While Toklas managed the house and served as her secretary, Stein wrote, among other works, *THE AUTOBIOGRAPHY OF ALICE B. TOKLAS* (1933). Only after Stein's death in 1946 did Toklas begin to write sketches and essays on her own. In the work for which she is best remembered, *The Alice B. Toklas Cookbook* (1954), she conveyed with wit and civility a richly diverse household and a way of life that could not survive World War II. Her recipe for 'Haschich Fudge (which anyone could whip up on a rainy day)' remains as popular as her account of 'Murder in the Kitchen', wherein she

dispatched a carp (stuffed with chestnuts), a pigeon (en croutons) and a duck (with orange sauce). A convert to Catholicism in her 80s, she died in penury at 90.   BF

Tomorrow and Tomorrow (1947) M. BARNARD ELDERSHAW's fifth and final novel provides an account of life in Australia, mainly in Sydney, from the 1920s to the 1940s, using the supposed perspective of a novelist writing 400 years in the future. Despite this futuristic frame, the novel is hardly science fiction, since much of it consists of Knarf's reading of his manuscript to his archaeologist friend Ord, allowing in part for a debate about the relative merits of fiction and history in representing the past. Knarf offers a detailed, REALISTIC story of how an ordinary Australian family experiences the Depression, after losing their farm and moving to the inner city, followed by the turmoil of World War II. The futuristic frame allowed MARJORIE BARNARD and FLORA ELDERSHAW to extend their story beyond the time in which it was being written, resulting in a graphic description of the takeover of Sydney, with the destruction of many of its famous buildings, and the escape of surviving inhabitants to the countryside. The 1947 version was, in consequence, heavily cut by the censor; in 1983 Virago published the original version, under its full Shakespearean title of *Tomorrow and Tomorrow and Tomorrow*.   EW

Top Girls (1982) CARYL CHURCHILL's play opens up a debate as to whether right-wing feminism is an oxymoron. Marlene, the main protagonist, is a businesswoman who hero-worships the recently elected Prime Minister, Margaret Thatcher; her sister, Joyce, left behind in rural poverty to bring up Marlene's child, Angie, as her own, already perceives Thatcher as 'Hitlerina'. The play defies contemporary theatrical conventions in its employment of overlapping dialogue, non-chronological sequence, and juxtaposition of fantasy and REALISM. In the striking opening scene, five women from fact and fiction across the centuries, ranging from the possibly apocryphal Pope Joan to Patient Griselda, are invited to celebrate Marlene's promotion. The festivities end sourly as the guests count the cost of their own achievements in terms of dead lovers, and lost or abandoned children. In Marlene's office, she and her female staff demonstrate that their 'success' has depended on internalizing masculine values. Churchill, however, avoids simplistic judgements through her unromanticized depictions of Joyce and the slow-witted Angie. The play throughout anticipated later internal debates within feminism.   WAP

Tostevin, Lola Lemire 1937– Bilingual Canadian poet and novelist born in Timmins, Ontario, who com-

bines English and French poetic conventions to create a double language that places women's experiences and voices within Canadian print culture. She has been actively involved with *Tessera*, a bilingual feminist periodical that was established in 1984 to foster a dialogue between women writers and artists from different cultural backgrounds across Canada. In *The Color of Her Speech* (1982) and *Gynotext* (1983) Tostevin reconstructs the feminine body in a poetic language that breaks down the phonemic elements of French and English words. And in *Double Standards* (1985) she registers the speaker's cultural and linguistic dislocation as a francophone woman living in Northern Ontario. Her concern with the erasure of the mother tongue in male-centred language and thought is continued in *'sophie* (1988), a collection of poetry that recuperates the voice of woman through the use of musical intonation, bilingual homophony and translation work.

Her first novel, *Frog Moon* (1994), recalls her childhood experiences in a strict, Catholic boarding school in North Ontario, and juxtaposes this with references to Algonquin myth, the stories of Ontario gold miners and Chinese folklore. By challenging the fixed meaning of literature and myth, the narrator subverts the repressive ethos and iconography of Catholicism, and gains control over her own language and sexuality. *Cartouches* (1994) explores the relationship between language and death, in a series of poems about Egyptian hieroglyphs and her own father's death.   SCM

Towers of Trebizond, The (1956) ROSE MACAULAY's last novel is a theological picaresque and, in a sense, one of her TRAVEL BOOKS. Laurie, the androgynously named narrator (whose sex is not made clear for most of the novel), goes to Turkey with her aunt Dot, Dot's camel and the Anglo-Catholic Father Chantry-Pigg. Laurie, an 'Angloagnostic', lapsed because of an adulterous love-affair, finds their missionary purposes more comic than her own self-excommunication. Her narrative is both farcical travelogue and elegiac meditation on the comic and tragic history of the Church. Trebizond, briefly the capital of the Byzantine Empire and Greek Christianity, figures (like Jerusalem) as two cities, earthbound and celestial. After Laurie's lover is killed in an accident partly caused by her insistence on her right of way, she is still enchanted by its towers but feels forever excluded from its pattern and hard core. 'Perhaps the pattern should be easier, the core less hard. This seems, indeed, the eternal dilemma.' The novel was a bestseller and won the James Tait Black Memorial Prize.   PMar

Townsend, Sue (Susan Lilian) 1946– British comic novelist and playwright who confronts large social issues through sharply observed characters forced to operate within narrow social and domestic confines. Her bestselling *The Secret Diaries of Adrian Mole Aged 13 3/4* (1982), and its sequels, personalize the socio-political culture of Thatcher's Britain to comic effect through the Pooteresque monologues of the adolescent anti-hero. *The Queen and I* (1992) juxtaposes working class and monarchy in an insightful and compassionate comedy of class and national identity. Of her plays, *Bazaar and Rummage* (1982) critiques health-care politics through the story of mental-health patients and social workers who hold a jumble sale; *Groping for Words* (1983), set in an adult-literacy class, probes class oppression imposed through the authority of language; *The Great Celestial Cow* (1984) portrays an Indian woman's confrontations with racial prejudice and traditional cultural restrictions.

A native and resident of Leicester, Townsend left school at 15, married young and divorced, and trained as a community worker after holding other jobs. She remarried and has four children.　　　　LDo

Traill, Catharine Parr 1802–99 One of the

STRICKLAND sisters who entered the London literary scene in the 1820s, Catharine married Lieutenant Thomas Traill in 1832. Like her sister SUSANNA MOODIE, she emigrated to Canada that year and sought to establish herself as a wife, mother, settler and writer amidst poverty and hardship. The first three years were the basis of her classic, *THE BACKWOODS OF CANADA: BEING LETTERS FROM THE WIFE OF AN EMIGRANT OFFICER* (1836). The rubric of 'letters' home to the family in England allows her to describe in detail the landscape, domestic life and inhabitants of the backwoods. These very pragmatic and practical letters are an interesting contrast to the sketches her sister Susanna published as *ROUGHING IT IN THE BUSH* in 1852. Catharine seems more optimistic and practical, Susanna introspective; however, the publication of selected correspondence by the sisters in recent years calls into question any direct reflection of the life and the individual in the writings. Ironically neither the Traill nor Moodie families prospered in the backwoods: the letters reveal the Traills in particular were reduced to abject poverty and destitution. Between 1833 and 1847 Catharine gave birth to nine children, two of whom died in infancy.

Traill's oeuvre needs to be considered in terms of both her class and her gender. Writing was a genteel way she could supplement the family's meagre income while fulfilling her duties as a wife, mother and settler. Traill wrote stories, nature sketches, autobiographical narratives, children's stories – *The Canadian Crusoes* (1852) and *Lady Mary and her Nurse: Or, A Peep into the Canadian Forest* (1856) – and *The Canadian Settler's Guide* (1855) for the market. The 'low' or 'feminized' genres of journal, handbook and sketch were eminently suited

to the representation of dislocation and settlement following emigration.

Traill is also renowned for her botanical knowledge. Like Georgiana Molloy and Ellis Rowan in Australia, Traill collected and catalogued specimens of flora; this later resulted in the nature works *Canadian Wild Flowers* (1868) and *Studies of Plant Life in Canada: Or, Gleanings from Forest, Lake and Plain* (1885). Like her sister Susanna Moodie, Traill has reemerged as a character and voice in contemporary Canadian writing, most notably in MARGARET LAURENCE's fiction, *THE DIVINERS* (1974).　　　　GWh

Transformations (1971) ANNE SEXTON's poetic

retellings of traditional FAIRY TALES have inspired a number of stage productions, including an opera. This disturbing collection, published three years before the author's suicide, turns comforting children's narratives into adult horror stories. Sexton's jazzed versions of chestnuts like 'Cinderella', 'Red Riding Hood' and 'Hansel and Gretel' bring the tales into the adult world of parenthood, ageing and quiet desperation, via quotidian references (to 'Chuck Wagon' dog food, for example) and allusions to contemporary tragedies (Thalidomide babies, the Holocaust). The result is a jarring contrast between childhood innocence and adult experience. Drawing mainly on the Grimm versions of various well-known tales, Sexton frames the narratives with sadly ironic riffs on adult discontents that shift perspective and figure prominently in the narration itself. 'Rapunzel', for example, takes the witch's point of view, presenting her as a lonely old woman filled with sexual longing who plays 'mother-me-do' with her young captive. This theme of sexual predation runs through the collection, culminating in a vision of incestual rape in 'Briar Rose (Sleeping Beauty)'. In light of these dark musings, it thus becomes clear that, in keeping with her assertion that 'I hold back nothing', Sexton has turned the fairy tale into a strikingly original form of proto-CONFESSIONAL poetry.　　　　LC

Transit of Venus, The (1980) SHIRLEY HAZZARD's

third and best-known novel, draws on the elegant prose and characters of her earlier fiction, but is, perhaps, chiefly memorable for its carefully controlled exploration of the expanding possibilities of the novel form. Here Hazzard's finely articulated bourgeois sensibilities are located in a more critically precise cultural and historical field, with events (and characters) self-consciously recalling specific novels (most explicitly *Great Expectations*) as well as broader patterns and traditions of ROMANCE, FAIRY TALE, melodrama, history and myth.

While the central narrative is concerned with the fortunes of two Australian sisters in England, Europe and the United States, secondary characters divert much of the novel's interest and energy toward unexpected and marginal experiences. Together with the novel's proleptic structure, this has the effect of diverting readerly attention from the satisfactions of traditional narrative and toward a sense of the centrality of the unexpected. Thus the experiences in love and loss of Caro Bell are explicitly compared to those of explorer James Cook, throughout the novel and without irony: 'The calculations were hopelessly out . . . Calculations about Venus often are.'   BO

Trapido, Barbara (Louise) 1941– Novelist, born in Cape Town of European parents, educated in South Africa but left with her husband for political reasons in 1963. Her non-English upbringing – in a reconstructed colonial English ethos – gives her observations of the English class system a peculiar piquancy. Her novels are comic in tone and structure, but her flippant, sometimes mocking tone masks a serious engagement with major issues of personal life: love, death, friendship, loss, parenthood, power, violence, religious faith. Her novels are, as she says, 'character based', with a preponderance of arty women, charismatic men and shrewdly observed children, who interact within intricately plotted narratives. Her comedy overtly owes much to Shakespeare, and to opera. Her acclaimed first novel, *Brother of the More Famous Jack* (1982), was awarded a special prize for fiction in the 1982 Whitbread Awards. *Noah's Ark* followed in 1984. *Temples of Delight* (1990), drawing on Mozart's *The Magic Flute*, with a protagonist mesmerized first by a story-spinning schoolfriend and later by a mysterious enchanter, includes a poignant evocation of loss. Its sequel, *Juggling* (1994), is dizzyingly Shakespearean in its multiple plot resolutions, and *The Travelling Hornplayer* (1998) uses a conceit spun out of a Schubert song cycle. Her recurring use of symbols and motifs and their patterning and balance owe as much to drama and to music as to her preoccupation with romantic – often unrequited – love.   SAS

Trapnel, Anna Daughter of a Stepney shipwright, a Fifth Monarchist and 'PROPHETESS'. She published four of her six texts in 1654, when the radicalism of the early Interregnum, and especially of the Barebones parliament of 1653, was being forcefully curbed by Cromwell and his associates. Radical sectarian thought stimulated an extraordinary political, verbal and personal licence in Trapnel, as it did in many other male and female 'saints'. This enabled her to 'prophesy' publicly, in a combination of prayer and spiritual songs, under what she claimed was the inspiration of the Holy Spirit, voicing direct and extremely dangerous criticisms of the Church, the Army, the Justices, the Universities, and Cromwell himself which resulted in temporary imprisonment in Bridewell. Most of Trapnel's prophesyings occurred while she was in trance and in bed, observed by her friends and other interested parties. But she was also capable of forthright speech in the waking state, as when tried by a magistrate in Cornwall. Trapnel's most famous prophesying, described in *THE CRY OF A STONE* (1654), took place at Whitehall in early January 1653.   PJB

travel writing It goes without saying that women's travel writing was predicated on two things: the freedom to leave home, and enough education to be able to write about what happened afterwards. Before the 19th century, there were vanishingly few women who could claim both. If you are prepared to sift through the previous centuries, they are there, just a few. But it was the new conditions of the Victorian era that allowed their numbers to increase exponentially, like mammals at the end of the dinosaur age. Those Victorian women set the tone for what came to be seen as a separate, strongly bounded, genre.

And what an astonishing lot they were. MARY KINGSLEY, extolling the virtues of a good strong skirt, after having fallen into an African game pit complete with spikes; the missionary, Mary Slessor, suffering breakdowns and chronic malaria in Calabar, yet never considering return; ISABELLA BIRD, plagued by spinal disease, insomnia and 'nervous debility' at home, yet managing to scamper up mountains in the Rockies, struggle through *taiphoons* in Japan and, at the age of 70, set off on a black stallion through Morocco. So many of them, each more doughty, more formidable, more irritating and more lovable, than the last.

They were singular women, but one thread that runs through the genre they created, is the passion for freedom – the sense of exultation not only in the heading forth, but in the *escape*. Isabel Eberhardt perhaps expressed it best, 'vagrancy is deliverance, and life on the open road is the essence of freedom . . . to take up the symbolic stick and bundle and *get out*! Leaving, she wrote, 'is the bravest and finest act of all.'

Which raises the question: is women's travel writing different from men's? Rather than limiting literature with generalizations, it is better to think of 'tendencies', always aware that there are far too many exceptions to prove any rule.

A woman traveller sets out into a world whose public domain is organized by, and for, men. How far can she claim a freedom of action taken for granted by her male counterparts, knowing that she is always, and everywhere, potentially prey? How is she to protect herself not just from aggression, but from being misperceived? Eberhardt solved the problem by dressing as a man. Some took a male companion – usually a servant. Others waited to reach an age when their sex was no longer so desirable, when they could become, as it were, honorary men. Most just took their chances. But it is internalized fear that is most crippling to spontaneity – the necessary reining-in, the ceaseless attention to modesty, to the body and, therefore, to the self.

It is perhaps because of this self-consciousness that women's travel writing often tends to be concerned as much with inner journeys as with outer, with not just what is seen, but who is doing the looking. At its worst, this kind of writing can be solipsistic and tedious. At its best, it can create a richness and intimacy lacking in more so-called objective texts. An added potential benefit might be a deeper insight into the sensibilities and bigotries of the author's era. Of course there were and are plenty of women who write in the objective mode, just as there are plenty of men who write in the subjective: generalizations are dangerous.

T.E. Lawrence, in his introduction to Doughty's *Travels in Arabia Deserta*, said: 'Here you have all the desert, its hills and plains, the lava fields, the villages, the tents, the men and animals.' Notice anything missing? Whatever difficulties women face because of their sex, there is one asset they have which is unassailable – access to both the male and female realms of the people they find themselves among. As anthropologists, they have opened up the hitherto hidden half of human consciousness.

But what of travel writing now? It is an irony that, just at the moment when both journeying and publishing are more available to women, there should be a decay in the quality of the genre as a whole. There are many reasons for this that have nothing to do with literary talent.

Travel literature was always the product of privilege, and of empire. As purveyors of cultural arrogance, women have been no different from men. These days travel has become, rightly, vexed by such concerns – who has the right to say what about whom, when the power to describe and misdescribe is in the hands of the powerful. We still have a plethora of books from the centre describing the periphery; very few, as yet, coming in the other direction. And even if we stick to the Victorian model, where is there left to 'discover'? The homogenization of the world's cultures, thanks to global capitalism, has meant that there is very little periphery left for the centre to explore. And the need of publishers to commercialize the genre to exploit the commerce of tourism diminishes it to travelogue, to the trivial, or the kitsch. All 'genres' are fuzzy sets, but travel writing defies its boundaries more than most. And if the genre is fuzzy, how much more the subgenre? Was Clara Schumann a travel writer when she described, in her diaries and letters, her exhausting journeys through Europe and Russia in a horse-drawn coach, to give her concerts? Does DORIS LESSING qualify when she writes of a return to Africa? In going on a lion hunt? MARGARET MEAD in the Pacific?

SIMONE DE BEAUVOIR in the United States? Nadezdha Mandelstam exiled to Voronezh with her husband? GERMAINE GREER going to Australia to find out about her father?

The wonderful feminist publishing of the seventies, which unearthed so many buried works, a counterforce to the obliteration of women's history in general, and their literature in particular, contained within it the possibility of another kind of marginalization. The idea that there should be separate sections in bookshops, not just for travel books, but for women's travel books, herds writers and readers alike into pens. It limits the adventure of reading – the ability to dip and browse and go to places you never knew you wanted to visit. RD

Travelling Ladies

Travelling Ladies (1990) The epigraph for JANICE KULYK KEEFER's fifth book of fiction – 'The real traveller is the one who never arrives', from Edgar Degas – is an apt compression of the collection's central themes, for the titular ladies embark on wayward journeys. All twelve stories explore female protagonists set in motion (often despite themselves) for uncertain destinations. Through a mode of REALISM always undercut by the imposition of dreams, memories, fantasies and madness, the author explores the dynamics of family, nationality and identity. Kulyk Keefer's ironically decorous title belies the frequent anxiety, discomfort and peril of her protagonists, who are often positioned between dual forces in opposition: a girl between quarrelsome parents, a widow between social convention and her own desires, an adolescent between disparate cultures. In keeping with her suspended protagonists, Kulyk Keefer's stories resist resolution and neat closure; they allow for the possibility of travel but do not guarantee safe arrival. BJG

Travers, P.L. (Pamela Lyndon Goff)

Travers, P.L. (Pamela Lyndon Goff) 1899–1996 CHILDREN'S AUTHOR, poet and journalist, best known as the creator of *Mary Poppins* (1934), especially since the film version appeared in 1964. Born in Queensland, she grew up there and in New South Wales and worked as a journalist and actor, two of the few professions then open to Australian women, before travelling to England in 1924. Perhaps because of her father's Irish background, she became friendly with 'A.E.' (George Russell) who published her poetry in his *Irish Statesman*. She also wrote theatre and film reviews, poems and travel essays for the *New English Weekly* in the 1930s and 1940s. It was Mary Poppins, the eccentric English nanny who flies with the aid of her large umbrella, however, who provided the cornerstone of Travers's literary career. Altogether, she published eight 'Mary Poppins' books, including *Mary Poppins Comes Back* (1935), *Mary Poppins in the Park* (1952)

Restoration   *A Novel*

ANITA: **1. THE FIVE BEGINNINGS**   USE BOLD FOR CHAPTER HEADINGS

USE
SIMILAR
L-(DE
MARGIN
AND

I am, I discover, a very untidy man.

    Look at me. Without my periwig, I am an affront to neatness.
My hair (what is left of it) is the colour of sand and wiry as
hogs' bristles; my ears are of uneven size; my forehead is
spattered with freckles; my nose, which of course my wig can't
conceal, however low I wear it, is unceremoniously flat, as if I
had been hit at birth.

Rose Tremain: an extract from the manuscript of *Restoration*, 1990.

and *Mary Poppins and the House Next Door* (1988). She also produced a number of travel and gift books, some of which were based on her Australian childhood, and some reworkings of FAIRY and other traditional STORIES. She later developed a strong interest in the area of myths and symbols, publishing *What the Bee Knows* (1989), working as a consultant editor for the magazine *Parabola*, and giving many lectures.   EW

Trefusis, Violet 1894–1972 English exile who wrote arch, bitter-sweet fiction in French and English. Her mother, Alice Keppel, was a prominent Edwardian hostess and mistress of the Prince of Wales, and Violet grew up a privileged child of the aristocracy. Her life was shaped by her affair with VITA SACKVILLE-WEST which began in 1918; but their marriages and (even more) their mothers prevented their elopement turning into the permanent liaison Violet wanted. Except for the World War II years spent in England, her time was divided between her house in France and a Florentine villa her mother bought in 1927. She frequented Paris salons and knew Winaretta Singer, Anna de Noailles, COLETTE and Proust. In 1929 she published her first novel, *Sortie de secours*, written, like *Echo* (1931), in French. *Tandem* (1933), in English, was followed by *Broderie anglaise* (1935), a witty and jealous *roman à clef* about Vita's affair with VIRGINIA WOOLF. (Woolf had based the character Sacha in ORLANDO (1929), on Vita's stories about Trefusis.) Further novels included *HUNT THE SLIPPER* (1937) and *Les Causes perdues* (1941). In 1952 she published a discreet autobiography, *Don't Look Round*, which, like her love letters to Vita and the best of the 1930s fiction, has a certain camp distinction.   LS

Tremain [née Thomson], Rose 1943– English novelist, short-story writer and playwright. Born in London, and educated at the Crofton Grange school, Tremain spent a year at the Sorbonne before attending the University of East Anglia from 1964 to 1967, where she studied under Angus Wilson. She taught, worked as an editor and had written two works of non-fiction by the time she published her first novel, *Sadler's Birthday*, in 1976. The story of an ageing butler looking back on his life, it signalled what was to become Tremain the novelist's main preoccupation: life experienced by people at the margins, including the old, the young and those whose class, gender, religion or sexuality leave them isolated. Variations on this theme endure throughout her work, despite its diversity of settings and styles.

Sadler's Birthday was followed by *Letter to Sister Benedicta* (1978), *The Cupboard* (1981) and *The Swimming Pool Season* (1985). Then in 1989, Tremain published *Restoration*, an extraordinary and extravagant novel set at the court of Charles II. It follows the rise and fall in the fortunes of Robert Merivel, appointed physician to the King's spaniels, and married off to one of his mistresses. Banished from the court for falling in love with his wife, the flawed Merivel embarks on a painful journey of self-discovery, which encompasses a Quaker lunatic asylum, before achieving a personal restoration. Although it includes accurate accounts of the Plague and the Great Fire of London, *Restoration*'s powerful psychological content broadened its appeal; it was short-listed for the Booker Prize and won the *Sunday Express* Book of the Year Award. Another highly personal journey is the subject of *Sacred Country* (1992), whose central character seeks to change sex. It won the James Tait Black Memorial Prize. *The Way I Found Her*

(1997) is narrated from the point of view of an adolescent boy at large in Paris.

Tremain has also published three volumes of short stories, a children's book and numerous radio and TV plays. AC

Trench [née Chenevix], Melesina (St George)

1768–1827 Irish author, philanthropist and traveller. Orphaned at 4, Melesina passed a lonely childhood in the care of an elderly grandfather. At 18 she married Richard St George, who died in 1790. She visited Germany in 1799–1800, recording her impressions in her JOURNAL. In 1802 she went to Paris for 'a short vacation ramble', but when war with Britain resumed in 1803 she and her second husband, Richard Trench, were trapped in France.

In 1807 Melesina and her husband were allowed to return to England, and her later years were spent quietly in Hampshire. She published, anonymously, a number of collections of poetry, including *Laura's Dream* (1816) and *Aubrey* (1818). She supported the anti-slavery and prison reform movements, and had a life-long interest in education. Her *Thoughts of a Parent on Education* appeared in 1837.

Her *Remains* (1862) were edited by her son, Richard Chenevix Trench. These extracts from her journals and correspondence describe her travels and her encounters with celebrities such as Lady Hamilton, Madame de Recamier and the Empress Josephine, as well as her responses to marriage and motherhood, and her friendships, particularly that with MARY LEADBEATER. RR

Trick is to Keep Breathing, The (1989) In a moving,

yet often savagely funny, account of a woman close to complete mental collapse, JANICE GALLOWAY subverts orthodox form, mirroring her heroine's resistance to the inadequate treatment of her condition. The tragedy haunting the narrator, the inappropriately named Joy, unfolds slowly as her mind throws up fragmentary episodes from the past, intruding into her attempts to function now. Bulimia, barely acknowledged self-mutilation, and other forms of compulsive behaviour lead her to become a voluntary patient in a psychiatric ward. Her sense of self-alienation is manifest in the frequent rendering of encounters, particularly with officialdom, in play-script form, as if she were a sardonic spectator of her own life. Grammatical and typographical violations further emphasize the fragility of Joy's hold on reality; most notably, half-formulated thoughts stray into the conventionally pristine margins and gutters.

The novel won the 1990 Mind Book of the Year / Allen Lane Award for an outstanding piece of writing dealing with the experience of emotional distress. WAP

Trimmer [née Kirby], Sarah 1741–1810 English

CHILDREN'S and educational WRITER. When her father became instructor of perspective drawing to the future George III, Sarah's family moved from Ipswich to London and entered literary and artistic circles. A precocious reader, Sarah impressed Samuel Johnson by pulling *Paradise Lost* from her pocket one evening. In 1762, Sarah married brickmaker James Trimmer and settled in the poor parish of Brentford. Educating her twelve children at home with the help of a cleric only in Latin and Greek, Sarah found her vocation; inspired by ANNA LAETITIA BARBAULD'S work, she wrote *An Easy Introduction to the Knowledge of Nature and Reading the Holy Scriptures, Adapted to the Capacities of Children* (1780), based on stories created for her own children. An Evangelical Anglican, Sarah devoted herself to promoting religious and practical education for poor children, establishing a highly successful Sunday school at Brentford. Her prolific publications include *The Oeconomy of Charity* (1786), a guide for women to open similar institutions and 'schools of industry'.

Her most famous work, *Fabulous Histories* (1786), pioneered the teaching of kindness to animals through stories of personified creatures. Frequently reprinted as *The History of the Robins* or *The Robins*, the work followed French educationalist Madame de Genlis in its early use of pictures to educate children. Sarah's other projects included the *Family Magazine* (1788–9) – a patriotic and didactic journal for servants, cottagers and recent readers – and the *Guardian of Education* (1802–6) – a review of current children's books and educational issues. JHP

Tristan, Flora [Flore Céleste Thérèse Henriette Tristan y Moscoso] 1803–44 A French writer and

social activist. Tristan was the technically illegitimate daughter of a Spanish-Peruvian father and French mother, and had no formal education until the age of 17, when she was apprenticed to the artist and lithographer André Chazal, whom she married in 1821. On her separation from Chazal in 1825, she earned her keep as a ladies' companion, travelling to Switzerland, and to England, where she found inspiration for *Promenades en Londres* (1840; *The London Journal of Flora Tristan*, first published in translation in the UK in 1982) which, along with *Pérégrinations d'une paria* (1838; *Travels of an Outcast*), made her a celebrated champion of workers' and women's rights. The latter tells of her journey to Peru to claim her inheritance from her paternal uncle, while the former is a description of what she termed the 'monster city' of London, where the 'commercial supremacy of England and her oppression of India' displayed, to her eyes, an 'arid egotism and gross materialism'. The *Journal* takes the form of sketches and descriptions of the social rituals of the upper classes and the contrasting situation of the poor. She found the difference between the 'brilliant light upon the intellectual scene' of writers such as MARY SHELLEY and FRANCES TROLLOPE and the conditions of life of their working-class female counterparts 'a revolting contrast'. She was the maternal grandmother of the painter Paul Gauguin.   SD

Trollope, Frances 1779–1863 British writer who began her career late in life, but soon produced over a hundred volumes, including thirty-five novels and many TRAVEL accounts. At the age of 47, she travelled to America in search of a utopian community in Tennessee. She had left behind in England her husband, a chronically indebted barrister, but was accompanied by three of the children whom her writing would later support, as well as by her future illustrator, Auguste Hervieu. Trollope soon fled the struggling experimental settlement for Cincinnati, where she tried various money-making schemes culminating in an ambitious 'bazaar' built in a flamboyant mixture of Gothic, Moorish and Egyptian styles. Combining a ballroom, an art gallery, a concert hall, a bar and a coffee-house with a fancy-goods shop, the venture failed disastrously and left her in debt. Trollope's first book, DOMESTIC MANNERS OF THE AMERICANS (1832), reflects her boredom in a society where women did nothing but 'mix puddings and cakes one half the day, and watch them baking the other half'. Published amidst the debate surrounding the Reform Bill, *Domestic Manners* attracted much partisan polemic in Britain, and inspired vicious counter-attacks in America; according to one critic, the book 'made the Old World laugh, and the New World howl with rage'.

Her £600 profit on *Domestic Manners* encouraged Trollope to undertake more travel books (*Paris and the Parisians*, 1836; *Vienna and the Austrians*, 1838), and to recycle her American experiences in several novels. Her fiction ranged from comedy (*The Widow Barnaby*, 1839) to GOTHIC romance (*The Abbess*, 1833) to anti-Catholic polemic (*Father Eustace, A Tale of the Jesuits*, 1847) to anti-Evangelical satire (*The Vicar of Wrexhill*, 1837) and to social-problem novels (*Michael Armstrong, the Factory Boy*, 1839; *Jessie Phillips*, 1843) which were widely criticized. Her later works aroused less controversy, and were largely forgotten even before her son Anthony's *Autobiography* (1883) memorialized her as an industrious hack.   LPr

Trollope, Joanna 1943– British writer of novels unofficially christened 'Aga Sagas', highlighting the lives of educated, articulate provincial Englishwomen of a class associated with these appliances and their specious air of permanence and stability. The product of an upper-middle-class upbringing, educated privately and at Oxford, Trollope writes histori-

cal ROMANCES under the name 'Caroline Harvey' (e.g. *Parson Harding's Daughter*), as well as contemporary fiction. She received critical recognition with *The Choir* (1986), a novel centred on cathedral-close politics and its domestic ramifications. This work exemplifies typical Trollope ingredients: minute DOMESTIC observation, romantic interest and sharp characterization – angst-ridden parents, formidable grandparents and sensitive children busily absorbing their own parents' unhappiness.

Trollope's forte is describing the minutiae of domestic life, infusing myriad details into convincing portraits of individuals working and living amongst friends and family. Rarely leaving the provincial and domestic, her work is descriptive rather than analytical – a close scrutiny of women's lives and the struggle to conciliate contradictory demands of marriage, motherhood and career. All her books contain mismatched couples, miserably embrangled in mutual misunderstanding and incompatible longing. The more ambitious include *A Village Affair* (1989), revolving around a lesbian affair in a small rural community, and *The Men and the Girls* (1992), examining relationships between younger women and older men; the latter also touching, albeit somewhat superficially, on battered women. More typical are *The Rector's Wife* (1991), her first serious success, where the eponymous heroine escapes to a new and secular life, and *The Best of Friends* (1995), scrutinizing a marriage collapse and its pervasive consequences. Three of Trollope's books have been televised. She was awarded the OBE in 1996.
                    CT

Trotter [née Cockburn], Catherine 1679–1749 British playwright, poet and essayist, whose early life in London was one of genteel poverty. After publishing poetry, she went on to write several plays. *Agnes de Castro* (1695) attracted much attention, mainly due to the author's youth and because it was the first tragedy penned by a woman after the death of APHRA BEHN. *The Fatal Friendship* (1698), a domestic tragedy in blank verse, revolved around the central theme of money, whilst *The Unhappy Penitent* (1701) focused on the complications of love and honour. *Love at a Loss: Or Most Votes Carry it* (1702), a conventional intrigue comedy, was less successful and later revived under another name. Although satirized in THE FEMALE WITS (1696) alongside two other contemporary female dramatists, MARY PIX and DELARIVIÈRE MANLEY, Trotter was not so bawdy, and in the tragic *The Revolution of Sweden* (1707) declared herself a reformer of the stage. Marrying the Revd Cockburn in 1708, she went on to write moral and philosophical essays, and corresponded with luminaries like John Locke and John Norris. Her collected works were posthumously published in 1751.   RDM

Truth, Sojourner *c.*1797–1883 American orator, abolitionist. Born a slave in Ulster County, New York, she was sold three times before she was 12. In 1827, a year before slavery was outlawed in New York, she escaped with one of her children, worked as a domestic servant, and sued for custody of another of her children who had been sold into slavery. As Isabella van Wagener, she was converted to Methodism. In 1843, in response to a vision, she renamed herself 'Sojourner Truth' and set out as a traveller and missionary. By 1850, she had already dictated her autobiography, *Narrative of Sojourner Truth*. Although there is some disagreement about whether Sojourner was literate, there is no question that she was a commanding orator. Nearly six feet tall, she was strikingly strong and spoke with a deep resonant voice. Relying on this image, she argued repeatedly against the notion that women were inferior and needed coddling because of their delicacy. 'And a'n't I a woman? Look at me! Look at my arm! I have ploughed and planted and gathered into barns, and no man could head me!' Accused in 1858 of being a man, she bared her breast at a convention. Her unorthodox insistence on the centrality of women in religion was based on her idea that a woman produced the Saviour without any involvement from men. Made famous as the 'Lybian Sibyl' by HARRIET BEECHER STOWE in the *Atlantic Monthly* (1863), her narrative was included by STANTON in the *History of Woman Suffrage* (1881).   SP

Tucker, Charlotte Maria see A.L.O.E. (A LADY OF ENGLAND)

Tudor, Margaret 1489–1541 Queen of Scotland and letter-writer. Her father, Henry VII, began negotiations before she was 6 for her marriage to James IV of Scotland. After it took place in 1503, to confirm a treaty, she wrote plaintively to her father. Five children died in infancy, and childbirth made Margaret dangerously ill, but one son survived, the future James V.

After James IV's death at Flodden in 1513 Margaret married twice more, to handsome younger men, but both marriages ended acrimoniously. She was now a dominant presence in volatile Scottish politics, unpopularly promoting alliance with England rather than France, and battling with the Scottish nobility for the regency and control of her son. Her biographer, Hester W. Chapman (1969), writes that her contemporaries found her 'capricious, hysterical, monstrously selfish, and impossible to deal with or understand'. Her prolific and strident correspondence is an important source for the history of Anglo-Scottish relations in the period.   HH

Tuite [née Cobbe], Eliza Dorothea 1764–1850 As the daughter of Thomas Cobbe of Newbridge House, County Dublin, and his wife, Lady Elizabeth, daughter of the Earl of Tyrone, Eliza was a member of a distinguished Anglo-Irish family, whose members held leading positions in church and state. Her father was an MP, who achieved distinction when he sought, in return for his vote in favour of the Union between Ireland and Britain, not a peerage or financial reward, but funding for educational projects in his locality.

Tuite's *Poems*, which appeared in London in 1796, showed signs of this inheritance. They included lyrics, ballads and tales, on themes such as love and friendship, the injustice and violence of contemporary society, and man's inhumanity toward animals, which she contrasted with God's graciousness toward man.

Tuite was also the author of a story for children, *Edwin and Mary* (1818); a further volume of poems appeared in 1824, and her *Miscellaneous Poetry* was published in Bath in 1841.   RR

Turkish Embassy Letters, The (1763) Originally entitled *Letters of the Right Honourable Lady M – y W – y M – e. Written, during her Travels in Europe, Asia and Africa, To Persons of Distinction, Men of Letters, etc. in different Parts of Europe. Which contain . . . Accounts of the Policy and Manners of the Turks; Drawn from Sources that have been inaccessible to other Travellers*. These posthumously compiled and edited letters were written by LADY MARY WORTLEY MONTAGU during her travels across Europe to Turkey. Her husband, with whom she had eloped some years earlier, was appointed ambassador to Turkey in 1716. The ambassadorial party sailed to Rotterdam, travelled through Holland, Germany and Austria to settle in Constantinople in 1717. The letters are detailed descriptions of these local manners and customs. Montagu criticizes the partial accounts of other travel writers of the time on account of their predominantly masculine concerns and emphasizes her first-hand experience of domestic life in these countries. Although she, too, is seduced by the mythical lavishness of Turkish life, she shows great curiosity and willingness to adapt to different cultures and provides an unprecedented insight into Islamic life and culture.   NBP

Turner [née Burwell], Ethel (Sybil) ['Dame Durden'] 1872–1958 Australian children's author and mother of Jean Curlewis. Born Ethel Burwell in Yorkshire, England, she took her stepfather's surname, Turner, when her widowed mother remarried and, following his death in 1878, the family moved to Australia. She was educated at Sydney Girls' High School where she co-founded and ran the *Parthenon*, a journal for young people, with her sister Lilian Turner. When it closed she wrote the children's columns for the *Illustrated Sydney News*, and later for the *Town and Country Journal*, as 'Dame Durden'. In 1896 she married

Herbert Raine Curlewis who was later to become a judge.

A prolific writer, her output included almost thirty CHILDREN'S BOOKS. However, she is chiefly remembered for her highly successful first book, SEVEN LITTLE AUSTRALIANS (1894), a children's novel celebrating the independent qualities of exuberant Australian youth, which opens with the caveat 'in Australia a model child is – I say it not without thankfulness – an unknown quantity'. In 1915 it was dramatized in Australian theatres and in 1953 it became the first Australian book to be serialized by BBC Television. JSte

Turner, Jane fl.1653 An English Baptist, married to army captain John Turner, Turner published her SPIRITUAL AUTOBIOGRAPHY, *Choice Experiences*, in 1653. It is prefaced by several male-authored dedicatory epistles which applaud and authorize her writing as an acceptable manifestation of feminine spirituality, in that it will be useful to many 'precious souls'. However, Turner's relationship to her writing and her spirituality is more active and autonomous than such gatekeeping might suggest: she is pleased by her text's originality, 'having never seen anything written before in this manner and method', and she does not refrain from castigating her fellow-Baptists for their discouragement of her work. The autobiography itself gives a sense of the flux and excitement of the radical religious sects in the 1640s and 1650s, as Turner recounts her movement from Anglicanism to Presbyterianism, Quakerism and, finally, to the Baptists. Each 'note of experience' is accompanied by a more general commentary, drawing broader spiritual precepts from her personal experiences. HAH

Tuttle, Lisa 1952– American-born writer resident in the UK since 1980. Tuttle trained as a journalist and worked for five years on a daily paper in Austin, Texas, while also being one of the founder members of the Clarion Writers' Workshop. She sold her first story in 1971 and won the John W. Campbell Award for Best New Writer in 1974. Most of her short stories, collected as *A Nest of Nightmares* (1986) and *A Spaceship Built of Stone* (1987), and her mature novels are to some degree fabulations which use material from SCIENCE FICTION and horror to dramatize aspects of the human, and specifically the female, condition. Aliens are constrained to strap themselves into approximately human shapes as sex objects for human male colonists; the Wrong Man is literally demonic. These dramatic effects work in short stories, even when the mapping of the fantastic over the mundane is crude; the most satisfactory of her novels, *The Pillow Friend* (1996), trades more on ambiguities in its use of imaginary friends, phantom pregnancies and edible boyfriends. RK

27th Kingdom, The (1982) ALICE THOMAS ELLIS's third novel is a story about good and evil, encompassing vengeance, retribution and reparation, but is deceptively cast as a comedy of manners whose plot turns on the joke figure of a mysterious tax inspector. Set in Chelsea, the novel is peopled with outsiders: Aunt Irene from Eastern Europe and her viciously camp nephew Kyril; her *faux*-genteel charlady with dipsomaniac husband; a persecuted neighbour; the semi-criminal, astute and virtuous O'Connors; and Valentine, a West Indian postulant who is sent on a visit by Aunt Irene's abbess sister for a dose of sordid reality to temper her miraculous goodness before she enters the order. In Aunt Irene, this outwardly comic novel, like much of Ellis's work, features a woman who enjoys playing games and relishes oblique and encoded power, often in its negative and puncturing aspect. Tightly plotted, witty and economical, the narrative moves lightly but disturbingly to a dramatic conclusion, while its moral hierarchy points to Ellis's Christian convictions: goodness involves at least a modest recognition of the numinous. SAS

Two Serious Ladies (1943) JANE BOWLES infuses autobiographical material into this novel about dysfunctional people who engage in destructive relationships. The wealthy, neurotic Miss Christina Goering collects sycophants of both genders, who become room-mates and companions. Her eccentric views of sin and salvation induce her to sell her family mansion and to move with her companions into a cold and decrepit house on an island. Shortly thereafter she abandons them for a mainland journey, where her pursuit of salvation leads her away from female companionship into abusive heterosexual relationships. Miss Goering describes the second serious lady, Mrs Frieda Copperfield, as courageous for having lived with Mr Copperfield. Frieda unwillingly accompanies her husband to Panama, where she eventually achieves her independence and develops an intense, one-sided relationship with Pacifica, a Colon prostitute. Society, Bowles suggests, regards the independent woman as marked by a certain degree of insanity. This insanity is manifested by woman's inherent vulnerability in conflict with the steeled perspective on life she must adopt in order to survive. JAHa

Two Women of London (1989) In EMMA TENNANT's reworking of *Dr Jekyll and Mr Hyde*, the nature of the criminal/vice, spotlighted in Stevenson's original as buried under the hypocritical Victorian moral/virtue, is put into radical query. The wretchedly vicious-looking woman Mrs Hyde is the murderer of the rapist prowler at the crescent garden. In this urban/feminist GOTHIC, the real horror is anchored in the everyday lives of the patriarchal City. Mrs Hyde is a victim of society: a single mother deserted by her husband, desperately poor and dependent on tranquillizers. Her fate begins to change when a certain drug metamorphoses her into youthful and beautiful Ms Jekyll. The case of Mrs Hyde is a favourite topic among the Yuppie feminists, gathering at the fashionable boarding-house-*cum*-club for women in West London. Another doubling at work is that of two opposite types of feminist: a radical artist, Mara Kaletsky, and a writer and good wife and mother, Jean Hastie. They function together as sense-and-sensibility sisters, mirroring each other and keeping watch over 'our new Victorian values' in pairs.   CY

Tyler, Anne 1941– American novelist often descibed as a Southern writer, born in Minneapolis. She wrote from childhood onwards, majored in Russian at Duke University where she won a number of creative-writing prizes, and published her first novel, the dreamlike *If Morning Ever Comes*, in 1965. Her characters are familiar to us in their oddities and their ordinariness, the everydayness of their concerns; buying chicken from the supermarket to feed everyone during a family crisis, leaving an indelible mark on a coffee table in a house where you shouldn't even be. There is a low-key drama to the disappointments and embarrassments of her characters.

She creates an entire world, one always centred on Baltimore, in which similar characters and situations recur throughout the novels: the competent ex-wives and rootless young women, the stay-at-home younger sons who can't quite cope, the up-till-now reliable mothers whose heads get turned overnight.

We are far from the world of radical sexual politics in Anne Tyler's Baltimore, but she shows us, in tender, tiny detail, how the old families drop apart and new ones get reconstructed or, rather, cobbled together, from a ragbag of drifting character types. She is a very patient chronicler of social change, siding instinctively with those who find such things difficult; those pushed onto the margins of their expectations and those whose circumstances force them into changing everything about their lives and buoying themselves up with hope.

Hugely popular, especially after winning the Pulitzer in 1989 for *Breathing Lessons*, she was neglected as a subject for serious critical study until comparatively late. Her experimentalism is never flashy. In novels of the 1970s, such as *Celestial Navigation* (1975) and *Searching For Caleb* (1976), her customary form is stretched to cover greater spans of time, to incorporate more and disparate points of view.

More hotly debated than her form or structure, however, are the ultimate fates of her heroines. In *Earthly Possessions* (1977) Charlotte is kidnapped and dragged bodily from her unsatisfying life, and in LADDER OF YEARS (1995) Delia simply wanders away from her family one day as they picnic on the beach. She hitches a ride and reinvents herself elsewhere. Public reaction to the eventual recapitulations of these characters are amongst the strongest to Tyler's fiction. We get the sense that much is invested in these characters; their stories are mapping out our own capacity for escape and reinvention.

Her best books are, perhaps, *DINNER AT THE HOMESICK RESTAURANT* and *SAINT MAYBE*, published in 1982 and 1992 respectively. Here, the big, tragic events are never overdone and we are always left with the survivors muddling on in the wake of disaster and deprivation. Ian, the brother who adopts his orphaned nephew and niece in *Saint Maybe*, and Pearl, with her dogged resilience in holding together her wayward family *just enough* in *Dinner at the Homesick Restaurant* are never sentimentalized as particularly heroic figures. They are afforded one or two compromised epiphanies in amongst the jostling, but what Tyler concentrates on is giving us these characters who have made various choices and have to live with them. What she is charting is the day-to-day effort of existing within that self-invented version of yourself.   PM

Tyler, Margaret fl.1578 Translator and pioneer of ROMANCE writing by women. Tyler's translation from Spanish of *The Mirror of Princely Deeds and Knighthood*, a chivalric romance by Diego Ortuñez de Calahorra, was published in 1578. In a spirited prefatory epistle Tyler defends her choice of 'a story profane, and a matter more manlike than becometh my sex'. She notes that diverse secular works are dedicated to women, and asserts 'that it is all one for a woman to pen a story, as for a man to address his story to a woman'. This was a radical claim: although secular fictions were becoming associated with female readers, they were invariably written by men, while women writers usually chose devotional genres. No other female writer of romance in English is known until MARY WROTH in 1621.

Tyler's *Mirror of Knighthood* generated numerous editions and sequels and initiated a trend for translated Iberian romances. In the 17th century it became conventional, as in the drama of Jonson, to denigrate these fictions as the foolish reading of tradeswomen and maidservants.

Tyler states in the prefaces to the *Mirror* that she is elderly, and that she is indebted to the Howard family. We have no other biographical information.   HH

Tynan, Katharine 1861–1931 Irish poet and novelist. When she was a young woman, Tynan's family home at Clondalkin was a meeting-place for the young writers of the Irish Literary Revival, and W. B. Yeats in particular was a frequent visitor and later correspondent. Her first volume of poetry, *Louise de la Vallière* (1885), was enthusiastically received and she was considered one of the major talents of her generation. Following her marriage and move to England in 1893 her output accelerated, and she became staggeringly prolific. There are more than 190 entries in her name in the *British Museum General Catalogue of Printed Books*. She herself described much of her work, with the exception of her poetry, as falling into the 'potboiler' category, necessary for the financial support of her family.

She wrote journalism, novels, poetry and sketches as well as 4 volumes of memoirs/autobiography from *Twenty-Five Years* (1913) to *The Wandering Years* (1922). Her major contribution to the Revival is in the form of the 4-volume *Cabinet of Irish Literature*, an anthology which she edited, revised and extended in 1902–3. There are many valuable entries in this anthology which preserves a record of many forgotten writers and their work.

LM

U

Ulasi, Adaora Lily 1932– Nigerian novelist, who also worked as a journalist in her own country and in Great Britain. Her first four novels are set in the colonial Nigeria of the 1930s: *Many Thing you no Understand* (1970), *Many Thing Begin for Change* (1971), *The Man from Sagamu* (1978) and *Who is Jonah?* (1978). *The Night Harry Died* (1974) is set in the American South. In her African fiction, she broke new ground by adapting the genre of the crime thriller to an Igbo or Yoruba context. She exposes the efforts of the British Administration to enforce their laws, in a complex world of ritual murders, curses and secret societies, as futile, using an urban journalist as a cultural mediator. Her own childhood memories of law courts in pre-independence days help to give life to the uneasy dialogue between rulers and ordinary citizens. Such scenes come successfully to life in a stylized, pidginized English which is an interesting stylistic creation. The novels however remain paradoxically close to the kind of COLONIAL popular fiction written for metropolitan readers. There is little sympathy for country people. Their beliefs are exoticized into 'unspeakable rites', they are corrupt and ignorant and the improbable pseudo-pidgin used for their conversations when together, as an equivalent to the African languages they would normally use, makes of them uncouth figures of fun, in great contrast to the works produced by other African novelists at the time.   JB

Uncle Piper of Piper's Hill: An Australian Novel

(1889) This lively first novel by 'Tasma' (JESSIE COUVREUR) deals with the *nouveau riche* and the impecunious aristocracy in Melbourne, Australia. Uncle Piper is a poor immigrant butcher-made-good, who imports his sister, her aristocratic husband, and their two daughters to share his luxury home and garden, and temper his dissatisfaction with the existing household occupants. He hopes that his beautiful niece Sara will distract his gambling son George from the pink-and-white charms of his step-daughter Laura. By novelistic coincidence, Laura's clergyman brother, Francis Lydiat arrives on the same boat with the Cavendish family. Atheist Laura is initially unimpressed with him but, wounded by George's attentions to Sara, she accompanies Francis to his new country parish. George is briefly persuaded to propose to his cousin, despite his commit-

ment to Laura. All these complications are sorted out, and the characters' priorities made clear to them when Uncle Piper's youngest daughter, Louie (half-sister to Francis, Laura and George), is badly injured and Laura is disfigured in a buggy accident.   SKM

Uncle Tom's Cabin (1851–2) An international best-

seller, HARRIET BEECHER STOWE's anti-slavery epic was the most influential novel of its time. Repudiated in the South, subsequently condemned for racism and sentimentality, the book compels strong interest today for its woman-centred politics and rhetorical complexity. Triggered by the Fugitive Slave Law, written out of visionary anger and pity, the book created images of suffering and heroism, rousing abolitionist sympathy worldwide. Combining domesticity and dissent, Stowe wrote from her 'heart's blood', appealing to the women of America to set right the house of the nation. The sweeping emotional narrative, spanning the continent, stirred readers' feelings, through suspense, tears and indignation. Stowe believed there was no arguing with 'pictures': people must *see* the evil of an economy founded on slave-holding. The vivid reality of Eliza crossing the ice to save her child, of little Eva on her death-bed, giving away her curls to a sobbing household, of Aunt Chloe working for a husband who would never return, of Cassy outwitting her hideous abuser, and of Uncle Tom reaching the end of his journey: all these, and more, seared the abolitionist cause into the hearts of its readers.   PEK

Under My Skin: Volume I of my Autobiography,

to 1949 (1994) First volume of author DORIS LESSING's autobiography. The period of life covered in this first volume, from her birth in 1919 to her departure from Zimbabwe in 1949, had been fictionalized in Lessing's work, most notably in the 'Children of Violence' series. Lessing claims to have written the autobiography as a form of 'self-defence' against biographers. While she has often said that her fiction (especially the fiction set in Zimbabwe) is not autobiographical, this first volume of the autobiography draws in many ways on the Martha Quest novels. In the autobiography, Lessing herself goes so far as to make explicit comparisons, and to draw distinctions between herself and her fictional character, thereby reinforcing the intertextual links and encouraging readers of the autobiography to consider the extent to which Martha Quest's experiences are based on Lessing's own. A second volume, *Walking in the Shade, Volume II of my Autobiography (1949-1962)* appeared in 1997, and suggests, given the relatively short period covered, that the whole story will fill many volumes.

CCo

Under the Net (1954) IRIS MURDOCH's first novel immediately signals the preoccupation with contemporary philosophy which runs through most of her work (reflecting her vocation as an academic as well as a novelist). On the surface, it is the story of Jake Donaghue, a highly intelligent young translator with literary aspirations, who has published an unreadable philosophical dialogue based on his friendship and conversations with the enigmatic magnate Hugo Belfounder. The novel follows Jake through a series of entertaining if implausible adventures, during which he searches for Hugo, his former lover Anna, artistic and political enlightenment, and money. Heavily symbolic and highly allusive, *Under the Net* draws on contemporary French existentialism and the philosophy of Wittgenstein, who provides the title image of the 'net': the network of theories under which we must crawl to get close to the particularity of lived experience. Concerned with the relationship between the individual and society – specifically where the individual feels himself to be alienated – and the pitfalls of trying to pattern experience through theory, the novel possesses an originality and humour which is largely undiminished by the weightiness of its themes. AC

Union Street (1982) Winner of the 1983 Fawcett Prize, English novelist PAT BARKER's début is a triumph of gritty REALISM. Set in her native North-East during the 1973 'winter of discontent', it explores the lives of seven working-class women (from Kelly, the youngest, a girl of 11, to Alice, the 'old one', who dies at the close). Barker's 'compound-eye approach' (her term) allows each character to function as the centre of consciousness and the resulting form can be read as a novel or as a group of interconnected stories. She came upon her subject after ANGELA CARTER, tutoring her on a course, read a story about her grandmother and suggested she write about her working-class past instead of her middle-class present. Hence this vibrant, grim, depressing yet heartening insight into women's lives and the issues which matter to them – menstruation, men, pregnancy, rape, ageing, the struggle to survive in hard times – which is at once harshly circumstantial and profoundly archetypal.

Transplanted to New England, *Union Street* was loosely adapted for the 1989 film *Stanley and Iris* (director Martin Ritt). MO'D

Unsuitable Job for a Woman, An (1972) P. D. JAMES's richly allusive DETECTIVE NOVEL introduced her pioneering female investigator Cordelia Gray. Partly modelled on DOROTHY L. SAYERS's Harriet Vane, Gray is young, vulnerable and inexperienced but also clever, tough and determined to see justice done when she is hired by Sir Ronald Callender to discover the cause of his son Mark's suicide. Male power and legitimation frame her activities, from her father's neglect to the detective agency left to her by her dead partner, Bernie, and the procedural homilies he has passed on, picked up in turn from his former partner Adam Dalgliesh (James's favoured detective, who interrogates Gray at the close). But female power is also enacted, most poignantly in the moral compact made, between Cordelia and Elizabeth Leaming, to withhold facts from the police: 'What is there to be frightened of? We shall be dealing only with men.'

The 1997 TV version cast rising star Helen Baxendale in the leading role, adding an older female assistant and removing Dalgliesh from the plot. MO'D

Up Country (1972) MAXINE KUMIN's fourth poetry collection won the Pulitzer Prize for depicting life on a farm in New Hampshire. Kumin remembers the mundane, familiar moments of natural life, finding strength in the ordinary and power in the cycle of life. Mortality – animal as well as human – thematically connects these formal, metrically regular explorations of the interconnectedness of natural existence. A sense of place, both as locale and as the local spaces of our lives in the world, in history and in nature, grounds the poems. About the several 'hermit' poems that open the collection, Kumin has said: 'I didn't think anyone could take a female hermit seriously, so I invented the [male] hermit, who, of course, is me.' These ostensible studies in isolation in fact stress the hermit's relationship with the world. Devoutly secular poems, colloquial, anecdotal, deceptively familiar, they engage with honesty and practicality the endurance of life, family and memory. The original edition was illustrated with pen-and-ink drawings by Barbara Swan. SC

Up the Country (1928) This is the first of MILES FRANKLIN's successful series of rollicking Australian pioneer yarns, written in Britain and published under the pseudonym 'Brent of Bin Bin'. Franklin kept her authorship of this series a secret until the 1950s. The novel recounts the Mazere family's establishment of a station in the High Country region of Victoria and New South Wales. Commencing with the arrival of Richard Mazere and his young wife, it describes the trials and joys of this family and their neighbours through three generations. The story is a nostalgic representation of heroic pioneers battling a hostile landscape, and contains stock 'pioneer' incidents including floods and attacks by bushrangers. It deviates from ear-lier male pioneer tales in its insistence that white women pioneers were braver than their male counter-parts, particularly stressing the endurance of women in childbirth. It also counters masculine Australian 'mateship' with depictions of female solidarity in extremes. The pioneer myth is brought into question by the contemporary ending of the 1928 version (unjustifiably edited out of the 1984 edition).   SKM

Urquhart, Jane 1949– Canadian poet and novelist born in Geraldton, Ontario, who combines evocative imagery and classic REALIST conventions to excavate the untold stories of Canadian and European history. Her first book, *I Am Walking in the Garden Of His Imaginary Palace* (1982), is inspired by Louis XIV's gar-den at Versailles; this short sequence of nature poems subverts the geometry of the Sun King's garden. The poems in *The Little Flowers of Montespan* (1983) similarly traverse 'the rooms and gardens of Versailles in the persona of Louis' mistress'. By contrast, her second col-lection of poetry, *False Shuffles* (1982), documented the personal narratives of various figures, from her Canadian grandmother to Niagara Falls daredevils. And the Niagara Falls also provided the backdrop for THE WHIRLPOOL (1986) – a novel rich in symbolism and visual metaphors – which explores a Victorian poet's tragic obsession with a married woman. *Changing Heaven* (1990) is a self-referential novel inspired by EMILY BRONTË's WUTHERING HEIGHTS (1847), while in *Away* (1993) Urquhart weaves together

oral story-telling modes and evocative, haunting imagery in a narrative that maps the lineage of a fifth-generation Canadian woman, living on the shore of Lake Ontario. Her 1997 novel, *The Underpainter*, marries her fascination with family history and visual art in a recursive narrative documenting the life of a palimp-sest painter.   SCM

Uttley [née Taylor], Alison (Alice Jane) 1884–1976 Popular British children's author (see CHILDREN'S BOOKS) of nearly a hundred works in the tradition of English pastoral, notably the classic 'Little Grey Rabbit' series, in which engaging animal characters provide comic opportunities for gentle lessons about life. Closely observed details of natural history and nostalgic recreations of English country life (including Victorian class structures) also charmed adult readers.

Uttley's fictional world owes much to her childhood in rural Derbyshire (and to her training as a scientist – she was the second woman to graduate in Physics from Owens College in Manchester, 1906). She married in 1911 and began writing, despite discouragement from her husband, but did not publish her first book (*The Squirrel, the Hare, and the Little Grey Rabbit*) until 1929. Her husband committed suicide in 1930 and she began writing in earnest to support her son, with whom she later had a painful relationship. She wrote autobio-graphical accounts of country life (*The Country Child*, 1931) and was an avid DIARIST, producing over forty volumes. She received an honorary doctorate from Manchester University in 1970.   LDo

V

Valentine, Jean 1934– American poet born in Chicago, Valentine gained considerable attention by winning the Yale Series of Younger Poets Award for *Dream Barker* (1965). Her poems read as meditative studies of life; of human interactions and imaginings. They sometimes appear irrational, built on *non-sequiturs*, but Valentine's poems weave a web of language still intimate and magical: 'How deep we met, how dark, / How wet! before the world began' opens 'First Love'. Often abstract, reaching beyond the obvious, Valentine's poems are nevertheless grounded in the world, in physicality and human wonderings. In 1988 she published *Home, Deep, Blue: New and Selected Poems* (1988) which won the Beatrice Hawley Award that year. She has won several other major awards for her collections of poetry, which include *Pilgrims* (1969), *Ordinary Things* (1974) and *The Messenger* (1979). Later poems become a little more fractured in form: 'the play of the breath of the world / they he she you', but remain faithful to the everyday and familiar. She writes of loss, of affirmation and also the ellipses in between.   ACH

Valleys of the Assassins, The (1934) Describes FREYA STARK's journeys in eastern Iraq and Persia (Iran), undertaken in the early 1930s (see TRAVEL WRITING). The central section of the travelogue describes Stark's quest for the Persian castles of the Assassins, a medieval sect of Ismaili (Shia) Muslims. She also charts the little-known territories of Luristan in western Persia and provides an account of an archaeological expedition, a 'treasure hunt' for Bronze Age relics in Pusht-i-Kuh, which she organized single-handedly. In the final section, Stark describes her failed attempt to climb Takht-i-Suleiman, the 'Throne of Solomon', a mountain north of Teheran. Alongside detailed descriptions and maps of the land – she studied surveying in preparation for her journeys – Stark's work offers vivid, frequently humorous accounts of her dealings with the Persians, and particularly memorable portraits of her guides, her sole companions throughout much of her travels.   VG

van Herk, Aritha 1954– Born in Alberta, Canada, in 1954, the daughter of Dutch immigrants, Van Herk has worked as a farm hand, tractor driver, secretary, researcher, teacher and bush cook. She achieved international recognition when, at the age of 24, her novel *JUDITH* – produced from her MA in English at the University of Alberta – won the $50,000 First Novel Award in 1978. *The Tent Peg* followed in 1981, charting the transgressions and transformations brought about by its heroine J.L. on a uranium prospecting camp in the Yukon. *NO FIXED ADDRESS: AN AMOROUS JOURNEY* (1988) continues the theme of female trespassing into traditionally male preserves and is a deliberate feminist reworking of the picaresque genre. Tracing the never-ending journey of Arachne Manteia, travelling underwear saleswoman, who shuttles back and forth across the Canadian prairie, this novel consolidates the themes of TRAVEL and cartography, landscape and place, textuality and representation, which are so prominent in Van Herk's work. It also highlights her recurring feminist reworkings of myth.

PLACES FAR FROM ELLESMERE (1990), a 'geograficfione', continues her explorations of alternative mappings, of re-readings and re-writings. *In Visible Ink* (1991) and *A Frozen Tongue* (1992) both mix fiction, autobiography and criticism in the determined blurring of genres which is characteristic of Van Herk's writing and of her position as both critic and 'fictioneer'. *Restlessness* (1998) extends her considerations of immigration. As well as teaching, Van Herk has published a wealth of stories and essays, and has co-edited three, and edited two, collections of western Canadian fiction. Her own work has also been widely translated.

CSt

van Rensselaer, Mariana Griswold 1851–1934 New York author on architecture, landscape and the environment who did much to reform American attitudes toward visual culture. Her parents were prominent in the upper reaches of New York society, and in 1873 she married the metallurgical engineer Schuyler van Rensselaer, whose distinguished family descended from the original Patroon of Rensselaerswyck. After her husband's death in 1884, Van Rensselaer settled at 9 West 10th Street in Manhattan, where she resided for many years. A prolific contributor to magazines, Van Rensselaer achieved her greatest success writing on architecture. Her *Henry Hobson Richardson and His Works* (1888) was the first monograph on a modern American architect. *English Cathedrals* (1892) was often reprinted.

She was an advocate of the naturalistic landscape architecture of Frederick Law Olmsted, and wrote extensively about American and European gardens. Although without a formal education in art history, she also wrote intelligently on a diversity of artistic subjects, witness *The Book of American Figure Painters* (1886). Her *History of the City of New York in the Seventeenth Century* (1909) did much to move the historiography of the city beyond antiquarianism. Although she was out of sympathy with the more progressive thinking about the place of women in modern society, she was the leading writer on visual culture in late 19th-century New York City. Her reputation as a historian–critic has steadily risen.　　　　　　　　　　　　　　EH

Vane, Frances, Lady 1715–88 Scandalized contemporaries by recounting her love-affairs and escapades in 'Memoirs of a Lady of Quality', inserted by Smollett, controversially, in *Peregrine Pickle* (1751), and which, despite rumours that she seduced or paid him, initially accounted for his novel's popularity (see SCANDALOUS MEMOIRS). A spurious *History of a Woman of Quality* preceded the novel's publication, while derogatory pamphlets followed. Horace Walpole and Lady Luxborough ridiculed her frankness, and Samuel Richardson deplored her excuses for infidelity, but LADY MARY WORTLEY MONTAGU believed her memoirs 'contained more Truth and less malice' than any. An approving review by John Cleland (in the *Monthly Review*) supported Lady Vane's assertion that she was prompted by SENSIBILITY not ambition or crude sensuality.

Lady Vane wrote rapturously of her first marriage for love to Lord Hamilton in 1733, but after his death she immediately regretted her next marriage in 1735 to Lord Vane. Accusing him of impotency, her flights and his pursuits entertained their contemporaries, but she failed in all her attempts to divorce him.　　　LMT

Vavasour [Finch, Richardson], Anne fl.1580–1622 Poet and figure of court notoriety. In 1580 she became one of Elizabeth I's Gentlewomen of the Bedchamber, and had an affair with Edward de Vere, Earl of Oxford. In 1581 she gave birth to a son at court and was committed to the Tower. Two poems which appear among Oxford's works are attributed to her in some manuscripts. In 'Though I seem strange sweet friend', a woman reassures her lover of her concealed devotion: women at court 'must in our hearts a secret meaning bear'. In 'Anne Vavasour's echo', a female complaint in the form of an echo-poem, a lady asks 'who was the first that bred in me this fever?' and the echo replies 'Vere'.

By 1590 Vavasour had married John Finch, but became the acknowledged mistress of 57-year-old Sir Henry Lee, Elizabeth I's retired champion. She cared for him through old age until his death in 1611. In 1621 she was convicted of bigamy, having married John Richardson although John Finch was still alive.　　HH

Vera (1921) ELIZABETH VON ARNIM's blackly comic novel, based on her disastrous second marriage to Earl Russell, is a mordant analysis of the romantic delusions through which wives acquiesce in husbands' tyrannies. In outline the story of this utterly unromantic novel anticipates DU MAURIER's influential ROMANCE, REBECCA. Naive Lucy Entwhistle, mourning her beloved father, and swept into marriage by masterful widower, Everard Wemyss, finds his mansion, 'The Willows', pervaded by his dead wife, Vera, with whom she becomes increasingly obsessed. In this version, however, the secret is the spirited Vera's suicide, humiliated by Everard's unctuous tyrannies. Here the servants are partisan for both wives, and lose no opportunity of disrupting Everard's oppressive household routines. Lucy neglects the proffered support of servants and her aunt for Everard's monopolizing and, presumably, eventually lethal, affection. An extraordinarily black vision of marriage, which is also continuously funny, the novel's power lies in the wit and economy with which the usually prolix Von Arnim distorts the ordinary details of household routine into horror.　　　　　　　　　　　　　　AT

Vera, Yvonne 1964– Born in Bulawayo, Yvonne Vera is considered one of Zimbabwe's most promising writers. After training as a school teacher in her country, she studied film at York University in Toronto, obtaining a doctorate in Literary Studies there. She later became the director of the National Gallery in Bulawayo.

Vera's work is striking for its symbolism and cryptic exploration of gendered relationships. Like the Zimbabwean writer, Chengerai Hove, she uses minimalist and lyrical techniques which differ from the REALISTIC strategies of many other Zimbabwean writers. Her first published work was *Why Don't You Carve Other Animals?* (1992), a collection of short stories. *Nehada* (1993), her first novel, is an allegory of colonialism which focuses on the messianic role of Nehada, a powerful woman leader in Zimbabwe's anti-colonial struggle. *Without a Name* (1994) explores the psychological experiences of a woman character as she travels through her country at the height of its civil war. In this novel, the protagonist's lonely questing is wholly disconnected from a national struggle against colonial domination. Vera's focus on the emotional anguish of a solitary woman character is continued in *Under the Tongue* (1996), for which she won the Commonwealth Writers' Prize for Africa in 1997. Dealing with incest, this novel probes the secrets that conceal oppressive relationships within families.　　　　　DLe

Vernon, Barbara 1916–78 Australian dramatist, best known for her work for the Australian Broadcasting Company's drama department, both in radio and later as a television script editor. Born in the New South Wales country town of Inverell, she served in the Women's Auxiliary Australian Air Force during World War II and then studied for a BA at the University of Queensland. While working in Inverell as a professional radio announcer, she staged many amateur productions including some of her own plays. Her most widely produced play, *The Multi-Coloured Umbrella* (1961), forms part of the saga of the Donnellys, the family of a selfmade bookmaker. After moving to Sydney in 1959 she began working for the ABC and in 1967 originated one of the first popular Australian television serials, *Bellbird*, set in a small country town. She later published two novels based on the series, *Bellbird: The Story of a Country Town* (1970) and *A Big Day at Bellbird* (1972). EW

Victoria 1819–1901 Queen, whose voluminous letters and JOURNALS record the longest reign in British history from the unprecedented double perspective of constitutional monarch and family-oriented woman. She succeeded William IV in 1837, and married her cousin, Albert of Saxe-Coburg, in 1840. Her correspondence is invaluable for understanding the dynamics of government as British politics and the monarchy negotiated the age of reform and expanded into imperialism. Conventional but forthright (and addicted to emphatic underlining), she wote the equivalent of 700 volumes of prose, in letters to prime ministers, subjects, family and friends (notably Tennyson) and in daily journal-entries bluntly assessing public figures or pouring out her emotions. The journals survive in a heavily edited transcription by her daughter Beatrice, who burned all the originals. As a memorial to Albert (d. 1861), she originated and largely compiled *The Early Years of the Prince Consort* (1865), but it was not until *Leaves from the Journal of our Life in the Highlands* (1868) that Disraeli graciously admitted her to literary status with 'We authors, Ma'am . . .'. Royalty had never revealed its domestic heart so intimately before. 'Balmorality' found a deep response in middle-class ideology, and the book re-stabilized the monarchy, threatened by her reclusive early widowhood. *More Leaves from the Journal of a Life in the Highlands* (1884) revealed a familiarity with her ghillie, John Brown, which worried her advisors, and her additional 'little memoir' was also burned. MSM

Victoria of England (1936) When EDITH SITWELL's sympathetic portrait of the Queen came out, nobody really expected it to become a bestseller, least of all Sitwell herself. The similarities between *Victoria of England* and Lytton Strachey's earlier book, *Queen Victoria*, were easily identified, to the point of Sitwell having to write a detailed preface acknowledging her debt to Strachey in order to avoid accusations of plagiarism. Sitwell, however, differentiates herself from Strachey by focusing a lot more on the later years of the Queen, after the death of the Prince Consort. It is an account of Queen Victoria the private person and her relation to her family rather than Victoria the sovereign, although a more general commentary on the social conditions that England was undergoing due to the Industrial Revolution is also at work. Though it has *longueurs*, the book is entertaining at times, when Sitwell decides to use her critical and ironic faculties. Her rather weak scholarship is compensated for by her powerful and imaginative descriptions. MPe

Vidal, Mary Theresa 1815–69 Her *Tales for the Bush* (1845), an instructional work for servants, was the first locally published fiction by a woman to treat of life in COLONIAL Australia. Mrs Vidal spent five years from 1840 to 1845 in the country west of Sydney, where she had settled with her young family and her clergyman husband in the hope of restoring his health. After their return to England she established herself as a writer. Using this Australian experience in her major novel *Bengala: Or, Some Time Ago* (1860), she drew attention to her choice of a 'transient period' in the life of the colony, the gold rush, with its particular 'hopes, fears, evils and enjoyments'. The novel itself concentrates on change at the level of individual lives, including those of several convicts and servants. Their presence transforms the JANE AUSTEN aspect of this novel about several genteel country families, with its central tale of a bright young woman growing to maturity. SMS

Viidikas, Vicki 1948–98 Poet and prose writer, born in Sydney to an Australian-Irish mother and an Estonian violin maker. Educated at a number of schools, she entered the workforce at the age of 15 when she also began writing. Her work has been published widely in literary journals and anthologies in Australia and overseas. Among her volumes of poetry and prose, all published in Australia, are *Condition Red* (1973), followed by *Wrappings* (1974) – a collection of short prose and stories – and *Knabel* (1978), a poetry collection. The poems which appear in *India Ink* (1984) were written in India, where Viidikas travelled and lived, and reflect her close engagement with Indian life and religion. She also travelled widely in other parts of Asia and lived in Australia and England. The effect and influences of these travels, displacements and other cross-cultural engagements, as well as living in urban Australia in the 1970s, are evident in her writing which constructs a persona in a passionate search for place, language and identity. MF

Villette (1853) CHARLOTTE BRONTË uses her experiences of teaching in Brussels as a framework for the setting of this novel, renaming the Belgian capital as 'Villette'. This rooting of the narrative in reality anticipates what is to follow, for here the author systematically undercuts the ROMANTIC devices of her earlier fiction. GOTHIC motifs are constructed only to be dismantled and even the strange figures of the spectral nun and the sinisterly named Mme Walravens are explained without recourse to the supernatural. Similarly, romantic love is no longer the telepathic union of souls, as in *JANE EYRE*, but a muted affair of kindness and mutual profit, with the un-Byronic lover, M. Paul Emmanuel, leaving the heroine Lucy in moderate comfort, in an ironically understated twist on the Victorian convention of the inheritance. Only in the teasing equivocation of the novel's ending is doubt cast upon the reliability of the narrator, the plain and frosty Lucy Snowe, and the pervasive ambience of dry rationalism relieved only by the author's irrationally fervent distrust of Catholicism.   MM

Vindication of the Rights of Woman: with strictures on political and moral subjects (1792)

Addressing women as 'rational creatures', MARY WOLLSTONECRAFT's second *Vindication* is a devastating critique of middle-class femininity: of the 'false refinement' and 'over-exercised SENSIBILITY' of women educated only to 'marry advantageously'. Unlike men, whose professional training encourages 'flights of ambition', women internalize their status as sexual objects: 'the mind . . . only seeks to adorn its prison'. Instead, Wollstonecraft argues for a controlled balance of reason and feeling, stressing women's civic responsibility as rational mothers (a playing-down of female sexuality which has worried some recent feminists). Echoing Tom Paine's *Rights of Man*, *Rights of Woman* followed Wollstonecraft's attack on Burke, *Vindication of the Rights of Men* (1790), and brings French Revolutionary sympathies into dialogue with 18th-century debates on women's education and conduct, and with a Christian humanist belief in the rational perfectibility of souls. Aligning herself with CATHERINE MACAULAY's defence of female education, Wollstonecraft attacks influential conduct-book writers and Rousseau's gendered education programme in *Emile*. Though the reactionary political climate meant that it had a comparatively limited impact when published, *Rights of Woman* became a key historical text for modern feminism.   VJ

Vine, Barbara see RENDELL, RUTH

Viramontes, Helena Maria 1954– Native of California, fiction writer, editor. She first reached national and eventually international attention with

Mary Wollstonecraft, author of *Vindication of the Rights of Woman.*

The Moths and Other Stories (1985), a collection that sketches the lives of Chicana, Mexican and Latin-American women in a dreamlike style that blends flashback, multiple point of view, surrealism and magical realism. Her first novel, *Under the Feet of Jesus* (1995), impressionistically follows the life of a young woman on the California migrant farming circuit, exposing the horror, despair and fragility of the Latino/a worker caught in the oppressive agricultural economy of the Southwestern USA. She has been awarded a 1989 NEA and the 1995 John Dos Passos Prize for Literature. Viramontes also co-edited one of the central critical texts of Chicano/a literary criticism and theory, *Chicana Creativity and Criticism: New Frontiers in American Literature* (1991), as well as *Chicana (W)Rites on Word and Film* (1995).   SMSt

Virgin in the Garden, The (1978) A.S. BYATT's third novel, the first of a projected quartet, and the beginning of an ambitious undertaking to chronicle England in the second half of the 20th century. Set in Yorkshire during 1952 to 1953, at the Coronation of Elizabeth II, a production of a pseudo-Spenserian verse drama is being mounted, based on the life of the first Elizabeth. Frederica Potter, a fiercely intelligent schoolgirl, is chosen to play the Virgin Queen, whilst her elder sister Stephanie, a Cambridge graduate, finds herself drawn into marriage. Richly allusive, and unabashedly erudite, *The Virgin in the Garden* investigates the lives and preoccupations of the burgeoning middle classes. It has a sense of a community's postwar celebration, but also of the frustrations and isolation of individuals. Populated with a substantial cast of complex characters who recur in the sequels, *Still Life* (1985) and *Babel Tower* (1996), the new Elizabethan age is depicted in a fusion of REALISM and symbolism, in a major work of 1970s fiction that brought A. S. Byatt to a wide audience.   CS

Volcano Lover, The (1992) SUSAN SONTAG's sweeping and ruminative HISTORICAL NOVEL concerns the many forms of passion, including the longing for it. Set during the French Revolution and Napoleonic Wars, the novel begins with the eponymous volcano lover, Sir William Hamilton, a collector who would become the most famous cuckold of his day. Half of the novel passes before Hamilton meets his notorious second wife, Emma, who lives by sexual passion and will fall in love with the man Sontag contemptuously tags 'the Hero', Admiral Horatio Nelson. The meaning of passion soon expands to include suffering as revolution erupts, tyranny reacts, and the age of Enlightenment draws to a painful close. The romantic triangle of the Hamiltons and Nelson stands at the centre of Sontag's excursions into philosophical questions of history, romance, heroism, feminism, love, idealism and the political forces bending our lives. Sontag continually stops her ostensible story to ask questions, answer them, and offer the myriad points of view that comprise her actual subject matter. The novel ends with the voice of a previously 'marginal' character, an executed female revolutionary who despises and damns all women who don't seek a glory greater than personal happiness.   SC

Von Armin [née Beauchamp], Elizabeth [Mary Annette, Countess Russell] 1866–1941 A brilliantly witty, incisive British writer whose novels chronicled comic marital mismatches. Born Mary Annette Beauchamp in Australia, in 1891 she married Count Henning August von Armin, a wealthy Prussian aristocrat, with whom she had five children. Von Armin made her family and home famous in the semi-autobiographical ELIZABETH AND HER GERMAN GARDEN (1898), in which she called her husband 'The Man of Wrath'. A paean to the beauty of nature, *Elizabeth and Her German Garden* also chronicled her own difficulty adjusting to life in Germany and her husband's authoritarian attitude. Subsequently, she was known as 'Elizabeth' after her heroine.

Von Armin wrote twenty other books. *The Solitary Summer* (1899) and *The Adventures of Elizabeth in Rugen* (1904) continue the story of Elizabeth's life in Germany, but Von Armin also wrote caustic accounts of German customs in *Fraulein Schmidt and Mr Anstruther* (1907) and the very funny *The Caravaners* (1909). Her most ambitious novel is the deeply chilling VERA (1921), about a girl entrapped into marriage with a vicious bully; it was based on her own second marriage to the unstable John Francis Stanley, Earl Russell (brother of Bertrand Russell). *The Enchanted April* (1923) remains probably her best-known novel. Von Armin also had an affair with H. G. Wells. Although often considered a merely popular novelist, Von Armin's caustic wit, sharp emotional insights and concise language make her work comparable to work by her admirers, who included REBECCA WEST and her cousin KATHERINE MANSFIELD   TS

Voyage Out, The (1915) VIRGINIA WOOLF's first embarkation on novelistic writing. It is about a sea expedition aboard the cargo boat *Euphrosyne*, setting off from London to the imaginary tropical South American island of Santa Marina. Parallel to this journey, the book sets up an intensive versatile scholarly programme for the *Bildung* (see BILDUNGSROMAN) of the 24-year-old Rachel Vinrace. Rachel's education, centred mainly around the classics and carried out by a microcosmic group of educators (relatives and friends), proves beyond her synthesizing capability. As Rachel becomes engaged to a young ambitious writer (Terence Hewet) in the heat of a jungle excursion, the novel looks set for a conventional marriage ending. Against all narrative expectations, Rachel is suddenly struck down with a devastating fever. Her death, preceded by moving descriptive scenes of her delirium and hallucinations, leaves the novel on the brink of narrative crisis. Rachel's psychodrama, written simultaneously with Woolf's bouts of madness, is stylistically the best writing in the book, although the reader is left with an inconclusive vision of Woolf's MODERNIST venture.   AA

W

Waciuma, Charity ?– Kenyan writer of BOOKS FOR CHILDREN and of one autobiographical novel, *Daughter of Mumbi* (1969). She grew up during the violent decade before Independence at the time of the 'Mau Mau' anti-colonial movement. Like the famous novel by Ngugi wa Thiong'o, *Weep not, Child* (1964), her novel tells of the confusion of an adolescent caught in civil strife, torn between the desire for modern education and an assertion of Kenyan and Kikuyu identity. Whereas Ngugi writes from the perspective of landless peasantry, Waciuma is aware of her privileged position in a prosperous 'loyalist' family. The novel is constructed on oppositions with no resolution: she is daughter of 'Mumbi' (the woman figure who is the mythical founder of the Kikuyu), but also of a well-loved father who looms large in the book and was probably poisoned for his allegiance to the British. The book is dedicated to him. The narrative is a balanced account of her conflictual emotions. She finds comfort in her warm modern family but suffers from feeling excluded from friendship and love because she is uncircumcised, and thus considered as impure by the majority. Waciuma's other works are four novels for adolescents written between 1966 and 1973 in a competent and relaxed vein.   JB

Waddell, Helen 1889–1965 Literary historian and poet–translator. Born in Japan of a Northern Irish missionary family, graduate of Queen's University Belfast, her academic career was impeded by duty to an exacting stepmother. On the latter's death, she enrolled at 31 for Oxford's new D. Phil., undertaking the research which was to make her famous. *The Wandering Scholars*, published in 1927 to general acclaim, was one of the first texts to argue that the human-centred focus of classical poetry was kept alive through the Dark Ages to flower again in the secular Latin verse of the goliards. Its style was controversial (drawing the accusation that she had 'jazzed the Middle Ages') – driven by narrative immediacy, it avoided interposing scholarly expertise between the reader and the sources. Waddell assumed an enduring human essence emerging in the poetry of medieval scholars, which she translated into late-Victorian idiom (as she did with her adaptations, *Lyrics from the Chinese* (1913)) so lyrically as to attract the title of poet herself.

These translations were expanded in *Medieval Latin Lyrics* (1929), of which more were published posthumously (*More Latin Lyrics*, 1976). She also translated the less ascetic legends of the early Christians in *Beasts and Saints* (1934) and *The Desert Fathers* (1936). Her interest in the humanist scholar and famous lover led to the celebrated novel *Peter Abelard* (1933), highly commended by no less an expert than Etienne Gilson. From the mid 1920s her home was in London, where she died after several years of 'anaemic amnesia'.   JFG

Wakefield, Priscilla (Bell) 1751–1832 English educational writer and philanthropist, who was born into a Quaker family in Tottenham, near London. She started writing to support her London merchant husband, Edward, and her three children. Like her niece Elizabeth Fry, Wakefield was driven by a sense of Quaker duty and social reform. She wrote seventeen books in twenty years, as well as founding several charities, including a maternity hospital, a Female Benefit Club, and a Penny Bank for children, which developed into the first savings bank in England. She published reports on her philanthropic projects, as well as a number of educational reform books for children, parents and governesses, such as *Mental Improvement: Or, the Beauties and Wonders of Nature and Art* (1794) and *Juvenile Anecdotes, Founded on Facts* (1795–8). Other works included books on natural history and TRAVELOGUES like *Domestic Recreation: Or, Dialogues Illustrative of Natural and Scientific Subjects* (1805), and her best-known work, *The Juvenile Travellers: Containing the Remarks of A Family During a Tour Through the Principal States and Kingdoms of Europe* (1801). Although Wakefield's books argue that women can improve themselves through education, she still believed in gender and class distinctions, a point brought out in her one book specifically written for an adult audience, *Reflections on the Present Condition of The Female Sex, With Suggestions for Its Improvement* (1798).   RDM

Wakoski, Diane 1937– American poet born in Whittier, California. *Coins and Coffins*, her first book of poetry, published in 1962, began a long career of verse steeped in the Whitman tradition of an autobiographical, spontaneous, mythic voice that speaks for self and others. Wakoski suggests that her use of autobiography is 'surface' and that her work is a 'precise shaping of trope'. Some of this shaping appears in her well-received collection, *The Motorcycle Betrayal Poems* (1971), whose infamous epigraph reads, 'to all those men who betrayed me at one time or another, in hopes they will fall off their motorcycles and break their necks'. Some critics cite this sentiment as representative of Wakoski's poetry, ignoring her sardonic self-consciousness. She rhapsodizes an 'I' that repudiates harm to that self, often with characteristic repetition of imagery and expression.

En route, her work ranges in ideas and form – from personal narrative to surreal imagism. This transmogrification is central to *Inside the Blood Factory* (1968), which she considers her first definitive collection:

> A woodpecker with a fresh broody crest
> knocks
> at my mouth. Father, for the first
> time I say
> your name

She has published over thirty other titles, including: *Discrepancies and Apparitions* (1966), *The George Washington Poems* (1967), *Greed Parts One and Two* (1968) and *Dancing on the Grave of a Son of a Bitch* (1973), a book ensconced in her characteristic belief in freedom – personal and political. Other books of poetry published in the 1970s include *Looking for the King of Spain* (1974) and its follow-up, *Waiting for the King of Spain* (1976). Her interest in imagery as transformative act is evinced in *The Collected Greed Parts 1–13* (1984) where she writes,

> If only life left us with metaphors.
> But we are lucky if life
> leaves us
> with life

Following collections include *Emerald Ice: Selected Poems* (1988), and a trilogy: *Medea the Sorceress* (1991), *Jason The Sailor* (1993) and *Argonaut Rose* (1998). She has also published several volumes of prose-writing about writing, including *Towards a New Poetry* (1979). Among her other teaching posts, Wakoski has served as writer-in-residence at Michigan State University.   ACH

Walford [née Colquhoun], Lucy (Bethia)

1845–1915 Scottish novelist whose writing was admired by QUEEN VICTORIA and Coventry Patmore (who recommended Walford and Thomas Hardy as little-known writers who ought to have greater followings). Walford's strict Presbyterian family belonged to Edinburgh society, and Walford was educated at home. When she began to publish her writing openly five years after her marriage (she had previously published stories secretly in *Blackwood's Magazine*), her family disapproved, but her first novel, *Mr Smith: A Part of his Life* (1874), was popularly successful. Walford wrote more than forty-five novels and stories, most of them love stories with domestic settings. Her 1893 novel *The Matchmaker* was the last triple-decker novel ordered by the great circulating library, Mudie's. Although Walford continued to write novels and two volumes of memoirs (1910's *Recollections of a Scottish Novelist* and 1912's *Memories of Victorian London*), she had outlasted her fame by the time of her death.   KW

Walker, Alice

1944– African-American novelist, poet, short-story writer and essayist, born in Eatonton, Georgia, to sharecropping parents. She lost sight in her right eye at 8 when she was accidentally shot with a BB gun by her brother. The immediate impact of the accident was to underscore her sense of difference, but, like some of the heroines she would later create in her fiction, she triumphed over adversity. She entered Atlanta's Spelman College in 1961, but she left after two years for Sarah Lawrence College in New York where she began writing.

Writing literally saved Walker's life. She was pregnant in her senior year at college, and when she could not find an abortionist, she kept a razorblade under her pillow and practiced the slicing motions that she intended to use to kill herself. A doctor was found later and the abortion was done, but that week when she was anticipating death she wrote almost all the poems in *Once*, her first book published three years later in 1968. Writing was '[her] way of celebrating with the world that [she had] not committed suicide the evening before'. Writing also 'clarified for me how very much I love being alive', and it is this feeling that informs 'To Hell With Dying', her first published short story. The poetry and short story deal with the awareness that the despair that could lead to literal and symbolic death could also feed an intense love for living. The author comes of age when that awareness is linked to an understanding of 'how alone woman is, because of her body'.

The survival of woman and her body, free from abuse and mutilation in a world that is better served by a commitment to the preservation of 'entire people, male AND female', is a life-and-death issue for Walker in the novels she is best known for (*The Third Life Of Grange Copeland*, 1970; *Meridian*, 1976; THE COLOR PURPLE, 1982; *The Temple of My Familiar*, 1989; POSSESSING THE SECRET OF JOY, 1992; and *By The Light Of My Father's Smile*, 1998); in her collections of essays (IN SEARCH OF OUR MOTHERS' GARDENS, 1983; *Living By The Word*, 1988; and *Anything We Love Can Be Saved*, 1997); in her collections of short stories (*In Love and Trouble*, 1973; and *You Can't Keep A Good Woman Down*, 1981); and in the collected poems (1965–90), *Her Blue Body Everything We Know* (1991). Her recent campaign in writing and in film (with Pratibha Parmar) against female genital mutilation is rooted in a dedication to civil and human rights that dates back to the 1960s; the campaign also re-affirms her preoccupation with wholeness in life and in art.

In the 1970s, Walker's search for ZORA NEALE HURSTON, the writer and the woman, unearthed a literary foremother and contributed to a resurgence of interest in Hurston's work. Walker's own place as one of the most versatile and influential authors in African-American, American, and feminist–womanist writing in the 20th century is assured.   KO

Walker, Brenda 1957– Academic, feminist critic and fiction writer, Walker was born in northern New South Wales, wrote a Ph.D. on Samuel Beckett and teaches in English at the University of Western Australia. Walker's first novel, *Crush* (1991), uses an epigraph from Roland Barthes – 'Isn't storytelling always a way of searching for one's origin, speaking one's conflicts with the law, entering into the dialectic of tenderness and hatred?' – to establish its writerly concerns with the need to narrate, the difficulties of narration, and the search for the father. A POSTMODERN thriller, set in Perth where Walker lives, it has an elliptical, teasing plot. *One More River* (1993) is the parable-like story of an ambivalent relationship between an elderly woman, Faith, and Winton, an escaped prisoner, to whom she gives sanctuary on the island where she lives alone. The two journey together to Sydney. Walker's third novel is an imaginative retelling of the last days of Virginia Poe. She has edited a collection of original work by younger Australian writers, *Risks* (1996), whose title indicates her interest in fiction that challenges boundaries and conventions.   DB

Walker, Kath see OODGEROO

Walker (Alexander), Margaret (Abigail) 1915–98 African-American poet, novelist and essayist, whose work addresses the 'black and poor and small and different'. Born to college faculty members, Jamaican theologian Sigismund C. Walker and musicologist Marion Dozier, Walker was raised with very high academic expectations. Her first publication was the 1932 essay, 'What Is to Become of Us?' After joining the Federal Writers' Project in Chicago in 1935 (where she worked with GWENDOLYN BROOKS and Richard Wright), her first book, *For My People* (1942), appeared in the prestigious Yale Younger Poets series, its first by an African-American poet. She wrote the title poem in what she calls 'strophic free verse', sonorous and sermonic phrases. As she notes in her first poem in 1937, 'I Want to Write': 'I want to write the songs of my people / I want to hear them singing melodies in the dark.' In 1943 she married and became the breadwinner for a disabled husband and four children. Finally in 1966, after three decades of intermittent writing, her HISTORICAL folk NOVEL *Jubilee*, appeared, based upon

family stories of her great-grandmother's life and validating matrofocal family structure, as had FRANCES ELLEN WATKINS HARPER earlier. Walker documents its writing in the essay 'How I Wrote *Jubilee*' (1972). Additionally she published *A Poetic Equation: Conversations Between Nikki Giovanni and Margaret Walker* (1974), *Richard Wright, Daemonic Genius: A Portrait of the Man, a Critical Look at His Work* (1988) and *This Is My Century: New and Collected Poems* (1988), comprising four earlier volumes plus recent work. In her essay, 'On Being Female, Black, and Free' (1980; now available in a book of the same title (1997)), she writes that 'freedom is a philosophical state of mind . . . In my mind, I am absolutely free.'   CFK

Wallace, Bronwen 1945–89 Canadian poet, essayist, writer of short fiction and film-maker, best known for her conversational poems which move between the worlds of celebration and elegy. Wallace was born in Kingston, Ontario, Canada, and attended Queen's University. She lived for four years in Windsor where she worked organizing unions and women's groups and where she studied creative writing. She returned to Kingston with her son Jeremy and began to publish her books of poetry: *Marrying into the Family* (1980), *Signs of the Former Tenant* (1983; which includes her best-known work 'A Simple Poem for Virginia Woolf'), *Common Magic* and *The Stubborn Particulars of Grace* (1987). She also made two films with her partner, Chris Whynot: *All You Have to Do*, a documentary about a friend's illness and death, and *That's Why I'm Talking*, conversations with four Canadian poets: Giorgio di Cicco, MARY DI MICHELE, Robert Priest and Carolyn Smart.

Three more books appeared after her premature death from cancer of the mouth: *Arguments with the World* (essays), *Keep That Candle Burning Bright* (1991; poems), and *People You'd Trust Your Life To* (1990; short fiction).

Bronwen Wallace wrote of the beauty and terror of the everyday, especially in women's lives. In her last poetry and fiction, she blurred the boundaries between science and art, natural and supernatural, life and death.   EG

Walshe, Dolores 1949– Irish playwright, and now novelist, who writes with impassioned skill on major issues of social conflict and injustice. She was born in the Liberties, a historic inner-city area of Dublin, and has lived and worked in many countries. She began writing short stories when in her late thirties. She is the winner of numerous prizes for stories, plays and poems, including the O.Z. Whitehead Award and the Jerusalem Bloomsday Award. *In The Talking Dark* (1989) was short-listed in the international section of the Mobil–Royal Exchange Theatre Playwriting

Competition and was performed at the Manchester Royal Exchange; it is set in South Africa and portrays an extended family blown apart by its confrontation with Apartheid. *The Stranded Hours Between* is also set in South Africa. *A Country in Our Heads* was produced by the Dublin Theatre Festival in 1991. Other plays include *Seeing an Angel in Hades*, *The Sins in Sally Gardens* and *All Kinds of Trinity*. Recently she has concentrated on fiction, returning to South Africa to set *Where the Trees Weep* (1992). A collection of short stories, *Moodmad* (1993), was followed by *Fragile We Are* (1996). She lives in Dublin.   CL

Walwicz, Ania 1951– Australian poet and visual artist, born in Poland, who immigrated to Australia in 1963, is well known as a performance poet, and has also produced pieces for the theatre. Her first book, *Writing*, a collection of prose/poetry pieces, was published in 1982 (later published as *Travel/Writing* with Philip Hammial (1989)), was followed by *Boat* (1989) which won the New Writing category of the Victorian Premier's Literary Awards, 1990, and *Red Roses* (1992). Her work is best known for its exploration of the migrant experience, and its concentration on the performative nature of ethnicity and gender. Much anthologized, her poems 'Australia' and 'Europe' are typical of her work in their deployment of a series of migrant interlocutors who question received ideas about Australia and Europe, and the experience of the migrant who moves between both. Her poetry, in its use of fractured or broken English, its deployment of a minimalist discontinuous style, and the substitution of voices and discourses for plot, has been aligned with other experimental or avant-garde writers like GERTRUDE STEIN.   JAM

Wanderer: Or, Female Difficulties, The (1814) FANNY BURNEY's fourth and last novel recounts the intricate life of Juliet Granville. It opens with Juliet's desperate flight from France during the reign of terror in 1793. Her true identity is only slowly revealed. She is the daughter from a first marriage of Lord Granville, who, due to her claims to the family fortune, is pursued and silenced by the family of Granville's second wife. Having being brought up in France, Juliet escapes to England after a forced marriage, in order to save her guardian from the guillotine. Her life in England is characterized by a desperate struggle for survival. Whilst she tries to earn her own living honourably, she faces the 'female difficulties' of impoverished and genteel women of the time. Burney places her often naive heroine in a number of situations which portray the severe hardship of governesses, teachers, milliners and semi-professional 'companions'. Further, through her nameless protagonist, Burney investigates critically the question of female identity and thus continues this theme from her earlier novel *Cecilia* (1782) and her own private DIARIES. Generically, the book is a sophisticated version of the contemporary anti-Jacobin novel with elements of ROMANCE and the GOTHIC.   NBP

Wandor, Micheline 1940– British feminist critic and author of experimental and political plays, poems and stories. Born in London to Russian Jewish parents, Micheline Wandor attended Chingford Secondary Modern and High Schools and Cambridge University. Her plays, which were mainly premièred by women's theatre groups, include *The Day After Yesterday* (1972), *Spilt Milk* (1973), *The Old Wives' Tale* (1977) and *Aid Thy Neighbour* (1978). Addressing issues ranging from the Miss World Beauty Contest to lesbian motherhood, her rich and varied creative output reflects her belief in the diversity and centrality of women's experience.

During the 1970s, she became heavily involved with the increasingly vociferous feminist movement, and edited the proceedings of a pivotal conference on Women's Liberation held at Ruskin College, Oxford, in 1970. *The Body Politic* (1972) was the first collection of British feminist writing, and was followed in 1990 by *Once a Feminist*, a series of retrospective interviews covering the two previous decades. The documentation of her generation's consciousness in these two volumes is an invaluable sociohistorical resource. Her association with feminism led to several collaborative projects, notably with ZÖE FAIRBAIRNS, SARA MAITLAND and MICHÈLE ROBERTS. She was on the advisory group of the Virago Press and edited a series of contemporary *Plays by Women* for Methuen in the 1980s. She has also written about theatre and sexual politics in *Carry On Understudies* (1981) and *Look Back in Gender* (1987), adapted various classic novels for radio serialization and worked as a newspaper and radio critic. CS

War Between the Tates, The (1974) ALISON LURIE's wryly comic satirical novel of gender- and generation-conflict unfolds against the background of Vietnam and the anti-war movement and the US campus upheaval of the late 1960s and early 1970s. Written in the present tense, the novel begins with the dejection of Erica Tate: academic (house)wife in a rural suburb progressively despoiled by developers, mother of two adored children inexorably mutating into revolting adolescents and wife of Brian, lecturer in Political Science who succumbs to the devotion of a tenaciously infatuated graduate student, Wendy. The plot turns on Wendy's pregnancy and Erica's and Brian's separate and opposed attempts to deal with this, the affair and their related life changes. In doing so, they migrate from the American nuclear family idealized in the 1950s through a period of 'hippy' sexual and cultural liberation which includes Brian Tate's non-smoking participation at a dope party and a mind-opening acid trip for Erica. Largely favouring Erica, point of view fluctuates between the protagonists, but the narrative voice remains unfailingly ironic. SAS

Ward, Harriet 1808–1873 British novelist, TRAVEL WRITER, journalist, military commentator on the wars with the Xhosa on the Eastern Cape frontier. Daughter of a colonel and wife of a captain in the 91st regiment, with her small daughter she accompanied her husband to St Helena and to the Cape, where she found rich material for her writing. *Five Years in Kaffirland* (1848) was based on journal entries she had converted into monthly contributions over five years to the *United Service Journal*; these begin conventionally, and then become outspoken in their condemnation of British colonial policy and the treatment by the army of soldiers and their wives. Having established an attentive audience, she returned to England to continue to publish in journals such as *Bentley's Miscellany* and *Ainsworth's Magazine*. Her most important novel was *Jasper Lyle: A Tale of Kaffirland* (1851), in which her sympathies for the marginalized – the Xhosa, the Boers, and women in particular in a patriarchal society – are made clear. In this text, she begins her sympathetic examination of the difficulties of 'miscegenation' (begun in her first novel, *Helen Charteris* (1848), the story of a young creole woman in provincial England, composed on the Eastern Cape frontier), which was to become a 'flood-subject' in South African literature. She discovers too the symbolic power implicit in the landscape. Committed and energetic, unexpectedly subversive of established authority, and conscious of her role as a woman writer, she is a significant early Victorian voice from the colonies. VHL

Ward [née Arnold], Mrs Humphry (Mary) 1851–1920 English novelist whose work combines romantic interest with themes reflecting contemporary theological and moral debate. The niece of Matthew and Thomas Arnold, her writing disseminated a liberal vision of an ecumenical English Church made more pressing by her father's final conversion to Rome in 1876.

Separated from her parents in early life, Mary rejoined them in Oxford aged 16, and in 1872 married the Brasenose tutor, T. Humphry Ward. Pater's aestheticism and Jowett's challenge to biblical authority informed the intellectual milieu for her continuing self-education. The Ward family, now including three children, moved to London in 1881 where T. Humphry became art critic of *The Times*. Mary concentrated on writing fiction, and her novel of ideas, *ROBERT ELSMERE* (1888), brought her widespread recognition. In it the young clergyman of the title comes under the influence of sceptical scholarship and can no longer adhere to the Church's Thirty-Nine Articles. His wife, Catherine, continues as a staunch Anglican while loyally supporting him in the establishment of an alternative religious brotherhood in the slums of London. Gladstone's review article expressed his unease with Elsmere's agnosticism and sparked a journalistic debate about the future of Anglicanism which ensured exceptional sales of the book on both sides of the Atlantic.

Other novels with religious themes followed, including *Helbeck of Bannisdale* (1898) in which the heroine drowns herself when torn between her Catholic lover and the spirit of her atheist father. With the new century, however, Ward's popularity declined and her role in the foundation of the Women's National Anti-Suffrage League in 1908 did little to confound contemporary views of her as embodying the worst aspects of Victorian prudery. Compelled by mounting debts and slumping sales, she produced a series of romantic potboilers such as *Daphne* (1909), on a divorce theme, and *Delia Blanchflower* (1913), on suffragism. The 1911 sequel, *The Case of Richard Meynell*, in which Elsmere's Anglican daughter Mary marries Rector Meynell despite his impending trial for heretical modernism, was also a flop. Patriotic writings during the war briefly revived her reputation although their propagandist tone was later parodied by her nephew, Aldous Huxley, in *The Farcical History of Richard Greenow* (1920). JSpi

Ward Jouve, Nicole 1938– French writer living and working in England who, being completely bilingual in French and English, can write and translate with ease and elegance in both languages, and whose nonfiction, as much as her fiction, demonstrates the literary power, grace and blossoming that can result from such a doubling of tongues. What might have been a painful split becomes for Ward Jouve an opening, an invitation.

She has been part of, and influenced by, the school of French criticism – Roland Barthes, Julia Kristeva, Luce Irigaray and HÉLÈNE CIXOUS. Her own criticism is characterized by close reading, a worrying-away at her subject until she creates a meaning, a poetic and passionate way of putting things which admits and explores its own subjectivity. Her non-fiction includes *Baudelaire: A Fire to Conquer Darkness* (1981), *The Street-Cleaner: The Yorkshire Ripper Case on Trial* (1986) and *Female Genesis* (1997). Her fictions use puns, associations, layers of metaphor, dream and snatches of personal narrative to create multi-faceted webs of women moving through their social, familial and historical contexts. She writes in French, then translates herself into English so that each book is truly doubled in size and language. Her first novel was *Shades of Grey* (1980), whose form of linked episodes announced her interest in short forms unconventionally narrated. Since then she has written stories characterized by their passionate commitment to their subject matter, their wit and jokes, and richly detailed backgrounds.　　MBR

Warner, Marina 1946– English novelist and critic whose half-Italian background and cosmopolitan education and early life may perhaps be credited with her love of art, art history, fairy tale and folklore, and also her prose style, which is more rich, poetic and wrought than often found among British writers. Warner's work, both fictional and non-fictional, is that of a consummate stylist. Her achievement is to have explored issues of female representation, myth and history, both in fiction and non-fiction. She has helped to create a new sort of cultural history, concerned with the human body and the unconscious as well as material processes such as economics and family structures, alongside a very contemporary kind of novel, in which the forces of symbolism are given their due.

She became well known for her study *Alone of All Her Sex : The Myth and Cult of the Virgin Mary* (1976), and followed this with other works of cultural history: *Joan of Arc* (1981), *MONUMENTS AND MAIDENS* (1985), *Managing Monsters* (1994, the BBC Reith Lectures), and *From the Beast to the Blonde: On Fairy Tales and Their Tellers* (1994). Her interest in FAIRY TALES is also evinced in the edited collection *Wonder Tales*, fairy stories collected by the BLUESTOCKINGS satirized by Molière. Warner has also written her own re-told tales, collected in *Mermaids in the Basement* (1993). The fascination for myth informs her novels too – myth in the ancient Greek sense of the ordering, disruption and re-ordering of the structures of family life. *THE LOST FATHER* (1988), which was a Regional Winner (Eurasia) in the Commonwealth Writers' Prize, interweaves the actual and psychic search of a daughter for her own father with an investigation of Fascism's appeal to Italian women, and its evocation of a certain kind of phallus-worshipping, self-sacrificing femininity which had so far been mainly explored only in feminist psychoanalytical literature. Her novel *Indigo* (1992) gave a fresh twist to her characteristic themes, looking at how the imagination is crucially linked to memory and history. It investigates imperialism through the story of a colonial family with roots in the slavery society of the West Indies, intercut with a poetically charged narrative concerning Sycorax, the witch in Shakespeare's *Tempest*. Magic, it turns out, has to do not only with men's powerful wands, but also with women's ancient skills and spells.　　MBR

Warner, Susan 1819–85 Bestselling American novelist. Born to a prosperous New York City family, Warner received an elite education, which was curtailed with her father's financial failure in 1838 and the family's retreat to Constitution Island near West Point, New York. To make money, Warner and her sister Anna Bartlett Warner began their writing career with the children's *Game of Natural History* (1848), and for the next sixty years between them produced some 100 books, including novels, CHILDREN'S BOOKS and devotional guides. Warner's first and most famous novel, the bestselling *The Wide, Wide World* (1850), is a Christian BILDUNGSROMAN with a little girl at its centre, an evangelized *JANE EYRE*. The appeal of this novel, reprinted in over 100 editions, is not only in the wrenching spiritual quest of little Ellen Montgomery, but also in a rich evocation of New England rural life, which earned Warner a reputation as an early regionalist. This success led to a series of children's books, 'Ellen Montgomery's Bookshelf', and many sentimental novels, notably *Queechy* (1852), *Letter of Credit* (1881), *Melbourne House* (1864), *The Old Helmet* (1863). Often semi-autobiographical, Warner's plots tend to embark girls and young women on quests for spiritual, emotional and financial well-being. Never married and since youth active in the evangelical American Tract Society, Warner devoted time in her later years to Bible classes for West Point cadets.　　PCr

Warner, Sylvia Townsend 1893–1978 English novelist and poet who excelled in the satirical HISTORICAL NOVEL. Educated at home by her Harrow schoolmaster father, she worked in a munitions factory in World War I, and from 1918 to 1930 for the Carnegie-funded Tudor Church Music project. Her poems in her first book, *The Espalier* (1925), and in *Time Importuned* (1928), are mostly pastoral, often pastiche, especially of Hardy or, in her long satire of rural poverty, *Opus 7* (1931), of Crabbe. Her first, most popular, novel, *LOLLY WILLOWES* (1926), uses witchcraft as metaphor to explore an unregarded spinster's secret life. *Mr Fortune's Maggot* (1927) is the tragicomedy of a deluded missionary. *The True Heart* (1930) transposes Psyche's legend to Victorian Norfolk.

From 1930 Warner lived mostly in rural Dorset with her partner, the poet VALENTINE ACKLAND. In 1935 they published a joint volume, *Whether a Dove or Seagull*, with unattributed poems. Both joined the Communist party and campaigned vigorously against the exploitation of agricultural workers. *SUMMER WILL SHOW* (1936), first of the three historical novels which are Warner's major achievement, celebrates a genteel Englishwoman's liberation by communism and lesbianism in Paris during the 1848 Revolution. In 1937 Warner and Ackland travelled twice to Spain; the Civil War inspired some of Warner's best poems, and the novel *After the Death of Don Juan* (1938), set in 18th-century Spain, which moves from aristocratic comedy to the heroic tragedy of popular revolt. Political disillusionment and war-time office experience informed her finest novel, *The Corner that Held Them* (1948), which reconstructs the everyday politics of a 14th-century Fenland convent. A high comedy, it fuses the 'complete worldliness' she admired in AUSTEN with an intense poetic imagining of landscape and material life. Thereafter Warner wrote the biography, *T.H. White* (1967), her most popular work since *Lolly Willowes*, but which she considered too 'auntlike'; never completed her projected biography of her friend T.F. Powys; wrote the pastiche Victorian family novel, *The Flint Anchor* (1954), many poems and short stories, notably for the *New Yorker*, a major financial support in her hard-up old age. Her most distinctive stories are satirical fantasy, as in the tales of chilly, elitist, vulnerable beings in *Kingdoms of Elfin* (1977). Her best work, witty imaginative exploration of the interactions of the political and personal life, remains under-rated.   AT

Warren, Mercy Otis 1728–1814 American historian, playwright, poet, pamphleteer. Daughter of a prominent Massachusetts family, sister of James Otis (said to have coined 'taxation without representation is tyranny'), wife of Revolutionary James Warren, Mercy Otis Warren helped shape American republican discourse through both her published work and her network of friends and correspondents, including John and ABIGAIL ADAMS, George and Martha Washington, John Dickinson, Thomas Jefferson, JUDITH SARGEANT MURRAY and CATHERINE MACAULAY. While her house in Boston became a patriots' salon, Warren joined the pre-Revolution newspaper debates through anonymous publication of dramatic political satires: *The Adulateur* (1773), *The Defeat* (1773) and *The Group* (1775); two more ribald satires, *The Blockheads* (1776) and *The Motley Assembly* (1779), may also be hers. More polished, but less dynamic, are the two admonitory tragedies, *The Sack of Rome* and *The Ladies of Castile*, published with her neoclassical poems in 1790. She participated in the constitutional debates with an anti-federalist pamphlet by a 'Columbian Patriot' (1788), but her major work is the three-volume *History of the Rise, Progress, and Termination of the American Revolution* (1805), one of few contemporary histories of the Revolution and the most comprehensive anti-federalist account. Her focus on character, in her dramas and in the *History*, allows her to promote public and private virtues desirable for and accessible to both men and women, including the virtue of tender feeling. Across genres, Warren writes with one ethical goal, to transmit the values of leading the republican life: one bound up with membership in and responsibilities toward the polis.   PCr

Waters, Alice [Singer] 1944– American COOKERY writer and restaurateur. Born and raised in Chatham, New Jersey, Waters earned a degree in French Studies at the University of California in Berkeley before travelling for a year in France. In 1971 she embodied her passion for France in a Berkeley restaurant she named 'Chez Panisse' after the hero of Marius Pagnol's fictional and cinematic trilogy, *Marius, Fanny* and *César*. In designing a place where she could meet her friends, Waters created a set menu for each day to guarantee produce of the highest quality for each season. Her kitchen was seminal in generating a crop of young chefs in the 1970s and in establishing a network of farmers to supply quality ingredients. In 1984 she opened 'Café Fanny', named for her daughter from her first marriage, and later wrote a cook book for her. Long an advocate of sustainable agriculture, Waters has spearheaded a number of public gardening and teaching projects that connect the growing of food with the cooking and eating of it. Her five cook books, beginning with *The Chez Panisse Menu Cookbook* in 1982, continued the revolution wrought by JULIA CHILD in translating French culinary traditions into the American idiom.   BF

Watson, Jean 1935– New Zealand novelist. Her first novel, STAND IN THE RAIN (1965), described by one critic as 'a woman's "on-the-road" novel', was followed by *The Balloon Watchers* (1975) which, to the central question in Watson's universe, 'Why anything?', answers, 'Because there can't be nothing'. *The World is an Orange and the Sun* (1978) is more conventionally realist, as the narrator, a housewife, ponders, 'The "me" that I see in the full length mirror seems dissassociated from the one that I'm used to.' *Flowers from Happyever* (1980) and *Address to a King* (1986) reflect Watson's increasing interest in Vedanta philosophy, as does *Three Sea Stories* (1994). *Karunai Illam: The Story of an Orphanage* (1992) is an autobiographical account of her involvement with the founding of an orphanage in southern India.

Watson's work deals with mundane circumstances, filtered through a central female observer, who displays an acute and at times quasi-mystical perception of reality. The novels – or novellas: they are very short – are often organized around central symbols of transcendence and epiphany: balloons, an orange, a flower, or, in *Address to a King*, the figure of mythical Indian King Aravinda whose exoticism contrasts with and informs the life of the narrator, a 47-year-old librarian living in Wellington.   JSt

Waves, The (1931) This highly experimental 'novel' was VIRGINIA WOOLF's 'most difficult and complex' book, as she herself said in her diary. In it she challenges conventional plot and character representation, especially with regard to the voiceless Percival, omnipresent in the consciousness of the text, although he has no living voice on the page.

The book is constructed as an alternating combination of interludes and monologues. The interludes are short poetic descriptions of a seashore landscape, tracing the movement of the sun from sunrise to sunset, while the monologues are a set of six chronologically arranged dramatic 'soliloquies' communicating fragmented scenes, impressions and sketches from the lives of six characters. These six speaking voices are those of close friends who grew up together, went to the same kinds of school, but had different destinies: Susan married a farmer and had two children, Jinny followed the pleasures of the body, Rhoda committed suicide, Louis became a successful businessman, Neville suffered badly from Percival's death, and Bernard is obsessed with words, phrases and telling stories. AA

We of the Never-Never (1908) Mrs Aneas (JEANNIE) GUNN drew upon her own letters to family in Victoria from the Northern Territory of Australia in writing what proved to be an extremely popular and influential narrative of her experience as 'the Little Missus', the bride of the manager of a remote cattle station where she was the only white woman. The book, like her CHILDREN'S STORY, *The Little Black Princess* (1906), gives a reassuring, genteel, sanitized picture of pioneering life: her white men are chivalrous, 'lovable' characters; the Aborigines are childlike; the Chinese cook is comic; the hardships of 'roughing it' in the bush are treated humorously; and the uglier aspects of the white–black encounter are carefully ignored. The narrative ends with the death of her husband, who is idealized throughout as a wise, authority figure, revered by both black and white. With its racial stereotyping, its sentimental tone and its image of indomitable and resourceful white men overcoming all obstacles with apparent ease, the book persuasively reinforced the imperialist myth of the benevolent British colonizers (see COLONIAL WRITING). JBa

Weamys, Anna fl.1651 British author of a pastoral prose ROMANCE, *A Continuation of Sir Philip Sidney's Arcadia*, published in London in 1651. Taking up Sidney's invitation to continue his *Arcadia*, the romance builds on the unfinished *New Arcadia* of 1593. It opens with Sidney's central figure, Basilius (King of Arcadia), his Queen and their family. Unlike Sidney, Weamys provides an ending, sending her characters to end 'their days in Peace and Quietness'. Little is known about Weamys's life. Indeed, her name first appears in the second edition (1690), the first being ascribed only to 'A.W.' This identification is confirmed by a letter from James Howell to 'Dr Weamys', probably a divine, suggesting that he was 'Father to a Daughter that *Europe* hath not many of her equals'. Information in this letter and the names of those who wrote dedicatory verses to her volume suggest that she was a gentle-woman, wrote the romance when she was relatively young, and may have been one of a circle of writers grouped around the Marquis of Dorchester, a Royalist who had compounded for his estates. SW

Weather in the Streets, The (1936) Mirroring societal shifts in the between-the-wars period, Olivia Curtis, introduced to readers by ROSAMOND LEHMANN in her novel of adolescence, *INVITATION TO THE WALTZ* (1932), has exchanged her comfortable, middle-class country life for a failed marriage, a London bed-sit, a badly paid job and a bohemian circle of friends. The account of her impassioned affair with Rollo, the married scion of minor aristocracy close to her parents' home, highlights and often effectively satirizes nuances of class, but finally emphasizes Olivia's impotence against gender and power structures. The unmelodramatic description of the abortion that Olivia is forced to seek (Harley Street rather than back-street, the abortionist an urbane aesthete rather than an ancient crone) nevertheless ruptured the contemporary tacit silence on the subject. The central section of the novel switches mainly to first-person interior monologue, conveying Olivia's isolation even when the affair is at its most intense. The difficulty of reproducing the immediacy of this narrative technique in another medium was evident in two BBC Television productions (Prudence FitzGerald, 1962; Gavin Millar, 1984). WAP

Webb [née Potter], Beatrice 1858–1943 Essayist, economist, sociologist and DIARIST. The eighth daughter of wealthy parents who wanted a son, Webb experienced an unhappy childhood and grew up searching for what she called 'creed' and 'craft', or belief and work.

Serving as a social investigator for Charles Booth's *Inquiry into the Life and Labour of the Poor of London* provided the meaningful focus she craved. In 1887 her essay 'Dock Life in the East End of London' appeared in the *Nineteenth Century*; later that year she disguised herself as a seamstress to gather information on East End sweat shops. In 1892, against the objections of friends and family she married Sidney Webb, a London tradesman she described as 'very small and ugly'. For the next fifty years they enjoyed an emotional and intellectual partnership devoted to the Fabian ideals of gradual reform and collectivism organized by an intellectual elite. They founded what became the London School of Economics and wrote a series of what she called 'solid but unreadable books' including *The History of Trade Unionism* (1894) and *Industrial Democracy* (1897).

By contrast the diaries she began keeping at the age of 15 reveal her 'longing to create characters and move them to and fro among fictitious circumstances'. Webb used the diaries as the basis for *My Apprenticeship* (1926), her autobiography up to her marriage, which F.R. Leavis recognized as 'one of the classics of English literature'. She completed only one volume of its anticipated two-volume sequel, *Our Partnership* before her death in 1943.   MAD

Webb [née Meredith], (Gladys) Mary 1881–1927

English novelist and poet. Born in Leighton in Shropshire, the daughter of a schoolmaster, Webb formed an intense and intimate relationship with the Shropshire countryside throughout her life, which was reflected in all of her work. She was educated largely at home and began writing poetry and prose in her teens. In 1912, she married schoolmaster Henry Webb, and they worked as market gardeners before moving to Hampstead in London in 1921.

Webb's first novel, *The Golden Arrow*, was published in 1916. It was followed by *The Spring of Joy* (1917) – a collection of essays – and the novels *Gone to Earth* (1917), *The House in Dormer Forest* (1920), *Seven for a Secret* (1922) and her most famous work, *Precious Bane* (1924), which won the Prix Femina Vie Heureuse in 1924–5, and decades later became a BBC dramatization. An unfinished novel, *Armour Wherein He Trusted*, was published posthumously in 1928. The dominant force in all Webb's writing is the power of nature, which is expressed both in terms of local settings and in a generalized pantheistic and animistic mysticism. Her work is peopled with 'simple-hearted' countryfolk, who are open to nature's forces, but who are also prone to superstition and prejudice; for example, they mount a witch-hunt against Prue Sarn, the heroine of *Precious Bane*, because she can read and write and has a hare-lip.

Webb's work was largely overlooked throughout her life, which ended prematurely after decades of ill health through Graves' disease. After her death, she achieved greater prominence, in part because of the endorsement of the Prime Minister, Stanley Baldwin.   AC

Webster [née Davies], Augusta 1837–94 English

poet and novelist whose REALIST verse made her one of the major women poets of the Victorian period. Born in Poole, Dorset, she was the daughter of Vice-Admiral George Davies and Julia Hume and was educated at the Cambridge School of Art, Paris and Geneva. In 1863 she married Thomas Webster, solicitor and law lecturer at Cambridge, and they had one daughter. From 1870 they lived in London where Augusta became involved in the Women's Suffrage movement and campaigned for women's education. She wrote a novel, *Lesley's Guardian* (1866), which was published under the pseudonym 'Cecil Home', but she is now most well known for her poetry and particu-

Illustration by Jean Webster from *Dear Enemy*, 1916.

larly her development of the female dramatic monologue to explore such issues as the marriage market, spinsterhood and motherhood. Both *Dramatic Studies* (1866) and *Portraits* (1870) reveal the influence of the monologues of Browning and FELICIA HEMANS, the latter volume including the highly regarded study of prostitution, 'A Castaway'. Other poetic works include *A Woman Sold* (1867), and the unfinished sonnet sequence *Mother and Daughter*, published posthumously in 1895. She also wrote a collection of essays entitled *A Housewife's Opinions* (1879), various plays, and articles for the *Examiner* and the *Athenaeum*.   SA

Webster, Jean [Alice Jane Chandler Webster]

1876–1916 Although Mark Twain was her great-uncle, and her father's publishing partner, Jean established herself as an American humorist and campaigning novelist in her own name. While studying at Vassar, she wrote for college journals and local newspapers. Soon after graduating (with a BA in English and Economics) in 1901, she published stories featuring the first of her sparky, witty, inquiring heroines, Patty Wyatt, turning her adventures into a series of novels (1903 onwards) based on Patty's activities in school and college. Patty, who declares, 'I never pay attention to "No Trespassing" signs. You'd never get anywhere in this world if you let *them* bother you' (*Just Patty*, 1911), is an energetic proponent of commonsense, whether leading her Latin class in a strike against excessive work-loads, or challenging a robber baron's misogyny. Travelling round the world in 1906–7, investigating economic deprivation and racial injustice at home, Jean was equally venturesome.

Her most famous activists are orphan Judy and Social-Register Sallie in the phenomenally successful *Daddy-Long-Legs* (1912) and its sequel, *Dear Enemy* (1914), both EPISTOLARY NOVELS, illustrated with Jean's lively stick-drawings. With echoes of JANE EYRE, these moving comic crusades for the rights of the child, the humanization of institutions, and the fulfilling power of administrative work for women, had a wide influence. (Judy's story was frequently adapted for stage and screen.)

Having married Glenn Ford McKinney in 1915, Jean died within the year, after giving birth to a daughter.

PEK

Weeton, Ellen [Mrs Stock] 1776–1845 British DIARIST, an abused wife and a devoted mother. After conducting a small school and becoming a governess, in 1814 Weeton married a nearly bankrupt widower, Aaron Stock of Wigan, who needed her small savings but could not stand her proud nature and was to subject her to more than seven years of verbal and physical abuse before casting her out entirely. By threatening her with starvation, further imprisonment, or a Lunacy Commission hearing, her brother Tom and Stock in 1822 forced her to accept unread a deed of separation banishing her from Wigan and limiting her to three supervised visits a year with her daughter Mary, in return for a meagre stipend paid irregularly. Refusing separation from her child, Weeton regularly walked almost eight miles each way just to view Mary at her boarding school and sometimes join the file of children going to chapel. After Stock left Wigan in 1827, Mary was returned to her mother, possibly through the offices of Hope Chapel, after Weeton became a member. The diaries and letter journals Weeton kept from 1807 to 1825 include an eloquent record of her sufferings and growth out of self-pity.

HB

Weil, Simone 1909–43 French political and philosophical theorist and religious writer, Weil was born a Jew but was later drawn to Catholicism by a belief in Christ, as well as to other religions. Most of her writings were published after she died, in England, while she was working for Charles de Gaulle's Free French. A distinguished graduate of the Ecole Normale Supérieure, Weil took the *agrégation* and became a teacher in the provinces. It was at this stage that she came to identify herself with manual workers and the

unemployed, taking this to extremes during World War II when she accepted no more than the minimum food rations, and refused to heat her home. Albert Camus hailed her *L'Enracinement: Prélude à une déclaration des devoirs envers l'être humain* (1948; *The Need for Roots*, 1952) as a necessary part of the spiritual rebirth of France after the war. Much of her other work is concerned with the construction of an aesthetic and moral system, where a balance between honesty in lived experience and philosophical belief is prized above all else (similar to the Existentialists' 'good faith'). Her *Notebooks* (*Cahiers*, 1970, 1972, 1974) contain the development and expression of this system, in their exploration of her terms, particularly 'gravity' and 'grace'.

SD

Weld, Angelina (Emily) Grimké 1805–79 American abolitionist and feminist. Like her older sister SARAH GRIMKÉ, she grew up in a wealthy planter's household in Charleston, where from childhood she felt the 'outrages and pollutions' of slavery. By 1829, at the age of 24, she had converted to Quakerism and moved to Philadelphia, where she began reading anti-slavery newspapers and attending abolitionist meetings. When in 1835 William Lloyd Garrison printed a letter of support she had written him, in the *Liberator*, she found herself publicly identified as an abolitionist, a role she soon prosecuted with vigour through both platform and pen. In 1836 she published *An Appeal to the Christian Women of the Southern States*, urging her 'respected friends' to overthrow slavery even if it required breaking the law; later that year she began lecturing for the American Anti-Slavery Society. A printed attack by CATHARINE BEECHER on both abolitionism and the propriety of women exerting extradomestic influence brought from Angelina a series of *Letters* (1837) passionately defending the movement and a woman's right to a public voice, declaring the 'present arrangements' of society regarding the latter a '*violation of human rights, a rank usurpation of power*'. In 1838 she married abolitionist Theodore Weld and began work on his *American Slavery as It Is* (1839), a detailed account based largely on Sarah's and Angelina's research. Though she continued her activism after her marriage, she published little and appeared only sporadically in public, devoting her energies to her children and schoolteaching. She died after a series of strokes at 74.

WG

Weldon, Fay 1933– Writer of blackly funny cautionary tales chronicling the ills of modern Britain, particularly those of wives and mistresses: a moralist with a delinquent streak. The groundwork for Weldon's feminism was laid by her childhood in an all-female household with sister, grandmother and a divorced writer-mother. After studying Economics and

Philosophy at St Andrews University, she worked on the problem page of the *Daily Mail* and as an advertising copywriter (Weldon invented the slogan 'Go to work on an egg', a classic of the genre). She has been married three times, and has four sons, the youngest of whom was born when she was 46.

Weldon's prolific writing career began in the mid sixties. From the start she delivered sharp commentary on current social issues. Her smart, dialogue-driven style owes much to her work as a television dramatist and in advertising, which made her an apt diagnostician of consumer society. Her first novel, *The Fat Woman's Joke* (1967), began as television drama. It was a 'summary of the complaints of women' and an anti-diet polemic. She writes of male and female relations, particularly in the media and advertising belts, with hard-edged economy and bleak wit. Her earlier novels – see DOWN AMONG THE WOMEN (1971), FEMALE FRIENDS (1975) and REMEMBER ME (1976) – tend to divide the world up into dolly birds (the mistress type) and doormats (wives). *LIFE AND LOVES OF A SHE-DEVIL* (1983) described the revenge of a 'doormat'. A satire on the hypocrisies of women's romantic fiction, it was made into a film starring Roseanne Barr and Meryl Streep. Weldon has written over forty television plays and adaptations, including one of PRIDE AND PREJUDICE (1980). She has attacked AUSTEN's co-optation into a nostalgic English idyll in *Letters to Alice on First Reading Jane Austen* (1984). Her belief in the writer's moral role has made her something of a pulpit rhetorician. This found extended expression in *Sacred Cows: A Portrait of BRITAIN, post-RUSHDIE, pre-UTOPIA* (1989), a left-leaning critique of contemporary British institutions and attitudes.

Weldon's novels have been emblematic of numerous contemporary themes; female physiology (*Puffball*, 1980), colonialism and militarism (*The Shrapnel Academy*, 1986), swinging London (*The Hearts and Lives of Men*, 1987), genetic experiment and nuclear energy (*The Cloning of Joanna May*, 1989), hopes for the future (*Darcy's Utopia*, 1990) and therapy culture (*Affliction*, 1994). She has a robustly dark view of the world, underlining the limits on her characters' autonomy and understanding by holding them at arms' length with authorial intrusions and ironic, distancing devices. Once an icon of sixties feminism, she is now critical of the era's hedonism and sees the 'emotional correctness' of therapy culture as oppressing men and women alike.   KE

Well, The (1986) ELIZABETH JOLLEY's discontinuous narrative recounts the intensifying relationship between Hester Harper, a wealthy landowner in rural Australia, and Katherine, an orphan teenager she brings home to live with her. Hester's intimate connection to her land is gradually broken by her increasing preoccupation with Katherine, and she sells up most of the property, moving with Katherine to an isolated farmhouse. The underlying tensions between the women erupt when Katherine drives the utility home one night and hits something unspecified on the track to the house. Hester dumps the body down the disused well on the property, but then discovers that money is missing from the house and insists Katherine climb down the well and retrieve it from the supposed thief. At this point Katherine becomes delusional. Rain breaks the drought, and more than the contents of the well threaten to rise to the surface. The novel ends at a moment of immanence, as Hester seems poised to break out of the relationship and re-enter her community by recounting a version of the story we have just read.   SKM

Well of Loneliness, The (1928) The history of RADCLYFFE HALL's fifth novel, banned on publication by the British courts, has been nothing but sensational. Recognized as the first lesbian novel, it has been described as notoriously obscene, surprisingly enlightening and ludicrously melodramatic. BILDUNGSROMAN by genre, the novel follows the life and adventures of an invert, Stephen Gordon, in her battle for compassion and acknowledgement. Its didactic and moralistic tone is hard to miss and the treatment of its subject matter constitutes a mixture of religiosity, popular beliefs and the newly emerging science of sexology. The language, rich and passionate in places, tedious and overworked in others, borrows its dramatic element from the long tradition of romantic fiction, yet without quite rising up to its level and consequently losing its overall effect. Contrary to the author's earnest attempt to educate the public and advocate the invert's right to 'a niche in the creation' the novel leaves the contemporary reader with little to dwell on. In a POSTMODERN age of multiple and diverse identities, *The Well of Loneliness* can contribute little apart from its historical significance.   MPe

Wellesley, Dorothy (Dorothy Violet Ashton)

1889–1956 British poet, patron, memoirist. Her father, Robert Ashton, who – as she recalled in her 1952 autobiography, *Far Have I Travelled* – lived mainly on his yacht, died when Dorothy was 7, and her mother remarried Lord Scarborough. Growing up at Sandbeck, Yorkshire, Dorothy (now called Dottie, a nickname she hated) roamed the Capability Brown landscaping and began writing poetry as a young teenager. Married in 1914 to Gerald Wellesley, she travelled with him to his diplomatic posting in Constantinople; during World War I, the Wellesleys moved to Rome, where their son Valerian was born. A daughter, Elizabeth, followed. Wellesley's first volume, *Poems*, was published in 1920. *Genesis* (1926) and *Deserted House*

(1931) brought her to the attention of W. B. Yeats. Yeats and Wellesley maintained a friendship, and an extensive correspondence about poetry, from 1935 until his death in 1939. Often a guest at Wellesley's home at Penns in the Rocks and the Mediterranean villas she took, Yeats included her poems in his (in)famous *Oxford Book of Modern Verse*, praising her work for its noble style and 'masculine rhythm'.

Wellesley would write poetry and memoirs, edit other English poets as well as her own letters, and entertain friends there until her death. *Rhymes for the Middle Years* (1954) was the last volume of poetry she published. AMD

Wells-Barnett, Ida B. 1862–1929 Led a crusade against lynching in the USA, that lasted for almost four decades. Her campaign began in 1892 when she, a part-owner of a black newspaper in Memphis, wrote an editorial protesting at the lynching of three black businessmen. In the editorial she advised local blacks to 'leave a town which will neither protect our lives and property, nor give us a fair trial in the courts'. When lynching continued, and was predominantly rationalized as justice due to black men for raping white women, Wells-Barnett took a controversial stance which incited the white community to destroy her newspaper office and run her business manager out of town.

What roused local white anger was Wells-Barnett's claim that white justification for lynching was based upon a 'thread bare lie that Negro men rape white women'. In the same year she published *Southern Horrors: Lynch Law in All its Phases*, boldly claiming that white women would willingly marry black men if miscegenation laws were not enforced. The real sexual aggressor, she said, is the white man who 'free(ly) . . . seduce(s) all the colored girls he can'. Wells-Barnett became an international figure for the campaign against lynch law, and went on to write several books on the subject. GG-R

Welty, Eudora (Alice) 1909– American imaginative writer, essayist and photographer whose unwavering subject is 'human life'. She was born in Jackson, Mississippi, one of the poorest of the United States, to a father of Ohio farming stock and a self-reliant West Virginian mother. Welty's was a sheltered and sociable childhood, avid for reading and for the drama, gossip and exuberant monologue of never-ending Southern talk. She graduated from the University of Wisconsin in 1929 and studied advertising in New York, where Depression-generated mass unemployment motivated her return to Jackson.

In the mid 1930s, Welty travelled Mississippi as junior publicity agent for a Federal relief organization, writing news stories and photographing hundreds of her largely impoverished fellow-citizens, whose complex human dignity emerges from her unstudied 'snapshots'. The best of these capture a moment, as she recognized, when 'people reveal themselves'. But she sensed that for her, the meaning of such apprehended transience could better be sought through fiction. Her early short stories were collected as *A Curtain of Green* (1941).

Continuing to live in her family's Jackson home, Welty produced further collections of stories – *The Wide Net* (1943), *The Golden Apples* (1949), *The Bride of the Innisfallen* (1955) – interspersed with a novella – *The Robber Bridegroom* (1942) – and four novels: DELTA WEDDING (1946) in which the dense complexities of 'the everyday' resound through a large clan gathered for an Old South wedding, THE PONDER HEART (1954), *Losing Battles* (1970) and THE OPTIMIST'S DAUGHTER (1972) – the latter, whose middle-aged 'daughter' plumbs depths of mortal understanding after cumulative family deaths, receiving the Pulitzer Prize for fiction. Welty's Mississippi photographs were first brought together in *One Time, One Place* (1971), and her autobiographical *One Writer's Beginnings* (1984) became a bestseller. A spirited traveller with multitudinous friends, Welty, as a writer, has gained numerous admirers, including William Faulkner, ELIZABETH BOWEN and Salman Rushdie.

All of Welty's fiction proceeds from 'within', beyond that photographer's 'crucial moment' to an empathetic and imaginative perception that illuminates the soul. Her stories are almost exclusively of Mississippi people whose emotions are rooted in their physical 'place', where events and tragedies 'live as long as the place does, though they are unseen'; and 'the new life' – the lives of her characters – springs from legends of their pre-statehood past, gathers power from the classical, Celtic and Germanic myths in which Welty discerned human 'interconnectedness', and takes voice in the Southern idiom of 20th-century small-town beautician ('Reach in my purse and git me a cigarette without no powder in it if you kin, Mrs Fletcher, honey'), hotel-keeper, racist gunman ('It looks like the town's on fire already, whichever ways you turn, . . . And a thousand cops crowding ever'where you go, half of 'em too young to start shaving, . . . I'm getting tired of 'em'), adolescent girl ('I'll tell on him, in Morgana tomorrow. He's the most conceited Boy Scout in the whole troop; and's bowlegged'), former slave. A dislocator of time in the MODERNIST vein, Welty has rejected the epithet 'regional', but influenced many Southern writers. (See THE EYE OF THE STORY.) AWS

Wentworth, Anne fl.1676–9 An English Baptist, who wrote texts combining PROPHECY and SPIRITUAL AUTOBIOGRAPHY in the 1670s, a time of increased persecution for sectaries. Wentworth's arguments depend on the skilful integration of the personal and the spiritual/political: she explains in *A Vindication of Anne Wentworth* (1677) that she was forced to leave her husband because he stole her writings from her, thereby hindering her in the fulfilment of God's work. However, the hostility she experienced from her fellow-Baptists as a result of this – 'I am reproached as a proud, wicked, deceived, deluded, lying woman' – and the succour she received from her friends and from God had, she argues, a broader significance: 'my oppressions and deliverance had a public ministry and meaning wrapped up in them', for God had 'revealed to me what wrath shall fall upon the same spirit throughout the whole nation, which everywhere oppresses the true seed as I have been oppressed by it'. The fate of the nation is thus prefigured by Wentworth's own experiences of oppression and deliverance. She also published *A True Account* (1676) and *The Revelation of Jesus Christ* (1679). HAH

Wertenbaker, Timberlake ?– Playwright and journalist of Anglo-American parents, bilingual, she was brought up in the Basque country, France, has taught French, and works as a writer in New York City and London. She has been prominent as a significant radical woman dramatist in the period of the flowering of women's drama after MAUREEN DUFFY's *Rites* of 1969, and the work of PAM GEMS, CARYL CHURCHILL and MICHELINE WANDOR. She made an impact with her work in a period – the 1970s, 1980s and 1990s – which was one of political statement and technical experimentation, but which financially squeezed women's theatre companies and radical feminist productions. Her first plays, including *This is No Place for Tallulah Bankhead* (1978), were performed in Greece. *Case to Answer* (1980) followed. *Breaking Through* (1980) and *New Anatomies* (1981) about the 19th-century adventurer Isabelle Eberhardt, were written for the Women's Theatre Group. *Abel's Sister* (1984) alters the biblical tale to make Abel a woman, while the award-winning *The Grace of Mary Traverse* (1985), at the Royal Court, concentrated on a transgressive theme using a female character. The award-winning *Our Country's Good* (1988) adapts Thomas Keneally's novel set in 1789 looking at a group of Australian convicts staging Farquahar's *The Recruiting Officer* (1706). Her *Love of the Nightingale* (1988) looks at the effects of silence, rewriting the terrible myth of Procte and Philomela, who lost her voice after a brutal rape. She has translated numerous plays by, for example, Anouilh and Lorca. *New Anatomies* was produced in a London pub in 1990 and her collected plays appeared in 1996. A radical playwright, Wertenbaker focuses on rewriting women's lives in myth and history. GW

Wesley, Mary (Mary Aline Siepmann, née Farmar) 1912– Novelist and mildly rebellious member of the British upper classes, who came late to writing, publishing her first in a line of genially amoral black comedies at 71. She has since become celebrated, and a number of her books have been adapted for television; perhaps her fame has been enhanced by the perceived incongruity of a woman of her age and background writing so candidly and enthusiastically about sex.

Wesley's first novel, *Jumping The Queue* (1983) set a pattern for her later books; clever, funny, mildly shocking, a little snobbish and dealing insouciantly with multifarious forms of deviance, from incest to drug smuggling and murder. Her subsequent novels have also focused on seemingly respectable people behaving unconventionally, but within a conventional framework: thus there is much discreet adultery but no divorce or tiresome emotional scenes in *The Camomile Lawn* (1984); in *Harnessing Peacocks* (1985), the school fees are paid by the heroine's work as a prostitute and cook; and in *Not That Sort of Girl* (1987), a widow looks back with quiet satisfaction on a double life and still untarnished reputation. Wesley's characters, mostly drawn from her own narrow social sphere, keep the little rules of life – good manners, kindness to animals – whilst cheerfully breaking all the big ones. In *An Imaginative Experience* (1994), Wesley attempts to describe raw pain occasioned by the death of her child, but in this, as in her other books, her liking for a happy ending and her emphasis on the healing power of love point to an optimistic view of life. CT

West, Dorothy 1907– Dorothy West calls Oak Bluffs, the elite African-American community on the Massachusetts island of Martha's Vineyard, 'the yearning place', and she writes about its inhabitants with elegance and subtlety. West, the last survivor of the Harlem Renaissance, quit her home in Boston's affluent black community in the 1920s to take up residence in Harlem. Despite her privileged upbringing, West had little use for the middle-class conservative wing of Harlem's black elite and sided instead with the iconoclasm of such writers as Wallace Thurman. After Harlem's glory days faded in the 1930s, West remained to work as an investigator for the Department of Welfare, an experience she dramatized in the story, 'For Richer, For Poorer'. She also edited the little magazine *New Challenge*, which published many of the major progressive black voices of the day.

West's two novels, *The Living Is Easy* (1948) and *The Wedding* (1995), show a sensitivity to the class aspirations of African-Americans struggling with the legacies of racism, miscegenation and class bias; her exploration of the psychological workings of the elite link her to such novelists of manners as EDITH WHARTON. Unlike Wharton, however, West always decries the snobbery of an elite that elevates 'false distinctions' – class privilege, inherited wealth or light skin – over love. While the world West depicts has been largely passed over by literary and social observers, her subtle exploration of the anxieties, and the rage, of a privileged elite merits further critical attention. MG

West, Jane 1758–1852 British novelist, poet and playwright, who was born in London and moved to Northamptonshire when she was 11. Wholly self-educated, she started writing poetry from an early age and her writing eventually helped to support her family. She married a yeoman farmer, Thomas West, and had three sons. Whilst espousing the importance of housewifery for women, she was a prolific author, and in a poem published in 1791 claimed that time spent on writing was defensible because of its moral aims. Various collections of poetry and drama appeared from the 1780s onwards, along with three novels in the 1790s: the heroine of *The Advantages of Education: Or The History of Maria Williams* (1793) rejects an attractive but unsuitable lover for a virtuous husband; *A Gossip's Story* (1796) foreshadows JANE AUSTEN's SENSE AND SENSIBILITY in its rejection of excessive sensibility; and *A Tale of the Times* (1799) is an anti-radical tale which condemns marriage for economic reasons. She also wrote conduct books, five more novels, including *Ringrove: Or Old-fashioned Notions* (1827), a translation and a collection of scriptural essays. RDM

West, Mae 1893–1980 American sex icon of stage and film whose verbal wit was integral to her magnificent creation , 'the Mae West character'. Born in Brooklyn of immigrant parents, she had little formal education, growing up a sexually adventurous 'tough girl' (she married in 1911 but it didn't last) and honing her skills in the sensational popular theatre and vaudeville. West's plays brought a little-known sexual underworld to Broadway: *Sex* (1926) drew charges of obscenity which excited public attention; *Diamond Lil* (1928) showcased her wisecracking, shimmying, Belle-of-the-Nineties persona, drawing on the burlesque and female impersonation traditions; and *The Drag* (1927) and *Pleasure Man* (1928) featured gay male cross-dressers. Her novel *The Constant Sinner* (1930), set in Harlem, centred on the taboo of inter-racial love. She wrote her own lines and collaborated on the script and dialogue for most of her Hollywood films: *She Done Him Wrong* (1933, based on *Diamond Lil*, also novelized) and *I'm No Angel* (1933), in particular, immortalized her predatory but good-humoured one-liners which we quote and – marking their mythical status – misquote today. West's role as writer was a rare and vital ingredient in her legendary control over her own image. MO'D

West, Rebecca (Cicily Isobel Fairfield) 1892–1983 Distinguished British woman of letters, the daughter of Isabella and Charles Fairfield, born in London and educated at George Watson's Ladies' College in Edinburgh. A passionate believer in women's rights, she wrote at the age of 14 to the *Scotsman* supporting votes for women. She left school to attend the Academy of Dramatic Art in London for a year. West joined the staff of the feminist journal, the *Freewoman*, as a journalist in 1911 and changed her name to Rebecca after the strong-minded heroine of Ibsen's *Romsersholm* in which she had acted, in 1912. She wrote for several socialist and radical papers including the *New Statesman* and the *Clarion* at about this time. After reviewing his novel, *Marriage*, she began a long and troubled relationship with H.G. Wells. Their son, Anthony West, was born in 1914. In 1930 West married the banker, Henry Maxwell Andrews.

Both the essays and fiction of the early years explore radical and feminist ideas, although West's politics moved to the Right in later life and she became virulently anti-Communist. Over the years she developed an interest in Manichean notions of good and evil and a range of intellectual interests including Hegelian aesthetics which sometimes inform her fiction. Selected essays and journalism from the period 1911–16 were published as *The Young Rebecca* (1982). *The Strange Necessity* (1928) is a collection of critical essays on literary and other topics.

Many of Rebecca West's novels are about relationships between the sexes. Her first, THE RETURN OF THE SOLDIER (1918), deals with the fracturing of a man's psyche after World War I and how this is repaired by an unassuming woman friend. *The Judge* (1922) engages with the trials of a young, unmarried mother who is a suffragette. *Harriet Hume: A London Fantasy* (1929) is a romantic, humorous meditation; its heroine a fictional embodiment of West's ideas about femininity and her lover the epitome of masculine qualities. *The Thinking Reed* (1936) dramatizes the lives of the indolent rich in France, depicting a symbiotic relationship between a husband who is a compulsive gambler and a wife who saves his fortune but suffers a miscarriage as a result. West's fiction is often polemical with vivid and painful passages of dialogue in which sex antagonism is explored. She is a gifted stylist whose post-war writing includes THE FOUNTAIN OVERFLOWS (1956), a semi-autobiographical novel of childhood with a fictional portrait of West's genteel, impoverished, piano-playing mother. THE BIRDS FALL DOWN (1966) is a novel of intrigue and duplicity set among expatriate Russians before the Russian Revolution.

Rebecca West's non-fiction includes the widely admired BLACK LAMB AND GREY FALCON: A JOURNEY THROUGH YUGOSLAVIA (1941), which describes her TRAVELS in Yugoslavia in 1937, offering perceptive insights into the growth and origins of nationalist feelings and the country's landscape and history. *The*

Meaning of Treason (1949) arose from West's reporting of the trial of William Joyce ('Lord Haw-Haw'). Later editions were expanded to deal with the traitors Maclean and Burgess, who defected to the Soviet Union in the 1950s. Three works were published posthumously: *This Real Night* (1984), *Cousin Rosamond* (1985) and *Sunflower* (1986). West is a writer of range and complexity and an important pioneering figure in early 20th-century feminism. She was created an OBE in 1949 and a DBE in 1959.   MJ

Weston, Jessie Edith

Weston, Jessie Edith 1867–1944 New Zealand novelist. Her only novel, *Ko Méri: Or, A Cycle of Cathay: A Story of New Zealand Life* (1890), is one of the earliest to deal with the issue of the place of Maori or part-Maori in 19th-century New Zealand society. The novel shares the common assumption of the time that the Maori race will die out. The central character is Mary Balmain, a half-Maori who has been brought up and educated by white people. Weston glamorizes Mary, describing her in exotic terms, emphasizing her 'magnetism', 'nobility' and 'dark, rich beauty', while believing she is doomed because of her mixed blood. When her fiancé dies, the crisis has the effect on Mary which most expect. Despite her upbringing, with 'the veneer of civilization fallen off, and the Maori blood surging wildly through her veins', she joins her mother's tribe. Mary laments the effect colonization has had on the Maori – 'Slowly but surely they are disappearing, and from being a brave, honourable people, they have become idle, sullen, and full of absurd superstitions' – and believes: 'Before long the Maori will cease to stand in the path of the white man . . . They are not adapted for that civilization which has taken the pakeha (white man) hundreds of years to attain.'   MMac

Wetherell, Elizabeth

Wetherell, Elizabeth see WARNER, SUSAN

Wharton, Anne

Wharton, Anne 1659–85 British poet and dramatist, who was an orphan and an heiress from her birth in Ditchley, Oxon. No offspring resulted from her marriage in 1673 to Thomas Wharton, later Marquis of Wharton. Much of his time was spent involved with horseracing and Whig politics, and Wharton was later stopped from leaving him by Bishop Gilbert Burnet. Apart from a year in Paris (1680–1) she settled quietly in Winchendon where she exchanged verses with Burnet, Edmund Waller and Robert Wolseley. A defender of her sex, Wharton was criticized for her association with the 'abominably vile' APHRA BEHN, a panegyric to whom was posthumously published in *A Collection of Poems* (1693). Her work was considered melancholic, powerful and pious, and her lyric poems were eagerly circulated amongst a large group of admirers. After her death they began to appear in several collections, including Nahum Tate's edition of *Poems by Several*

Hands in 1685 and Edward Young's *Idea of Christian Love*, three years later. Further poems were printed in Gildon's *Miscellany Poems* (1692) and Dryden's *Miscellany Poems* (1702). Other works included a translation of the 'Epistle of Penelope to Ulysses', reproduced in Tonson's *Ovid's Epistles* (1716), and an unperformed blank-verse tragedy, *Love's Martyr: Or Witt Above Crowns* (1679–80).   RDM

Wharton [née Jones], Edith (Newbold)

Wharton [née Jones], Edith (Newbold) 1862–1937 American novelist who celebrates and satirizes social changes and shifts in sexual mores. She was born into a distinguished family belonging to the 'old' New York, a world whose gradual decay and absorption by new money forms one of the main themes of her fiction. Between 1866 and 1872 she travelled widely in France, Italy and Spain with her parents, and she read widely too (including SENSATION NOVELISTS like RHODA BROUGHTON, forbidden by her mother). In 1877, aged 15, she wrote a parodic tear-jerker, *Fast and Loose*, accompanied by cruel mock-reviews. She went on, however, to the career of a conventional debutante, and in 1885 married Teddy Wharton and launched into a life focused on socializing, houses and pets, punctuated by illness and depression.

In 1897, with the architect Ogden Codman, she published her first book, *The Decoration of Houses*, and in 1899 a collection of short stories, *The Greater Inclination*: 'thereafter I never questioned that story-telling was my job', she wrote in her autobiography, *A Backward Glance* (1934). She took on the profession of writer with great success, becoming a friend of Henry James and (like him) an eventual exile from the USA. She and Teddy established a second home in Paris from 1907 on, they separated in 1911 and she divorced him in 1913; meanwhile between 1908 and 1910 she was involved in a passionate love-affair with American journalist Morton Fullerton. After 1913 she returned to the States only once, to receive a Doctorate of Letters from Yale in 1923.

Her first bestseller – also a critical success – was THE HOUSE OF MIRTH in 1905; ETHAN FROME (1911), THE REEF (1912) and THE CUSTOM OF THE COUNTRY (1913) mark the apogee of her confidence and creativity, though it was in 1920 with THE AGE OF INNOCENCE that she won the Pulitzer Prize. During World War I she had worked with refugees and orphans, and was awarded the Cross of the Legion d'honneur in 1915. In many ways a most modern woman (she adored motor cars), she was not a MODERNIST writer, though she lived on the Left Bank in Paris at the same time as GERTRUDE STEIN. Nonetheless, she does inject into the tradition of SOCIAL REALISM a distinctive irony. She enjoyed predetermined plots – 'It is always a necessity to me that the note of inevitableness should be sounded at the very opening of my tale' – a trait which reflects the influence of Darwinian ideas about evolution. Wharton saw her own class caught up in the struggle to adapt and survive, many of them unsuccessfully. She herself belonged to both old and new worlds, and observed their mingling with sensitivity and also cruel humour. Her later admirers include writers as diverse as Gore Vidal and ANITA BROOKNER.

The Age of Innocence has been filmed several times, most recently in 1993 by Martin Scorsese as a lush costume drama. LS

What Remains (1990; UK 1993) The title of CHRISTA WOLF'S controversial novella, only published ten years after it was written, refers to the situation of the individual in East Germany. The problem is perceived through the eyes of a woman writer, trying to find a new language which would release her from the impasse created by the different degrees of control she experiences: from state-induced surveillance to self-imposed censorship. Wolf's character seems uncompromising in her refusal to collaborate with the state apparatus. 'The opposite of soft isn't hard. The opposite of soft is unyielding, firm' is her motto. She is nevertheless conscious of the potential danger excessive outspokenness can bring in her situation, and thus, rather than advocate outright militancy, she concentrates on little acts of inner resistance. Refusing to be paralysed into silence, she resorts to irony, humour and interior monologue – which often turns into dialogue – to acknowledge, finally, that 'there is no misfortune other than that of not being alive.' JZ

Wheathill, Anne fl.1584 Composer of prayers. In 1584 she published *A Handful of Wholesome (though Homely) Herbs Gathered out of the Goodly Garden of God's most Holy Word*, a volume of forty-nine prayers directed 'to all religious ladies, gentlewomen, and others'. She describes herself as an unmarried gentlewoman who has undertaken the enterprise 'without the counsel or help of any', but asserts that her 'small handful of gross herbs' will be as acceptable to God as the 'fragrant flowers' of the learned.

The prayers are Reformist in doctrine, and often resonant in their phrasing. In contemplation of her own sinful state, she writes, 'I cannot but lament, mourn, and cry for help, as doth a woman whose time draweth near to be delivered of her child; for she can take no rest, till she be discharged of her burden.' A meditation on the Fall blames Adam and Eve equally while laying the emphasis slightly on the man: 'by Adam, death came to mankind'. HH

Wheatley, Nadia 1949– Australian CHILDREN'S AUTHOR and historian; born and educated in Sydney, where she completed postgraduate research in history. Her historical interests, and particularly the influence of E. P. Thompson and his emphasis on recording the

histories of 'ordinary' people, are reflected in much of her work. *My Place* (1987), a much-awarded picture book for younger children, with illustrations by Donna Rawlins, tells the story of a house in inner Sydney and its various occupants, moving back decade by decade from 1988 to 1788, so beginning and ending with Aboriginal families. Her first two novels, *Five Times Dizzy* (1982) and *Dancing in the Anzac Deli* (1984), set in much the same locale, also show the influence of the five years she spent living in Greece, in their focus on the problems faced by a Greek migrant family. *The House that Was Eureka* (1984) again uses as its setting two inner-city terrace houses, contrasting and comparing the events which occurred there in 1931, at the height of the Depression, with those of fifty years later. In contrast to her earlier novels, *The Blooding* (1987) is set in a rural logging community and involves a battle with conservationists, while the stories in *The Night Tolkien Died* (1994) depict many different settings and themes. Wheatley has also helped adapt *Five Times Dizzy* for television and has edited two volumes of essays by the novelist CHARMIAN CLIFT: *Trouble in Lotus Land* (1990) and *Being Alone with Oneself* (1991). EW

Wheatley, Phillis *c.*1753–84 Author of the second known book by a woman in the North American colonies, an especially enormous achievement for a young African-American slave woman who had learned English barely a decade before publishing *Poems on Various Subjects, Religious and Moral* (1773).

Kidnapped from West Africa and sold in Boston to Susanna and John Wheatley, Phillis began publishing poetry when she was about 13 years old. Her 'On the Death of Mr George Whitefield' (1770) appeared as a broadside in the colonies and England, leading the Countess of Huntingdon to sponsor the London publication of Wheatley's book. Fêted by luminaries such as Brook Watson, Granville Sharp and Benjamin Franklin, and judged by Voltaire as writing 'very good English verse', Phillis remained a slave until sometime in 1773 when 'friends in England' convinced the Wheatleys to manumit her. In 1778, she married John Peters, a free African-American. Despite their best efforts, they could not escape poverty and none of their three infants survived. On 5 December 1784, Phillis Wheatley Peters died from childbirth complications.

Wheatley's most-anthologized poems are eulogies and religious poems such as 'On the Death of the Rev. Dr. Sewell, 1769', 'To the University of Cambridge, in New England' and 'On Being Brought from Africa to America'. As John Shields and others have pointed out, they present a complex of African hierophantic solar worship, Greek and Roman mythology, and radical Great Awakening Protestantism. As important, however, are her political proclamations, including 'To the King's Most Excellent Majesty. 1768', 'To His

POEMS

ON

VARIOUS SUBJECTS,

RELIGIOUS AND MORAL.

BY

PHILLIS WHEATLEY,

NEGRO SERVANT to Mr. JOHN WHEATLEY,
of BOSTON, in NEW ENGLAND.

LONDON:

Printed for A. BELL, Bookseller, Aldgate; and sold by
Messrs. COX and BERRY, King-Street, BOSTON.

M DCC LXXIII.

Published according to Act of Parliament, Sept.ʳ 1, 1773 by Arch.ᵈ Bell,
Bookseller Nº 8 near the Saracens Head Aldgate.

Phillis Wheatley: frontispiece and title-page of *Poems*, 1773.

Excellency General Washington' and 'Liberty and Peace', and her aesthetic and philosophical meditations such as 'On Imagination' and 'To S(cipio) M(oorhead)'. Scholars have long recognized influences of Ovid, Milton and Pope, her predilections for heroic couplets and panegyrics, but recent studies illuminate pervasive West African poetic techniques as well.

Many of Phillis Wheatley's elegant and eloquent letters to British royalty, colonial leaders and personal friends were published during her lifetime. Her letters to Samson Occum, a Mohegan Indian writer and minister, and to Obour Tanner, a slave in Newport Rhode Island, give rare insight into the lives, politics and aesthetics of 18th-century colonialists of colour.   FSF

Wheeler, Anna 1785–1848 A radical author, born in County Tipperary, Ireland, whose father was a Protestant Archbishop and whose godfather was Henry Gratton, and who is said to have introduced the notion of women's equality to Daniel O'Connell, the leader of Catholic Emancipation. Wheeler co-

authored, with William Thompson, one of the most influential and pioneering texts on the rights of women, called *The Appeal of One Half the Human Race Women Against the Pretensions of the Other Half Men* (1825).

Years earlier, she had given herself an education in female radicalism at Ballywire, a remote country house in County Tipperary, Ireland, where she was unhappily married to Francis Massy Wheeler. Leaving her husband, she set sail with her sister and her children for Guernsey, where her uncle was Governor. During the early 1820s, she spent time in France with the circle of radical socialists that had formed around Count Claude-Henri de Rouvroy de Saint-Simon where she was known as 'the Goddess of Reason'. In 1823, Wheeler established a salon where she first became acquainted with the French Utopian socialist, Charles Fourier.

She was also involved in the English circle surrounding the socialist Robert Owen. Under the name of 'Vlasta', she published articles attacking marriage and other inequalities for women in Owen's paper, the

Crisis. In 1829, Wheeler gave a lecture in Finsbury Square in London on 'Rights of Women' in which she advocated harmony between the sexes.　　　MM-R

Whirlpool,　The (1986) By Canadian JANE URQUHART, this won the Best Foreign Book Award in France in 1992. The last days of Robert Browning, in Venice in December 1889, frame the tale. He is obsessed with Shelley's romantic death by water, and comforted by the knowledge that a gondola will take him to his grave. The novel centres on the summer of 1889, where Fleda reads Browning in the woods above the whirlpool at the foot of the Niagara Falls. Into her life comes the young poet Patrick who idealizes but cannot accept her: he sees her as part of the landscape and whirlpool, 'the art of poetry', that both seduce him and terrify him. The poet also forges a connection with the child of Maud, the undertaker's widow. The danger of the falls and whirlpool is underlined by catalogues of deaths by accident or intent. In a strange, hypnotic manner, the author creates a situation in which Patrick's 'swimmer's moment at the whirlpool' liberates both Fleda, who finally leaves her meaningless relationship with her husband, and Maud, who at last lets go of her obsession with cataloguing the possessions of the dead. The commitment of the poet inspires us all, the author suggests, in a novel that shimmers with her own poetry.　　　FD

White, Antonia [Eirene Adeline Botting] 1899–

1980 Autobiographical novelist, identified with her classic novel of convent-school life, FROST IN MAY (1933), based on her experiences at the Convent of the Sacred Heart, Roehampton, where her Classics master father sent her in 1908 after his conversion to Roman Catholicism. In 1914 he removed her to St Paul's School, London; her belief that she had been expelled is central to the novel. She worked as teacher, governess and advertising copywriter in 1916–18, studied at RADA in 1919, and toured briefly as an actress. She was married three times: to Reggie Greene-Wilkinson in 1921–3, to Eric Earnshaw, a civil servant, in 1925–9, and to the journalist Tom Hopkinson in 1930–8; she had two daughters. She spent 1924 in a mental hospital, and in 1925 she left the Church, eventually returning in 1948. In the 1920s she worked for an advertising agency and for Harrods.

Frost in May was an immediate critical success. The inter-war period was the heyday of the GIRLS' SCHOOL STORY, and, although much male reminiscence discussed the destructive effects of boarding-school on the young psyche, there had been no comparable female account. White's novel, with its sharp focus, childlike clarity and painful nostalgia, supplied this lack. The experience of writing it plunged White into a nervous crisis, and from 1935 to 1938 she was in analy-

sis, recalling further painful childhood memories, including sexual abuse by her father.

From 1933, like the heroine of DORIS LESSING's *THE GOLDEN NOTEBOOK*, she kept several notebooks, including an analysis diary, agonizing about her writer's block and her many love-affairs. She worked for various journals, including *Time and Tide*, *Picture Post* and, as fashion editor, the *Sunday Pictorial*, and, during World War II, for the BBC's Overseas Service. After the war she published three more novels, effectively sequels to *Frost in May*, though without that novel's distinctive power: *The Lost Traveller* (1950), *The Sugar House* (1952) and *BEYOND THE GLASS* (1954), respectively based on her post-convent teens, her acting experiences and her year in a mental hospital. White translated many novels from French, beginning with Maupassant's *Une vie* (1949). *The Hound and the Falcon* (1965) is a memoir of her reconversion. Her important achievement was *Frost in May*; her life, lavishly recorded in her diaries and in the memoirs of her daughters, Susan Chitty and Lyndall Hopkinson, is troublingly suggestive of the insecurities of women writers.　　　AT

Whitney, Isabella *c*.1540 – after 1580 Elizabethan

poet. Possibly the first known professional woman poet writing in English, she published two collections: *Copy of a Letter* (*c*.1567) and *A Sweet Nosegay* (*c*.1573). What little is known of her life is derived from her poetry. She tells us in 'Wyll and Testament', an astonishing poem addressed to the City of London and written in 1573, that her parents lived in Smithfield. Apparently from minor gentry stock, she seems to have suffered financially in her life; the same poem talks poignantly of debtors' prisons and of being 'weake in Purse'. Her highly secular poetry may well have been an attempt to raise money. She certainly praises the bookbinders of St Paul's.

'Wyll and Testament', written in the style, as its title suggests, of a will, of which she makes the City of London the 'sole executor, because / I lov'de thee best', is a veritable survey of the Elizabethan capital. Its subject matter, with its urban focus, is unusual in the canon of early modern women writers. Readers are taken on a journey around the city and its streets and shops. We pass butchers, brewers and bakers, and see wool and linen shops. We even hear the streetboys' cries: those who 'wil aske you what you lacke'. Inevitably there are less desirable elements: there will be 'Some Roysters styll' who will fight in the streets and to them she bequeaths surgeons and plasters. To Inns of Court lawyers she leaves books for study but also means of recreational pursuit. There is a sense here (the speaker is apparently leaving the city, possibly to die) of a poet acknowledging her rich source material, although Whitney stresses: 'I little brought / but nothyng from thee tooke.'

Whitney's work is elsewhere characterized by an equally vibrant voice and style. 'To Her Inconstant Lover' (?1567) rails against a former partner about to get married, comparing him to such classical betrayers as Aeneas, Theseus and Jason.   JS

Who Do You Think You Are? (1974) ALICE MUNRO's fourth collection of short stories won her a second Governor General's Award for Fiction in Canada and, under the title of *The Beggar Maid*, was short-listed for the UK Booker Prize. Interweaving themes of violence, alienation and the tensions of social class, these linked stories follow the life of Rose from precocious child to struggling actress. Looking back on the ordeals of both home and school, Rose says: 'Learning to survive, no matter with what cravenness and caution, what shocks and forebodings, is not the same as being miserable. It is too interesting.' This spirited attitude leads her to hear the title question on the lips of guardians, teachers and strangers. The words also hint at the quest for some truer sense of self than angry rebel or safe conformist, roles she toys with as she hurtles through a landscape of memorable characters whose engaging pretensions and dangerous weaknesses Munro strips bare. Finally, when Rose meets briefly with the schoolmate who first inspired her with the idea that mimicry might be the route to self-transformation, Munro challenges the reader to feel superior to these fragile, expertly created and memorable human beings.   FD

Wickham, Anna [Edith Mary Alice Harper] 1884–1947 Combative feminist poet who said 'I may be a minor poet but I am a major woman.' With her piano-salesman father and ex-actress mother she emigrated to Australia in 1890, and attended schools in Brisbane and Sydney. She studied singing in Paris in 1904, but a proposed operatic career ended with her marriage to Patrick Hepburn, a lawyer. Back in London, they settled in Hampstead, where she had four sons and worked for the St Pancras School for Mothers. The marriage was turbulent; Hepburn had Wickham confined in a mental hospital for six weeks after the publication of her first volume of poems, *Songs by John Oland* (1911). The Poetry Bookshop published *The Contemplative Quarry* (1915). In this and subsequent volumes – *The Man with a Hammer* (1916), *The Little Old House* (1921) and *Thirty-Six New Poems* (1936) – Wickham treated her poems as reports from the gender war. The poems, free verse, ballads, epigrams, all short, adopt a range of dramatic personae to explore sexual tensions and incompatibilities, and women's distinctive experience and creativity. She was friendly with the Lawrences, and in the 1920s became a frequent visitor to NATALIE BARNEY's Paris salon. Her 1935 fragmentary autobiography, 'Prelude to a Spring-Clean', ago-

nized about the incompatibility of motherhood and poetry, and her inadequacy in both. In 1947, after a wartime worrying about her sons who all survived, she hanged herself. Her poems are notable in anticipating many later feminist debates.   AT

Wicks, Susan 1947– British poet and prose writer who grew up in Kent and studied French at Hull and Sussex Universities. Wicks's first collection, *Singing Underwater* (1992), is full of the muted outbursts that its title suggests. Like DENISE LEVERTOV, Wicks looks for the moment when an altered state offers access or connection. This can be the fluid made concrete as in a frozen lake, or the upset of illness or dancing. For Wicks, intimacy is echo-location: 'I touch you and feel myself / touched'. The gesture carries weight, and her response is further slowed by the line break. Wicks can also be sharp, funny and surreal. In poems about nosebleeds, headlice and clock radios, dull surfaces distort and irridesce.

Open Diagnosis (1994) and *The Clever Daughter* (1996) show Wicks pushing harder and deeper into her themes, exploring the shadows of mysticism, violence and desire. Loss and separation are acknowledged, even longed for but sometimes viscerally opposed. These are poems of accusation and protection in which proportions veer as relationships blur:

> Clearing my father's house, I have room
> only for miniatures: his freezer,
> its little lid propped open, the thumbnail
> meat-safe, three barley-twist tables that nest
> in my hand.   'Leaf-storm'

Wicks is a controlled writer who also makes much of control as a subject. It is a disturbing game in her novels, *The Key* (1996) and *Little Thing* (1998), and central to the threat and promise of family life in her memoir, *Driving My Father* (1995).   LG

Wicomb, Zoë 1948– South African author living in England. Wicomb was born in a small town in Namaqualand, a semi-arid region on the west coast of South Africa, in a community classified 'coloured' by the then racial classification laws of South Africa. She is a graduate of the University of the Western Cape, and went on from there to study at Reading University in England. In Wicomb's only published fiction, *You Can't Get Lost in Cape Town* (1987), she writes sensitively about themes that recur in many South African texts. Her narrator recounts events and impressions from her youth. The stories are arranged chronologically; the twin focuses are the body (racialized and female) and the effects of education on those who leave their community to better themselves through learning. In the story called 'Bowl Like Hole' the narrator reflects on her mother's ambitions for her daughter, revealed

through her interest in 'correct' pronunciation and proper behaviour. Disobedience, in the form of fraternization with children from the village, as well as shyness, are described as 'Griqua' behaviour – a racial slur indicative of the mother's distaste for her own racial identity, and her aspirations for her daughter. In the story 'Behind the Bougainvillea' a visit to the doctor becomes a vehicle for the author to depict the various levels of estrangement and dislocation experienced by the returnee. The Virago edition of the short-story collection describes it as a novel, and indeed the stories do form a coherent whole, although there are some internal contradictions which discourage seeing the text as a unitary narrative.   CCo

Widdemer, Margaret 1884–1978 American poet, novelist. Prolific in many genres, Widdemer became famous in 1915 for her poem, *The Factories* – a passionate lament about young female factory workers – and her best-selling novel, *The Rose Garden Husband*. In 1919, she was awarded the Pulitzer Prize for Poetry (along with Carl Sandburg) for *The Old Road to Paradise*. She was part of American literary life through the 1970s, teaching and speaking at various colleges and writers' workshops from Breadloaf to Boulder, contributing regularly to the *New Yorker* and other magazines, and producing in that time eight volumes of poetry, thirty-four novels and several books of advice to writers. Beginning her career at a time 'when the young poets were occupied with social wrongs', Widdemer saw a stanza from her 'God and the Strong Ones' deleted without her permission because it seemed too extreme for the radical journal publishing it: '"They will break the world in twain when their hands are on the rein –" / "What is that to me?" saith God'. In her memoir, *Golden Friends I Had* (1964), she characterizes the American poetic tone as shifting from 'cheerfully cynical' between the World Wars to the 'ferocious despair that is now called irony' afterwards.   SP

Wide Sargasso Sea (1966) JEAN RHYS's widely acclaimed revision of the fictional life of Mrs Rochester, the 'madwoman' who wed CHARLOTTE BRONTË's Rochester (he later attempts to bigamously marry JANE EYRE in the novel by that name). Rhys's narrative unfolds in a highly impressionistic style recalling the MODERNIST ethos she'd shared with Ford Madox Ford, with whom she had once had an affair. In its opening section, Bertha Mason (whom Rhys renames 'Antoinette Cosway') tells us of growing up in the West Indies amid social unrest and family insanity. Rochester, who arrives from England to make his fortune, narrates the middle section of the book, revealing insecurities accentuated by his unfamiliarity with the lush, decadent atmosphere of his new wife's home. The final section takes place in England and is

again narrated by Bertha/Antoinette, culminating in a fiery dream which prefigures the inferno in which Brontë's Bertha Mason kills herself and maims Rochester. The novel's COLONIAL themes have made it the focus of much recent scholarly attention, but its vivid reimagining of Brontë's famous and lopsided sexual triangle remains its most striking achievement.   BWB

Wier, Dara 1949– American poet born in New Orleans, she continues to reference her origins in her poetry. She has published a number of collections: *Blood, Hook and Eye* (1977), *The 8-Step Grapevine* (1980), *All You Have In Common* (1984), *The Book of Knowledge* (1988), *Blue for the Plough* (1992). Critics use words like 'insight' and 'luminous vision' in talking about Wier's poetry, and unique observations about people characterize her writing. She writes about ordinary folk and mythological characters: Creole women, a man with a goitre, Lot's wife (with her 'storehouse of sorrow') and herself – here as a child: 'I pictured the dark / house shrink around us like a muscle.' *Our Master Plan*, her most recent collection, was published in 1998. She has won several awards, including a Guggenheim Fellowship in 1991 and currently lectures at the University of Massachusetts – Amherst, in the MFA Creative Writing programme.   ACH

Wiggins, Marianne 1947– American novelist with a bold intelligence and an ear for hidden comedy. Wiggins's early novels – *Babe* and *Went South* – featured striving single mothers somewhat like herself. *Separate Checks* (1984) and the sharp, fast-talking stories of *Herself in Love* (1987) earned her more widespread critical attention, but her commercial and aesthetic breakthrough was *John Dollar* (1989): a searing, splintered account of English girls going savage on a Burmese island – a female reworking of Golding's *Lord of the Flies*. Iran issued its notorious *fatwa* on Wiggins's second husband, Salman Rushdie, in February 1989, and *John Dollar*'s significant achievement was to some extent buried by the events that followed. For several months she went with Rushdie into hiding and issued loyal defences of him, but by August the marriage had ended in bitter divorce. She resumed her public life, teaching and reviewing, and another volume of stories, *Bet They'll Miss Us When We're Gone*, was published in 1991 (as *Learning Urdu* in the USA). Her 1995 novel *Eveless Eden* was a complex, ambitious tale of love, war and journalism set across Paris, London and Bucharest.   SB

Wijenaike, Punyakante 1933– Sri Lankan author born in Colombo into an affluent family, educated at a private school for girls. She began publishing in the 1950s, after her marriage to a civil servant. Wijenaike's early writing deals with rural life in Sri Lanka, sometimes with a tendency to idealization, such as in *The Third Woman and Other Stories* (1963), a collection of short fiction dealing with village life. A more mature and balanced vision of Sri Lankan rural life is present in *The Waiting Earth* (1966), one of her most accomplished works. The novel focuses on the disintegration of rural culture and the role of women who are often tied down by customs and rituals. Because of her gender and privileged background, critics in the 1960s were surprised at the forceful and serious nature of her writing. In *Giraya* (1971) Wijenaike narrates the decline of Sri Lankan aristocracy and the transference of power from one social class to another. Probably because of her deep knowledge of the social milieu she describes, she succeeded in creating stronger characters and in rendering the claustrophobic atmosphere of a decaying feudal manor-house. Some of her numerous short stories, published in newspapers and journals, have been collected in *Betel Vine* (1976), *The Rebel* (1979) and *Yukthi and Other Stories* (1991). In 1986 she published *A Way of Life*, an account of upper-middle-class society in Colombo from the 1930s to the 1950s, with sketches drawn from the author's own childhood and adolescence. Her novel *Amulet* was the winner of the prize for the Best Sri Lankan Book in English in 1994.   SPo

Wilcox, Ella Wheeler 1850–1919 American popular poet and sexual pioneer. She was born in Johnstown Center, Wisconsin, the youngest of four children in a farming family. Her mother encouraged her to read popular novelists OUIDA, MARY J. HOLMES and E.D.E.N. SOUTHWORTH. She attended public schools and the University of Wisconsin. She wrote her first novel at the age of 9 and published her first essay at 15. By 18 she was helping to support her family with her literary earnings. Her first book, *Drops of Water* (1872), was a collection of temperance verse. By 1880 she was part of Milwaukee's literary circle. Her *Poems of Passion* (1883) were initially rejected by a publisher because of their erotic content but, accepted by another, sold 60,000 copies in two years. She married Robert Marius Wilcox, a silversmith, in 1884, and moved to Meriden, Connecticut. Their only child died in infancy. They travelled widely in Europe and Asia and became involved with theosophy and paranormal exploration. Her early views on gender roles were conservative, but she became a pioneering and influential advocate for women's sexual pleasure. She was a prolific poet, for a time writing daily poems for a newspaper syndicate. She published forty-six books and sustained wide popularity through the 1920s. Though lines such as 'Laugh, and the world laughs with you, / Weep, and you weep alone' have been condemned as platitudinous, Wilcox's verse often expresses cynicism ('Feast, and your halls are crowded; / Fast, and the world goes by') alongside a manic drive to be part of the pulsing world. Near the end of her life she suffered a nervous breakdown after touring World War I army camps reciting poems and lecturing on sexually transmitted diseases.   JSG

Wild Irish Girl, The (1806) By SYDNEY OWENSON, later Lady Morgan, an EPISTOLARY ROMANCE which tells the story of a young Anglo-Irish law student, the Hon Horatio M, banished to Ireland by his absentee landowner father, to distract him from the dissipations of London. He falls in love with Glorvina, the golden-haired, harpist, daughter of an ancient Irish Prince. She and her father are reduced to squatting, humiliatingly, in the ruins of their own castle at Inismore, on the rocky Atlantic shore, land which is now owned by M's father. During the course of M's courtship, the reader is introduced to the beauties and the natural dignity of the ancient Irish, and, after much discussion, the hero even declares himself reconciled to the superior sensibility of the loyal Roman Catholic priest, Father John. Rousseauistic SENSIBILITY is shot through with nationalist propaganda. Glorvina was rapidly conflated with her creator, Owenson (who also played the harp), and was adopted as a cult stereotype in early 19th-century London. Charles Robert Maturin's novel, *The Wild Irish Boy* (1808), satirized this vogue for Celtic kitsch amongst the aristocracy.   VS

Wild Nights (1979) Dedicated to her brother Colin, EMMA TENNANT's sixth novel is, in her own words, a 'fictional childhood memoir'. Certainly it is a potent fantasy, set mainly in an imaginary version of her father's stately family home in Scotland – here described as a 'mock castle' – where she grew up as a child. The narrator is the unnamed daughter of the household, who makes no distinctions between the literal and the metaphorical, the natural and the supernatural, history and myth. The annual arrival of her Aunt Zita, whom she perceives as a magical being controlling the North wind and flying her to riotous balls, sparks off old family rivalries, incurs the local villagers' wrath and ensures that the seasonal cycle continues. Incest, murder and metamorphosis are perfectly normal (if sometimes terrible) in this baroque yet elemental world. Inspired by the work of surrealist Bruno Schulz, and with diverse echoes of Laurence Sterne, EMILY BRONTË, Mervyn Peake, ANGELA CARTER and J.G. Ballard, *Wild Nights* is a darkly revelrous *tour de force* in the female GOTHIC tradition.   MO'D

Wilde [née Elgee], Jane (Francesca) 1821–96 Irish nationalist poet, translator and essayist. Born in Wexford, she was educated at home and gained an extensive knowledge of European languages and literature. This led to widely admired translations of Meinhold, Lamartine and Dumas. In 1851 she married William Wilde, a distinguished surgeon and President of the Irish Academy who was knighted in 1864, and they had three children, including the writer Oscar. From 1847 she contributed highly influential and vehemently nationalist poems and prose to the *Nation*, the newspaper of the Young Ireland Movement, under the pseudonym 'Speranza'. Her *Poems* (1864) has a strong republican tone and is dedicated to Ireland: 'My country, wounded to the heart'. She also wrote works on folklore which appeared under her own name. Widowed in 1876, she moved to London where she established a popular literary salon. Despite the granting of a civil pension, she died in poverty during the year of Oscar's public humiliation and imprisonment.

SA

Wilder, Laura (Elizabeth) Ingalls 1867–1957

American CHILDREN'S NOVELIST and journalist whose autobiographical 'Little House' novels describe pioneer experience in the American Mid-west. Born in Pepin, Wisconsin, she travelled West with her family and was educated at schools in Minnesota, Iowa and the Dakota Territory. At 15 she became a teacher and in 1885 married Almanzo James Wilder. After farming in De Smet, South Dakota, and experiencing several hardships, in 1894 they settled on a farm in Mansfield, Missouri, where she became a newspaper columnist. In her sixties, at her daughter's urging, she began work on her memoirs which became the nine-novel 'Little House' series for children published in the 1930s and 1940s.

Narrated in the third person and linguistically 'growing-up' as Laura does, the novels trace her girlhood, youth and marriage as her family move West during the 1870s and 1880s. Important for both literary and historical content, the series contains detailed descriptions of the difficulties and skills of pioneer life, including a covered-wagon journey and the building of a log cabin in *Little House on the Prairie* (1935), the perils of farming in *On the Banks of Plum Creek* (1937) and the severe effects of blizzards in *The Long Winter* (1940). Centring on frontier life, family and girlhood, the novels are classics whose popularity has been enhanced by a television series based loosely upon them. Wilder received an American Library Association Award named in her honour in 1954.

AEG

Wilder Shores of Love, The (1954)

This quartet of exotic biographies was an instant success for LESLEY BLANCH, whose multi-translated first book has added a phrase to the English language and never gone out of print. Escape, ROMANCE and headlong adventure in the 19th-century 'East' link disparate women of diversely colourful European backgrounds: Isabel Burton was the dazzled, very Catholic spouse of Richard, reprobate explorer of Arabia, Africa and beyond; Jane Digby, much-married and -liaised to European noblemen and swaggerers, found fulfilment in Syria as a celebrated Bedouin wife; Aimée Dubucq de Rivery was a pirates' captive whose enlightened Sultan son brought reform to Turkey; Isabelle Eberhardt, mystic, libertine and self-invented 'Arab' nomad, chronicled North Africa with unique understanding and scope.

The Wilder Shores combines solid research with highly charged conjecture, an imaginative method which renders history *and* its atmosphere. The style is opulent, with a characteristic edge of the piquant or absurd: 'When banished from Syria, along with other Arabic habits, such as puffing at the *tchibouk*, they both continued to rim their eyes sootily with *kohl*, the Oriental and Western maquillage struggling oddly for supremacy on the plump pink planes of Isabel's face'.

AWS

Wilkinson, Anne (Gibbons) 1910–61

Canadian poet, editor, writer of memoirs. She was born in Toronto, daughter of Mary Osler Boyd Gibbons whose family settled in the backwoods of Ontario in 1837 and produced the four famous Osler men whose lives this author chronicled in LIONS IN THE WAY (1956). In this work she included an account of her own childhood in the family mansion – one of the 'Four Corners of my World' (1961) – the privileged childhood that involved summers on Lake Simcoe, winters in Santa Barbara, private tutors and finishing school. In 1932, she married a paediatrician, had three children, and was divorced in 1952. She began to write poetry seriously when her children were grown, and published two volumes of poetry, *Counterpoint to Sleep* (1951) and *The Hangman Ties the Holly* (1955), as well as writing voluminous journals, and founding and editing the *Tamarack Review*. Her poems are finely chiselled lyrics, full of wit, natural imagery and, especially in later years, honest confrontation of death. 'I could substitute the word "poetry" for "honour"', she wrote in her journal. 'My poetry is "my word of honour".' She was very beautiful, shy and much loved by friends; she died of cancer.

FD

Willard, Frances Elizabeth Caroline 1839–98

American temperance and suffrage activist. She was born in Churchville, New York, and grew up in Oberlin, Ohio, and on the Wisconsin frontier. She attended college in Evanston, Illinois, and remained there for much of her life after graduating in 1859. She taught in school and college, then travelled to Europe from 1868 to 1870. She served as Dean of Women and Professor of Aesthetics at Northwestern University but resigned in 1873 to become a leader of the Women's Christian Temperance Union; she served as its national president from 1879 to 1898. In the WCTU journal, *Our Union,* she linked suffrage and other women's issues to temperance, a strategy that garnered widespread support. With Mary A. Livermore, she wrote *Woman of the Century* (1893), which remains a valuable source on the achievements of 19th-century women. Her autobiography, *Glimpses of Fifty Years,* was published in 1889.

JSG

Williams, Helen Maria 1762–1827 British poet, novelist and letter-writer, born in London but brought up and educated at Berwick-on-Tweed by her Scottish mother, where she began writing verses at an early age. Returning to London in 1781, her long verse legend, *Edwin and Eltruda,* was published the following year. She socialized and corresponded with a number of literary luminaries, including ELIZABETH MONTAGU, ANNA SEWARD and FANNY BURNEY. Prolific, popular and profitable, Williams's work tapped into the current revolutionary fervour. Her sentimental verses, such as *Peru* in 1784, centred on the evils of the slave trade and often idealized political victims. A great believer in the tenets of the French Revolution, she wrote a first-hand account, *Letters written from France in the summer of 1790,* and provided a fictionalized version in her novel of the same year, *Julia.* Williams's Paris salon provided a meeting-place for Revolutionary sympathizers, including MARY WOLLSTONECRAFT, and her shocking political stance was compounded when she began to live with John Hurford Stone, a divorcee. Williams continued to write about French politics, later severely criticizing Napoleon for his imperialism.

RDM

Williams, Pauline see SHANGE, NTOZAKE

Willis, Sara Payson see FERN, FANNY

Wilmot, Catherine 1773–1824 Irish TRAVEL WRITER. Raised near Cork by an Irish mother and an English father, Catherine travelled in 1802–3, through Europe with Lord and Lady Mount Cashell. She recorded her trip in journal-letters to her brother. Although Catherine considered travel writing stale and heavy, she was encouraged to publish her correspondence in 1812. Catherine's younger sister MARTHA WILMOT travelled to Russia in 1803 to visit the family's friend Princess Daschkaw or Dashkova, a writer and director of the St Petersburg Academy; Martha remained in Russia until war forced her return in 1808.

Joining her sister, Catherine travelled to Russia in 1805–7. After convincing the Princess to write her memoirs, Martha translated and published the work in 1812, along with her own account of the country, and Catherine's letters from her visit. The two sisters' interests complemented each other: Catherine focused mainly on descriptions of locations and landscapes, while Martha explored people and living conditions. Martha described, for instance, a visit to the Jewish synagogue and meeting the parents of her servant girl. Characterizing the country as 'but in the 12th Century', Catherine wrote of the Russian sky, 'So vaulted, & so blue; so cloudless & so ethereal!'

JHP

Wilmot [Bradford], Martha 1775–1873 Irish DIARIST and translator born in County Cork, she spent five years in Russia, from 1803 to 1808, as the guest of Princess Yekaterina Dashkova (1744–1810). A participant in the *coup d'état* that placed Catherine the Great on the Russian throne, Princess Dashkova was a prominent intellectual figure, a friend of Voltaire and Diderot, and a director of the St Petersburg Academy of Arts and Sciences, who established the Russian Academy in 1783. An intimate relationship quickly developed between the young, inquisitive Irishwoman and the ageing Russian Princess, whose memoirs were translated and later published by Martha (1840). In 1805, Martha's older sister CATHERINE WILMOT (1773–1824) joined her in Russia. While Martha's descriptive passages frequently reflect GOTHIC influences, in their letters and JOURNALS, the two Irishwomen recorded vividly the Russian court society that Tolstoy would later immortalize in *War and Peace.* Due to increasing political uncertainties, Martha was forced to leave Russia in 1808. She married William Bradford, chaplain to the British Embassy in Vienna (1819–29), and her Viennese journal and letters are admired for their sociopolitical details. The Wilmots' letters and journals have been variously edited and published.

BTF

Wilson, Anne Glenny, Lady 1848–1930 New Zealand novelist and poet. Born in Victoria, Australia, she had a good education and was renowned for her intellect. In 1874 she married James Glenny Wilson and moved to New Zealand. They owned a farm at Bulls that was never very profitable, and struggled through the Depression, bringing up five children. She is reported to have been the driving force behind her husband's political involvement – he was a member of the House of Representatives, supporting women's suffrage. *Alice Lauder, A Sketch* (1893) and *Two Summers* (1900) are both ROMANCES, humorously contrasting New Zealand and English societies. They touch on issues of the day such as women's suffrage and the perceived dying out of the Maori race, but do not put forth strong opinions. *Alice Lauder* tells of a woman who must choose between her career or marriage, but eloquent arguments for the former are consumed by the need to fit the novel into the romance mould. Her two collections of poetry, *Themes and Variations* (1889) and *A Book of*

Verses (1901), were well received in New Zealand and Britain and later reprinted. Several of her poems were included in the government-produced series of reading books used in New Zealand schools for many years. She published stories and poetry in various New Zealand, Australian, English and American journals, sometimes under the pseudonym 'Austral'.   MMac

Wilson [née Evans], Augusta Jane 1835–1909

American novelist. Born into wealthy Southern society, she retrieved her family from the bankruptcy caused by her father's unwise investments with the publication of *Beulah* (1859), her second novel. One of the most celebrated Confederates of Mobile, Alabama, she served as a nurse during the Civil War and was reportedly consulted by statesmen and generals on matters of policy. *Macaria: Or Altars of Sacrifice* (1864), her passionate defense of the Old South, was smuggled through military blockades via Cuba for publication in the North. At the age of 33, she married Lorenzo Madison Wilson, a 60-year-old widower. Critics in her own time and since have made much of the heavily erudite, allusion-laden style in her novel *St Elmo* (1867), whose publishers boasted a million readers just four months after it appeared. A female BILDUNGSROMAN of the type that dominated the US literary market in the mid 19th century, *St Elmo* is the sentimental tale of a moral exemplar and the Byronic hero she transforms and finally marries. The novel's anomalous style, however, marks it as a departure from the genre, presaging the discursive complexities of MODERNISM and its descendants.   VC

Wilson, Harriet E. [Adams] 1828?–70? Believed to

be the first African-American woman to publish a novel in the United States. Up until the early 1980s, Wilson's place in literary history was hardly recognized, in part because her identity had never been authenticated. With the recovery project of Henry Louis Gates, Jr, Wilson, sometimes suspected to have been a white writer by critics, was recovered from years of obscurity. Born in Milford, New Hampshire, Wilson is believed to have been an indentured servant up to the age of 18. She married in 1851, but her husband deserted her before the birth of their son, leaving her in ill health. Unable to provide for her son, Wilson relinquished him to foster care. She writes in her preface that she wrote the book to earn enough to retrieve her son from his foster family. Unfortunately her son died only months after the publication of *OUR NIG: OR, SKETCHES FROM THE LIFE OF A FREE BLACK, IN A TWO-STORY HOUSE, NORTH, SHOWING THAT SLAVERY'S SHADOWS FALL EVEN THERE* (1859), a fictional autobiography. The novel bears many characteristics of sentimental fiction, however its emphasis on the inequities of American culture, especially issues of race and gender oppression, thwart the sentimental tradition as well. In addition, *Our Nig* recalls conventions of the slave narrative, though the novel's plot structure manipulates the bondage-to-freedom plot that slave narratives follow, suggesting a more complex representation of life.   CJ

Wilson, Harriette 1786–1845 English autobiographer and SCANDAL-WRITER, whose career began – as,

famously, do her *Memoirs* (1825) – with her escape from a violent father at 15, only to find her first lover, Lord Craven, equally threatening. Written in a brash, sardonic tone and including her own sharp repartee, her memoirs were bestsellers, greeted with libel actions and moralizing pamphlets. Sir Walter Scott, recalling she had 'the manners of a wild schoolboy', decried her as a 'punk' who set out to blackmail aristocratic lovers, but he appreciated her 'good retailing of conversations . . . exactly imitated'. Wilson asserted her own code of honour, arguing wryly that even if she was not the 'steady, prudent, virtuous woman' society approved, she maintained 'strict probity and love of truth', never going against her conscience, even if it was 'a very easy one'. She later wrote a novel, *Clara Gazul* (1830), and from Paris a *roman à clef*, *Paris Lions and London Tigers* (1825). Her letters to Byron were published in 1935.   LMT

Winchilsea, Anne Finch [née Kingsmill], Countess of 1661–1720 English poet born in

Hampshire and orphaned at the age of 3. Her aristocratic birth nonetheless dictated a loyalty to the Stuart monarchy that influenced her philosophical and material world. In 1684, while serving as a maid of honour to Queen Mary of Modena, she met and married Colonel Heneage Finch, described by Finch as 'The much loved husband of a happy wife', to whom she dedicates many love poems. After refusing to swear oaths of allegiance to William and Mary in 1688, the couple were forced to leave London for the family seat in Kent presided over by Heneage's nephew, the Earl of Winchilsea, a title her husband would eventually inherit. In Kent, Finch found a stimulating social group of women and in London incited the admiration of such literary celebrities as Gay, Pope and Swift.

Fables, satires, burlesques, dialogues and meditations, Finch's poetry ranges from unflinching criticism of the 'Unequal Fetters' of marriage to the beauty of 'A Nocturnal Reverie', whose sensitive depiction of the sights and sounds of nature contributed to her revival by Wordsworth and other Romantic poets. Her stint at court no doubt inspired such whimsical allegory as 'The Lord and the Bramble', in which an unfeeling nobleman refuses to hear the pleas of an unwanted bramble and suffers for his neglect. The moral, 'Appease the Man, if you'd prevail, /Who some sharp

Satire writ', suggests Finch's recognition of the power of poetry, a power about which she expressed ambivalence and insecurity. She was writing poetry as early as 1660 but it wasn't widely noticed until 1701 when her Pindaric ode 'The Spleen', – an exploration of grief and self-pity inspired by her own bouts of depression – was published. In 1713, her *Miscellany Poems* appeared, and a volume of manuscript poems discovered posthumously was not published until 1903.   JRS

Wingfield [née Claude], Sheila (Viscountess Powerscourt)

1906–95 British poet whose self-declared subject matter is the 'Irish and English countryside . . . this blows through my work'. Wingfield was born in Hampshire and educated at Roedean School. She married the Honourable M. Wingfield, later Viscount Powerscourt (d.1973), in 1932 and had one daughter and two sons. Her first book, *Poems* (1938), was praised by no less than W. B. Yeats ('Your remarkable poems . . . have style, distinction, and a precise and subtle vocabulary').

Her later verse – all represented in *Collected Poems 1938-1983* (1983) – has admirers, but her verse as a whole is little-known and hardly ever anthologized. The sections 'Women in Love' and 'Women at Peace' from her long poem *Beat Drum, Beat Heart* (1946) show her at her strongest; here she releases her grip on rhythm and writes more personally than is her custom. ELIZABETH JENNINGS has argued: 'At her best [Wingfield] has a sense of the heraldic, the emblematic which can produce glittering lines'. A reader more used to the natural orders of MODERNISM and POSTMODERNISM may be inclined to dismiss her work as outmoded or precious, yet her poems repay re-reading and her output deserves a reassessment.   DM

Wings, Mary

1949– American novelist from Chicago, who settled in Amsterdam. Published three comic books – *Come Out Commix, Dyke Shorts* and *Are Your Highs Getting You Down?* (1980) – but is better known for her lesbian DETECTIVE FICTION, which provides both rich crime narratives laced with undercut romance and a Chandleresque satirical style parodying patriarchal norms. Her novels destabilize the conventional confirmation of a patriarchal status quo, challenging the genre's comfortable, logical deduction and conventional closure. *She Came Too Late* (1986) introduces investigator Emma Victor, raises social issues of reproductive technology, social hierarchies, vice and unions, and plays with sexual innuendo amid rich metaphors and descriptions. A 'Strong Woman', Emma views dressing up for parties in pantyhose and skirt as a cross-dressing exercise: 'High heels make you do that sort of thing, the feet don't think for themselves any more. The dress circled out slightly with the movement, the platform shoulders were balanced by my fluffy hair. I saw it was

good. I was a girl . . . in drag'. Spare, witty, sophisticated and perceptively descriptive, this novel won the *City Limits* Award. *She Came in a Flash* (1988) investigates the Divine Vishnu Inspiration Commune and portrays New Age religion as a version of benevolent patriarchal power dependent upon its followers' blindness. *She Came By the Book* (1995) begins with the opening of the memorial archives of her flamboyant former boss, Howard Blooming, and sees the loss of her relationship with Frances Cohen, and deaths by cyanide and gunshot. Other work includes a bestselling GOTHIC detective novel, *Divine Victim* (1992). The Gothic challenges and reverses conventions and crosses boundaries. Mary Wings's combination of the Gothic and a challenge to the conventions of crime fiction enables boundaries of gender, life and death to be crossed.   GW

Winkworth, Catherine

1827–78 British author, daughter of a London silk merchant, and, like her sister SUSANNA WINKWORTH an early feminist. The family moved to Manchester when she was 2. Catherine took lessons from James Martineau, HARRIET MARTINEAU's brother, and William Gaskell, ELIZABETH GASKELL's husband. A friendship developed with the Gaskells and many of Elizabeth Gaskell's letters are written to 'My dearest Katie'. From 1845 to 1846, Catherine stayed with an aunt in Dresden and improved her German. She made her own translations of German hymns and published these in her very successful *Lyra Germanica* in 1853. After suffering financial losses, the Winkworth family moved in 1862 to Clifton where Catherine became involved in the movement for the promotion of higher education for women. In 1870, she became secretary of a committee formed for this purpose, and set up a series of lectures and classes for women. She was also governor of Red Maids' School in Bristol and one of the promoters of the Clifton High School for Girls, and, from 1875, she was a member of the council of Cheltenham Ladies' College. In 1872, with her sister Susanna, she went as a delegate to a German conference on women's work. In 1878 she died suddenly in Geneva of a heart attack. Her writings were largely inspired by her interest in Germany – *The Christian Singers of Germany* appeared in 1866, for example, and *Prayers from the Collection of Baron Bunsen* in 1871.   CPe

Winkworth, Susanna

1820–84 British translator, biographer, campaigner for women's rights and elder sister of CATHERINE WINKWORTH. Susanna lived in Bonn for a year between 1850 and 1851 and there decided to translate and expand the German *Life of Niebuhr* (1852). In 1854, she published her translation of *Theologica Germanica* with a preface by Charles Kingsley. She finished and published Archdeacon Hare's *Life of Luther* in 1855 and the following year she translated

Bunsen's *Signs of the Times*, and became his literary secretary. In 1858 she translated Max Müller's *German Love from the Papers of an Alien*, followed by her three-volume translation of Bunsen's *God in History* (1868–70). Like her younger sister, Susanna was very committed to plans for social improvement and, in 1874, she formed the company which built Jacob's Wells industrial dwellings, which she managed herself. After Catherine's death in 1878 she took over her work on the committees concerned with women's education. Susanna herself died in Clifton in 1884.   CPe

Winnemucca (Hopkins), Sarah 1844–91 Native American writer and activist who chronicled the dramatic changes in her own life and that of her people, from early contact with whites to life on reservations. A liaison between whites and Paiutes, Winnemucca became a controversial figure. During the Bannock War, she was an interpreter who did more than just translate messages: she is said to have convinced some of her people to return to their reservation. While she worked as an interpreter to government agents, she also criticized those whose corrupt practices caused Native Americans to starve. Winnemucca's activism included opening and running a school for Native American children and lecturing in San Francisco and in cities of the eastern United States. Her lectures detailed the sufferings of the Paiutes in their removal to, and hardships on, reservations and called for changes in government policy. Winnemucca's personal life seems to have been less successful than her public life; she was married briefly three times.

Winnemucca is best known for *Life Among the Piutes: Their Wrongs and Claims* (1883), a combination autobiography and history of the Paiutes in the 19th century. Edited by philanthropist Mrs Horace (Mary) Mann, the text is notable for its unique use of voice, influenced by oral story-telling traditions, and for its attention to the place of women in Paiute life. Winnemucca's work uses a tactic employed by other 19th-century Native American writers: that of overturning stereotypes by depicting white actions as 'savage' and Native American actions as 'civilized'.   KMP

Winter, John Strange [Henrietta Eliza Vaughan Stannard] 1856–1911 Prolific journalist, editor, business-woman and novelist, specializing in military stories. Her father was an officer in the Royal Artillery and came from several generations of soldiers. She adopted the pseudonym 'John Strange Winter' when the magazine the *Family Herald*, refused to publish *Cavalry Life* (1881) and *Regimental Legends* (1883) under a woman's name. In 1885 she published *Bootle's Baby*, which sold 2 million copies within ten years. It is the story of a kindly cavalry officer who adopts and adores a baby girl, a good deed which unexpectedly facilitates his marriage. Winter produced almost 100 novels, ten books of short stories, and uncounted articles, including many praising Dieppe, which she is credited with making into a popular tourist resort. Winter edited a weekly magazine in 1891–5, was the first president of the Writers' Club (1892) and president of the Society of Women Journalists (1901–3). She single-handedly supported her husband and three children. After the turn of the century, Winter ran a successful business manufacturing and selling cosmetic lotions; *The Little Vanities of Mrs Whittaker* (1904) praises a feminist activist for getting a makeover. Although her fiction has not caught the interest of later generations, Winter deserves respect for an astonishingly energetic, varied and original career.   TS

Winter Sun (1960) MARGARET AVISON's first collection of poetry won her a Governor General's Medal and quickly confirmed her reputation as one of Canada's most technically innovative poets. Avison's poems contain intricate networks of metaphor that resist easy consumption, but reward deeper investigation. Insisting that 'Nobody stuffs the world in at your eyes. / The optic heart must venture: a jail-break / And re-creation', Avison's often cryptic images demand the reader's analytical as well as imaginative involvement. While influenced by Romanticism and the Black Mountain poetics of Charles Olson, Avison's craft nonetheless challenges self-aggrandizing notions of the poetic subject and the self-referentiality of literary forms. Her rapid transitions, organic forms, ellipses and multiple narratives defy the temptation to 'Limn with false human clarity / A solar system with its verge / Lost'. Instead of appealing to reason or emotion, Avison's meditative style 'shows the terrain comprehended' by a faculty attuned to spiritual presence. A non-linear perspective, which rarely acknowledges distance and saturates every perceived object with potential significance, is Avison's principal means of 'lighting up' her unique literary terrain.   IR

Winterson, Jeanette 1959– Experimental British novelist who combines 'magical realist' fantasy with dense play on religious, poetic and philosophical ideas: a self-styled visionary who identifies with Blake, the Bible, revolutionaries and idealists. As the adopted daughter of Pentecostal Evangelists, Winterson wrote sermons at 8 and prepared to become a preacher at school. She left home at 15, after being punished by her parents and community for a love-affair with a woman. She read English at Oxford between 1978 and 1981 and then worked in publishing until 1987, when she became a full-time writer. Her autobiographical first novel, ORANGES ARE NOT THE ONLY FRUIT (1985), brought her acclaim as a young literary star and was made into a highly successful television serial. Its tale

of a girl growing up gay in a close-knit Lancashire religious sect takes place in a world poetically distorted by biblical certainties. Biblical language runs through all Winterson's work. Equally, the powerful figure of Jeanette's mother in *Oranges*, who 'hung out the largest sheets on the windiest days', recurs in her gallery of outrageous women – the androgynous, web-footed Villanelle in *The Passion* (1987) and the immense, whip-cracking Dog Woman of SEXING THE CHERRY (1989). Never less than ambitious and at times outright grandiose, Winterson's 'tendency towards the exotic [which] has caused me many problems, just as it did Blake', has left her increasingly impatient with REALISM. Her freewheeling narratives use interludes, digressions, revisionary FAIRY TALES and relativist theories of time and physics. In *Art and Lies* and her essay collection *Art Objects*, she became excessively abstruse and self-referential. *Gut Symmetries* (1987) brought disparate theories of the universe (quark theory, astrology) to bear on one of Winterson's favourite plots (three-way love between two women and a man) in a witty, poetic and convincingly visionary novel. KE

Wise Blood (1952)

The recurring plot of FLANNERY O'CONNOR's fiction – the possibility of grace achieved through violence and often death – is fully present in her first novel. It recounts the blasphemous and barely articulate attempts of young returning war veteran Haze Motes to defy his vocation as a fundamentalist preacher in America's Bible-belt South; but the anti-sect he founds, the Church Without Christ, is a mere parodic inversion of his obsession with redemption in a fallen world. O'Connor's harsh and vibrant prose seeks out the allegorical dimensions of concrete situations and experiences; the blindness/sight opposition, in particular, cords together levels of meaning here. Coming from a deeply Catholic family and already suffering, in the early fifties, from the lupus which would eventually kill her, she was acutely aware of the desire for salvation: the well-known grotesque and freakish 'GOTHIC' dimensions of her writing vividly dramatize a serious religious purpose.

A film version of *Wise Blood* (director, John Huston) was released in 1979; quite well received, it strongly emphasized the story's tragi-comic dimensions. MO'D

Wiseman, Adele

1928–92 Jewish Canadian writer whose chief subjects are the immigrant experience, 'otherness', creativity and, as she put it, 'the best possible reason for doing the worst thing'. She was born in Winnipeg, Manitoba, third child of Pesach and Chaika Waisman, who had recently emigrated from the Ukraine. In 1947 she met MARGARET LAURENCE, who became a lifelong friend. (Laurence drew on that friendship when creating the character of Ella in THE DIVINERS.)

Wiseman's first novel, THE SACRIFICE (1956), won the Governor General's Award. Her next two works were plays, one unpublished, one printed privately. Her second novel, *Crackpot* (1974), follows Hoda, a prostitute/socialist/artist of love, and her blind father, Danile, through about thirty years. Wiseman's memoir of her mother, *Old Woman at Play*, explores the creative process through examining Chaika Waisman's dolls (made from scraps of material and unused bits of almost anything), Wiseman's own writing, and her daughter Tamara's drawing and painting. Generally, in Adele Wiseman's work, it takes three generations to tell a story. Her last book, *Memoirs of a Book-Molesting Childhood* (1987), brings together essays on her childhood, on Canadian writing and women writers, on Henry James, on 'the forest' and on suffering – and so restates many of the themes of her thought and work. The poetry written in her last decade remained largely unpublished.

In 1986 Adele Wiseman became director of the Writing Programmes at the Banff Centre for the Arts, where her talents for creating community and nurturing writing could express themselves fully. She died of cancer in 1992, shortly following the publication of her long story 'Goon of the Moon and the Expendables' in the *Malahat Review*. EG

Wister, Sally (Sarah)

1761–1804 Revolution-era DIARIST. Born in 1761, Wister is primarily known for the journal she kept when she was 16 years old. Wister grew up in Philadelphia among the city's most influential Quaker families, receiving formal education at Quaker schools such as the one run by Anthony Benezet. Although her early personal writings describe her romantic leanings, she never married, but instead cared for her mother. Wister died in 1804, just two months after her mother's death.

Wister's journal is most noted for its strong personal voice and occasionally literary style as well as its descriptions of war-time from the unique perspective of a young woman. While historical events such as the invasion of Philadelphia are described in the journal, they are overshadowed by Wister's interpretations of such events – the fear inspired by armies and skirmishes nearby, but also the personal excitement of enjoying the company and conversation of young officers. Other writings by Wister became available in print in 1987. They include her devotional journal, written about twenty years after the Revolution-era journal and focused on spiritual rather than social concerns; occasional poetry reflective of the styles and themes of the age; and selected letters between Wister and friends and relatives. KMP

Wittig, Monique

1935– Born in the Haut-Rhin region of France, Wittig won the Prix Médicis in

673

France at the age of 24 with her first novel, *The Opoponax* (transl.1964). *Les Guérillères* (transl. 1971) is an epic celebration of the destruction of patriarchal institutions and language and the birth of a new feminist order achieved by a tribe of warrior women. *The Lesbian Body* (transl. 1975) is a poetic anatomy of the female body, eulogizing its skin and bones, its muscles and nerves, secretions and excretions and celebrating relationships between women.

Wittig argues that the 'generic feminine subject can only enter by force into a language which is foreign to it'. Enacting guerrilla tactics of a distinctly lesbian 'violence by writing', this work challenges the literary canon and the very act of reading itself. Wittig expounds, controversially, a new speaking subject, neither man nor woman but lesbian, 'the only concept I know of which is beyond the category of sex'. *Across the Acheron* (transl. 1987) rewrites and parodies Dante's *The Divine Comedy* in a surreal journey through Hell and Limbo, from San Francisco's dyke bars to the deserts of SCIENCE-FICTION landscapes. *Lesbian Peoples: Material for a Dictionary* (1976, with Sandy Zeig) continues Wittig's explorations of an alternative lesbian lexicon and her reclaiming and reconstructing of language, myth and culture. Her extremely influential essays, 'One is Not Born a Woman' , 'The Mark of Gender' and 'The Straight Mind', are collected in *The Straight Mind and Other Essays* (1992) and attack the assumed naturalness of heterosexuality and the social construction of femininity. Wittig's linguistic experimentation is matched by a highlighting of the materiality of women's oppression and an intense commitment to lesbian feminist politics.   CSt

Witting, Amy [Joan Levick, née Fraser] 1918–
Australian REALIST novelist and poet, whose style employs irony and dark humour. Her philosophy of life was shaped by the most basic instinct – survival – but tempered by her chosen work, writing: 'Indeed my central thought is that work (not slavery, or drudgery!) is the antidote to despair' – 'the one small god who does not fail'.

Witting was born in Annandale, then a 'tough' inner suburb of Sydney. These difficult years provided 'an inexhaustible subject' and her writing reveals the power of a personality pitted against adverse circumstance. Educated at the local Catholic school and then the selective Fort Street High School, in the 1930s she became part of the 'sourly brilliant literary group' at Sydney University that included James McAuley, Harold Stewart and DOROTHY GREEN [née Auchterlonie], where she was known for her sharp intellect and acerbic wit. Her colleagues went on to become well-known academics and poets, but difficult family circumstances forced Witting into the workforce. She taught French and German in high schools,

but 'was never too busy to write'. Witting published her first short story, 'Goodbye Ady, Goodbye Joe', in the *New Yorker* (1965) and others followed in Australian journals. She also co-wrote two French textbooks. Retiring from teaching in 1974, Witting turned to a back-log of material and published her first novel, *The Visit* (1977).

The self-published poetry collection, *Travel Diary* (1985), gained critical acclaim, but it was the autobiographically influenced *I for Isobel* (1989) and the short stories collected in *Marriages* (1990) that brought her to the attention of a contemporary audience. They revealed her capacity for pin-pointing life's foibles, her deep psychological understanding and empathy. Her second book of poetry, *Beauty is the Straw* (1991), made plain Witting's strength as a poet. In 1993 she received the Patrick White Award for her life's work.

Witting has maintained her teaching interest by helping migrant women learn English. Her *Collected Poetry* was published in January 1998, to coincide with her 80th birthday, and a fourth novel, *Maria's War*, later in the year.   YEM

Wives and Daughters 1864–6 ELIZABETH
GASKELL's last novel, serialized in *Cornhill* and left unfinished at her death, has enjoyed a shifting status among her other works. Much admired by critics like David Cecil who saw her as the quintessential 'lady novelist', it later lost ground against the gritty REALISM of her early 'social problem' novels. Molly Gibson is indeed a heroine possessed of conventional nurturing virtues, a dutiful daughter spending her girlhood among the gentry and aristocracy of a more peaceful, older rural world. Gaskell, though, does not offer nostalgia, but rather uses this representation of England to engage with current questions of social change: her hero, Roger Hamley, is modelled on her cousin Darwin. The novel offers an interesting counterpoint to GEORGE ELIOT's *MIDDLEMARCH* (1872), that other novel of the provincial 1830s which is, more overtly, concerned with the implications of Darwinian theory.   EA

Wolf, Christa 1929–   East German novelist, widely respected for her work's ethical concerns, and its vivid intimacy with everyday existence. Translations into English may obscure the rhythms, and allusiveness, of her style. *The Quest for Christa T.* (1968; sensitively translated by Christopher Middleton, 1970) led to increasing appreciation outside Germany. Like much of her later work, it is critical of both capitalism and actually existing socialism.

Educated under the Nazi regime, she fled with her family in 1945 from Landsberg, now part of Poland. Studying Literature at university, she committed herself to making a world which would not be Fascist 'even if it meant building ourselves into the foundations' (*The Quest for Christa T.*). She worked in publishing and editing, and was an executive member of the GDR Writers' Union (1955–76). Married in 1951, she has two daughters. Her essays and fictions increasingly engage in dialogue with a younger generation; about technology, ecology and gender inequalities, with a keen sense that parental silences had damaged identity and values.

Her own reputation was damaged after the fall of the Berlin Wall in 1989. From 1968–80 the security police (the Stasi) kept files on Wolf, but in 1993 it was discovered that (like other 'dissident' East German writers) she had informally collaborated with the Stasi years before (1959–62). Publication of *What Remains* (1989), drawing on her experiences of surveillance and restraint, had prepared for this furore. However, censorship, and self-censorship, was already signalled and questioned in her work, particularly *A Model Childhood* (later translated in the USA as *Patterns of Childhood* (1980/4)) and *Cassandra: A Novel and Four Essays* (1983/4). Essays in *Cassandra* were censored for failing to represent NATO (Greeks?) as worse than the Warsaw Pact (Trojans?). The narrative itself, overtly archaic, concerned painful disengagement from disappointed loyalties. *NO PLACE ON EARTH* (1979/82) had also used 'another time, another place' to explore disillusioned remainders of hope, in a dialogue between male and female writers from the Romantic period (highly valued, like the Greek classics, in German culture). *Accident* (1987/9) combines a terrifying day's news about the Chernobyl nuclear disaster with an operation on a benign brain tumour on her scientist brother. *Medea: Stimmen* (1996; *Medea: A Novel*, 1998) maintains her historical scope and immediacy of concern. In her intense care about past, future and present she is one of the most moving and exemplary writers of the 20th century.

EJ

Wollstonecraft, Mary

Wollstonecraft, Mary 1759–97 English Enlightenment thinker who wrote a variety of innovative feminist books for the age of the French Revolution. Her formation as social critic resembled that of many others of her time, involving aspirations of upward mobility but experience of decline in status and marginalization. Encouraged by leading English Dissenters and close women friends, she educated herself in the progressive ideology, politics and poetics of SENSIBILITY and engaged in the few occupations open to women of her class, including writing. *Thoughts on the Education of Daughters* (1787) impressed Joseph Johnson, who became her employer, publisher, advisor and banker. She completed her political and literary education in his circle of reformist writers and artists, including the painter Henry Fuseli. Their shared enthusiasm for the French Revolution inspired

P. 24

The Dog strove to attract his attention. — He said, Thou wilt not leave me!

Mary Wollstonecraft: 'The Dog strove to attract his attention. He said, Thou wilt not leave me!', illustration by William Blake from *Original Stories from Real Life*, 1791.

her to counter Edmund Burke's attack on it. *A Vindication of the Rights of Men* (1790) brings together her education in the politics and poetics of sensibility. Written in a highly personal, self-authorizing style appropriate for the Revolutionary ideology of individual rights, it was well received. She then swiftly wrote *A VINDICATION OF THE RIGHTS OF WOMAN* (1792), now arguing that unless women were educated for citizenship, though predominantly domestic, they would remain intellectually trivialized and thereby undermine the Revolution.

In early 1793 she joined expatriate pro-Revolutionary circles in Paris and formed a relationship with the American entrepreneur Gilbert Imlay, bearing a daughter, Fanny. During the Jacobin Terror, Wollstonecraft surreptitiously produced a large overview of the early Revolution (1794), based on principles of Enlightenment cultural and economic analysis. Her faltering relationship with Imlay led to a suicide attempt, however, followed by a trip to Scandinavia on business of his. The journey produced a powerful and innovative book in the line of sentimental TRAVELS, in which Wollstonecraft represents herself as the 'female philosopher' – both woman and intellectual, lover and social critic, mother and representative revolutionized consciousness – afflicted by the failed Revolution on the one hand and an unrevolutionized sexist society on the other. Back in England, failure to reconcile with Imlay led to another suicide attempt, followed by slow recovery, resumption of her writing career, and a new and constructive relationship with the eminent political theorist and novelist, William Godwin. She became pregnant and they married, but only to avoid harming her usefulness as a public voice for women in the increasingly conservative political climate. She started an innovative feminist novel modelled on the form developed by the Godwin circle. In August 1797 she bore a girl, later to become MARY SHELLEY, but mishandling of the delivery led to infection and Wollstonecraft's death on 10 September. In 1798 her distraught widower published her incomplete novel, as MARIA: OR, THE WRONGS OF WOMAN, with other works and a memoir illustrating the link between her politics and her personal life. The disclosures there enabled counter-Revolutionary journalists to smear her and her feminist politics, however, and her name remained under a cloud for some decades, except in reformist circles. Revival of open interest in her and her work began with mid-Victorian feminism.   GK

Wolstenholme-Elmy, Elizabeth (Clark) 1834–1913
British feminist whose writing advocated women's suffrage, changing discriminatory laws toward women, and other progressive causes. Little is known about her parents beyond the fact that her father was a Methodist minister, and that they shared the prevailing Victorian attitude toward women's education: Elizabeth Wolstenholme was taught at home (unlike her brother, later a brilliant Cambridge mathematician). Her parents died by the time Elizabeth was 14, and she went to school for two years, though her guardians prevented her from attending a women's college. At 19 she opened a school near Manchester, and while working for women's higher education met JOSEPHINE BUTLER and other prominent feminists. Wolstenholme championed women's enfranchisement from the movement's early days, and later fought

for the Married Women's Property Act. Her opposition to Victorian marriage laws at first discouraged her from marrying her lover, Ben Elmy, a fellow-radical whom she met after moving to London in 1872. In 1874 Elizabeth, who was visibly pregnant, was persuaded to marry by fellow feminists who argued that the scandal surrounding the relationship was damaging feminist causes. The couple wrote books and poetry together (using the pseudonym Ellis Ethelmar), including the 'Human Flower' series, accessible books on human physiology. Wolstenholme-Elmy published many polemical pieces – among them *The Criminal Code in its Relation to Women* (1880), *The Emancipation of Women* (1888) and *Woman's Franchise: The Need of the Hour* (1907) – but was perhaps most effective behind the scenes, particularly in her voluminous correspondence with political colleagues and opponents.   KW

Woman in the Nineteenth Century (1845) This
dense and resonant exploration of women's unrealized potential was the culmination of MARGARET FULLER's feminist insights. Fuller argues that man's search for truth and harmony will remain flawed until women are allowed to develop themselves. Being naturally more 'electrical' or 'magnetic' than man, woman has the capacity to make a unique contribution, a necessary complement, to society.

The numerous citations in *Woman in the Nineteenth Century* revise, rather than substantiate, largely masculine sources of authority. This feminist declaration challenges America to live up to the Declaration of Independence's pledge that, in Fuller's words, 'All men are born free and equal.' In an imaginary dialogue between a slave trader and his unidentified antagonist, the national union's dependence on slavery is correlated with the patriarchal family's dependence on the domination of women.

Anticipating later arguments distinguishing sex from gender, Fuller contends that men and women possess both masculine and feminine traits. These traits must be harmonized in the individual before concordant unions can be created with other individuals and before truth can be found in life.   VM

Woman on the Edge of Time (1976) MARGE
PIERCY's fourth and most highly regarded novel is a principal work of seventies socialist-feminist SCIENCE-FICTION. The 37-year-old Mexican-American Connie Ramos, abused on account of her marginalization within the hierarchies of gender, class and race, is deprived of her young daughter by state authority and forced into a psychiatric hospital. Discovering that she can communicate telepathically with a future *alter ego*, Luciente, she time-travels mentally to alternative societies. Piercy develops a rich contrast between present, grim reality and the

back-to-nature *and* high-tech utopia of Mattapoisett, Massachusetts, in 2137. Here relationships are non-exploitative, childbirth and rearing arrangements are separated from any basis in gender, and all waste is recycled. Mattapoisett is derived from ideas then circulating in the Students for a Democratic Society organization and the Womens' Liberation movement, to which Piercy belonged. Connie also visits a dystopia where contemporary sexism and commodification are grotesquely exaggerated. Piercy's method is polemical and melodramatic; the novel remains a passionate plea for progressive social change.   MO'D

Woman Warrior: Memories of a Girlhood Among Ghosts, The (1976) MAXINE HONG

KINGSTON's first book, winner of the National Book Critics Circle Award, tells a powerful story of a cross-cultural encounter. Trying to reconcile her Chinese background with her American present, the narrator embraces the memories of the female members of her family – she talks about the suicide of her relative, No Name Woman; the sudden madness of another aunt; and the interruption of her mother's medical career. Contesting the rigid norms of life and the position of woman in a traditional Chinese family, she has recourse to children's tales or stories. Rather than adopt a servile attitude, the narrator identifies with a powerful heroine, a warrior woman, only to find herself in a double bind: 'Marriage and childbirth strengthen the swordswoman . . . Do the women's work; then do more work, which will become ours too.' The book illustrates a painful but rewarding process of forming an identity taking place at the border of two different cultures, value-systems and temporalities. JZ

Women in a Lampshade (1983) This collection of

ELIZABETH JOLLEY's short stories dates from the late 1970s and early 1980s, when many of them were published in a range of Australian literary journals. The stories are oddly entangled with each other and with the rest of her work in many ways. 'Pear Tree Dance' tells of how the domestic Weekly, a central character in *The Newspaper of Claremont Street*, buys a tiny country property, where she can revel in the sensuous parts of her self that nobody else recognizes. Several of the stories are autobiographical fragments, and several of the stories share characters. Motifs are shared between stories: the dream of a tiny weatherboard cottage in the middle of a paddock, sunlit bush spaces, the veil or lampshade or cloak of blossom thrown transformingly over the everyday shoulders of a protagonist. Sudden violence erupts between family members; silent, clumsy people have passionate dreams. In general, the stories feature fractured narrative structures and problematically shifting points of view. Sometimes tender and celebratory, sometimes bleak in the extreme, all the stories consider the passions of relatedness, isolation and family tensions.   KTS

Women in the Wall (1975) JULIA O'FAOLAIN's HIS-

TORICAL NOVEL, set in 6th-century Gaul and peopled by characters drawn largely from chronicles of the period, resonates with contemporary and still unresolved issues of sexual politics. Situated in a convent founded by Queen Radegunda, wife of Clotair, King of Gaul, this account of interlocking institutions of sexual oppression begins with Clotair's abduction of 11-year-old Radegunda. Tortured by her treasonous sexual response to her captor, Radegunda finds relief and expiation in her fervently held Christianity. She eventually persuades Clotair to release her and to finance the founding of a convent to which she retreats with Agnes, a young woman whose ambivalence about the retreat echoes Radegunda's earlier self-dividedness. Against a background of political and ecclesiastical intrigue and unrest, Radegunda, subject to ecstatic visions and self-mortification, becomes more unearthly and remote as Agnes, whom Radegunda has made abbess, becomes more troublingly worldly. The competing models of devotion represented by foundress and abbess fissure the young nuns' loyalties, and one renegade faction uncovers a sexual scandal with disastrous results.   MO'C

Women of Brewster Place, The (1980) GLORIA

NAYLOR's first work was 'a novel in seven stories', each the tale of a different resident of a neglected street in an unnamed American city. Naylor chooses a range of black women characters who, in her words, express 'the complexity of our lives, the richness of our diversity, from skin colour on down to religious, political and sexual preference'. They include a displaced Southern mother, an activist who has renamed herself Kiswana, and a lesbian couple. Naylor's lyrical descriptions show a stylistic debt to TONI MORRISON, the multivocal structure to NTOZAKE SHANGE, though the novel is weakened by moments of melodrama. A more distinctive interest elaborated on elsewhere in Naylor's tetralogy of black life, of which this was the first volume, was in the political and social forces that shape communities. The story was made into a television movie in 1989, starring and produced by Oprah Winfrey. Though Naylor resisted the criticism, also lobbed at ALICE WALKER, that black women writers should show more sympathy to men, in 1998 she brought out a companion novel, *The Men of Brewster Place*.   SB

Women's Room, The (1977) MARILYN FRENCH's

best-known, and most controversial, novel is an uncompromising, monumental depiction of the debilitating conditions of women's social, economic and political inequality. Through the disillusioning experiences of the all-too-representative Myra and her peers, the lot of the mid 20th-century American woman is shown to be a choice between the suburban miseries of meaningless affairs, alienation and exploitation or the 'liberated' hell of rape, betrayal and abuse. Although one character notoriously claims that 'all men are rapists and that's all they are', the novel demonstrates how generations of women have conspired with the violence done to their autonomy. The documentary qualities of the novel are underlined by the narrator who, addressing the reader, insists on the reality of her story and argues that the insignificance of the male characters is only a response to male novelists whose female characters are also 'stick figures'. In reversing these conventions, French shows too how men are trapped in the same patterns of conformity, and how they, like women, lose out in a patriarchal society. MM

Wong, Jade Snow 1919– The first Chinese-American woman writer to be born in the United States. She was born into a Christian family in the San Francisco Chinatown, from which she moved away in order to integrate herself into more culturally diverse areas of the city. She was educated at Mills College and worked as a potter. Her most famous work, the autobiography *Fifth Chinese Daughter* (1945), has been cited by MAXINE HONG KINGSTON and AMY TAN as the main influence on their writing. It was republished in 1989 with a new retrospective introduction by Wong in response to the project by Chinese-American critics to identify a literary tradition. Her second book, *No Chinese Stranger* (1975), has not received the same critical coverage. Her work holds a controversial position in literary history, since her promotion of the idea of assimilation into dominant American culture and her Christianity have been interpreted as a slur against the maintenance of Chinese tradition in America. MAB

Wood, Ellen 1814–87 British novelist, the eldest daughter of Thomas Price, a well-to-do Worcester glove-maker. From girlhood, she suffered from curvature of the spine, a condition which affected her health throughout life. She wrote in a reclining chair with the manuscript on her knees. Ellen Price married, in 1836, Henry Wood, a banker and shipper in the consular service. They spent twenty years abroad, largely in France; her contributions during that time to *Bentley's Miscellany* and Colburn's *New Monthly Magazine* in London earned her the nickname of 'Scheherezade' amongst the editors, because she had been keeping both journals afloat.

In 1861, *EAST LYNNE* began running in *Bentley's*, and was enthusiastically reviewed in *The Times* of 25 January 1862. This novel, which went through five editions by 1862, and was to sell 140,000 copies by 1895, was translated into most European and some oriental languages and was the subject of many dramatic adaptations; it became an oft-quoted example in copyright disputes because the author received no royalties from these adaptations. The agony of the aristocratic adulteress, Isabel Vane, who returns in disguise to work as governess to her own children in the household of her former husband, himself now married again, helped fix the conventions of the Victorian SENSATION NOVEL, a mixture of REALISM and melodrama, of secrets (often kept from the reader) and shocks to the nerves ('sensations').

Mrs Wood produced her best work in the early 1860s, in *The Channings* (1862) and (her own favourite) *The Shadow of Ashlydyat* (1863). Like her rival ELIZABETH BRADDON, she went on to become proprietor of a magazine, the *Argosy*, in 1867, and published the rest of her work in its pages, including the 'Johnny Ludlow' papers, which some regard as her most interesting project. She died of heart failure in 1887 and was buried in Highgate Cemetery in a red granite monument which is a copy of the tomb of Scipio Africanus in Rome. VS

Woodhull, Victoria Claflin 1838–1927 American reformer, editor. Born in Ohio, Victoria and her sister Tennessee performed feats of mesmerism and psychic healing in their parents' travelling show. At the age of 15, she was married for the first time and had two children. Later divorced, in 1866 she married Col. James Blood, who is said to have written many of her later essays. When she and Tennessee moved to New York in 1868, they immediately gained the support of Cornelius Vanderbilt, who established them as stockbrokers and helped to underwrite their *Woodhull and Claflin's Weekly*, devoted to issues of socialism, free love and women's rights. In 1872, the *Weekly* gained notoriety for publishing the first English translation of the *Communist Manifesto*, as well as a story about the scandalous Ward-Tilton affair, the lurid story of which briefly landed them in prison for obscenity. That same year, Woodhull was nominated for president by the Equal Rights party, with Frederick Douglass as her running-mate. In 1877, she and her sister moved to England, where they both married wealthy bankers and remained until their deaths. SP

Woolf [née Stephen], (Adeline) Virginia 1882–1941 Novelist, short-story writer, journalist, critic and DIARIST. Woolf is a central figure within English MODERNISM. Her continuing formal and thematic experimentation and her reflections on the nature of prose fiction have had a profound influence on the development of English prose in the 20th century, and her engagement with issues of gender and sexuality has made her works of particular interest to feminist critics. Woolf was the daughter of Leslie Stephen, a formidable Victorian man of letters. Her childhood was marked by tragedy, in particular the death of her mother and of her half-sister. It was also marred by sexual abuse perpetrated by her two half-brothers, the children of her mother Julia's marriage to Herbert Duckworth. From an early age she felt compelled to write, contributing many stories to the family 'newspaper', the *Hyde Park Gate News*. (See also DIARY OF VIRGINIA WOOLF). From 1904 she published critical essays in a range of journals and newspapers. She moved to Bloomsbury where she became friendly with a number of prominent writers, artists and intellectuals, and in 1912 she married Leonard Woolf.

Her first novel, THE VOYAGE OUT, was published in 1915. She and Leonard founded the Hogarth Press in 1917: this was to allow Woolf the artistic and economic space for experimentation in her writing in the following years. She published *Night and Day* in 1919 and *Jacob's Room* in 1922. In the early 1920s a number of her essays, including 'Modern Fiction' and 'Mr Bennett and Mrs Brown' analysed the challenges facing modern novelists. Woolf stressed the importance of subjective complexity, of associative metaphors and of 'moments of being' as aspects of the literary representation of modern life. MRS DALLOWAY (1925) focuses on the temporal density and emotional fluidity of personal identity and explores the psychic legacy of World War I. It draws on metaphor and parallel imagery to construct connections between characters who are otherwise separate. TO THE LIGHTHOUSE (1927) offers an innovative architecture of the novel, with two sections detailing the minute patterns of familial and social interaction connected by a brief but symbolically highly charged section exploring the rhythms in which 'time passes'.

Woolf's affair and intense friendship with VITA SACKVILLE-WEST provided the theme and the context for ORLANDO (1928), a fascinating yet disturbing blend of fantasy, biography and cultural history. *Orlando's* exploration of the social and psychic meanings of gendered identity was developed in A ROOM OF ONE'S OWN (1929) where she considers: 'women and what they are like'; 'women and the fiction that they write'; and 'women and the fiction that is written about them'. Woolf's fictional engagement with the temporal complexity and the precariousness of personal identities continued in THE WAVES (1931). From 1932 she began working on an experimental hybrid form, the novel–essay. Her aim was to interweave a fictional text exploring historical and cultural changes in family life with a polemical essay on forms of gendered inequality. In the end the two strands of this experiment appeared as a novel, THE YEARS (1937), and a long essay, THREE GUINEAS (1938) which argued for a profound connection between patriarchal forms of culture and

Woodcut by Vanessa Bell in Virginia Woolf's *Kew Gardens*, second edn 1919, Hogarth Press.

the rise of Fascism. Her final novel, BETWEEN THE ACTS, appeared in 1941. Having suffered frequent episodes of mental instability throughout her life, Woolf drowned herself in 1941. MS

Woolfe, Sue (Suzanne) 1950– Australian novelist who grew up in the Blue Mountains outside Sydney, which provide the setting for her first novel, *Painted Woman* (1989), and for part of her second, *Leaning Towards Infinity* (1996). Both deal with the dilemma of the exceptional woman growing up in a household which refuses to acknowledge and/or exploits her genius. In *Painted Woman*, the famous artist has, years before, killed his wife who, it is suggested, had more talent than he. Their daughter, who has inherited her mother's genius, is eventually able to break free from her father and create her own art. *Leaning Towards Infinity* complicates this story of suppressed female talents by extending it over a number of generations and making the mother(s) more complicit in the suppression. Its central character, Frances Montrose (which, incidentally, is also the name of the heroine of *Painted Woman*), is a mathematical genius who eventually is able to prove that her mother has discovered a new number. Woolfe has also written versions of both her novels for the stage. She is a highly experienced teacher of creative writing and, with her friend KATE GRENVILLE, has edited *Making Stories: How Ten Australian Novels were Written* (1993). EW

Woolley, Hannah 1622?–75 Author and printer of several manuals on housewifery, covering topics from COOKERY and cleaning through to medicine and social etiquette. Self-authored prefaces to her works offer autobiographical details. Born in Essex into a family of middling status, she was a working woman all her life. Aged 15 she went to work as a teacher and later as a servant in a noble household, where many of the skills she recounts in her books were no doubt acquired. Aged 24, she married Benjamin Woolley, Master of a grammar school near Saffron Walden, going on to run an educational establishment with him in Hackney, London, until his death in 1661. It was to support herself as a widow that she began to publish books from her own house (a not untypical measure for women of her social status in urban areas at this time, although the extent of her output is impressive). Amongst the works she had published by the mid 1670s were *The Ladies Directory* (1661), *The Cooks Guide* (1664) and *The Queen-like Closet* (1670). Their contents include recipes, beauty tips and folk remedies.

The work most often quoted in association with Woolley is *The Gentlewoman's Companion* (1673) but her authorship of this guide has been persuasively challenged of late. The speaker of the text appears to be male, the picture and biography of Woolley attached to original printings is erroneous in a number of respects and she herself attacked plagiarism of her work around this time. Her oeuvre remains, however, a remarkable insight into the life, experience and expected knowledge of a late 17th-century housewife.

JS

Woolson, Constance Fenimore 1840–94 American essayist, poet and writer of REALIST and DOMESTIC FICTION. Grand-niece of novelist James Fenimore Cooper, she was born in New Haven, grew up in Cleveland, Ohio, and was educated at private girls' schools. After her father's death in 1869, she travelled with her mother through the eastern and southern states writing TRAVEL sketches for leading periodicals. These were collected in *Castle Nowhere: Lake Country Sketches* (1875) and *Rodman the Keeper: Southern Sketches* (1880). When her mother died in 1879, she moved to Europe with her sister. She met novelist Henry James in 1880 and began a close lifelong friendship. Before leaving the States, Woolson published a children's novel, *The Old Stone House* (1872); poetry, including the innovative verse narrative *Two Women* (1877); and a novel for adults, *Anne* (1880). Her later publications include a novella, *For the Major* (1883), and three novels; *East Angels* (1886), *Jupiter Lights* (1889) and *Horace Chase* (1894). She died from what was probably a suicidal fall from her apartment window in Venice. *Dorothy and Other Italian Stories* (1895), *The Front Yard and Other Italian Stories* (1896) and a book of collected travel writing, *Mentone, Cairo, and Corfu* (1896), were published posthumously.

JSG

Worboise, Emma Jane [Mrs Guyton] 1825–87 Biographer, editor of an evangelical journal and writer of fiction in which favoured female characters display 'patience . . . gentleness, and meek womanly fortitude', this British author's first novel, *Alice Cunningham*, was published in 1846. It was followed by nearly fifty others.

Many of these are anti-Catholic and anti-ritualist in tone, rather advocating the personal faith and extempore prayer characteristic of the Dissenting churches. The Church of England, whether for its preoccupation with the Oxford Movement (regarded as the Church of Rome under another name) or for its empty forms, is criticized accordingly. *Father Fabian, the Monk of Malham Tower* (1875) is especially notable for its anti-Catholic polemic. Jesuit conspirators are to be found everywhere; people are cynically persuaded to enter convents, regardless of vocation; and most of the major Catholic protagonists ultimately turn Protestant!

More straightforwardly DOMESTIC NOVELS include *A Woman's Patience* (1879), the story of an heiress married for her money who has to combat both her husband's contempt and the hostile presence of the woman he loves, and *Married Life: Or the story of Phillip and Edith* (1863), which concerns two young wives whose marriages are put under strain when another woman unduly influences their husbands.

EMH

Wordsworth, Dorothy 1771–1855 British DIARIST, letter-writer and poet, she was brought up in a conventional and restricting environment after her mother died in 1778. Eventually moving in with her brother William, in 1794, she became his constant companion. Unconventionally, they chose to live without servants, and their daily routine was based around work and long walks in the surrounding countryside. Descriptions of the changing landscape and the minutiae of her everyday activity, in Alfoxden, Germany and Grasmere, formed the basis of her *Diaries*, which showed a keen sense of observation and poetic imagination; they greatly influenced the work of her brother and his friend Coleridge. Although hating 'the idea of setting myself up as an Author', she wrote several poems which anonymously appeared alongside William's during her lifetime. Some of her prose writing was published in his *Guide to the Lakes* (1820), and she wrote several narrative accounts of her journeys (see TRAVEL WRITING), including *Recollections of a Tour Made in Scotland AD 1803*, posthumously published in 1874. In 1829 she suffered a breakdown in health which foreshadowed her premature senility and was looked after by her brother and his family. Her letters, published recently along with William's, vividly describe a life of struggle and worry.

RDM

Wright, Frances [Madam d'Arusmont] 1795–1852 British letter-writer, autobiographer, dramatist, social campaigner and orator who was, in her advocation of birth control, religious toleration and universal suffrage, an enlightened and radical thinker. Distantly related to the writer ELIZABETH MONTAGU, she was born in Scotland into a family that supported Thomas Paine, and was orphaned at a very young age. She and her sister Camilla were raised for a while by their great-uncle, a lecturer in philosophy. In 1818 she went with Camilla to the United States, where she was to spend long periods of her life. Her experiences there are recounted in letters published as *Views of Society and Manners in America* (1821). In 1824 she toured the United States with Lafayette. She married the French doctor Phiquepal d'Arusmont in the 1830s, divorcing him in 1851.

Her political ideals are evident in her verse drama on Swiss independence, *Altorf* (1819), and her witty Socratic dialogue, *A Few Days in Athens* (1822), as well as in the many lectures and articles she published. Her 1825 *Plan for the Gradual Abolition of Slavery in the United States* was received enthusiastically by Thomas Jefferson, and she attempted to put her ideas into practice by establishing a slave community called 'Nashoba' near Memphis. The experiment failed after a few years, but her zeal for her utopian vision did not waver, and was still in evidence in her extensive lecture tours and in her last publication, *England the Civilizer* (1848). In 1844 she published a third-person autobiography, *Biography, Notes, and Political Letters of Frances Wright D' Arusmont*. Her outspoken views meant that she was not universally popular, as her newspaper nicknames 'The Priestess of Beelzebub' and 'The Great Red Harlot of Infidelity' suggested. She died in Cincinnati at the age of 57, and her works and philosophy remained largely ignored until the 1960s.　　ELER

Wright [McKinney], Judith 1915– Australian poet, critic, essayist and activist, who has become as eminent for her public campaigns for Aboriginal rights and conservation as for her poetry. Wright was born to a pioneering grazing family in the New England area of New South Wales. Her mother died when she was 11, and she was sent to boarding school in Armidale before attending the University of Sydney. After the outbreak of World War II, she returned for a time to assist her father on the land. In 1943 she moved to Brisbane where she assisted in the early establishment of *Meanjin* magazine. With her husband, the philosopher Jack McKinney, she settled at Mount Tamborine in the ranges outside Brisbane. They had one daughter.

Wright's experiences on the land during the war, and the questioning of Australian culture among intellectuals at the time, influenced her first book of poetry, THE MOVING IMAGE (1946). *Woman to Man* (1949) was more overtly metaphysical in its interests, and contains some of her most famous poetry. During the 1950s she began to study the work of earlier Australian poets, and her critical book *Preoccupations in Australian Poetry* (1965) represents a landmark reassessment of Australian poetry. She also began research into

her own family history, the source of her *Generations of Men* (1959) which she later rewrote, as a result of a growing awareness of Aboriginal history, as *The Cry for the Dead* (1981).

Wright became more involved in public activities after her husband's death in 1966. She moved to the Canberra district after 1974, where she advised the Whitlam Federal Government on conservation issues, and served on the Aboriginal treaty committee during the 1980s. Wright has not allowed an increasing deafness to inhibit her campaigning on conservation issues and for Aboriginal rights. At times, she has been criticized for writing propaganda poetry, but even her most political work seems to come out of deep-felt emotion. Wright has always maintained that humans need to recognize that they are 'part of nature' and her poetry calls for us to acknowledge our bond with the natural world.　　SPL

Wright, L(aurali) R. 1939– Canadian writer and journalist mostly known for her Karl Alberg mysteries. She attended a number of Canadian universities and received an MA in Liberal Studies from Simon Fraser University, Burnaby, British Columbia, in 1995, and is the mother of two daughters. After starting her career as a fiction writer with three non-mystery novels (1979–84), she published her first crime novel, *The Suspect*, in 1985. It was the outset of a popular mystery series based on the characters Karl Alberg – Royal Canadian Mounted Police Staff Sergeant in rural Sechelt, British Columbia – and Cassandra Mitchell – the local librarian and Alberg's lover. With this novel, Wright became the first Canadian author to win the prestigious American Edgar Allan Poe Award. Since then, she has published seven sequels and one more non-mystery novel. Twice she received the Crime Writers of Canada Arthur Ellis Award for Best Mystery Novel, for *A Chill Rain in January* (1990) and *Mother Love* (1995); the latter also gained the Canadian Author's Association 1995 Literary Award for Fiction. Wright is praised for her psychological insight into human relationships as well as for complex plots and sub-plots. Several continuing characters add elements of humour and love. Alberg's investigations into the motivation of the murderer become more important than the crime itself. Physical violence is mainly restricted to the acts of murder. Wright's detailed depictions of fictionalized Sechelt and its environs, of the landscape and weather specific to British Columbia's Sunshine Coast, create a very special atmosphere.　　GWi

Wright, Susanna 1697–1785 American poet. Susanna Wright was born in England of Quaker parents; she completed her education there before she joined her family who had emigrated to Pennsylvania in 1714. The Wrights formed long-lasting friendships with prominent Quaker families, the LOGANS and Norrises of Philadelphia. In 1726, after her mother's death, the Wrights moved to the Pennsylvania frontier in Lancaster County where they operated a ferry over the Susquehanna river. Although Susanna Wright feared that she would be 'estrang'd' from 'all the social world', especially 'books and engaging friends', she overcame the loneliness of the frontier by exchanging letters, books and poetry with her friends. The recipients of her extensive correspondence included James Logan, Charles Norris, Deborah and Benjamin Franklin, HANNAH GRIFFITTS and MILCAH MARTHA MOORE's extended family.

Wright became one of the most celebrated writers of her day. Unfortunately only about thirty of her poems are extant, the majority of them preserved by Milcah Martha Moore in her commonplace book. She wrote in many different genres and styles, including brief epigrams, elegies and epistles. One of her most powerful poems is on marriage and the single life and is addressed 'To Eliza Norris – at Fairhill'. Wright praised Norris for her ability to resist 'seducing tales' about marriage which 'yield obedience'; instead, Norris reigns in freedom 'o'er your own thoughts'. Neither woman ever married. In her outspoken defence of the single life, she had much in common with the younger poet that she encouraged, Hannah Griffitts. Wright's energy extended to many areas of intellectual enterprise – politics, medicine, law and horticulture. Books and learning, however, were probably her first love, as she confided to Benjamin Rush before her death 'that pleasure of reading was to her a most tremendous blessing'. Hannah Griffitts remembered her friend and mentor in an elegy, praising her 'striking sense and energy of mind'. CLB

Wrightson, Patricia 1921– One of Australia's best-loved contemporary writers for children. Wrightson's first novel, *The Crooked Snake* (1955), was awarded the 1956 Children's Book of the Year Award, and in 1986 she won the Hans Christian Andersen Medal. She has since published eighteen CHILDREN'S BOOKS, among them *An Older Kind of Magic* (1972), *The Nargun and the Stars* (1973) and the 'Wirrun' books: *The Ice is Coming* (1977), *The Dark Bright Water* (1978), *Behind the Wind* (1981) and *Song of Wirrun* (1987). In many of her books Wrightson evokes the mystical role of the Aboriginal people as guardians of the land, incorporating Aboriginal myths into her narratives and reinterpreting them to suit a modern, urban readership. In *An Older Kind of Magic*, Rupert, Selina and Benny discover the ancient beings who live within the earth – the Nyol, Net-Net, Pot-Koorok and Bitarr – emerging in the Sydney Botanical Gardens in an attempt to save the park from developers. Throughout Wrightson's work is an attempt to inspire within her readers a respect for

and love of the ancient mysteries of the Australian land: 'For stone is stone; and men whose drills break into the living stone should take care. They may find what they do not expect.' SS

Wrongs of Woman: Or, Maria, The (1798) MARY WOLLSTONECRAFT's fictionalized version of her most famous work, *VINDICATION OF THE RIGHTS OF WOMAN* (1792), was left incomplete when she died, and published posthumously the following year. Imprisonment is used here as a metaphor for the female condition, mirroring the view in *Vindication* that the world is 'a vast prison, and all women born slaves', and the novel is suffused with images connected to the French Revolution, which Wollstonecraft supported. The plot centres on Maria's confinement in an asylum by a brutal and uncaring husband who also seized, and she believes, killed, her baby daughter, whilst fleeing the marital home. During her incarceration she encounters the working-class wardress, Jemima, whose story of poverty and prostitution is presented in a sympathetic fashion, and Darnford, with whom she falls in love. Maria's relationship is presented as a dangerous romantic folly, swayed by her reading of Rousseau rather than rational thought. However, the free expression of female sexuality is also championed, an idea which brought the author and her work considerable condemnation. RDM

Wroth, Mary *c.*1586 – *c.*1651 Wrote *Urania*, a pastoral ROMANCE with a sonnet sequence appended: the first significant body of secular love literature to be published by an Englishwoman. She was born into the foremost literary family of the Elizabethan age. Her uncle and aunt were Philip Sidney and the influential patroness MARY SIDNEY. She was lady-in-waiting to Queen Anne at the Jacobean court and well known in literary circles. She performed at court in a masque by Ben Jonson, who dedicated *The Alchemist* to her. She married Robert Wroth in 1604 but the marriage was not happy and she was encumbered by debts when he died in 1614. Mary Wroth's affair with her cousin, William Herbert, by whom she bore two children, seems to have affected her standing at court. She spent her last twenty years in straitened circumstances on her country estate at Penshurst.

It was here that she wrote *Urania* (1621), an intricate pastoral romance modelled on Philip Sidney's *Arcadia* but imbued with an ironic REALISM closer to Cervantes. Its tone is typified by a Queen who cries 'I am not a Nimphe . . . nor a Goddesse, but a distressed woman'. *Urania* was an outspoken work that dramatized Wroth's alienation from the Jacobean court. Its veiled allusions to her contemporaries led to a bitter and very public dispute with Lord Denny, who claimed she had slandered him. Wroth gave a spirited reply but withdrew the book from sale; and then went on to write an unfinished sequel. *Urania* foregrounds female lovers, writers and readers. At its centre is Pamphilia, a poet–lover whose loyalty is polemically used to accentuate male infidelity. Pamphilia writes of the torments of secret love in a public court environment. Wroth made further use of pastoral, with its contrast between idealized retreat and the world of the court, in her unpublished tragi-comedy, *Love's Victorie*.   KE

Wuthering Heights (1847) EMILY BRONTË's novel was initially believed to be an awkward first attempt by her sister CHARLOTTE. The characters of this quintessentially romantic book are splendidly oblivious to everyday concerns. The language is violent and extreme and the plot bold and simple. It features the uncouth, changeling-like Heathcliff who is adopted into a family where he excites the most violent emotions. When Heathcliff's adoptive sister, Cathy, opts to marry not him but the mild-mannered Edgar Linton, Heathcliff is set on implacable revenge. At the core of *Wuthering Heights* is the mystical love of Cathy and Heathcliff. As Cathy says, 'My love for Linton is like the foliage in the woods: time will change it . . . as winter changes the trees. My love for Heathcliff resembles the eternal rocks beneath . . . I *am* Heathcliff!' The book is patterned with primal oppositions. The fair-haired, civilized Lintons and the temperate environs of their home contrast with bleak, dark-haired Heathcliff and the wildness of Wuthering Heights. Brontë's picture of romantic love, which is characterized by total honesty, hysterical emotion and implacable need, is not an attractive one. Love here is neither civilizing nor a force for good; it is a force of nature.   KE

Wylie, Elinor Hoyt 1885–1928 American poet, novelist, critic. Born to a wealthy and socially prominent Philadelphia family, Elinor was educated at schools in Philapdelphia and Washington, D.C., groomed for the aristocracy and introduced into society as a debutante. Prevented from continuing her education, she married the unstable Philip Hichborn in 1905 but eloped to England with the also-married Horace Wylie in 1910, leaving her husband and son behind. The ensuing scandal was so highly publicized that she published her first book of poems, *Incidental Numbers* (1912), anonymously in England. They show the beginnings of the remarkable balance she struck in her poems between romantic grace and technical precision. That year,

Hichborn committed suicide, but Wylie was not divorced until 1916, when he and Elinor moved back to the United States and were married. In 1919, Elinor began to publish in *Poetry* magazine, which served as her introduction to American literary society. Leaving Wylie, she moved to New York in 1921, published her prize-winning *Net to Catch the Wind*, and was eagerly celebrated by figures like Carl van Vechten, Edmund Wilson and William Rose Benét. A whirlwind year, 1923 saw her publish her first novel, *Jennifer Lorn: A Sedate Extravaganza*, divorce Wylie and marry Benét. *Jennifer Lorn* and her next novel, *The Venetian Glass Nephew* (1926), both depict fragile heroines forced into positions of mere decoration by callous men. Although generally considered overwrought in their style, the novels were praised for their satire. Still, Elinor's great contribution was her poetry, exemplified in the dark and powerful *Black Armour* (1923). Her lifelong fascination with Percy Shelley inspired her to write two novels about him (*The Orphan Angel* and *Mr Hodge and Mr Hazard*) and dedicate a book of poetry to him (*Trivial Breath*). Leaving Benét in 1927 for her final great love, Henry de Clifford Woodhouse, she died suddenly of a stroke in 1928.   SP

Wynter, Sylvia 1932– Jamaican playwright, novelist and critic. Born in Cuba, at 2 Wynter moved to Jamaica where she received her early education. She gained her BA and MA at the University of London and afterwards taught Modern Languages at the University of the West Indies, Jamaica. She is now professor in the Department of Spanish and Portuguese at Stanford University. Her only published novel, *Hills of Hebron: A Jamaican Novel* (1962), examines a Jamaican spiritual community moving toward self-definition after the death of its leader. Her plays, including *Ballad for a Rebellion: Epic Story of Morant Bay Rebellion* (premiered in Jamaica 1965) and *Rockstone Anancy: A Magical Morality* (Jamaica 1970), reflect her interests in Caribbean history and folklore. Wynter has co-written plays for radio and television with her ex-husband, Jan Carew. Her scholarly publications cover a wide range of subjects including the relationship of African culture to the Caribbean, the legacy of colonialism and the reception of Caribbean literature; the most notable of these being 'Let Us Sit Down and Talk About a Little Culture: Reflections on West Indian Writing and Criticism' (1968) and 'Beyond Miranda's Meanings: Un/silencing the "Demonic Ground" of Caliban's "Woman"' (1990).

AD

Yamamoto (DeSoto), Hisaye [Napoleon] 1921–
Second-generation ('Nisei') Japanese-American short-
story writer, in 1986 given the American Book Award
for Lifetime Achievement by the Before Columbus
Foundation. Born in Redondo Beach, California, to
immigrants from Kumamoto, Japan, she was the only
daughter among three sons. Interned in Poston,
Arizona, during World War II, she wrote for the camp
newspaper, and, during the 1950s, for the *Catholic
Worker* in New York, where she met and in 1955 married
Anthony DeSoto. She is the mother of an adopted son
and four other children, born in Los Angeles after she
moved there with DeSoto.

Her first published story, 'The High-Heeled Shoes: A
Memoir', in *Partisan Review* (1948), exemplifies her feminist critique of women's lives, as do her much-anthologized 'Seventeen Syllables', appearing the following
year in the same outlet, and three stories also listed as
'distinctive' in Martha Foley's *Best American Short Stories*
collections: 'The Brown House' and 'Yoneko's
Earthquake' (both 1951), and 'Epithalamium' (1960).
'The Legend of Miss Sasagawara' (1950) derives from
her internment camp experience. All of her stories
reveal a catholicity of empathy – for both sexes and

'Martyrdom of Profane Love', from O. Vaenius,
Amorum emblemata, 1608. One of the occult images
Frances Yates revisited.

sundry ethnicities. 'Seventeen Syllables' and 'Yoneko's
Earthquake' were produced as *Hot Summer Winds* for
PBS 'American Playhouse' (1991). Her work can be com-
pared to ANN PETRY's for its portrayal of racism, to
FLANNERY O'CONNOR's for its irony, and to GRACE
PALEY's for its wit. *Seventeen Syllables and Other Stories*
was reprinted in 1998. CFK

Yates, Frances (Amelia) 1899–1981 British scholarly
pioneer, a specialist on the occult, who demonstrated a
formidable range of learning. Her contribution to
decoding the elaborate iconography of Renaissance
Hermeticism/Platonism is one of her major achievements, and her arguments in that field have been at
once provocative and tantalizing. Startlingly original,
sometimes dangerously assertive, she matched its
encyclopaedic eclecticism.

The youngest child of a naval architect, Frances grew
up surrounded by a high-minded family of devoted
Shakespeareans and Francophiles. Her love of French
Renaissance poetry – nurtured in the library she grew
up in – inspired her early promise (she gained a First in
an external degree in French at London University)
and led to the publication of *The French Academies of the
Sixteenth Century* in 1959. Her subsequent research
ranged over a broad and fascinating field and produced, among her most notable works, *Theatre of the
World* (1969), *Giordano Bruno and the Hermetic Tradition*
(1964) and *The Art of Memory* (1966). Her association
with the Warburg Institute began informally in 1937
and she later joined the staff, becoming Reader in the
History of the Renaissance at the University of London
between 1956 and 1967. She brought to life the traditions of Hermetic philosophy from the inside, intent
on recreating the sensibility and retracing the intellectual currents of Renaissance thought and belief. JCr

Years, The (1937) VIRGINIA WOOLF's eighth novel
was a new departure from the MODERNIST poetics she
had pursued so far. *The Years* chronicles the Pargiter
family from 1880 to the mid 1930s. In a deliberately
REALIST manner (reminiscent of Arnold Bennett, her
former literary adversary), Woolf describes the emotional, intellectual and financial difficulties of the
daughters of the respectable family, but nevertheless
emphasizes that they are not necessarily hopeless, for

Ann Yearsley.

their lonely struggles are not closed to new awareness. Eleanor, a 'spinster' who spends thirty years looking after her widowed father as the eldest daughter is expected to, learns how to dream a new world under the air raids on London in World War I, and holds out her hands to her beloved brother Morris on the eve of World War II. The novel reaches its climax here, suggesting that a woman's self-realization has a potential to prevent the repetition of history (a theme further developed in *THREE GUINEAS*, 1938). Sophocles' *Antigone*, a champion of private love (especially a sister's love of her brother) over public duty, is in the background.   AK

Yearsley [née Cromartie], Ann 1752–1806 English poet, novelist and playwright. Born in poverty, Ann was taught to write by a brother. Like her mother, Ann delivered milk from door to door, and, in 1774, she married John Yearsley, an illiterate labourer. After producing six children, the couple sank into destitution. Introduced to Ann's verse by her cook, HANNAH MORE gave the 'heaven-taught' poet volumes on grammar and spelling. With ELIZABETH MONTAGU, More assembled 1,000 subscribers for *Poems on Several Occasions* (1785), establishing Ann's fame as 'Lactilla' or the 'poetical milkwoman' within the 18th-century vogue for celebrity 'unlettered' poets, including Stephen Duck ('the thresher poet') and MARY COLLIER (the 'washerwoman'). When her patrons established a trust to oversee the volume's £600 profits, Ann's initial gratitude turned to outrage. In a caustic public feud, she attacked More's 'guilty blandishments' and meddling 'corrections'. Eventually gaining control over her funds, Ann added an 'Autobiographical Narrative' repudiating More to later editions.

Ann clearly relished the 'Lactilla' persona. Highly conventional and derivative, her verse favours tones of woe and self-pity, extols nature over education and poetic rules, and fawns over various patrons. Her later volumes, *Poems on Various Subjects* (1787) and *The Rural Lyre* (1796), range from domestic to political themes, such as 'Poem on the Inhumanity of the Slave Trade' or 'An Elegy on Marie Antoinette'. Remembered mainly as a poet, Ann also wrote a play, *Earl Goodwin* (produced 1789, published 1791), and a GOTHIC novel, *The Royal Captives* (1795). She died in obscurity.   JHP

'Yellow Wallpaper, The' (1892) CHARLOTTE PERKINS GILMAN's most celebrated and widely read short story is the tale of a depressed woman with a young baby who has been prescribed a period of social exclusion and mental inactivity, a 'rest cure' that precipitates the very collapse it was designed to avoid. The (unnamed) narrator becomes obsessed with her own condition and the 'torturing' pattern and 'repellant ... unclean' colour of the wallpaper in her room, which symbolizes both her incarceration and her disturbance. She becomes convinced that a woman – with whom she progressively identifies – is trapped within the wallpaper. Her husband eventually comes upon her acting this out. The story has strong GOTHIC elements and a clear feminist message concerning the infantilizing and constriction of women within marriage. Gilman herself had suffered a similar treatment after the birth of her daughter, counselled to have no intellectual or artistic and little social stimulus; as a result, she records, she 'came so near the borderline of utter mental ruin that I could see over'. In *Why I wrote the 'Yellow Wallpaper'* she maintained that the story 'was not intended to drive people crazy, but to save people from being driven crazy, and it worked'.   SAS

Yezierska, Anzia 1880?–1970 Polish Jew who landed at Ellis Island as an immigrant and escaped the squalid sweatshops to become a leading author of REALISTIC social fiction which reflected the hopes and horrors of Jewish immigrants such as herself. In 1920, Edward J. O'Brien, editor of the 'Best Short Stories' series, chose 'Fat of the Land' as the best short story of 1919 and dedicated the year's collection to her. Her first novel, *Hungry Hearts*, was published in 1922 and the film rights were immediately purchased by Samuel Goldwyn. Her disillusioned Hollywood experiences are found in *All I Could Never Be* (1932) and the fictional autobiography *Red Ribbon on a White Horse* (1950). She wrote a number of other works besides novels, but she is most often recognized as initiating an understanding of the Jewish-American experience which was, as yet, an undefined and uncharted cultural territory.

MRA

Yonge, Charlotte Mary 1823–1901 English novelist. The daughter of a minor country gentleman and author of some 160 books, Yonge was a committed High Church spinster whose inspiration is obvious in her writings, the profits of which she gave to charity. A Sunday school teacher from the age of 7, she was enormously influenced by John Keble, who was appointed vicar of a neighbouring parish in 1835. He not only prepared her for confirmation but recognized her talent and encouraged it, editing her work in manuscript and successfully warning her against preaching too overtly in it.

Nonetheless, a strong and untroubled faith pervades all Yonge's writing; her characters are unashamedly measured against the Christian ideal. Her first success was THE HEIR OF REDCLYFFE (1853), an enormously popular novel examining the distinction between real and specious virtue, whose central theme is the idea of redemption through another's example and ultimate sacrifice. Yonge believed in the weakness and subordination of women, holding their proper role to be supportive – as is neatly illustrated in *The Daisy Chain* (1853). Sons are educated and make their way in the world; daughters escape, if at all, through marriage. But greatest approval goes to the academically brilliant Ethel, who sacrifices her interests to the role of 'home daughter', the tending of her widowed father and charitable labour in the parish.

Yonge's other notable novels include *The Clever Woman of the Family* (1865), a sensitive and sympathetic treatment of female adolescence, and *The Pillars of the House* (1873), another detailed family chronicle. She also wrote a number of children's historical tales, among them *The Little Duke* (1854), the story of William the Conqueror's great-grandfather. For thirty-nine years she edited the *Monthly Packet*, a magazine designed to promote the principles of the Oxford Movement among the young. She died of pleurisy. CT

Yonnondio: From the Thirties (1974) In the mid thirties TILLIE OLSEN laid aside this work and only rediscovered her manuscript forty years later. In this story of the working-class poor during the twenties, Olsen offers striking commentary on women and motherhood, seeking to locate woman's potential outside her sexuality. Anna Holbrook struggles to hold her family together in the harsh climate of a Wyoming coal-mining community. After her husband, Jim, survives a terrifying mine accident, the family moves to a tenant farm in South Dakota, where Anna gives birth to their fifth child, Bess. In spite of the lush and fertile land, they are driven by poverty to the city, where Jim finds employment in the slaughterhouses. In the multi-national slum community, Anna is raped by her husband, suffers a miscarriage and survives mental and physical illness. Olsen frequently focuses her story on the oldest daughter, Mazie, implying not merely the cyclical nature of life but rather woman's recurrent struggle to find recognition and identity beyond her singular, stereotypical role as childbearer. JAHa

Young, E(mily) H(ilda) 1880–1949 British novelist Young led a seemingly conventional middle-class life – growing up in a large well-to-do family in Northumberland, marrying a Bristol solicitor, J.A.H. Daniell (killed in World War I), then lodging in London during the inter-war years with a respectable headmaster, Ralph Henderson, and his wife. But Henderson was her lover, and her home a *ménage à trois*. In her eleven novels published under the gender-neutral 'E.H. Young', she created eccentric characters who battle the inevitability of a diminished life in the face of conventional social demands. Judith in *A Corn of Wheat* (1910) is a spirit of the woods who spurns the confines of domesticity. In subsequent novels, the protagonists leave the moors for suburban Radstowe (Young's name for Bristol), and their forays into solitary nature occur only at moments weighted with significance, until in *Chatterton Square* (1947), her last novel, the setting is reduced to two adjacent claustrophobic houses on the eve of World War II. Young views relationships from an odd angle; romance may be a possibility but it is nudged out of sight while other relationships take centre stage – mothers and daughters, a housekeeper and her charges, two sisters. Although curates and vicars abound, religion is mocked and hypocrisy reviled. Young was no experimentalist, but both her narrative form and her characters continually surprise: spinster Hannah Mole in *Miss Mole* (winner of the 1930 James Tait Black Prize) turns out to have intimate sexual knowledge, and shipowner William Nesbitt (*William*, 1925) supports his daughter's decision to desert her husband for her novelist lover. The darker side of Young's fiction portrays the disappointments of marriage, the despair of physical revulsion, and the narrowing of horizons. CBr/KM

Z

Zitkala-Ša (Gertrude Simmons Bonnin) 1876–1938 Native American writer and reformer. Zitkala-Ša was born on a Sioux reservation and educated far from home at schools run by whites. Rather than return to reservation life, difficult after learning white ways, she resumed her education, enjoying success as a musician and orator, attending Earlham College, and becoming a teacher at Carlisle Indian School. Zitkala-Ša would later criticize sharply the practices of Indian boarding schools, highlighting the tragic loss of tribal culture their assimilationist practices entailed.

Zitkala-Ša's first book, *Old Indian Legends* (1901), retold stories of Sioux mythical and trickster figures, preserving the oral tradition of her people. She published stories and autobiographical essays in periodicals such as *Harper's* and *Atlantic Monthly* and collected them in her second book, *American Indian Stories* (1921). This work focused not on myths of the past but rather on present-day conditions and struggles of Native Americans. She also collaborated with William Hanson on the opera *Sun Dance* (1913), which centred around Sioux dances and songs.

In 1902 Zitkala-Ša married Raymond Bonnin, a Sioux agent in the Bureau of Indian Affairs; they had a son, Ohiya (Raymond). She became a key member of the Society of the American Indian, an organization for the advancement of Native American interests, and in 1926 established the National Council of American Indians, which she ran until her death. Her reform work included co-authoring *Oklahoma's Poor Rich Indians: An Orgy of Graft and Exploitation of the Five Civilized Tribes–Legalized Robbery*, published in 1924, the same year Native Americans finally won the vote. KMP

Zwicky, Fay 1933– Australian poet, born in Melbourne; some of her most memorable poetry evokes the life of a Jewish family, notably in 'Kaddish', from her award-winning collection *Kaddish and Other Poems* (1982). Fay Zwicky has had a varied career, beginning as a concert pianist, then becoming an academic and later editor as well as poet. *The Lyre in the Pawnshop* (1986) is a collection of her essays, reviews and articles that reflects the breadth of her life and professional experience. Her poetry volumes include *Isaac Babel's Fiddle* (1975), *Ask Me* (1990), *A Touch of Ginger* (1991, with Dennis Haskell) and *Fay Zwicky: Poems 1970-1992* (1993). Sometimes her poems record with acerbity and barely suppressed anger the needless waste of female middle age, as in the poem 'Forbearance – Coolgardie, 1898':

> Aunt Phoebe spent her
> Rocky middle years inside
> A tent upon the goldfields,
> Swore at tardy camel trains
> And waterless, she rued the day
> Of comfort's banishment,

and more exhaustively, in 'A Midwestern Wife', which catalogues a life-time where family members, things and meanings are relentlessly taken away. She has edited anthologies of poems by a number of distinguished women writers: JUDITH WRIGHT, GWEN HARWOOD, ROSEMARY DOBSON and DOROTHY HEWETT. A collection of short stories, *Hostages*, was published in 1983. Zwicky's is a strong, distinctive voice that focuses on women's experience, and particularly their silencing by patriarchal myth. She addresses a wide range of topics, one of them the relation between art and the artist. HTh

Contributors

AA	**AHMED ABDELMOHCINE** *University of Meknes, Morocco*		ABl	**ANN BLAKE** *La Trobe University, Melbourne*
FA	**FLEUR ADCOCK** *Poet*		LB	**LESLEY BLANCH** *Writer*
EA	**ELIZABETH ALLEN** *Regent's College, London*		CLB	**CATHERINE BLECKI** *San José State University*
MA	**MARGARET ALLEN** *University of Adelaide*		HB	**HARRIET BLODGETT** *California State University, Stanislaus*
IA	**ISOBEL ARMSTRONG** *Birbeck College, University of London*		EBo	**ELLEKE BOEHMER** *Writer/University of Leeds*
SA	**SIMON AVERY** *Anglia Polytechnic University, Cambridge*		WJB	**JOHN BOLLAND** *Manchester Metropolitan University*
MRA	**MARK R. AXELROD** *Chapman University, Orange, California*		MAB	**MAGGIE ANN BOWERS** *UIA, University of Antwerp*
MLA	**MARIE-LOUISE AYRES** *University College, University of New South Wales*		AB	**ARABELLA BOXER** *Food writer*
CB	**CRISTINA BACCHILEGA** *University of Hawai'i–Manoa*		MSB	**MARGARET SOENSER BREEN** *University of Connecticut*
DZB	**DOROTHY Z. BAKER** *University of Houston, Texas*		ILB	**IRIS BREUER** *Editor and publisher, Victoria*
EB	**ELAINE BANDER** *Dawson College, Montreal*		CBr	**CHIARA BRIGANTI** *Carleton College, Minnesota*
JB	**JACQUELINE BARDOLPH** *University of Nice, Professor Emerita*		RB-S	**RHONDA BROCK-SERVAIS** *University of South Carolina – Columbia*
JBa	**JOHN BARNES** *La Trobe University, Melbourne*		JLB	**JULIA LACEY BROOKE** *Renaissance Drama Research Group, Shakespeare Institute, Stratford-upon- Avon*
JHB	**JULIA BELL** *Writer*		RB	**RUTH BROWN** *Freelance researcher/University of Sussex*
LBe	**LIZ BELLAMY** *Open University, United Kingdom*		SB	**SYLVIA BROWNRIGG** *Writer*
LBer	**LAUREL BERGMANN** *Scholar and researcher, Brisbane*		SBB	**SARAH BRYANT-BERTALL** *University of Washington*
PJB	**PHILIPPA BERRY** *King's College, University of Cambridge*		BWB	**BRAD BUCHANAN** *Stanford University*
MB	**MIRELLA BILLI** *Università degli Studi della Tuscia, Viterbo/ Writer*		CBu	**CLIVE BUSH** *King's College, University of London*
DB	**DELYS BIRD** *University of Western Australia*		LMC	**LICIA MORROW CALLOWAY** *University of Michigan*

KC	**KATE CAMPBELL** *University of East Anglia*		JD	**JUDITH DALE** *Victoria University of Wellington*
LCa	**LORRAYNE CARROLL** *University of Southern Maine*		AMD	**ANNE MARGARET DANIEL** *Princeton University*
LC	**LEONARD CASSUTO** *Fordham University*		SD	**SIGRID DANIEL** *Corpus Christi, postgraduate*
JC	**JOCELYN CATTY** *Freelance researcher, London*		RD	**ROBYN DAVIDSON** *Writer*
EC	**ELLEN M. CHAFEE** *Washington DC*		KD	**KATE DAVIES** *University of York*
ACh	**ANN CHARTERS** *University of Connecticut*		FD	**FRANCES DAVIS** *Vanier College, Montreal*
SC	**SARAH B. CHURCHWELL** *Princeton University*		MAD	**MARGARET DEBELIUS** *Princeton University, postgraduate*
AC	**ALEX CLARK** *Freelance writer*		MDeK	**MARIANNE DEKOVEN** *Rutgers University*
TC	**THEKLA CLARK** *Publisher and writer*		HMD	**HELEN M. DENNIS** *University of Warwick*
CC	**CHERRY CLAYTON** *University of Guelph*		RDM	**REBECCA D MONTÉ** *University of Southampton New College*
VC	**VICTORIA CLEMENTS** *Community College at St Mary's County*		AD	**ALISON DONNELL** *Nottingham Trent University*
CCl	**CATRIONA CLUTTERBUCK** *University College Dublin*		LDo	**LAURA DONOHUE** *Writer and editor*
CCo	**CARLI COETZEE** *University of Cape Town*		SDo	**SARA DOWSE** *Writer*
LCo	**LISA COLLETTA** *Claremont Graduate University*		MD	**MAUREEN DUFFY** *Novelist and poet*
RJC	**ROBYN COLWILL** *University of Queensland*		LD	**LINDSAY DUGUID** *Times Literary Supplement*
RCo	**RACHEL CONNOR** *North East Wales Institute of Higher Education*		CD	**CHRIS DUNTON** *University of North-West, South Africa*
JCo	**JON COOK** *University of East Anglia*		ESE	**ELIZABETH S. EGER** *University of Warwick*
PLC	**PATTIE COWELL** *Colorado State University*		RE	**REBECCA EGGER** *University of Michigan, Ann Arbor*
PC	**PATRICIA CRAIG** *Freelance writer*		REi	**RENATE EIGENBROD** *Lakehead University, Ontario*
PCr	**PATRICIA CRAIN** *Princeton University*		MRE	**MARY R. ELLEN** *University of East Anglia*
JCr	**JULIA CROCKETT** *University of East Anglia, postgraduate*		CE	**CATH ELLIS** *University of Wollongong*
CCr	**CHARLOTTE CROFTS** *University of Manchester*		KE	**KATY EMCK** *Freelance writer*
NC	**NORA CROOK** *Anglia Polytechnic University, Cambridge*		AE	**ANNA ENGLE** *Emory University*

REn	**RIEMKE ENSING** *Poet/University of Auckland*		MG	**MEREDITH GOLDSMITH** *Bilkent University, Ankara, Turkey*
FE	**FAITH EVANS** *Literary agent, editor and translator*		VG	**VESNA GOLDSWORTHY** *Writer*
REv	**RUTH EVANS** *University of Wales Cardiff*		AG	**ALEX GOODY** *Falmouth College of Arts*
EF	**EILEEN FAUSET** *Bretton Hall College of the University of Leeds*		JVG	**JULIE V. GOTTLIEB** *University of Toronto*
ARF	**ANNETTE R. FEDERICO** *James Madison University*		JAG	**JUDITH GRAHAM** *Roehampton Institute, London*
PRF	**PAULA R. FELDMAN** *University of South Carolina*		JSG	**JANET GRAY** *Princeton University/The College of New Jersey*
CF	**CAROLE FERRIER** *University of Queensland, Brisbane*		EG	**ELIZABETH GREENE** *Queen's University, Kingston, Ontario*
JFG	**JENNIFER FITZGERALD** *Queen's University of Belfast*		JGr	**JODY GREENE** *University of California, Santa Cruz*
BTF	**BETSEY TAYLOR FITZSIMON** *University College Dublin, postgraduate*		LG	**LAVINIA GREENLAW** *Poet and critic*
KFl	**KATE FLINT** *University of Oxford*		GG	**GERMAINE GREER** *University of Warwick*
SF	**STEPHANIE FORWARD** *St Augustine's School, Redditch*		BJG	**BRETT JOSEF GRUBISIC** *University of British Columbia*
FSF	**FRANCES SMITH FOSTER** *Emory University*		BH	**BARBARA HABER** *Curator of Books, The Schlesinger Library*
MF	**MARCELLE FREIMAN** *University of New South Wales, Sydney*		HH	**HELEN HACKETT** *University College London*
SFu	**SARAH FULFORD** *University of Kent at Canterbury, postgraduate*		JH	**JANE HARRIS** *Writer*
KF	**KATE FULLBROOK** *University of the West of England, Bristol*		EMH	**ELAINE HARTNELL** *University of Leicester*
DF	**DANIELLE FULLER** *University of Birmingham*		JAHa	**JUDY A. HAYDEN** *University of East Anglia*
BF	**BETTY FUSSELL** *Writer, New York*		AH	**ANN HEILMANN** *Manchester Metropolitan University*
MBG	**MAGGIE B. GALE** *University of Birmingham*		PRH	**POWHIRI RIKA-HEKE** *University of Osnabrück*
EDG	**ELISABETH D. GARRETT** *Christie's, New York*		HAH	**HILARY HINDS** *Cheltenham & Gloucester College of Higher Education*
AEG	**ADRIENNE E. GAVIN** *Canterbury Christ Church University College*		RH	**RUPERT HODSON** *Accademia Britannica, Florence*
CG	**CAROLE GERSON** *Simon Fraser University, Canada*		ACH	**ANDREA HOLLAND** *Writer/Norwich School of Art & Design*
GG-R	**GENELLE GERTZ-ROBINSON** *Princeton University, postgraduate*		GH	**GERALDENE HOLT** *Writer*
JG	**JOAN GIVNER** *University of Regina, Professor Emerita*		EH	**ERIC HOMBERGER** *University of East Anglia*
WG	**WILLIAM GLEASON** *Princeton University*			

DH	**DAVID HOPES** *University of North Carolina at Asheville*		PEK	**PAMELA KNIGHTS** *University of Durham*
JAH	**JAMES A. HOPKIN** *Writer*		DKo	**DENISE KOHN** *Greensboro College, North Carolina*
JTH	**JANETTE TURNER HOSPITAL** *Novelist/University of South Carolina*		GKr	**GREG KRATZMANN** *La Trobe University, Melbourne*
BHu	**BARBARA HUGHES** *University College Dublin*		MLK	**MARK L. KRUPNICK** *University of Chicago*
EHu	**EAMONN HUGHES** *Queen's University of Belfast*		JL	**JOANNA LABON** *Birkbeck College, University of London*
CLI	**C. L. INNES** *University of Kent at Canterbury*		AL	**ALEXANDRA LAVAU** *Editor, Australian Broadcasting* *Corporation*
CJ	**CASSANDRA JACKSON** *Emory University*		DL	**DAVID LAWTON** *Washington University in St Louis*
JJ	**JASBIR JAIN** *Institute for Research in Interdisciplinary* *Studies, Jaipur, India*		EL	**EVE LECKEY** *UNICEF, Florence*
MJ	**MARY JOANNOU** *Anglia Polytechnic University, Cambridge*		SL	**SALLY LEDGER** *Birkbeck College, University of London*
MCJ	**MELISSA JOHNSON** *University of South Carolina, postgraduate*		CL	**CATHY LEENEY** *National University of Ireland, Dublin*
SJ	**SUSANNA JOHNSTON** *Writer*		RL	**REBECCA LEMON** *University of Warwick*
VJ	**VIVIEN JONES** *University of Leeds*		VHL	**VALERIE H. LETCHER** *Edgewood College of Education, Durban*
EJ	**ELAINE JORDAN** *University of Essex*		SPL	**SUSAN LEVER** *University of New South Wales, Canberra*
NWJ	**NICOLE WARD JOUVE** *Writer/York University*		DLe	**DESIREE LEWIS** *University of the Western Cape*
AK	**AKI KATAYAMA** *University of East Anglia, postgraduate/* *Toho University*		ELi	**ELSBETH LINDNER** *Editor and novelist*
RK	**ROZ KAVENEY** *Freelance writer*		MM	**MARINA MACKAY** *University of East Anglia, postgraduate*
JK	**JONATHAN KEATES** *Writer and teacher*		MMac	**MORAG MACKAY** *University of Auckland, postgraduate*
DK	**DEBORAH KELLAWAY** *Gardening writer*		JMcK	**JOY MCKENZIE** *Freelance writer, Auckland*
GK	**GARY KELLY** *University of Alberta*		SMcK	**SARAH MCKENZIE** *University of Warwick, postgraduate*
CFK	**CAROL FARLEY KESSLER** *PennState, Delaware County Campus*		AM	**AOREWA MCLEOD** *University of Auckland*
SLK	**SUSANNAH L. KETCHUM** *Writer, Boston*		HM	**HELEN MCNEIL** *Independent scholar/University of East Anglia*
KK	**KERRY KILNER** *Australian Studies Centre, University of* *Queensland*		HSM	**HEIDI SLETTEDAHL MACPHERSON** *University of Central Lancashire*
			PM	**PAUL MAGRS** *Writer/University of East Anglia*

PMa	**PAOLA MARCHIONNI** *Wasafiri magazine/Commonwealth Institute, London*
JMM	**JAN MARK** *Freelance writer*
SM	**SIGRID MARKMANN** *University of Osnabrück*
GM	**GAIL MARSHALL** *University of Leeds*
PMar	**PRISCILLA MARTIN** *St Edmund Hall, University of Oxford*
SKM	**SUSAN K. MARTIN** *La Trobe University, Melbourne*
JBM	**JOEL MARTINEAU** *University of British Columbia*
EM	**EMMA MASON** *University of Warwick*
JFM	**JEREMY MAULE** *Trinity College, University of Cambridge*
GMe	**GERARDINE MEANEY** *Centre for Film Studies, University College Dublin*
JSM	**JESLYN MEDOFF** *University of Massachusetts, Boston*
PMM	**PINKIE MEKGWE** *Poet/University of Sussex, postgraduate/ University of Botswana*
RM	**RITU MENON** *Writer and independent scholar/ co-founder of Kali for Women Press*
CM	**CAROL MERLI** *La Trobe University, Melbourne*
PJM	**PETER MERRINGTON** *University of the Western Cape*
KM	**KATHY MEZEI** *Simon Fraser University, Canada*
C-AM	**CHERYL-ANN MICHAEL** *University of the Western Cape*
YEM	**YVONNE E. MIELS** *Flinders University, Adelaide*
MSM	**MARY S. MILLAR** *Co-editor of Disraeli Letters/Queen's University, Ontario*
JM	**JANE MILLER** *Institute of Education, University of London*
LM	**LIA MILLS** *Novelist/research associate, WERCC, University College Dublin*
DMM	**DUNJA M. MOHR** *University of Trier/journalist*
DM	**DAVID MORLEY** *Poet/University of Warwick*
MMo	**MARK MORRIS** *Trinity College, University of Cambridge*
SCM	**STEPHEN MORTON** *University of Leeds, postgraduate*
MMos	**MERRITT MOSELEY** *University of North Carolina at Asheville*
VM	**VALARIE J. MOSES** *University of Michigan, postgraduate/writer*
LMu	**LISA MUIR** *University of Wisconsin, Green Bay*
MMu	**MEENAKSHI MUKHERJEE** *Independent scholar, Secunderabad, India*
JAM	**JULIE ANN MULLANEY** *University of Leeds*
MM-R	**MARIE MULVEY-ROBERTS** *University of the West of England*
DdeCN	**DENISE deCAIRES NARAIN** *University of Sussex/Guyana*
EJN	**EMMA NEALE** *University College London, postgraduate*
GHN	**GRETA HOFMANN NEMIROFF** *Writer/Dawson College, Montreal*
JN	**JENNY NOBLE** *University of New South Wales, Sydney, postgraduate*
SN	**SARAH NUTTALL** *University of Stellenbosch*
EO'C	**EVELYN O'CALLAGHAN** *University of the West Indies, Barbados*
MO'C	**MAUREEN O'CONNOR** *Claremont Graduate University*
MO'D	**MARC O'DAY** *Suffolk College*
FJO'G	**FRANCIS O'GORMAN** *Cheltenham & Gloucester College of Higher Education*
SO	**SYBIL OLDFIELD** *University of Sussex*
BO	**BRIGITTA OLUBAS** *University of New South Wales, Sydney*
CCO	**CLARISSA CAMPBELL ORR** *Anglia Polytechnic University, Cambridge*
KO	**KOFI OWUSU** *Carleton College, Minnesota*